Peter Brown, Rita L

Pagans and Christians in
The Breaking of

CHRISTIANITY AND HISTORY

Series of the John XXIII Foundation
for Religious Studies in Bologna

edited by

† Prof. Dr. Dr. h.c. mult. Giuseppe Alberigo
Prof. Dr. Alberto Melloni

(Fondazione per le scienze religiose Giovanni XXIII, Bologna)

Scientific Board

Prof. Dr. Claus Arnold, Frankfurt
Prof. Dr. Paolo Bettiolo, Padova
Prof. Dr. Philip Denis, KwaZulu-Natal
Prof. Dr. Hyacinthe Destivelle, Paris
Prof. Dr. Étienne Fouilloux, Lyon
Prof. Dr. Giovanni Miccoli, Trieste
Prof. Dr. Kenneth Pennington, Washington DC
Prof. Dr. Paolo Pombeni, Bologna
Prof. Dr. Adriano Prosperi, Pisa
Prof. Dr. Yan Li Ren, Bejing
Prof. Dr. Joachim Stieber, Northampton
Prof. Dr. Christoph Theobald, Paris
Card. Roberto Tucci, Città del Vaticano

Volume 9

LIT

Pagans and Christians in the Roman Empire: The Breaking of a Dialogue

(IVth- VIth Century A. D.)

Proceedings of the International Conference
at the Monastery of Bose
(October 2008)

edited by

Peter Brown and Rita Lizzi Testa

LIT

Cover image:
Elisabetta Pizzichetti, *Torre di Babele*, 2008, 120 × 50, tecnica mista su tela (per gentile concessione dell'artista)

With the generous support of:
Compagnia di San Paolo, Torino
Fondazione Cariplo, Milano

Bibliographic information published by the Deutsche Nationalbibliothek
The Deutsche Nationalbibliothek lists this publication in the Deutsche Nationalbibliografie; detailed bibliographic data are available in the Internet at http://dnb.d-nb.de.

ISBN 978-3-643-90069-2

A catalogue record for this book is available from the British Library

©LIT VERLAG GmbH & Co. KG Wien,
Zweigniederlassung Zürich 2011
Klosbachstr. 107
CH-8032 Zürich
Tel. +41 (0) 44-251 75 05
Fax +41 (0) 44-251 75 06
e-Mail: zuerich@lit-verlag.ch
http://www.lit-verlag.ch

LIT VERLAG Dr. W. Hopf
Berlin 2011
Fresnostr. 2
D-48159 Münster
Tel. +49 (0) 2 51-620 320
Fax +49 (0) 2 51-922 60 99
e-Mail: lit@lit-verlag.de
http://www.lit-verlag.de

Distribution:

In Germany: LIT Verlag Fresnostr. 2, D-48159 Münster
Tel. +49 (0) 2 51-620 32 22, Fax +49 (0) 2 51-922 60 99, e-mail: vertrieb@lit-verlag.de

In Austria: Medienlogistik Pichler-ÖBZ, e-mail: mlo@medien-logistik.at

In Switzerland: B + M Buch- und Medienvertrieb, e-mail: order@buch-medien.ch

In the UK: Global Book Marketing, e-mail: mo@centralbooks.com

In North America by:

Transaction Publishers
New Brunswick (U.S.A.) and London (U.K.)

Transaction Publishers
Rutgers University
35 Berrue Circle
Piscataway, NJ 08854

Phone: +1 (732) 445 - 2280
Fax: + 1 (732) 445 - 3138
for orders (U. S. only):
toll free (888) 999 - 6778
e-mail: orders@transactionpub.com

Indice

RITA LIZZI TESTA
    Introduzione   p. 9

Il cristianesimo di A. Momigliano

PETER BROWN
    Back to the future: pagans and christians at the Warburg Institute in 1958   17

ALBERTO MELLONI
    Momigliano «in conflict». Un'indagine nell'Archivio Einaudi, 1952-1968   25

AVERIL CAMERON
    Thoughts on the «Introduction» to «The Conflict between Paganism and Christianity in the Fourth Century»   39

GUIDO CLEMENTE
    Pagani, ebrei, cristiani nella riflessione storica di Arnaldo Momigliano   55

GIANMARIA ZAMAGNI
    Theology and history. A retrospective on the «End of the Constantinian Era» in the works of F. Heer, E. Buonaiuti and E. Peterson   69

«Ma come tutti i grandi libri...»

HERVÉ INGLEBERT
    L'historiographie au IVe siècle entre païens et chrétiens: faux dialogue et vrai débat   93

JOHANNES HAHN
    Julian and his partisans: supporters or critics?   109
FEDERICO FATTI
    Il principe, la «Tyche», i cristiani: Giuliano a Cesarea   121
JAN WILLEM DRIJVERS
    Religious conflict in the Syriac «Julian Romance»   131
SERGIO KNIPE
    Recycling the refuse-heap of magic: scholarly approaches to theurgy since 1963   163
FRANCISCO MARSHALL
    The late antique hero   171

« Contiene in se stesso i germi delle più vere critiche future»

MAIJASTINA KAHLOS
    The importance of being pagan   187
GIANFRANCO AGOSTI
    Cristianizzazione della poesia greca e dialogo interculturale   193
PIERRE CHUVIN
    Homère christianisé. Esthétique profane et symbolique chrétienne dans l'œuvre de Paul le Silentiaire   215
GIOVANNI A. CECCONI
    Contenuti religiosi delle discipline scolastiche e prassi d'insegnamento come terreno di conflitto politico-culturale   225
KATE COOPER
    Reti di famiglia, reti di evangelizzazione: la famiglia tra paganesimo e cristianesimo nella «Passio Sebastiani»   245

«Appunto perché impone ricerche nuove»

CLAUDE LEPELLEY
    De la réaction païenne à la sécularisation: le témoignage d'inscriptions municipales romano-africaines tardives   273

ARNALDO MARCONE
   Persistenze classiche e innovazioni cristiane: iconografia e epigrafia nelle Venezie   291

WOLF LIEBESCHUETZ
   The view from Antioch: from Libanius via John Chrysostom to John Malalas and beyond   309

GIORGIO BONAMENTE
   Dall'imperatore divinizzato all'imperatore santo   339

CHRISTOPHE J. GODDARD
   Au cœur du dialogue entre païens et chrétiens: l'«aduentus» des sénateurs dans les cités de l'Antiquité tardive   371

«I documenti si scoprono se si cercano»

LELLIA CRACCO RUGGINI
   «Pontifices»: un caso di osmosi linguistica   403

SILVIA ORLANDI
   Gli ultimi sacerdoti pagani di Roma: analisi della documentazione epigrafica   425

RITA LIZZI TESTA
   Legislazione imperiale e reazione pagana: i limiti del conflitto   467

CARLOS MACHADO
   Roman aristocrats and the christianization of Rome   493

ALAN CAMERON
   Vergil and his commentators   517

Silenti epiloghi

PAOLO LIVERANI
   I vescovi nell'edilizia pubblica   529

BÉATRICE CASEAU
   Le crypto paganisme et les frontières du licite: un jeu de masques?   541

GIORGIO CRACCO
    Un conflitto dentro il cristianesimo. L'apporto di Gregorio Magno alla storia religiosa dell'Occidente   573

PETER BROWN
    Concluding remarks   599

Indice dei nomi antichi (*a cura di Alessandra Bravi e Rita Lizzi Testa*)   611

Indice dei nomi moderni (*a cura di Giulia Marconi e Silvia Margutti*)   621

Autori   641

RITA LIZZI TESTA

Introduzione

L'idea di un convegno sulle relazioni tra pagani e cristiani negli ultimi secoli dell'Impero è maturata all'interno del comitato di direzione di «Cristianesimo nella Storia», discutendo il progetto per un futuro Quaderno monografico della Rivista. Poiché proprio cinquanta anni fa, nel corso del 1958-1959, furono tenute al Warburg Institute di Londra le conferenze che Arnaldo Momigliano raccolse nel volume *The Conflict between Paganism and Christianity in the Fourth Century* (Oxford, 1963) – pubblicato in traduzione italiana dopo un decennio con il titolo *Il conflitto tra paganesimo e cristianesimo nel secolo IV* (Torino, 1968) – si è pensato che studiare quel tema avrebbe pure offerto l'occasione di tracciare un bilancio degli orientamenti assunti dalla ricerca storica in mezzo secolo di studi. Accettata la proposta, Alberto Melloni propose di riunirci a Bose – in quel monastero cresciuto sulle prealpi biellesi, tra i dioriti della Serra d'Ivrea e l'altipiano petroso della Bessa, un tempo costellato di miniere d'oro a cielo aperto (le *Victimularum aurifodinae* di Plinio, *N.H.* 33, 21,12 e di Strabone, *Geogr.* V,1,12) – ove il dialogo tra le religioni è oggetto vivo di confronto.

Per tre giornate, dal 20 al 22 ottobre 2008, in un tempo scandito dai momenti di preghiera dei confratelli della comunità, illustri maestri e più giovani allievi hanno presentato le proprie ricerche con passione, trattando argomenti trasmessi e accolti nella discepolanza. Il nostro tema, antico quanto l'origine del cristianesimo, si è fatto attuale, mentre lo scambio di idee tra almeno tre generazioni ha reso consapevoli delle enormi prospettive apertesi dall'epoca delle *Warburg Lectures*, molte delle quali impensabili prima della loro pubblicazione.

Mentre una piccola selezione dei contributi recitati a Bose è già confluita nell'ultimo volumetto monografico di «Cristianesimo nella Storia»[1],

---

[1] *Le relazioni tra pagani e cristiani: nuove prospettive su un antico tema*, a cura di R. Lizzi Testa, in «Cristianesimo nella Storia» 30 (2009)/2, 255-481.

in questi Atti sono raccolti tutti i lavori presentati al convegno[2]. Ispiratore e anima dell'incontro è stato Peter Brown, giovanissimo uditore delle *Warburg Lectures*, nonché primissimo recensore del volume in inglese a cura di A. Momigliano[3]: con generosa disponibilità ha accettato l'onere di condividerne la curatela, di rivedere il testo con cui aveva introdotto il convegno, ora in apertura dei saggi della prima sezione di questi Atti (*Back to the future: pagans and christians at the Warburg Institute in 1958*), nonché di tracciarne le conclusioni (*Concluding remarks*).

I contributi non sono editi nell'ordine in cui sono stati recitati perché, nel leggere i testi che i vari autori hanno rielaborato anche tenendo conto della vivace discussione suscitata, è parso opportuno darne una diversa disposizione a soggetto, in differente sequela. Uguale, invece, è rimasto il titolo, e ciò benché già prima del convegno la scelta di eliminarvi qualunque riferimento al «conflitto» avesse suscitato qualche perplessità e sebbene la discussione abbia variamente confermato di non eludere il modello del «conflitto», così centrale nell'opera di Momigliano[4]. Non saprei dire se l'immagine di «pagani e cristiani in dialogo» sia un'illusoria proiezione di come vorrei che fosse andata la storia dei rapporti tra quanti alla fine dell'Impero professarono scelte religiose diverse. È indubbio che «fare storia consiste essenzialmente nel guardare al passato con gli occhi del presente», come suggeriva Benedetto Croce sostenendo che «ogni storia è storia contemporanea»[5]. Eppure, al di là di quanto i fattori soggettivi possano condizionare la ricostruzione del passato, resto convinta che il cristianesimo divenne il «discorso dominante», perché tra le sue molte correnti prevalse quella in cui più spiccata era la disposizione dialogica, a sua volta riflesso della cultura entro cui la nuova religione si era sviluppata. Tale capacità di assimilare il diverso, che era pure componente strutturale della Romanità, non fu totalmente persa quando nel IV secolo il cristianesimo fu sostenuto e poi imposto dall'Impero, cosicché le relazioni tra pagani e cristiani – persistendo anche negli ultimi due secoli la volontà

---

[2] Pur non potendo partecipare al convegno, SILVIA ORLANDI ha gentilmente mantenuto la sua promessa di preparare il proprio testo per gli Atti.

[3] P. BROWN, *Review* «*The Oxford Magazine*», 16 maggio 1963, 300-301, confluita in ID., *Religione e società nell'età di sant'Agostino*, Torino 1975, 137-140.

[4] Esplicito nel titolo, esso è riproposto nell'*Introduzione* e, in modo implicito, in quasi tutti gli altri saggi del volumetto, come sottolinea Averil Cameron, *infra*.

[5] L. CRACCO RUGGINI, *Perché e come si studia oggi la storia del mondo antico*, in *Storia Antica. Come leggere le fonti*, a cura di L. CRACCO RUGGINI, Bologna 2000², 14.

di far progredire la conversione – mantennero un carattere prevalentemente «dialogico»[6].

Vari lavori del nostro convegno, peraltro, hanno mostrato che piccoli e grandi conflitti interruppero il dialogo tra cristiani e pagani nella fase in cui la cristianizzazione si fece processo dinamico, investendo l'intera società romana. W. Liebeschuetz ha suggerito che il conflitto tra sistemi religiosi (*Il conflitto tra paganesimo e cristianesimo...*) corrispose, quasi inevitabilmente, al dialogo tra gli uomini (*Pagani e cristiani in dialogo...*). C'è molto di vero in tale considerazione, purché essa resti ancorata alla storia e, dunque, alla consapevolezza della fatale contingenza dei conflitti e del dialogo. Il problema è strettamente connesso con quello del prevalere della tolleranza e dell'intolleranza, fenomeno che non credo si possa spiegare con i caratteri intrinseci dell'uno o dell'altro sistema religioso: né il politeismo, che si era fatto più volte persecutorio, né il cristianesimo, che giunse spesso a chiedere l'intervento della mano armata dell'Impero – in altri momenti invocando entrambi la tolleranza[7] – furono per loro natura tolleranti o intolleranti. Mutamenti economici, politici e istituzionali influirono potentemente sulla capacità di allargare o restringere la tolleranza degli uomini, ora scatenando sopraffazione e violenza, ora rendendo ancora possibile il dialogo.

In tali termini, molte novità sono emerse dalle relazioni che i vari autori, «lasciati liberi di scegliere il loro argomento»[8], hanno offerto sul tema: alcune riguardano l'origine di *The Conflict* – che non raccoglie gli Atti di un Convegno, né conferenze progettate e decise da A. Momigliano, bensì *papers* dati al Warburg (e non tutti alla presenza del futuro curatore) per volere e su invito di Gertrud Bing, allora *Director* dell'*Institute*. Altre pro-

---

[6] Esemplificazioni e fonti in R. Lizzi Testa, *L'Eglise, les domini, les païens rustici: quelques strategies pour la christianisation de l'Occident (IVe-VIe siècle)*, in *Quid sit christianum esse. Le problème de la christianisation du monde antique*, colloque organisé par H. Inglebert, B. Dumézil et S. Destephen à l'Université de Paris X-Nanterre, les 26-27-28 mai 2008, in corso di stampa.

[7] Per la celebre requisitoria simmachiana, all'indomani della rimozione dell'altare della Vittoria dalla curia del senato e dell'abolizione dei privilegi delle Vestali, R. Lizzi Testa, *Introduzione. Le relazioni tra pagani e cristiani: nuove prospettive su un antico tema*, in *Le relazioni tra pagani e cristiani...*, 263 ss. ed ora, più in generale sul problema della tolleranza, Ead., *Il terrore delle leggi in difesa dell'insatiabilis honor della Chiesa: la retorica della rappresentazione cristiana dell'Impero*, in *Entre política, religión y legislación (ss. IV y V d.C.): convergencias, antagonismos y rectificaciones. Coloquio Internacional hispano-italiano, Zaragoza, 29-30 oct. 2009*, in corso di stampa.

[8] Seguendo l'esempio di A. Momigliano, *Prefazione all'edizione originale*, in *Il conflitto...*, XII.

vengono dall'analisi inedita del carteggio tra Momigliano e Giulio Einaudi in vista della traduzione italiana del volume, in un contesto di trattative durate anni (dal 1962 al 1968), durante i quali fu progettata e realizzata la pubblicazione anche di altri famosi testi. Né è mancata una lucida analisi del modo in cui si sviluppò – a partire dalla fine degli anni Trenta fino agli anni Sessanta e ben oltre[9] – la peculiare visione momiglianea del ruolo del cristianesimo nell'Impero, in un contesto europeo dominato dalle riflessioni di grandi storici della religione come E. Bonaiuti, F. Heer e E. Peterson, per i quali divenne centrale tornare a Costantino per capire come il cristianesimo (o meglio le differenti articolazioni del pensiero cristiano) avrebbe potuto reagire quando il *princeps* romano si fosse fatto *Führer*.

Al di là della sezione propriamente storiografica, su molti argomenti affrontati in *The Conflict* – sia che ivi fossero oggetto di singoli saggi o solo di brevi note – i contributi di questi Atti offrono riflessioni originali, non di rado con spirito critico. Per lo studio dell'età tardoantica, del resto, disponiamo ormai di una mole incredibile di nuovo materiale. Ma, soprattutto, una percezione diversa dei fenomeni religiosi, in gran parte suggerita dalla fiducia momiglianea del ruolo centrale che essi ebbero nella vita dell'Impero, ha consentito negli anni di riappropriarsi di fonti inedite, o che nessuno mezzo secolo fa avrebbe ritenuto versabili in un discorso storico.

In tal senso, riguardo a molti temi, la ricerca, per quanto già matura e variamente articolata, sembra ancora foriera di sviluppi. La consapevolezza che per parlare di cristianizzazione della storiografia sia prioritario stabilire dei criteri di definizione dei testi storiografici antichi rende questo settore di studi un'area suscettibile di ulteriori indagini. Il fatto che Giuliano, figura quasi elusa in *The Conflict*, abbia ricevuto un'attenzione straordinaria negli ultimi decenni è spia non solo della complessità dell'uomo e del principe, ma pure della ricchezza e dell'elusività del politeismo tardo, un sistema ibrido di dottrine, valori civici, speculazioni filosofiche, tentativi sperimentali di agire sulla trasformabilità della materia per attingere al divino, di cui solo qualche aspetto (tra cui la valorizzazione del culto eroico o delle pratiche magico-teurgiche) è oggi un po' meglio conosciuto. In un contesto effervescente di letture inedite secondo ottiche molteplici, le stesse relazioni tra pagani e cristiani risultano interpretabili, oltreché nella loro dimensione oggettiva, anche come proiezione di processi identitarî: pagani e paganesimo, nel corso degli ultimi secoli dell'Impero, divenne-

---

[9] Cfr. in G.M. ZAMAGNI, *infra*, il riferimento al saggio del 1986 sul problema del monoteismo in uno stato universale: A. MOMIGLIANO, *The Disadvantages of Monotheism for a Universal State*, in «Classical Philology» 81 (1986), 285-297.

ro un oggetto reso necessario dal bisogno cristiano di creare e ricreare un'identità smarrita o confusa e di mantenere viva l'evangelizzazione per il tramite dei consueti legami familiari e di amicizia, nonostante strutture e istituzioni imperiali profferissero la loro disponibilità a tal fine.

Il diffondersi del cristianesimo nella società romana, dunque, non provocò – come un tempo si credeva – uno scontro epocale tra due mondi diversi e in profondo contrasto, ma interazioni sottili, reazioni a volte minimali che favorirono l'osmosi, conflitti e scontri violenti, che in alcuni casi resero più rapida la conversione di intere masse rurali o civiche, nonché un deciso cambiamento che dette il significato della svolta. Ciò è parso chiarissimo nello studio delle trasformazioni provocate nelle manifestazioni culturali, che – pur costituendo una base unitaria irrinunciabile per pagani e cristiani – furono assoggettate a stridenti cambiamenti, magari favoriti dallo spirito di competizione artistica, più che da un dichiarato conflitto. Lo stesso sistema scolastico, creduto immutabile attraverso i secoli perché fortemente conservativo nei programmi e nei testi utilizzati, fu nella sostanza modificato dall'esigenza cristiana di imporre le sue distinzioni identitarie, sebbene tali operazioni fossero condotte in modi non sempre resi perspicui dalle fonti.

Allo stesso modo, molteplici fattori intervennero in ambito urbano – nelle città dell'Africa romana, ovvero in alcune metropoli siriache meglio documentate come Antiochia – a favorire la convivenza tra pagani e cristiani. I maggiorenti locali agirono su più registri, per lo più con la volontà di ridurre gli scontri rendendo l'ambiente civico uno spazio di neutralità religiosa meglio gestibile. Nondimeno i conflitti scoppiarono anche virulenti, catalizzati da motivazioni religiose, sebbene più spesso causati da altro; talvolta esagerati nella loro portata da fonti partigiane, furono spesso acuiti dalle emissioni legislative, per lo più vòlte a risolvere situazioni specifiche e quasi mai tali, comunque, da operare come fattore di conversione. Nell'Urbe stessa, l'aristocrazia senatoria seppe conservare più a lungo di quanto immaginato il controllo di culti e rituali che, per la loro intrinseca qualità pubblica, investivano aree di potere non facilmente, né troppo presto delegabili ai nuovi attori cristiani, anche se alla fine del IV secolo si cessò di dare pubblicità epigrafica ai sacerdozi tradizionali. Le osmosi linguistiche, riflesso della traslazione di ruoli un tempo gestiti dai sacerdoti pagani e poi dai funzionari pubblici (come in campo edilizio), gli slittamenti semantici tra divinizzazione e santità (come per gli imperatori cristiani) campeggiano chiari nelle fonti ma la loro esegesi, come per le brillanti tessere dei pavimenti musivi o per le scene di sarcofagi e altri imponenti pezzi architettonici, continua a sfidare la sensibilità moderna di cogliere in pieno i mutamenti che allora si verificarono.

La cristianizzazione, fattore comunque imponente nel suo divenire storico, fu processo lento e variegato, fatto di ripensamenti e contraddizioni, accelerazioni e tempi lentissimi a seconda delle regioni dell'Impero: ebbe modalità diverse nel centro e alla periferia; fu polimorfica nelle città e nelle campagne. I pagani costituirono infine un'alternativa reale sempre meno importante, in un mondo popolato anche da eretici, giudei, arabi, dei quali solo lentamente la ricerca odierna riesce ad apprezzare la consistenza e non solo in termini di alterità. L'epilogo naturalmente continua ad apparire scontato, sebbene rimeditare sul problema delle relazioni tra pagani e cristiani, mettendo in discussione facili modelli di «resistenza pagana» o di trito «eclettismo religioso», faccia scorgere non uno ma più epiloghi alla storia del divenire cristiano. Il politeismo mantenne, infatti, spazi importanti nell'immaginario comune e persino nelle pratiche di culto: alcune sono bene leggibili dietro la sommaria verniciatura cristiana, altre continuarono ad essere celebrate in segreto da nostalgici criptopagani, la cui entità è infine valutabile dalla circospetta lettura di molte nuove fonti archeologiche e vecchi testi letterari, fino a poco fa del tutto trascurati. Il conflitto pagani/cristiani, infine rimosso o attenuato, sullo scorcio del VI secolo si spostò all'interno della cristianità, quale contrasto tra modi diversi di concepire il cristianesimo, caricandosi della nuova alterità tra l'Occidente barbarico e l'Oriente bizantino.

Una riappropriazione storiografica dei contributi pubblicati in *The Conflict* ne ha dunque mostrato la peculiare natura di *summa* delle prospettive storiche, consolidatesi tra Ottocento e prima metà del Novecento, sul rapporto tra cristiani e pagani. Valutando la gamma di ricerche inedite che essi suggerirono, si ha la misura di quale fermento abbia creato nella cultura internazionale. In tal senso, nessuna migliore definizione potrebbe applicarsi al volume di quella che, a suo tempo, A. Momigliano usò per il libro di R. Syme, *The Roman Revolution* (Oxford, 1940), nell'*Introduzione* all'edizione italiana presso Einaudi (Torino, 1962, XIV): «Ma come tutti i grandi libri questo di Syme contiene in se stesso i germi delle più vere critiche future, appunto perché impone ricerche nuove».

Prima di congedare questo volume vorrei ringraziare Pino Ruggieri e Alberto Melloni, che hanno speso molte energie perché il convegno si realizzasse e avesse luogo a Bose: tutti noi, per alcuni giorni, abbiamo partecipato di una sorta d'incanto intellettuale e spirituale, di cui siamo grati alla Comunità di confratelli. Un grazie del tutto speciale va a Federico Ruozzi: umile, determinato, sempre cordiale, perfettamente organizzato, capace di coordinare tutti gli aspetti del Convegno e della pubblicazione dei suoi Atti.

Il cristianesimo di A. Momigliano

PETER BROWN

Back to the future: pagans and christians at the Warburg Institute in 1958

To return to the Warburg Lectures of 1958 on *The Conflict between Paganism and Christianity in the Fourth Century* is to return to a Britain (indeed, to a Europe) that still lay on the edge of deep shadows of tyranny and war. It was a Post-War world, set against the further, spreading shadow of the Cold War. The opening words of Herbert Bloch, as he began to speak on *The Pagan Revival in the West at the End of the Fourth Century*, made this plain:

> «Saint Bernard of Clairvaux says: *Habet mundus iste noctes suas, et non paucas* ("this world of ours has its nights, and not a few of them"). We ourselves have been passing through such a period of darkness for nearly half a century, uncertain even now as to whether the present respite will end in a true dawn or whether it is just another *hupoptos anokôkhé* – in Thucydides' words – of the kind that intervened between 1918 and 1939»[1].

Conflict was in the air. It was time to visit again the conflict between Christianity and Paganism. As Bloch made clear:

> «In times like ours, it becomes easier to understand kindred periods in which long-established traditions and values disintegrate... There has been no more momentous breakdown in the history of mankind than the one which marked the end of the ancient world and the final conflict between paganism and Christianity»[2].

And a conflict it had to be. The word «struggle» occurs frequently. Arnaldo Momigliano evoked the fierce energies deployed by Christians in creating, for themselves at the expense of the Roman empire, a «*civitas Dei* – a

---

[1] H. BLOCH, *The Pagan Revival in the West at the End of the Fourth Century*, in *The Conflict between Paganism and Christianity in the Fourth Century*, ed. A. MOMIGLIANO, Oxford 1963, 193-218, at 193.
[2] *Ibid.*, 193.

new commonwealth of men for men»[3]. With electrifying common sense, Hugo Jones showed how the «triumph of Christianity» was aided by social changes which had shaken the very foundations of the Roman Ancien Régime[4]. Henri-Irénée Marrou laid bare the inner struggles of Synesius of Cyrene:«It is a typical case of what Arnold Toynbee has taught us to call "schism in the soul"»[5].

Only the Marxist, E.A. Thompson told us, with his accustomed *grisaille* good sense, that, as far as the relations between Christianity and the northern barbarians were concerned, there was neither conflict nor triumph. The history of Christianity among the barbarians began only with «their transference from the wilds of *barbaria* into the social relationships of *Romania*»[6].

But, around the Mediterranean, it was agreed that a conflict had occurred and that each of the protagonists in this conflict had played their role with gusto. They did this according to a script that had been part of the master narrative of European history since the nineteenth century. Christians were predictably fierce. Their bishops were energetic: «They could tell both the learned and the unlearned how they should behave»[7]. And, of course, none did this better than did Saint Ambrose. He threw «the whole weight of his powerful and fearless personality into the struggle»[8].

For we must remember that, in 1958, Ambrose still weighed in as a heavyweight. We had to wait 36 years (that is, until 1994) for the nimble lightweight presented to us in Neil McLynn's *Ambrose of Milan. Church and Court in a Christian Capital*[9]. Pagans, by contrast, lacked the sinister intensity of their rivals. They were gentlemen: «Their mood was altogether that of generous and fair-minded liberalism»[10].

Our own experience of the fate of liberalism in an age dominated by ideologues and bullies, caused us to fear for the last pagans. Like amiable dodo birds, they were creatures doomed to extinction. But, before they

---

[3] A. MOMIGLIANO, *Introduction*, in *The Conflict...*, 1-16, at 6.
[4] A.H.M. JONES, *The Social Background to the Struggle between Christianity and Paganism*, in *The Conflict...*, 17-37, at 34-36.
[5] H.-I. MARROU, *Synesius of Cyrene and Alexandrian Neo-Platonism*, in *The Conflict...*, 126-150, at 128.
[6] E.A. THOMPSON, *Christianity and the Northern Barbarians*, in *The Conflict...*, 56-78, at 77.
[7] A. MOMIGLIANO, *Introduction...*, 9.
[8] *Ibid.*, 10.
[9] N. MCLYNN, *Ambrose of Milan. Church and Court in a Christian Capital*, Berkeley 1994.
[10] A. MOMIGLIANO, *Pagan and Christian Historiography in the Fourth Century*, in *The Conflict...*, 79-99, at 94-95.

vanished, they did what they were supposed to do, according to the script of the grand narrative of European civilization. They saved the classics[11].

They had copied manuscripts. They had spent no time, that I can see, worshipping – either God or the gods. In an Institute which bore the name of Aby Warburg, there was hardly an echo, in these lectures, of Paganism as a perpetual reminder of dark forces of the soul untamed by centuries of Christianity – such as is summed up by an entry in the index of Ernst Gombrich's *Aby Warburg. An Intellectual Biography*: «Paganism, see Frenzy, Myth, Primitive Mentality»[12].

Indeed, the principal protagonists were congratulated for having had as little as possible to do with such dark things[13]. And this is not surprising if much of Late Roman religion was anything like the world conjured up by A.A. Barb, speaking on *The Survival of the Magical Arts* in late antiquity: «The syncretistic, rotting refuse-heap of the dead and dying religions of the whole ancient world grew to mountainous height»[14].

It is as if it were Naples in the grip of a garbage strike.

And so the conflict ended, as it should have done, among gentlemen surrounded by their books. As Herbert Bloch concluded: «But the last Romans did not leave the stage of history without having made a lasting contribution [...] they devoted special attention to the preservation of Latin literature»[15].

No sooner had the lecturers and their heroes left the stage, than brisk stage-hands, of a younger generation, invaded it. Within a decade they had removed almost every stage-prop on which the drama had been based. In 1961, it was suggested that the last pagans of Rome may have paid more attention to their Christian wives and in-laws and to those subdued social interchanges which make up the *histoire de moeurs* in any period[16]. Only occasional moments of tension occurred; and these were provoked by the intervention of distant emperors and were amplified out of all proportion by strident Christian texts. By 1964, the «circle of Symmachus» had been disbanded[17]. By 1966, Macrobius had been moved a full generation away

---

[11] *Ibid.*, 98.
[12] E. GOMBRICH, *Aby Warburg. An intellectual biography*, London 1970.
[13] H.-I. MARROU, *Synesius of Cyrene*, in *The Conflict...*, 138.
[14] A.A. BARB, *The Survival of the Magical Arts*, in *The Conflict...*, 100-125, at 114.
[15] H. BLOCH, *The Pagan Revival in the West*, in *The Conflict...*, 213.
[16] P. BROWN, *Aspects of the Christianization of the Roman Aristocracy*, «Journal of Roman Studies» 51 (1961), 1-11.
[17] A. CAMERON, *The Roman Friends of Ammianus*, «Journal of Roman Studies» 54 (1964), 15-28.

from the world of Praetextatus and Nicomachus Flavianus[18]. By 1968, the author of the *Historia Augusta* had been revealed to be a «rogue *grammaticus*»[19]. The anonymous Christian poem, confidently ascribed to the stormy days of Nicomachus Flavianus, in 394, began to slither all over the place: in 1960, it broke loose and made an unsuccessful dash for 408; it has been known to wander as far as 431; it seems to have come to rest in 384, thanks to the discoveries of François Dolbeau and the erudition of Lellia Cracco Ruggini[20]. As for the famous conflict around the Altar of Victory, the recent articles of Charlotte Roueché[21] and, especially, that of Rita Lizzi Testa[22] have shown that the central issue in the *Relatio III* of Symmachus had nothing to do with the altar itself and even less with the winged statue which hovered above it.

And so the story continues. I trust that you will forgive my concentration on the somewhat limited field of fourth century Rome. I do this because the conflict between pagans and Christians in Rome has been held in the unusually strong grip of a master narrative. As Rita Lizzi says, this approach has ensured that we «tend to emphasize contingent situations and to invest them with absolute meanings»[23].

Every time such a contingent situation is divested of the ominous overload of meaning which it had been made to bear in conventional narratives of the end of paganism, scholars heave a sigh of relief. Each such article is a breath of pure oxygen, inhaled with gratitude in an atmosphere still heavy with false certainties.

So, to conclude, what shall we do with *Conflict*? I have come here largely to learn from you whether it is a concept that is still of use to us. For I do not think that it is any longer possible to isolate the conflict between paganism and Christianity as the principal and privileged motor force of change in the last centuries of the ancient world. It was one factor among others. We need both to re-read the evidence and to find a theo-

---

[18] A. CAMERON, *The Date and Identity of Macrobius*, «Journal of Roman Studies» 56 (1966), 25-38.

[19] R. SYME, *Ammianus and the Historia Augusta*, Oxford 1968, 103.

[20] L. CRACCO RUGGINI, *Il paganesimo romano tra religione e politica (384-394): per una reinterpretazione del Carmen contra paganos*, Rome, Accademia Nazionale dei Lincei 1979; F. DOLBEAU, *Damase, le* Carmen contra paganos *et Hériger de Lobbes*, «Revue des etudes augustiniennes» 27 (1981), 38-43.

[21] C. ROUECHÉ, *The Image of Victory. New Evidence from Ephesus*, in *Mélanges G. Dagron*, «Travaux et Mémoires» 14 (2002), 527-546.

[22] R. LIZZI TESTA, *Christian Emperors, Vestal Virgins and Priestly Colleges: reconsidering the end of paganism*, «Antiquité tardive» 15 (2007), 251-252.

[23] *Ibid.*, 253.

retical model, which will enable us to chart more accurately the extent to which this conflict impinged on the later Roman world as a whole.

Let me make a few suggestions based on modern experience. In 1997 two social scientists (a Russian and a Finn) published an article in the Russian journal, «Voprosy Filosofii». It was entitled *Believers, Atheists and Others: The Evolution of Russian Religious Feeling*. It examined the results of a series of public opinion polls conducted on attitudes to religion in the decade which followed the *Perestroïka* of Gorbachev – the Constantinian revolution of our age. The results merit our attention. They did not show a sudden, triumphant upsurge of Orthodoxy, consequent to the fall of Communism (as many religious persons claimed). Rather, the polls showed that the two «marked» categories – Atheist and Orthodox (each consciously embraced by the informants, and always in sharp contradistinction to each other) – remained stable. Neither was anywhere near a majority. Both stood at 25% each in 1987. These proportions – 25% and 25% – did not change throughout the entire decade. The real changes happened in the middle. Those who answered the first polls were content to offer, with Slavonic prudence, vague terms such as «waverer», «seeker» or «agnostic». But by the end of the decade, the middle ground had blossomed into a confident profusion of new age cults, astrology, palm-reading and evangelical Protestantism. Furthermore, the answers of those in the middle were distinguished by their vigor and confidence, compared with the somewhat gray antithesis invoked, against each other, by Orthodox believers and atheists[24].

It is for us, also, to recapture something of the warmth and color of a world not entirely given over to the two «marked» categories of pagan and Christian. In this matter, I think that we have made enormous strides since 1958. We know that, beside paganism and Christianity, there is an elephant in the room. This is the *saeculum*. We have come to appreciate the sheer vigor of a great imperial society, the rhythms of whose public life, whose civic excitements open to all classes, and whose shared upper class culture frequently pushed Christianity and paganism alike to the margins.

The issue is not only the size of this elephant: it is the ancient, warm blood that still flowed in its veins. In the fourth and fifth centuries, the saeculum could still endow with a suffused numinosity – with what Edward Shils has aptly termed a sense of «Awe-Inspiring Centrality»[25] – phenom-

---

[24] K. KAARIAINEN, D.E. FURMAN, *Veruiushschie, ateisti I prochie (evoliutsiia rossiiskoi religiozhnosti*, «Voprosy filosofii» 6 (1997), 35-52, esp. at 37-39.

[25] E. SHILS, *Center and Periphery. Studies in Macrosociology*, Chicago 1975, 257.

ena as diverse as the ceremonial of the court, the heavy roar of the Circus Maximus, the delicious dance of the Seasons in the newly discovered mosaic in the Via D'Azeglio in Ravenna, or the rich harvest of fifty years of archaeological discoveries of Middle Eastern mythological mosaics, garnered in the scintillating little book of Glen Bowersock, *Mosaics as History*[26].

We have come closer to answering the question which Henri-Irénée Marrou had posed a year before the Warburg Lectures, in 1957: *Civitas Dei, civitas terrena, num tertium quid?*[27]. Put briefly: in the last 50 years, we have discovered a lot of *tertium quid*. We have found, between the marked categories of pagan and Christian, a solid middle ground, bathed in a radiance all of its own.

Yet we must also make room for conflict. In order to find this room, we must know where to place our elephant on the map of late Roman society. Put very briefly; in Rome and elsewhere, both in the East and in the West, one cannot help noticing that common codes, which tended to push religious identities to one side, most usually crystallized around the upper classes[28]. They bore the menacingly serene smile of power and wealth. The discipline which they imposed did not always hold in all places, at all times and among all classes. To dismantle the notion of a conflict between pagans and Christians in the upper classes of the Roman world is a very real achievement of modern scholarship. But this may mean that we have been seeking for conflict in the very areas of late Roman society where we would be least likely to find it.

Altogether, we still need a more nuanced sociology of the later empire. My own recent work on the problems of wealth and poverty have convinced me that we have almost unconsciously committed ourselves, in the past half century, to an excessively «aristocratized» view of late Roman society. We look for Roman senators everywhere. We often fail to see the little big men, whose proliferation in every province of the empire is one of the most blatant features of the remodeling of Roman society to which A.H.M. Jones already drew attention in his path-breaking lecture in 1958. Nor have we followed through as pertinaciously as we should have done, Jones' observation that

---

[26] J.R. CURRAN, *Pagan City and Christian Capital. Rome in the Fourth Century*, Oxford 2000; M.G. MAIOLI, *Il complesso archeologico di Via d'Azeglio a Ravenna*, «Corso di cultura sull'arte ravennate» 41 (1994), 45-61; G.W. BOWERSOCK, *Mosaics as History. The Near East from Late Antiquity to Islam*, Cambridge 2006.

[27] H.-I. MARROU, «*Civitas Dei, civitas terrena, num terium quid?*», in *Studia Patristica* 2, Berlin 1957, 342-350.

[28] P. BROWN, *Power and Persuasion in Late Antiquity*, Madison, Wisconsin, 1992, 35-70.

«the main strength of Christianity lay in the lower and middle classes of the towns, the manual workers and clerks, the shopkeepers and merchants»[29].

Yet these *mediocres* were there in larger numbers and with a greater say in the affairs of their cities and their villages than we had once thought[30].

Altogether, we have to ask a basic question. Why do societies who seemed to have possessed tried and true methods of cohesion seem to opt, at times, for sharper identities, so that we can sense a novel, almost electric crackle in their atmosphere? I am struck by the case of modern Brazil. Here the remarkable spread of intransigent evangelical Protestantism has, in many circles, destroyed a previous consensus between Catholicism and alternative cults, such as *candomblé* and various forms of New Age religion. This consensus went by the name of *cortejão* – of cordiality. It was a code of conduct that was calculated to «avoid clashes [...] and exclusive affirmations of identity». But it did so on clear terms: «The myth of Brazilian cordiality [...] values relations of proximity between those who are different and of unequal status: masters and slaves, whites and blacks, Catholics and the followers of African religions»[31].

Cortejão was linked to firm notions of deference in a hierarchical society. Its basic social metaphor was «proximity between those who are different and of unequal status».

In some parts of the late Roman world, deference was an exacting school of tolerance. But it did not always work. We need only read the essays assembled by Johannes Hahn under the title of *From Temple to Church. Destruction and Renewal of Local Cultic Topography in Late Antiquity* to appreciate how varied was the map of pagan-Christian conflict. Issues of new patronage asserted and old deference withheld emerge as crucial variables in the different patterns of violence which appear on this map. The rhetoric of Shenoute of Atripe, intent on shaming a civic notable and former Duke of the Thebaid in front of the Christian congregation in the church of Panopolis (published by Stephen Emmel)[32], and the chilling manner in which Theophilos, patriarch of Alexandria, wrested control of the patronage networks

---

[29] A.H.M. JONES, *The Social Background*, in *The Conflict...*, 21.
[30] P. BROWN, *The Study of Elites in Late Antiquity*, «Arethusa» 33 (2000), 321-346, at 338-345.
[31] P. BIRMAN, M. PEREIRA LEITE, *Whatever happened to what used to be the largest Catholic country in the world?*, «Daedalus» 129 (2000), 271-290, at 273.
[32] S. VAN EMMEL, *Shenoute of Atripe and the Christian Destruction of Temples in Egypt: Rhetoric and Reality*, in *From Temple to Church. Destruction and Renewal of Local Cultic Topography in Late Antiquity*, ed. J. HAHN, S. VAN EMMEL, U. GOTTER, Leiden 2008, 161-201.

of the city from its traditional leaders, in the wake of the destruction of the Serapeum (as described by Johannes Hahn) takes us to a world considerably more frightening than the Rome we knew in 1958[33]. And yet, who in 1958, would have dreamt of the three cornered competition between Christians, Jews and pagans which we meet in the fifth-century Aphrodisias of Angelos Chaniotis[34]? We need a model of an entire society, as it changed relentlessly over the centuries, to do justice to the true dimensions of incidents of conflict between pagans and Christians and to their exact place on the social map of the late Roman world.

So let me conclude with the words of an *Altmeister* – William Lowther Clarke, author of *Saint Basil the Great: A Study in Monasticism* of 1913: «But it is just in this that the fascination of history lies; the student feels himself confronted by forces too mighty to be measured by any instruments at his disposal»[35].

O, come diceva il nostro Simmaco:
Uno itinere non potest perveniri ad tam grande secretum.
«Non si può giungere per un'unica via a un segreto così sublime»[36].

---

[33] J. HAHN, *The Conversion of Cult Statues: The Destruction of the Serapeum in 392 A.D. and the Transformation of Alexandria into a «Christ Loving» City*, in *From Temple to Church...*, 335-365.

[34] A. CHANIOTIS, *The Conversion of the Temple of Aphrodite at Aphrodisias in Context*, in *From Temple to Church...*, 243-273.

[35] W.K. LOWTHER CLARKE, *Saint Basil the Great. A Study in Monasticism*, Cambridge 1913, 14.

[36] SYMMACHUS, *Relatio* 3.10, transl. D. VERA, *Commento storico alle «Relationes» di Quinto Aurelio Simmaco*, Pisa 1981, 392.

ALBERTO MELLONI

Momigliano *in conflict.* Un'indagine nell'Archivio Einaudi, 1952-1968

La bibliografia su Arnaldo Momigliano è ormai una biblioteca a sé stante, e *pour cause*[1]. Il suo percorso intellettuale e spirituale rappresenta infatti le sfumature e più d'uno dei possibili esiti della vicenda italiana negli anni del fascismo: anni ai quali approda adolescente e dai quali viene espulso dalle leggi razziali per un esilio che non sarà interrotto col 1945, ma appena attenuato a metà anni Sessanta dal trasferimento della sua cattedra torinese, rimasta deserta, alla Normale di Pisa, nel segno d'una prudenza che tutti i ragazzi piemontesi conoscevano dall'autobiografia di D'Azeglio che mentre parla col re si ripete «Massimo, non ti fidare...».

Il rapporto destinato a divaricarsi con Croce e quello con De Sanctis[2], d'altronde, avevano inserito Momigliano dentro un filone nel quale la storia e la riflessione sulla storiografia non sapevano separarsi: e lo avevano legato ad un mondo romano nel quale, nonostante tutto, conserverà con-

---

[1] *L'archivio Arnaldo Momigliano, Inventario analitico*, a cura di GIOVANNA GRANATA, Roma 2006, XXXV-LVI. Lo stesso volume fornisce un bell'inventario analitico delle carte pisane del maestro, che, come si vedrà dai documenti che di seguito citerò dall'Archivio Einaudi, apertomi dalla incondizionata fiducia di Roberto Cerati che di cuore ringrazio, è tutt'altro che completo. Sulle carte cfr. anche *Omaggio ad Arnaldo Momigliano. Storia e storiografia sul mondo antico. Convegno di studio (Cuneo-Caraglio, 22-23 ottobre 1988)*, a cura di L. CRACCO-RUGGINI, Como 1989; *The Presence of the Historian: Essays in Memory of Arnaldo Momigliano*, ed. M.P. STEINBERG, in «History and Theory» 30 (1991); vari riferimenti nei saggi raccolti dalla «Rivista storica italiana» 100 (1988)/2, tutto dedicato a Momigliano e in «Storia della storiografia» 16 (1989).

[2] È in corso l'edizione del carteggio De Sanctis-Momigliano; sui loro rapporti cfr. L. POLVERINI, *Momigliano e De Sanctis*, in *Arnaldo Momigliano nella storiografia del Novecento*, a cura di L. POLVERINI, Roma 2006, 11-35 e G. CLEMENTE, *Arnaldo Momigliano e la storia della cultura*, «Archivio di storia della cultura» 2 (1989), 85-88. In S. BERTI, *Autobiografia, storicismo e verità storica in Arnaldo Momigliano*, «Rivista storica italiana» 100(1988)/2, 297-312 una fine analisi del distacco da Croce; più generale la ricostruzione di M. GIGANTE, *Momigliano e Croce*, in *Arnaldo Momigliano nella storiografia del Novecento...*, 37-67.

tatti decisivi, come quello con don Giuseppe De Luca, il dottissimo prete della storia della pietà che sarà anche il primo editore dei *Contributi*. Ma non avevano spezzato quel vincolo con l'ebraismo piemontese e italiano che era stato così forte – sia sul piano della letteratura teologica, sia sul piano di quella filosofica – in una giovinezza apertasi, quando Arnaldo aveva sedici anni, col suicidio di Felice[3] – quello la cui morte era stata salutata dal p. Gemelli con le agghiaccianti parole pubblicate nel 1924 su *Vita e pensiero* che tutti ricordano:

> «Un ebreo, professore di scuole medie, gran filosofo, grande socialista, Felice Momigliano è morto suicida [...]. Ma se insieme col Positivismo, il Socialismo, il Libero Pensiero e con il Momigliano morissero *tutti i giudei* che continuano l'opera dei giudei che hanno crocifisso Nostro Signore, non è vero che al mondo si starebbe meglio?»[4].

Cito questi elementi solo per giustificare il fatto che non mi misurerò con l'insieme di questa figura[5], anche se – anticipo qui una conclusione – la tesi di *The Conflict* e l'impianto di quelle lezioni tenute al Warburg Institute nel 1958[6], confluite nel volume edito in inglese e poi nel 1968 in italiano, non è *solo* una tesi storiografica sul IV secolo, ma è un *modo* di riflettere sull'atteggiamento del cristianesimo così come Momigliano l'aveva letto e capito fra gli anni Trenta e la fine della Seconda guerra mondiale[7] e di cui – vedremo alla fine una illuminante lettera a Dionisotti – lo stesso maestro dà ragione nel quadro di un programma di ricerca articolato.

Ciò che vorrei proporre, dunque, è una lettura del carteggio che Momigliano intrattiene con la casa editrice e poi con l'editore Einaudi, spesso mediato e sostituito dal rapporto epistolare con Bollati e con Vivanti – nel

---

[3] Momigliano lo commemora nel 1949 nel XXV della morte, cfr. G. CLEMENTE, *Arnaldo Momigliano*...

[4] G. MICCOLI, *L'atteggiamento delle chiese durante l'Olocausto*, in *Storia della Shoah*..., 1077-1120.

[5] R. DI DONATO, *Materiali per una biografia intellettuale di Arnaldo Momigliano*, I: *Libertà e pace nel mondo antico*; II: *Tra Napoli e Bristol*, «Athenæum», 83 (1995), 213-244 e 86 (1998), 231-244.

[6] Cfr. A. GRAFTON, *Momigliano's Method and the Warburg Institute: Studies in His Middle Period*, in *Momigliano and Antiquarianism. Foundations of the Modern Cultural Sciences*, ed. P.N. MILLER, Toronto 2007, 97-126.

[7] Lettera non firmata del 12/11/1952, 1 f. ds r. Sono particolarmente utili le indicazioni di L. SCHIROLLO, *Per Arnaldo Momigliano*, «Storia della storiografia» 16 (1989), 36 per l'influsso di Eric Weil sulla categoria del «rivolgimento radicale» nella interpretazione momiglianea.

quale si radica la decisione della pubblicazione in Italia di quel volume. Anche perché – ammesso che l'inventario dell'Archivio Momigliano edito di recente non abbia pecche – non tutto il coté einaudiano della vicenda è noto.

1. «Ci permettiamo di chiederle il suo avviso»

I rapporti con la più prestigiosa casa editrice del tempo, infatti, sono lunghi: iniziano attraverso contatti informali ancora negli anni Quaranta, quando Piero Treves parla a Momigliano in un dialogo fra condiscepoli di De Sanctis di una raccolta di storici dell'Ottocento[8]; si prolungano nel primo dopoguerra attraverso Venturi (che ad esempio, nel 1947 riceve dall'antichista il volume di Lewis B. Namier sul 1848[9]) e soprattutto nei primissimi anni Cinquanta passano dalla stima di Delio Cantimori[10] per disperdersi nelle discussioni sul progetto della storia universale.

Rapporti diretti e formali con la casa torinese s'avviano in forma impersonale il 12 novembre 1952, quando qualcuno (Solmi?) chiede parere allo storico sulla traduzione di alcune opere di storia romana (R. Syme, H.H. Scullard, H. Berve, M.P. Charlesworth) nelle quali gli è riconosciuta assoluta competenza[11]. In cambio gli vengono spediti a Bristol *Il Rinascimento* di Piero Pieri e *Il populismo russo* di Franco Venturi, avviando una pratica che nei suoi tratti essenziali (richieste, doni, controproposte) rimarrà aperta per oltre un trentennio. Momigliano, infatti, scrive a Torino a stretto giro di posta, il 15 novembre, dando i suoi responsi al «Caro Editore» *per puncta*: è positivo su Syme («un classico»), secco su Scullard («una imitazione di Syme senza l'aspro realismo», anche se mostra «maggior accuratezza nei particolari»), duro su Berve («un egregio nazista che ha cessato di scrivere cose serie nel 1926 [...]; è tutt'altro che uno stupido e sa scrivere, ma io lo lascerei alle cure dei missini»), franco su Charlesworth («un mediocre storico»). Ma l'occasione che gli viene offerta spinge

---

[8] L. MANGONI, *Pensare i libri. La casa editrice Einaudi dagli anni Trenta agli anni Sessanta*, Torino 1999, 196.
[9] *Ibid.*, 473.
[10] *Ibid.*, 632. Anche se lo stesso Cantimori, in un appunto del 4/12/1951 sulla traduzione del *Feudal Order* di Marion Gibbs raccomanda di «non domandare il parere su di lei a Momigliano!», *ibid.*, 793.
[11] A. GRAFTON, *Arnaldo Momigliano e la storia degli studi classici*, «Rivista storica italiana» 107 (1955), 91-109.

Momigliano a fare anche[12] una sua proposta, che diventerà l'occasione di quel negoziato infinito sul quale si inseriscono altre proposte e altre idee. Scrive in coda alla sua lettera Momigliano:

> «È strano che con una piccola eccezione niente sia stato tradotto in italiano del più grande storico dell'antichità di questo secolo, E. Meyer. Non suggerirei naturalmente di tradurre la *Geschichte des Altertums*. Ma ci sono delle *Kleine Schriften* e nel secondo volume delle *Forschungen zum Alten Geschichte* delle cose tuttora luminose».

Momigliano dovrebbe saperlo: ma la macchina editoriale dell'Einaudi ha le sue regole e formalità politico-culturali inflessibili. Il 23 dicembre gli si risponde che, con l'assenso di Chabod e Cantimori, Eduard Meyer si tradurrà e si chiede a Momigliano di esserne curatore[13]. Cosa che Momigliano accetta facendo proposte sul traduttore[14], ma poi evadendo fino a novembre dell'anno dopo la consegna di un indice. Giulio Einaudi nel frattempo prende in mano personalmente la corrispondenza con lo storico londinese: lo consulta su Ostrogorski e Vasiliev[15], sull'idea di Chabod che possa curare le *Causes de la grandeur et décadence des Romains* di Montesquieu, su quella di Petazzoni di tradurre la *Römische Religionsgeschichte* di Altheim[16]: trova in Momigliano un interlocutore aperto sul piano culturale[17], meno sul piano più aziendale, nel quale lo vorrebbe implicare

---

[12] Momigliano a Einaudi («Caro Editore»), 15/11/1952, biglietto di 1 f. ms r/v e 1 f ms r su carta intestata dell'University College London (come anche tutti i successivi biglietti citati, con una sola variante di cui *infra*); il maestro chiede che gli si mandi R. Treves e Kelsen.

[13] Ne cita qualche passo L. MANGONI, *Pensare i libri...*, 813.

[14] Momigliano a Einaudi, 30/12/1952, biglietto ms di 2 pp s 1 ff: propone Caterina Caprino o in subordine i nomi ben noti a Chabod di Gigante o Giarrizzo. Dopo altri scambi Einaudi propone un contratto di curatela a Momigliano del valore di £ 100 mila e un conto presso Charles Bode, il libraio di Clive Court a Londra per l'acquisto dei libri da usare.

[15] Momigliano a Einaudi («Caro Editore»), 6/10/1953, 1 f.ms r/v.

[16] Sui rapporti con la religionistica italiana cfr. C. GINZBURG, *Momigliano e de Martino*, «Rivista storica italiana» 100 (1988)/2, 400-413 e G. STROUMSA, *Arnaldo Momigliano and the History of Religions*, in *Momigliano and Antiquarianism...*, 286-311: sull'influsso di De Martino in Einaudi, via Pavese, cfr. G. TURI, *Casa Einaudi. Libri uomini idee oltre il fascismo*, Bologna 1990, 236 e i riferimenti dello stesso A. MOMIGLIANO, *Per la storia delle religioni nell'Italia contemporanea: Antonio Banfi ed Ernesto De Martino tra persona ed apocalissi*, «Rivista storica italiana» 99 (1987), 444.

[17] Suggerisce il libro di Iris Murdoch su Sartre, Momigliano a Solmi, 23/11/1953, 1 f.ms r/v: «Non è la mia partita, ma val la pena di conoscerlo e farlo conoscere traducendolo».

offrendogli di sottoscrivere le azioni per la ricapitalizzazione della società nel marzo 1955.

La vicenda delle *Forschungen zur alten Geschichte* di Meyer però si dilunga a non finire; solo a dicembre 1955 Momigliano trova la copia per la Caprino, la traduttrice; poi scrive per accertarsi che sia pagata[18]; e a novembre del 1957 Giulio Einaudi gli scrive per ricordargli che vorrebbe «pubblicare nel 1958 la raccolta di scritti di Meyer curata da Lei e tradotta, se ben ricordo, sotto il Suo patrocinio[19]».

Ma l'editore ha anche capito che ben altro è da chiedere: e in quella occasione dice che la sua Casa vorrebbe avere un libro propriamente suo, foss'anche una «raccolta tutta in italiano» di saggi usciti in inglese e tedesco. Momigliano svicola: propone un'aggiunta al Meyer e chiede altre 20-30mila lire per la Caprino per tradurre il discorso autobiografico pronunciato da Meyer per il suoi 75 anni, rinvia alla parola di Franco Venturi, che fa la spola con Londra. Finché le cose si chiariranno con la lettera di Giulio Einaudi del 29 novembre: «Venturi mi ha detto che possiamo sperare di essere gli editori non di una raccolta di Suoi scritti, ma d'un libro sulla storiografia dell'antichità al quale sta lavorando[20]».

Poi un silenzio che s'interrompe nel 1959 con la richiesta di un parere su *Hellenism* di Toynbee che, pur in partenza per Chicago dove ha iniziato una presenza nuova e altamente stimolante sul piano scientifico, Momigliano accetta. Nel frattempo, mentre le altre proposte bollono in pentola[21], Meyer resta al palo: la richiesta di Einaudi di aver l'introduzione il 4 marzo 1960 resta sospesa[22] fino a gennaio 1961. Anno in cui finalmente

---

[18] Momigliano a Einaudi («Caro Editore»), 30/1/1956 e 12/3/1956, entrambi brevi biglietti di 1 f.ms r.

[19] Einaudi a Momigliano, 14/11/1957, 1 f.ds r.

[20] Einaudi a Momigliano, 29/11/1957, 1 f.ms r/v (sulla stessa carta intesta dell'University College indicata *supra*, ma da qui in poi con il dipartimento e il nome di Momigliano a stampa). Sui saggi di *Studies in Historiography*, London 1966 e *Essays in Ancient and Modern Historiography*, Oxford 1977 (poi in *La storiografia greca*, Torino 1982), cfr. in *Omaggio ad Arnaldo Momigliano*...

[21] Momigliano a Einaudi, 7/3/1960, 1 f.ms r/v su carta intestata del dipartimento dell'University College London: lo studioso dà parere favorevole alla storia greca di Hermann Bengston, «un po' la caricatura del professore tedesco: gioviale (debitamente nazista in giovinezza), onesto, paziente, bene informato, chiaro e competente»; entusiasta invece su Wilamowitz.

[22] L'editore vuole l'originale per controllare la traduzione ma Momigliano non vuole mandare la sua preziosa edizione, antecedente la censura post-bellica.

esce Syme – il libro capostipite di questo carteggio – al quale Momigliano appone qualche pagina di prefazione[23].

2. Tutto tranne Meyer

Altri consigli, altre richieste arrivano e partono da Torino, spesso (la prima di questo genere è del novembre 1962) legate al «caro Bollati». Lettere scherzose[24], in parte perdute o sostituite dagli ormai frequenti viaggi in Italia e a Torino in ispecie. Lo sappiamo proprio dalla prima lettera nella quale Momigliano accenna alla traduzione di *The Conflict*[25] e nella quale si mostra assai aperto alle scelte del suo nuovo editore: «Intanto le volevo dire questo. Toccherà a voi decidere quale priorità intendete dare al volume su *Paganism and Christianity* in confronto all'altro che G. Lepschy deve tradurre per voi».

In realtà l'accenno non serve solo a dire che Giulio Lepschy deve essere pagato regolarmente, – «queste traduzioni sono parte essenziale del suo pane quotidiano»[26] – ma anche a precisare che «nella trad. italiana del volume su *Paganism etc.* potremmo fare qualche opportuna aggiunta[27]».

La traduzione delle *Lectures* al Warburg viene affidata, su proposta di Momigliano[28], ad Anna Davies Morpurgo, «pronta a passare a Torino» per chiudere un contratto di cui è ancora referente Bollati. Da dicembre 1963, infatti, appaiono nuovi interlocutori nel rapporto fra la casa editrice e il maestro: gli scrivono Caprioglio[29], Ponchiroli che vorrebbe aggior-

---

[23] R. SYME, *La rivoluzione romana*, introduzione di Arnaldo Momigliano, Torino, Einaudi, 1962 (1974); Momigliano a Einaudi, 26/10/1961 accetta e le promette per il 5/11 e che arriva a Torino il 10.

[24] Ad es. Momigliano a Bollati, 8/11/1962, 1 f.ms r che chiede copia della traduzione di Dumézil: «L'ho spedita a suo tempo ma ora vedo che Dumézil la indica come l'unica versione legittima delle sue diatribe teoriche. E perciò necessaria per i miei esorcismi. Voi sarete inclusi nei suffumigi. Abracadabra, bracdabr, racadad...».

[25] *L'archivio Arnaldo Momigliano. Inventario analitico...*, 199 e 397, identifica, secondo me equivocando, con una stipula con Einaudi del 21/2/1968 il contratto per l'edizione italiana di *Il conflitto*.

[26] Momigliano a Bollati, 10/3/1063, 1 f.ms r/v; Bollati a Momigliano, 25/3/1963, 1 f.ds r, dà conferma che la richiesta di Momigliano è stata accolta.

[27] Momigliano a Bollati, 10/3/1063, cit.

[28] Momigliano a Bollati, 19/7/1963, 1 f.ms r.

[29] Non unico: la stroncatura nel biglietto di Momigliano a Caprioglio del 10/2/1964, 1 f.ms r, liquida Claudio Masetti come orientalista («la sostanza del commento è che Masetti è approssimativamente competente, ma non appieno informato e padrone del

nare Wilamowitz[30], Guido Davico Bonino che si scusa del triste destino della Qaballah di Scholem[31] – e poi Corrado Vivanti, che nel periodo di svolta del 1963-64[32] diventa il principale referente dello storico anglopiemontese, intessendo con lui un dialogo alla pari, nel quale Momigliano si muove con libertà. Al giovane studioso mantovano che aveva rimbalzato con entusiasmo le voci su un rientro del maestro in patria[33], il 3 maggio 1964 Momigliano risponde in modo secco e duro. Nessun rientro, solo una docenza: «Falso il mio ritorno in Italia, naturalmente. Probabile il mio passaggio in forza alla Normale di Pisa con varie conseguenze pratiche (del resto già andavo ogni anno a predicarci)»[34].

Nel frattempo, però, nel carteggio con Bollati riappare *The Conflict*, ormai associato di fatto all'eterno sogno degli scritti di Meyer: a fine novembre 1964 il maestro scrive:

> «Caro Bollati, spero ci vedremo durante il mio breve passaggio a Torino il 9-10 dicembre prossimo. Potrebbe forse combinare con Franco [Venturi] il 10. Ma mi preoccupa che la Morpurgo a Oxford non sia stata ancora pagata per la traduzione del volume *Paganism and Christianity*. Vorrei anche sapere quando e come lo farete uscire. Dopo la triste sorte del Meyer (Ed.) sono diventato sospettoso e pessimista»[35].

Bollati, punto sul vivo, dà mandato di pagare la Morpurgo: ma sette mesi dopo, il 30 giugno 1965, sono necessarie ulteriori rimostranze...

---

suo argomento») e suggerisce di usarlo per traduzioni o revisioni di traduzioni dal russo, come accadrà.

[30] «Aggiornamento? Nemmeno per ridere: non si aggiornano le Bibbie, o sconsacrati del centro-sinistra!», Momigliano a Ponchiroli, 16/3/1964, 1 f.ms r.

[31] Lettera dell'editore a Momigliano, 27/4/1964, 1 f.ds r (siglato CDB.csm).

[32] Così lo identifica R. Di Donato, *Gli anni di Londra*, in *Arnaldo Momigliano nella storiografia del Novecento...*, 125.

[33] Vivanti a Momigliano, 2/4/1964, 1 f.ds r: «Mi è giunta voce di un Suo rientro in Italia e – se ciò fosse vero – ne sarei estremamente lieto, non solo per la possibilità di incontrarla forse più spesso, ma per il beneficio che ne deriverebbe alla scuola italiana. È vero che gettati «parmi la tyrannie des Loyolites» – come scriveva Gillot allo Scaligero, di cui si ventilava il ritorno a Parigi, nei primi tempi di ritorno alla pace civile – «nous ne méritons point cela». Ma proprio il suo insegnamento potrebbe evidentemente giovare moltissimo».

[34] Momigliano a Vivanti, 3/3/1964, f.ms r/v: nella lettera propone Simonsohn «ma non a Giulio».

[35] Momigliano a Bollati, 29/11/1964, 1 f.ms r con allegato un foglio di bloc-notes ms con un indice degli *Scritti scelti* di E. Meyers.

3. *Paganism*

Nel frattempo, però, emergono i problemi di una traduzione nata male, le cui lacune vengono inizialmente sottovalutate. Scrivendo a Vivanti, nell'ottobre 1965, Momigliano scherza sulla proposta di tradurre Epstein – «è da rabbino per i rabbini. Non roba per voi, o per me» – e suggerisce per pure ragioni pratiche di rimandare la traduzione di *Paganism* alla Morpurgo perché «riveda la forma»; un rapido accenno in una lettera nella quale sogna che E.R. Dodds, *Pagan and Christian in an Age of Anxiety* sul III secolo possa «utilmente supplementare il mio tomo»[36]. Ma la lentezza einaudiana qualche irritazione deve averla suscitata, se a febbraio 1966 tocca a Giulio Einaudi in persona scrivere a Gower Street per domandare una prefazione *ad hoc* all'edizione italiana di *The Conflict*.

> «Stiamo per mettere ai fornelli *Conflict between Paganism and Christianity* e ci viene spontaneo farle una richiesta che spero non risvegli il Suo risentimento (siamo, per restare in tema, dei figlioli prodighi e vorremmo essere riammessi nella casa del padre). Non pensa che sarebbe opportuno presentare al lettore questa raccolta di studi, che Lei apre in modo così drammatico? Le propongo questo perché Lei, in questo modo, potrebbe far cenno, se la cosa Le sembra utile, a studi apparsi in questi due anni[37]».

La lettera – che fa vanto di tre libri fatti per onorare il parere dello storico, ma nei quali imprudentemente Einaudi menziona il Meyer – va a segno solo parzialmente. Momigliano punge appena su Meyer, ma si sottrae all'idea di una nuova introduzione, anche se usa un tono di confidenza («ci davamo del tu? posso continuare?») che vuole appianare la tensione: ma la sostanza è chiara.

> «Bene per i fornelli sotto il *Conflict* – cerchiamo di tenerli per eterno brucianti! Ma veramente sconsiglio una introduzione alla introduzione del medesimo. Per una ragione semplice di buon gusto. Non è un libro mio: è un libro in collaborazione. Io già canto due volte, mentre i miei colleghi cantano una volta sola. Se canto tre volte, prendo un'aria da prima donna, che se ricordi i miei

---

[36] Momigliano a Vivanti, 26/10/1965, 1 f.ms r/v; già il 25/6/1965 in una comunicazione a Santoni, Guido Davico Bonino allegava «un mandato per la traduzione consegnata nel settembre '64, delle *Lotte tra paganesimo e Cristianesimo nell'antica Roma*, curata da Momigliano. Costui, in un recente incontro col nostro Vivanti, ha fatto ampie rimostranze sull'incidente. Vivanti ne ha avvertito E[inaudi], che ieri sera mi ha raccomandato il pagamento».

[37] Einaudi a Momigliano, 11/2/1966, 1 f.ds r. Einaudi presenta la lista di tutte le cose fatte «in onore» di Momigliano, cioè Ostrogorski in riedizione, Meyer da ripubblicare anche nella «Nuova Universale», Tacito, ecc.

"connotati personali" non mi si confà. Il libro ha un suo reale interesse com'è, senza pretese. Qui è alla 2^{nda} edizione»[38].

Pochi giorni dopo Einaudi ringrazia (accettando il «tu»), incassando la lettera del maestro come una manifestazione della volontà di non rompere i rapporti, pur davanti ad un saldo non proprio positivo dei rapporti con la casa editrice torinese[39]. Ma Momigliano ha già scritto a Vivanti, per sapere com'è la traduzione e se può «risparmiarsi il travaglio» di una correzione delle bozze[40]. La risposta che riceve (passata al vaglio di Giulio Einaudi...) introduce un tema che sarà causa di ulteriori ritardi e litigi: Vivanti spiega al maestro «che non sarebbe inopportuno apporre in calce alla *Preface* un'altra mezza pagina di nota all'edizione italiana»[41].

La risposta di Momigliano arriverà in una lettera del 9 ottobre, a meno d'un mese dalla morte di Cantimori alla quale gli «è impossibile rassegnarsi», piena di preoccupazione per Emma Cantimori. Passando al lavoro Momigliano risponde alle proposte su Gibbon, pur protestando ancora su Meyer, e accetta con qualche stizza la richiesta d'inizio anno: «Vedrò un po' di aggiungere una prefazione alla prefazione della prefazione del Pagani e Crist. Più che si ritarda, più ahimè diventa inevitabile»[42].

A novembre 1966 – c'è sempre la questione della revisione della traduzione in ballo – pare ricredersi, quasi rassegnato davanti a quello che sembra una replica del Meyer: «Ci penseremo un po' più tardi a un'eventuale seconda introduzione. Ma veramente bisogna che il libro *esca* non più tardi di aprile prossimo: altrimenti è tutto vecchio. Aveva una sua freschezza, che si perde di giorno in giorno»[43].

Il pessimismo di Momigliano davanti allo sfiorire di *The Conflict* viene però confermato a dicembre a Vivanti quando gli prospetta una raccolta

---

[38] Momigliano a Einaudi, 19/2/1966, 1 f.ds r/v.
[39] Einaudi a Momigliano, 1/3/1966, 1 f.ds r.
[40] Momigliano a Vivanti, 20/2/1966, 1 f.ms r: «Caro Vivanti, com'è la trad. della Morpurgo del *Conflict*? È il caso che le bozze siano riguardate anche dal sottoscritto? Spererei di risparmiarmi questo travaglio» e chiede che gli si mandi «il Vico di Fubini», le *Lettere dal carcere* di Gramsci e «*[Il problema del]L'origine e della natura del linguaggio [nel Cratilo di Platone]* di M. Fano».
[41] Vivanti a Momigliano, 17/3/1966, 1 f.ds r/v con una nota ms (per Einaudi?) che dice «Ho pensato di scrivere a Momigliano: dai per piacere un'occhiata? E pensi tu, per piacere, a farla imbustare?».
[42] Momigliano a Vivanti, 9/10/1966, 1 f.ds r/v. Le richieste di libri – Pavese, Löwith e Adorno – sono interessantissime.
[43] Momigliano a Vivanti 1/11/1966, 1 f.ms r/v: qui la proposta di una biografia di Cantimori scritta da Emma.

di saggi per la «storica» einaudiana[44], che fa capire come *The Conflict* non fosse diventato ancora una priorità.

4. «E accidenti»

In una delle pochissime lettere senza data del carteggio, ma collocabile a fine 1966, Momigliano prende finalmente in mano la traduzione di *The Conflict* ormai in bozze e s'infuria. S'infuria con l'editore (che annota a mano sulla lettera «Mi piace, perché la traduttrice ce l'ha mandata lui!»), ma anche con un progetto che pare a questo punto traballare:

> «Ho letto il primo e parte del secondo dei miei due capitoli del *Paganesimo e Cristianesimo*. Il primo capitolo contiene vari *errori* e per di più traduzioni infelici. Il secondo, se va avanti così, dovrà semplicemente essere ricomposto: incredibile. Io non ho tempo per rivedere tutto il volume, e in verità non ho nemmeno tempo da perdere con i miei capitoli. Suggerirei intanto di mandare ciascun capitolo al suo autore. Qualcuno capirà poco; ma almeno Barb, Bloch, Marrou e Courcelle – e forse anche Jones si accorgeranno delle marronerie più grosse. La Morpurgo sa l'inglese come un inglese ma probabilmente ha tradotto tutto in fretta e forse va dimenticando l'italiano. Con tanta perdita di tempo l'ispirazione per una nuova prefazione va al diavolo. Potreste tuttavia per i miei capitoli aggiungere intanto le poche indicazioni bibliografiche che si trovano nel testo inglese così come ristampato nel mio *Terzo contributo*, tomo I: questo vi darà un aggiornamento bibliografico per i due capitoli che, essendo a carattere generale, più si prestano. Vi manderò il conto delle ore bestialmente perdute: spero me le paghetere a 1000 lire l'ora, che è quanto mia sorella prende per le lezioni di latino ai ragazzini. E accidenti. Con affettuosi (tuttavia) saluti, Arnaldo»[45].

Giulio Einaudi riesce ancora una volta a farsi perdonare: lo ingolosisce con richieste di pareri, gli manifesta interesse («abbiamo avviato la lettura dell'*Agostino* di Brown, che tu cortesemente mi segnalasti»[46]), si adopera con zelo per far uscire Gibbon con la sua prefazione (tre volumi sul cui

---

[44] Vivanti a Momigliano, 12/12/1966, 3 ff.ds r, con 3 ff.ds allegati di indice.
[45] Momigliano a Vivanti, fra il dicembre 1966 e il gennaio 1967, 1 f.ms r/v.
[46] Einaudi a Momigliano, 5/5/1967, 1 f.ds r. Una vivace difesa contro un anonimo detrattore in Momigliano a Einaudi, 11/5/1967, 1 f.ms r: «Nei termini in cui sono state poste le obiezioni all'Agostino di P. Brown sono assurde: il libro è sottile e originale, proprio il contrario d'un manuale, ed è fondato su una eccezionale conoscenza di storia sociale del Basso Impero. Bisogna che tu conosca un giorno P. Brown, uno dei più bei tipi di questo noioso mondo». Si veda per converso il ricordo di P. BROWN, *A. Dante Momigliano*, «Proceedings of the British Academy» 74 (1988), 405-442.

prezzo Momigliano ironizzerà pesantemente[47]). Ma di *The Conflict* nessuna notizia, fino al 26 giugno, quando Vivanti gli annuncia che «il *Conflict* dovrebbe inaugurare la ripresa autunnale, e spero che non ci siano altri incidenti»[48].

Annuncio avventato. Il 6 novembre Momigliano chiede lumi, dando un esempio di come la complicazione della sua bibliografia abbia indotto Routledge ad una gaffe imperdonabile:

> «Spero che il tomo sul conflitto tra Paganesimo e Crist. si avvicini in porto: ho ricevuto una lettera di Routledge e Kegan Paul che mi offrono di comprarlo per una traduzione in inglese! Ho risposto che siffatti esercizi di ritraduzione non sono economici e per di più vietati dagli accordi internazionali. Ma vedete voi quali aspettative desta la vostra fatica»[49].

Da Torino Vivanti deve informarlo che un eccesso di zelo tarda ancora una volta l'uscita già molte volte procrastinata:

> «Paganesimo e cristianesimo è la fola dello stento. La traduzione, rivista da persona di fiducia, è caduta sotto gli occhi di Carena, il quale ha trovato che molti passi (soprattutto nelle traduzioni dal latino) lasciavano a desiderare. Motivo per cui lo si sta rivedendo: la domanda di chi rivede il revisore, come noterà, viene largamente applicata. In ogni modo a gennaio il libro dovrebbe proprio uscire. Ma la storiella della ritraduzione in inglese è pero molto divertente. Il medesimo Carena ha già visto un paio di prove di traduzione dell'amico Peter Brown, che non lo hanno per niente soddisfatto. E invece il testo merita proprio una persona di fiducia»[50].

Nonostante l'irritazione per Carena (colpevole innanzi agli occhi di Momigliano dell'irredimibile colpa di aver definito l'Agostino di Brown una compilazione[51]), anche la mancata prefazione, la cui ispirazione era naufragata sulle marronerie della Morpurgo riprende quota: la promette entro il 20 gennaio una lettera del 7 gennaio nella quale il maestro conferma a Vivanti che manderà «una prefazione al *Pagan.+Crist.* in cui tra l'altro darò in nota un elenco delle rec. più importanti alla edizione inglese

---

[47] E. GIBBON, *Storia della decadenza e caduta dell'Impero romano*, tr. di G. FRIZZI, con un saggio di Arnaldo Momigliano, Torino 1967.
[48] Vivanti a Momigliano, 26/6/1967, 1 f.ds r/v.
[49] Momigliano a Vivanti, 6/11/1967, 1 f.ms r/v.
[50] Vivanti a Momigliano, 11/11/1967, 1 f.ds r/v.
[51] Momigliano a Vivanti, 2/1968 [n. 108], 1 f.ms r/v: «non capisco perché voi vi siate resi prigionieri di Carena sia per il mio tomo sia per quello di Peter Brown. Non è quel Carena che riteneva Peter Brown un compilatore? Saprà il latino...».

– e qualche altra notizia utile e dilettevole. Spero spedire *prima del 20 gennaio*[52]».

Il manoscritto della prefazione italiana effettivamente arriva per tempo e il 6 febbraio, sentendosi certo dell'uscita dell'opera, Momigliano dà disposizioni per gli invii di dovere delle prime copie al Warburg, e ai collaboratori[53]. Ormai, dice lui, è chiaro che molti non scriverebbero più come hanno scritto nove anni prima. Non certo Momigliano la cui visione delle cose ha subito significativi sviluppi. Ma finalmente si arriva in porto. Il 20 marzo solennizza la consegna Giulio Einaudi:

> «Caro Momigliano, con piacere ti ho fatto spedire la prima copia della nostra edizione de *Conflitto tra paganesimo e cristianesimo*. Dico "nostra" giacché in questo caso la tua collaborazione si è rivelata determinante. Mi auguro che tu voglia ancora lavorare con noi con eguale lena: la prossima meta, per non dire di altre iniziative, dovrebbe essere la raccolta dei tuoi saggi»[54].

Momigliano reagisce solo a maggio chiedendo fra l'altro che si regoli il pagamento dell'introduzione nuova[55]: ma comunicare nell'Italia del 1968 è difficile e le incomprensioni crescono. Momigliano partecipa con pena al crollo di Garzetti, che «dopo le persecuzioni degli studenti, soffre di un esaurimento nervoso grave». E il manifesto di Giulio Einaudi nel primo numero di *Libri nuovi* pone

> «per me e non solo per me problemi seri di collaborazione. Il manifesto è vago – e naturalmente in astratto c'è poco con cui non si sarebbe d'accordo. Ma o l'articolo non vuol dire niente o vuol dire una rottura con il passato di casa Einaudi, che è in molta misura il passato di noi tutti intellettuali italiani antifascisti. Bisognerà dunque vedere che cosa casa Einaudi intende fare. È il meno

---

[52] Momigliano a Vivanti, 7/1/1968, 1 f.ms r/v. È allegata a questa lettera e datata «gennaio 1968» la prefazione: 3 ff.ms r, con ampia grafia, in carta bianca.
[53] Momigliano a Vivanti, 6/2/1968, 1 f.ms r/v.
[54] Einaudi a Momigliano, 20/3/1968, 1 f.ds r: il volume *Il conflitto tra paganesimo e cristianesimo nel secolo IV*, saggi a cura di A. Momigliano, Torino 1968 sarà ristampato nel 1971[2] e nel 1975[3].
[55] Momigliano a Vivanti, 14/5/1968, 1 f.ms r/v: «sono tornato dall'America e ho per lei i saluti di Braudel incontrato in quel di Chicago. Vorrei domandare: 1) anzitutto, è vero che Einaudi ruppe un contratto già firmato con Getto per disaccordo ideologico? La cosa mi è stata riferita; mi pare incredibile e spero venga smentita e spero di poter contribuire a smentirla. 2) è avvenuto il versamento di 100.000 lire per Miss Meyer? 3) è previsto un pagamento, sia pure modesto, per la mia prefazione all'ed. italiana del *Conflitto*? Se non altro per la mia efficienza (e vostra in...)».

che possa dire in questo momento. Marcuse non è il sostituto per la filologia, cioè per il rispetto ai fatti, da qualunque parte siano scoperti»[56].

Ancora pochi mesi è un nuovo articolo sulla «delinquenza accademica» dei professori apparso su *Libri nuovi* fa indignare Momigliano, anche con Vivanti che risponde[57] cercando di salvare un rapporto che si salverà e andrà poi avanti per altre vie[58]. Un passaggio amaro del 25 novembre spiega l'amara rassegnazione/indignazione di Momigliano[59]: «Ciò che mi preoccupa è che quando si abbandona l'unico criterio valido in cultura – che è quello della discussione spassionata dei risultati della ricerca – si va oggi giorno di filato nel Nazismo: lo si chiami contestazione o altrimenti».

5. Il senso d'una ricerca

Per quanto legate ad un periodo felice del lavoro momiglianeo, i saggi suoi su *The Conflict* non rappresentano né il principale lavoro di Momigliano né quello che gli resta più caro anche se, è lui stesso a dirlo, la funzione di quell'analisi nel *Terzo contributo* gli pare centrale[60]. Era una

---

[56] Momigliano a Vivanti, 2/7/1968, 1 f.ms r/v.
[57] Momigliano a Vivanti, 11/10/1968, 1 f.ds r, e Vivanti a Momigliano, 18/10/1968, 1 f.ms r/v.
[58] Dei saggi si riparla per il *Terzo contributo* in italiano, di cui i carteggi einaudiani conservano note per un indice.
[59] Momigliano a Vivanti, 25/11/1968, 1 f.ds r: dichiara che nelle ultime settimane «abbastanza fatti si siano accumulati per chiarificare il nostro dissenso». In primo luogo Momigliano attacca la pubblicistica della rivista icona della ribellione giovanile: «La *New Left Review*, che è esplicitamente vostra alleata, ha attaccato in massa gli intellettuali "stranieri" in Inghilterra dal defunto Namier al vivente Gombrich (autori di casa Einaudi) come reazionari al servizio della società reazionaria di Gran Bretagna. L'attacco, di ovvio carattere xenofobo e anti-semita, è la più chiara indicazione delle implicazioni di una politica populista che subordina la cultura alla ideologia del momento. Poiché ogni antisemita (Dr. Goebbels incluso) ha il suo *Hausjude*, Piero Sraffa, come avrà visto, è stato scelto come *Hausjude* di circostanza»; poi elenca l'attacco di Previtali a Gombrich «non perché le teorie sull'arte di Gombrich siano giuste o sbagliate, ma perché sono "conservatrici". Il criterio di falsificabilità del borghese Popper deve essere evidentemente radiato dal mondo della nuova cultura populista di contestazione»; poi polemizza con un saggio di Giuliano su *Parola del Passato* e sulla definizione di Tacito come «storico in rivolta», che anziché una semplice stonatura fa chiedere a Momigliano se «rivolta è diventata l'equivalente di paranoia». La chiusa è quella citata nel corpo del discorso.
[60] Cfr. *Terzo contributo alla storia degli studi classici e del mondo antico*, I, Roma 1966.

pista d'indagine che aveva annunciato a Dionisotti da Oxford nel 1946 rimaneva centrale per lui: mettere in opera in un primo momento un esame sistematico delle linee eterodosse della morale antica, che costituiva «già di per sé una critica dello stato etico e chiuso»; da lì andare avanti con una ipotesi di lavoro assai forte in due tempi:

> «Il secondo passo è un esame della situazione per cui il cristianesimo, pur derivando la sua forza rivoluzionaria dalle linee non ortodosse del pensiero pagano, in sostanza accettò e rafforzò con la sanzione divina qualsiasi tipo di stato pagano che desse mano libera alla Chiesa. Il terzo passo è un esame delle difficoltà che su origini romane e cristiane si è creata in noi nei rapporti tra stato e famiglia (o ogni altra società fondata sull'amore e sulla carità): libertà sembra oggi coincidere con amore, una cosa che avrebbe stupito un Greco»[61].

Una rivendicazione che chiude il cerchio aperto all'inizio di questo saggio: giacché sbatteva in faccia a quella cultura, di cui l'antisemitismo di un padre Gemelli era l'espressione, quella contraddizione che non aveva cessato di produrre frutti velenosi e che Momigliano sapeva di poter affrontare in modo appassionatamente «spassionato»[62], smentendone con la ricerca le presunzioni di nobiltà.

---

[61] C. DIONISOTTI, *Ricordo di Momigliano*, Bologna 1989, 105-107.
[62] S. BERTI, *Autobiografia, storicismo e verità storica in Arnaldo Momigliano...*, 297-312.

AVERIL CAMERON

Thoughts on the *Introduction* to *The Conflict between Paganism and Christianity in the Fourth Century*

Not long ago I was at a memorial service for an archetypal English patristic scholar, Henry Chadwick, quintessentially Oxbridge, Regius Professor of Divinity, Dean of Christ Church, Oxford, Master of Peterhouse, Cambridge, spokesman for the Anglican church in its conversations with Roman Catholicism[1]. One can hardly think of anyone less like Arnaldo Momigliano, Italian Jew and passionately serious historian of the ancient world. And yet their friendship was mentioned in the address at the service, and when I first came into contact with him in the early 1960s, Momigliano sent me to Oxford to meet Henry Chadwick and ask for his advice. That is a measure of the breadth of approach which is illustrated in the volume which is the starting point of this collection. I want in this short contribution to draw attention to Momigliano's *Introduction*, a part of the book that is often overlooked.

The seminar which formed the basis of the eventual volume entitled *The Conflict between Paganism and Christianity in the Fourth Century*[2] took place in London during the academic year 1958-59. It was held at the Warburg Institute, an institution which, having been forced to move from Hamburg in the 1930s, continued the European tradition of scholarship in England, and which naturally attracted refugee scholars. Here Momigliano found a home in his post-war years in London, both before and after his retirement from the chair of ancient history at University College, and it was a natural place for an invitation to the European scholars whose lectures

---

[1] The Very Revd H. CHADWICK (1920-2008) was the author of many books including *Origen, Contra Celsum*, Cambridge 1953; *The Sentences of Sextus*, Cambridge 1959; *Early Christian Thought and the Classical Tradition*, Oxford 1966; *The Early Church*, London 1967; *The Church in Ancient Society: from Galilee to Gregory the Great*, Oxford 2001 and *East and West: the Making of a Rift in the Church*, Oxford 2003.
[2] *The Conflict between Paganism and Christianity in the Fourth Century*, ed. A. MOMIGLIANO, Oxford 1963.

are included in the published volume³. We know now much more clearly from Momigliano's Cambridge lectures of spring 1940 on the subject of peace and liberty, published by Riccardo Di Donato in Italian and soon to be published in English⁴, about his interest in and indeed respect for, Christianity. He went so far in the last lecture in the series as to tie in the western concept of liberty to the ideals of Christianity, contrasted with the decadence of the Roman state⁵. According to these lectures, the Christian ideal of peace was new and comprehensive. It opposed itself to what was offered by the state, and Momigliano believed that the contrast could not persist indefinitely. Either one of the two bodies must destroy the other or state and church must recognize each other. Such a dramatic formulation makes striking reading now, and an understanding of the earlier history of Momigliano's thinking about Christianity is essential in order to explain the nature of the volume under discussion.

It is against this background that we can understand what may otherwise seem surprising in the *Introduction*. Momigliano referred at the end of his life to his triple heritage – Jewish, classical and Christian – as a Jew and an Italian⁶, and expressed a passionate belief elsewhere that the ancient world could only be understood in terms of the successive impacts of Judaism and Christianity. «Peace and liberty» was a poignant choice of theme for the series of eight lectures given at Cambridge in the early months of World War II, when he had lost the chair he had briefly held at Turin because of the race laws, and been forced to move to the unfamiliar circumstances of England and of Oxford. However, it was a theme on which he had already reflected for some time, and it took up again the subject of «peace» which had been the topic of his unpublished inaugural

---

³ It was also at the Warburg Institute that he later held his own regular seminar, as has been described for instance by M. CRAWFORD, *L'insegnamento di Arnaldo Momigliano in Gran Bretagna*, in *Omaggio ad Arnaldo Momigliano. Storia e storiografia sul mondo antico*, ed. L. CRACCO RUGGINI, Como 1989, 27-41; R. DI DONATO, *Gli anni di Londra*, in *Arnaldo Momigliano nella Storiografia del Novecento*, ed. L. POLVERINI, Rome 2006, 125-36; A. GRAFTON, *Momigliano's method and the Warburg Institute. Studies on his middle period*, in ID., *Worlds made by Words. Scholarship and Community in the Modern West*, Cambridge, MA, 2009, 231-54.

⁴ For the Italian version see R. DI DONATO, *Pace e Libertà nel mondo antico. Lezioni a Cambridge: gennaio-marzo 1940*, Firenze 1996; cf. ID., *Materiali per una biografia intellettuale di Arnaldo Momigliano I. Libertà e pace nel mondo antico*, «Athenaeum» n.s. 83 (1995), 213-44; ID., *Gli anni di Londra*...

⁵ See also A. CAMERON, *Momigliano and Christianity*, forthcoming.

⁶ Preface to *On Pagans, Jews and Christians*, Hanover, NH, 1987, dated December 1986.

lecture given in Turin in 1936[7]. Guido Clemente has brilliantly shown in a recent paper how this complex of ideas had its roots in Momigliano's exposure in his youth to the thinking on the topic by other scholars in his circle, including Croce and De Sanctis[8]. In the early 1950s in London Momigliano had continued these themes in lectures at the Warburg Institute on impiety and heresy and at the Institute of Classical Studies on *parrhesia* and *isegoria* as aspects of freedom of speech in the ancient world[9]. The problem of freedom in relation to ancient history occupied him from an early stage and continued to do so. He was to come to the view, which lies behind the *Introduction* that we are considering and which had already been expressed in his inaugural lecture at Turin and in his Cambridge lectures, that Christianity, developing out of Judaism and impacting on the Roman empire, offered the freedom of the individual conscience that could not be provided by the imperial Roman state. If the *Introduction* seems in some ways to put forward a rather stark and even schematized view of the relation of Christianity to that of the fate of the Roman empire, it is because behind it lay many years of developing and complex reflection on the topic, of which only a part had at the time been published[10].

The original Warburg seminar in 1958-59 assembled a group of scholars including H.-I. Marrou, for whom Momigliano already had a high respect, having known him since the early 1930s[11]. As Marcone has pointed out, Marrou's *St Augustin et la fin de la culture antique* had appeared in 1938, only two years after Momigliano's papers of 1936, but at the most difficult period in the latter's life; Marrou's famous *Retractatio,* in which he set the agenda for a reversal of his earlier emphasis on decline, came out in 1949, thus ten years before the Warburg seminar[12]. Having been cut off from continental scholarship during the war years Momigliano was now in a position from the security of his chair at University College in which he might look forward to visits from Marrou and other European

---

[7] For this period see L. CRACCO RUGGINI, *Gli anni di insegnamento a Torino*, in *Arnaldo Momigliano nella Storiografia...*, 77-123.
[8] G. CLEMENTE, *Between Hellenism and the Roman empire*, forthcoming.
[9] See R. DI DONATO, *Gli anni di Londra...*, 130.
[10] See G. CLEMENTE, *Between Hellenism...*; A. CAMERON, *Momigliano...*
[11] For the high estimation with which Momigliano regarded Marrou see L. CRACCO RUGGINI, *Arnaldo Momigliano e il tardoantico*, in *Omaggio ad Arnaldo Momigliano...*, 159-184, at 162; see also A. MARCONE, *Un treno per Ravenna. Riflessioni sulla Tarda Antichità*, in *Arnaldo Momigliano nella storiografia del Novecento*, ed. L. POLVERINI, Rome 2006, 219-233, at 227 and further below. The influence of Marrou on the young Peter Brown is also evident.
[12] A. MARCONE, *Un treno per Ravenna...*, 229-230.

scholars, although it is interesting that Marrou is not included in his list in the *Introduction* of «the most recent contributions» on the later Roman empire, and he does not point out the difference between Marrou's original book and his later comments[13]. Although he had felt earlier that he himself still lacked the deep acquaintance with Christian writings that he would have liked, Momigliano's exposure to and engagement with the historical role played by Christianity in the Roman empire went back to his youth. More recently, he had recognized the fundamental importance for the understanding of Constantine, and therefore of relations between church and state in the fourth century, of a papyrus in the British Museum discussed by A.H.M. Jones in an article of 1954 that seemed to confirm the authenticity of Eusebius's reporting of one of Constantine's most important documents, and thereby undermined Burckhardt's highly sceptical view of both Constantine and Eusebius[14].

Contrary to what might have been the impression given in the volume, it was not Momigliano who invited the speakers, at least officially, but his friend Gertrud Bing, the Director of the Warburg Institute. In a letter dated 10 June, 1959, she invited him to edit the lectures for publication (for fee), and to add a short introduction; she had already discussed this with Colin Roberts and had suggested Momigliano's name[15]. In his reply, dated 15 June, Momigliano said that he agreed in general, despite having a great deal of other work, but about the proposed *Introduction* he wrote:

> «As for the short introduction, it raises problems; it is easy to run against the intentions and convictions of the individual authors. However the first thing I want to do is read the lectures! Three of them I do not know. Then we must discuss the subject together, and even may think of the fee».

Not only had he not himself decided whom to invite for the seminar in 1958-59, though he had given some advice on this point; he had not even

---

[13] *Introduction*, 6, n. 1.
[14] *Sulla stato presente degli studi di storia antica (1946-54),* in *Secondo contributo alla storia degli studi classici,* Rome, 1960, 319-353 (= *Relazioni del X Congresso Internazionale di Scienze Storiche,* Rome, 4-11 Nov. 1955, VI: *Relazioni generali e supplementari,* 3-40), at 340; it is worth noting that this wide-ranging bibliographical paper includes recent works on Christianity in the Roman empire. In fact the article in question was by A.H.M. Jones, with an appendix by T.C. Skeat, not Jones and C.E. Stevens, as Momigliano has it: A.H.M. JONES, *Notes on the genuineness of the Constantinian elements in Eusebius's Life of Constantine,* «Journal of Ecclesiastical History» 5 (1954), 196-200, with an Appendix by T.C. Skeat at 200.
[15] I owe this vital point to my friend Professor John North; the letters are held in the Warburg Institute Archive.

attended all the papers. Nevertheless, as Oswyn Murray and Anthony Grafton have shown, the Warburg Institute had been familiar to him since the 1930s; and he had had dealings with it in its first London home in the 1940s, published in its journal and lectured there in 1949[16].

Momigliano is quite explicit in his *Introduction* about the fact that the thinking about Christianity expressed here was not new: in a footnote he refers to his contribution on «Roma: Impero» in the *Enciclopedia Italiana*, xxix, of 1936, and to an article published in «Rivista Storica Italiana» in same year[17], recently reprinted in 1955 in the first volume of the *Contributi*, and states clearly that «my point of view was already formulated»[18]; the «more recent contributions» he mentions had not therefore caused him to change his approach. In agreeing to write the article on the Roman empire in the *Enciclopedia Italiana* he had resisted the temptation to focus on classical Greek city-states and insisted on the transforming effect of Christianity in the Roman empire. Likewise he saw his early focus on the history of liberty in the ancient world as necessarily leading to the attempt to understand the effect on the ideal of liberty associated with the Greek city-states through the impact of universalism, Judaism and Christianity[19]. The relation between liberty and empire was needless to say a tense subject in Fascist Italy, and Lellia Ruggini has described the hesitation which Momigliano's recent articles had produced in the minds of the jury in the *Concorso* for the chair at Turin in 1936[20]. The 1940 lectures, as yet still unpublished when Momigliano wrote the *Introduction* in 1959, had developed the theme of the relation of Christianity to the history of the Roman empire, and the commission for the *Introduction* caused him to return to it, although in the intervening period he had famously turned his attention in a different direction, towards the history of historiography, in itself a topic influenced by his contacts with the Warburg Institute and the scholars connected with it[21].

---

[16] A. GRAFTON, *Momigliano's method and the Warburg Institute...*, 246-251.

[17] *La formazione della moderna storiografia sull'impero romano*, in *Contributo alla storia degli studi classici*, Rome 1955, 107-164.

[18] *Introduction*, 6, n. 1.

[19] As early as 1931 he had reviewed Croce's *Constant e Jellinek intorno alla differenza tra la libertà degli antichi e quella dei moderni*, Naples, 1930, «RFIC» 9 (1931), 262-264 (= *Quinto Contributo* II, 906-907): see M. CRAWFORD, *L'insegnamento di Arnaldo Momigliano in Gran Bretagna...*, 29; L. CRACCO RUGGINI, *Arnaldo Momigliano e il tardoantico...*, 177.

[20] L. CRACCO RUGGINI, *Gli anni dell'insegnamento a Torino...*, 108-109.

[21] See A. GRAFTON, *Momigliano's method and the Warburg Institute...*, 246; O. MURRAY, *Arnaldo Momigliano in England*, in *The Presence of the Historian. Essays in Memory*

The *Introduction* to *The Conflict between Paganism and Christianity in the Fourth Century* begins with an elegance that is highly characteristic (one of the most extraordinary things about Momigliano was indeed his combination of a beautiful English style with a heavy Italian accent): «I may perhaps begin with a piece of good news. In this year 1959 it can still be considered an historical truth that the Roman empire declined and fell. Nobody as yet is prepared to deny that the Roman empire has disappeared»[22]. As Arnaldo Marcone has recently pointed out[23], this famous assertion was directly challenged in a well-known paper by Glen Bowersock, whose position is shared by the many other scholars who have followed Momigliano's pupil Peter Brown in extending the coverage of late antiquity up to the eighth century or even longer. But an emphasis on «fall», now receiving approval from revisionist historians (see below), is crucial for the argument of the *Introduction* and for the whole conception of the Warburg seminar of 1958-59 and the volume that ensued. For Momigliano it is very clear that the rise of Christianity, or what we now tend to call «Christianization», was connected with the fate of the Roman empire, and specifically with its decline, and that the fourth century was a crucial phase in this process. We may compare the last of his Sather lectures, delivered in 1962, a year before the publication of the *Conflict* volume[24], and thus between the seminar held in 1958-59 and its publication in 1963. The last Sather lecture dealt with the origins of ecclesiastical historiography, a theme related to his own paper in *The Conflict between Paganism and Christianity in the Fourth Century*[25]. It credits Eusebius, «simple and majestic», with being the real founder of the genre, but ranges much more widely; we also find here also references to the «Church» under Constantine as «victorious», and as «a separate body

---

of Arnaldo Momigliano, ed. M. STEINBERG, «History and Theory» Beiheft 30 (1991), 49-64, at 53-54.

[22] Contrast his paper of 1973, *La caduta senza rumore di un impero nel 476 d. C.*, «Annali della Scuola Normale di Pisa», ser. III, 3 (1973), 397-418.

[23] A. MARCONE, *A long late antiquity? Considerations on a controversial periodization*, «Journal of Late Antiquity» 1 (2008)/1, 4-19, at 4, with 8, n. 13; see G.W. BOWERSOCK, *The vanishing paradigm of the fall of Rome*, «Bulletin of the American Academy of Arts and Sciences» 49 (1996), 29-43.

[24] Published posthumously as *The Classical Foundations of Modern Historiography*, Berkeley 1990; R. DI DONATO, *Gli anni di Londra...*, 128, points to the coherence of Momigliano's thinking in the period 1962-1964.

[25] *Pagan and Christian historiography in the fourth century A.D.*, in *The Conflict...*, 79-99.

within the Roman Empire»[26]. The last sentence of the concluding Sather lecture commends the comparison made in 1834 between Eusebius and Herodotus by F.C. Baur: «We can accept this comparison and meditate on his remark that both Herodotus and Eusebius wrote under the inspiration of a newly established freedom»[27]. When he returned to the subject much later, for instance in his paper *After Gibbon's «Decline and Fall»*, published in 1978[28], it was to insist again that while by then the question of why Rome fell had seemed to have lost its urgency, a nuanced return to Gibbon's themes was needed, including the role which the latter attributed to Christianity. Here again Momigliano discusses the various theories put forward for the fall of the empire and concludes with the observation that the Church had become «state within a state», as he had earlier predicted, after which the empire could not be the same as before; «anything which happened in the fourth and fifth centuries A.D. had to be fitted into a new frame».

The entire first section of the *Introduction* is concerned with the debate about the decline and fall of the Roman empire. Various explanations and dates are majestically surveyed, with the history of debates about decline, from the time of the Romans onwards. It is intriguing to see that, 20 years or more before the publication of Geoffrey de Ste Croix's *Class Struggle in the Ancient Greek World* (1981), Momigliano regarded as discredited even in the Soviet Union the idea that decline started with the Peloponnesian war and the dependence on slavery in classical Greece[29]. He surveys the theories of Dopsch and Pirenne, and acknowledges as signs of a move away from the concentration on the end of the Roman empire the vitality of Byzantium, referring to the work of Norman Baynes, a predecessor at University College London, and the impact of Islam on society[30]. In this he admitted that the older debates on the fall of the Roman empire were being modified. Nevertheless, for him the missing element was a full realization of the role played by Christianity, even if not «a simple

---

[26] *The Classical Foundations of Modern Historiography*, 138, 141.
[27] *Ibid.*, 152. His turn to ecclesiastical history, and especially to Eusebius's place in its development, grew out of a magisterial series of papers dealing with ancient historiography which he published in the years 1944 to 1957, many of which can be found in his *Contributo*, published in 1955 (see A. GRAFTON, *Momigliano's method and the Warburg Institute...*, 234-235).
[28] *After Gibbon's «Decline and Fall»*, «Annali della Scuola Normale di Pisa», ser. 3, 8 (1978), 435-54.
[29] *Introduction*, 2, 4.
[30] *Ibid.*, 4, 5.

return to Gibbon». The section ends with a resounding affirmation: while Harnack and Troeltsch had written about early Christianity as a social phenomenon, they remained theologians. It was now for historians to give Christianity its due as the «most important social change of all». Christianity must be understood on its own terms as a dynamic force and not merely as a destructive one in relation to the empire. Momigliano's own aim is stated with uncompromising clarity, and in stating it he reiterates the notion of decline: «It is the modest purpose of this paper to reassert the view that there is a direct relation between the triumph (sic) of Christianity and the decline of the Roman empire»[31]. He also employs another characteristic and very recognizable stylistic trope: «So far nobody has written a realistic evaluation of the impact of Christianity on the structure of pagan society. I shall not attempt such a task here. I shall confine myself to a few elementary remarks on the impact of Christianity on political life between the fourth and sixth centuries A.D. We all know the basic facts»[32]. Momigliano's English style is one of his more striking features, and has often received comment[33], and I suspect that a study of the structures of his arguments in his published papers in terms of the impact of rhetoric (especially their opening remarks and their conclusions) would also be revealing. The extract just quoted ends a section, not the whole *Introduction*, but the phraseology of the disclaimer, and the use he makes of such formulations in general, would be well worth considering further.

Section II presents a very recognizable picture of third-century crisis and fourth-century structural and economic problems, reminiscent of both Rostovtzeff and Jones. As we have seen, and as Arnaldo Marcone remarks, Momigliano had predictably observed the changes in attitudes to the later Roman empire that were taking place after World War II; nevertheless I will argue that his thought on the relation between Christianity and the end of the empire remained consistent. It is also instructive to place the *Introduction* and the seminar series more fully in their historical context[34]. In his Cambridge lectures of 1940 Momigliano had spoken of Christianity as offering a relief from the difficulties of the third century.

---

[31] On this issue see also A. MARCONE, *Un treno per Ravenna...*, 227-229.
[32] *Ibid.*, 6.
[33] A. GRAFTON, *Momigliano's method and the Warburg Institute...*, 237, remarks on his characteristic openings but suggests that his rhetorical flights were rare; all the same, the lucidity of his arguments and the care which he gave to style are remarkable, given the well-known difficulties he had had with English in his early years in the country.
[34] A. MARCONE, *A long late antiquity?...*, 13; cf. ID., *Un treno per Ravenna...*, 219-233 (on the *Introduction* to *The Conflict...*, see 222).

He referred to the dry spiritual life of the Empire and the new content of Christianity. We might remind ourselves that 1963, the year of publication of the *Conflict* volume, was also the publication year of E.R. Dodds's *Pagan and Christian in an Age of Anxiety*, with a similar psychological message. In the following year A.H.M. Jones published his *Later Roman Empire*[35], which acknowledged the appeal of Christianity to able minds and the drain this represented on the bureaucratic and official classes of the Empire. Indeed we find a similar argument in Momigliano's *Introduction*, where the argument is traced back to the influence of Edward Gibbon and before him to Voltaire and Montesquieu: «the [...] equilibrium changed... to the disadvantage of the ancient institutions of the empire»[36]. Christians were simply «superior» to pagans in dynamism and efficiency, better able to adapt to the new political and social situation and to deal with barbarians[37]. It was a formulation which owed much to Rostovtzeff's insistence on the chaos of the third century (the English revised edition of Rostovtzeff's *Social and Economic History of the Roman Empire* had been published in 1957)[38], even while contrasting this Christian dynamism with Rostovtzeff's static and rigid Dominate.

I was still a student in Oxford at the time of the original Warburg seminar in 1958-59, but this section reminds me vividly of the way such questions were formulated when I started teaching the history of the Roman empire in London in 1970. This was also before the rise of late antique archaeology as a discipline; no-one could write today, as Momigliano does here, that «one has the impression that long-distance trade was increasingly in the hands of small minorities of Syrians and Jews»[39], a remark prefaced by reference to a supposed decline of the bourgeoisie and lack of prosperous traders in the fourth century. It was a formulation which not only antedated Jones's *Later Roman Empire*, but also Peter Brown's seminal *World of Late Antiquity*, published in 1971.

One could carry this contextualization further, and I believe it is important. I will mention now only Santo Mazzarino's *La fine del mondo antico* of 1959 (cited in the *Introduction*) and Marrou's *Saint Augustin et la fin de la culture antique*, which had appeared in its 4th edition with Marrou's

---

[35] A.H.M. Jones, *The Later Roman Empire, 284-602. A Social, Administrative, and Economic Survey*, 3 vols, Oxford, 1964.
[36] *Introduction*, p. 9.
[37] *Ibid.*, 15.
[38] M. Rostovzeff, *Social and Economic History of the Roman Empire*, 2nd ed., rev. P.M. Fraser, Oxford 1957.
[39] *Introduction*, 8.

Rectractatio in the previous year⁴⁰. As Momigliano rightly remarks⁴¹, even leaving out the Romans themselves, «since Flavio Biondo each generation has produced its own theory or theories on the decline and fall of Rome». This is in part what the original 1959 seminar was about.

In some ways it seems like a modern discussion. The questions are about culture wars and conversion, and these continue. But seen from a twenty-first century perspective, why only pagans? Where is the vibrant Judaism of late antiquity, and where are the Arabs, pre-Islamic or otherwise? Where are the questions about heresy, orthodoxy and identity, not to mention constructivism or symbolic power, with which the pages of journals on late antiquity and early Christianity now abound? Or church councils, and hagiography? Again, the model is in essence that of a conflict of religions, at least in ideological terms, in contrast with many, if certainly not all, formulations prevailing today. Indeed Momigliano's own paper in the volume applies to the Christians of the era of Constantine and Eusebius, terms such as «fierceness», «determination», «resentment» and «aggressiveness»⁴².

We may also now be tempted to ask, why only the fourth century? For a generation or more, «late antiquity» in its later formulation by Brown and others has embraced a far longer stretch, and admits of regional studies and a far wider range of subjects than are covered in Momigliano's volume. Yet despite Marrou, despite Riegl and others, and despite a mass of discussion about the origins of the concept⁴³, in 1959 «late antiquity» as we have known it since the work of Momigliano's student Peter Brown had not yet been invented. Momigliano's own periodization is still the periodization of Dopsch versus Pirenne. It is all the same surprising to a modern reader to find such confident references to the «dying State» and the declining empire⁴⁴. Compare also «the superiority of Christianity over paganism in dynamism and efficiency was already evident in the fourth

---

[40] S. MAZZARINO, *La fine del mondo antico*, Milan 1959 (=*The End of the Ancient World*, Eng. trans., London 1966); H.-I. MARROU, *Saint Augustin et la fin de la culture antique*, 4ᵗʰ ed., also containing MARROU's *Retractatio* of 1949), Paris 1958. For more on the overall context see A. CAMERON, *A.H.M. Jones and the end of the ancient world*, in *A.H.M. Jones and the Later Roman Empire*, ed. D.H. GWYNN, Leiden-Boston 2008, 231-249.

[41] *Ibid.*, 3.

[42] *Pagan and Christian historiography in the Fourth Century A.D.*, in *The Conflict...*, 79-99, at 80, 94.

[43] On which see A. MARCONE, *A long late antiquity?...*, 11-13.

[44] *Introduction*, 15, 16.

century»[45]. It is not just that the vocabulary is that of decline, but that Monigliano assumed that the decline set in so early and was so incontrovertible.

The next section of the *Introduction*[46] is also striking, given the emphasis which Jones's *Later Roman Empire* was to place so soon afterwards on the theory of «idle mouths» as a factor in the decline of the empire[47]. Momigliano puts it rather differently; he offers a social and religious explanation instead of an economic one, and the army does not come into the equation. Moreover he puts forward a very positive assessment of the impact of Christianity in terms of «creativity», energy, and local pride. Not only did the «best men»[48] look to the Church rather than the state; the new churches and new structures also gave ordinary people something to be proud about[49], even though that meant diverting money away from necessary projects like building aqueducts. Many were attracted to the monastic movement, which is described here in terms of «monasticism» and «hermits» (the «holy man» of Peter Brown is not yet present). Momigliano admits that hermits (that is, as we might now say, ascetics) could be a nuisance, and were a kind of diversion from the state, but he answers this potential objection to his thesis with what would now seem too blanket an appeal to the influence of organized monastic structures and rules; most scholars would now argue that «monasticism» in late antiquity was a far more varied phenomenon, and that the development of some kinds of «monastic» rules by no means controlled this variety. The actual violence in which some monks were to be involved and the trouble they were to cause is also passed over[50]. Momigliano admits that monks were a subversive force, «but they provided an alternative to pagan city life»[51]; and above all they too represented a set of new and attractive personal aspirations.

Even in the last section, which has barbarian invasions as its starting point, the emphasis is on the Church's capacity to offer psychological

---

[45] *Ibid.*, 15.
[46] *Ibid.*, 9-12.
[47] See further A. CAMERON, *A.H.M. Jones and the end of the ancient world....*
[48] *Introduction*, 11.
[49] *Ibid.*, 9.
[50] For this theme see for instance M. GADDIS, *There is no Crime for Those who have Christ*, Berkeley 2005; *Violence in Late Antiquity*, ed. H.A. DRAKE, Aldershot 2006; B. SHAW, *War and violence*, in *Late Antiquity: a Guide to the Post-Classical World*, eds. G.W. BOWERSOCK, P. BROWN, O. GRABAR, Cambridge, MA, 1999, 130-169.
[51] *Ibid.*, 11.

help, whether through conversion of barbarians, or to the existing Roman populations that were threatened. The figure of St Severinus, whose activities in Noricum are chronicled by Eugippius, is made to stand for the capacity of the Church to negotiate a way through the new situations and offer something to all sides[52]. The argument is not quite put in terms of democratization, in the formulation of Santo Mazzarino, but Momigliano is concerned, like Mazzarino, with «ordinary people», and with the idea of a preservation of Roman civilization at ground roots level by the very fact that barbarians lived side by side with and rubbed along with the ordinary citizens of the Roman empire[53].

It is easy enough to point out the various agendas which have changed the picture since the early 1960s, in particular the debate between «catastrophists» and «continuists» which is still very much in progress. Yet this would not be fair to Momigliano. What is more intriguing is how positive (and perhaps how optimistic) is the view he presents here of the advantages of Christianity; he even uses the term «triumph of Christianity»[54], a term which would give many scholars pause today. It is less surprising in the light of his Cambridge lectures of 1940, published in Italian only in 1996[55], but only in the sense that the lectures confirm his own reference in the *Introduction* to the continuity of his thinking since 1936.

In the remaining section of this paper I would like briefly to make a few further general observations about this extremely interesting *Introduction*.

The first is to repeat that the model implicit in the *Introduction*, as in the very title of the volume, is one of conflict. Christians and pagans are envisaged as being in competition, with the Christians being better poised to emerge on top. Several of the individual papers in the volume, including that by Jones, adopt the same kind of approach. It is not one adopted by most historians of late antiquity since the 1970's[56]. Nor, though much of the volume is in fact about social and cultural issues rather than economic,

---

[52] For a recent use of the figure of Severinus see J. O'DONNELL, *The Ruin of the Roman Empire*, London 2009, 101-104.
[53] *Introduction*, 13.
[54] *Introduction*, 4.
[55] R. DI DONATO, *Pace e Libertà nel mondo antico*...
[56] Though now see J. HAHN, *Gewalt und religiöser Konflikt. Studien zu den Auseinandersetzungen zwischen Christen, Heiden und Juden im Osten des römischen Reiches (von Konstantin bis Theodosius II)*, Berlin 2004, and see below. For the idea of a religious «marketplace» see R. STARK, *The Rise of Christianity. A Sociologist Reconsiders History*, Princeton 1996.

military or administrative, is Momigliano's approach one of cultural history, a term now used explicitly by many historians of late antiquity, especially historians of religion. The latter is a tendency which Momigliano would probably have rejected, and indeed, it is a common criticism of cultural history that it finds it difficult to accommodate or explain change, let alone conflict. Momigliano in contrast apparently had no qualms about accepting the conflict model, or even, it seems, in assuming the inevitability of conflict between Christians and pagans.

Again, the range covered by the essays in the volume is restricted by today's standards. Although Momigliano says in the *Introduction* that he intends to consider the period from the fourth to the sixth century, the thrust of the volume is actually about the fourth century, and as such, it places a heavy weight of explanation on that early phase of what many now refer to as «late antiquity». One might perhaps argue that the original seminar was not about Christianization as such, but rather about the conflict situation in the fourth century itself – were it not that in suggesting a tie between Christianity and the end of the Roman empire, the *Introduction* does seem to imply a wider scope. But even within the chronological range of the fourth century one might have expected a wider net to be cast, to include Jews and Judaism, «heretics», and even Arabs, or at least «Saracens». The field has broadened, even exploded[57], since the early 1960s, not least because many more young scholars have entered it. Judaism, and the literary presentation of Jews in Christian texts, are major subjects[58]; so, certainly is the whole huge arena of orthodoxy and heresy and the wider but related question of «identity»; so too is the search for pre-Islamic Arabs amid the references in the sparse but tantalizing literary and epigraphic record[59]. It is difficult today, with an enormously increased interest in Islam, not

---

[57] See A. GIARDINA, *Esplosione di tardoantico*, «Studi Storici» 40 (1999), 157-180.

[58] E.g. S. SCHWARZ, *Imperialism and Roman Society, 200 B.C.E. to 640 C.E.*, Princeton 2001; A.S. JACOBS, *Remains of the Jews. The Holy Land and Christian Empire in Late Antiquity*, Stanford 2004; D. BOYARIN, *Border Lines: the Partition of Judaeo-Christianity*, Philadelphia 2004.

[59] All three issues are reflected in recent papers by F. MILLAR, for example *The Theodosian empire (408-450) and the Arabs: Saracens or Ishmaelites?*, in *Cultural Borrowings and Ethnic Appropriations in Antiquity*, ed. E.S. GRUEN, Stuttgart 2005, 297-314; *Libanius and the Near East*, «Scripta Classica Israelica» 26 (2007), 155-180; *The Syriac Acts of the Second Council of Ephesus (449)*, in *Chalcedon in Context*, eds. R. PRICE, M. WHITBY, Liverpool 2009, 45-69. They have been the subject of several edited volumes, including *Constructing Identities in Late Antiquity*, ed. R. MILES, London, 1999; *Orthodoxie, christianisme, histoire*, eds. S. ELM, E. REBILLARD, A. ROMANO, Rome 2000. The re-interpretation of ethnicity has also been a major trend in recent

to read back, or at least to have in mind, what we all know was to come. Some scholars have particular reasons to want to argue that Islam was a religion rooted in Hellenism and in late antiquity[60]. It seems somewhat ironic now that the 1960's, when Momigliano's collection was published, also saw the beginnings of a vast expansion of range among late antique historians, both geographically and chronologically, into the Near East and well into the Islamic period[61].

To return then to this question of period. Late antiquity as defined by Peter Brown and others in the generation after Momigliano is much longer than Momigliano allowed for, extending in many central works as late as the fall of the Umayyads, or even as late as AD 800[62]. In response, some have reacted to what they see as an excessive emphasis on the cultural sphere by re-emphasizing the importance of violence and catastrophe and by returning to the theme of the fall of empires[63]. A further charge made against the idea of a «long» late antiquity by its critics is that while it may fill a cultural space it does not help us understand real historical change[64]. But it is a fallacy to imagine that culture can be so easily separated from political and economic structures, and I would counter with some words from Aziz al-Azmeh, who is one of those who are quite specifically «writ-

---

writing about barbarians in the later Roman empire: see the discussion by G. HALSALL, *Barbarian Migrations and the Roman West 376-568*, Cambridge 2007, 35-62.

[60] A. AL-AZMEH, *Rom, das Neue Rom und Bagdad. Pfade der Spätantike* (with English translation), Berlin 2008; the current emphasis on late antique monotheism helps support such a view. In contrast, I. SHAHID's multi-volume work on *Byzantium and the Arabs*, Washington, DC, 1984-95), seeks to emphasize a non-Islamic Arab identity as an important component of Roman history from the third century to the beginning of the seventh.

[61] There is a large bibliography discussing this periodization: see A. CAMERON, *The «long» late antiquity: a late twentieth-century model*, in *Classics in Progress. Essays on Ancient Greece and Rome*, ed. P. WISEMAN, London 2002, 165-191; A. MARCONE, *A long late antiquity?...*; C. ANDO, *Decline, fall and transformation*, ibid., 30-60; also A. AL-AZMEH, *Rom, das Neue Rom...*, especially 58-61; further debate in «Studi Storici» 45 (2004).

[62] See especially *Late Antiquity: a Guide...*; A. MARCONE, *A long late antiquity?...*, 17-19.

[63] For instance B. WARD-PERKINS, *The Fall of Rome and the End of Civilization*, Oxford 2005, with G. FOWDEN, *410 and all that*, «Journal of Roman Archaeology» 19 (2006), 706-708; P. HEATHER, *The Fall of the Roman Empire: A New History*, London 2005; A. GOLDSWORTHY, *The Fall of the West. The Death of the Roman Superpower*, London 2009; J. O'DONNELL, *The Ruin...*

[64] See the opening remarks directed at the alleged inability of cultural history to deal with «big topics with intellectual coherence» in M. WHITTOW, *Beyond the cultural turn: economic history revived?*, «Journal of Roman Archaeology» 20 (2007), 697-704.

ing backwards», looking back from the vantage point of knowing what came next, in fact writing Islam into late antiquity; in this of course he differs fundamentally from Momigliano. «My approach backwards in time», al-Azmeh says, «goes beyond culture, for culture overall is premised on empire, the substratum of late antiquity»[65].

That brings us back to Momigliano's *Introduction*, with its confident assumption that the story of Christianisation, and the role of Christianity in the post-Constantinian world, are quite simply connected with the fate of the empire itself. In a way it is of its time. But for Momigliano it was a view formed in his early years, and one that he was to maintain throughout his life.

---

[65] A. AL-AZMEH, *Rom, das Neue Rom...*, 68.

GUIDO CLEMENTE

Pagani, ebrei, cristiani
nella riflessione storica di Arnaldo Momigliano

«The treble tradition – Jewish, Classical and Christian – that I have inherited as a Jew and as an Italian invited exploration and clarification, but did not carry inside it the seeds of any dramatic conflict. The spirit of the Risorgimento is still active in Italy. The conflicts in which I have been involved during my life – and the resulting cruelties – have other origins». Ho scelto questa frase, contenuta nella breve premessa alla raccolta *On Pagans, Jews, and Christians*, scritta da Momigliano nel dicembre 1986, fra le molte notazioni autobiografiche degli ultimi anni, perché essa mi permette di indicare subito almeno due aspetti essenziali utili a definire il tema di queste riflessioni, e di orientarmi in un complesso di problemi nei quali non è facile districarsi: il richiamo al Risorgimento è la riproposizione della italianità dell'ebreo e piemontese Momigliano, particolarmente significativa perchè viene, con molta chiarezza, proposta negli anni di intenso interesse per l'ebraismo; quindi, il richiamo alla «treble tradition», che imponeva una «esplorazione» e «chiarificazione» da parte di chi, ebreo, si sentiva parte, a pieno titolo, della cultura greca, romana e cristiana; e questa partecipazione, non assimilazione, non generava conflitti.

I saggi raccolti nell'*Ottavo* e *Nono Contributo*, entrambi postumi, rispettivamente 1987 e 1992 (ma il primo ancora organizzato dall'autore), le *Pagine ebraiche* (1987), le raccolte di saggi sulla religione, oltre a quello già citato, la raccolta per il pubblico italiano *Saggi di storia della religione romana* (1988), scelti dallo stesso autore poco prima della scomparsa, la prefazione ai saggi raccolti in *Storia e storiografia antica* (1987) documentano queste essenziali preoccupazioni, e sono volte a chiarire le motivazioni profonde delle sue ricerche, e quindi la loro sostanziale unità, che nasceva dalla sua personale esperienza, e di questa si nutriva[1].

---

[1] Wesleyan University Press, Middletown 1997; la prefazione a p. IX; nell'*Ottavo Contributo alla storia degli studi classici e del mondo antico* vd. la sezione *Religione dell'impero romano*, che contiene dodici saggi elaborati tra il 1984 e il 1987 (pp. 193-358);

La sua personale esperienza era, fin dagli anni della sua formazione in famiglia, caratterizzata dalla coesistenza di educazione religiosa e di educazione laica: l'una nel rispetto della tradizione, l'altra quale era impartita ad ogni studente. Una condizione che non doveva essere comune a molti.

In questo ambito, le questioni che mi sembrano essenziali per una discussione di qualche utilità sono almeno tre: il rapporto tra la sua educazione negli anni della adolescenza e della giovinezza, e la rilevanza che la religione assume nei suoi studi; quella, evidentemente connessa, del peso delle sue drammatiche vicende personali nella evoluzione della sua ricerca, le direzioni, complesse e molteplici, che tale ricerca stava prendendo fin negli ultimi mesi della sua attività; a queste la morte ha conferito un carattere definitivo che non erano destinate ad assumere; i suoi ultimi studi proponevano con particolare insistenza il rapporto tra esperienza religiosa individuale e società, in sostanza tornando ai temi della giovinezza, ora indagati con una capacità e esigenza di chiarificazione ben maggiori e consapevoli[2].

Mi limito a indicare i nodi problematici che mi paiono più rilevanti.

---

nel *Nono Contributo* vd. i numerosi saggi nelle sezioni *Conferenze e lezioni inedite 1939-1987* e *Ultimi saggi*; nelle *Pagine ebraiche* vd. la *Prefazione* dell'autore, XXIX ss.; la *Prefazione* in *Storia e storiografia antica*, 7 ss. Tutti questi interventi hanno un forte carattere autobiografico. Deve essere considerato nel giusto valore, nel brano citato all'inizio, il richiamo al Risorgimento, che implica il riconoscimento, da parte di Momigliano, dell'adesione ai valori nazionali della sua famiglia e di gran parte degli ebrei italiani. Si tratta di una posizione che riprende, a distanza di mezzo secolo, quanto lo storico aveva sostenuto nel 1933, nella recensione a C. ROTH, *Gli Ebrei in Venezia* (ora in *Quinto Contributo*, II, 1975, 1022 ss.), e riformulato con ampiezza in *The Jews of Italy*, nel 1985, in *Ottavo Contributo*, 361 ss. e in traduzione italiana nelle *Pagine ebraiche*, 129 ss. La politica della monarchia sabauda, favorendo l'integrazione, aveva posto le basi per una lealtà degli ebrei italiani alla causa nazionale che ebbe nel processo risorgimentale e nella successiva partecipazione alla costruzione dello stato unitario il suo compimento.

[2] Momigliano ha descritto la sua educazione in famiglia come caratterizzata da rispetto per l'ortodossia e le cerimonie del sabato, e insieme improntata a grande libertà di discussione e tolleranza (*Pagine ebraiche*, XXX); questa formazione, permeata di rispetto per valori tradizionali conservati in famiglia, e accompagnata da ampie letture e discussioni su temi etici e filosofici, dovette avere grande importanza; basti vedere le lettere a De Sanctis, pubblicate da L. POLVERINI, *Momigliano e De Sanctis*, in *Arnaldo Momigliano nella storiografia del Novecento*, a cura di L. POLVERINI, Roma 2006, 13 ss., scritte nel 1930; qui sono evidenti le preoccupazioni spirituali di Momigliano in costante rapporto dialettico con il maestro, e con un significativo rinvio dalla sfera personale a quella degli studi; vd. anche una lettera a C. Dionisotti, del 1926, citata in *Ricordo di Arnaldo Momigliano*, Bologna 1989, 11, e le considerazioni dello stesso Dionisotti su quegli anni giovanili.

La riflessione di Momigliano, negli anni '30, si era concentrata particolarmente su due temi di valore generale, trattati in parallelo: la importanza dell'ellenismo, che introduceva la questione dello stato nazionale come superamento della *polis*, e creava una società cosmopolita, luogo di incontro delle culture classica, ebraica, cristiana; l'impero romano, universale, che creava le condizioni per il trionfo dello stesso cristianesimo; quindi il tema della libertà e della pace nel mondo antico, dalla *polis* classica all'impero romano[3].

In questo ambito si iscrivono gli studi sui Maccabei e su Flavio Giuseppe nei primissimi anni '30; in essi appare con evidenza la preoccupazione di indagare la specificità della reazione ebraica, tra accettazione dell'ellenismo e suo rifiuto. Giuseppe non capiva più la cultura giudaica, poiché voleva spiegarla ai romani con gli strumenti concettuali e la lingua dei greci. Nel moto maccabaico gli ebrei ellenizzanti erano stati una componente importante nel determinare l'intervento di Antioco, e il conflitto era analizzato come interno all'ebraismo. Queste preoccupazioni emergono, nello stesso periodo, nelle prese di posizione dello studioso sui problemi dell'ebraismo contemporaneo in Italia, che mostravano la sua totale disapprovazione delle correnti sioniste ostili alla integrazione; ma erano preoccupazioni che motivavano, non inquinavano, la autonomia del ricercatore rispetto ai problemi storici che indagava[4]. Poiché si fa autobiografia parlando di altri, può tornare utile ricordare qui ciò che Momigliano scrisse nel 1949 nell'anniversario della morte del cugino paterno, Felice

---

[3] Si veda quanto Momigliano scrive nella ristampa di *Filippo il Macedone*, Milano 1987, XV ss., sul contesto delle sue ricerche sull'Ellenismo e sul tema della libertà antica; oltre al *Filippo*, scritto nel 1932 ma pubblicato nel 1934, essenziali per la definizione degli orientamenti degli studi del Momigliano in quegli anni *La koiné eiréne dal 386 al 338 a.C.*, «Rivista di Filologia e Istruzione Classica» n.s. 12 (1934), 482 ss., e in *Terzo Contributo* I, 493 ss.; *Genesi storica e funzione attuale del concetto di Ellenismo*, «Giornale critico della filosofia italiana» 16 (1935), 10 ss., e in *Contributo alla storia degli studi class*ici, Roma 1955, 165 ss.

[4] Vd. soprattutto *Prime linee di storia della tradizione maccabaica*, Città di Castello 1930, rist. Torino 1931, e Amsterdam 1968, e *Un'apologia del giudaismo: il* Contro Apione *di Flavio Giuseppe* (1931), in *Terzo Contributo* I, 513 ss. e *Pagine ebraiche*, 63 ss.; per le posizioni di Momigliano sulla questione ebraica vd. i documenti, con dure prese di posizione, in R. Di Donato, *Materiali per una biografia intellettuale di Arnaldo Momigliano*, «Athenaeum» 83 (1995), 219 ss.; vd. L. Ventura, *Ebrei con il duce. La «Nostra Bandiera», (1935-1938)*, Torino 2002, per un'analisi delle posizioni dell'ebraismo di quegli anni. Non condivido l'impostazione di S. Levis Sullam, *Arnaldo Momigliano e la nazionalizzazione parallela:autobiografia, religione, storia*, «Passato e Presente» 25 (2007), 59 ss., che sopravvaluta il taglio «politico» del giovane Momigliano: vd. le mie osservazioni in «Rivista Storica Italiana» 119 (2007), 1051 ss.

«non fu mai uno studioso capace di fare oggetto di indagine scientifica gli argomenti della sua fede». Ciò che, evidentemente, aveva cercato di fare il nipote[5].

Il cosmopolitismo dell'impero di Alessandro aveva creato le condizioni per questo confronto tra culture diverse, e per le conseguenti implicazioni sulla religione.

La più compiuta e durevole forma universalistica assunta dall'impero romano favorì l'affermarsi del cristianesimo, fino alla sua vittoria finale. L'interpretazione che Momigliano dava in quegli anni dell'impero presentava vari aspetti, ma analizzava tra l'altro i modi nei quali il cristianesimo aveva creato un rapporto del tutto nuovo tra pace e libertà, in collegamento evidente con le ricerche di storia ellenistica. L'impero aveva determinato il superamento del conflitto tra libertà politica della città classica, che era conquistata attraverso l'oppressione di altri, e la pace romana, che aveva eliminato la libertà dei vincitori, parificati infine ai vinti; si era così affermata la libertà più alta, interiore, della coscienza cristiana; lo stato divenuto cristiano, eliminando il conflitto tra lo stato stesso e libertà politica, consentiva di raggiungere la forma più elevata di libertà, e quindi la pace interiore, che superava ogni altro conflitto; la pace esterna era così anche pace della coscienza individuale.

La voce *Impero Romano* nell'*Enciclopedia Italiana*, nel 1936, formulava questo problema come chiave interpretativa generale: l'universalismo cristiano, la pace come valore spirituale resa possibile dalla pace romana, e il cristianesimo che, assorbendo le migliori energie e intelligenze dell'impero, mentre ne favoriva il declino se ne appropriava. Una chiave di lettura che non era comune nella ricerca di quegli anni, ripresa nella prolusione su pace e libertà dello stesso anno nella Università di Torino; e che torna nei saggi suoi ne *Il conflitto tra paganesimo e cristianesimo*[6].

---

[5] *Felice Momigliano*, in *Terzo Contributo* II, 843 ss., e in *Pagine ebraiche*, 153 ss.

[6] Vd. tra l'altro *L'opera dell'imperatore Claudio*, Firenze 1932, e i contributi per la *CAH* 10 (1934), 702 ss. e 887 ss.; *La formazione della moderna storiografia sull'impero romano*, «Rivista Storica Italiana» 48 (1936)/1, 35 ss. e (1936)/2, 19 ss., e in *Contributo...*, 107 ss.; importanti per le ricerche su pace e libertà, oltre ai saggi sulla *koiné eiréne*, la prolusione letta nella Università di Torino nel 1936, pubblicata in C. DIONISOTTI, *Ricordo...*, 109 ss., e in *Nono Contributo*, 409 ss.; *Pace e libertà nel mondo antico. Lezioni a Cambridge: gennaio marzo 1940*, a cura di R. DI DONATO, Firenze 1996, ove un'ampia analisi del tema nella riflessione di Momigliano in quegli anni; su questo tema vd. la importante discussione di E. GABBA, *Arnaldo Momigliano: pace e libertà nel mondo antico*, «Rivista Storica Italiana» 111 (1999), 146 ss., ora in *Riflessioni storiografiche sul mondo antico*, Como 2007, 215 ss. Nel volume su *Il conflitto* (Oxford 1963, trad. it.

Si trattava di problemi di attualità concreta e drammatica allora in Italia; appresi dal Momigliano nella scuola di De Sanctis, in dialogo con l'idealismo crociano e gentiliano, si nutrivano nel giovane studioso di una acuta preoccupazione filosofica, ma anche arrivavano a una sostanziale autonomia rispetto ai risultati specifici della ricerca antichistica di quegli anni. Era urgente per il giovane ricercatore fare i conti con le correnti prevalenti della storiografia e della filosofia della storia hegeliana ripensata dall'idealismo italiano, ma anche, fin dai primi studi, cercare una sua strada. La discussione dell'ellenismo del Droysen, in discussione con la filosofia della storia di Hegel, e il saggio sulla formazione della moderna storiografia sull'impero romano servivano, al Momigliano, a prendere posizione su questi problemi.

Ho richiamato questi aspetti, del resto ben noti, per sottolineare un punto: i temi di ricerca del giovane Momigliano lo impegneranno tutta la vita, ma il loro sviluppo, le differenti soluzioni prospettate nel corso del tempo, e infine negli ultimi anni, richiedono precisazioni non semplici. La sua educazione, la sua famiglia, la sua appartenenza ebraica, in una parola i problemi del suo tempo erano alla base della sua attività di ricercatore; in questo, egli rimase sino alla fine crociano. Sarebbe tuttavia un esercizio fuorviante individuare rotture e continuità nella formulazione dei problemi, basate principalmente sulla sua biografia. La insistenza autobiografica, divenuta così evidente, e ingombrante per noi, negli anni '80, non deve trarre in inganno: lo studioso continuava a verificare nei suoi studi l'origine dei propri problemi, in un rapporto dialettico tra esperienza personale e indagine storiografica. Momigliano, in sostanza, era fedele a se stesso sul piano delle regole del gioco, ma proprio questa fedeltà lo induceva a ripensamenti, chiarificazioni e controllo dei risultati[7].

Torino 1968), vd. l'Introduzione su *Il cristianesimo e la decadenza dell'impero romano*, 3 ss.

[7] Una diversa formulazione del rapporto tra vicende autobiografiche e orientamento degli studi propongono M. ISNARDI PARENTE, *Arnaldo Momigliano, la VII epistola e l'autobiografia*, «Belfagor» 43 (1988), 245 ss., e F. PARENTE, rec. a *Pagine ebraiche*, «Quaderni di Storia» 15 (1989), 171 ss. e *Arnaldo Momigliano e il giudaismo. Tra storia e autobiografia*, «Storia della storiografia» 16 (1989), 65 ss. (su cui vd. la replica di S. BERTI, *Autobiografia, storicismo e verità storica in Arnaldo Momigliano*, «Rivista Storica Italiana» 100, 1988, 300, n. 6, da leggersi con la *Introduzione* in *Pagine ebraiche*, IX ss.). Non convince la tesi di una frattura negli studi di Momigliano determinata da avvenimenti traumatici come la Guerra dei sei giorni, in quanto non tiene conto della ovvia continuità dei temi di fondo della sua ricerca, e della loro ispirazione; importante, in questa ottica, G. FUBINI, *Storicismo, storia della storiografia ed ebraismo*

Questo modo di procedere lo portava a volte su strade che si rivelavano impervie o non percorribili, altre volte apparentemente ai margini del tema principale.

In particolare, il tema di pace e libertà accompagnò Momigliano per molti anni dopo l'esilio; nato nel vivo della situazione italiana, culturale e politica, e già forse datato in quel momento, il libro che aveva progettato e continuamente modificato nel suo impianto non fu mai scritto; a leggere le lettere dei primi anni di Inghilterra appare chiara la difficoltà dello studioso: i due temi, libertà e pace, non potevano trovare una composizione, una unità concettuale. La libertà politica della *polis*, che nasce dall'oppressione, e la pace romana divenuta cristiana, che è etica e che rende possibile la pace dell'anima, e raggiunge quindi una forma superiore di libertà, erano due problemi distinti e non conciliabili nel concreto sviluppo storico. Momigliano non affrontò compiutamente la questione della libertà politica, ad esempio non fece che un accenno marginale alla questione assai complessa delle libertà municipali nell'impero romano, di contro alla soppressione della libertà politica a Roma e al conseguente trovare rifugio nella filosofia degli intellettuali e delle classi alte; le sue riflessioni sul rapporto tra intellettuali, come Seneca o Tacito, e l'opposizione o la collaborazione al regime, che avevano implicazioni assai serie negli anni '30, ripresero negli anni '80 con accenti diversi, che mostrano una compiuta consapevolezza della insufficienza delle formulazioni giovanili, pur senza invalidarle[8].

Questa difficoltà portò Momigliano a abbandonare il libro, ma non il tema. Alla fine degli anni '60 egli raccolse una quantità di schede sulle assemblee antiche, che utilizzò per le *Jerome Lectures*, del 1971, e per il saggio sulla struttura sociale della città antica. Le *Jerome Lectures* trattavano in definitiva due problemi: la libertà di parola nelle istituzioni poli-

---

in Arnaldo Momigliano, in *Appartenenza e differenza: ebrei d'Italia e letteratura*, Firenze 1998, 43 ss.

[8] Importante, per i rapporti con Croce, G. Sasso, *Il guardiano della storiografia*, Bologna 2002², 211 ss.; C. Dionisotti, *Momigliano e Croce*, «Belfagor» 43 (1988), 617 ss., ora in Id., *Ricordo...*, 27 ss.; Momigliano si è occupato della questione del rapporto tra intellettuali e potere a lungo negli anni del dopoguerra: è significativa la lettera a Dionisotti da Oxford del febbraio 1946: «Le lezioni su Tacito e il Tacitismo vorrei trasformare presto in volume: un contributo, inevitabilmente, alla fenomenologia della opposizione senza programmi positivi e collaboratrice sul terreno amministrativo, che ha solo il difetto di accompagnarsi di troppa esperienza personale». In queste affermazioni si riassumono anni di discussioni sul fascismo e sull'antifascismo nell'ambiente torinese degli anni '30 e '40. In tale contesto sono di grande interesse le pagine di C. Dionisotti, *Scritti sul fascismo e sulla Resistenza*, Torino 2008.

tiche, e il tema della empietà ed eresia, che definivano la libertà religiosa. La mia impressione è che questa fosse la strada intrapresa dal Momigliano, a distanza di anni, per tornare a riflettere sulla questione che aveva occupato i suoi anni giovanili, e che di nuovo si trovasse di fronte a una difficoltà: i due temi sono svolti, in definitiva, in modo autonomo, e nel suo svolgimento storico la libertà di parola del santo nei confronti di ogni potere terreno non si collega senza una qualche fatica alla libertà di parola delle assemblee[9].

Intanto, Momigliano si rivolgeva a un altro campo di indagine, il passaggio dall'antichità al medioevo; le forme culturali nuove prodotte dal rapporto tra paganesimo e cristianesimo prendevano le mosse dalla riflessione sulla fine dell'impero; il tema veniva esplorato in direzioni molto diverse; il problema storiografico, con la riflessione su Gibbon, si accompagnava alla identificazione di fondamentali passaggi nella formazione di una visione cristiana della storia, nella biografia dei santi e nella storia ecclesiastica come storia e come autorappresentazione.

Sono i temi maturati intorno alle lezioni del Warburg (1959), che ancora daranno, nel 1973, il saggio famoso sulla caduta senza rumore dell'impero. Le trasformazioni culturali prodotte dal conflitto religioso erano, ancora una volta, la chiave privilegiata di lettura di un fondamentale problema storico; un approccio che ripropone quello sull'ellenismo, ha le sue radici nella sua giovanile ricostruzione dell'impero romano, ma se ne distacca per la concretezza e la eliminazione di preoccupazioni filosofiche. Si tratta di una chiarificazione della tesi del ruolo della religione, e della chiesa come istituzione, nel determinare la creazione di un mondo nel quale il cristianesimo era divenuto elemento decisivo[10].

---

[9] *La libertà di parola nel mondo antico*, «Rivista Storica Italiana» 83 (1971), 499 ss. e *Empietà ed eresia nel mondo antico*, ibid., 771 ss., e in *Sesto Contributo* II, 403 ss.; allo stesso ordine di problemi si riferisce *The Social Structure of the Ancient City: Freedom of Speech and Religious Tolerance in the Ancient World*, «Annali Scuola Normale Superiore di Pisa» s. III, 4 (1974), 331 ss., e in *Sesto Contributo* II, 459 ss. Questo approccio, istituzionale e politico-sociale, non ebbe tuttavia continuazione, e la ricerca prese altre direzioni.

[10] Si veda, per la riflessione storiografica, *Ancient History and the Antiquarian* (1950), in *Contributo*, 67 ss., quindi in trad. it. in *Sui fondamenti della storia antica*, Torino 1984, 3 ss.; qui a 294 ss. i saggi rilevanti su Gibbon, a partire dal 1954, e la ristampa del saggio del 1936 sulla *Formazione della moderna storiografia...*, nel quale è impostato il problema del rapporto tra erudizione, critica delle fonti e ricostruzione storica tra '600 e '700; *La caduta senza rumore di un impero nel 476 d.C.* (1973), in *Sesto Contributo* I, 159 ss.

Tra gli anni '70 e '80 torna in primo piano la *treble tradition*; l'indagine assume direzioni sempre più articolate, che da un lato portano a una ulteriore chiarificazione delle sue posizioni, e dall'altro offrono sintesi di questioni essenziali. Nel 1975 con *Alien Wisdom* Momigliano riprende il tema del confronto tra culture nel mondo ellenistico, ma lo propone da una prospettiva rovesciata rispetto a quella degli anni '30: i greci, in definitiva, non comprendevano le altre culture, e quindi la loro capacità di assimilazione era molto limitata[11]. Alcuni saggi, tra cui *The Fault of the Greeks*, e *The Greeks and the Jews*, precisano ulteriormente il concetto, che verrà ripreso in una lezione a Chicago nel 1987; questa era la prima di una serie, sulla *Self-Awareness of the Protagonists*, e riprendeva la riflessione sulle origini della storiografia e della letteratura romane. Alla cultura ellenistica resistettero quelle società che avevano una identità forte, e fra queste il giudaismo aveva le maggiori possibilità; il monoteismo, il rigore dell'osservanza della legge, la sinagoga che con i rabbini ne era la custode, furono decisivi nel separare gli ebrei della diaspora, dopo la distruzione del secondo Tempio. Momigliano rivisita i temi della sua giovinezza, il moto maccabaico, e attribuisce importanza maggiore all'intervento esterno di Antioco, più che ai giudeoellenisti, già sostanzialmente incapaci di influire su scelte di fondo della società ebraica, proprio perchè, da questa prospettiva, essi erano privi di interlocutori; ne escono confermate, e rafforzate, le convinzioni sull'abbandono della storia da parte degli ebrei dopo il I secolo d.C., sul loro isolamento, e la fine di una creatività che stava invece caratterizzando i cristiani; Flavio Giuseppe parlava agli altri; culture meno attrezzate, come quella celtica, rinacquero solo col cristianesimo, che ne valorizzò, quasi paradossalmente, la identità nazionale, a cominciare dalla lingua; quasi paradossalmente, poiché il cristianesimo aveva ereditato l'universalismo romano, ma era capace di parlare alle realtà provinciali a lungo omologate nella cultura imperiale egemone e elaborata, e rivolta, alle classi alte[12]. Gli approcci alla storia religiosa dominanti sino agli anni

---

[11] *Alien Wisdom. The Limits of Hellenization*, Cambridge 1975; *The Fault of the Greeks* (1975), in *Sesto Contributo* II, 509 ss.; *Ebrei e Greci*, trad. it. in «Rivista Storica Italiana» 88 (1976), 425 ss., ora in *Sesto Contributo* II, 527 ss.; *The Self-Awareness of the Protagonists* (1987), pubblicato postumo nel *Nono Contributo*, 609 ss., rappresenta una riflessione sulle origini della storiografia romana vista nella prospettiva dominante in quegli anni nell'autore sulla reazione delle culture altre alla cultura greca.

[12] Esemplari di questo ordine di problemi *Il secondo libro dei Maccabei* (1975), in *La storiografia greca*, Torino 1982, 308 ss., e *Pagine ebraiche*, 41 ss.; quindi *The Romans and the Maccabees*, pubblicato postumo nel 1988, ora in *Nono Contributo*, 747 ss.; *Ciò che Flavio Giuseppe non vide*, «Rivista Storica Italiana» 91 (1979), 564 ss., e in *La*

'60, eredi della tradizione ottocentesca, non potevano spiegare i processi cui era interessato Momigliano, che vide negli studi più recenti la apertura di nuove strade. Approcci sociologici e antropologici, che aveva studiato nella loro prepotente apparizione in Francia, continuavano a interessarlo, ma non a convincerlo, e tantomeno li fece suoi come metodo d'indagine. Vale la pena di ricordarlo, dopo l'uscita di un curioso quanto ampio libro su *Momigliano and antiquarianism. Foundations of the Modern Cultural Sciences*; la tesi di fondo del curatore è che Momigliano avrebbe guardato a queste scienze come alla soluzione per fuoriuscire dalle secche dello storicismo, come aveva guardato alla antiquaria come antidoto alla storiografia dei *philosophes*: due tesi discutibili, che si sostengono, e smentiscono, a vicenda[13].

È significativo il fatto che lo sforzo di comprensione e approfondimento della religione portò a nuove indagini su Dumézil, Bachofen, Cumont e la antropologia anglosassone di Warde Fowler e altri, ancora una volta secondo il metodo di indagare il problema nella sua dimensione storiografica, essenziale per la sua comprensione e ricostruzione storica.

Questa riflessione conclude un ciclo, e apre una serie di altri interrogativi e percorsi.

Negli stessi anni, il ritorno a Droysen lo induceva a precisarne e approfondirne la interpretazione, dando maggiore spazio all'ambiente di ebrei convertiti che lo studioso, per via della moglie, si era trovato a frequen-

---

storiografia greca, 322 ss. e *Pagine ebraiche*, 73 ss.; *Daniele e la teoria greca della successione degli imperi*, «Accademia Nazionale dei Lincei» (Atti, XXXV) 1980, 157 ss., e in *La storiografia greca*, 293 ss. e *Pagine ebraiche*, 33 ss.

[13] *Momigliano and antiquarianism. Foundations of the Modern Cultural Sciences*, ed. P.N. MILLER, Toronto 2007; nel volume ci sono alcuni contributi di valore, volti a un esame critico della posizione di Momigliano, ma sfugge la motivazione ultima della raccolta; il saggio del 1950 affrontava il problema dell'antiquaria da un'angolazione del tutto diversa (vd. ad es. T. CORNELL, *Ancient history and the Antiquarian Revisited: Some Thoughts on Reading Momigliano's Classical Foundations*, in *Ancient History and the Antiquarian*, a cura di M.H. CRAWFORD e C.R. LIGOTA, Londra, 1995, 1 ss., e la rec. di O. MURRAY, «English Historical Review» 123, 2008, 414 ss.); le conclusioni di Miller sono in definitiva fuorvianti, in quanto indicano nell'interesse di Momigliano per le scienze sociali una sua scelta di metodo in funzione del superamento dello storicismo, che non avvenne se non parzialmente, e non per quella via; tra le molte discussioni di Momigliano in proposito basti rinviare al sintetico *Epilogo senza conclusione* (1980), in *Settimo Contributo*, 37 ss. Per la storiografia della religione in questi anni vd. *Premesse per una discussione su Georges Dumézil* (1983), «Opus» 2 (1983), 329 ss. (con qualche variante in *Ottavo Contributo*, 135 ss.); *From Bachofen to Cumont* (1986), in *Nono Contributo*, 593 ss.; *Bachofen tra misticismo e antropologia* (1987), in *Nono Contributo*, 767 ss.

tare; ma precisava anche che la assoluta predilezione per la cultura greca classica gli aveva impedito di svolgere l'ellenismo sul piano culturale, come sarebbe stato necessario per comprenderlo[14].

Accanto a Droysen, si fa prepotente l'esigenza di ripercorrere l'ebraismo attraverso medaglioni biografici di alcuni fondamentali studiosi: Bernays, Scholem, Leo Strauss, Benjamin, Finley, Bickerman, per citare alcuni particolarmente significativi, rappresentano una galleria che dà modo a Momigliano di individuare le molteplici influenze sugli studi, e le risposte individuali alla appartenenza ebraica, in una connessione a volte non facile da determinare tra biografia e orientamento della ricerca. Su questo si innesta la riflessione autobiografica. La rivendicazione della propria unitaria identità, di ebreo, piemontese, italiano, non è mai venuta meno,e si è accentuata, cercando indizi nelle biografie di altri. La ricerca di una identità ebraica, le diverse reazioni, dal rifiuto della assimilazione in Scholem, al suicidio di Benjamin, alla negazione di Finley e alla reticenza del terzo Bickerman, all'antistoricismo e alla ermeneutica di Strauss, percorre la riflessione storiografica di questi anni[15]. Ed è accompagnata dal ritorno alla riflessione sull'ebraismo italiano; visto ancora nella sua compiuta integrazione «nazionale» promossa dalla monarchia sabauda e dal Risorgimento, e negata tragicamente dal razzismo del regime fascista.

D'altro canto, l'indagine si fa più penetrante, e urgente, sul piano storico-culturale: i cicli di lezioni tra il 1977 e il 1982 sul giudaismo ellenistico, che dovevano dare luogo a un libro, *From Synagogue to Apocalypse*, che come tale non fu mai scritto, mostrano un continuo ripensamento e riordinamento di materiali; i temi erano uno sviluppo dell'approccio concettuale presentato in *Alien Wisdom*, arricchito da altri elementi più specifici[16].

---

[14] *J.G. Droysen between Greeks and Jews* (1970), in *Quinto Contributo*, 109 ss.; trad. it. in *Tra storia e storicismo*, Pisa 1985, 211 ss.

[15] *Jacob Bernays* (1969), in *Quinto Contributo* I, 127 ss.; *Gershom Scholem's Autobiography* (1980), in *Settimo Contributo*, 349 ss.; *Ermeneutica e pensiero politico classico in Leo Strauss*, «Rivista Storica Italiana» 79 (1967), 1164 ss., e in *Quarto Contributo*, 117 ss. e *In memoriam. Leo Strauss* (1977), in *Sesto Contributo* II, 841 sg.; *Walter Benjamin*, «Rivista Storica Italiana» 92 (1980), 815 ss., e in *Settimo Contributo*, 509 ss.; *Moses Finley*, in *Belfagor* 41 (1986), 25 ss. e *Moses Finley on Slavery: a Personal Note* (1987), in *Nono Contributo*, 657 ss. e 663 ss.; *L'assenza del terzo Bickerman*, «Rivista Storica Italiana» 94 (1982), 527 ss., in *Settimo Contributo*, 371 ss. Vd. anche *Storie e memorie ebraiche del nostro tempo*, «Rivista Storica Italiana» 92 (1980), 191 ss., e in *Settimo Contributo*, 361 ss.

[16] G. GRANATA, *La resistenza all'ellenizzazione. Il corpus di inediti momiglianei sul giudaismo ellenistico (1977-1982)*, «Studi Ellenistici» 12 (1999), 73 ss.; ID., in *L'Archivio Arnaldo Momigliano. Inventario Analitico*, Roma 2006, LXXXVI ss. Lo schema di

L'indagine sulla identità ebraica assume un rilievo straordinario negli ultimi anni, ed è da collegare alla urgenza di definire anche se stesso, la sua vicenda umana, in rapporto con la validità dei suoi studi. Tuttavia, in Momigliano la rivendicazione personale non diventa adesione acritica a questa o quella corrente dell'ebraismo. La collocazione dell'ebraismo nei confronti della cultura classica e del cristianesimo è questione primaria, per riproporne la legittimità, attraverso la dimostrazione della sua importanza e della sua appartenenza alla nostra cultura tutta; questo preoccupa Momigliano, e questa è la conclusione alla quale la sua vita e i suoi studi lo portano: rimanere ebreo, piemontese e italiano è un diritto, e forse anche un dovere; purtroppo, troppe volte a molti, e in moltissime circostanze storiche, questo non è stato possibile; la condanna dell'antisemitismo è prima di tutto etica, e poi culturale, non implica un giudizio storico privo di comprensione per quanti, da Giuseppe Flavio a Scholem, hanno scelto strade diverse. Solo nel chiarimento, senza indulgenze, della storia intera dell'ebraismo è la risposta possibile dello studioso alla sua condizione; Momigliano lo aveva detto per tutti gli anni '30, con i diversi accenti, le asprezze, i compromessi su scelte personali cui la situazione italiana allora induceva o costringeva. A distanza di decenni questo problema rimaneva intatto, più consapevoli erano le risposte, ma anche intatte le ansie e aumentate le incertezze. La questione, cruciale, della identità di un popolo che rifiuta la assimilazione, ha prodotto tragedie, e la integrazione senza identità non è mai stata una soluzione, né collettiva né individuale, priva di conflitti e contraddizioni insanabili. Di questo problema si nutrivano i suoi studi.

A questo ordine di idee mi pare di poter collegare l'interesse degli ultimi saggi di Momigliano per la persona; un interesse per il quale lo studioso riteneva importante misurare i risultati della sua indagine storica con la indagine antropologica e filosofica di due autori, Ernesto De Martino e Antonio Banfi, incentrate appunto sulla persona, in un saggio del 1987, preceduto da quello, del 1985, su Marcel Mauss e la persona

---

lavoro è stato ripetutamente modificato da Momigliano, con successivi ampliamenti, e solo alcuni testi sono stati pubblicati; fra questi assumono particolare rilievo, per le considerazioni svolte qui, *Indicazioni preliminari su apocalissi ed esodo nella tradizione giudaica*, «Rivista Storica Italiana» 98 (1986), 353 ss.; in *Ottavo Contributo*, 211 ss. e *From the Pagan to the Christian Sibyl: Prophecy as History of Religion*, in *Nono Contributo*, 725 ss. (versione italiana in «Annali Scuola Normale Superiore di Pisa» s. III, 17, 1987, 407 ss.).

nella biografia greca[17]. Lo stesso Momigliano sente il bisogno di spiegare il collegamento con i suoi interessi specifici degli ultimi anni; tale collegamento non era ovvio. Gli studi sulla biografia greca degli anni '70 non facevano intravedere questi sviluppi; essi si comprendono se guardiamo alla preoccupazione di Momigliano per la religiosità individuale, presente nei suoi ultimi lavori, e per il rilievo che assumono, in questo ambito, le ricerche sulla letteratura apocalittica giudaico-cristiana, sugli oracoli sibillini, sul messianesimo.

La mediazione tra gli interessi e il metodo di De Martino e Banfi non è compiuta del tutto, ma si comprende l'esigenza, che Momigliano sentiva, di esplorare queste potenzialità di analisi, che lo avevano incuriosito, ma erano rimaste fuori dagli interessi più immediati degli anni del dopoguerra.

Queste preoccupazioni dello studioso sono la formulazione più problematica di temi presenti nel suo ritorno alla storia religiosa, che vede anche la sua intensa collaborazione alla *Encyclopedia of Religion* di Mircea Eliade e i cicli di lezioni alla Università di Chicago. Mi pare di poter affermare che la sua preoccupazione di comprendere se stesso in rapporto all'ebraismo lo aveva portato a esplorare la nozione stessa di persona in culture anche lontane. Era il suo modo di chiarificare una questione che lo aveva accompagnato tutta la vita[18].

E proprio in questo ordine di problemi si iscrive la domanda su cosa realmente pensasse, in termini religiosi, l'uomo della strada nel mondo ellenistico e romano; si tratta di una accentuazione nuova del problema del comune sentire delle masse e degli individui. Il cosmopolitismo e

---

[17] *Marcel Mauss e il problema della persona nella biografia greca*, «Rivista Storica Italiana» 97 (1985), 253 ss. e *Ottavo Contributo*, 179 ss.; *Per la storia delle religioni nell'Italia contemporanea: Ernesto De Martino tra persona ed apocalissi* (1987), in *Nono Contributo*, 701 ss.; vd. G. BOWERSOCK, *Momigliano's Quest for the Person*, «History and Theory» 30 (1991), 27 ss.; C. GINZBURG, *Momigliano e De Martino*, «Rivista Storica Italiana» 100 (1988), 400 ss.

[18] Vd. tra l'altro *Ancient Biography and the Study of Religion in the Roman Empire*, «Annali Scuola Normale Superiore di Pisa» s. III, 16 (1986), 25 ss., e in *Ottavo Contributo*, pp. 193 ss.; *Religion in Athens, Rome and Jerusalem in the First Century B.C.*, «Annali Scuola Normale Superiore di Pisa», s. III, 14 (1984), 873 ss. e *Ottavo Contributo*, 279 ss.; *How Roman Emperors became Gods* (1986), in *Ottavo Contributo*, 297 ss.; *The Disadvantages of Monotheism for a Universal State*, «Classical Philology» 81 (1986), 285 ss. e *Ottavo Contributo*, 313 ss.; *Some Preliminary Remarks on the «Religious Opposition» to the Roman Empire*, in «Entretiens Fondation Hardt» 33 (1986), 103 ss. e *Nono Contributo*, 681 ss.; a questi saggi si collega una nutrita serie di recensioni e altri interventi, volti a chiarire singoli aspetti del problema che Momigliano stava affrontando in quegli anni.

l'universalismo sono ora collocati in una prospettiva che va oltre la impostazione degli anni '30, e li pone alla base di un'analisi di problemi concreti: il monoteismo in un impero universale, il culto dell'imperatore in relazione al politeismo, la educazione religiosa di ebrei e cristiani, di cui sappiamo poco, ma che aveva una base dottrinaria e dei libri, e la difficoltà di comprendere cosa significava essere nati, e formati, nel paganesimo, la possibilità di individuare una specifica religiosità popolare, il ruolo della religione nella opposizione all'impero, e la considerazione del fatto che il cristianesimo potesse più facilmente alimentarsi di alcuni contenuti della cultura classica che non di un ebraismo che si era chiuso nella difesa di sé, le conseguenze del superamento della storia classica da parte di ebrei e cristiani nella visione apocalittica e messianica; sono tutti aspetti di un modo di calare la storia religiosa nella visione complessiva di una triplice tradizione che non si lascia ridurre a schematismi, ricca di contraddizioni, chiaroscuri e rimescolamenti. Questo approccio, che pone al centro ancora una volta la religione come elemento essenziale collettivo e individuale, è nutrito della fede laica del ricercatore, che crede nel metodo per l'accertamento della verità storica, e nel dubbio che alimenta la ricerca, e dunque non beneficia, direbbe Momigliano, di una fede ricevuta una volta per tutte.

GIANMARIA ZAMAGNI

Theology and history. A retrospective on the *End of the Constantinian Era* in the works of F. Heer, E. Buonaiuti and E. Peterson

1. Starting from Momigliano: Cincinnati, 1959

In his introductory essay to *The Conflict between Christianity and Paganism in the Fourth Century*, Arnaldo Momigliano sought to summarise that work through a formula, according to which «no interpretation of the decline of the Roman empire can be declared satisfactory if it does not also account for the triumph of Christianity». This statement has rightly become famous. Immediately after, however, he also stressed a certain divergence from the history of Christianity:

> «It may seem ridiculous to have to emphasize this proposition so many years after A. Harnack and E. Troeltsch. But a careful study of their works can perhaps explain why they failed to impress their fellow historians. Though both Harnack and Troeltsch were well aware that the Church was a society competing with the society of the Roman empire, they remained theologians to the end. They were more interested in the idea of Christianity than in Christians. Rostovtzeff and Pirenne, who loved the cities of men, may be excused if they remained unimpressed by theologians who talked or seemed to talk about the idea of the city of God»[1].

This essay will not seek to discuss this aspect of Momigliano's work more closely[2]. It is interesting to note, however, the way in which in the period from the 1930s to the 1950s a series of historians, Friedrich Heer, Ernesto Buonaiuti and Erik Peterson, in works written either side of the Second World War, dealt with issues of late antiquity: of pagans and

---

[1] A. MOMIGLIANO, *The Conflict between Paganism and Christianity in the Fourth Century*, Oxford 1963, 6.
[2] On this, see G.G. STROUMSA, *Arnaldo Momigliano and the History of Religions*, in *Momigliano and Antiquarianism. Foundation of the Modern Cultural Sciences*, ed. P.N. MILLER, Toronto-Buffalo-London 2007, 286-311; see 298-300 and 304-306 in particular.

Christians, the city of God and the city of men, and the «end of the Constantinian era»[3].

2. Vienna, 1953: Friedrich Heer's *Europäische Geistesgeschichte*

In the same year in which Momigliano began that focus on late antiquity which would lead to *The Conflict between Paganism and Christianity in the Fourth Century*[4], the Austrian historian Friedrich Heer published his *Europäische Geistesgeschichte*[5], in which he, a medievalist by training, went for the first time beyond the strict chronological limits of that discipline by starting his history of ideas with the birth of Christianity. The aim, as he wrote in the preface, was to study the intellectual history of post-classical Europe or, to be more precise, «between Constantine and Hitler»[6].

---

[3] I refer here to Marie-Dominique Chenu, who was the subject of my *La «Fine dell'era costantiniana» in F. Heer e M.-D. Chenu (1938-1963). In tre quadri e un epilogo al Concilio vaticano II*, «Cristianesimo nella storia» 29 (2008), 113-138. This essay represents a continuation of themes investigated in that article; these studies are preparatory to my post-doctoral dissertation, *«Fine dell'era costantiniana». Retrospettiva genealogica di un concetto critico*, Bologna 2010.

[4] A. MARCONE, *Un treno per Ravenna. Riflessioni sulla Tarda Antichità*, in *Arnaldo Momigliano nella storiografia del Novecento*, ed. L. POLVERINI, Rome 2006, 219-233; compare also L. CRACCO RUGGINI, *Arnaldo Momigliano e il Tardoantico*, in *Omaggio ad Arnaldo Momigliano. Storia e storiografia sul mondo antico*, ed. L. CRACCO RUGGINI, Como 1989, 159-184, and A. FRASCHETTI, *Trent'anni dopo Il conflitto tra paganesimo e cristianesimo*, in *Pagani e cristiani da Giuliano l'Apostata al sacco di Roma*, ed. F.E. CONSOLINO, Cosenza 1995, 5-14.

[5] F. HEER, *Europäische Geistesgeschichte*, Stuttgart 1953; the *Vorwort* has the date as 22nd April. Reviews of this work have been published by: W. VON DEN STEINEN, «Historische Zeitschrift» 179 (1955), 93-99; J. KRUEGER, «Deutsche Zeitschrift für Philosophie» 3 (1955) 2, 268-277; H.J. SCHOEPS, «Zeitschrift für Religions- und Geistesgeschichte» 7 (1955) 1, 89-91; C. BRINTON, «The American Historical Review» 60 (1955) 4, 856-857; «Philosophischer Literaturanzeiger» 14 (1961) 3, 97-100; more generally, it is interesting to note that the work was translated in 1966 into English by Jonathan Steinberg for the publishers Weidenfels and Nicolson: F. HEER, *Intellectual History of Europe*, London 1966.

[6] F. HEER, *Europäische Geistesgeschichte...*, 6: «[Dieser Essay] ist ein Versuch, zwischen gestern und morgen, zwischen alter und neuer Geistesgeschichte, einige Kraftlinien aufzuzeigen, und einige Punkte festzuhalten, die für das geistige Schicksal Europas bestimmend waren. "Europa" wird hierbei in einem engen Sinne begriffen, als das nachgriechische Westeuropa zwischen Konstantin und Hitler». This book immediately followed F. HEER, *Aufgang Europas. Eine Studie zu den Zusammenhängen*

Heer begins with the description of a society in which there was still no precise distinction between Christians and pagans, in the same way as there was no distinction between «pre-» and «post-» Christian. If, at its most intimate, the word «tradition» designated the passing of a secret revelation within a cultural community, Paul – the Apostle to the Gentiles – had, in his letters to the Ephesians and Colossians, transferred the language of the ancient mysteries onto Christian liturgy, contributing to a similarity of gestures, rituals, customs, and also abuses[7].

In defining Christ as the «true Orpheus» or the «true Logos», in highlighting similarities with Odysseus, with Socrates and with Plato, Christianity had no uniqueness (*Einzigartigkeit*). On the other hand (as had already been stated by Buonaiuti), there were still no «new people of God», before a divinity given sacred names, cultural symbols, the same colours (Peterson) and dress as a Hellenistic emperor. The greatest risk to Christians came not from persecution but from the possibility of being reabsorbed – through familiarity, through connaturality – into the pagan world, into the many cults existing in late antiquity[8].

For the Viennese historian, the traumatic possibility of disappearing into the Graeco-Roman ecumene would have had extremely long-term effects. Above all, it would have led to the expulsion of sects from the

---

zwischen politischer Religiosität, Frömmigkeitsstil und dem Werden Europas im 12. Jahrhundert, Vienna-Zurich 1949 and F. HEER, *Die Tragödie des Heiligen Reiches*, Stuttgart 1952, both of which drew on studies completed prior to the outbreak of the Second World War, when Heer became a member of the *Institut für Österreichische Geschichtsforschung* (Institute for Austrian historical research) of Vienna. For a bibliography and biography of Heer see respectively: A. GAISBAUER, *Friedrich Heer (1916-1983). Eine Bibliographie*, Vienna-Cologne 1990, and E. ADUNKA, *Friedrich Heer (1916-1983). Eine intellektuelle Biographie*, Innsbruck-Vienna 1995. These works have been followed by W.F. MÜLLER, *Die Vision des Christlichen bei Friedrich Heer*, Innsbruck-Vienna 2002; *Offener Humanismus zwischen den Fronten des Kalten Krieges. Über den Universalhistoriker, politischen Publizisten und religiöse Essayisten Friedrich Heer*, ed. R. FABER, Würzburg 2005; and lastly, *Die geistige Welt des Friedrich Heer*, eds. R. FABER and S.P. SCHEICHL, Vienna-Cologne-Weimar 2008.

[7] F. HEER, *Europäische Geistesgeschichte...*, 10: «Tischsitte, Gebetsgeste und Totenmahl, alle Sitten und Unsitten [...] teilen vom 2. bis 5. Jhdt. die Christen mit den "Heiden"»; the reference essay on this theme was O. CASEL, *Zur Kultsprache des heiligen Paulus*, «Archiv für Liturgiewissenschaft» 1 (1950), 1-64.

[8] F. HEER, *Europäische Geistesgeschichte...*, 10: «Das Schockerlebnis der Christen, ihre hohe und berechtigte Angst, verschlungen und aufgesogen zu werden von den Kulten der "heidnischen" spätantiken Gesellschaft, die auch sie, die Christen, barg und aufzog, vermochte dennoch in den stärksten Geistern nicht das Bewußtsein der großen Einheit der vor- und nachchristlichen Menschheit zu überdecken».

womb of the church herself (1 Cor. 11:19), «heresies» that found their own origins in popular enthusiasm, in learned gnosis or in the Hellenistic philosophical school. The exclusion of old and new sects started the process of self-comprehension of the «Great Church»: a process through which many different Christianities matured into a single «dialectic complex» church-heresy, which would last for centuries[9].

In the world of late antique education (*heidnisch-christliche Bildungswelt*), it was difficult to distinguish between Christian, non-Christian, or even anti-Christian, versions of Platonism, Stoicism, and especially Gnosticism; concepts that could have led to a clear subordination and devaluation of the second person of the Holy Trinity – and ultimately the role of Jesus in history[10]. Heer describes this phase as a «*pre-Constantinian and pre-Theodosian union of Christian intellectuals with their pagan brothers*» which dramatically went into crisis with the entrance of religion into politics, (or rather, of politics into religion), «*from the moment when their spirit was bewitched by the pleasures and the promises of power*»[11].

It is against the backdrop of the great spiritual and intellectual currents of late antiquity, principally Origenism and Arianism – understood as attempts to give a theological shape to the gospel, (in a similar way to the Greek-Hellenistic philosophy, which had been able to integrate Christian theology into

---

[9] *Ibid.*, 12: «Sie [*scil.* die Christen] vermochten dergestalt nicht zu erkennen, wie "Kirche" und "Häresien" zusammengehören, wie der geheimnisvolle, vom *Geist* überschattete Wachstumsprozeß der Christenheit zu ihrem Selbstverständnis und ihrer Selbstbehauptung als „Kirche" gebunden ist an das Entlassen von Häresien aus ihrem eigenen Schoße»; see also above this quotation: «"Europa": das sind zunächst Heere und geschlossene politische Gebilde und Organisationen; der "Osten": das ist ein Sich-Begegnen, Zusammenströmen, Verschmelzen und Wiedertrennen religiöser Bewegungen, philosophische Ideen, politischer Erfahrungen und volkhafter Bedingtheiten vieler "Völker", "Nationen" und "Reiche", aus denen sich im Prozeß des 2. bis 5. Jhdt. die Christentümer durchringen zu jenem Komplex, der als "Kirche" und "Häresien" das geistige Geschehen bis zum heutigen Tage bestimmen wird» (9). This is the crux of Heer's work; the very word *Geist* (italicised in the text) does not only serve to identify the (holy) Spirit, but it is a key to Heer's critique of the *Geistesgeschichte* of the protestant school; on this, see the preface (*ibid.*, 5-6), and also E. ADUNKA, *Friedrich Heer...*, 444 («Das Gegenstand einer solche "Histoire spirituelle" sieht Heer im Zusammenwirken von Gottes Geist und Menschengeist»), and W.F. MÜLLER, *Die Vision...*, 223 («In seiner "Europäische Geistesgeschichte" wehrt sich Heer gegen diese "Säkularisierung" des Geistes»).

[10] F. HEER, *Europäische Geistesgeschichte...*, 16: «Da entpuppen sich heidnische Philosophen als christliche Apologeten, Bischöfe konzipieren rein immanente Weltdeutungsversuche, in denen Christus gar keine, eine zweideutige oder sehr untergeordnete Rolle spielt».

[11] *Ibid.*, 17.

pagan divinity[12]) – that the political-religious actions of Constantine stand out, themselves very common in the society of late antiquity:

> «This process is incomprehensible only to posterity, which can no longer understand the role and functions of ancient gods in the political community of men, for their salvation, health, peace and political security, assured by the power of the presence, and for which, on the other side, Christ was also reduced to an "idea"»[13].

It was therefore natural that Constantine held the position of bishop within the council, to ensure the rights and salvation of his subjects, as well as peace; on the other hand, Heer did not find anything opportunistic in the Arian confession of faith signed under Constantius II by Hosius of Cordoba, adviser to the First Council of Nicea, who had long resisted Arianism. However, Eusebius of Caesarea was the true «patriarch of the political theologians»: his monotheistic ideas, focusing on «one God, one emperor, one land, one (religious-political and national) faith», and according to which «the one God is enthroned as the Great King in his royal residence, in his celestial palace. On Earth, he is represented by Constantine»[14] showed an Origenian and Arian pedigree more deeply rooted in a Graeco-Roman context than in Jewish monotheism[15].

---

[12] *Ibid.*, 19. Heer was cross-referencing here to: H. BERKHOF, *Kirche und Kaiser. Eine Untersuchung der Entstehung der byzantinischen und der theokratischen Staatsauffassung im vierten Jahrhundert*, Zürich 1947 (see *ibid.*, 200: «Origenismus und Arianismus sind zum guten Teile als Versuche zu verstehen, dem Evangelium eine theologische Form zu geben»); and to M. WERNER, *Die Entstehung des christlichen Dogmas problemgeschichtlich dargestellt*, Berne-Leipzig 1941, 271 and 371.

[13] Heer – quoting the review of W. SESTON, *La vision païenne de 310 et les origines du chrisme constantinien*, in «Annuaire de l'institut de Philologie et d'Histoire orientales et slaves», IV [=*Mélanges Fr. Cumont* (Brussels 1936)], 373-395, published in *Archiv für Liturgiewissenschaft*, 1 (1950), 311 – was making a blunt remark on *labarum* with a method typical of the history of religions: see F. HEER, *Europäische Geistesgeschichte...*, 20.

[14] This is how Heer (agreeing with and quoting Erik Peterson), saw Eusebius' *Triakontaétérikos* I.1-6, ed. I.A. HEIKEL, *Eusebius Werke* I (*Tricennatsrede an Constantin*), in GCS 7, Leipzig 1902, 196-199; compare this to EUSÈBE DE CÉSARÉE, *La théologie politique de l'Empire chrétien. Louanges de Constantin (Triakontaétérikos). Introduction, traduction originale et notes*, ed. PIERRE MARAVAL, Paris 2001; Maraval, whilst concedingto J.-M. Sansterre that the theory of a proto-Bizantine Eusebius «semble devoir être abandonnée» (n. 62), still concludes «qu'avec cet ouvrage et la *Vie de Constantin* il en a posé le fondements», and that his political theology has had «une longue postérité dans tout l'Occident chrétien» (65).

[15] F. HEER, *Europäische Geistesgeschichte...*, 21: «Die weltbewegende Formel: Ein Gott – ein Kaiser – ein Land – ein (religiös-politischer Staats-)Glaube wurzelt mehr noch

For Heer, the protection of the absolute uniqueness (*Einzigartigkeit*) of the Son of God against the Arian idea of *logos* and the protection of the mystery of the Trinity, (the conflicts of Pope Liberius and Lucifer of Cagliari, of Eusebius of Vercelli, of Ambrose and Hilary of Poitiers), were at the root of the Western, popular aversion towards a Christian-pagan development, science and philosophy in the centuries to follow: the human and historical nature of Christ were the proof enough of God's existence[16].

After the war, Heer's work, which had its origins in the context of occupied Austria[17], warned against attempts at restoration that, echoing Constantine, proclaimed the political and religious dogma: «One faith, one people, one *Führer*, one culture, one sword»[18].

---

als im jüdischen Monotheismus in der politischen Wirklichkeit und der geistigen Welt der griechisch-hellenistischen Ökumene»; therefore «Eusebius wird zum Erzvater der politischen Theologie von Byzanz, Aachen und Moskau, nicht einfach nur aus politischen Opportunismus, sondern als griechischer Monotheist, als Schüler des Origenes und Arius»; again, Heer was referring to E. PETERSON, *Der Monotheismus als politische Problem*, in ID., *Theologische Traktate*, Munich 1951, 45-147.

[16] *Ibid.*, 23: «*Für den Osten hat der historische Christus keine Beweiskraft, für den Westen wird die geschichtliche Tat der Gottesbeweis*» (author's italics). Heer was quoting in these pages the first volume of *Storia del cristianesimo* by E. Buonaiuti, who will also be mentioned elsewhere: with the unification of Italy Heer noted the «beginnende Befreiung des Katholizismus von der Ideologie der antikischen, mittelalterlich-barokken Kosmosstadt Rom», and listed him alongside Don Sturzo, Papini, Gramsci and Croce, to show «wie fruchtbar dieser Aufbruch geworden ist» (*ibid.*, 369).

[17] This is visible, for example, when he writes in the introduction to his first work, *Aufgang Europas*: «Diese Arbeit ist *cum ira et studio* geschrieben: in Bedrängnis durch ein Zeitalter, das für den frei schaffenden geistigen Arbeiter Pressalien und Terror aller Art zur Verfügung stellt» (7); for information on Heer's early career, see his *Jugend zwischen Haß und Hoffnung*, Munich-Eßlingen 1971; see also E. ADUNKA, *Friedrich Heer...*, 18.

[18] F. HEER, *Europäische Geistesgeschichte...*, 656, where he outlines his fears over «die Bemühungen, auf katholischer Grundlage einen neuen Nationalismus, technisch durchorganisiert in totalitären Systemen, als Heilslehre und Heilsmacht anzubauen. [...] Unter Berufung auf Konstantin, Karl der Großen, Donoso Cortes usw. wird hier das religiös-politische Dogma verkündet: Ein Glaube, ein Volk, ein Führer, eine Kultur, ein Sabel»; Heer alludes here to the work of C. SCHMITT, *Donoso Cortés in gesamteuropäischer Interpretation*, Köln 1950.

3. Rome, 1942: E. Buonaiuti's *Storia del cristianesimo*

Among the direct references made in the text, the name of Ernesto Buonaiuti appeared most frequently and was most often quoted in the first chapter of *Europäische Geistesgeschichte*. His *Storia del cristianesimo*, which had only recently been made available in Germany[19], should be understood as starting from the eternal dualism that for the Roman priest forms the basis of the Christian tradition (as of every genuine religious experience[20]). The reason behind the preaching of John the Baptist and of Jesus was, in this way, identified as a prophetic reaction – at the same time ethical and eschatological – to the politics of conquest, violence and injustice[21]. The

---

[19] E. BUONAIUTI, *Storia del cristianesimo*, Milan 1942/XX-1943, or rather only the first two volumes, had been translated in 1948 by Hans Markun, working for the publishers Francke in Berne; see also H. MARKUN, *Geleitwort des Übersetzers*, in E. BUONAIUTI, *Geschichte des Christentums* I, Berne 1948, 7-11; Heer always felt he owed a debt to Buonaiuti: in 1973, Heer dedicated an episode of the radio transmission «Erst verfemt und dann geehrt» from the Saarlandischer Rundfunk (Saarland Broadcasting) to him; during the series, Buonaiuti followed Origen, St. Francis of Assisi, Jan Hus and Felicité de Lamennais; see also A. GAISBAUER, *Friedrich Heer...*, 300.

[20] On this, see M. RAVÀ, *Introduzione*, in *Bibliografia degli scritti di Ernesto Buonaiuti*, Preface by L. Salvatorelli, ed. M. RAVÀ, Florence 1951, XV: «Il Buonaiuti è nettamente dualista. [...] Questa concezione lo conduce di rimbalzo a una visione della società basata su una netta dicotomia fra valori politici e valori religiosi, dicotomia che si manifesta in pieno nel cristianesimo»; and, more recently, G. GAETA, *Introduzione* to E. BUONAIUTI, *Pellegrino di Roma. La generazione dell'esodo*, Rome 2008³ (first edition being 1945), XI: «Certo non fu Buonaiuti il primo a rilevare la matrice escatologica del cristianesimo, ma gli va dato il merito di averne assunto il dualismo implicito a chiave di lettura della storia, grandiosa e tragica, del cristianesimo; dualismo a cui non ci si può sottrarre senza cadere in una idealità disincarnata oppure di adeguarsi alla logica di questo mondo». Directly regarding the work examined here, compare: R. MORGHEN, *Il modernismo e la storia del cristianesimo di Ernesto Buonaiuti*, in *Ernesto Buonaiuti storico del cristianesimo. A trent'anni dalla morte*, Rome 1978, 7-22; ID., *Tradizione cristiana e civiltà mediterranea nel pensiero storico di Ernesto Buonaiuti, ibid.*, 23-41; A. PINCHERLE, *Buonaiuti storico dei primi secoli, ibid.*, 43-53; and F. PARENTE, *Ernesto Buonaiuti e gli altri storici del cristianesimo e della chiesa antica, ibid.*, 159-188. See also R. MORGHEN, *Louis Duchesne e Ernesto Buonaiuti storici della chiesa e del cristianesimo*, in *Monseigneur Duchesne et son temps (Actes du colloque organisé par l'École Française de Rome, Palais Farnèse 23-25 mai 1973)*, Rome 1975, 375-393; and *Ernesto Buonaiuti*, in the *Appendix* to E. BUONAIUTI, *Pellegrino di Roma...*, Rome 2008³, 621-638.

[21] E. BUONAIUTI, *Storia del cristianesimo...*, I, 25: «Ma quando, appunto, tutta la violenza malefica di cui è capace un'organizzazione statale, sul cui fondamentale egoismo non esercitino la loro virtú di freno e di correttivo la visione degli inviolabili diritti della coscienza e la fede dell'Infinito, affiori e stranipi nello svolgimento della vita associata;

preaching of Paul, consisting of the transferring of Moses' values onto the pagan liturgies of mysteries, found its reason for being in the blocking of the cult on the part of the religious Jerusalemite powers, and its polemic target in the Roman imperial domination, which dared to present itself with the insignia of celestial sovereignty[22]. The millenarian element, taking its basis from chapter 20 of the Book of Revelation was – more than the reason for its success – a symbol of the theoretical effort of early Christianity. In particular, Buonaiuti set great store by the «first theorist of millenarianism», Papias (in this, Buonaiuti was against an ecclesiastical tradition which still found itself in the twentieth century «under the woeful impression given by the disdainful judgment of Eusebius of Caesarea»[23]) and by the *The Shepherd of Hermas*. This work, charismatically effervescent, would soon be superseded by «a refined system of philosophical and theological speculation, destined to influence the thought and attitudes of European society»[24].

---

quando l'intreccio dei fatti storici dia la sensazione esasperante della impossibilità di opporre un margine alla perversità di un potere, giunto in pari tempo al massimo grado della sua degenerazione e della sua forza bruta; gli spiriti acquistano, improvvisa, la consapevolezza di una sanzione ultraterrena e, affrancandosi dal fosco fascino degli interessi e della materialità su cui s'innalzano le gerarchie politiche, intuiscono l'incommensurabile virtú etica e sociale della rinuncia e concretizzano, d'istinto, il loro anelito di liberazione, nella fede del soprannaturale, che sa abbattere e rinnovare con armi ignote alla perfidia e all'inganno delle potestà umane»; see also *ibid.*, 29-45.

[22] On the first idea, see *ibid.*, 46-59 and 49: «Non sarebbe stato per caso cómpito provvidenziale d'Israele l'innestare, sulle amorali credenze dei misteri, la coscienza dei valori morali, nella celebrazione dei quali era il vanto della legislazione Mosaica?»; on the second, see page 51: «quei Cesari [...] con la loro blasfema pretesa di ricevere onori divini appaiono inequivocabilmente, all'Apostolo, quali mostruosi e insani profanatori di quanto v'è di sacro nello spirito dell'uomo e della vita associata. [...] vale a dire il Sovrano Imperiale, nella cui persona divinizzata e nelle cui temerarie prerogative Roma pagana aveva sintetizzato tutte le capacità malefiche della sua politica sopraffattrice». For Buonaiuti, imperial power and pharisaism were «due forze difformemente ostili» to the original ethical messianism of Christian preaching (see *ibid.*, 61); see also E. BUONAIUTI, *Il messaggio di Paolo*, Rome 1933, IX: «il legalismo farisaico e il paganesimo hanno saggiato tutte le vie, da due millenni, per separare Cristo da Paolo o Paolo da Cristo».

[23] Controversially, it continues: «Ma l'aulico biografo costantiniano aveva le sue buone ragioni per deprezzare il millenarismo, egli che era capace di scoprire una pregustazione del regno di Dio in un banchetto offerto a corte ai vescovi di Nicea» (*ibid.*, 76, but see also 83).

[24] E. BUONAIUTI, *Storia del cristianesimo...*, I, 95. Buonaiuti however, explicitly refused to include Christian thought in the broader evolutionary process of Hellenistic inquiry: «il passaggio del cristianesimo da religione di messianismo e di escatologia a religione

This development, the first trace of which Buonaiuti found in the writings of Basilides as given by Clement of Alexandria, existed at the time of the «original» Gnosticism, since this had been the «speculative attempt to move the moral dualism on which evangelical preaching depends into the realm of cosmogony»[25]. In the writings of various second century apologists, *Storia del cristianesimo* found in common a theoretical need (from time to time more or less linked to the eschatological character of early Christianity) that aimed to translate the Gospel into a terminology that might be more easily understood by the sensitivities of the cultured classes of the pagan world. This took place through, for example, the study of Justin on the *logos*, or the repudiation of Tatian and the scorn of Hermias for philosophy[26]. For Buonaiuti, the mirror of this irresistible trend was Tertullian, who had in his *Apologeticum* argued against polytheism (and in defence of Christians), but had done so using a metaphysics based on parallels to Hellenistic cults. He argued that: «Christianity created not only the aggressive weapons used for its defence and

---

della dommatica e del rito offre un cosí caratteristico modello di quel che è, nella storia delle religioni, il solidificarsi e il cristallizzarsi repentino dei vasti entusiasmi mistici, nelle formole paralizzanti del pensiero e della liturgia, che è straordinariamente istruttivo cogliere tale processo, di trasformazione e di transizione, nei suoi confini circoscritti e nella sua cornice isolata» (*ibid.*, 96).

[25] *Ibid.*; moreover, he wrote that through Gnosticism «il messaggio cristiano iniziale si viene trasformando in una visione integrale e composita del mondo, delle sue origini, delle sue vicende, delle sue trasfigurazioni nel pensiero e nella esperienza dell'uomo, del destino della vita e del raggiungimento della salvezza attraverso il mistero della iniziazione e della grazia» (*ibid.*, 109); regarding the importance of this development, see page 530 of the Bibliography *ibid.*: «lo gnosticismo ha rappresentato veramente il primo passo, e passo decisivo, verso l'elaborazione disciplinare cattolica dell'atteggiamento apocalittico della prima forma di conversione e di rinnovamento, in cui è l'essenza della parola neotestamentaria», but see also E. BUONAIUTI, *I frammenti gnostici*, Roma 1923. From what he says here it seems clear how strongly he felt that Christianity and Gnosticism did not simply overlap: «Se parallelamente al formarsi del pensiero gnostico teniamo di mira il movimento proselitistico del millenarismo cristiano, anch'esso tutto pervaso di senso dualistico della vita e di aspettativa di una palingenesi cosmico-sociale, noi comprendiamo perfettamente come nel decorso della civiltà romano-mediterranea, il cristianesimo costituisse una forza di ascensione e di progresso, destinata infallibilmente a scardinare la vecchia struttura sociale del mondo romano per trapiantarla su altre basi e su altri sostegni» (*ibid.*, 114).

[26] *Ibid.*, 136, where the apologists, aside from their various differences, are described as «tutti intenti a purgare la figura morale dei cristiani dalle accuse inverecondi che il mondo pagano circostante scagliava contro la loro professione di fede, e tratti da un istinto quasi inconsapevole a rivestire il messaggio cristiano di una patina filosofica che lo facesse accetto alle classi colte dell'Impero»; compare also the relevant part of the Bibliography *ibid.*, 532.

attack, but also offered a systematic forging to a Christian teaching that was still shapeless and fluid. From this forging arose the dogma of the ecclesiastical tradition»[27].

However, it was in the historical work of Eusebius (written soon after the Edict of Toleration by Galerius), and in particular in the apostolic succession, that Buonaiuti found the first traces of the process of centralisation towards Rome: in this way the inheritance of jurisdiction and the supremacy of the apostolic succession (see also the case of Hegesippus[28]) replaced a charismatic and prophetic doctrine of early Christianity (the *didaché*). This formed part of a historical-philosophical framework, very different to that of the expectation of the kingdom of Heaven, and because of which – albeit slowly – «charismatic Christianity became a bureaucratic hierarchy» (the *diadoché*)[29].

According to *Storia del cristianesimo*, first Tertullian's *Adversus Praxean* showed the fusion between the original apocalypticism (which made a strong return with montanism) and the metaphysical rebuttal of the errors which could already be termed Trinitarian. Accordingly, Buonaiuti saw this fusion in an economic conception of the Trinity, which is defined as «a unity that refracts into multiple hypostases, corresponding to the variable cycles in the historical process of humanity»[30].

---

[27] *Ibid.*, 146. On this theme, Buonaiuti had already written *L'apologetica cristiana: Tertulliano*, Milan 1926 and *Il cristianesimo nell'Africa romana*, Bari 1928.

[28] *Ibid.*, 168: «Se dunque, secondo Egesippo, la pulviscolare secessione delle eresie si rinnova nel seno del cristianesimo, come già aveva imperversato in seno al giudaismo, il cristianesimo, continuazione del giudaismo, doveva, per difendersi, seguire la prassi del giudaismo stesso, e fare ricorso ad un sacerdozio organizzato e ad un pontificato legittimamente legiferante e amministrante le realtà sacre». In these pages Buonaiuti went as far as to propose Hegesippus as the author of Mt 16,18 (*ibid.*, 172).

[29] *Ibid.*, 159, which continues, observing the degree to which this centralisation was assisted by «la formazione di quella filosofia della storia, di cui Eusebio stesso si costituisce testimone e patrocinatore eminente, la filosofia cioè che vede nella storia la manifestazione ininterrotta di un immanente Verbo divino, di un Logos astratto, di cui il cristianesimo è la suprema incarnazione [...] Ed una trasformazione di questo genere non rappresentava una attenuazione sensibilissima dell'atmosfera messianico-apocalittica nella quale erano vissute le prime generazioni cristiane?»; the phrase «inheritance of jurisdiction» («eredità di giurisdizione») is used *ibid.*, 165; the *didaché/diadoché* juxtaposition is reaffirmed later (*ibid.*, 169).

[30] *Ibid.*, 193, which continues «d'altro canto, millenarista convinto, Tertulliano ha dinanzi ai suoi occhi una amministrazione divina ben definita e esaurientemente ripartita. Il piano dell'azione divina è tutto conchiuso nella raffigurazione trinitaria. [...] Fenomeno strano: ci volle un eretico montanista per dare alla Chiesa latina la formula del suo dogma trinitario». On Tertullian and the «economic» conception of the Trinity,

The dualistic outlook of Christianity, which led it to place greater emphasis on the kingdom to come than on earthly power, led inexorably to the community of Christians being the designated victims – «also in this sense heir and successor to the Hebrew religious community»[31]– of a new way of exercising the power of Rome. This was even more true from the moment when the evolutionary trajectory of the Roman Empire had sealed a partnership between West and East that had led the sovereign to take on, like the Eastern tyrants, the traits of a god incarnate[32], a «Tunic of Nessus» to which the emperors were attracted, almost despite themselves:

> «Every time the West has found itself politically close to the East, the latter, while accepting the cultural and legislative predomination of the former, has imposed on it both its techniques of monarchical government and its conception of the venerable divinity of the sovereign»[33].

In Tertullian, Buonaiuti found an «irreconcilable» antithesis between, on the one hand, communal awareness, moral superiority, and the millenarian zeal typical of Christianity and the Imperial Roman constitution on the other[34]. The Constantinian «revolution» was to be, in this sense, the water-

---

see also E. BUONAIUTI, *Il cristianesimo nell'Africa romana...*, 168 and E. BUONAIUTI, *Gioacchino da Fiore. I tempi – la vita – il messaggio*, Rome 1931, 204.

[31] E. BUONAIUTI, *Storia del cristianesimo...*, I, 216.

[32] *Ibid.*, 223: «La grande novità e la grande scoperta del cristianesimo è la separazione netta dei valori politici dai valori religiosi. Di fronte ad una concezione dura, assoluta, della vita politica e del suo organo direttamente rappresentativo, lo Stato, il cristianesimo ha praticato nel mondo una super-politica, anch'essa assoluta, la quale implicava la svalutazione completa, dal punto di vista morale e religioso, della organizzazione statale. E un impero romano che per logica fatale di cose tendeva automaticamente a rivestirsi, al modo delle monarchie orientali, di forme ieratiche e di pretese divine, era automaticamente tratto a scorgere nel cristianesimo il suo irriducibile avversario e ad assumere quindi un atteggiamento di difesa che si riversava immediatamente in una pratica persecutrice». Compare, also, *ibid.*, 324: «Nella storia del Cristianesimo [Costantino] ha segnato una data fatale perché ammettendo la legalità del Vangelo che in tutto il suo contenuto sociale è separazione di valori politici dai valori religiosi, ha iniziato un ciclo di civiltà, in completa difformità dalla mentalità del Cristianesimo antico».

[33] *Ibid.*, 215; in the *Bibliography* (*ibid.*, 535), Buonaiuti found a fundamental problem in the contrast in political forms between early Christianity and the Empire: in this sense, he was making a reference to L. SALVATORELLI, *Lo stato e la vita sociale nella coscienza religiosa d'Israele e del cristianesimo antico* I, Pavia 1913.

[34] Here the contrast between paganism and Cristianity was reduced to a truely civil and political debate: «Contro questa coscienza federativa del cristianesimo primitivo, contro questa non dissimulata pretesa di superiorità morale, spirituale e religiosa; la massa pagana si ribella. Il cristianesimo, nelle sue espressioni più audacemente innovatrici

shed of Christian antiquity, an epochal transition, and – moreover – the central theme in the history of Mediterranean civilisation[35]. In his reconstruction of past events, the roman priest emphasized the political/military and sociological reasons for the «conversion» of Constantine above all others: through his religious policy, he had succeeded in winning over the educated, and increasingly important, Christian classes of Africa and then the Middle East[36]. Through the resolution of the Donatist schism, the foundation of the new capital and the outbreak of the Arian crisis, he obtained supremacy.

Thanks in particular to the latter development, two possible interpretations of the second person of the Trinity (and hence of Christianity itself) faced each other: a soteriological-prophetic and a philosophical interpretation, the latter for Buonaiuti entirely practical as part of a totalitarian system of government:

> «At the root of the discussions provoked by Arius there was a simple problem: did not Christianity, now the state religion, need to be neatly treated as one of those philosophical and cultural forms that had never truly irritated or hindered the absolutist nature of the pagan state?»[37].

---

come la millenaristica, non rappresentava la corrosione minacciosa della costituzione imperiale? Cristianesimo e vita imperiale non si rivelavano come i due termini di una antitesi irreconciliabile?»; E. BUONAIUTI, *Storia del cristianesimo...*, I, 234.

[35] *Ibid.*, 236: «Nell'evo antico valori politici e valori religiosi sono strettamente associati gli uni agli altri, perché la religione rappresenta, né piú né meno, che un dovere civico come gli altri. [...] Nell'evo nuovo invece la sfera dei valori religiosi è bruscamente scissa da quella dei valori politici». Compare *ibid.*, 269: «La storia della civiltà mediterranea sarebbe stata d'ora in poi la storia del contrasto fra Cesare Augusto e i rappresentanti di quel Maestro galileo che Roma, per bocca del suo rappresentante in Giudea, aveva condannato»; and, again, see *ibid.*, 324. The bibliography regarding this point (*ibid.*, 536) refers above all to A. DE BROGLIE, *L'Église et l'Empire Romain*, Paris 1856, but also to the work of A. Piganiol, W. Seston, J.-R. Palanque and E. Staehelin.

[36] *Ibid.*, 320: «Istintivamente diffidente verso tutti coloro che avevano avvicinato il debellato rivale Licinio, Costantino si appoggia dunque nel primo momento del suo trionfo orientale alle correnti cristiane dell'Egitto alessandrino, come per l'Occidente, nelle sue prime diffidenze per tutto quello che era romano, dopo la vittoria *ad Saxa Rubra*, si appoggia all'episcopato dell'Africa romana»; see later 324: «Il suo grande sogno politico, l'unificazione cioè dell'Impero, non piú possibile ormai senza la preponderanza incontrastata dell'elemento orientale, non si sarebbe potuto attuare senza che egli entrasse sempre piú in dimestichezza con le classi nuove che, cristiane, rappresentavano in Oriente la cultura e il potere».

[37] This is the terminology used, on 298: «L'arianesimo rappresentò un tentativo audace di fare della teodicea e della teologia cristiana un puro sistema dialettico umano. L'Impero totalitario ne avrebbe potuto comodamente attingere le idee piú atte a quella disciplina intellettuale che è in fondo il piú squisito e valido strumento di governo».

In contrast, the Trinitarian mystery was inseparable from that of the prophetic claim, and necessarily implied an apocalyptic aspect; the text continues:

> «Or rather, had Christianity not, within the sphere of its beliefs and its doctrinal transcripts, to maintain and enhance that atmosphere of mystery, and therefore of indifference, to the usual expressions of culture, which had automatically made it an opposition force to the absolutism of the pagan state?»[38].

It was highly significant for the history of the church, then, that at the Council of Nicea it was the anti-Arian party led by Alexander and Athanasius of Alexandria that had the upper hand, since the true reason for the *homoousia* dispute was a question of cultural and theological dominance, balanced between Rome as the cradle of Christianity and Constantinople as the seat of Imperial power[39]. Hence while undergoing many metamorphoses, Caesar, the Empire, and the Roman papacy (which gradually became theologically more dogmatic[40]) would survive. A history that Buonaiuti lived through until the Lateran Accords of 11th February 1929, and afterwards[41].

4. Rome, 1936-35. Two essays of Erik Peterson

The analysis offered in *Europäische Geistesgeschichte* also owed, in various points, a debt to a pair of then-recently republished essays by Erik

---

[38] *Ibid.*, 508.
[39] *Ibid.*, 347: «La conversione dell'Impero al Cristianesimo non aveva fatto altro che scatenare nel seno dell'episcopato cristiano il prurito scandaloso per un predominio apparente, che in realtà non era altro che un asservimento nettamente antievangelico ai poteri politici e alle loro finalità».
[40] *Ibid.*, 406: «L'impero è sopravvissuto, sotto le più strane e imprevedibili reincarnazioni, a Cesare, per diciotto secoli. Pietro sopravvive ancora. [...] Anche il papato ha subíto le sue profonde metamorfosi e l'aumento del suo potere si attua di pari passo con una elaborazione sempre più complessa della dogmatica teologale e con un irrigidimento sempre più meccanico e sempre più legalistico e burocratico della sua disciplina».
[41] See, for example, this extract from E. BUONAIUTI, *Pellegrino di Roma*, Bari 1964², 503: «Il vitello d'oro era levato su tutte le vie, per ricevere le prostrazioni degli incoscienti. Le contaminazioni della coscienza e della cultura, ormai da decenni e decenni accostumate alla fornicazione più sfacciata con gli ideali politici e con le contraffazioni pseudo-morali di correnti spirituali aliene da ogni disciplina e da ogni ispirazione evangeliche, davano il loro risucchio nella insensibilità universale alla catastrofe immane, in cui andavano ad inabissarsi i titoli più insigni del nostro passato».

Peterson[42]. In particular, the short 1936 essay *Christus als Imperator* had an influence on the very beginning of Heer's book, while another segment a little further on owes a debt to *Der Monotheismus als politisches Problem*[43].

Christ as Imperator analysed the theme of the title in ancient Christian literature, through quotes from Tertullian, Cyprian and Lactantius, amongst others[44]. For Peterson, however, the value that the term took on in St. Augustine's *City of God* was exemplary, because in it was a particularly explicit reference to eschatological time. Therefore, a Christ *imperator* could not only be understood in the sense of the Christian *militia*, but also, and above all, in the sense of transcendency, which erupted into opposition to the pagan *imperium*:

---

[42] F. HEER, *Europäische Geistesgeschichte...*, 10, 20 and 24 (though the latter is a little less pronounced) refers to E. PETERSON, *Theologische Traktate*, Munich 1951; but evidence of Peterson's influence is already visible in 1949, in the first comment in *Aufgang Europas... Kommentarband*, 25, which took the lead in a critical analysis of political religiosity: «Die "politische Religiosität" als Grundphänomen der abendländische Geschichte ist zum erstenmal entscheidend herausgestellt worden in den Arbeiten Erik Petersons».

[43] E. PETERSON, *Christus als Imperator*, «Catholica» 5 (1936), 64-72, later republished in the *Appendix* to E. PETERSON, *Zeuge der Wahrheit*, Leipzig 1937, a text which has also been published in French (*Les témoins de la Vérité*, Paris 1948) and in Italian (*I testimoni della verità*, Milan 1955). See also E. PETERSON, *Der Monotheismus als politisches Problem. Ein Beitrag zur Geschichte der politischen Theologie im Imperium Romanum*, Leipzig 1935, published in Italian as *Il monoteismo come problema politico*, Brescia 1983, and in French as *Le monothéisme: un problème politique*, Paris 2007: they are both included in *Theologische Traktate*, Munich 1951 (45-147 and 149-164 respectively), and as such republished by B. NICHTWEISS, in *Ausgewählte Schriften* I, Würzburg 1994. On the life and work of Peterson see: F. BOLGIANI, *Dalla teologia liberale alla escatologia apocalittica. Il pensiero e l'opera di Erik Peterson*, «Rivista di storia e letteratura religiosa» 1 (1964), 1-58; *Monotheismus als politisches Problem? Erik Peterson und die Kritik der politischen Theologie*, ed. A. SCHINDLER, Gütersloh 1978, the *Appendix* of which has reviews of *Der Monotheismus*; of these, I would recommend that of N. TURCHI, in *Studi e materiali di storia delle religioni*, 12 (1936), 225; G. RUGGIERI, *Resistenza e dogma. Il rifiuto di qualsiasi teologia politica in Erik Peterson. Editoriale*, in E. PETERSON, *Il monoteismo come problema politico...*, 5-26; B. NICHTWEISS, *Erik Peterson. Neue Sicht auf Leben und Werk*, Freiburg-Basel-Vienna 1992; B. NICHTWEISS, *Zur Einführung*, in E. PETERSON, *Ausgewählte Schriften* I, Würzburg 1994, VII-XXIII; *Vom Ende der Zeit. Geschichtstheologie und Eschatologie bei Erik Peterson (Symposium Mainz 2000)*, ed. B. NICHTWEISS, Münster 2001, which contains a further *Bibliography* on Peterson in the *Appendix*.

[44] E. PETERSON, *Christus als Imperator...*, 152: «Jedenfalls ist die Beziehung dieser Akklamation auf Christus in der patristischen Literatur häufig».

«When one considers all these contexts, it also becomes possible to understand where early Christian literature speaks of Christ not only as *imperator* regarding the authority over his *militia*, but of how at the same time the Christ-Imperator is the lord of an empire that transcends all earthly empires. The empire of Christ has superseded the pagan empire»[45].

The language of Revelation itself testifies to the correlations with the Roman model – among others, Heer referred to the colours of the Four Horses and the factions of the Roman Circus[46] – but only to show the opposite meaning of these reflections. Ancient exegesis, to give only Peterson's principal example, had interpreted the declaration of loyalty owed to Him who sits on the throne (see Rev. 4) as being in opposition to the oath of allegiance to the secular ruler[47]. The conclusion, in this sense, was clear: in the parallel between Christ and the Emperor no symbology serving as an apology for the Empire should be found, regardless of the context in which it originated; rather, a symbolism of explicit, open conflict[48].

With this text, Peterson was engaging in a direct confrontation with Harnack's *Militia Christi* of thirty years before: the sense of protochristian martyrdom was not to be understood morally (as had Harnack), but eschatologically, and so the struggle in question was that of earthly empires, *all* earthly empires, and the transcendent heavenly empire which had opposed them[49]. It was not therefore a simple, mundane comparison between

---

[45] *Ibid.*, 153, referring to A. von Harnack, *Militia Christi. Die christliche Religion und der Soldatenstand in den ersten drei Jahrhunderten*,Tübingen 1905.

[46] E. Peterson, *Christus als Imperator*..., 156: «Der Antritt der Herrschaft Christi wird mit kosmischen Zirkusspielen eingeleitet, die das Proömium zum Ende dieser Welt darstellen».

[47] *Ibid.*, 155.

[48] *Ibid.*, 156: «Es ist klar, daß in der Parallelisierung Christi mit dem Imperator keine zeitlose Symbolik, sondern eine Kampfsymbolik vorliegt». It should be remembered that the terminology used by Peterson was that of a contraposition (*entgegenstellen, Gegengestalt, Gegenstück, Gegenkundgebung* and *passim*).

[49] *Ibid.*, 157: «In seinem bekannten Buch über die Militia Christi, Tübingen 1905, S. 10, hat Ad. Harnack behauptet, das militärische Element in der christlichen Stimmung sei nicht aus der christlichen Apokalyptik, sondern aus der sittlichen Ermahnung abzuleiten. Ich halte das für eines jener Mißverständnisse Harnacks und der liberalen Theologie, das auf einer mangelnden theologischen Einsicht beruht. Man kann den altchristlichen Begriff des Märtyrers nicht verstehen, wenn man nicht den Zusammenhang mit der urchristlichen Eschatologie erkennt»; on this, see F. Bolgiani, *Dalla teologia liberale...*, 35: «Lo scritto *Testimoni della verità* è appunto l'attacco piú diretto, sul piano teologico, come fu giustamente notato, contro la concezione di uno stato totalitario».

church and state, to be solved finding some sort of *modus vivendi*[50], but a real «struggle» (*Kampf*) between the kingdom of God and the Empire, which had taken place when the Roman *princeps* had become a *Führer* who had united all power under himself[51]. This was the theme of Peterson's short essay: a theological critique, historically based, on the cult of the charismatic leader, written a few months after the moment in August 1934 when Hitler had assumed all the main offices of the German Reich with the name of *Führer und Reichskanzler*[52].

Therefore, although quotes from John's gospel repeated this eschatology (for example, when Jesus says «my kingdom is not of this world» in Jn 18:36), the *Christus Imperator* formula could find a conceptual space in a world where the Jews were now without a king, and the Romans only had Caesar[53]. Here, Peterson was not indulging in a «dialectic» theological scheme: in fact, he well understood how for a community, a militant church which was living through a period of martyrdom, the acclamation of Christ as Emperor should have a truly terrestrial meaning.

The most important theoretical reference in the work of Heer was, however, to be identified in Peterson's famous earlier essay, *Der Monotheismus als politisches Problem*, the basic thesis of which had already

---

[50] Note that on the 20th July 1933 Hitler's Germany and the Holy See had agreed the *Reichskonkordat*; see F. BOLGIANI, *Dalla teologia liberale...*, 27.

[51] E. PETERSON, *Christus als Imperator...*, 157: «Der Christus, der Imperator ist, die Christen, die zur *militia Christi* gehören, sie sind Symbole eines Kampfes um ein eschatologisches *imperium*, das sich allen *imperia* dieser Welt entgegenstellt. Es handelt sich hier nicht um eine Auseinandersetzung zwischen Staat und Kirche, die sich als zwei Institutionen gegenüberstehen und als Institutionen nun auch einen *modus vivendi* finden müssen, sondern der Kampf (und nicht die Auseinandersetzung) ist nötig geworden, weil die Basis des Institutionellen im Imperium verlassen ist. Als mit der Vergrößerung des Imperiums die Massen nicht mehr einfach mit den Institutionen der Polis zu regieren waren, mußte der *princeps* als Führer alle Macht in sich vereinen».

[52] Compare this to B. NICHTWEISS, *Zur Einführung*, in E. PETERSON, *Ausgewählte Schriften*, I, VII-XXIII: «Eine durchaus passende Zusammenstellung, denn dieser Text ist nur auf den ersten Blick eine rein historische Studie über einen patristischen Christus-Titel. Auf den zweiten Blick enthüllt sie sich als die anhand eines sorgsam ausgewählten historischen Stoffes geführte Kritik an einem totalitären "Führer"-Kult, den die Kirche als "militia Christi" im "blutigen Krieg der Märtyrer" überwinden müsse. Der Text ist eine Paradebeispiel für Petersons Kunst, im Willen zur Wirksamkeit in einer konkreten, (kirchen-)politischen Situation der Gegenwart historische Forschung und theologische Deutung zu verbinden»; *ibid.*, XVIII.

[53] E. PETERSON, *Christus als Imperator...*, 160: «In einer Welt, die notwendigerweise von allem Institutionellen gelöst ist, da die Juden ohne König sind und die Heiden nur den Cäsar haben, muß auch der König der kommenden Welt in dem Kampf um den zukünftigen Äon etwas von einem Imperator annehmen».

been anticipated in an invocation to Augustine: «for Christians, political actions can only exist in the context of faith in the Triune God. This faith is beyond Judaism and paganism»[54].

Peterson surveyed the different values attributed to the concept of divine monarchy, beginning with Aristotle and the unknown author of *De mundo*, according to which the monarchical *constitution* of the universe expressed an objection to the metaphysical pluralism of the heavenly powers[55]. The concept would nonetheless acquire theological-political values only with Philo: in Alexandrian Judaism[56] and later for the Apologetic Fathers, monotheism and divine monarchy coincided closely in a Hellenistic context[57] (so much so that the adjective «divine» was omitted). This formed the basis for the mission (or *propaganda*[58]) to the Gentiles.

---

[54] E. PETERSON, *Der Monotheismus...*, 47; in the first part of *Der Monotheismus* Peterson returned to the theme of his *Göttliche Monarchie*, «Theologische Quartalschrift» 112 (1931), 537-564; see also *Der Monotheismus als politisches Problem?...*, 14.

[55] This was the terminology given: «Für der Verfasser der Schrift von der Welt hat der Kosmos eine monarchische *Verfassung*» (my italics), E. PETERSON, *Der Monotheismus...*, 52.

[56] *Ibid.*, 58: «Für ihn steht aus der konkreten Situation seines Judentums heraus das theologisch-politische Problem im Vordergrund [...] Dabei wird das metaphysische Problem, ob es ein odere mehrere Prinzipien gibt, nicht eigentlich mehr diskutiert, die Entscheidung scheint auch in der metaphysischen Welt *vom* Politischen *her* erfolgt zu sein» (my italics); note, however, the terminology used to describe the passage of the concept from Aristotle to Philo of Alexandria: «Der Begriff des Homerischen Königtums nicht eigentlich mehr einen sprachlichen Ausdruck gefunden hat, vielmehr steht der Königstitel anscheinend unorganisch neben der Beamtentitulatur der griechischen Polis, die auf Gott *übertragen* worden ist. Wir finden eine solche *Übertragung* der Beamtentitular auf Gott in der hellenistischen Literatur [...] öfter» (*ibid.*, 61, my italics, but see also *Ibid.*, 117, n. 57). On Peterson's view on Philo of Alexandria, see H.-U. PERELS, *Philo von Alexandrien*, in *Monotheismus als politisches Problem?...*, 28-32.

[57] See *ibid.*, 60, which observed how «Dabei ist ohne weiteres deutlich, daß es wohl möglich war, auf dem Boden des Heidentums von einer göttlichen Monarchie zu sprechen, die sich erst im Kampf gegen die Gewalten der Unordnung im Kosmos konstituiert, aber von den Voraussetzungen des jüdisch Gottes- und Schöpfungsbegriffes aus war das nicht möglich».

[58] E. PETERSON, *Der Monotheismus...*, 64: «Das Bedeutsame ist, daß auch hier, in dem Beweis des "Monarchie"-Begriffes aus der griechischen Dichtung, der Zusammenhang der christlichen mit der älteren jüdischen *Propaganda*literatur wieder deutlich ist. Der "Monarchie"-Begriff des Alexandrinischen Judentums war letzthin ein politisch-theologischer Begriff, dazu bestimmt, die religiöse Überlegenheit des jüdischen Volkes und seine Sendung an das Heidentum zu begründen». This was how the apologists Tatian and Justin retranslated the phrase – naturally the church found itself among the Jewish population.

An examination of the anti-Gnostic arguments of Theophilus of Antioch (although here the concept had no theological or political value) makes it possible to assess a further aspect of Peterson's text. To contemporary poets and Gnostics, Theophilus argued that enthusiasm and dualism of gender (Adam and Eve) should not to give rise to doubts about the monarchy of God:

> «It is poetic enthusiasm and women which can bring us to make this mistake [of metaphysical pluralism], but both are surmountable temptations. It is clear from the words of Theophilus that his concept of monarchy, precisely because it is always shown in real situations, cannot be turned into politics, which in its concept of unity must always, necessarily, be placed above a particular situation»[59].

This showed the degree to which the concept of divine monarchy had originated in tangible circumstances, (even from physical, bodily causes) and could not be distanced from them, unlike attempts to give an extra-temporal, non-contextual meaning to the divine monarchy.

Within Christian literature, the more overtly political problem would be created only in the struggle. The concept of *monarchia* – ultimately denoting a group within the church (*monarchiani*) – was heavily debated because with Praxeas, this had found a powerful new function, entirely within the sphere of metaphysics, which involved the identification of the Son with the Father[60]. In these circumstances, Tertullian contrasted his legal and statutory construction against that of the grammarian Praxeas, in order (again, quite casually and pragmatically) to «understand the relationship between Christ and God *originating from* the joint rulers of Rome»[61], a construction that went as far as to prevent Tertullian from see-

---

[59] *Ibid.*, 66; the problem of the two genders was to be read as reflection of Gnostic theories which related procreation to the material principle; in this sense Peterson was also referring to Theophilus the analysis on Marcion of Sinope of the *Pseudo-clementines*.

[60] *Ibid.*, 69: «Praxeas scheint der Erste gewesen zu sein, der den Begriff der "Monarchie" – wenngleich polemisch – auf das Verhältnis des Sohnes zum Vater angewandt hat, während der Ausdruck bisher immer nur in der kosmologischen Sphäre Verwendung gefunden hatte».

[61] *Ibid.*, 70, my italics. A few lines before Peterson had defined this as a *polemische Gelegenheitschrift*. Such an explanation rendered it possible to justify Roman polytheism: not only the Son, but a myriad of divinities could be included, like «gods who govern with God» (Maximus of Tyre), or like «vice-sovereigns and satraps» (Aelius Aristides), in a true Christian pantheon, modelled on a Persian or Imperial Roman despotism; compare E. PETERSON, *Der Monotheismus...*, 72. On this part and the similarities, highlighted by Athenagoras of Athens, with the joint reign between Marcus

ing how the concept of monarchy was inapplicable to that of a triune God: «it is impossible to simply *transfer* the secular concept of the monarchy of pagan theology onto the Trinity»[62].

Having concluded that the attempts – of Praxeas like those of Tertullian – to unite the doctrine of divine monarchy with the Trinitarian dogma had failed[63], Peterson went on to examine the christological debate between Dionysius of Alexandria and Dionysius of Rome. Against the theories of Marcion of Sinope, but against, at the same time, the subordinationism of Dionysius of Alexandria, «the Pope said that God has never existed without the divine Logos (θεῖος λόγος) and the Holy Spirit. This is the only way "one can save the Trinity of God and the sacred proclamation of the monarchy"».

At the time of the *edict of tolerance,* issued by *Gallienus* in A.D. 260, the difficulties of merging the two semantic constellations were finally overcome; Dionysius of Rome above all was able to transfer (*übertragen*) not the legal-constitutional construction of Tertullian, but the philosophical concept of monarchy (which he defined σεμνότατον) onto the Trinity, thus paving the way for attempts at conciliation and compromise[64].

Therefore, for Peterson, talking of a divine monarchy was not only a *rhetorical figure*, a *metaphor* («*Bild*»)[65]: Celsus, for example, despite being against it, had fully grasped the political significance of Judeo-Chris-

---

Aurelius and Commodus, compare J. BADEWIEN, *Die Apologeten und Tertullian*, in *Monotheismus als politisches Problem?...*, 32-36, which seeks to explain this process in the philosophical terms of *analogy*, a concept not used by Peterson.

[62] E. PETERSON, *Der Monotheismus...*, 72, my italics. See also shortly before: «Es ist nun erstaunlich, daß Tertullian, der, wie die Auseinandersetzung im Apologeticum beweist, dieses Bild aus der heidnischen Verteidigung des Polytheismus kannte, dennoch es wagen konnte, sich desselben zur Bestimmung des trinitarischen Verhältnisses zu bedienen».

[63] *Ibid.*, 76: «Unsere Ausführungen haben gezeigt, daß die ersten Versuche, die überkommene Lehre von der göttlichen Monarchie mit dem Trinitätsdogma zu verknüpfen, gescheitert waren. Das gilt von dem Versuch des Praxeas so gut wie von dem Tertullians».

[64] *Ibid.*, 77: «Er hat vielmehr [...] die philosophische Ausdeutung des Begriffes der "Monarchie" [...] auf das trinitarische Verhältnis [...] übertragen und damit einen Ausgleichversuch zwischen dem Monarchie-Begriff und dem Trinitäts-Dogma angebahnt»; the quotation given by Peterson was from Dionysius' letter to the Sabellians, in Athanasius, *Epistola de Decretis Nicænæ Synodi*, PG 25, 461D ff.

[65] *Ibid.*, 79: «Es handele sich im Grunde nur um ein "Bild", dem keinerlei politische Bedeutung beizumessen sei. Ein Hinweis auf die Polemik des Celsus gegen die Christen wird nun aber zeigen, daß der politische Sinn des jüdisch-christlichen Monotheismus im Altertum durchaus nicht verborgen geblieben ist».

tian monotheism. He judged it to be an impulsive metaphysical revolt of he who «ultimately *transfers* his own emotions onto God», thereby jeopardizing the multinational balance of the Empire[66].

Through the theory of the *logos* would come the attempt to realise what Celsus had pronounced to be, as desirable as it was impossible, namely the subordination of all peoples within a single legal-religious sphere[67]. Thus, even if Origen operated within the limits of eschatological prophecy (Zep 3:9, Ps 71:7), the reference to the *pax augusta* showed that a tendency to overcome national differences already existed[68]. Eusebius, unlike Origen, led to the complete «de-eschatologisation» of the problem of monotheism, and therefore to political Arianism: Constantine was, in this sense, the perfect reflection of a heavenly monarchy made into a god on earth.

For Peterson, with the wording of the dogma of the Trinity it had become impossible to transfer the image of the Roman Empire onto divinity, so at the same time the doctrinal debate became a political struggle[69]. St. Augustine, on whom the essay began, also heralded its conclusion. Thanks to this renewed understanding of the eschatological meaning of the prophecies of peace and the (non-) political meaning of the Trinity,

> «a doctrine of divine monarchy had to fail before the Trinitarian dogma, as did the interpretation of the *Pax Augusta* before Christian eschatology. In this way, not only was monotheism as a political problem closed theologically, and the Christian faith freed from its ties to the Roman Empire, but also the break was made with any "political theology" which misused the Christian message to justify a certain political situation[70]».

However, if the assumption of Carl Schmitt's *politische Theologie* consisted in the consideration that all significant concepts of the modern

---

[66] *Ibid.*, 79.

[67] *Ibid.*, 80: «Gewiß, das wäre etwas, "wenn es möglich wäre, daß Asiaten, Europäer und Libyer, Hellenen sowohl wie Barbaren, die bis an die Grenzen der Erde verteilt sind, in einem einzigen Gesetze übereinstimmten. Aber wer so etwas annimt, der weiß im Grund gar nichts"».

[68] E. PETERSON, *Der Monotheismus...*, 84: «der Glaube an die eschatologische Aufhebung der nationalen Unterschiede zu der Tendenz führt, diese Differenzierung schon jetzt als im Verschwinden begriffen zu konstatieren».

[69] *Ibid.*, 102: «Der Monotheismus ist eine politische Forderung, ein Stück der Reichspolitik. In dem Augenblick, in dem der Begriff der göttlichen Monarchie, der nur die Widerspiegelung der irdischen Monarchie im Imperium Romanum war, in einen Gegensatz zum christlichen Trinitätsdogma trat, mußte der Streit um dieses Dogma zugleich zu einem eminent politischen Kampf werden».

[70] *Ibid.*, 104.

theory of the state are secularized theological concepts, Peterson's essay did more than just rebut this view through his demonstration of how this was inapplicable to the Trinity. In fact, Schmitt's ideas were literally upturned: all previous ideas on the monarchy of God had been nothing more than occasional transferences (*Übertragungen*) onto the divinity of tangible, everyday constitutions.

Epilogue: London, 1986, and some thoughts on theology and history

Twenty-three years after *The Conflict between Christianity and Paganism in the Fourth Century*, Arnaldo Momigliano returned to this theme, publishing an article devoted to the problems of monotheism in a universal state[71] in the journal «Classical Philology». Here, mentioning *Der Monotheismus als politisches Problem*[72], he expressed his high regard for the *theologian* Peterson: his was rated «the most remarkable book ever produced on the subject»[73].

(1) The impossibility of the transference from the city of men to the city of God, (and *vice versa*) also manifested through the opposition to acquiescences and conciliations between Church and political power; (2) the refusal to reduce the humanity of Jesus to a disembodied *logos* and (3) the impossibility of reducing history to the history of salvation (and *vice versa*), were shown – in the historical context of three countries crushed by Fascism – by these concepts: (1) what Peterson saw as the absolutely immeasurable gap between transitory, earthly powers and the divine Trinity (but, at the same time, the effectiveness of the faith of those who believed in the latter) – *contra* Constantine; the dualism with which Buonaiuti expressed the eschatological tension of Christian morality – *contra* Arius;

---

[71] A. MOMIGLIANO, *The Disadvantages of Monotheism for a Universal State*, «Classical Philology», 81 (1986), 285-297 (later reproduced in ID., *On Pagans, Jews, and Christians*, Middletown, CT, 1987, 142-158); from the introduction: «If we want to know what the Roman Empire was and why in the East it survived until 1453, we must of course turn to military history, not to religious history»; on this essay see J. ASSMANN, *Herrschaft und Heil. Politische Theologie in Altägypten, Israel und Europa*, Munich/Vienna 2000, 21 and G.G. STROUMSA, *Arnaldo Momigliano...*, 300.
[72] A. MOMIGLIANO, *The Disadvantages...*, in particular 291-293.
[73] *Ibid.*, 292. The essay completes Peterson's argument by noting the (for the «costantinians» providential) destruction of the temple and of the nation of Israel in view of the *pax augusta*.

and Heer's express refusal to idealistically identify (or isolate) spirit and *Spirit* – *contra* Eusebius.

As for the history of the church, it becomes then possible to think, in fact, of an «"open" secularisation, in the sense that this discipline aims at scientific knowledge of forms of Christian life which follow one another; forms that are, to the believer, also signs»[74].

---

[74] G. ALBERIGO, *Nuove frontiere della storia della chiesa?*, «Concilium» 7 (1970), 82-102, quotation from *ibid.*,102. On Alberigo see also: *Fede nella chiesa e fede nella storia*, in *Chiesa della fede. Chiesa della storia. Saggi scelti*, ed. H. JEDIN, Brescia 1972, VII-XV; *Cristiani nella storia*, in G. ALBERIGO, G. RUGGIERI, G. PIANA, *La chiesa italiana nell'oggi della fede*, Casale Monferrato 1979, 11-40; and G. ALBERIGO, *Cristianesimo come storia e teologia confessante*, in M.-D. CHENU, *Le Saulchoir. Una scuola di teologia*, Casale Monferrato 1982, VII-XXX. On this part of Alberigo's research see now A. MELLONI, *Giuseppe Alberigo (1926-2007). Appunti per un profilo biografico*, «Cristianesimo nella storia» 30 (2008), 665-701, particularly 667.

«Ma come tutti i grandi libri...»

HERVÉ INGLEBERT

L'historiographie au IVe siècle entre païens et chrétiens: faux dialogue et vrai débat

Pour étudier l'écriture de l'histoire entre Constantin et Théodose, on doit partir de la communication qu'Arnaldo Momigliano fit lors du colloque de 1958 (publié en 1963) du Warburg Institute: *Pagan and Christian Historiography in the Fourth Century A.D.* Cela signifie qu'il faut insérer l'historiographie contemporaine dans le processus actuel de la construction de la connaissance historique sur l'Antiquité, en mêlant trois strates de données et de réflexion: le jadis des œuvres historiques tardoantiques, l'hier historiographique (celui d'une conférence tenue voici 50 ans) et le présent de la recherche. Tenant compte de ces trois states temporelles, on partira du texte de Momigliano pour réfléchir sur la manière dont on a traité l'historiographie du IVe siècle de 1958 à 2005[1], puis on verra comment on pourrait décrire autrement l'historiographie du IVe siècle, on reviendra sur les relations entre les historiographies chrétienne et païenne, et on conclura sur la question de la christianisation de l'historiographie.

Momigliano avait étudié la période 312-395[2], avait cité la quasi totalité des sources historiographiques subsistantes, et était parvenu à six conclusions principales:

---

[1] On peut le faire à partir de quatre textes: A. MOMIGLIANO, *Pagan and Christian Historiography in the Fourth Century A.D.*, dans *The Conflict between Paganism and Christianity in the Fourth Century*, éd. A. MOMIGLIANO, Oxford 1963, 79-99; A. MOMIGLIANO, *L'età del trapasso fra storiografia antica e storiografia medievale (320-550 d. C.)*, dans *Settimane di studio del Centro italiano di studi sull'alto Medioevo* XVII, *10-16 aprile 1969*, Spoleto 1970, 89-118, repris dans «Rivista Storica Italiana» 81 (1969)/2, 286-303 (version française dans A. MOMIGLIANO, *Problèmes d'historiographie ancienne et moderne,* Paris 1983, 120-144); G. ZECCHINI, *La storiografia cristiana latina del IV secolo (da Lattanzio ad Orosio)*, dans G. ZECCHINI, *Ricerche di storiografia Latina tardoantica*, Roma 1993, 7-28; *Greek and Roman historiography in Late Antiquity*, ed. G. MARASCO, Leiden-Boston 2003.

[2] Il exclut, 81, les années 395-410 de son étude, et ne mentionna qu'en passant Eunape, l'*Histoire Auguste*, Sulpice Sévère, Augustin et Orose.

1) il faut distinguer (p. 81) deux phases historiographiques: l'une, chrétienne, de 312 à 360 (avec Lactance, auteur du *De mortibus persecutorum*, Eusèbe de Césarée auteur de la *Chronique*, de l'*Histoire ecclésiastique*, de la *Vita Constantini*, et Athanase d'Alexandrie, auteur de la *Vie d'Antoine*), suivie d'une phase païenne de 360 à 400, avec les *Césars* d'Aurelius Victor vers 360, les *Bréviaires* d'Eutrope et de Festus vers 370, les *Histoires* d'Ammien Marcellin vers 395, l'*Histoire Auguste* vers 400. Pour Momigliano, les chrétiens attaquèrent les premiers et les païens se défendirent;

2) l'originalité chrétienne au IVe siècle réside dans la création de nouveaux genres historiographiques religieux (p. 88: histoire ecclésiastique, hagiographie) et dans la récupération des données des abrégés païens (p. 86: Jérôme et Eutrope, le Chronographe de 354 et la *Chronica urbis Romae*) ou juifs (p. 88: la traduction latine du *Livre des Antiquités bibliques* du Pseudo-Philon). L'insistance sur les aspects religieux explique l'agressivité des chrétiens envers le paganisme;

3) l'histoire ecclésiastique, inventée par Eusèbe, crée une nouvelle manière d'écrire de l'histoire, sans discours (qui expliquent les actions), mais avec insertion de documents (qui prouvent les faits) (p. 92);

4) les chrétiens ne s'intéressent pas aux formes littéraires classiques d'écriture historique (ils n'écrivent pas d'histoire politico-militaire classique ni de biographies impériales), et ne cherchent pas à les christianiser (p. 88); la *Vie de Constantin* d'Eusèbe n'eut pas de suite;

5) les historiens païens manifestent de diverses manières leurs réticences devant la manière chrétienne, religieuse et apologétique, d'écrire l'histoire (p. 94): choix des modèles historiographiques de Salluste, Tite Live, Tacite; rejet des valeurs chrétiennes d'humilité et de pauvreté; présence de quelques remarques ironiques (*Histoire Auguste*) ou critiques envers certains chrétiens (Ammien), mais jamais envers le christianisme ou l'empereur chrétien; de manière générale, insistance sur les *virtutes* et non sur la dimension religieuse. L'historiographie païenne au IVe insiste sur l'amour du passé romain (d'où les éditions des classiques, et les résumés de Tite Live), et l'érudition classique antiquarienne (commentaires de Virgile);

6) au IVe siècle, il n'y a pas eu de conflit entre païens et chrétiens dans le domaine historiographique (p. 94); les chrétiens inventent leurs voies (histoire ecclésiastique, hagiographie), et laissent les païens suivre les leurs (histoire classique avec Ammien, biographies impériales avec *Histoire Auguste*). Ils ne discutent pas ensemble, non par ignorance, mais par mépris mutuel; à l'agressivité religieuse des chrétiens, les païens répondent par un silence condescendant (p. 96) et l'exaltation

du passé païen, celui-là qu'attaquèrent ensuite Augustin et Orose. Pour Momigliano, dans le champ historiographique, il n'y eut au IVe siècle ni conflit, ni dialogue.

La plupart de ces conclusions, sauf la première³, seraient encore recevables aujourd'hui, sous réserve de nuances et de compléments⁴. Si on peut admettre que la taille de l'article explique l'absence de certaines sources hypothétiques⁵, certaines appréciations, sur l'importance at-

---

³ H. INGLEBERT, *Les Romains chrétiens face à l'histoire de Rome: histoire, christianisme et romanités en Occident dans l'Antiquité tardive (IIIe-Ve siècles)*, Paris 1996, 6-7; 13-14, avec note 43;131-132, avec les notes 281 et 282, pour la critique de cette conclusion, tant sur la périodisation (la prise en compte de la tradition chrétienne grecque et latine d'utilisation des exemples historiques, des traductions latines des oeuvres d'Eusèbe et des chroniques du Ve siècle permet de proposer une autre périodisation) que sur la succession dialectique des deux phases (car Aurelius Victor, Eutrope, Festus, Ammien Marcellin n'écrivent pas pour répondre à Eusèbe ou Athanase, et ne sont pas sur la défensive par rapport à une historiographie chrétienne qu'ils ignoraient ou qu'ils n'auraient pas considérée comme de l'histoire; seule l'*Histoire Auguste* peut être considérée comme une réponse païenne aux chrétiens, mais elle date de la fin du IVe siècle).

⁴ La conclusion 3 est discutable, car Rufin d'Aquilée n'a pas cité de documents comme l'avait fait Eusèbe, cf. Y.-M. DUVAL, *Les métamorphoses de l'historiographie aux IVe et Ve siècles. Renaissance, fin ou permanence de l'empire romain*, dans *Actes du VII Congrès de la FIEC*, Budapest 1983, 137-182. Et l'originalité d'Eusèbe dans l'utilisation des documents peut être contestée, R. MORTLEY, *The idea of universal history from Hellenistic philosophy to early Christian historiography,* Lewiston, NY, 1996, 154-155.

⁵ Les lacunes de l'article de Momigliano s'expliquent en grande partie parce qu'il ne pouvait pas citer tous les textes en 20 pages. L'ouvrage collectif *Greek and Roman historiography in Late Antiquity* consacre environ 200 pages au IVe siècle et au début du Ve siècle: F. WINKELMANN, *Historiography in the Age of Constantine*, 3-41; G. SABBAH, *Ammianus Marcellinus*, 43-84; G. BONAMENTE, *Minor Latin Historians of the Fourth Century A.D.*, 85-125; A.R. BIRLEY, *The Historia Augusta and Pagan Historiography,* 127-149; P. VAN DEUN, *The Church Historians after Eusebius*, 151-176; W. LIEBESCHUETZ, *Pagan Historiography and the Decline of Empire*, 177-218. On trouvera dans ces articles la plupart des références manquantes chez Momigliano: la *Vie de Constantin* de Proxagoras d'Athènes, la *Ennmansche Kaisergeschichte*, la *Leoquelle* (parfois datée plus tard, si on l'identifie avec l'œuvre de Pierre le Patrice), les *Annales* de Nicomaque Flavien. Certes, ces textes n'ont pas été conservés et leur contenu ainsi que leur datation restent hypothétiques. Toutefois, leur existence est avérée ou probable et remet en cause l'idée selon laquelle il n'y aurait pas d'historiographie païenne avant 360, surtout si l'on accepte une datation haute de l'*Origo Constantini imperatoris*. A cela, on peut ajouter des oeuvres chrétiennes disparues, comme la continuation antiochienne de la *Chronique* d'Eusèbe (R.W. BURGESS, *Studies in Eusebian and Post-Eusebian Chronography*, Stuttgart 1999) ou l'*Histoire ecclésiastique* de Gélase de Césarée (ou sa source si on date Gélase du Ve siècle). De plus, même s'ils ne sont guère

tribuée au *De mortibus persecutorum* de Lactance[6] ou la succession des deux phases chrétienne et païenne de l'historiographie[7], sont discutables. Mais le plus important est en réalité de réfléchir sur le titre, *Pagan and Christian Historiography in the Fourth century A. D.*, car si cette formule était évidente voici un demi-siècle, aujourd'hui, chaque mot en est discutable. D'abord, pourquoi opposer des historiens païens et chrétiens, alors qu'une appartenance confessionnelle ne se manifestait pas nécessairement par un militantisme historiographique? Ensuite, le IVe siècle défini de 312 à 395 n'est pas une donnée de l'historiographie antique, mais un choix de l'historiographe contemporain[8]. Enfin, que recouvre le terme d'histo-

---

pris en compte par les historiens de l'historiographie, il faudrait également mentionner les computs (la version de 362 de la *Computatio a. CCCCLII*, le *Prologus Paschae ad Vitalem* de 395, le *De duratione mundi* d'Hilarianus, de 397), et les dossiers de documents d'archives qui ont servi dans les polémiques des crises subordinatianiste (ceux d'Athanase et d'Hilaire de Poitiers contre les «ariens») ou donatiste (celui d'Optat de Milev). Enfin, on pourrait aussi mentionner les aspects historiques présents dans certaines sources chrétiennes syriaques, comme le memrè *Sur les guerres*, d'Aphraate, daté de 337; sur ce point, voir H. INGLEBERT, *Aphraate, le «sage persan»: la première historiographie syriaque*, «Syria» 78 (2001), 179-208.

[6] G. ZECCHINI affirme avec raison dans *La storiografia cristiana...* que l'œuvre du Chronographe de 354 était en réalité plus importante pour l'historiographie chrétienne latine que le *De mortibus*.

[7] Il y eut des textes historiques païens avant 360, mais surtout des textes historiques chrétiens après 360 avec Gélase de Césarée ou Jérôme. La surestimation du *De mortibus persecutorum* par Momigliano ou Winckelman fausse la perspective historiographique; en fait, le développement de l'historiographie chrétienne à partir du IVe siècle se comprend par 1) l'œuvre d'Eusèbe de Césarée et de ses successeurs grecs (chronique, histoire ecclésiastique, mais aussi apologétique historique, jusqu'à Théodoret de Cyr, dérivée de la *Préparation évangélique* et, secondairement, de la *Démonstration évangélique*); 2) la *Vie d'Antoine* d'Athanase et la tradition hagiographique; 3) les traductions du grec au latin (*Chronique* d'Hippolyte dans l'œuvre du Chronographe de 354, traduction de la *Vie d'Antoine* d'Athanase, de Flavius Josèphe, du Pseudo-Philon) et en particulier les traductions d'Eusèbe (la *Chronique* par Jérôme vers 380, l'*Histoire ecclésiastique* par Rufin vers 401-402). L'existence de textes historico-apologétiques est souvent liée à des moments difficiles: Eusèbe et Lactance avaient connu la persécution; ensuite, les chrétiens se sentirent en position de force et il fallut attendre 410 pour voir apparaître de nouveaux textes apologétiques contre les païens et s'appuyant sur l'histoire: la *Cité de Dieu* d'Augustin et les *Histoires* d'Orose. Entre temps, les chrétiens purent se contenter d'écrire entre eux et pour eux, comme le Chronographe de 354.

[8] Après tout, le IVe siècle n'existe pas en soi, car le siècle n'est qu'une convention d'historiens qui date du XIXe siècle, et on peut douter de la pertinence des dates de 312 et 395. L'essentiel de la *Chronique* d'Eusèbe et les premiers livres de l'*Histoire ecclésiastique* avaient été écrits avant cette date. 312 n'est pertinent que pour le *De mortibus*

riographie? Pour Momigliano qui fut avec Mazzarino celui qui a le plus réfléchi sur l'historiographie antique, la définition explicite de l'historiographie reposait sur les genres littéraires, ce qui n'est plus nécessairement une évidence. C'est ce décalage du discours historiographique depuis un demi-siècle qu'il faut comprendre, ce qui est d'ailleurs possible à partir de Momigliano même, car son érudition supérieure l'a amené à des intuitions fécondes qui n'ont pas toujours été reprises ensuite.

Dans sa préface à la traduction italienne de *The Conflict between Paganism and Christianity* (1968), Momigliano affirma que les contributeurs de 1958 n'auraient plus écrit alors comme ils l'avaient fait dix ans plus tôt. Il montra l'exemple l'année suivante dans *L'età del trapasso fra storiografia antica e storiografia medievale (320-550 d. C.),* beaucoup moins cité, mais tout aussi important que la communication de 1958 qu'il complète. Momigliano avait lu à peu près toutes les sources historiographiques païennes, juives ou chrétiennes, ce qui lui permettait de pouvoir écrire des articles de synthèse ou un ouvrage comme *Alien Wisdoms* (1975). Le point le plus fascinant dans les articles de 1958 et 1969 est que certaines de ses intuitions, liées à sa culture générale, contredisaient les catégories qu'il utilisait pour penser l'historiographie antique. En effet, Momigliano raisonnait essentiellement à partir des genres littéraires tels qu'ils avaient été définis au XIXe siècle: l'histoire classicisante, l'histoire ecclésiastique, la chronique, le bréviaire, la biographie, l'hagiographie. Mais certaines œuvres ne rentraient pas dans ces cadres: le *De mortibus persecutorum*, l'œuvre du Chronographe de 354, la traduction du *Livre des Antiquités bibliques* du Pseudo-Philon. Momigliano les connaissait et ne pouvait pas ne pas les citer, mais ne pouvant les interpréter par les catégories des genres historiographiques, il se contenta d'y faire des allusions (sauf pour Lactance, trop utile pour les historiens d'aujourd'hui pour être négligé, ce qui fait oublier que le *De mortibus persecutorum* n'a pas eu de postérité, et que donc il n'inaugure en rien une nouvelle phase de l'historiographie). Or, s'il avait poussé ses intuitions jusqu'au bout de leur logique, il aurait

---

persecutorum, un pamphlet ponctuel qui reprenait un thème ancien déjà attesté chez Méliton de Sardes et surtout chez Denys d'Alexandrie, et qui n'eut guère de successeur, et pour les derniers livres de l'*Histoire ecclésiastique*, où le thème principal devient la politique impériale de Constantin, ce qui réintègre l'histoire politique et militaire dans l'histoire ecclésiastique; mais Eusèbe ne fut également continué dans cette voie que bien plus tard. 312 et 395 ont certes une signification dans le contexte général de l'histoire de l'empire romain et du christianisme, mais le lien avec la production historiographique ne fut pas automatique; 363, 378 ou 410 eurent bien plus d'impact sur les contemporains.

dû prendre en compte d'autres traductions (celle de la *Guerre des Juifs* du Ps-Hégésippe, celle de la *Chronique* d'Eusèbe par Jérôme), les computs chrétiens, les dossiers historiques et tous les autres textes à teneur historique (comme ceux liés au *Roman d'Alexandre*). D'ailleurs, c'est ce qu'il fit en partie en 1969, où il cita les épigrammes biographiques traduites du grec par Ausone ou que voulait écrire Symmaque pour prolonger les *Imagines* ou *Hebdomades* de Varron.

Le fait que Momigliano ait cité certains textes sans pouvoir les analyser réellement et plus encore, qu'il en ait omis d'autres, est le symptôme d'une contradiction entre sa culture universelle et les outils historiographiques qui formaient le discours de son époque. Or ces limites posent une question essentielle: qu'est ce que l'historiographie? Quels sont les critères utilisés pour définir la dimension historiographique d'un texte, et donc pour établir le corpus des textes historiographiques d'une époque? Cette question est primordiale, mais si on n'y répond pas, on ne peut pas réfléchir sur la christianisation de l'historiographie au IVe siècle. Or, Momigliano n'a pas posé cette question, et ses successeurs non plus, puisque l'ouvrage collectif récent *Greek and Roman historiography in Late Antiquity* conserve les genres historiographiques traditionnels, omettant même d'intégrer certains textes cités par Momigliano. On peut certes déduire ce que les historiens d'aujourd'hui pensent être l'historiographie en étudiant les textes qu'ils étudient, mais il manque là une réflexion explicite. Or cette lacune réflexive amène de fait à retenir des textes comme historiographiques parce qu'ils ont été définis comme tels par le XIXe siècle (selon certaines traditions antiques et certaines traditions modernes). Mais après Foucault, Kosseleck et Hartog, on ne peut plus penser ainsi, car l'historiographie en soi, cela n'existe pas. On peut même aller plus loin et poser que l'historiographie définie par les genres littéraires n'est qu'une représentation de l'écriture du passé. Dans ce cas, considérer aujourd'hui une représentation du XIXe siècle (où l'on supposait qu'il existait des genres historiques selon la définition du XIXe siècle, en outrepassant, au nom du progrès des sciences historiques, les définitions antiques de l'historiographie, ce qui était anachronique) comme une évidence est une erreur de méthode. Il faudrait soit s'en tenir à l'usage strict des Anciens (mais qui est également une représentation: et alors, que faire des chroniques et des biographies qui ne sont pas de l'histoire d'un point de vue littéraire, mais qui étaient considérés comme en faisant partie au XIXe siècle?), soit accepter consciemment de poser le problème autrement, par exemple en termes de connaissances du passé (y compris dans la poésie ou l'exégèse), d'usages du passé (y compris dans un panégyrique), de régimes de vérité ou de véridicité historique (y compris dans des textes chrétiens apocryphes et hagiographiques), ou en termes d'histoire culturelle des structures mentales ou des représentations. Dans tous les cas, il est nécessaire d'inclure d'autres textes dans la discussion, en fait tous ceux qui portent sur certains thèmes (principalement politiques, militaires et religieux) du passé et du présent. Car au-delà de la définition littéraire et de la circulation sociologique antique des textes historiographiques traditionnels se pose le problème d'une histoire implicitement connue, classique ou biblique, que l'on voit affleurer dans des textes très nombreux et divers en dehors des genres historiques (au sens antique ou moderne).

Ainsi, outre les descriptions habituelles de l'historiographie antique à partir des genres historiographiques, qui ont leur pertinence et leur utilité, il existe d'autres manières d'écrire l'histoire de cette historiographie, et donc l'histoire de sa christianisation.

D'abord, on peut étudier la matière de la rédaction historique. En 1969, Momigliano avait étudié la place de la corruption, du christianisme et des barbares. Si on analyse le thème de l'histoire de Rome, sujet central pour tous nos auteurs, on s'aperçoit qu'il existait sous l'Empire trois manières différentes, urbaine, latine et grecque, de concevoir le passé romain[9]. Or, ces trois manières se retrouvent aussi bien chez les auteurs païens que chrétiens, car les choix culturels idéologiques furent aussi essentiels que les appartenances religieuses. Cette façon d'écrire l'histoire de l'historiographie conduit à retenir des textes souvent négligés, des manières différentes d'écrire sur le passé (des computs, l'histoire rhétorique par citations ou par jugement sur le présent, les traductions modifiées), et à une périodisation autre. On pourrait réaliser une étude similaire en faisant une histoire de la causalité historique dans l'historiographie tardoantique.

Puis, on peut analyser les modalités des évolutions de l'historiographie, ce qui ne se réduit pas aux transformations de l'historiographie (ce qui privilégierait les nouveautés) et encore moins à la christianisation de l'historiographie (qui n'en est qu'un aspect). Pour analyser le devenir d'une évolution culturelle, on peut partir de la méthode du filtre, avec ses quatre modalités[10]: la création (ex. l'histoire ecclésiastique, l'hagiographie, la chronique chrétienne latine mais aussi l'histoire religieuse païenne et la biographie/hagiographie philosophique néoplatonicienne); la perma-

---

[9] H. INGLEBERT, *Les Romains chrétiens...*, 43-54.
[10] H. INGLEBERT, *Interpretatio Christiana. Les mutations des savoirs (cosmographie, géographie, ethnographie, histoire) dans l'Antiquité chrétienne (30-630 après J.-C.)*, Paris 2001.

nence (ex. l'histoire classicisante ou la biographie impériale, païennes au IVe siècle, mais reprises par des chrétiens au VIe siècle; mais aussi l'histoire rhétorique exemplaire ou l'histoire des hérésies chez les chrétiens); la synthèse, sous diverses formes (l'histoire pouvait être christianisée par ajouts, cas de l'*Origo Constantini* complétée à partir d'Orose, mais il pouvait également y avoir une réinterprétation chrétienne de genres existants: *Chronique* d'Eusèbe, *Histoires* d'Orose, ou des thèmes: l'histoire de Rome); l'abandon de certaines traditions (la fin de l'histoire ecclésiastique au VIIe siècle).

On peut ensuite partir des événements tels qu'ils ont été compris par les contemporains. Ainsi, pour les élites du IVe siècle, celles qui réfléchissaient sur l'histoire et qui écrivaient de l'histoire, on peut penser que la mort de Julien et la perte de Nisibe en 363, la défaite et la mort de Valens à Andrinople en 378[11], ou le sac de Rome en 410, eurent bien plus de répercussions dans les mentalités que la bataille du Pont Milvius en 312 ou la mort de Théodose en 395. Si on considère la date de 363, l'étude du débat politico-religieux-historique qui s'ensuivit doit prendre en compte les écrits rhétoriques et théologiques d'Ephrem, de Grégoire de Nazianze ou de Libanios, les bréviaires d'Eutrope et de Festus, qui privilégient la question d'Orient, les récits de la guerre de 363, dont celui d'Ammien, mais aussi les débats sur la vaine puissance du dieu Terminus dans la *Cité de Dieu*, IV, 29. Les événements de 363 eurent un écho dans les textes durant 50 ans, et sélectionner certaines œuvres pour les qualifier d'historiographiques risque d'amener à une compréhension incomplète de ce qu'était l'historicité de cette époque, qui incluait aussi bien l'histoire militaire que les réflexions eschatologiques[12]. On peut d'ailleurs aller plus loin, car l'expédition de 363 s'inscrit dans un contexte de tensions avec la Perse qui remonte à 337 et qui avait déjà assombri le règne de Constance II. Or, c'est dans ce contexte qui construisait la Perse comme ennemi héré-

---

[11] En particulier, c'est l'événement qui est choisi par Jérôme pour achever sa continuation de la *Chronique* d'Eusèbe et par Ammien Marcellin pour terminer ses *Histoires*; le chrétien et le païen avaient une conscience partagée de l'importance de la bataille. Sur cette dernière, A. BARBERO, *Le jour des barbares. Andrinople, 9 août 378*, Paris 2006.

[12] Ces dernières pouvaient d'ailleurs être païennes comme les spéculations sur les 365 ans de durée du christianisme ou sur les 12 siècles de Rome liés aux 12 vautours aperçus par Romulus (avec la réponse de Polemius Silvius dans son *Laterculus*); cf. Y.-M. DUVAL, *Les douze siècles de Rome et la fin de l'empire romain. Histoire et arithmologie*, dans *Colloque Histoire et Historiographie*, «Clio, Caesarodunum» 15 bis, Paris 1980, 239-254. et J. DOIGNON, *Oracles, prophéties, «on-dit» sur la chute de Rome (395-410). Les réactions de Jérôme et d'Augustin*, «REAug» XXXVI (1990), 120-146.

ditaire de Rome que se développèrent des thèmes autour d'Alexandre, que l'on retrouve aussi bien dans les textes liés au *Roman d'Alexandre* étudiés par Jean-Pierre Callu[13] que dans les rêves d'hellénisation de la Perse de Julien et de Libanios. Que ces textes ne soient pas de la même nature que les récits d'Ammien Marcellin ou Eutrope est une évidence; mais que les contemporains les aient considérés comme de l'histoire, c'est-à-dire comme des récits vrais sur le passé lointain ou proche, n'est pas discutable. Or, si l'on prend en compte cette historicité, on écrirait autrement l'histoire de l'historiographie au «IVe siècle»; car 363, 378 et 410 furent assurément par leur retentissement de plus grands événements que 312 ou 395. Une telle méthode, applicable également à l'instauration du principat, permet de comprendre pourquoi il faut prendre en compte aussi bien le *Roman d'Alexandre* qu'Ammien à propos de Julien, comme on le fait avec l'*Enéide* et Tite Live à propos d'Auguste. Car ce n'est pas seulement dans l'*historia* littéraire que l'on parle des *res gestae*. Déjà le grand poème d'Ennius s'appelait les *Annales*; et on trouve d'importantes réflexions méthodologiques sur l'*historia* dans la *Cité de Dieu*[14].

Une autre manière d'écrire l'historiographie serait d'analyser les régimes d'historicité. Momigliano en avait eu l'intuition dès 1969, en remarquant que le sens de l'observation du détail concret était plus fort aux IVe-VIe siècles. De même, il avait noté que la notion de vérité historique devenait plus floue à partir du IVe siècle; il pensait surtout à ce qui était retenu comme vrai dans un récit, comme certains éléments apocryphes ou miraculeux. Jean-Pierre Callu a fait des études remarquables sur ce qu'il appelle la *mythistoria*[15], montrant que le genre historique déteignait sur tous les textes, mais aussi qu'après 200 l'histoire comme genre littéraire n'aidait plus à vivre (comme *magistra vitae*), et qu'elle fut en partie remplacée par le romanesque. En effet, comme on ne pouvait plus s'inspirer des modèles du passé, ni imiter un bios impérial, on s'intéressa à d'autres modèles d'identification possibles: les héros du roman grec pour les élites, et ensuite le *theios aner*, réel ou non (ceux des apocryphes chrétiens), que tous pouvaient admirer grâce à la dimension religieuse. Cette approche a

---

[13] Voir J.-P. CALLU, *Culture profane et critique des sources de l'antiquité tardive. Trente et une études de 1974 à 2003*, Rome 2006: 5) *Les Constitutions d'Aristote et leur fortune au Bas-Empire (Symm., Ep. 3, 11)* (1975); 23) *Julius Valère, le Pseudo-Libanius et le tombeau d'Alexandre* (1997); 24) *Alexandre dans la littérature latine de l'Antiquité Tardive* (1999).

[14] H. INGLEBERT, *Les Romains chrétiens...*, 399-408.

[15] Voir J.-P. CALLU, *Culture profane...*: 21) *Propos sur l'imaginaire latin au Bas-Empire* (1992).

des conséquences sur la compréhension de l'évolution des genres littéraires et en particulier sur la place grandissante de la biographie[16].

On pourrait aussi analyser les usages de l'histoire. Il y eut un usage polémique entre chrétiens (de Tatien à Théodoret de Cyr) et païens (Celse, Porphyre, Julien); ou entre chrétiens et juifs (sur l'exégèse des prophéties ou sur l'histoire du peuple juif); ou entre chrétiens (les catalogues d'hérésies, les dossiers conciliaires, les listes épiscopales fondant la primauté de certaines églises). On connaît aussi un usage politique de l'histoire (les *Actes de Pilate* au temps de Maximin Daia; l'argumentation de Symmaque lors du conflit de l'autel de la Victoire en 384; la mention du laraire d'Alexandre Sévère dans l'*Histoire Auguste*). L'intention polémique (et la réponse apologétique) politique et religieuse n'était pas nouvelle, mais elle prit selon les époques des formes historiographiques diverses.

En changeant les hypothèses de définitions historiographiques, on modifie les corpus et les chronologies et on transforme les interprétations, ce qui permet de reprendre le débat sur la christianisation de l'historiographie sur des bases totalement nouvelles. Par exemple, Eunape peut apparaître comme le premier à développer une histoire religieuse païenne; mais si on prend en compte le *Banquet des Césars* de Julien, cela est moins

---

[16] Le problème peut être posé dans une perspective plus vaste. Depuis Caton, voire depuis Ennius, jusqu'à Tite Live et Florus, l'histoire de Rome était celle du peuple romain, avec ses variantes urbaine et latine; l'histoire dominante était celle des dieux, du Sénat et du peuple romain, justifiant les conquêtes passées et fondant la domination présente et future. Tacite posa autrement le problème, car depuis *Actium*, l'histoire ne pouvait en réalité plus être que celle du prince qui cumulait les pouvoirs politique, militaire et religieux; le fait de conserver la forme annalistique (Tacite, ou ensuite Dion Cassius et Ammien Marcellin) n'y changeait rien. Avec Auguste, il y a eu impérialisation de l'historiographie, passage de la vie politique du peuple romain à la description du pouvoir impérial et personnalisation du récit. Ceci a favorisé le rapprochement entre histoire et biographie, car le règne d'un empereur devenait l'unité chronologique de description et d'intelligibilité de l'histoire romaine. Plutarque pouvait encore distinguer *historia* et *bios*, mais Suétone pouvait penser que la série chronologique des biographies des Césars résumait l'essentiel de l'histoire romaine récente, ce qui fut accepté ensuite dans la production historiographique latine, avec Marius Maximus, l'*Enmannsche Kaisergeschichte* et l'*Histoire Auguste*. Et la tradition historique romaine de langue grecque (Hérodien, Dexippe) tint également compte des règnes impériaux. Or, cette contamination de l'histoire romaine par la dimension biographique, ou au moins personnelle, des empereurs favorisait l'éloge (Alexandre Sévère dans l'*Histoire Auguste*) ou le pamphlet (Galère dans le *De mortibus persecutorum*, Elagabal dans l'*Histoire Auguste*), les deux versants de la rhétorique épidictique; cf. *Geschichtsschreibung und politischer Wandel im 3. Jh. N. Chr.*, éd M. ZIMMERMANN, Stuttgart 1999. Ceci s'accompagnait d'une présence constante, depuis Auguste, des *exempla* dans la production littéraire en relation avec l'empereur, dans la poésie (l'*Énéide*) ou l'éloquence (les panégyriques).

évident. De même, si on considère la *Chronique* d'Eusèbe comme un ouvrage d'histoire malgré sa portée apologétique, alors il devient gênant d'oublier la *Préparation évangélique* qui se présente comme une réflexion sur l'histoire religieuse de l'humanité (avec une relecture de toute la tradition savante de Diodore à Porphyre); mais alors comment considérer comme des œuvres non historiques le *Contre les Chrétiens* de Porphyre, où l'argumentation méthodologique fondée sur l'histoire est primordiale, le *Contre les hérésies* d'Epiphane de Salamine, qui est une histoire religieuse générale de l'humanité, voire la *Cité de Dieu*, qui argumente sur le statut de l'*historia* ou sur l'histoire romaine et sur l'histoire de l'humanité à travers celle des deux cités? On répondra peut-être que l'histoire n'est là que comme argument et qu'elle n'est pas étudiée pour elle-même. Mais outre le fait que ce serait également le cas pour certaines œuvres «historiographiques» (le *De mortibus persecutorum* de Lactance ou l'*Histoire Auguste*), il suffit de lire le début de la *Préparation évangélique* ou de la *Cité de Dieu* pour voir que c'est bien l'interprétation du passé qui est le thème de ces ouvrages. Déjà Lucien s'insurgeait contre la confusion entre le récit historique et l'éloge, rejetant au nom de la vérité la définition rhétorique, acceptée par Cicéron, de l'histoire comme un récit de grand style. Or, comment expliquer que parler véridiquement du passé (au moins en intention) n'est pas écrire de l'histoire? Car si l'histoire est un récit sur les événements (*negotia, praxeis*) humains vrais du passé, alors pourquoi tout récit sur ces événements ne serait-il pas aussi historiographique? Sans aller si loin[17], il reste que l'*historia* au sens classique n'épuise pas l'historicité, qui inclut non seulement les autres genres littéraires historiques, mais aussi l'histoire implicite, celle qui est la référence des récits sur le temps passé et présent et que l'on peut retrouver également dans de la poésie (l'*Énéide*), dans un panégyrique impérial ou un apocryphe chrétien. En 50 ans, le questionnement historique a été profondément transformé: on est passé de l'intérêt pour les descriptions (le problème des genres littéraires historiographiques) du passé (supposé exister de manière absolue dans des domaines divers: politique, militaire et religieux au sens chrétien) aux

---

[17] D. ROHRBACHER, *The Historians of Late Antiquity*, London 2002, rappelle, 150-151, un critère formel qui reste utile: l'historien est celui qui se définit comme tel car ce qu'il rapporte est important et ne doit pas être oublié; mais on n'a pas conservé toutes les préfaces et cela est surtout vrai pour les historiens de l'histoire présente. Les autres critères, finalité morale (Eunape, Théodoret, Socrate), diversion face aux malheurs du temps (Rufin), plaisir du lecteur (Sozomène), édification du lecteur (Orose), sont moins spécifiques. Et le critère du style persiste; Olympiodore ne se prétendait pas historien, mais disait avoir rassemblé des matériaux pour l'histoire.

représentations (dans de très nombreux textes, mais aussi parfois dans les sources iconographiques) des passés (désormais définis comme ce qui est supposé avoir eu lieu pour un groupe donné). La question de la christianisation de l'historiographie est donc à repenser totalement. Il y faudra bien un autre demi-siècle.

On se contentera ici de reprendre le dossier des genres littéraires historiographiques. Momigliano écrivait qu'au IVe siècle, il n'y avait eu ni conflit ni dialogue entre païens et chrétiens dans le domaine historiographique, car chacun avait suivi sa voie, les païens suivant leurs traditions (histoire classique, biographies impériales) et les chrétiens inventant les leurs (histoire ecclésiastique, hagiographie) tout en utilisant les données de l'historiographie classique. Le problème est qu'il n'y a pas eu un Yalta de l'écriture de l'histoire: les thématiques n'ont pas été partagées, les chrétiens prenant le religieux et les païens le politique et le militaire. Il était de toute façon impossible de partager les domaines, car tout le monde convenait que la victoire militaire avait une signification divine, même si pour les chrétiens, il s'agissait surtout de la *vittoria incruenta*, l'absence de sang versé étant la preuve de l'intervention divine (défaite de Gildon chez Orose, défaite de Radagaise à Fiesole chez Prudence). De même, il fallait faire nécessairement une place au pouvoir impérial, persécuteur ou protecteur, dans l'histoire chrétienne. La ligne de partage n'était donc pas entre païens et chrétiens, mais entre ceux, militants païens, comme Julien ou Eunape, et militants chrétiens, comme Orose et Prudence, qui pensaient que l'histoire politique ou militaire avait forcément une signification religieuse providentielle, et ceux, païens et chrétiens, qui pensaient que la compréhension de l'histoire politique et militaire ne se réduisait pas à la sphère religieuse, qui existait mais qui n'englobait pas tout. Ammien considérait que Julien avait eu tort de ne pas écouter les augures lors de son expédition en Perse, et Libanios admettait que les dieux avaient abandonné les Romains à Andrinople; mais tous les détails de l'histoire politique et militaire n'étaient pas régis par les dieux. De même, la croyance en la providence divine chez Augustin ne l'amenait pas à tout expliquer de manière providentielle, ou alors, d'une manière si subtile qu'elle mêlait les fins dernières (le salut de l'âme) aux réalités politiques et militaires, ce qui brouillait tout[18]. La question, bien posée par Robert Markus, est

---

[18] AUGUSTIN, *De civitate Dei*, V, 24-26, avec l'éloge des empereurs chrétiens de Constantin à Théodose.

de savoir si on pouvait laisser une place au profane[19], que l'on pouvait concevoir chez les païens soit comme une zone neutre areligieuse (Aurélius Victor), soit comme une zone de coexistence religieuse (Ammien, Symmaque); soit, chez les chrétiens, comme une zone neutre areligieuse (par exemple, la cité), comme une zone inexistante (car ce qui n'est pas chrétien est païen ou juif) ou comme une zone de confusion théologique (le *saeculum permixtum* d'Augustin, qui englobe tout). Les choix retenus s'expliquent parfois par la sociologie, car, hormis Lactance, ce ne sont pas seulement des chrétiens, mais aussi des clercs et des ascètes/moines qui, au IVe siècle, écrivirent de l'histoire chrétienne. Inversement, cette dimension cléricale ou ascétique a pu amener ces auteurs à s'intéresser au problème du pouvoir ailleurs que dans la sphère politique traditionnelle, et en particulier dans l'Eglise déchirée par les conflits doctrinaux (Eusèbe, Sulpice Sévère).

Il est vrai que les chrétiens ne s'intéressèrent que tardivement à l'histoire classicisante; cependant, on trouve chez eux, mais pas forcément dans des œuvres historiques de type classique et toujours en relation avec l'histoire religieuse, de nombreuses réflexions sur l'histoire politique de Rome: le thème de la succession des 4 empires de *Daniel* et la place de Rome dans l'histoire divine, l'alliance entre l'empire de Rome et le christianisme (Eusèbe, Prudence), la signification des persécutions ou des empereurs hérétiques, le rôle des empereurs chrétiens, le lien entre la fin de Rome et la fin du monde. Bien entendu, cela est fait selon un point de vue particulier, car il faut y ajouter les «guerres des chrétiens» contre le diable – les persécutions et les hérésies – la «politique des chrétiens», – celle des grands sièges épiscopaux entre eux ou envers l'empereur –, et la «chronologie des chrétiens», – celle des successions épiscopales et des écrivains ecclésiastiques (comme dans le *De viris illustribus* de Jérôme en 393). Mais chez les païens aussi, on trouvait une attention aux aspects religieux; c'était déjà vrai chez Tite Live à propos de la seconde guerre punique et cela le reste chez Ammien avec l'expédition de Perse. Simplement, le religieux va devenir prépondérant chez Eunape et Zosime.

Les chrétiens affirmaient que l'histoire chrétienne était doublement universelle, car englobant la totalité du passé et concernant la totalité des nations présentes. Et ils pensaient que l'histoire de Rome avait connu deux ruptures récentes: le Christ (Auguste-Tibère) et Constantin. Mais

---

[19] Sur cette question essentielle de la bipartition païen-chrétien ou de la tripartition païen-profane-chrétien, voir R. MARKUS, *The End of Ancient Christianity*, Cambridge 1990.

si Constantin fut évident pour Eusèbe, cela fut moins net ensuite à cause de la crise subordinatianiste qui amena les nicéens à nuancer a posteriori les jugements sur le premier empereur chrétien; et la conscience des *tempora christiana* ne fut nette qu'avec Théodose, car pour les païens, les temps chrétiens n'étaient pas ceux des empereurs chrétiens, mais ceux de l'abandon des sacrifices. Avant 391-92, la vraie question chronologique est donc l'affirmation de la rupture christique de l'histoire romaine, sous une double forme; le lien privilégié entre la naissance du Christ et la monarchie impériale romaine fut affirmé par Eusèbe et repris par Ambroise et Prudence; le lien privilégié entre le christianisme et la ville de Rome fut affirmé par le *Liber generationis II* (avec le catalogue pontifical libérien) ou par Damase qui voyait en Pierre et Paul les véritables fondateurs de Rome.

Contre cette prétention chrétienne à réécrire l'histoire universelle et romaine, de la Ville et de l'empire, être païen pouvait s'exprimer de deux manières: par une contre histoire religieuse païenne qui apparut après 360 (Julien, Eunape avec ses *Histoires* et ses *Vies des Sophistes*, la prophétie des 365 ans de durée du christianisme), ou par une réaffirmation de la tradition idéologique romaine. Car l'histoire de Rome était aussi une histoire universelle dans le temps passé et dans l'espace présent. Pour ceux qui acceptaient le fait que Rome était bien le dernier empire universel, l'histoire était terminée: l'*imperium sine fine* s'était achevé en *Roma aeterna*; et on pouvait encore affirmer jusque vers 400 que le pouvoir de Rome s'étendait jusqu'en Inde, et donc sur la terre entière. Face au défi chrétien de tentative de mainmise sur la signification de l'histoire, rappeler la tradition romaine, en marquant sa fidélité au passé de la République (les *Periochae* de Tite Live), en écrivant une histoire des origines de Rome (l'*Origo gentis Romanae*), en refusant toute césure chronologique au temps d'Auguste (Eutrope, Festus), en poursuivant Tacite (Ammien Marcellin), en réaffirmant la continuité idéologique (sénatoriale) de la tradition romaine (avec la compilation regroupant l'*Origo gentis Romanae* de Saturne à Romulus et Rémus, le *De viris illustribus urbis Romae*, de Procas, roi d'Albe à Octave et les *Caesares* d'Aurelius Victor), étaient autant de manière de s'opposer consciemment au discours historique clérical. Ces auteurs ne se souciaient pas de dialogue (puisque aucun compromis religieux n'était envisageable) et évitaient le conflit (car la plupart des historiens païens ne mettaient pas en avant leurs valeurs religieuses, mais des valeurs civiques profanes), mais prenaient part au débat sur ce que devait être la société romaine du temps et l'attitude du pouvoir en réaffirmant leurs positions. Et comme ils ne pouvaient guère le faire en critiquant le présent chrétien, ils le firent en louant le passé civique: contre la continuité de l'histoire sainte chrétienne, ils réaffirmaient la continuité de l'histoire civique romaine. Ceci supposait une présentation classique de l'histoire, où le religieux, quoique présent et païen, restait subordonné au politique; ceci visait surtout à inclure la plus grande partie de l'histoire dans la sphère de neutralité profane. Ceci a pu être accepté au Ve siècle par des historiens chrétiens laïcs, comme le rédacteur de la *Chronique gauloise de 452*. En effet, l'histoire politique de l'empire romain chrétien restait obscure, surtout en Occident, et une conception chrétienne de l'histoire, par exemple de type augustinien, pouvait s'accommoder d'une histoire classicisante écrite par des chrétiens. Même une histoire ecclésiastique n'était pas forcément cléricale, comme le prouva Socrate. Et seule la cléricalisation des historiens, qui fut une évolution sociologique plus que religieuse, amena la fin de l'histoire classicisante, qui avait été païenne au IVe siècle, mais qui a pu ensuite être chrétienne aux Ve et VIe siècles[20].

En conclusion, on peut dire qu'au IVe siècle, il y eut bien deux phases historiographiques, mais il ne s'agit pas de celles, successives, auxquelles avait pensé Momigliano en 1958, car il y eut en fait chevauchement de ces deux phases, définies chacune par une opposition. Lors de la première, qui alla de Constantin à Honorius, il y eut opposition non entre deux écritures, païenne et chrétienne, de l'histoire, mais entre deux écritures, classique et chrétienne cléricale, de l'histoire. Et ceci conduisit à une vraie tension entre deux systèmes de valeurs différentes, l'un civique, où le religieux restait subordonné au politique, et l'autre ecclésiastique, où le religieux l'emportait sur le politique. Dans cette première configuration, l'entre-deux, lorsqu'il existait, mêlait les aspects classiques civiques et chrétiens ecclésiastiques, comme dans l'œuvre du Chronographe de 354, et ne pouvait être le fait que des chrétiens. Ensuite, à partir de 360, une autre opposition, plus conflictuelle, vint s'ajouter à la précédente, l'opposition entre deux écritures historiques religieuses militantes, une païenne «hellène» et une cléricale chrétienne. Dans cette seconde configuration, l'écriture classique civique devint un entre-deux, ce qui explique qu'elle put être reprise par des païens modérés au IVe siècle (les abréviateurs, Ammien Marcellin, l'*Histoire Auguste*) ou par des chrétiens laïcs (aux Ve-VIe siè-

---

[20] Si la cléricalisation des historiens limite la possibilité de l'histoire classicisante, elle n'implique pas le triomphe perpétuel de l'histoire ecclésiastique, car celle-ci, sous la forme eusébienne d'une histoire commune entre le christianisme et l'empire romain, n'est plus possible après 407 en Occident ni après 632 en Orient; restera le genre de la chronique, qui dominera l'historiographie chrétienne ultérieure.

cles). Car la valeur des productions historiographiques n'existe pas en soi à partir de valeurs religieuses, mais dans un contexte politique précis qui fixe la valeur idéologique, ici principalement religieuse, des débats. Mais cette présentation ne serait valable que pour les genres historiographiques traditionnels, et on a vu que d'autres définitions de l'historiographie seraient possibles.

On comprend donc toute la complexité de la question de la «christianisation de l'historiographie». Car si, d'une part, la définition de l'historiographie est devenue problématique, de l'autre, celle de la christianisation est encore plus complexe, comme le montrent les remarques suivantes[21]. D'abord, dans le terme de christianisation, il faut distinguer les processus et le résultat (lequel dépend des critères de jugement). Ensuite, si on s'intéresse aux processus, la «christianisation de l'historiographie» peut signifier diverses choses: la transformation chrétienne de l'historiographie existante (via par exemple les modalités culturelles du filtre); le fait que de plus en plus de chrétiens écrivaient de l'histoire; le fait qu'à un moment donné, seuls des clercs écrivirent l'histoire; mais il faut éviter de confondre les aspects culturels, religieux et sociologiques. Enfin, puisque la christianisation est toujours christianisation de quelque chose, il faut savoir comment on définit ces items. Dans le cas de l'historiographie, on a vu non seulement que de nombreuses définitions et approches sont possibles, mais de plus, on peut penser que les contenus même de l'histoire (ses domaines, ses régimes d'historicité) ont changé avec les chrétiens. Dans ce cas, il est possible que l'expression «christianisation de l'historiographie» n'ait pas de sens, car le terme d'historiographie n'aurait plus la même signification au début et à la fin du processus. Il faudrait parler en réalité de «redéfinition chrétienne du discours sur le passé» ou de «christianisation de la relation au passé», voire même de «christianisation de la relation au discours sur le passé» Néanmoins, la christianisation de la relation au passé, qui signifie une relecture biblique du passé (y compris classique) et une compréhension religieuse du présent, n'est pas totalement séparable de l'existence d'une conception païenne de l'histoire passée et présente; car c'est par exemple le même régime d'intelligibilité religieuse du monde qui permettait d'accepter les miracles du saint chrétien et du *theios aner* païen. Cela permet de penser que la christianisation de la relation au passé fut le résultat d'un processus religieux global d'histoire des mentalités (ou des représentations) qui n'était pas que chrétien, mais bien tardo-antique.

---

[21] Sur ce thème, les contributions rassemblées dans *Quid est christianum esse? Le problème de la christianisation du monde antique*, éd. H. INGLEBERT, Paris 2010.

JOHANNES HAHN

Julian and his partisans: supporters or critics?

Christian contemporaries, and no less the powerful Christian tradition, have taught us that Julian's successful usurpation of imperial power resulted in an unparalleled eruption of religious tensions between pagans, Christians and Jews. The publication of his religious program – comprising the reopening of the pagan temples, the restitution of former temple property and the restoration of pagan worship through sacrifices[1] besides proclaiming an universal religious toleration including an amnesty for exiled Christian leaders (both of which were aimed to antagonize the Christian church) – soon led to open conflict, later sometimes to violence and murder, among religious groups in many communities of the Greek East. In particular, Julian's measures were greeted, we are told, with widespread enthusiasm among pagans and Jews alike. According to Ephraem of Nisibis «the Jewish people raged and raved and sounded the trumpets; they rejoiced because he was a diviner, they were overjoyed because he was a Chaldaean»[2].

Such enthusiasm and widespread support, in particular among the curial elites, was no doubt crucial for Julian's ambitious attempt to strengthen the cities, their economies and councils, and to re-establish pagan culture and, even closer to his heart, pagan worship in their midst. But no less important were Julian's efforts to win over eminent intellectuals and

---

[1] AMM. MARC. 22,5,2, LIB. *or.* 18,126. For concise, reliable and persuasive treatments of Julian's religious program see G.W. BOWERSOCK, *Julian the Apostate*, London 1978; P. ATHANASSIADI-FOWDEN, *Julian and Hellenism: An Intellectual Biography* (Oxford 1981), London 1992²; K. BRINGMANN, *Kaiser Julian*, Darmstadt 2004.

[2] EPHR. SYR. *Hc Jul.* 1,16 with S.N.C. LIEU, *The Emperor Julian. Panegyric and Polemic. Claudius Mamertinus, John Chrysostom, Ephrem the Syrian*, Liverpool 1989², 93-104 (trl. 108). For Ephraem, his polemics and bias, see S.H. GRIFFITH, *Ephraem the Syrian's Hymns «Against Julian». Meditations on History and Imperial Power*, «Vigiliae Christianae» 41 (1987), 238-266, and now C. SHEPARDSON, *Anti-Judaism and Christian Orthodoxy. Ephrem's Hymns in Fourth-Century Syria*, Washington, DC, 2008.

prominent public figures as political counsellors and spiritual leaders at his court, to recruit competent advisors and efficient administrators that could implement and execute the enormous number of political initiatives and volume of legal matter emanating from the restless young emperor. The task of recruiting suitable officials and functionaries for a wide variety of jobs was even more urgent as Julian had broken down and cleared out much of the imperial court he encountered in Constantinople at his arrival in late 361[3].

Surprisingly little we learn from the sources how successful Julian was in managing this task. At any rate, very early and consciously, in his days as Caesar in Gaul, he had defined the circles that should stay in the focus of his recruiting efforts. In the centre of his mind stood a particular group of intellectuals: in his letter to the philosopher and rhetorician Themistius, he unmistakably requested aid from philosophers in his divine mission to re-establish a shaken public order and «to extirpate the vices of the past»[4].

From Gaul he sent letters to friends from his student days and, even more important, to several of his former Neoplatonic teachers and influential pagan sages – men he had met in the few periods of his life when he was allowed to leave the strict isolation that had been imposed on him in his youth, men who had shaped his intellectual and personal development. Still, it would be a gross exaggeration to speak of political, social or intellectual networks upon which Julian was now able to draw. The loneliness of his youth and his solitary personality let him always first look for support among former acquaintances – all of them, it appears, teachers or fellow students – or, otherwise, to rely on recommendations from a very small circle of proven intimates.

The more remarkable is how little success Julian enjoyed in drawing people of the same mind to his side. His former and much-beloved teacher in Pergamon, the Neoplatonist Chrysanthius, obstinately refused to join him. Another philosopher of the school of Iamblichus, Eustathius, showed

---

[3] AMM. MARC. 22,4,1-10.

[4] CIL 3, 10648 = Dessau 8946 (from ancient Mursa in Pannonia Inferior): ...*ob deleta vitia / temporum pr(a)eteri/torum*. See S. CONTI, *Die Inschriften Kaiser Julians*, Stuttgart 2004, no. 74 with commentary and reference to other relevant epigraphical texts. Julian's plea, expressed well before his later usurpation, that he would need the support of all intellectuals in order to act as their leader, in *ep. ad Them.* 266D-267A. For the evident exchange of letters with Themistius in the early 350s see Julian's *ep. ad Them.* 253C, 257D, 259C, 260A, 266A. See *Politics, Philosophy, and Empire in the Fourth Century. Select Orations of Themistius*, ed. P. HEATHER, D. MONCUR, Liverpool 2001, 138-142.

up in Constantinople but soon asked for permission to return to his home province Cilicia[5]. From the wide circle of addressees who had received Julian's invitations only a small group of intimates were indeed later to form the emperor's *consilium*: his former teachers and Neoplatonic mystics Maximus and Priscus, and the physician Oribasius[6].

Some former teachers and associates who Julian tried hard to recruit for his ambitious plans were, perhaps, less suitable choices. Arguably some of them pursued rather their own than the young emperor's agendas. The Athenian sophist Himerius, for instance, left Athens in the winter of 361/62 and attached himself to the court of Julian. Probably he was summoned by a now lost imperial letter, much like the one to Maximus which has survived[7]. Julian would have been pleased to see that this leading Athenian intellectual immediately took sides with him and, more importantly, with his religious program. Soon after his arrival Himerius de-

---

[5] IUL. *ep.* 34; two invitations to Chrysanthius: *ep.* 27 and 37. Return of Eusthatius to Cappadocia: *ep.* 35 and 36. We also hear of invitations to one Hermogenes and one Basilius, who both had fallen into disgrace with Constantius before: *ep.* 33 and 32. For the identity of the latter see K. BRINGMANN, *Kaiser Julian...*, 216 n. 58 contra G.W. BOWERSOCK, *Julian...*, 64 who thinks that this was the Christian fellow-student of Julian from former days in Athens, the later bishop of Caesarea, Basil the Great.

[6] For Maximus see 33-37 and K. ROSEN, *Julian. Kaiser, Gott und Christenhasser*, Stuttgart 2006, 96-104; 231-234, for Priscus P. ATHANASSIADI-FOWDEN, *Julian...*, 49 f. and K. ROSEN, *Julian...*, 119 f., 172 f. These philosophers found opposition even among sympathizers of Julian as Ammianus Marcellinus (22,7,3; 29,1,42) and Eunapius, the biographer and historian (*vit. soph.* 7,1,1-4, 473), and no less among declared partisans of Julian: U. CRISCUOLO, *Libanios et les philosophes de Julien: le cas de Maxime d'Éphèse*, in *Melanges A.F. Norman*, ed. A. GONZALEZ-GALVEZ, P.-L. MALOSSE, Lyon 2006, 103-112. Oribasius (PLRE I 653f.) again is one of Julian's earliest and closest friends, doubtlessly from his student times. As Caesar he entrusted Oribasius with the supervision of his library and took him – Constantius was allegedly unaware of their close friendship – as his personal physician on his mission to Gaul where Oribasius was the only one who shared the secret of Julian's hidden devotion to the pagan gods (IUL. *ep. ad Ath.*, 277 BC). Their intimate relationship is documented in *ep.* 14 as well. On Oribasius, a highly educated member of the pagan intelligentsia of the time, also see the biography devoted to him by EUNAP. *vit. Soph.* 7,3,8 [498f.]. Later, Oribasius – if this tradition reflects not later Christian legend – occupied himself in Delphi with the the restoration of the temple of Apollo and the attempt to revive the famous oracle; *Artemii passio* 35; GEORG. CEDR. I 532, 1; PHILOSTORG. *hist. eccl.* 77, 21-26. 37-40.

[7] Himerius may have been a former teacher of Julian in the latter's student days in Athens in 355; T.D. BARNES, *Himerius and the Fourth Century*, «Classical Philology» 82 (1987), 206-225, esp. 221 f. The scholiast's opening notes to *Oration* 39, 40 and 41, held in Thessalonici, Philippi (on the way to the capital) and Constantinople make clear that Himerius had been summoned to court by the emperor; H. VÖLKER, *Himerios, Reden und Fragmente. Einführung, Übersetzung und Kommentar*, Wiesbaden 2003, 6 f.

livered a speech in the capital with the opening words: «I have cleansed my soul through Mithra the Sun, and through the gods I have spent time with an emperor [Julian] who is a friend of the gods»[8]. As a fresh initiate of one of Julian's favourite cults he no doubt found acclaim with the emperor. However, contemporaries understood this as an attempt to win favour in order to outdo his Athenian rival Prohaeresius and to dispossess this Christian sophist of his chair[9]. Himerius' speeches under Julian do not reveal any specific religious leanings in accordance with Julian's program of Hellenism. This intellectual never turned to a pagan propagandist as, for example, Julian's close friend and pretorian prefect Saturninus Secundus Salutius, the author of the pamphlet *On the God and the Universe*[10].

Opportunism, no doubt, claimed its toll in Julian's entourage – or rather propelled flexible men into the centre of power. Julian's uncle from the mother's side, named Julian as well, is a noteworthy case in point. His apostasy from Christianity, immediately after the young Caesar's successful bid for supreme power, brought him high office: Julian entrusted him with a most powerful job and made him *comes Orientis*. Here, among other duties, he was commissioned with the restoration of pagan cults and temples and, consequently, the occasional persecution of Christian iconoclasts[11].

The cooperation of some intellectuals was not welcomed by Julian: the sophist Prohaeresius, a Christian, whom Julian had heard in Athens and who now approached the emperor with a long letter was turned away in a very unkind manner[12]. But even prominent representatives of the pagan cause with immaculate Hellenic credentials occasionally fared no better. Rather well documented and revealing is the case of the philosopher and rhetorician Themistius.

---

[8] HIMER. *or.* 41 (trl. R.P. PENELLA). R.P. PENELLA, *Himerius. Man and the Word. The Orations of Himerius*, Berkeley-Los Angeles 2007.

[9] EUNAP. *vit. Soph.* 14 [494] asserts that Himerius went to the emperor's Julian's court «in the hope that he would be regarded with favour on account of the emperor's dislike of Prohaeresius». See T. BARNES, *Himerius...*, 220-223 and R.P. PENELLA, *Himerius...*, 4 f. (with modifications) and 33-35. Years later, on the news of his rival's Prohaeresius death, he should immediately return to Athens in order to claim his position.

[10] G.W. BOWERSOCK, *Julian...*, 125; *De deis et mundo*, by *Sallustius*, ed. A.D. NOCK, Cambridge 1926. For the character of Himerius' speeches under Julian see R.P. PENELLA, *Himerius...*, 34 ff. and, pointedly with regard to religion, H. GÄRTNER, *s.v. Himerios*, in *Reallexikon für Antike und Christentum* 15, Stuttgart 1991, 167-173 at 170 f.

[11] PHILOSTORG. *hist. eccl.* 7,10; *Passio Artemii* 23. Compare *PLRE* I, 470.

[12] IUL. *ep.* 31. On this eminent Christian sophist (*PLRE* I, 731) see in particular EUNAP. *vit. Soph.* 10 with E.J. WATTS, *City and School in Late Antique Athens and Alexandria*, Berkeley-Los Angeles 2006, 48-78.

Themistius was a dominating figure in the cultural and political life of Constantinople from the mid 350s on, advising – and praising – Roman emperors for decades. It was Constantius II. who adlected this intellectual to the city's senate in 355 and chose him as representative of the eastern capital and personal company when he left for his famous visit to Rome in 357 A.D. Themistius successfully secured privileges for the city from this emperor, as he did later from several successors constantly drawing imperial attention to Constantinople[13]. It appears that his relationship with Constantius was an intimate one and that under this emperor his career reached a pinnacle[14]. Themistius public profile, despite his renown as a panegyrist, was that of a philosopher: this is what the Codex Theodosianus 6,4,12 from the year 361 A.D. calls him explicitly. Libanius, a couple of years later, regarded him as «the best of philosophers»[15]. Themistius owed this title not least to his pioneering *Paraphrases* of Aristotle's works. Hence it is not surprising that Julian encountered him early, indeed already during

---

[13] For details see P.J. HEATHER, *Themistius. A Political Philosopher*, in *The Propaganda of Power. The Role of Panegyric in Late Antiquity*, ed. M. WHITBY, Leiden 1998, 125-150, in particular 125 f.; P. HEATHER and D. MONCUR, *Politics...*, 71-113; see 138-142 on Themistius' relationship with Julian.

[14] J. VANDERSPOEL, *Themistius and the Imperial Court. Oratory, Civic Duty, and Paideia from Constantius to Theodosius*, Ann Arbor 1995, 71ff. The other period of substantial influence and office holding would have been under Theodosius. Themistius seems to characterize his relationship with Constantius (the emperor is not named but can hardly be Julian) as late as in the mid 380s with the words «he often took advice from me in council while I was wearing my philosopher's cloak, and he also often made me his dinner guest and his traveling companion. He gently endured it when I admonished him and did not take it badly when I rebuked him» (*or.* 34 [XIV]; cf. LIB. *ep.* 66,2). For the identification of the emperor with Constantius cf. R.P. PENELLA, *The Private Orations of Themistius*, Berkeley 2000, 3; J. VANDERSPOEL, *Themistius...*, 71-113 in detail on the relationship between Themistius and Constantius. For Themistius' prestige and influence under Constantius II. see also G. DAGRON, *L'Empire romain d'orient au IVe siècle et les traditions politiques de l'hellenisme. Le témoinage de Themistios*, «Travaux et Memoires» 3 (1968), 23ff.; P. HEATHER and D. MONCUR, *Politics...*, 43 ff. and R.M. ERRINGTON, *Themistius and his Emperors*, «Chiron» 30 (2000), 861-904, especially 865-872 (*ibid.*, 900-902 on behalf of Themistius' *praefectura urbis* (*or.* 34, 13) – versus T. BRAUCH, *The Prefect of Constantinopel for 362 A.D.: Themistius*, «Byzantion» 63 (1993), 37-78, who does not want to exclude holding this office under Julian.

[15] LIB. *ep.* 1186,2 (364 A.D.). Gregory of Nazianzus refers to him under the same title, *ep.* 24. This is how Themistius sees himself: *In anal. post.* 1,2-12, cf. *or.* 23 (89,20-90,9). In his first speech in front of Constantius II (*or.* 1,1a) he opens as follows: «Now, for the first time, your majesty, there comes on the scene for you an independent speech and a truthful admirer, who would not willingly utter any word, however insignificant, for which he shall not render account to philosophy».

his education, as is clear from his letter to Themistius where he notes that he had studied with Themistius and other philosophers[16].

After Julian's appointment as Caesar, one would expect that relations between the two would have prospered: Themistius sent him a formal *protrepticus* which served as a basis of a philosophical exchange between the men. Despite the respect they showed for each other – Julian called Themistius friend and master[17] – philosophical differences on various points are evident[18]. This is, in particular after Julian's assumption of sole power, of significance as Themistius, in the early phase of his Constantinopolitan career, had been attacked by influential Christians and later, under Constantius, had encouraged the influx of Greek intellectuals from the provinces to Constantinople. Now he represented the key figure of Hellenism in the capital.

We might imagine that for Julian, the young emperor with a hellenic vision, the elder man would have been a natural and immediate choice in his search for suitable advisors and comrade-in-arms in his enormous task of reforming imperial government and society, in particular of revitalizing the rapidly waning vigour of Hellenism.

However, this seems not to have been the case. There are good reasons to think that this was due to differences on important philosophical issues, issues as the suitable actions for philosophers and kings, the role of wisdom and virtue *versus* Tyche in public life, the nature of kingship and the question of divinity for a ruler[19]. Themistius can not have been happy with Julian's blatant declaration of protest against his own positions and even less pleased with the emperor's criticism of the philosopher's interpretation of Aristotle. Even more hurtful must have been the way this disapproval was expressed: Julian sent his letter to the court-philosopher as a circular letter to numerous intellectuals in the East, thus responding to Themistius' *protrepticus* of four years earlier[20]. It is therefore unsurprising that Themistius plays no distinctive role in Julian's short reign. Indeed, he hardly appears in the sources and seems to have been without

---

[16] Iul. *ep. ad Them.* 257D, where Julian, quoting from Plato's Laws, adds: «You know it well and indeed taught it to me» (trl. W.C. Wright): J. Vanderspoel, *Themistius...*, 118-119; P. Heather, *Themistius...*, 127-130.

[17] Iul. *ep. ad Them.* 263D.

[18] See the discussion by R.P. Penella, *Private Orations...*, 120 ff.; J. Bouffartigue, *L'empereur Julien et la culture de son temps*, Paris 1992, 296-300, P. Athanassiadi-Fowden, *Julian...*, 90-96, J. Vanderspoel, *Themistius...*, 119-123.

[19] P. Athanassiadi-Fowden, *Julian...*, 90-93.

[20] J. Vanderspoel, *Themistius...*, 118-127, P. Athanassiadi-Fowden, *Julian...*, 90-96.

any responsibility in Julian's political program[21]. Evidently, this intellectual with widely differing views to Julian's and the emperor's entourage was dispensable in carrying out the enormous task of a pagan revival – the emperor's religious zeal was, no doubt, not reconcilable with Themistius' convictions of religious tolerance and the desirability of religious plurality which brought him so much approval from contemporaries and modern scholars[22]. But there was surely just as much reluctance on Themistius' part to join Julian's cause with enthusiasm – and we may ask whether this crucial figure of Constantinopolitan Hellenism and declared *politikos philósophos*[23] should be counted among Julian's partisans at all.

Here as elsewhere early in Julian's reign, however, we never hear of an articulate protest against the emperor's religious declarations and measures under the label of a revival of Hellenism. We probably have occasionally to allow the possibility of pagan dissidence and of withdrawal from meaningful silence.

On his way through Asia to Antioch one can see the emperor continue with his endeavour to recruit suitable men and women, now for his visionary project of a new universal pagan church with a strict ecclesiastical hierarchy. Again appointing various philosopher friends, mostly Neoplatonists, to regional high priests Julian personally tried to recruit local priests as well. Not all of his choices were lucky ones. One appointment he was proud of, a former Christian bishop, Pegasius, had to be defended publicly and passionately by the emperor[24]. Besides, the clear impression is that it was often difficult or impossible to find any candidates in the local elites at all. Julian soon complained about the slow progress of Hellenism (in his preferred, religious sense): «The Hellenic religion does not yet prosper as I desire, and it is the fault of those who profess it»[25]. However, it may

---

[21] His panegyric for Julian's consulship in 363 on behalf of the senate clearly has to be understood as a duty mandated by his position as *princeps senatus* in Constantinople. Besides J. VANDERSPOEL, *Themistius...*, 115 ff. see the laconic but accurate assessment by M. ERRINGTON, *Themistius...*, 873.

[22] L.J. DALY, *«In a Borderland». Themistius' Ambivalence Toward Julian*, «Byzantinische Zeitschrift» 73 (1980), 1-11.

[23] As Themistius defined himself in the extant preface of his now-lost *Philopolis*, an oration delivered under Julian; O. SEECK and H. SCHENKL, *Eine verlorene Rede des Themistius*, «Rheinisches Museum» 61 (1906), 554-566, at 557.

[24] IUL. *ep.* 79. For the convert and former bishop Pegasius, see G. SCHÖLLGEN, *Pegasios Apostata. Zum Verständnis der «Apostasie» in der 2. Hälfte des 4. Jahrhunderts*, «Jahrbuch für Antike und Christentum» 47 (2004), 58-80.

[25] IUL. *ep.* 84, probably in June 362 while on his way to Antioch, in his letter to Arsacius, high-priest of Galatia (*PLRE* I, 110). Note also Julian, in *ep.* 78 (to some Aristoxenus):

instead have been the austere and rigid concept of priesthood that Julian established and developed in detail for his church which disinclined aristocrats to devote, under the new regime, their services to a highly demanding, strictly regulated and mostly separated existence in their communities. Religious enthusiasm and pagan support were most likely difficult to kindle with such job description. And sympathizers with the new regime and its program will have hesitated to stand for priestly offices which forbade simultaneous political participation and no longer guaranteed unquestioned social distinction as it also allowed humble members of their community to qualify as a priest simply by merit of ascetic and moral virtues and, at the same time, placed them under strict control of provincial high priests[26].

Julian's ideas of the key personnel of his religious reform and his recruiting policy proved to be idiosyncratic. They most likely alienated, apart from the hard core of his Neoplatonic friends, not a few of his partisans. And there is little indication that the emperor ever realized the pitfalls of his new priesthood's design.

But to what extent did Julian's friends and partisans who were also his political advisors, share his views, in particular his religious vision and zeal? The reservations of an Ammianus Marcellinus, for example, are well known. But much more interesting is the case of a truly public figure, Libanius. I shall only be able to sketch a more detailed argument here[27].

«Show us a man among the Cappadocians who is a pure Hellene» (with Hellenism in the religious sense) or, on Pegasius, «For so far I have seen only those who do not wish to sacrifice, or else a few who want to but do not know how» (*ep.* 79).

[26] Julian on pagan priesthood (his programmatic description, however, has not survived: see *ep.* 47, in particular 453A): *epp.* 84, 88 and 89b. On Julian's concept J. HAHN, *Kaiser Julians Konzept eines Philosophenpriestertums. Idee und Scheitern einer Vision*, in *Formen und Funktionen von Leitbildern*, ed. J. HAHN and M. VIELBERG, Stuttgart 2007, 147-161. See also M. MAZZA, *Giuliano o dell'utopia religiosa: il tentativo di fondare una chiesa pagana?*, in *Giuliano imperatore. Le sue idee, i suoi amici, i suoi avversari* (*Atti Convegno, Lecce 10-12 Dicembre 1998*), Galatina 1998 [2000], 17-42.

[27] The best treatment of Libanios' religion still is J. MISSON, *Recherches sur le paganisme de Libanius*, Louvain 1914. However, Misson abstains from embedding the results of his analysis into wider horizons, e.g. by linking them to the religious situation in Antiochia and to contemporary imperial politics of religion: such perspectives would deserve thorough treatment. See also A.-J. FESTUGIÈRE, *Antioche païenne et chrétienne. Libanius, Chrysostome et les moines de Syrie*, Paris 1959, 229 ff., and, more recently, R. SMITH, *Julian's Gods. Religion and Philosophy in the Thought and Action of Julian the Apostate*, London 1995 and G. WÖHRLE, *Libanios' Religion*, in *Publications du Centre Universitaire de Luxembourg, Dép. des Lettres et Sc. Hum.*, «Études Classiques» 7 (1995), 71-89.

This sophist and influential representative of the curial class of Antioch is regularly regarded and labelled as «propagandist of paganism» or «zealous champion of the old religion» and seen as a protagonist of the pagan cause in his home town[28]. Libanius' vain self-stylization in his autobiographical speeches and in his correspondence is less crucial for this historical judgment than are his extraordinary role and well-known commitment during Julian's stay in Antioch. As the emperor's intimate advisor he was later appointed to the small investigating committee that had to discover the allegedly Christian arsonists who burned down the great Apollon temple of Daphne[29].

But how important were pagan religion and temple cult in Libanius' thought? Which religious aims did he pursue and what zeal stood behind his political attitudes and action? To consider these questions one has to go beyond Libanius' standardized evocations of gods in his work which are dictated by rhetorical rules.

At first glance, Libanius' religiosity is strongly marked by his intense belief in Tyche. She is omnipresent in his life[30]. However, this goddess is his personal Tyche. In marked contrast, the sophist shows very little attention and even less enthusiasm for the local cult of the goddess, the Tyche of Antioch. Furthermore, aside from the special case of his speech *Pro templis* of 385 AD, one clearly discerns that cults and gods, even their temples, play an astonishingly marginal role in his speeches, indeed. This observation is no less accurate for speeches given under Julian's reign. It is true, in his *Antiochikos* gods and temples are named, together with their myths, as basics of the city's foundation. However, turning in this

---

[28] A.F. NORMAN, *Introduction: Oration 30*, in *Libanius, Selected Works* II, ed. A.F. NORMAN, Cambridge-London 1977, 97; *The Emperor Julian. Panegyric and Polemic. Claudius Mamertinus, John Chrysostom, Ephrem the Syrian*, ed. S.N.C. LIEU, Liverpool 1989², 43.

[29] LIB. *ep.* 1376. The two other members of the commission were Libanius' compatriots Heliodorus (on him O. SEECK, *Die Briefe des Libanius zeitlich geordnet*, Leipzig 1906, 166) and Asterius (see O. SEECK, *Daie Briefe...*, 143). To this letter also see O. SEECK *Die Briefe...*, 314 and S.N.C. LIEU, *Emperor Julian...*, 51 and 81. For the historical context and various political as well as religious implications see J. HAHN, *Gewalt und religiöser Konflikt. Studien zu den Auseinandersetzungen zwischen Christen, Heiden und Juden im Osten des Römischen Reiches (von Konstantin bis Theodosius II.)*, Berlin 2004, 168-180.

[30] Libanius' Tyche dominates *or.* 1, where the sophist looks back at his life. Already in antiquity this speech, now often called Libanius' autobiography, received the title *Bios or about his own Tyche*. On Tyche in Libanius' thought and religion see J. MISSON, *Recherches*, 50 ff. and 93 ff.

panegyric to the Roman period and the contemporary history of his home town, Libanius gives only very meagre hints about the sacred appearance of the city in his day and has nothing to say about her cults at all.

Libanius' interest in the concrete situation of the contemporary urban cults and temples is strikingly limited. When Julian was on his way to Antioch, he assured the emperor that many of the great temples were still standing – but only to add that their destruction had been just narrowly averted (and most of them were actually in a deplorable state). Later, in the presence of Julian, Libanius' personal contribution to the problems of temples was to be of a rather different kind. He repeatedly pleaded on behalf of prominent fellow citizens that they be spared from prosecution for illegal spoliation and occupation of temples and their conversion in private palaces. The purely pragmatic arguments brought forward are highly revealing – they do not suggest that they were spoken by a well-known pagan at all. No hint is given that Libanius himself ever hastened to the newly lighted altars. On one occasion, he blatantly refused – and is proud to tell of it – to join Julian and his entourage when they were carrying out public sacrifices[31].

Perhaps the most striking text is Libanius' *Epitaphius* on Julian where he offers, in the context of an obituary, his personal appreciation of Julian's life and political achievements. The restoration of the temples and cults is given pride of first place; they are characterized as *tà prôta kaì mégista*[32]. Here, Libanius simply follows traditional political thought and a standard rule of contemporary rhetorical handbooks. Then he explores, in much more detail, Julian's fight against corruption at court and the emperor's promotion of city life and *curiae*. The true climax of his argument – and the pinnacle of Julian's patronage of the cities – is only reached with the final focus on the emperor's promotion of *paideia*, again culminating in the art of rhetoric[33]. In what follows Libanius defines *polis* and *logoi* as the two corner pillars of his political and spiritual world[34]. Religion and cult, however, have somehow faded from prominence, owing their principal importance to the weight and patina of tradition and myth, these again of elementary significance for his beloved *logoi*.

---

[31] *Or.* 1,121, an episode that gives a remarkable glimpse of Libanius' sense of self-esteem in contrast to his religious feelings.
[32] *Or.* 18,126ff.; see also 18,114 ff.
[33] *Or.* 18,282ff.; in particular the dense version in 284.
[34] M. FRANCESIO, *L'idea di città in Libanio*, Stuttgart 2004.

Libanius was, as his speeches and the *Epitaphius* show, an ardent admirer and partisan of Julian. But he was no congenial spirit. He did not appreciate all the complexity of the emperor's endeavour to restore and reform Hellenism – the Hellenism Julian believed in, that is, a Hellenism focused primarily on religion, not on culture[35]. It is for that reason that Julian's efforts spun around the resuscitation of cult praxis in ritual and sacrifice[36], along with promoting, of course, traditional city life and *paideia*. But for Libanius the latter counted most and he was unable to follow Julian into his universalistic Neoplatonic thought world or to grasp his syncretistic ideas. For the sophist, religion and cult could primarily claim their due as the historic bedrock of cities and as an instrumental part and indispensable stage of city life and culture – and here, in particular, of his *logoi*: This helps to explain the remarkable dominance of gods that are closely related to the world of the *polis* in Libanius' *pantheon*.

In one regard Libanius' attitude, we may assume, stands for the religious indifference among pagan members of his class in Antioch: Though he set, in one letter, great store on the statement that he belonged to those who work for the restoration of the temples, his single documented action is a recommendation letter for a hierophant[37]. Besides this, in all his correspondence, one can find no hint of any personal engagement in the cult life of his home polis. The same is true for all his correspondents, many of them likewise representatives of the cultivated pagan elite of Antioch.

Julian's failure in his grandiose attempt to reform and to re-establish paganism as the dominant religious power in public life in the Empire has – as far as the traditional Greek elites, the indispensable political instrument for such an enterprise, is concerned – to be explained with his failure to dominate the contemporary discourse on Hellenism and with various breathtakingly revolutionary elements of his religious agenda: the new type of pagan priesthood and pagan church, the spiritualisation of ritual etc.

---

[35] See the excellent analysis by G.W. BOWERSOCK, *Hellenism in Late Antiquity*, Ann Arbor 1990, 6-13; compare J. BOUFFARTIGUE, *L'empereur Julien...*, 658-669. For a famous critique of Julian's distinctive but one-sided concept of Hellenism, see GREG. NAZ. *or.* 4,103.

[36] N. BELAYCHE, *Sacrifice and Theory of Sacrifice during the «Pagan Reaction»: Julian the Emperor*, in *Sacrifice in Religious Experience*, ed. I. BAUMGARTEN, Leiden 2002, 101-126.

[37] *Ep.* 718,3; seen by E. PACK, *Städte und Steuern in der Politik Julians. Untersuchungen zu den Quellen eines Kaiserbildes*, Bruxelles 1986, 297. See, however, contrary endeavours as in *ep.* 724. 763. 819 and 1364.

That Julian lost his battle for the religious hearts and minds of his pagan sympathizers among the elites, that he could not win them over to his belief in sacrifice and religion as the heart and soul of Hellenism meant that no reformed and lively religious paganism could blossom. The deep hatred the emperor was to earn from his Christian enemies, however, did not derive from their fear of a lasting effect of his religious program. The ensuing antagonizing and invocation of a vibrant pagan-Christian conflict by Christian leaders and authors in the following decades was not owed to a real threat of a continuing and perilous pagan challenge that Julian had planted. For explaining the unceasing polemics against the dead emperor one has to turn to other aspects of his efforts: namely the devastating example to the common faithful that baptism and the Christian truth could simply be thrown away – and that the apostate had written, with his *Contra Galilaeos,* a seducing, indeed to many educated Christians a convincing refutation of the Christian faith[38]. These elements mark the truly poisonous bequest of Julian's reign. The pagan-Christian conflict, if it ever had had been seriously dominating public life on the local level in the empire at some scale, was a thing of the past due to the unwillingness of the traditional elites and pagan leaders to support and identify with Julian's Hellenism.

---

[38] R.L. WILKEN, *Cyril of Alexandria's Contra Iulianum,* in *The Limits of Ancient Christianity. Essays on Late Antique Thought and Culture in Honor of R.A. Markus,* ed. W.E. KLINGSHIRN and M. VESSEY, Ann Arbor 1999, 42-55; R.P. PENELLA, *Julian the Persecutor in Fifth Century Church Historians,* «Ancient World» 24 (1993), 31-43; H.-G. NESSELRATH, *Kaiserlicher Held und Christenfeind. Julian Apostata im Urteil des späteren 4. und des 5. Jahrhunderts n.Chr.,* in *Die Welt des Sokrates von Konstantinopel,* ed. B. BÄBLER, H.-G. NESSELRATH, München 2001, 15-43.

Federico Fatti

Il principe, la *Tyche*, i cristiani: Giuliano a Cesarea*

Un uomo implacabilmente ostile ai cristiani. Questo è il ritratto che, di Giuliano, usciva in filigrana dalle celebri conferenze lette al Warburg Institute, nessuna della quali – tanto evidente era la cosa – fu dedicata espressamente al principe, presto assurto a simbolo di quel «conflitto tra paganesimo e cristianesimo» che i relatori del '59 intendevano indagare.

Osservandolo a quasi cinquant'anni di distanza, non è difficile accorgersi che quel ritratto è molto cambiato. Esaminato da prospettive differenti, sottoposto ad effetti di luce molteplici, esso ha rivelato ogni volta un volto diverso: persino quello dell'imperatore tollerante, o del politico preoccupato, anzitutto, di moralizzare e di rinvigorire gli apparati dello Stato. Ancora poco conosciuto, mi pare, è rimasto però il Giuliano cristiano: non solo quello nato ed educato nella nuova fede, ma pure l'erede di una dinastia che aveva scelto il cristianesimo come religione della corona, e che perciò non poteva non dialogare con i suoi capi neanche volendolo.

Riflettendo su *questo* Giuliano, Hans Christof Brennecke ha scoperto due decenni orsono un fatto importante, accuratamente minimizzato già dalle fonti coeve di parte: e cioè che l'odio dell'Apostata, in teoria generalizzato, fu, nella pratica, un odio selettivo, del quale furono oggetto non *tutti* i cristiani, ma solo *alcuni* di loro. In particolare, Brennecke ha messo in rilievo che i martiri della cosiddetta «persecuzione» giulianea furono, nella stragrande maggioranza dei casi, martiri omei, martiri cioè di quella Chiesa che il predecessore dell'Apostata, suo cugino Costanzo II, aveva incaricato nel 360 di sostenere il proprio progetto politico e religioso. La persecuzione che costoro subirono fu dunque la persecuzione di una classe dirigente della quale un uomo come Giuliano, che era asceso al trono a seguito di un'usurpazione, si fidava molto poco, essendone cordialmente

---

* Il tema del presente contributo è affrontato in forma più ampia e particolareggiata in F. Fatti, *Giuliano a Cesarea. La politica ecclesiastica del principe apostata*, Roma 2010.

ricambiato. Completamente diversa, invece, la sorte di quei cristiani che dal piano di Costanzo erano rimasti esclusi, e ai quali il nuovo imperatore poteva rivolgersi – e in taluni casi effettivamente si rivolse – sperando nella loro collaborazione[1].

Benché abbia ormai compiuto vent'anni, il Giuliano di Brennecke resta un Giuliano decisamente nuovo. Dinanzi a noi, infatti, non si staglia più il «rinnegato» assetato del sangue dei suoi antichi compagni di fede. Ma non c'è più nemmeno il principe munito soltanto del suo senso civico, sostanzialmente indifferente alla sorte degli «empi Galilei». Invece, c'è uno statista politicamente sensibile al fatto cristiano, capace perciò di una politica ecclesiastica degna di un costantinide, fatta di amici da coinvolgere e di nemici da ostacolare, in funzione di un progetto di governo non riducibile al già di per sé ambizioso obiettivo della restaurazione degli antichi dèi.

Quanto accadde nell'estate del 362 a Cesarea di Cappadocia – ove il principe fece tappa nel corso del suo viaggio da Costantinopoli ad Antiochia, effettuato in funzione della prevista spedizione persiana – conferma la bontà di questo nuovo ritratto, ma al tempo stesso lo complica, mostrando che l'Apostata, se è vero che non si procurò i suoi avversari cristiani soltanto a motivo delle sue preferenze religiose, non se li procurò nemmeno per ragioni dettate esclusivamente dalla grande politica. Piuttosto, le sue scelte in fatto di collaboratori – pur'essi cristiani – ebbero talora ripercussioni così gravi, nelle relazioni di potere esistenti a livello locale, da innescare tensioni e squilibri che si ritorsero contro di lui a prescindere tanto dalla sua fede pagana quanto dalla sua volontà di conquistare alla propria causa la Chiesa emarginata da Costanzo.

1. Cesarea 362

Sostiene dunque Sozomeno che, in occasione del passaggio di Giuliano in città – non sappiamo esattamente se prima, durante o dopo –, qualcuno ebbe l'idea di danneggiare il tempio della *Tyche*[2]. La famiglia di Sozomeno era stata tra le vittime della persecuzione giulianea[3]: l'episodio che questi racconta, perciò – uno dei tanti raccolti dallo storico per celebrare coloro che a quella persecuzione avevano resistito – risente del livore di

---

[1] Cf. H.C. BRENNECKE, *Studien zur Geschichte der Homöer. Der Osten bis zum Ende der homöischen Reichskirche*, Tübingen 1988, 87-91; 96-107.
[2] Cf. Soz. *h.e.* V, 4, 1-5.
[3] Cf. *ibid.*, 15, 13-17.

qualcuno che aveva ragioni personali per demonizzare il principe apostata. La natura dell'aggressione, però, non fu – o, perlomeno, non fu soltanto – di tipo religioso.

Per provare a comprendere di che cosa si sia trattato veramente occorre tener presente che l'attacco al *Tycheion* di Cesarea si verificò in concomitanza con un altro evento, che dispiacque anch'esso all'imperatore: l'elezione del nuovo vescovo della città, nella persona di Eusebio[4].

Per quale motivo quest'uomo fosse sgradito a Giuliano non è perfettamente chiaro. Secondo Brennecke, il principe lo sospettava considerandolo espressione della Chiesa di osservanza omea favorita da Costanzo[5]. Ma non si hanno né prove né indizi che consentano di determinare l'appartenenza confessionale del vescovo. Per il momento, perciò, dobbiamo rinunciare a chiederci *perché* Giuliano non lo volesse, tenendo invece a mente il dato, di per sé molto importante, *che il principe assolutamente non lo voleva*[6].

Per fortuna di Eusebio, Giuliano non poté occuparsi della questione di persona. L'Apostata aveva fretta di arrivare ad Antiochia, e viaggiava veloce[7]. Perciò, lasciò che a risolvere le cose fosse il governatore della provincia. Il quale, non appena ebbe ricevuto notifica del desiderio imperiale, immediatamente lo trasmise ai vescovi convenuti a suo tempo per l'elezione, invitandoli a riunirsi di nuovo e ad annullare quanto avevano fatto[8]. Fu a questo punto che, in città, un settore del clero locale si sollevò contro l'eletto: un settore guidato dall'allora presbitero Basilio.

Immediatamente dopo che l'imperatore ebbe reso di dominio pubblico il suo disappunto circa la nomina di Eusebio, tra Eusebio e Basilio sorse infatti «una divergenza»[9]. Per quale motivo, ancora una volta non è chiaro. Secondo la nostra fonte sulla vicenda – Gregorio Nazianzeno – i rapporti tra i due

---

[4] In proposito, GREG. NAZ. *or.* 18, 34 (PG 35, 1029, B).
[5] Così H.C. BRENNECKE, *Studien...*, 151 e n. 195.
[6] «Assolutamente» è avverbio che va inteso *stricto sensu*. Secondo il Nazianzeno, infatti, quando l'Apostata conobbe il risultato dell'elezione, perse letteralmente le staffe, minacciando rappresaglie: «La nomina fu accolta con collera, e colui che era stato promosso venne minacciato. La città era sul filo del rasoio: o non sarebbe esistita più, dopo quel giorno, oppure si sarebbe salvata e avrebbe ottenuto una qualche benevolenza» (GREG. NAZ. *or.* 18, 34 [PG, 35, 1029, B, 2-5]).
[7] Sul viaggio e le sue tappe, da ultimo K. ROSEN, *Julian. Kaiser, Gott und Christenhasser*, Stuttgart 2006, 275-280. Sull'accelerazione della marcia dopo il passaggio a Pessinunte, vd. LIB. *orr.* 17, 17; 18, 162 FOERSTER.
[8] Cf. GREG. NAZ. *or.* 18, 34 (PG 35, 1029, B).
[9] Così di nuovo GREG. NAZ. *or.* 43, 28, 1 BERNARDI: τις ... διαφορά.

si sarebbero rovinati a causa di non meglio specificate questioni personali[10], della cui natura siamo completamente all'oscuro. Nel 1968, Jean Bernardi suggerì che potesse essersi trattato di qualcosa di offensivo che sarebbe stato detto, nei confronti del proprio vescovo, da un Basilio già da qualche anno al servizio di Eusebio, ipotesi che ci porterebbe in un'epoca di qualche anno posteriore a quella in cui si svolsero i fatti di cui stiamo parlando[11]. Un'ipotesi del genere, però, non ha fondamento. Sul punto in questione, Gregorio è infatti chiarissimo: quell'attrito si verificò in concomitanza con la «persecuzione» – così si esprime testualmente il Nazianzeno – che Eusebio subì da parte di Giuliano[12]. Questa circostanza ci assicura che il dissidio non sorse né nel 363, come creduto da Bernardi, né tantomeno nel 364, come proposto da altri[13], ma appunto nel 362, cioè precisamente al momento del passaggio del principe – e di un principe che si era espresso in modo inequivocabile sul conto di Eusebio.

Naturalmente, che Basilio avesse manifestato il proprio dissenso per far piacere a Giuliano la nostra fonte non lo dice. Quel che è certo, però, è che esso creò al vescovo parecchi problemi: intorno al presbitero dissidente si coagulò infatti il malcontento di molti altri dissidenti – la maggioranza dei vescovi elettori; alcuni cittadini «in vista», membri di certo della classe dirigente della città; nonché i «Nazirei», che vedremo tra poco chi fossero –, i quali diedero luogo ad uno scisma che per poco non fece perdere davvero ad Eusebio la cattedra appena conquistata[14]. Anche se non era sorto per far piacere a Giuliano, perciò, *di fatto* il dissenso basiliano veniva incontro alla volontà del principe, il quale poteva legittimamente guardare al fronte guidato da Basilio come ad un fronte di suoi fiancheggiatori.

---

[10] Secondo GREG. NAZ. *or*. 43, 28, 5-6 BERNARDI, nell'occasione Eusebio avrebbe provato nei confronti di Basilio τι ... ἀνθρώπινον.
[11] Cf. J. BERNARDI, *La prédication des Pères Cappadociens. Le prédicateur et son auditoire*, Montpellier 1968, 19; 58-59.
[12] «Si verificò un disaccordo tra quest'uomo e colui che l'aveva preceduto nella guida della Chiesa. Sulle origini e sulle circostanze di questo disaccordo è meglio tacere, dicendo solo che si verificò con una persona per il resto non priva di valore e ammirevole quanto a pietà [τὴν εὐσέβειαν, gioco etimologico sul nome di Eusebio], *come mostrò la persecuzione di allora e la resistenza che questi le oppose*, ma che tuttavia provò nei suoi confronti qualcosa di personale» (GREG. NAZ. *or*. 43, 28, 1-6 BERNARDI).
[13] Per esempio, da P. GALLAY, *La vie de Saint Grégoire de Nazianze*, Lyon 1943, 77 e n. 4.
[14] In tal senso, ancora GREG. NAZ. *or*. 43, 28, 11-23 BERNARDI.

2. Il *Tycheion*

È tenendo conto di questa situazione che si capisce l'attacco alla *Tyche*: perché molto alte sono le probabilità che l'operazione sia stata orchestrata proprio da quella cattedra nel cui organico Basilio figurava e verso la quale costui maturò il proprio dissenso.

Della vicenda i contemporanei parlarono tra molte reticenze. Gregorio Nazianzeno si limitò ad ironizzarci sopra[15]. Libanio non si spinse, dal canto suo, oltre una velata allusione[16]. Già nel V secolo, perciò, molti dettagli erano andati irrimediabilmente perduti. Sozomeno, tuttavia, era ancora in grado di riferire qualcosa sul conto di almeno uno dei responsabili, del quale poteva citare anche il nome: non Basilio – del quale, curiosamente, non si conosce nessun atto antigiulianeo – ma un certo Eupsichio, «eupatride» di Cesarea, che aveva pagato il suo coinvolgimento con la vita[17]. A dire dello storico, quest'uomo non era un fanatico isolato. Al contrario, era stato denunciato all'imperatore insieme ad altri, di concerto coi quali aveva certamente agito. Alcuni di costoro se l'erano cavata con l'esilio. Ad altri, invece, era toccata la pena di morte: evidentemente, quelli le cui responsabilità erano risultate maggiori. Il fatto che Eupsichio sia stato tra questi ultimi, mostra con sufficiente chiarezza che egli fu identificato appunto come una delle menti dell'operazione.

Se dovessimo credere a Sozomeno, dovremmo concludere che il movente che spinse un uomo del genere a rischiare e a pagare così tanto fu lo stesso che animò tutti gli altri martiri della persecuzione giulianea, vale a dire l'avversione provata spontaneamente da ogni vero cristiano nei confronti del principe rinnegato. Le cose, tuttavia, sono molto più complicate di come lo storico le descrive.

Da una fonte tarda, ma attendibile – il vescovo di Cesarea, Areta (902-944 ca) – sappiamo infatti che quell'uomo, proprio come Basilio era anch'egli un presbitero della Chiesa della metropoli cappadoce[18]. Eupsichio, cioè, apparteneva anch'egli al clero del vescovo Eusebio – lo stesso che Giuliano cercò in ogni modo di ostacolare al momento dell'elezione. Il suo gesto, perciò, dal momento che costituiva un atto di protesta contro

---

[15] In *or.* 18, 34 (PG, 35, 1029, B 5-8), risalente al 374, ma già dieci anni prima, in *or.* 4, 92, 16-22 BERNARDI.
[16] Cf. LIB. *or.* 16, 14 FOERSTER.
[17] Così SOZ. *h.e.* V, 11, 7-8.
[18] Cf. ARET. CAES. *Ep. ad Eustathium episc. Sid.* 33-35 WESTERINK: Εὐψύχιος, ὁ τοῦ Χριστοῦ μάρτυς, πρεσβύτερος.

l'Apostata, è molto probabile che non sia dispiaciuto affatto al presule che l'Apostata voleva togliere di mezzo.

Ciò che è più importante, però, è che Eupsichio apparteneva ad un settore di quel clero le cui convinzioni ideologiche erano diametralmente opposte a quelle del collega Basilio. Areta ci informa infatti che, al momento di essere consacrato sacerdote, Eupsichio aveva da poco preso moglie; egli era, insomma, un presbitero sposato[19]: dal punto di vista di uno come Basilio, il peggio che potesse capitare ad un uomo di Chiesa.

In effetti, oltre che un membro del clero di Cesarea, all'epoca dei fatti Basilio era pure un seguace dell'ascesi di Eustazio di Sebastia, il cui codice, tra le altre cose, vietava qualsiasi rapporto con i chierici ammogliati[20]. Ora, noi sappiamo che quando Basilio si mobilitò contro Eusebio lo fece precisamente in questa veste, vale a dire nella veste di «capo» di coloro che Gregorio Nazianzeno definì «i nostri Nazirei» – i membri, cioè, della locale comunità eustaziana[21]. Fu in qualità di capo di costoro che Basilio si guadagnò, in particolare, il sostegno di quei cittadini «in vista» che si dissero disposti a sostenerne la protesta[22]. È evidente che, tra questi cittadini, l'eupatride Eupsichio non c'era.

Costui, deve essere appartenuto piuttosto a quel settore della Cesarea bene che – ci informa un'epistola dello stesso Basilio – nei confronti della vita ascetica di Eustazio, anziché ammirazione, provava un sincero disgusto[23]. Deve aver rappresentato, insomma, la voce e la mente di una parte

---

[19] Cf. *ibid.*, ove si legge che Eupsichio era uno che «si era sposato dopo la consacrazione», «un presbitero che aveva cinto la corona del martirio quando era ancora fresco di nozze».

[20] Cf. C. Gangr. *Epistula synodica* JOANNOU I/2, 88, 4-7: «Disprezzano i presbiteri sposati e non toccano le liturgie fatte da loro»; *can.* 4 (91, 1-7): «Se uno ha da eccepire a scapito di un presbitero sposato, sostenendo che, quando costui celebra la liturgia, non si debba prender parte all'offerta, sia anatema»; e inoltre SOCR. *h.e.* II, 43, 5; SOZ *h.e.* III, 14, 33. Sul discepolato eustaziano di Basilio e i problemi che esso suscitò nell'ambiente basiliano, vd. F. FATTI, *Nei panni del vescovo. Gregorio, Basilio e il filosofo Eustazio*, in *Le trasformazioni delle élites in età tardoantica*, ed. R. LIZZI TESTA, Roma 2006, 177-238.

[21] Così GREG. NAZ. *or.* 43, 28, 8-14 BERNARDI (ove Basilio è descritto come κράτος dei Ναζιραῖοι, con F. FATTI, Nei panni..., 213-216 e n. 102.107.110.

[22] Sono infatti i Nazirei che «si mettono in mente una secessione, una rottura del grande corpo della Chiesa alieno da ribellioni, guadagnando a sé una parte non piccola di popolo cristiano, sia di bassa condizione che dignitari» (GREG. NAZ. *or.* 43, 28, 13-17 BERNARDI).

[23] «Quanti motivi per ridere di noi procureremo a quanti in questa sventurata città dicono sempre male della vita devota, e dichiarano che la finzione dell'umiltà è un artificio per convincere e una posa per ingannare, la tua intelligenza lo sa benissimo, senza che

dell'*élite* dirigente della città che era attestata su posizioni antitetiche a quelle sulle quali si trovavano Basilio e quanti erano disposti ad appoggiarlo; una parte – questa di Eupsichio – in cui si riconosceva evidentemente anche il vescovo Eusebio – il quale, accogliendo quell'uomo nella sua Chiesa, si era automaticamente mostrato indifferente alle eccezioni che gli eustaziani sollevavano sul conto dei presbiteri sposati, esponendosi in tal modo al loro disappunto.

Il fatto che proprio *questa* parte, restìa ad apprezzare l'eustaziano Basilio, si sia resa responsabile dell'aggressione al *Tycheion* sembra dunque potersi spiegare come un'operazione pianificata per colpire non tanto l'Apostata, come invece si è detto anche di recente[24], quanto l'ambiente civico sul cui sostegno l'Apostata contava, e che, conoscendo la sensibilità del principe per simili questioni, si poteva facilmente prevedere che avrebbe pagato anch'esso le conseguenze del sacrilegio; se non altro perché non aveva fatto nulla per impedirlo.

Per esser certi di ottenere questo risultato, del resto, gli aggressori avevano scelto il loro obiettivo con grande cura. Colpendo un tempio pagano essi avevano commesso, naturalmente, un reato contro la religione dell'imperatore, già così esponendosi alla sua ira – dal momento che, notava Libanio, il principe «si compiaceva [...] nel vedere quelle città che avevano i loro templi ancora in piedi e le riteneva meritevoli di ricevere benefici, mentre chiamava corrotte quelle città che avevano demolito tutti o gran parte dei loro templi»[25]. Colpendo il tempio della *Tyche*, ossia della divinità tutelare della città, dal punto di vista dell'imperatore – e di un imperatore che considerava la devozione templare parte integrante del suo piano di rinvigorimento delle *poleis*[26] – essi avevano compiuto, inoltre, un

---

noi stiamo a spiegartelo. Perché ormai nessuna occupazione è così sospetta di cose cattive, per la gente di qui, come la professione di vita ascetica». Così Bas. *ep.* 119, 28-35 Courtonne, scritta ad Eustazio nell'inverno 372-373, a seguito di gravi incomprensioni sorte tra maestro e discepolo.

[24] Cf. per esempio R. Van Dam, *Kingdom of Snow. Roman Rule and Greek Culture in Cappadocia*, Philadelphia 2002, 101, per cui «[i]n Cappadocia Julian had [...] discovered [...] a city that ignored his religious preferences»; e S. Métivier, *La Cappadoce (IVe-VIe siècle). Une histoire provinciale de l'Empire romain d'Orient*, Paris 2005, 396, la quale crede che «la destruction du temple de la Fortune fait connaître [...] la difficulté du ralliement, voire l'hostilité de la cité au nouvel empereur».

[25] Lib. *or.* 18, 129 Foerster (trad. Angiolani).

[26] Sul punto, G. Bonamente, *Le città nella politica di Giuliano l'Apostata*, «Annali della Facoltà di Lettere e Filosofia dell'Università di Macerata» 16 (1983), 35-96, partic. 55-64; 88-90; E. Pack, *Städte und Steuern in der Politik Julians. Untersuchungen zu den Quellen eines Kaiserbildes*, Bruxelles 1986.

attentato contro la salute del corpo civico, tanto più grave in quanto nel recente passato i cristiani avevano già demolito i templi di Zeus «protettore della *polis*» (*poliuchos*) e di Apollo «patrio» (*patròos*), cioè delle altre divinità poliadi che vigilavano su Cesarea[27]. Attaccando la *Tyche*, però, gli attentatori avevano fatto ancora di peggio. *Tyche*, infatti, non era una divinità qualunque, ma la divinità alla quale Giuliano credeva di dovere il suo impero.

Questo, almeno, fu quanto Giuliano stesso volle far credere quando, entrato a Costantinopoli e cinto ufficialmente il diadema imperiale, egli sacrificò, in segno di ringraziamento, nel locale *Tycheion*[28]; o quando, ad Antiochia, fece lo stesso nel giorno dell'assunzione del suo quarto consolato[29]. Questo fu quanto sostenne la propaganda del principe, ben rappresentata da Mamertino[30] e, più tardi, da Ammiano, secondo cui se c'era una cosa di cui l'imperatore era sicuro era «che a lui, che ormai reggeva senza alcuna opposizione l'impero romano, la Fortuna favorevole, come se portasse una cornucopia terrena, concedeva gloria e successo in tutte le imprese»[31].

Coloro che, a Cesarea, avevano attaccato il tempio della *Tyche* avevano fatto dunque qualcosa di più che attaccare un sacrario pagano: essi avevano messo in discussione il carattere divino della missione del principe, macchiandosi del reato di lesa maestà; un reato tanto grave da innescare una reazione che – almeno fin quando le indagini certamente avviate dopo l'incidente non avessero fatto luce sulla vicenda, distinguendo tra colpevoli e innocenti – avrebbe travolto non solo i diretti responsabili ma anche i fiancheggiatori dell'Apostata, rei quantomeno di non averne difeso apertamente gli interessi.

Sozomeno, in effetti, ricorda che l'ira del principe – abbattutasi sulla città come previsto: Cesarea fu privata del titolo di *polis* e declassata a *kome*, con i conseguenti oneri fiscali – non aveva risparmiato nessuno, nella metropoli, nemmeno gli elleni, considerati pur'essi colpevoli precisamente per la loro inerzia e inefficienza[32]: a maggior ragione era prevedibile che non avrebbe risparmiato, quell'ira, nessuno del clero, nemmeno il fronte «filogiulianeo» guidato dal presbitero dissidente Basilio. Il quale, guarda caso, nonostante i suoi sforzi dovette ad un certo punto rassegnarsi

---

[27] Secondo la notizia di Soz. *h.e.* V, 4, 2.
[28] Cf. Socr. *h.e.* III, 11, 4; Soz. *h.e.* V, 4, 8.
[29] Cf. Iul. *misop.* 15, 6-7 Prato; Lib. *or.* 15, 79 Foerster; Amm. Marc. 23, 1, 6.
[30] Mamert. *pan.* 27, 2.
[31] Amm. Marc. 22, 9, 1.
[32] Così Soz. *h.e.* V, 4, 3.

a rinunciare alla cattedra metropolitana, finendo addirittura con l'abbandonare Cesarea[33].

Attentando al *Tycheion*, dunque, Eupsichio non aveva messo a rischio la sua vita per niente, ma per uno scopo che valeva il prezzo pagato per raggiungerlo: vanificare i progetti dell'Apostata relativi alla metropoli e, soprattutto, i piani di quel settore del clero locale che dalla volontà dell'imperatore aveva cercato di trarre profitto.

Se questo è vero, allora Cesarea costituisce un'opportunità eccezionale per capire un po' meglio la breve stagione giulianea – e, con essa, il rapporto pagani-cristiani che essa riportò alla ribalta. In effetti, se, come ho provato a dimostrare, è vero che un settore della Chiesa locale si ribellò al principe non a motivo della sua apostasia ma a motivo delle alleanze che questi si era procurato in città, è possibile che qualcosa del genere sia accaduto anche altrove.

Cesarea può costituire insomma un esempio di metodo: dove ci sono nemici cristiani dell'Apostata, conviene perlomeno sospettare che possano esserci pure amici, disposti, in cambio di aiuto, ad appoggiarlo.

---

[33] Cf. GREG. NAZ. *or.* 43, 29, 6-8 BERNARDI.

JAN WILLEM DRIJVERS

Religious conflict
in the Syriac *Julian Romance*

Arnaldo Momigliano's *The Conflict between Paganism and Christianity in the Fourth Century* and the 1958 Warburg Lectures on which it was based are a monument of scholarship of its age. All contributions have survived the ravages of time and still are of great scholarly importance in spite of the fact that the study of Late Antiquity has made immense progress in the past fifty years. Surprisingly, in *The conflict* Julian the Apostate is only mentioned in passing[1]. Julian's attempts at injecting new life into the cults of the old gods after five decades of gradual christianization of the empire were a source of conflict and provoked fierce reactions from Christian authors and church leaders, in particular after the short period of his rule. Consideration of Julian and the Christian reactions to his rule would therefore have fitted in perfectly in Momigliano's volume. In spite of the breath of approach, the great majority of the contributions in *The Conflict* are concerned with the Latin west; paganism and Christianity in the Greek east receive hardly any attention. Moreover, the contributors predominantly use accepted (pagan and Christian) historical sources: Eusebius, Orosius, Ammianus Marcellinus, Aurelius Victor to name just a few. The importance of less obvious historical sources – such as martyr acts, the *vitae* of holy men and women, or legendary material for the reconstruction of interaction and conflict between religious movements as well as for social, cultural and political developments in general – still had to be discovered and appreciated by historians at the time Momigliano's volume was published.

This paper focuses on a topic, a part of the Roman Empire and a type of source that remained underexposed in *The Conflict*, namely Julian, one of the most remarkable and controversial emperors of the fourth century,

---

[1] *The Conflict between Paganism and Christianity in the Fourth Century*, ed. A. MOMIGLIANO, Oxford 1963, 24, 30-31 (Julian's law against Christian teachers), 52 (Julian's *De Caesaribus* and his indictment of Constantine), 95, 96, 110, 115, 195, 204.

and the reactions to his rule in the eastern regions of the Empire from the perspective of the so-called *Julian Romance*, a rather unknown Christian source of historical fiction in Syriac.

1. The *Julian Romance*

The *Julian Romance* falls into three parts. The first part is about the reign of the Christian-loving emperors Constantine and his son, the persecution of the Christians initiated by Julian and the perseverance and eventual victory of Eusebius, bishop of Rome, against the pagan emperor. This section is only partially preserved and fills a mere two-three pages[2].

The second part, which I call the «History of Eusebius», tells at great length about the many vain attempts of Julian to have Rome's bishop Eusebius, who is already ninety-seven years old, renounce his Christian conviction and become a venerator of the old gods[3]. To that end Julian first sends his representative Adoctus with a letter offering to let Eusebius become the chief priest of the pagan cults. Eusebius, of course, refuses even under the threat of death and tears up the emperor's letter. Adoctus, in his efforts to win Rome for the pagan side, talks to the senators of Rome, for whom Julian also had letters. The senators, represented by Volusianus, refuse to support Julian and recognize his rule since they are Christians and in support of Eusebius. The people of Rome also do not favour Julian's efforts to repaganize their city, apart, of course from the pagan part of the population and the Jews. In his letter to the Roman senate Julian orders a great altar to be built before the great church of Rome. Pagans and Jews work together harmoniously in constructing this altar. The senators, who are saddened about the affairs, inform the rectors of the convents in and around Rome. These assemble all the monks, who subsequently enter Rome and start a great massacre among the pagans and Jews. The pagan priests who accompanied Adoctus are burned on the altar, after which it is demolished. After these affairs, the senators of Rome enter into a covenant and take oaths that they would never renounce their Christian belief and would be willing to

---

[2] J.G.E. HOFFMANN, *Iulianos der Abtrünnige. Syrische Erzählungen*, Leiden 1880, 3-5; H. GOLLANCZ, *Julian the Apostate. Now translated for the first time from the Syriac original*, Oxford 1928, 7-9. Part of this introduction is missing in Add. MS 14641, but it is at least partly preserved in the palimpsest of the MS Syr. 378 in Paris.

[3] J.G.E. HOFFMANN, *Iulianos der Abtrünnige...*, 5-59; H. GOLLANCZ, *Julian the Apostate...*, 10-65.

sacrifice their wealth and power for that. On the 25th of the month of Adar of the year 673, i.e. 25 March 362, Julian himself enters Rome accompanied by his army. The emperor, enraged by what happened but wanting to give the impression that he is a clement ruler, orders shows to be given. When the people, assembled in the theatre, ask for religious tolerance and peace concerning all cults, Julian demands worship and veneration of the gods. He has Eusebius imprisoned in order to have him sacrificed at the festival for the gods that Julian has ordered to give. At the day of the festival Julian, dressed in royal garments and surrounded by soldiers, intends to do honour to his gods. A large crowd has also assembled, extremely hostile to the emperor, in order to save Eusebius from being burnt on the restored altar in front of the great church. When Eusebius is brought forward, the crowd becomes even more hostile and demands pardon for the bishop. A discussion between Julian and Eusebius follows, with accusations and insults back and forth. Eusebius blames Julian for having fallen away from God and omitting to look after pressing matters such as the war against Persia. Julian accuses Eusebius of being mad and having an impure belief. The executioner, with the name of Plato, instantly drops dead when he approaches the bishop to bring him to the altar to be burnt. Eusebius is imprisoned again and Julian commands that all churches be closed and all bishops be sent into exile. Eusebius is put to torments of all sorts, but they do not afflict the bishop in any way. In an ultimate attempt to have Eusebius removed from out of his way, Julian condemns him to the sword. But when the executioner lifts the sword to strike Eusebius, the instrument of execution miraculously melts away. Ashamed, disillusioned, and angry, Julian leaves Rome to campaign against the Persians. Eusebius prophesies the emperor's death in this campaign as an act of God's justice. Eusebius survives Julian by several years and dies in the year 367.

The third part of the *Romance*, which I call the «History of Jovian», is the longest of the three[4]. In its introduction it is said that the text was written as a letter by a certain Aploris, who is called «confidential minister to Jovian the King» at the request of Abdel, «chief of the convent»[5]. It tells the story of Julian's journey from Rome via Constantinople, Antioch, Harran and Nisibis to Persia, in order to wage war on Shapur for the reason that the Persian king has stopped persecuting the Christians. Julian's anti-Christian measures are elaborately described. The other key-figure of this narrative is

---

[4] J.G.E. HOFFMANN, *Iulianos der Abtrünnige...*, 59-242; H. GOLLANCZ, *Julian the Apostate...*, 66-255.
[5] *Ibid.*, 66.

Julian's general Jovian, or Jovinian as he is called in the *Romance*. Jovian secretly favours the Christian cause and through the confidence Julian has in him he is able to restrain the emperor's anti-Christian measures and come to the help of individual Christians. This part of the *Romance* is, like the «History of Eusebius», characterized by dialogues between Julian and his supporters on the one hand, and Jovian and the emperor's opponents on the other, as well as by the exchange of letters, the contents of which are elaborately described, between Julian, Jovian and others. Also in this third part, Julian not only wants to reintroduce paganism but also seeks recognition of his rule. Whereas he did not receive acknowledgment from the city of Rome, his reign was ultimately recognized by Constantinople, the second Rome. Jovian has regular contact with Shapur's chief general, Arimhar, who, through his exchange of information with Jovian, converts to Christianity. When in the fatal campaign Julian is killed by an arrow sent by God, Jovian is made emperor. Both Julian's death and Jovian's emperorship are predicted and are seen as acts of God. Interestingly, both the pagan Julian, who on his deathbed had designated Jovian as his successor, as also the non-Christian Shapur, who had written a letter to recommend Jovian, are instrumental in making Jovian emperor. Subsequently Shapur and Jovian enter on a peace treaty, which includes the voluntary cession of Nisibis and the eastern provinces to Shapur, together with the cessation of the persecution of Christians in the Sassanian empire for a period of hundred years.

In the «History of Jovian» Jovian is the instrument of God who restores the Christian rule of his predecessor Constantine, and who turns the nightmare of Julian's reign into the reality of the Christian dream, in which Christianity is favoured by the emperor, an end is made to the pagan cults, and the Jews are punished. Edessa plays a central role in this third part of the Romance. The city is presented as «the mother of believers»[6], and uniquely of the cities in the East stays firm in its faith, irrespective of Julian's threats to devastate the city and kill its inhabitants. As a reward for the city's firmness Jovian visits Edessa on his return to Constantinople. The Edessenes receive the emperor with great joy, and he amazes everybody, including himself, by performing a healing miracle.

Christian reactions to Julian's reign were vehement – fed possibly by the fear of the revival of polytheism at the cost of Christianity –, in particular in the eastern part of the empire where no doubt the emperor's anti-Christian measures were felt more directly than in the western provinces. The east was also directly confronted with the consequences of the disastrous Per-

---

[6] H. GOLLANCZ, *Julian the Apostate*...,138.

sian campaign. Julian's successor Jovian had to arrange a shameful peace settlement with Shapur, which implied the loss of important cities such as Nisibis and regions which had been under Roman rule since the end of the third century[7]. This was not only a tremendous shock for public opinion but had also an immediate effect on the populations of these cities and regions, many of which had to leave their homes and settle elsewhere. Shortly after Julian's death, polemical writings against the emperor appeared, of which *Orations* 4 and 5 by Gregory of Nazianzus were the first[8]. Gregory's extreme hostility towards Rome's last pagan emperor was repeated in other Greek Christian writings, among them the fifth-century *Ecclesiastical Histories*. Not only did Julian's reign provoke vehement reactions by Greek Christian authors, also in Syriac literature Julian and his reign are described in extremely negative terms. Ephrem Syrus, who was forced to leave his native Nisibis because of the peace settlement and move to Edessa, wrote his *Hymns contra Julianum* in 363/4, which breathe a vehement abhorrence of Julian and his reign. After Ephrem had set the tone, later Syriac writings regularly refer to Julian in hateful terms[9]. Probably the fiercest polemical work against Julian in the Syriac-speaking regions was the so-called *Julian Romance*.

The *Julian Romance*, preserved in the ms. BL 14.641, was first brought to attention by the famous German orientalist Theodor Nöldeke in 1874. In a long article he presented an extensive summary of the text based on the manuscript, and dealt with several fundamental issues such as the date, author, original language, and place of origin of the text. In the same year he published the translation of another, much shorter text about Julian, found in the Syriac ms. BL Richmond 7192 dating from the seventh century; this much shorter text, called by Nöldeke the second *Julian Romance*, deals with Julian's apostasy, sorcery and veneration of idols and demons[10]. Nöldeke

---

[7] AMM. MARC. 25.7.9-14 with commentary by J. DEN BOEFT, J.W. DRIJVERS, D. DEN HENGST, H.C. TEITLER, *Philological and Historical Commentary on Ammianus Marcellinus XXV*, Leiden 2005, 233-250.

[8] See e.g. J. BERNARDI, *Les invectives contre Julien de Grégoire de Nazianze*, in *L'empereur Julien. I. De l'histoire à la légende (331-1715)*, ed. R. BRAUN, J. RICHER, Paris 1978, 89-98; J. MCGUCKIN, *Saint Gregory of Nazianzus. An Intellectual Biography*, New York 2001, 119ff.

[9] R. CONTINI, *Giuliano imperatore nella tradizione Siriaca*, in *Da Costantino a Teodosio il Grande. Cultura, società, diritto*, ed. U. CRISCUOLO, Naples 2003, 119-145.

[10] T. NÖLDEKE, *Über den syrischen Roman von Kaiser Julian*, «Zeitschrift des Deutschen Morgenländischen Gesellschaft» 28 (1874), 263-292; ID., *Ein zweiter syrischer Julianusroman*, «Zeitschrift des deutschen morgenländischen Gesellschaft» 28 (1874), 660-674. According to Nöldeke (pp. 671-674), whose article is the only scholarly pub-

was the first to call the text a Romance. Six years later J.G.E. Hoffmann published the complete Syriac text under the title *Syrische Erzählungen*; in 1928 Hermann Gollancz published an English translation, which is the only translation available to date[11]. Thereafter the text received no attention from scholars for some six decades. In the 1980s interest in the *Julian Romance* arose again, which led to new publications and novel and different views on various aspects of the text[12]. Notwithstanding this renewed interest it is fair to say that, on the whole, the *Julian Romance* is understudied and deserves more attention[13]. The text is of importance for the un-

---

lication about the second *Julian Romance*, the latter text is not older than the sixth century and was originally published in Syriac but by an author other than that of the first *Julian Romance*.

[11] J.G.E. HOFFMANN, *Iulianos der Abtrünnige...*; H. GOLLANCZ, *Julian the Apostate...* In between selections of the *Romance* were published by R.J.H. GOTTHEIL, *A Selection from the Syriac Julian Romance*, Leiden 1906. A new English translation is being prepared by Emmanuel Papoutsakis for the Liverpool series Translated Texts for Historians.

[12] M. VAN ESBROECK, *Le soi-disant roman de Julien l'Apostat*, in *IV Symposium Syriacum 1984. Literary Genres in Syriac Literature*, ed. H.J.W. DRIJVERS ET AL., Rome 1987, 191-202; G.J. REININK, *The Romance of Julian the Apostate as a source for seventh century Syriac Apocalypses*, in *La Syrie de Byzance à l'Islam. Actes du Colloque international, Lyon-Paris 11-15 Septembre 1990*, ed. P. CANIVET, Damas 1992, 75-86; repr. in G.J. REININK, *Syriac Christianity under Late Sasanian and Early Islamic Rule*, Aldershot 2005, ch. XI; H.J.W. DRIJVERS, *The Syriac Romance of Julian. Its Function, Place of Origin and Original Language*, in *VI Symposium Syriacum 1992*, ed. R. LAVENANT, Rome 1994, 201-214; A. MURAVIEV, *The Syriac Julian Romance and its Place in the Literary History*, «Khristianskii Vostok» 1 (1999)/7, 194-206; J.W. DRIJVERS, *The Syriac Julian Romance. Aspects of the Jewish-Christian Controversy in Late Antiquity*, in *All those Nations... Cultural Encounters within and with the Near East. Studies presented to Han Drijvers at the occasion of his sixty-fifth birthday*, ed. H.L.J. VANSTIPHOUT ET AL., Groningen 1999, 31-42; S. BROCK, A. MURAVIEV, *The Fragments of the Syriac Julian Romance from the Manuscript Paris Syr. 378*, «Khristianskii Vostok» 2 (2001)/8, 14-34. J.W. DRIJVERS, *Julian the Apostate and the City of Rome: Pagan-Christian Polemics in the Syriac* Julian Romance, in *Syriac Polemics. Studies in Honour of Gerrit Jan Reinink*, ed. by W.J. VAN BEKKUM, J.W. DRIJVERS, A.C. KLUGKIST, Louvain 2007, 1-20; J.W. DRIJVERS, *The Emperor Jovian as New Constantine in the Syriac Julian Romance*, in *Studia Patristica. Papers presented at the Fifteenth International Conference on Patristic Studies held in Oxford 2007*, Louvain (in press). J. RICHER, *Les romans syriaques des sixième et septième siècles:* I. *Histoire d'Eusèbe.* II. *Histoire de Jovien.* III. *Julien le magician*, in *L'empereur Julien.* I. *De l'histoire à la légende (331-1715)*, ed. R. BRAUN, J. RICHER, Paris 1978, 233-268 offers summaries of the second and third part of the *Julian Romance* and of the so-called second *Julian Romance*.

[13] Studies on Julian, even those published in recent years, do not refer to the *Romance*. The exception is K. ROSEN, *Julian. Kaiser, Gott und Christenhasser*, Stuttgart 2006, 399. Unfortunately, Rosen presents incorrect information by dating the text to the fourth century and ascribing it to a Greek author.

derstanding of later Syriac literature and for the reception of Julian's reign and the image which was created of the pagan emperor in the eastern part of the Roman Empire. The *Romance* reflects the fear and anxiety which the presence of pagans and Jews inspired in Christians in Late Antiquity, even many years after Julian's death. The Romance possibly also reflects the fear that Christians had for another non-Christian emperor on the Roman throne who would, like Julian, attempt to restore the old polytheistic cults at the expense of Christianity.

In spite of the renewed attention, modest as it is, scholars differ on a variety of issues concerning the text. Concerning the date of origin, the author, its purpose, its sources, the genre it belongs to, and even the language in which it was originally composed there is no *communis opinio*. There is, however, agreement on a few things. The text as we have it is accepted as having been been composed in Edessa. Edessa has a special place and a prominent role in the *Julian Romance* (see below) and it is mainly for this reason that the *Romance* is thought to have its origin in this north-Mesopotamian city. Also the influence of the writings of Ephrem Syrus, in particular his *Hymns against Julian*, the *Doctrina Addai* – the official foundation myth of Christianity in Edessa – on the *Romance*, the animosity towards Harran, the incorporation of local Edessene tradition (e.g. Constantine's letter to Edessa) are reasons for believing that the text was composed in Edessa[14]. An Edessene provenance almost automatically implies that the *Romance* is an authentic Syriac text and not a translation from the Greek. However, while Nöldeke has convincingly argued that the text does not show indications of translation, the opinion of a Syriac original text is not universally accepted[15]. On internal grounds Nöldeke proposes as date of composition the beginning of the sixth century, more precisely the years 502-532[16]. This date coincides nicely with that of the

---

[14] T. NÖLDEKE, *Über den syrischen Roman...*, 283-284; H.J.W. DRIJVERS, *The Syriac Romance of Julian...*, 202-203, 213; A. MURAVIEV, *The Syriac Julian Romance...*, 205 («Edessan background is evident in the Romance»).

[15] T. NÖLDEKE, *Über den syrischen Roman...*, 284: «Kein Zeichen führt darauf, dass eine griechische Urschrift vorgelegen, während sich sonst doch die Spuren der Ueberzetzung im Syrischen nicht leicht ganz verwisschen». Cf. M. VAN ESBROECK, *Le soi-disant roman...*, 196, who suggests that it had a Greek predecessor; A. MURAVIEV, *The Syriac Julian Romance...*, 200-201 thinks the question of the original language should be left open, although he does not refute Syriac as its original language.

[16] T. NÖLDEKE, *Über den syrischen Roman...*, 281-283. Nöldeke used the following passage for the establishment of the date: «Fourteen weeks of years the kingdom of Persia will be powerful over your kingdom... then both the powers shall dwell in peace for seven weeks of years, and after that there will be war between the two powers during

manuscript, which W. Wright on palaeographical grounds dates to the sixth century[17]. Nöldeke's proposed date was not challenged until 1994, when Han Drijvers' article was published. He was the first to approach the text from a historical rather than a philological perspective. In his article he dealt exclusively with the «History of Jovian», i.e. the third part of the *Romance*. He argued that the purpose of the text was to come to terms with and justify the Roman surrender of Nisibis by the Christian emperor Jovian to Shapur, and that the text was written not long after Shapur's death (379 C.E.), therefore at the end of the fourth century. This date has been challenged as too early but has also encouraged scholars to propose other dates[18]. In particular the fifth century has come into view[19]. As to the author of the *Romance* we remain in the dark. The text itself mentions a certain Aploris who wrote the «History of Jovian» on the request of Abdel, but he is generally considered a fictitious person. Various suggestions for authorship have been put forward. Because of the anti-judaism of the text Nöldeke suggested that the author was a former Jew who had converted to Christianity. Baumstark considers the author to have been «ein edessenischer Mönch... auf monophysitischem Boden»[20]. Because of the strong influence of the writings of Ephrem Syrus, Han Drijvers believes the author to belong to the School of the Persians[21]. I myself have suggested an author belonging to the circle of Rabbula, bishop of Edessa (412-436)[22]. An interesting suggestion is that of A. Muraviev. He considers Aploris, whom the text mentions as author, not as a fictitious figure, as all other scholars do, but thinks that he can be identified with Jovian's counterpart in the *Romance*, i.e. Shapur's general Hwarra-mir (Arimhar in Gollancz' translation). In Muraviev's view he

---

two weeks of years, and then Persia will be subjected to the tribute of the Romans during ten years» (H. GOLLANCZ, *Julian the Apostate...*, 191-192). Taking 363 C.E. as a starting point the total of twenty-three weeks of years and ten years brings us to the beginning of the sixth century.

[17] W. WRIGHT, *Catalogue of the Syriac Manuscripts in the British Museum*, London 1887, vol. I, 1042.

[18] M. PAPOUTSAKIS, *The Making of a Syriac Fable: From Ephrem to Romanos*, «Le Muséon» 120 (2007)/1-2, 29-75, at 38-40 remains in favour of Nöldeke's date; he adds that the text was «heavily influenced by the formulaic style and phraseology characteristic of the verse homilies of Jacob of Serugh».

[19] G.J. REININK, *The Romance of Julian the Apostate as a source...*, 171, n. 9: «In my opinion there are reasonable grounds for the assumption that the work originated in Edessa in the fifth century»; J.W. DRIJVERS, *The Syriac Julian Romance...*, 38.

[20] A. BAUMSTARK, *Geschichte der syrischen Literatur*, Bonn 1922, 183.

[21] H.J.W. DRIJVERS, *The Syriac Romance of Julian...*, 203 ff.

[22] J.W. DRIJVERS, *The Syriac Julian Romance...*, 38.

is the same as Xwarrabût (Khorohbut), who occurs in Moses of Khorene's *History of Armenia* (seventh century), where he is mentioned as a scribe of Shapur. Moses reports that Xwarrabût (Khorohbut) returned with Jovian to the Roman Empire, converted to Christianity and wrote a history of Shapur and Julian[23].

The sources for the «History of Jovian» used are hard to establish. We may assume that the author employed a mix of writings for the composition of his work. Since it is evident that he wrote in the anti-Julian tradition initiated by Ephrem Syrus, he is likely to have known Ephrem's *Hymns against Julian*. The author must also have been familiar with the *Doctrina Addai*, a central text for Edessene Christians. He must also have used other (now lost) Syriac and possibly Greek sources about Julian and Jovian. The character of these sources is hard to define but they were of various kinds. The *Romance* clearly has a hagiographical imprint and the author may therefore have used hagiographical writings. He was also reasonably well informed about Julian's journeys and Persian campaign, and he probably consulted historiographic sources as well.

The genre of the *Romance* is another matter of debate. Nöldeke was the first to characterize the text as a romance, a name by which it has since been known. The text bears some resemblance to the genre of the romance or novel, including the Christian novel, as we know it from Antiquity. Such works were often set in the past and are marked by invention and fantasy[24]. Baumstark's characterization as a «durchaus romanhafte, von Übertreibungen und freien Erfindungen strotzenden Darstellung» is therefore not inaccurate[25]. Han Drijvers' description of the text as a religious «propaganda tract»[26] is less adequate, not because the *Romance* should

---

[23] A. MURAVIEV, *The Syriac Julian Romance...*, 205-206. MOSES OF KHORENE, *Hist. Arm.* 2.70 = MOSES KHORENATS'I, *History of the Armenians*, tr. R.W. THOMSON, Cambridge-London 1978, 217: «This Khorohbut was the scribe of Shapuh, the Persian king, and he fell into the hands of the Greeks when Julian, also called the Apostate, went with an army to Ctesiphon. When he [Julian] was killed there, he [Khorohbut] returned to Greece in the company of the royal officers with Jovian and, having been converted to our faith, was named Eleazar. He learned the Greek language and wrote a history of the deeds of Shapuh and Julian».

[24] According to B.E. PERRY, *The Ancient Romances. A Literary-Historical Account of Their Origins*, Berkeley-Los Angeles 1967, 78, Greek romances set in the past are comparable with what we today call historical novels. See also G.W. BOWERSOCK, *History as Fiction. Nero to Julian*, Berkeley-Los Angeles 1994, 139-141. The *Julian Romance* can be seen as a historical novel.

[25] A. BAUMSTARK, *Geschichte der syrischen Literatur...*, 183.

[26] H.J.W. DRIJVERS, *The Syriac Romance of Julian...*, 202.

not be seen as such but because it is far too general a term. Van Esbroeck proposed to define the text as hagiography. Even though the *Romance* evidently has hagiographical elements, in particular the second part about Eusebius, it is more than mere hagiography. Perhaps it is best not to attempt to characterize the text as a particular art of literature and rather to speak of «Erzählungen» (i.e. narrations) as Hoffmann does, and to consider the *Romance* as narrative fiction in the form of history of a Christian propagandistic nature with hagiographical elements. Characterizing the text as «Erzählungen» also has the advantage of reflecting the synthetic nature of the *Romance*, because one of the things that is not sufficiently realised is that the *Julian Romance* as we have it is a compilation of three texts. Even though the *Romance* may seem to be a single literary piece and reflect unity of style and ideology, i.e. the condemnation of Julian and the glorification of Christianity, it remains a synthesis of three different narrations[27]. I consider it possible that the three constituent texts of the *Romance* originated independently from each other, before they were brought together in a synthetic narrative. The author, date of composition and background of each of the three texts may have been different. However, the synthesis which Nöldeke labelled *Julian Romance* may well have been composed in the first decades of the sixth century, and its composer may have brought unity of style to the various texts and borrowed phraseology from his contemporary Jacob of Serugh[28]. In discussing the *Julian Romance* we should therefore not put the three texts in one box, but deal with them separately.

Muraviev has called attention to the eschatological character of the text and its function in a Roman-centred eschatological milieu which was a complex of ideas concerning the destiny of the Christian Empire[29]. In this respect it is of interest that the *Romance* left its traces in Syriac apocalyptic texts; it was, for instance, one of the main sources for the *Apocalypse* of Ps. Methodius[30]. Also on other than Syriac texts did it leave its traces, such as on the Georgian *Life of Vakhtang Gorgasal* and the Armenian *Agath-*

---

[27] See also A. MURAVIEV, *The Syriac Julian Romance...*, 197.

[28] M. PAPOUTSAKIS, *The Making of a Syriac Fable...*, 38.

[29] A. MURAVIEV, *The Syriac Julian Romance...*, 200; see also H.J.W. DRIJVERS, *The Syriac Romance of Julian...*, 212-213.

[30] G.J. REININK, *The Romance of Julian the Apostate as a source....*

angelos[31]. It also served as source for the *Life* of S. Basil the Great[32]. The *Romance* was translated into Arabic albeit in a much shortened version[33].

This paper focuses on the «History of Jovian», which is the best studied of the three parts of the *Romance*[34]. This part is of considerable length – almost 200 pages in the English translation – and complexity. Like the *Julian Romance* as a whole it is about the confrontation between paganism personified in the person of the emperor Julian and Christianity represented by Jovian and other *dramatis personae*. Jovian is clearly the key figure and hero of the text. In the context of this paper I will deal with three aspects of this part of the *Romance*: 1. the way in which Julian and Jovian are represented, and in particular the image of Jovian as New Constantine; 2. the way in which cities are characterized, in particular regarding their attitude towards Julian's religious policy; 3. the Jewish reaction to Julian's policy of de-christianization. At the end I hope to be able to offer some new insights concerning the purposes of the text and the date of composition of this third part of the *Julian Romance*.

2. Julian and Jovian

It comes as no surprise that the way in which Julian is portrayed in the «History of Jovian» is entirely negative. The emperor is characterized as a viper, a wicked and wretched tyrant, a madman, and someone who was already dead in life. He is portrayed as a man without composure; he is full of rage – not the best of qualities for a Roman emperor – for everyone who opposes him and the peoples under his dominion were full of fear for him. He is portrayed as a ruler who has made the restoration of the cults of the old gods his primary aim. In order to reach that goal he persecutes Chris-

---

[31] M. VAN ESBROECK, *Le soi-disant roman...*, 199-201; A. MURAVIEV, *The Syriac Julian Romance...*, 197-198.

[32] A. MURAVIEV, *The Syriac Julian Romance as a Source of the Life of St. Basil the Great*, in *Studia Patristica* 37. *Papers presented at the Thirteenth International Conference on Patristic Studies held in Oxford 1999*, ed. M.F. WILES, E.J. YARNOLD, Louvain 2001, 240-249.

[33] U. BEN-HORIN, *An Unknown Old Arabic Translation of the Syriac Romance of Julian the Apostate*, «Studia Hierosolymitana» 9 (1961), 1-10; also A.S. ATIYA, *The Arabic Manuscripts of Mount Sinai*, Baltimore 1955, 19; T. NÖLDEKE, *Über den syrischen Roman...*, 291-292.

[34] *Ibid.*, 264, without underpinning his opinion, considers this part of more importance («Wichtiger ist die Geschichte Jovian's») than the second part concerning Eusebius and Julian.

tianity in all possible ways. Not only are temples restored and old cults revived at the expense of the Church, but the Christian clergy are made subservient to his rule; the sisters of the church are forced to marry and have children, the bishops are made generals and the forces under their command financed by the riches of the Church. Those who remain firm in their Christian conviction are tortured and eventually put to death[35]. Many atrocities are committed by pagans against the Christians and by Julian himself[36]. The emperor is said to have cut out the hearts of little children and snatch unborn children from the wombs of their mothers for use in divination and magical arts[37]. Julian allows pagans to persecute Christians in their cities and villages and execute them without trial[38].

A few times Julian receives premonitions about his death and defeat by the Persians[39]. When leaving the pagan city of Harran his crown falls from his head when he bows to the image of the god Sîn which was set up over the city gate. Moreover, his horse does not want to go any further and when Julian steps down and takes hold of the bridle to make the horse go, the beast tears the emperor's purple robe after which it falls dead[40]. After his initial victories over the Persians, Julian has a dream, in which his death is predicted and the end of paganism foretold[41].

Throughout the text Julian's reign is unfavourably compared to that of Constantine[42]. Julian's intention was to undo the work of Constantine and to return to the religious situation of the days of Diocletian and Maximian, which included persecution of the Christians[43]. Julian is only king in name whereas Constantine was a real king; Julian wanted to raise anew

---

[35] H. GOLLANCZ, *Julian the Apostate...*, 67-69.
[36] Cf. e.g. SOCR. *Hist. Eccl.* 3.13; SOZ. *Hist. Eccl.* 5.4ff.; THDT. *Hist. Eccl.* 3.3.
[37] H. GOLLANCZ, *Julian the Apostate...*, 100.
[38] *Ibid.*, 107.
[39] *Ibid.*, 108, 130, 160.
[40] *Ibid.*, 157-159.
[41] *Ibid.*, 188-189. Just before the decisive battle between Julian and Shapur a voice from heaven pronounces: «The arrow of salvation in the camp of the Romans! The wicked shall be taken from its midst! Peace shall reign between the kingdoms!»; *ibid.*, 197. Unfavourable *omina* are not only characteristic for Christian texts about Julian. The opening chapter of Ammianus' Book 23 reports several unpropitious signs about the result of Julian's Persian expedition; J. DEN BOEFT, J.W. DRIJVERS, D. DEN HENGST, H.C. TEITLER, *Philological and Historical Commentary on Ammianus Marcellinus XXIII*, Groningen 1998, 1-19.
[42] In the «Eusebius narrative» also, Julian is contrasted with Constantine; J.W. DRIJVERS, *Julian and the City of Rome...*, 11-13.
[43] H. GOLLANCZ, *Julian the Apostate...*, 82, 187.

the persecution of Christians in Persia, which had quietened down thanks to a letter of Constantine[44]. Julian is wicked and mad whereas Constantine is called just, stable and wise. In a speech to his soldiers Julian contrasts himself with Constantine, mentioning that his predecessor had never been able to defeat the Persians because he had denied the pagan gods; now, because of his honouring of the gods, Julian has won victories over the Persians[45]. Furthermore, Julian is presented as the wolf who intends to kill Christianity whereas Constantine is the shepherd who protects his Christian flock[46]. Julian is also compared to the paltry fox who presumes to be a king whereas Constantine is a robust lion[47].

The way in which Jovian is portrayed is in complete contrast to Julian[48]. He is a man of knowledge and sense[49]. As a man of God – he conceals his Christianity for Julian – he is in constant distress about Julian's measures against the Christians. He frequently prays to God for advice and assistance, and asks Him to grant peace to the Church. As Julian's main adviser he is in regular contact with the emperor by way of personal meetings and the exchange of letters. Jovian is always able to talk sense into Julian and to mitigate the initial harsh anti-Christian measures that the emperor has decided

---

[44] Possibly a reference to Constantine's letter to Shapur included in Eusebius' *Vita Constantini* (4.9-13).

[45] H. GOLLANCZ, *Julian the Apostate...*, 86-7, 111, 132-3, 134-5, 186-188 for comparisons between Julian and Constantine.

[46] *Ibid.*, 135-136.

[47] *Ibid.*, 68-69. M. PAPOUTSAKIS, *The Making of a Syriac Fable...*, 30 ff., in particular 37-42, convincingly argues that the antagonism between the lion and the fox became a feature of the Syriac polemic literature against Julian since the time of EPHREM SYRUS' *Hymn on Nativity* VI, 19-20. In this hymn king Herod is called a paltry fox but in late antique Syriac literature Herod and Julian are considered as being of the same stock.

[48] The contrast between the legendary Jovian of the *Romance* and the historical emperor Jovian, who ruled only for some eight months (363-364) is great. T. NÖLDEKE, *Über den syrischen Roman...*, 290 goes too far in calling him «in der Wirklichkeit eine recht elende Figur», but he was not an emperor who left his mark. The primary source for Jovian is Ammianus Marcellinus (25.5-10), who considers him inferior in every respect to Julian and criticizes him for the disgraceful capitulation to Shapur. On Jovian see e.g. G. WIRTH, *Jovian. Kaiser und Karikatur*, in *Vivarium. Festschrift Theodor Klauser sum 90. Geburtstag*, ed. E. DASSMANN, K. THRAEDE, Münster 1984, 353-384; J. VANDERSPOEL, *Themistius and the Imperial Court. Oratory, Civic Duty, and Paideia from Constantius to Theodosius*, Ann Arbor 1995, 135-154. See further J. DEN BOEFT, J.W. DRIJVERS, D. DEN HENGST, H.C. TEITLER, *Philological and Historical Commentary on Ammianus Marcellinus XXV...*, 169-343. Jovian has a more positive press in Christian writings, in particular the fifth-century *Church Histories*.

[49] H. GOLLANCZ, *Julian the Apostate...*, 67.

upon. Let me give one example. In the first dialogue of the text[50], included after Julian has decreed a Christian persecution, Jovian is able to persuade the emperor that a policy of persecution is to the disadvantage of Julian and the empire but to the advantage of the Christians, by arguing that Christians seek death, preferably a martyr's death. Moreover, a great number of the soldiers were Christians and killing them would jeopardize the Persian expedition. The destruction of churches was, according to Jovian, also unwise because many of them were former pagan temples, and why demolish these structures when they could be put to good use for honouring the gods. As a consequence of Jovian's reasoning Julian revises his anti-Christian measures. Jovian intercedes not only with the emperor on behalf of the Christians but also on behalf of the Persians. He prevents the leading into captivity of Persian women and children, the killing of men, the destruction of cities, and he convinces Julian to show mercy to the Persian captives[51]. However, Jovian is also able to kill for the preservation of his faith. He strangles the Egyptian diviner Galas in his sleep and then has him hung up on the statue of Apollo for advising Julian to persecute the Christians and to destroy their churches[52]. Whereas Julian is visited with premonitions about his defeat and death, Jovian has dreams and visions, in which his coming rule and the freedom of religion for Christianity is predicted. Even Faith, in the form of a modest woman, manifests herself to him and predicts that the success of his combat will soon be apparent[53]. Jovian is favoured by God and he is an instrument in His plan, which entails Jovian's rule over the empire and peace between the Romans and Sassanians[54]. The martyr Mercurius prophesies to Jovian in dreams that not Julian but Shapur will be victorious, that Julian will meet his end on the Persian campaign through an arrow shot by the same Mercurius, and that Christianity will be restored[55]. In one

---

[50] H. GOLLANCZ, *Julian the Apostate...*, 72-75.
[51] *Ibid.*, 175, 179, 182.
[52] *Ibid.*, 99-100.
[53] *Ibid.*, 98-99.
[54] *Ibid.*, 197 about God's wish for a peaceful existence between the two empires. His Persian counterpart Arimhar had a vision in which «he saw a right hand holding a crown over the head of Jovian, and he knew that the kingdom and government of the Romans would belong to him»; *ibid.*, 166.
[55] *Ibid.*, 153-155, 190. Mercurius is called «one of those forty blessed ones who were martyred in the ice in the time of Maximinian the wicked» (153). St. Mercurius is also in other sources referred to as killer of Julian; MALAL. *Chron.* 13.333-334; *Chron. Pasch.* a. 363; see further T. NÖLDEKE, *Über den syrischen Roman...*, 287. In the *Romance* the pagan Mercurius, messenger of the Olympian gods, is merged with the third-century Christian martyr of the same name.

of his dreams Jovian is also told that Nisibis is to be handed over to the Persians[56].

While Julian is contraposed to Constantine, Jovian is presented as the New Constantine[57]. Jovian's many visions and dreams, which evidently present him as part of God's plan, bring him close to Constantine, who also received divine messages and prophecies by way of dreams and visions. In addition, like Constantine Jovian held the symbol of the Cross in high esteem. After Julian's death Jovian publicly avowed his Christianity. Even though the soldiers and officers wished to proclaim him emperor, Jovian declined and hid himself. When he was finally found, he demanded that he only would become emperor when the whole army would adore the sign of salvation, i.e. the Cross, and convert to Christianity. In a mass ceremony Jovian inclined his head before the Cross, that is the *labarum* which since Constantine's time went in front of the army[58], and the royal crown descended and placed itself on his head. The soldiers marvelling at this miracle cried out: «Henceforth, Christ is our King in heaven, and Jovian is our king on earth»[59]. Jovian restores the continuity of Christianity that started with Constantine and was interrupted by Julian. The *Romance* emphasizes that Jovian «walked in the ways of Constantine»[60]. He restored the treasures which Julian had taken from the church, he re-installed the tax privileges for the Christian clergy, he wrote letters of peace and reconciliation to the churches in his realm and even to other governments concerning the peace of the church in their countries, he ordered the release of believers and he

---

[56] H. GOLLANCZ, *Julian the Apostate...*, 192.

[57] J.W. DRIJVERS, *The Emperor Jovian as New Constantine...*. See also H.J.W. DRIJVERS, *The Syriac Romance of Julian...*, 208.

[58] H. GOLLANCZ, *Julian the Apostate...*, 212. Curiously, according to the text Julian had not abrogated the custom that the Cross should go in front of the army; GREG. NAZ. *Or.* 4.66.

[59] H. GOLLANCZ, *Julian the Apostate...*, 214. Also the Church Historians have the story that Jovian declined the emperorship because he did not want to command an army consisting of pagans; thereupon the soldiers replied that they were Christians like himself. See also RUF. *Hist. Eccl.* 11.1; SOCR. *Hist. Eccl.* 3.22.2; SOZ. *Hist. Eccl.* 6.3.1; also ZON. 13.14.2-4. Most elaborate is THDT. *Hist. Eccl.* 4.1.4-6: «Jovian... said: "I am a Christian. I cannot govern men like these. I cannot command Julian's army trained as it is in vicious discipline. Men like these, stripped of the covering of the providence of God, will fall an easy and ridiculous prey to the foe". On hearing this the troops shouted with one voice, "Hesitate not, O emperor; think it not a vile thing to command us. You shall reign over Christians nurtured in the training of truth; our veterans were taught in the school of Constantine himself; younger men among us were taught by Constantius"» (tr. NPNF 3, 107-108).

[60] H. GOLLANCZ, *Julian the Apostate...*, 252-253.

ended the pagan sacrifices[61]. Under Jovian peace reigned in the churches as in the days of Constantine.

While the story develops, Jovian turns into a saintly figure. At the end of the narrative the holy emperor even performs a healing miracle. In Edessa he cures a woman by the name of Maria who had been seriously ill for eight years and prayed for death. Through his faith in God and God's support of him, Jovian is able to heal the woman[62].

An interesting feature of Jovian, who is called «son of Orninus»[63], is his portrayal as an easterner. He has very good relations in Nisibis, in particular with the city's bishop Valgash, and it is evident from the text that he is a native of this city[64]. Jovian also has good contacts with the Persians and is held in esteem by them. He exchanges information with Shapur's general Arimhar; after the death of Julian Shapur too recommends Jovian as successor to the Roman throne and the two rulers maintain good relations. Shapur calls Jovian a wise king[65]. The Persian nobles are so impressed by Jovian that they want him to become Shapur's deputy, marry a Persian wife, and become heir to the Persian throne[66]. While Julian is portrayed as a stranger and foreigner[67], Jovian evidently belongs to the East as a representative of both civilizations: the Roman, which is equal to the Christian world, and the Persian world[68].

---

[61] With these measures Jovian reactivates Constantine's enactments: e.g. *CTh* 16.2.2.; Eus. *VC* 2.63-73, 3.16-20, 4.8-13, 3.44-45, 4.23. See also Socr. *Hist. Eccl.* 3.24 and Soz. *Hist. Eccl.* 6.3 who mention *inter alia* that Jovian closed pagan temples, prohibited pagan sacrifice, and restored immunities to the churches and clergy, which had been granted by Constantine and his sons, and by these measures returned to the situation of the time of Constantine.

[62] H. Gollancz, *Julian the Apostate...*, 247-251.

[63] *Ibid.*, 100, 164.

[64] There are several indications for this. It is said that he had many kinsmen in Nisibis (H. Gollancz, *Julian the Apostate...*, 163 and 165); when Julian was looking for Jovian in Nisibis after he been released him his service, only the chief of his tribe Saragdanus knew where he was hiding (*ibid.*, 169-170); the Nisibenes are called «the children of your [Jovian's] nation» (*ibid.*, 192). In reality Jovian was of Illyrian origin; N. Lenski, *Failure of Empire. Valens and the Roman State in the Fourth Century A.D.*, Berkeley-Los Angeles-London 2002, 16-17.

[65] H. Gollancz, *Julian the Apostate...*, 220. The portrayal of Shapur is interesting. Although he is the enemy he is described in mild terms, obviously to blacken Julian even more; T. Nöldeke, *Über den syrischen Roman...*, 289-290.

[66] H. Gollancz, *Julian the Apostate...*, 227-228.

[67] M. Papoutsakis, *The Making of a Syriac Fable...*, 43-44.

[68] The Jovian of the *Romance* may be considered as an example of the multicultural character and adaptability which in «historical reality» characterised social relations

3. Cities

Cities have a prominent role in the *Romance*. In the «History of Eusebius» the city of Rome figures as a setting for Julian's efforts at re-introducing paganism and as a stage of Christian opposition against the emperor's plans and his emperorship. In the «History of Jovian» it is not one city but several which have this function: Constantinople, Antioch, Harran, Edessa and Nisibis. Julian visits these cities, or intends to visit them, on his march to Persia for his war against Shapur. Of these five cities, the historical Julian had visited Constantinople, Antioch and Harran.

When Julian is still in Rome, he sends his uncle Julian to Constantinople, bearing a letter from the emperor, in which the latter announces his intention to name the city Byzantium again after its original founder, king Byzas – evidently intended to erase the connection between the city and Constantine – and to return to the habits of Diocletian and Maximian, i.e. to make the city pagan again, and to wipe the Christian cult from off the surface of the earth[69]. The historical Julian indeed made some important decisions on religious matters when in Constantinople from December 361 to the summer of 362. His religious policy was aimed at restoring the old cults and breaking the power of Christianity[70].

Julian's letter is interesting because it presents a clear, but of course hostile, characterization of Julian's paganism. The emperor explains that there is a Ruler of Creation who is the leader of demons and devils, who created the gods and who turned all the peoples to the adoration of these gods. The Ruler bestowed upon the peoples love, joys, gifts, and pleasures, not least among them sexual pleasure. Furthermore, as is reported also elsewhere in the *Romance*, paganism is a religion of divination, en-

---

and conduct in the Roman-Persian frontier zone. Ammianus Marcellinus mentions Antoninus, a merchant who had been in Roman service (18.5), and Cragausius, a *nobilis Nisibenus* (19.9.3-8), who both defected to Persia and continued their life and career without a hitch at the other side of the frontier. See also J.F. MATTHEWS, *The Roman Empire of Ammianus*, London 1989, 68.

[69] Julian's letter refers to Constantinople as a city built ons even hills; H. GOLLANCZ, *Julian the Apostate...*, 82. See for this myth, W. BRANDES, *Sieben Hügel. Die imaginäre Topographie Konstantinopels zwischen apokalyptischem Denken und moderner Wissenschaft*, «Rechtsgeschichte» 2 (2003), 58-71, esp. 69.

[70] AMM. MARC. 22.5 with commentary J. DEN BOEFT, J.W. DRIJVERS, D. DEN HENGST and H.C. TEITLER, *Philological and Historical Commentary on Ammianus Marcellinus XXII*, Groningen 1995, 51-62. For Julian's stay in Constantinople see e.g. AMM. MARC. 22.2-7; R. BROWNING, *The Emperor Julian*, London 1975, 123-143; K. ROSEN, *Julian...*, 236ff.; K. BRINGMANN, *Kaiser Julian*, Darmstadt 2004, 93-105.

chantment, magical practices, and sacrifices to meaningless idols. Above all, it is a religion of feasts, dancing, music, and sexual licentiousness[71]. Julian's letter inspires the Constantinopolitans with fear and only a certain Maximus, who is called one of the most distinguished citizens of the city and a convinced Christian, has the courage to react[72]. In a speech he derides not only Julian for his paganism but also the pagan gods, whom he characterizes as empty, corrupt, wanton and obscene, and as adulterers and fornicators – as, he says, can already be read in the works of Homer[73]. Maximus does not consider Julian as a true king but sees his government as conducted by demons and devils. After his speech he tries to kill Julian's uncle, but he is carried away by his friends. When Julian is near Constantinople and participating in a feast in honour of Aphrodite, Maximus approaches the emperor and knocks him down, whereby the crown falls from Julian's head. He is immediately arrested and killed by the emperor's guards. While he is dying, a voice speaks from heaven that he has done well, and when he is dead the sky darkens and there is a hailstorm by which many are killed[74]. Jovian has him buried secretly. In the story Maximus is an interesting figure: he represents the Christians of Constantinople and is the only one who dares to oppose Julian openly. For his opposition he dies a martyr's death. Maximus can be seen as the Constantinopolitan counterpart of Eusebius in Rome. However, where Eusebius receives support from the senate and most of the people of Rome, the senate and people of Constantinople do not oppose Julian but receive him with honour and joy. They even recognize him as their emperor, a recognition which Julian had sought in vain in Rome[75].

---

[71] References to the character of paganism: H. GOLLANCZ, *Julian the Apostate...*, 78, 82-85, 127, 183-184, 188.

[72] Maximus is a fictitious figure. He makes an effective contrast with the historical pagan philosopher Maximus of Ephesus (*PLRE* I, 21), who was enthusiastically received by Julian when he resided in Constantinople (AMM. MARC. 22.7.3) and received an outstanding position at the imperial court (EUN. *V. Soph.* 477).

[73] H. GOLLANCZ, *Julian the Apostate...*, 87.

[74] For the Maximus story, see *ibid.*, 81-93, 101-106.

[75] *Ibid.*, 108: «When he was ready to arrive in their city, all the Senate went out to receive him with honours... When he entered Constantinople, he threw presents to the crowds of the city, and again sowed in their ears the echoes of ease and reconciliation. With this disturbing cunning he gained from them the acclamations of royalty, and sat on the throne of Constantinople, and was counted among the kings of the Romans for one year and eight months».

The following great city that Julian visits is Antioch, in the *Romance* called «the residence of the gods»[76]. The Antiochenes also did not oppose Julian, and they even rejoiced when they heard the news of the emperor's arrival: they adorned their city with brilliant cloths of all colours, and put up altars in all the city's streets and quarters[77]. Two great altars were set up on either side of the city gate through which Julian would enter. When Julian arrived in Antioch the people went wild and mad, and were not far from committing shameful acts, i.e. sexual acts, openly in the streets. The treasury of the Church of Antioch had to be handed over[78]. The emperor expresses his gratefulness to the Antiochenes by promising them gifts, and strengthening and adorning their city. The only protests come from a certain Elpidius, like Jovian an official in the imperial service who conceals his Christianity. When witnessing the pagan folly and madness of the Antiochenes he makes the sign of the cross – something noticed by the emperor – and, when during a sacrifice the pagan priest spills oil on Elpidius' garment, he kills the priest. After a fierce argument with Julian in the course of which Elpidius calls him wicked and a venerator of demons and in which he predicts Julian's defeat against Persia because of his turning away from God, he is arrested and thrown into prison[79]. The *Romance* presents Julian's stay in Antioch as a great success. In reality this was not the case. Julian, who sojourned in Antioch from July 362 to the beginning of March 363 to prepare his Persian campaign, was criticized by the Antiochenes for his excessive offering and ridiculed for his behaviour and appearance. This induced Julian to write his *Misopogon*[80].

---

[76] H. GOLLANCZ, *Julian the Apostate*..., 128.
[77] *Ibid.*, 126 ff.
[78] *Ibid.*, 128-130.
[79] Helpidius is by M. VAN ESBROECK, *Le soi-disant roman*..., 198 identified with the monk Helpidius mentioned by Egeria (*It. Eg.* 20.5) who died a martyr's death in Harran: «saint Helpidius de Carrhes le 24 Avril, moine et martyr selon Égérie, est incontestablement le personnage du Roman de Julien, Helpidius dans le roman syriaque est celui qui, vers le fin du Mars 363, s'est oppose violemment et éloquemment au paganisme de Julien, face à l'empereur». Cf. P. DEVOS, *La date du voyage d'Égérie*, «Analecta Bollandiana» 85 (1967), 165-194, at 168 n. 2 who rejects this identification.
[80] For Julian's stay in Antioch see e.g. AMM. MARC. 22.12-14 with commentary J. DEN BOEFT ET AL., *Commentary on Ammianus Marcellinus XXII*..., 213-252; R. BROWNING, *Julian*..., 144-158; G.W. BOWERSOCK, *Julian the Apostate*, London 1978, 94-105; P. ATHANASSIADI, *Julian. An Intellectual Biography*, London-New York 1992², 195-196, 201 ff.; K. ROSEN, *Julian*..., 280-285, 293-296; K. BRINGMANN, *Kaiser Julian*..., 152-168.

Harran, Edessa's pagan rival, is presented as the «mother of paganism» which longed for a visit by the emperor[81]. Julian, who intended to visit Edessa on his way to Persia but was not welcome there, visited Harran instead, but the text reports that «How Harran received its mad king it is superfluous to insert in our history... We will, therefore, desist from telling what unjustifiable things happened at Harran, and rightly praise the faith of the Edessenians»[82]. Apart from the fact that Julian robbed the church of Harran of its treasures for the benefit of idol-worship, that sacred books were burnt and many Christians were restored to paganism, it is left unmentioned what happened in Harran[83]. In Harran the incident of the crown falling from Julian's head occurred (see above p. 142). In reply to this unfortunate divine message, the pagan priests advised him to send away the Christian soldiers in his army; twenty-two thousand military left and were gladly received by the city of Edessa[84]. The historical Julian spent several days in Harran while on his way to Persia, as Ammianus Marcellinus reports, to offer sacrifices according to the native rites to the Moon (Sîn)[85]. Harran was especially known for its Moon cult, but it had also been the residence of Abraham[86]. For that reason the Christian pilgrim Egeria visited the place c. 385; she reported that the city had a bishop and a few clergy, but that no Christians lived in the city[87]. While in Harran Julian divided his forces and left 30.000 soldiers in northern Mesopotamia in order to protect the regions near the Tigris[88]. The sending away of Christian soldiers as reported in the *Romance* probably is based on this historical fact.

---

[81] H. GOLLANCZ, *Julian the Apostate...*, 133.
[82] *Ibid.*, 147.
[83] *Ibid.*, 156.
[84] *Ibid.*, 158-159. «There returned from the army that was with Julian nearly twenty-two thousand men that were warriors. They made in a crowd for Edessa, and they were received therein with joy» (159).
[85] AMM. MARC. 23.3.1. For Harran see e.g. S. LLOYD and W. BRICE, *Harran*, «Anatolian Studies» 1 (1951), 77-111; W. CRAMER, *Harran*, in *Reallexikon für Antike und Christentum* 13, Stuttgart 1986, 634-650.
[86] *Gen.* 11:31, 24:4, 28:2.
[87] *It. Eg.* 20.8.
[88] AMM. MARC. 23.3.5. See also J. DEN BOEFT, J.W. DRIJVERS, D. DEN HENGST and H.C. TEITLER, *Philological and Historical Commentary in Ammianus Marcellinus XXIII*, Groningen 1998, 41-45.

Most pages of the text are dedicated to Edessa[89]. The city is called «blessed» and the «mother of believers»[90], and the only city of all the cities in the East that stands firm in her rectitude against Julian and keeps to the Christian faith. The Roman officers who have defected from Julian support Edessa, and they cleanse the city from Jews and pagans still living there. When the emperor intends to visit Edessa in order to punish the Edessenes for their opposition to his rule and for their Christian conviction, he sends an embassy headed by a certain Callimachus to announce his coming. The emperor, however, is not allowed to enter and is met outside the city wall by the Edessene chief Arorita[91]. He declares that Edessa cannot open her gates to Julian because the city is Christian. Constantine himself had blessed the city in a letter, which is read aloud to Julian's envoys. Especially in this part of the text is the contrast between Julian and Constantine emphasized: the Christian Constantine is just, stable and wise, while the infidel Julian is wicked, mad and a famished wolf thirsting for Christian blood. The Edessenes show no fear for Julian: they refuse to recognize him as their king because he does not honour the King of Truth. These actions anger Julian so much that he plans to destroy the city and kill its Christian population. The letters that Julian subsequently sends to Edessa are immediately thrown away into the city's latrines. In their reply to the emperor, the Edessenes write *inter alia* that they owe their city's greatness to Christ, who has bestowed many benefits on Edessa[92].

The hostility of the Edessene Christians towards Julian as described in the «History of Jovian» may very well be founded on more than just Christian animosity towards a pagan emperor. In a letter, possibly addressed to the Edessenes, the historical Julian punished the Christians of Edessa for their sectarian strives by confiscating all their money and property[93].

---

[89] H. GOLLANCZ, *Julian the Apostate...*, 131-139, 147, 238-252. On Edessa, J.B. SEGAL, *Edessa. «The Blessed City»*, Oxford 1970, is still the standard work. See also H.J.W. DRIJVERS, *Hatra, Palmyra und Edessa. Die Städte der syrisch-mesopotamischen Wüste in politischer, kulturgeschichtlicher und religionsgeschichtlicher Beleuchtung*, in *ANRW* II.8 (1977) 799-906, esp. 863ff.; F. MILLAR, *The Roman Near East 31 BC-AD 337*, Cambridge-London 1993, *passim*.

[90] H. GOLLANCZ, *Julian the Apostate...*, 138.

[91] *Ibid.*, 131 ff.

[92] *Ibid.*, 137-138.

[93] IUL. *Epist.* 115 (ed. Bidez), 424c: «I have ordered that all their funds, namely, that belong to the church of the people of Edessa, are to be taken over that they may be given to the soldiers, and that its property be confiscated to my private purse. This is in order that poverty may teach them to behave properly and that they may not be deprived of that heavenly kingdom for which they still hope» (tr. Wright). See also G.W. BOWER-

Moreover, in contrast to the *Romance* the historical sources present quite another picture. The Edessenes were eager to receive Julian in their city and they sent an embassy to Batnae when the emperor was staying there to invite him. However, Julian declined the invitation because Edessa was too Christian for his taste. He insulted the Edessenes even more by visiting Harran instead[94].

After Julian's death the new emperor Jovian honours the Edessenes by praising in letters their firmness of faith. When he expresses his intention to visit the city, the Edessenes gladly agree and honour the new Christian emperor, who «walks in the ways of Constantine»[95]. Jovian's visit to Edessa is elaborately described and a great success; it is crowned by a healing miracle performed by the new emperor[96].

The last city that plays an important role is Nisibis[97]. It is implied that this is the native city of Jovian[98]. Jovian has good relations with the Christian community of Nisibis and in particular with its bishop Valgash. Jovian consults the bishop and appreciates him for his advice. He does so, for instance, when Julian gives him the order to destroy Edessa, after new troubles between the Edessenes and the emperor[99]. Nisibis is also the scene for the only serious conflict between Julian and Jovian[100]. When Julian is on his way to the city he is informed by Nisibene Jews that Jovian is protecting the Christians and allowing them to hold their assemblies. Therefore Julian, urged by the pagans and Jews of Nisibis, dismisses him from his service. When he later regrets his decision, Jovian is reinstated and made general over all the forces and ruler next to Julian himself[101]. Nisibis of

---

sock, *Julian...*, 92. The author of the «History of Jovian» may also have been inspired by the conflict between the emperor Valens and the Christians of Edessa about the Arian heresy of which the emperor was an adherent but was opposed by the Edessene Christians; SOCR. *Hist. Eccl.* 4.18; THDT. *Hist. Eccl.* 4.15.

[94] LIB. *Or.* 18.214; SOZ. *Hist. Eccl.* 6.1.1; THDT. *Hist. Eccl.* 3.26.2. For the embassy see ZOSIMUS (3.12.3) with F. PASCHOUD's note 32 ad loc. in the Budé edition.

[95] H. GOLLANCZ, *Julian the Apostate...*, 238 ff., 252. It is likely that Jovian in reality visited Edessa; according to PHILOST. *Hist. Eccl.* 8.4-7 he had a meeting in the city with Arrianus and Candidus, two Arian bishops from Lydia.

[96] H. GOLLANCZ, *Julian the Apostate...*, 247-249.

[97] On Nisibis, see J.-M. FIEY, *Nisibe: métropole syriaque orientale et ses suffragants des origines à nos jours*, Louvain 1977.

[98] See above n. 65.

[99] H. GOLLANCZ, *Julian the Apostate...*, 150-153 and 161-162 for Jovian asking Valgash for advice.

[100] *Ibid.*, 163-165.

[101] *Ibid.*, 169-172.

course also plays an important role in the peace agreement between Rome and Persia. Even before he became emperor Jovian has a dream in which he is told that Nisibis has to be ceded to the Persians[102]. Nisibis is indeed given by Jovian to the Persians, but on the condition that the Christians in the Persian Empire will not be persecuted but enjoy liberty of religion for a hundred years, and that their churches are to be restored to them[103]. King Shapur gladly agrees to this condition and orders that persecutions against Christians in his realm should cease, churches be returned or rebuilt on state expense, stolen goods be given back to the Christians, and the relics of the dead, i.e. of the martyrs, be handed over so that memorial chapels may be built for them[104].

Cities figure as stages for Julian's reintroduction of polytheism and festivities in honour of the gods. In connection with this, they also serve as the scenes for confrontations with Christians who have had the courage to oppose the emperor and to stand up for their faith, in particular in Constantinople and Antioch. However, these latter cities also easily gave in to Julian, and their inhabitants enthusiastically participated in his pagan religious festivities. In that sense they do not differ that much from Harran, «the mother of paganism», which did not oppose Julian at all and eagerly received him. Interestingly, however, Harran is also the city where Julian received the clearest premonition about his coming death and defeat by Shapur. Jovian's city Nisibis, although it has pagan and Jewish residents who collaborate with Julian, is presented in a positive way. In particular its bishop and Christian community are described favourably. The Nisibene Christians pray for their brethren in Edessa when the latter are threatened by Julian; in this way a connection is established between the Christian communities between the two cities. Clearly, the most attention is given to Edessa, which is presented as the only city in the East that resisted Julian and kept firm to its Christian faith. Its Christianity is underscored by the contrast with the paganism of Edessa's neighbour city and pagan opponent Harran, but even more so by the comparison of Edessa to the demeanour of Constantinople and Antioch towards Julian. As «mother of

---

[102] «You will make peace between the kingdoms by agreement, and you will place the children of your nation [i.e. Nisibis] under the tribute of Persia...»; H. GOLLANCZ, *Julian the Apostate...*, 192.

[103] «And Nisibis had been given to the Persians for a hundred years together with its provinces on its eastern side. That had been done voluntarily and without compulsion»; *ibid.*, 233.

[104] *Ibid.*, 234-236. It is furthermore stated that by making peace with the Persians and giving over Nisibis, Jovian was able to rescue his troops.

believers» and Constantine's blessed city, Edessa supersedes both capital cities and claims for itself the status of the Christian city *par excellence*.

4. Jews[105]

The *Romance* is extremely hostile towards the Jews. They are said to be full of hatred against the Christians, and they support Julian's religious policy[106]. Two longer passages in the «History of Jovian» stand out. The first is a meeting in Tarsus between Julian and the Jewish high priests from Tiberias[107]. The priests intend to show the subservience of the Jews to the pagan emperor by presenting him with a golden crown[108]. In a discussion between the emperor and the Jews it becomes clear that the priests are more than willing to conform to the paganism of Julian, because their forefathers likewise sacrificed to various gods. Jacob, head of the tribes of Israel, sacrificed under the terebinth to strange gods[109], and Solomon sacrificed and put incense on the altar of the gods of his wies[110]. The Jewish priests dine with the emperor and indulge themselves in non-kosher food. When the priests have satiated themselves with this food, the emperor requests them to sacrifice to the idols. The following day an altar and a throne for Julian are erected in the centre of Tarsus. The emperor commands the Jews to come forward. He speaks harshly to them, and condemns their false doctrine. The priests, being very afraid, say that they are not Nazarenes (i.e. Christians) opposing the will of his (Julian's) divinity, and moreover that distress has been removed from their hearts and that their souls have leapt for joy at the prospect of Julian's reign. Julian, who is very happy with their

---

[105] This paragraph is based on my *The Syriac Julian Romance*.

[106] H. GOLLANCZ, *Julian the Apostate...*, 68-69: «The children of the Cross had for long shown intense hatred against us [the Christians], and vehemently they spoke slanders against us to the tyrant». Anti-judaism is also prominenty present in the second part of the *Romance*; see J.W. DRIJVERS, *Julian and the City of Rome...*, 19.

[107] H. GOLLANCZ, *Julian the Apostate...*, 117-126.

[108] This is the *aurum coronarium*, originally offered to rulers and conquerors in the ancient near east and the Hellenistic world. In the Roman Empire it became an irregular form of taxation, indicating the submission of communities; F. MILLAR, *The Emperor in the Roman World (31 BC-AD 337)*, London 1977, 140ff. In this respect it is interesting to note that Julian abolished the *aurum coronarium*; see W. ENSSLIN, *Kaiser Julians Gesetzgebungswerk und Reichsverwaltung*, «Klio» 18 (1923), 104-199, at 104-109.

[109] Cf. *Gen.* 35:2-4.

[110] I *Kings* 11.

words, accepts the golden crown and invites the Jews to sacrifice to the pagan gods[111]. Subsequently, the Jews present Julian with a letter, in which they pledge unconditional allegiance to the emperor and call Julian the king of Jacob and the leader of Israel. Now that they have performed the emperor's will and have sacrificed to the idols, the priests furthermore petition Julian that he direct his benign eyes upon Jerusalem, where the Temple lies in ruins. Julian, who cannot refuse this request, promises to protect the Jews and gives them permission to lay bare the foundations of the Temple. Having gained this promise, the priests return to their country in shame and with their faces hidden in disgrace.

The second passage describes a meeting not far from Edessa between Julian and the Edessene Jews[112]. The Jews, some 700 in number, having had a hard time in Christian Edessa, have secretly left their city to meet the emperor. At first, Julian wants nothing to do with the Jews, thinking that because they come from Edessa they must be against him[113]. However, the Chief of the Synagogue, Humnas[114], explains that they have incurred the hatred of their city because they have accepted Julian's reign. In Edessa they have been insulted, physically maltreated, their synagogues seized, their homes plundered and their possessions taken. Humnas also explains that

---

[111] A similar story can be found in the *Nestorian History*, PO 5, 238-239, where is related that 400 rabbis from Tiberias went to Constantinople at Julian's accession to offer the new emperor a golden crown, which was fashioned with seven idols by way of decoration. Julian demanded that they should worship the idols and partake of a meal of pork, to which the Jews happily consented.

[112] H. GOLLANCZ, *Julian the Apostate...*, 143-146.

[113] Julian's reluctance to meet with the Jews may have some basis in the emperor's own writings, which do not demonstrate a high opinion of the Jewish faith and god; c. *Galilaeos* 75A-86A, 93E, 99E ff., 100C, 134D ff., 141C, 148C, 155C ff., 176A-C ff., 201E, 221E. Only when the emperor learns that the Jews are willing to venerate more than one god, that the Edessene Jews are living in conflict with the Christians, and that they are happy with his reign, is he prepared to receive them. This does not make the emperor an unconditional friend of the Jews as becomes most obvious from the measures which the emperor takes against the Jews of Nisibis for slandering his second-in-command, Jovian. Six of the Jewish leaders are crucified, all other Jews are expelled from Nisibis, their goods are given as booty and their synagogues burnt (H. GOLLANCZ, *Julian the Apostate...*, 169). Apart from Julian's attempt at rebuilding the Temple in Jerusalem, the meeting between Julian and the Jews in Tarsus, the neglect of dietary laws, the bringing of sacrifices to pagan gods, the recognition of Julian as the Jewish redeemer, and the coming of the Edessene Jews to Julian are stories which are not founded on historical reality and which are evidently invented for the sake of religious propaganda.

[114] His name is not mentioned in this passage but has already been referred to several pages before; H. GOLLANCZ, *Julian the Apostate...*, 131.

the Jews of Edessa would be willing to serve the gods of Julian, since their ancestors likewise had served a multitude of gods. Again, Julian is requested to remember Jerusalem and the Temple, which he promises to do after his return from Persia. Humnas expresses his gratitude for Julian's promises, and offers the emperor the help of the Jews whenever Julian should decide to turn his army against Edessa. However, Julian dismisses the Jews, saying that now is not the time for vengeance. Their sortie and meeting with the emperor ended dramatically for the Jews. The governors of Edessa did not dare to harm these Jews out of fear that Julian might take revenge on their city. However, some 1800 Roman soldiers who had served under Julian and who were disgusted with paganism were willing to come openly out for their Christian faith by killing the Jews who had met with Julian. And so happened; those who returned to Edessa were all murdered while those who had not gone out to meet the emperor were expelled from Edessa (and so were all pagans) so that there was not a single soul left in Edessa that was not Christian[115].

A few aspects of these passages deserve closer examination. At first, the Jews are presented as a people who are willing to give up their monotheism and dietary laws in order to gain the support of Julian. In presenting them in this way the author of the text reduces the Jews to the level of pagans, thereby depriving them of their exclusivity and special position in the Graeco-Roman world. Secondly, the Jews call Julian their Divinity, the king of Jacob, and the leader of Israel[116]. Julian is seen by the Jews as their Redeemer[117]. This presentation of the emperor as the saviour of the Jews forms an interesting contrast with the Christian view in the *Romance*, according to which Julian was a wicked, accursed and wretched tyrant. Perhaps most important is that the Jews' recognition and honouring of Julian serves only one purpose, i.e. the restoration of the Temple in Jerusalem[118].

---

[115] H. GOLLANCZ, *Julian the Apostate*..., 147-149.

[116] *Ibid.*, 124: «Your graciousness has manifested itself mightily over our people in public, for after more than nine hundred years the Kingdom of David has shone forth in you, and at your hands the headship of the Israelites has been confirmed. You are the king of Jacob, and the leader of Israel».

[117] Cf. RUF. *Hist. Eccl.* 10.38 where it is reported that to some of the Jews it seemed that with the reign of Julian the days of the prophets had returned, and that the days of their kingdom had arrived.

[118] Some recent studies on the Temple's restoration: R.J. PENELLA, *Emperor Julian, the Temple of Jerusalem and the God of the Jews*, «Koinonia» 23 (1999), 16-31; G. STEMBERGER, *Jews and Christians in the Holy Land, Palestine in the Fourth Century*, Edinburgh 2000, 201-216; J.W. DRIJVERS, *Cyril of Jerusalem. Bishop and City*, Leiden

During Julian's reign there was a genuine attempt to rebuild the Temple. Although it is not clear from whom the initiative for this project came, it seems more likely that it was Julian's idea rather than that of the Jews. Julian's motive may have been, as alleged by Christian sources, to refute the prophecy of Daniel and the prediction of Jesus that of the buildings of the Temple not one stone should be left standing upon the other[119]. An attraction of the Jewish faith for Julian was the ritual offering of animal sacrifices. In order to make it possible again for the Jews to sacrifice, the emperor was willing to rebuild the Jewish Temple in Jerusalem. Contrary to what is said in the Romance, the restoration actually began before the Persian expedition. This restoration, which ended in failure, had a tremendous impact on the Christians, who considered the attempt to rebuild the Temple as an extremely threatening act that undermined the very foundations of Christianity. Shortly after Julian's death Ephraem Syrus' *Hymns against Julian* and Gregory of Nazianzus' *Orations* 4 and 5 appeared, in which anti-Judaism and the rebuilding of the Jerusalem Temple are central themes. These two writers set the pace for later fourth- and fifth-century Christian stories concerning the Temple's restoration[120]. However, the Christian literary tradition about the restoration attempt is closer to legend than to a historical report of what had actually happened, and should be considered religious propaganda directed against Julian and the Jews. The author of the «History of Jovian» clearly had knowledge of this literary tradition and incorporated it in his narration[121].

2004, 127-152; D.B. Levenson, *The Ancient and Medieval Sources for the Emperor Julian's Attempt to Rebuild the Jerusalem Temple*, «Journal for the Study of Judaism» 35 (2004), 409-60; J. Hahn, *Kaiser Julian und ein dritter Tempel? Idee, Wirklichkeit, Wirkung eines gescheiterten Projekts*, in *Der Jerusalemer Tempel und seine Zerstörungen*, ed. by J. Hahn (Tübingen 2002), 237-262; F. Millar, *Rebuilding of the Jerusalem Temple: Pagan, Jewish and Christian Conceptions*, «вестник древней истории. Journal of Ancient History» 264 (2008), 19-37; H. Sivan, *Palestine in Late Antiquity*, Oxford 2008, 204-210.

[119] Daniel 9:26-27; Matth. 24:1-2; cf. Luke 19:44, 21:6 and Mark 31:2.

[120] Joh. Chrys., *Jud.* 5.11, *Jud. et gent.* 16, *Pan. Bab.* 2.22, *De Laud. Pauli* 4, *Exp. in Ps.* 110.4, *Hom. in Mt.* 4, *Hom. in Acta Apost.* 41.3; Ambr. *Epist.* 40.12; Ruf. *Hist. Eccl.* 10.38-40; Philost. *Hist. Eccl.* 7.9; Socr. *Hist. Eccl.* 3.20; Soz. *Hist. Eccl.* 5.22; Thdt. *Hist. Eccl.* 3.20. The only pagan source to report the rebuilding is Ammianus Marcellinus; see J.W. Drijvers, *Ammianus Marcellinus 23.1.2-3: The Rebuilding of the Temple in Jerusalem*, in *Cognitio Gestorum. The Historiographic Art of Ammianus Marcellinus*, ed. J. den Boeft, D. den Hengst, H.C. Teitler, Amsterdam 1992, 19-26.

[121] Apart from the writings of Ephrem against Julian and the Jews, there was also the letter in Syriac allegedly by Cyril of Jerusalem on the restoration of the Temple; S.P. Brock, *A Letter Attributed to Cyril of Jerusalem on the Rebuilding of the Temple*, in

5. Concluding remarks

The Syriac *Julian Romance* is narrative fiction. Most of the persons that occur in the story are not historical and the events described will never have happened. Nevertheless, the *Romance*, and in particular the «History of Jovian», has a foundation in historical events such as Julian's sojourns in Constantinople, Antioch and Harran, his war against Persia, his good relations with the Jews, his participating in pagan festivities, his discussions with his opponents, etc.; these events are the framework for the «History of Jovian».

The *Romance* serves several purposes. In the first place it is a polemical narrative in the late-antique anti-Julian tradition which started with Ephrem Syrus and Gregory of Nazianzus, and it is a Christian propaganda tract against paganism. Paganism is personified in Julian and is considered mad, foolish, wicked, intolerant, licentious, and identified with death. Christianity, on the other hand, is personified in Jovian and stands for wisdom, judiciousness, tolerance, humaneness, and life. Apart from a polemical text against Julian and paganism, it is also an anti-Jewish treatise. For the sake of the victory of Christianity violence against pagans and Jews is not shunned and even applauded[122]. Secondly, it is a text that emphasises the uniqueness of Edessa as a Christian city of old as the only city in the East that dares to oppose Julian. It is evidently written to enhance the status of Edessa in the Christian East, not only because the city kept firm in its faith but also because of its connection with Constantine. Thirdly, the text serves as an explanation and justification for the loss of Nisibis and large parts of the Roman East to Persians, after Julian's fatal campaign. Jovian's peace settlement and the loss of Roman territory served the higher purpose of freedom of religion for Christians in the Persian Empire. Fourthly, the text expresses the wish for peace in the Roman-Persian frontier zone, as well as for peaceful coexistence between peoples on both sides of the border. This wish is exemplified by the peace arrangement Jovian made with

---

«Bulletin of the School of Oriental and African Studies» 40 (1977), 267-286, repr. in ID., *Syriac Perspectives on Late Antiquity*, London 1984; J.W. DRIJVERS, *Cyril of Jerusalem...*, 137-152, 191-193. The author of the *Romance* does not display knowledge of Cyril's letter.

[122] T. NÖLDEKE, *Über den syrischen Roman...*, 290: «Gradezu widerartig ist die Glorificierung jeder Gewaltsamkeit gegen Heiden oder gar Juden».

Shapur and by the character of Jovian himself, who as a native of Nisibis belongs to both the Roman and the Persian cultures[123].

The prominence of Edessa in the «History of Jovian» makes it almost impossible that the text was composed in any other city than Edessa. Its author (or authors) clearly were well acquainted with the work of Ephrem Syrus, who had to leave Nisibis and came to Edessa in 363. There are undeniably resemblances between Ephrem's *Hymns against Julian* and the *Romance*. The hymns allude to Julian's pagan unchastity and immodesty, they demonstrate a violent anti-Judaism, they applaud the peace that Jovian concluded, they present Jovian as the associate of Constantine, and they describe Shapur in a favourable way[124]. The *Romance* also has remarkable resemblances with the *Doctrina Addai* (*DA*), which tells how Christianity was brought to Edessa by the apostle Addai shortly after Christ's crucifixion[125]. In its final form the *DA* was composed well after the beginning of the fifth century by an unknown author who made use of earlier legendary Edessene traditions. The reference that Edessa thrice withstood a Persian siege refers to the *DA*, where Christ had promised that no enemy would have power over Edessa[126]. There is furthermore a clear similarity between Christ's letter to king Abgar, as mentioned in the *DA*, and Constantine's letter to the Edessene community in the *Romance*: Constantine's letter is a counterpart of that of Christ[127]. In both the *DA* and the «The History of Jovian» Edessa has a central position and is considered the «Blessed City » and the Christian city *par excellence*. Both texts connect the city with the imperial power and express Edessa's loyalty to the Roman Empire. In the *DA* king Abgar has good contacts with the emperors Tiberius and Claudius while in the «History of Jovian» the authorities in Edessa express their undivided loyalty to the Christian emperors Constantine and Jovian. In both texts the pagans and Jews are considered

---

[123] This wish for peace was also expressed by the prophetess Dinosa who was consulted by Julian: «This is the result of your war: peace between the frontiers, reconciliation between the kingdoms...The East and West will be happy, and rejoice that they are at peace through you»; H. GOLLANCZ, *Julian the Apostate* ..., 160.

[124] H.J.W. DRIJVERS, *The Syriac Romance of Julian...*, 207: «All the basic themes of Ephrem's Hymns *contra Julianum* return in this treatise [the *Julian Romance*]». Cf. A. MURAVIEV, *The Syriac Julian Romance and its Place...*, 199 who is not convinced of Ephrem's influence on the *Romance*.

[125] H.J.W. DRIJVERS, *Abgarsage*, in *Neutestamentliche Apokryphen* I. *Evangelien*, ed. by W. SCHNEEMELCHER, Tübingen 1990⁶, 389-395.

[126] H.J.W. DRIJVERS, *The Syriac Romance of Julian...*, 211. Also Egeria, when she visited Edessa c. 385, refers to this; *It. Eger.* 19.9.

[127] H. GOLLANCZ, *Julian the Apostate...*, 212.

the main adversaries of Christian Edessa. Moreover, from a christological point of view the *DA* expresses the full divinity of Christ and its author clearly takes position in favour of the christology of Cyril of Alexandria and hence against the Antiochene views about the nature of Christ[128]. The author of the integral version of the *DA* clearly composed his text «for the purpose of making a historical and doctrinal claim in his own day»[129]. As such, the *DA* has a function in the polemical debate in Edessa as it took place in the fifth century between what after the Council of Chalcedon of 451 came to be called monophysites and dyophysites. In this debate the author of the *DA* took the monophysite side.

The correspondences as regards contents between the *DA* and the *Romance* may also bring us closer to establishing a date of composition for the «History of Jovian». As mentioned above, several suggestions have been made for a date – ranging from the second half of the fourth century to the beginning of the sixth century. The many ideological resemblances between the *DA* and the «History of Jovian» make it likely that they were composed in more or less the same period and a similar milieu in Edessa. Unfortunately, the «History of Jovian» does not express christological views. However, what is striking is the portrayal of the city of Antioch. Although Antioch was one of the first and foremost cities of the Christian world, the author of the «History of Jovian» describes it as pagan and calls it "the residence of gods". This antagonistic characterization of Antioch may have a connection with its predominant dyophysite theology as formulated by Theodore of Mopsuestia. This theology had considerable influence in Edessa and led to internal christological dissensions in that city, in particular in the time of bishop Rabbula (412-436) and the years thereafter. The presentation of Edessa as the only city that stood firm in its faith as opposed to Constantinople and Antioch, may reflect the christological conflict between dyophysites and monophysites at the time. Edessa's bishop chose for monophysitism whereas Constantinople and Antioch inclined towards dyophysitism.

Sidney Griffith has recently argued that the final version of the *DA* was probably composed during Rabbula's episcopate[130]. The «History of Jovian» may date from around the same time. I have suggested elsewhere

---

[128] S.H. GRIFFITH, *The Doctrina Addai as a Paradigm of Christian Thought in Edessa in the Fifth Century*, in *Hugoye. Journal of Syriac Studies* 6.2 (2003); online publication: http://syrcom.cua.edu/Hugoye/Vol6No2/HV6N2Griffith.html#FNRef92, 29-30, 38-40.
[129] H. GOLLANCZ, *Julian the Apostate...*, 28.
[130] *Ibid.*, 40.

that because of its fierce anti-Judaism the «History of Jovian» may have been composed in the time of Rabbula[131]. Rabbula was known for his anti-Jewish attitude and he is said to have converted thousands of Edessene Jews and heretics, in the process of which he did not shrink from using violence and from the devastation of Jewish places of worship[132]. Under his ecclesiastical authority the synagogue of Edessa was converted into a church and dedicated to the protomartyr St. Stephen[133]. Rabbula was heavily involved in the christological debate of his time. After the Council of Ephesus in 431, he chose the monophysite side, which brought him into conflict with Ibas, the head of the so-called School of the Persians in Edessa[134]. The doctrinal strife over Christ's nature continued in Edessa for many years after Rabbula's death, and throughout the fifth century there were struggles between monophysites and Chalcedonians[135]. Furthermore, the anti-Judaism of the «History of Jovian» may have a christological aspect; in Syriac literature the Chalcedonian dyophysites or Nestorians were branded as Jews because according to their enemies they denied Christ's divinity[136]. I consider it therefore possible that like *DA* the «History of Jovian» was composed either in the 430s during Rabbula's lifetime or thereafter in the context of Christian conflict about doctrinal dogma.

---

[131] J.W. DRIJVERS, *The Syriac Julian Romance...*, 37-38.

[132] J.J. OVERBECK, *S. Ephraemi Syri, Rabulae Episcopi Edesseni, Balaei aliorumque opera selecta*, Oxford 1865, 193, *l.*14 - 194, *l.*18; G. BICKELL, *Ausgewählte Schriften der syrischen Kirchenväter Aphraates, Rabulas und Isaak von Ninive*, Kempten 1874, 196-198. See further for Rabbula, P. PEETERS, *La vie de Rabboula, évêque d'Édesse (mort 7 août 436)*, in *Mélanges de Grandmaison* = «Recherches de science religieuse» 18 (1928), 170-204 = P. PEETERS, *Recherches d'histoire et de philologie orientales*, I, in *Subs. Hagiogr.* 27, Brussels 1951, 139-170; G.G. BLUM, *Rabbula von Edessa. Der Christ, der Bischof, der Theologe, CSCO Subs.* 31, Louvain 1969; H.J.W. DRIJVERS, *The Man of God of Edessa, Bishop Rabbula, and the Urban Poor. Church and Society in the Fifth Century*, «Journal of Early Christian Studies» 4 (1996), 235-248.

[133] *Chronicum Edessenum*, ed. I. GUIDI, *Chronica Minora* I, *CSCO Script. Syr.* 1, Louvain 1903, 6, sub LI.

[134] E.g. E. SEGAL, *Edessa...*, 94ff.; A.H. BECKER, *Fear of God and the Beginning of Wisdom. The School of Nisibis and the Development of Scholastic Culture in Late Antique Mesopotamia*, Philadelphia 2006, 47ff.. On Ibas and the theological controversies in Edessa in the fifth century, see now C. RAMMELT, *Ibas von Edessa. Rekonstruktion einer Biographie und dogmatischen Position zwischen den Fronten*, Berlin-New York 2008.

[135] E. SEGAL, *Edessa...*, 93ff.

[136] E.g. SIMEON OF BĒT ARŠAM, *Epist.* 347 = *Simeonis epistola de Barsauma episcopo Nisibeno, deque haeresi nestorianorum*, in *Bibliotheca Orientalis Clementino-Vaticana* I, ed. and tr. J.S. ASSEMANI, Rome 1719-1728, 246-258, repr. Hildesheim 2000.

Another argument for the origin of the «History of Jovian» in a milieu favourable to monophysitism may be the connection between Edessa and Constantine and the presentation of Jovian as the New Constantine. Constantine himself had confided Edessa to Christ, and had blessed the city in a letter. The Edessenes held this letter in high regard[137]. Constantine is of course identified with the Nicene orthodoxy that is close to the monophysitism of the fifth century. Jovian, who was greatly honoured in Edessa, is described as an emperor who «walks in the ways of Constantine» and may therefore be considered as an adherent of doctrine that God and Son were of one nature. Like Constantine he blessed Edessa, he visited the city and even performed a miracle there. The portrayal of Jovian as the New Constantine and his special relationship with the city may therefore also have served in the christological debate which was going on in Edessa in the fifth century.

The *Julian Romance* is a polemical narrative of considerable importance for the Christain image of Julian the Apostate as it developed in Late Antiquity, and for Christian conflict with and fear of paganism and Judaism. The *Romance* raises many questions and deserves a more thorough treatment than I have been able to do in this paper, in which I have only dealt with a few, albeit important, aspects of the «History of Jovian». This third part of the *Romance* was written at least six decades after the death of Julian and at its centre are Jovian as the New Constantine and the city of Edessa. The text serves various political and religious purposes in order to come to terms with the political situation of the time and to propagate Christianity in a verbally aggressive way by attacking Julian, paganism and Judaism. The text was also meant to emphasize the status of Edessa as a Christian city of old and its connection with the imperial power of Rome; in addition, it may have served in the christological conflict that was taking place in Edessa itself in the fifth century[138].

---

[137] H. GOLLANCZ, *Julian the Apostate...*, 134-135.
[138] I am grateful to Alasdair MacDonald for correcting my English.

Sergio Knipe

Recycling the refuse-heap of magic: scholarly approaches to theurgy since 1963

One of the essays included in *The Conflict between Paganism and Christianity in the Fourth Century* is devoted to the survival of magic arts[1]. When first presenting this essay as a lecture, in 1959, A.A. Barb made his intentions quite clear: «I have not come to bury the term "Magic", but neither do I want to praise what it denominates (as certain neo-gnostic occultists are nowadays inclined to do)»[2]. While the nature of «neo-gnostic occultism» escapes me, the purpose of my paper is not to deliver any eulogy of «magic». It is not the scholarly debate on magic that I am directly concerned with, but something more specific: the debate surrounding Neoplatonist theurgy. Barb's essay provides a useful starting point to consider how the scholarly perception of theurgy has changed over the past forty-five years, and what difference this makes to the study of pagan religiosity in late Antiquity. My aim in what follows is not to provide a complete bibliographical survey, but to highlight some significant scholarly trends.

Providing a straightforward definition of theurgy is a challenging task. As outlined by Porphyry's disciple Iamblichus in his treatise *De mysteriis* (*On the Mysteries of Egypt*), theurgy was a philosophical doctrine that promoted ritual practices – the manipulation of material objects, sacrifices, the recitation of prayers and sacred formulas – as means to elevate the human soul to the divine. As such, theurgy has been described as «a sacramental system and a form of revelation»[3], «une technique révélée par les dieux eux-mêmes pour permettre à l'homme d'entrer en contact avec

---

[1] A.A. Barb, *The Survival of Magic Arts*, in *The Conflict Between Paganism and Christianity in the Fourth Century*, ed. A. Momigliano, Oxford 1963, 100-25.
[2] *Ibid.*, 100-101.
[3] J. Bregman, *Judaism as Theurgy in the Religious Thought of the Emperor Julian*, «AncW» 26 (1995), 135.

eux»⁴. Whether Barb would have subscribed to any of these definitions is hard to tell. The view he adopted in his 1963 paper, at any rate, was a very different one: «All the fashionable pagan philosophers of the [fourth] century, headed by the divine Iamblichus, believed in the magical arts of *theurgia* as part and parcel of their theosophic systems»⁵. While the meaning of the word «theosophic» in this context is somewhat obscure, Barb's approach to theurgy in *The Survival of Magic Arts* is unequivocal: he describes it as a form of white magic – a decadent degeneration of religion. By consciously revising evolutionist paradigms, Barb argues that:

> «Religion does not evolve from primitive magic; on the contrary magic derives from religion, which, as it becomes tainted by human frailty, deteriorates into so-called white magic (the Greeks called it *theurgia* – working things divine), gradually losing its whiteness and turning from more or less dirty grey into black magic, called in Greek *goēteia*, from the evil-sounding recitation of spells»⁶.

In support of his conflation between sorcery (γοητεία) and theurgy (θευργία) Barb goes on to quote the words of Augustine: *quam uel magiam uel detestabiliore nomine goetiam uel honorabiliore theurgiam uocant*⁷.

Like Augustine, Barb is quite frank in telling the reader just what he thinks of pagan magic (and, by extension, theurgy): he presents it as a heterogeneous mix of practices essentially deriving from the putrefaction of proper religious standards. This bag of magic nonsense contained a little bit of everything, including – in the case of theurgy – «a large proportion of philosophy run wild»⁸. Barb's description of magic is delightfully graphic: comparing it to a refuse heap, he argues that: «To complain that the current use of the word magic is libellous would be [...] as if we were to complain that the authorities concerned condemn rotten food to the refuse-heap as unfit for human consumption»⁹. Certainly, sometimes quite good food is wasted, but the risk of food poisoning is too great to attempt to salvage anything from the rubbish. Adding a politically incorrect twist, as it were, Barb also adds that: «Food-poisoning is caused more

---

⁴ P. HADOT, *Théologie, exégèse, révélation, écriture dans la philosophie grecque*, in *Les règles de l'interprétation*, ed. M. TARDIEU, Paris 1987, 27 (reprinted in P. HADOT, *Études de philosophie ancienne*, Paris 1998, 27-58).
⁵ A.A. BARB, *The Survival...*, 115.
⁶ *Ibid.*, 101.
⁷ AUGUSTINE, *De ciuitate Dei*, 10, 8.
⁸ A.A. BARB, *The Survival...*, 124.
⁹ *Ibid.*, 101.

frequently by imported food than by home-grown stuff; just so we find again and again that the closest connection exists between magic and alien imported cults»[10].

While theurgy is not given much credit by Barb, who ultimately agreed with Augustine in his scholarly verdict, it should also be noted that his portrayal of ancient magic was unusually harsh for the academic milieu of the late 1950s. In his attempt to defend the use of «magic» as a category to describe inferior, superstitious, alien and decadent forms of religiosity, Barb was fighting a losing battle – and consciously so[11]. What is most interesting for the purposes of the present enquiry, however, is not the fact that Barb was particularly fierce in his condemnation of ancient magic, but that he took it for granted that no distinction could – or should – be drawn between ancient magic and theurgy, between γοητεία and θευργία. Far from being exceptional, this was the most common approach to theurgy until quite recently, even among scholars who stood on less critical ground than Barb when it came to expressing moral judgments on ancient magical practices.

In *The Survival of Magic Arts*, theurgy is presented as the product of religious despair: as something developed by late-antique philosophers to fill a spiritual void. By returning to his initial metaphor, Barb remarks that:

> «The task of a Roman emperor as health officer in things supernatural became increasingly difficult when the syncretistic, rotting refuse-heap of the dead and dying religions of the whole ancient world grew to mountainous height while wholesome supernatural food became scarce. It was perhaps never more difficult than in the fourth century»[12].

Parallels for Barb's rationalist dismissal of theurgy can be found in almost all early works on the subject[13]. Without stretching too far back in time, an important name that springs to mind is that of E.R. Dodds, who would happily have concurred with another historian of the fourth

---

[10] *Ibid.*, 101-102.
[11] For a recent discussion of the way in which scholarly use of «magic» as a semantic category in religious discourse has changed, I refer to S. TRZCIONKA, *Magic and the Supernatural in Fourth-Century Syria*, London and New York 2007, ch. 2; K.B. STRATTON, *Naming the Witch: Magic, Ideology, and Stereotype in the Ancient World*, New York 2007, ch. 1; J.N. BREMMER, *Greek Religion and Culture in the Bible and the Ancient Near East*, Leiden-Boston 2008, 347-352.
[12] A.A. BARB, *The Survival...*, 104.
[13] A useful overview of the negative reception of Iamblichean theurgy among nineteenth- and early twentieth-century scholars can be found in B.D. LARSEN, *Jamblique de Chalcis: Exégète et philosophe*, Aarhus 1972, 18-19.

century, Campbell Bonner, that this was an era «darkened by the most degrading of superstitions in a manner that can only be compared to the benighted condition of western Europe in the later Middle Ages»[14]. Dodds, not unlike Barb, unceremoniously referred to theurgy as «theosophical rubbish»[15]: an inferior kind of mysticism not essentially different from sorcery, «the refuge of a despairing intelligentsia which already felt *la fascination de l'abîme*»[16]. Dodds, once a member of the Society for Psychical Research, at best considered theurgy to be a pursuit akin to contemporary spiritualism. Mostly, however, like Barb, he approached theurgy from a psychological rather than psychic angle, seeing it as the angst-ridden product of an «age of anxiety»[17] – what Gilbert Murray had famously referred to as the «failure of nerve» of the Hellenes[18].

Other names could be mentioned aside from those of Barb and Dodds to illustrate the rationalist and psychoanalytical approach to theurgy once prevalent amongst ancient historians[19]. In the 1950s and 60s, theurgy was generally regarded as a later degeneration of Neoplatonism, so much so that scholars dealing with Iamblichus could feel almost embarrassed: «Comment se fait-il – A.-J. Festugière asked in 1968 – qu'un philosophe, qui use de la purification par le λόγος et de la contemplation par le νοῦς, se laisse aller à ces pratiques de sorcellerie...? Comment se fait-il donc que Proclus, diadoque officiel de Platon, s'abaisse aux rites de la théurgie et de la magie?». No doubt, as Garth Fowden has observed, «the essentially intellectual character of Plotinos' writings [...] made him more congenial than his successors [...] to modern western scholars»[20]. In the years when Barb was delivering his lectures at the Warburg Institute, the kind of questions rhetorically posed by Festugière were on the mind of all those concerned with later developments in Neoplatonism. The answer that Barb and Dodds provided had a Spenglerian ring to it: the rise of theurgy, as they saw it, was ultimately a matter of historical involution.

---

[14] C. BONNER, *Witchcraft in the Lecture Room of Libanius*, «TAPA» 63 (1932), 44.
[15] E.R. DODDS, *Numenius and Ammonius*, in *Les sources de Plotin*, eds. E.R. DODDS ET AL., Geneva 1960, 11.
[16] E.R. DODDS, *The Greeks and the Irrational*, Berkley 1951, 288.
[17] E.R. DODDS, *Pagan and Christian in an Age of Anxiety: Some Aspects of Religious Experience from Marcus Aurelius to Constantine*, Cambridge 1965.
[18] M. MURRAY, *Five Stages of Greek Religion: Studies Based on a Course of Lectures Delivered in April 1912 at Columbia University*, Oxford 1925, ch. 3.
[19] Particularly noteworthy, in this respect, is R. MACMULLEN's article *Sfiducia nell'intelletto nel quarto secolo*, «RSI» 84 (1974), 1-16.
[20] G. FOWDEN, *Late Antique Paganism Reasoned and Revealed*, «JRS» 71 (1981), 178.

Yet alternative strategies in the study of fourth-century Neoplatonism had been available even in the 1950s. Not all commentators, like Barb, had been willing to describe theurgy as merely a variety of ancient magic. In the 1940s, Samson Eitrem and L.J. Rosan had attempted to salvage the philosophical credibility of theurgy by distinguishing two forms of the practice: Eitrem distinguished between theoretical and practical theurgy, while Rosan simply spoke of higher theurgy and lower[21]. Higher theurgy was regarded as being effectively identical to contemplative philosophy (Plotinus' θεωρία): a practice free of any ritual components and ultimately aimed at bringing about the soul's union with the divine. By contrast, lower or practical theurgy was understood as a practice involving material rites and concerned with more mundane goals. On this perspective, the theurgy Barb refers to in his article – that which makes use of formulas and rituals – may be seen as identical to lower theurgy and, by extension, magic. The identity between lower theurgy and magic was explicitly affirmed by both Rosan and Eitrem. The latter, in his comparative study of Greek Magical Papyri and Neoplatonist writings, argues that: «L'évolution de la philosophie grecque dans la dernière phase est caractérisée par l'influence toujours croissante de la magie»[22]. Like Barb, Eitrem further quotes Augustine to suggest that: «Il sera difficile de séparer ces pratiques des magiciens gréco-égyptiens de celles de théurges»[23]. He concludes by observing that from the time of Iamblichus magical practices came to influence Greek philosophy profoundly, to the point that Proclus may be seen as wavering between an adherence to ordinary paganism and occult, theurgic rites[24].

The notion of the existence of different «theurgies», or different levels of theurgy, was given new impetus, some thirty years later, by Andrew Smith[25]. In his book *Porphyry's Place in the Neoplatonic Tradition*, Smith speaks of Iamblichean doctrine in far more favourable terms than either Barb, Dodds, Rosan or Eitrem – an indication of the broader shift towards a positive re-evaluation of later Neoplatonism that took hold in the 1970s,

---

[21] S. EITREM, *La théurgie chez les néoplatoniciens et dans les papyrus magiques*, «SO» 22 (1942), 49-79; L.J. ROSAN, *The Philosophy of Proclus: The Final Phase of Ancient Thought*, New York 1949.
[22] S. EITREM, *La théurgie...*, 49.
[23] *Ibid.*, 59.
[24] *Ibid.*, 74 («il semble bien que Proclus ait vacillé de temps à autre entre la théurgie et le culte traditionnel et officiel»).
[25] A. SMITH, *Porphyry's Place in the Neoplatonic Tradition*, The Hague 1974, 90 ff. and 111-121.

particularly thanks to the work of D.B. Larsen and Jean Trouillard[26]. Smith does not dismiss theurgy as «theosophical rubbish», but regards it as an attempt to redefine Neoplatonic soteriology on the basis of a new religious sensibility. Like Eitrem and Rosan, Smith distinguishes between two levels of theurgy, a higher and a lower, but believes that both involve some kind of ritual practices. While this may seem like a minor development, it actually signals an important change in perspective: Smith, unlike his predecessors, does not envisage the distinctive ritual practices of theurgy as subordinate or irrelevant to the higher goals of Neoplatonism; rather, he sees them as articulating these philosophical goals in a new way. At the same time, Smith continued to refer to theurgy as a form of magic, arguing that Iamblichus «believed and accepted the magico-religious practices of his times and attempted to incorporate them into Neoplatonism»[27]. While not dismissing theurgy as an alien and irrational offshoot of Neoplatonism, he ultimately agreed with Barb that it was best understood as a form of white magic[28].

Trouillard appears to have gone one step further in his book *L'un et l'âme selon Proclos* (1972), where he suggests theurgy be firmly distinguished from what is commonly termed magic, given that it serves not a mundane purpose but a transcendent goal: not to compel daemons for material gain, but to awaken the presence of the gods[29]. Yet for all their divergences, the works of both Smith and Trouillard usefully serve to illustrate how by the 1970s theurgy was no longer regarded as an unfortunate «borrowing» from the oriental world of magic, but as a coherent development within Neoplatonism. In the same period, established scholars such as A.H. Armstrong, L.G. Westerink and J.M.P. Lowry came to describe Iamblichus' «theurgical Platonism» as a conscious attempt to preserve Plotinus' belief in the superiority of intuition to reason (the «mystical side of Plotinus»)[30]. Since the mid-1970s, scholarly literature on theurgy has

---

[26] D.B. LARSEN, *Jamblique de Chalcis...*; J. TROUILLARD, *L'un et l'âme selon Proclos*, Paris 1972.

[27] A. SMITH, *Porphyry's Place...*, 89.

[28] An interesting parallel for Smith's analysis can be found in HANS LEWY's book *Chaldaean Oracles and Theurgy* (Paris 1978. First edition: Cairo 1956). While Lewy does not mention different theurgic levels, he describes theurgy as an occult practice based on «the correct ritual performance of certain magical actions» aimed at attaining the same goal traditionally assigned to philosophy: «Union with the gods» (462).

[29] J. TROUILLARD, *L'un et l'âme...*, 174.

[30] J.M.P. LOWRY, *The Logical Principle of Proclus' ΣΤΟΙΧΕΙΩΣΙΣ ΘΕΟΛΟΓΙΚΗ as Systematic Ground of the Cosmos*, Amsterdam 1980, 21; A.H. ARMSTRONG, *Tradition, Reason, and Experience in the Thought of Plotinus*, «Accademia Nazionale dei Lin-

largely continued in this direction. Gregory Shaw's research over the past twenty-five years, leading to the publication of *Theurgy and the Soul* in 1995, has shed invaluable light on the philosophical, theoretical grounds behind Iamblichus' embrace of ritual[31]. The two most recent monographs on the subject, by Carine van Liefferinge and E.G. Clarke[32], have followed closely in Shaw's steps, approaching theurgy as a sophisticated attempt to engage with important metaphysical issues. In the light of this scholarly trajectory, it is easy to imagine how surprised – and possibly irritated – Barb would be at the way in which theurgy appears to have been salvaged from the rotten heap of fourth-century religion gone awry. To draw some conclusions from the short survey provided so far, the major changes that have taken place in the scholarly approach to theurgy since 1963 might be summarised as follows: theurgy, and the committed embrace of ritual it entails, is now seen as deriving from articulate philosophical positions; consequently, the place of theurgy as a genuine expression of Platonist thought has been re-evaluated; in turn, this has led to a treatment of theurgy as a specific phenomenon to be understood in its own terms rather than as another manifestation of late-antique «occultism»; theurgy is now generally studied separately from the nebulous underworld of «magic»: *pace* Augustine, few scholars today would contend that to describe «theurgy» as another form of γοητεία is helpful in any way[33].

The greatest impact of this shift in the scholarly treatment of theurgy has been on the contemporary reception of Neoplatonist writings. If the advancements made since Barb's day in the study of Iamblichus and Proclus have been so considerable, this is at least partly due to a re-evaluation of the religious thought of these philosophers. Yet, to accuse Barb of not having grasped the subtleties of Iamblichean metaphysics would be to miss the point: his paper in *The Conflict between Paganism and Christianity*

---

cei», Quaderno 198 (1974) (*Atti del Convegno internazionale sul tema: Plotino e il Neoplatonismo in Oriente e in Occidente*, Roma, 1974), 187 (reprinted in *Plotinian and Christian Studies*, London 1979, XVII); L.G. WESTERINK, *The Greek Commentaries on Platos' Phaedo I: Olympiodorus*, Amsterdam-Oxford-New York 1976, 15.

[31] G. SHAW, *Theurgy and the Soul*, University Park (Penn.) 1995, with review by J.F. FINAMORE in «Speculum» 73 (1998)/3, 894-896.

[32] C. VAN LIEFFERINGE, *La Théurgie: Des Oracles Chaldaïque à Proclus*, Liège 1999; E.G. CLARKE, *Iamblichus' De Mysteriis: A Manifesto of the Miraculous*, Aldershot 2001.

[33] Particularly significant are the remarks by the most recent translators of Iamblichus, emphasising how it is the philosopher's «determination to distinguish between worthless magic and divine theurgy that dominates and defines the subject matter of the *De mysteriis*»: E.R. CLARKE, J.M. DILLON, J.P. HERSHBELL, *Iamblichus: On the Mysteries*, Leiden-Boston 2003, XXVI.

in the Fourth Century was never intended to be a study of Neoplatonism; its purpose was to outline how religious practice had degenerated in late Antiquity. In moving towards a conclusion, therefore, it is worth considering how changes in the approach to theurgy may be seen to affect the historical engagement with late-antique religiosity more broadly. I would here suggest that some of the implications of this shift in perspective are only starting to be appreciated by those exploring later pagan thought. In particular, the fact that theurgy has come to be regarded as a coherent philosophical doctrine, rather than merely a set of esoteric practices, suggests that it may also be seen as an intellectual attempt to reaffirm the efficacy and legitimacy of pagan ritual in centuries of mounting Christianisation. Theurgy may thus be understood as an attempt to preserve what was best in the religious traditions of all peoples, to re-conceptualise or re-fashion pagan identity by developing a holistic spiritual outlook. Nicole Belayche's work on Julian proves highly revealing in this respect: by tracing the philosophical basis of the emperor's commitment to ritual practice, it shows how the study of theurgy can contribute to drawing light on socio-religious dynamics that fall well outside the cloudy boundaries of ancient «magic»[34]. The increasing emphasis laid over the past four decades on the theoretical foundations of theurgy, its philosophical grounding and its relevance towards the pursuit of spiritual goals has delivered a fatal blow to the notion that the Neoplatonist embracing of ritual in the fourth century was an escapist fall into the sub-rational realm of the «occult». By assigning theurgic doctrine its rightful place in the history of philosophy, modern scholarship has contributed to define theurgy as one of the great intellectual discourses that shaped the religious landscape of late Antiquity.

---

[34] N. BELAYCHE, *«Partager la table des dieux». L'empereur Julien et les sacrifices*, «RHR» 218 (2001)/4, 458-486. English translation: *Sacrifice and Theory of Sacrifice during the «Pagan Reaction»: Julian the Emperor*, in *Sacrifice in Religious Experience*, ed. A.I. BAUMGARTEN, Leiden-Boston-Cologne 2002, 101-126.

FRANCISCO MARSHALL

The late antique hero*

Flavius Philostratus voiced his *Heroikos* from amid the ruins of the temple of Protesilaos, in the Chersonesos, and claimed for its relevance, and restoration. It would be easy, then, to place him in that scenario of «shrunken or ruined cities, deserted villages, roofless temples, shrines without images, and pedestals without statues, faint vestiges of places that once had a name and played a part in history», which James Frazer described as his impression of Pausanias[1]. Although Frazer is a landmark editor of Pausanias, and although, also, Pausanias has been a good source for writing about Greece in ruins[2], such impressions have been challenged, especially in what concerns the standing of the hero cult in the late antique Greek landscape. Despite the state of degradation experienced by many traditional Greek places after c. 380 years of Roman domain, in his ten books, Pausanias refers to more than 100 heroes and heroines with active cult places like temples[3], tombs, shrines, altars, and monuments[4]. From this universe, he chooses and describes more than 50 cases of hero cult, all of them with active practice of sacrifice. It was easy and even pleasant for him to archaize the narrative, but the consistency of his vocabulary helps to endorse his opinion that a great part of these cults of heroes belonged to ancient cults, still active in his times. By the second half of the second

---

* *This work was possible due to a research grant from the Alexander von Humboldt Foundation, enjoyed at the Ruprecht-Karls-Universität Heidelberg, in 2008-2009, under the cordial cares and friendship of Reinhard Stupperich, which I hereby thank. Many thanks also to Carlos Machado, who offered clever insights and precise topic indications to the earlier versions of this paper, as well as to Peter Brown, for the general appreciation and topic inspiration, and to Alexandra Eppinger, in Heidelberg, who offered wonderful help on heraclean matters.*
[1] J. FRAZER, *Pausanias's Description of Greece*, London 1898, 1, XIV (introd.).
[2] S.E. ALCOCK, Graecia Capta: *The Landscapes of Roman Greece*, Cambridge 1993.
[3] C.H. WELLER, *May a hero have a temple?*, «Classical Philology» 12 (1917)/1, 96-97.
[4] G. EKROTH, *Pausanias and the Sacrificial Rituals of Greek Hero-cults*, in *Ancient Greek Hero Cult*, Stockholm 1999, 145-158.

century, the smoke of hero cult was still part of the landscape, and one could not ignore that, even when aiming to do so.

Despite the surveys of Pausanias, and the efforts of Philostratus, however, after the third century, the fate of hero cult in the Greco-Roman world was more complicated. We can suppose that amid the smoke of sacrifices that so much annoyed Constantine, and his Christian successors in the fourth century, there should be also smoke signals of heroic cult; nevertheless, it is not that easy to distinguish by the smokes' smell which is the ritual represented, even when we have intriguing references such as those in the last book of the *Codex Theodosianus* (L. 16,10)[5]. The predominant mainframe of Late Antique teleologies, assuming the progressive fading and later collapse of hero cult, can easily mistake the historian, since this institution, and its transformation, are of a very much complex nature. Also, one can easily get trapped by the enthusiasm of an apologist of hero-cult in the third century, as was Philostratus, and assume, as the historical consequence of his work, a revival of such culture[6]. Behind those risks and traps, lies a set of questions very much neglected in the bibliography, and for which it is difficult to provide evidence: what is the standing of hero cult in late antiquity? What is the historical reality of hero cult, beyond its rhetorical, artistic, and propagandistic forms? Which were its transformations, both face to the Greek religious traditions, and vis-a-vis the Christians? Hereby, our effort to advance this quest will comprehend, first, the earlier context of cultural contact between Christians and Pagans, mediated by hero myth and cult, followed by a consideration of the main work of hero cult apology written in Late Antiquity (and ever), Philostratus's *Heroikos*, its features and contextualization in the social and religious history of the Roman empire; as a conclusion, follows a survey of the later fortune of hero cult in the fourth century, and its aftermaths.

The emergence of Christianity was embedded in ancient heroic myth and cult, especially in what concerns the patterns of narrative, and its relations to the ancient folklore[7]. Serious discussion on this cultural closeness

---

[5] See especially *CTh* 16, 10, 2; 16,10,9 and 16,10,10; the references can point also to domestic religion, mystery cults, religious fraternities and other forms of non heroic cults, including Olympic.

[6] So was H.D. BETZ, *Hero worship and Christian beliefs: observations from the History of Religion on Philostratus's Heroikos*, in *Philostratus's Heroikos. Religion and Cultural Identity in the Third Century C.E.*, eds. A.B. AITKEN, J.K. BERENSON MACLEAN, Atlanta 2005, 25-48.

[7] A. DUNDES, *The Hero Pattern and the life of Jesus*, in R. SEGAL, *In quest of the Hero*, Princeton 1990, 179-223; M. HADAS, N. SMITH, *Heroes and Gods: Spiritual Biogra-*

started already in Antiquity (c. 156), when Justin of Caesarea, addressing hellenic audience, had to struggle to the best of his imagination trying to set Jesus Christ apart from the Greco-Roman tradition of hero-cult[8]; then, he even endorsed standards of comparison, since the coincidences approaching the life of Christ to the fates of Hermes, Asclepius, Dionysus, Herakles, the Dioscuri, Perseus, Bellerophon, and even (!) Ariadne, were too clear to be disdained in such a context of justification. The shadow of Herakles, especially, was an overwhelming burden to any quest for Christian originality. Celsus, in the pagan side and by the same epoch, teased the Christians upon these kind of similarities, what provoked, later, a compromising comment by Origenes[9], where the bishop would simultaneously reject and cancel the argument of his pagan antagonist, assuming that it wasn't a cardinal sin to work on such comparisons. Besides the patterns of mythic narrative, and the similarities in the «biographies» of Greek heroes and Christ, there was also, to some extent, an intromission of hero cult and tomb cult expression in some Christian sacred books, notably in the Revelation of John (1,7)[10], as well as in other early Christian texts, like, e.g., the Acts of Peter[11].

It is not clear to which extent Justin succeeded with his claim. There is the famous and intriguing note of the *Historia Augusta* (SHA II, 29), telling that the young emperor Severus Alexander (205-222/235) worshiped every morning, in the same *lararium*, his ancestors, and a selection of the best emperors, altogether with Jesus Christ, Abraham, Orpheus, Apollon-

---

phies in Antiquity, New York 1965. See also R.H. FULLER, *The Foundations of New Testament Christology*, New York 1965, 184-97.

[8] Especially in the First Apology, chapters XXI to XXIV, LIV to LVII, i.a.

[9] Celsus raises the cases of Zamolxis among the *Getae*, the Sicilian worship of Mopsus, Amphilochus among the Acarnanians, the Theban cult of Amphiarus, and the cult of Trophonius by the Lebadians. For Origenes, more than the risk of mistaking Jesus with pagan figures, here what matters is to underline that Celsus, with these comparisons, accepts «that Jesus was a person of a similar nature» (ORIGENES, *Cels*. 3, 34-35).

[10] L.L. THOMPSON, *Lamentation for Christ as a Hero: Revelation 1,7*, «JBL» 119 (2000)/4, 683-703.

[11] Cf. H.D. BETZ, *Hero worship...*; there's a good *compte-rendu* of the discussion in J.K. BERENSON MACLEAN, *Jesus as a Cult Hero in the Fourth Gospel*, in *Philostratus's Heroikos..*, 195-218; cf. also the reference paper by S. EITREM, *Heroes*, in *RE* 8 (1913)/1, 1111-1145; F. Pfister (*Herakles und Christus*, «Archiv für Religionswissenschaft» 34, 1937, 42-60) tried to show the dependence of Christ on Hercules by showing (some very questionable) parallels in their lives and that the *Urevangelium* was dependent on a written biography of Hercules; his theories were refuted in H.J. ROSE, *Herakles and the Gospels*, «Harvard Theological Review» 31 (1938), 113-142.

ius of Tyana, Alexander the Great, and others[12]. Despite the problematical interpretation of the *Historia Augusta*, it is a hint on the persisting rhetorical tangibility of such approaches. In a papyrus discovered in World War II near Toura, Egypt, containing, i.a., Didymus's *Commentary on Ecclesiastes*[13], there's a quotation where Porphyry of Tyre analyses, in an allegorical interpretation, the standards to compare the combat between Achilles and Hector, and the combat between Christ and Devil[14]. The quotation of such a comparison in a fourth century author like Didymus the Blind (c.310/c.395) is hereby equally relevant. Also, in his *Philosophy of Oracles*, quoted by Augustine four or five generations later, Porphyry, evoked the authority of an oracle of Hecate to concede to Jesus an honor equivalent to that of other deified men[15]. Then, if we keep in mind all this collection of cross-references whenever visiting places like the IV century catacomb of Santi Marcellino e Pietro, in Rome, with its beautiful fresco of Christ as Orpheus, then we can really know and feel that there is much room for varied and ancient comparisons between Jesus and Greek heroes. There are many ways to show, then, a context of cultural contact in between Pagans and Christians mediated by the heroic myth and cult, a context of contact sometimes critical, sometimes positive, as perceived and commented by both sides. There are many Christian ways, also, to deny such contact, especially when it comes to theological justification, but this scrutiny doesn't belong to this paper.

Severus Alexander was raised in a court fed by the lessons of Philostratus, who most likely wrote also[16] the biography of Apollonius of Tya-

---

[12] For Jesus in hero cult among the gnostics, see W. SPEYER, *Heros*, in *RAC* 14, Stuttgart 1988, 861-77.

[13] M. GRONEWALD, *Didymos der Blinde: Kommentar zum Ecclesiastes (Tura-Papyrus)*, 5 (*Zu Eccl. 9.8-10.20*), Bonn 1979; G. BINDER, *Eine Polemik des Porphyrios gegen die allegorische Auslegung des Alten Testaments durch die Christen*, «ZPE» 3 (1968), 81-95.

[14] The passage is translated and commented in P. SELLEW, *Achilles or Christ? Porphyry and Didymus in Debate over Allegorical Interpretation*, «HTR» 82 (1989)/1, 79-100.

[15] AUGUSTINE, *De civitas dei*, XIX, 23. It is impossible to assume the identification, carried by P. SELLEW, *Achilles...*, 97, of the «pious men» referred by Porphyry (apud Augustine) as any specific Greek hero, like Orpheus or Asclepius. Living humans deified due to pious excellence, however, belong to hero myth and cult.

[16] There is an unconclusive discussion on the precise identity and works of the several Philostrati, belonging to the same family and writing on similar topics, with similar style. I assume, with Solmsen, that, as the Suidas also understands, the so-called Philostratus the Elder (Flavius Philostratus) the authorship of both the *VA* and the *Heroikos*, altogether with other books, including the *Vitae Sophistarum*. F. SOLMSEN, *Some Works of Philostratus the Elder*, «TAPhA» 71 (1940), 556-572.

na (the *VA*) at the request of the empress Julia Domna, the great-aunt of Severus Alexander, and wife of Septimius Severus[17]. It is clear that Flavius Philostratus sustained a campaign in favor of the Greek hero myth and cult tradition, fostered earlier in the biography of the magus from Tyana, and fulfilled later with the dialogue *Heroikos*[18]. As a man involved with the court life[19], his propositions gained in status, and qualified to find some imperial audience[20], and the consequent historical fortune. We can even imagine the shadow of this sophist behind the visit that Caracalla paid to the tomb of Achilles in Illium, in 215; in the *VA*, it is within this tomb that Achilles appears to Apollonius and, among other things, asks for the restoration of the tomb of Palamedes, another hero disdained by Homer, and patron hero of the sophists. Endorsing his campaign with imperial exempla, the sophist remembers, in the *Heroikos*, how Hadrian embraced the bones of Ajax in his tomb in Illium, and then proceeded to its restoration (*Her.* 8,1). Imperial support to the restoration of heroic cult places was one of the main targets of Philostratus. Besides these signals and pushes, it is still to be properly evaluated the extension and the concrete consequences of the input of Philostratus in the imperial policies, especially in terms of temple restorations and hero cult enforcement.

Written in between the year 217 and a little before 230[21], the *Heroikos* can be considered the first systematic approach to the religious tradition of hero cult; it is also the first treaty of pagan apologetics, for it concentrates on explaining and justifying the mechanics of Greek religion in one of its main features, the hero cult. Then, it belongs to a late lineage of pa-

---

[17] J.J. FLINTERMAN, *Power, Paideia & Pythagoreanism*, Amsterdam 1995, 15-29 and 217-219.

[18] The study of the *Heroikos* has been greatly improved after the recent work of Ellen Brandshaw Aitken and Jennifer K. Berenson Maclean, first for their translation: *Flavius Philostratus – Heroikos*, eds. A.B. AITKEN, J.K. BERENSON MACLEAN (Society for Biblical Literature), Atlanta 2001, followed by a very much complete set of studies (vd. *supra, Philostratus's Heroikos...*), coming from a conference held at Harvard Divinity School in 2001.

[19] G. BOWERSOCK, *Greek Sophists in the Roman Empire*, Oxford 1969, 101-109; and F. GHEDINI, *Giulia Domna tra Oriente e Occidente: Le fonti archeologiche*, Roma 1984, 10-11.

[20] Indeed, to gain and involve the imperial attention was one of the main rethorical goals of this sophist, as Flinterman illustrates very well commenting the *VA* (*Power, Paideia...*, ch. 4, 128-230); it applies also to the *Heroikos*.

[21] For the *terminus post quem*, there's inside evidence; see C. JONES, *Philostratus' Heroikos and its Setting in Reality*, «JHS» 121 (2001), 141-149; for the *terminus ante quem*, see *Heroikos...*, LXXXXV.

gan theological writings, finished in the IV century with Sallustius' «*Peri theon kai kosmou*» (On the Gods and the Universe), which doesn't talk about heroes, but explains and justifies the Olympic religion in terms of neoplatonic mysticism, tuned with Julianus's campaigns. First and foremost, the Heroikos is a very much typical work of the Second Sophistic, written by the very author who invented this expression[22] with the explicit goal of including himself in a tradition that started by the late classical age, and extended up to his own age. This means that author and book are self-included in the main genealogy of Greek culture, which he aims to defend and to restore in Roman imperial times[23]. In this case, it is done through the confrontation and emendation of no one less than Homer himself, whose bias pro-Odysseus and Achilles the writer then denounces, and tries to fix through the promotion of a concurring leading hero person, Protesilaos, defended as the true hero. The proficiency in the *quaestiones homericae* can here appear not only as the performance of a sophistic virtuoso, but also as a means of gaining authority, setting light in the alleged shadows of the main source of classical tradition. It is also a most typical work of the Second Sophistic in the fancy way it mixes myth and history, disdaining the earlier criticism of myth, but nevertheless aiming to stand as historical discourse[24].

In the *Heroikos*, the didactics of hero cult has the platonic form of a dialogue, where a Vinedresser, who works as a priest in the ruins of the temple of Protesilaos, in the Chersonesos, receives the visit of a Phoenician merchant in search of omen for obtaining good winds. Then, the Vinedresser subjects the visitor to an extensive and detailed exposition on the fundamentals of hero religion, myth and cult, as well as, in the second part, extended heroic mythography. Along his explanation, most of the fundamental concepts of this tradition is rescued and commented, what results in an updating of a universe of pagan beliefs and practices never demonstrated before, but very much performed since the late Dark Ages of Greece, and very much developed, after more than ten centuries.

Despite the broader cultural circumstances of the Severan age, and of the earlier Late Antiquity, and some semantic similarities approaching the imagery and the vocabulary of the *Heroikos* to Christian discourses[25], it

---

[22] PHILOSTRATUS, *Lives of the Sophists*, 1, 481.
[23] E.L. BOWIE, *Greeks and Their Past in the Second Sophistic*, «P&P» 46 (1970), 3-41.
[24] G.W. BOWERSOCK, *Fiction as history: Nero to Julian*, Berkeley and Los Angeles 1994; E.L. BOWIE, *Greeks and Their Past...*, *passim*.
[25] Explored by B. MACLEAN, *Jesus as a cult hero...*

is not easy to assume that Philostratus was addressing a Christian reader, even as a secondary reader, and even if we consider that Protesilaos was a hero famous for his resurrection, as it was already referred in Petronius' *Satyricon*, much earlier. We must, however, give up the temptation to christianize his readership, for the text offers no clear evidence of that kind. Rather, he imagines an ideal reader invested of fundamental knowledge of the Greek tradition, as even the Phoenician merchant appears to be. To the Greek reader and to the Roman rulers, also in Philostratus' array of readers, the quest was for attention and cares towards the sacred places, whose abandonment he deplored.

Among Philostratus's conceptions and ideologies of hero and hero cult, we can summarize at least seven main points:

1. The hero has a body, in Protesilaos' case, a resurrected body, but even though, a concrete body that the Vinedresser could feel, embrace, measure, and feed in several ways (*Her.* 10-11); that was the condition of Protesilaos, a resurrected hero, but so happened also to Achilles, who is also described in his recurrent talks, visits, and hunts in the other side of the Hellespont, in the Trojan plains (*Her.* 22). The bodily presence of the heroes helps to understand how Philostratus conceives the intervention of the hero in the living world of human affairs, not as a *skias* or an *eidolon*. This argument for the materiality of the heroic body should be taken into consideration when we see the neoplatonic complains about body and purity, in terms of the opposition body-soul, and in the context of the attacks on Christian materialism; there was a Pagan version of this materialism, even if it was not the option of Porphyry or of Julianus;

2. The heroic body is oversized, much higher than the average man; heroes have greater bodies, accordingly to their power. We know it from the ancient iconography, which was a source also for Philostratus (the author of the *Peri eikones*). The Vinedresser specifies the monumental measures of several different heroes, considering the large bones that have been found in Tegea, Sigeon, the river Orontes, Lemnos, Imbros, Cos, Phrygia (Hyllos), the Alôadai (Thessaly), Napoli, Pallene (Phlegra), and Olympia. With this graphic representation, the notion of the heroic gigantism, a main feature of the ancient imagination[26], here gains a positive description and justification;

---

[26] And beyond. See W. TRAVIS, *Representing «Christ as Giant»*, «Early Medieval Art. Zeitschrift für Kunstgeschichte» 62 (1999)/2, 167-189. See also C. JONES, *The Emperor and the Giant*, «Cl. Ph.» 95 (2000)/4, 476-481.

3. The bones constitute a crucial proof of the historical presence of the heroes. The Phoenician takes for grant the bone evidences reported by the Vinedresser in detail; then, religious discourse and casual paleontology meet and, blended, become history, or, better, sacred history. Also, we must consider how much the bones belonged both to an experience in the landscape, and to the encyclopedia then available to interpret casual paleontological finds. With this full documentation on the osteoarchaeology of the heroic, Philostratus tries to assure the field for the interpretation of such a phenomenon. Also, this is one more device to connect with the cosmology of Hesiod (*EkH*, 109-201), although it implies the syncope between silver and heroic ages. It is not out of purpose, also, to ask how much similarly bone evidence wasn't to become one of the main supports for the historicization of saints, as well as to their respective faith;

4. The hero was a potency full of prophetical and practical wisdom. Sharing the vision of the gods, like a rhapsode or a prophet, Protesilaus could update his friend, the Vinedresser, with full knowledge of what happened after his own death, in the Trojan war. Ancient Muse-like inspiration is here seasoned with neoplatonic cognitive standards:«To be cleansed of the body is the beginning of life for divine and thus blessed souls» (*Her.* 7, 3). Naturally, as it is the Second Sophistic discourse, the contradiction of this neoplatonic epistemology with the materialist ontology does not matter (above, item 1). Philostratus manage to associate his hero to the high rank of such heroes like Orpheus and Asclepius, resurrected and healing heroes; then, he can offer not only omens in propitiating winds, but also advise for erotic, eye, and skin diseases, as well (*Her.* 16, 1-5). Also, the hero was able to afford the Vinedresser the proper botanical knowledge useful to the maintenance of the small farm where the temple is located (*Her.* 11). Then, it is not just about praising a powerful warrior from the homeric times, but also stressing the connection between the divine and the human mediated by the heroic, with holistic applications: «The gods know everything; but the heroes know less than the gods but more than humans» (*Her.* 16). In a glance, the prophetic powers of Herakles are also reminded (*Her.* 7, 5);

5. The hero is a *daimon* connected to the space. His proper and local position is coordinated to a larger sacred landscape; in this case, he faces the planes of Troas, located right in front of Protesilaus's temple in the Chersonesos, in triangulation with the tombs of Achilles and Ajax. Nowadays, the hero surrounding this area is Heinrich Schliemann, who perfectly understood this space coordination, and then, informed by the *Heroikos*, located the tomb of Protesilaos and added it to his cartography

of Troy[27]. Consistently, in the *Heroikos* all heroes are reported by their toponymics, instead of the epic patronymics, enhancing the perception of local belonging, associated with all heroes referred in the book. The geography of Greco-Roman Mediterranean can be represented not as a geography of cities and lands, but especially as the living scenario of the ancient heroes, a sacred geography;

6. The hero is also a patron and a defense force in social conflicts on land and land tenure. As the earlier tombs of heroes of the late Dark Ages already did, helping to set landmarks and to ensure property in a world of land disputes[28], Protesilaos is said to have taken active part in the conflict with the neighboring greater landowners (*Her.* 4, 2), helping to assure to the Vinedresser the right to the temple property, in the very much strategic, and disputed land of the Chersonesos. He does it not through arbitration, but throughout a hierophany, frightening and then dispelling the local opponents[29]; it shows how much hero cult and the daimonic force of the local cults were active religious references in the agrarian conflicts;

7. The heroic temple is in the periphery of the urban center. In the archaic ages, it would help establishing the limits of the inhabited area (*chora*), and then, the identitary space of the *polis*; as Elaious, the city connected to the temple of Protesilaus, is a colony of Athens, we have to consider here an *imitatio metropolis*, and the active role of the space demarcation described by François de Polignac in relation to hero cult, and the origins of the Greek city[30]. Several oppositions between the urban, the rural, and the wild (Thrace), belong to the semantic fabric of the *Heroikos*; in reality, those are not true oppositions, but complementarities, making clear what was the extension of the neighboring city, Elaious, which had just minted in Commodus's time (180-192) a coin showing Protesilaos armed and standing at the prow of a ship in the reverse, precisely as described by Philostratus (*Her.* 9, 6)[31]. Indeed, the tomb of Protesilaos is located at a short distance from the beach in the Bay of Morto, half way

---

[27] H. SCHLIEMANN, *Troja. Ergebnisse meiner neuesten Ausgrabungen*, Leipzig 1884, 286-292.

[28] A. SNODGRASS, *The Archaeology of the Hero*, in R. BUXTON, *Oxford readings in Greek religion*, Oxford 2000, 180-190; J. WHITLEY, *Early States and Hero Cults: A Re-Appraisal*, «JHS» 108 (1988), 173-182.

[29] The Vinedresser tells how Protesilaos blinded the former owner of the land, a certain Xeinis, through the bright of his apparition (*Her.* 4,2).

[30] F. DE POLIGNAC, *La naissance de la cité grécque*, Paris 1995.

[31] There's a reproduction of this coin in *Flavius Philostratus...*, VIII; the coin is in the Münzkabinett der Staatlichen Museen zu Berlin-Preußischer Kulturbesitz.

in between the site of the former Elaious (Heiki Hissarlik) and the most southern cape of the Chersonesos (Seddul Bahr). Such location, in Late Antiquity, would mean displacement, and then require another coordination, no longer political, but daimonic. Then, with no necessary correlation to Elaious, the place of the temple can be enhanced as an attraction for peregrination, integrating the late antique web of sacred touristic places.

It is necessary here to consider that the re-enactment of hero and landscape could lead, in this context, to the reinforcement of a traditionally pagan sacred landscape, which Tim Withmarsh calls «a hyperhellenic landscape»[32], with its proper and traditional Greek signature. Then, the defense of hero cult is *per se* a manifesto for the daimonic identity of the place, or, in a broader sense, of the places marked by the presence of hero cult. Besides the stress in the strategic region connecting Europe and Asia, and the reminiscence of Homer and of the heroic age of the Trojan cycle, Philostratus draws a large cartography, displaying the presence of bone remains and heroic presence upon a vast area of the Roman empire (see item 2, above). We must consider, on the other side, the earlier difficulties of the Christian communities to build their own landscape in a world full of gods – and heroes (to add to Keith Hopkins' title)[33]. Then, it is easier to understand the offensive of Martin of Tours to seize the pagan cult places, especially the much revered altar of Asclepius in Tours, as well as all the movements of naoclasty of the late IV and early V century.

Hero cult means also the reverberation of a whole set of formulas singing and praising the heroes, from Homer to Pindar, from Sophocles to Virgil, and beyond, but means, above all, the reinforced connection with a world of deep numinous roots and smoking actuality. Philostratus added to the late antique circuits two consistent and much provoking works, ready to be used as ideological devices in the battlefield. In the case of Apollonius of Tyana, besides its topic impact and influence[34], we know how this work was adopted by Hierocles, the loyal governor of Egypt in the times of Diocletian, as the source for the diffusion of an exotic pagan credo, where the pythagorean hero would play the pagan messiah; Hierocles's program is known from Eusebius's refutation[35]. However, it is very

---

[32] T. WITHMARSH, *The Harvest of Wisdom: Landscape, Description, and Identity in the Heroikos*, in *Philostratus's Heroikos...*, 237-249.

[33] K. HOPKINS, *A World Full of Gods: The Strange Triumph of Christianity*, New York 1999.

[34] J.J. FLINTERMAN, *Power, Paideia...*, 15-51.

[35] *Contra Hieroclem*; PHILOSTRATUS, *The Life of Apollonius of Tyana and the Treatise of Eusebius against Hierocles*, ed. and tr. F.C. CONYBEARE, 2 vol., London 1912, 483-605.

much likely that Apollonius of Tyana has more devotes nowadays, in Los Angeles or London, than it ever had in Hierocles's times. In this case, as in many other, hero myth and cult wasn't a bridge of dialogue, but most likely a weapon for confrontation.

Hero myth and cult has been, since ever, an expression of power and, as such, developed a whole structure of narratives, signals, rituals and possibilities connected to leadership and sovereignity. Although there is a great variety of local forms of power and prestige related to hero cult, since Alexander Magnus the image of the pan-hellenic hero Herakles became the main heroic icon associated to imperial power. Consequently, there's a long history of the presence of Herakles in Roman domains[36], consecrated in the temple of Hercules Victor (or Olivarius), of the late II century BC, by the Tiber, near the Forum Boarium[37]. This tradition flourished by the end of the Republic, and was strategically updated by Virgil in the book VIII of the Aeneid (the foundation of Rome, and the story of Hercules and Cacus), as well as by Propertius, in an elegy (Prop. 4, 9) where the poet remembers (as Virgil) the early arrival of Hercules at the site of Rome, and then weaves the ideological bonds between Hercules and Augustus[38]. Well established as an imperial tradition, with especial relevance in the reigns of Caligula, Nero, Domitian, and Trajan, the incrustation of Hercules's figure in imperial imagery and piety attained its acumen by the end of the second century; who will ever forget the figure of Commodus, the emperor dressed as Hercules (or the Hercules invested as emperor), in that outstanding sculpture in the Museo Capitolino, in Rome? More than personal and dramatic self-fashioning, or propaganda, this tradition talks about the sound actuality of this major figure of the Greek tradition within heart and head of the Roman empire. Beyond the Imperial tradition, nobody can ever doubt of the widespread diffusion of the imagery of Hercules (and its regional correlates) in the whole Roman world in Late

---

[36] S. RITTER, *Hercules in der römischen Kunst von den Anfängen bis Augustus*, Heidelberg 1995. Cf. also H. BOWDEN, L. RAWLINGS, *Herakles and Hercules. Exploring a Graeco-Roman Divinity,* Swansea 2005, 254. In this text I use the name *Herakles* when the stress is on Hellenic tradition, and *Hercules* when it refers to Roman and/or Latin context.

[37] The temple of *Hercules Musarum*, its reconstructions and reconsecrations, is also worth reference: L. RICHARDSON JR., *Hercules Musarum and the Porticus Philippi in Rome*, «AJA» 81 (1977)/3, 355-361.

[38] M. BERRY, *Hercules and Augustus Propertius 4.9: a political reading.* Research Master thesis, University of Tasmania, 2006; D. SPENCER, *Propertius, Hercules, and the Dynamics of Roman Mythic Space in Elegy 4.9*, «Arethusa» 34 (2001), 259-84.

Antiquity[39], a presence most of the time embedded in different types and levels of religious intention.

A supplemental challenge, however, is to evaluate how much of these representations of Herakles/Hercules convey religious meaning, or can be connected to ritual practices, or are expressions of the Greek tradition of hero myth and cult. Indeed, Hercules had such a religious status in many places and moments in the late Roman empire, including the Roman aristocracy of the IV century[40], that enables him to be considered, altogether with Asclepius, as the main surviving hero receiving cult in Late Antiquity. In broader political sense, one of the last relevant expressions of the Herculean tradition seem to have been the use of *Herculius* as a *cognomen* and as a military *signum*, first by Maximian (first as a Caesar, but then as Augustus) in the diarchy, by the times of Diocletian and Maximian, and later by Julianus Augustus, amid larger revivals of the heroic. In the diarchy, the correlation of *Jovius* and *Herculius* represented a formal operation grounded on clear symbolic meaning, especially in what concerns the imperial hierarchy and the tradition of hero cult and Greco-Roman religion[41]. There were, also, especial circumstances related to the history of Maximian and to the situation in the germanic provinces, after the period of the Gallic Empire (260-273) and the extensive use of herculean imagery by Postumus. In a context of recovery, it was of particular need to work on this inheritance[42]. As to the religious meaning of the signature of *Herculius* (and *Jovius*, as well), it is enough to remind the reaction of

---

[39] A wonderful analysis of such imagery, accompanied by its catalogue, appears in A. EPPINGER, *Hercules in der Spätantike Der Heros im Spannungsfeld von Heidentum und Christentum*, Heidelberg 2007 (M.A. Dissertation under supervision of Tonio Hölscher).

[40] See esp. the catacomb in *Via Latina*. M. JACZYNOWSKA, *Le Culte d'Hercule romain au temps du Haut-Empire*, in *ANRW* II 17/2, Berlin-New York, 1981, 661. Vettius Agorius Praetextatus was also *curialis Herculis* (*CIL* VI 1779a), although it is not clear if this was an active priesthood or a just one more honorific title. Cf. also AL. CAMERON, *The Last Pagans in Rome*, in *The Transformations of VRBS ROMA in Late Antiquity*, ed W.V. HARRIS, JRS suppl. 33, Portsmouth RI 1999, 110 f. 112, and P. BRUGGISSER, *Symmaque et la memoire d'Hercule*, «Historia» 38 (1989), 380-383.

[41] Marcel Simon considered that the use of the signum of Hercules in the diarchy and the tetrarchy «could be called heracleology and served as a doctrinal basis for the cult of the hero»; M. SIMON, *Early Christianity and Pagan Thought: Confluences and Conflicts*, «Religious Studies» 9 (1973)/4, 385-399, esp. 397.

[42] R. REES, *The Emperors' New Names. Diocletian Jovius and Maximian Herculius*, in H. BOWDEN, L. RAWLINGS, *Herakles and Hercules...*, 223-239.

Lactantius, in his *De Mortibus Persecutorum* (of 314-315)[43]; celebrating Christian triumph in the earlier Constantinian times, he perceived the end of the tetrarchic rule, and of the consequent use of those *signa* (...even after c. 25 years!), as a theodicy, punning the hybristic use of such titles[44]. So, even if we speculate on some remote shades of cultural and religious contact between Pagan and Christian with the adoption of a divine father-son representation to describe the head of the empire[45], the clearer result of that was, in the first instance, one more step in the confrontation, a burden increased by the historical context of the great persecutions.

The last ground of the late antique history of the hero cult concerns the particular features of heroic religion in Julianus's age. Although his philosophical and theological concernments were much more motivated by the developed forms of late antique neoplatonism, Julianus, as a defender of the traditional Greek patrimony, couldn't avoid assuming names, formulas, symbols, and postulates belonging to the heroic culture. In his work, there isn't a hint of reception of Philostratus, or of such a level of concernment with heroic religion, but, nevertheless, he stands in defense of the positive effects of the heroic models in a classical paideia, and adheres to the canonic forms of heroic representation of the age, Hercules and Asclepius. Also, he restituted the *signa* of *Jovius* and *Herculius*, what granted him supplemental troubles with part of his troops[46]. Besides the honors paid to Hercules in his Hymn to the Sun, it seems that the major compromise of the emperor Julianus with hero cult was his defense of Asclepius against Christ, in his *Contra Galileos* (1387): «Asclepius heals our bodies, and the Muses with the aid of Asclepius and Apollo and Hermes, the god of eloquence, train our souls»[47]; this program fed the unsuccessful efforts of restoration of the temple os Asclepius in Tarsus, which best represents the policy of Julianus on hero cult, in the frame of his general policy towards Greek temples and ritualistics. As a healing hero, Asclepius was,

---

[43] P. MONAT, *La polémique de Lactance contre Hercule. Tradition orientale et culture occidentale*, in *Hommages à Lucien Lerat 2*, ed. H. WALTER, Paris 1984, 575-583.

[44] R. REES, *The Emperors' New Names...*, 225-226.

[45] H. MATTING, *Jovius and Hercules*, «Harv. Theol. Rev.» 45 (1952), 131-134, refuted by F. KOLB, *Preasens Deus: Kaiser und Gott unter der Tetrarchie*, in *Diokletian und die Tetrarchie. Aspekte einer Zeitenwende*, ed. A. DEMANDT ET AL., Berlin-New York 2004, 33.

[46] D. WOODS, *The Emperor Julian and the Passion of Sergius and Bacchus*, «Journal of Early Christian Studies» 5 (1997)/3, 335-367, esp. 348.

[47] Also *Oration* 4, 144b, where Julianus, as here, opposes Asclepius to Christ; and 153b for Asclepius the saviour.

indeed, in permanent route of collision with Christ the healer, and that, more than syncretism or more than a key for eventual transcultural transformations, meant a territory of dispute and conflict. As a late trait of herculean signals, it was in the Battle on the River Frigidus, in September 5 and 6, 394, the last time in antiquity an army marched under the standard of Hercules[48]. In Late Antiquity battlefields it is not clear if the combat was between men, heroes or gods, or heroes and God, but it is clear that the end was decided after several sets of contacts, confrontations, mimesis, translation, and refusal, which properly shaped the face of Christianity after the IV century.

There is a subsection of the ancient Greek hero cult tradition, the tomb cult, that could survive intermingled with other Christian beliefs and behaviors, but that is a different phenomenon. After the IV century, the practice of hero cult was fated to survive just as a small and ever declining share of medieval cryptopaganism, related much more to the Hermetic pray of the king, the wise man and the magician. Devoid of its religious and social consequences, the heroic tradition could survive as a myth, and, as such, assuming heterogeneous narrative forms and functions, what includes also the cosmologies, and visual patterns so wisely studied by Aby Warburg in his *Atlas Mnemosyne*[49]. The heroic myth could survive, as well, in the broad heroic imagery of the indo-european community, including its persian and hindi counterparts and, lately, the Americas, but especially in the world of the ruling aristocracies in Europe. Then, heroic tradition, as a myth, became one of the core traditions of art history, the imagery of the city, and the expression of power. That historical fortune was the most beautiful epitaph produced for this personage, after many centuries of heroic performance in the Mediterranean: the *late* antique hero.

---

[48] THEODORET, *Hist. Eccles.*, 5, 24, 4.

[49] A. WARBURG, *The renewal of pagan antiquity: contributions to the cultural history of the European Renaissance*. Los Angeles 1999.

**«Contiene in se stesso i germi
delle più vere critiche future»**

Maijastina Kahlos

The importance of being pagan

It has been remarked that «Late Antiquity saw, as a tool of Christianization, the creation of "paganism"»[1]. I will discuss – using a few cases from the fourth and fifth centuries – what the pagans were needed for and the use of paganism in Christian texts. In other words, I will consider the use of polytheism and polytheistic practices in Christian literature for creating and polarizing cognitive boundaries between Christian and non-Christian. This demarcation of boundaries was part of the project of constructing and clarifying Christianity in the constantly changing circumstances of the fourth and fifth centuries.

As is well known, there was no such thing as a uniform religion called paganism in Greco-Roman antiquity but rather a wide assortment of diverse cults and beliefs, practices and attitudes (therefore, the words pagan and paganism are to be read as if in inverted commas throughout this article). Nonetheless, it was convenient for Christian polemicists to group religious rivals together under a single blanket-term[2].

Pagans and paganism were needed in the demarcation of boundaries. This demarcation was done with regard to doctrine as well as rituals. By treating rival religions and practices as a collective concept, Christian writers aimed at defining Christianity. Paganism functioned as a mirror for Christianity. However, this polarizing view restricted the possibility for nuance in Christian identity: Christian authors simplified the religious other but at the same time they of course simplified Christians themselves as well.

---

[1] R. Rothaus, *Christianization and De-Paganization: The Late Antique Creation of a Conceptual Frontier*, in *Shifting Frontiers in Late Antiquity*, eds. R.W. Mathisen, H.S. Sivan, Aldershot 1996, 299-307, esp. 305.
[2] For the conceptual birth of paganism, see M. Kahlos, *Debate and Dialogue. Pagan and Christian Cultures c. 360-430*, Aldershot 2007, 18-26.

1. Vigilantius, Jerome and Burning Tapers

My first example comes from Vigilantius, a fourth-century presbyter, who is known to have written a work (around 400) in which he attacked several practices common in the mainstream church, for example, the reverence paid to the relics of holy men, vigils held in honour of martyrs and the burning of tapers (candles)[3]. His attack is not extant but fragments are known through Jerome's reply *Contra Vigilantium* in which Jerome attacks his rival.

In an interesting passage Jerome quotes Vigilantius who labels burning tapers as well as kissing and worshipping the relics of martyrs as pagan practices: «Under the cloak of religion (*sub praetextu religionis*) we see almost pagan rituals (*prope ritum gentilium*) introduced into the churches: while the sun is still shining, masses of tapers are lighted, and everywhere a little bit of powder *(pulvisculum)*, wrapped up in a costly cloth, is kissed and worshipped. People of this sort pay great honour to the blessed martyrs, who, they think, are to be made glorious by skimpy tapers...»[4].

Here pagans and the label of paganism are used as a means of condemning the rivalling views of what is a proper, correct and decent Christian practice or belief. Jerome takes great pains to refute Vigilantius' views and labels him a heretic. (That is another method of reviling a rival). Jerome states that Christians never adore martyrs or any humans as gods. Concerning the burning of tapers in honour of martyrs, Jerome admits that some persons, being ignorant and simple-minded laymen (*aliqui per imperitiam et simplicitatem saecularium hominum*) or, in any event, religious women (*vel certe religiosarum feminarum*) have zeal for God but not according to knowledge (*non secundum scientiam*) and adopt this practice in honour of the martyrs. «But what harm is thereby done to you?», Jerome asks Vigi-

---

[3] Vigilantius was possibly protesting against the cult of martyrs advocated by Victricius of Rouen in *Praising the Saints* (*De laude sanctorum*, ed. J. MULDERS, in CCSL 64, Turnhout 1985). G. CLARK, *Christianity and Roman Society*, Cambridge 2004, 58. Clark sees the form of veneration of saints expressed by Victricius as extreme for the time. For Victricius, Vigilantius and Jerome, see also C. WALKER BYNUM, *The Resurrection of the body in Western Christianity, 200-1336*, New York 1995, 93-107.

[4] HIER. *c. Vigil.* 4, 7: «Prope ritum gentilium videmus sub praetextu religionis introductum in ecclesiis, sole adhuc fulgente, moles cereorum accendi, et ubicumque pulvisculum nescio quod, in modico vasculo pretioso linteamine circumdatum osculantes adorant. Magnum honorem praebent huiusmodi homines beatissimis martyribus, quos putant de vilissimis cereolis illustrandos; quos Agnus, qui est in medio throni cum omni fulgore maiestatis suae, illustrat».

lantius[5]. Jerome defends the rituals of these people, writing that «all those who light these tapers have their reward according to their faith» and asks whether Vigilantius calls these kinds of people idolaters (*Idololatras appellas huiusmodi homines?*). Jerome admits that not all those who believe in Christ have passed from the error of idolatry (*de idololatriae errore*). However, he continues, their former worship of idols should not deter Christians from worshipping the Christian God now. Christians should not be afraid of having similar rituals and abstain from the rituals for fear of appearing to worship the Christian God similarly to idols (*ne simili eum videamur cum idolis honore venerari*). The ritual observed for idols is to be abhorred but the same ritual observed for the martyrs is to be allowed (*Illud fiebat idolis, et idcirco detestandum est; hoc fit martyribus et idcirco recipiendum est*)[6].

Here we have two representatives of the ecclesiastical elite disputing over the authority of defining what is acceptable and what is not. Jerome verifies his interpretation of the proper Christian cult with arguments of authority: from the authority of Christian emperors such as Constantius II and Arcadius, promoting the cult of martyrs, as well as from the authority of the bishop of Rome, offering «sacrifices to the Lord», as Jerome puts it, «over the venerable bones of the deceased Peter and Paul»[7].

Jerome was by no means lenient in regard to the demarcation of boundaries. As is well known, he was keen on fixing cognitive boundaries between the acceptable Christian behaviour elsewhere in his writing, for instance, by forbidding the reading of classical literature, especially poetry, and branding his rivals as dedicated to idolatry and the cult of demons. He regarded classical poetry, secular philosophy and rhetoric as the food of

---

[5] HIER. *c. Vigil.* 7: «Quod si aliqui per imperitiam, et simplicitatem saecularium hominum, vel certe religiosarum feminarum, de quibus vere possumus dicere: "Confiteor, zelum dei habent, sed non secundum scientiam", hoc pro honore martyrum faciunt, quid inde perdis?». The «zeal for God» is a reference to *Rom*. 10, 2.

[6] HIER. *c. Vigil.* 7: «Et quicumque accendunt cereos, secundum fidem suam habent merdecem, dicente Apostolo: "Unusquisque in suo sensu abundet" [Rom. 14:5]. Idololatras appellas huiusmodi homines? Non diffiteor omnes nos qui in Christo credimus de idololatriae errore venisse. Non enim nascimur, sed renascimur christiani. Et quia quondam colebamus idola, nunc deum colere non debemus; ne simili eum videamur cum idolis honore venerari? Illud fiebat idolis, et idcirco detestandum est; hoc fit martyribus et idcirco recipiendum es».

[7] HIER. *c. Vigil.* 8: «Male facit ergo Romanus episcopus, qui super mortuorum hominum Petri et Pauli, secundum nos ossa veneranda, secundum te vilem pulvisculum, offert domino sacrificial, et tumulos eorum Christi arbitrator altaria?».

demons and insisted upon the choice between «the chalice of Christ» and «the chalice of demons» (*calicem Christi et calicem daemoniorum*)[8].

Ecclesiastical leaders aimed at creating a conceptual and intellectual frontier between the Christian and the pagan: in order to clarify what made Christians Christian they needed a division between things Christian and things pagan[9]. In the case of martyr cults Jerome's boundaries ran along different lines from those set by Vigilantius.

There are a number of similar cases concerning rituals practiced in fourth- and fifth-century Christian communities that Christian bishops and prominent writers condemned as superstitious or pagan. These constructions of reality served to redefine and reinforce the sort of Christianity that these church leaders advocated. To reinforce proper Christian conduct was to cordon off what was defined as pagan.

For instance, in the case of the funerary and martyr cults, the need to draw boundaries led church leaders such as Ambrose of Milan and Augustine of Hippo to condemn funerary banquets as inappropriate for Christians[10]. The funerary customs or rituals of the cult of martyrs that they disapproved of for various reasons were labelled as pagan, superstitious and demonic practices. Augustine, for example, stated that the dances at the *martyria* were performed to worship and delight demons (that is, the Greco-Roman gods)[11]. Ordinary Christians taking part in local popular

---

[8] HIER. *epist.* 21, 13. «Daemonum cibus est carmina poetarum, saecularis sapientia, rhetoricorum pompa verborum», and *epist.* 22, 29: «Tamen simul bibere non debemus calicem Christi et calicem daemoniorum».

[9] Cf. R. ROTHAUS, *Christianization...*, 299-307.

[10] Ambrose forbade Christians to offer food and wine at the tombs and justified his prohibition with two arguments: first, there should be no opportunity for drunkenness, and second, the habit of offering food and wine at the tombs of the martyrs was too similar to the superstition of pagans, the *Parentalia* (AUG. *conf.* 6, 2, 2). Gaudentius of Brescia (*tract.* 4, 14) also condemned the feasting of *Parentalia* as the foremost error of idolatry. *S. Gaudentii episcopi Brixiensis tractatus*, ed. A. GLÜCK, in CSEL 68, Wien 1936. For the disapproval of church fathers towards funeral feasting, see M. KAHLOS, *Comissationes et ebrietates. Church leaders against banqueting at* martyria *and at tombs*, in *Studi in onore di Anne Helttula*, ed. O. MERISALO, R. VAINIO, Jyväskylä 2007, 13-23.

[11] AUG. *sermo* 311, 6: «Cum ergo modo hic ista Deo propitio non fiant, quia non celebramus daemoniis ludos, ubi solent ista fieri in eorum delectationem qui coluntur, et immunditia sua solent suos depravare cultores, sed celebratur hic sanctitas et solemnitas martyrum».

feasting at the tombs and *martyria*, on the other hand, regarded their funerary customs and martyr cult as completely and properly Christian[12].

2. Maximus of Turin and Kalendae Ianuariae

My second example comes from the fifth-century discussion on the celebration of *Kalendae Ianuariae* (the New Year) and *Saturnalia* that in Late Antiquity formed an extensive and socially important series of feasts at the turn of the year. The bishop of Turin, Maximus, condemns the celebration of *Kalendae Ianuariae* and *Saturnalia*, in which his parishioners are accustomed to take part, as gloomy superstitions of errors (*inter ipsas tenebrosas superstitiones errorum*). The nativity of the Lord, Christmas, occurs exactly midway between these errors in order to shine the true light. Maximus denounces the festivities of pagans (*gentilium festivitates*; *vanitas gentilium*) as sacrilege, superstition, drunkenness (*ebrietas*) and intemperance (*lascivia*). He stresses that the one who has fellowship with the vanity of pagans shall not have communion with the truth of the saints (*qui societatem habuerit cum vanitate gentilium, copulam non possit habere cum veritate sanctorum*)[13].

Thus, in a manner similar to Jerome and his chalices, Maximus of Turin insists upon the choice between things he regards as Christian and those he considers pagan or superstitious. In Maximus' case this includes refraining from the traditional banqueting with wine and food (*vino et epulis*) as well as from giving gifts (*strenae*) and taking auspices (*auspicia*)[14].

Maximus of Turin was by no means the only ecclesiastical leader to reprimand Christians for celebrating the Saturnalia and Kalendae Ianuariae. Augustine of Hippo rebukes Christians for having a good time during

---

[12] Aug. *ep.* 29, 8. For general discussion on the Christian funerary customs before the fourth century, see, e.g., H. Kotila, Memoria Mortuorum. *Commemoration of the Departed in Augustine*, Roma 1992, 65-73; P.A. Février, *Approches de fêtes chrétiennes (fin du IVe s. et Ve s.)*, in *La fête, pratique et discours d'Alexandre hellénistique a la mission de Besançon*, Paris 1981, 149; P.A. Février, *Le culte des morts dans les communautés chrétiennes durant le IIIe siècle*, in *Atti del IX congresso internazionale di archeologia cristiana, Roma 21-27 settembre 1975*, Roma 1978, 241-256, 271-274 and C. Lepelley, *Formes païennes de sociabilité en Afrique au temps de Saint Augustin*, in *Sociabilité, pouvoirs et société. Actes du Colloque de Rouen 24/26 nov. 1983*, éd. F. Thélamon, Rouen 1987, 101.

[13] Max. Taur. *sermo* 98, 1, quoting *2 Cor.* 6, 14.

[14] Max. Taur. *sermo* 98, 2-3.

the Kalendae Ianuariae as people had done in earlier generations – even as Christians[15]. Augustine compares the celebration of the Kalendae Ianuariae with offering incense to the demons (that is, the pagan gods). Again, defining and redefining the concept of being Christian was an issue of authority, in Maximus' and Augustine's case authority over congregation[16]. With his episcopal authority Maximus redefines what constitutes appropriate behaviour for Christians. Since the construction of a Christian identity was done in reference to a perceived «other», pagans were vital in this cognitive process. In John Chrysostom's words, «There would be no pagans if we were such Christians as we ought to be»[17].

We see early Christianity under constant negotiation. This negotiation has by no means ended – it continues even today. Just to mention one example that comes from recent events in Finland: an ethnographic museum organised for school children workshops on the Latin American rituals of the cult of the dead[18]. Then, some parents objected to these workshops, maintaining that teachers should not take their pupils there (or at least that they should ask permission from the parents first): these Lutheran parents insisted that their children should not take part in what they thought were pagan and demonic superstitions. There was a lively dispute in newspapers, in the editorials and on the internet. Then, in the whirlpool of the dispute, it was pointed out that, in fact, these so-called pagan and demonic superstitions were part of the Christian rituals of Catholic Latin Americans. Thus, we see that pagans are needed even today in the construction of the idea of a Christian self – in this case a Lutheran self[19].

---

[15] AUG. *sermo* 198, 3.

[16] For the issue of authority, see P. BROWN, *Christianization and religious conflict*, in *The Late Empire, A.D. 337-425. The Cambridge Ancient History* 13, eds. A. CAMERON, P. GARNSEY, Cambridge 1998, 662-663; P. BROWN, *Authority and the Sacred. Aspects of the Christianization of the Roman World*, Cambridge 1995, 23-24 and T.E. KLUTZ, *The Rhetoric of Science in The Rise of Christianity: A Response to Rodney Stark's Sociological Account of Christianization*, «Journal of Early Christian Studies» 6 (1998)/2, 183-184.

[17] IOH. CHRYS. *hom.* 10 in 1 Tim. 3.

[18] The museum is *Helinä Rautavaaran museo*; see the internet home page http://www.helinamuseo.fi/.

[19] Cf. J.Z. SMITH, *Drudgery Divine. On the Comparison of Early Christianities and the Religions of Late Antiquity*, London 1990, 43, who remarks that, in the modern comparison of early Christianity and the religions of Late Antiquity, the latter have often become «code-words for Roman Catholicism and it is the Protestant catalogue of the central characteristics of Catholicism, from which it dissents, which provides the categories for comparison with Late Antiquity».

GIANFRANCO AGOSTI

Cristianizzazione della poesia greca e dialogo interculturale

È possibile misurare l'influenza di *The Conflict between Pagans and Christians in the Fourth Century AD* anche in un settore un po' inatteso degli studi, quello della storia letteraria tardoantica, dove per decenni si è recepita una visione conflittuale dei rapporti fra gruppi religiosi e culturali della Tarda Antichità, privilegiando le opposizioni ideologiche come sono presentate dalle fonti, soprattutto dalle fonti cristiane, e accreditando anche equivalenze esclusive del tipo «classico» = «pagano», e dunque «cristiano» = «non classico»[1]. È noto che negli ultimi anni, grazie alla *esplosione* del paradigma «postmoderno» del Tardoantico[2], il modello conflittuale, che si era iniziato a intendere in modo meno rigido a partire dagli anni '70, è stato spesso modificato[3], e termini come «dialogo», «coa-

---

[1] E nelle storie della letteratura greca si continua di regola a perpetuare il modello che separa nettamente la letteratura «pagana» da quella cristiana. Assai opportunamente avverte S. Averincev, *L'anima e lo specchio. L'universo della poetica bizantina*, ed. it. Bologna 1988, 329-330: «Quando si parla di poetica antico-bizantina è particolarmente importante assumere a pari titolo materiale pagano e cristiano; in tal modo affiorerà il carattere oggettivo delle forme della cultura sottomesse a necessità interna ed entro un certo limite indipendenti da ciò che avviene nella testa del lettore». Personalmente sono profondamente convinto che in una storia della letteratura greca tardoantica non avrebbe senso separare gli autori sulla base della confessione religiosa.

[2] Una bella analisi dello sviluppo di questo paradigma storiografico e delle recenti controversie si trova in due recenti contributi di P. Athanassiadi, *Antiquité tardive: construction et déconstruction d'un modèle historiographique*, in «Antiquité Tardive» 14 (2006), 311-324 e in A. Marcone, *A Long Late Antiquity? Considerations on a Controversial Periodization*, in «Journal of Late Antiquity» 1 (2008), 4-19.

[3] Sino a giungere ad affermazioni recise, come «the construction of a fierce battle between opposing forces or even a religious war is entirely modern» (P. van Minnen, *The Letters (and Other Papers) of Ammon: Panopolis in the Fourth Century A.D.*, in *Perspectives on Panopolis*, a cura di A. Egberts, P.B. Muhs e J. van der Vliet, Leiden-Boston-Köln 2002, 177-199, spec. 181). Per la progressiva definizione del concetto di una «zona grigia» intermedia fra pagani e cristiani si veda M. Kahlos, *Dialogue and Debate: Christian and Pagan Cultures c. 360-430*, Aldershot 2007, 26-41; Ead.,

bitazione», «interazione» si sono imposti anche nella ricerca letteraria, soprattutto nell'analisi della grande letteratura storica e oratoria. Questo modello ermeneutico (anch'esso, peraltro, non esente da ripensamenti) è stato tuttavia poco applicato alla produzione poetica, che è ancora prevalentemente studiata da un punto di vista strettamente filologico, nonostante alcuni importanti lavori di studiosi come Alan Cameron, Glen Bowersock, Pierre Chuvin[4].

Nel libro curato da Momigliano la poesia è praticamente assente[5]: non è fatto di cui stupirsi. Nel dibattito sul rifiuto ideologico, o sull'accettazione pragmatica della cultura classica da parte dei Cristiani nell'Oriente tardoantico, essa all'epoca non rivestiva ruolo alcuno, visti anche i pregiudizi sul suo valore letterario e la sua oggettiva inferiorità quantitativa rispetto alla prosa. A parte la poesia epica e mitologica, etichettata senz'altro come pagana, opere come i *Centoni* eudociani o la *Parafrasi del vangelo di Giovanni* di Nonno di Panopoli, o anche i poemi di Gregorio di Nazianzo, difficilmente erano considerati qualcosa di diverso da un semplice *divertissement* letterario, o – nel migliore dei casi – da una episodica, ovvero nostalgica, compromissione con la cultura profana a fini puramente estetici. Cinquant'anni più tardi, il lavoro editoriale e di esegesi della poesia classicistica tardoantica[6], così come la rivalutazione dal punto di vista letterario della produzione cristiana[7], hanno cambiato pro-

---

Forbearance and Compulsion. The Rethoric of Religious Tolerance and Intolerance in Late Antiquity, London 2009.

[4] Di Cameron ricordo, fra gli altri, due articoli che in qualche modo delimitano un periodo degli studi: AL. CAMERON, *Wandering Poets. A Literary Movement in Byzantine Egypt*, «Historia» 14 (1965), 470-509; AL. CAMERON, *Poets and Pagans in Byzantine Egypt*, in *Egypt in the Byzantine World 300-700*, a cura di R. BAGNALL, Cambridge 2007, 21-46; e i libri assai innovativi di G.W. BOWERSOCK, *Hellenism in Late Antiquity*, Ann Arbor 1990 e di P. CHUVIN, *Chronique des derniers païens*, Paris 1990. Le edizioni della *Parafrasi* nonniana promosse da E. LIVREA (vd. *infra* nota 63) uniscono alla severa analisi filologica una notevole attenzione alla contestualizzazione storica, indispensabile per capire un poeta così complesso.

[5] Eccezion fatta per una allusione agli *Inni* di Sinesio nell'articolo di HENRI-IRENÉE MARROU, e per la citazione degli *Epigrammata Bobiensia* del *Carmen contra Paganos* nel lavoro di HERBERT BLOCH.

[6] Soprattutto in Francia e in Italia (le edizioni dei poemi di Nonno, dirette da F. VIAN, P. CHUVIN, E. LIVREA, D. GIGLI; e quelle di poeti «minori», a cura E. LIVREA e di J.-L. FOURNET).

[7] Si veda per un penetrante bilancio generale AV. CAMERON, *New Themes and Styles in Greek Literature, A Title Revised*, in *Greek Literature in Late Antiquity. Dynamism, Didacticism, Classicism*, a cura di S.F. JOHNSON, Aldershot 2006, 11-28.

fondamente la visione della poesia greca dei secoli IV-VI d.C[8]. Al punto che oggi si è più disposti a riconoscere che anche una letteratura altamente formalizzata come quella in versi era concepita per rispondere a questioni di ordine pratico, tanto da poter essere veicolo di rappresentazione di ideali di comportamento e di programmi al tempo stesso religiosi e culturali.

Vorrei dunque mostrare, attraverso una selezione necessariamente sommaria delle questioni, l'apporto che la poesia cristiana greca dei sec. IV e V può dare alla questione del «dialogo» (o del «conflitto») fra pagani e cristiani.

1. Cristianizzazione come classicismo

La poesia cristiana greca in metri classici[9], dopo alcuni incerti tentativi epigrafici e innici, nasce compiutamente alla metà del IV secolo in Egitto con caratteristiche *tematiche* già ben definite e senza quelle preoccupazioni di giustificazione, che invece mostra verso la fine del secolo Gregorio di Nazianzo (autore pure di un *corpus* di più di sedicimila versi). Sul piano formale la poesia cristiana in Egitto non mostra alcuna incertezza nell'adozione del linguaggio e delle *strutture retoriche* dell'epica profana. È grazie a tale adattamento che, ad es., può accadere di rilevare una identità

---

[8] Panorami recenti: D. GIGLI, *Nonno di Panopoli. Le Dionisiache. Canti I-XII*, Milano 2003, 8-13; M. HOSE, *Poesie aus der Schule. Überlegungen zur spätgriechischen Dichtung*, München 2004 (poco aggiornato e adugggiato da vecchi stereotipi); AL. CAMERON, *Poetry and Literary Culture in Late Antiquity*, in *Approaching Late Antiquity*, a cura di S. SWAIN e M. EDWARDS, Oxford 2004, 327-3; G. AGOSTI, *La voce dei libri: dimensioni performative dell'epica greca tardoantica*, in *Approches de la Troisième Sophistique. Hommage J. Schamp*, a cura di E. AMATO, A. RODUIT e M. STEINRÜCK, Bruxelles 2006, 33-62; sulla poesia egiziana vd. ora L. MIGUÈLEZ CAVERO, *Poems in Context: Greek Poetry in the Egyptian Thebaid 200-600 AD*, Berlin-New York 2008.

[9] Esametri, distici e giambici principalmente: ho tentato un esame complessivo di questa produzione in alcuni recenti lavori, G. AGOSTI, *L'epica biblica nella tarda antichità greca. Autori e lettori nel IV e V secolo*, in *La scrittura infinita. Bibbia e poesia in età medioevale e umanistica*, a cura di F. STELLA, Firenze 2001, 67-104; ID., *Late Antique Iambics and iambikè idéa*, in *Iambic Ideas. Essays on a Poetic Tradition from Archaic Greece tao the Late Roman Empire*, a cura di A. ALONI, A. BARCHIESI e A. CAVARZERE, Lanham-Boulder-New York-London 2001, 217-254; si veda anche AL. CAMERON, *Poetry and Literary Culture...*, 333-339. Minoritaria, ma di grande livello, la produzione in metri ionici (gli *Inni* di Sinesio) e quella delle anacreontiche della cerchia di Gaza (edite e commentate da F. CICCOLELLA, *Cinque poeti bizantini*, Alessandria 2000). Tralascio, per motivi di spazio, di trattare degli esperimenti accentuativi e della linea che porterà alle omelie versificate di Romano.

di strutture fra testi lontanissimi come una pafrasi esegetica in versi di *Genesi* 4.13-14, contenuta in un papiro della fondazione Bodmer (*P.Bodmer* 33) e un passo delle *Dionisiache* di Nonno di Panopoli (2.114-162)[10]: nel poemetto cristiano (metà del IV sec. d.C.) Caino non sa dove nascondersi dopo il suo terribile delitto e lamenta che cercherà inutilmente rifugio nella terra, nel mare, nel cielo. Il passo delle *Dionisiache* (metà del V sec. d.C.) presenta l'accorato discorso di una ninfa Amadriade, che cerca di scappare allo sconvolgimento cosmico portato da Tifeo ipotizzando di nascondersi nelle colline, sui monti, in mare, in aria o persino sottoterra. In ambedue i testi ricorrono i medesimi *topoi*, la stessa struttura con l'interrogazione patetica (πῇ... πῇ, «dove... dove»?), la ripetizione di πῇ δὲ φύγω («dove posso fuggire?») e due parti dominate prima dal motivo del *luogo in cui nascondersi* e poi dal motivo della *metamorfosi*[11]. Naturalmente non si tratta di un rapporto diretto, di imitazione: i due poeti utilizzano la medesima struttura retorica che avevano appreso a scuola, quella dell'etopea[12], alla quale era pressoché obbligatorio ricorrere per descrivere con patetismo un discorso[13], e che il pubblico si aspettava di riconoscere. Il poeta cristiano si limita ad adattare a un contenuto nuovo il *linguaggio* su cui si era formato e che evidentemente non aveva motivo di cambiare. L'autore del *P. Bodmer* non era un letterato di primissima qualità: ma proprio il confronto con Nonno mostra che utilizza le strutture retoriche tradizionali non per incapacità creativa, ma per obbligata adesione alle regole del genere. Analoga osservanza della *generic composition*, del resto, si trova in un poeta cristiano di ben altra levatura come Gregorio di Nazianzo, che ad es. nel carme a Vitaliano (*carm.* 2.2.3, *PG* 37.1480-1505), epistola in esametri rivolta dai figli diseredati a un alto funzionario statale

---

[10] Una discussione più estesa e il confronto analitico fra i due testi si trova in G. Agosti, *L'etopea nella poesia greca tardoantica*, in ΗΘΟΠΟΙΙΑ. *La représentation des caractères dans la littérature de l'Antiquité Tardive*, a cura di E. Amato e J. Schamp, Fribourg-Salerno 2005, 33-60.

[11] Per il passo di Nonno si veda anche F. Vian, *Nonnos de Panopolis. Les Dionysiaques. Chants I-II*, Paris 1976, 73-74.

[12] Basata sul riprodurre le possibili parole pronunciate da un personaggio (mitologico, storico o fittizio) in una situazione critica; si tratta di uno dei προγυμνάσματα, «esercizi preliminari», base dell'insegnamento scolastico.

[13] In questo caso le parole di un personaggio che cerca di fuggire: qualcosa come τίνας ἂν λόγους εἴποι ὁ δεῖνα ἐκφυγεῖν θέλων «che cosa potrebbe dire uno che vuole fuggire?». Dal punto di vista letterario la situazione ha origine in passi tragici come, *ex. gr.*, Eur. *Or.* 1375-1380 (discorso di un servitore frigio di Elena).

per chiederne il perdono, costruisce il suo lungo carme esattamente come una *suasoria*[14].

L'episodica messa in discussione da parte cristiana dell'insegnamento basato sulla παιδεία tradizionale[15] non ha portato a proporre (almeno per quanto risulta dalla nostra documentazione) un sistema realmente alternativo a quello tradizionale: semmai è più spesso ribadita l'opportunità di servirsi della cultura profana anche in prospettiva antagonistica (è la posizione espressa da Socrate, *HE* 3.16.1-7 nel giudizio sulle parafrasi degli Apollinarii)[16]. Su tale scia si colloca anche la posizione di Gregorio di Nazianzo, che mostra al contempo come per la poesia cristiana la questione di fondo non fosse espressiva, ma ovviamente tematica. È assai esplicita a tal proposito la *recusatio* nel carme *in silentium ieiunii* 2.1.34a.71-78, *PG* 37.1312-1313, che nel 382 delinea gli ambiti tematici del poeta cristiano:

μέλπω δ' οὐ Τροίην, οὐκ εὔπλοον οἷά τις Ἀργώ,
   οὐδὲ συὸς κεφαλὴν, οὐ πολὺν Ἡρακλέα,
οὐ γῆς εὐρέα κύκλα ὅπως πελάγεσσιν ἄρηρεν,
   οὐκ αὐγὰς λιθάκων, οὐ δρόμον οὐρανίων·
75 οὐδὲ πόθων μέλπω μανίην, καὶ κάλλος ἐφήβων,
   οἷσι λύρη μαλακὸν κρούετ' ἀπὸ προτέρων.
μέλπω δ' ὑψιμέδοντα Θεὸν μέγαν, ἠδὲ φαεινῆς
   εἰς ἓν ἀγειρομένης λάμψιν ἐμῆς Τριάδος...[17]

---

[14] Vd. K. DEMOEN, «*I Am a Skilful Poet*». *Persuasion and Demonstration in Gregory Nazianzen's Ad Vitalianum*, in *Approches de la Troisième Sophistique...*, 431-440. In questo lungo carme sono presenti anche etopee. Per la presenza delle strutture declamatorie nella prosa di Gregorio si veda ora C. MILANOVIC, *Sailing to Sophistopolis: Gregory of Nazianzus and Greek Declamation*, «Journal of Early Christian Studies» 13 (2005), 187-232.

[15] Si veda negli Atti di questo convegno la relazione di GIOVANNI ALBERTO CECCONI, *Contenuti religiosi delle discipline scolastiche e prassi d'insegnamento come terreno di conflitto politico-culturale. Alcune annotazioni*, che pone importanti questioni da questo punto di vista.

[16] I quali per reagire all'editto giulianeo avrebbero composto prodigiose parafrasi secondo i principali generi letterari classici (epos, tragedie, dialoghi platonici) delle Scritture. Le fonti principali, non concordi fra di loro, sono Socrate e Sozomeno (*HE* 5,18): ho discusso più ampiamente queste testimonianze in G. AGOSTI, *L'epica biblica...* Sul passo di Socrate vd. H.-G. NESSELRATH, *Die Christen und die heidnische Bildung: Das Beispiel des Sokrates Scholastikos (hist. eccl. 3,16)*, in *Leitbilder der Spätantike – Eliten und Leitbilder*, a cura di J. DUMMER e M. VIELBERG, Stuttgart 1999, 79-100.

[17] «Non canto Troia, né come altri Argo veloce, né la testa del cinghiale, né il forte Eracle, né come l'ampio cerchio della terra sia connesso al mare, né lo splendore delle pietre, né il corso degli astri; non canto la follia amorosa, la bellezza dei giovani, per i quali molle suonava la lira degli antichi. Canto Dio grande che regna nei cieli, lo splendore della mia lucente Trinità che si raccoglie nell'Uno...». Sul passo si veda K.

Nessuna concessione alla materia iliadica, del tipo di quella cantata da Quinto Smirneo autore di *Posthomerica*, o da Taziano l'amico di Libanio autore di un fortunatissimo centone omerico[18]; del pari è dismessa la poesia argonautica, quella mitologica, quella cosmogonica e l'epos litologico o erotico[19]. L'unico oggetto degno di canto è Dio onnipotente, la Trinità, il Figlio e il mistero dell'incarnazione, il riscatto dell'uomo. La lingua e i generi della poesia di Gregorio sono peraltro assolutamente tradizionali: a parte la diversità tematica, che porta con sé anche una inevitabile costellazione di «tecnicismi» (evidente soprattutto negli epiteti divini)[20] e *mots-outils*[21], i suoi poemi sono connotati in sostanza il robusto esperimento di adattare al Cristianesimo il *classicismo*, inteso come condivisione e accettazione delle forme espressive classiche. Una caratteristica condivisa da tutta la poesia cristiana dei secoli IV-VI, ciò che spiega fra l'altro perché in certi ambienti più conservatori la poesia sia stata guardata con sospetto[22]: l'adozione del linguaggio convenzionale poteva essere considerata come pericolosa idolatria letteraria. In realtà – lo vedremo più avanti – ai detrattori, che vedevano l'aspetto bellettristico come una forma di criptopaganesimo, sfuggiva, o non interessava, il suo carattere saliente, vale a dire la possibilità di instaurare un dialogo con chi si riteneva depositario di quel linguaggio convenzionale.

Parlare semplicemente di classicismo per la poesia cristiana greca reca anche il vantaggio sul piano storiografico di riconoscere, al di là dei nostri giudizi e dei nostri gusti, che opere come i poemetti del codice Bodmer, quelli dell'imperatrice Eudocia (V sec.), del notaio Dioscoro di Afrodito

---

DEMOEN, *The Attitude towards Greek Poetry in the Verse of Gregory Nazianzen*, in *Early Christian Poetry. A Collection of Essays*, a cura di J. DEN BOEFT e A. HILHORST, Leiden-New York-Köln 1993, 240-242; G. AGOSTI, rec. a D. Gigli, «Atene&Roma» 38 (1994), 30.

[18] Liban. *Epist.* 990, 2-3; 11,120-121 Foerster.

[19] Generi attestati nel IV e V secolo: lo testimoniano le *Argonautiche orfiche* (V sec.), i πάτρια di Hermupolis noti come *Cosmogonia di Strasburgo* (IV sec.), e i *Lithica* orfici (IV sec.); per l'epos erotico Gregorio poteva avere in mente le gigantesche *Teogamie Eroiche* di Pisandro (III sec.).

[20] Si veda ad es. C. MORESCHINI e D.A. SYKES, *St Gregory of Nazianzus* Poemata Arcana, Oxford 1997, *passim*.

[21] Com'è il caso di termini come Ade, Erebo etc. Per una documentazione vd. G.L. PRESTIGE, *Hades in the Greek Fathers*, in «Journal of Theological Studies» 24 (1923), 476-485 e, per la poesia, il mio commento a NONN. *Par.* 5.97.

[22] Eloquenti le riserve di Nilo di Ancira nei confronti degli ἀκερδῆ τῶν ἐπῶν, delle inanità della poesia (*epist.* 2.49, *PG* 79.221, ad un monaco letterato).

(VI sec.), nelle intenzioni di chi le componeva erano «classiche» esattamente come il *Ratto di Elena* di Colluto (V-VI sec.), o la *Presa di Ilio* di Trifiodoro (IV sec.)[23]: i loro autori volevano fare della poesia classica, che il pubblico riconoscesse come tale. Il che, a sua volta, implica l'abbandono della tradizionale categoria ermeneutica «alto *vs* basso», in favore di una analisi che tenga contro degli orizzonti d'attesa del pubblico e dei *contesti* della poesia cristiana[24].

2. Forme e intenzioni della poesia cristiana nel IV secolo: il Codice delle Visioni

Naturalmente un simile approccio non è teso a ridimensionare le peculiarità tematiche della poesia cristiana, né ciò che la differenzia dall'epos profano. Anzi, il punto chiave è proprio l'individuzione della *specificità cristiana*, che risiede piuttosto nel passaggio da un'estetica autonoma ad una eteronoma, il cui scopo non è tanto la scontata sostituzione delle Muse col Cristo, quanto quello di mostrare le *altrettanto lecite* possibilità del soggetto cristiano espresso in metri classici.

Abbiamo sopra accennato al fatto che non ci sono stati modelli di scuola cristiana autonoma. È peraltro un fatto che gran parte della poesia cristiana greca pratica generi legati alla scuola, come la parafrasi e l'*ekphrasis*[25], ciò che – unitamente all'eccessivo credito dato alla storia sui due Apollinari e delle loro prodigiose parafrasi sotto Giuliano[26] – ha contribuito alla dismissione di questa poesia come generico «prodotto scolare', o addirittura nato per alternativi apprendimenti cristiani della lingua dell'epos (come se fossero una sorta di antesignani del programma educativo di Antonio Possevino). A parte la difficoltà di tracciare netti

---

[23] Anche se la metrica e la prosodia di questi poeti cristiani non è classica *stricto sensu*: analisi in G. AGOSTI e F. GONNELLI, *Materiali per la storia dell'esametro nei poeti cristiani greci*, in *Struttura e storia dell'esametro greco*, a cura di M. FANTUZZI e R. PRETAGOSTINI, I, Roma 1995, 289-434.

[24] Cfr. anche Av. CAMERON, *New Themes*..., 14-15. Si tratta anche di mettere da parte l'ottica della tradizionale filologia classica, che privilegia i rapporti con i modelli letterari e la permanenza della tradizione finendo così per accreditare l'immagine di una poesia libresca ed epigonale.

[25] I due maggiori rappresentanti del genere sono Giovanni di Gaza (ecfrasi della croce e della raffigurazione cosmica di un edificio di Gaza, V-VI sec.) e Paolo Silenziario (ecfrasi della chiesa di Santa Sofia a Costantinopoli); ma ci sono anche molti epigrammi ecfrastici cristiani conservati nell'*Antologia Palatina* o su supporto epigrafico.

[26] Vd. *supra* n. 16.

confini fra prodotti scolastici e prodotti influenzati dalla scuola, come ha mostrato in alcuni fondamentali lavori R. Cribiore[27], gli studi più recenti hanno mostrato come i poemi cristiani di Gregorio, di Nonno, dello Ps.-Apollinario, siano caratterizzati da un notevole impegno letterario ed esegetico che mal si accorda con la qualifica di testi scolastici. La questione di una poesia concepita per l'insegnamento di un epos cristiano alternativo a quello classico si è riproposta con la pubblicazione di un codice papiraceo del IV/V sec., conservato alla Bibliothèque Bodmer a Ginevra, una scoperta che ha permesso di farci un'idea molto più precisa della nascita della poesia cristiana in metri classici e di liberarci di alcuni luoghi comuni[28].

P.Bodmer 29-37 è un codice copiato da mani differenti, di formazione diacronica e perizia diseguale; esso conteneva le prime quattro visioni del Pastore di Erma (nei fogli perduti), e una serie di poemetti cristiani aperti dalla *Visio Dorothei* (di qui il nome di «codice delle visioni»): tutti poemetti sconosciuti, composti in esametri e in distici elegiaci e risalenti più o meno alla metà del IV secolo[29]. Le prime ipotesi avanzate (quando

---

[27] R. Cribiore, *Gymnastics of the Mind. Greek Education in Hellenistic and Roman Egypt*, Princeton 2001, 228-244; per il caso paradigmatico dell'etopea si veda G. Agosti, *L'etopea nella poesia ...*

[28] Edizione: *Papyrus Bodmer XXIX. Vision de Dorothéos*. Édité avec une introduction, une traduction et des notes par A. Hurst, O. Reverdin, J. Rudhardt. En appendice: Description et datation du Codex des Visions par R. Kasser et G. Cavallo, Cologny-Genève 1984; *Papyri Bodmer XXX-XXXVII. «Codex des Visions» Poèmes divers*, édités avec une introduction générale, des traductions et des notes par A. Hurst et J. Rudhardt, München 1999. Discuto più estesamente alcuni temi qui toccati in G. Agosti, *I poemetti del codice Bodmer e il loro ruolo nella storia della poesia tardoantica*, in *Le Codex des Visions,* a cura di A. Hurst - J. Rudhardt, Genève 2002, 73-114; Id., *Considerazioni preliminari sui generi letterari dei poemi del Codice Bodmer*, «Aegyptus» 81 (2001) [ma 2003], 115-147; Id., *Sul ruolo e la valutazione dei «minori» nella poesia tardoantica*, in *Incontri triestini di filologia classica V*, a cura di L. Cristante, Trieste 2006, 209-223.

[29] Ecco l'elenco degli otto testi (con le abbreviazioni usate nell'*ed. pr.*): *1. VD* = ὅρασις Δωροθέου, *Visione di Dorotheos* (P.Bodmer 29): 343 esametri (colofone: τέλος τῆς ὁράσεως / Δωροθέου Κυίντου ποιητοῦ. []). 2. *Abr.* = Πρὸς Ἀβραάμ, *Ad Abramo* (P.Bodmer 30): 30 esametri (acrostico; parafrasi di *Gen.* 22.1-19). 3. *J.* = Πρὸς δικαίους, *Ai Giusti* (P.Bodmer 31): 164 vv. (distici elegiaci sul male e la teodicea; al v. 160 Δω[ρόθ]εον Κύντου). 4. *Jes.* =]τοῦ δεσπότου Ἰησοῦ, *<Elogio> del Signore Gesù* (P.Bodmer 32): 25 esametri (acrostico). 5. *C.* = τί ἂν εἴποι ὁ Καιν ἀποκτείνας τὸν Ἀβελ; *Che cosa avrebbe detto Caino dopo l'assassinio di Abele* (P. Bodmer 33): 19 esametri (etopea, parafrasi di *Gen.* 4.13-14). 6. *D.* = ὁ δεσπότης πρὸς τοὺς πά[σχο]ντας, *Il Signore a coloro che soffrono* (P.Bodmer 34): 27 esametri (acrostico). 7. *A.* = τί ἂν εἴποι ὁ Ἀβελ ἀναιρηθεὶς ὑπὸ τοῦ Καιν; *Che cosa avrebbe detto Abele*

il codice era stato pubblicato solo parzialmente) suggerivano appunto la possibilità di un esercizio di scrittura (data l'eterogeneità delle mani e del contenuto) o di un testo per una scuola cristiana (J. van Haelst). Ma pare ormai chiaro che il codice, opera probabilmente di più autori, è l'espressione poetica di una comunità dalla fisionomia quasi-monastica, che praticava la poesia in metri classici sull'esempio del proprio fondatore (o guida spirituale), cui vanno ascritti i primi tre poemetti. La presenza nel codice di parafrasi bibliche e di etopee, cioè di generi e strutture insegnate a scuola, non è sufficiente per connotarlo come concepito per una scuola cristiana, dato che sono tratti che caratterizzano tutta la poesia tardoantica (lo abbiamo accennato sopra). A ciò si aggiunga la complessità dei testi, specie della *Visione* e dell'elegia *Ai Giusti*, per i quali mal si immagina una destinazione scolastica[30]. Il codice Bodmer è una *raccolta di poesie epiche cristiane*, incentrate su una figura esemplare (Doroteo, il protagonista/autore della *Visione*), che designa una storia della salvezza, individuale e collettiva[31].

A chi erano rivolti questi poemetti? I destinatari e i fruitori di questa raccolta (come si evince anche dalla sue caratteristiche bibliologiche) appartenevano sicuramente alla comunità che li ha espressi, simile a quelle create da Basilio e Gregorio ad Annesi, a quella di Ieraca a Leontopoli[32].

---

ucciso da Caino (P.Bodmer 35): 69 esametri (etopea, parafrasi di *Ps.* 101 partendo da *Gen.* 4.10). 8. *X.* = *Poema senza titolo* (P.Bodmer 36): 75 esametri (parafrasi di vari salmi), 9. *Hy.* = *Inno* (P.Bodmer 37).

[30] La lingua è inoltre assai curiosa, per la presenza di latinismi burocratici e di parecchie glosse esichiane, fenomeno che sia pure in misura inferiore riappare anche nei nuovi poemetti. Cfr. E. LIVREA, *La Visione di Dorotheos come prodotto di consumo*, in *La letteratura di consumo nel mondo greco-latino*, a cura di O. PECERE e A. STRAMAGLIA, Cassino 1996, 71-95: 75; G. AGOSTI, *Contributi critico-testuali all'esegesi della* Visio Dorothei, «*Analecta Papyrologica*» 8-9 (1996-97), 47-60, con bibliografia.

[31] La *Visione* narra la storia di una duplice erranza, di un battesimo rigeneratore e di una consacrazione ad un compito elevato; poi viene *Abr.*, con l'*exemplum* di Abramo e Isacco, a mostrare la serena accettazione della volontà di Dio e la ricompensa per il fedele. Segue una riflessione sul male, sull'inganno del demonio e la perniciosità delle ricchezze (*J.*). In intermezzo si colloca un encomio di Cristo (*Jes.*), che insiste soprattutto sul suo ruolo salvifico. La successiva etopea di Caino (*C.*) serve a dimostrare l'esiziale sorte dei peccatori (ulteriore sviluppo di uno dei temi di *J.*), ed è seguita da una *exhortatio* di Gesù a coloro che soffrono (*D*.) accompagnata da un'etopea di Abele (*A.*), lamento di un giusto che soffre. Ritornano infine i temi caritatevoli annunciati già in *J.*, la cura delle vedove e degli orfani e la rinuncia alle ricchezze (*X*).

[32] G. AGOSTI, *I poemetti* ..., 85-87 e, per simili circoli a Bisanzio, G. CAVALLO, «*Foglie che fremono sui rami». Bisanzio e i testi classici*, in *I Greci. III. I Greci oltre la Grecia*, a cura di S. SETTIS, Torino 2001, 614-616.

I suoi membri, caratterizzati da forti propensioni ascetiche, si autodefinivano δίκαιοι ed erano impegnati nella rinuncia alle ricchezze e nella cura dei più deboli[33]; e soprattutto non disdegnavano la cultura greca (nella biblioteca che si ricostruisce dal fondo Bodmer, oltre ai testi cristiani, sono presenti anche Menandro, Tucidide e Omero; ed ad esso vanno aggiunti i testi dei *P.Beatty* e del codice miscellaneo di Barcellona, che allargano alla letteratura latina gli interessi di questa biblioteca)[34]. Il Doroteo protagonista della *Visione*[35] era probabilmente uno dei personaggi più illustri[36], passato attraverso una vicenda esemplare di caduta e riscatto, raccontata attraverso la diegesi simbolica della visione e allusa poi nel *Ai Giusti* e forse in *Ad Abramo*.

La pubblicazione di questi poemetti ha modificato sensibilmente il quadro letterario del IV secolo: Gregorio di Nazianzo non appare più una personalità isolata; la presenza nel codice Bodmer di parafrasi bibliche mostra che anche nell'Oriente greco si era sperimentato uno dei generi peculiari della produzione cristiana, l'epica biblica, pressoché contemporaneamente all'Occidente latino (gli *Evangeliorum libri* di Giovenco risalgono al 329-330): è stato dunque cancellato quel che appariva come un inspiegabile ritardo culturale ed è stato colmato lo iato fra i pochi esempi di Gregorio[37] e i poemi del V secolo: la *Parafrasi di Giovanni* di Nonno, la

---

[33] In *J.* 111-118 si consiglia la rinuncia ai beni materiali, all'impegno politico, al matrimonio; in *X.* si insiste sulla cura di orfani e vedove, sulla povertà: sono temi comunque che attraversano tutti i poemetti e che sono presenti anche nel *Pastore di Erma*. Si veda E. NORELLI, *Quelques conjectures sur le* Poème au titre mutilé, in *Le* Codex des Visions..., 203-217.

[34] Vd. E. CRISCI, *I più antichi codici miscellanei greci. Materiali per una riflessione*, «Segno&Testo» 2 (2004), 109-144, spec. 115-132. Si aggiunga ora il commentario tachigrafico pubblicato da S.T. TOVAR e K.A. WORP, *To the Origins of Greek Stenography. P.Monts.Roca I*, Barcelona 2006.

[35] Il colofone di *VD*, Δωροθέου Κυΐντου ποιητοῦ, mi sembra vada inteso nel modo più piano «Doroteo figlio del poeta Quinto», come è confermato da *J.* 160 Δω[ρόθ]εον Κύντου. La qualifica ποιητοῦ nel colofone potrebbe addirsi sia a Doroteo che al padre: in ogni caso ciò non significa che Doroteo fosse figlio di Quinto Smirneo (vd. F. VIAN, *À propos de la Vision de Dorothéos*, «Zeitschrift für Papyrologie und Epigraphik» 60, 1985, 45-49).

[36] Come testimoniato ora dalla recentissima pubblicazione di un codice tachigrafico proveniente dalla stessa biblioteca, che ne reca appunto il nome, *P.Monts.Roca* I inv. n. 149v, p. 49 (J.-L. Fournet ha in preparazione un lavoro sull'argomento), come già nel codice miscellaneo di Barcellona (f. 242: vd. CRISCI, *I più antichi codici...*, 131).

[37] Sui suoi carmi biblici vd. R. PALLA, *Ordinamento e polimetria delle poesie bibliche di Gregorio Nazianzeno*, «Wiener Studien» 102 (1989), 169-185.

Metafrasi del Salterio, le *Metafrasi* dell'*Ottateuco* e di Zaccaria e Daniele (perdute) di Eudocia e i *Centoni omerici*.

Inoltre (ciò che per il nostro tema è più importante) i papiri Bodmer (più *P.Beatty* e *P.Monts.Roca*) provengono da una biblioteca nelle vicinanze di Panopoli[38]: ciò che conferma, ancora una volta, l'incoercibile amore degli egiziani per la poesia, testimoniato dall'intensa attività poetica fiorita soprattutto ad Alessandria e nella zona attorno a Panopoli nei secoli IV-VI[39]. Tale attività finora ci era nota solo attraverso i poemi mitologici o «pubblicistici» (encomi, poemi patriografici etc., tipici dei *Wandering Poets*): ma la scoperta dei poemetti Bodmer ha riportato alla luce il *coté* cristiano della poesia panopolitana, mostrando che l'esponente di spicco di questa poesia, Nonno di Panopoli, autore di una parafrasi esametrica del Vangelo di Giovanni, e il poeta della *Metrafrasi del Salterio* (attivo a Costantinopoli, ma di origine egiziana) ebbero dei precedenti nella Tebaide del IV secolo. Un tale panorama di poesia cristiana e pagana nella Tebaide mi sembra che porti ulteriore conferma a ciò che negli studi italiani è sostenuto da diversi anni, vale a dire che la maggior parte dei poeti egiziani, anche quelli autori di carmi «profani», era in realtà cristiana, e che comunque i temi mitologici ed epico-storici non sono indizio di un paganesimo militante, bensì semplicemente soggetti attesi della *paideia*: opinione che recentemente ha ribadito anche Alan Cameron[40].

Tutto ciò evidentemente indirizza a delineare un quadro culturale improntato all'interazione e al dialogo piuttosto che al conflitto. Ed è in tale prospettiva che, oltre alla scelta dei temi, riacquistano rilevanza anche le forme espressive: i poemetti infatti mostrano molte delle caratteristiche

---

[38] Vd., fra gli altri, P. SCHUBERT, *Contribution à une mise en contexte* du *Codex des Visions*, in *Le Codex des Visions...*, 19-25.

[39] AL. CAMERON, *Wandering Poets...*; G.W. BOWERSOCK, *Hellenism...*, 87-107; AL. CAMERON, *Poetry and Literary Culture...*; AL. CAMERON, *Poets and Pagans..*, 21-46.

[40] Sul cristianesimo di Nonno vd. E. LIVREA, *Nonno di Panopoli. Parafrasi del Vangelo di S. Giovanni, Canto B*, Bologna 2000, 51-70; G. AGOSTI, *Nonno di Panopoli. Parafrasi del Vangelo di S. Giovanni. Canto Quinto*, Firenze 2003, 52-70; D. GIGLI, *Nonno Dionisiache I-XII...*, 33-44; D. ACCORINTI, *Nonno di Panopoli, Le Dionisiache. Canti XL-XLVIII*, Milano 2004, 7-37; AL. CAMERON, *Poets and Pagans...*, 36-38 (il quale nota anche, *ibid.*, 39: «I suspect that mythological art and poetry helped many educated people to embrace a Christianity that did not involve rejecting too much of the past. Not the least important aspect of the relations between poet and community in late antiquity is that, by keeping alive the forms and motifs of classicizing poetry, and above all by reviving mythological epic, they eased the transition from Hellenism to Christianity»); Cameron nel lavoro sui *Wandering Poets* aveva legato invece la poesia egiziana alla sopravvivenza del paganesimo impegnato.

peculiari della poesia cristiana, come la risemantizzazione del lessico epico, l'*imitatio homerica* coonestata dall'interpretazione allegorica, la creazione di un sistema formulare per gli epiteti divini[41]. E rientra in gioco anche il rapporto con i modelli, che da mero fatto imitativo si trasforma in dialettica ideologica.

Faccio un paio di esempi molto semplici, che riguardano due procedimenti tipici, l'*Usurpation* cioè l'utilizzo per Dio o Cristo di termini tipici delle divinità pagane, e la *Konstrastimitation* che rovescia il contesto del modello[42]. Nel codice ritorna più volte il nesso ἄγγελος ὠκύς[43] per designare l'arcangelo Gabriele: formalmente si tratta del riutilizzo di un sintagma omerico[44], il quale nella lingua epica diviene formulare di Hermes[45]. Tale impiego ne favorisce l'uso nella poesia cristiana, in quanto permette un implicito parallelo fra Gabriele ed Hermes (è il caso di *P.Bodmer* 30.2 e 31.71), o anche – secondo le prospettive delle *Engelchristologie* – fra il Cristo e Hermes, secondo una lettura figurale di Hermes come tipo di Cristo diffusa fin da Iustin. *apol.* 21[46].

Palese l'imitazione contrastiva che viene proposta nel poema *Jes.* (P.Bodmer 32) 21-24:

φήνατο δ' ἐν δικαίοις ἅγιον φάο[ς ἰσόθε]ος φώς
χρηστὸς ἄναξ, μέγ' ἄγαλμα θεόσπ[ορον
ψυχὰς δ' ἐξ Ἐρεβεὺς πολέας προέη[κε φό]ωσδε
ὠΐσθη φάος αἰνὸν Ἄιδῃ νεκύ[ε]σσι φ[ορῆσαι[47]

---

[41] Una disamina dettagliata in G. AGOSTI, *I poemetti...*
[42] Per la definizione di queste due categorie imitative si vd. K. THRAEDE, *s.v. Epos*, in *Reallexicon für Antike und Christentum* 5, Stuttgart 1962, coll. 1039-1042.
[43] *Vis. Dor.* (P. Bodm. 29) 159 ἄ[σχε]τρον οὐκέτ' ἔπαυσεν ἐὸν μένος ἄγγελος ὠκύς; *Vis. Dor.* 169 ἤλυθε δ' ἄγγελος ὠκύς, ὃς ἄφθιτος ἔπλετ[ο πάντω]ν; Abr. (P.Bodm. 30) ἐκπροΐαλλε τῷ Ἀβραὰμ ἄγγ[ελον] ὠκύν; Just. (P.Bodm. 31) 71 καί τ[ότ]ε δ' αὖ προΐησι πατὴρ θεὸς ἄγγελον ὠκύν.
[44] *Od.* 16.468 ὡμήρησε δέ μοι παρ' ἑταίρων ἄγγελος ὠκύς.
[45] Fin da *Hymn. Hom. Cer.* 407 Ἑρμῆς ἦλθ' ἐριούνιος ἄγγελος ὠκύς; cfr. ad es. *Cosm. Strasb.* 9ᵥ Gigli (= 24.9 Heitsch) πατρῴου καθαροῖο νοήματος ἄγγελος ὠκύς, Nonn. *Dion.* 3.374 ταχὺν ἄγγελον etc.
[46] Eloquente la resa in [Apol.] *Met.Pss.* 34.9 e 11 διάκτορος ὀξύς (dove διάκτορος è epiteto di Hermes, inteso come «messaggero» e «servitore») dell'ἄγγελος κυρίου di *Ps.* 34.5-6; ne discuto più estesamente nel mio comm. a Nonn. *Par.* 5.22; vd. anche K. SMOLAK, *Beobachtungen zur Darstellungsweise in den Homerzentonen*, in «Jahrbuch für Österreichische Byzantinistik» 28 (1979), 29-49: 32. L'autorità scritturale era l'ἄγγελος τῆς βουλῆς di *Is.* 9.6 interpretato in senso cristologico.
[47] «Si mostrò fra i Giusti, santa luce uomo pari a Dio, Cristo Signore, immagine sublime nato da Dio. Condusse alla luce molte anime dall'Erebo, concepì il disegno di portare una luce tremenda ai morti nell'Ade».

Il verso 23 combina un emistichio odissiaco con il riconoscibilissimo inizio dell'*Iliade*[48], suggerendo che mentre Achille mandava i guerrieri alla morte, il Cristo li libera dall'Ade e li porta alla luce.

Pensati in primo luogo per la comunità i poemetti Bodmer volevano guidare i seguaci all'esaltazione di Dio attraverso il canto ispirato da Cristo-Gabriele (*Vis. Dor.* (P.Bodm. 29) 168-177, un passo che è un bell'esempio della nuova estetica eteronoma):

ἤλυθε δὲ Χρηστὸς φαεσίμβροτος ἐν δικ[αίο]ισι
ἤλυθε δ' ἄγγελος ὠκύς, ὃς ἄφθιτος ἔπλετ[ο πάντω]ν.
170 Γαβριήλ, μάλα χαῖρε, σὺ γὰρ πατὴρ ἔπλε[υ ἀοιδῆς
οὔτι κατήφησας τὸν ἐμὸν νόον· ὡς ὅτε μή[τηρ
ἀμφιχυθεὶς φίλον υἷα κινύρεται, ὡς σύ [παρέστης
δείξας σήματα πάντα, βαλὼν χαρίεσσαν ἀοι[δὴν]
ἐν στήθεσσιν ἐμοῖσιν, ὄπιν χέα[ς] ωγ[...]εφ[
175 ἐν λιμέσιν μαλακοῖσιν ἐφεζόμενον λιτα[νεύειν.
τοῖα δ' ἐνὶ στήθεσσιν ἐμοῖς ποτικάμβαλες αὐδ[ὴν
θέσπιν, ἵνα κλείοιμι τά τ' ἐσσόμενα π[ρ]ό τ' ἐόντα[49].

È assai significativo che una simile dichiarazione di poetica si chiuda, ai vv. 176-7, con una patente citazione della *Teogonia* di Esiodo (31-2): si tratta di una strategia espressiva che stabilisce un dialogo con il modello classico, e dunque con coloro che si riconoscono in tale modello. Più avanti nella *Visione* (il testo chiave della raccolta) il poeta/protagonista chiede a Dio di essere inviato «presso genti straniere», ἄνδρας ἐπ' ἀλλοδαποὺς (310), risemantizzando un'espressione omerica (*Il.* 24.382; *Od.* 14.231; 20.220), che più tardi nella *Parafrasi del vangelo di Giovanni* (6.213) Nonno reimpiega per coloro che abbandonano Cristo[50]. La *Visione* si chiude con l'indicazione di un «programma poetico»: narrare l'esperienza visionaria e cantare le opere dei giusti e di Cristo signore, un compito definito «sempre

---

[48] *Od.* 11.37 ψυχαὶ ὑπὲξ Ἐρεβεὺς νεκύων κατατεθνηώτων + *Il.* 1.3 πολλὰς δ' ἰφθίμους ψυχὰς Ἄϊδι προΐαψεν.

[49] «Venne il Cristo, luce degli uomini, fra i Giusti, venne l'angelo rapido, che è immortale (fra tutti): «Salve Gabriele, giacché tu sei il padre del (canto), e non hai rattristato la mia anima; come quando la (madre), tenendo il figlio fra le braccia piange, così tu (sei stato al mio fianco) mostrandomi tutti i segni, dando al mio cuore un canto pieno di grazia, versando la voce... approdato a un porto tranquillo levare una preghiera. Ecco, tu hai versato nel mio cuore un canto divino, perché cantassi il futuro e il passato».

[50] Nonno era certo consapevole del processo di risemantizzazione subito dal sintagma omerico nella poesia cristiana.

più dolce di anno in anno per un poeta», con un'altra patente citazione, stavolta da Apollonio Rodio (*P. Bodmer 29* 339-343):

εὐξάμην ὑψίστοιο θεοῦ ἕνεκ᾽ ἄγγελ[ος εἶναι
340 πάντων ὧν μ᾽ ἐφέηκε καὶ ἐν στή[θεσσιν ἀ]οιδὴν
παντοίην ἐνέηκε παρεστάμενα[ι καὶ ἀειδ]ειν
ἔργων δικαίων ἠδ᾽ αὖ Χρηστοῖο ἄνακτος
εἰς ἔτος ἐξ ἔτεος γλυκερώτερον αἰὲν [ἀοιδῷ[51].

Due considerazioni si impongono: da una parte, il riuso scoperto di modelli così prestigiosi presuppone che i fruitori all'interno della cerchia li riconoscessero, apprezzando il gioco letterario; dall'altra tale *lusus* letterario diventa anche ideologico (è il fine della *Kontrastimitation*) e dunque esso si rivolge a chi era stato educato su quei modelli e li riconosceva come parte essenziale della *paideia*, vale a dire ai pagani colti invitati a riconoscere la liceità della poesia cristiana a livello formale[52] e la sua superiorità a livello contenutistico.

Una simile dialettica fra il destinatario immediato e un destinatario ideale caratterizza anche altri poemi cristiani, nei quali il destinatario ideale sono i pagani colti. Ad es. il *Carmen Paschale* di Sedulio (prima metà del V sec.) è rivolto in immediato al colto uditorio cristiano del circolo di Macedonio, ma contempla anche l'istanza evangelizzatrice presso i pagani[53]; a un gruppo di intellettuali pagani era rivolto il carme a Nemesio di Gregorio di Nazianzo (2.2.3)[54]. Gli ἄνδρες ἀλλοδαποί sono contemplati in un testo di poco posteriore ai *P.Bodmer*, la *Vita di Antonio* di Atanasio, in cui è esplicitamente prevista l'istanza evangelizzatrice presso gli ἐθνικοί

---

[51] «Ho pregato di essere nunzio per Dio altissimo di tutto quanto mi ha ispirato; e Lui mi ha ordinato nel cuore di esser presente e di cantare un canto vario, celebrando le opere dei Giusti e di Cristo signore, un canto di anno in anno più dolce per il poeta». Per il v. 343 si veda Ap. Rh. *Arg.* 4.1744 ἀοιδαὶ / εἰς ἔτος ἐξ ἔτεος γλυκερώτεραι εἶεν ἀείδειν.

[52] Naturalmente si parla delle *intenzioni* degli autori e non dei *risultati*: qualsiasi lettore di buona cultura avrebbe storto la bocca dinanzi alla prosodia di questi poemi (G. AGOSTI e F. GONNELLI, *Materiali per la storia dell'esametro...*) e non è un caso se essi non abbiano avuto alcun ruolo semiotico attivo nella posteriore poesia cristiana.

[53] C.P.E. SPRINGER, *The Gospel as Epic in Late Antiquity. The* Paschale Carmen *of Sedulius*, Leiden-New York-København-Köln 1988, 28-33.

[54] K. DEMOEN, *Gifts of Friendship that Will Remain for Ever. Persons, Addressed Characters and Intended Audiences of Gregory Nazianzen's Epistolary Poems*, «Jahrbuch für Österreichische Byzantinistik» 47 (1997), 1-11 (9-10: «Nemesius should be considered as an actual reader of this (...) pamphlet, but certainly not as the only one: the text was probably directed at a public of open-minded pagan intellectuals»).

e circa un secolo dopo un altro poeta cristiano indirizza la sua metafrasi esametrica dei *Salmi* τοῖς ἄλλοις⁵⁵.

3. La poesia biblica del V secolo

Il problema cruciale, naturalmente, risiede nel capire se il destinatario ideale fosse anche immediatamente concreto. Come sappiamo la zona attorno a Panopoli resterà teatro di tensioni religiose per tutto il quinto secolo[56] ed era un fiorente centro di cultura ellenica e di produzione poetica (cioè aveva una radicata tradizione di insegnamento): in queste condizioni il progetto di dare contenuti cristiani alla poesia epica compiuto dagli autori dei poemetti del codice Bodmer difficilmente si può considerare avulso dalla realtà circostante. I destinatari ideali di questa poesia potevano appartenere a una *élite* colta ancora pagana, o anche essere rappresentanti della *upper class* cristiana: coloro, insomma, che per appartenenza sociale[57] o per convinzione ideologica guardavano alla *paideia* tradizionale come a un valore. Si tratta della medesima ambivalenza che occorre tener

---

[55] ATHAN. *Vit. Ant.* 94.2 ἐὰν δὲ χρεία γένηται, καὶ τοῖς ἐθνικοῖς ἀνάγνωτε, ἵνα κἂν οὕτως ἐπιγνῶσιν, ὅτι ὁ Κύριος ἡμῶν Ἰησοῦς Χριστὸς οὐ μόνον ἐστὶ θεὸς καὶ τοῦ Θεοῦ Υἱός, ἀλλ' ὅτι καὶ οἱ τούτῳ γνησίως λατρεύοντες καὶ πιστεύοντες εὐσεβῶς εἰς αὐτόν, τοὺς δαίμονας, οὓς αὐτοὶ οἱ Ἕλληνες νομίζουσιν εἶναι θεούς, τούτους οἱ Χριστιανοὶ ἐλέγχουσιν, οὐ μόνον μὴ εἶναι θεούς, ἀλλὰ καὶ πατοῦσι καὶ διώκουσιν, ὡς πλάνους καὶ φθορέας τῶν ἀνθρώπων τυγχάνοντας («Se si presenta il caso, *leggete questo scritto anche ai pagani,* affinché riconoscano che non solo il nostro Signore Gesù Cristo è Dio e Figlio di Dio, ma anche che coloro che lo servono con purezza di cuore e credono con devozione in Lui, i Cristiani possono non solo dimostrare che i demoni, che i pagani considerano dèi, non lo sono, ma anche possono calpestarli e scacciarli come ingannatori e corruttori dell'uomo»). Per il poema del Metafraste salmico si veda più avanti, p. 18.

[56] Cfr., per un caso specifico all'interno della comunità cristiana, D. FRANKFURTER, *Things Unbefitting Christians: Violence and Christianisation in Fifth-Century Panopolis,* «Journal of Early Christian Studies» 8 (2000), 273-295; AL. CAMERON, *Poets and Pagans...,* 39-41 suggerisce, riprendendo un'idea di J. Timbie, che la polemica di Shenoute contro l'Ellenismo sia diretta in realtà contro Cristiani colti e che sia da intendere come un fatto di rigorismo, che non distingue fra cultura classica e culto pagano.

[57] Sulla *paideia* classica come fattore sociale d'obbligo il rimando a P. BROWN, *Potere e persuasione nella tarda antichità,* ed. it. Roma-Bari 1995 (Madison - London 1992), 51-102.

presente nelle opere d'arte a soggetto mitologico[58]. I poemi Bodmer non presuppongono una conflittualità fra Ellenismo e Cristianesimo[59], ma semmai considerano l'Ellenismo il linguaggio con cui instaurare un dialogo a fini evangelizzatori. Non c'è quella irriducibilità fra fede e cultura che era invece percepita fra il popolo della *chora* e i monaci di Shenoute[60].

Il dialogo con i pagani, che supera le possibili accuse di bellettrismo esasperando la funzione didascalica, appare anche nella breve stagione dell'epica biblica greca del V secolo[61]. Alan Cameron[62] ha mostrato come questi esperimenti di poesia biblica sembrino legati a un dibattito sulla liceità della poesia cristiana, in cui erano coinvolti soprattutto gli intellettuali del *milieu* costantinopolitano, Socrate e Sozomeno e soprattutto l'imperatrice Eudocia. A questi si deve aggiungere l'anonimo autore (di origine egiziana) di una metafrasi esametrica dei Salmi, e Nonno che da Alessandria non ha mancato di far pervenire il suo apporto al dibattito.

Il poema biblico di quest'ultimo, la *Parafrasi del vangelo di Giovanni*[63], è un'opera ideologicamente impegnata in cui è riversato un intenso sforzo esegetico e dottrinario. Nonno ha cercato di costruire un elaborato progetto culturale, in cui trovassero posto sotto nuova forma sia la componente più specificamente classica che quella cristiana. Un progetto che trovava nel clima culturale alessandrino il terreno più adatto. L' *audience* che si siedeva nei θέατρα alessandrini (del tipo di quelli scoperti dalla

---

[58] Vd. J. ELSNER, *Art and the Roman Viewer. The Transformation of Art from the Pagan World to Christianity*, Cambridge 1995, 251-255; G. AGOSTI, *Due note sulla convenienza di Omero*, in *Società e cultura in età tardoantica*, a cura di A. Marcone, Firenze 2004, 38-57; A. MARCONE, *Tra paganesimo e cristianesimo. Le persistenze classiche nell'iconografia tardoantica*, in ID., *Di Tarda Antichità. Scritti scelti*, Firenze 2008, 184-203.

[59] Una antitesi fra Ellenismo e Cristianesimo è negata anche per l'arte copta da L. TÖRÖK, *Transfigurations of Hellenism. Aspects of Late Antique Art in Egypt AD 250-700*, Leiden-Boston 2005, 86-96 e 269-334.

[60] Sulla quale vd. AL. CAMERON, *Poets and pagans* ... , 43.

[61] Segnatamente la *Parafrasi di Giovanni* di Nonno, le metafrasi dell'Ottateuco e di Zaccaria e Daniele e i centoni testamentari in esametri omerici dell'imperatrice Eudocia, la metafrasi in esametri del Salterio.

[62] AL. CAMERON, *The Empress and the Poet*, «Yale Classical Studies» 17 (1982), 217-289; G. AGOSTI, *L'epica biblica...*, 92-99.

[63] L'unica edizione completa è ancora quella di A. SCHEINDLER, Nonni Panopolitani *Paraphrasis S. Euangelii Joannei*, Lipsiae 1881; singole edizioni con ampi commenti sono uscite in Italia a cura di E. LIVREA (canto 18, Napoli 1989; canto 2, Bologna 2000), C. DE STEFANI (canto 1, Bologna 2000), G. AGOSTI (canto 5, Firenze 2003), C. GRECO (canto 13, Alessandria 2005), M. CAPRARA (canto 4, Pisa 2005), D. ACCORINTI (canto 20, Pisa 1996).

missione archeologica polacca nel quartiere di Kom el-Dikka)[64], ad ascoltare la lettura dei poemi di Nonno era un pubblico misto (come quello che seguiva le lezioni dei professori di filosofia, quale ci è noto ad es. dalla *Vita Severi* di Zaccaria Scolastico[65]), interessato allo straniamento stilistico provocato dal vangelo in versi barocchi. Non sorprende, dunque, di trovare nel poema molti passi in cui il dettato si espande rispetto alla falsariga del modello giovanneo, per instaurare un dialogo con i pagani simile a quello che abbiamo visto nei poemi Bodmer. Nel quarto canto il miracolo del figlio del centurione sembra una «risposta» ad un analogo miracolo di Proclo, nel quinto il poeta adotta una sottile imitazione contrastiva fra il Vero Salvatore e l'ingannevole Salvatore Asclepio[66]; tutto il canto secondo esprime la superiorità del vino cristiano su quello dionisiaco[67]; sempre nel quarto canto c'è una polemica esplicita contro il sacrificio cruento pagano[68]; nel sesto canto la distesa *amplificatio* del Cristo che cammina sulle acque ne mostra in filigrana la superiorità su Iside οἶδμα καθιππεύουσα; la parafrasi dei versetti del Logos nel primo capitolo è un virtuoso brano di poesia neoplatonica[69]. Il poema di Nonno è di un livello stilistico assai elevato, incomparabile con quello dei poemi Bodmer, e l'imitazione contrastiva è utilizzata con grande raffinatezza. Il dialogo coi pagani colti è posto sulla terreno dell'alta παιδεία: conseguente, del resto, alla scelta di parafrasare proprio il quarto evangelo, il più «greco», e il cui prologo aveva da tempo interessato gli ambienti neoplatonici[70]. Ma forse non è del tutto esatto considerare questa poesia solo come un dialogo cortese fra intellettuali: certe scelte culturali di Nonno, *in primis* quella di utilizzare l'esegesi giovannea di Cirillo Alessandrino, lo portavano ad assumere un atteggiamento ben schierato nell'Alessandria degli anni '40 del V secolo e dunque nella contrapposizione con il paganesimo neoplatonico (l'*affaire*

---

[64] Si vedano i saggi raccolti in *Alexandria. Auditoria of Kom el-Dikka and Late Antique Education*, a cura di T. DERDA, T. MARKIEWICZ e E. WIPSZYCKA, Warsaw 2007.

[65] Cfr. su questo punto G. AGOSTI, *La voce dei libri...*, 49-50; R. Cribiore, *Higher Eucation in early Byzantine Egypt*, in R. Bagnall (cur.), *Egypt in the Byzantine...* , 47-66: 51.

[66] L'analisi dettagliata dei due episodi si trova in G. AGOSTI, *Parafrasi Canto Quinto...*, 83-90.

[67] E. LIVREA, *Parafrasi Canto Secondo...*, 76-90.

[68] M. CAPRARA, *Nonno e gli Ebrei. Note a Par. IV. 88-121*, «Studi Italiani di Filologia Classica» 17 (1999), 195-215: 212-213; EAD., *Nonno di Paonopoli. Parafrasi del Vangelo di San Giovanni Canto Quarto*, Pisa 2005, 15-20.

[69] Analisi in C. DE STEFANI, *Nonno di Panopoli. Parafrasi del Vangelo di Giovanni. Canto Primo*, Bologna 2002, 14-21.

[70] H. DÖRRIE, *Une exégèse néoplatonicienne du prologue de l'Évangile de Saint Jean (Amélius chez Eusèbe, Prép. Év. 11, 19, 1-4)*, in *EPEKTASIS. Mélanges patristiques offerts au cardinal J. Daniélou*, Paris 1972, 75-87.

di Ipazia) e quello della pietà popolare (la traslazione delle reliquie di Ciro e Giovanni nel tempio di Iside a Canopo)[71].

Gli altri poemi biblici hanno scelte strade meno autonome, preferendo portare agli estremi il riuso di Omero: ad es. l'autore della *Metafrasi dei Salmi* propone una operazione squisitamente linguistica, caratterizzando nella prefazione dell'opera il suo sforzo come una «traduzione» dei *Salmi* nella lingua primigenia del canto (quella omerica appunto)[72], comprensibile a tutti, per recuperare la perduta χάρις μέτρων dei Salmi e convertire così i pagani con un linguaggio accettabile. Quel che è detto nella προθεωρία, infatti, una volta tanto non lascia dubbi sul fatto che il poema è indirizzato anche ai pagani (32 ἵνα γνώωσι καὶ ἄλλοι, dove «gli altri» è termine tecnico per indicare i pagani):

15 οἶσθ᾽ ὅτι Δαυίδου μὲν ἀγακλέος ἤθεα μέτροις
Ἑβραίοις ἐκέκαστο καὶ ἐκ μελέων ἐτέτυκτο
θεσπεσίων τὸ πρόσθεν, ὅθεν φόρμιγγι λιγείῃ
μέλπετο καὶ μελέεσσιν· ἀτὰρ μετ᾽ Ἀχαΐδα γῆρυν
αὖτις ἀμειβομένων κατὰ μὲν χάρις ἔφθιτο μέτρων,
20 μῦθοι δ᾽ ὧδε μένουσιν ἐτήτυμοι· οὐ γὰρ ἀοιδῆς,
ἀλλ᾽ ἐπέων Πτολεμαῖος ἐέλδετο, ἔνθεν Ἀχαιοί
μείζονα μὲν φρονέεσκον ἐπὶ σφετέρῃσιν ἀοιδαῖς,
ὑμετέρας δ᾽ οὐ πάμπαν ἐθάμβεον. [...]
29   τά περ πρότεροι λίπον ἄνδρες
30 ἐκ μελέων, μέτροισιν ἐνήσομεν, εἰς δὲ μελιχρὴν
Δαυίδου βασιλῆος ἐγείρομεν αὖτις ἀοιδήν
ἐξατόνοις ἐπέεσσιν, ἵνα γνώωσι καὶ ἄλλοι,
γλῶσσ᾽ ὅτι παντοίη Χριστὸν βασιλῆα βοήσει
καί μιν πανσυδίῃ γουνάσσεται ἔθνεα γαίης[73].

---

[71] Vd. J. Rougé, *La politica di Cirillo di Alessandria e l'uccisione di Ipazia*, in *L'intolleranza cristiana nei confronti dei pagani*, a cura di P.F. Beatrice, Bologna 1993, 57-78; J.A. McGuckin, *The Influence of the Isis Cult on st. Cyril of Alexandria's Christology*, in «Studia Patristica» 24 (1992), 191-199; G. Agosti, *Parafrasi Canto quinto...*, 88 e 92-93.

[72] 107 ἐκ παλαχῆς, «dall'antichità», espressione che in *Met. Pss.* 24.12 = ἀπὸ τοῦ αἰῶνος dei *LXX*. Naturalmente lingua ionica qui significa anche metro epico, vd. G. Agosti – F. Gonnelli, *Materiali...*, 359-361. La prefazione si legge in J. Golega, *Der homerische Psalter*, Ettal 1960; F. Gonnelli, *Il Salterio esametrico. I-II*, «Κοινωνία» 13 (1987), 51-60 e 127-151.

[73] «Sai che i canti del glorioso Davide erano adorni di metri ebraici e che di carmi divini erano fatti in passato, e si cantavano con la cetra sonora e in versi; ma tradotti nella lingua degli Achei persero la grazia dei metri. I contenuti rimangono veri: ma Tolemeo voleva non il canto, bensì le parole. Perciò gli Achei vanno fieri dei propri canti e non ammirano i nostri [...] ciò che gli antichi tralasciarono dai canti, noi lo metteremo in metro e risveglieremo di nuovo il dolce canto del re Davide coi versi esametrici, affin-

4. *Homerus christianus*

L'assunzione della lingua epica in quanto lingua originaria della poesia aveva in realtà dietro di sé la tradizione della lettura allegorica e della «spiritualizzazione» del testo omerico. Una tradizione frutto del lavoro d'esegesi sul «testo sacro» che trova un parallelo nell'impegno ermeneutico dei cristiani sulle Scritture. Del resto la comune formazione grammaticale e scolastica dei commentatori di Omero e di quelli della Bibbia si riflette in una sostanziale similarità di metodi, che si possono riassumere nel principio ossimorico di una polisemia inesauribile ma al contempo accessibile a tutti i livelli e continuamente rinnovantesi[74]. Già i poemetti del codice Bodmer mostrano esempi di risemantizzazione e di centonatura veicolata dall'esegesi allegorica di Omero, inaugurando una linea che trova la sua realizzazione nella poesia di Eudocia, la moglie di Teodosio II. L'imperatrice ha cercato costantemente una mediazione fra cristianesimo e cultura greca[75], componendo parafrasi veterotestamentarie (perdute, ma apprezzate da Fozio), la parafrasi di una vita di *S. Cipriano*, scelta non casuale vista la forza evangelizzatrice che la vicenda del mago iniziato ai misteri pagani e poi convertito poteva avere (e nel II libro c'è un elenco dei perniciosi riti pagani che meriterebbe uno studio dettagliato sul piano storico-religioso), e infine collaborando a una redazione dei *Centoni omerici*. L'itinerario in Omero di Eudocia ha trovato il suo punto d'arrivo proprio negli *Homerocentones*, attingendo agli *ipsissima verba* chiamati senza intermediari ad esprimere la verità biblica. I *Centoni* (nei quali Eudocia dice di aver portato a termine l'opera del predecessore Patricio) sono un'opera di letteratura alta che si rivolge a un pubblico competente delle Scritture, ma anche esperto di Omero; ma essi sono inoltre, proprio per quest'ultima caratteristica, un'opera anche di dialogo, in quanto disvelano le potenzialità del santo Omero. Il libro viene a concentrare su di sé due santità, quella delle Scritture e quella di Omero, e perciò stesso si poneva come un formidabile punto di contatto fra i due mondi. Non a

---

ché anche gli altri sappiano che ogni lingua canterà Cristo re e che i popoli della terra a lui obbediranno».

[74] Di questo aspetto ho trattato in G. AGOSTI, *Interpretazione omerica e creazione poetica nella Tarda Antichità*, in *Koruphaio andrì. Mélanges A. Hurst*, a cura di A. KOLDE, A. LUKINOVICH e A.L. REY, Genève 2005, 19-32; analoghi risultati ha raggiunto nello studio della terminologia scoliastica D. ZORODDU, *Escursioni scoliastiche*, «Athenaeum» 95 (2007), 597-632.

[75] M. HAFFNER, *Die Kaiserin Eudokia als Repräsentantin des Kulturchristentums*, «Gymnasium» 103 (1996), 216-228.

caso, dunque, nella prefazione (ἀπολογία, trasmessa dal *Par. suppl. gr.* 322) si trova un accenno polemico al centone omerico di Taziano[76] che apparentemente accampa motivazioni di ordine tecnico (la maniera giusta di applicare le regole della centonatura), ma che riguarda ovviamente il buon uso di Omero e che richiama i lettori di Taziano a confrontarsi con i nuovi centoni di Patricio ed Eudocia e ad apprezzarne la pari qualità e dignità, e soprattutto la superiorità tematica (vv. 19-33):

> εἰ δέ τις ὑμνοπόλοιο σαόφρονα Τατιανοῖο
> 20 μολπὴν εἰσαΐων σφετέρην τέρψειεν ἀκουήν,...
> οὐ ξένον, οὕνεκα κεῖνος Ὁμηρείης ἀπὸ μολπῆς,
> κεῖνος δ' ἐξ ἐπέων σφετέρων ποίησεν ἀοιδήν
> 25 Τρώων τ' Ἀργείων τε κακὴν ἐνέπουσαν αὐτήν,
> ὥς τε πόλιν Πριάμοιο διέπραθον υἷες Ἀχαιῶν,...
> 30 Πατρίκιος δ', ὃς τήνδε σοφὴν ἀνεγράψατο δέλτον,
> ἀντὶ μὲν Ἀργείων στρατιῆς γένος εἶπεν Ἑβραίων,
>   ἀντὶ δὲ δαιμονίης τε καὶ ἀντιθέοιο φάλαγγος
>   ἀθανάτους ἤεισε καὶ υἱέα καὶ γενετῆρα[77].

5. Conclusioni

Quanto fin qui esposto è naturalmente una selezione assai parziale delle problematiche. In particolare sarebbe interessante analizzare il *coté* cristiano della poesia «pubblicistica» e pragmatica: penso in particolare agli epigrammi epigrafici, o alla produzione patriografica (sappiamo che ad Alessandria un certo Teodoro alla metà del V sec. aveva composto dei

---

[76] A noi noto da Libanio, che in *epist.* 990.2-3 FOERSTER ne parla in termini entusiastici.
[77] «E se qualcuno si rallegra ad udire il canto del sapiente poeta Taziano..., non è strano perché lui, partendo dalla poesia di Omero ha composto i propri poemi con quei versi, un poema che racconta la funesta guerra dei Troiani e degli Argivi, come i figli degli Achei distrussero la citta di Priamo... Patricio invece, che ha redatto questo libro pieno di saggezza, invece dell'esercito degli Argivi ha cantato la stirpe degli Ebrei, invece della schiera dei demoni opposti a Dio ha cantato il Figlio e il Padre immortali». Il testo si legge nelle edizioni di A.-L. REY (*Patricius, Eudocie, Côme de Jérusalem, Centons Homériques (Homerocentra)*, Paris 1998) e di R. SCHEMBRA (*Homerocentones*, Turnhout 2007); lo studioso italiano ha pubblicato due importanti lavori esegetici, R. SCHEMBRA, *La prima redazione dei centoni omerici. Traduzione e commento*, Alessandria 2006; *La seconda redazione dei centoni omerici. Traduzione e commento*, Alessandria 2007.

πάτρια cristiani della città)⁷⁸. Ma mi sembra che alcuni punti si possano enucleare.

Quel che emerge dai testi non è sufficiente per legare la produzione di poesia cristiana classicistica a scopi esclusivamente didattici, vale a dire a tentativi di proporre programmi scolastici alternativi. La presenza di generi tipicamente scolastici è tratto comune alla poesia profana ed è dovuta all'uso delle medesime strutture retoriche che informano tutta la letteratura tardoantica: un fatto di *langue*, insomma. L'abbondanza di poemi parafrastici non è legata all'insegnamento, ma piuttosto a una volontà di adagiare il linguaggio della poesia classica sui soggetti biblici, per conferire liceità alla versificazione cristiana. Un progetto di assorbimento della poesia omerica che appare già nel IV secolo nei testi del codice Bodmer e che arriva alle sue estreme conseguenze nella produzione centonaria. Ciò non toglie, va da sé, che certi testi potessero trovare anche una collocazione in programmi d'insegnamento cristiano: ma, ripeto, un eventuale utilizzo scolastico non implica che i poemi cristiani fossero nati per l'insegnamento.

La poesia cristiana classicistica è programmaticamente volta al dialogo con i pagani, proponendo una forma di interazione culturale tesa naturalmente a mostrare la superiorità del soggetto del canto, ma con un linguaggio accettabile per l'interlocutore. Tale istanza dialogica ed evangelizzatrice costantemente presente è un aspetto fondamentale: questi poemi, al di là del giudizio di valore che oggi ne diamo, intendevano inserirsi in un dibattito culturale e religioso, non erano astratte esercitazioni o astrusi esperimenti. La diffusione (e dunque l'impatto) di questa poesia fu senz'altro maggiore di quanto generalmente si ammette: ad es. la *Parafrasi* nonniana e la *Metafrasi del Salterio* sono presenti in un autore di mediocre formazione culturale, come il notaio e poeta dilettante Dioscoro di Afrodito (VI sec.), come documenta l'edizione di J.-L. Fournet; mie ricognizioni nelle epigrafi metriche hanno rilevato una altrettanto sorprendente presenza di riecheggiamenti di questi due poemi⁷⁹.

---

[78] J.-L. FOURNET, *Théodore, un poète chrétien alexandrin oublié. L'hexamètre au service de la cause chrétienne*, in *Des Géants à Dionysos. Mélanges de mythologie et de poésie grecques offerts à Francis Vian*, a cura di D. ACCORINTI e P. CHUVIN, Alessandria 2003, 521-539.

[79] J.-L. FOURNET, *Hellénisme dans l'Égypte du VIᵉ siècle. La bibliothèque et l'œuvre de Dioscore d'Aphrodité*, Le Caire 1999, 298-300; G. AGOSTI, *Il ruolo di Dioscoro nella storia della poesia tardoantica*, in *Les Archives de Dioscore d'Aphrodité cent ans près leur découverte. Histoire et culture dans l'Égypte byzantine (Actes du Colloque de Strasbourg, 8-10 déc. 2005)*, a cura di J.-L. FOURNET e C. MAGDELAINE, Paris 2008,

Infine se il termine «dialogo», evitando ogni drammatizzazione, è quello che meglio rappresenta gli scopi della poesia cristiana classicistica nei confronti dei pagani, forse è altrettanto bene ricordare che il tentativo di annettere al cristianesimo Omero può non essere stato percepito come indolore da parte pagana. Potrebbe dunque essere proficuo verificare se ci sono poemi dichiaratamente pagani che rappresentano una reazione a questa evangelizzazione letteraria. È un terreno su cui per ora si procede per tentativi (non esiste alcuno studio sistematico), ma nel IV e V secolo poemi come i *Lithica* orfici, il carme astrologico di Manetone, le *Argonautiche Orfiche* veicolano una ideologia convintamente pagana (e trattano tematiche che Gregorio rifiuta, non a caso). Sono poemi che risentono di influssi neoplatonici (specie i primi due, legati probabilmente all'ambiente di Massimo di Efeso); le *Argonautiche Orfiche* propongono una rilettura delle reliquie del viaggio argonautico chiaramente in chiave pagana, forse anche anticristiana[80]. Attraverso il linguaggio formalizzato la poesia tardoantica riflette, nelle modalità peculiari della comunicazione letteraria, le tensioni contemporanee: una lettura che ne consideri solo gli aspetti bellettristici non rende giustizia alla sua natura di documento storico.

33-54: 44-48; Id., *Miscellanea epigrafica I. Note letterarie a carmi epigrafici tardoantichi*, «Medioevo Greco» 5 (2005), 1-30; *Note a epigrafi tardoantiche (Miscellanea epigrafica II)*, «Zeitschrift für Papyrologie und Epigraphik» 161 (2007), 41-49.

[80] G. Agosti, *Reliquie argonautiche a Cizico. Un'ipotesi sulle* Argonautiche orfiche, in *Incontri triestini di filologia classica X*, a cura di L. Cristante e I. Filip, Trieste 2008, 17-36.

PIERRE CHUVIN

Homère christianisé. Esthétique profane et symbolique chrétienne dans l'œuvre de Paul le Silentiaire

Je commencerai en soulignant un paradoxe si évident qu'il cesse d'être visible: les poèmes de Paul le Silentiaire, *Description de la Grande Église* et *Description de l'Ambon*[1], furent lus pour la première fois en 562 ap. J.-C.; le poème de Nonnos de Panopolis, les *Dionysiaques*, est daté avec vraisemblance dans la période entre 450 et 470, «plutôt vers la fin de cette période» (F. Vian, 1976, XVII), donc un siècle plus tôt. Or ces deux auteurs, tout en s'obstinant à se placer sous l'invocation d'Homère (largement plus d'un millénaire auparavant), forgent une langue en perpétuelle création, dans son vocabulaire, sa métrique, voire sa syntaxe, et la mettent au service d'une sensibilité «moderne». Ils sont ainsi amenés à ce qui pourrait sembler un grand écart: un très long processus d'évolution linguistique et un changement radical dans la spiritualité les séparent du modèle qu'ils invoquent l'un et l'autre expressément. Pourtant, l'auditoire de Paul, composé en partie de dignitaires de la cour (ce qu'était Paul lui-même) et non d'érudits de cabinet, avait un accès direct à ce texte qui nous paraît difficile. Paul montre en effet un grand souci d'être compris et apprécié, s'adresse à plusieurs reprises directement à son public et fait état du succès remporté par une première audition[2].

Le poète invoque le patronage d'Homère aux vers 617-618 de la *Description de la Grande Église*, au moment de faire un catalogue éblouissant des marbres qui revêtent les parois et le sol de l'église: «*Et qui, à plein gosier, avec les bouches retentissantes d'Homère, chantera...*». Or le vocabulaire de Paul, en général, doit moins à Homère qu'à Nonnos et même ici l'écart est sensible avec le passage homérique auquel il est fait allusion (*Il.*, II, 488-493): «*Quant à la foule, je ne saurais la dénombrer, même si j'avais dix langues, dix bouches, une voix que rien ne brise, une poitrine d'airain, si les Muses ne me rappelaient...*» En fait, la même référence

---

[1] Ces titres seront désormais abrégés en *Grande Église* et *Ambon*.
[2] Cf. *Grande Église*, v. 411-416; *Ambon*, Prologue, notamment v. 11-14.

homérique figurait déjà dans les *Dionysiaques*, de manière tout à fait naturelle car il s'agit là d'une œuvre totalement profane, sur laquelle nous nous arrêterons un peu en raison de l'influence qu'elle a eue sur Paul[3]. On verra d'abord de quelle manière Nonnos se réfère à cet Homère qu'il proclame son maître, pour préciser ensuite l'attitude de Paul par rapport à l'un et à l'autre.

1. Homère chez Nonnos

Dans le grand poème de Nonnos, Homère est nommé dans cinq chants, soit six passages (le chant 25 en comportant deux). Il apparaît notamment dans les deux prologues que comporte l'œuvre: au chant 1 puis, ouvrant la seconde partie de l'épopée, au chant 25.

Dans les deux prologues:
– au chant 1, les v. 36-38 font des allusions mi-plaisantes mi-sérieuses à l'*Odyssée*: le parfum exquis du vin de Maronée, qui sera capable d'apaiser même le Cyclope, d'une part (*Od*. IX, v. 196-211), de l'autre la puanteur des phoques de Pharos parmi lesquels Ménélas se cache (*Od*. IV, 435-443);
– et au chant 25, v. 8, au seuil de ce qui constitue l'*Iliade* des *Dionysiaques*, pour proclamer, sur un ton en apparence sérieux, «Homère, mon modèle», puis adapter le prodige des oisillons dévorés par un serpent qui est ensuite pétrifié, *Il*., II, 308-320; avec de nouveau une pointe d'humour relevée par F. Vian *ad loc*., car les oisillons «piailleurs» prophétisent les années de la guerre, le dernier faisant ainsi figure du conteur qui instruit le poète sur la dernière année... Il n'est plus question de pétrification terrifiante;
– toujours au chant 25, après une série de trois comparaisons avec d'autres fils de Zeus (Persée, Minos, Héraclès), Nonnos invoque à nouveau Homère, le nomme à trois reprises («Homère, mon père»), mais récuse la comparaison entre Dionysos et Achille, entre Dériade et Hector (v.

---

[3] Mon point de vue ici est différent de celui de R. SHORROCK, *The Challenge of Epic. Allusive engagement in the Dionysiaca of Nonnus*, Leiden 2001. Je ne m'attacherai qu'aux mentions explicites d'Homère, qui ne font pas l'objet d'une étude spéciale de la part de Shorrock, la question de l'émulation homérique «allusive» chez Nonnos dépassant largement le cadre de cet exposé.

253-270), l'expédition des Achéens à Troie restant bien inférieure à celle de Dionysos aux Indes (cf. déjà *ibid.*, v. 26-27).

Il est clair que ces deux prologues ont fait l'objet d'une composition raisonnée, par couples antithétiques: les allusions prises à l'*Odyssée* dans le premier, à l'*Iliade* dans le second, correspondent (en gros) au contenu des chants qui suivent: le voyage de Dionysos vers l'Inde (ch. 13-24) opposé à la dernière année de combat en Inde (ch. 25-40); les contrastes sont voulus: dans le premier prologue, entre l'arôme du bon vin et la puanteur des phoques; dans le second, entre les héros qui ont l'honneur d'une *syncrisis* (Persée, Minos, Héraclès), même dépréciative, et ceux qui sont évincés (Achille, Hector: précisément les principales figures homériques).

En dehors des prologues:
– au chant 13, v. 47-52, au seuil du catalogue des alliés de Dionysos, Nonnos «transpose le prélude homérique au Catalogue des Vaisseaux»[4] qui a été cité plus haut: «*Car moi, aurais-je dix langues, verserais-je par dix bouches une voix toute bruissante d'airain, je ne saurais chanter...*». Dans ces vers, Nonnos s'inspire du même passage que Paul un siècle plus tard, mais il se tient beaucoup plus près que Paul du texte homérique. Il poursuit par une métaphore maritime, Homère, «*havre parfait de toute belle poésie*», développée pour en faire une comparaison, invoquant Homère comme les marins dans la tourmente invoquent Poseidon; Paul de son côté, à la fin de la description proprement dite de Sainte-Sophie, présente la basilique comme le repère infaillible qui guide les marins (*Grande Église*, v. 906-920);
– au chant 32, v. 184, pour un catalogue de victimes de Dériade, Nonnos appelle les «Muses homériques» qui ouvrent un catalogue de victimes des guerriers achéens dans l'*Il.*, XIV, 511-522;
– au chant 42, v. 181, l'expression «*le livre d'Homère en a menti*» fait référence à l'*Il.*, XIII, 636-637, pour une question que nous qualifierons de fantaisiste (se lasse-t-on de désirer les femmes?).

Sauf peut-être dans les deux ouvertures de catalogues (chants 13 et 32, mais l'emphase des v. 47-52 du ch. 13 n'est-elle pas teintée d'ironie?), toutes les références faites par Nonnos à Homère le sont sur un mode plaisant, ce qui n'exclut pas, au moins dans les deux prologues, un certain sérieux de l'intention.

Paul, lui aussi, sait à l'occasion manier l'humour érudit, par exemple dans les prologues iambiques, lorsqu'il évoque l'Athénien «rongeur de

---

[4] F. VIAN dans son édition, t. V, 1995, 114 et note aux v. 46-49a (214).

fèves»⁵. Mais, dans une œuvre beaucoup plus brève et descriptive, non narrative, il disposait de moins de place pour se référer au Père fondateur de la poésie grecque et avait moins d'occasions de le faire. Pour exalter son sujet, il n'en évoque pas moins «les bouches» d'Homère (*Il.*, II, 489), son pluriel renvoyant aux «dix bouches» de son modèle, et l'épithète qui les qualifie, ἐρίγδουπος (*Grande Église*, v. 617), est naturellement un terme homérique; c'est une épithète de Zeus dans l'*Iliade*, bien adaptée ici à la solennité de la circonstance. Certes, Paul est plus loin d'Homère que Nonnos, mais il fait bien référence directe à Homère plutôt qu'à Nonnos: les deux seuls emplois de l'épithète ἐρίγδουπος chez Nonnos, tout en restant fidèles à son sens précis, sont d'un registre moins soutenu (elle sert à caractériser un bruit confus, clameur guerrière ou grondement de tambour: *Dion.* 17, 227 et 18, 106).

Un autre exemple de *variatio* sur une expression homérique, et très significatif, est fourni par l'emploi du participe πεπαρμένον, «percé, transpercé» de clous au v. 883. Cette forme n'est pas rare chez Nonnos (dix-huit exemples) mais Paul ici se modèle directement sur une formule de l'*Il.* I, 246 et XI, 633 («incrusté de clous d'or» pour désigner un sceptre, une coupe). L'expression retenue par Paul mérite qu'on s'y arrête: un luminaire «sur le modèle de la croix immortelle brûle d'une lumière qui éclaire les mortels, transpercée par les attaches de clous aux belles prunelles». Le texte ne va pas sans difficultés: Comment une lumière peut-elle être transpercée⁶? L'expression «les attaches des clous» désigne-t-elle les têtes de ces clous, comme des cabochons renvoyant la lumière? Quoi qu'il en soit, une allusion aux clous de la croix se superpose à l'évocation d'un objet précieux et on passe du sens d' «incrusté» à «transpercé».

Nonnos et Paul ne pouvaient avoir la même attitude vis-à-vis de leur sujet. Nonnos, bien que certainement d'origine chrétienne, traite un sujet profane et peut se permettre une grande liberté de langage. Paul traite un sujet de l'ordre du sacré, et dans une cérémonie officielle. Tout au plus fait-il intervenir la personnification de Rome ou encore évoque-t-il le Léthé (*Grande Église*, v. 181), les Géants entassant Pélion sur Ossa⁷ (*ibid.*, v.

---

⁵ *Grande Église*, Iambes au Patriarche, v. 125; le terme vient d'ARISTOPHANE, *Cavaliers*, v. 41.

⁶ On serait tenté de corriger πεπαρμένον en πεπαρμένος, mais le parallèle homérique n'y encourage pas.

⁷ Les Roches Errantes (*Planctai*, v. 909) n'entrent pas dans cette catégorie car elles correspondent à un site bien réel au débouché du Bosphore dans la mer Noire. Banalité du thème des Géants entassant Pélion sur Ossa: voir ma note à NONNOS, *Dion.* 6, 328, et cf. Claudien dans les célébrations du 4ème consulat d'Honorius et du consulat de Stilicon.

302-310). En revanche, il montre son habileté à adapter à un sens chrétien les expressions homériques.

Mais dans ce contexte, certaines références, rares sinon absentes ailleurs dans la littérature chrétienne, peuvent surprendre. Paul détourne des épithètes divines consacrées par l'usage[8] (outre ἐρίγδουπος, citons γλαυκῶπις, *ibid.*, v. 294 et 924), mentionne les Telchines ou Mégaira (*ibid.*, v. 195 et 221); et lorsque le ciel est qualifié d'*astrochitôn*, «à la tunique d'étoiles» (*ibid.*, v. 288), l'usage est encore moins conventionnel si l'on se souvient que cette épithète qualifie l'Héraclès tyrien qui joue un si grand rôle à la fin du chant 40 des *Dionysiaques*, aussitôt après la victoire de Dionysos sur les Indiens, pour ouvrir la «marche vers l'apothéose» des derniers chants. Or Astrochitôn est une épithète rare (dans le *TLG*, en tout 15 exemples dont 7 chez Nonnos) dont on n'a aucune attestation sûre avant Nonnos: cf. *Argon. Orph.*, 513, 1028; Jean de Gaza, *Descr.*, I, 193; Jean d'Antioche (d'après Nonnos?); *Etym. Magnum*, 805, 54 Gaisford[9]. Autant que nous puissions voir, c'est donc Nonnos qui a mis, si l'on peut dire, l'expression à la mode. Plus étonnante encore est chez Paul l'évocation du déluge (Genèse, 6-8) et de la destruction de Sodome et Gomorrhe par le feu (*ibid.*, 19, 12-29), calquée, pour l'ordre des catastrophes et pour les termes employés, sur l'embrasement universel et le déluge consécutifs au meurtre de Zagreus chez Nonnos, ch. 6, v. 206-313, ce qui amène Paul à modifier la nature et à inverser l'ordre des deux châtiments bibliques[10] (*Grande Église*, v. 208-213).

Une caractéristique saillante du style homérique est la grande comparaison développée, avec le balancement ὡς... οὕτω... et surtout ὡς δ'ὅτε et sa forme «emphatique»[11] ὡς δ'ὅταν. J'ai relevé quatre exemples de cette tournure solennelle dans l'ensemble des deux poèmes de Paul. Dans chaque poème, ils se trouvent à la fin de la description proprement dite, avant l'envoi.

---

[8] Il conviendrait de relever les variations sur des formules homériques, par ex., sur l'Aurore «aux chevilles de rose» plutôt qu'«aux doigts de rose»...

[9] L'expression citée dans l'*Etym. Magnum*, πόλῳ ἀστροχίτωνι, très proche de JEAN DE GAZA, *loc. cit.*, πόλον ἀστροχίτωνα, figurait dans les *fragmenta anonyma* à la suite de l'édition SCHNEIDER de CALLIMAQUE (*fr. anon.* 107), d'où elle est passée dans le *Suppl. Hell.* 1051. «*Silentio praeterii*» écrit à propos de ce fragment R. PFEIFFER, t. I de son édition de CALLIMAQUE, 498.

[10] Cf. PAUL LE SILENTIAIRE, *Description de Sainte-Sophie de Constantinople*, prés. et trad. M.-C. FAYANT, P. CHUVIN, Paris 1997, et notre note *ad loc.*, suivie par M.-L. FOBELLI, *Un tempio per Giustiniano. Santa Sofia di Costantinopoli e la «Descrizione» di Paolo Silenziario*, Roma 2005.

[11] P. CHANTRAINE, *Grammaire Homérique*, t. II, *Syntaxe*, Paris 1963, par. 370.

Dans la *Grande Église*, v. 866-870, en 5 v., c'est tout d'abord le cercle des flambeaux de la corniche, au moment où on les allume, qui est comparé à un collier d'or et de pierreries passé au cou d'une jeune princesse. Si la forme de la comparaison est homérique, le geste d'offrande d'un objet précieux a de lointains échos pindariques et peut rappeler le début si célèbre de la VIIème *Olympique*; cependant que le collier, lui, rappelle le collier passé au cou d'Harmonie chez Nonnos, *Dion.* ch. 5, v. 136-137.

Dans ce poème destiné à accompagner des fêtes de la nuit et de l'aube, Paul décrit ensuite la forêt des luminaires de l'église, qui lui inspire une seconde comparaison homérique, avec un ciel «sans nuages» où brillent les constellations qu'observent les voyageurs pour se repérer; c'est la seconde comparaison «formelle», *ibid.*, v. 895-905, prolongée en 906-920 par un εὖτε, très développée puisqu'elle compte vingt-six vers en tout: de la joie du voyageur qui voit les constellations, on passe à l'assurance du marin à voir au loin les lumières de l'église[12]. Les éloges finaux de l'empereur et du patriarche suivent immédiatement, v. 921-1028, de sorte qu'on peut bien dire que cette majestueuse comparaison clôt la description «avec l'aide du Dieu vivant» (selon la formule du v. 920 fin), donc de manière très solennelle.

La fin de la description de l'*Ambon*, elle aussi, offre une paire de comparaisons en forme. C'est d'abord, v. 224-239, en seize vers, la comparaison de la chaire avec une île, vue depuis la mer par les voyageurs qui la longent «et la disent bénie». Paul la décrit en la dotant de toutes les prospérités: blé, vignes, prairies, forêts... Les voyageurs sont évidemment les fidèles qui, au long de leur existence, «se repaissent des peines» d'une traversée maritime, et l'opulence nourricière de l'île, sa beauté, sont la richesse et la beauté des Évangiles qui sont lus en chaire, en même temps que celles de l'édifice réel avec sa «prairie de pierres» selon une métaphore affectionnée de Paul[13]. Le goût du symbole n'élimine pas le souci de précision, et Paul a soin de rectifier la comparaison: il ne s'agit «pas tout à fait» d'une île, mais d'une presqu'île. Pour l'évoquer, Paul se souvient très certainement de Nonnos décrivant la presqu'île de Tyr (ch. 40, v. 311-326 et 338-352) comme une jeune nageuse dont les pieds touchent encore la terre ferme, mais les indices d'humanisation du paysage sont ténus,

---

[12] On relève de telles accumulations de comparaisons dans l'*Iliade*, par ex. à la fin du ch. XVII.

[13] La «prairie de pierres» chez Paul: *Grande Église*, v. 618; *Ambon*, v. 226, 231, 256; cf. *Grande Église*, v. 288 (la prairie des astres), 1016 (la prairie de la piété).

ainsi ἐπιπροθέουσα, «accourant au-devant [des flots]» et la comparaison s'établit plutôt avec une barque amarrée.

La seconde comparaison de Paul, *ibid.*, v. 283-293, en onze vers, porte sur les marbres colorés de Hiérapolis ornant la balustrade de la soléa; ils sont tels un vêtement de pourpre broché d'or. Le congé, après trois vers d'une grande sécheresse, suit presque immédiatement, v. 297-304.

La fin de chaque poème propose, dans une structure formelle identique, des comparaisons analogues: deux concernent des éléments de la parure de Sainte-Sophie (l'éclairage de la corniche de la coupole) ou de l'ambon (la soléa), l'un semblable à un collier de pierreries, l'autre à des broderies sur un vêtement de pourpre, parures régaliennes (la seconde est celle du Christ sur une tenture du chancel); deux ont un cadre naturel, maritime et agreste, et présentent Sainte-Sophie ou l'ambon comme des repères pour les fidèles vus comme des voyageurs spirituels. L'image du voyage, et plus spécialement de la navigation, est très présente dans le poème, à la faveur d'un mot parfois, par ex. au v. 445a, «comme en haute mer». Les quatre grandes comparaisons sont disposées en chiasme:

Grande Église: fin de la description, v. 920; fin du poème, 1028	v. 866-870 pierreries au cou d'une princesse	v. 895-920 ciel étoilé
Ambon: fin de la description, v. 296; fin du poème, 304	v. 224-239 île luxuriante	v. 283-293 pourpre brochée d'or

Le registre de ces comparaisons correspond à ce que l'on trouve dans le reste du poème. Comme le fait remarquer Marie-Christine Fayant, 37, «globalement, Sainte-Sophie est décrite non comme un monument mais comme un être humain». De nombreuses comparaisons ou métaphores la font voir en effet comme un être humain tantôt debout (et la coupole centrale est sa tête) et tantôt allongé (et l'abside est sa tête), comme l'ont relevé Marie-Christine Fayant et à sa suite Maria Luigia Fobelli. Il s'y ajoute, pour caractériser les mosaïques à fond d'or des absides et demi-coupoles, la comparaison avec un paon et avec l'arc-en-ciel. Les couleurs dominantes dans les marbres sont le vert et le rouge, couleurs impériales du porphyre. Mais le poète, dans ce catalogue solennel pour lequel il invoque Homère (v. 617-646), ne se limite pas à un tableau de l'Empire romain reconstitué: l'édifice figure l'univers dans son ensemble, grâce au contraste entre l'or du soleil de midi sur la coupole, le blanc gris du pavement et la variété florale des parois; un univers dépouillé de tout élément anecdotique (v. 286-299).

Sainte-Sophie est donc un microcosme: la coupole appelle inévitablement la comparaison avec la voûte céleste, le sol en marbre de Proconnèse, blanc festonné de gris, la surface de la mer; en témoigne, chez le biographe de Mehmet II, Tursun bey, qui n'avait probablement pas lu Paul, cette remarque faite à l'entrée du souverain dans Sainte-Sophie: «Si on regarde du sol vers le sommet, c'est une aube constellée que l'on voit; et si on regarde d'en haut vers le sol, on examine une mer houleuse»[14].

J'ajouterai que dans la zone intermédiaire, la corniche avec sa décoration en *opus sectile*, ses rinceaux animés, évoque la végétation, nourricière et exubérante, qui recouvre l'île/ambon, et les arbres de lumière qui éclairent la basilique (v. 741 s., *al.*). Il y a ainsi deux types de paysage très proches par leurs composantes: un paysage naturel dont on peut se lasser, *Grande Église*, v. 286-299, où un vaste panorama depuis la voûte céleste jusqu'à la mer donne l'image d'une nature florissante, généreuse, tout en affirmant la supériorité du ciel mystique où brille la Croix sur la simple voûte céleste. Et le paysage dont on ne saurait se lasser, métaphore de la parole divine : le thème est en effet repris par la comparaison explicite que nous avons relevée dans *Ambon*, 224-229 et 240: cette île, havre d'abondance et de sûreté, au milieu de la mer des périls de l'existence, est le lieu d'où la «bonne nouvelle» est annoncée aux hommes. Le parallélisme des deux passages me paraît clair. La place du premier dans la composition générale du poème est significative. Au seuil de la description architecturale proprement dite, forcément austère avec ses indications techniques, c'est une présentation générale de l'effet produit, sans que la comparaison soit formellement introduite. La comparaison remplit bien cette «fonction d'encadrement et de mise en valeur» définie par Annie Bonnafé à propos du Catalogue des Vaisseaux: les comparaisons encadrent le Catalogue, mais sont absentes du corps même de celui-ci[15].

Or, dans la description de l'ambon, on trouve aussi, *avant* la description «technique» proprement dite, une série de brèves comparaisons qui méritent de retenir l'attention par leur contenu, unique dans le poème. Ces comparaisons (*Ambon*, v. 84-94) caractérisent les marbres de la dalle de la chaire, que les fidèles ne peuvent pas voir (d'où peut-être cette abondance d'images?), successivement par rapport à des ongles humains, à du buis,

---

[14] Tursun beg, *Târîh-i Ebül-Feth*, 51a (p. 6 de l'éd. Mertol Tulum, 1977).
[15] A. Bonnafé, *Quelques remarques à propos des comparaisons homériques de l'Iliade; critères de classification et étude statistique*, «RPh» LVII (1983), 79-97.

à de la cire, à de l'ivoire[16]. Il s'agit de variations sur des nuances de blanc tirant sur le jaune; ou de jaune passant au blanc. Ces nuances sont très proches les unes des autres. Y a-t-il une raison à cette accumulation de matériaux? L'un d'eux est évoqué plus longuement que les autres, c'est la cire, «lavée à l'eau pure des montagnes» et «séchée aux rayons du soleil». Or la cire, pour être blanchie, fait bien l'objet d'un traitement, mais celui-ci est gauchi par Paul: la cire est lavée dans la saumure plutôt que dans l'eau des torrents et elle sèche, soit à l'obscurité soit exposée au soleil et à la lune[17]. Ce qui importe pour Paul, c'est la pureté (de l'eau du torrent, du blanc) et la lumière. De la cire on fait les cierges et la surface d'écriture des tablettes, notamment, qui ont l'un et l'autre un usage liturgique[18]. Or, curieusement, on a ici plusieurs éléments d'un diptyque: le buis, très dur, est l'un des bois de prédilection pour la confection de tablettes, cf. les termes *pyxinos*, *pyxion*, dérivés de *pyxos*, «buis», pour désigner celles-ci (et il a beaucoup servi, plus tard, dans l'Occident chrétien pour les crucifix); l'ivoire est le matériau des diptyques d'apparat, si prisés, dont il subsiste quelques exemplaires dans nos musées; la cire sert, on l'a dit, à enduire pour la rendre propre à l'écriture la face non ornée de la tablette. Les ongles pourraient figurer ici par synecdoque pour les doigts, mais le terme de στόνυξ («pointe», «griffe») que Paul utilise mériterait d'être étudié (s'appliquerait-il à un stylet?). L'évocation des éléments d'une forme de livre, par un jeu de correspondances colorées, convient bien à l'ambon, lieu par excellence de la lecture. Les images ont une fonction à la fois pédagogique et «psychagogique»; elles doivent à la fois instruire et plaire.

Dans les passages qui entourent celui-ci, on remarquera aussi l'apparition, toujours par le biais des matériaux employés, du corps souffrant et du corps triomphant du Christ, «incarnés» dans le marbre; cette humanisation est marquée dans la description de l'ambon, à propos des marbres, par la reprise insistante – trois exemples dans les v. 95-104 – de l'adjectif «livide» ou «blême», πελιδνός, qui ailleurs dans la littérature grecque ne s'applique qu'à la peau; Paul parle d'ailleurs plusieurs fois de l'épiderme du marbre, de ses veines, bien sûr, et aussi de ses «nerfs» ou «nervures»;

---

[16] Seule la comparaison avec l'ivoire pourrait avoir une origine homérique (*Il.* IV, 141-147).

[17] Voir PLINE, *N.H.*, XXI (49), 83-84, pour la description la plus détaillée de la préparation et du blanchiment de la cire; article *cera* du *Dict. Ant.*, I, 2, col. 1019a – 1020 a, par E. SAGLIO; art. «Wachs» de R. et E. MOSER, *Real-Enc.*, Suppl. XIII (1973), col. 1347-1416 (col. 1352-1353 sur la préparation).

[18] Le diptyque jouait un rôle dans la liturgie, mais à l'autel, non à l'ambon semble-t-il (SAINT AUGUSTIN, *Lettres*, 78, 4).

le contraste du rouge et du blanc est exploité de deux manières: comme *topos* de la poésie érotique, pour célébrer la beauté[19]; et comme signe du martyre lorsqu'il s'agit du sang qui ruisselle sur les suppliciés, évoqués au début de l'*Ambon*[20]. Dans la *Description de la Grande Église*, v. 631, pour les marbres, on rencontre aussi l'alliance du sanglant et du livide, version «sinistre» des «fleurs de pierre», roses et lis, *Ambon*, 140-147, avec la réapparition d'un vocabulaire anatomique, veines, nerfs, sang...

Paul fait preuve d'une grande virtuosité dans le traitement du matériau homérique, tant sur le plan du lexique que des images. Se tenant tantôt plus près tantôt plus loin du Maître que Nonnos, il crée un langage poétique, concret et évocateur, presque entièrement épuré de réminiscences païennes, et préservant cependant une culture millénaire. Paul part d'une comparaison simple, coupole/voûte céleste, et d'une métaphore courante dans diverses langues, le marbre et la chair. Il en tire ici des effets d'une grande force pour suggérer la présence du Sauveur, à la fois au sommet de la coupole de l'univers et présent en ce monde par sa Parole, pleinement homme dans la souffrance de sa Passion et pleinement Dieu dans la gloire de sa Résurrection, traduites au regard du poète par le jeu des couleurs répandues sur les marbres de la basilique.

---

[19] C'est déjà le cas chez Nonnos dans le portrait de Cadmos, *Dion.*, IV, v. 128-132, et ma note au v. 132 dans *Nonnos de Panopolis. Les Dionysiaques,* III *(Chants III-V)*, éd. et tr. P. Chuvin, Paris 1976.

[20] Au début de la description de l'ambon, l'évocation très doloriste des martyrs amène la métaphore usuelle à leur propos «baignés, lavés dans le sang» (*Ambon*, 41-45), qui rappelle les paroles de félicitations adressées aux personnes qui sortent des bains. L'acclamation «tu t'es bien baigné!» a été étudiée par L. Robert, *Une vision de Perpétue martyre à Carthage en 203*, «CRAI» (1982), 229-276 (237, n. 39; repris dans *OMS*, V). À l'origine elle appartient au registre de la vie quotidienne. Ici elle est criée aux martyrs victimes des ours et autres fauves, ruisselant de sang sous les coups de griffe et les morsures.

Giovanni A. Cecconi

Contenuti religiosi delle discipline scolastiche e prassi d'insegnamento come terreno di conflitto politico-culturale

Vista dalla parte dei fruitori della scuola (famiglie, studenti), è spesso ammessa una distinzione tra adozione del sistema educativo profano, in larga misura data per scontata e fatta propria dai cristiani, e accettazione dell'humus culturale sul quale quello stesso sistema si fondava, più contrastata, in particolare al di fuori delle cerchie dei raffinati letterati che ricorrevano, indipendentemente dalle tendenze religiose, alla citazione, alla reminiscenza di autori canonici, all'immagine tratta dal patrimonio mitologico e dal pantheon greco-romano[1].

In questa sede mi soffermerò sugli atteggiamenti dei cristiani verso la didassi secolare tradizionale e cercherò di valutare se la distinzione appena accennata si configuri diversamente, per esempio come una polarità radicale, o se dinamiche conflittuali potessero insorgere sino a fare del comparto formativo, pur in situazioni transitorie e secondo ogni apparenza in via minoritaria, un terreno di antagonismo serrato fra le due grandi categorie socio-culturali al centro del presente volume. Una ricerca – questa dei fattori e delle forme di conflittualità – che da un lato, per quanto mi riguarda, è stata sollecitata dagli scontri religiosi del mondo attuale, mentre dall'altro, e su un piano storiografico, nasce dallo stimolo a vagliare la zona d'ombra meno «dialogica» nel quadro di un dibattito odierno che appare talvolta privilegiare nella scelta dei suoi temi legittime e più generali aspirazioni alla edificazione di relazioni interculturali privilegiate, alla convivenza, alla coabitazione.

Il tema della simbiosi culturale, dopo Costantino, è stato opportunamente enfatizzato negli ultimi decenni. Ricordare che ambienti, o indivi-

---

[1] Distinzione già evidenziata da H.-I. Marrou (sulla cui opera si veda di recente *Que reste-t'il de l'éducation classique? En relisant l'«Histoire de l'Education dans l'Antiquité» de H.-I. Marrou*, a cura di J.-M. Pailler, P. Payen, Toulouse 2004); cfr. L. Lugaresi, *Studenti cristiani e scuola pagana. Didaskaloi, logoi e philia nel discorso di ringraziamento a Origene e nell'orazione funebre per Basilio di Gregorio Nazianzeno*, «Cristianesimo nella Storia» 25 (2004), 779-832.

dui, pagani e cristiani erano formati e compartecipavano con tolleranza reciproca a una stessa cultura – di matrice pagana e colta – ha il vantaggio di denunciare come tutto si determina lungo un crinale più sottile che quello dello scontro epocale fra due mondi, di un conflitto di valori etici e di modelli comportamentali inteso come alterità totalizzante e prodromo di esplosioni di violenza (alla Herbert Bloch, per intendersi)[2]. Talvolta però le argomentazioni di supporto a tale prospettiva sembrano quasi dare la sensazione che non solo l'antinomia irriducibile ma la stessa distinzione identitaria fra pagani e cristiani si attenui in una sorta di dissolvenza, quasi a farceli sentire immersi in un «vaste "marais" de conformistes inoffensifs de deux bords, de païens peu convaincus et de chrétiens mal convertis». Riprendo per comodità queste efficaci parole di Jacques Fontaine (1976) in quanto credo molti, anche a svariati lustri di distanza, le sottoscriverebbero. Esse alludevano ai destinatari di una certa letteratura – anche cristiana – diffusa o letta in Occidente, alla «Repubblica dei letterati», se posso esprimermi con siffatto anacronismo, ma anche, più in generale, alle comunicazioni sociali tardo antiche. Lo stesso studioso vedeva nel fatto che i ragazzi condividessero le attività, i programmi, i metodi della scuola classica tradizionale un fattore di condizionamento e di costruzione di una mentalità e di un'impronta estetica unitaria[3].

Posto in altri termini, non si può far discendere, dal clima della cultura d'élite tardoantica caratterizzato da un flessibile e trasversale paganesimo letterario, l'idea che – *presso tutti i fruitori della formazione scolastica* – divinità, miti classici, stilemi letterari costitutivi della *paideia* fossero quasi *adiafora*, e che in generale, intorno ai contenuti religiosi e agli interessi materiali che concernevano la scuola e l'insegnamento, pagani e cristiani si fossero dal IV secolo accontentati di una composizione pacifica fondata su un patrimonio letterario e morale pagano che si pretende irrinunciabile, utilizzato sia nell'allenamento disciplinare sia nelle metodiche

---

[2] Il rinvio è in primo luogo alla celebre e influente conferenza *La rinascita pagana in Occidente alla fine del secolo IV*, pubblicata nella raccolta di saggi a cura di A. MOMIGLIANO, *Il conflitto tra paganesimo e cristianesimo nel secolo IV*, Torino 1968 (1975), 199-224; cfr. già H. BLOCH, *A New Document of the Last Pagan Revival in the West*, «Harvard Theological Review» 38 (1945), 199-244.

[3] J. FONTAINE sulla relazione di AL. CAMERON in *Christianisme et formes littéraires de l'antiquité tardive en Occident (Vandoeuvres-Genève, 23-28 août 1976)*, Genève 1977, 31; J. FONTAINE, *Unité et diversité du mélange des genres et des tons chez quelques écrivains latins de la fin du IVe siècle: Ausone, Ambroise, Ammien*, ibid., 425-482 (compresa la discussione); cfr. spec. 434-436. Per l'opposizione, nelle sue variegate morfologie sia contenutistiche che cronologiche, nel campo delle scritture storiografiche si veda in questa sede il contributo di H. Inglebert.

d'insegnamento e come base delle conoscenze tecniche. In un quadro di incertezza e di dubbi anche sulla stessa identità di pagani e cristiani, sono preziosi riesami chiari e distesi, come quello di Karen Piepenbrink (2005) per il IV e l'inizio del V secolo[4].

Toccherò con l'aiuto di un florilegio di riferimenti documentari pochi aspetti interconnessi.

1. Riserve e attitudini radicali dei cristiani verso l'istruzione tradizionale

Genitori cristiani «consapevoli», in grado di garantire ai propri figli l'accesso all'istruzione nelle scuole dovevano porsi delle domande su come impostarla. Come rapportarsi dinanzi agli studi liberali dei propri rampolli, quali spazi anche di tempo trovar loro per la preparazione sulle Sacre Scritture, e in definitiva come conciliare le esigenze dell'identità e della sensibilità religiosa con la presenza inesauribile del politeismo nei diversi stadi della *paideia*? L'offerta formativa tradizionale, quella delle scuole cittadine e dei centri di studio delle capitali, conservava nel tardo IV secolo e oltre una relativa stabilità ma le fonti lasciano cogliere anche superfici di attrito e sfere di tensione che avranno potuto contribuire o a una flessione della domanda del sistema scolastico o a un suo riadattamento in senso cristiano.

Iniziamo con un passo dell'orazione funebre di Gregorio per Basilio di Cesarea (Or. 43, 11), nel quale il Nazianzeno rievoca la formazione di Basilio, dopo averne elogiato i genitori:

> «La cultura (*paideusis*) detiene il primo posto tra tutti i beni umani. Non solo, però, quella più nobile e che ci appartiene, che, tenendo in dispregio ciò che nell'eloquenza è ornato e in cerca di plauso, si cura soltanto della salvezza e della bellezza dei pensieri, ma anche quella estranea a noi (*exothen*), che *la maggior parte dei Cristiani* rifiuta (*diaptuousin*), ritenendola, a torto, nociva, pericolosa e causa di allontanamento da Dio (trad. M. Vincelli)».

Con un'ampia, erudita nota, Al. Cameron e J. Long[5] hanno rilevato la frequenza dei riferimenti degli autori cristiani di IV e V secolo alla

---

[4] K. PIEPENBRINK, *Christliche Identität und Assimilation in der Spätantike. Probleme des Christseins in der Reflexion der Zeitgenossen*, Frankfurt am Main 2005; si veda in part. 340-391.

[5] AL. CAMERON, J. LONG, *Barbarians and the Politics at the Court of Arcadius*, Berkeley-Los Angeles 1993, 35-36 e nota 90. Cfr. C.M. CHIN, *Grammarian and Christianity in the late Roman World*, Philadelphia 2008, 72-109, sul tema della creazione delle

filosofia o a altre discipline a loro «estranee, straniere», e come in essi il vocabolo *exothen* assuma il senso principale di «pagani, secolari» (opposto a «cristiani»). Il contesto del passo citato di Gregorio è in stretta relazione con le tematiche della educazione e della scuola: lo è sia per la collocazione nel corpo dell'orazione sia per il lessico impiegato[6]. Non è probabilmente possibile dar seguito alla domanda su quale proporzione di cristiani, e quali cristiani, fossero i *polloi* che, fra i cristiani, assumevano tale atteggiamento di diniego assoluto, accompagnato da disprezzo (in prevalenza dei *logoi*, il verbo greco anch'esso di largo impiego è *diaptuo* ed è verbo altrove impiegato a rimarcare consapevoli ripulse culturali e religiose), che peraltro lo scrittore invita nel prosieguo del brano a modificare, sottolineando la necessità di selezionare quanto della *paideia* tradizionale debba essere accolto e quanto respinto. Mi pare tuttavia che la formulazione meriti qualche attenzione per le implicite allusioni a materie e docenti non cristiani. Espressioni di rifiuto in blocco della *paideia* classica, verosimilmente con la conseguenza concreta che ad essa si saranno opposti in parte anche coloro che avrebbero potuto recarsi alle scuole tenute da *magistri publici*, erano sempre esistite, ma è di qualche rilevanza aggiuntiva che qui si tratti di un fenomeno apparentemente diffuso e in larga misura svincolato dalle influenze del monachesimo o da invocazioni di principi ascetici nella società cristiana del tardo IV secolo, in un quadro non a torto ritenuto in genere meno oppositivo quanto a attitudini cristiane verso le arti liberali classiche e il loro insegnamento.

In altra orazione gregoriana (*Or.* 21, 6-7), Atanasio è detto essersi limitato a un'infarinatura minima della *enkyklios paideia* per dedicarsi poi serratamente e unicamente allo studio dell'Antico e del Nuovo Testamento: importa qui meno che Gregorio non negasse l'utilità della *paideia* per la futura carriera episcopale del grande presule filoniceno rispetto al fatto che quest'ultimo era fra i cristiani che avevano sostanzialmente rinunziato a approfondirla con studi regolari. Non era proprio di Gregorio un atteggiamento univocamente ostile nei confronti dell'ellenismo negli studi scolastici. Egli, piuttosto, si collocava sulla scia intellettuale del dedicatario della sua orazione funebre nel suo celebre *Discorso ai giovani* – apparentandosi anche con autori di analoghi opuscoli come i c.d. *Iambi ad Seleu-*

---

barriere disciplinari, «linguistic spoliation», ecc. da parte dei cristiani del mondo occidentale latino, e in particolare 72 sulle implicazioni dell'espressione *apud nos*.

[6] Espressioni quali *ta exothen mathemata* o *exothen paideia* si trovano anche nell'*Ad adulescentes* basiliano: 2; 4; 10.

cum di Amphilochio Iconiense, un allievo di Libanio[7]. Ma anche di simili proposte di riformare l'apprendimento tradizionale mediante un'opera di selezione sui suoi contenuti religiosi dovremmo forse considerare come, accanto all'elemento di apertura e rispetto verso la parte buona della cultura profana, esse incidevano di sicuro nel favorire novità per la prassi didattica, quantunque dal nostro osservatorio tali novità rimangano implicite e potenziali.

Compilati nello stesso periodo, ebbero diffusione nelle chiese orientali i *Canoni Apostolici*, conservati in appendice alle *Costituzioni Apostoliche*: un passaggio abbastanza noto istituisce una serie di antinomie irriducibili: «Vuoi leggere opere storiche? Vi è il Libro dei Re. Scritti di *sophistikà* e poesia?[8] I Profeti, Giobbe, l'autore dei Proverbi... Lirica? I Salmi. Opere sulle antiche origini del mondo? La Genesi. Diritto e morale? La legge gloriosa del Signore Iddio».

La Chiesa molto a lungo non strutturò sul territorio una rete di scuole alternative, se non per chi aveva in mente di dedicarsi alla carriera ecclesiastica. Ci si può tuttavia di nuovo chiedere se anche prese di posizione come quella richiamata, certo solo ufficiose ma precise e a loro volta esprimenti trasformazioni di sensibilità già emerse nella società cristiana, lasciassero sostanzialmente inalterate le metodiche educative delle scuole «laiche» e con sedi in spazi appositi, oppure se, come qui si ritiene, tali dettami imponessero a esse innovazioni sul piano organizzativo e delle letture. Viene qui spontaneo pensare alle rilevazioni quantitative su base prosopografica fatte oltre cinquanta anni fa da Paul Petit sugli studenti di Libanio, in un contesto cristianizzato quale Antiochia: fra quelli di cui era nota l'appartenenza religiosa solo 12 su 100 sarebbero stati cristiani[9], un calcolo comunque significativo per quanto possa essere da aggiustare e da soppesare alla luce vuoi dell'esimia qualità della scuola del retore e l'alta estrazione media delle pecore del suo gregge, vuoi della possibilità che i cristiani siano sottorappresentati nell'epistolario. Un qualche ruolo in tale disaffezione potrebbe anche averlo avuto la ritrosia delle famiglie

---

[7] Testo consultato nella ed. di E. Oberg, *Amphilochii Iconiensis Iambi ad Seleucum*, Berlin 1969.

[8] *Sophistika* è forse nel senso di sapienziali, anche se il contesto polemico suggerirebbe un confronto con un genere secolare-profano. A.H.M. Jones, *The Later Roman Empire*, Oxford 1964, 1005, traduce il vocabolo con «Eloquence».

[9] P. Petit, *Les étudiants de Libanius. Un professeur de faculté et ses élèves au Bas Empire*, Paris 1957, sul reclutamento, le origini, l'appartenenza religiosa degli studenti di Libanio si ved la parte terza del libro, 95 ss.

cristiane a inviare i loro ragazzi presso un professore così connotato culturalmente e religiosamente[10].

Spostandoci dall'altra riva del Mediterraneo, la documentazione relativa al grado di compatibilità tra libri cristiani e formazione fondata sulle discipline profane è più esile. L'installazione germanica incise sul restringimento (peraltro di disagevole misurazione) dell'educazione scolastica tradizionale concentrata nelle città, che pare aver preso corpo già nel V secolo, mentre nascevano le prime scuole episcopali e monastiche[11]. L'Occidente latino è stato vagliato in un importante libro pubblicato nel 2007 da Peter Gemeinhardt (*Das lateinische Christentum und die antike pagane Bildung*, Tübingen), che ho conosciuto troppo tardi per poterne fare pieno uso in questa sede: Gemeinhardt accoglie lo schema che vede una separazione tra gli atteggiamenti di principio dei cristiani e le loro effettuali condotte verso la *Bildung* antica, la quale non avrebbe mai cessato di costituire una parte integrante della loro essenza culturale e formativa; da ciò sarebbe dipeso anche la sostanziale mancata cristianizzazione delle istituzioni scolastiche canoniche, «pubbliche» (con professori stipendiati dalle municipalità o dallo stato) o «private» (con docenti che si organizzavano da soli e i cui redditi erano tratti principalmente dagli esborsi delle famiglie degli studenti). Agostino fornisce esempi di esposizioni di pedagogia cristiana che toccano il rapporto con i metodi e le arti liberali nel *de magistro* e specialmente nel *de doctrina christiana* ma occorrerebbe procedere con uno spoglio sistematico tra le pieghe del sermonario e dell'epistolario del vescovo ipponense per carpire, verosimilmente, almeno alcuni dati più vividi, ossia con riflessi di storia sociale. Paolino da Nola nel suo epistolario fornisce per parte sua qualche spunto utile. In partico-

---

[10] Nel suo recente *The School of Libanius in Late Antique Antioch*, Princeton 2007, sul quale ho in c.d.s una recensione per «Athenaeum» 98 (2010), Raffaella Cribiore non interviene sulla questione sollevata dalla statistica di Petit. Una certa influenza sui comportamenti dovettero avere le polemiche e le iniziative di cristiani aggressivi con i loro ex-professori e con i metodi trasmessi dalla loro scuola (noi conosciamo le punte dell'iceberg, come Giovanni Crisostomo verso Libanio nella sua orazione *Su Babila*, 98-113, *Jean Chrysostome – Discours sur Babylas*, a cura di M.A. SCHATKIN, Paris 1990, 225-251). Cfr. anche le proposte fra loro convergenti di un Pomerio, orientale di origine ma scrivente in latino, nel *De vita contemplativa* I, 23 e degli *Statuta Ecclesiae Antiqua*, canone 79, sulla necessità di trasmettere, per farsi capire, un linguaggio più semplice rispetto a quello appreso nelle scuole: un tema che fu declinato da vari altri interpreti e che incideva direttamente sul rapporto tra retorica e insegnamento, cfr. oltre § 4.

[11] Sul tema si veda W. LIEBESCHUETZ, *The Decline and Fall of the Roman City*, Oxford 2001, 318-341, spec. 318-320.

lare nella epistola 16, al suo parente Giovio, pagano non solo nel nome, dalle spiccate attitudini razionalistiche ma incuriosito dagli usi e dalle dottrine del cristianesimo, Paolino rimprovera l'influenza di cattivi maestri e il tempo dedicato alle arti liberali, pratica che potrà non essergli di danno solo se deciderà finalmente di volgersi esclusivamente a Cristo. Il filo rosso di questa lettera è, appunto, *il buon impiego del tempo*, collegato all'idea di recuperare il tempo perduto – a scuola e altrimenti – nelle vane letture profane (e in effetti a giudicare dalla messe di allusioni e citazioni ininterrotte da Vecchio e Nuovo Testamento, che caratterizza l'opera in prosa di Paolino, la sua personale conversione era stata senza alternative, e comprensibilmente aveva lasciato interdetti molti dei suoi amici). Si può pensare inoltre all'epistola a Apro, che aveva lasciato l'attività forense (*Ep.* 38, 6: *Sibi habeant litteras suas oratores, sibi sapientiam suam philosophi...*; cfr. *Ep.* 7)[12].

Per far progredire il nostro mosaico con un ultimo tassello fra quelli a disposizione, per l'Oriente come per l'Occidente si può postulare una relativa diffusione del fenomeno, frammentariamente attestato, di opposizione cristiana alla educazione tradizionale mediante il ritiro individuale di grammatici e retori che dopo la conversione ritennero loro dovere abbandonare la professione docente, per ragioni morali, e dedicarsi a una vita contemplativa[13].

Di quanto sin qui detto, più della disomogeneità dei materiali, il limite è nella difficoltà a individuare le ricadute sociali delle dinamiche che essi consentono almeno di intravedere, una determinazione che sarebbe fondamentale per generalizzazioni meno rozze. Possiamo però tentare di rafforzare l'inchiesta spostandoci su un piano più direttamente politico.

---

[12] Incidentalmente, sia aggiunto che Paolino cercava di autorappresentarsi fra coloro che ritenevano Virgilio, da lui peraltro assai ben conosciuto, «escluso ormai dai nostri studi», *non nostri iam studii*, *Ep.* 22, 3. In generale su Paolino, la cultura classica, l'amicizia cristiana vd. D. TROUT, *Paulinus of Nola. Life, Letters, and Poems*, Berkeley 1999, 198-251.

[13] L'elemento del *topos* biografico e ascetico non implica che il fenomeno non avesse addentellati reali; cfr. Origene in Eusebio *H.E.* VI 3, 8-9; il sofista di inizio IV secolo Asterio di Cappadocia, *PLRE* I, Asterius 2 è un altro caso. Lo stesso Agostino, come è noto, ebbe esperienze di insegnamento prima di attraversare la protratta fase di crisi che lo condusse a convertirsi e a assumere poi il clericato. Si veda anche, per fasi più tarde, P. RICHÉ, *La scuola e l'insegnamento nell'Occidente cristiano*, trad. it. Roma 1984, 40-41.

2. La politica scolastica e le forme letterarie

Come è noto, nel periodo della propagazione del cristianesimo, fra II e III secolo, alcuni pubblicisti cristiani sottolinearono la problematicità del ruolo dell'insegnante e posero in questione la legittimità di una partecipazione dei fedeli alle attività di una scuola dai contenuti profani, ventilando la possibilità di ritirare i ragazzi del tutto da essa, per non essere contaminati e per non compromettersi con le tematiche religiose e le devianze etiche che vi erano inscindibilmente connesse[14]. Non sappiamo se questo modo di contestare la scuola rimase un puro fatto di élite, una protesta «di testimonianza», o se il controllo delle autorità sulle attività formative delle scuole municipali e metropolitane si rafforzò di conseguenza. Esso comunque deve essere stato percepito come un problema rilevante già prima di Giuliano l'Apostata. Eusebio di Cesarea racconta che Massimino Daia avrebbe usato le scuole per indottrinare: paradossalmente autorizzando i ragazzi a discutere di Gesù e di Pilato e ordinando ai maestri di far circolare nelle classi, al posto dei loro testi abituali, versioni spurie e manipolate degli *Acta Pilati* (Eus. *H. E.* IX 5, 1; IX 7, 1). Un altro noto documento sulla scuola (immaginata come) sede di esasperate tensioni religiose è la versione della passione di Cassiano in Prudenzio, la prima di questo santo pervenutaci: *Peristephanon* 9, col maestro cristiano Cassiano ucciso in un imprecisato tempo *vetustum* rispetto a quando scriveva il poeta, forse nel periodo della grande persecuzione, dai suoi scolari, a colpi di stilo. Per la temperie post-tetrarchica, sarebbe interessante saperne di più sulle motivazioni e i contenuti di una epistola-trattatello sull'educazione del politeista convinto Giamblico di Calcide, scritta probabilmente in età costantiniana[15].

Per quel che riguarda l'editto del 362 e le considerazioni di Giuliano sulla vocazione e le attitudini morali dei docenti delle scuole di grammatica e retorica, tali (pur ragionevoli) prese di posizione non devono essere raccordate esclusivamente con una situazione di eccezionalità e con la politica di rilancio religioso un po' fondamentalista[16] dell'imperatore. Esse

---

[14] Mi riferisco in particolare a Tertulliano, *De idololatria* 10; *Tradizione Apostolica* di Ippolito di Roma (II 16, 3); Celso in Origene (*Contra Celsum* 3, 55 e 3, 58). Polemiche aspre contro la filosofia pagana e la scuola classica erano contenute anche nell'opera di Taziano il Siro (II secolo).

[15] A.-M. PALMER, *Prudentius on the Martyrs*, Oxford 1989, 242-243; J. BIDEZ, *Le philosophe Jamblique et son école*, «REG» 32 (1919), 29-40, spec. 34-35.

[16] Cfr. per la nozione *Fondare i fondamentalismi. Esplorazioni critiche dei diversi modi del fondamentalismo nella storia*, a cura di F. SQUARCINI, L. TAVARNESI, Firenze 2007.

sono del resto perfettamente speculari ai timori e alle proteste dei cristiani prima di lui[17].

Che il prestigio e il fascino di un professore fosse in grado di influenzare sino a coartarle le propensioni degli studenti è detto esplicitamente da alcune fonti – Giuliano stesso attaccava l'opportunismo dei maestri cristiani con le loro finalità di proselitismo attuate mentre insegnavano cose in cui non credevano – ma è anche un dato universalmente constatabile. Anche Mario Vittorino, l'oratore convertitosi in vecchiaia, verso il 354, nelle *Confessioni* agostiniane (VIII 2, 3) è citato come «maestro di tanti nobili senatori» il quale per quasi tutta la vita «s'era attardato a difendere» gli idoli pagani «con tuonante eloquenza», il che avveniva dalla sua cattedra romana oltre che dai discorsi e dagli scritti di sua produzione. Sappiamo, e ci si attarda sino al V secolo inoltrato, di retori e filosofi pagani che, in circostanze riconducibili alle loro funzioni di docenza caldeggiavano il ritorno alle antiche divinità o che rifiutavano di convertirsi. Materiali suggestivi si trovano nella *Vita di Santa Tecla*, illustrati nella magistrale introduzione di G. Dagron alla sua edizione[18].

Un caso merita un richiamo più disteso. Da Alessandria si trasferì nel tardo V secolo ad Afrodisia, ad insegnare ed operare, Asklepiodotos (*PLRE* II, Asclepiodotus 3), colto e efficace reclamizzatore di miracoli pagani, autore di inni religiosi. Secondo R.R.R. Smith alla sua scuola forse appartenevano gli spazi ove erano installati numerosi ritratti di pensatori classici e altri ritrovamenti archeologici legati alla promozione del neoplatonismo e con esso anche ad attività più propriamente cultuali. Siamo dinanzi a un contesto focalizzato nella scuola di «tense co-existence and conflict between Platonists and Christians»[19]. Ma questo caso di mobilità intellettuale mi spinge a porre un'altra domanda non oziosa, nonostante sia forse inadatta a ricevere risposta dalla nostra *evidence*: se anche una

---

[17] Recentemente E. GERMINO, *Scuola e cultura nella legislazione di Giuliano l'Apostata*, Napoli 2004, con discussione sulla fonti a 51-110.

[18] G. DAGRON, *Vie et miracles de Sainte Thècle. Texte grec, traduction et commentaire*, in «Subsidia Hagiographica» 62 (1978), p. es. 90-94; cfr. l'interessante testimonianza di NILO, *Ep.* I 75 (*PG* 79, col. 116). Su Hegias e il suo amico Isidoro di fine V secolo, filosofo autore di inni pagani verosimilmente fatti conoscere ai suoi scolari: *PLRE* II, Isidorus 5.

[19] R.R. SMITH, *Late Roman Philosopher portraits from Aphrodisias*, «Journal of Roman Studies» 80 (1990), 127-155. Gli ambienti di quella che può essere identificata come la scuola ateniese di Proclo contenevano anch'essi rilievi e sculture di sicuro richiamo pagano, come dalla ricostruzione su base archeologica di L. BAUMER (conferenza tenuta nell'ambito dei seminari EPHE diretti da F. QUEYREL nel gennaio 2009, *La ville tardo-antique dite «de Proclus» au sud de l'Acropole d'Athènes*).

famiglia cristiana desiderava avviare il proprio figlio a studi liberali in sedi prestigiose, tali che potessero essere un buon viatico professionale: cosa poteva accadere una volta finiti gli studi, quando – come spesso attestato – l'ex studente se ne tornava in patria o si trasferiva in centri minori a fondare scuole, e a impartire lui l'insegnamento? Almeno a quel punto l'identità religiosa produceva qualche modifica rilevabile nella docenza, o tutto si perpetuava tralatiziamente con la ripetizione di tecniche e contenuti appresi nei centri di alta formazione? Insistiamo su un punto di metodo. Possiamo definire i professori tardo antichi, sulla base della loro appartenenza religiosa, come pagani e cristiani. Che una parte essenziale della loro vita, l'esercizio del mestiere, rimanesse area sostanzialmente sterilizzata dalle convinzioni religiose e culturali, è, in linea anche solo astratta, storicamente inattendibile.

La scuola non era un catalizzatore di atti di violenza materiale fra pagani e cristiani. Le attestazioni in tal senso sono scarse, sebbene non del tutto inesistenti (si pensi a episodi raccontati nella *Vita di Severo* di Zaccaria di Mitilene; alle amputazioni forse mirate alla gola delle sculture della scuola di Afrodisia, mentre i locali continuarono a essere usati). Divergenze più sottili riguardavano la selezione delle letture – si può ben ipotizzare, fra le altre, gli *exempla* rappresentati dalle vite e dalle figure dei martiri – i cambiamenti (o all'opposto la conservazione) degli ordinamenti didattici e dei programmi curriculari tradizionali, coi loro costanti richiami al culto degli dèi, e i più neutri soggetti mitologici, forse moralmente ripugnanti ma sostanzialmente percepiti come anodini, almeno nella pratica ripetitiva dell'esercizio scolastico[20]. Molto discussa è la «riforma» della didattica consistente nel riadattamento nei generi letterari greci delle Scritture pro-

---

[20] Non sorprende la centralità della presenza del paganesimo – ma di un paganesimo affabulato e meccanico – nelle produzioni tecnico-pedagogiche come i *progymnasmata,* in particolare attestati nella tradizione bizantina; peraltro glossatori e copisti non si esimevano a volte dal precisare che le divinità menzionate negli eserciziari erano un inganno. Sul tema delle persistenze del paganesimo nei livelli più elementari dell'apprendimento ho avuto una proficua conversazione con Maria Tanja Luzzatto, che ringrazio vivamente. Analoghe valutazioni per l'Occidente medievale, per manuali largamente adottati come le *Institutiones grammaticae* di Prisciano (VI sec.), nei quali le citazioni degli autori classici non potevano essere purgate dai riferimenti alle divinità (su Prisciano, per prospettive più sofisticate alla luce di analisi delle strutture testuali, cfr. ora C.M. CHIN, *Grammarian...*, es. 15-16). Per alcune osservazioni sulla differenza tra mitologia come «one of the indispensable components of a liberal education» e aspetti cultuali nella letteratura tardoantica, a proposito di Servio e Servio *auctus* vd. AL. CAMERON, *Poetry and Literary Culture in Late Antiquity*, in *Approaching Late Antiquity. The Transformation from Early to Late Empire*, a cura di S. SWAIN, M. EDWARDS, Oxford 2004, 327-354, 342.

posta dai due Apollinari, padre grammatico e figlio sofista, con una *grammatike Christianiko typo* e poi la trasposizione epicizzata dei libri storici della Bibbia, la composizione di drammi con vari schemi prosodici a uso cristiano, dialoghi con la narrazione dei Vangeli. Socrate Scolastico in un lungo excursus del III libro della sua storia ecclesiastica, secondo abituali schemi indulgente verso l'uso della *paideia* ellenica (III, 16), la giudica negativamente, come una reazione sbagliata circoscritta al contesto della politica scolastica giulianea. Ma si noti qui bene che Socrate argomenta l'utilità delle arti liberali in prima istanza con un'idea (che ritroviamo in altri scrittori), ossia che siccome le Scritture non fornirebbero ammaestramenti sul ragionamento logico, le opere degli autori profani permetterebbero invece di operare in tal senso rivelandosi assai vantaggiose per confutare i nemici della verità, pagani e senza dubbio anche eretici[21]; l'idea sembra essere quella di una *strumentalizzazione della paideia per finalità contrarie a quelle da cui proviene la paideia medesima*. Sarebbe stata proprio di questo tipo la motivazione profonda dell'editto giulianeo del 362: privare i cristiani di ottenere mediante l'educazione degli Elleni armi dialettiche troppo efficaci. Potrebbe avere inciso nella critica dello storico ecclesiastico la volontà di porre in cattiva luce due esponenti di un cristianesimo eretico (apollinarista, appunto). Si è anche messo in dubbio (con argomenti *ex silentio*) che l'iniziativa degli Apollinari sia mai esistita davvero; ma la sua sola verosimiglianza storica, rafforzata da notizie assimilabili – come quella relativa al programma scolastico cristianizzato proposto da Protogene di Edessa sotto Valente – rimane significativa[22].

---

[21] Eretici caratterizzati dall'abilità nei discorsi, p.es. GREG. NAZ. *Or.* 27, 1; 27, 10 sugli attacchi dialettici da allestire contro pitagorici, epicurei, peripatetici, platonici, stoici e tutto quel che riguarda gli dèi e i sacrifici, idoli e demoni.

[22] W.V. HARRIS, *Lettura e istruzione nel mondo antico*, trad. it. Roma-Bari 1991, 349; P. SPECK, *Sokrates scholastikos über die beiden Apolinarioi*, «Philologus» 141 (1997), 362-369; nel mio senso C. MARKSCHIES, *Lehrer, Schüler, Schule: zur Bedeutung einer Institution für das antike Christentum*, in *Religiöse Vereine in der römischen Antike*, a cura di E. GAISER, A. SCHÄFER, Tübingen 2002, 97-120, spec. 109-110; cfr. però H.-G. NESSELRATH, *Die Christen und die heidnische Bildung: Das Beispiel des Sokrates Scholastikos (hist. eccl. 3,16)*, in *Leitbilder der Spätantike – Eliten und Leitbilder*, a cura di J. DUMMER, M. VIELBERG, Stuttgart 1999, 79-100.

3. Polemiche sulla superiorità culturale

Entrambi gli universi religiosi a confronto proclamavano, sin dall'età della prima apologetica, una loro autentica superiorità culturale. Prevalevano accuse quali per esempio: da un lato, ridicolaggine e vacuità del politeismo tradizionale nelle sue rappresentazioni letterarie-figurative-rituali[23], inanità della scienza della natura con le sue spiegazioni razionali del mondo, incapaci di cogliere il senso profondo della realtà e dell'esistenza[24], anteriorità di Mosè rispetto a Omero e Platone; dall'altro lato, mancanza di maestri di filosofia e oratoria, eccessiva semplicità del messaggio etico-religioso, rozzezza dei veicoli di trasmissione dello stesso, *rusticitas* di chi rifiutava in nome della propria dottrina religiosa la civiltà urbana di matrice classica.

Aspetti della diatriba sono riproposti dal prologo del *De viris illustribus* di Gerolamo, risalente al 395-396. Siamo negli anni cruciali di poco posteriori alla grande offensiva legislativa antipagana e antieretica attuata da Teodosio Magno. L'opuscolo è dedicato a Nummius Aemilianus Dexter, senatore di origine spagnola dalla brillante carriera pubblica[25], figlio del vescovo di Barcellona Paciano e in rapporti di amicizia con la famiglia imperiale. Destro aveva invitato Gerolamo a seguire il precedente svetoniano per redigere un elenco ordinato cronologicamente di autori ecclesiastici e che avevano scritto di materia religiosa e di storia della chiesa: l'obiettivo era dimostrare agli avversari il prestigio di questo filone. Lo stesso Destro risulta nominato come 132° personaggio illustre in quanto autore di una *Omnimoda historia* (una *Storia Varia*) di cui Gerolamo, pur essendone il dedicatario, non aveva avuto ancora modo di prendere visio-

---

[23] P. es. TERTULL. *Apol.* 14-15; MIN. FEL., *Octav.* 4; ARNOB. *Disp.* IV; LACT. *Inst.* I, 9-21; FIRM. MAT. *Err. profan. relig.* 12; AUG. *Civ. Dei* VII, *passim*, ma, beninteso, l'elenco potrebbe continuare.

[24] M.L.W. LAISTNER, *Christianity and Pagan Culture in the Later Roman Empire*, Ithaca, N.Y. 1951, 52-53; R. MACMULLEN, *Christianity and Paganism in the Fourth to Eight Centuries*, New Haven-London 1997, 88-89. Si veda specialmente di Giovanni Crisostomo l'*Adversus oppugnatores vitae monasticae*; E. DI SANTO, *Giuliano l'Apostata nel pensiero di Giovanni Crisostomo: imperatore, filosofo, persecutore*, «Augustinianum» 45 (2005), 349-387, 354 nota 16; 357 con nota 27; 377 nota 88; G. RINALDI, *La Bibbia dei pagani, I. Quadro storico*, Bologna 1997, 136-137; IOH. CHRYS. *De s. Babyla contra Iulianum*, 40-50.

[25] Proconsole d'Asia dal 379 al 387, quando divenne *comes rerum privatarum* in Oriente, infine prefetto al pretorio d'Italia nel 395, *PLRE* I, Dexter 3. Cfr. HIER. *adv. Rufin.* II 23, sulla carica prefettizia ricoperta da Dexter al momento della stesura geronimiana del *de viris illustribus*.

ne[26]. L'autore di Strìdone (*oppido Stridonis*: di se stesso in *de vir. ill.* 135) non abbandona mai del tutto i suoi (pre)giudizi retorici[27] – tant'è che gli apprezzamenti sugli autori cristiani, per lo più appartenenti alle gerarchie ecclesiastiche[28], contrapposti ai pagani fanno spesso uso di parametri quasi ciceroniani[29] – ma le sue pagine danno ben conto sia delle più comuni accuse ricevute sia di possibili strategie di risposta[30]. Nelle ultime righe del prologo c'è il riferimento più puntuale alla contesa in atto:

> «Discant igitur Celsus, Porphyrius, Iulianus, rabidi adversus Christum canes, discant sectatores eorum qui putant ecclesiam nullos philosophos et eloquentes, nullos habuisse doctores, quanti et quales viri eam fundaverint, struxerint, adornaverint, et desinant fidem nostram rusticae tantum simplicitatis arguere, suamque potius imperitiam recognoscant».

> «Imparino dunque Celso, Porfirio, Giuliano, cani rabbiosi contro Cristo, imparino i loro seguaci che pensano che la Chiesa non abbia avuto filosofi e oratori, né maestri, quanti e quali uomini l'abbiano fondata, edificata, adornata, e cessino di accusare la nostra fede di rozza semplicità, riconoscendo piuttosto la propria ignoranza».

All'interno del testo, colpiscono notizie come quella su Lucio Anneo Seneca (*de vir. ill.* 12), di cui si ricorda lo stoicismo e si ammette l'inseri-

---

[26] In modo analogo, Gerolamo si scusa preventivamente per eventuali assenze di scrittori che non aveva potuto conoscere vivendo – come dice nella prefazione del *de viris illustribus* – *in hoc terrarum angulo*.

[27] Osservazioni succinte sul dibattito sulla simbiosi fra cultura classica e cultura biblica e sui suoi limiti nell'opera di Gerolamo in *Gerolamo. Gli uomini illustri*, a cura di A. CERESA-GASTALDO, Firenze 1988, 29-30.

[28] Comprensivo degli eresiarchi: un dato che fa riflettere, specialmente se si pensa che spesso la pamphlettistica fra correnti cristiane faceva ricorso all'accusa di connivenza coi pagani dei leader o del pensiero eretico-scismatici.

[29] *Gerolamo. Gli uomini...*, 30-31. Il caso di Origene (citato anche come esempio di insegnante che usava le *saeculares litterae* per attrarre molti a sé e quindi al cristianesimo) è emblematico perché di lui Gerolamo sottolinea con forza – nella più lunga notizia dell'opuscolo – la grandezza intellettuale di cui offriva dimostrazione grazie alle sue conoscenze nei campi «secolari» di dialettica, geometria, aritmetica, musica, grammatica, retorica, filosofia (*de vir. ill.* 54); cfr. su Anatolio di Alessandria, per le sue capacità negli stessi settori, *ibid.* 73.

[30] Sulla difesa da parte di Gerolamo della cultura cristiana si veda anche per esempio la lettera 70 (397-398 d.C.), S. PRICOCO, *Storia letteraria e storia ecclesiastica dal «De viris illustribus» di Gerolamo a Gennadio*, Catania 1979, spec. 22-23. In generale F. THÉLAMON, *Païens et chrétiens au IVe siècle*, Paris 1981; per una trattazione più rapida dei rapporti culturali tra pagani e cristiani e le polemiche sui contenuti del contrasto cfr. A. QUACQUARELLI, *Reazione pagana e trasformazione della cultura (fine IV secolo d.C.)*, Bari 1986, spec. 13-29.

mento in ragione del carteggio con Paolo di Tarso. A proposito di Giusto di Tiberiade (*de vir. Ill.* 14): «Della provincia di Galilea, tentò anche lui di comporre una *Storia delle vicende giudaiche* e certi brevi commenti alle Scritture, ma Giuseppe lo accusa di falsità. È noto del resto che egli scrisse nello stesso periodo in cui scrisse anche Giuseppe». Un personaggio del IV secolo è così presentato: «Gelasio, vescovo di Cesarea di Palestina dopo Euzoio, si dice che scriva alcune opere in stile accurato e preciso [*accurati limatique sermonis*], ma non le pubblichi». Si potrebbero citare svariati altri esempi[31]. Cosa potevano rappresentare notizie così brevi e insignificanti per un detrattore della religione cristiana, ipotetico destinatario o lettore del catalogo, che adduceva la superiorità culturale del suo mondo? Gerolamo evidentemente fa del suo meglio (i risultati di questa sorta di agone saranno stati fatti circolare) per rivendicare appartenenze e «iscrizioni» al suo elenco, la sua operazione mirava cioè ad avere un impatto quantitativo per realizzare il quale, accanto agli scrittori, apologeti e ecclesiastici, menzionò anche personaggi solo molto poco noti o solo forzosamente ascrivibili alla *pars* cristiana[32].

---

[31] Il modo in cui viene presentato Erma (*de vir. ill.* 10) mostra come alcune personalità di *illustres viri* cristiani vengano inserite nell'elenco senza alcun tipo di giustificazione o di caratterizzazione tale da potere avere una efficacia dimostrativa: «Si dice che Erma, di cui fa menzione l'apostolo Paolo scrivendo *Ai Romani*: – Salutate Flegonte, Erme, Patroba, Erma ed i fratelli che sono con loro –, sia l'autore del libro che si intitola *Il pastore* ed è anche letto in pubblico presso alcune chiese della Grecia, un libro veramente utile, da cui molti antichi scrittori attinsero testimonianze, ma presso i Latini quasi sconosciuto». Un tal Pinito di Creta (*de vir. ill.* 28) viene ricordato unicamente per una *valde elegans epistula* nella quale spiegava come occorre somministrare ai fedeli non solo latte ma anche cibi solidi necessari «per progredire verso la piena maturità spirituale». Vd. anche *de vir. ill.* 64; 131.

[32] Nell'ambito delle rivendicazioni identitarie e delle polemiche tipiche del clima culturale di IV e V secolo, i pagani cercavano di uscire dalle secche di un mero e fragile politeismo cercando con maggior vigore che in passato, ora che era in gioco la loro stessa sopravvivenza, una contaminazione fra esso e forme di enoteismo di natura filosofica-platonica e solare. Divinità ancillari o virtù del dio Sole che si manifestano come divinità sono lungamente catalogate e spiegate ai convitati da Pretestato in Macrobio *Sat.* I 17-23; sull'identificazione di Giove con il Sole, *ibid.* I 23. Coglie bene «le souci prosélyte» della valorizzazione, da parte di alcuni autori cristiani come Saturnino di Thugga, delle potenzialità monoteistiche racchiuse nel paganesimo cfr. N. BELAYCHE, «*Au(x) dieu(x) qui régne(nt) sur...*». *Basileia divine et fonctionnement du polythéisme dans l'Anatolie impériale*, in *Pouvoir et religion dans le monde romain en hommage à Jean-Pierre Martin*, dir. A. VIGOURT, X. LORIOT, A. BÉRENGER-BADEL e B. KLEIN, Paris 2006, 257-269, 266-267. Uno, come mente divina, nella filosofia di un autore anonimo di III secolo considerato pagano e apprezzato da Lattanzio: R. MACMULLEN, *Christianity...*, 85.

4. Retorica e scuola

Le *disputationes* fra pagani e cristiani sulla superiorità culturale oscillavano tra due estremi: le disquisizioni molto amichevoli tra uomini e ambienti accomunati da un senso di appartenenza alle élites (che decisamente prevaleva sulla divisione provocata dalla loro distanza religiosa) e i livelli di effettivo e più aggressivo scontro culturale nei singoli contesti, da parte cristiana sollecitato peculiarmente dagli obblighi del proselitismo e dell'evangelizzazione. Fondamentale fra le arti liberali era la retorica, una disciplina verso la quale i cristiani ebbero un rapporto sfaccettato. Elementi di persistenza erano legati alla sua funzione di strumento di preparazione professionalizzante e in tal senso non stupisce la frequentazione dei giovani discenti cristiani delle scuole di retorica né la presenza di retori-professori cristiani. Con una solo parziale contraddizione, i cristiani ammettevano che la retorica era una materia mal conciliabile con la loro dottrina (oltre ai contenuti con i quali la si esercitava, c'erano implicazioni morali, quali la vanità del retore, l'elemento eccessivamente competitivo della disciplina, ecc.) e precocemente procedettero soprattutto in ambiti episcopali a rifunzionalizzare i *logoi*, per potere interloquire meglio con le folle che ascoltavano i sermoni al limite adattando verso il basso il registro dell'eloquio, a scopi di edificazione e conversione, educazione religiosa *ad intellegendas sacras scripturas*. Testo chiave per la riflessione sull'«altra retorica», più spiritualmente elevata, quella biblica, è il IV libro del *De doctrina christiana* di Agostino. Già maestro di retorica, egli distingueva fra un'arte dell'eloquenza resa nobile dai contenuti e una al contrario più fine a se stessa o comunque utile solo per andare incontro a esigenze pratiche.

Le attitudini di opposizione radicale come quella critica geronimiana fra «ciceroniano» e «cristiano» non raggiunsero una capacità di penetrazione nel corpo sociale: contraddizioni e critiche culturali e etiche non ebbero mai forza tale da modificare in profondità l'organizzazione dell'insegnamento. Si deve al tempo stesso riconoscere che le nostre fonti concernono soprattutto le realtà metropolitane, nel campo delle *litterae liberales* più conservative per vari motivi. Un Cassiodoro, parlando di Roma, nella prefazione alle *Institutiones divinarum et saecularium litterarum* poteva dichiararsi... *dolore permotus ut Scripturis divinis magistri publici deessent cum mundani auctores celeberrima procul dubio traditione pollerent*. E in effetti alcuni decenni prima, nell'Italia ostrogota della prima metà del VI secolo, Magno Felice Ennodio, che sarà vescovo di Pavia dal 513, nella *Paraenesis didascalica* evocava Cicerone come modello di eloquenza preziosa per i cristiani e in altro luogo menziona l'Arpinate in un contesto di elogio dell'educazione grammaticale (e fra le sorgenti di sapere cui attinge il *grammaticus*) con altri autori profani come Sallustio e Virgilio. Ma Ennodio, nelle *Dictiones*, oltre che nella *Paraenesis* stessa può essere considerato un caso degno di considerazione per capire come i programmi scolastici e i metodi di allenamento retorici non fossero affatto rimasti cristallizzati e bloccati alla situazione di secoli addietro, e del resto i modelli stilistici e gli argomenti della poetica ennodiana contaminavano sacro e profano, mitigavano (presi nel complesso della produzione) la tradizione «libertaria» classica con la prudenza virtuosa degli approcci cristiani[33].

Il meccanismo che probabilmente salvò la retorica tardoantica da condanne senza appello si raccorda con la appena evocata teorizzazione cristiana secondo cui essa poteva essere destinata «a fin di bene» per combattere senza mediazioni sul piano tecnico e dialettico chi cristiano non era. Dunque non si trattò di una sopravvivenza anodina e inerziale, priva di spigoli. Così, anche la tesi (A. Bartalucci) del *Carmen contra paganos* come *vituperatio* di provenienza scolastica antipagana, ipotesi che pure non ha incontrato successo, e anch'io credo giustamente, suscita qualche interesse per l'idea che simili finalità fossero contemplate e che analoghi pamphlet potessero altrimenti essere composti in ambienti di scuola[34].

5. Conclusioni

È opportuno non deporre la nozione di conflitto, in generale, per l'analisi politica e sociale dei rapporti tra pagani e cristiani del IV-V secolo[35]. Si è cercato qui di riargomentarne la funzionalità, nei limiti consentiti da una documentazione frammentaria e spesso poco esplicita, per fornire un profilo interpretativo delle relazioni tra i due gruppi avendo come sfondo di inda-

---

[33] Per un avviamento vd. G. POLARA, *Letteratura latina tardoantica e altomedievale*, Napoli 1987, 46-49. Traendo spunto in particolare dall'attività poetica ennodiana (49), l'autore chiarisce efficacemente in che senso fosse «ancora irrisolto, in Ennodio, il conflitto tra cristianesimo e tradizione classica». Cfr. *La Paraenesis didascalica di Magno Felice Ennodio*, a cura di R.A. RALLO FRENI, Firenze 1981², spec. 7-32.

[34] «*Contro i pagani*» – *Carmen cod. Paris. Lat. 8084*, a cura di A. BARTALUCCI, Pisa 1998.

[35] Esso è ripreso nel cap. 3 del libro (che mi è stato possibile sfogliare del tutto parzialmente e solo in rete) di A. KALDELLIS, *Hellenism in Byzantium: The Transformations of Greek Identity and the Reception of the Classical Tradition*, Cambridge 2008, cfr. *ibid.*, 5.

gine la scuola³⁶. Le critiche cristiane alla *paideia* classica, che scaturivano da un effettivo disagio sulla compatibilità tra una corretta formazione religiosa e i programmi della scuola «secondaria» pagana, ebbero conseguenze di qualche rilievo sull'impianto sia concettuale sia pratico che stava alla base dell'insegnamento delle discipline secolari. Ove anche queste ultime erano accettate, il complesso delle relazioni sociali, culturali, religiose non ne riceveva necessariamente un impulso al dialogo, alla coabitazione con il diverso da sé, giacché l'esigenza rimaneva quella di consolidare un'identità cristiana che non era inclusiva. Da analoga angolazione, in un recente studio italiano si è parlato, con una generalizzazione interessante ma non del tutto convincente, di un avvicinamento dei cristiani al bagaglio culturale e alle strutture della scuola classici come una sorta di «cavallo di Troia», deliberata manovra di aggiramento a scopi di predominio³⁷: ciò che implica una sottovalutazione di dati essenziali come quello della nostalgia letteraria, della soggezione ammirata verso la cultura tradizionale, dell'autorevolezza sociale e della realizzazione professionale di cui a lungo fu pre-condizione e simbolo; in un senso opposto, si è parlato (per Cesario di Arles) di una strategia di cristianizzazione consistente direttamente nell'ostilità spinta al sabotaggio di letteratura e pensiero classici³⁸. Tralasciando di versare nel dibattito il problema di come la legislazione imperiale e le politiche culturali dello stato tardoantico abbiano potuto incidere sui cambiamenti della scuola³⁹, in vari modi, l'assetto di studio tràdito poteva essere trasformato, come esito di dinamiche non più dialogiche che conflittuali: sul piano delle

---

[36] G. STROUMSA, *La fine del sacrificio. Le mutazioni religiose nella tarda antichità*, trad. it. Torino 2006: prospettiva conflittuale a tutto tondo, ma cristianizzazione culturale e educativa con risistemazione del patrimonio classico in subordine a quello biblico (sistema della «doppia elica»), spec. 56-57.

[37] M.G. LA CONTE, *L'Occidente romano fra alterità e mediazione: strategie di potere*, «Acta Classica Univ. Scient. Debrecen.» 34-35 (1998-1999), 367-388.

[38] W.E. KLINGSHIRN, *Caesarius of Arles: The Making of a Christian Community in Late Antique Gaul*, Cambridge 1994. C'è anche da tener conto, quale ulteriore elemento di complessità, del valore positivo attribuito in ambienti cristiani all'ignoranza accompagnata dalla fede (e come prova di fede), cfr. HARRIS, *Lettura e istruzione...*, 339.

[39] Istituzionalmente la legislazione imperiale si occupava soprattutto di garantire con regolamenti e sussidi il buon funzionamento di pochi grandi e tradizionali centri di eccellenza metropolitani (Roma, Costantinopoli, Atene, Berito: A.H.M. JONES, *The Later Roman Empire...*, 997-1000, per l'essenziale), mentre meno controllate dall'alto erano le attività di molte sedi municipali disseminate nelle province e ancora attive almeno nel IV e V secolo. Altra questione teorica da porre è se un potere imperiale tutt'altro che immune da tendenze alla intolleranza religiosa e artefice della legislazione della prima metà del V secolo, con la quale si ostacolava ai pagani l'accesso alle attività pubbliche e anzi si metteva al bando la semplice professione di paganesimo (*CTh* XVI

metodologie e dei fini dell'insegnamento, dei programmi, della partecipazione stessa dei cristiani. Fra le prime, alcuni schemi letterari di matrice cristiana o riadattati cristianamente, i centoni, la poesia parafrastica, l'uso degli inni nella liturgia[40], l'uso stesso della poesia (altrimenti sospetta) e dell'esametro, secondo tendenze sviluppatesi tra IV e V secolo, possono forse essere interpretati quale ricerca di registri e generi identitariamente definiti e competitivi[41]. Si potrebbe ribadire quanto osservato in altra sede, prendendo in considerazione le comunità studentesche del Mediterraneo tardo antico: gli studenti cristiani potevano adeguarsi più o meno ai comportamenti richiesti loro, erano sottoposti a forme di controllo sociale, potevano costituire orgogliosamente dei gruppi a sé caratterizzati dalla loro fede[42].

Per concludere. È fuori di dubbio: abbiamo maggiori riscontri delle dinamiche di continuità di una tradizione educativa pagana e di una tipologia di erudizione secolare nella quale le grandi aristocrazie e i più raffinati artisti e scrittori si riconoscevano indipendentemente dalla loro professione religiosa. La più fitta presenza di tali riscontri corrispondeva a una effettiva centralità della meccaniche di simbiosi e permanenza nell'ambito tematico qui indagato, nel ricomporre le quali altri fattori qui non esplicitamente evocati dovevano entrare in gioco con ritmi e incidenze spazio-temporali non sintetizzabili, per esempio l'incoerenza delle spiritualità, le incertezze sui culti da professare, il carattere religiosamente misto degli aggregati familiari. In un tentativo di analisi di storia sociale sulle realtà locali e sugli strati dove agiva la cultura cristiana non si dovrà tuttavia sottovalutare che agli elementi di amalgama e dialogo, coesione, acculturazione reciproca, simbiosi, si associavano, e con un'incidenza mal

---

10, 21-24; *Sirmond.* 6; *Nov. Theod.* 3), potesse vedere negativamente le forme con le quali avveniva una cristianizzazione del sistema formativo.

[40] Ambrogio vantava che quest'uso riuscisse a equiparare a un maestro chi non era stato neppure studente, per la facilità che tutti avevano allo stesso modo di memorizzare le strofe cantate: *Ep.* 75, 34; cfr.i versi iniziali del I libro del *Carmen Paschale*.

[41] Per una disamina sulla poesia greca tardoantica in rapporto all'accettazione della cultura classica da parte dei cristiani, con brevi notazioni (non necessariamente coincidenti con le mie) anche sul problema dell'elaborazione di programmi scolastici alternativi si veda in questa sede il saggio di G. Agosti.

[42] GREG. NAZ. *Or.* 43, 21; G.A. CECCONI, *Mobilità studentesca nella tarda antichità: controllo amministrativo e controllo sociale*, «MEFRIM» 119 (2007), 137-164; alle fonti qui citate per esemplificare il fenomeno delle raccomandazioni di vescovi per studenti amici o parenti (150-151) si aggiungano p.es. quelle indirizzate al pagano, ma ben introdotto nel mondo ecclesiastico, Isokasios da Teodoreto, indicate in G. DAGRON, *Vie et miracles...*, 91 nota 5.

misurabile e mischiandosi secondo «posologie» non ricostruibili, tensioni, rivalità, antagonismi, legati sia a spinte pagane in tal senso, sia a forme di relativa chiusura e boicottaggio verso le *artes* tradizionali e le *litterae mundanae*, riserve sui contenuti religiosi dell'insegnamento, sui disvalori e sulle attitudini comportamentali di chi era educato a vivere secondo il modello classico. Si può ipotizzare che tali elementi siano sottorappresentati nella nostra evidenza documentaria e che lo siano perché il loro impatto potrebbe essere stato più significativo in segmenti sociali al di sotto della crema dell'élite politica e letteraria e nelle numerose scuole municipali di richiamo minore rispetto ai centri di alta formazione «universitaria» che perpetuarono fra IV e VI secolo la loro esistenza nelle due parti dell'impero.

KATE COOPER

Reti di famiglia, reti di evangelizzazione: la famiglia tra paganesimo e cristianesimo nella *Passio Sebastiani*

«I discepoli di Cristo non considerano come andranno le cose davanti ai giudici. Per questo egli ci avvertì, dicendo: "quando vi metteranno nelle loro mani, non preoccupatevi di come parlare o cosa dire; ciò che direte vi sarà dato quando verrà il momento; perché non sarete voi a parlare, ma lo Spirito del Padre che parlerà attraverso di voi!"»[1].

Queste sono le parole di sfida del martire Tranquillino ad Agrestio Cromazio, prefetto urbano della città di Roma sotto Diocleziano, così come sono riportate nella *Passione di san Sebastiano*, testo del V secolo o dell'inizio di quello successivo. Lettori e ascoltatori del VI secolo, ripensando a questo colloquio, erano al corrente di un fatto che lo spettatore contemporaneo non ricorda, cioè che nella storia del primo cristianesimo sarebbero poi emersi come figure eroiche non solo Sebastiano ma anche lo stesso pagano Cromazio: infatti, secondo la *Passio*, il prefetto stesso esitava sulla soglia della conversione al cristianesimo; egli sarebbe stato ricordato non come il severo giudice dei cristiani, ma come uno di essi, come padre di Tiburzio, anch'egli martire sotto Diocleziano.

Con la *Passio Sebastiani* siamo in presenza dell'idea, molto influente nella prima comunità cristiana, che il martire fosse il paradigma del predicatore cristiano, capace in modo unico, attraverso il suo completo sacrificio della carne per la Parola, di servire da cassa di risonanza, con un fenomeno che potrebbe essere chiamato «ventriloquismo divino». Oltre al dono della resistenza di fronte alla morte, il martire gode del pieno potere

---

La presente è una versione rielaborata di un'articolo originalmente pubblicato come Ventriloquism and the Miraculous: Conversion, Preaching, and the Martyr Exemplum in Late Antiquity, *in* Signs, Wonders, and Miracles, Studies in Church History 41, *eds.* K. COOPER, J. GREGORY, *Woodbridge 2005, 22-45. Ringrazio Riccardo Bof per la collaborazione nel rendere migliore la versione italiana, ma la colpa è mia se sono rimaste inesattezze o errori.*

[1] Matt. 10, 19, citato in *Passio Sebastiani* 45. La *Passio Sebastiani* (BHL 7543) è edita negli *Acta Sanctorum*, secondo volume di gennaio (AASS II Ian., 265-78: qui, 272).

della parola, della capacità di trasmettere un messaggio mandato dallo Spirito del Padre. Questa idea aveva solide basi bibliche, ma – come molte altre idee ricavate dalla Scrittura per utilità delle comunità cristiane – la sua apparizione nel testo in considerazione è anche espressione di interessi e ansietà specificamente propri della generazione contemporanea alla stesura della *Passio*. Quando assistiamo alla scena in cui Sebastiano predica agli ufficiali pagani, il cui compito è perseguitarlo, siamo testimoni di una raffigurazione tardo romana – per quanto idealizzata – del processo della conversione cristiana.

Nell'analisi di questo testo è di capitale importanza l'approccio della *Passio* alla relazione tra discorso e miracolo, col fine di mostrare come almeno un gruppo di cristiani alla fine dell'antichità interpretava l'intervento divino che portava all'adesione alla fede di nuovi proseliti. Il testo non mette in contrasto in alcun modo due aspetti della fede, quello «razionale» e quello «miracoloso»: al contrario, essi sono visti come operanti in una sorta di sinergia di ispirazione divina. La professione di fede chiara e accurata fatta da un membro della comunità si integra perfettamente nel panorama mentale del miracoloso: il dono della conversione – la capacità del martire di attirare i persecutori alla fede – non era niente di meno che un miracolo.

Ho sostenuto altrove che nel periodo precedente la conversione di Costantino gli scrittori cristiani facevano un uso immaginativo delle convenzioni della pratica forense romana, con il fine di descrivere e interpretare l'apparentemente miracolosa forza d'animo dei martiri come garanzia della verità della propria fede. La volontà – e la capacità – di fronteggiare risolutamente la morte era vista come prova del fatto che la fede cristiana fosse fondata su una realtà incontestabile[2]. Proprio questo spinse a porre molta enfasi sulle professioni di fede pronunciate dai martiri, come appaiono registrate nei testi.

***

Incominciamo con il problema del miracoloso: se gli anonimi autori dei *Gesta martyrum* non sono visti come testimoni preziosi di un'interpretazione autenticamente tardo romana del fenomeno della conversione dei loro antenati, il motivo è da cercare nell'imbarazzo di noi moderni di fron-

---

[2] K. COOPER, *The Voice of the Victim: Gender, Representation, and Early Christian Martyrdom*, «Bulletin of the John Rylands Library» 80 (1998), 147-157.

te alla retorica del miracolo presente in quelle fonti. Nel suo influente studio del 1981, *The cult of the Saints*, P. Brown suggerì che chi nel XX secolo si era interessato alla religione popolare nella Tarda Antichità doveva molto ai modelli proposti nel XVIII secolo da David Hume sulla persistenza dell'opposizione tra le idee religiose del popolo e quelle dell'*élite* – una visione che da quel momento è nota come modello a due livelli[3]. D. Hume vedeva nel «volgo» della Tarda Antichità una manifestazione della perenne e immutabile forza che si oppone allo sforzo esercitato dalla società umana per avanzare sulla strada della ragione. A causa di questa resistenza il cristianesimo postcostantiniano conobbe una sorta di inerzia che condusse la massa appena cristianizzata a rimanere fedele alle proprie antiche credenze, nonostante i migliori sforzi profusi dai vescovi. A sua volta P. Brown vide nel *The natural history of religion* di D. Hume l'opera che fornì la «struttura mentale» del classico approccio al cristianesimo delle origini e della Tarda Antichità, dal *Decline and fall of the Roman empire* di Edward Gibbon alla *History of Latin Christianity* di Dean Milman. Celebre è l'affermazione di E. Gibbon, secondo la quale il cristianesimo fu corrotto, in quanto religione monoteistica, dal «volgare». Occasione di questa corruzione fu ovviamente l'ascesa del culto dei santi, «una mitologia popolare che tendeva a restaurare il regno del politeismo»[4].

P. Brown prese il modello a due livelli come punto di partenza per una critica ormai celebre: l'accusa che l'attività di culto presso le tombe dei defunti riflettesse «pratiche precristiane», alle quali i vescovi dovevano opporsi, era collegata con l'idea, condivisa dai vescovi stessi, che l'appartenenza al cristianesimo fosse stata corrotta dalle mutazioni introdotte durante il regno di Costantino. Secondo P. Brown sia i vescovi del IV secolo sia gli storici moderni hanno spiegato con la conversione di massa il fatto che la maggioranza dei fedeli non fosse, secondo il loro parere, sufficientemente cristiana. Secondo questa visione, il gruppo di clienti che ruotava attorno ad un aristocratico, o la folla che seguiva una persona in grado di fare miracoli, avrebbe preso improvvisamente il nome di cristiano senza alcun processo di istruzione culturale o etica.

P. Brown sospettava che i vescovi di IV secolo avessero inventato il fenomeno della «conversione di massa» per reagire alla loro preoccupante percezione che stesse avendo luogo una trasformazione del cristianesimo.

---

[3] P. BROWN, *The Cult of the Saints: its Rise and Function in Latin Christianity*, Chicago 1981, 13-15.
[4] E. GIBBON, citato da P. BROWN, *The Cult of the Saints...*, 15, n. 55.

L'idea di «volgo» non era così un'invenzione dell'Illuminismo, ma degli stessi autori del IV secolo.

> «Il modello a due livelli ha fatto pensare ad una valanga che potrebbe non essere mai esistita; e ciò perché solo l'irruzione del «volgo» dentro la Chiesa cristiana poteva soddisfare le esigenze del suo sistema di spiegazione, se messa di fronte all'ascesa all'interno della Chiesa stessa di nuove forme di – apparente – sentimento religioso popolare»[5].

Tuttavia P. Brown pensava che la radice del cambiamento avesse poco a che vedere con i misteri della «religione popolare» (un fenomeno che egli, con Momigliano, pensava non esistesse). Piuttosto, gli sgradevoli sviluppi del IV secolo riflettevano una tensione tra la famiglia biologica e la Chiesa in quanto «gruppo di parentela artificiale»:

> «Dobbiamo ricordare che la Chiesa cristiana era giunta ad una posizione preminente soprattutto perché le sue pratiche rituali centrali e la sue sempre più centralizzate organizzazione e amministrazione finanziaria si presentavano al mondo pagano con un ideale di comunità che pretendeva di modificare, ridirigere e anche delimitare i limiti della parentela. La Chiesa era un gruppo di parentela artificiale. Dai suoi membri ci si aspettava che rivolgessero adeguatamente alla nuova comunità il proprio senso di solidarietà, delle lealtà e degli obblighi che prima erano rivolti alla famiglia fisica»[6].

Nel quadro dipinto da P. Brown era il vescovo, in quanto *impresario* del culto dei santi, a simboleggiare le istituzioni «pubbliche» cristiane, in contrasto con le alleanze «private» della famiglia biologica. Sebbene in questo studio non sia centrale la sostituzione da parte di P. Brown dei rapporti tra «pubblico» e «privato» per quanto riguarda la conversione di massa, si dovrà tornare ai testi in cui incombe minacciosa la famiglia romana di recente conversione. Inoltre si vedrà che devono ancora essere comprese pienamente le scene di conversione di massa, rese disponibili dalla letteratura del primo cristianesimo, in cui un aristocratico si converte insieme alla famiglia e ai dipendenti.

***

Ho dato ampio spazio a P. Brown e D. Hume in parte perché, nonostante la storiografia recente metta grande enfasi sul «volgo» e sulla critica di

---

[5] P. Brown, *The Cult of the Saints...*, 29-30.
[6] *Ibid.*, 31.

P. Brown a D. Hume, rimane ancora qualcosa da imparare dallo stesso Hume. É possibile che lo Hume del miracoloso *per se* sia più costruttivo dello Hume sulla religione popolare in generale[7]. Certamente egli scriveva in un momento storico in cui si cominciava a sfidare l'uso, da parte delle istituzioni, di occultare con il mistero le relazioni di potere. Questo progetto di demistificazione, che contribuì alla nascita delle teorie ottocentesche sulla religione come proiezione, ha avuto molteplici conseguenze sulla nostra abilità di pensare analiticamente il miracoloso. Tuttavia, quando l'analisi non viene affiancata dal riduzionismo che spesso la accompagna, essa riflette un vivido senso di cosa fosse in gioco nelle istituzioni cristiane. Nonostante la sua suscettibilità all'accusa di «ateismo dogmatico»[8] e la sua riluttanza a prestare fede al miracoloso, D. Hume vide come una questione di competenza professionale il fatto di dare conto di cosa avrebbe indotto una persona ragionevole a credere a ciò che lui stesso rifiutava.

D. Hume può fare preziosa luce sugli antichi resoconti cristiani di miracoli grazie all'enfasi da lui posta sul problema dell'affidabilità della testimonianza. Egli isolò il problema della prova indiretta – esperienza riportata, sentito dire, e altre forme di conoscenza di seconda mano – come il tipo specifico di documentazione le cui proprietà devono essere comprese perfettamente dal filosofo, in particolare quando si tratta di discutere prove in favore o contro una sospensione delle leggi della natura. «Nessuna testimonianza è sufficiente per stabilire un miracolo, a meno che la testimonianza stessa non sia tale che la sua falsità non sia più miracolosa del fatto stesso che si tenta di stabilire»[9]. Diversamente dai primi vescovi cristiani, D. Hume dava per assodato che ai suoi giorni a nessun filosofo avrebbe potuto essere fornita in modo convincente la prova diretta di un miracolo.

Certamente per D. Hume era impossibile stabilire la veridicità di una testimonianza in modo convincente, dal momento che riportare un miracolo come Verità poteva essere interpretato come prova della debolezza della fonte. Non si deve comunque essere così ingenui da credere che gli scrittori del primo cristianesimo avessero dimenticato il problema della veridicità delle fonti, quando si interessavano al miracoloso. La letteratura

---

[7] D. Hume elaborò la sua idea di miracolo nella sezione X, «Of Miracles», del suo *Enquiry Concerning the Human Understanding: an Enquiry Concerning the Human Understanding, and an Enquiry Concerning the Principles of Morals*, ed. L.A. SELBY-BIGGE, Oxford 1894.

[8] Discusso da M.SAINSBURY nella sua recensione *(TLS* 15.10.04, 4-5) di R.J. FOGELIN, *A Defense of Hume on Miracles*, Princeton 2004.

[9] D. HUME, *Enquiry...*, X.J.91, ed. SELBY-BIGGE, II. 5-16.

antica, sia pagana che cristiana, abbonda di suggerimenti sul metodo con cui riconoscere la circonvenzione religiosa, e la presenza di pretese di miracoloso tendeva a generare un confronto con un profilo criminale[10]. Ciò potrebbe spiegare perché la *Passio Sebastiani*, come gli altri *Gesta martyrum*, si occupa di stabilire le credenziali del martire come testimone nelle prime parti della narrazione, molto prima che questi sigilli le proprie buone intenzioni affrontando la morte per la fede, che conferisce il titolo di *martyr*, derivante dal greco *martyros*, il cui significato è *testimone*.

Sorprendentemente la veridicità del messaggio cristiano avrebbe potuto non essere la principale preoccupazione degli uomini e donne che si univano come convertiti adulti alla comunità cristiana dei primi secoli. Tuttavia era fondamentale nel raccontare, nel significato attribuito in retrospettiva al duello della conversione. É questa tensione tra eventi storici e invenzione pastorale che deve essere attentamente osservata e altrettanto attentamente rispettata. Si vedrà in seguito che si presta molta attenzione alle parole del martire, e al problema di resuscitare per gli spettatori della *Passio* la forza – e la verità – della predicazione in essa contenuta.

***

Quando ci dedichiamo al secondo tema, quello della conversione, incontriamo un panorama storiografico anche più spinoso di quello del miracoloso. Ad esempio, nel *Martirio di Policarpo* (II secolo), il vescovo di Smirne, legato al palo del rogo, pronuncia un discorso che serve non solo a registrare le sue istruzioni alla folla raccolta ad assistere alla sua esecuzione, ma anche ad un ulteriore scopo, cioè istruire e fortificare spiritualmente coloro che leggono o ascoltano il resoconto della sua morte. Il coraggio di Policarpo di fronte alle fiamme è il sigillo di Dio sulla veridicità del suo messaggio, anche se essa non era ancora riconosciuta da tutti.

Dopo la conversione di Costantino, i modelli narrativi sui martiri continuarono ad essere replicati nonostante la fine delle persecuzioni. Per i cristiani postcostantiniani, come l'autore della *Passio Sebastiani* o di altri romanzi tardo romani riguardanti i martiri (noti come *Gesta martyrum*)[11],

---

[10] Per esempio, un paragone tra la *Vita di Alessandro di Abonuteico* di Luciano di Samosata, con il Simone Mago dei quasi contemporanei *Riconoscimenti Clementini* mostra quanto pagani e cristiani abbiano condiviso il loro giudizio sul profilo del ciarlatano.

[11] Su data e contesto dei *Gesta martyrum*, vedere K. COOPER, *The Martyr, the Matrona and the Bishop: Networks of Allegiance in Early Sixth-Century Rome*, «Early Medieval Europe» 8 (1999), 297-317.

l'incontro tra il martire cristiano e i suoi inquisitori e carnefici divenne l'occasione per esplorare il significato del cambiamento avvenuto. Per semplificare, autori e spettatori del periodo successivo a Costantino sapevano che il loro mondo era cambiato, e ritenevano che ciò fosse avvenuto grazie ai martiri. Essi immaginavano che in qualche modo il luminoso discorso dei martiri avesse reso frutti sia celesti che terreni, in particolare con la conversione dei persecutori stessi. Tornare ripetutamente ai martiri e al loro predicare aveva il fine di comprendere come queste potenti parole avessero agito sui loro ascoltatori, ottenendo la trasformazione dell'impero.

Nel tentativo di comprendere la conversione del mondo antico al cristianesimo gli storici moderni aderiscono generalmente a uno di due modelli. Il primo, fatto proprio da Arthur Darby Nock nel suo studio sulla conversione (1933), suggerisce essenzialmente che il cristianesimo abbia provocato le conversioni grazie ad una sorta di magnetismo etico. Nock interpretava la conversione come una questione tra un individuo e la sua coscienza. Consisteva nel

> «riorientare l'anima di un individuo, nel suo passaggio dall'indifferenza o da uno stadio precedente di pietà ad un altro, in un passaggio implicante la coscienza che esso coinvolge un grande cambiamento, che il vecchio è sbagliato e il nuovo è giusto»[12].

L'idea della conversione come «riorientazione dell'anima» era certamente debitrice all'idea di conversione come «esperienza spartiacque», quale era stata descritta una generazione prima da William James[13]. Non si può dire che questa idea fosse intrisa della sensibilità dell'*élite* maschile formata da individui dotati di razionalità.

Tuttavia, in un influente studio del 1983, Ramsay MacMullen si domandava cosa rimanesse della conversione, una volta che fosse stata esclusa l'*élite* maschile che era in realtà al centro del processo. Egli suggeriva che nelle fonti del primo cristianesimo potessero essere distinti almeno due diversi tipi di conversione. Un tipo era quello dell'uomo ragionevole,

---

[12] A.D. Nock, *Conversion: the Old and the New in Religion from Alexander the Great to Augustine of Hippo,* Oxford 1933,7. D. Praet, *Explaining the Christianization of the Roman Empire: Older Theories and Recent Developments*, «Sacris Erudiri» 33 (1992-3), 5-119, 8-9, situa il lavoro di A.D. Nock nel contesto delle discussioni europee a lui contemporanee.

[13] Nelle sue *Gifford Lectures* del 1901-02, pubblicate col titolo *The Varieties of Religious Experience: a Study in Human Nature,* London 1902. Il rapporto tra A.D. Nock e W. James è discusso da F. Parente, *L'idea di conversione da Nock ad oggi*, «Augustinianum» 27 (1987), 7-25, 7-8.

componente delle *élites*, cui si interessavano W. James e A.D. Nock, mentre un altro riguardava le folle che rispondevano al contatto con il miracoloso, diretto o mediato, ed erano messe in moto dalle performances del potere divino. R. MacMullen ricorda come sin dal tardo secondo secolo il pagano Celso avesse ridicolizzato il cristianesimo per la tendenza dei suoi praticanti a giocare sull'eccessiva credulità del «semplice popolo»[14].

R. MacMullen concludeva il suo ragionamento con il suggerimento, apparentemente logico, che il modello della conversione elitaria potesse rendere conto solo di una parte della popolazione, che in realtà doveva essersi unita al movimento nel momento in cui esso guadagnava forza: «se dobbiamo... valutare il cristianesimo in quanto forza storica, che attrasse decine di migliaia di persone, dobbiamo tener conto anche dell'Uomo qualunque (anche se non possiamo certo entrare nei suoi pensieri)»[15]. Ho usato l'espressione «apparentemente logico» perché nel ragionamento si può rilevare una mancanza. R. MacMullen non considera la possibilità che le conversioni dell'*élite* e del popolo fossero in qualche modo interdipendenti. Piuttosto, il suo «Uomo qualunque» è un'anima indipendente che, pur essendo influenzabile dalla demagogia, prendeva tuttavia le proprie decisioni in base a dati indiscutibili, piuttosto che in base alla pressione dei suoi pari o ai desideri del suo *patronus*.

Nel suo tentativo di essere equilibrato nei confronti dell'Uomo qualunque, R. MacMullen evita accuratamente di attribuirgli motivazioni che non siano riconducibili all'etica o al soprannaturale. Egli intende essere corretto nei confronti delle «credenze» religiose per come egli le interpreta, e vuole allontanarsi, per quanto reso possibile dalla sua sensibilità iconoclastica, dal riduzionismo o da una grossolana valutazione delle motivazioni materiali. Così R. MacMullen descrive il suo punto di partenza:

> «Escludendo la considerazione di ogni ricompensa che aspettasse le nuove reclute – ricompense spirituali, sociali, emozionali e finanziarie – che giungeva solo *dopo* la conversione; perciò sembra corretto definire il nostro argomento, la conversione, come l'esperienza tramite la quale i non-credenti prima si convincevano che il Dio Cristiano fosse onnipotente, e che essi dovessero compiacerlo»[16].

---

[14] R. MACMULLEN, *Two Types of Conversion to Early Christianity*, «Vigiliae Christianae» 37 (1983), 174-92, spec. 187. Vedere anche il suo *Christianity and Paganism in the 4th to 8th Century*, New Haven 1997.
[15] R. MACMULLEN, *Two Types of Conversion...*, 188.
[16] *Ibid.*, 184.

Tuttavia il lettore dovrebbe soffermarsi sulla frase «prima si convincevano». Per le *élites* come per l'Uomo qualunque, R. MacMullen chiaramente pensa ad uno scenario in cui l'individuo è colto dallo strale della convinzione – tramite un messaggio – prima che lui o lei sappia molto a riguardo del gruppo che era ad esso connesso. Per quanto ambivalente R. MacMullen possa essere nei confronti del modello della conversione in risposta alla predicazione, la sua visione della conversione è centrata sulla fede.

Avrebbe dovuto essere tra i poteri dell'eloquenza il semplice saper intrattenere la gente trattando questioni di fede. Era forse un tema così difficile? Invece, ciò che è generalmente presente nelle scene di conversione sono le risposte alle dimostrazioni di poteri sovrumani: percepite come miracoli, alternativamente erano intese come prove di genuina origine divina connesse con qualunque divinità fosse invocata e creduta[17].

Qui come altrove, R. MacMullen ha contribuito in maniera fondamentale alla nostra comprensione di ciò che potrebbe essere chiamata una «teologia» tardoantica «del conferimento divino dei poteri», in cui figure come Costantino accordavano la loro fedeltà al Dio che sembrava più capace di servire da protettore e campione. Si vedrà in seguito, comunque, che una volta ampliata la nostra base documentaria fino ad includere atti di martirio e i più tardi *Gesta martyrum*, incontriamo numerose scene di predicazione. In questi testi la predicazione e il miracoloso operano all'unisono invece che in opposizione. Il perché rimane una domanda senza risposta. Forse gli autori postcostantiniani dei *Gesta* erano consapevoli del potere immaginativo del miracolo e volevano assicurarsi che esso venisse strettamente collegato con un messaggio cristiano accettabile. In alternativa, avrebbero semplicemente potuto non percepire i due modelli di conversione come in opposizione. Prima di prendere in considerazione questa domanda, tuttavia, bisogna considerare il cambiamento di prospettiva verificatosi negli studiosi di quelle «regole» sociali tramite le quali i gruppi religiosi raggiungono quella sorta di sorprendente espansione demografica che caratterizza il cristianesimo del IV secolo.

***

Uno dei principali obiettivi di R. MacMullen, nel suo lavoro sulle conversioni, era quello di dare conto in termini razionali di come il cristianesimo

---

[17] R. MacMullen, *Christianity Shaped through its Mission*, in *The Origins of Christendom in the West*, ed. A. Kreider, Edinburgh 2001, 97-117, spec. 98-9.

potesse essere cresciuto così rapidamente come nel corso del IV secolo. I dati sull'affiliazione cristiana sembrano indicare un'*escalation* a partire da circa un decimo della popolazione dell'Impero, circa 6 milioni di persone, all'inizio del secolo, fino a circa la metà del totale, circa 30 milioni – entro la fine del secolo se non ancora prima[18]. Comprensibilmente R. MacMullen si domandò se due o tre milioni di persone per decade (o forse molto di più se il numero di 30 milioni fu raggiunto, come ritengono alcuni studiosi, entro il 350) si convertirono al cristianesimo in seguito a una comprensione profonda della predicazione cristiana. Per mettersi ripetutamente in contatto con milioni di nuove reclute, egli riteneva che i cristiani avrebbero dovuto spingersi ben oltre quella particella di popolazione che prendeva le proprie decisioni spirituali sulla base di una sofisticata adesione a concetti teologici.

Ma per raggiungere un'ampia *audience* non sempre si ha bisogno di folle o di miracoli. Nel suo studio del 1996, *The rise of Christianity: a sociologist reconsiders history*, Rodney Stark ha richiamato l'attenzione sull'importanza, nel primo cristianesimo, di due elementi che emergono da studi demografici, basati su ricerche sul campo, condotti su alcune comunità religiose americane che avevano conosciuto nel XIX e XX secolo una crescita esplosiva. Il primo è una questione di aritmetica: se un gruppo fosse in grado di sostenere costantemente un ritmo di crescita di circa il 40 per cento per decennio – raggiunto, per esempio, dai Mormoni – al terzo secolo di crescita i numeri coinvolti raggiungerebbero i milioni[19]. Il punto è che incrementi apparentemente modesti – con ogni membro della comunità che guadagni a quest'ultima meno di un nuovo convertito ogni due decenni – nel tempo giungerebbero a sommarsi, attraverso un processo simile ad una capitalizzazione di interessi. Convertire centomila anime sembra dover implicare eventi ampi e drammatici, ma se un milione di fratelli portati all'evangelizzazione si fossero impegnati singolarmente in una tranquilla conversazione con amici e parenti, la crescita sembrerebbe accaduta «da sola». Dal punto di vista di R. Stark un migliaio di conversazioni sottotono valgono più di una rappresentazione spettacolare dello stile di Cecil B. De Mille.

---

[18] Le cifre sono tratte da *ibid.*, 10. Sono comunque simili a quelli citati da R. STARK, *The Rise of Christianity: a Sociologist Reconsiders History*, Princeton 1996, 5-11, anche se Stark crede che i cristiani avessero raggiunto il 50 per cento della popolazione anche in precedenza, verso il 350, e ha tutt'altra idea sulle modalità della crescita.

[19] R. STARK, *Rise of Christianity...*, 5-11, citando R. STARK, *The Rise of a New World Faith*, «Review of Religious Research» 26 (1984), 18-27.

Il secondo (e forse più importante) punto di R. Stark è che la reazione iniziale di un individuo al «messaggio» di un movimento religioso non stabilisce se lui o lei alla fine si convertirà. Senza dubbio, dopo il fatto sia il convertito che l'agente della conversione ritengono che il «messaggio» sia stato il fattore fondamentale, ma la ricerca sul campo intorno alle percezioni del «prima» e «dopo» mostra che, presso i gruppi che alla fine si convertono, non c'è inizialmente un'alta valutazione del messaggio dopo il primo contatto sostanziale, in confronto alla reazione di altri individui che non si convertiranno. R. Stark descrive i primi seguaci americani del reverendo Sun Myung Moon, che furono oggetto della sua ricerca con John Lofland nei primi anni '60 del Novecento:

> «Se non fossimo usciti a vedere la gente quando convertivano, avremmo perso completamente il punto, perché quando retrospettivamente descrivono la propria conversione, le persone tendono a mettere l'accento sulla teologia. Quando interrogati sul motivo della loro conversione, i seguaci di Moon rilevavano sempre l'irresistibile attrazione dei Principi Divini... Ma Lofland e io sapevamo bene [...] potevamo ricordare quando la maggior parte di loro riteneva piuttosto strane le credenze religiose dei loro nuovi amici»[20].

A questo stadio iniziale anche il futuro convertito è spesso saldo nella convinzione che la sua reazione negativa al «messaggio» sia incrollabile.

Ciò che sembra distinguere coloro che non si convertono da coloro che lo fanno è un'intesa sociale con i membri del gruppo. Nella loro ricerca sul campo sui seguaci di Moon, J. Lofland e R. Stark scoprirono che le conversioni di successo e permanenti tendevano a costituire una rete parallela di famiglia e amicizia, sia che un seguace di Moon avviasse un'amicizia con un estraneo al gruppo, sia che un neoconvertito iniziasse ad influenzare altri estranei che erano già suoi amici prima della conversione. Se un familiare «estraneo» comincia a passare più tempo con un neoconvertito nella speranza di allontanarlo dal gruppo, è altrettanto probabile che ci riesca quanto che egli o ella stessa si unisca al gruppo.

Il principio in azione in questi casi è che le persone tendono a «razionalizzare» le loro affiliazioni, religiose come di altra natura, con il fine di riflettere e rinforzare i loro legami sociali, come famiglia e amicizia. «In effetti, la conversione non è cosa che riguardi cercare o abbracciare un'ideologia, ma piuttosto allineare il proprio comportamento religioso

---

[20] R. STARK, *Rise of Christianity...*, 19, citando J. LOFLAND, R. STARK, *Becoming a World-Saver: a Theory of Conversion to a Deviant Perspective*, «American Sociological Review» 30 (1965), 862-75.

con quello di amici e membri della famiglia»[21]. R. Stark rafforza le sue spiegazioni menzionando una varietà di casi empirici riguardanti altre tradizioni religiose, fino a concludere facendo riferimento ad una sola, evocativa statistica, estratta ancora dai suoi lavori sui Mormoni. In una missione mormone, il tasso di conversioni di successo raggiunto attraverso visite porta a porta non preannunciate presso estranei era di uno a mille. Ma se i missionari stabilivano il primo contatto da ospiti a casa di amici o parenti di un individuo, il tasso di successo era di uno su due[22].

Se seguiamo R. Stark, il momento di R. MacMullen in cui il convertito «si convince per la prima volta» è il risultato, invece che la causa, di una forte relazione con i membri del gruppo. Certo, può comunque accadere *nonostante* – invece che a causa di – il messaggio portato dal gruppo. Si può anche chiedersi se la predicazione pubblica alla folla – supponendo che essa avesse luogo – non fosse di fatto un modo di «pregare al coro», ma di fornire un punto focale per il «networking» fatto in maniera meno visibile ed evidente dai membri del gruppo[23]. Senza dubbio le teorie derivate dalla ricerca sul campo nel XX secolo possono al massimo offrire uno strumento euristico atto ad esaminare le testimonianze antiche. È tuttavia utile riconoscere che una rilevante crescita demografica avrebbe potuto avvenire tramite piccoli incrementi, attraverso un tipo di canali informali che non necessariamente apparirebbe nella documentazione storica, piuttosto che attraverso occasioni documentate che coinvolgevano intere folle.

I vescovi, anche se soddisfatti del numero di convertiti che la fede attraeva, potevano domandarsi se anche gli entusiasti convertiti in realtà avessero un'idea chiara del contenuto della tradizione. Se, tramite il risalto dei poteri miracolosi o attraverso il «networking» laico, i nuovi membri entrassero nella comunità cristiana per vie che erano al di fuori del «controllo sul messaggio» di cui essi, i vescovi, godevano. Entro il primo V secolo, Agostino di Ippona si preoccupava del fatto che i cristiani che conoscevano e si interessavano delle tradizioni etiche della Chiesa potessero trovarsi marginalizzati in quanto estremisti. Alan Kreider descrive così questo fenomeno:

---

[21] R. STARK, *Rise of Christianity*..., 17-18.
[22] *Ibid.*, 18; vedere anche R. STARK and W.S. BAINBRIDGE, *Networks of Faith: Interpersonal Bonds and Recruitment to Cults and Sects*, «American Journal of Sociology» 85 (1980), 1376-1395.
[23] R. MACMULLEN stesso ha notato questo fatto, e.g. in *Christianity Shaped through its Mission*, 106-109.

«Agostino pensava ai primi tempi della Chiesa, narrati negli Atti 2, quando le persone erano «completamente e perfettamente convertite». Anche ai suoi giorni egli sapeva di alcune persone che cercavano di seguire Cristo, di pregare per i propri nemici, e di distribuire i loro beni ai bisognosi. Al loro comportamento... la risposta di molti dei battezzati era incredula: «Perché ti comporti come un pazzo? Stai estremizzando; gli altri, non sono cristiani?»»[24].

Se «estremizzare» era quello che la Chiesa aveva sempre fatto, era la stessa Chiesa quella in cui gli estremisti diventavano sempre di più una minoranza? Questa la domanda che si ponevano Agostino e altri.

In un noto passaggio del *De catechizandis rudibus*, il suo trattato su come gestire chi chiedeva informazioni sulla fede – potenziali convertiti – Agostino riconosceva che le motivazioni di un potenziale candidato alla conversione potevano essere ben poco onorevoli. Poteva essere «la speranza di derivarne qualche beneficio da uomini a cui pensa di non poter piacere altrimenti, o di evitare i colpi di persone di cui teme la disapprovazione o l'inimicizia»[25]. Il trucco consisteva nell'assecondare questo inganno, nella speranza di aiutare il candidato a divenire effettivamente ciò che lui o lei voleva sembrare di essere – una persona per la quale l'insegnamento cristiano aveva significato un'esperienza in grado di cambiare la vita. A questo fine, avverte Agostino, il processo di preparazione per l'ammissione al catecumenato doveva includere, per usare un'espressione di A. Kreider, «60 minuti di esposizione della storia della salvezza dalla creazione al giorno del giudizio, culminanti in un'esortazione al corretto comportamento»[26]. Questa *narratio* o «compendio della fede» avrebbe dovuto servire da avvertimento pubblico per il candidato, che avrebbe dovuto comprendere di cosa stava per entrare a far parte.

La *narratio* di Agostino avrebbe offerto un modello per gli ambiziosi ecclesiastici delle generazioni successive, particolarmente nel periodo carolingio, sebbene ci sia motivo di credere che la sua funzione abbia conosciuto uno slittamento dall'essere un preludio al catechismo al costituire il catechismo in sé. Non c'è traccia nelle fonti altomedievali di alcuna istruzione formale per i bambini nati da famiglie cristiane – quelle cioè che non arrivavano al cristianesimo attraverso la conversione[27]. Certamente questo non significa che non ci sia testimonianza della trasmissione delle idee cri-

---

[24] A. Kreider, *Changing Patterns of Conversion in the West*, in *The Origins of Christendom...*, 3-46 (here, 34), citando i sermoni di Agostino 88.12-13 e 14.4 rispettivamente.
[25] *De catechizandis rudibus*, 5.9, trad. e cit. Kreider, *Changing Patterns...*, 32.
[26] *Ibid.*, 32. basato su *De catechizandis rudibus*, 13.18 e 16.25-25.49.
[27] A. Kreider, *Changing Patterns...*, 41.

stiane ai fedeli. Vedremo in seguito che l'agiografia potrebbe aver preso il sopravvento in quanto mezzo attraverso il quale i «contenuti» cristiani venivano sia introdotti per i nuovi membri della comunità sia ripetuti per coloro che erano entrati nella Chiesa per via «ereditaria».

***

Ricordando questo fatto, si torni alla *Passio Sebastiani*. Sebbene il racconto pretenda di descrivere un martirio avvenuto ai tempi di Diocleziano e Massimiano, che abdicarono entrambi nel 305, è probabile che esso sia stato scritto nel quinto secolo o anche nei primi decenni del secolo successivo: abbiamo dunque di fronte un documento romanzato, più che un resoconto storico. Come gli altri *Gesta martyrum* scritti dopo gli anni di Costantino, la *Passio Sebastiani* ha suscitato poco o nessun interesse negli studiosi interessati alla conversione e al miracoloso nel primo cristianesimo. Ciò è forse dovuto al fatto che c'è un intervallo di almeno un secolo tra i giorni dell'autore e quelli dell'evento descritto. Questi testi, dunque, non possono essere letti come una immediata riflessione di realtà precedenti al regno di Costantino. Tuttavia il processo di mediazione, tramite il quale uno scrittore di quinto o sesto secolo tentava di comprendere l'eroismo dei suoi fratelli della generazione di Diocleziano, fornisce un indizio interessante, come si vedrà in seguito, per lo studio di un problema più ampio, cioè come i cristiani antichi e medievali percepissero i tempi in cui secondo loro c'era stata la grande età della conversione.

Studiosi e teologi sono stati a lungo concordi sul fatto che le *passiones* postcostantiniane dei martiri fossero un prodotto di fertili immaginazioni letterarie, basate almeno in alcuni casi su nomi ricordati grazie a liste di martiri tramandate dalle Chiese. I dettagli presenti in questi testi sono molto probabilmente un prodotto di invenzione, fatto rilevato già nei tentativi dei Bollandisti di separare i «fatti» dalla «finzione» nelle vite dei santi. In ciò fu molto influente la massima di Hippolyte Delahaye, tratta da Gregorio il Grande, secondo la quale c'è una sola vita dei santi, della quale le vite individuali solo semplici esempi. Ciononostante, comunque siano modellati dalle pie forze dell'invenzione, i *Gesta martyrum* servirono come uno dei più importanti mezzi di comunicazione tramite i quali i pensatori cristiani poterono esplorare il processo storico che portò l'Europa ad essere cristiana[28].

---

[28] Sui *Gesta* come risposta alla letteratura cristiana primitiva vedere K. COOPER, *The Virgin and the Bride: Idealized Womanhood in Late Antiquity*, Cambridge, MA, 1996, 16-19.

Sembra appropriato, perciò, lasciare in sospeso la domanda se i *Gesta* siano una relazione attendibile sugli eventi precostantiniani, e invece concentrarsi su come essi riflettano gli interessi e le preoccupazioni degli scrittori e del pubblico postcostantiniani. Invece di vedere un approccio etico o razionale alla fede come posizione in tensione con la credenza nel miracoloso, nella *Passio* si mette l'accento sulla dimensione etica del miracolo, che riflette l'intervento divino nella storia che fu l'ascesa del cristianesimo. Segni e meraviglie si potevano trovare non solo nelle *virtutes* – atti di potere miracoloso – ma anche nella vita etica a cui erano chiamati i cristiani, il miracolo quotidiano dell'amicizia, e la Parola divenuta carne nella persona non solo di Gesù ma anche nei suoi santi.

Ha anche importanza un altro aspetto dell'interpretazione proposta dei *Gesta martyrum*, cioè il loro interesse per i legami familiari come reti di comunicazione e di influenza personale, attraverso i quali poteva diffondersi la nuova fede. È un aspetto che deve essere messo in luce, perché il problema della famiglia come luogo della cristianizzazione è un problema irrisolto da decenni. Anche in questo contesto possiamo ricollegarci al lavoro di Peter Brown. Cinquant'anni fa P. Brown ha sostenuto la tesi, all'epoca sorprendente, che la cristianizzazione dell'aristocrazia romana sia stata compiuta non tramite dibattiti filosofici tra uomini colti, ma attraverso network di parentela ed amicizia in cui le donne ricoprivano un ruolo fondamentale[29]. L'ipotesi rendeva conto di un filo narrativo visibile in tantissime fonti dell'epoca: vediamo infatti ripetutamente la prontezza della fede di una madre, moglie o figlia di un uomo influente proposta a lui o ad altri come modello al quale conformarsi[30]. Se questa ipotesi non ha convinto ogni lettore, essa ha tuttavia aperto una discussione importante[31]. Per la presente discussione, offre un contesto molto evocativo per il nesso tra la famiglia e la conversione nei *Gesta martyrum*.

Nel descrivere la storia della carriera di Sebastiano, dal momento in cui si scopre che è cristiano fino alla sua morte e sepoltura, la *Passio*

---

[29] P. BROWN, *Aspects of the Christianization of the Roman Aristocracy*, «Journal of Roman Studies», 51 (1961), 1-11.

[30] K. COOPER, *Insinuations of Womanly Influence: An Aspect of the Christianization of the Roman Aristocracy*, «Journal of Roman Studies» 82 (1992), 113-127; EAD., *Poteri invisibili: La matrona cristiana tra obsequium e autorità legittima all'epoca di sant'Agostino*, in *Agire da Donna: Modelli e pratiche di rappresentazione (secoli VI-X)*, ed. C. LA ROCCA, Turnhout 2007, 7-21.

[31] Un approccio critico alla tesi di Brown, con discussione della relativa bibliografia, si trova in M.R. SALZMAN, *The Making of a Christian Aristocracy: Social and Religious Change in the Western Roman Empire*, Cambridge, MA 2002.

Sebastiani mostra un intenso impegno immaginativo sul problema della predicazione e della conversione, e sugli effetti della fede cristiana sulla famiglia, cristiana come pagana. La *passio* pone al centro dell'attenzione una sequenza di conversioni, e in ciascun caso il nuovo convertito ha una singolare costellazione di relazioni familiari che deve essere ristrutturata alla luce del passaggio alla nuova fede. Ciò che deve essere notato qui è che non è necessariamente il *pater familias* a convertirsi per primo, portando con sé tutti i suoi dipendenti (sebbene questo paradigma sia certamente presente). Invece diverse famiglie vengono raggiunte attraverso un «primo contatto» stabilito attraverso uno dei dipendenti del *pater*.

La storia si apre con Sebastiano, un comandante militare che godeva del favore imperiale, nell'atto di confortare due *viri inlustri* cristiani, i gemelli Marco e Marcelliano, accusati di essere cristiani e perciò imprigionati insieme ai loro servi. Le loro famiglie ottengono dal prefetto urbano, Agrestio Cromazio, una sospensione della pena di 30 giorni, nella speranza che la misericordia o la persuasione di mogli e figli potessero convincere i due giovani uomini a desistere dalla propria folle convinzione. In questo modo la *Passio* esordisce con il tema della conversione, con due gemelli cristiani che tentano di rimanere coerenti con le proprie idee contro le suppliche dei loro stessi amici, che tenevano in maggior conto le loro responsabilità familiari – verso i genitori, le mogli e i figli che avrebbero pianto la loro morte. Di fronte alla persecuzione, secondo gli amici, i due giovani hanno la responsabilità di abbandonare la propria fede, ritornare alle loro case e compiere il proprio dovere. La *Passio* sottolinea più di qualsiasi altro racconto martiriale precostantiniano la difficoltà di non cedere di fronte a questo tipo di suppliche, anche più del celebre diario di prigionia di Vibia Perpetua, che dà conto pienamente delle richieste del padre di lei affinchè ella avesse pietà della sua veneranda età.

Tutto ciò conduce ad uno scontro verbale in cui le famiglie si misurano con Sebastiano, che ha la meglio con la sua lode delle gioie dell'eternità, confrontate con i piaceri passeggeri della vita terrena. Ciò che salva gli uomini dall'arrendersi è la costante predicazione di Sebastiano, che ricorda loro continuamente quanto brevi saranno le loro sofferenze terrene – e quelle delle loro famiglie – e quanto grande la gioia nel regno della luce eterna. Ancora non si sa se i loro genitori Tranquillino e Marcia avrebbero seguito i gemelli nell'adesione alla fede, ma alla fine anche essi si convertono. Sebastiano comincia a guadagnare alla fede prima Zoe, la moglie dell'ufficiale nella cui casa i due gemelli sono tenuti in arresto, e alla fine convince 68 persone tra gli abitanti della casa, molte delle quali saranno futuri martiri di Roma.

Mentre i due gemelli sono imprigionati, Sebastiano si reca a predicare a loro e a coloro che sono radunati in quel luogo. Il discorso è accompagnato da segni miracolosi: «Per quasi un'ora fu illuminato da una straordinaria luce che veniva dal cielo. Al di sotto di questo splendore, fu ricoperto da un mantello interamente bianco da sette angeli risplendenti. E un giovane apparve al suo fianco, dandogli la pace e dicendo: "Sarai sempre con me"»[32].

Sebastiano comincia allora a curare i malati. Prima Zoe, che era muta da sei anni. Dice infatti Sebastiano: «Se io sono un vero servo di Cristo, e se è vero tutto quello che questa donna ha udito e creduto dalla mia bocca, che il mio Signore Gesù Cristo faccia sì che le ritorni la capacità di parlare, e che Colui che aprì la bocca del profeta Zaccaria schiuda la sua bocca»[33].

Le prime parole di Zoe sono «sei benedetto, e ben detto è il sermone sulla tua bocca»: il discorso miracoloso, in quanto guarisce il silenzio della donna, echeggia e amplifica quello di Sebastiano. La guarigione in sé è prova della validità della predicazione di Sebastiano, un test del suo status di canale del potere divino che gli giunge attraverso la luce soprannaturale. Così il miracolo serve da punteggiatura spirituale, per confermare la veridicità dell'insegnamento di Sebastiano.

La professione di fede di Zoe conduce immediatamente ad uno sviluppo che sembra riflettere il modello di conversione relazionale discusso da R. Stark. «Inoltre Nicostrato, suo marito, quando vide che tale era la virtù di Cristo nella sua austera moglie, cominciò a dirigere il suo passo verso Sebastiano»[34]. Nicostrato allora parla ai due giovani imprigionati nella sua casa, domandando loro di permettergli di nasconderli o almeno di essere giustiziato al loro posto. I gemelli lodano la sua solerzia «la tua fede è sorta dal Maestro, e tutto ciò che può a malapena essere dato da molti anni di educazione, tu lo hai imparato in un'ora»[35]. Non bisogna ignorare

---

[32] *Passio Sebastiani* 23 (*AASS*, II Jan., 268): *per unam fere horam splendore nimio de caelo veniente illuminatus est, et sub ipso splendore, candidissimo pallio amictus est ab angelis septem clarissimis, et iuvenis apparuit iuxta eum dans ei pacem, et dicens: Tu semper mecum eris.*

[33] *Passio Sebastiani* 24 (*ibid.*): *Tunc B. Sebastianus dixit: Si ego verus Christi servus sum, et si vera sunt omnia, quae ex ore meo haec mulier audivit et credidit, iubeat Dominus meus Jesus Christus, ut redeat ad eam officium linguae, et aperiat os eius qui aperuit os Zachariae Prophetae sui; et fecit crucem in os eius. Atque ad hanc vocem S. Sebastiani, exclamavit mulier voce magna, dicens: Beatus es tu, et benedictus sermo oris tui...*

[34] *Passio Sebastiani* 24 (*ibid.*).

[35] *Passio Sebastiani* 26 (*AASS*, II Jan., 269).

che Nicostrato non ha dato alcuna prova di essere a conoscenza di alcun «contenuto» della fede cristiana, e infatti non c'è alcuna indicazione del fatto che egli fosse presente alla predica di Sebastiano.

Con le altre conversioni, tuttavia, sembra di essere nel terreno di R. MacMullen: quando si converte un altro alto ufficiale, Claudio il *commentariensis*, non solo egli si porta con sé i suoi due figli per la guarigione, ma è accompagnato al battesimo dalla moglie e dalla famiglia estesa. Nel frattempo Nicostrato porta al fonte battesimale 33 membri della sua stessa casa. Il modello di conversione qui operante è quello che vede nel capo della famiglia la voce dei membri di questa – nonostante il fatto che Nicostrato sia stato guidato dall'esempio di sua moglie. Tranquillino, il padre di Marcelliano e Marco, si converte, in questo caso seguendo l'esempio dei suoi figli. Con un distacco radicale dal suo ruolo di *pater familias* – nell'adottare la convinzione dei suoi figli – Tranquillino ha permesso al giovane di guidare l'anziano, invece di essere guidato dalla saggezza e autorità del più vecchio. Ma nel rispondere con prontezza alla rivelazione portata dai suoi figli, il padre ha dimostrato la grandezza della sua saggezza.

Quando scadono i 30 giorni i due giovani vengono portati di fronte al prefetto urbano Agrezio Cromazio, con il quale abbiamo cominciato questo articolo: ora Tranquillino deve rendere conto per i propri figli e per i propri tentativi per farli rinunciare alla superstizione cristiana. Quando Cromazio chiede a Tranquillino se i suoi figli siano pronti ad offrire il sacrificio, l'uomo risponde rivelando di essersi anch'esso convertito al cristianesimo.

La conversazione quindi si trasforma in uno scontro verbale tra i due uomini, con Cromazio che accusa Tranquillino di pazzia, e questi che risponde vantando la propria sanità mentale e fisica. Poi Tranquillino sottolinea i fallimenti del paganesimo come sistema religioso, e si passa dunque ad una discussione il cui tema è se le Storie di Livio dimostrino o meno il fallimento degli dei nel proteggere l'impero anche nei giorni in cui il culto tradizionale era seguito con attenzione e precisione. La scena sembra intesa quasi come un florilegio di esempi di conversioni elitarie, con due letterati aristocratici che provano l'un l'altro la propria conoscenza della storia e dell'etica romane.

Alla fine Cromazio viene piegato da una elaborata spiegazione della metafora dell'anima come un anello perso in una fogna, che sarebbe il corpo (l'ironia che il corpo di Sebastiano stesso sarebbe stato gettato dentro la grande fogna di Roma, la Cloaca Massima, non doveva passare inosservata al pubblico della *Passio*). Cromazio, malato da tempo, chiede di essere guarito, dietro pagamento di una ricompensa in denaro, dal potere miracoloso già dimostrato da Sebastiano: ma Tranquillino risponde che il suo corpo sarebbe stato guarito solo una volta che la sua mente si fosse rivolta alla Verità. Egli dunque ordina che Sebastiano sia portato di fronte a lui. Tuttavia, una volta che è chiaro che Cromazio si convertirà insieme al figlio, Sebastiano lo ammonisce di non tentare di abusare dei suoi poteri: «Bada! Non voler divenire cristiano, indotto solamente dalla salvezza del tuo corpo! Piuttosto purifica la tua mente, cosicché tu possa vedere la ragione della verità. Perché, a meno che tu non riconosca chi è il tuo Creatore, non potrai trovare la salute che cerchi»[36].

È importante notare che nonostante stia parlando al prefetto di Roma, uno dei più alti ufficiali dell'impero, Sebastiano in questo passo tratta la conversione come finalizzata ad accedere ai vantaggi offerti dall'essere membro di una comunità della fede – l'accesso alla guarigione miracolosa, dunque, una volta che la sua efficacia sia accettata, risulta essere simbolo dei benefici dell'appartenenza, benefici visti da Agostino e R. Stark come motivazione importante all'interno del processo di conversione. Secondo la *Passio*, la distinzione operata da R. MacMullen tra «*élite*» e «massa» risulta essere troppo stretta.

Tenendo a mente questo punto, ci dedichiamo in conclusione alle caratteristiche verbali e narrative della predicazione del martire nella *Passio*. Il momento del «ventriloquismo» – in cui il martire è rappresentato mentre parla con potere o autorità divine – è riflesso in due distinti tipi di discorso. Il primo tipo è quello in cui l'oratore riassume un'ampia mole di informazioni sul cristianesimo, tratta da fonti bibliche o liturgiche, spesso usando un vocabolario specialistico. Questo primo tipo richiama la *narratio* proposta da Agostino, il «sommario della fede» da fornire ai catecumeni prima che siano ammessi all'istruzione formale. La *narratio* ricapitola il «significato» della tradizione cristiana per un pubblico che poteva incontrare la *Passio* una volta all'anno, nel giorno della commemorazione del santo. Potrebbe essere utile comprendere il discorso del santo in questo modo, come un resoconto idealizzato della predicazione alla conversione, un discorso in grado di mettere in moto un «circolo di riscontro» che coinvolgesse il pubblico che leggeva o udiva il testo. In questo senso la ripetizione della narrativa agiografica su Sebastiano e gli altri martiri romani avrebbe svolto una funzione simile al rinnovamento dei voti del battesimo, ricordando al laicato cristiano o alle comunità mo-

---

[36] *Passio Sebastiani* 51 (*AASS*, II Jan., 273).

nastiche i termini della fede – o persino istruendo da capo coloro che erano appena entrati nella comunità.

Il secondo modo riflette la preoccupazione per un «discorso evidente», in cui fossero utilizzate brevi costruzioni paratattiche e un vocabolario non aulico. La brevità degli elementi sintattici conferisce a questi discorsi un effetto ritmico stupefacente, che compare spesso al momento della *climax* della conversione o della guarigione[37]. Possono prendere questa forma sia il discorso miracoloso del martire sia le parole della professione di fede fatta da parte di chi è appena stato guarito o convertito. L'effetto ritmico può fungere sia da innesco che da interpunzione: esso fornisce una vivida illustrazione del potere della parola cristiana – spesso formulata in un linguaggio derivato direttamente dalle parole di Gesù – che sembra potersi accordare a preoccupazioni probabilmente nuove nel raggiungere un pubblico attraverso un fraseggio acuto e vivo, in un modo simile a quello rilevabile nel caso dei sermoni contemporanei.

Dire che il miracoloso era percepito come «causa» del credere, tuttavia, non è del tutto corretto, poiché la fede a sua volta era vista come fonte di potere miracoloso. Gli scrittori dell'Alto Medioevo erano profondamente interessati alla percezione di una sinergia tra l'azione extra-umana di Dio e la sua abilità di agire attraverso gli esseri umani. La loro fede stimolava il loro interesse nella comprensione della struttura sociale di questo processo, e la narrativa postcostantiniana sui martiri offre una testimonianza diretta di questo loro tentativo. Certamente la fede di chi riceve il miracolo e la *virtus* o il potere miracoloso del martire o del santo creava una forma di circolo virtuoso nella narrativa altomedievale, la cui forza era amplificata dalle dinamiche narrative e rappresentative quando la storia veniva raccontata ad un nuovo pubblico[38].

Ricordando questo fatto, può essere opportuno vedere i due tipi di discorso presenti nella *Passio Sebastiani* come il riflesso di due strategie, differenti e complementari, di fronte a quella che si intendeva essere

---

[37] Per approcci comparativi, vedere S. TAMBIAH, *The Magical Power of Words*, «Man» 3 (1968), 177-206; P.L. RAVENHILL, *Religious Utterances and the Theory of Speech Acts*, in *Languages in Religious Practice*, ed. W.J. SAMARIN, Rowley, MA, 1976, 26-39; P. COX MILLER, *In Praise of Nonsense*, in *World Spirituality, 15: Classical Mediterranean Spirituality*, ed. A.H. ARMSTRONG, New York 1986, 481-505.

[38] Simon Yarrow afferma che «il miracolo viene compiuto ogni volta che viene nuovamente raccontato»: S. YARROW, *The Negotiation of Community in Twelfth-Century English Miracle Narratives*, in *Elite and Popular Religion, Studies in Church History* 42, eds. K. COOPER, J. GREGORY, Woodbridge 2006, citando M. GILSENAN, *Recognizing Islam: Religion and Society in the Modern Middle East*, London 1982, rist. 2000, 75.

l'*audience* del testo. Il tentativo di comprimere il contenuto sostanziale del cristianesimo in un riassunto in cui fosse presente una frequente ripetizione dei temi trattati doveva agire, in senso lato, allo stesso modo in cui operava la ripetizione liturgica del Credo. Per contrasto, il linguaggio acuto e vivido del discorso ritmico può essere stato progettato per stimolare un nuovo livello di impegno – rapporto potrebbe essere un termine più adatto – verso Dio attraverso i suoi santi. Questo potrebbe richiamare una distinzione fatta da Agostino tra ciò che egli chiamava «le lunghe, tortuose vie del discorso» in questo mondo[39] e l'epifania del discorso che sarà possibile nella Gerusalemme celeste[40]: il *locus classicus* di questo secondo modo trasparente di comunicazione escatologicamente pregna tra i cristiani è contenuto nel nono libro delle *Confessioni*, nella sua conversazione con Monica ad Ostia, appena prima della morte di lei. Si può ritenere che la *Passio Sebastiani* abbia dato il suo contributo alla discussione postagostiniana della *disciplina* cristiana offrendo una distinzione tra le due modalità, confessionale da una parte ed escatologica dall'altra, del discorso didattico.

Senza dubbio le strategie testuali della *Passio* si impegnano in un più ampio cambiamento nel comportamento verso retorica e autorità vigenti in questo periodo. Tra la fine del quinto e l'inizio del sesto secolo, i cristiani erano profondamente preoccupati dalla difficoltà di raggiungere nei loro discorsi ciò che uno scrittore chiamò *puritatis index loquella*, «la piccola voce che dà la misura della purezza»[41]. Fonti così diverse come la *Regola di san Benedetto* e l'anonimo *Manuale per Gregoria*, scritto per una laica sposata, testi entrambi provenienti dall'Italia centrale del primo sesto secolo, descrivono monaci e donne sposate che abitualmente misuravano il numero e il tono delle loro parole. In questo modo essi si mostravano come praticanti del *sermo humilitatis*, uno stile modesto che li segnava come «democratici» linguistici[42]. Nel fare ciò essi si ribellavano alla tradizione latina che faceva di ogni sillaba un modo per distinguersi per classe sociale, regione di provenienza e qualità letterarie – o loro man-

---

[39] Citazione da *De catechizandis rudibus,* 10, 15, in P. BROWN, *Augustine of Hippo*, London 1967, 161.

[40] Idea che sarà ripresa da Gregorio Magno: C. LEYSER, *Asceticism and Authority from Augustine to Gregory the Great*, Oxford 2000, 177-81.

[41] *Liber ad* Gregoriam, 4. ed. G. MORIN, in Études, textes, découvertes, Paris 1913, 383-439, in part. 389 (rist. in PLS 3, 221-256).

[42] C. LEYSER, *Asceticism and Authority...*, 59-61, fornisce un resoconto della letteratura secondaria successiva a E. AUERBACH, *Literary Language and its Public in Late Antiquity*, trad. R. Mannheim, London 1965.

canza. Un'estetica puritana della semplicità stava emergendo nella letteratura devozionale, tanto che Eugippio di Lucullanum, scrivendo attorno al 511 al diacono Pascasio per introdurre la sua *Vita* del sant'uomo Severino, trova difficile trattenersi dal vantarsi della sua incapacità di emulare lo «stile alto» dell'elegante *Vita di Basso*, scritta da un dotto laico a lui contemporaneo, testo ora perduto ma allora ancora noto[43].

Nel mondo della spiritualità monastica, si punta a massimizzare negli ascoltatori l'impatto delle parole usate nelle istruzioni e ancora si fa ricorso all'idea che Dio parli direttamente attraverso coloro che sono scelti per essere suoi intermediari. La prefazione della anonima *Regula magistri*, per esempio, composta in Italia centrale attorno all'anno 500[44], mette alla base dell'insegnamento dell'autore una visione di ispirazione divina, simile a quella del passaggio «ventriloquo» della *Passio Sebastiani* con cui abbiamo cominciato[45]. Questo è ancora più rilevante quando ricordiamo che le citazioni della *Passio* nella *Regula magistri* offrono quella che di fatto è la più antica attestazione per la composizione del primo testo.

Questo gruppo di fonti centroitaliane di inizio VI secolo può facilmente riflettere le preoccupazioni presenti in un contesto cronologico e geografico particolare; il crogiolo di esperienze e sperimentazioni da cui tutti questi testi sembrano emergere, tuttavia, potrebbe aver avuto un impatto di vasta portata sul cristianesimo latino. Sia la *Regola di san Benedetto* che i *Gesta martyrum* stessi, che costituirono il modello della successiva agiografia latina, esercitarono un'influenza virtualmente incommensurabile sullo sviluppo della letteratura devozionale latina.

***

---

[43] Sulla relazione tra Eugippio e i *Gesta martyrum*, vedere K. COOPER, *The Widow as Impresario: the Widow Barbaria in Eugippius' «Vita Severini»*, in *Eugippius und Severinus: Der Autor, der Text, und der Heilige*, eds. W. POHL, M. DIESENBERGER, Vienna 2000, 53-64.

[44] Per la discussione sulla datazione e l'autore della *Regula Magistri*, vedere C. LEYSER, *Asceticism and Authority...*, 103, 108-17.

[45] Questo si vede all'inizio della Regola: *Oh, homo, primo tibi qui legis, deinde et tibi qui me ausculatas dicentem, dimitte alia modo quae cogitas, et me tibi loquentem et per os meum Deum te convenientem cognosce* (Prologus, I), e oltre, *Et intellige tu, homo, cuius admonemus intuitum, quia te per hanc scribturam [sic] admonet Deus [...]* (Prologus, 16): *La Regle du maître*, ed. A. DE VOGÜÉ, SC 105, Paris, 1964, 288 e 290.

I tentativi di comprendere la funzione sociale delle idee religiose sono tradizionalmente associati a riduzionismo e demistificazione – e certo, come si vede nel caso di D. Hume, questo accostamento è talvolta eloquente. Conseguentemente l'analisi funzionale è spesso messa da parte con l'affermazione che la fede era «genuina» o che le motivazioni erano «religiose», come se questo significasse che idee e pratiche religiose autentiche non abbiano una dimensione sociale. Nel caso in questione abbiamo visto che D. Hume e l'autore della *Passio Sebastiani* avevano motivazioni uguali e contrarie per riflettere sulla validità di una conoscenza di seconda mano di fatti in cui fosse coinvolto il soprannaturale; tuttavia entrambi erano fondamentalmente interessati ai meccanismi di questo fenomeno. Analogamente, abbiamo visto Rodney Stark e Agostino di Ippona condividere un profondo interesse per il fatto che i nuovi membri di una comunità religiosa fossero in grado o meno di comprendere le sue «regole base», anche se per motivi ancora differenti.

Il presente contributo è basato su una struttura analitica funzionalista, intendendo con funzionalismo una visione secondo la quale le idee sono inserite socialmente in un sistema di comunicazione, attraverso il quale gli individui possono tentare di influenzare – o anche controllare – il loro comportamento reciproco. Alternativamente le idee sono state intese come messe in gioco per incoraggiare alcune tendenze e scoraggiarne altre. In questo studio siamo partiti dall'idea che l'accusa di riduzionismo contro l'analisi funzionalista sia in conclusione mal diretta. Certo, come scrisse Mary Douglas nel 1970, «le possibilità di un'analisi funzionalista non sono state esaurite. Come l'etica cristiana, può essere difesa contro i suoi critici sulla base del fatto che non è mai stata realmente tentata»[46].

Storicamente, come abbiamo tentato di suggerire, i più abili utilizzatori dell'approccio strutturale-funzionalista sono infatti stati gli agenti storici, gli individui a cui era addossata la responsabilità di istituzioni e comunità. All'interno del discorso cristiano questo desiderio di dirigere energie e risorse è stato generalmente classificato sotto la categoria dell'amministrazione. In questa forma ciò che potrebbe essere definito «funzionalismo pastorale» riflette il pensiero pragmatico dei leader religiosi nel loro tentativo di dirigere i membri della comunità col fine di incanalare i loro sforzi dove si percepiva avrebbero dato il miglior frutto, o dove avrebbero funzionato da «moltiplicatore» degli sforzi di altri. I «buoni amministratori» si sono sempre impegnati nell'analisi funzionalista non perché ci credono,

---

[46] M. DOUGLAS, *Introduction*, in Witchcraft Confessions and Accusations, ed. M. DOUGLAS, *ASA Monographs* 9, London 1970, XXV.

ma perché lo fanno. Dal momento che le risorse istituzionali nella Tarda Antichità e nell'Alto Medioevo erano tanto esigue da non poter esser concepite secondo i criteri moderni, gli sforzi per sviluppare anche solo una rudimentale continuità sociale richiedevano quanto più possibile supporto ideologico.

Forse il più grande «funzionalista strutturale» all'interno della tradizione cristiana fu Agostino, che ricorda nel decimo libro della *Città di Dio* che anche i rapinatori devono cercare di stabilire la pace tra loro – cioè che anche nell'angolo più disfunzionale dell'ordine sociale gli esseri umani devono cercare una base di complicità al di sopra della quale costruire strutture di obbligo reciproco e mutua assistenza, anche se esse stesse sono destinate ad essere messe in crisi e perfino a fallire. Che i cristiani dovessero utilizzare idee di natura teologica per rinforzare tali strutture era una faccenda di urgenza pastorale.

Nel suo *De catechizandis rudibus* Agostino si mostra cosciente della fragilità di tali strutture. Egli non rifiuta di rendersi conto della piccolezza delle motivazioni di piccoli uomini:

> «Se infatti ha intenzione di diventare cristiano perché attende qualche vantaggio dalle persone che gli stanno intorno, alle quali ritiene altrimenti di non essere gradito, oppure perché vuol evitare danni da altre, dalle quali teme offesa o inimicizia, questi non vuole diventare veramente cristiano quanto piuttosto fingere di esserlo. Giacché la fede non è espressa da un corpo che si prostra, ma da un animo che crede. Spesso però, tramite l'opera del catechista, subentra la misericordia di Dio, cosicché il candidato, colpito dal discorso, vuol ormai diventare ciò che aveva stabilito di fingersi: quando un tale desiderio abbia preso in lui il sopravvento, allora possiamo ritenere che egli sia mosso da motivi genuini. Certo a noi rimane nascosto il momento in cui aderisca con il cuore quegli che già vediamo presente con il corpo; nondimeno dobbiamo agire con lui in modo che nel suo animo si sviluppi questo desiderio, seppure non c'è»[47].

---

[47] AUGUSTINUS, *De catechizandis rudibus*, 5.9, CCSL 46: *Si enim aliquod commodum exspectando ab hominibus, quibus se aliter placiturum non putat, aut aliquod ab hominibus incommodum devitando, quorum offensionem aut inimicitias reformidat, vult fieri Christianus; non fieri vult potius quam fingere. Fides enim non res est salutantis corporis, sed credentis animi. Sed plane saepe adest misericordia Dei per ministerium catechizantis, ut sermone commotus iam fieri velit, quod decreverat fingere: quod cum velle coeperit, tunc eum venisse deputemus. Et occultum quidem nobis est quando veniat animo, quem iam corpore praesentem videmus: sed tamen sic cum eo debemus agere, ut fiat in illo haec voluntas, etiamsi non est* (trad. it. www.augustinus.it/italiano).

I rapporti tra uomini e il rapporto uomo-Dio erano entrambi impenetrabili; l'arte del vescovo stava nell'invitare i suoi seguaci a percepire il legame tra parola umana e Parola divina.

L'approccio al discorso e al miracolo nella *Passio Sebastiani* può anche allargare la nostra percezione delle diverse posizioni verso l'appartenenza e la conversione cristiana nel corso del periodo preso in considerazione. È stato suggerito, come abbiamo visto sopra, che le generazioni postcostantiniane videro un progressivo degradarsi del significato della conversione, cioè, in altre parole, del tipo e della qualità dell'esposizione dell'insegnamento cristiano che si pensava dovesse essere condiviso dal convertito presentato al battesimo. Potrebbe essere che i termini dell'appartenenza cristiana stessero mutando in un altro senso, cioè che la funzione sociale dei network cristiani assumesse sempre maggiore importanza mano a mano che le altre strutture di reciprocità del mondo tardo e post-romano entravano in crisi.

Questo ci lascia, finalmente, con un paradosso. Nel quinto secolo e all'inizio di quello successivo, nell'Italia della *Passio Sebastiani*, è un errore mettere in opposizione un cristianesimo dei valori etici e un cristianesimo comparativamente povero nei contenuti ma basato sul più primitivo valore della fedeltà, dell'*appartenenza*. Perché nel paesaggio immaginario della *Passio* l'appartenenza è etica. Forme nuove e obbligatorie di appartenenza, forme garantite dalla Parola e dal suo potere miracoloso, emergono dalla *Passio* come una nuova strategia di difesa contro la crisi dei legami sociali di reciprocità e autorità, come un raggio di speranza nella sopravvivenza di un mondo fragile.

«Appunto perché impone ricerche nuove»

CLAUDE LEPELLEY

De la réaction païenne à la sécularisation: le témoignage d'inscriptions municipales romano-africaines tardives

L'Afrique romaine tardive nous a transmis un nombre considérable d'inscriptions révélant une vie urbaine et municipale active, toujours très enracinée dans la tradition civique classique, et impliquant une évidente prospérité économique. J'avais pu recenser à la fin des années 1970 environ 500 de ces documents[1], et une bonne cinquantaine d'autres, souvent d'un grand intérêt, ont été publiés depuis[2]. Mon propos est d'examiner, à travers une sélection d'exemples, ce que cette riche documentation épigraphique nous apprend sur le paganisme en Afrique au temps de l'empire chrétien, et donc sur la fin de l'ancienne religion. Au cours du IVe siècle, après le règne de Dioclétien, on constate en effet une disparition progressive des hommages épigraphiques aux dieux païens, des dédicaces de leurs statues, des évocations de constructions de temples, des mentions de sacerdoces traditionnels (l'augurat, le pontificat) assumés par les dirigeants des cités, à l'exception du flaminat perpétuel municipal et du sacerdoce provincial, prêtrises d'un culte impérial réduit depuis Constantin à un hommage

---

Abréviations: AE: L'Année Épigraphique (Paris). Ant. Afr.: Antiquités Africaines (Aix-en-Provence). BCTH: Bulletin archéologique du Comité des travaux historiques et scientifiques (Paris). CIL: *Corpus Inscriptionum Latinarum* (Berlin). CRAI: Comptes-rendus des séances de l'Académie des Inscriptions et Belles-Lettres (Paris). CTh: *Codex Theodosianus*. CEFR: Collection de l'École française de Rome. ILAlg: Inscriptions latines de l'Algérie. ILCV: *Inscriptiones latinae christianae veteres* (Berlin). ILS: *Inscriptiones latinae selectae* (H. Dessau éd.). IRT: Inscriptions of Roman Tripolitania. MEFRA: Mélanges de l'École française de Rome – Antiquité (Rome). MGH AA: *Monumenta Germaniae Historica. Auctores antiquissimi*. PLRE: *Prosopography of the Later Roman Empire* (Cambridge) I, 1971; II, 1980. SC: Collection Sources Chrétiennes.

[1] C. LEPELLEY, *Les cités de l'Afrique romaine au Bas-Empire*, I-II Paris 1979-1981.
[2] Recension de quatorze de ces inscriptions dans C. LEPELLEY, *Nouveaux documents sur la vie municipale dans l'Afrique romaine tardive*, in *Actes du VIIIe Colloque International sur l'histoire et l'archéologie de l'Afrique du Nord*, éd. M. KHANOUSSI, Tunis 2003, 215-228.

solennel sans sacrifices, donc assumé sans problème par des chrétiens[3]. Notons d'emblée un silence: cette riche documentation n'évoque jamais le christianisme. Comme je l'ai écrit[4], «si l'on ne disposait que de cette série de sources, passerait totalement inaperçu l'événement majeur que fut la christianisation de l'Empire», ainsi que l'exceptionnelle vitalité des églises africaines, attestée par de multiples autres sources. Les mentions des cultes païens se raréfiant, jusqu'à disparaître dans le dernier quart du IVe siècle, c'est donc un silence global sur les affaires religieuses qu'on voit s'établir dans cette riche épigraphie municipale. Ce silence s'explique, à mon sens, par la volonté des dirigeants des cités de rester à l'écart des violentes controverses entre païens et chrétiens et entre catholiques et donatistes qui déchiraient la population.

On constate qu'au cours du long règne de Constantin, l'exercice des cultes traditionnels demeurait libre, ainsi que son expression publique par les inscriptions, qui se raréfie mais ne disparaît pas. Je citerai deux exemples, dont la dédicace d'action de grâce à Esculape et Hygie pour sa guérison, faite en 320 à Lambèse par le sénateur Domitius Zenofilus, alors gouverneur consulaire de Numidie, et plus tard proconsul d'Afrique, ouvertement païen, comme le montrent ses titres officiels mentionnés sur l'inscription.

a) **AE 2003, 2022. Lambèse (Numidie) – M. Christol, M. Janon, «Ant. Afr.», 38-39 (2002-2003), 79-84 (nouvelle édition améliorée de AE 1915, 30)**

Dis salutari/bus Escolapio (sic) *et Hygiae quo/rum ope adver/sae valetudines / propelluntur, Domi/tius Zenofilus, v(ir) c(larissimus), / cons(ularis) sexfascalis /p(rovinciae) N(umidiae) , sacrum reli/gionis suae iux/ta eos indici/un dedit. / Curetii.*

«Aux dieux salutaires Esculape et Hygie, grâce au pouvoir desquels les maladies nocives sont repoussées, Domitius Zenofilus, homme clarissime, consulaire à six faisceaux de la province de Numidie, a donné cet objet sacré, preuve de sa dévotion à leur égard. Curetius» (d'après la traduction de Christol et Janon).

Date: 320 (d'après Optat, Appendice, I, *Gesta apud Zenofilum*).

---

[3] Résumé de la question dans C. LEPELLEY, *Cités*..., I, 362-369. Sur cette sécularisation du culte impérial, voir J. GASCOU, *Le rescrit d'Hispellum*, «MEFR» (1967), 609-659, commentant CIL XI, 5265 = ILS 705. Ce rescrit de Constantin instaurant pour l'Ombrie un culte impérial sans sacrifices est datable des années 333-335. Sur les *flamines* et *sacerdotales* chrétiens en Afrique, cf. A. CHASTAGNOL, N. DUVAL, *Les survivances du culte impérial dans l'Afrique du Nord à l'époque vandale*, in *Mélanges William Seston*, Paris 1974, 87-118.

[4] C. LEPELLEY, *Le lieu des valeurs communes. La cité terrain neutre entre païens et chrétiens dans l'Afrique romaine tardive*, in *Idéologies et valeurs civiques dans le monde romain. Hommage à Claude Lepelley*, éd. H. INGLEBERT, Paris 2002, 272.

Curetius: ce *signum* de Zenofilus, se lit déjà sur l'inscription de Lilybée CIL X, 724, gravée quand il était *corrector* de Sicile. *Curetius* pourrait dériver du grec *Kourètes*, nom désignant les prêtres crétois de Zeus, ce qui constitue un autre indice des convictions païennes du personnage (selon Christol et Janon). Proconsul d'Afrique (au cours des années 326-332), il présida à la restauration du capitole de Cingaris[5]. Il devint consul ordinaire en 333 (*PLRE* I, 993).

Un second exemple d'adhésion affichée au paganisme de la part d'un haut dignitaire au temps de Constantin est donné par une inscription carthaginoise datant de la dernière partie du règne, évoquant la restauration du portique du temple de la Mère des Dieux à Carthage, sur décision du proconsul Lucius Aradius Valerius Proculus, en fonction vers 331-333. L'inscription expose son cursus sénatorial, dont ses sacerdoces païens (*pontifex maior, quindecemvir sacris faciundis,* et probablement *augur, pontifex flavialis*), ainsi que sa double fonction de proconsul et de vicaire des préfets du Prétoire *per provincias africanas*. Il devint préfet de la Ville en 337-338, puis consul ordinaire en 340 (*PLRE* I, 747-749).

b) CIL VIII 24521. Carthage

> *[Matri deum magnae Ideae et] Atti / [L. Aradius Valerius Proculus v(ir) c(larissimus), augur], pont(ifex) mai(or), XV v(ir) s(acris) f(aciundis), / [pontifex Flavialis, praetor tutelaris, legat(us)] propraetore provinciae Numid(iae), / [peraequator cens(us) p]rov(inciae) Gallae[c(iae), p]raeses prov(inciae) Bizac(enae), consular(is) / prov(inciae) Europae, consula]r(is) prov(inciae) Thrac(iae), consular(is) prov(inciae) Sicil(iae), com(es) / [ordinis secundi et pri]mi, procons(ul) prov(inciae) Afr(icae), agens iudicio sacro / [pe]r provincias africana[s, / porticum templi (?) ab ut]roque latere [res[tituit d[- - - - curante ? - - - -] C. filio [Karth]aginie[n - - - -].*

Inscription trouvée sur l'emplacement du temple, à l'angle nord-est de la colline de Byrsa. Restitutions dues à A. HÉRON DE VILLEFOSSE («CRAI» 1897, 723) par comparaison avec les *tituli urbani* de Proculus (CIL VI, 1690-1691 = ILS 1240).

Au temps des fils de Constantin, on constate à la fois une raréfaction des inscriptions municipales et une absence de témoignages épigraphiques sur les cultes païens. L'Afrique fut sous l'autorité de Constance II de 350 à 361. Sa politique anti-païenne fut résolue, et elle explique le silence des

---

[5] AE 2003, 2004. Cincaris (Henchir Singaris) – Proconsulaire: J. PEYRAS, in *Itinéraires de Saintes à Dougga. Mélanges Louis Maurin*, éd. J.-P. BOST, J.-M. RODDAZ, Bordeaux 2003, 278-279. Plaque de marbre brisée en 12 morceaux. Date: 326/333. La restauration d'un temple païen était alors devenue rare.

inscriptions. L'évêque contemporain Optat de Milev a évoqué, en s'en félicitant, la fermeture des temples, à cette époque[6]. Les païens, qui demeuraient assurément nombreux parmi les dirigeants des cités, allaient donc accueillir avec faveur la politique religieuse de Julien.

1. La réaction païenne sous Julien

L'autorité de Julien ne fut pas reconnue en Afrique avant l'extrême fin de l'année 361, car Constance II avait préposé le notaire Gaudentius pour défendre la contrée contre toute tentative d'invasion après la proclamation de Julien comme Auguste à Paris en février 360[7]. Jusqu'à la mort de Julien en juin 363 au cours de son expédition contre les Perses, moins de 20 mois s'écoulèrent. Pourtant, quelques inscriptions parvenues jusqu'à nous montrent que sa politique religieuse fut, durant cette brève période, accueillie par des notables Africains païens comme une divine surprise.

c) ILAlg II, 2, 4674 (AE 1893, 87). Thibilis (Announa; Numidie)

D(omino) n(ostr)o Fl(avio) Cl(audio) Iuliano / Pio Felici vi/ctori ac trium/fatori sem/per Aug(usto), / restituto/ri sacrorum, / ordo splen/didissimus / Thib(ilitanorum) p(osuit) d(edicavit).

«À notre Seigneur Flavius Claudius Julien, Pieux, Bienheureux victorieux et triomphateur toujours Auguste, restaurateur des rites sacrés, l'ordre très splendide des Thibilitains a élevé et dédié ceci».

Cette inscription a été gravée et dédiée par l'ordre des décurions du municipe de Thibilis: l'adhésion à la politique religieuse de Julien est donc ici exprimée officiellement, au nom de la cité, et elle paraît refléter un consensus de l'ensemble des décurions. Est exaltée dans cette dédicace la restauration des *sacra,* soit des rites de l'ancienne religion, ceux là mêmes que Constance II avait voulu abolir.

---

[6] OPTAT DE MILEV, *Contre les donatistes,* II, 16-17. Optat dit que «le diable s'ennuyait» dans ses temples fermés!

[7] AMMIEN MARCELLIN, XXI, 7, 2-4. Selon Ammien (XVII, 9, 7), Gaudentius avait déjà été envoyé par Constance en Gaule pour surveiller et espionner Julien César. Il fut mis à mort sur l'ordre de Julien en 362 (AMMIEN, XXII, 11, 1).

d) **CIL VIII, 4326 = ILS 752. Casae (Numidie; El Mahder, à 20 km au nord-est de Lambèse) – Meilleure lecture (d'après Gsell): CIL VIII, 18529**

D(omin)o n(ostro) Fl(a)v(io) (sic) *Clau/dio Iuliano / Pio Felici, / omni ge/nere pote/nti virtu/tum, invicto / principi, res/titutori li/be[r]tatis et romana(rum) re/ligionum ac tr[i/umfat]ori or/bis.*

«À notre Seigneur Flavius Claudius Julien Pieux, Bienheureux, puissant par toutes sortes de vertus, prince invaincu, restaurateur de la liberté et de la religion romaine et triomphateur du monde».

Les *religiones*, comme les *sacra* dans l'inscription de Thibilis, sont les pratiques religieuses, les rites interdits antérieurement, sous les fils de Constantin. On constate que cette inscription en l'honneur de l'empereur ne mentionne pas de dédicants, ce qui peut surprendre. D'ordinaire, ce type de dédicace, donnant la titulature de l'empereur et exaltant ses vertus, est fait au nom de toute la cité, ou, comme à Thibilis, de l'ordre des décurions. À mon sens, ce silence n'est pas fortuit.

e) **AE 1988, 1110. Bou Arada[8] (Proconsulaire) – N. FERCHIOU, in L'Africa Romana 5, Sassari 1988, 143-147. C. LEPELLEY, Nouveaux documents sur l'histoire municipale de l'Afrique romaine tardive. Éléments d'un supplément épigraphique aux «Cités de l'Afrique romaine au Bas-Empire», in Actes du VIIIe congrès d'hist. et d'archéol. de l'Afrique du N., éd. M. KHANOUSSI, Thabarca 2000, [Tunis 2003], 224-225**

Soli invicto Aug(usto) sacrum / pro salute imp(eratoris) d(omini) n(ostri) Iuliani / victoris ac triumfatoris sem/per Augusti, devoti num/ini magestati (sic) *eorum.*

«Consacré au Soleil Invaincu Auguste, pour le salut de l'empereur notre Seigneur Julien, victorieux et triomphateur toujours Auguste. Ceux qui sont voués à leur puissance divine et à leur majesté».

Le dernier mot se lit sur la pierre *forum*: la rectification s'impose. L. 5: *magestati*; il faudrait *maiestatique*.

Le Soleil Invaincu était le dieu de prédilection de Julien, qui lui consacra un traité (*Sur Hélios Roi*). Le libellé du texte me paraît digne d'attention. La formule finale, gravée de manière incorrecte (il faudrait, à la dernière ligne, *maiestatique* et non *magestati*; le E de *eorum* a la forme

---

[8] L'identification du site de Bou Arada (au nord de la plaine du Fahs) avec l'antique Aradi, ville connue par les listes épiscopales de 484 et de 525, ne reposait que sur une supposée permanence du toponyme. Aradi est en fait le site de Sidi Jdidi, à 14 km d'Hammamet. Cf. AE 1974, 693; voir *infra*, n. 16.

d'un F), correspond à celle des nombreuses inscriptions officielles en l'honneur des empereurs rédigées par des dignitaires ou des cités se disant *devoti numini maiestatique eorum*, «voués à leur puissance divine et à leur majesté». Ici, les dédicants anonymes se disent voués à la puissance divine et à la majesté tant du dieu d'élection de l'empereur que de celui-ci[9]. Je pense qu'il faut comprendre qu'à Bou Arada, au temps de Julien, un groupe de païens a fait graver cette inscription pour manifester leur adhésion à la politique religieuse de l'empereur, mais qu'ils l'ont fait à titre privé, car les chrétiens du lieu, peut-être majoritaires, se seraient opposés à la gravure d'une inscription officielle au nom de toute la cité, comme ce fut le cas à Thibilis pour la dédicace précitée à Julien *restitutor sacrorum*, faite officiellement par l'ordre des décurions. C'est assurément pour une raison identique qu'aucune mention de dédicant ne figure sur l'inscription de Casae citée précédemment, exaltant Julien en tant que «restaurateur de la liberté et de la religion romaine».

f) **P. Salama, *Une couronne solaire de l'empereur Julien*, in *Acts of the fifth epigraphic congress*, Cambridge 1967, 279-286 = *Promenades d'antiquités africaines*, Paris 2005, 191-200. Borj Medjana, Maurétanie Sitifienne (à 75 km à l'ouest de Sétif)**

Borne milliaire
DN
IVLIANI
VICTO
RISSE
MPAVG

D(omini) n(ostri) / Iuliani / victo/ris se/mp(er) Aug(usti).

Au dessus de la première ligne figure un arc de cercle avec rayons extérieurs, soit la couronne radiée ou couronne solaire. L'inscription, signalée par St. Gsell en 1893, fut publiée par Massiéra dans «BCTH» 1934-1935, 226, n° 13. Ces éditeurs n'avaient pas remarqué la couronne radiée. Ce symbole solaire, comme Pierre Salama l'a bien vu, renvoie à la dévotion de Julien pour *Sol Invictus*/Hélios-Roi, et il remplace le chrisme, habituel

---

[9] L'éditrice, N. Ferchiou, suppose que le rédacteur du texte, habitué à la mention de plusieurs empereurs sur les inscriptions, aurait écrit par erreur *eorum* au lieu de *eius*. Je pense qu'il faut comprendre le texte littéralement, donc constater une juxtaposition et de la puissance divine et de la majesté du dieu, et de celles de l'empereur, même si une telle formulation est inhabituelle.

en tête des inscriptions de milliaires depuis Constantin. C'était comme un *signum* personnel de Julien, le chrisme ayant été au départ, selon Salama, un *signum* personnel de Constantin.

Hors d'Afrique, citons deux dédicaces à Julien. À Césarée (Caesarea Paneas; Palestine) – AE 1969-1970, 631, on lit:

> *Romani orbis liberatori, templorum restauratori, curiarum et rei publicae recreatori, barbarorum extinctori, domino nostro Iouliano* (sic) *perpetuo Augusto, Alamannico maximo, Francico maximo, Sarmatico maximo, pontifici maximo, patri patriae, Foenicum ---ius ---ob impet---*

(*Coenum Phoenices*: le conseil provincial – *koïnon* – de Phénicie)

À Beyrouth – AE 1907, 191. – Base de statue, dédicace à Julien, *recreatori sacrorum et extinctori superstitionis*. Dans ce contexte, la *superstitio* ne peut être que le christianisme.

Les mesures anti-chrétiennes de Julien ne lui survécurent pas, car elles furent vite abolies par ses successeurs. Toutefois, Valentinien Ier (364-375) ne revint pas à la politique agressivement anti-païenne de Constance II, et il voulut établir une liberté religieuse, comparable à celle qu'avait d'abord instaurée Constantin (CTh IX, 16, 9, de 371). Optat de Milev, dans son traité contre les donatistes (OPTAT II, 16-17), déplore que, sous le règne de Valentinien Ier, les temples soient restés ouverts, comme ils l'avaient été sous Julien. Dans les années 364-367, la Numidie fut gouvernée par le consulaire Publilius Ceionius Caecina Albinus, qui était un fervent païen, membre du cercle de Symmaque selon Macrobe (MACROBE, *Saturnales*, XII, 15). Il présida à de nombreux chantiers publics dans les cités de sa province: une quinzaine sont connus par les inscriptions, dont quatre concernent des temples. Toutefois, les travaux à des temples municipaux pouvaient fort bien concerner l'entretien d'un patrimoine monumental public dont la fonction religieuse était oubliée. C'est net pour la restauration, sur l'ordre du gouverneur Albinus, des portiques du capitole de Timgad, toujours dans les années 364-367. L'inscription (CIL VIII, 2388 = ILS 5554 – *Cités* II, 447) précise que furent relevées les colonnes effondrées des quatre portiques, lesquels entouraient une très grande cour, plus vaste, comme le montrent les fouilles, que le forum de la ville. Il s'agissait donc d'une opération d'urbanisme sans caractère religieux explicite. Ajoutons que le principal responsable du chantier fut le curateur en exercice Aelius Julianus, lequel était chrétien, puisqu'il reçut une tablette de patronat où figurait un chrisme (AE 1913, 25 = ILCV 387). En revanche, la construction à Cirta d'un mithreum avec sa décoration sculptée sur l'ordre du même gouverneur Albinus concernait directement l'exercice d'un culte païen.

g) CIL VIII, 6975; ILAlg II, 1, 541. Cirta

Speleum cum sig[nis] / et ornament[tis] / Publilius Ceion[ius] / Caecina Albinu[s] / [faciendum curavit ?.....].

On l'a dit, Albinus était un païen convaincu (MACROBE, *Saturnales*, XII, 15). Toutefois, la disparition de la fin de l'inscription empêche de savoir s'il avait agi dans l'exercice de ses fonctions de gouverneur, ou s'il avait accompli un acte d'évergétisme privé en faveur d'une communauté de fidèles de Mithra. Toujours à Cirta, l'inscription fragmentaire CIL 19502 = ILAlg II, 1, 618 montre Albinus intervenant en tant que consulaire de Numidie dans des travaux à un temple.

C'est du règne de Valentinien Ier que datent les dernières mentions en Afrique d'augures et de pontifes municipaux. Quatre pontifes et quatre augures figuraient sur l'album municipal de Timgad, datable de 363. Le dernier augure connu en Afrique était *curator rei publicae* de Calama dans les années 364-367 (CIL VIII 5335 et 5337 = ILAlg I, 256 et 254). Le dernier pontife africain connu fit graver une dédicace à Valentinien Ier (364-375) à Sicca Veneria, où il était *curator rei publicae* (CIL VIII, 1636). Par la suite, les seuls prêtres de l'ancien culte mentionnés étaient des flamines perpétuels municipaux et des *sacerdotales* provinciaux, mais, on l'a dit, leur fonction étaient désormais vidée de toute signification religieuse.

Deux inscriptions, sans évoquer l'exercice d'un culte païen, manifestent pourtant un attachement certain à la tradition religieuse ancienne. La première, trouvée à Cuicul (Djemila), date toujours des années 364-367, mais le consulaire de Numidie en fonction était le successeur d'Albinus, Ulpius Egnatius Faventinus (*PLRE* I, 325).

h) ILAlg II, 3, 7914 - AE 1946, 108. Cuicul (Djemila; Numidie)

Ulpius Egnatius Faven/tinus v(ir) c(larissimus) cons(ularis) / p(rovinciae) N(umidiae), quod vel amplitudi/ni vel ornatui basilicae Tisediacor(um) / tribunalium / defuerat, Victoriae simula/crum consti/tuendum con/locandumque / curavi.

«Moi, Ulpius Egnatius Faventinus, homme clarissime, consulaire de la province de Numidie, j'ai veillé à ce que fût élevée et mise en place une statue de la Victoire, car cela manquait à la grandeur ou à l'ornementation des tribunes de la basilique des Tisediaci (?)».

Cette inscription figurait sur un cippe trouvé dans l'abside de la basilique civile construite peu auparavant à Cuicul sur l'ordre de Publilius Ceionius Caecina Albinus (ILAlg II, 3, 7876 et 7877 – AE 1946, 107). Cette basilique était construite sur l'emplacement d'un temple de Saturne Frugifer, dont subsistent des colonnes et une inscription de dédicace.

> l. 4: *Tisediacor(um)* – aucune explication satisfaisante n'a été proposée pour ce terme.
> l. 5: *Tribunalium*: pluriel, dû probablement à la présence de deux estrades ou tribunes (ou pluriel emphatique pour désigner l'unique estrade).

Païen convaincu, Ulpius Egnatius Faventinus reçut à Rome le taurobole et le criobole de Cybèle le 13 août 376, d'après CIL VI, 504 = ILS 4153, où sont énumérés ses sacerdoces (augure public du peuple romain des Quirites, *hieroceryx* et *Pater* de Mithra, *archibucolus* de Liber Pater, hiérophante d'Hécate, prêtre d'Isis). L'installation de cette statue de la Victoire dans la basilique de Cuicul est présentée ici comme ayant un but uniquement esthétique. Compte tenu des fortes convictions religieuses de Faventinus, il semble bien qu'il faille voir ici une transposition de la présence de la statue de la Victoire dans la curie sénatoriale romaine, qui devait être l'objet d'une âpre controverse[10].

L'autre inscription est plus tardive (années 379-383). Elle a été trouvée à Lambèse.

i) CIL VIII, 18328; ILS 5520. Lambèse (Numidie)

J'ai reproduit cette inscription dans mes *Cités* II, 420-421, mais je n'ai pas relevé alors la signification religieuse de la formule *templum ordinis*, non plus que la simultanéité avec le conflit romain sur l'autel de la Victoire.

> *Aureis temporibus / ddd(ominorum) nnn(ostrorum) Gratiani, Va/lentiniani et Theo/dosi(i) perpetuorum / et divinorum princi/pum, non solum labsa /reparantur sed et nova / pro felicitate con/struuntur. Curia igi/tur ordinis quam maio/res nostri merito tem/plum eiusdem ordinis vo/citari voluerunt, vetustate / immo incuria verum in / odiu(m)* (sic) *f(o)eda[ta] iacuisse [v]ide/batur, qua(e) nunc ex novo / opere in eo-*

---

[10] C. LEPELLEY, *Cités...*, II, 406, n. 21: «Assurément, les notables de Cuicul ont accueilli favorablement cette initiative du gouverneur, ce qui montre une persistance païenne certaine dans les familles dirigeantes de la cité. On remarque cependant que l'érection de la statue est présentée comme due uniquement à des motif esthétiques [...]. Ces considérations étaient peut-être destinées à dissimuler auprès des citoyens chrétiens et des autorités les aspects religieux de l'opération».

dem solo egregi/a{e} cognoscitur. Nam etiam in / tam splendidissima civitate / meatus fluentorum deesse vi/debatur, qui ex integro opere /ad usum uitlitatemque (sic – corriger en *utilitatemque*) *eiusde(m) / urbis extructus videtur. Quae / omnia pro splendore felicis/sim(a)e urbis sub fascibus Luci(i) Ae/mili(i) Metopi(i) Flaviani clarissimi / viri, consularis sexfascalis / p(rovinciae) N(umidiae), perfecta sunt, curante / L. Silicio Rufo du/oviral[i]c(io), cu(ratore) r(ei) p(ublicae), / sum(p)tu proprio.*
L. 13-14:Schmidt, CIL: *verum in odiu(m).*
L. 21: *Ad usum utilitatemque.*
Publication par Schmidt d'après estampage.

«À l'âge d'or de nos Seigneurs Gratien, Valentinien et Théodose, princes éternels et divins, non seulement les édifices tombés en ruine sont restaurés, mais de nouveaux sont également édifiés en raison de la félicité des temps. C'est pourquoi la curie de l'Ordre (des décurions), dont nos ancêtres ont voulu à juste titre qu'elle fût appelée le temple de ce même Ordre, et qu'on voyait effondrée, défigurée, par la vétusté, ou plutôt par l'incurie, jusqu'à devenir un véritable objet de répulsion, maintenant, à la suite de travaux nouvellement menés, on la découvre belle, sur le même emplacement. De plus, quant à la conduite des eaux courantes qu'on voyait manquer à cette très splendide cité, on la voit construite pour l'usage et l'avantage de cette même ville, à la suite de travaux complets. Tout cela a été mené à bien, pour la splendeur de cette ville très heureuse, sous les faisceaux de Lucius Aemilius Metopius Flavianus, homme clarissime, consulaire à six faisceaux de la province de Numidie, par les soins de Lucius Silicius Rufus, duoviralicien, curateur de la République, à ses propres frais» (traduction établie avec la collaboration de Valérie Fauvinet-Ranson).
Date: entre janvier 379 et août 383.

Cette inscription est un témoignage éloquent sur la prospérité de l'Afrique au temps de la dynastie valentinienne, sur le maintien dans l'élite dirigeante des cités d'un ardent patriotisme municipal, sur la volonté de maintenir et même d'enrichir le patrimoine monumental des villes. Les deux chantiers, la restauration de la curie et la construction d'une canalisation pour les eaux courantes correspondent au programme énoncé en préambule: les édifices tombés en ruine sont restaurés, et de nouveaux sont également édifiés. Le dirigeant municipal, curateur et ancien duumvir, L. Silicius Rufus a non seulement assumé la responsabilité (*cura*) des travaux, mais il les a également financés (*sumptu proprio*); c'est un bel exemple du maintien en Afrique au IVe siècle de la pratique et de l'idéal évergétiques. Je retiendrai surtout ici la formule sur «la curie de l'Ordre (des décurions) dont nos ancêtres ont voulu à juste titre qu'elle fût appelée le temple de ce même ordre». Cette expression est très notable: elle exalte éloquemment l'attachement des rédacteurs de ce texte à l'idéal civique, à la vie municipale traditionnelle, et, indissociablement, à la tradition civique païenne.

On trouve déjà l'expression *templum ordinis* pour désigner une curie municipale africaine dans la célèbre inscription dite «du Moissonneur de Mactar», qui est datable du IIIe siècle (probablement après le milieu de ce siècle)[11]. C'est l'épitaphe métrique d'un paysan parvenu, qui exalte son enrichissement et sa réussite sociale, couronnée par une carrière municipale ainsi relatée: *Ordinis in templo delectus ab ordine sedi / et de rusticulo censor et ipse fui,* «choisi par l'Ordre (des décurions), j'ai siégé dans le temple de l'Ordre, et de petit paysan, je devins censeur» (censeur signifiant ici duumvir quinquennal).

Ce terme de temple pour désigner la curie fut donc repris plus d'un siècle après à Lambèse. On doit rappeler que l'édifice de la curie (celle du Sénat à Rome, la *Curia Iulia,* mais aussi celles des diverses cités de l'Occident latin) avait la forme d'un temple: une construction rectangulaire avec souvent des colonnes en façade (prostyle), laquelle façade était surmontée d'un fronton triangulaire. Plus encore que le plan architectural, la présence de la statue de la Victoire, et surtout celle de l'autel, faisaient de la curie de Rome un temple. Il semble bien que les sénateurs entrant en séance jetaient des grains d'encens sur l'autel, assimilant ainsi la séance sénatoriale à un sacrifice. Symmaque, dans sa *Relatio* III, 5, évoque un serment prêté par les sénateurs sur l'autel: *Ubi in leges vestras et verba iurabimus?* Les sénateurs juraient d'être loyaux envers l'empereur et ce *sacramentum publicum* contenait une invocation à la déesse Victoire. Et nous devons ici souligner une coïncidence chronologique qu'il est bien difficile de croire fortuite. La fourchette de datation de l'inscription, et donc de la restauration de la curie de Lambèse, est assez restreinte: entre l'avènement de Théodose en janvier 379 et l'assassinat de Gratien à Lyon fin août 383. Or c'est l'époque de la querelle sur l'autel de la Victoire au Sénat de Rome, affaire bien connue grâce à la *Relatio III* de Symmaque, document officiel du Sénat, et aux lettres 72 (l'*ep.* 17 de l'édition des Mauristes) et 73 (l'*ep.* 18 de l'édition des Mauristes) adressées à Valentinien II par saint Ambroise. Gratien ordonna l'enlèvement de l'autel en 382. Il avait déjà été enlevé sous Constance II, en tout cas lors de la visite de cet empereur à Rome en 357 (AMBROISE, lettre 18, 32). Il fut évidemment rétabli sous Julien, et il était resté en place sous Valentinien I. Les démarches oppo-

---

[11] CIL VIII, 11824 = ILS 7457. Cf. G. PICARD, H. LE BONNIEC, J. MALLON, *Le cippe de Beccut*, «Ant. Afr.» 4 (1970), 125-165. Paléographie: J MALLON, *ibid.*, 162; G. PICARD, *ibid.*, 148, date le texte vers 270. L'inscription du cippe de Beccut est gravée en lettres onciales comparables à celles de l'inscription du Moissonneur.

sées de Symmaque et d'Ambroise, à Milan, datent de 383[12]. L'inscription de Lambèse est contemporaine, et elle fait assurément écho à cette affaire romaine. Elle implique, chez les rédacteurs de l'inscription – et d'abord le curateur évergète Lucius Silicius Rufus –, sinon une affirmation explicite de paganisme, du moins une grande nostalgie pour l'ancienne religion, liée à un vif attachement à la tradition civique romaine.

On doit constater dès les années 380 une disparition des mentions de temples dans les inscriptions municipales africaines, pourtant toujours nombreuses, sauf pour deux cas (à Madaure et à Abthugnos) où des temples étaient affectés à des usages profanes[13]. C'est assurément un indice de l'efficacité des mesures impériales anti-païennes, dont la sévérité allait croissant, jusqu'à l'interdiction radicale de toute pratique «idolâtre», décidée par Théodose en 391 (CTh XVI, 10, 10), et effective en Afrique en 399[14]. Demeurait toujours vivante l'exaltation de la cité, du patriotisme municipal, mais sans aucune implication religieuse, même chrétienne: on était dans un domaine profane, séculier. Les valeurs exaltées sur les inscriptions officielles étaient purement séculières, on dirait, non sans anachronisme, laïques en langage contemporain: c'était la gloire de l'Empire et des empereurs, le prestige de la cité, le bien public, la vertu et la générosité des dignitaires, gouverneurs ou dirigeants municipaux, toujours supposés parfaitement intègres et bienfaisants. La cité est *splendidissima*, adjectif qualifiant aussi l'ordre des décurions, Carthage est féconde (*alma Carthago*), un monument public servira «à la splendeur tant de la patrie

---

[12] Voir la bonne mise au point récente de RITA LIZZI TESTA, sur les mesures prises par Gratien en 382 contre certains aspects du paganisme (affaire de l'autel de la Victoire, 253; privilèges financiers des Vestales et autres collèges sacerdotaux): *Christian emperors, Vestal Virgins and priestly colleges: reconsidering the end of Roman paganism*, «Antiquité Tardive» 15 (2007), 251-262. Y sont critiquées des extrapolations des historiens, depuis le XIXᵉ siècle, exagérant l'ampleur de ces mesures dans le domaine financier. De la même historienne, cf. *Legislazione imperiale e reazione pagana: limiti del conflitto*, dans le présent ouvrage, 467-491.

[13] Madaure (Numidie proconsulaire): ILAlg I, 2103; restauration entre 379 et 383, d'un temple de *Fortuna*, dans lequel avaient lieu des opérations commerciales (*res venales*). Abthugnos (Proconsulaire): CIL VIII, 11205 = 928. Cette inscription très mutilée évoque probablement des réunions de collèges dans les *cellae Capitolii*. La loi d'Honorius CTh XVI, 10, 19, de 407, prévoit l'utilisation des temples désaffectés *ad usum publicum*.

[14] Mission des comtes Gaudentius et Jovius, envoyés en Afrique, selon Augustin, «sous le consulat de Mallius Theodorus» (399), «pour renverser les temples et briser les idoles» (*Cité de Dieu*, XVIII, 54). Le même événement est relaté par QUODVULTDEUS, *Livre des promesses et des prédictions de Dieu*, III, 38, 4, in SC 102, 568; cf. aussi *Consularia Constantinopolitana*, MGH AA, 19, ann. 399.

que de la province»[15]. Ainsi des inscriptions tardives de Lepcis Magna sont dédiées *principali integerrimo*; *amatori patriae et civium suorum*; *ob amorem incomparabilem in patriam et cives suos*; *ob insignem iustitiam et integritatem eius erga rem publicam* (IRT 564; 567; 568). Cette image idéalisée de la vie de la cité s'inscrit dans la tradition la plus classique, tout en l'exprimant avec une emphase nouvelle. Mais dans cet univers profane, ce monde séculier, le christianisme ne s'était nullement substitué, en tant que religion civique, au paganisme disparu.

Pour illustrer ce processus, je citerai deux inscriptions trouvées au capitole d'Abthugnos (en Proconsulaire, près de la frontière de la Byzacène).

l) **AE 1991, 1641-1643. Abthugnos (Henchir Souar, Proconsulaire) – N. FERCHIOU, in *L'Africa Romana* 7, Sassari 1989, 754-758. Trois bases, sur le podium du Capitole – Textes à peu près identiques (est donné ici le texte d'AE 1643)**

Compellente tem/porum felicitate / ddd(ominorum) nnn(ostrorum) Valentis, / Gratiani et Valenti/niani invictissimo/rum semper Auggg(ustorum), / Publicius Felix Hor/tensius, fl(amen) p(er)p(etuus), cur(ator) r(ei) p(ublicae), / rostra ad ornatum / patriae in meliorem / statum redducxi (sic) */ itemque dedicavi.*

«Contraint par la félicité des temps de nos Seigneurs Valens, Gratien et Valentinien très invaincus, toujours Augustes, moi, Publicius Felix Hortensius, flamine perpétuel, curateur de la République, j'ai remis en meilleur état les rostres, pour l'ornementation de la patrie, et j'en ai également fait la dédicace».
Date: 375/378.

Le podium du capitole, qui pouvait de fait servir de tribune, est ici qualifié de rostres (*rostra*), terme se référant explicitement au vieux forum romain. Cette expression met en valeur la culture latine du rédacteur, et elle permet aussi d'exalter la cité locale et l'attachement civique qui lui était porté (*ad ornatum patriae*), mais sans implications religieuses.

m) **AE 1991, 1644. Abthugnos (Henchir Souar, Proconsulaire) – Autre base, au même endroit. N. FERCHIOU, in *L'Africa Romana* 7, Sassari 1989, 754-758**

Temporum fe/licitate compellen/te ddd(ominorum) nnn(ostrorum) / Valentis, Gratiani / ac Valentiniani, in/victissimorum sem/per Augg(ustorum) (sic), *aeternam / Urbem*

---

[15] AE 1911, 217, Mascula (Numidie); date: 364/367: *ad splendorem tam patriae quam provinciae.*

Romam Publi/cius Felix Hortensi/us, fl(amen) p(er)p(etuus), cur(ator) r(ei) p(ublicae) / cum ordine posui.
À la ligne 7, *Augg* pou*r Auggg.*

«Contraint par la félicité des temps de nos Seigneurs Valens, Gratien et Valentinien très invaincus, toujours Augustes, moi, Publicius Felix Hortentius, flamine perpétuel, curateur de la République, j'ai élevé avec l'ordre (des décurions la statue de) la Ville éternelle de Rome».
Ann. 375-378.

La base portait une statue de l'*Aeterna Urbs Roma*, la Ville éternelle de Rome, c'est à dire la déesse Rome désignée d'une manière désacralisée ne pouvant choquer les chrétiens. La statue, représentant assurément une femme coiffée d'un casque, avait probablement été sculptée antérieurement et elle avait été simplement installée (*posui*) sur l'emplacement restauré du podium du capitole.

Une grande inscription récemment publiée illustre éloquemment cette idéologie et cette évolution.

n) AE 2004, 1798. Aradi[16] (Sidi Jdidi, Byzacène) – Plaque brisée en deux morceaux jointifs, en remploi dans le coffrage de la tombe d'un chrétien nommé Felix, comme l'atteste une mosaïque funéraire avec inscription (AE 1993, 1743). A. BEN ABED-BEN KHADER, M. FIXOT, M. BONIFAY, S. ROUCOLE, in *Sidi Jdidi I. La basilique sud* (CEFR, 339), Rome 2004, 24-30. Les améliorations apportées à la lecture du texte et à sa traduction, pour la publication dans L'Année Épigraphique, sont dues à M. Corbier, M. Ducos, X. Dupuis, J. Gascou et O. Salomies.

Beatissimis florentissimisq(ue) [tem]poribus ddd(ominorum) nnn(ostrorum) Arcadi(i), / Honori(i) et Theodosi(i) / ppp(erpetuorum) Auggg(ustorum), administrante M[an]lio Crepereio Scipione Vincentio, v(iro) c(larissimo), / consulare p(rovinciae) Fl(aviae) Valeriae Byz(acenae), plateam quae splendori est civi/tati et huic natura loci denecabat ornatum, aegestis (sic) *ruderib(us), inaequalitate (s)ilicibus coequa/ta{m}, additis quoq(ue) columnis arcib(us) circumclusis, in meliorem faciem T. F(lavius) Dyscolius / Therapius, ex t(ribuno), fl(amen) p(er)p(etuus), c(urator) r(ei) p(ublicae), liberalitatem ob amorem civicum patriae inpendens, proprio / sumptu excoluit, perfecit et ludos scaenicos praemiales edidit et cum splendi/dissimo ordine feliciter dedicavit.*

---

[16] A. Ben Abed Ben Khader et M. Fixot ont montré, dans leur publication du site mentionnée ci-après (17-18), que Sidi Jdidi est l'antique Aradi, ville connue par les listes épiscopales de 484 et 525. Il convient de lire Aradi, et non Asadi, sur l'inscription AE 1974, 693, trouvée à Sidi Jdidi, et d'abandonner l'identification d'Aradi avec l'actuel Bou Arada, (cf. *supra* n. 8), qui n'était fondée que sur une prétendue permanence du toponyme.

«Aux temps très heureux et très florissants de nos Seigneurs Arcadius, Honorius et Théodose Augustes perpétuels, sous l'administration de Manlius Crepereius Scipio Vincentius, homme clarissime, consulaire de la province Flavienne Valérienne de Byzacène, la *platea* qui est pour la cité sa splendeur, et à laquelle la nature du lieu refusait l'élégance, une fois déblayés les décombres, une fois les irrégularités aplanies avec des pierres, une fois ajoutées tout autour des colonnades fermées par des arcs pour embellir son apparence, cette *platea* Titus Flavius Dyscolius Therapius, ancien tribun, flamine perpétuel, curateur de la République, répandant sa libéralité en raison de son amour de citoyen pour sa patrie, l'a embellie à ses frais et l'a achevée d'une manière parfaite, il a donné des représentations scéniques pourvues de prix et il a fait avec joie la dédicace avec le très splendide *ordo*».

Date: entre janvier 402 (naissance et avènement de Théodose II) et mai 408 (mort d'Arcadius).

l. 2- 3: gouverneur de Byzacène nouveau dans les fastes.

l. 3: *platea*: vu le contexte, plutôt sens classique (place publique) que sens habituel tardif (avenue à portiques). *Aegestis*: faute pour *egestis*.

l. 4: la lecture *(s)ilicibus*, due à O. Salomies, dans AE 2004 *loc. cit.*, s'impose: les inégalités de la place ont été aplanies grâce un empierrement (cf. *viam silice sternere*, «niveler une route en l'empierrant», LIV. XXXVIII, 28, 3). *Ilicibus* est l'ablatif pluriel de *ilex*, le chêne vert ou yeuse: mais on ne voit pas comment une plantation d'arbres pourrait aplanir une place. Pour niveler cette place, l'empierrement était moins coûteux qu'un dallage.

l. 5: *arcibus*: corriger en *arcubus*: les arcs (arches) ferment (*circumclusis*) la colonnade du portique. *Arcibus* est une graphie fautive: on ne voit pas comment des forteresses ou des collines pourraient fermer une colonnade.

Dernière ligne: *ludos praemiales*: «dotés de prix». Les spectacles théâtraux offerts par l'évergète sont mis au concours et reçoivent des prix.

Ce texte est la plus tardive des grandes inscriptions municipales que nous a transmises l'Afrique romaine du Bas-Empire. Elle révèle, en ce début du Ve siècle, le maintien d'une généreuse pratique évergétique de la part d'un dirigeant local, dont est exaltée la libéralité due à «son amour de citoyen pour sa patrie». On a noté la précision de l'évocation des travaux d'urbanisme, manifestant la volonté résolue des Romano-Africains de maintenir et même de développer à l'époque tardive la parure monumentale classique de leurs villes. La fouille n'a pas permis de retrouver les monuments mentionnés par l'inscription, car celle-ci a été trouvée hors de son contexte archéologique, remployée dans le coffrage d'une tombe chrétienne. On constate, ici, une absence totale d'allusion à une quelconque vie religieuse, sauf le titre de flamine perpétuel porté par l'évergète, mais on a vu que, dès le règne de Constantin, ce sacerdoce municipal du culte impérial n'était plus qu'une dignité reçue par les notables locaux et dépourvue de contenu proprement religieux, au point que des chrétiens l'acceptaient volontiers.

En un temps où les tensions, les conflits religieux entre païens et chrétiens et entre catholiques et donatistes étaient forts, et même souvent violents, les institutions et les espaces publics de la cité étaient essentiels pour maintenir un consensus séculier commun. La cité était un terrain neutre où tous étaient censés pouvoir se retrouver autour d'un idéal collectif[17]. Comme l'a écrit Robert Markus, le *secular* était «un secteur de la vie qui n'était pas considéré comme ayant une signification religieuse»[18]. L'absence, à coup sûr délibérée, de toute référence au christianisme dans ce corpus épigraphique, et la disparition progressive des références au paganisme, ne laissaient subsister qu'un idéal culturel, politique et social séculier, c'est à dire profane. Le monde où vécut Augustin, se caractérisait, selon Markus, par une «massive secularity»[19].

Un article récent de Richard Miles[20] a brillamment démontré comment à l'époque du royaume vandal, Dracontius et les poètes carthaginois dont les écrits ont été transmis par l'*Anthologia Latina* révèlent un projet conscient et cohérent de la part de l'élite romano-africaine de promouvoir une vision séculière, permettant l'établissement d'un *modus vivendi*, en une époque de très grave tension religieuse, non plus entre païens et chrétiens ni entre catholiques et donatistes, mais entre les rois vandals ariens et l'église catholique africaine qu'ils persécutaient. La sécularité exprimée par les inscriptions municipales du IVe siècle et du début du Ve siècle, se retrouvait désormais dans les productions poétiques de l'élite romano-africaine de l'époque vandale, où les multiples références à la mythologie classique manifestaient une adhésion enthousiaste à une culture classique désormais vidée de toute signification religieuse, devenue pleinement séculière, c'est à dire profane, donc étrangère au conflit religieux contemporain.

Toutefois, Robert Markus, toujours dans *The End of Ancient Christianity*, a mis en lumière le processus inverse, ce qu'il appelle la «désécularisation», soit l'éclipse de la dimension séculière dans la conscience chrétienne, l'absorption du séculier dans le sacré, l'avènement d'une société totalement sacrale (*wholly sacral*), animée par le pouvoir grandissant de l'Église[21]. Mais, montre Markus, ce processus n'advint que lorsque les traditions politiques, institutionnelles et culturelles antiques se trouvèrent affaiblies et en voie de disparition, ce qui fut le cas dans le troisième tiers du VIe siècle et au siècle

---

[17] C. LEPELLEY, *Le lieu des valeurs communes...*, 271-285.
[18] R.A. MARKUS, *The End of Ancient Christianity*, Cambridge 1990, 15.
[19] *Ibid.*, 227.
[20] R. MILES, *The* Anthologia Latina *and the Creation of Secular Space in Vandal Carthage*, «Antiquité Tardive», 13 (2005), 305-320.
[21] R.A. MARKUS, *The End of Ancient Christianity...*, 218-222.

suivant. «L'univers mental de Grégoire le Grand et de ses contemporains, écrit Markus, était le résultat d'une immense mutation dans les horizons intellectuels et mentaux des chrétiens d'Occident»[22]. Le contraste était radical avec l'époque d'Augustin, caractérisée selon Markus, on l'a dit, par une «massive secularity». C'est alors, et non avant, qu'il faut situer la fin du monde antique et le début du Moyen Âge[23].

---

[22] *Ibid.*, 227.
[23] Citons encore R.A. MARKUS, *The End of Ancient Christianity...*, 222: «In Western Europe, the late sixth century marks a real break with the world of Antiquity, closed off access to most of its intellectual culture, and even more drastically, to its ways of looking at, understanding and speaking about that world».

Arnaldo Marcone

Persistenze classiche e innovazioni cristiane: iconografia ed epigrafia nelle Venezie

Da un punto di vista strettamente storiografico sembra guadagnare consistenza la prospettiva che, al di là delle formule inevitabilmente semplificatrici di «rivoluzione costantiniana» e simili, valorizza l'idea di una conversione tutto sommato pacifica del mondo antico. Il «conflitto» tra paganesimo e cristianesimo, per riprendere il titolo del convegno organizzato da Arnaldo Momigliano che ha costituito il punto di riferimento costante di queste giornate di convegno, appare sempre più una definizione di comodo che implica dei presupposti ormai superati soprattutto quando ci si confronta con le tradizioni culturali proprie dei ceti elevati[1].

Forse non ci sono parole migliori, per introdurre l'argomento che intendo trattare, di quelle di Peter Brown: «In the past several decades the history of early Christian art and of the late-antique world in which this art developed have been subject to a series of surprises, all of them profoundly disruptive of previous certitudes». Così ha scritto pochi mesi fa Peter Brown in una recensione al catalogo di una bella mostra *Picturing the Bible. The earliest Christian Art* che si è appena svolta al Kimbell Art Museum a Fort Worth[2].

Riprendo in parte in questo lavoro mie riflessioni già svolte in occasione della XXXVIII settimana di studi aquileiesi (Aquileia, maggio 2007): La cristianizzazione dell'Adriatico, *a cura di G. Cuscito, Trieste 2008, 19-44; si veda anche la versione di quell'intervento con il titolo* Tra paganesimo e cristianesimo. Le persistenze classiche nell'iconografia tardoantica, *in A.* Marcone, Di Tarda Antichità. Scritti scelti, *Firenze 2008, 184-203. Desidero ribadire il mio debito di riconoscenza per Giuseppe Cuscito, Paolo Liverani e Valentino Pace.*

[1] Vorrei solo sottolineare la prudente e autocritica considerazione, segno di una sensibilità che si direbbe infallibile nel cogliere il mutare delle temperie storiografiche, premessa da Arnaldo Momigliano alla traduzione italiana del libro (Einaudi, Torino, 1968, XI): «È probabile che nessuno di noi collaboratori scriverebbe esattamente ora come scrivemmo nel 1959. Profondamente riveduto dovrebbe essere soprattutto il mio saggio iniziale».

[2] «The NewYork Review of Books», 55 (20 march 2008): *Picturing the Bible: The Earliest Christian Art*, Kimbell Art Museum, Fort Worth, November 18, 2007-March 30,

Un singolare mosaico, che ritroviamo nel catalogo di questa mostra, rinvenuto casualmente in un piccolo villaggio del Dorset, Hinton St. Mary, agli inizi degli anni '60, merita attenzione (fig. 1). In due locali contigui di quella che si presume dovesse essere una villa abbiamo due grandi mosaici. In uno di questi è raffigurato Bellerofonte che uccide la chimera a tre teste mentre nell'altro, nel rosone centrale, campeggia un busto contrassegnato dal monogramma cristiano con un melograno a destra e l'altro a sinistra. Ai lati ci sono scene di caccia e agli angoli quattro teste forse raffiguranti le stagioni[3].

Anche se si accetta l'identificazione del personaggio del rosone con Cristo come è stato fatto perentoriamente sin dalla prima pubblicazione del mosaico[4], rimane suggestivo l'accostamento nei saloni di un medesimo edificio di soggetti così radicalmente diversi. Il fatto che la scena di Bellerofonte che uccide la chimera sia presente anche nella vicina villa di Lullingstone ha ovviamente suscitato attenzione e varie interpretazioni[5].

Credo che ormai si debba prender atto dell'elusività di molti manufatti e di molte rappresentazioni (è inevitabile pensare, ad esempio, al bellissimo ritratto di dama nimbata dipinto sul soffitto dell'aula costantiniana di Treviri) spesso presentati, forse con troppa facilità, come documenti di resistenza pagana, intesa come manifestazione consapevolmente agguerrita e religiosamente motivata di circoli di pagani irriducibili: se ne ha un'esemplificazione molto convincente, oltre che nella mostra già ricordata del Kimbell Art Museum, in una appena precedente che si è svolta nel 2007, a Vicenza, nella bella sede di palazzo Leoni Montanari: *La rivoluzione dell'immagine. Arte paleocristiana tra Roma e Bisanzio*.

Si pensi, tra i tanti esempi che si potrebbero fare per il IV secolo, alla *Corbridge lanx* (fig. 2), interpretata ora come traduzione iconografica di un mito sconosciuto, per quanto affine al giudizio di Paride, oppure come congresso di divinità in una sorta di *sacra conversazione pagana* in santuari localizzati in sedi diverse, oppure ancora in altro modo. In realtà come aveva già scritto a suo tempo Brendel: «The lanx tells no story and

---

2008. Catalog of the exhibition ed. by J. Spier, New Haven 2007.

[3] Non credo che sia corretto sminuire il significato dei motivi non cristiani ipotizzando per essi finalità allegoriche o sincretistiche: così P. Salway, *Roman Britain*, Oxford 1981, 725.

[4] J.M.C. Toynbee, *A new Roman mosaic pavement found in Dorset*, «JRS» 54 (1964), 1-14.

[5] Cfr. M. Henig, *Art, religion and letters in a fourth-century villa: the Lullingstone Villa mosaic*, «Mosaic» 24 (1997), 4-7.

proclaims no mysterious allegory»[6]. Si pensi ancora alla fortuna, come soggetto di raffigurazione in mosaici negli ambienti più diversi, di Dioniso e del suo entourage tra IV e VI secolo[7].

Quanto alla diffusione del cristianesimo nell'area nordorientale in età precostantiniana questa pone problemi di non semplice soluzione[8]. Aquileia, dove non si ha documentazione archeologica relativa al primo insediamento della comunità cristiana, è uno dei centri più ricchi di iscrizioni cristiane dell'Occidente cristiano – oltre cinquecento. Di questo patrimonio si è occupato con capacità e rigore uno studioso triestino, Giuseppe Vergone, in un libro appena pubblicato, *Le epigrafi lapidarie del museo paleocristiano di Monastero*[9].

È assai pertinente la valorizzazione fatta da lui sulla scia del suo maestro Giuseppe Cuscito dei caratteri della fede e della religiosità popolare – un concetto questo assai delicato sul piano storiografico – che emerge dalle formule più tipiche delle iscrizioni in cui si ripropone, in forma semplificata, uno dei contenuti più specifici dell'escatologia cristiana, ove la morte appare come «un transito da una condizione precaria a uno stato gioioso e beato». Giusta considerazione hanno meritato di recente, soprattutto per merito di Fabrizio Bisconti, le scene in qualche modo realistiche, che hanno a che vedere con aspetti di vita quotidiana rispetto ad altre con aspettative di tipo escatologico in cui la figura è colta nella tensione dell'aspettativa verso il mondo ultraterreno. Ne è un buon esempio quella che accompagna l'iscrizione 36 della raccolta in cui compare un tal Flavius Saturninus.

Le iscrizioni cristiane aquileiesi, per quanto numerose, sono relativamente tarde. La più antica con datazione certa, fornitaci dall'indicazione del nome dei consoli, risale al 336: si tratta del *titulus* di un certo Antonius[10].

---

[6] «JRS» 31 (1941), 126.
[7] D. PARRISH, *Dionysos and his circle in mosaics of Late Antiquity*, in *Mélanges d'Antiquité tardive. Studiola in honorem N. Duval*, a cura di C. BALMELLE, P. CHEVALIER, G. RIPOLL, Turnhout 2004, 75-84.
[8] Cfr. G. CUSCITO, *Il primo cristianesimo nella «Venetia et Histria». Indagini e ipotesi*, Reana del Rojale-Udine 1986.
[9] Trieste 2007. Ho discusso di questo libro in «Aquileia Nostra» in c.d.s.
[10] Cfr. D. MAZZOLENI, *L'epigrafia cristiana ad Aquileia nel IV secolo*, «AAAd» 22 (1982)/1, 301-325. Quanto scrive C. SOTINEL, *Identité civique et christianisme. Aquilée du IIIe au VIe siècle*, Rome 2005, 91-93 va letto insieme a quanto osserva G. CUSCITO in «Riv. di Arch. Cristiana» 83 (2007), 469-489.

Questa peculiarità spiega probabilmente il fatto che esse presentano moduli formulari già relativamente stabili mentre a Roma si può verificare un'evoluzione dal cosiddetto laconismo arcaico, vale a dire le iscrizioni con il solo nome del defunto, sino alla riappropriazione cristiana del patrimonio classico[11].

Ad Aquileia è particolarmente evidente una caratteristica peculiare dell'epigrafia cristiana, dei *tituli* cristiani di pieno IV secolo e oltre, vale a dire l'inserimento negli spazi di scrittura di eterogenei elementi figurativi. Ne è un buon esempio l'iscrizione di *Tertio* (la nr. 35) che già Wilpert, a fine '800, considerava un gioiello della collezione epigrafica (fig. 3). Si tratta di una lastra marmorea di medie dimensioni rinvenuta a Monastero da Gregorutti nel 1874. Vi è un epitaffio posto dai genitori per il figlio morto dodicenne da battezzato (*fidelis* è il termine che nelle iscrizioni ricorre per indicare il battezzato). Al centro della lastra è delineato, come osserva Vergone, con tratti eleganti un orante vestito di calzari, tunica e clamide fissata da una fibula. Sul capo è bene evidente il monogramma cristologico. Elementi sicuri di datazione non ce ne sono ma si oscilla, plausibilmente, tra la metà e la fine del IV secolo. Per dare un'idea di come questo e altri *tituli* siano organizzati si consideri come la figura dell'orante sia al centro della lastra mentre il testo dell'iscrizione che è disposto su sei righe, tranne la prima, è letteralmente diviso in due al punto che addirittura due parole, una della quinta e una della sesta riga (*depo/situs* e *Au/gustas*), sono separate dalla figura.

I testi lasciano talvolta intravedere realtà specifiche rispetto alle quali, non di rado, si sente ancora il pulsare della vita. Prendiamo il caso della già ricordata iscrizione nr. 36 della raccolta, rinvenuta nel 1875 a S. Martino di Terzo. Si tratta di un testo semplice che commemora Flavius Saturninus di cui si ricorda soltanto, oltre al nome, gli anni di vita, il giorno della sua sepoltura e che è morto da *fidelis*, da battezzato (fig. 4). Al centro, in basso, è delineata, in modo alquanto schematico e grossolano, la figura di un fabbro: anche in questo caso la figura divide in due il testo dell'epigrafe. Il fabbro appare munito di calzari ai piedi e vestito di una tunichetta succinta nel pieno del lavoro: con la destra sta per colpire sull'incudine quanto è tenuto dentro il forcipe retto dalla sinistra. Verrebbe da dire che qui abbiamo una delle ultime sopravvivenze di arte popolare romana, o meglio, plebea, secondo la definizione di Bianchi Bandinelli, che aveva alle sue spalle una lunga tradizione.

---

[11] Cfr. G. Cuscito, *L'epigrafia cristiana dell'Alto Adriatico tra ripresa e trasformazioni*, in *Società e cultura in età tardoantica*, a cura di A. Marcone, Firenze 2004, 162-180.

Un cenno merita anche il *titulus* che è riprodotto nella copertina del libro di Vergone, il nr. 139, una lastra marmorea rinvenuta alla Beligna. Il testo, quasi integro salvo nella parte superiore malgrado le fratture del marmo, è un epitaffio di un defunto oriundo della Dardania e morto nel 352 (fig. 5). Il defunto parla in prima persona e racconta in breve le tappe della sua vita trascorsa in larga parte nell'esercito. Di specificamente cristiano in questa breve autobiografia non c'è invero quasi nulla. Di veramente notevole in questa iscrizione c'è il fatto che il testo sia interrotto da tre figure virili. A sinistra si vede raffigurato il defunto nella sua veste di *protector*, di guardia del corpo dell'imperatore, carica con la quale aveva preso il congedo. Nella figura di profilo vediamo un uomo, seduto su di una sedia pieghevole, che beve da un bicchiere a forma cilindrica, un gesto che è interpretato come raffigurante il *refrigerium*, inteso come il banchetto ristoratore che il defunto trova nell'aldilà, un segno di augurio per il defunto. La parte superiore della figura di destra è andata perduta ma va notato che è separata dalla precedente tramite un vistoso ramo di palma. È suggestivo, ma credo indimostrabile, che in questa successione di figure si ritrovi una sintesi della vita terrena e ultraterrena del defunto.

Una breve riflessione merita anche il contenuto di un testo (nr. 88). L'iscrizione è stata incisa per volere dei genitori che ricordano la loro figlioletta morta a poco più di tre anni, la cui anima è stata accolta *ad spirita sancta*. Il neutro è usato, come in altri casi, al posto del maschile in testi che rivelano spesso un evidente processo in corso di involuzione linguistica. È oggetto di studio il grado di alfabetizzazione che si può dedurre da queste e altre iscrizioni: elementi utili per un confronto sono forniti dalle ricerche di Danilo Mazzoleni a proposito delle iscrizioni concordiesi. Vorrei sottolineare la peculiarità del sentimento di questi genitori straziati dal dolore. Da una parte confidano che la figlioletta goda già della beatitudine celeste. Dall'altra manifestano il loro sconforto, tanto umano, con la formula finale: *posuerunt filiae inpiae* (posero alla figlia priva di pietà) che mi sembra una variante della formula corrente *contra votum*.

È legittimo chiedersi che cosa ci sia di specificamente cristiano in questi testi, quali siano i caratteri distintivi dell'epigrafia della nuova religione, visto che si tratta di epitaffi e, quindi, hanno implicazioni immediate con la vita ultraterrena. Almeno apparentemente c'è abbastanza poco. O meglio, quello che di specifico c'è è proprio quello che si è appena ricordato. Nei testi si trovano ricorrenti attributi come *dulcis/dulcissimus, carus/carissimus, castus/castissimus, innocens/innocentissimus, fidelis, incomparabilis*. Emerge quindi nel quadro complessivo di questo lessico formulare la sostanziale assenza di uno specifico cristiano nella rievocazione degli elementi della vita vissuta, cioè di tutti quegli aspetti direttamente o indirettamente connessi ai comportamenti e agli atteggiamenti individuali e collettivi della comunità.

La tradizione, la prassi, la consuetudine non si possono cancellare e così rilevanti appaiono le abitudini e gli usi dell'epoca che noi possiamo chiamare tardoantichi, vale a dire peculiari di un'epoca ancora impregnata di valori classici ma ormai percorsa di una nuova sensibilità e di nuovi valori. È dunque bene evitare quelle conclusioni che sono alla fine più impressionistiche che realmente documentabili, essendo spesso espressione di un desiderio di cogliere a tutti i costi in queste testimonianze epigrafiche «un linguaggio tutto nuovo», consapevolmente funzionale ad esprimere l'idea o l'ideale dell'uomo rinnovato dei *christiana tempora*. Quello che possiamo considerare uno specifico cristiano in realtà si manifesta solo episodicamente e quindi è bene non amplificarne la portata.

In buona sostanza conviene accettare l'idea che l'epigrafia cristiana di età postcostantiniana conservi intatta la sua peculiare finalità di memoria scritta da trasmettere ai superstiti. La funzione, invece, di bilancio consuntivo di un'esistenza, di una sorta di attestazione che il defunto ha meritato, con quanto da lui fatto in nel corso della sua esistenza terrena, la vita eterna sembra circoscritta. È stato ben osservato da Carletti e da altri come in questo caso la sua forma espressiva sia prevalentemente in versi e, dunque, ne presuppone un uso ristretto nell'ambito delle élites (molti dei nostri testi presentano una chiara involuzione linguistica, segno forse anche di decadenza scolastica). Merita riprendere quanto ha ben scritto Cuscito nella sua prefazione al libro di Vergone: «Quanto ai contenuti, si può dire che la commemorazione del defunto, l'identificazione della sepoltura e la sua protezione dipendano da una tradizione secolare più che da un'autonoma iniziativa della nuova fede che tuttavia suggerisce, pur senza sistematicità e rigore, espressioni e segni tesi a costituire uno specifico genuinamente cristiano».

C'è probabilmente stato un eccesso di fiducia nel riconoscere come esplicitamente cristiane e, al contrario, come manifestazioni di credo pagano, delle raffigurazioni che invece, a una lettura più attenta e spassionata, possono essere interpretate, con maggiore verosimiglianza, come manifestazioni di conservatorismo e di tradizionalismo culturale e sociale.

Per questa ragione parlerei appunto di «persistenza» di tradizioni classiche ma non di paganesimo in quanto religione – che implica per associazione automatica un'opposizione e una resistenza al cristianesimo – ed essenzialmente come quadro di riferimento di un codice artistico condiviso. La creatività in questo campo è relativa. Forse è opportuno ricordare quanto ebbe a scrivere André Grabar una quarantina di anni fa:

«It is important to keep in mind that creativity in this area consists in appropriating existing figurations by shifting the meaning of repeated formulas, by taking over known iconographic formulas, or composing similar ones by analogy». Non a caso «the same iconographic term – the orant, the Good Shephard – has different meanings according to the context»[12].

C'è un'unità di fondo nella cultura tardoantica che sintetizza i valori comuni dei ricchi proprietari desiderosi di dare visibilità al proprio status sociale e, in taluni casi peculiari, anche alla loro personalità. Ci sono indubbiamente temi e figure proprie della tradizione classica che erano particolarmente suscettibili di essere recepiti e utilizzati con connotazioni cristiane. La figura di Orfeo si prestava già nella cultura pagana a un interscambio con la figura di Apollo musageta e fu quindi assimilato alla raffigurazione di Davide salmista[13].

La compresenza di Cristo-Orfeo e di Davide nel cunicolo di Domitilla a Roma suggerisce l'intenzione di sottolineare la relazione tra Antico e Nuovo Testamento. I Padri della Chiesa si impegnarono nell'esegesi della figura di Orfeo fatto assurgere addirittura a simbolo del *Logos*, che è il vero Orfeo capace di ammansire le bestie feroci: così già Clemente Alessandrino, che lo paragona al *Logos* di Dio capace di ammansire le bestie feroci e, soprattutto Eusebio, in un testo politicamente e ideologicamente impegnativo come le *Laudes Constantini*: se Orfeo con il suono della lira ammansì le fiere... il Verbo di Dio fece di più: ammansì i costumi dei barbari e dei pagani» (*Laud. Const.* 14). Nella pittura cimiteriale l'immagine inizia a comparire nella seconda metà del III secolo. In un cubicolo di Callisto Orfeo è raffigurato, nella volta, quasi a sottolinearne il valore simbolico di immagine di figura di Cristo, tra due ovini. Non mancano le varianti nella raffigurazione di Orfeo.

Nell'arcosolio della catacomba dei santi Marcellino e Pietro, della seconda metà del IV secolo, per quanto Orfeo sia seduto con gli strumenti musicali, non compie l'atto di suonare ma è raffigurato con le braccia aperte in un gesto che può apparire simbolico mentre lo sguardo è rivolto verso l'alto forse per suggerire un riferimento trascendente (fig. 6). È interessante come la figura di Orfeo risulti chiaramente funzionale in diversi

---

[12] Cfr. A. GRABAR, *Christian Iconography. A Study of its Origins*, Princeton 1968, XLVIII.

[13] Per un esempio della fortuna del mito di Orfeo in tutt'altro contesto si pensi a quello di Rottweil (seconda metà del II sec. d.C.), il mosaico meglio conservato dell'attuale Baden-Württemberg. Cfr. L. JESNICK, *The Image of Orpheus. An Exploration of the Figure of Orpheus in Graeco-Roman Antiquity with special Reference to its Expression in the Medium of Mosaic in Late Antiquity*, Oxford 1997.

contesti, con peculiari slittamenti semantici, alla celebrazione della figura del *dominus* per la quale doveva essere secondario lo stretto riferimento religioso.

Basterà fare qualche esempio. A Rimini, nello scavo recente di piazza Ferrari, il cantore tracio è raffigurato al centro di un pavimento di una *domus* in cui in sei esagoni disposti intorno a lui sono rappresentati vari animali attratti dalla musica. Poiché, in ragione degli attrezzi chirurgici che sono stati ritrovati nella casa, si può ritenere che il proprietario fosse un medico sembra plausibile che le competenze del committente fossero messe in parallelo con quelle di Orfeo che, secondo una versione del mito, era riuscito a strappare Euridice alla morte[14]. A Piazza Armerina la figura di Orfeo sembra presupporre una serie complessa di rimandi alla cultura del proprietario, idealmente concepito come *mousikós anér*, con la musica celebrata per il suo potere spirituale[15].

I soggetti latamente mitologici, che possono essere sottoposti a processi di desemantizzazione o di risemantizzazione in quanto utilizzati a celebrare la persona del committente, sono i più vari. Prendiamo il caso di una *domus* di IV secolo recentemente scavata a Faenza in piazza Dogana di cui sono venuti alla luce degli ambienti di rappresentanza[16]. A noi interessa la scena che adornava un vestibolo che precedeva una sala absidata, probabilmente di ricevimento. Nella fascia perimetrale si susseguono una serie di figure virili in armi, alternate da altre femminili. La raffigurazione principale è incentrata su un personaggio maschile, parzialmente coperto da un mantello fermato sulla spalla destra, seduto su una sorta di trono, circondato da uomini in armi mentre ai suoi piedi si vedono corazze e scudi. Sembra accettabile l'idea di vedervi un'immagine riassuntiva delle imprese di Achille (fig. 7). È naturalmente impossibile immaginare quale concreto legame ci potesse essere tra il proprietario e la scena mitologica da lui voluta riprodurre con tanta evidenza nella sua casa. Ma certo lascia intendere le sue ambizioni culturali per le quali il tradizionalismo del quadro di riferimento non ha di per sé nette implicazioni religiose.

Se posso introdurre un termine di riscontro vorrei prendere in considerazione il caso del mosaico di Leda rinvenuto nel pavimento di una casa

---

[14] Cfr. J. ORTALLI, *La* domus *riminese del chirurgo: un percorso di ricerca*, «Atti e Memorie della Deputazione di Storia Patria per le Province di Romagna» 51 (2000), 171-192.

[15] Cfr. H.I. MARROU, *Mousikòs anér: étude sur les scènes de la vie intellectuelle figurant sur les monuments funéraires romains*, Rome 1968.

[16] Cfr. M.G. MAIOLI, *Mosaici di epoca tardo romana in Faenza*, in *Archeologia a Faenza. Ricerche e scavi dal Neolitico al Rinascimento*, Faenza 1990, 63-75.

romana a Trier. Faccio mia l'interpretazione che ne ha dato un giovane studioso, Marcello Ghetta, in una monografia appena pubblicata: *Spätantikes Heidentum. Trier und das Trevererland*[17]. Il mosaico di Leda è organizzato in due grandi campi figurativi di cui uno è dedicato alla raffigurazione del mito vero e proprio mentre l'altra è una scena di un banchetto, forse una sorta di scena di cucina di commedia, una parodia del mito (fig. 8). In questa secondo campo siamo nel contesto rilassato del banchetto, della gioia della tavola con Quodvultdeus, i medaglioni con i domestici e le ballerine. Contrariamente all'interpretazione che ha avuto fortuna che vi vede una scena di culto con gli adepti di un rito misterico, la scena con Quodvultdeus appare interpretabile in un senso profano. In realtà tutto lascia pensare a una scena di cucina: c'è una persona con un cucchiaio e un pollo nelle mani, un'altra che tiene pronto un tegame per l'animale e una terza con un contenitore per l'uovo. Il legame tra le due scene, se c'è, è molto labile. La scena con il mito di Leda vuol far presupporre un proprietario colto, che ha familiarità con la cultura classica; il banchetto presuppone rilassatezza e simbolizzare gioia di vivere. Dunque questo mosaico non sembra interpretabile come una professione di fede ma piuttosto come manifestazione di appartenenza a un livello sociale agiato e culturalmente elevato rispetto al quale la fede religiosa del committente è secondaria. Come S. Muth ha indicato, spesso la rappresentazione di un mito serviva a dare espressione a concetti-guida come *virtus*, *concordia* o *pulchritudo* senza che rispetto a questi l'effettivo contenuto narrativo del mito giocasse un ruolo[18].

Ma torniamo all'area nordorientale, con qualche esempio. Basterà solo un cenno al mosaico aquileiese di Licurgo e Ambrosia, che sembra da attribuirsi a botteghe locali[19], della *domus* del fondo CAL, che rappresenta una delle testimonianze più tarde della persistenza di soggetti classici – a prescindere dall'eventuale intenzione religiosa dei committenti che, in mancanza di un contesto, è difficile da valutare – in un'Aquileia ormai cristianizzata (escluderei interpretazioni di tipo psicologico sulla crisi del mondo antico: se mai mi sembra vero il contrario e, cioè, che ci si possa vedere una consapevole affermazione di identità nel riproporre temi col-

---

[17] Trier 2008.
[18] *Erleben von Raum-Leben im Raum. Zur Funktion mythologischer Mosaikbilder in der römisch-kaiserzeitlicher Wohnarchitektur*, Heidelberg 1998.
[19] Cfr. F. GHEDINI, *L'età romana* in *Storia di Venezia. Dalle origini alla caduta della Serenissima*, I: *Origini. Età ducale*, a cura di L. CRACCO RUGGINI, M. PAVAN, G. CRACCO, G. ORTALLI, Roma 1992, 271-320.

ti)[20]. È evidente che i medesimi artigiani servivano indifferentemente i ricchi proprietari, ancora sensibili ai richiami della tradizione classica, e l'importante committenza cristiana nella quale dovevano essere comunque ben presenti coloro i quali si compiacevano di riproporre i temi mitologici colti, per i quali presumibilmente si prescindeva dalla valenza religiosa.

D'altra parte l'utilizzazione del mito in chiave personale, con evidenti riferimenti alla cultura dei committenti, ha un riscontro nel noto mosaico della *domus* conosciuta come di Caliendo e Iovina, raffigurati come Amore e Psiche, un tema favolistico idoneo, attraverso un processo di cristianizzazione, a essere reso compatibile con la nuova fede[21]. È interessante come il significato di questa scena, che suggerisce un immediato rimando al romanzo di Apuleio, datata in genere alla seconda metà del III secolo, possa risultare rafforzato da quello delle Stagioni nel vano accanto.

Che, d'altra parte, l'arte cristiana attingesse al repertorio di quella classica è ben comprensibile soprattutto nel campo dell'ideologia della gloria e del trionfo (ma anche a quella del circo)[22] per il quale la nuova religione mancava di espliciti e fruibili modelli iconografici[23]. È il caso della Vittoria che compare nella monetazione di IV secolo per celebrare la vittoriosità degli imperatori in virtù della loro adesione al culto cristiano. L'uso allegorico della Vittoria, soprattutto in ambito funerario, nel senso del premio della vita eterna riservato al buon cristiano al termine della sua esistenza terrena, è in qualche modo un corollario di un tema ben presente nell'immaginario tardoantico. È dubbio che si possa leggere la nota raffigurazione nella basilica aquileiese della «Vittoria», raffigurata come una fanciulla che reca la palma e una corona di alloro con ai suoi piedi un canestro con pani e forse un altro con spighe, come «Vittoria Eucaristica» (fig. 9)[24]. Appare preferibile vedervi un'immagine di genere, familiare, e dunque facilmente apprezzabile, al di là di un immediato ed esplicito riferimento religioso, che si prestava a una rilettura in chiave cristiana.

La delicatezza dell'intreccio dei temi figurativi sembra particolarmente evidente proprio nella basilica teodoriana di Aquileia che, nella sua artico-

---

[20] L. BERTACCHI, *Licurgo e Ambrosia*, «Aquileia Nostra» 45-46 (1974-75), coll. 535-550.
[21] Cfr. G.L. GRASSIGLI, *La scena domestica e il suo immaginario. I temi figurati nei mosaici della Cisalpina*, Napoli 1999, 231-232.
[22] Cfr. A. GRABAR, *Christian Iconography...*, 16-17.
[23] Cfr., peraltro, T. MATHEWS, *Scontro di dei. Un'interpretazione dell'arte paleocristiana*, Milano 2005.
[24] Cfr. F. MIAN, *La «Vittoria» di Aquileia. Il battezzato come competitore vittorioso*, «AAAd» 8 (1975), 131-153. Si veda anche la copertina del libro di C. Sotinel (n. 9) che la riproduce.

lata e complessa struttura, si colloca in una tappa precoce nell'evoluzione dell'edificio di culto cristiano. Pare dunque conveniente interrogare con prudenza filologica le polisemie delle raffigurazioni mosaicali e verificare in che misura esse possano essere ancora essere portatrici di temi propri della decorazione pavimentale domestica delle *domus* tardoantiche. Anche nei mosaici teodoriani, prima di pensare a messaggi intenzionalmente orientati in senso religioso, è lecito vedere un repertorio neutrale su cui la simbologia cristiana si sarà progressivamente inserita. Alcuni temi appaiono innocentemente profani: e la stessa convergenza di temi bucolici e marini non è estranea alla fortuna di un genere che ha precisi riscontri nell'iconografia funeraria tra la fine del III e l'inizio del IV secolo, in un'epoca dunque vicina a quella di realizzazione dei mosaici aquileiesi quando il tema del *locus amoenus* acquista un rinnovato favore (fig. 10)[25].

Abbiamo a che fare con una concezione di fondo che non sembra diversa da quella che ritroviamo all'origine del pavimento musivo della basilica aquileiese dove l'ispirazione generale, tradizionalmente paradisiaca, è come riorientata in senso cristiano dalla storia di Giona e dalla figura del Buon Pastore (fig. 11)[26]. Credo che per un osservatore medio fosse spontaneo prescindere, almeno a un primo sguardo, dalla lettura allegorica della storia di Giona e vedere nella raffigurazione di lui beatamente dormiente sotto un pergolato da cui pendono delle zucche nell'ultima campata dell'aula teodoriana meridionale quella di una scena realistica e, tutto sommato, banale di ozio campestre[27]. E lo stesso mare, in fondo, è troppo ricco di pesci, e di pescatori impegnati nella pesca, perché essi non richiamino in primo luogo su di loro l'attenzione. Non è fuori luogo ricordare come in una coppa in vetro di Cartagine del IV secolo la tradizionale immagine

---

[25] L'affresco conservato nel ninfeo sotto la chiesa dei SS. Giovanni e Paolo ne è un esempio eloquente: cfr. B. BRENK, *Le costruzioni sotto la chiesa dei ss. Giovanni e Paolo*, in *Aurea Roma. Dalla città pagana alla città cristiana*, a cura di S. ENSOLI, E. LA ROCCA, Roma 2000, 156-158.

[26] Cfr. SICHTERMANN, *Der Jonaszyklus*, in *Spätantike und frühes Christentum. Katalog der Ausstellung*, Frankfurt 1983, 241-248.

[27] La fortuna del tema nell'iconografia cristiana tardoantica emerge bene nel catalogo della mostra *Rivoluzione delle immagini* 2007 (vd. tav. 15, 132, tav. 43, 184). Merita di segnalare, in particolare, la sua presenza nella parte inferiore della copertura di Evangelario detta «dittico di Murano» (214, tav. 55). Cfr., da ultimo, L. DELMAS, *La rappresentazione di Giona nel complesso cultuale di Teodoro ad Aquileia: nuove ipotesi*, «Num. e Ant. Class.» 36 (2007), 287-299.

di idillio marino sia cristianizzata con l'aggiunta dei nomi degli apostoli Pietro e Giovanni ai pescatori che vi sono raffigurati[28].

I possibili livelli di lettura delle scene dei mosaici sono diversi ma è del tutto plausibile che la fonte di ispirazione fosse condivisa e tradizionale[29]. In realtà la pluralità dei motivi iconografici che sono alla base dei temi sviluppati nei mosaici delle due aule della basilica aquileiese è oltremodo eloquente: essi derivano, oltre che da fonti vetero e neotestamentarie, dall'iconografia aulica e imperiale, dalla mitologia pagana, da repertori generici ellenistici e, addirittura, dalla criptografia misterica[30]. Tale pluralità suggerisce, a mio modo di vedere, non tanto la spregiudicatezza intellettuale dell'ambiente ecclesiastico aquileiese quanto il forte radicamento nella tradizione antica di un messaggio iconografico che proprio ad essa attingeva la sua forza per farsi recepire[31]. In questo io vedo la persistenza di quello che più che «paganesimo» chiamerei tradizionalismo culturale e la forza del suo valore di tessuto connettivo anche in ambiente cristiano. Perché davvero, se posso utilizzare una bella formulazione di Peter Brown, «the IVth century was not a tidy age»[32].

---

[28] J. VILLETTE, Mon. Piot 46 (1952), tav. 15. Cfr. H. BRANDENBURG, *Die Darstellung maritimes Lebens* in *Spätantike...*, 253.

[29] Come risulta dal mosaico di Oderzo (cfr. G.L. GRASSIGLI, *La scena domestica e il suo immaginario...*, 307-308).

[30] Così è talvolta interpretato il motivo della lotta del gallo con la tartaruga: cfr. G.C. MENIS, *Il complesso episcopale teodoriano di Aquileia e il suo Battistero*, Udine 1986, 489.

[31] Tra i tanti esempi che si potrebbero fare da altri contesti basterà pensare ai mosaici dai temi mitologici scoperti a Madaba sotto la chiesa della Vergine, in particolare la cosiddetta sala dell'Ippolito: qui il mosaico rappresenta la scena, ispirata al ben noto *Ippolito incoronato* di Euripide, di Fedra che manda, per tramite della vecchia nutrice, un biglietto a Ippolito con la sua dichiarazione d'amore mentre nel registro superiore campeggia Afrodite, con Adone al suo fianco, simbolo dell'onnipotenza di Amore: cfr. J. BALTY, *La place dei mosaiques de Jordanie au sein de la production orientale*, in *Les églises de Jordanie et leur mosaiques*, a cura di N. DUVAL, Beyrouth 2003, 154-188 (178 fig. 38); cfr. anche C. DAUPHIN, *La Palestine byzantine. Peuplement et Populations*, I, cap. VI, *Peuplement et religion en Palestine byzantine. La lutte pour la suprématie*, Oxford 1998, 167-225.

[32] «Art Bulletin» 77 (1995)/3, 501.

Appendice. Figure

FIG. 1. *Mosaico di Hinton St. Mary.*

FIG. 2. *Corbridge lanx.*

Fig. 3. *Iscrizione di Tertio (Aquileia)*.

Fig. 4. *Iscrizione di Flavius Saturninus (Aquileia)*.

FIG. 5. *Epitaffio di Oriundo della Dardania (Aquileia)*.

FIG. 6. *Orfeo: catacomba Santi Marcellino e Pietro*.

Fig. 7. *Imprese di Achille (Faenza)*.

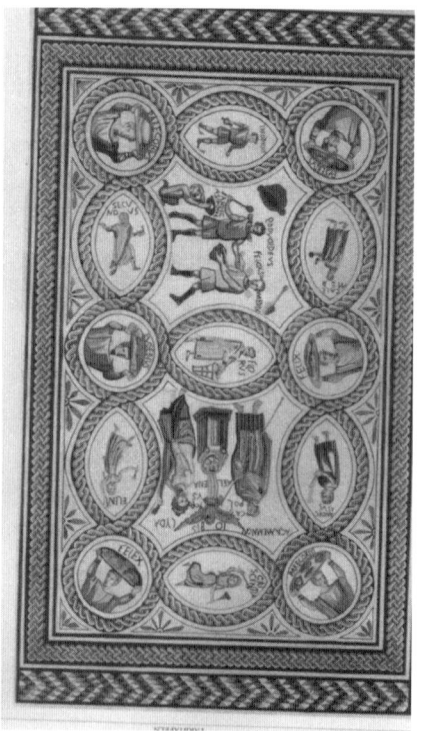

Fig. 8. *Mosaico di Leda (Treviri)*.

Fig. 9. *Cosiddetta «Vittoria Eucaristica» (Aquileia).*

Fig. 10. *Ninfeo (Roma, chiesa SS. Giovanni e Paolo).*

Fig. 11. *Giona dormiente (Aquileia – basilica)*.

WOLF LIEBESCHUETZ

The view from Antioch:
from Libanius via John Chrysostom
to John Malalas and beyond

1. Pagans, Jews and Christians at Antioch in the mid fourth century

That by the mid-fourth century Christians had become the most powerful and influential religious group in the city was demonstrates very clearly by the well documented failure of Julian's pagan revival[1]. The evidence allows only one conclusion: Antioch rejected the apostate emperor's restoration of paganism. This was what Julian thought when he claimed that the citizens had adopted Christ as the guardian of their city instead of Zeus[2]. Libanius too accuses the citizens of having abandoned the gods[3]. Most of our detailed evidence concerns the ruling elite. Julian thought that the governing body had simply given up its duty of maintaining the public cults of the city. He does not say that the majority of the *curiales* were Christians, but he claims that their wives were[4]. Analysis of individuals mentioned in the writing of Libanius shows that some of the leading families in the city, notably the families of Argyrius[5] and Letoius, and the fam-

---

I want to thank Robert Markus for reading, and generally much improving, my text. Remaining errors and infelicities are mine not his.

[1] For a general survey see J. HAHN, *Gewalt und religiöser Konflikt. Studien zu den Auseinandersetzungen zwischen Christen, Heiden, und Juden im Osten des römischen Reiches von Konstantin bis Theodosius II*, Berlin 2004, 54-177.

[2] *Misopogon* 357 C.

[3] LIB. *Or* XVI, 47-48. Orations XV and XVI in which Libanius apologises to Julian for the behaviour of the Antiochenes, emphasises that there were some good pagans in the city, but also implies that the majority, certainly the vocal and influential majority, were now Christians, cf. I. SANDWELL, *Religious Identity in Late Antiquity. Greeks, Jews and Christians at Antioch*, Cambridge 2007, 169-173.

[4] It is true that statistics drawn from Libanius' writings suggest that Christians were even then still a minority in the *curia* (P. PETIT, *Libanius et la vie municipale à Antioche*, Paris 1955, 202). But the collective behaviour of the *curiales* suggests that in Petit's sample, essentially friends of Libanius, pagans are over-represented.

[5] B. CABOURET, *Les Argyrioi une famille de notables*, in *Mélanges A.F. Norman*, Lyon 2006, 343-360.

ily of Libanius' friend Olympius, were still pagans. But the same analysis also shows that leading pagan families including Libanius' own[6] had close relatives who were Christians. So pagans and Christians in the civic elite had strong motives to be tolerant of each other's religious differences. Libanius was a consistent and dedicated upholder of the ancestral cults[7], and most of his closest friends were pagans, but he corresponded with plenty of Christians, and Christian fathers sent their sons to his school[8]. So religious differences do not appear to have led to hostility in private life[9]. The religious conflict we hear about – though not from Libanius – is conflict among Christians, between those who accepted the creed of Nicaea and those who did not. We do not know how far this division divided lay-people at Antioch.

We have no statistics to assess the numerical strength of different religious groups at Antioch at this, or any other time. We have altogether very little information about the religious behaviour of the silent majority. But one thing is clear, the high proportion of Christians, and the considerable Jewish population, together with the fact that the administration of the empire now consistently favoured Christianity, and was biased against the traditional religion, meant that the old cults could not continue as the religious voice of the citizen-body. Antioch no longer had a pagan identity. Julian admitted that he had failed to restore a religious meaning to the public festivals of Antioch. He distinguishes the truly sacred festivals (which he had failed to revive) from the festivals which mattered not only to those who worshipped the gods, but to the entire people[10]. The latter were spectacles like the animal chases, the Olympic Games, chariot races and theatricals, many of which had once had a religious significance[11], but were now regarded by most people simply as public entertainments.

---

[6] See J. WINTJES, *Das Leben des Libanius Das Leben des Libanius,* in *Historische Studien der Universität Würzburg* 2, Rahden Westfalen 2005, 43-62.

[7] There is abundant evidence that Libanius was a committed pagan, particularly in *Or.* XVIII; (*Funeral Oration for Julian*, AD 365); *Or.* XXIV (*On the avenging of Julian*, 378/9 AD) ; *Or.* XXX (*For the temples*, AD 386); *Or.* V (*Artemis*); also the concluding chapters the *Autobiography* (*Or.* I, 283-85), and many passages elsewhere, both in *Or.* I and in other writings.

[8] See prosopographical detail in P. PETIT, *Les étudiants de Libanius*, Paris 1957.

[9] W. LIEBESCHUETZ, *Antioch, City and Imperial Administration in the Later Empire*, Oxford 1972, 226-228.

[10] *Misopogon* 346 A & C.

[11] Animal chases had been linked to the imperial cult. The Olympic Games were instituted in honour of Zeus. Chariot-race meetings were originally linked to pagan festivals, e.g. that of Poseidon and that of Calliope, and the celebration of the New Year.

They had been completely secularized[12]. Clearly there still were many convinced followers of the old cults among the citizens of Antioch. But the focus of paganism had changed. It had ceased to be the public religion of the city. It had been forced out of the public sphere, and had become largely a private and personal religion. One might compare what is happening to Christianity in western Europe today, where the very concept of public religion is becoming unintelligible[13].

The evidence therefore strongly suggests that when Julian arrived there in 362, Christianity, even if it had not yet triumphed completely, already had very much the upper hand at Antioch[14]. This is not surprising. After all Christianity had a long history in the city. It was there that followers of Jesus were first called «Christians». Furthermore Antioch had for something like twenty years, between 340 and 360, been the principal residence of a committed Christian emperor and his court[15], so that men could hope for secular advancement if they converted to Christianity. Furthermore the emperor Constantius had actually prohibited sacrifices[16], and his law was widely enforced[17]. In the 350s pagan altars had been attacked, and temples destroyed and their stones carried off to be re-used in private buildings[18].

It is noteworthy that Constantius' prohibition of blood-sacrifices does not appear to have caused the widespread riot and protest that one would expect to follow the prohibition of the central rite of traditional paganism. Perhaps the recent prohibition of smoking provides an instructive parallel. For many years a large part of the population in Britain and elsewhere in Europe had enjoyed smoking, though the number of smokers, noticeably among students was declining. At that point the political leadership issued a prohibition of smoking in all public places. One might have expected protests at so blatant an infringement of liberty. But in fact prohibition has been quietly accepted. Why was that? Partly because the new law was imposed by the overwhelming power of the government, but also because public opinion was already turning against smoking, because the facts of

---

[12] At least for Julian, for Libanius the Olympic Games still honoured Zeus. Many Antiochenes evidently did not think attendance incompatible with Christianity.
[13] The transformation of paganism into a private religion is a principal theme of I. SANDWELL, *Religious Identity...*
[14] Otherwise E. SOLER, *Le Sacré et le salut à Antioche au IVe siècle apr. J.C.*, Beirut 2006, 240.
[15] P.-L. MALOSSE, *Antioche et le Kappa*, in *Antioche de Syrie*, Lyon 2004, 77-96.
[16] *CTh* XVI,10,4 (354); 10,6 (356).
[17] LIB. *Or.* I, 27; XXX, 6; XIV, 41.
[18] LIB. *ep.* 695, 2; more references in P. PETIT, *Libanius...*, 196-198.

its unhealthiness were beginning to sink in. Smoking had lost the moral high ground. Perhaps something similar had happened to the sacrificial rites[19], and so the temples fell into disuse and ruin, just as many public houses in England to day. However it must also be remembered that neither the law of Constantius, nor its repetition by Theodosius I and again by later emperors, succeeded in stamping out blood sacrifices by private individuals, and occasionally at least in the fourth century even by imperial officials[20].

I have maintained that the elite at Antioch, that is the people we hear about and who had most influence in the public life of the city, were already largely Christian. Though we lack the evidence to assess the importance of the Christian elite in numerical terms, it would seem that already in the mid-fourth century Christians in the *curia* of Antioch were more influential than Christians in the *curiae* of some of the cities of Numidia decades later[21]. We have another indicator of the relatively high proportion of Christians among the leading citizens of Antioch. Among the imperial governors of oriental provinces in the fourth century whose religion is known, at all but the highest level more than half were pagans, and the proportion was significantly higher in the mid fourth century than in the 390s. This suggests that pagans were more numerous in the elite of cities of the East generally, than at Antioch[22].

We have some evidence about Christianisation at a lower social level in the epigraphy of villages in the limestone massif to the east of Antioch, Christian inscriptions on lintels of houses and tombstones begin in the

---

[19] E. FERGUSON, *Spiritual sacrifice in early Christianity and its environment*, in *ANRW* II, 23, 2, Berlin-New York 1980, 1151-1189; R.P.C. HANSON, *The Christian attitude to pagan religion up to the time of Constantine the Great*, ivi, 910-973; S.F.R. PRICE, *Ritual and Power. The Roman Imperial Cult in Asia Minor*, Cambridge 1984, 229: the feast becomes more important than the sacrifice, enabling festal slaughter to continue in a secularised form.

[20] F.R. TROMBLEY, *The legal status of sacrifice to 529 AD* in his *Hellenic Religion and Christianization*, I, Leiden-New York-Cologne 1993, 1-97. I am not convinced that the undated *CI* I, 11, 9 & I, 11, 10, which seem intended to finally crush paganism, and which are usually dated to 529, were in fact issued c.481-84, soon after the rebellion of Illus, to punish the pagans for their participation.

[21] See paper of C. LEPELLEY, *infra*, and ID., *Les cités de l'Afrique romaine au Bas-Empire*, I, Paris 1979, 352-414.

[22] The argument is based on P. PETIT, *Libanius...*, 202, and assumes that the proportion of pagan officials is related to the proportion of pagans in the *élites* of the cities from which they were drawn.

330s. Inscriptions that are explicitly pagan soon become rare[23]. The emperor Julian noticed that inhabitants of the countryside between Antioch and Beroea (Aleppo) were markedly unenthusiastic about paganism[24]. But the territory can be said to have been fully Christianised only between 365 and 425[25].

The fact that Christianity was now the predominant religion of Antioch did not of course mean that all traces of paganism had disappeared from the city's culture. Far from it! In fact the division of the population into sharply divided religious groups is certainly misleading. It is likely that at Antioch as elsewhere many individuals had not decisively opted for any one particular religious allegiance, but hedged their bets by placing their hopes now in the rituals of one group, now in those of another[26]. Some twenty years later Chrysostom was to complain that individuals who belonged to his congregation nevertheless thought that oaths taken in a synagogue or attention to the sick by a rabbi were particularly effective. People continued to observe many practices which were certainly of pagan origin[27]. At the same time the annual cycle of festivals which gave variety and entertainment to the inhabitants of Antioch was still that of the pagan religious calendar. Traditional festivals continued to be popular. Best documented of all are the Kalends[28], the celebrations marking the New Year. But evidently the May festival, the Maiouma, was still very much alive in the mid-fourth century. This was a water festival which may have once been associated with Dionysus and Aphrodite. It was celebrated with nocturnal processions and theatrical shows involving dancing and water[29]. The festival of Artemis too was still being celebrated in May, with a boxing competition for which each of the eighteen tribes of the city pro-

---

[23] W. Liebeschuetz, *Epigraphic evidence on the Christianisation of Syria*, in *Akten des XI Internationalen Limeskongresses*, Budapest 1981, 485-508.

[24] Julian, *ep.* 58 (ed. Wright in Loeb library = 98 ed. Bidez).

[25] See F.R. Trombley's thorough survey: *The Antiochene and the Apamene* in his *Hellenic Religion...*, 246-295.

[26] L. Brottier, *Jean Chrysostome: un pasteur face à des demi-chrétiens*, in *Antioche de Syrie*, Lyon 2004, 439-57. For example Chrysostom, *Hom. in ep. ad Titum* 3, 2 in PG 62. 679, warning not to visit sanctuary of Saturn in Cilicia, or the grotto of Matrona at Daphne. For an empire – wide view of this problem see Majastina Kahlos on what she calls the *incerti*, in her *Debate and Dialogue, Christian Pagan Cultures c. 360-430*, Aldershot 2007, 30-48.

[27] J.I. Maxwell, *Christianization and Communication in Late Antiquity*, Cambridge 2006, 148-161; and below.

[28] Lib. *Or* IX, vol. 1.472ff (ed. Forster).

[29] See n. 36, below.

vided a boxer[30]. Early in summer there followed the festival of Calliope with theatrical shows and chariot races[31], and the mourning for the death of Adonis in July[32]. In autumn at the time of the wine harvest came the festival of Dionysus when hymns to Dionysus were still sung everywhere[33]. In the time of Libanius the Olympic Games, originally held in honour of Zeus, continued to take place regularly every four years.

We do not have information about the ultimate history of most of these festivals, but Robert Markus has shown that the celebrations of pagan festivals, in a «disinfected» form, that is without the explicit worship of pagan deities, and above all without animal sacrifices, continued in many cities in the West well into the 5th century[34]. At Rome the Lupercalia were still being celebrated at the end of the fifth century[35]. In the East too the old festivals continued, no doubt in a modified form. For example the Maiouma was observed through the fifth, and even into the sixth century, in various places all round the Mediterranean, at a variety of dates, and in the name of a variety of gods. At Antioch, although the festival was morally suspect even to some pagans, it was still being celebrated, indeed even received new endowments, as late as AD 431, in the reign of the pious Christian emperor Theodosius II. By then it must have shed all connections with the worship of pagan divinities[36]. In the early sixth century Severus, patriarch of Antioch (512-18), and Jacob of Serugh attacked chariot racing and theatricals very much as Chrysostom had done in the 4th century[37]. In the long run the attacks of the clerics were not without effect. The Olympic Games at Antioch were stopped in AD 520[38]. It seems that

---

[30] LIB. Or. V, 43-51.
[31] LIB. ep. 811.
[32] AMMIANUS XXII, 9, 14; XIX, 1, 11. Julian entered the city in 362 amid women wailing for Adonis, a bad *omen*.
[33] LIB. epp. 661, 1480, 1288, 1212.
[34] R.A. MARKUS, *The End of Ancient Christianity*, Cambridge 1990, 107-123. On the East see the important book of H. SARADI, *The Byzantine City in the Sixth Century*, Athens 2006, 293-324.
[35] R.A. MARKUS, *End of Ancient Christianity...*, 131-135.
[36] N. BELAYCHE, *Une panégyrie antiochéenne: «le maïouma»*, in *Antioche de Syrie*, Lyon 2004, 401-415.
[37] F.N. ALPI, *Société et vie profane à Antioche sous le patriarcat de Sévère (512-518)*, in *Antioche de Syrie*, Lyon 2004, 519-542, relevant 531-533; C.A. MOSS, *Jacob of Serugh's homilies on the spectacles of the theatre*, «Le Muséon» 48 (1935), 87-112; F. GRIFFIN, *La vie à Antioche d'après les homélies de Sévère. Invectives contre les courses de cheveaux, le theatre et les jeux Olympiques*, in *Erkenntnisse und Meinungen*, ed. G. WIESSNER, Wiesbaden 1978, 115-130.
[38] MALALAS XVII, 13, 417.

from the late fourth century floor mosaics decorated with scenes drawn from pagan mythology went of fashion. Gods and heroes were replaced by personified abstractions of virtues and by geometric patterns[39]. But cultural transformation naturally was a very slow process. Festivals and their customs tend to outlive their gods. Customs that were associated with the Kalends, as it was celebrated at Antioch in the time of Libanius, have survived linked to Christmas even until today[40]. The dominant religion had changed, but civic culture changed much more slowly[41].

2. The Christian reaction

The fact that the gods had obviously not supported Julian certainly was a heavy blow to paganism. The restoration of the old cults was discredited. There followed a certain Christian reaction with prosecution of some followers of Julian and the mass treason trial of 371, which involved the condemnation of a number of philosophers, and and the burning of books[42]. Libanius himself was in great danger[43]. Neither letters nor orations[44] survive from this period. Libanius evidently was determined not to leave any writings around which could be used to incriminate him. Antioch was filled with fear. The affair certainly did involve attacks on men who had been prominent under Julian, but it can nevertheless not be diagnosed as simply religious persecution. Religion was mixed with politics. The trials were to some extent an aftermath of the usurpation of Procopius, the

---

[39] W. LIEBESCHUETZ, *From Antioch to Piazza Armerina and back again*, in *Mélanges de l'université Saint-Joseph*, 60 (2007), *Mélanges en l'honneur de Jean-Paul Rey-Coquais*, 135-151, esp. 145-148; J. BALTY, *Mosaïques antiques du proche Orient*, Paris 1995.

[40] LIB. *Or.* IX, in *Libanios Discours* II-X, ed. J. MARTIN, Paris 1988, 196-200. JOHN CHRYSOSTOM, *In Kalendas*, in PG 48, 954 ff.; E. SOLER, *Le sacré et le salut...*, 24-27; M. MESLIN, *La fête des Calendes de Janvier dans l'empire romain*, Brussels 1970, describes the «after-life» of some of its customs.

[41] On persistence of pagan festivals see M.R. SALZMAN, *Religious Koine and Religious Dissent in the Fourth century*, in *A Companion to Roman Religion*, ed. J. RÜPKE, Oxford 2007, 109-125.

[42] F.J. WIEBE, *Kaiser Valens und die heidnische Opposition*, Bonn 1995.

[43] AMMIANUS XXIX, 1, 1- 2.16; LIB. *Or.* I, 156-178 deal with this troubled period, cf. J. WINTJES, *Das Leben des Libanius...*, 163-76.

[44] No orations between *Or.* XVIII (the funeral oration on Julian) and 374 *Or.* I, the first edition of the Autobiography. The next speech is *Or.* XXIV, *On avenging of Julian* of 378/9. This begins the long sequence of late political speeches.

unsuccessful usurper who had been a relative of Julian, and no doubt was hoping for support from men who had followed Julian. The main issue was about who was to rule the Empire, not whether the ancestral cults were to be replaced by Christianity. These events are not well documented. We do not know whether there was any deterioration in the previously good relations between Christians and pagans in the city.

3. Pagans and Christians in the age of John Chrysostom

Our evidence about the religious situation at Antioch becomes extremely abundant again in the 380s when the orations of Libanius are supplemented by the writings and, after 386, the sermons of John Chrysostom (c349- 407). Chrysostom wrote the greater part of his very large output at Antioch. He was ordained in 386, and his sermons date from that time. But some of his treatises are earlier. Among his earliest writings is the treatise on St Babylas composed around 380 when Julian's attempt to revive paganism was still an issue. Chrysostom's treatise is designed to show, among other things, that Julian was wrong and that Christianity is the true religion[45]. The *De Sancto Babyla* is rather discursive but it falls essentially into two halves, the legendary story of how Babylas prevented a wicked emperor from entering a church and the saint's subsequent martyrdom and the power demonstrated by his relics during Julian the Apostate's stay at Antioch. The first half is remarkable for the extraordinarily forceful assertion of the priest's right and duty to reprimand even an emperor, to expel him from his church, as a shepherd would chase a diseased sheep from his fold, or a landlord a dog, or unruly slave from his yard[46]. It is an ideological anticipation of the way Ambrose compelled the emperor Theodosius to do penance after the massacre at Thessalonica, though the language is much more radical than that used by Ambrose in his famous letter. The story, though legendary, was no doubt an essential part of the tradition about Babylas, and its point that a priest must rebuke even an emperor who has committed a serious sin, even if he is a Christian, is relevant to a treatise which culminates in an account of the conflict of the Church with Julian the Apostate. One wonders nevertheless why Chrysostom has made so much of the story, which was legendary – as he may well have conjec-

---

[45] JEAN CHRYSOSTOM, *Discours sur Babylas*, éd. et trad. par M.A. SCHATKIN, C. BLANC, B. GRILLET, suivi de *Homélie sur Babylas*, éd. et tr. B. GRILLET, J.-N. GUINOT, Paris 1990.
[46] *Ibid.*, 30 and 47 in PG 50, 6, 541 and 9, 546.

tured[47] – and concerned a conflict not with a pagan but with a supposedly Christian emperor. Perhaps he was thinking not so much of the position of the Church under the pagan Julian, as under Valens, the *homoian* Christian[48].

The second half of the work describes how the relics of Babylas defeated the paganism of Julian. The Caesar Gallus transferred the relics of Babylas to a new martyrium at Daphne. The arrival of the relics immediately raised moral standards in what had previously been the notoriously easy going and licentious life at Daphne. More impressively still, the relics silenced the oracle of Apollo. Julian had the relics of Babylas moved back to their old resting place in a cemetery outside Antioch. Almost immediately after, the temple of Apollo at Daphne caught fire. The flames destroyed the timber roof, and the famous cult-statue of Apollo. In his monody Libanius had regretted that the pagan gods, especially Apollo and Zeus, were mourning the destruction of their sanctuary, but had done nothing to save the temple. Chrysostom gleefully points out that this proved the hopeless weakness of the supposed gods when faced by an act of God, and the foolishness of the Hellenes who had allowed themselves to be so deceived by demons. God gave Julian a chance to repent, but the emperor continued his campaign against Christianity and paid the penalty: he was killed and his huge army destroyed.

Chrysostom wrote a second apology, *Christ's divinity proved against Jews and pagans*. This like *De Sancto Babyla* represents a late response to Julian's attempt to restore paganism. It bears a definite resemblance to the *De Sancto Babyla* and was therefore probably written about the same time. Its argument is that the expansion and triumph of Christianity proves the truth of its teaching, and thus the divinity of Christ. The title of the treatise is misleading in that the pamphlet has no separate section directed against the Jews. So it probably either is a fragment or was never completed. Chrysostom continued to think that the Jews of Antioch presented him with a problem. But the problem was not the Jews themselves, but the Christians who insisted on combining Christian worship with participation in some ceremonies of the Jews, in other words tried to get the benefit of both religions[49]. This Chrysostom would not tolerate, and on the eve

---

[47] Chrysostom leaves the emperor anonymous.
[48] He may also have thought that the murder of the boy hostage by the anonymous emperor of the third century resembled in wickedness the murder of the young Armenian king Pap by the officers of Valens (AMMIANUS XXX, 1, 1-23).
[49] R.WILKEN, *John Chrysostom and the Jews. Rhetoric and Reality in the Late Fourth Century*, Berkeley-Los Angeles 1983.

of the Jewish high festivals in autumn 386 he interrupted a series of sermons against the Anomoeans to deliver the first of a series of quite vicious sermons to deter members of his congregation from judaising; a second sermon in January 387 warned members of his congregation against celebrating Easter at the same time as the Jewish Passover, and in autumn of the same year he delivered no less than five sermons telling his auditors that their participating in a variety of Jewish rites was totally incompatible with their Christianity[50].

It is however significant that as a priest after 386 he only very occasionally preached whole sermons against pagans and paganism, and references to paganism in sermons directed at other objectives are relatively rare[51]. Chrysostom compares the pagans to children who are happy to spend their lives playing on the floor, and who merely laugh when an adult tries to talk to them about serious matters[52]. Compared with Judaism, and of course the community of *homoian* Christians, whom he, like other upholders of the Nicene creed, describes as Arians, Chrysostom evidently did not consider the traditional cults any longer as serious rivals to Nicene Christianity. Chrysostom had noticed that paganism as a public religion was no longer self-sustaining. It needed support of a pagan emperor, which it had briefly regained under Julian[53]. Without that it was helpless, and would presumably fade way. It was no longer necessary to refute it.

Chrysostom of course remained very much involved in the conflicts dividing the Christian community at Antioch, the conflict between those who accepted the Creed of Nicaea (Nicenes, *Homoousians*) and those who did not (*Homoians* or for their opponents, Arians), and the schism dividing the Nicenes between those who recognised Flavianus as their bishop, and those who recognized Euagrius. Chrysostom was strongly engaged on the side of the Nicenes, and in the rivalry of Flavianus and Euagrius he was commited to the side of Flavianus, and surely the most effective

---

[50] *Ibid.*: texts in PG 48. 843-942; english tr. by P.W. HARKINS, *Discourses against Judaizing Christians*, Washington 1977. See also R. ZADÉ, *Les martyres Maccabées. Les homélies de Grégoire de Nazianze et de Jean Chrysostome*, Supplement to «Vigiliae Christianae» 80, Leiden 2007.

[51] E.g. *Hom. in ep. ad Ephes.* 12. Chrysostom argues that neither the sun nor water are gods, and that pagans consider things sinful that are not, such as filthiness of the body, the pollution of a funeral, the keeping of particular days, but take no account of real sins such as unnatural lust, adultery, fornication.

[52] *Hom. in ep. 1 ad Cor.* 4, 6 in PG 61, 38-40.

[53] *De St Babyla* 41-42 in PG 50, 7, 544. In contrast Christianity flourishes under persecution.

preacher of that group. A paper on pagans and Christians is not the place to go into detail about the complicated story of the Antiochene schisms. It must suffice to point out that Chrysostom's principal contribution to the Nicene cause did not consist in theology and dogmatic arguments, but of the bond he managed to build up between himself and his congregation by his passionate and eloquent preaching.

But if the religious ceremonies and theology – if that is the right word – of paganism did not worry Chrysostom, the many secularized relics of the traditional religion conspicuous in the life and culture of Antioch did trouble him. Chrysostom was concerned not so much with conversion, as with Christianisation. He wanted to make Antioch and the whole culture totally Christian. What his sermons are generally about is not to prove that Christianity is true, but to thoroughly Christianise the life of his congregations. It was not enough to go to church on Sundays, though that was of course important, but every aspect of life should shaped in a specifically Christian way. Monks had developed a way of life which aimed at living the morality of the New Testament in its totality. In the majority of the sermons he seems principally concerned to persuade his congregation that the way of life which had been pioneered by Christian ascetics could be, and indeed must be, adopted by lay-people. Of course the ordinary Christians of Antioch were far from doing this. Their customs had been shaped by many centuries of urban life, and adherence to Christianity and even baptism did not, and could not, shake their instinctive sense of what was right and proper, and what was not. They thought nothing wrong in attending chariot races or the theater, or in women to wearing attractive dresses and make up, in swearing oaths, and thus from a Christian point of view taking the name of God in vain, in dubbing mud on the foreheads of children to guard them from the evil eye, in traditional ways of choosing names for children[54] or the traditional license and merry-making of wedding ceremonies[55], or during the celebrations of the New Year[56], or the simple the enjoyment of dancing[57]. Chrysostom accepted the established custom of the funeral banquets, but he disapproved of subsequent mourn-

---

[54] *Hom. in 1 Cor.* 12,7 in PG 61,106, instead mark them with sign of the cross. Cf. E. SOLER, *Le sacré et le salut...*, 27-29 on more traditional «superstitions» practised by Christians.
[55] *Hom. in Coloss.* 12; *In 1Cor.* 12, 5 in PG 61,103.
[56] *Hom. in Kalend.* in PG 48, 953-962.
[57] *Hom. in Matth.* 48, 3 in PG 58, 491: «Where there is dancing, the devil is also there... For God did not give us feet for that purpose, but to walk with discipline... not for us to leap like camels».

ing, because this implied a denial of the Christian teaching of an after-life. Mourning was appropriate for one's sins, but not for deaths[58].

The mass of the Christians of Antioch evidently did not see any incompatibility between such ancestral customs and habits, and their considering themselves Christians, attending church on Sundays more or less regularly, and eventually having themselves baptized. But from the point of view of Chrysostom, inspired as he was by the idealism of the ascetic movement, this state of affairs was intolerable, and required fundamental reform[59]. So in his sermons Chrysostom demanded self-critical introspection, study of the Bible, an ascetic life-style, and above all charitable giving. He required his hearers to abstain from all the secularized relics of paganism and superstitions, and above all to stay away from the public games. He preached at the festivals of the martyrs whose martyria were situated around the walls of the city, and at festivals commemorating Nicene bishops. He delivered a sermon when Christmas was for the first time celebrated at Antioch on 25 December, in 386[60]. We have three brief sermons[61] which Chrysostom preached on the festival of the Maccabee martyrs, presumably in the church, which according to a late tradition was a confiscated synagogue[62]. A Christian festival calendar was coming into being, which would eventually replace the traditional pagan one.

Chrysostom's objectives have been well summarized by J.I. Maxwell: «Chrysostom's immediate objective in preaching was [...] the inculcation of Christian habits. Chrysostom's goal was not social change but to encourage a life conductive to collective salvation... Everyone would have a Christian response to any situation». The Christian ethos had to become all embracing, to become common sense, to become habit, and so to be taken for granted. Only if he or she achieved this, could a Christian be sure of salvation.[63] But this was inevitably a very slow process.

---

[58] *Hom. in Matth.* 27, 3 in PG 57, 347-50; *Hom. in Gen.* 45, 2 in PG 54, 416; *Hom. de stat.* 5, 6 -14 in PG 49, 70-8. More references in J.I. MAXWELL *Christianization...*, 160.
[59] *Ibid.*, 148-161.
[60] PG 49, 351-362.
[61] PG 50, 617-628.
[62] Chrysostom says nothing about the confiscation, or indeed about the location where he was speaking. See J. HAHN, *Gewalt und religiöser Konflikt...*, 180-188 for a very plausible argument that the building over the supposed graves of the Maccabee martyrs had never been a synagogue. The graves were probably only near the synagogue, and the building over them was a Christian church from the beginning, as is stated by AUGUSTINE, *Sermo* 300, 6 in PG 38, 1379, of 391 or later.
[63] J.I. MAXWELL *Christianization...*, 147-148.

4. Creation of a Christian identity was the result, not the purpose of preaching

One is bound to ask why Chrysostom, and so many of his colleagues, insisted that it was necessary for society to be totally Christianised, moreover Christianised in accordance with their own particular brand of Christianity. I do not think it at all helpful to describe his efforts as a directed at the creation of a particular religious identity, an unmistakable identity which would differentiate Christians, or simply Nicene Christians from every other groups, as has been argued in an important recent book: «Chrysostom stood at the end of a long line of Christian leaders who sought [...] to construct a Christian identity. Chrysostom wanted to define clearly what it meant to be a Christian. This meant preaching the meaning of Christian identity at every possible opportunity»[64]. This description of the objective of Chrysostom and of other Christian leaders[65] is not helpful, because it does not describe what the preachers thought that they were doing, and it does not explain why congregations found their preacher's demands persuasive. First of all Chrysostom and his colleagues did not think that they were creating something new. They thought that they were propagating New Testament teaching. Of course there was innovation too. The situation of Christianity had been radically changed by the conversion of the emperor Constantine and the numerous conversions that followed, and now the ascetic movement was making new demands. This required a great deal of adaptation and clarification. But adaptation to a changing environment was merely acceleration of a continuing more or less subconscious process.

The objective of Chrysostom, and his collegues, was much wider, and their purpose was after all much grander than the creation of a new identity. What he asked of his congregation was what he thought was full implementation of the Christian religion, and Christian religion was not something that Chrysostom, or any of his contemporaries, were construct-

---

[64] I. SANDWELL, *Religious Identity*..., 277. The book is full of interesting information about the religious situation at Antioch in the fourth century, especially about the «privatisation» and internalisation of the traditional cults. But the application of the discourse of identity, in the sense in which the word is currently used by sociologists and many historians, ignores what the individuals concerned were fearing, thinking and doing, and therefore does not help to understand the causes of change.

[65] M. HARL, *La denunciation des festivities profanes dans les discourse episcopal et monastique en Orient chrétien à la fin du IV*[e] *siècle*, in *La fête, pratique et discours*, «Annales littéraires de l'Université de Besançon» 262 (1981), 41-84.

ing, but a body of teaching founded on the Bible and expanded and developed in the traditions of the Church. The dynamics of their campaign was derived from the fact that they felt that they were doing God's will. When the great pagan senator Symmachus had insisted that the great mystery of that great a secret (that is God) could be reached by more than one route, Ambrose, bishop of Milan, replied «you have admitted that you are ignorant of what you worship... we know with certainty, directly from the wisdom and truth of God» (i.e. the Bible). Chrysostom, like Ambrose and the other Church Fathers, was certain that there was only one correct belief, and one correct way of life; and this conviction had been part of Christianity, at least of the Christianity preached by leaders of the Churches from the beginning, as it already had been that of the compilers of the Old Testament. These people did not advocate plain living, giving away riches to the poor, the staying away from the circus and theater, and they did not recommend that girls should dedicate their virginity to Jesus, that widows should not remarry, that everybody should give up swearing, and so on, in order to make Christians different from their fellow citizens, but because they believed that the behaviour they taught was commanded by God, and necessary for salvation and as far as these sermons were persuasive, it was by and large[66], because the hearers believed that they were being correctly informed about the purposes of God. Preachers wanted their congregation to be distinguishable from pagans but not because difference was good in itself, but because it was better to be seen doing what is right than what is wrong, and because mingling endangered salvation[67].

Human motivation is mixed. At one level the demand for total Christianisation was about God's will being fulfilled on earth, but at another and less conscious level, it was about power. Chrysostom and many of his colleagues were participating in a wider offensive on the part of Christianity, and particularly Nicene Christianity, against paganism and heresy. In the 380s, while Chrysostom was preaching in the city, monks were destroying pagan temples in the countryside east of Antioch, and the bishop of the neighbouring city of Apamea was demolishing the principal temple of that city[68]. The Western emperor Gratian had cut the connection between the Roman state, and the old Roman religion, and both he in the West, and Theodosius in the East had put the whole weight of the Roman

---

[66] Allowing for the fact that decisions about how to live are always influenced by a range of factors.
[67] M. KAHLOS, *Debate and Dialogue...*, 133 (on Augustine).
[68] See F. R.TROMBLEY, *Hellenic Religion...*, I, 123-129.

state behind Nicene Christianity. Laws were issued penalizing paganism and non-Nicene Christianity. One factor behind these developments was the ascetic movement which was radicalizing Christianity[69]. At the same time the fact that the emperor and many of his leading officials[70], and in cities like Antioch a large part of the population, was now Christian made the objective of a totally Christianised society seem achievable.

Chrysostom himself was well aware that he was demanding a lot. He therefore advised his congregation that they should start by trying to observe those commandments that are relatively easy to fulfill[71]. So he repeatedly, seemingly obsessively, tells his congregation that they should make an effort to obey the Third Commandment[72]: «You shall not take the Lord' name in vain» and stop themselves from swearing. Moreover his regular urging that his hearers must give up going to the theatre, or in the case of women to stop wearing make up, are fairly superficial changes in life style, and therefore relatively easy to adopt. To judge by the number of times the same demands are repeated in sermon after sermon, Chrysostom did not believe that he was changing the habits of his congregation, never mind the culture of his city, very much. In fact the transformation of a century old culture cannot be achieved quickly. It is bound to be a very slow process, drawn out over centuries. The end of the public spectacles attacked by Chrysostom and generations of Christian preachers was only brought about by the decline and fall of the classical city itself.

5. Christian numbers

How numerous were Christians at Antioch in the 380s? Chrysostom claimed that Christians at Antioch amounted to 100,000 persons[73], perhaps half the population of the city[74]. We don't know whether this is just a rhetorical claim, or an estimate based on evidence. In any case we don't know by what criteria Chrysostom would have classified an individual

---

[69] One might compare the influence of «intransigent evangelical Protestantism» in Brazil referred to in paper of Peter Brown, *infra*.

[70] J. MATTHEWS, *Western Aristocracies and Imperial Court AD 364-425*, Oxford 1975, 101-153.

[71] *Hom. in Act.* 8.

[72] *Exodus* 20,7.

[73] *Hom. in Matth.* 85, 4 in PG 58, 762: cf. W. LIEBESCHUETZ, *Antioch...*, 93-94.

[74] 200.000 inhabitants according to *Hom. in Ignatium* 4 in PG 50, 59; on population of Antioch, see W. LIEBESCHUETZ, *Antioch...*, 92-96.

as a Christian, i.e. what precisely in the way of church-linked activities he considered the minimum necessary to qualify. He could hardly have insisted on regular church attendance. Antioch did not have enough churches. There was the Old, or Apostolic, Church which had been rebuilt between 314 and 324, after its destruction during the Great Persecution[75]. There was the octagonal cathedral, the Great Church, on the Island near the palace, dedicated in 341[76]. These were the only churches of which we can be certain that they existed at the time of Julian. Around 380 there was a church over the tomb[77]. Between 379 and 381 bishop Meletius built the cruciform church of St Babylas. These churches presumably had regular weekly services.

Antioch was surrounded by *martyria*. We know that the Caesar Gallus built a *martyrium* for St Babylas in Daphne in the neighbourhood of the temple of Apollo in the 350s. The *martyria* nearer to Antioch cannot be dated. They were situated in Christian cemeteries. There was a collective *martyrium* in the Christian cemetery outside the Daphne Gate where St Julianus was buried, among the relics of other saints. Another collective *martyrium* was situated in a cemetery beyond the Romanesian Gate. A third *martyrium*, that of St Drosis, was somewhat further out[78]. We do not know whether any of the sanctuaries that housed the sacred remains were large enough to house a significant congregation. The sites of none have so far been identified. But *martyria* certainly attracted large crowds to the festival of their martyr. They also regularly attracted families for funerals, and the banquets that commemorated the anniversary of the dead buried *ad sanctos*. In addition it can surely be taken for certain that many men and women came to pray at the tombs of the martyrs[79].

The Church's social work provided another link between the population of the city and the Church. The church fed three thousand virgins every day and gave aid to prisoners[80]. It provided food and clothing to men whose names were entered on a register and who presented themselves day by day[81]. Chrysostom complained that many of the clergy spent so

---

[75] G. DOWNEY, *A History of Antioch in Syria*, Princeton 1961, 336.
[76] *Ibid.*, 358.
[77] *Ibid.*, 448, but see n. 62 above.
[78] On *martyria* and their festivals see also E. SOLER, *Le Sacré et le salut...*, 201-208, see also (*honoris causa*), H. DELEHAYE, *Les origins du culte des martyres*, Brussels 1933, 192-207.
[79] E. SOLER, *Le scaré et le salut...*, 209-210 on Chrysostom's *In martyres*, in PG 50, 664.
[80] *Hom in Matth.* 66 in PG 57, 658.
[81] *Hom. in I Ep ad Cor.* 15 in PG 61, 179.

much time in the administration of almsgiving that few were left for the care of souls[82]. We can be sure that very many inhabitants of Antioch had some contact with the Church. The size of the Christian community of Antioch in the later fourth century should therefore not be underestimated on the ground that there were possibly only two or three churches inside the city at that time. Chrysostom claimed that there were 100.000 Christians at Antioch[83]. What we do not know is how many of the «the ordinary men or women» who considered him or herself a Christian accepted that adherence to Christianity was incompatible with participation in any other cult. Certainly many could have identified themselves as Christians and thought nothing wrong in participating in other cults. Indeed not all individuals who now and again participated in Christian activities necessarily identified themselves simply as Chistians.

While there are too many uncertainties for us to reach a meaningful estimate of the numerical strength of the Christian population of Antioch, there can be no doubt that Christianity was now a very powerful force in the city. This was shown clearly on the occasion of the Riot of the Statues. The riot started as a protest against a new tax. A large number of notables crowded into the governor's courtyard to proclaim the city's inability to pay, and to obtain relief from the new burden. They were heard to call on the god of the Emperor Theodosius, i.e. Jesus, for aid. When the demonstration at the governor's palace met with no response, a larger crowd marched to the residence of the bishop Flavianus to obtain his support. When they could not find him, the peaceful protest turned to a riot which culminated in the overthrow of imperial images[84]. When the city was threatened with terrible punishment for this act of rebellion, bishop Flavianus travelled to Constantinople to plead for the city[85]. Antioch had begun to speak with a Christian voice[86].

---

[82] *Hom. in Matth.* 85 in PG 57, 761-62.
[83] *Hom. in Matth* 85, 4 in PG 57, 762.
[84] LIB. *Or.* XIX, 25-27.
[85] FRANS VAN PAVERD, *St John Chrysostom, the Homilies on the Statues*, Rome 1991. Flavianus' supposed speech to Theodosius: *Hom. de statuis* 21, in PG 49, 211-220. While Chrysostom gives all credit for the pardon to the bishop, Libanius gives it to the imperial officials. See *Ors.* XIX–XXXIII in *Libanius Selected Works* II, ed. and tr. A.F. NORMAN, Loeb Library, Cambridge-London 1977, 237-407.
[86] Cf. P. BROWN, *Power and Persuasion in Late Antiquity*, Wisconsin 1992, 105-108.

6. Christians and Pagans in the Fifth Century and John Malalas

We have no sources which are as informative about conditions at Antioch in the fifth century as the works of Libanius and John Chrysostom are for the second half of the fourth century. Above all we have no letter-collection. This means that we have no information about the religion of individuals. The pagans of Antioch have become almost invisible. But paganism was certainly far from extinct. In the middle of the century the sophist and philosopher Isocasius seems to have occupied a position at Antioch comparable to that of Libanius in the previous century. He achieved the high office of *quaestor* at Constantinople, but was eventually compelled to convert to Christianity[87]. Theodoret, bishop of Cyrrhus who originated from Antioch, and presumably received his very full traditional education in that city, wrote a large treatise defending Christianity against pagan critics[88]. So presumably such critics existed and were worth answering[89].

Religion caused considerable disturbances at Antioch in the last quarter of the century. But these involved anti-Jewish rioting by the Green faction in the hippodrome, and conflict between upholders of the canons of the Council of Chalcedon and opponents of the Council, the so-called Monophysites. As far as our evidence goes, pagans as such played no part[90]. We have a remarkably detailed account of persecution of pagans instigated by students at Alexandria, Beirut and Aphrodisias between 485 and 491[91]. This led to the desecration of a sanctuary of Isis, prosecutions on charges of magic, book burning and forced conversions. Both the Christian instigators and the pagan victims were highly educated intellectuals. It is likely that the Christian students received official backing for their anti-pagan activities because of the dangerous contemporary rebellion of the Isaurian

---

[87] *PLRE* II. 633-34 s. v. Isocasius; cf. G. Downey, *A History of Antioch...*, 483-484. No writings of his have survived.

[88] Théoderet de Cyr, *Thérapeutique des maladies helléniques,* texte, introduction et trad. par P. Canivet, 2 vols, Paris 1958; also 12 orations translated into French by Y. Azéma: *Théodoret de Cyr. Discours sur la providence,* Paris 1954. Both works would repay longer discussion in the context of Christian/Pagan dialogue.

[89] For an interesting discussion on apologetic and Christian/Pagan dialogue generally see M. Kahlos, *Debate and Dialogue...*, 55-92.

[90] G. Downey, *A History of Antioch...*, 484-99; 504-507.

[91] In these cities paganism was still very much alive in the late fifth century. See Zacharie le Scholastique, V*ie de Sévère*, ed. and tr. M.-A. Kugener, *POr.* 2/1, Paris 1903, 7-115, and the excellent discussion in F.R. Trombley, *Hellenic Religion and Christianization...*, II, 1-73.

general Illus[92] in the years AD 484-88, whose rebellion received strong support from pagans who evidently hoped that pagans would be better off if he replaced Zeno the current emperor with his nominee, Leontius[93]. Illus and Leontius[94] for a time controlled Antioch, but we do not know how, if at all, Antiochene pagans were affected by this usurpation[95]. The rebellion of Illus is the last political episode in which pagans, upholding the cause of paganism, are reported to have played a part[96]. However that maybe, when the imperial government launched offensives against remaining adherents of the cults of the gods in the later sixth century, they still found individuals at Antioch to prosecute.

7. The Chronicle of John Malalas[97]

The story of the zealous Christian students who launched attacks on pagan cults first at Alexandria, then at Beirut, illustrates the fact that throughout the fifth century, and for much longer, Christians continued to attend the traditional secular schools, that is schools where the education was based on the Greek or the Roman literary classics, of which classical mythology with its stories of the doings of gods and goddesses was an integral part. Every boy who was to make a name for himself in the law courts or the city council, or the Church, or above all in the imperial service would have to undergo this education, and in the course of it would inevitably acquire a profound familiarity with these throughly pagan stories. For at this time, and for long after, the traditional education was still the only one available. There were no Christian schools. But it was not only the educated who had their heads filled with stories about the pagan gods. Much of entertainment in the theatre was based on mythological stories. Libanius, who was almost as critical of what happened in the theatre as Chrysostom,

---

[92] *PLRE* II, 586-90, s. v. Illus 1.
[93] F.R. TROMBLEY, *Hellenic Religion and Christianization...*, II, 20-29.
[94] *PLRE* II, 670- 71 s. v. Leontius 17.
[95] G. DOWNEY, *A History of Antioch...*, 490-92.
[96] F.R. TROMBLEY, *Hellenic Religion and Christianization...*, I, 81-97.
[97] New edition by I. THURN, in the *Corpus Fontium Historiae Byzantinae*. An English translation based on the Oxford manuscript of Malalas, but taking into account other Greek, Latin Slavonic and Syriac texts which preserve material derived from Malalas: E. JEFFREYS, M. JEFFREYS, R. SCOTT, *The Chronicle of John Malalas*, Melbourne 1986. The same team has produced *Studies in Malalas*, eds. E. JEFFREYS, R. SCOTT, B. CROKE, Sydney 1990.

nevertheless defended the dancers against criticism by austere moralists like himself with the argument that they provided an education for those who could not afford to go to school[98]. This situation was of course extremely unsatisfactory from the point of view those who were trying to establish a totally Christian culture.

This problem must have caused much discussion. It also produced a literature, most of which has been lost, but some of the lost authors are summarized in the *Chronicle* of Malalas. Malalas was probably a citizen of Antioch, and his *Chronicle* was almost certainly compiled at Antioch early in the sixth century[99] from a wide range of sources, though certainly less wide than suggested by names dropped in the text[100]. So Malalas gives us an Antiochene slant of a dialogue which must have been carried on all over the Greek East. What is more it presents the dialogue from the point of view of an Antiochene layman.

Though written from a strongly Christian point of view, Malalas's *Chronicle* is not in any sense an ecclesiastical history. Malalas view of history is biblical, in that he always sees the hand of God rewarding, and especially punishing, behind the events of history. He shows remarkably little interest in the contemporary religious conflict between those who accepted the decrees of Chalcedon and those who did not, the Monophysites[101]. He does not record the development of the monastic movement. Of the famous St Symeon Stylites he records only the death and burial[102]. The accession and deaths of bishops of Antioch, Constantinople, and occasionally elsewhere, are sometimes noted, but there is no attempt to record the history of the Church, its divisions, its councils, and its holy men, which we find in ecclesiastical historians. Malalas's focus is on secular events.

8. Malalas' Biblical perspective

Following in the tradition of Eusebius, Malalas has fitted the events of early Greco-Roman history and of biblical history into a common chronol-

---

[98] *Or.* LXIV and on it J. HAUBOLD, R. MILES, *Communality and theatre in Libanius*, in *Culture and Society in Later Antioch*, eds. I. SANDWELL, J. HUSKINSON, Oxford 2004, 24-34.

[99] The original edition may have ended around 528, see B. CROKE, *The Early Development of Byzantine Chronicles*, in *Studies in Malalas...*, 17-19.

[100] E. JEFFREYS, *The sources of Malalas*, in *Studies in Malalas...*, 167-216.

[101] See B. CROKE, *The Early Development...*, 15-17.

[102] MALALAS XIV, 369 (37).

ogy[103]. So David is said to have been a contemporary of Priam of Troy[104]. Solomon founded Palmyra to commemorate David's slaying of Goliath, which Malalas tells us took place on the site of that city[105]. When Croesus of Lydia consulted Apollo about his prospects against Kyros of Persia, Kyros was putting the same question to the Biblical prophet Daniel[106].

Since the Bible tells us that all mankind, with the exception of the family of Noah, was annihilated in the Flood, it inevitably follows that all subsequent human beings, including the Greek heroes and those individuals worshipped by pagans as gods were descendants of Noah[107]. Of course the pagan gods could not remain gods. So the pre-history of Malalas's Chronicle, like earlier Christian Apologies[108], refutes paganism by claiming that the so-called gods had really been human rulers and benefactors, and that their worship was in fact the cult of dead kings. But he goes further. The story of the gods transformed into human rulers is fitted into the framework of biblical history. Kronos (Saturn) is made into a descendant of Noah[109]. He becomes ruler of the West, and has a son Zeus Picus. He is called Zeus Picus because in Virgil and elsewhere the Latin god/ruler Picus is said to be a son of Saturn, and Saturn is identified with the Greek Kronos, the father of Zeus. So Zeus and Picus are identified. We see that this version manages to combine Roman and Greek mythologies – just as the Empire combined Greece and Italy. Subsequently Kronos/Saturn remained in the West, but his son Zeus Picus and his descendants became rulers in the East. Between them Kronos/Saturn and Zeus/Picus thus anticipated the divided Roman Empire[110]. With perfect Christian logic Kro-

---

[103] B. CROKE, *The Early Development...*, 27-38; S. MUHLBERGER, *The historiographical background of the fifth-century chronicles,* in his *The Fifth Century Chronicles. Prosper, Hydatius and the Gallic Chronicle of 452,* Leeds 1990, 8-23. A. MOMIGLIANO, *Pagan and Christian historiography,* in *The Conflict of Paganism and Christianity in the Fourth Century,* ed. A. MOMIGLIANO, Oxford 1963, 79-99, supplemented by H. INGLEBERT above.

[104] MALALAS V, 91.

[105] MALALAS V, 143.

[106] MALALAS VI, 156.

[107] MALALAS I, 9-12.

[108] MINUCIUS FELIX, *Octavius,* 21; LACTANTIUS, *Inst. Div.* I, 14-15, 18.

[109] MALALAS I,12-13.

[110] That this extraordinary tale (MALALAS I, 8-17; II, 28; II, 34; VI, 16-18) was not invented by Malalas is shown by. B. GARSTAD, *The* excerpta Latina Barbari *and the Picus – Zeus narrative,* «Jahrbuch für internationale Germanistik» 34 (2002), 252-313. Garstad dates the original narrative to the fourth century, and tentatively assigns it to Bouttios of Antioch. See also his *The Assyrian hero's romantic interlude in Libya. A*

nos and Zeus Picus, being descended from Noah, are then shown to have been the ancestors of all the principal gods and heroes, whose deeds in a somewhat reinvented form fill the first two book of Malalas' *Chronicle*. All mythological allusions to supernatural intervention by pagan gods are made harmless by giving them a naturalistic explanation[111].

In the process of being fitted into a Christian world view the characters and interests of some mythological individuals have been strangely changed. Aphrodite and Adonis are said to have been philosophers[112]. Heracles is said to have «conquered the seductive thoughts of evil desire with the club of philosophy»[113]. To Hephaestus[114] is attributed a law that Egyptian women must to be monogamous, and live chastely. It is difficult to take this seriously. Surely humour is intended. In the same spirit we are not only told that women wrestled at the Olympic Games[115], but also that the women who took part in the games practised philosophy, wrestled in leggings, i.e. did not perform naked like male athletes, and that they took part only after swearing a vow of chastity. We are also told that anyone, man or woman, who was crowned victor in the Olympic Games would remain chaste for the rest of his life, for he would be ordained and become a priest immediately after the end of the contest[116]. It is difficult not to smile. Once again humour is surely intended[117].

The Antiochene synthesis of Biblical history and Greek mythology involves an interesting change of perspective. Neither Greece, nor Italy, but the Near East was the source of human kind and human civilisation. This new perspective abolishes the classical superiority of Greeks and Romans

---

topos from Virgil in Pisander of Laranda, the Picus-Zeus narrative, and Nonnus of Panopolis, «Eranos» 101 (2003)/1, 6-16.

[111] The technique closely resembles that of Palaephatus, probably a contemporary of Aristotle, whom Malalas cites several times. See J. STERN, *Palaephatus* ΠΕΡΙ ΑΠΙΣΤΩΝ: *on Unbelievable Tales*, Teubner 1902 (text, translation introduction and commentary), Wauconda 1996. E. HÖRLING, *Mythos und Pistos in der christlichen Weltchronik des Johannes Malalas*, Lund 1980.

[112] MALALAS I, 13.

[113] MALALAS I, 17-18.

[114] MALALAS I, 19.

[115] MALALAS XII, 288. This is in fact unlikely, as women were not even allowed to watch the games (LIB. *Or.* X, 30).

[116] MALALAS XII, 288.

[117] For a perhaps comparable combination of seriousness with humour, see P. CHUVIN, *Nonnos de Panopolis et la «deconstruction» de l'épopé*, Genève 2006, 249-270, esp. 260-263. See also W. LIEBESCHUETZ, *Pagan mythology in the Christian Empire*, «Int. J. Class. Trad.» 2 (1995)/2, 193-208.

over barbarians[118], The doctrine of the essential unity of all mankind was not invented at Antioch, but it was perhaps particularly relevant in that city of a very mixed population.

Though Malalas has few straightforward attacks on paganism, he does claim that several statues of a young women at Antioch and elsewhere commemorate the sacrifice of a maiden at the start of a building project[119]. The passages all seem to come from the same source, and to have been inserted by Malalas into appropriate places in his own narrative. It has been suggested that they are derived from a work by the Antiochene Bouttios, and that they represent rather crude anti-pagan pagan polemic directed against Julian[120]. Malalas engages in something like dialogue with pagans when he cites passages from the Hermetic corpus[121]. These writings expounded a religious philosophy that was up to a point common to Christians and pagans. This had enabled Earlier Christian apologists, notably Lactantius, to quote Hermes, in support of Christian teachings. Malalas continues this tradition. He quotes a passage from the Hermetic writings which seems to reveals Hermes Trismegistus to have been a monotheist, and prophet of the coming into the world of «the Word», the *logos*. In the same spirit Malalas made use of the so-called Orphic writings. These writings had been closely linked with the mysteries of Dionysus, and they were incorporated into the Neo-Platonism of the last pagans. But Malalas cites a long passage in which Orpheus appears to echo the biblical account of the creation, and to proclaim the Christian doctrine of the Trinity[122].

We see that Malalas tried to harmonise what had been conflicting traditions: pagan and Christian, Greek and Roman[123]. There is no compromise

---

[118] As also in THEODERET, *Curatio affectionum Graecarum* I, 1-46, 50-52; V, 58 -78.

[119] X, 234 at Antioch by Tiberius; X, 268 by Zarbos at foundation of Anazarbos; XI, 276 by Trajan at Antioch; Perseus sacrifices Parthenope at Tarsus (II, 37), Alexander a virgin at foundation of Alexandria (VIII, 192), Augustus at foundation of Ancyra (IX, 222). C. SALIOU, *Statues d'Antioche de Syrie dans la Chronographie de Malalas*, in S. AUGUSTA BOULAROT, J. BEAUCAMP ET AL., *Centre de recherches d'histoire et civilization de Byzance. Monographies 24*, Paris 2006, 69-95, relevant 78-85.

[120] B. GARSTAD, *The Tyche sacrifices in John Malalas: Virgin sacrifice and Fourth-Century polemical history*, in «Illinois Classical Studies» 30 (2005), 83-136. Garstad suggests that Bouttios may also have been the source for the Zeus-Picus narrative.

[121] MALALAS I, 26-27.

[122] MALALAS IV, 73-6 = O. KERN, *Orphicorum fragmenta*, Berlin 1922, 62, 65, 233, cited by Malalas as from Timotheus, on whom *Studies in Malalas...*, 194-5.

[123] The same strategy is also found in *The Tübingen Theosophy*. See H. ERBSE, *Fragmente griechischer Theosophie*, Leipzig (1941) 1995², and S. BROCK, *A Syriac collection of prophecies of pagan philosophers*, «Orientalia Lovaniensia Periodica» 14 (1983),

with polytheism and sacrifice, but a sustained attempt to reinterpret accepted stories and traditions and beliefs to make them compatible with a Christian world picture. Moreover this was clearly an important part of his project: for no fewer than six of Malalas' eighteen books are concerned with «prehistory», that is pagan mythology and biblical narrative merging into what we would call history proper.

9. Christians and Pagans at Antioch in the Sixth Century

There is no doubt that the accession of Justinian marked a new epoch in relations of pagans and Christians. In 529 the emperor Justinian issued some ferocious laws against the pagans, which if the empire had had the administrative strength to enforce them would have amounted to a prohibition of the old religion and forceful conversion of such individuals as still adhered to it[124]. Of course the government was not able to enforce these laws systematically, but they furnished a legal basis for several waves of prosecution of alleged pagans in high positions. The first took place at Constantinople in 529. High officials were charged and their property confiscated. Some were executed[125]. There was a second wave of persecution of pagans at Constantinople in 545/46. Most of the victims were prominent intellectuals, sophist, lawyers and doctors[126]. Two men alleged to have been pagan priests at Antioch and two from Hierapolis were prosecuted in 562[127]. At Constantinople pagans were arrested and paraded, and books, statues and pictures of gods publicly destroyed in the arena[128]. These actions were unprecedented in that the charge was no longer the use of magic for treasonous purposes, but simply adherence to paganism, i. e. alleged evidence of having performed some kind of pagan ritual. The

---

204-46; also *Some Syriac excerpts from Greek collections of pagan prophecies*, «Vig. Christ.» 38 (1984), 77-90. P.F. BEATRICE, *Pagan wisdom and Christian theology according to the Tübingen Theosophy*, «Journal of Early Christian Studies» 3 (1995), 403-418. A combination of pagan and biblical material is also used in the Sybilline Oracles. See J.L. LIGHTFOOT, *The Sybilline Oracles*, Oxford 2007.

[124] *CI* 1,11, 9-10.
[125] MALALAS XVIII, 449 (AD 529); THEOPHANES 6022 (AD 528).
[126] JOHN OF EPHESUS in *Pseudo-Dionysus of Tel Mahr* (tr. W. WITAKOWSKI), 77-78 (pp. 71-72).
[127] MICHAEL THE SYRIAN 2, 271 (tr. CHABOT).
[128] MALALAS XVIII, 491.

government now set out to compel what in the fourth century preachers like Chrysostom had tried to achieve by preaching[129].

Why did this happen? There is not enough evidence to see clearly the background to these persecutions. Some of the victims may have been Christians who had not given up belief in the effectiveness of some of the old cults. It is likely that in some cases the accusation was simply a convenient weapon to destroy political or private enemies. This was a period when a sequence of terrible disasters struck Antioch. In 526 a calamitous earthquake destroyed much of the city and killed many thousands (Malalas XVII,19-22). There was another earthquake in 528 (Malalas XVIII, 442-43). In 540 the city was captured and burnt by the Persians who proceeded to deport a large number of inhabitants (Malalas XVIII, 480; Procopius II, 8, 20ff.). There were further earthquakes in 551, 557, 587, and 588. The year 542 saw the first of a series of empire-wide outbreaks of plague. Justinian's wars which had started so successfully proved very difficult to finish. The schism between those who with the emperor accepted the Council of Chalcedon, and those who rejected it, turned out impossible to resolve. A separate Monophysite Church was being set up. It might be suggested that in these circumstances pagans (and Jews and dissenting Christians) were seen as convenient scapegoats. But of course the laws on which the prosecutions relied preceded most of the disasters. One must conclude that Justinian and his ministers gave the enforcement of religious a higher priority than his predecessors had done.

Most of our not very abundant information about these prosecutions is from Constantinople[130], although we do hear of accusations of pagans at other cities too[131]. A series of prosecutions of alleged pagans was launched between 554 and 559 at Antioch. Some of the accused were condemned to work in hospitals, others interned in monasteries. Some were put to death[132]. We are also told that certain pagans were miraculously foiled when they tried to pull down a picture of Symeon Stylites the Younger which a shopkeeper at Daphne had set up over his shop and honoured with lighted candles[133]. That is not very much. In fact we are not very well informed about the inter-

---

[129] PROCOPIUS *HA* 19, 11 suggests that Justinian's prosecution of pagans were motivated by a desire to confiscate their property.
[130] MALALAS XVIII, 449; THEOPHANES 6022 (AD 528); PSEUDO-DIONYSUS OF TEL-MAHRÉ 77-78 (pp. 71-72).
[131] *C* 138 *IG* 8645 = *Sardis VII*, ed. W.H. BUCKLER, D.M. ROBINSON, Leiden 1932, no 19.
[132] *Vita Symeonis iunioris*, ed. VAN DEN VEN, 2 vols., Brussels 1962-70, 146; F.R. TROMBLEY, *Hellenic Religion and Christianisation*..., II, 181.
[133] *Vita Symeonis iunioris* 172.

nal affairs of the city under Justinian. The last book of Malalas's *Chronicle* (AD 527-563) is no longer centred on Antioch. Apart from accounts of the great disasters that struck the city what we are told about affairs at Antioch mainly concerns ecclesiastical affairs. On the face of it Antioch was now a Christian city. After the second earthquake the acclamations in the hippodrome demanded that the city's name be changed to Theoupolis. The emperor agreed to the change, though the new name did not stick[134].

However, the city still housed some followers of the old religion, or at least individuals who could be put on trial for adhering to the old cults. Good evidence is provided in accounts of persecution of pagans later in the sixth century recorded in the *Ecclesiastical Histories* of Euagrius[135], and of John of Ephesus[136]. This episode which began in 578/9 and was only concluded in 587/8 is interesting from several points of view. The prosecuting authority was as earlier the imperial government, but in this episode the large parts of the population were evidently passionately involved in the attack on the pagans. The government's action was clearly popular. Then the persecution was directed against members of the elite, especially at Antioch and Baalbek in Syria and at Edessa in Mesopotamia. The government's prosecutions were launched by local accusations. So it looks as if there were some regional factors and local factions behind the accusations. It is notable that some of the accused were at least outwardly Christian. More extraordinary still, Gregorius, the «Diphysite» bishop of Antioch, was among those accused. There is evidence that Monophysites added their voice to the accusations against the «Diphysite» patriarch[137]. The prosecution of real and alleged pagans, or perhaps *incerti* or demichristians[138] were only part of a situation of increasing conflict and disorder in the eastern provinces of the Empire in the late 6th century, in the years leading up first to the Persian and then the Arab invasions[139].

---

[134] MALALAS XVIII, 443 (AD 528).

[135] P. ALLEN, *Evagrius Scholasticus, the Church Historian*, Louvain 1981, 320-322. EVAGRIUS, *HE* (ed. BIDEZ and PARMENTIER), 5, 17-18.

[136] JOHN OF EPHESUS, *Ecclesiastical History*, in CSCO, Ser. Syr. 55, Louvain 1936; English translation *The Third Part of the Ecclesiastical History of John, bishop of Ephesus*, tr. R. PAYNE SMITH, Oxford 1860, relevant III, 27-34.

[137] Cf. I. ROCHOW, *Der Vorwurf des Heidentums als Mittel der innenpolitischen Polemik in Byzanz*, in *Paganism in the Later Roman Empire and in Byzantium*, ed. M. SALAMON, Crakow 1991, 133-156.

[138] On the problematic aspects of concepts like «Christianization» and «pagan survivals» cf. R. MARKUS, *The end of ancient Christianity...*, 8-12.

[139] W. LIEBESCHUETZ, *The Decline and Fall of the Roman City*, Oxford 2001, 260-269.

It is likely enough that among the individuals hit by this persecution were some real pagans. Some citizens surely remained loyal to their old cults. Many more, one would imagine, refused to recognise the total incompatibility of the old religion and the new, and hoped for supernatural help from a combination of both[140]. After all even today there are around two million and a half Alawites (Nusayri) in Syria, a sect allied to Shiite Islam, whose ritual and theology nevertheless has important elements clearly derived from Christianity, from Gnosticism and from ancient sun-worship[141].

10. Conclusion

Momigliano entitled his volume *The Conflict between Paganism and Christianity*. If we look exclusively at the two religious systems, the traditional cults of the Greeks and Romans on the one hand, and Christianity on the other, there was indeed a conflict, a conflict from which Christianity emerged triumphant. But if we look at the interaction of the people involved, that is the Christians and the pagans themselves, it becomes clear that the word conflict does not describe the situation adequately[142]. As far as we can see, Antiochene society was not divided into conflicting groups, split on the basis of conflicting religious allegiances. We get the impression that many aspects of civic life continued unaffected by religious differences. At Antioch in the fourth century, and probably more widely in the ruling classes of the empire, relations between Christians and pagans appear to have been mostly, though not always, good. Nevertheless this impression must be qualified. The competition between the religions was certainly not played out on a level playing field. The centuries following

---

[140] Cf. E. SOLER, *Le Sacré et le salut...*, 240: «Beaucoup d'Antiochiens n'avaient pas une mais plusieurs religions et, sans les confondre, sans démarche à proprement parler syncrétiste, ils participaient à leurs fêtes, dans le but d'avoir plus de moyens et de chances d'atteindre ce à quoi ils aspiraient par-dessus tout, le salut». Soler refers to the 4th century, but his assessment may well still valid, if to a lesser extent, for the sixth century.

[141] See *Encyclopaedia of Islam* VIII, 145-48, s. v. Nusayriyya; also M. MOOSA, *Extremist Shiites, the Ghulat Sects*, Syracuse-New York 1988, 255-431. They have a trinity of Mohammed, Ali and Salman al Farisi. They celebrate Christmas, and have a communion service. Ali, the divinity, is closely linked to the sun. Before the fall, mankind were points of light contemplating the sun. Eventually, after repeated metempsychosis, they will return to their original condition.

[142] So also the Roman view of the paper of R. LIZZI TESTA, *infra*.

the conversion of Constantine saw steadily growing pressure by bishops and government on sectarian Christians, Pagans and Jews. There were occasions of violent conflict, riots, destruction of temples, mutilation of images, and trumped up prosecutions, and eventually forced conversions. Since our literary sources only provide a very incomplete picture, episodes of violence were probably more common than we would conclude from the surviving evidence. Violence was however episodic, not continuous, and the exception rather than the rule[143]. The reason for this was that the balance of power was very one-sided. Pagans had to be extremely careful. There is plenty of evidence, from our own times and throughout history, that legal discrimination against a religious group, verbal abuse in legislation and sermons, and the threat, and from time to time the reality, of interference with religious practices, produces resentment and hostility. But as the bulk of our evidence is Christian and much of it ecclesiastical, it does not allow us to reconstruct in full the reaction of remaining pagans to the discrimination against their cults and the sustained promotion of Christianity in the Christian empire. It of course also tells us very little about what the ordinary Christian thought about his pagan neighbours.

As its title indicates, this volume differs from its famous predecessor in that its focus is on dialogue rather than conflict. I have found little or no evidence from Antioch[144] of direct dialogue between Christian leaders and representative pagans on the subject of their differing religious views. There could be no real dialogue between them, because they did not recognize each other's claims. However in order to win support, the religious contenders had to adapt to their cultural environment. The emperor Julian thought that to revive paganism he would have to introduce elements of organization and social work obviously derived from Christianity[145]. As Christianity was the party of change, its leaders had to clarify the Christian position towards the cultural heritage. We can observe the creation of a calendar of Christian festivals to replace the pagan calendar. Malalas shows us how Christian writers tried to reconcile the prehistory of classical mythology with the narrative of the Bible. He also cites Hermetic and «Orphic» writings, that is pagan texts, in support of Christian doctrin[146]. Chrysostom recommends the morality of the ascetic movement

---

[143] See M.R. SALZMAN, *Pagan-Christian religious violence*, in *Violence in Late Antiquity, Perception and Practices,* ed. H.A. DRAKE, Aldershot 2006, 266-296.

[144] For a wider view of dialogue see M. KAHLOS, *Debate and Dialogue...*, especially 62-83.

[145] *Epp.* 16, 20 & *Fragment of a Letter to a Priest*.

[146] Theodoret too argued for Christian truth from Hellenic philosophy, see n. 89.

by presenting this as a philosophy which realizes the ethical objectives of secular philosophy far more effectively than classical philosophy had ever been able to do[147].

This paper has traced the Christianisation of Antioch. But once again it must be remembered that our evidence has important gaps. We have abundant information about what John Chrysostom and Theodoret and their contemporary fathers of the Church thought was required for an individual to be a Christian. We know that some aspects of their teaching, for instance the call to stay away from the public spectacles, were widely disregarded. But we really don't know what the «ordinary» Christian thought was essential in the way of Christian observance. Indeed we cannot even know what proportion of the people whom Chrysostom included in his estimate of the Christian population of Antioch would have defined themselves as Christians.

As far as the politics of religion are concerned Julian's Antioch was probably, the Antioch of Chrysostom certainly, a Christian city. Pagans continued to exist, but our sources tell us very little them. So we have little information about the nature and extent of surviving pagan beliefs and practices. The Alawites (Nusayri) of contemporary Syria, who are actually today the most important political grouping in the country, do however provide a suggestive analogy, though only an analogy[148]. Islam has been the dominant religion in Syria for more than a millennium. Yet the Alawites adhere to a form of Islam which includes important elements derived from Christianity, from the mythology of Late Antique Gnosticism, and also an ancient sun cult.

---

[147] Most fully in *Adversus oppugnatores vitae monasticae*, in PG 57, 519-86, tr. by D. G. HUNTER, *A Comparison between a King and a Monk & Against the Opponents of the Monastic Life*, Lewiston-Queenstown-Lampeter 1988.

[148] Analogy, not continuity. The similarities seem to be with the ancient cults of Harran in Mesopotamia, not with any specifically Antiochene cult, see M. MOOSA, *Extremist Shiites...*, 339-341.

GIORGIO BONAMENTE

Dall'imperatore divinizzato all'imperatore santo

Il libro di Lucien Cérfaux e di Julien Tondriau, che considerarono il culto imperiale come concorrenziale al cristianesimo[1], seguì a breve distanza di tempo l'VIII Congresso internazionale di Storia delle religioni tenutosi a Roma nell'aprile 1955, che aveva dato origine al volume collettivo su *The Sacral Kingship – La regalità sacra*, pubblicato nel 1959; fra i contributi inerenti il culto imperiale almeno tre, di Jean Bayet, di Kurt Aland e di Friedrich Heiler, richiamavano l'attenzione sui motivi e sui modi in cui il cristianesimo poté assimilare elementi del culto imperiale romano[2].

Ma da più di trenta anni un altrettanto celebre testo, di Pierre Batiffol e di Louis Bréhier, aveva colto i vari aspetti della sopravvivenza del culto imperiale all'interno della Chiesa, a partire da Costantino e per tutta l'età bizantina[3]. In effetti nel momento stesso in cui un imperatore romano adottò come propria *religio* il cristianesimo, accettando il battesimo, si impose il problema di ridefinire tanto il cerimoniale funerario, quanto la concezione relativa alla sua sorte nell'al di là, essendo i due aspetti interdipendenti fin dal tempo di Giulio Cesare e di Augusto. Nella sua «teologia politica», infatti, Eusebio di Cesarea formulò con circospezione non solo

---

[1] L. Cérfaux, J. Tondriau, *Le culte des souverains dans la civilisation romaine: un concurrent du christianisme*, Tournai 1957.
[2] Cfr. *La regalità sacra – The sacral Kingship. Contributi al tema dell'VIII Congresso internazionale di Storia delle religioni (Roma, aprile 1955)*, Leiden 1959. I tre contributi: J. Bayet, *Prodromes sacerdotaux de la divinisation impériale*, 418-434; K. Aland, *Der Abbau des Herrscherkultes im Zeitalter Konstantins*, 493-512 (ora in *Kirchengeschichtliche Entwürfe*, Gütersloh 1960, 240 ss.); F. Heiler, *Fortleben und Wandlungen des antikes Gottkönigtums im Christentum*, 543-580; cfr. G. Bonamente, *L'apoteosi degli imperatori nell'ultima storiografia pagana latina*, in *Studien zur Geschichte der römischen Spätantike. Festgabe für Professor Johannes Straub*, hg.von E. Chrysos, Athen 1989, 19 nota 1.
[3] Cfr. P. Batiffol, L. Bréhier, *Les survivances du culte impérial romain*, Paris 1920: i due contributi, rispettivamente P. Batiffol, *L'Église et les survivances du culte impérial*, 5-33; L. Bréhier, *Les survivances du culte impérial à Byzance*, 35-73.

le tematiche inerenti la sacralità del potere imperiale in quanto tale, ma anche quelle, strettamente connesse, della sorte dell'imperatore dopo la morte, indicando gli elementi ed i limiti della compatibilità tra la divinizzazione tradizionale degli imperatori e la dottrina cristiana[4]. Nella *Historia ecclesiastica* l'apoteosi di Costanzo Cloro appariva motivata sia dalla clemenza e benignità verso i sudditi, sia dalla sua favorevole disposizione verso la dottrina cristiana[5]; quando nel *Triaconteterico* tornò sul tema generale della «divinizzazione di uomini mortali», facendone una motivata contestazione[6], Eusebio aveva già sviluppato, riguardo a Costantino, quella definizione dell'imperatore come «icona» del Padre ed «imitazione» del Figlio, che avrebbe poi dispiegato nella *Vita Constantini*. A sua volta il riconoscimento dell'imperatore come costruttore del «regno di Dio» era una premessa alla sua proiezione nell'assoluto dopo la morte, in ragione della propria *pietas/eusebèia*, dunque delle sue virtù, e del fatto di essere stato scelto espressamente da Dio[7].

Nella *Vita Constantini* l'assunzione in paradiso ha un rilievo fondamentale, fin dall'inizio dell'opera, ove si insiste sulla permanenza della «presenza» di Costantino, il quale, vivendo ormai in una dimensione ultraterrena, veglia sui propri figli ed opera attraverso di loro, conservando intatta, ed anzi accresciuta, la propria potenza. Viene quindi sviluppato il tema di un «regno dopo la morte», concessogli da Dio «nell'eternità senza fine del tempo»[8]. Tale carattere è stato colto in modo significativo da

---

[4] Cfr. R. FARINA, *L'impero e l'imperatore cristiano in Eusebio di Cesarea. La prima teologia politica del cristianesimo*, Zürich 1966; E. PRINZIVALLI, *Storia ed escatologia in Eusebio di Cesarea*, in *Costantino il Grande nell'età bizantina. Atti del Convegno internazionale di studi, Ravenna, 5-8 aprile 2001*, a cura di G. BONAMENTE, A. CARILE, «Bizantinistica» 5 (2003), 97-112 (con bibliografia precedente); A. PINZONE, *Eusebio e la storiografia profana. Il caso della* Praeparatio Evangelica, in *Storiografia e agiografia nella tarda antichità. Alla ricerca delle radici cristiane dell'Europa. Atti del Convegno, Roma 21-22 gennaio 2005*, a cura di G. AMATA, G. MARASCO, «Salesianum» 67 (2005), 653-655.

[5] EUSEB. *Hist. eccl.* 8, 13, 12; cfr. G. BONAMENTE, Optimi principes – principes divi *nell'*Historia Augusta, in stampa in *Historiae Augustae Colloquium Genevense* II, nota 16.

[6] EUSEB. *Log. Basil.*13, 1-5; cfr. *Praepar. Evang.* 2, 8, 1-13 (riguardo Romolo).

[7] R. FARINA, *La «pietas» del servo di Dio Costantino imperatore. Santità e culto di Costantino imperatore nella «Vita di Costantino» di Eusebio di Cesarea*, in *Poteri religiosi e istituzioni: il culto di San Costantino imperatore tra Oriente e Occidente*, a cura di F. SINI, P.P. ONIDA, Torino 2003, 302 s. (con indicazione di tutti i passi significativi); cfr. G. BONAMENTE, *Costantino santo*, «CrSt» 27 (2006), 738.

[8] EUSEB. *Vita Const.* 1, 1, 2-3: «Sia ad Oriente sia ad Occidente, sia verso qualsiasi punto della terra sia verso il cielo stesso, in ogni luogo e dappertutto [...] quel principe benedetto è tuttora presente nell'impero... egli stesso è ancora vivo in potenza e governa

quanti, giudicando la *Vita di Costantino* una sorta di agiografia, l'hanno considerata una *Vita di San Costantino* sia sotto il profilo formale che del contenuto⁹.

La concezione di un imperatore cristiano comportava quindi un confronto ineludibile con l'istituto secolare della *consecratio* degli imperatori defunti in termini di «vita beata» dopo la morte, non solo in quanto uomo, ma specificamente per la funzione politica e religiosa da lui esercitata. Alla sua morte Costantino il Grande ricevette pertanto sia onori propri della *relatio in numerum divorum* tradizionale in Roma, sia un'inedita quanto solenne *depositio* nella Basilica degli Apostoli in Costantinopoli, due rituali che esprimono da un canto la continuità e dall'altro l'evoluzione della concezione e della ritualità in direzione della santificazione dopo la morte.

La *Vita Constantini* presenta lo svolgimento di un cerimoniale di impronta tradizionale svolto in Roma «con il concorso del senato e del popolo», articolato nel *iustitium* (*luctus publicus*) e nella *probatio* (*laudatio*), che erano componenti essenziali della *relatio in numerum divorum*; ancora più esplicita è l'esposizione di *tabulae pictae* di Costantino collocato «nello spazio etereo al di sopra della volta celeste» e l'esplicito riferimento alla legittimazione dei successori¹⁰.

La *Vita Constantini* testimonia che nella «città regina» l'imperatore fu proclamato *divus* ed indica quali siano stati gli aspetti della divinizzazione

---

tutto il mondo in modo migliore di prima, come se si fosse moltiplicato nella successione dei figli... risplendono cinti degli ornamenti che furono del padre loro». Cfr. 4, 67, 3: «E così quel principe benedetto fu il solo sovrano che continuò a regnare anche dopo la morte». Cfr. P. PICCININI, *Ideologia e storia in termini del lessico politico eusebiano: il tempo eterno della* basileia *di Costantino*, in *Costantino il Grande dall'antichità all'umanesimo. Colloquio sul Cristianesimo nel mondo antico, Macerata 18-20 dicembre 1990*, a cura di G. BONAMENTE, F. FUSCO, I-II, Macerata 1992-93, 769-790.

⁹ H. INGLEBERT, *Renommée et sainteté. Historiographie et hagiografie dans les chroniques tardo-antiques latines et dans le* De ortu et obitu patrum *d'Isidore de Seville*, in *Storiografia e agiografia...*, 980. Si può ricordare che Salvatore Calderone si era ripromesso di pubblicare con tale titolo una traduzione ed un commento della *Vita Constantini*; cfr. G. BONAMENTE, *Sulla conversione di Costantino*, in *Salvatore Calderone. Atti del Convegno Internazionale di Studi, Messina-Taormina 19-21 febbraio 2001*, a cura di L. DE SALVO, in stampa, nota 15.

¹⁰ *Vita Const.* 4, 69: «Gli abitanti della *città regina*, sia il senato che il popolo romano... con grida e suppliche chiesero insistentemente che il corpo del loro imperatore venisse trasportato presso di loro, per essere sepolto nella *città regina*». Cfr. W. KIERDORF, *«Funus» und «consecratio». Zu Terminologie und Ablauf der römischen Kaiserapotheose*, «Chiron» 16 (1986), 43-69; M. CLAUSS, *Kaiser und Gott. Herrscherkult im römischen Reich*, Stuttgart 1999, 358.

tradizionale che Eusebio riteneva compatibili con la prospettiva cristiana: sono quelli ai quali viene data maggiore evidenza nell'esposizione, come la «vita dopo la morte»[11] ed il consenso, espresso dal popolo di Roma, alla soluzione dinastica adottata dagli eserciti orientali: «Anche gli abitanti di Roma proclamarono i figli di Costantino, essi soltanto e non altri, imperatori e augusti...» (4,69,2).

Eusebio registra con cura che l'assenza del corpo dell'imperatore venne considerata lesiva dell'istituto da parte degli abitanti della «città regina»[12]; considerazione capziosa, in quanto sapeva bene che esisteva da secoli il rituale del *funus imaginarium*[13], che surrogava in modo pieno tale, peraltro ricorrente, carenza rituale, ma che comunque sortiva l'effetto di sottolineare che il vero funerale era quello svolto a Costantinopoli.

Nella nuova capitale, la «città preferita», fu celebrato infatti il *funus* vero e proprio, alla presenza di Costanzo II, con un cerimoniale decisamente innovativo nella sua bipartizione tra la *pompè* funebre guidata da Costanzo II (componente tradizionale – politica) e la celebrazione del sacrificio della messa all'interno della Basilica degli Apostoli, dopo che si fu allontanato l'imperatore (non ancora battezzato)[14].

Anche a proposito degli onori conferitigli a Costantinopoli Eusebio volle rimarcare che la successione imperiale era garantita dal favore divino (4,71,2); il richiamo agli apostoli è una chiara allusione al fatto che Costantino continuava a detenere il potere imperiale anche dopo la morte, un'argomentazione che si conclude con un'immagine particolarmente ardita: l'imperatore «tre volte benedetto» si sarebbe moltiplicato «come Cristo» nella successione dei figli (4,72).

Ma il modello costantinopolitano del funerale imperiale può essere colto solo se si osserva la forma della sepoltura: il sarcofago di porfido dell'imperatore posto all'interno della Basilica degli Apostoli, al centro

---

[11] EUSEB. *Vita Const.* 4, 69, 2: «Onorando il defunto sovrano con la dedica di ritratti, proprio come se fosse ancora in vita: tali dipinti raffiguravano la distesa del cielo con l'imperatore che dimorava nello spazio etereo al di sopra della volta celeste». Si veda *infra* nota 19 a proposito delle monete di consacrazione.

[12] Oltre al fondamentale L. DE GIOVANNI, *L'imperatore Costantino e il mondo pagano*, Napoli 2003², si veda P.P. ONIDA, *Il divieto di sacrifici di animali nella legislazione di Costantino. Una interpretazione sistematica*, in *Poteri religiosi e istituzioni...*, 163 ss.

[13] H. CHANTRAINE, *«Doppelbestattungen» römischer Kaiser*, «Historia» 29 (1980), 71, 77, 84 s.; G. BONAMENTE, *Il ruolo del senato nella divinizzazione degli imperatori*, in *Humana sapit. Études d'antiquité tardive offertes à L. Cracco Ruggini*, ed. J.-M. CARRIÉ, R. LIZZI TESTA, Turnhout 2002, 5.

[14] EUSEB. *Vita Const.* 4,71,1; cfr. P. FRANCHI DE' CAVALIERI, *I funerali e il sepolcro di Costantino Magno*, Paris 1916-17, 245 ss.

delle dodici stele che li rappresentavano. Il valore simbolico era forte e costituiva un messaggio coerente con l'operato e con la pubblicistica riguardante Costantino, per ciò che concerneva la funzione da lui svolta nei confronti della Chiesa e la sua potenziale assimilazione agli apostoli[15]. Al contempo era ambiguo, in quanto esso evocava tanto la *depositio ad martires* (con la celebrazione dell'eucaristia) quanto l'imitazione di Cristo: in ambedue le direzioni si trattava di significati imbarazzanti per la dottrina cristiana, tanto che Eusebio volle sottolineare che era stato direttamente Costantino ad averlo voluto[16].

Pur nella loro evidente asimmetria, gli onori tributati a Roma ed a Costantinopoli avevano profonde analogie e concorrevano a ribadire il nesso tra il buon governo e la sorte celeste dell'imperatore dopo la morte. Ne sono indizio le monete di consacrazione, nelle quali Eusebio stesso trovò adeguatamente espresso il passaggio di Costantino in una dimensione escatologica; l'iconografia prevalente recava infatti sul recto l'immagine di Costantino *capite velato* (con tanto di epiteto *divus*) e al verso l'imperatore che ascendeva al cielo su una quadriga, mentre era chiamato da una mano dall'alto.

Se è opportuno, ed anzi necessario, ricercare i precedenti sia nell'iconografia tradizionale degli *honores caelestes* e del *katasterismos* dei *boni*

---

[15] EUSEB. *Vita Const.* 4, 60, 1-2. Cfr. G. DAGRON, *Naissance d'une capitale. Constantinople et ses institutions de 330 à 451*, Paris 1974 = G. DAGRON, *Costantinopoli. Nascita di una capitale* (330-541), trad. a cura di A. SERAFINI, Torino 1991, 411 ss.; CALDERONE, *Eusebio di Cesarea e l'ideologia imperiale*, in *Le trasformazioni della cultura nella tarda antichità*, a cura di M. MAZZA, C. GIUFFRIDA, Roma 1985, 1-25; AV. CAMERON, S.G. HALL, *Eusebius. Life of Constantine*, Oxford 1999, 339 ss.; S. REBENICH, *Vom dreizehnten Gott zum dreizehnten Apostel? Der tote Kaiser in der Spätantike*, «ZAChr» 4 (2000), 300-324, 318; M. AMERISE, *Eusebio di Cesarea, Elogio di Costantino. Discorso per il trentennale. Discorso regale*, Milano 2005, 233-236.

[16] EUSEB. *Vita Const.* 4, 71, 2. Cfr. A. KANIUTH, *Die Beisetzung Konstantins des Großen. Untersuchungen zur religiösen Haltung des Kaisers*, Breslau 1941 [Aalen 1974], 9; R. FARINA, *L'impero e l'imperatore cristiano...*, 108. Sulle procedure con cui si attribuiva nel IV secolo il culto proprio dei martiri cfr. H. LECLERCQ, s.v. *Saint*, in F. CABROL, H. LECLERCQ, *Dictionn. d'archéol. chrétienne et de liturgie*, V¹, Paris 1950, 406 ss.; P. BROWN, *Il culto dei santi. L'origine e la diffusione di una nuova religiosità*, Torino 1983, 101 ss.; G. BONAMENTE, *Apoteosi e imperatori cristiani*, in *I Cristiani e l'Impero nel IV secolo. Colloquio sul Cristianesimo nel mondo antico, Atti del Convegno Macerata 17-18 dicembre 1988*, ed. G. BONAMENTE, A. NESTORI, Macerata 1988, 115.

principes[17], sia in due *Panegirici* di pochi anni prima[18], resta fuori discussione che Eusebio poté e volle mettere in rilievo che il messaggio divulgato dalle monete di consacrazione coniate per Costantino fu recepito dai contemporanei come espressione della svolta religiosa da lui impressa all'impero. Invero la prospettiva di Eusebio va messa a confronto con il dato di fatto che le monete di consacrazione di Costantino furono anche le ultime ad essere emesse per gli imperatori romani; questo significa che esse conservavano un equilibrio tra vecchio e nuovo, tanto precario che non si mantenne dopo la morte del primo imperatore cristiano. La loro tipologia fu infatti frutto di un'accorta selezione degli elementi tràditi (presenza della legenda *divus* ed eliminazione di *consecratio*; assenza dei simboli più esplicitamente legati al culto, quali l'altare, il tempio, il levarsi dell'aquila; obliterazione del rogo)[19], ai quali si contrapponeva l'elemento innovativo costituito dal tipo con la quadriga di Costantino che sale al cielo accolto da una mano dall'alto, come si è già detto.

La *ratio* dell'esposizione di Eusebio è comunque che la divinizzazione tradizionale (*consecratio*) era compatibile per alcuni dei suoi aspetti e poteva essere recepita all'interno della concezione cristiana. In modo specifico poteva essere condiviso proprio il nesso sostanziale e strutturale:

---

[17] La quadriga è presente nelle monete da Adriano a Valeriano; cfr. E. BICKERMANN, *Die römische Kaiserapotheose*, «ANRW» 27 (1929), 1-31, ora in *Römischer Kaiserkult*, ed. A. WLOSOK, Darmstadt 1978, 94; P.N. SCHULTEN, *Die Typologie der römischen Konsekrationsprägungen*, Frankfurt a. M. 1979, 28.

[18] I precedenti immediati riguardavano Costanzo Cloro: *Paneg. Lat.* 6, 14, 3 (307 d.C.): *dive Constanti, quem curru paene conspicuo, dum vicinos ortus repetit occasu, Sol ipse invecturus caelo eccepit*; 7, 7, 1, 165 (310 d.C.): *vere enim profecto illi superum templa patuerunt receptusque est consessu caelitum, Iove ipso dexteram porrigente*; cfr. J.R. FEARS, *Princeps a diis electus: the Divine Election of the Emperor as a political concept at Rome* (Papers and Monographs AAR, 36), Rome 1977, 181; S.G. MACCORMACK, *Art and Ceremony in Late Antiquity* (1981) = *Arte e cerimoniale nell'antichità*, Torino 1995, 158 ss.; G. BONAMENTE, *Apoteosi e imperatori cristiani...*, 124 s.; K. ROSEN, *Constantins Weg zum Christentum und die Panegyrici Latini*, in *Costantino il Grande...*, 858 ss.; A. AMICI, *La divinizzazione imperiale in età tetrarchica*, «CrSt» 27 (2005), 355-363 (le attestazioni epigrafiche dell'epiteto *divus*).

[19] Nelle monete (le ultime che possano essere definite «di divinizzazione») coniate in tutte le zecche dell'impero, ad eccezione di quella di Roma e delle altre due sottoposte al controllo di Costante (Aquileia e Siscia), restò la legenda consueta *divus,* ma scomparve *consecratio*. Cfr. S. CALDERONE, *Teologia, politica, successione dinastica e «consecratio» in età costantiniana...*, 215 ss.; 248 s.; P.N. SCHULTEN, *Die Typologie der römischen Konsekrationsprägungen...*, 526, nn. 407-410; ARCE, *Funus imperatorum...*, 163 ss.; G. BONAMENTE, *Apoteosi e imperatori cristiani...*, 121 s. (con bibliografia precedente); M. CLAUSS, *Kaiser und Gott...*, 203 ss.

quello tra l'approvazione dell'operato del *bonus princeps*, ivi compresa la conferma della successione (*probatio*)[20], e la collocazione cosmico-religiosa (*caelestis religio*), consistente nell'ingresso in una dimensione divina (*in deorum numerum recipere*). A conciliare la divinizzazione con la «santificazione» era proprio l'elemento centrale del modello tradizionale, quello per cui l'imperatore era chiamato nei cieli in ragione della sua funzione istituzionale.

Malgrado il collaudo positivo con il primo imperatore cristiano, questa sintesi fra le due concezioni non poté svilupparsi però con i successori, ed anzi nell'anno 359 si verificò un momento di svolta: mentre Costanzo II esercitava una prova di forza con i vescovi per far accettare loro il «credo datato» in due concili, a Oriente e ad Occidente, in Costantinopoli il vescovo Macedonio fece rimuovere il sarcofago di Costantino dal centro della Basilica degli Apostoli, adducendo a pretesto i danni riportati dall'edificio durante il terremoto del 24 agosto 358. Traslato momentaneamente nel *martyrium* di S. Acacio[21], il sarcofago del primo imperatore cristiano sarebbe tornato nel complesso di edifici connessi con la Basilica degli Apostoli, ma in un contesto trasformato, inaugurato il 9 aprile del 370, sotto Valente, nel quale il Mausoleo era nettamente distinto dalla Basilica[22].

---

[20] Su questa tematica si rinvia a M. STROTHMANN, Sepultura more perfecta. *Zur legitimatorischen Funktion des Totenkultes in der römischen Kaiserzeit*, «Arch. Religionsgesch.» 2 (2000), 103 ss.

[21] Il 1 gennaio 360 Macedonio fu deposto e sostituito da Eudossio di Antiochia (*Chron. Pasch.* A. 360, 224, 11-225, Bidez-Winkelmann); cfr. SOCR. *HE* 2, 38; SOZOM. *Hist.eccl.* 4, 21, 6; R. LIZZI, Discordia in urbe. *Pagani e cristiani in rivolta*, in *Pagani e cristiani da Giuliano l'Apostata al sacco di Roma. Atti del Convegno Internazionale di Studi, Rende 12-13 novembre 1993*, a cura di F.E. CONSOLINO, Soveria Mannelli 1995, 122 e nota 30; G. BONAMENTE, *Chiesa e impero nel IV secolo: Costanzo II fra il 357 e il 361*, in *La comunità cristiana di Roma. La sua vita e la sua cultura dalle origini all'Alto Medio Evo*, a cura di L. PANI ERMINI, P. SINISCALCO, Roma 2000, 113-138; G. BONAMENTE, *La figura dell'imperatore in Giovanni Crisostomo*, in *Omaggio a Rosario Soraci. Politica retorica e simbolismo del primato: Roma e Costantinopoli (secoli IV-VII). Atti del Convegno Internazionale (Catania 2001)*, ed. F. ELIA, II, Catania 2004, 195; F. FATTI, *Giuliano a Cesarea. La politica ecclesiastica del principe apostata*, Roma 2010, 35.

[22] Il processo è chiaro soltanto nelle sue linee fondamentali: dalla sepoltura del primo imperatore cristiano all'interno della Basilica degli Apostoli/Mausoleo si passò a quella degli imperatori in un Mausoleo (a pianta circolare), cui ne sarebbe stato aggiunto un altro a pianta cruciforme sotto Giustiniano. Si ritiene che sia stato Costanzo II ad iniziare la costruzione del primo Mausoleo (e con ogni probabilità anche il restauro della originaria Basilica degli Apostoli) già nell'anno 359. L'opera fu completata il 9 aprile 370 ed alla stessa data si ascrive anche la riapertura al culto della Basilica; cfr.

L'intervento del vescovo di Costantinopoli aveva interrotto il rapporto simbolico tra gli Apostoli e l'imperatore, ma anche quello reale tra vescovi ed imperatore, quest'ultimo definito con formule emblematiche sia al tempo di Costantino (*epìskopos tòn ektòs*) che di Costanzo II (*episcopus episcoporum*). Il suo significato risulta interpretato in modo articolato, con forte intento apologetico, in testi di Giovanni Crisostomo ai quali offrono riscontro sia la testimonianza di Giuliano l'Apostata, che a brevissima distanza di tempo dalla rimozione del sarcofago di Costantino, nel *Discorso contro il cinico Eraclio*, fece riferimento alla tomba che Costanzo II aveva preparato per sé e per i suoi per ispirazione del Fato[23], sia Agostino di Ippona, come si vedrà in prosieguo.

Giovanni Crisostomo trattò espressamente il tema in due omelie pronunciate in Antiochia, l'*Adversus Iudaeos et Gentiles quod Christus sit Deus*, databile fra il 386 ed il settembre 387[24], e l'*Homilia XXVI in Epistulam II ad Corinthios*, datata fra il 386 ed il 397[25], intervenendo su due versanti: da un canto contestando il senso della sepoltura di Costantino nella Basilica degli Apostoli in nome della differenza incommensurabile tra il carisma proprio degli apostoli e il potere degli imperatori, dall'altro

---

HIERON. *Chron. ad a. 358*; SOCR. *Hist. eccl.* 2, 38; SOZOM. *Hist. eccl.* 4, 21, 3-6; ZONAR. *Ep. h.* 13, 11, 24; R. KRAUTHEIMER, *Zu Konstantins Apostelkirche in Konstantinopel*, in *Mullus. Festschr. Th. Klauser*, «JAChr», 1 (1964), 228; G. DAGRON, *Naissance d'une capitale...*, 407-415; C. MANGO, *Constantine's Mausoleum and the translation of relics*, «Byz. Zeitschr.» 83 (1990), 56; R. LIZZI, Discordia in urbe. *Pagani e cristiani in rivolta...*, 122 e nota 30; G. DAGRON, *Empereur et prêtre. Étude sur le «césaropapisme» byzantin*, Paris 1996, 151 ss.; 372 nota 43 (con bibliografia precedente); S. REBENICH, *Vom dreizehnten Gott...*, 300-324.

[23] Giuliano l'Apostata sembra avere fatto riferimento al Mausoleo annesso alla Basilica degli Apostoli, quando notava con sarcasmo che Costanzo II non aveva fatto altro che preparare una tomba per sé e per i suoi: IULIAN. *Adv. Heracl. Cyn.* VII 228 b-c. Sul contesto cfr. G. BONAMENTE, *Sviluppo e discontinuità nella legislazione antipagana: da Costantino il Grande ai figli*, in *Istituzioni, carismi ed esercizio del potere (IV-VI sec. d.C.). Atti del Convegno internazionale Perugia 25-27 giugno 2008*, a cura di G. BONAMENTE, R. LIZZI TESTA, in stampa, 63, nota 14; vd. *infra*, nota 111.

[24] IOHANN. CHRYS. *Homil. adversus Iudaeos* (PG 48, 843-942); cfr. G. BONAMENTE, *La figura dell'imperatore in Giovanni Crisostomo...*, 191 ss.; W. PRADELS, R. BRÄNDLE, M. HEIMGARTNER, *The sequence and dating of the series of John Chrysostom's eight discourses Adversus Judaeos*, «ZAC» 6 (2006), 90-116; G. BONAMENTE, *Teodosio il Grande e la fine dell'apoteosi imperiale*, in *Entre política, religión y legislación (ss. IV y V d. C.): convergencias, antagonismos y rectificaciones. Coloquio Internacional hispano-italiano, Zaragoza, 29-30 oct. 2009*, in stampa.

[25] L'arco cronologico va dal 386 al 397; per la datazione è considerata importante la menzione delle città di Roma e di Costantinopoli; cfr. C. TIRONE, *Giovanni Crisostomo. Commento alle lettere di S. Paolo ai Corinti*, II, Siena 1962, 5.

investendo con le sue argomentazioni la *consecratio* stessa degli imperatori col proporre un confronto a tutto campo tra le sepolture imperiali e quelle degli apostoli[26].

Sotto il profilo dottrinale si trattava di distinguere tra il potere di re ed imperatori (tra i quali egli sceglie quale simbolo Alessandro Magno), fondato sugli eserciti, ed il carisma degli apostoli e dei loro successori, dotato di un fondamento ed una dimensione trascendenti. Il Crisostomo aveva buon gioco a mettere a confronto diretto i mausolei degli imperatori e dello stesso Alessandro Magno, di cui denunciava il degrado e l'incuria, rispetto alle sepolture degli apostoli e dei martiri, mèta di visite e di pellegrinaggi[27]; ciò gli consentiva di puntare infine l'indice sul Mausoleo di Costantinopoli, per concludere la sua tesi con una formula non precisamente consequenziale, ma di grande efficacia: dopo la morte, gli imperatori diventano *portinai del pescatore*[28].

L'argomentazione aveva fondamento dottrinale in quanto si richiamava al *novissimum* della morte e riceveva particolare efficacia nel riferirsi ad un fatto recente: se la traslazione di Costantino il Grande dalla Basilica degli Apostoli alla chiesa di S. Acacio risaliva ormai a circa trenta anni prima, il completamento del Mausoleo era avvenuto nel 370, ed erano ormai numerosi gli imperatori che vi erano stati sepolti: oltre a Costantino, Costanzo II[29], Gioviano[30] e Valentiniano I[31]. Vi sarebbero stati sepolti suc-

---

[26] IOHANN. CHRYS. *Hom. XXVI in Epist. II ad Corinth*. 5: dal principio secondo cui prestigio e autorità sono riconducibili alla grazia divina derivava che il carisma proprio degli apostoli era incommensurabilmente superiore a quello dell'imperatore: il primo era capace di superare la barriera della morte e di dominare gli spiriti, il secondo rimaneva circoscritto al periodo ed ai poteri propri del regno.

[27] IOHANN. CHRYS. *Homil. XXVI in Ep. II ad Corinth*. 5, PG 582; cfr. *supra* e *Adversus Iudaeos et Gentiles* 9, PG 48, 825.

[28] IOHANN. CHRYS. *Hom. XXVI in Epist. II ad Corinth*. 5, PG 61, 580-582.

[29] GREG. NAZ. *Orat. In Iulianum* 5, 17, 5; HIER. *Chron. ad a. 361*; AMMIAN. 21, 16, 20 (fu Gioviano, allora *protector domesticus*, a ricondurre le spoglie di Costanzo II dalla Cilicia fino a Costantinopoli, ove le cerimonie funebri furono presiedute da Giuliano); J. ARCE, *Los funerales del emperador Constancio II (a. 361 d. C.)*, in *Homenaje al prof. Fr. R. Adrados*, Madrid 1987, 29-39. Quanto ad Elena, sepolta in un mausoleo imperiale a Roma, fu traslata successivamente in Costantinopoli; cfr. EUSEB. *Vita Const*. 3, 47, 1; CONSTANT. PORPH. *De caeremoniis aulae Byzantinae libri duo*, PG 112, 1, Bonn 1829, 42, coll. 1190-1209; J. ARCE, Funus imperatorum..., 115; C. MANGO, *Constantine's Mausoleum...*, 51 ss.; S.G. MACCORMACK, *Arte e cerimoniale nell'antichità...*, 190.

[30] Morto il 17 febbraio 364, Gioviano fu traslato a Costantinopoli nel complesso dei Santi Apostoli; cfr. AMMIAN. 26, 1, 3; ZONAR. 13, 14, 23 Bonn III 72.

[31] Morto in Pannonia nel 375, fu anch'egli traslato a Costantinopoli e sepolto nel mausoleo il 21 febbraio 382; cfr. AUS. *Grat. actio* 7, 2: *pater divinis honoribus consecratus*;

cessivamente anche Teodosio[32], nonché – ma solo nel secolo successivo – Giuliano[33]; degli altri imperatori del IV secolo non vi risultano sepolti Valente, il cui corpo non fu ritrovato dopo la rotta di Adrianopoli, mentre Graziano era stato sepolto a Milano e altrettanto sarebbe poi accaduto a Valentiniano II[34].

Nelle Omelie sopra indicate il Crisostomo faceva un uso apologetico di una dottrina sui rapporti tra il potere imperiale e l'autorità dei vescovi, che si andava consolidando, sia nelle opere esegetiche e dottrinali sia nella prassi, ad opera di vescovi autorevoli, quali Ambrogio e Damaso, attirando gli ascoltatori verso una prospettiva particolare, quella di confrontare i carismi di re e di imperatori rispetto a quelli degli apostoli nel tempo successivo alla morte: poteva contrapporre così l'inerzia e l'oblio dei primi all'efficacia taumaturgica ed alla frequentazione dei sepolcri degli altri.

Le esperienze conflittuali con Costanzo II, l'aperta ostilità di Giuliano l'Apostata, quindi la politica di equilibrio di Valentiniano I, contraddetta dall'aperta preferenza di Valente per gli omèi, avevano indotto i vescovi a contestare la tutela sulla Chiesa esercitata da Costantino, nella misura in cui essa aveva comportato un'intromissione nelle questioni dottrinali e disciplinari. Il fallimento della guerra di Costanzo II e di Giuliano contro i Persiani, poi la grave sconfitta di Adrianopoli, subita il 9 agosto 378, diedero anche il senso di una crisi politica grave, di un impero che non riusciva a mantenere saldi i confini.

In questo quadro storico variarono i rapporti di forza con una Chiesa che radicava la propria struttura organizzativa entro l'impero ed era guidata, sia in Roma, sia nelle grandi sedi episcopali, da personalità di grande rilievo il cui prestigio era concorrenziale a quello dei funzionari di più alto grado e degli stessi imperatori[35]. La funzione carismatica assunta e riconosciuta a Costantino appariva sempre più priva di senso: non erano più gli imperatori il tramite del favore divino per l'impero, i custodi e i tutori della fede cristiana, ma era la legge divina a costituire il parametro del

---

AMMIAN. 30, 10, 1: *corpusque curatum ad sepulturam, ut missum Constantinopolim inter divorum reliquias humaretur*.

[32] Dopo il funerale solenne in Milano, Teodosio fu traslato nel Mausoleo di Costantinopoli il 9 nov. 395 a cura di Arcadio; cfr. J. ARCE, Funus imperatorum..., 116.

[33] Giuliano fu sepolto in un primo momento a Tarso. Nel 457 l'imperatore Leone ne decise la traslazione a Costantinopoli; J. ARCE, *Estudios sobre el emperador Fl. Cl. Julianus*, Madrid 1984, 171 ss.

[34] AMBROS. *De obitu Valentiniani*, 79, *PL* 16, 1382-3.

[35] Si veda ora *Le relazioni tra pagani e cristiani: nuove prospettive su un antico tema*, a cura di R. LIZZI TESTA, «CrSt» 31 (2009), 255-481.

governo imperiale e in subordine era la fede – cristiana nicena – ad assicurare il successo dell'imperatore, secondo l'assioma formulato da Gregorio di Nazianzo, che considerò provvidenziale la morte di Giuliano[36], quindi da Ambrogio, nella *Expositio evangelii secundum Lucam*, all'indomani della sconfitta di Adrianopoli: *Dei minister sit qui bene potestate utitur*[37].

Nel volgere di pochi decenni la stessa figura di Costantino, duramente contestata in prospettiva anticristiana al tempo di Giuliano[38], venne messa in discussione anche per la funzione di tutore della fede cristiana, che egli aveva espletato nella guida del Concilio di Nicea, ma che risultava compromessa – agli occhi degli atanasiani – dai suoi successivi tentativi di recuperare Ario. In realtà Costantino aveva perseguito con coerenza il suo compito di garantire l'unità dell'impero sotto il profilo del culto e della religione e altrettanto aveva fatto il figlio Costanzo II con la formulazione di un credo omèo noto come «credo datato»[39]; ma nella prospettiva della Chiesa ciò era apparso sempre più chiaramente come intromissione indebita, riassunta nell'espressione polemica *episcopus episcoporum*, addirittura come persecuzione, e la Chiesa, con Damaso e con Ambrogio, aveva prevalso.

---

[36] La parte iniziale della prima *Invettiva contro Giuliano* è uno scomposto tripudio per la morte dell'Apostata; cfr. *infra* nota 116.

[37] AMBROS. *Exp. Ev. sec. Lucam* 4,29; cfr. *Epist.* 20, 21; 40,41; 51; F. KOLB, *Das Bussakt von Mailand: Zum Verhältnis von Staat und Kirche in der Spätantike*, in *Geschichte und Gegenwart. Festschrift für K. D. Erdmann*, hg. von H. BOOCKMANN, K. JÜRGENSEN, G. STOLTENBERG, Neumünster 1980, 41-74; M. SORDI, *La concezione politica di Ambrogio*, in *I Cristiani e l'Impero nel IV secolo...*, 150 ss.; K. GROSS-ALBENHAUSEN, *Imperator christianissimus. Der christliche Kaiser bei Ambrosius und Johannes Chrysostomus*, Frankfurt a. M. 1999, 144 ss.; M. SORDI, *L'impero romano-cristiano al tempo di Ambrogio*, Milano 2000, 36 ss.

[38] Cfr. V. NERI, *Medius Princeps. Storia e immagine di Costantino nella storiografia latina pagana*, Bologna 1992; R. LIZZI TESTA, *Alle origini della tradizione pagana su Costantino e il senato romano (Amm. 21, 10, 8 e Zos. 2, 32, 1)*, in *Transformations of Late Antiquity. Essays for Peter Brown*, ed. P. ROUSSEAU, M. PAPOUTSAKIS, Farnham (Surrey)-Burlington 2009, 85-128.

[39] Cfr. D. BARNES, *Athanasius and Constantius. Theology and Politics in the Constantinian Empire*, Cambridge, MA, 1993; P. BARCELÓ, *Constantius II. Und seine Zeit. Die Anfänge des Staatskirchentums*, Stuttgart 2004; R.M. ERRINGTON, *Roman Imperial Policy from Julian to Theodosius*, Chapell Hill 2006; S. DIEFENBACH, *Kaiser, Kirche, Konfession: zum Verhältnis von Reichskirchenpolitik und politischer Integration im römischen Imperium unter Constantius II (337-361)*, in *Contested Monarchy. Integrating the Roman Empire in the 4th Century AD*, Intern. Conference, Konstanz, July 9-11, 2009, hg. von J. WIENAND, in stampa.

Girolamo teneva conto dei tentativi di appropriazione della figura di Costantino da parte degli ariani e denunciava, intorno al 380, che questi non costituiva un modello, ricordando espressamente il battesimo impartito dal vescovo ariano Eusebio di Nicomedia[40]. Ma gli negava anche il ruolo di tutore della Chiesa al punto da indicarlo come responsabile delle sue discordie interne. Così facendo inficiava i presupposti della sua santificazione: sul piano della fede ne metteva in dubbio l'ortodossia, sul piano etico registrava temi della tradizione storiografica ostile a Costantino – peraltro fondati – quali lo spergiuro nel far uccidere il cognato Licinio, la condanna a morte del figlio Crispo e l'uccisione della moglie Fausta[41].

Nel *Chronicon* veniva quindi registrato un fatto storico veritiero, quanto al battesimo impartito da Eusebio di Nicomedia, e veniva riportata una valutazione storica fondata, che riassumeva quanto si pensava di Costantino il Grande nell'età di Damaso, di Ambrogio e di Giovanni Crisostomo. Ma queste testimonianze non erano funzionali alle esigenze della Chiesa, né sotto il profilo dottrinale né sotto il profilo storiografico e solo il prestigio dell'Autore e la specifica funzione del genere letterario in cui esse comparivano, ne hanno assicurato la conservazione.

Alla Chiesa nicena serviva un Costantino semplificato, depurato degli aspetti più crudeli della sua azione politica, da identificare con le formule teologiche del concilio del 325, ma senza ricordare la funzione di controllo esercitata su quel concilio[42], che fosse insomma il primo imperatore cristiano e come tale fosse esempio di quella «vera fede» che la Chiesa ancorò al simbolo niceno-costantinopolitano proprio nell'età di Teodosio il Grande. Questo equivale a dire che mentre Girolamo ha presentato un Costantino autentico, era già forte la propensione a semplificarne ed assolutizzarne la figura, strappandola dal suo contesto storico e facendone un simbolo disponibile anche per le più ardite manipolazioni, che si sarebbero verificate nei secoli successivi, a cominciare dagli *actus Sylvestri*, per finire con la *Donatio*.

---

[40] HIERON. *Chron. ad aa. 306, 327, 334, 337* (*Constantinus extremo vitae suae tempore ab Eusebio Nicomedensi episcopo baptizatus in Arrianum dogma declinat. A quo usque in praesens tempus ecclesiarum rapinae et totius orbis est secuta discordia*).

[41] Eutropio, autore del *Breviarium*, ma anche *magister scrinii memoriae* sotto Valente e prefetto del pretorio sotto Teodosio (a lui è indirizzata la costituzione *CTh* 16, 5, 6 del 10 gennaio 381), è tra le fonti di Girolamo; cfr. V. NERI, *La figura di Costantino negli scrittori cristiani dell'età di Onorio*, «Simblos» 1 (1995), 231 ss.

[42] Cfr. K.M. GIRARDET, *Kaisertum, Religionspolitik und das Recht von Staat und Kirche in der Spätantike*, Bonn 2009 (con riferimenti ai numerosi studi precedenti).

Esemplare, anche per la sua precocità, è il trattamento di Rufino di Aquileia, che proprio all'inizio del V secolo, tra silenzi sui punti controversi (uccisione di Crispo e di Fausta, fondazione di Costantinopoli e battesimo), contraffazione della cronologia (attribuzione della reintegrazione di Ario a Costanzo II)[43] e dissimulazione del ruolo svolto da Costantino nel Concilio di Nicea[44], riuscì a presentare un Costantino appiattito sull'ortodossia nicena, utile simbolo all'interno della «storia sacra», ma già disancorato dal contesto storico. Né mancavano le premesse, visto che Liberio, negli anni 353/4, aveva indicato a Costanzo II il rapporto inscindibile Costantino-Nicea quale esempio da seguire[45], che nel concilio di Rimini, del 359, l' iniziale resistenza dei vescovi niceni alle pretese di Costanzo II si era richiamata al precedente di Costantino[46] e che nel *Contra Constantium* Ilario aveva proposto il padre – quale custode della dottrina nicena – come termine di paragone per Costanzo II[47].

Il *De obitu Theodosii* offrì ad Ambrogio l'occasione, il 25 febbraio 395, per riformulare su nuove basi la figura di Costantino e per imporgli un confronto con Teodosio dalla prospettiva del secondo. Non solo Costantino venne svuotato della sua fisionomia storica, con l'obliterazione di ogni riferimento all'opera di governo ed alla sua stessa personalità, mentre gli si riconosceva come unico merito l'aver professato la fede, essendo per questo premiato con la «pace di Dio»; ma la sua esaltazione e la sua esemplarità furono imposti dall'esterno e consistettero nella scoperta della croce di Cristo – da parte della madre Elena – e nella grandiosa metafora

---

[43] RUFIN. *Hist eccl.* 1, 12-13; analogo il procedimento di Sulpicio Severo in *Chron.* 2, 36, 5-6 (attribuì a Costantino la volontà di richiamare Atanasio nel 343, sei anni dopo la morte!); cfr. V. NERI, *La figura di Costantino...*, 231 ss.; V. AIELLO, *La fortuna della notizia geronimiana su Costantino «eretico»*, «Messana», 13 (1992), 225; G. BONAMENTE, *Sull'ortodossia di Costantino. Gli* Actus Sylvestri *dall'invenzione all'autenticazione*, «RSBS» 2, 6 (2004), Spoleto 2005, 11-12.

[44] RUF. *Hist. eccl.* 1, 2; 5.

[45] HILAR. PICTAV. *Coll. Antiar.* A 7, 1, CSEL 65, 89; cfr. K. M. GIRARDET, *Kaiser Konstantius II. als «episcopus episcoporum» und das Herrscherbild des kirchlichen Widerstandes (Ossius von Corduba und Lucifer von Caralis)*, «Historia» 26 (1977), 95 ss. ora in K.M. GIRARDET, *Kaisertum...*, 295 ss.; K. ROSEN, *Ilario di Poitiers e la relazione tra la chiesa e lo stato*, in *I Cristiani e l'Impero nel IV secolo...*, 63 ss.

[46] HILAR. PICTAV. *Coll. Antiar.* 5, 1, 1, CSEL 65, 79; cfr. M. SIMONETTI, *s. v. Liberio*, in *Enciclopedia dei Papi*, Roma 2000, 341 ss.

[47] HILAR. PICTAV. *Contra Const.* 27; ATHAN. *Apol. de fuga sua* 26, PG 25, 678; *De syn.* 10; *H. A.* 51, PG 25, 754.

dell'uso di due chiodi della crocifissione, rispettivamente come corona e come freno (del cavallo) dell'imperatore[48].

Sono questioni ben note nella loro potente carica ideale e per l'eco propagatasi nei secoli; qui importa notare che il Costantino di Ambrogio è configurato come prototipo di Teodosio ed è proposto come un simbolo autonomo, snaturato dalla cornice di fatti non autentici, tutti efficaci sul piano esegetico e pastorale, ma per l'appunto estranei alla sua dimensione storica e di indimostrata veridicità[49].

A questo Costantino venne comunque confermata la collocazione nella pace eterna, in paradiso, anche se è naturale che sia stata la chiamata di Teodosio «nelle tende di Cristo, nella Gerusalemme celeste» a tenere la scena[50]; ma ciò che appare significativo è altro, cioè una «eticizzazione»[51] dei motivi della santificazione dell'imperatore Teodosio, del quale Ambrogio mise in primo piano le virtù morali, segnalandole già al par. 12 («un imperatore devoto, un imperatore misericordioso, un imperatore fedele»), insistendo nel richiamarsi alla sua *misericordia* ed alla sua *humilitas*[52].

---

[48] M. SORDI, *La concezione politica di Ambrogio...*, 143 ss.; V. NERI, *La figura di Costantino...*, 243-252 (con un puntuale confronto fra i due imperatori); K. ROSEN, *Geschichte der politischen Ideen. Von der Antike zur Gegenwart*, Frankfurt a. M. 1996 = *Il pensiero politico dell'antichità*, Bologna 1999, 174; R. LIZZI TESTA, *Legislazione imperiale e reazione pagana. I limiti del conflitto*, in *Le relazioni tra pagani e cristiani...*, 390.

[49] F.E. CONSOLINO, *Il significato dell'*inventio crucis *nel* de obitu Theodosii, «Ann. Fac. Lettere e Filosofia Firenze» 5 (1984), 176.

[50] AMBROS. *De obitu Theodosii* 2; 31-32: annunciata fin dall'inizio (par. 2), ripetuta durante l'omelia, viene ripresa con enfasi al par. 31 – che costituisce la conclusione della prima parte – nella forma del ritorno di Teodosio «nella pace».

[51] Il termine è stato adottato da Elias Bickermann a conclusione del suo contributo del 1929 (*supra*, nota 17); esso mette in rilievo lo sviluppo di un tema che affiora ripetutamente nella tradizione antica sull'istituto della divinizzazione degli imperatori, da Svetonio (*Vesp.* 23, 8: *Vae, puto deus fio*) a Cassio Dione, il quale sostiene, in un contesto significativo, che l'uomo avrebbe semmai potuto diventare simile agli dèi grazie alla virtù, ma non per decreto del senato (Dio Cass. 52, 35, 5); cfr. G. BONAMENTE, *L'apoteosi degli imperatori nell' ultima storiografia pagana latina...*, 22-25.

[52] *Dilexi virum misericordem, humilem in imperio, corde puro et pectore mansueto praeditum, qualem Dominus amare consuevit*: cfr. N. DUVAL, *Formes profanes et formes bibliques dans les orations funèbres de saint Ambroise*, in *Christianisme et formes littéraires dans l'Antiquité tardive en Occident*, ed. M. FUHRMANN, Genf 1977, 235-301; F.E. CONSOLINO, *L'*Optimus princeps *secondo S. Ambrogio: virtù imperatorie e virtù cristiane nelle orazioni funebri per Valentiniano e Teodosio*, «RSI» 96 (1984), 1025-1045; M. BIERMANN, *Die Leichenreden des Ambrosius von Mailand. Rethorik, Predigt, Politik*, Stuttgart 1995, 93 ss.; K. ROSEN, *Geschichte der politischen Ideen...*, 174; M.

In realtà il *De obitu Theodosii* è un'originale riflessione su un modello sostanzialmente inedito, di un imperatore battezzato da tempo[53], che aveva fatto professione di appartenenza alla Chiesa, che aveva sostenuto in modo decisivo la dottrina nicena[54], che si era adeguato – talora invero non di buon grado – a confrontare le sue scelte politiche con la dottrina ecclesiale. Ambrogio doveva quindi indicare entro quali termini Teodosio entrava nella casa del Padre come uomo o come imperatore, ed optò decisamente per la prima dimensione, privilegiando il tema del rapporto diretto, personale, tra l'imperatore e Dio.

Il valore di questa connessione tra la morte del buon imperatore e la sua «santificazione» va meglio compreso nel confronto con la definizione coeva della sorte ultraterrena dei buoni vescovi, come si può osservare nei casi di Cipriano, Atanasio, Gregorio il Taumaturgo e Basilio, ma in modo particolare si imponevano all'attenzione i casi del vescovo di Tessalonica Acolio, cui Ambrogio stesso aveva attribuito carattere di esemplarità, di Eusebio di Vercelli, definito *confessor*, e di Filastrio[55].

Le argomentazioni di Ambrogio riguardo Teodosio trovavano un solido punto di appoggio nella recente vittoria su Eugenio, nel settembre del 394, che il vescovo stesso aveva accreditato pubblicamente e platealmente

---

SORDI, *La morte di Teodosio e il* De obitu Theodosii *di Ambrogio*, «ACD» 36 (2000), 131-136.

[53] Fu battezzato da Acolio poco dopo l'assunzione del titolo di Augusto; cfr. SOCRAT. *Hist. eccl.*, 5, 6; SOZOM. *Hist. eccl.*, 7, 4.

[54] Cfr. *CTh* 16, 1, 2, sul cui significato si veda ora R. LIZZI TESTA, *Legislazione imperiale e reazione pagana...*, 391 s.

[55] AMBROS. *Epist.* 51, 7-8; 12 (ed. M. ZELZER, CSEL 82, 2, Wien 1990); cfr. L. CRACCO RUGGINI, *Il tempo per la santità e per i miracoli*, in *Quinto Seminario sobre el monacato. El monasterio en su vida cotidiana: el espacio y el tiempo, Aguilar de Campoo, Julio de 1991*, «Codex Aquilarensis» 6 (1992), 113 s. (per l'appropriazione del culto della reliquia di Giovanni Battista da parte di Teodosio); M. FORLIN PATRUCCO, *Modelli di santità e santità episcopale nel IV secolo: l'elaborazione dei padri cappadoci*, in *Modelli di santità e modelli di comportamento. Contrasti, intersezioni, complementarità*, a cura di G. BARONE, M. CAFFIERO, F. SCORZA BARCELLONA, Torino 1994, 65-77; R. LIZZI TESTA, *I vescovi e i potenti della terra: definizione e limite del ruolo episcopale nelle due partes imperii fra IV e V secolo d.C.*, in *L'évêque dans la cité du IVe au Ve siècle. Actes de la table ronde organisée par l'Istituto Patristico Augustinianum et l'École française de Rome (1-2 déc. 1995)*, Roma 1998, 86; C. RAPP, *Holy Bishops in Late Antiquity. The nature of Christian Leadership in an Age of Transition*, Berkely-Los Angeles-London 2005; R. LIZZI TESTA, *Martino vescovo santo: un modello di santità nell'Occidente tardoantico*, «CrSt» 29 (2008), 324-332; EAD., *Il vescovo santo come mediatore divino per la città degli uomini*, in *Mediadores con lo divino en el mundo mediterráneo antiguo. Actas Congreso Internacional de Historia de las Religiones, Palma 13-15 octubre 2005*, in stampa.

come opera dell'intervento divino e come effetto della *fides* dell'imperatore (*recognoscitis nempe quos vobis Theodosii fides triumphos adquisiverit*)[56]. La rielaborazione in termini provvidenzialistici della vittoria finì per stravolgere la realtà, per cui nel volgere di pochi anni la dura e sanguinosa battaglia al Frigido, durata ben due giorni, fu fatta apparire come una «vittoria incruenta» conseguita dalla fede e dalle preghiere di Teodosio[57]; ma ancor più significativo fu il procedimento espositivo e narrativo messo in atto nell'orazione funebre, per cui al centro della battaglia venne collocato un Teodosio che pregava il «suo» Dio in assoluta solitudine, dopo essersi svestito delle armi.

Questa riproduzione di modelli biblici[58] aveva una assoluta attualità culturale e dottrinale, che connotava la figura del vescovo «santo»[59] per il

---

[56] Durante l'usurpazione di Eugenio Ambrogio aveva rinvenuto le reliquie dei santi Vitale e Agricola; subito dopo la vittoria di Teodosio aveva proclamato che essa era frutto dell'intervento divino; cfr. AMBROS. *Epist. Extra coll.* 2 e 3; 10 [57], 6 (ad Eugenio); 61, 1 (a Teodosio); *De obitu Theodosii* 7; M. BIERMANN, *Die Leichenreden des Ambrosius von Mailand...*, Stuttgart 1995, 93 ss.; F. PASCHOUD, *La figure de Théodose chez les historiens païens*, in *Actas Congreso internacional La Hispania de Teodosio (Segovia-Coca, 3-6 octubre 1995)*, Madrid 1997, I, 193 ss.; ID., *Eunape, Olympiodore, Zosime. Scripta minora. Recueil d'articles, avec addenda, corrigenda, mise à jour et indices*, Bari 2006, 353 ss. (con bibliografia precedente).

[57] Nella *Gratiarum actio* per il consolato di Probino e di Olibrio del 395 era ancora menzionato un grande numero di caduti: CLAUDIAN. *Carmina* 1, 110-112; nell'orazione che Giovanni Crisostomo tenne a Costantinopoli per il quarto anniversario della morte di Teodosio, il 17 gennaio 399, il momento cruciale della battaglia al *Frigidus* diventò un'epopea divina, con Teodosio in atto di pregare, in solitudine e addirittura spogliato delle insegne imperiali (IOHANN. CHRYS. *Om.* 6, 2, 355, PG 63, 491-2); a circa venti anni di distanza Orosio avrebbe affermato che la battaglia al Frigido si era conclusa con la morte di due persone soltanto, Eugenio ed Arbogaste (OROS. *Hist. adv. Pag.* 7, 35, 19). Cfr. G. ZECCHINI, *S. Ambrogio e le origini del motivo della vittoria incruenta*, «Rivista di Storia della Chiesa in Italia» 38 (1984), 391-404; R. PERELLI, *La vittoria «cristiana» del Frigido*, in *Pagani e cristiani da Giuliano l'Apostata al sacco di Roma...*, 258 ss.; F. PASCHOUD, *Pour un mille six centième anniversaire: le Frigidus en ébullition*, «AnTard» 5 (1997), 275-280 (con una complessiva analisi critica); G. BONAMENTE, *La figura dell'imperatore in Giovanni Crisostomo...*, 210 ss.

[58] Esempi pertinenti sono quello di Mosé, che sosteneva con la preghiera i soldati di Giosué mentre combattevano contro Amalek (*Es.* 17, 9-11), oppure di Eliseo, che difese con la sola preghiera la città di Dotan dall'assedio degli Aramei (*Re* 6, 17-23); cfr. L. CRACCO RUGGINI, *Il profeta Eliseo, modello episcopale fra IV e V secolo*, in Historiam perscrutari. *Miscellanea di studi offerti a Ottorino Pasquato*, ed. M. MARITANO, Roma 2002, 239-253; R. LIZZI TESTA, *Il vescovo santo...*, supra.

[59] R. LIZZI TESTA, *Tra i classici e la Bibbia: l'*otium *come forma di santità episcopale*, in *Modelli di santità e modelli di comportamento: contrasti, intersezioni, complementarietà*, a cura di G. BARONE ET AL., Torino 1994, 43-64.

suo *otium,* inteso come distacco dal mondo attivo e atto di comunicazione diretta con Dio, un carattere che in quegli stessi anni, e proprio ad opera di Ambrogio, era stato sviluppato come motivo di distinzione del vescovo[60].

La suggestiva interpretazione della recente vittoria come risultato della protezione divina era coerente con la dottrina ambrosiana sulla funzione imperiale e dava un contenuto dottrinale all'immagine di un *princeps* cristiano che ascendeva in paradiso in quanto dotato delle principali virtù morali e sottomesso ai dettami della legge divina, che aveva avuto già in vita i segni del compiacimento di Dio sia nel vincere i propri nemici, sia nell'assicurarsi la successione dei figli all'impero: Teodosio diventava così un modello alternativo agli antichi imperatori, ma anche allo stesso Costantino il Grande[61].

Nel *De obitu Theodosii* affiora un vero e proprio canone degli imperatori «santi», proiettati nella pace eterna: al centro ci sono Graziano e Teodosio[62] insieme ai membri della famiglia imperiale (il padre Teodosio Sr., la prima moglie Flaccilla, i due figli Graziano [da distinguere dall'Augusto][63] e Pulcheria); degli Augusti precedenti c'è solo Costantino, ma risulta assente Costanzo II e non vengono menzionati nemmeno Valentiniano I e il figlio Valentiniano II, sebbene fossero stati considerati assunti in cielo nell'orazione funebre tenuta per la morte di quest'ultimo[64]. A questi «buo-

---

[60] R. Lizzi, *Il vescovo santo...*, *supra.*

[61] Nel panegirico che Claudio Claudiano indirizzò ad Onorio nel 396 la divinizzazione di Teodosio il Grande assunse la forma di un *katasterismos* di grande suggestione, che proiettava l'imperatore, scomparso recentemente, nel cielo delle stelle fisse; l'azione «cosmica» del *divus* si esercitava nel vegliare sui regni dei figli (*III cons. Honorii*, vv. 167 s.; 178, 182). Sulla centralità del tema della successione nell'orazione di Ambrogio: cfr. V. Aiello, *Il tempo del potere negli auspici di Ambrogio vescovo di Milano*, in *Tempo sacro e tempo profano. Visione laica e visione cristiana del tempo e della storia*, a cura di L. De Salvo, A. Sindoni, Soveria Mannelli 2002, 119 ss.

[62] Ambros. *De obitu Theodosii.* 39; 51-52.

[63] *De obitu Theodosii* 40; cfr. S. Rebenich, *Gratian, a Son of Theodosius, and the Birth of Galla Placidia*, «Historia» 34 (1985), 372-385; A. Amici, *Imperatori* divi *nella decorazione musiva della chiesa di san Giovanni Evangelista*, «Ravenna. Studi e ricerche» 8 (2000), 35.

[64] Nel *De obitu Valentiniani* era stata proposta l'immagine di Graziano, già accolto nei cieli, che andava incontro ed accoglieva il fratello Valentiniano II (54; 71-78), non battezzato, ma che aveva manifestato la volontà di ricevere i sacramenti dell'iniziazione cristiana (par. 51; 79-80). Anche il padre Valentiniano I era considerato presente in cielo (55): se ne ricordava la coraggiosa testimonianza della fede cristiana quando era tribuno militare, ma non il regno; cfr. anche Ambros. *Ep.* 21, 3; che la politica di equilibrio di Valentiniano I non sia stata apprezzata da parte dei cristiani suggeriscono J. Gaudemet, *L'église dans l'empire romain (IVe et Ve siècles)*, Paris 1958, 499; R. Soraci,

ni imperatori» si contrappongono quelli *damnati*, gli usurpatori Massimo ed Eugenio, che sono collocati all'inferno[65].

I criteri che sono alla base di questa specie di giudizio divino sugli imperatori da Costantino in poi possono essere identificati con buona approssimazione: Costanzo II appare escluso per il suo aperto sostegno alla dottrina omèa, Valentiniano II, imperatore legittimo, era morto non battezzato ma aveva manifestato l'intenzione di ricevere il sacramento, secondo la testimonianza di Ambrogio; per il giudizio su Massimo e su Eugenio, può aver prevalso invece il criterio politico, in quanto si trattava di usurpatori[66].

Eugenio era cristiano ma era stato molto legato al generale Arbogaste e soprattutto al prefetto del pretorio Nicomaco Flaviano ed aveva sviluppato una politica sempre più filo-pagana, per cui Ambrogio stesso aveva preso le distanze da lui, affrettandosi anche, una volta sconfitto al Fiume Freddo, ad enfatizzare la vittoria di Teodosio come dono divino, come si è già notato; il caso di Massimo era più complicato, sia per quanto concerne i suoi rapporti con Teodosio, sia quelli con Ambrogio stesso, che si era recato più volte da lui dopo l'uccisione di Graziano ed aveva motivi di tensione non lievi con Giustina e il figlio Valentiniano II; ma anche in questo caso la posizione del vescovo di Milano era stata ostile a Massimo e legittimista, come è agevole notare nel *Commento al Salmo 61* dell'anno 387, in cui Massimo era paragonato a Pilato, e nel *De apologia prophetae David* dello stesso anno, in cui definiva l'usurpazione non lecita e l'uccisione di Graziano come un «pubblico parricidio»[67].

Anche per contrasto, emerge pertanto che la legittimità del potere ed il suo esercizio in conformità con la legge divina sono i parametri su cui Ambrogio ha misurato un buon imperatore come Teodosio. Rispetto ai criteri che il senato adottava nel decretare la *probatio* degli imperatori per procedere alla loro *relatio in numerum divorum*, l'analogia riguarda punti

---

L'imperatore Valentiniano I, Catania 1971, 167 ss.; R. LIZZI TESTA, *Senatori, popolo, papi. Il governo di Roma al tempo dei Valentiniani*, Bari 2004, 229-235.

[65] AMBROS. *De obitu Theodosii* 39: *Maximus et Eugenius in inferno... docentes exemplo miserabili quam durum sit arma suis principibus inrogare*; cfr. G. BONAMENTE, *Potere politico ed autorità religiosa nel* De obitu Theodosii *di Ambrogio*, in *Studi storici in onore di P. Ilarino da Milano*, I, Roma 1979, 91;117; C.R. RASCHLE, *Ambrosius in psalm 61,16-27: eine Predigt gegen den Usurpator Magnus Maximus*, «GFA» 5 (2002), 225-243.

[66] G. BONAMENTE, *Potere politico ed autorità religiosa nel* De obitu Theodosii..., 116.

[67] Cfr. PACAT. *Paneg.* 23, 1-4; 43, 4; AMBROS. *In Ps. 61*; *De apol. proph. David* 26 s. (è indirizzata a Teodosio); Y.-M. DUVAL, *Les ambassades de Saint Ambroise auprès de l'usurpateur Maxime en 383 et 384*, in Humana sapit..., 239 ss.

essenziali: il riconoscimento della legittimità del regno, la convalida degli acta del *divus princeps*, la legittimazione del successore. Ma il porsi su un piano di valutazione religioso-etico faceva la differenza, provocando, nel caso di Teodosio, una significativa divaricazione tra la funzione imperiale e la persona dell'imperatore divinizzato/santificato. In primo luogo si impose un mutamento radicale della ritualità, in quanto da Costantino in poi il funerale aveva previsto, accanto alla spettacolarità della pompè nel Palazzo imperiale e nella città, anche la celebrazione del Sacrificio divino e quella speciale forma di *laudatio* che consisteva nell'omelia di un vescovo, come si è verificato appunto per Valentiniano II e per Teodosio. Ma il mutamento sostanziale concerneva la definizione delle virtù dell'imperatore che, sebbene articolata nei canoni di una retorica encomiastica condivisa da cristiani e pagani, doveva ormai confrontarsi in modo più diretto con gli *exempla* vetero- e neo-testamentari, riformulando i concetti tràditi come *pietas, fides, clementia* ed introducendone di nuovi come *humilitas, misericordia* e *fidelitas*; nell'insieme ne usciva fuori un modello imperiale decisamente coerente con la dottrina ambrosiana, nel quale i valori etici e la caratterizzazione della persona dell'imperatore assumevano un rilievo primario[68].

Sotto questo aspetto la panegiristica e l'omiletica sugli imperatori condividevano un elemento innovativo della storiografia, quello dello sviluppo della biografia, che nel corso del IV secolo venne decisamente sollecitato in primo luogo dal diffondersi di quel particolare genere letterario che sono state le vite dei santi, in decisa concorrenza con il filone delle biografie dei filosofi. L'immissione di parametri di valutazione legati alla sfera della psicologia, del sentire individuale, della continenza e del dominio delle passioni, del rapporto mistico con la divinità, spostavano il registro dell'etica, anche nel caso degli imperatori, verso l'individualità e l'interiorità riflettendosi – nel fatto specifico – sui criteri da adottare per definire se essi fossero *boni, optimi* oppure *sancti*, a seconda dei contesti[69].

---

[68] AMBROS., *De obitu Theodosii* 12: *imperatoris pii, imperatoris misericordis, imperatoris fidelis.*

[69] Nella sua caratterizzazione di Giuliano, Ammiano mise in evidenza le quattro virtù canoniche quali *temperantia, prudentia, iustitia, fortitudo*, integrandole con la *scientia rei militaris*, l'*auctoritas*, la *felicitas* e la *liberalitas* (25, 4, 1) e dando particolare rilievo alla *temperantia* (ed alla *inviolata castitas*: 25, 4, 2-6). Cfr. C.J. CLASSEN, Virtutes *und* vitia *in Claudians Gedichten*, in Humana sapit..., 166; BONAMENTE, Optimi principes – principes divi..., 71 (ivi un elenco delle *virtutes* corrispondenti a parametri cristiani).

Anche Agostino di Ippona affrontò in più occasioni il tema della sacralità del potere e degli imperatori, adottando parametri coerenti con la sua chiara definizione della trascendenza del regno di Dio rispetto alla realtà storica, ivi compreso l'impero romano. La sua valutazione dell'istituto della divinizzazione degli imperatori va colta all'interno delle sue considerazioni di matrice evemeristica sul pantheon romano, che nel suo insieme gli appariva implementato nella prima fase della civiltà romana (*tempora rudia et indocta*) dalla divinizzazione di capi politici tra cui Romolo; successivamente questo procedimento non sarebbe stato più adottato: per Agostino infatti la *relatio in numerum divorum* era un fenomeno che andava definito come un eccesso di ossequio, ma non come vero e proprio *error* di natura teologica e religiosa: *mortuum Romulum... in deos rettulere Romani... nec postea nisi adulando, non errando, factum est temporibus Caesarum*[70].

La sua posizione dottrinale nei confronti dell'apoteosi imperiale può essere definita ulteriormente alla luce di una considerazione fatta a proposito di Romolo, di cui i Romani non avrebbero mai dimenticato la natura «eroica» e non pienamente divina (*semideum potius quam deum*)[71], considerazione di cui non si trova riscontro nella tradizione cultuale[72], ma che è speculare alla precisa definizione coeva di Servio *Ad Aen.* 5, 45: *quamquam sit discretio, ut deos perpetuos dicamus, divos ex hominibus factos, quasi qui diem obierint: unde divos etiam imperatores vocamus*)[73].

Con questo atteggiamento appare coerente il fatto che Agostino non abbia fatto nessun altro riferimento all'apoteosi imperiale nel *De civitate Dei*, mentre mise ripetutamente in discussione la divinizzazione dei due eroi Ercole e Quirino; tale atteggiamento trova riscontro in autori cristiani come Arnobio, che in età dioclezianea aveva contestato divinizzazioni di *tyranni ac reges*, oppure degli eroi più famosi come Ercole, Romolo,

---

[70] AUGUSTIN. *De civ. Dei*, 18, 24; G. BONAMENTE, *L'apoteosi degli imperatori nell' ultima storiografia pagana latina...*, 29. Cfr. *infra*, n. 113.

[71] AUGUSTIN. *De civ. Dei* 2, 15.

[72] E. BICKERMANN, *Die römische Kaiserapotheose...*, 83 ss.; J. BÉRANGER, *L'expression de la divinité dans les panegyriques latins*, «MH» 27 (1970), 242-254, ora in *Principatus*, Genève 1973, 443 nota 96; E. BICKERMANN, *Consecratio*, in *Le culte des souverains dans l'empire romain*, Vandoeuvres-Genève 1973, 22.

[73] SERV. *Ad Aen.* 5, 45; cfr. W. ENSSLIN, *Gottkaiser und Kaiser von Gottes Gnaden*, München 1943, 31; L. CRACCO RUGGINI, *Apoteosi e politica senatoria nel IV sec. d. C.: il dittico dei Symmachi al British Museum*, «RSI» 89 (1977), 452; PH. BRUGGISSER, *Romulus Servianus. La Légende de Romulus dans les Commentaires à Virgile de Servius: mythographie et idéologie à l'époque de la dynastie théodosienne*, Bonn 1987, 227-241 (datazione dopo il sacco di Alarico); M. CLAUSS, *Kaiser und Gott...*, 30 s.

Esculapio, Dioniso, Enea, senza però toccare quella degli imperatori[74], mantenendosi sulla falsariga della critica evemeristica e pervenendo alla conclusione che si trattava di una venerazione eccessiva di uomini, di cui si poteva condividere un presupposto fondamentale, quello della valutazione e della individuazione dei *boni principes*. Il declassamento dell'istituto tradizionale dal piano istituzionale-religioso a quello etico gli consentiva di accoglierne un elemento importante, quello della valutazione degli imperatori, elemento compatibile con la dottrina cristiana[75].

Nel V libro del *De civitate Dei* affiora un catalogo delle virtù proprie del buon imperatore:
– *iuste imperaverunt*;
– *non extolluntur*;
– pongono il potere *ad Dei cultum maxime dilatandum*;
– temono, amano e onorano Dio;
– sono ponderati nel comminare le pene;
– sono inclini a perdonare;
– compensano la severità con la misericordia;
– ritengono il dominio delle *pravae cupiditates* preferibile alle conquiste militari;
– operano *non propter ardorem inanis gloriae sed propter caritatem felicitatis aeternae*;
– offrono a Dio il sacrificio dell'umiltà e della preghiera.

Significativo è il riferimento a Costantino ed a Teodosio: distinguendo tra la *felicitas* (che è effetto non necessario della provvidenza divina) e la *aeterna felicitas* (che è una condizione assoluta e trascendente), Agostino valutò infatti in modo diverso l'esemplarità di Costantino (ricolmo di doni divini per la sua azione politica) rispetto a Teodosio, che egli propose invece come modello di imperatore *pius* e *misericors*[76].

---

[74] ARNOB. *Adv. nat.* 1, 64, 2; 3, 39, 1.

[75] Cfr. L. CRACCO RUGGINI, *Apoteosi e politica senatoria...*, 452; G. BONAMENTE, *L'apoteosi degli imperatori nell'ultima storiografia pagana latina...*, 31.

[76] Cfr. AUGUSTIN. *De civ. Dei* 5,24 (ivi il catalogo delle virtù dell'imperatore); 5, 25: *(Constantinus) diu imperavit, universum orbem Romanum unus Augustus tenuit et defendit; in administrandis et gerendis bellis victoriosissimus fuit, in tyrannis opprimendis per omnia prosperatus est, grandaevus aegritudine et senectute defunctus est, filios imperantes reliquit*; 5, 26, 1 (su Teodosio); cfr. F. PASCHOUD, *Roma aeterna. Étude sur le patriotisme romain dans l'Occident latin à l'époque des grandes invasions*, Neuchatel 1967, 234 ss.; L. CRACCO RUGGINI, *Simboli di battaglia ideologica nel tardo Ellenismo (Roma, Atene, Costantinopoli; Numa, Empedocle, Cristo)*, in *Studi storici in on. O. Bertolini*, I, Pisa 1972, 177 ss.; G. BONAMENTE, *Eutropio e la tradizione pagana su Costantino*, in *Scritti storico-epigrafici in memoria di Marcello Zambelli*, a cura di

Prima che il sacco di Alarico mettesse drammaticamente a nudo la crisi politica dell'impero, a poca distanza di tempo dalle omelie sopra ricordate di Giovanni Crisostomo, Agostino ne riprese il tema polemico, proponendo il confronto tra gli imperatori e gli apostoli/vescovi in una serie di *sermones*: mise infatti in rilievo il fatto che, in occasione del suo *adventus* a Roma nel 404, Onorio aveva mostrato venerazione per la memoria di s. Pietro (*sepulcrum piscatoris*) mentre aveva trascurato il Mausoleo di Adriano (*templum imperatoris*)[77].

Una testimonianza della continuità e della contaminazione del modello dei *boni principes* nel culto cristiano è offerta – a breve distanza di tempo dalle formulazioni agostiniane – da un catalogo di imperatori *divi* con le rispettive immagini, che – secondo una tradizione cinquecentesca – fu proposto nella chiesa dedicata a San Giovanni Evangelista nella città di Ravenna come voto per il ritorno di Galla Placidia e del piccolo Valentiniano III da Costantinopoli a Ravenna nel 423. Sull'estradosso dell'arco trionfale compariva in pieno rilievo una serie di dieci imperatori (per gli Augusti ricorreva l'epiteto *divus* e per i principi morti prematuramente quello di *nobilissimus puer*): *divus Constantinus* (Costantino il Grande), *divus Valentinianus* (Valentiniano I), *divus Gratianus* (Graziano), *divus Theodosius* (Teodosio il Grande), *divus Arcadius* (Arcadio), *divus Honorius* (Onorio), *divus Constantius* (Costanzo III), *Gratianus nobilissimus puer* (Graziano figlio di Teodosio), *Iohannes nobilissimus puer* (Giovanni figlio di Teodosio), *Theodosius nobilissimus puer* (Teodosio figlio di Ataulfo e Galla Placidia)[78].

L. Gasperini, Roma 1978, 50; S. D'Elia, *Storia e teologia della storia nel «De civitate dei»*, in *La storiografia ecclesiastica nella tarda antichità. Atti del Convegno di Erice, 3-8 dicembre 1978*, Messina 1980, 451 ss.; J. Szidat, *Constantin bei Augustin*, «Rev. Ét. August.» 36 (1990), 248; V. Neri, *La figura di Costantino...*, 248 ss. (con bibliografia e messa a punto del tema); A. Isola, *Agostino, un pastore di fronte al potere. Il contributo dei* sermones *Dolbeau*, in *Intellettuali e potere nel mondo antico*, a cura di R. Uglione, Alessandria 2003, 312 s.

[77] Augustin. *Serm.* D 22, 4, 557.

[78] Le iscrizioni erano collegate ai ritratti, collocati rispettivamente a destra: *d(ivus) Constantinus, d(ivus) Theodosius, d(ivus) Arcadius, d(ivus) Honorius, Theodosius n(obilissimus) p(uer)*; a sinistra: *d(ivus) Valentinianus, d(ivus) Gratianus, d(ivus) Constantius, Gratianus n(obilissimus) p(uer), Iohannes n(obilissimus) p(uer)*. Le iscrizioni sono di tradizione erudita; cfr. Girolamo Rossi, *Historiarum Ravennatum libri decem*, Venezia 1589, 101; W. Ensslin, *s.v. Galla Placidia*, in *RE*, XX, 2, 1915 (sul significato di *n. p.*).

La funzione di questa serie di imperatori, cui vanno aggiunti i dedicanti Galla Placidia ed i figli Valentiniano III e Giusta Grata Onoria[79], appare essere quella di legittimare le pretese di Valentiniano III, presentando le due linee dinastiche dei Teodosi e dei Valentiniani che a lui facevano capo; degli imperatori precedenti compare solo Costantino il Grande, mentre appare ignorato Costanzo II. Sui dati offerti da una tradizione incerta, sulla quale si è dovuto intervenire con emendamenti, si possono avanzare solo ipotesi aleatorie[80], ma resta interessante che nel terzo decennio del V secolo la legittimazione della dinastia teodosiana e valentiniana che faceva capo a Valentiniano III si richiamasse solo a Costantino il Grande, tralasciando la menzione di Costanzo II, proprio come aveva fatto Ambrogio nel *De obitu Theodosii*.

Nel coevo codice Teodosiano viene registrato l'impiego dell'epiteto *divus* nell'accezione giuridico-politica di «imperatore defunto, del quale sono considerati validi gli atti», un fenomeno rilevante di continuità (che permane anche nel Codice di Giustiniano), caratterizzato dalla perdita del significato sacrale originario, come indica l'alternanza delle formule in cui prevale il termine *memoria*[81]. Nello specifico, Costanzo II viene correntemente richiamato nel Codice Teodosiano con l'epiteto *divus*[82].

Ma se i cristiani elaboravano ed imponevano un proprio modello del buon imperatore, anche sul versante dei tradizionalisti si veniva riconsiderando la sacralità della figura imperiale, trovando un punto di forza proprio nell'istituto della *relatio in numerum divorum*, in cui si intersecavano la memoria storica, la tutela della tradizione religiosa nonché il prestigio del senato di Roma; fu infatti quest'ultimo, nel corso del IV secolo, consapevole del ruolo che gli competeva nella gestione della *relatio in numerum divorum*, a mantenerne in vita alcuni elementi, tra cui le celebrazioni dei *Natales divorum* in Roma stessa[83] e l'uso ufficiale del formulario della

---

[79] Menzionati nell'iscrizione del catino dell'abside: CIL XI 276e; ILS 818,1.
[80] Il *divus Constantius* ivi menzionato va identificato con Costanzo III, secondo marito di Galla Placidia e per l'appunto padre di Placido Valentiniano III e di Giusta Grata Onoria; cfr. CIL XI 276 c e ILS 818; A. AMICI, *Imperatori divi nella decorazione musiva...*, 34 nota 55. In una *Novella* di Valentiniano III del 452 ricorre l'epiteto *divus* per il padre Costanzo III: *Nov. Val.* 25.
[81] Per la permanenza dell'epiteto nei testi legislativi, cfr. G. BONAMENTE, *Apoteosi e imperatori cristiani...*, 134; A. AMICI, *Divus Constantinus: le testimonianze epigrafiche*, «RSA» 30 (2000), 206-208; 212, nota 78.
[82] *CTh* XIII, 5, 14, 2; XVI, 2, 18, 1; 8, 13, 6.
[83] Si pensi al Calendario di Filocalo; cfr. CIL I², 254-79; T. MOMMSEN, *Chronica Minora*, I, in *MGH AA*, 9, Berlin 1892 [1961], 15 s.; Inscr. Ital. XIII, 2, p. 374 s.; M.R. SALZMAN, *On Roman Time. The Codex-Calendar of 354 and the Rhythms of urban life in late*

probatio fino al caso di Teodosio seniore: Q. Aurelio Simmaco – avendo come referente il senato di Roma – si mostrò attento nel menzionare l'apoteosi degli imperatori, usando in modo appropriato l'epiteto *divus*: di Costanzo II proclamava che era stato *aeque relatus in caelum*[84]; ricordò la *relatio in numerum divorum* di Graziano e definì *consecratio inter prisca nomina* la riabilitazione del padre di Teodosio, durante la sua prefettura urbana del 384[85].

L'attenzione all'istituto della divinizzazione degli imperatori romani è attestata anche nell'opera coeva di Macrobio, i *Saturnaliorum libri VII* ed i *Commentarii*[86], ed appare puntualizzarsi nel commento al *Somnium Scipionis* ciceroniano, uno degli assiomi della cultura filosofico-politica romana, posto a conclusione del *De republica*, che dava un prestigioso fondamento alla concezione per cui i buoni «rettori» della *res publica* conseguivano una collocazione nell'ordine assoluto del cosmo[87].

L'istituto della *relatio in numerum divorum* trovò comunque la sua sede naturale nella storiografia pagana del IV secolo, da Aurelio Vittore a Eutropio, ad Ammiano Marcellino, mostrando il suo apice nella *Historia*

---

antiquity, Berkeley-Los Angeles 1990, 131-146; G. ZECCHINI, *Costantino e i* natales Caesarum, «Historia» 39 (1990), 349 s.; A. FRASCHETTI, *La conversione. Da Roma pagana a Roma cristiana*, Bari 1999, 294 ss.; P. ATHANASSIADI, *Ascent to heroic or divine status in late antiquity: continuities and transformations*, in *Thesaurus cultus et rituum antiquorum*, II, Los Angeles 2004, 212-214.

[84] SYMM. *Rel.* 40, 2; cfr. 3, 4 e 6; 34, 2 e 4 e 5; *Ep.* 9, 150, 1.

[85] Rispettivamente SYMM. *Rel.* 34, 6: [*divus Gratianus*] *novissime relatus in caelum* e *Rel.* 9, 4-5; cfr. P. BATIFFOL, *L'église et les survivances...*, 5 s.; 72; L. CRACCO RUGGINI, *Apoteosi e politica senatoria nel IV secolo d.C...*, 444 s.; 485; D. VERA, *Le statue del senato di Roma in onore di Flavio Teodosio e l'equilibrio dei poteri imperiali in età teodosiana*, «Athenaeum» 57 (1979), 383 s.

[86] Sulla datazione delle due opere intorno ai primi due decenni del V secolo e sull'identificazione dell'Autore cfr. A. CAMERON, *The date and the identity of Macrobius*, «JRS» 56 (1966), 25-38. Sull'ambientazione storica, al dicembre 383 di personaggi come Vettio Agorio Pretestato, Ceionio Rufio Albino, Quinto Aurelio Simmaco, Virio Nicomaco Flaviano, cfr. J. FLAMANT, *Macrobe et le néoplatonisme latin à la fin du IVe siècle*, Leiden 1977, 96-141; M. KAHLOS, *Vettius Agorius Praetextatus. A senatorial life in beetwen*, Roma 2002, 151-153.

[87] CIC. *De republ.* 6, 3, 13: *omnibus qui patriam conservaverint, adiuverint, auxerint, certum esse in caelo ac definitum locum, ubi beati aevo sempiterno fruantur.* Cfr. MACR. *Somn.* 1, 9, 6: *civitatum vero rectores ceterique sapientes caelum respectu, vel cum adhuc corpore tenentur, habitantes, facile post corpus caelestem, quam paene non reliquerant, sedem reposcunt: nec enim de nihilo aut de vana adulatione veniebat quod quosdam urbium conditores aut claros in re publica viros in numerum deorum consecravit antiquitas.* G. BONAMENTE, *L'apoteosi degli imperatori nell'ultima storiografia pagana latina...*, 30 s.

Augusta, nella quale esso è un elemento costitutivo delle biografie imperiali[88]. Ed è proprio in quest'ultima opera, collocabile appunto nel primo decennio del V secolo[89], che il rapporto di un buon imperatore con gli dei (*pietas erga deos*) si fa criterio determinante, alla pari della registrazione sistematica – naturalmente solo per i *boni principes* – per l'assegnazione dell'epiteto di *divus* e della conseguente ascesa al cielo, da dove l'imperatore può continuare ad esercitare la sua azione a favore dell'impero anche dopo la morte.

Che l'anonimo autore della *Historia Augusta,* pur attingendo ampiamente il materiale storico e biografico dalla tradizione[90], abbia mostrato peculiare interesse per la divinizzazione degli imperatori, può essere dimostrato almeno da tre fatti: la sistematicità con cui il tema viene affrontato per ogni imperatore, lo spazio riservatogli nell'economia dell'opera, infine la coerenza con cui esso viene trattato, sia quanto a precisione terminologica, sia quanto a finalità apologetica[91].

Prescindendo in questa occasione da alcune caratteristiche, quali l'impiego rigoroso della terminologia ufficiale e la descrizione puntigliosa del cerimoniale[92], nonché dal risalto dato alla funzione esercitata dal senato

---

[88] H. STERN, *Date et destinataire de l'Histoire Auguste*, Paris 1953, in particolare 92-96; J. SCHWARTZ, *À propos du vocabulaire religieux de l'Histoire Auguste*, in BHAC 1975-76, Bonn 1978, 187-193; A.R. BIRLEY, *Religion in the Historia Augusta*, in *Historiae Augustae Colloquium Parisinum*, Macerata 1991, 29-51; G. BONAMENTE, *L'apoteosi degli imperatori nell' ultima storiografia pagana latina...*, 61-73; ID., *L'apoteosi degli imperatori nella* Historia Augusta, in *XV Miscellanea greca e romana*, Roma 1990, 257-308; G. BONAMENTE, *Il canone dei* divi *e la* Historia Augusta, in *Historiae Augustae Colloquium Parisinum...*, 59-82.

[89] Sull'autore (anonimo) e sulla cronologia (intorno al primo decennio del V secolo) cfr. ora A.R. BIRLEY, *The* Historia Augusta *and Pagan Historiography*, in *Greek and Roman Historiography in Late Antiquity. Fourth to Sixth Century A. D.*, ed. G. MARASCO, Leiden-Boston 2003, 144 (e bibliografia relativa).

[90] Si tratta, come è ben noto, di Erodiano e Cassio Dione, nonché degli storici della EKG, tutti peraltro attenti alla divinizzazione imperiale. Il passo in cui è descritto dettagliatamente il cerimoniale dell'apoteosi (di Settimio Severo) è HERODIAN. 4, 2, 1-10. Cfr. F. KOLB, *Literarische Beziehungen zwischen Cassius Dio, Herodian und der Historia Augusta*, Bonn 1972.

[91] Essa occupa all'incirca il 15 per cento dello spazio dedicato alla religione; cfr. A.R. BIRLEY, *Religion in the Historia Augusta...*, 30.

[92] La menzione esplicita dei vari momenti del *funus publicum* e degli *honores caelestes* ricorre nella *Historia Augusta* con una frequenza non riscontrabile in alcuna altra opera; cfr. G. BONAMENTE, *Il canone dei* divi *e la* Historia Augusta..., 64, tabella 3 (le formule di consacrazione) e tab. 5; H. BRANDT, *De mortibus principum et tyrannorum. Tod und Leichenschändung in der Historia Augusta*, in *Historiae Augustae Colloquium Perusinum 2000*, Bari 2002, 65 ss.

nella *probatio*, si deve tenere conto di quegli elementi di più diretto contatto con la riflessione cristiana coeva, quali la «eticizzazione» dei motivi dell'apoteosi[93], l'obliterazione e la dissimulazione delle *consecrationes* dei *mali principes* con la finalità di tutelare meglio l'istituto in sé[94]; la rimozione dell'uso tradizionale dell'incinerazione insieme all'enfatizzazione dell'inumazione[95]; da ultimo l'uso del termine *sanctus* e di quelli ad esso connessi[96].

Se l'espediente di far apparire l'*Historia Augusta* come se fosse stata scritta sotto Diocleziano e Costantino consente all'Anonimo di esimersi dal confronto diretto con le figure incombenti di Costantino e di Giuliano, queste ultime riemergono comunque in controluce negli *optimi principes*, quali in prima istanza Marco Aurelio e Alessandro Severo, proposti come modelli per il loro costante rapporto con gli dei, per il rispetto scrupoloso del rituale religioso e per le modalità della loro divinizzazione.

La figura di Alessandro Severo è emblematica, essendo una creazione ideologica dell'*Historia Augusta*, che rielaborò in modo raffinato dati

---

[93] Cfr. *supra* nota 51 e G. Bonamente, Optimi principes..., 68. Il tema è sviluppato in S.H.A *AS* 29, 2 e in *A* 42, 3-4: *Quid hoc esse dicam, tam paucos bonos extitisse principes, cum iam tot Caesares fuerint? Nam ab Augusto in Diocletianum Maximianumque principes, quae series purpuratorum sit, index publicus tenet. Sed in his optimi ipse Augustus, Flavius Vespasianus, Flavius Titus, Cocceius Nerva, divus Traianus, divus Hadrianus, Pius et Marcus Antonini, Severus Afer, Alexander Mammaeae, divus Claudius et divus Aurelianus.*

[94] Esemplari sono i casi di Commodo, Caracalla e Geta; cfr. S.H.A. *C* 18-20; *Cc* 11, 5-7; *G* 2, 8-9; G. Bonamente, *L'apoteosi degli imperatori nella Historia Augusta...*, 290-295; Id., *Il canone dei divi e la* Historia Augusta..., 65.

[95] L'Anonimo attribuisce il rito dell'inumazione anche a casi che nelle sue fonti erano espressamente ricordati come incinerazioni, come per Settimio Severo (*S* 24,1-2; cfr. Herodian. 3, 15, 7; Cass. Dio 76, 15, 3) e per Caracalla (*Cc* 9, 12; *OP* 5,2; cfr. Herodian. 4, 13, 8; Cass. Dio 79, 9, 1). Cfr. R. Turcan, *Le culte impérial au IIIe siècle*, in *ANRW*, 2, 16, 2, 1978, 325-330; J. Arce, Funus imperatorum..., 93; G. Bonamente, *L'apoteosi degli imperatori nella Historia Augusta...*, 293; Id., *Il ruolo del senato nella divinizzazione degli imperatori...*, 377. Una questione a sé è costituita dalle forme di culto dedicate a personaggi discutibili, come nel caso di Antinoo, considerato *exemplum* in senso negativo sia dai cristiani che dai pagani; cfr. G. Bonamente, *Il ruolo del senato nella divinizzazione...*, 373 s.; J. Hammerstaedt, *Die Vergöttlichung unwürdiger Menschen bei den Heiden als apologestisches Argument in Schriften des Sokrates, Theodoret, Cyrill von Alexandrien und Johannes Chrysostomos*, «JbAC» 39 (1996), 76-101.

[96] Un'analisi sistematica dell'impiego dei termini connessi al concetto di *sanctitas* evidenzia riflessi dell'uso proprio di autori cristiani del IV e del V secolo quali Lattanzio, Girolamo e Agostino; cfr. J. Burian, *Sanctus als Wertbegriff in der Historia Augusta*, «Klio» 63 (1981), 630 s.; A.R. Birley, *Religion in the Historia Augusta...*, 49, nota 41.

storici autentici della politica religiosa dei Severi[97]. Questo imperatore, dalla personalità di basso profilo, venne trasformato in un esempio, poco credibile invero, di sincretismo religioso, sia nella direzione del rapporto pagani-cristiani (si pensi al fatto che avrebbe venerato nel suo *lararium maius*, accanto ai propri antenati e agli *optimi principes*, Orfeo, Apollonio di Tiana, Abramo e Cristo)[98], sia sul versante del mondo giudaico-cristiano[99]. Egli così diventava simbolo positivo, come antesignano di una politica improntata a sincretismo ed alla coesistenza delle varie *religiones*[100], ma anche come alternativa ideale a Costantino e, soprattutto, a Teodosio.

Centrale è comunque la figura di Marco Aurelio, cui era stata riconosciuta già in vita la natura di «uomo divino» capace di operare miracoli, come quello della pioggia durante la campagna contro i Quadi[101], ed era considerato simbolo di imperatore carismatico sia nelle dossografie neoplatoniche, sia nella tradizione storiografica. In lui l'Anonimo indicò il modello della *sanctitas vitae,* un carattere strettamente legato al suo vivere da filosofo[102]. La sua eccezionalità si manifestò in vita, per il rapporto co-

---

[97] La distanza fra realtà storica e uso ideologico di tale figura in E. DAL COVOLO, *Gli imperatori Severi e la «svolta costantiniana»*, in *Cristianesimo e istituzioni politiche. Da Augusto a Costantino*, a cura di E. DAL COVOLO, R. UGLIONE, Roma 1995, 75-87; L. CRACCO RUGGINI, *Simboli di battaglia ideologica nel tardo ellenismo...*, 181-187.

[98] Che la notizia relativa al larario imperiale possa essere una risposta alla lettera con cui Ambrogio, in polemica con Simmaco, si chiedeva se mai un imperatore romano avesse innalzato un'ara a Cristo (*Ep.* 18,10) è stato suggerito fondatamente; cfr. L. CRACCO RUGGINI, *Elagabalo, Costantino e i «culti siriaci» nella* Historia Augusta, in *Historiae Augustae Colloquium Parisinum* (Paris 1990), Macerata 1991, 133. Non meno rilevante è il passo della Vita di Alessandro Severo in cui si attribuisce all'imperatore l'intenzione di innalzare un tempio a Cristo (*AS* 43, 6: *Christo templum facere voluit eumque inter deos recipere*).

[99] *AS* 51,7-8; cfr. J. STRAUB, *Heidnische Geschichtsapologetik in der christliche Spätantike. Untersuchungen über Zeit und Tendenz der Historia Augusta*, Bonn 1963, 106 ss.; ID., *Il precetto aureo*, in *Atti del Colloquio patavino sulla Historia Augusta*, Roma 1963, 21-28; L. CRACCO RUGGINI, *Ambrogio e le opposizioni anticattoliche fra il 383 e il 390*, «Augustinianum» 14 (1974), 427 ss.

[100] Cfr. R. LIZZI TESTA, *Christian Emperor, Vestal Virgins, and Priestly Colleges: reconsidering the End of Roman Paganism*, «AnTard» 15 (2007), 251-262.

[101] Basti qui il riferimento alla Colonna Antonina, di poco successiva (176 d.C.); cfr. L. CRACCO RUGGINI, *Imperatori e uomini divini...*, 18-19.

[102] Si tratta dell'inizio della biografia: S.H.A. *Vita Marci* 1, 1: *Marco Antonino, in omni vita philosophanti viro et qui sanctitate vitae omnibus principibus antecellit*. L'impiego dell'epiteto *sanctus*, naturalmente con varie accezioni, e sempre in contesti rilevanti, va considerato un tratto originale; cfr. *MA* 15, 3 (*tantae autem sanctitatis fuit Marcus*); 19, 10 (*boni principis vita, sanctitas, tranquillitas, pietas*); *V* 8, 9 (*ut [scl. Marcus] fratri venerabilem morum suorum et imitandam ostenderet sanctimoniam*);

stante con gli dei[103] e per la sua divinizzazione, proposta come esemplare sia sotto l'aspetto teologico, in quanto il suo appariva come un «ritorno» in cielo, sia sotto l'aspetto rituale, in quanto nel suo caso la prassi della *consecratio* sarebbe stata potenziata da una partecipazione eccezionale del popolo alla deliberazione del senato[104]. La sua ascesa al mondo degli dei doveva essere considerata come un ritorno, in quanto egli era stato semplicemente «dato in prestito» agli uomini[105].

L'Anonimo mise in rilievo due questioni, che proiettavano la figura di Marco Aurelio nell'attualità: dalla sua sede celeste Marco Aurelio compiva miracoli, tra cui quello di essere fonte di vaticini veritieri[106]; il suo culto si era così diffuso, avendo avuto continuità nel tempo, che la sua statua era presente nel Larario di molte *domus*[107]. Con Marco Aurelio, l'Autore della

---

J. BURIAN, Sanctus als Wertbegriff in der Historia Augusta..., 626 s.; K. ROSEN, Sanctus Marcus Aurelius, in *Historiae Augustae Colloquium Argentoratense*, Bari 1998, 288 (nell'uso dell'Anonimo la *sanctitas,* pur mantenendo il significato etico, viene attratta dai contesti nella sfera religiosa).

[103] Viene messo in evidenza il rispetto dei *ludi* in onore di Giove, un *exemplum* di rispetto del *mos* che appare alludere, per contrasto, all'obliterazione dei *Ludi saeculares* nel 314 da parte di Costantino; cfr. ZOSIM. 2, 1-7; F. PASCHOUD, *Cinq études sur Zosime*, Paris 1975, 125 ss. Quando, allo scopo di far cessare la pestilenza, celebrò *peregrini ritus* facendo ricorso a sacerdoti stranieri, avrebbe avuto cura di concluderli con un lectisternio secondo l'uso tradizionale: cfr. *MA* 13, 1. I due episodi, del fulmine che distrugge la macchina da guerra nemica e della pioggia che disseta i soldati, erano nella Colonna antonina. Cfr. CASS. DIO 71, 8, 10; EUSEB. *Hist. eccl.* 5, 5 (versione cristiana dell'episodio).

[104] Cfr. *MA* 18, 3: *senatus populusque non divisis locis sed in una sede propitium deum dixit*. Il particolare ricorreva già in altri autori della EKG quali AUR. VICT. 16, 14-15; EUTR. 8, 14, 2 (*omnibus certatim adnitentibus inter divos relatus est*); *Epit.* 16,12-14; cfr. H. TEMPORINI, *Die Frauen am Hofe Trajans*, Berlin-New York, 1978, 205 s. (l'espressione riportata dall'Anonimo appare riprodurre un'acclamazione); S. G. MAC-CORMACK, *Arte e cerimoniale nell'antichità...*, 190 ss.; G. BONAMENTE, *Il ruolo del senato nella divinizzazione...*, 376; K. ROSEN, Sanctus Marcus Aurelius..., 289-290.

[105] *MA* 18, 4: *vir tantus et talis ac diis vita et morte coniunctus...*; *MA* 18, 2: *... ut nemo illum plangendum censuerit, certis omnibus, quod ab diis commodatus ad deos redisset.* Cfr. SEN. *De clement.* 1, 3, 5; 4, 1; G. BONAMENTE, *Il ruolo del senato nella divinizzazione...*, 375.

[106] *MA* 18,7.

[107] *MA* 19,12: *deusque etiam nunc habetur, imperator Diocletiane, et semper visus est et videtur, qui eum inter numina vestra non ut ceteros sed specialiter veneramini.* Cfr. K. ROSEN, Sanctus Marcus Aurelius..., 290-295 (con esame critico della notizia secondo cui sarebbe stato considerato *sacrilegus* chi non avesse avuto *in sua domo* una *imago* del *divus Marcus* [*MA* 18,5] e con l'ipotesi che l'Anonimo abbia tenuto conto di formule che ricorrevano nella legislazione antipagana coeva, come ad esempio *CTh* 16, 10, 12 dell'anno 392).

Historia Augusta integrava così la figura del sovrano carismatico: essa assicurava prestigio sia alla figura dell'imperatore in quanto tale, sia, più in particolare, a quella dell'imperatore divinizzato. Parlare di Marco Aurelio nei primi anni del V secolo, tuttavia, significava richiamare alla mente Giuliano, il quale lo aveva scelto come modello[108]; anche lui si era riproposto di vivere in costante rapporto con la divinità, da cui sarebbe stato ispirato nelle scelte decisive[109], dando nuovo impulso ai culti, e in particolare riportando in evidenza la sacralità della figura imperiale con l'iniziazione ai culti più importanti, tra cui quello di Serapide, che aveva costituito un nesso costante con la tradizione religiosa e politica egiziana[110].

Alla sopravvivenza dell'istituto dell'apoteosi Giuliano aveva dato un contributo indiretto, quando nel dicembre del 362 compose il *Symposion*: ne è tema centrale il giudizio divino (espresso da Zeus) sugli imperatori romani, a partire da Cesare ed includendo Alessandro Magno, con l'intento prevalente di mostrare che Costantino ed i suoi figli avevano tralignato gravemente, tanto da meritare un'aperta condanna[111], ma l'opera propone un vero e proprio catalogo dei *boni principes,* che corrisponde sia ai vari elenchi di *principes divi* a lui accessibili dalla tradizione storiografica, sia a documenti coevi quale il *Calendario di Filocalo*[112]. La caratterizzazione dei vari imperatori è accurata ed altrettanto precisa è la collocazione dei *divi* nel cielo – tra la terra e la luna – come avrebbe a breve ribadito Servio[113].

---

[108] IULIAN. *Caes.* 317 c; *Epist. ad Them.* 1, 253 a-b; EUTR. 10, 16, 3: *Marco Antonino non absimilis, quem etiam aemulari studebat*; cfr. G. BONAMENTE, *Giuliano l'Apostata e il Breviario di Eutropio*, Roma 1986, 139-140; K. ROSEN, *Kaiser Julian in der* Historia Augusta, in *Historiae Augustae Colloquium Bambergense*, Bari 2007, 319-330.

[109] Tra i momenti più significativi egli stesso indicava in primo luogo quello in cui accettò la proclamazione dell'esercito a *Lutetia Parisiorum* nel 360; anche la morte improvvisa di Costanzo II, che gli assicurò la vittoria «senza sangue», sarebbe avvenuta per volere divino. Cfr. IULIAN. *Misopogon* (28, 357 b); LIBAN. *Orat.* 18, 103; 118; ZOSIM. 3, 9, 6-7; 3,11,1-2; AMMIAN. 20, 5, 10 (*apparizione del Genius publicus populi Romani*); P. ATHANASSIADI FOWDEN, *Julian and Hellenism. An intellectual Biography*, Oxford 1981, 177; G. BONAMENTE, *Giuliano l'Apostata e il Breviario di Eutropio...*, 83; ID., *Eutropio e la tradizione su Giuliano l'Apostata*, in *Hestiasis. Studi di tarda antichità offerti a S. Calderone*, III, Messina 1989, 10 ss.

[110] L. CRACCO RUGGINI, *Imperatori e uomini divini...*, 12-23.

[111] Cfr. *supra*, n. 23. L'incidenza dei giudizi di Giuliano sulla formazione della tradizione anticostantiniana è delineata nei saggi di Valerio Neri e di Rita Lizzi citati *supra*, n. 38.

[112] Un riscontro analitico in G. BONAMENTE, *L'apoteosi degli imperatori nell'ultima storiografia pagana latina...*, 33 e 43-46.

[113] I *divi* non solo sono diversi per natura dagli dèi, ma hanno anche una sede diversa, nel cielo della Luna (LUCAN. *Phars.* 4, 6: *Quodque patet terras inter lunaeque meatus*;

Dei convincimenti di Giuliano è testimone il coevo *De deis et mundo* di Sallustio, il quale evitò di menzionare espressamente il culto dei *divi* e deplorò il culto degli imperatori viventi, sostenendo però che le anime capaci di esercitare la virtù sarebbero entrate in comunione con gli dei ed avrebbero collaborato con loro per governare il mondo[114]. Più in generale, la forte accentuazione giulianea del ruolo della *religio* nell'esercizio del potere aveva fatto sì che la divinizzazione, tributatagli subito dopo la morte, assumesse significato simbolico[115]: lo aveva percepito in modo evidente Gregorio di Nazianzo, deplorando che la tomba di Giuliano, in Tarso di Cilicia, fosse oggetto di culto[116]; lo aveva reso esplicito Libanio,

---

IULIAN. *Caes.* 307c). Cfr. *supra*, nn. 70 e 73, con i riferimenti ad Agostino e Servio; va altresì tenuto presente che Stobeo riporta un assioma della dottrina ermetica sulla natura mista, umana e divina, del re: Stob. 1,49,45, 407; G. BONAMENTE, *Il ruolo del senato nella divinizzazione degli imperatori...*, 360, nota 4.

[114] *De deis et mundo* 18, 3 e 21, 1. Cfr. G. RINALDI, *Sull'identificazione dell'autore del Perì theòn kaì kòsmou*, «Koinonia» 2 (1978), 119 ss.

[115] Lo esprime in modo emblematico Ammiano, sia introducendo il suo giudizio complessivo su Giuliano (25, 4, 1: *vir profecto heroicis connumerandus ingeniis*), sia quando denuncia l'inopportunità che Giuliano restasse sepolto a Tarso, mentre il suo posto era a Roma, lungo le sponde del Tevere (25, 10, 5). Sulla esperienza personale, di Eutropio e di Ammiano, che avevano visitato il sepolcro a Tarso cfr. G. BONAMENTE, *L'apoteosi degli imperatori nell'ultima storiografia pagana latina...*, 60.

[116] GREG. NAZ. *Or.* 4, 59; 5, 14, 2; 18 (a circa due anni dalla morte dell'imperatore, Gregorio prese di mira il tempio-sepolcro di Giuliano, avanzando il sospetto, nella seconda invettiva, che i cortigiani avessero tentato di far sparire il corpo dell'imperatore per accreditarne l'apoteosi). Cfr. altresì LIBAN. *Or.* 16, 35; 18, 242; 252; 304-308; 37, 4; SYMM. *Rel.* 40, 3; AMMIAN. 25, 10, 5 (Giuliano era stato sepolto presso un piccolo fiume dell'Asia e non lungo il Tevere dove erano i *divorum vetera monumenta*); 26, 10, 8; EUN. *Vitae Sophist.* 7, 2, 12; 7, 44; *Hist. fr.* 26 (ove è riportato un oracolo sul ritorno di Giuliano al cielo: «Quando avrai soggiogato i Persiani sotto il tuo scettro e li avrai messi disordinatamente in fuga fino a Seleucia con la spada, allora un carro di fuoco avvolto nella tempesta e nel turbine ti guiderà fino all'Olimpo, libero dal peso delle tue spoglie mortali. Raggiungerai i vestiboli atavici raggianti di luce, dai quali sei caduto per incarnarti in un corpo mortale»); Socr. *Hist. eccl.* 3, 23, 42. Al riguardo si vedano: A.D. NOCK, *Deification and Julian*, «JRS» 47 (1957), 115-123; J. STRAUB, *Die Himmelfahrt des Julianus Apostata*, «Gymnasium» 62 (1962), 310-326, ora in *Regeneratio imperii*, Darmstadt 1972, 164 ss.; J. BERNARDI, *Un réquisitoire: les invectives contre Julien de Grégoire de Nazianze*, in *L'empereur Julien. De l'histoire à la légende (331-1715)*, ed. R. BRAUN, J. RICHER, Paris 1978, 91 s.; M. REGALI, *Intenti programmatici e datazione delle* Invectivae in Iulianum *di Gregorio di Nazianzo*, «CrSt» 1 (1980), 401-9; L. CRACCO RUGGINI, *Imperatori romani e uomini divini..*, 21; J. BERNARDI, *Grégoire de Nazianze. Discours 4-5 contre Julien*, Paris 1983, XXX; G. BONAMENTE, *Giuliano l'Apostata e il Breviario di Eutropio...*, 152 s.; ID., *L'apoteosi degli imperatori nell'ultima storiografia pagana latina...*, 47 s.; *Gregorio di Nazianzo, Contro Giuliano*

proponendo la figura di Giuliano in termini apertamente concorrenziali con la concezione cristiana dei martiri, col sottolinearne i poteri taumaturgici[117].

Il modo in cui l'Anonimo affrontò i temi della religiosità, e specificamente quello della divinizzazione degli imperatori, mostra quanto fosse presente la necessità di confrontare valori ed istituti importanti della tradizione con valori e modelli cristiani. Il confronto comportava, però, un'attualizzazione nella quale le esigenze apologetiche finirono per prevalere sull'autenticità della tradizione, come rivela vistosamente la *Historia Augusta*, quando attribuì ai propri modelli ideali, quali Alessandro Severo o Marco Aurelio, doti personali ed indirizzi di governo nei quali riecheggiavano aspirazioni ed esigenze del tempo dell'autore, oppure quando fece dei *principes mali* – delineati quali esempio di malgoverno e di cattiva condotta personale, come per antonomasia Elagabalo – i simboli dell'intolleranza religiosa e della smania di innovazione: entrambe erano mal tollerate dal tradizionalista Anonimo, che ne vedeva l'inizio nel regno di Costantino[118].

Quanto è stato detto della *Historia Augusta*[119] può essere considerato anche come clausola dell'intera questione esaminata nel presente contributo: in tema di dimensione carismatica degli imperatori e specificamente

---

l'Apostata, Orazione IV, a cura di L. LUGARESI, Firenze 1993, 306; V. UGENTI, *La figura di Giuliano in Ambrogio e Agostino*, «Rudiae» 10 (1998), 381.

[117] LIBAN. *Orat.* 18, 304: «molte città hanno collocato la sua effige accanto alle statue degli dei e lo onorano come fanno con gli dei. Già la gente gli ha chiesto, con preghiere, qualche beneficio e non è rimasta inappagata. Così egli è salito realmente verso gli dei e ha partecipato del potere divino per volontà degli dei stessi». Cfr. altresì LIBAN. *Orat.* 18,177 (la sua unione mistica con il dio Poseidone aveva fatto cessare un terremoto in Tracia). Cfr. *Libanio. Epitafio per Giuliano (Orazione XVIII)*, ed. S. ANGIOLANI, Napoli 2000, 117 e nota 424 (con bibliografia); 125, nota 461 (la datazione è fissata fra la seconda metà del 365 e l'inizio del 366 per la menzione del terremoto che colpì Nicea il 21 luglio 365).

[118] L. CRACCO RUGGINI, *Elagabalo, Costantino e i culti «siriaci» nella* Historia Augusta..., 123-146; S.C. ZINSLI, *Gute Kaiser, schlechte Kaiser. Die eusebische* Vita Constantini *als Referenztext für die* Vita Heliogabali, «WS» 118 (2005), 117-138; R. VON HAELING, *Ignem perpetuum estinguere voluit: Heliogabal und der Vestakult in der* Historia Augusta, in *Historiae Augustae Colloquium Bambergense,* Bari 2007, 240 (solo nella HA Eliogabalo è messo in rapporto con il collegio delle Vestali).

[119] F. PASCHOUD, *Raisonnements providentialiste dans l'Histoire Auguste*, in *BHAC*, 1977-78, Bonn 1980, 163-178; ID., *Il problema del carattere letterario dell'*Historia Augusta, «AFLM» 17 (1984), 11-36; ID., *La Storia Augusta come testimonianza e riflesso della crisi d'identità degli ultimi intellettuali pagani in Occidente*, in *I cristiani e l'impero nel IV secolo...*, 155-168.

circa la loro sorte dopo la morte, i cristiani elaborarono rapidamente dei modelli efficaci, nel sessantennio che va da Costantino a Teodosio, provocando nei tradizionalisti una «crisi di identità» nel senso specifico che essi si lasciarono indurre a rielaborare addirittura la tradizione storica nel tentativo di resistere al confronto. Se sul finire del IV secolo Eunapio riprese le fila delle biografie dei filosofi nelle *Vite dei sofisti,* condizionato dalla necessità di contrapporsi ai nuovi modelli di vita proposti con crescente successo dai cristiani[120], pochi anni dopo l'*Historia Augusta*, nel parlare di apoteosi degli imperatori romani – in un contesto dominato dal magistero di un Giovanni Crisostomo e di un Agostino – non dovette soltanto accentuarne la dimensione etica, ma anche impiegare criteri innovativi rispetto alla tradizione. Introdusse, tra l'altro, un nuovo canone, più rigoroso, dei *principes divi*: quello degli *optimi principes,* ottenuto selezionando i migliori tra quanti erano stati proclamati *divi* nel corso di quattro secoli[121].

---

[120] Si veda U. CRISCUOLO, *Biografia e agiografia fra pagani e cristiani fra il IV e il V secolo: Le* Vitae *di Eunapio e la* Historia Lausiaca, in *Storiografia e agiografia nella tarda antichità...*, 778 ss. (con bibliografia precedente).

[121] L'Anonimo in un passo della Vita di Aureliano (*A* 42, 3-4) infatti afferma che all'indice ufficiale dei *divi*, definito come *series purpuratorum/index publicus*, andava preferito un diverso elenco, più rigoroso, quello dei *boni principes / optimi principes*, indicando soltanto Augusto, Vespasiano, Tito, Nerva, Traiano, Adriano, Antonino Pio, Marco Aurelio, Settimio Severo, Alessandro Severo, Claudio il Gotico e Aureliano; cfr. *supra*, n. 93.

CHRISTOPHE J. GODDARD

Au cœur du dialogue entre païens et chrétiens: l'*aduentus* des sénateurs dans les cités de l'Antiquité tardive

Si l'on y prend bien garde, l'*aduentus* des sénateurs fournit un observateur privilégié du dialogue entre païens et chrétiens dans les cités de l'Antiquité tardive, un dialogue dont j'aimerais montrer aujourd'hui qu'il fut constructif. Comme pour d'autres périodes – je pense bien entendu aux études fondamentales d'Ernst Kantorowitz[1] ou de Bernard Guénée et Françoise Lehoux[2] portant sur les entrées royales à l'époque médiévale, l'entrée solennelle d'un haut dignitaire nous révèle un système symbolique, car une entrée officielle était tout autant une cérémonie qu'un spectacle où une société toute entière et ses institutions se donnaient à voir. Cette approche s'appuie sur une tradition historiographique solidement établie pour notre période. L'étude de l'*aduentus* des empereurs dans les cités tardo-antiques ou byzantines a, en effet, donné lieu à de très belles études[3]. Toutefois, les

---

Je tiens à remercier Claude Lepelley, pour ses relectures patientes et son soutien indéfectible, Nicole Belayche, Lisa Fentress, John Scheid, Yan Thomas, Paolo Liverani, Ignazio Tantillo, Pierfrancesco Porena, Rita Lizzi-Testa, J.-M. Carrié, Peter Brown, Alan Cameron, R. Bagnall pour les suggestions, corrections et encouragements qu'ils m'ont apportés tout au long de l'élaboration de cette étude. Ils ne sauraient pour autant être tenus responsables des erreurs et des positions avancées ici. Les prémices de cette réflexion se trouvent dans le mémoire de l'Ecole française de Rome consacré à La pastorale des sénateurs païens dans les cités de l'Antiquité tardive et présenté devant l'Académie des Inscriptions et Belles Lettres en juin 2003. Un premier volet tiré de ce mémoire («Les sénateurs comme miroirs du Prince. Un marqueur symbolique de l'Antiquité tardive»), doit paraître à l'automne 2010 aux Publications de la Sorbonne, dans un ouvrage (Les transferts culturels et les droits dans le monde grec et hellénistique) placé sous la direction de Bernard Legras.

[1] E. KANTOROWICZ, *Les Deux corps du Roi. Essai sur la théologie politique au Moyen Age*, Princeton 1957, (tr. fr. Bibliothèques des Histoires, Paris 1989).
[2] B. GUENEE, F. LEHOUX, *Les Entrées royales françaises de 1328 à 1515*, Paris 1968.
[3] M. McCORMICK, *Eternal Victory. Triumphal Rulership in Late Antiquity, Byzantium, and the Early Medieval West*, Cambridge-Londres-New York-New Rochelle-Melbourne-Paris-Sydney 1986; S. MACCORMACK, *Art and Ceremony in Late Antiquity*, Berkeley, Los Angeles-Londres 1981; G. DAGRON, *Empereur et prêtre. Etude sur le*

entrées solennelles des sénateurs n'ont pas autant retenu l'attention des spécialistes, alors que les sources textuelles et iconographiques abondent. Le nombre même de sarcophages présentant l'*aduentus* comme le sommet d'une vie publique et privée, près d'une trentaine à ma connaissance[4], nous laisse même entendre son importance pour l'aristocratie sénatoriale romaine. Nous verrons que les sénateurs constantinopolitains étaient tout aussi attachés à cette forme d'hommage qui leur était adressé. En somme, ce système symbolique a su dépasser la frontière culturelle que Fergus Millar a voulu récemment décrire avec force entre les deux domaines impériaux «associés» d'Orient et d'Occident[5].

«*césaropapisme*» *byzantin*, Paris 1996; A. FRASCHETTI, *La conversione da Roma pagana a Roma cristiana*, Roma-Bari 1999, 5-127 et 243-269.

[4] G. WILPERT, *I sarcofagi cristiani antichi*, I, *Testo*, Rome 1929, 25 (pl. 21, 4) = R. AMEDICK, *Die Sarkophage mit darstellungen aus dem Menschenleben*, IV, *Vita priuata*, Berlin 1991, 153 (n. 191); G. WILPERT, *I sarcofagi cristiani...*, 27 (n. 2, pl. 21, 1) = R. AMEDICK, *Die Sarkophage...*, 146 (n. 149) et 158 (n.232); G. WILPERT, *I sarcofagi cristiani...*, 89 (pl. 27) = R. AMEDICK, *Die Sarkophage...*, 161 (n. 247); N. HIMMELMANN, *Typologische Untersuchungen an römischen Sarkophagreliefs des 3 und 4 Jahrhundert n. Chr.*, Mainz-am-Rhein 1973, 30; N. HIMMELMANN, *Typologische...*, 32 = R. AMEDICK, *Die Sarkophage ...*, 143 (n. 128); G. WILPERT, *I sarcofagi cristiani...*, 27 (pl. 21, 1) = R. AMEDICK, *Die Sarkophage ...*, 170 (n. 298); G. WILPERT, *I sarcofagi cristiani...*, 27 (n. 4; pl. 21, 3) = R. AMEDICK, *Die Sarkophage ...*, 170 (n. 297); G. WILPERT, *I sarcofagi cristiani...*, 28 (n. 7, pl. 22,4) = R. AMEDICK, *Die Sarkophage...*, 135 (n. 79); G. WILPERT, *I sarcofagi cristiani...*, 28 (n. 5; pl. 22,6); G. WILPERT, *I sarcofagi cristiani...*, 29 (n. 2; pl. 23, 2) = R. AMEDICK, *Die Sarkophage...*, 146 (n. 148); G. WILPERT, *I sarcofagi cristiani...*, 30 = R. AMEDICK, *Die Sarkophage...*, 126, n.30; G. WILPERT, *I sarcofagi cristiani...*, 66 (pl. 6, 2) = R. AMEDICK, *Die Sarkophage...*, 160 (n.244); G. WILPERT, *I sarcofagi cristiani...*, 62 (pl. 2,4) = R. AMEDICK, *Die Sarkophage...*, 165 (n. 272); G. WILPERT, *I sarcofagi cristiani...*, 28 (n. 9, pl. 22, 3) = R. AMEDICK, *Die Sarkophage...*, 162 (n. 255); G. WILPERT, *I sarcofagi cristiani...*, 30 (n. 7, pl. 22,5) = R. AMEDICK, *Die Sarkophage...*, 168 (n.290); G. WILPERT, *I sarcofagi cristiani...*, 28 (pl. 22, 7) = F. BARRATE, C. METZGER, *Catalogue des sarcophages en pierre d'époque romaine et paléochrétienne*, Paris RMN, 1985, 35 (n. 6); G. WILPERT, *I sarcofagi cristiani...*, 68 (pl. 5, 1) = R. AMEDICK, *Die Sarkophage...*, 135 (n. 83); G. WILPERT, *I sarcofagi cristiani...*, 30 (n. 5, pl. 23, 1) = R. AMEDICK, *Die Sarkophage...*, 148 (n. 163); G. WILPERT, *I sarcofagi cristiani...*, 30 (pl. 23, 3) = R. AMEDICK, *Die Sarkophage...*, 156 (n.222); = R. AMEDICK, *Die Sarkophage...*, 158 (n. 239); G. WILPERT, *I sarcofagi cristiani...*, 29 (pl. 23, 5) = R. AMEDICK, *Die Sarkophage...*, 148 (n. 164); R. AMEDICK, *Die Sarkophage...*, 127 (n. 40); R. AMEDICK, *Die Sarkophage...*, 165 (n.269); N. HIMMELMANN *Typologische...*, 31-54 (n. 34) = R. AMEDICK, *Die Sarkophage...*, 170 (n. 2999). Pour une bibliographie plus précise de ces différentes pièces, que l'on me permette de renvoyer à C.J. GODDARD, *La pastorale des sénateurs païens...*,108-154.

[5] F. MILLAR, *A Greek Roman Empire. Power and Belief under Theodosius (408-450)*, Berkeley-Los Angeles-London 2006.

Le bandeau historié du musée des thermes à Rome (fig. 1)[6] nous présente peut-être la représentation la plus complète de l'*aduentus* d'un haut dignitaire dans une cité de l'époque tardive, dont les dimensions mêmes (L 0,92, H, 0,35) permettent l'examen précis. Commençons par une simple description, en procédant de gauche à droite, du premier plan à l'arrière plan.

Au premier plan, tout à fait à gauche, une femme, dont la chevelure est couverte par un voile, se tient agenouillée ou assise (une lacune interdit de trancher) pour accueillir le cortège. Sa main droite, paume ouverte mais tournée vers l'intérieur, est dirigée vers le ciel, tandis qu'elle semble s'apprêter à saisir de l'autre, la main droite du premier homme du cortège, qui semble vouloir la relever. Ce dernier est vêtu d'une tunique courte, sur laquelle est jeté un manteau de voyage ou quelque *chlamyde*. Sous lui et vers lui, un enfant, habillé d'une simple tunique sans manche, lève les mains. A droite de ces trois personnages, l'on trouve un carrosse bige à quatre roues, conduit par un cocher à la barbe frisée, coiffé d'un capuche, qui porte une tunique courte mais aux longues manches. Il se trouve en contrebas de deux personnages, qui semblent avoir pris place sur une chaise au dossier surélevé, une sorte de cathèdre. Leurs visages se distinguent sans difficulté. Le premier, légèrement en retrait, dont l'âge avancé est signifié par la barbe et la partielle calvitie, et le rang par le rouleau qu'il tient de la main gauche, s'adresse au second plus jeune et encore imberbe, assis à sa droite. Tous deux sont vêtus d'une longue tunique, qui leur descend jusqu'aux pieds. Les plis d'une ample *chlamyde* leur couvrent le dos et les épaules.

A l'arrière-plan sont représentés les symboles d'une cité. A gauche, derrière la femme, un édifice, qui repose sur un beau portique orné de chapiteaux corinthiens, dont les feuilles d'acanthe sont à peine suggérées, et de colonnes sans cannelure. Au niveau supérieur, un homme imberbe, appuyé de la main droite sur une longue balustrade, se tourne vers le cortège. L'on distingue derrière lui deux fenêtres et au registre supérieur un toit en arrête. A droite de ce premier édifice, l'on trouve une tour, dont l'on voit nettement le crénelage et les deux meurtrières. Le quadrillage signifié par quelques traits, suggère que l'ouvrage solide était bâti en *opus quadratum*,

---

[6] G. WILPERT, *I sarcofagi cristiani...*, 25 (pl. 21, 4) = N. HIMMELMANN, *Typologische...*, 32 (pl. 52) = W. WEBER, *Die Darstellung einer Wagenfahrt auf römischen Sarkophagedeckeln und Loculusplatten des 3. und 4. Jahrhundert n. Chr.*, Rome 1978, 23 (n. 13); 41; 46; 53-58; 60; 68 (pl. 8) = F. BISCONTI, *Un nuovo coperchio di sarcofago dal cimitero di Novaziano*, «RACrist» 59 (1983), 71 (fig. 6); M.E. MICHELI, dans A. GIULIANO, 1985, 127 (n. III, 4, 2) R. AMEDICK, *Die Sarkophage...*, 153 (n. 191).

nous dirions en pierre de taille, à moins qu'il ne soit simplement revêtu de large plaques qui voulaient en donner l'apparence. Plus à droite, sur une colonne, est placée une sorte de disque ou de sphère, où l'on peut lire un «X», (qui représente selon les uns la distance qui sépare le cortège de la cité, pour les autres l'âge du défunt), un arbre et une dernière colonne surmontée d'une structure marquée par trois pointes triangulaires (dont celle placée au centre domine les deux autres), identifiée par Fabio Bisconti avec une méridienne, une horloge solaire[7]. De sa disposition variable sur les bas-reliefs de notre série, par rapport aux bâtiments symbolisant la cité, l'on pourra en déduire le sens de la procession et l'identifier soit comme un *aduentus* proprement dit, ou une *profectio*.

C'est à Josef Wilpert qu'est revenu le mérite en 1929 d'avoir attiré notre regard sur la série de bandeaux de sarcophages à laquelle appartient cette pièce, tout en nous en fournissant une lecture pour le moins improbable[8]. Elle représenterait l'arrivée catéchétique à Jérusalem du diacre Philippe, qui au terme d'un long voyage, était parvenu à obtenir la conversion du ministre eunuque de la reine Candace d'Ethiopie. Cette interprétation ne convainc guère pour deux raisons. Tout d'abord, elle ne s'appuie sur aucun parallèle textuel. Pire, elle fournit une explication erronée de nombreux détails. Passons en revue brièvement ces détails:

1. L'historien méconnaissait ainsi la variante dionysiaque que l'on trouve présente sur un sarcophage de la collection Chiaramonti du Vatican (fig. 2)[9] et que l'on pourrait difficilement interpréter de façon catéchétique, à moins de vouloir en faire une nouvelle preuve de la tendance religieuse syncrétique de l'Antiquité tardive. Nous nous refusons évidemment à recourir à ce type de facilité.

2. La femme agenouillée ou assise serait, selon Josef Wilpert, une mendiante à qui l'on ferait l'aumône[10], alors qu'il faut y voir une matrone romaine, telle qu'elle apparaît par exemple sur une monnaie datant de

---

[7] Cf. F. Bisconti, *Un nuovo coperchio di sarcofago*...,71, fig. 6
[8] N. Himmelmann, *Typologische*..., 32, tav. 54; suivi par G. Dalla Torre Del Tempio di Sanguinetto, *Una scena rara e controversa della sculptura paleocristiana*, «BMC» (1972), 22-26.
[9] Une pièce pourtant étudiée ailleurs par G. Wilpert, *L'ultimo viaggio nell'arte sepolcrale classico-romana*, «RendPontAcc» 1925, 62, pl. 2, 4. Cf. N. Himmelmann, *Typologische*..., 27; 31; 50 (n. 19; pl. 36b; 55a); W. Weber, *Die Darstellung*..., 28 (n. 18); 40-68; R. Amedick, *Die Sarkophage*..., 165 (n. 272).
[10] G. Wilpert, *I sarcofagi cristiani*..., 25.

88 apr. J.-C. et conservé au Cabinet des Médailles (BN, 1416)[11], c'est-à-dire en position de suppliante (fig. 3), et ici accompagnée de son enfant. Ailleurs, sur le bandeau du musée de Stockholm (fig. 4), la femme qui agite une tenture n'est pas non plus une «*nutrice col panno per asciugare l'infante nel bagno*» comme le pensait Josef Wilpert, mais encore une fois une matrone agitant l'une de ces lourdes tentures qui manifestait l'hommage d'une cité, comme lors de l'*aduentus* de Théodose à Hémona en Pannonie Supérieure en 388[12]. Claudien rappela lui aussi que Rome s'était parée des meilleurs atours pour accueillir Honorius à Rome en 404[13]. D'ailleurs, le rôle des femmes et des enfants lors d'une cérémonie d'*aduentus* a été régulièrement souligné par les contemporains. Ainsi Ménandre le Rhéteur à l'époque tétrarchique[14], le panégyriste Mamertin[15] et

---

[11] Cf. J. SCHEID, *Déchiffrer des monnaies. Réflexions sur la réprésentation figurée des Jeux séculaires*, dans *Images romaines. Actes de la table-ronde, ENS, 24-26 oct. 1996*, Paris 1998, 13-33 et 21, fig. 12.

[12] PACATUS, *Pan. Theodosio Dictus*, XXXVIII, éd. et trad. E. GALLETIER, Paris 1955, 104: *quid portas uirentibus sertis coronatas? Quid aulaeis undantes plateas accensisque funalibus auctum diem* («Et les portes couronnées de vertes guirlandes, les places ornées de mouvantes tapisseries, le jour accru par l'éclat des torches?»).

[13] CLAUDIEN, *Panegyricus de sexto consulatu Honorii Augusti*, v. 524-531. Voir P. LIVERANI, *Arco di Onorio – Arco di Portogallo*, «Bollettino della Commissione archeologica comunale di Roma» 104 (2003), 351-370.

[14] MÉNANDRE LE RHÉTEUR, *Le Discours d'arrivée*, 381, 5-23, dans *Menandor Rhetor*, éd. et trad. (anglaise) A. WILSON et D.A. RUSSEL, Oxford 1981, 100-101: «L'épilogue devrait être construit en tenant compte de la finalité même de ce type de discours, en représentant les habitants en train de saluer le gouverneur: "Nous sommes venus à ta rencontre, nous tous, avec nos familles complètes, nos enfants, nos anciens, nos collèges de prêtres, nos collèges de magistrats, le commun peuple, te saluant avec joie, te souhaitant la bienvenue avec les accents de la prière, t'appelant notre sauveur et notre gardien, notre étoile brillante: les enfants t'appellent leur père d'adoption et le sauveur de leur père". Si les cités pouvaient parler et prendre une silhouette féminine, comme sur une scène théâtrale, elles diraient: "O le plus grand des gouverneurs, quel jour merveilleux, le jour de ton arrivée! Désormais, le soleil brille de façon plus éclatante, désormais nous semblons voir un jour heureux émerger de l'obscurité. Bientôt nous érigerons des statues. Bientôt des poètes et des écrivains et des orateurs chanteront tes vertus et répandront ta gloire à travers l'humanité. Que les théâtres soient ouverts, que l'on organise des festivals, que l'on assure les empereurs et les dieux de notre gratitude"»; ibid., 97 (378) et 169-171; cf. PROCOPE DE GAZA, dans *Procope de Gaza, Priscillien de Césarée. Panégyriques de l'empereur Anastase I*er. *Textes traduits et commentés*, éd. A. CHAUVOT, Bonn 1986, 97.

[15] MAMERTINUS, *Panegyricus Genethliacus Maximiano Augusto dictus*, éd. et trad. E. GALLETIER, I, Paris 1949, 61: *Vt uero limine egressi per mediam urbem simul uehebamini, tecta ipsa se, ut audio, paene commouerunt, omnibus uiris feminis, paruulis senibus aut per fores in publicum proruentibus aut per superiora aedium lumina im-*

surtout Libanios évoquant l'entrée solennelle du préfet du prétoire Rufin à Antioche en août 393. Ce dernier[16] rapporta que les femmes avaient été les porte-paroles officiels de la cité, un rôle dévolu aux enfants sous la plume de Ménandre[17].

3. Quant aux personnages assis sur la sorte de cathèdre, on les identifie sans mal par leur costume et leur attitude avec des dignitaires, magistrats, fonctionnaires civils[18] ou militaires[19] tels qu'on les représentait depuis 317[20]. Leur costume nous fournit d'ailleurs un premier indice de datation,

---

  minentibus[...] Quam iunctini sedent! [...] Quam cito transeunt! («Mais lorsqu'une fois passé le seuil du palais vous vous êtes avancés tous deux sur le même char au milieu de la ville, les maisons elles-mêmes, me dit-on, furent près de se mouvoir, tandis que tout le monde, hommes et femmes, enfants et vieillards, se précipitaient dans les rues par les portes ou se penchaient sur vous par les fenêtres des étages supérieurs [...] Comme ils sont assis l'un près de l'autre! [...] Comme ils passent vite!»).

[16] LIBANIOS, *Epist.*, 97, 1106F, a. 393, éd. R. FOERSTER, Leipzig 1922, 212-214 (trad. B. Cabouret, LIBANIOS, *Lettres aux hommes de son temps*, Paris 2000), 203-206: εὔχονται δὲ γυναῖκες οὐ παροφθεῖσαι οὐδ' ἀμεληθεῖσαι οὐδὲ ἀπελαθεῖσαι, λόγων δὲ τυχοῦσαι πράων τε καὶ ἡμέρων, εὔχοντ' οὖν αἱ γυναῖκες σώζεσθαι μέν σοι τὴν τοῦ γενναίου βασιλέως εὔνοιαν, σώζεσθαι δὲ βασιλεῖ τοὺς σοὺς ὑπὲρ αὐτοῦ πόνους ἐλθεῖν τε αὖθις ὡς ἡμᾶς τὸν τῶν πόλεων ἰατρὸν ἀναβῆναί τε πάλιν εἰς Δάφνην δευτέρων ἀκριβεστέρων, ὡς νῦν γε ἱέραξ ἡμῖν ἦσθα τάχος τε πτεροῦ τοῦ 'κείνου μιμούμενος καὶ τῷ πᾶσαν ἐθέλειν εἰδέναι ἐν βραχεῖ τὸ μὴ πᾶσαν ἰδεῖν κεκωλυμένος ταῦτ' οὖν τὰ διαφυγόντα τῶν σῶν ὀφθαλμῶν τυχεῖν καὶ μὴ τῶν ὀφθέντων ἔλαττον ἔχειν· εἰ δὲ καὶ μετὰ τῶν ἀρίστων βασιλέων, ὧν πολὺς ἔρως τῇ πόλει («Et les femmes, qui n'ont essuyé ni dédain ni négligence ni manque de considération, mais ont reçu des paroles empreintes de douceur et de civilité, les femmes donc prient que te soit sauvegardée la bienveillance de notre noble empereur, que soient sauvegardés à l'Empereur les efforts que tu déploies pour lui, et que reviennent vers nous le médecin des cités, qu'il monte à nouveau vers Daphné, la seconde fois avec plus d'attention, car, dernièrement, tu étais pour nous un faucon dont tu imitais la vitesse de vol et, par ton désir de saisir la ville en raccourci, tu t'es privé de la voir tout entière. Elle souhaitent donc que ce qui t'a échappé s'offre à tes yeux et ne le cède pas à ce qui a été vu»).

[17] Voir supra n. 14.

[18] Dont l'exemple le plus ancien me semble être celui d'un *palatinus a memorialis* de Salone (cf. D. RENDIC-MIOCEVIC, *Nova kasnoanticka stela iz Salona*, «VAHD» 56-59 (1954-1957)/2, 156 sq.), dont je daterais volontiers la dédicace de la fin du règne de Licinius. Cr. *infra*, n. 20.

[19] Tels qu'on les trouve figurés sur les tombes d'Aquilée, qui doivent dater du début IVᵉ siècle, selon F. REBECCHI, *Le stele di età tetrarchica al museo di Aquileia. Documenti tardo-antichi per la storia della città*, «Aquileia nostra» 47 (1976), col. 65-142.

[20] Selon F. MILLAR, *The Emperor in the Roman World*, Londres, 108 sq., qui fournit l'étude la plus précise de l'introduction du costume militaire chez les palatins du IVᵉ siècle (une mesure de Licinius, reprise par Constantin en 326); cf. J.-M. CARRIE, A. ROUSSELLE, *L'Empire romain en mutation des Sévères à Constantin 192-337* (*Nouvelle Histoire de l'Antiquité*, 10), Paris 1999, 664-665; la première représentation d'un fonctionnaire

un indice qui n'a pas la fragilité des critères esthétiques trop souvent utilisés pour dater ces sarcophages, en l'absence d'ailleurs de tout contexte archéologique précis. Giuseppe Wilpert en 1929 a cru y voir la production d'un long IIIe siècle[21], alors que Nikolaus Himmelmann[22] en 1973 a soutenu à propos du relief d'Aquilée et de celui du musée des Thermes, que la coiffure des femmes laissait entendre une datation plus tardive, contemporaine des portraits féminins de l'époque de Constantin, à commencer par ceux attribués à sa mère, Hélène. Suivant les pièces, le savant allemand a retenu ainsi une période courte entre 270 et 315. A l'invitation de Winfried Weber[23], Catherine Metzger et François Baratte[24] ont préféré attribuer certaines pièces à une production postérieure à cette estimation d'un bon demi-siècle. Nous verrons que c'est l'hypothèse qui nous paraît la plus vraisemblable, même si en 1991, Rita Americk[25] est revenue à une datation plus haute.

L'élément je crois le plus important pour dater et comprendre ces documents reste l'utilisation du char bige à quatre roues doté d'une cathèdre. Dans les cités tardives, les dignitaires entraient manifestement assis, en adoptant une posture hiératique, tel le préfet du prétoire Rufin à Antioche en 393, selon Libanios: «Et nous apparaissent aussi les roses qui volaient, venues d'un côté, de l'autre, d'en haut, dont certaines se posaient sur tes genoux et qu'un mouvement élégant de tes doigts sous la chlamyde rejettait à terre»[26]. C'était bien parce qu'il était assis, que les pétales de rose pouvaient s'accumuler sur ses genoux. Cette attitude hiératique que relève le rhéteur d'Antioche, rappelle bien évidemment l'attitude de Constance II lors de l'*aduentus* romain du 28 avril 357, tel que nous le rapporte Am-

---

palatin me semble se trouver sur une stèle funéraire découverte à Salone et datant sans doute du règne de Licinius, que l'on me permette de renvoyer à C.J .GODDARD *136. Epitaphe d'Aur(elius) Valerinus,* exceptor Imp(eratorum) in officio memoriae *(IVe-Ve siècles apr. J.-C.),* dans N. GAUTHIER, E. MARIN, F. PREVOT, *Salona IV,* à paraître dans la Collection de l'Ecole française de Rome.

[21] G. WILPERT, *I sarcofagi cristiani...*, 25-31, suite à ses articles portant sur *La catechesi di S. Filippo,* «Riv. Arch. Crist.» (1924), 140 sq. et *L'ultimo viaggio nell'arte sepolcrale classico-romana,* «RendPontAcc» (1925), 61-72.
[22] N. HIMMELMANN, *Typologische...*, 30-34.
[23] W. WEBER, *Die Darstellung...*, 43.
[24] C. METZGER, F. BARATTE, *Catalogue des sarcophages en pierre d'époques romaine et paléochrétienne,* Paris 1985, n. 6, 35.
[25] R. AMEDICK, *Die Sarkophage...*, 46-58.
[26] LIBANIUS, *supra* n. 16: φαίνεται δ' ἡμῖν καὶ τὰ ῥόδα τά τε ἔνθεν καὶ ἔνθεν τά τε ἄνωθεν πετόμενα καὶ τούτων τὰν τοῖς γόνασιν ἱζάνοντα καὶ τοῖς ὑπὸ τῇ χλαμύδι μετ' εὐσχημοσύνης κινουμένοις δακτύλοις ἐπὶ τὰ κάτω φερόμενα.

mien Marcellin[27] dans un passage célèbre. L'empereur prenait la pause d'une statue et se donnait à voir ainsi dans une immobilité propre à la divinité, ce qui ne saurait surprendre à une époque où *numen* et *sacer* finirent par rimer avec empereur et maison impériale[28]. Si l'on en juge par les

---

[27] AMMIEN MARCELLIN, XVI, 10, 9-10, éd. et trad. E. GALLETIER et J. FONTAINE, Paris 1968, 166: *Augustus itaque faustis uocibus appellatus, non montium litorumque intonante fragore cohorruit, talem se tamque immobilem, qualis in prouinciis suis uisebatur, ostendens. Nam et corpus perhumile curuabat portas ingrediens celsas, et uelut collo munito, rectam aciem luminum tendens, nec dextra uultum nec laeua flectebat et (tamquam figmentum hominis) nec cum rota concuteret nutans, nec spuens, aut os aut nasum tergens uel fricans, manumue agitans uisus est umquam.* («Auguste, acclamé par des cris d'heureux augure, ne fut donc pas troublé par le bruit de tonnerre répercuté par les collines et les rives, mais il observa l'attitude immobile qu'on lui voyait prendre dans ses provinces. En effet, il inclinait sa taille minuscule au passage des hautes portes et, comme s'il eût le cou pris dans un carcan, il portait son regard droit devant lui, sans tourner le visage à droite ni à gauche et, semblable à une statue, on ne le vit jamais faire un mouvement aux cahots de son char, ni cracher, ni essuyer ou frotter son visage ou son nez, ni agiter la main»). Sur l'*aduentus* romain de Constance II en 357, voir A. FRASCHETTI, *La conversione da Roma pagana...*, 253 sq.; O. SEECK, *Regesten der Kaiser und Päpste für die Jahre 311 bis 476 n. Chr.*, Stuttgart 1919, 204; J. STRAUB, *Vom Herrscherideal in der Spätantike*, Stuttgart 1939, 325 sq.; R.O. EDBROOKE JR., *The Visit of Constantius II to Rome in 357 and its Effects on the Pagan Roman Senatorial Aristocracy*, «AJPh» 97 (1976), 1976, 40 sq.; M. CALTABIANO, *I trionfi di Costanzo II*, dans *Studi di antichità in memoria di C. Gatti*, Milan 1987, 37 sq.; N. BAGLIVI, *Ammianea*, Catane 1995, 55 sq.; A. ALFÖLDI, *Die monarchische Repräsentation im römischen Kaiserreiche*, Darmstadt 1970, 108 sq.; J. CURRAN, *Pagan City and Christian Capital. Rome in the Fourth Century*, Oxford 2000, 191 sq.; J.F. MATTHEWS, *The Roman Empire of Ammianus*, Londres 1989, 231-5; S. MACCORMACK, *Art and Ceremony...*, 40-3; D. VERA, *Commento storico alle* Relationes *di Quinto Aurelio Simmaco*, Pise 1981, 35-6; R. KLEIN, *Der Rombesuch des Kaisers Konstantius II im Jahre 357*, «Athenaeum» 57 (1979), 98-115; Y.M. DUVAL, *La venue à Rome de l'empereur Constance II en 357 d'après Ammien Marcellin*, «Caesarodunum» 2 (1970), 299-304; N.H. BAYNES, c. r. *J. Vogt et E. Kornemann, Römische Geschichte, Leipzig, Berlin 1933*, «JRS» 25 (1935), 87 sq.; M. VITIELLO, *Nuove prospettive sull'*aduentus *in età imperiale*, «MedAnt» III (2000)/2, 551-580, qui reprend et commente J. LEHNEN, Aduentus principis. *Untersuchungen zu Sinngehalt und Zeremoniell der KaiseranKunft in den Städten des Imperium des Imperium Romanum*, Frankfurt am Main-Berlin-New York-Paris-Vienne 1997.

[28] Cf. L. CRACCO RUGGINI, *Apoteosi e politica senatoria nel IV s. d.C.: il dittico dei Symmachi al British Museum*, «Riv. St. It.» 3-4 (1977), 425-489 et part. 425 et n. 3, qui montre la progressive sécularisation de ces qualificatifs et qualités divines; N. GAUTHIER, *Le* numen *des empereurs chrétiens: à propos de CIL III, 8710 (Salone)*, dans *Romanité et cité chrétienne. Permanences et mutations, intégration et exclusion du Ier au VIe siècle. Mélanges en l'honneur d'Yvette Duval*, éd. F. PRÉVOT, Paris 2000, 233-247, qui montre la permanence du sens religieux du *numen* au IVe siècle, sous l'influence de dédicants clarissimes païens.

panneaux qui furent consacrés aux *aduentus* de Galère à Thessalonique[29] en 311 et de Constantin à Rome[30], l'institution de ce type de cérémonie, où l'empereur se tenait non plus debout comme un *imperator* triomphant de la République, mais assis sur un char élevé, était une invention du tout début du IVe siècle. Sa plus ancienne mention littéraire se trouve dans le second panégyrique de Maximien, qui évoque l'entrée solennelle de Dioclétien et de Maximien pendant l'hiver 290-291 à Milan[31]. Selon

---

[29] Cf. K.F. KINCH, *L'arc de triomphe de Salonique*, Copenhague-Paris 1893; W. SESTON, *Dioclétien et la tétrarchie*, I, Rome 1946, 182-183; H.P. LAUBSCHER, *Der Reliefschmuck des Galeriusbogens in Thessaloniki*, Berlin 1975, 62 et pl. 48, 1; A. ALFÖLDI, *Die monarchische Repräsentation...*, 108 sq.; R. TEJA, *Il cerimoniale imperiale*, dans *Storia di Roma. L'età tardoantica. I luoghi e le culture*, edd. A. CARANDINI, L. CRACCO RUGGINI, A. GIARDINA, III-1, Turin 1993, 613-642 et plus particulièrement 625 sq.

[30] A. CAPODIFERRO, Arcus Constantini, dans, *LTVR*, éd. E. STEINBY, I, Rome 1993, 86-91 (qui rassemble la bibliographie antérieure); A. FRASCHETTI *La conversione da Roma pagana...*, 21 et n. 15. Le bas-relief évoquant l'*aduentus* romain de Constantin fut diversement apprécié: témoignage d'un art populaire et provincial pour les uns (G. RODENWALT, *Studi e scoperte germaniche sull'archeologia e l'arte del Tardo impero*, dans *Quaderni dell'impero. Roma e le provincie*, I, *Istituto di Studi Romani*, Roma 1937, 3-23 et part. 22 sq., qui renvoie à ses travaux antérieurs), témoignage d'un courant primitif pour les autres (O. WINCKELMANN, *Die Kunst der Antike*, Berlin 84 sq.), œuvre digne de la médiocrité des temps selon les autres (G. BECATTI, *L'arco di Costantino*, «CritdAJ», 1940, 45-58). R. BIANCHI BANDINELLI, *Roma. La fine dell'arte antica*, Milan, 73-83, a le premier insisté sur l'importance de la nouvelle étiquette, imposée par Constantin, une mode dont il croit trouver l'origine en Orient, ce que P. VEYNE, *L'Empire gréco-romain*, Paris 2004, a récusé très récemment. Sur cette frise historiée, J. RUYSSCHAERT, *Essai d'interprétation synthétique de l'arc de Constantin*, «RendPontAcc» 35 (1962-1963), 79-100; ID., *Unità e significato dell'arco di Costantino*, «St. Rom.» 11 (1963), 1-12, suivi A. FRASCHETTI, *La conversione da Roma pagana...*, 97 sq., a insisté sur l'absence de référence capitoline, sans remarquer que les arcs de Septime-Sévère et de Titus sur la zone forale n'en contenaient pas plus. Ce n'était donc pas un élément d'originalité et l'on ne saurait en tirer argument pour affirmer qu'à la première heure, dès 312, Constantin se refusa à monter au Capitole.

[31] MAMERTINUS, *Panegyricus Genethliacus Maximiano Augusto dictus*, 61: *Vt uero limine egressi per mediam urbem simul uehebamini, tecta ipsa se, ut audio, paene commouerunt, omnibus uiris feminis, paruulis senibus aut per fores in publicum proruentibus aut per superiora aedium lumina imminentibus [...] Quam iunctini sedent! [...] Quam cito transeunt!* («Mais lorsqu'une fois passé le seuil du palais vous vous êtes avancés tous deux sur le même char au milieu de la ville, les maisons elles-mêmes, me dit-on, furent près de se mouvoir, tandis que tout le monde, hommes et femmes, enfants et vieillards, se précipitaient dans les rues par les portes ou se penchaient sur vous par les fenêtres des étages supérieurs [...] Comme ils sont assis l'un près de l'autre ! [...] Comme ils passent vite»). LACTANCE, *De mort. Persec.*, XIX, affirme que lors de son abdication, Dioclétien quitta Nicomédie sur un char ordinaire, une *reda* gauloise,

Augusto Fraschetti[32], il fallait lire là – du moins dans le cas de Constantin – la volonté de proclamer une majesté conférée personnellement par la *diuinitas*, tout en cherchant pour des raisons religieuses à échapper au déroulement d'une cérémonie encore trop entachée de paganisme. Retenons pour l'heure que l'utilisation pour un *aduentus* impérial d'un char où l'empereur se devait de rester assis et immobile, était une innovation de l'époque tétrarchique habilement détournée par Constantin.

L'existence de ce type de carrosse tirerait son origine, selon Gabriele Lucchi[33], du *carpentum* utilisé lors de la cérémonie de la *consecratio* à Rome dès le IIe siècle apr. J.-C, coiffé d'un toit, soutenu par de majestueuses caryatides (fig. 5), qui lui donnait l'apparence d'un temple, tiré lentement par deux mulets. Lellia Cracco Ruggini[34] a retrouvé un dernier exemple de ces carrosses consécratoires sur le second dyptique des Symmaque (fig. 6), où se trouverait représentée l'apothéose de Théodose l'Ancien, le célèbre général et père de l'empereur homonyme: l'équipage était constitué d'éléphants[35], comme sur le relief contemporain d'un sarcophage, conservé dans la basilique romaine de Saint-Laurent-Hors-les-Murs, qui évoque très certainement l'une des processions liées au culte officiel de Magna Mater[36] (fig. 7).

---

abandonnant son carrosse impérial. Je dois ces références à l'amitié et l'érudition de Claude Lepelley.

[32] A. FRASCHETTI, *La conversione da Roma pagana...*, 97 sq. (qui contient la bibliographie antérieure), proche en cela de S. MACCORMACK, *Art and Ceremony...*, 17-92 sur l'*aduentus* impérial tardif et 62 sur sa christianisation; *contra* F. PASCHOUD, *Ancora sul rifiuto di Costantino di salire al Campidoglio*, dans, *Costantino il Grande dall'Antichità all'Umanesimo. Colloquio sul cristianesimo nel mondo antico. Macerata 18-20 décembre 1990*, 2, edd. G. BONAMENTE et F. FUSCO, Macerata 1993, 737-748; cf. A. MASTINO, A. TEATINI, *Ancora sul discusso «trionfo» di Costantino dopo la battaglia del ponte Milvio. Nota a proposito di CIL, VIII, 9356 = 20941 (Caesarea)*, dans *Varia Epigraphica. Atti del Colloquio internazionale di epigrafia, Bertinoro, 8-10 giugno 2000*, Faenza 2001, 272-327; et sur l'*aduentus* d'images impériales, voir le très riche C. ANDO, *Imperial Ideology and provincial Loyalty in the Roman Empire*, Berkeley- Los Angeles-Londres, 2001, 206 sq.

[33] G. LUCCHI, *Sul significato del* carpentum *nella monetazione romana imperiale*, «RitNum» 16 (1968), 131-141.

[34] L. CRACCO RUGGINI, *Apoteosi e politica senatoria...*, 425-489 et part. 452 sq.

[35] Selon L. Cracco Ruggini, *ibid.*, ces éléphants seraient une allusion à la victoire africaine de Théodose l'Ancien sur Firmus.

[36] Notons avec P. LIVERANI, *La topografia antica del Vaticano*, Città del Vaticano 1999, 31 sq., que sur ce sarcophage, le cortège est ouvert par deux *fercula*, le premier supportant une statue de Magna Mater, le second la Victoire, dont l'association renvoyait à l'association antique des deux déesses sur le Palatin. Le temple de la Victoire, voisin du temple de Cybèle accueillit la pierre aniconique de la divinité que l'Etat romain fit

Toutefois, le *carpentum* des IVe et Ve siècles se distinguait nettement de son lointain et funeste cousin, tant par l'apparence que par la fonction. Si le carrosse était tout aussi bige et supporté par quatre roues, il était en revanche toujours découvert, tiré par deux chevaux, conduit par un cocher assis à même le plancher, ce qui élevait davantage encore le dignitaire qui avait pris place sur un siège élevé, qui avait toute l'apparence d'un trône ou d'une cathèdre.

On devine aisément que l'adoption par les sénateurs de ce protocole d'entrée solennelle et l'utilisation de ce nouveau véhicule, dont le nom varie, *carruca*, *uehiculum* pour les uns et *carpentum iudiciale* pour les autres, devait être logiquement postérieure à son modèle impérial. Un dossier important mais complexe nous permet d'en retracer la chronologie.

La *Notitia dignitatum* au début du Ve siècle en faisait l'un des insignes des fonctionnaires impériaux les plus importants, les préfets de la Ville et du prétoire[37] et nous fournit un premier *terminus ante quem*. La plupart des historiens à la suite d'Andreas Alfoldi[38] se sont fondés sur la lecture de deux *relationes* (4 et 20) adressées par le préfet de la Ville, *Quintus Aurelius Symmachus*, à la fin 384 à l'empereur Valentinien II pour en

---

venir à grand frais de Pessinonte en 205-204 av. J.-C., cf. J. Scheid, *Religion et piété à Rome*, Paris 2001², 126 sq. Une lacune interdit de voir ce qui pouvait se trouver sur le *carpentum* à quatre roues tiré par quatre éléphants. P. Liverani, *La topografia antica...*, mentionne un passage de *SHA, V. Heliog.*, XXIII, 1, qui montre Elagabal sur un tel carrosse. On peut penser aussi au dyptique de Symmaque, qui placerait Théodose l'Ancien sur le même véhicule, selon L. Cracco Ruggini, *Apoteosi e politica senatoria...*, 436 et 453. Je formule l'hypothèse que pouvait s'y tenir le préfet de la Ville. Il suffit de lire l'*incipit* de la *Vita Aureliani* dans l'*Histoire Auguste*, où au terme des *Hilaria*, le préfet urbain accueillit sur son *carpentum iudiciale* le futur et imaginaire biographe d'Aurélien, revenant du Palatin et se rendant au temple de Sol d'Aurélien. Sur le bandeau du sarcophage de Saint-Laurent, les personnages qui précèdent le *carpentum*, habillés d'une digne toge sénatoriale, étaient à mon sens les *quindecemuiri sacris faciundis* (cf. C. Fevrier, *De l'usage des Livres: le décemvir, prêtre ou uates*, «Latomus» 61 [2002], 821-841, qui rassemble la bibliographie sur la question) qui surveillaient avec attention le déroulement de ce culte.

[37] O. Seeck, *Notitia Dignitatum, accedunt Notitia Vrbis Constantinopolitanae et Laterculi prouinciarum*, Berlin 1876, 9, 107 et 113; J.J.G. Alexander, *The Illustrated Manuscripts of the* Notitia Dignitatum, dans *The Aspects of the* Notitia Dignitatum. *Papers presented to the Conference in Oxford, December 13 to 15, 1974*, éds. R. Goodburn et P. Bartholomew, Oxford 1976, 11-50; P. Berger, *The Insigna of the* Notitia Dignitatum, Garland 1981.

[38] A. Alföldi, *Die monarchische Repräsentation...*, 109 sq.; cf. R. Turcan, *Les sarcophages romains à représentations dionysiaques. Essai de chronologie et d'histoire religieuse*, Rome 1966, 468 sq., pour qui la présence d'éléphants dans ce type de processions avait une origine dionysiaque.

faire l'une des nombreuses innovations introduites dans la vie religieuse et festive romaine par Gratien en 382-383[39]:

> «Falso creditum est, quod urbanae fastigium potestatis peregrini ac superbi uehiculi usus adtolleret; haec ratio sola nouum statutum benigno tunc persuasit ingenio, ut ueterem magistratum diues pompa gestaret. Recusat istius modi decus honor sobrius, quem numquam paenitet sui; cui si quid patimur accedere, fatemur hactenus defuisse. Itaque oculi quaerunt ciuitatis priuati uehiculi nobilem modum et degenerem praefecturam populus Romanus existimat, quae posteriora traxit exempla».

> «Il est illusoire de croire que l'utilisation d'un véhicule magnifique et étranger <à l'usage> porterait à un accroissement du pouvoir <de la préfecture> urbaine; ce fut pour cette seule raison, inspirée par sa bienveillance, qu'il (= Gratien) fut convaincu alors de prendre <cette> nouvelle disposition, afin qu'un riche équipage transportât l'antique magistrature. La sobriété attachée à cette charge, qu'elle (la préfecture urbaine) n'a jamais regrettée pour sa part, se refuse à une gloire de ce genre. Et si nous consentons qu'elle en soit doté, nous reconnaissons que jusqu'alors il (le carrosse de fonction) lui avait fait défaut. C'est pourquoi les yeux de la cité exigent le genre respectable d'un véhicule privé et le peuple romain estime la préfecture dégénérée, elle qui a conservé les modèles précédents (de carrosse)».

Pour Andreas Alfoldi[40], le préfet ne devait plus utiliser sa *carruca* privée mais son *carpentum iudiciale*, un véhicule de fonction, richement réhaussé de pierres précieuses et orné du plus bel argent. Wilhelm Ensslin[41] a contesté la nature de ce changement en remarquant que Symmaque, comme Ammien Marcellin, employait indifféremment *carpentum*, *curruca* ou *uehiculum* pour désigner le carrosse emprunté par le haut-fonctionnaire. En quelque sorte, cette révolution cérémonielle n'avait laissé aucune trace lexicale. Pour André Chastagnol[42], cette contestation reste sans valeur, car Symmaque évoque moins une évolution du vocabulaire qu'un changement radical du mode de propriété: selon le savant français, pour la première fois se trouvait mis à la disposition du préfet urbain un «char-insigne», qui était une propriété publique. Arnaldo Momigliano[43],

---

[39] SYMMAQUE, *Rel.* 4 .
[40] A. ALFÖLDI, *Die monarchische Repräsentation...*, 107 sq.
[41] W. ENSSLIN, *«Carpentum» oder «Curruca»*, «Klio» 32 (1939), 89-105.
[42] A. CHASTAGNOL, *La préfecture urbaine à Rome au Bas-Empire*, Paris 1960, 203-205 et ID., *Le problème de l'Histoire Auguste: état de la question*, dans *Bonner Historia-Augusta-Colloquium 1963*, Bonn 1964, 43-71 et part. 60-61.
[43] A. MOMIGLIANO, *Per la interpretazione di Simmaco*, «RAL» 19 (1964), 225-230.

suivi par Domenico Vera[44], lui rétorqua que les critiques de Symmaque ne visaient finalement que le caractère luxueux du nouveau véhicule préfectoral. Il est vrai que l'on peut diversement interpréter *itaque oculi quaerunt ciuitatis priuati uehiculi nobilem modum* («C'est pourquoi le regard de la cité réclame le mode noble d'un véhicule privé»). Et le terme de *modus* peut permettre aussi bien de préciser que la voiture de fonction se devait de ressembler au véhicule ordinaire d'un particulier, qu'indiquer qu'il fallait revenir à l'usage d'un véhicule privé pour les préfets. Ce seul témoignage ne permet pas de trancher, quoi qu'en ait pensé André Chastagnol[45]. Ce dernier me semble l'emporter sur ses confrères sur un point, le carrosse de fonction était bien une propriété publique. Le préfet urbain de 384 est on ne peut plus clair dans le second rapport qu'il consacra à cette question:

> «Cum clementia uestra meminisset faciendae carrucae inpendium de sacro aerario esse decretum, censuit, ut eius argentum publicis conditis redderetur, ddd imppp sed examinis repperit fides ex aliis titulis adsumptam speciem, quam uehiculi ornatus accepit. Cuius rei etiam uir industris predecessor meus Auchenius Bassus perennitati uestrae rationem dicitur intimasse».

> «Comme Votre Clémence s'est souvenu d'avoir décrété que la construction d'un carrosse soit à la charge du Sacré *Aerarium*, Elle a décidé, que l'argent serait rendu aux instances publiques qui avaient été assignées à la dépense, Vos Impériales Seigneuries, mais il est ressorti d'un solide examen que l'éclat que reçut la décoration du véhicule avait été empruntée à d'autres caisses, ce dont, semble-t-il, mon prédécesseur, l'illustre Auchenius Bassus, a informé aussi Votre Pérennité[46]».

La construction du carrosse faisait suite à une décision impériale de Gratien et le trésor impérial se devait d'en assurer le financement public. Le rapport ne dit pas pour autant que la mise à disposition du préfet de la Ville fut le fruit de cette même législation. En effet, André Chastagnol a, me semble-t-il, sous-estimé un passage fondamental d'Ammien Marcellin:

> «[...] paulo enim afuit quin filia caperetur Constanti, cibum sumens in publica uilla quam appellant Pistrensem, cum duceretur Gratiano nuptura, <ni> fauore propitii numinis, praesens Messala, prouinciae rector, eam iudiciali carpento inpositam, ad Sirmium uicensimo sexto lapide disparatam, cursu reduxisset».

---

[44] D. VERA, *Commento storico...*, 55 sq. et cf. p. 147 sq.
[45] A. CHASTAGNOL, *La préfecture urbaine...*, 204 et n. 6, où il en vient à qualifier d'anachronique la mention antérieure d'une voiture de fonction chez Ammien Marcellin, XXIX, 6, 7, Cf. *infra*.
[46] SYMMAQUE, *Rel.*, 20; Cf. D. VERA, *Commento storico...*, 208.

> «Et peu s'en fallut que la fille de l'empereur Constance ne fût capturée, en prenant son repas dans le domaine impérial nommé Pistrensis, alors qu'on la menait épouser Gratien, si, grâce à la protection de la divinité propice, Messala, le gouverneur de la province, présent sur les lieux, ne l'avait installée sur son char de fonction (*carpentum*) et ramenée à Sirmium, distante de vingt-six milles en une course effrénée»[47].

Cette scène se déroulait en 374, l'année du mariage de l'empereur Gratien avec Constantia[48], la fille posthume de Constance II, âgée d'à peine 15 ou 16 ans. Le nouveau *dux per Valeriam*, Marcellianus selon Ammien, Celestius selon Zosime (IV, 16, 4)[49] en faisant assassiner le roi quade Gabinius[50], venait de provoquer une révolte de son peuple et des *gentes circumsitae* – des Sarmates, selon Zosime (IV, 16, 4) – qui ravagea les régions danubiennes, et notamment Pistrensis, siège d'une *uilla* impériale inconnue par ailleurs, non loin de Sirmium, où se situe la présente scène[51].

Il paraît absurde d'imaginer qu'un *rector prouinciae*, tout clarissime qu'il était alors, avait pu bénéficier du privilège d'une voiture officielle avant le préfet de la Ville de Rome, d'autant que sur la *Notitia dignitatum*, le *carpentum* ne figure pas parmi les attributs de sa fonction[52]. L'*Histoire Auguste* vient troubler cette chronologie, en renvoyant cette disposition au règne de Sévère Alexandre:

---

[47] AMMIEN, XXIX, 6, 7, éd. et trad. G. SABBAH, t. XXX, Paris, CUF, 1999, 48

[48] S.v. *Constantia 2*, *PLRE*, I, 221; cf. D. KIENAST, *Römische Kaisertabelle. Grundzüge einer römischen Kaiserchronologie*, Munich 1996, 333 sq.; E. DEMOUGEOT, *La formation de l'Europe et les invasions barbares*, Paris 1969, t. II, 1, 303 et G. SABBAH, *Ammien...*, 204 et n. 191.

[49] S.v. *Marcellianus 2* (*PLRE*, I, 343 sq.) était le fils du préfet du prétoire Maximinus 7, pour le titre cf. *ND* Oc., V, 137 (éd. O. SEECK 1876, 121). Pour W. ENNSSLIN, s. v. *Marcellianus*, dans *RE*, XIV, 1930, col. 1439, suivi par F. PASCHOUD, éd. ZOSIME, *Histoire Nouvelle*, II, Paris 1979, 365 et. 135.

[50] Cf. aussi Zos. IV, 16, 4-6 (éd. F. PASCHOUD, Paris 1979, 277 et n. 135, 365); éd. et trad. G. SABBAH, *Ammien...*, 206 et n. 196 et *PLRE*, I, 377 et O. SEECK, s.v. *Gabinius 5*, dans *RE*, VII, 1, 1910, col. 1439 sq.

[51] A une quarantaine de km, sur «l'axe routier Singidunum-Cibalae-Mursa», si l'on en croit G. SABBAH, *Ammien...*, 20 6; U.-B. DITTRICH, *Die Beziehungen Roms zu den Sarmaten und Quaden im 4. Jahrhundert n. Chr. (nach der Darstellung des Ammianus Marcellinus)*, Bonn 1984, 102 et n. 68; A. MOCSY, *Pannonia and Upper Moesia*, Londres 1974, 300-306.

[52] Seules les préfectures de la Ville de Rome, du prétoire de l'Illyricum, et du prétoire de l'Italie-Afrique-Illyricum, ont pour attribut le *carpentum*.

«Leges innumeras sanxit. Carrucas Romae et redas senatoribus omnibus ut argentatas haberent, permisit, interesse Romanae dignitatis putans, ut his tantae urbis senatores uterentur».

«Il promulgua un nombre considérable de lois. Il autorisa tous les sénateurs à avoir à Rome des carrosses et des voitures pourvus d'ornements en argent, pensant qu'il était important pour le prestige romain que les sénateurs d'une si grande ville puissent en faire usage»[53].

L'*incipit* de la *Vie d'Aurélien* (dans *l'Histoire Auguste*) pouvait mettre en scène son biographe imaginaire, Flavius Vopiscus de Syracuse sur le *carpentum* tardif du préfet de la Ville dès le règne de Dioclétien[54]. Cette dernière référence a du moins le mérite de ne pas anticiper l'utilisation de ce véhicule par l'empereur lui-même. Toutefois ces deux mentions, n'étant corroborées par aucune autre source, doivent sans doute être rangées parmi les très subtils jeux anachroniques auxquels aimait à se livrer l'auteur de l'*Histoire Auguste*. Ils ne sauraient donc constituer à eux seuls des indices chronologiques sûrs. D'ailleurs, l'on notera que pour Symmaque le revêtement du carrosse en argent constituait l'innovation même de la loi de Gratien[55]. En résumé, la *relatio 20* indique clairement que

---

[53] *SHA, V. Seu. Alex.*, 43, 1, trad. A. CHASTAGNOL, Paris, 1994, 611
[54] *SHA, V. Aur.*, 1: *Hilaribus, quibus omnia festa et fieri debere scimus et dici, impletis sollemnibus uehiculo suo me et iudicali carpento praef. Vrbis, uir inlustris ac praefata reuerentia nominandus, Iunius Tiberianus accepit*: «A l'occasion des fêtes de Cybèle [*Hilaria*], pendant lesquelles nous savons que conduite et propos se doivent d'être joyeux, une fois les cérémonies terminées, le préfet de la Ville Junius Tibérianus, un homme illustre dont il faut citer le nom avec respect, m'invita dans sa voiture qui était son véhicule de fonction», dans la trad. d'A. CHASTAGNOL, Paris 1994, 969. Ce dernier, *ibid.*, cxvii, note qu'il y eut sous la tétrarchie deux préfets de ce nom, un père (18 février 291 – 3 août 292) et son fils (12 septembre 303 – 4 janvier 305). La fête des Hilaria tombant le 25 mars devrait faire pencher pour le père, mais prétend être composée en 305-306. Sur ces anachronismes, cf. les p. cxiv sq. de l'éd. d'A. Chastagnol.
[55] Si l'on veut bien comprendre *cum fiscus in tempore, quod praebendum fuerat, non haberet, ex arca quaestoria itemque ex formarum conditis, praetera ex argentariorum parsimonia argentum iusso operi ministratum est* [...] («comme à cette époque le fisc ne disposait pas du nécessaire, l'on s'est servi pour l'ouvrage requis de l'argent tiré de la caisse questorienne, comme de celles des acqueducs, puis du trésor des argentiers [...]», *Rel.* 20), comme une référence à un prélèvement d'argent brut et non à une ponction monétaire, comme A.H.M. JONES, *The Later Roman Empire*, Cambridge 1964, 429 et D. VERA, *Commento storico alle* Relationes *di Quinto Aurelio Simmaco*, Pise 1981, 147, *contra* A. CHASTAGNOL, *La préfecture urbaine...*, 204. Par *arca quaestoria*, il faut comprendre la caisse du sénat, soit l'ancien *aerarium populi Romani* (A.H.M. JONES, *The Later Roman...*, 709; A. CHASTAGNOL, *La préfecture urbaine...*, 75-78); sur celle des acqueducs, cf. D. VERA, *Commento storico...*, 151; sur celle des argentiers, la discus-

le véhicule du préfet de la Ville était bien une propriété publique dont la construction et la riche ornementation en argent décidée par Gratien devait être financée par la caisse impériale (*sacro aerario*). Ammien Marcellin laisse entendre qu'à Sirmium le gouverneur Messala disposait d'un *carpentum iudiciale*, d'un véhicule de fonction, dès 374. Le 30 janvier 386, l'utilisation d'un véhicule de fonction était rendue obligatoire par Théodose pour tous les *honorati*, qu'il soient de rang civil ou militaire lorsqu'ils étaient appelés à circuler dans Constantinople[56]. Retenons que les hauts dignitaires clarissimes eurent accès progressivement à partir de la seconde moitié du IVe siècle apr. J.-C. à ce type de véhicule de fonction, qui avait été adopté par les empereurs pour leurs entrées officielles dès la tétrarchie. Gratien rendit son utilisation obligatoire à Rome pour les préfets de la ville, sans doute en 381-382. Théodose étendit cette mesure à tous les «dignitaires» à Constantinople à partir de 386.

L'existence de ces *aduentus* sénatoriaux n'était pas le seul usage social, qui semble dériver d'une pratique aulique. Ammien Marcellin en évoque un autre :

> «Ex his quidam, cum salutari pectoribus oppositis coeperunt, osculanda capita in modum taurorum minacium obliquantes, adulatoribus offerunt genua sauianda uel manus».

> «Certains de ces personnages (i.e. les sénateurs), quand on s'apprête à les saluer poitrine contre poitrine, tournent de côté, à la manière de taureaux menaçants, la tête qu'ils devraient offrir aux baisers, et présentent aux flatteurs leurs genoux ou leurs mains à embrasser»[57].

L'historien glissa cette remarque dans le portrait au vitriol qu'il brossa des mœurs du Sénat et du peuple de Rome, dans l'une des célèbres digressions de ses *Res gestae*. L'historien décrit donc ce qu'il pense être une réalité des années 350-370[58].

---

sion continue entre ceux qui y voient une caisse de changeurs tel A. CHASTAGNOL, *La préfecture urbaine...*, 204, et ceux qui pensent aux artisans d'ateliers où l'on travaillait l'argent tel A.H.M. JONES, *The Later Roman...*, 435 et D. VERA, *Commento storico...*, 151.

[56] *CTh* XIV, 12, 1 (à Nébridius, PVC, 30 janvier 386): *Omnes honorati seu ciuilium seu militarium dignitatum uehiculis dignitatis suae, id est carrucis bijugis, intra urbem sacratissimi nominis semper utantur.* («Que tous les dignitaires de rang soit civils soit militaires se déplacent toujours à travers la Ville du Nom Très Sacré [= Constantinople] sur les véhicules de leur rang, c'est-à-dire des chars biges»).

[57] AMMIEN, XXVIII, 4, 10, trad. G. SABBAH, Paris, 1988, CUF, 97.

[58] Cf. *supra* n. 43-44.

Ce salut pectoral était, à en juger une remarque contemporaine du panégyrique du consul Mamertin (adressé à Julien), un signe de parité, que l'on faisait mine d'offrir, voire de requérir lors d'une rencontre[59]. Il ressortissait à la *salutatio* matinale que l'empereur adressait à ses visiteurs, tout d'abord aux sénateurs de haut rang, comme au reste de la société romaine, qui se présentait à lui en bon ordre. C'est bien le baiser entre égaux qui est refusé ici, celui que sous Auguste, Trajan ou Marc Aurèle, un sénateur offrait à l'empereur et que celui-ci devait lui rendre[60], le baiser que vraisemblablement les sénateurs se concédaient les uns aux autres.

Adulatoribus offerunt genua sauianda uel manus renvoie à un geste courant: embrasser les genoux d'une statue ou d'un prince, c'était depuis longtemps adopter l'attitude même du suppliant[61]. Fléchir le sien pour tenir la tunique de l'autre, c'était ce geste de génuflexion, la proskynèse ou en latin *adoratio*, réservée normalement à l'empereur. Selon Andreas Alföldi[62] et Robert Turcan[63], si les premières proskynèses, considérées par nos sources comme un vice perse, furent exigées par le modèle même du mauvais empereur, Caligula[64] ou par le père de l'empereur Vitellius[65], soit dès le Ier siècle apr. J.-C., il fallut attendre la Tétrarchie pour qu'il fût considéré comme la position ordinaire à adopter en présence de l'empe-

---

[59] S. ESTIENNE, *Les Dieux dans la Ville. Recherche sur les statues de dieux dans l'espace et les rites publics de Rome*, thèse de doctorat, Ecole pratique des Hautes Etudes, Paris 2001, 216 qui en fait le «geste de reconnaissance d'un certaine dignité», pratiquée surtout parmi les élites.

[60] Cf. PLIN. IUN. *Pan.* 23, 1; 24, 2; accompagné de l'accolade chez *SHA, MA*, 3, 4; FRONT. *Ad L. Verum*, II, 8, 1; voir les critiques contre Tibère qui s'en abstint par peur de quelque maladie contagieuse, PLIN. SEN. *N.H.* 26, 3; SUET. *Tib.* 34, 4; 68, 2; VAL. MAX. II, 16, 17; sur les réactions sénatoriales face à l'abandon de cette pratique par Néron selon SUÉTONE, *Ner.* 37, 6; cf. A. ALFÖLDI, *Die monarchische Repräsentation...*, 38 sq.; R. TURCAN, *Vivre à la cour des Césars: d'Auguste à Dioclétien (Ier – IIIe s. apr. J.-C.)*, Paris 1987, 138.

[61] Cf. les pages lumineuses de S. ESTIENNE, *Les Dieux dans la Ville...*, 224, qui montrent toute l'importance du genou, qui pour Pline l'Ancien et Servius, était le siège même de la vie ou de la miséricorde; F. GHEDINI, *Arte romana: generi e gesti*, dans *Civiltà dei Romani. Un linguaggio comune*, éd. S. SETTIS, Milan 1993, 161-178 et part. 170 qui montre que selon sa forme, l'agenouillement «esprime non più, o meglio, non solo sottomissione ma piuttosto devozione e gratitudine».

[62] A. ALFÖLDI, *Die monarchische Repräsentation...*, 45 sq.

[63] R. TURCAN, *Vivre à la cour des Césars...*, 132 sq.

[64] PHIL. *Leg. Ad Gaium*, 116; SEN. *Ben.* II, 12, 1; SUET. *Cal.* 56, 4; DION CASSIUS, LIX, 27, 1.

[65] SUET. *Vit.* II, 9.

reur, quel que fût son rang[66]. La remarque d'Ammien paraît d'autant plus cinglante, que les critiques contemporaines d'Eutrope[67], d'Aurelius Victor[68] ou de l'anonyme de l'*Histoire Auguste*[69] portant sur l'introduction de l'*adoratio*, trahissaient à l'évidence l'agacement de nombreux sénateurs du IVe siècle, qui prenaient mal de se voir refuser cette forme d'égalité socio-juridique, quoiqu'elle fût aulique et purement formelle[70]. Peu importe que l'anecdote rapportée par l'historien d'Antioche fût réelle ou non, il reste cette direction que semble suivre Ammien, de vouloir montrer chez les sénateurs romains de la fin du IVe siècle une diffusion des pratiques auliques[71]. Comment expliquer encore une fois cette diffusion sénatoriale? Ne constituait-elle pas un crime de lèse-majesté?

L'historiographie à l'instar d'Andreas Alfoldi[72] a trop longtemps compris les rapports entre le pouvoir impérial chrétien et le sénat romain, peuplé de païens irréductibles, sur un mode uniquement conflictuel. Or l'on ne pourrait comprendre l'efficacité des réformes institutionnelles engagées par Constantin, sans imaginer qu'elles connurent un certain succès parmi les membres des aristocraties sénatoriales romaines puis constantinopolitaines. C'est ce que j'ai voulu récemment éclairer en me penchant sur l'évolution de la position symbolique et sociale des membres l'ordre sénatorial[73]. Il me semble que Constantin et ses successeurs purent être exigeants, car ils avaient su rehausser le prestige de la curie romaine. Comme

---

[66] On en trouvera d'ailleurs l'illustration iconographique, découverte à Louxor dans une pièce de réception impériale d'époque tétrarchique; cf. I. KALAVREZOU-MAXEINER, *The Imperial Chamber at Louxor*, «DOP» 29 (1975), 225-251 et part. 242 sq.; cf. V. MAROTTA, *Liturgia del potere. Documenti di nomina e cerimonie di investitura fra Principato e Tardo Impero romano*, «Ostraka» 8 (1999), 180 sq.

[67] EUTROPE, IX, 26.

[68] AURELIUS VICTOR, XXXIX.

[69] *SHA, V. Seu. Alex.*, XVIII, 3; *V. Max.*, XXVIII, 7.

[70] Voir *Pan.* V, 1, 3 de 311 où *l'adoratio* était une manifestation d'autorité sur le Sénat et le confronter au *Pan.* III, 29, 4 où Julien semblait renouer avec une *salutatio* républicaine ou augustéenne.

[71] Cf. V. MAROTTA, *Liturgia del potere...*, 145-220, et 168 et n. 169; PHIL. *Vitae Soph.*, II, 10 (590); LUC. *Nigrinus*, 21; *P. Oxy.* II, 237, VI, l. 37 (186 apr.); *P. Teb.* 286, l. 22 (IIe s. apr.); *OGIS* I, 262, l. 26-27 (*pagus Baetocaece*, 253-259 apr.; HEROD. IV, 1, 3-4; PLOTIN. *Enn.* V, 5, 3; cf. *RIC*, V, 2 (1933), n.276, m. 277, pl. XIII, 12.

[72] A. ALFÖLDI, *A Conflict of Ideas in the Late Roman Empire; the Clash between the Senate and Valentinian I*, trad. H. Mattingly, Londres 1952.

[73] Que l'on me permette de renvoyer à mon étude, C.J. GODDARD, *Les senateurs comme miroirs...*

l'a montré Claude Lepelley[74], en prononçant la fin de l'ordre équestre – quoique que cette fin ait mis plus de 80 ans à se réaliser – Constantin rendit une large part de sa gloire au sénat, en lui offrant de nouvelles fonctions administratives et lui ouvrant accès à de nouveaux symboles. Il aurait été impensable au Haut-Empire de voir des sénateurs disposer des attributs liés au pouvoir impérial, tel que le *carpentum iudiciale* qui n'était rien d'autre, à y bien penser, qu'un trône impérial mobile. Cette situation était devenue normale entre le règne de Constantin et celui de Justinien, car les sénateurs étaient devenus les incarnations administratives du prince, ou pour reprendre une expression de la Seconde Sophistique, un reflet du soleil impérial, son miroir. C'est d'ailleurs ce qu'exprima en des termes très clairs Honorius le 4 septembre 397, en affirmant que non seulement les préfets, les membres de son consistoire, mais aussi les sénateurs étaient des «parties de son corps» (*pars corpori nostri*)[75]. La subtile distinction, la fiction dirons certains, entre magistrats élus et fonctionnaires nommés, qui avait été maintenue au Haut Empire, certes de façon symbolique, avait disparu dans l'Empire romain tardif. Il y eut une conséquence protocolaire et juridique de taille : du règne de Constantin à celui de Justinien (exclu), toutes les autorités, magistrats ou fonctionnaires, sénateurs ou curiales, devaient rendre leurs décisions devant le portrait impérial, comme l'expliqua très clairement Sévérien de Gabala au tout début du Ve siècle apr. J.-C[76]. Ce subtil équilibre symbolique et protocolaire entre pouvoir impérial et autorités sénatoriales, administratives, militaires et curiales fut rompu,

---

[74] C. LEPELLEY, *Du triomphe à la disparition. Le destin de l'ordre équestre de Dioclétien à Théodose*, dans *L'ordre équestre. Histoire d'une aristocratie (IIe siècle av. J.-C. – IIIe siècle ap. J.-C.). Actes du colloque international (Bruxelles-Leuven, 5-7 octobre 1995)*, éds. S. DEMOUGIN, H. DEVIJVER, M.-T. CHARLIER, Rome 1999, 629-646. Sur les réformes du sénat par Constantin et ses successeurs et l'évolution du statut des sénateurs, voir d'une manière générale, A. CHASTAGNOL, *Le Sénat romain à l'époque impériale*, Paris 1992, 293-344.

[75] *CTh* IX, 13, 3, 4 septembre 397: *[...] uirorum inlustrium, qui consiliis et consistorio nostro intersunt, senatorum etiam, nam et ipsi corporis nostri [...]* («(à la vie) des *illustres* qui participent aux conseils et à notre consistoire, comme à celle des sénateurs, car ils sont eux-mêmes une partie de notre corps [...]»).

[76] SÉVÉRIEN DE GABALA, *In Cosmogoniam*, VI, 5 (éd. B. DE MONTFAUCON, dans PG, 56, 489). ἐννόησον πόσοι εἰσὶν ἄρχοντες ἀνὰ πᾶσαν τὴν γῆν. Καὶ ἐπειδὴ Βασιλεὺς πᾶς οὐ πάρεστι, δεῖ παραστῆναι τὸν χαρακτῆρα τοῦ βασιλέως ἐν δικαστηρίοις, ἐν ἀγοραῖς, ἐν συλλόγοις, ἐν θεάτροις. Ἐν ταύτῃ οὖν πόπω, ἐν ᾧ πράττει ἄρχων δεῖ παρεῖναι ἄρχων, δεῖ παρεῖναι ἵνα βεβαιῶται τὰ γινόμενα («Considère combien d'autorités il y a dans le monde. Comme l'empereur ne peut se trouver avec eux tous, l'image de l'empereur doit être placée dans les cours de justice, sur les marchés, dans les salles de réunion, dans les théâtres. L'image de l'empereur doit être placée dans tous les endroits où une autorité exerce son pouvoir, pour qu'il délivre ses jugements»).

au grand dam de Jean Lydus[77], par Justinien. Les hommages impériaux que recevaient sénateurs et curiales étaient en fait adressés à travers eux aux empereurs, comme l'expliqua Athanase d'Alexandrie[78], suivi par Libanios[79] et Sévérien de Gabala[80]. Ils confortaient leur prestige respectif, tout en les liant de façon inextricable.

Le succès de ces *aduentus* et des réformes constantiniennes avait d'autres raisons. Le protocole impérial de l'*aduentus* auquel avaient accès les sénateurs durant l'Antiquité tardive présentait de multiples avantages symboliques, mais aussi religieux. On en prend conscience lorsque l'on cherche à donner une définition rituelle précise du protocole en utilisant les conceptions religieuses et politiques de l'époque.

---

[77] J. Lydus, *De Magistratibus*, II, 17, éd. et trad. (corr.) J. Schamp, Paris 2006, 22-23; cf. *Novella* 26. Justinien aurait exigé que le préfet du prétoire rende ses sentences sans présence du portrait impérial, afin qu'il assume lui-même ses propres décisions sans engager la responsabilité de l'empereur. Cette rupture de Justinien a été analysée avec finesse par J. Caimi, *Burocrazia e diritto nel De Magistratibus di Giovanni Lido*, Milan 1984, 360-361 et A.C. Bandy, *Ioannes Lydus, On Powers or The Magistracies of the Roman State. Introduction, Critical Text, Translation, Commentary and Indices*, Philadelphia 1983, 111. Sur la révolution juridique et judiciaire de Justinien, voir en dernier lieu C. Humfress, *Law and Legal Practise in the Age of Justinian*, dans M. Maas, *The Cambridge Companion of the Age of Justinian*, Cambridge 2005, 161-184 et C. Pazdernik, *Justinianic Ideology and the Power of the Past*, dans M. Maas, *The Cambridge Companion...*, 185-212.

[78] Athanase d'Alexandrie, *Discours contre les ariens*, 3, 5 (PG 26, 329), cité par Jean Damascène, *supra*, III, 114, dans *Die Schriften des Johannes von Damaskos*, III, *Contra imaginum calumniatores orationes tres*, éd B. Kotter, Berlin-New York 1975, 191, trad. A.L. Darras-Worms, M.H. Congourdeau, 1994, 153: ὁ γὰρ προσκυνῶν τὴν εἰκόνα, ἐν αὐτῇ προσκυνεῖ τὸν βασιλέα. Ἡ γὰρ ἐκείνου μορφὴ καὶ τὸ εἶδος αὐτοῦ ἐστιν ἡ εἰκών («Celui qui se prosterne devant l'image (de l'empereur) se prosterne à travers elle devant l'empereur, car l'image est sa forme et son apparence»).

[79] Libanios, *supra*, n. 16.

[80] Sévérien de Gabala, *Homélie sur le lavements des pieds*, éd. A. Wenger, 1967, 226 (§9) et 231 pour la traduction corrigée (nos corrections sont signalées par des crochets): Οὐδὲ γὰρ ὅταν βασιλικοὶ χαρακτῆρες καὶ εἰκόνες εἰς πόλιν εἰσφέρωνται καὶ ὑπαντῶσιν ἄρχοντες καὶ δῆμοι μετ' εὐφημίας καὶ φόβου, οὐ σανίδα τιμῶντες ἢ τὴν κηρόχυτον γραφὴν τοῦτο ποιοῦσι ἀλλὰ τὸν χαρακτῆρα τοῦ βασιλέως, οὕτω καὶ ἡ κτίσις οὐ τὸ γήϊνον σκεῦος τιμᾷ ἀλλὰ τὸν ἐπουράνιον χαρακτῆρα αἰδεῖται («Car lorsque les enseignes ou les images de l'empereur entrent dans une [cité] et que les autorités et le [peuple] viennent au-devant des acclamations mêlées de crainte, ils ne vénèrent pas la pancarte ni les modelages de cire, mais l'image de l'empereur. Ainsi, la création n'honore pas notre instrument terrestre mais elle révère en nous l'image céleste»); cf. *Die Schriften des Johannes von Damaskos...*, 193, trad. A.L. Darras-Worms et M.H. Congourdeau, 155.

A quelle tradition rituelle ces *aduentus* peuvent-ils être rattachés? Reprenons quelques caractéristiques du protocole, que nous avons déjà relevés, en croisant les données littéraires, épigraphiques et iconographiques:

1. l'accueil hors des murs;
2. les matrones en position de suppliantes qui font une prière publique et lancent l'invitation au nom de la cité;
3. les tentures placées sur les murs d'enceinte et certains bâtiments;
4. les proskynèses en cascade devant l'*imago* impériale;

On doit y ajouter:

5. la visite des monuments publics et notamment des temples de la cité, dont les portes étaient ouvertes pour l'occasion[81];
6. l'érection d'une statue du dignitaire auquel l'on a rendu hommage et l'organisation d'une cérémonie commémorative devant sa statue[82];

---

[81] MÉNANDRE LE RHÉTEUR, *Le Discours d'arrivée*, 381, 5-23, éd. et trad. (anglaise) A. WILSON et D.A. RUSSEL éd., *Menandor Rhetor*, Oxford 1981, 100, mentionne l'ouverture des théâtres; LIBANIOS, *Epist.*, 97, 1106F, a. 393, 212-214, trad. B. Cabouret, LIBANIOS, *Lettres aux hommes de son temps*, Paris 2000, 203-206, reprocha au chrétien zélote Rufin, le préfet du prétoire, de s'être abstenu de visiter certains temples de la cité et semble avoir visité le célèbre sanctuaire de Daphné en coup de vent. Il s'agit d'une tradition respectée par Constance II lui-même lors de son *aduentus* romain de 357: SYMMAQUE, *Rel.* III, 7; Prudence, t. III, *Psychomachie, Contre Symmaque*, éd. et trad. M. LAVARENNE, Paris 1948, 109: *Accipiat Aeternitas uestra alia eiusdem principis facta, quae in usum dignius trahat [...]. Et per omnes uias aeternae urbis laetum secutus senatum uidit placido ora delubra, legit inscripta fastigiis deum nomina, percontatus templorum origines est, miratus est conditores, cumque alias religiones ipse sequeretur has seruauit imperio* («Que votre Eternité se rappelle d'autres procédés de ce prince (i. e. Constance II), pour s'en inspirer plus dignement. [...] Il a suivi le Sénat plein d'allégresse à travers toutes les rues de la Ville éternelle, il a regardé les temples sans s'émouvoir, il a lu les noms inscrits sur leurs frontons, il s'est enquis des origines de ces sanctuaires, il a manifesté son admiration pour ceux qui les avaient construits, et, bien que lui-même suivît une autre religion, il a conservé la nôtre à l'empire»). Symmaque lui-même après avoir rendu visite à la cité de Bénévent, tout juste remise d'un tremblement de terre, pu se féliciter de la vigueur de la piété païenne municipale, sans doute après avoir vu la réparation des temples, dont celui d'Isis (SYMMAQUE, *Ep.* I, 3, 3-5 avant 375, éd. J.-P. CALLU, Paris 1972, 67-68). Les enquêtes régionales ont récemment constaté la restauration du célèbre Iseum de la cité. Sur ce point, voir R. PIRELLI, *L'Iseo di Benevento*, dans *Iside. Il mito, il mistero, la magia*, éd. E.A. ARSLAN, Milan 1997, 376-380.

[82] Ainsi Rutilius Namatianus évoquant les hommages rendus à son père, l'ancien gouverneur d'Emilie-Ligurie: RUTILIUS NAMATIANUS, *De red. suo*, v. 375-396, trad. corr. J. VESSEREAU et F. PRÉCHAC, Paris 1933, 30: *Hic oblata mihi sancti genitoris imago/Pisani proprio quam posuere foro./ Laudibus amissi cogor lacrimare parentis;/ Fluxerunt madidis gaudia maesta genis. / Namque pater quondam. Tyrrhenis praefuit aruis / Fascibus et senis credita iura dedit. / [...]/ Nec fallebatur, tam carus et ipse probatis:*

7. la présence de l'*urceus* et de la *patera* sur les dédicaces honorant ces hôtes de marque, rappelant l'offrande de vin et d'encens qui était régulièrement offerte aux dieux de la cité pour l'occasion[83].

Ces différents éléments correspondaient très exactement au déroulement d'une *supplicatio* impériale, une cérémonie d'hommage qui était réservée d'ordinaire à l'empereur durant le Principat. Comme l'a montré John Scheid[84], les matrones, femmes de magistrats, y jouaient un rôle fondamental, car, par leur biais, la cité pouvait se mettre à genoux devant le Prince, sans le faire tout à fait[85]. On jouait ainsi sur l'ambiguïté naturelle des matrones, citoyennes, femmes de sénateurs ou de décurions, mais femmes tout de même, « indispensables étrangères», pour reprendre l'expression de John Scheid[86]. Comme pour les dieux, l'on invitait officiellement et religieusement la divinité impériale ou à l'époque tardive son incarnation par une offrande de vin et d'encens accomplie par les

---

/ *Aeternas grates mutua cura canit,* / *Constantemque sibi pariter mitemque fuisse* / *Insinuant natis qui meminere senes.* / *Ipsum me gradibus non degenerasse parentis* / *Gaudent et duplici sedulitate fouent.* / *Haec eadem, cum Flaminiam regionibus irem,* / *Splendoris patrii saepe reperta fides.* / *Famam Lachanii ueneratur numinis instar* / *Inter terrigenas Lydia tota suos* («Ici s'offre à mes yeux l'image de mon vénérable père, dressée par les Pisans sur leur propre forum. Les éloges décernés à ce père qui n'est plus m'arrachent des pleurs... Mes joues ruisselèrent de larmes, de douleur et de joie. C'est que mon père gouverna autrefois les campagnes tyrrhéniennes; il y exerça la juridiction aux six faisceaux [...]. Il était payé en retour, également chéri de son côté par ceux qu'il estimait: l'éternelle reconnaissance inscrite dans leurs vers est inspirée par une mutuelle affection. "Il avait à la fois de la fermeté et de la douceur" confient à leurs enfants, les vieillards qui se souviennent de lui. Et moi, ils sont heureux que mes honneurs n'aient pas été indignes des siens, et ils redoublent à mon égard de soins affectueux. Tels étaient les témoignages qu'en traversant les régions bordées par la voie flaminienne, je trouvai, maintes fois, du mérite éclatant de mon père. Le renom de Lachanius était vénéré à l'égal d'un *numen* dans la Lydie tout entière, qui le place parmi ses enfants»). Ce *numen* vénéré par la Lydie toute entière faisait bien entendu référence à l'empereur dont le gouverneur Lachanius était l'incarnation.

[83] Ainsi la dédicace des *regiones* de Pouzzoles honorant le sénateur, respectable «augure du peuple romain et des Quirites», *Q. Flauius Maesius Egnatius Lollianus signo Mauortius*, en 334-342 (CIL X. 1695 = 2503 = ILS 1224a).

[84] J. SCHEID, *Indispensables «étrangères». Les rôles religieux des femmes à Rome*, dans *Histoire des femmes en Occident*, 1. *L'Antiquité*, éds. G. DUBY, M. PERROT, dirigé par P. SCHMITT-PANTEL, Paris 1991, 405-437.

[85] Ainsi sur le protocole des Jeux Séculaires, *De Ludis saecularibus populi Romani Quiritium, libri sex*, éd. G. B. PIGHI, Amsterdam 1965², 157, IV, l. 12-13: *Haec matres familias CX, p(opuli) R(omani) Q(uiritium) nuptae, genib[us nixae] precamur, o[r]amus obsecramusque.* («Nous, ces cent dix *matres familias*, nous les épouses du peuple romain des Quirites, c'est à genoux que nous prions, implorons et supplions»).

[86] Cfr. *supra*, n. 84.

magistrats de la cité. Comme l'expliquent John Scheid[87] et Paul Veyne[88], une *supplicatio* comme une action de grâce n'était jamais qu'une forme théâtralisée de la *praefatio* sacrificielle, de l'invitation faite aux dieux à participer à une cérémonie.

Durant l'*aduentus* tardo-antique comme la *supplicatio* medio-impériale, il fallait manifester le consensus par la présence de toutes les catégories sociales et symboliques de la cité : femmes, enfants, vieillards, collèges, magistrats, prêtres. Comme la cité s'offrait toute entière à son dieu d'un jour ou à son représentant, tous les monuments publics étaient ouverts. C'est ainsi qu'il faut comprendre l'importance de la disposition que Théodose adressa en 382 au duc d'Osrhoène Palladius: «Pour que l'on en dispose pour les assises de la ville et pour un rassemblement important, que ton Expérience permette que le temple soit ouvert pour chaque célébration des vœux par respect pour l'autorité de Notre Oracle» (*Ut conuentu urbis et frequenti coetu uideatur, exprentia tua omni uotorum celebritate seruata auctoritate nostri ita patere templum permittat oraculi*)[89]. On peut lire aussi la fréquence de ce genre de visites dans la Novelle de Majorien, qui restreignit à trois jours le séjour officiel des gouverneurs dans les cités de leur province, pour que la prise en charge financière ne pesât pas trop sur le budget municipal[90]. Le succès de ce type de cérémonie tenait précisément à la protection impériale derrière laquelle pouvaient se placer les païens et le caractère très malléable du rituel qui pouvait s'abstenir de tel ou tel élément. Les temples étaient ouverts? Symmaque s'y précipitait[91], faisant de ces *aduentus* à Bénévent et à Naples des véritables tournées pastorales païennes pour reprendre l'expression de Jean-Pierre Callu[92]. Quant au chrétien Rufin, il se tenait à l'écart de temples d'Antioche, essuyant ainsi les critiques, certes très feutrées, de Libanios, car il s'était envolé hors d'Antioche, sans respecter la durée du séjour protocolaire. Chacun pouvait en quelque sorte à loisir respecter tout à la fois son contrat protocolaire et ses convictions religieuses. La même cérémonie pouvait ainsi être considérée par les païens comme authentiquement païenne, romaine et traditionnelle, et séculaire, neutre pour des chrétiens aussi rigoristes que le préfet du prétoire Rufin. Elle pouvait permettre aussi aux curiales et à

---

[87] J. Scheid, *La religion des Romains*, Paris 1998, 92.
[88] P. Veyne, *Inviter les dieux...*, 3-42.
[89] *CTh* XVI, 10, 8.
[90] *Nouella*, 7, 17.
[91] Symmaque, *Lettres*, I, 3, 4, à son père (Bénévent); VIII, 27, 2, 3, à Censorinus (Naples).
[92] J.-P. Callu, *Symmaque, Lettres...*, 127 et n. 5.

leurs concitoyens de manifester leur respect des options religieuses de leur hôte de marque.

Avant de conclure, je voudrais faire une dernière observation. Les personnages sont souvent deux sur le *carpentum iudiciale*. A Rome, le préfet de la Ville honorait souvent ainsi un personnage, comme le suggère l'*Histoire Auguste* lors des *Hilaria* de Magna Mater[93]. Sur les bandeaux des sarcophages, les deux personnages assis sur la cathèdre portent souvent deux objets, soit un rouleau, soit une tablette. Valerio Marotta[94] a souligné récemment toute l'importance de ces rouleaux parmi les insignes des plus hauts fonctionnaires du IVe au VIe siècles apr. J.-C. La tablette faisait très vraisemblablement référence aux tables remises aux patrons et qu'ils se devaient d'afficher en bonne place dans leur demeure[95]. S'il y a une différence d'âge entre les occupants de la cathèdre, c'est toujours le plus jeune qui semble honoré, c'est lui qui paraît au premier plan et c'est lui qui focalise les regards. Cette paire évoque une succession, ou à vrai dire deux types de successions.

La première était patronale. N'oublions pas en effet que le patronat d'une cité était familial et héréditaire, comme nous le rappellent nombre d'inscriptions[96], qu'il supposait des échelons, qu'un jeune clarissime ou perfectissime commençait par être investi du patronat d'un *uicus*, d'un quartier ou d'une agglomération secondaire si l'on veut, avant d'embrasser sous son aile protectrice une cité toute entière, voire toute une province[97].

La seconde était administrative. Il faut commencer par noter, en effet, que c'est bien en Italie que ces représentations ont connu le plus grand succès, d'après ce que laisse entendre la concentration étonnante de sarco-

---

[93] *SHA, V. Aur.*, trad. A. CHASTAGNOL, Paris, 1994, 969: *Hilaribus, quibus omnia festa et fieri debere scimus et dici, impletis sollemnibus uehiculo suo me et iudicali carpento praef. Vrbis, uir industris ac praefata reuerentia nominandus, Iunius Tiberianus accepit* («A l'occasion des fêtes de Cybèle [*Hilaria*], pendant lesquelles nous savons que conduite et propos se doivent d'être joyeux, une fois les cérémonies terminées, le préfet de la Ville Junius Tibérianus, un homme illustre dont il faut citer le nom avec respect, m'invita dans sa voiture qui était son véhicule de fonction»). Je dois cette référence à Claude Lepelley.

[94] V. MAROTTA, *Liturgia del potere...*, 145-220; cf. ID., 1991.

[95] *Suppl. It.*, 9, 1992, n.35: *et in aedibu[s suis lo]/co sacrari praecipiat* («qu'il prescive de le consacrer à un endroit dans sa demeure») conclut le décret patronal des *Forulani* d'Amiternum en 335 et que l'on me permette encore une fois de renvoyer à mon article (C.J. GODDARD, *Les formes festives...*, 1025-1088) qui rassemble la bibliographie sur la question.

[96] Cf. *infra* n. 9.

[97] C'est ce qu'expliquent clairement les tables patronales d'Amiternum (*Suppl. It.*, 9, 1992, n.34 et 35). Cf. C.J. GODDARD, *Les formes festives...*, 1035 sq.

phages présentant ce type de double *aduentus*. Or c'est l'Italie qui connut une réforme administrative de grande importance[98], dont nous aurions ici en quelque sorte la conséquence protocolaire. Constantin avait en effet ajouté un échelon nouveau à la carrière sénatoriale en Italie, en nommant des gouverneurs clarissimes dans ces provinces de création récente[99]. Cette fonction était la première étape d'une carrière et l'on y accédait par une nomination impériale. Il ne serait pas étonnant, notamment sur les bas-reliefs romains, qu'ils figurent l'arrivée d'un jeune gouverneur et de son sénateur de père, d'autant que ces nominations venaient souvent raffermir sur le plan administratif d'antiques liens patronaux, comme l'a rappelé Giovanni A. Cecconi[100]. Rappelons avec Andrea Giardina et Francesco Grelle[101], à la lumière d'une inscription de Trinitapoli, qui reproduit un décret impérial de Valentinien Ier, que, les tournées dans les cités constituaient l'un des devoirs des gouverneurs, qui se devaient de procéder à l'*inquisitio* fiscale de leurs administrés et de veiller à régler leurs-mêmes d'éventuels litiges. Nous savons par ailleurs qu'eux devaient tenir des assises judiciaires dans des cités différentes, car un gouverneur était avant tout un *iudex*. Chacune de leurs tournées étaient très certainement marquée par l'une de ses majestueuses entrées. L'accession à ce char de fonction et le bénéfice d'un bel *aduentus* ou d'une solennelle *profectio* marquaient donc manifestement l'une des étapes les plus importantes de la vie sociale d'un noble sénateur ou d'un curiale, qui manifestait son autorité et son lien privilégié avec le pouvoir impérial. Cette scène a d'ailleurs sans doute partie liée au songe de Scipion, si populaire parmi les sénateurs païens comme chrétiens, puisqu'elle présentait en somme l'ultime voyage comme une sorte d'apothéose[102]. C'était la vertu exercée dans la détention d'une char-

---

[98] P. PORENA, *Riflessioni sulla provincializazzione dell'Italia tardo romana*, dans *Les Cités de l'Italie tardo-antique, IVe-VIe siècles: institutions, économie, société, culture et religion*, éds. M. GHILARDI, C.J. GODDARD, P. PORENA, Rome 2006, 9-21.

[99] G.A. CECCONI, *Governo imperiale e élites dirigenti nell'Italia tardoantica. Problemi di storia politico-amministrativa (270-476 d.C.)*, Côme 1994, 134 sq.,

[100] *Ibid.*, 134 sq., qui explique de façon pertinente que l'autorité d'un gouverneur devait beaucoup au croisement de sa délégation impériale et du prestige antique, dont il jouissait quand sa famille détenait le patronage héréditaire des cités et de la province qu'il était appelé à administrer.

[101] A. GIARDINA, F. GRELLE, *La tavola di Trinitapoli: una nuova costituzione di Valentiniano I*, dans F. GRELLE, *Canosa romana*, Rome 1993, 237, une table datée par les auteurs de 368-75, voire même de 368.

[102] Cf. C. LEPELLEY, *L'aristocratie païenne: une menace aux yeux d'Augustin (à propos du sermon Dolbeau 26 – Mayence 62)*, dans *Augustin prédicateur. Actes du Colloque internationnal de Chantilly, septembre 1996*, éd. G. MADEC, Paris 1998, 327-342 = ID.,

Fig. 1. *Sarcophage romain représentant un /aduentus/, Rome, Musée des Thermes, G. Wilpert, /I sarcofagi cristiani.../, pl. 21, 4.*

Fig. 2. *Procession dionysiaque, G. Wilpert, /L'ultimo viaggio nell'arte sepolcrale .../, pl. 2, 4.*

Fig. 3. *Supplication des matrones sous Domitien (88 apr.J.-C.), Paris, Bibliothèque Nationale, Cabinet des Médailles (BN 1416), J. Scheid, /Déchiffrer/ /des monnaies.../, 21*

Fig. 4. *Bandeau de sarcophage représentant un /aduentus/, musée de Stockholm, G. Wilpert, /I sarcofagi cristiani.../, pl. 24, 1.*

FIG. 5. *Monnaies consécratoires (1. Livie, 42 apr. J.-C. ; 2. Agrippine l'Ancienne, 33 apr. J.-C. ; 3. Fl. Domitilla, 90 apr. J.-C. ; 4. Flavia Iulia, 89. apr. J.-C. ; 5. Marciana, 112 apr. J.-C. ; 6. Faustine l'Ancienne, 140 apr. J.-C.), G. Lucchi, /Sul significato del /carpentum/...,/ 141.*

Fig. 6. *Second diptyque des Symmaque, dans L. Cracco Ruggini, /Apoteosi e politica senatoria/..., 452.*

Fig. 7. *Sarcophage représentant sans doute une procession en l'honneur de Magna Mater (350 apr. J.-C. environ), Rome, basilique de Saint-Laurent-hors-les-murs (DAI, Ist. Neg., 732422).*

«I documenti si scoprono se si cercano»

LELLIA CRACCO RUGGINI

«Pontifices»:
un caso di osmosi linguistica

Mi concentrerò qui su di un caso molto circoscritto, ma a mio avviso significativo per comprendere il modo di pensare delle persone (colte e non) nei secoli IV-VI. La discussione verterà su di un noto passo di Zosimo (IV, 36), ancora in tempi recentissimi affrontato da Alan Cameron con un'analisi ricca di riferimenti, rigorosa ed esaustiva[1]. Ne condivido l'interpretazione generale, come lui dissentendo da teorie precedenti (ancor oggi però vigorose), che leggiamo esemplarmente esposte e approfondite in numerosi contributi di François Paschoud (il dotto editore di Zosimo nella Collection «Guillaume Budé»)[2]. Non credo però che si possa liquidare

---

[1] AL. CAMERON, *The Imperial Pontifex*, «Harvard Studies in Classical Philolology» 103 (2007), 341-384.
[2] Cfr. spec. F. PASCHOUD, *Cinq études sur Zosime*, Paris 1975, 63-99 (3: *La fin du règne de Gratien dans l'«Histoire nouvelle» de Zosime*), Paris 1975; ID., ed. di Zosimo, II/2 (cit. oltre, nota 8), 419-422 (nota 174). Enumero qui di seguito altri contributi dello stesso Autore, particolarmente utili anche come rimando per la successiva nota 6: ID., *Eunapiana*, in Bonner Historia-Augusta-*Colloquium 1982-1983*, a cura di J. STRAUB, Bonn 1985, 239-303 = ID., *Eunape, Olympiodore, Zosime. Scripta minora. Recueuil d'articles, avec addenda, corrigenda, mise à jour et indices*, Bari 2006, 153-194 (*Retractatio*, 190-194); ID., *Zosime et la fin de l'ouvrage historique d'Eunape*, «Orpheus» n. s. 6 (1985), 44-61 = ID., *Eunape, Olympiodore, Zosime...*, 127-141 (*Retractatio*, 140-141); ID., *Sur Eunape de Sardes* (recensione a A. BALDINI, *Ricerche sulla «Storia» di Eunapio di Sardi. Problemi di storiografia filopagana*, Bologna 1984), «Revue des études grecques» 98 (1985), 395-398; ID., *Le début de l'ouvrage historique d'Olympiodore*, in «Arctos. Acta Philologica Fennica» (*Studia in honorem I. Kajanto*), Suppl. II, Helsinki 1985, 185-196 = ID., *Eunape, Olympiodore, Zosime...*, 144-151; ID., recensione a J.A. OCHOA, *La transmisión de la Historia de Eunapio*, Madrid 1990, «Orpheus» n.s. 13 (1992), 168-172 = ID., *Eunape, Olympiodore, Zosime...*, 241-245; Id., *Valentinien travesti ou: De la malignité d'Ammien Marcellin*, in Cognitio gestorum. *The Historiographic Art of Ammianus Marcellinus. Proceedings of the Colloquium (Amsterdam, 26-28 Agust 1991)*, a cura di J. DEN BOEFT, D. DEN HENGST, H.C. TEITLER, Amsterdam-Oxford-New York-Tokyo 1992, 67-84, partic. 86 ss. ID., *Nicomaque Flavien et la connexion byzantine (Pierre Patrice et Zonaras): À propos du livre récent de Bruno Bleckmann)*, «Antiquité Tardive» 2 (1994), 71-82 = ID., *Eunape, Olympiodore, Zosime...*, 293-316

come mera invenzione di Zosimo (o, meglio, come fraintendimento della fonte antiquaria che probabilmente gli soggiace con quella antiquaria) anche la notizia circa il rifiuto del pontificato massimo da parte di Graziano, contenuta nella digressione della *Storia nuova* sui *pontifices*.

(*Retractatio*, 315-316); ID., *Les descendants d'Ammien Marcellin (Sulpicius Alexander et Renatus Profuturus Frigeridus)*, in Nomen Latinum. *Mélanges de langue, de littérature et de civilisation latines offerts au professeur André Schneider à l'occasion de son départ à la retraite*, a cura di D. KNÖPFLER, con la collaborazione di M. BOILLAT, M. GENDRE LOUTSCH, C. JACOBS, T. CHÂTELAIN, C. TRIPET, Neuchâtel 1997, 141-147; ID., *Zosime et Constantin: nouvelles controverses*, «Museum Helveticum» 1 (1997), 9-28; ID., *Note sur les relations de trois historiens des IVe et Ve siècles: Sulpicius Alexander, Rénatus Profutus* [sic] *Frigéridus et Olympiodore*, «Antiquité Tardive» 6 (1998), 313-316 (ove non è chiaro perché l'Autore, dopo avere supposto che a monte di Olimpiodoro stia Renato Frigerido – uno storico che l'onomastica sembra suggerire cristiano –, senta poi il bisogno di attribuire a un'ulteriore fonte – questa volta pagana – il colorito pagano che poteva essere stato invece conferito all'interpretazione degli avvenimenti da Olimpiodoro medesimo, contemporaneo e pagano, il quale ben conosceva il latino, Roma e anche la *vulgata* filo-pagana orale allora circolante – con molteplici varianti – in entrambe le *partes Imperii* sugli avvenimenti più noti e quindi di maggiore impatto psicologico: l'Autore dimostra qui un accanimento «fontaniero» che, senza sufficiente giustificazione, nega a Olimpiodoro – come altrove a Zosimo, nonostante il titolo dell'opera di quest'ultimo, *Storia nuova*, attestazione eloquente di per sé sola della novità ideologica attribuita da Zosimo, per una ragione o per l'altra, alla propria composizione – la capacità intellettuale d'inserire fatti attinti a una fonte anche cristiana entro una cornice interpretativa pagana pensata in proprio); ID., *Propos sceptiques et iconoclastes sur Marius Maximus*, in Historiae Augustae Colloquium Genevense. *Atti dei Convegni internazionali sulla* Historia Augusta, a cura di F. PASCHOUD, Bari 1999, 241-254; ID., *Preuves de la présence d'une source occidentale latine dans la tradition grecque pur l'histoire du 4e siècle*, «Journal of Classical Studies (Classical Society of Japan)» 3 (2001), 7-17 = ID., *Eunape, Olympiodore, Zosime...*, 413-422; ID., *Chronique d'historiographie tardive*, «Antiquité Tardive» 14 (2006), 325-344 e spec. 337-344 (*IV. Jérôme, «EKG» aucta, Nicomaque Flavien, Eunape comme source de* l'Epitome de Caesaribus, *aliaque minuta eiusdem farinae*), a proposito di R.W. Burgess, *A Common Source for Jerome, Eutropius, Festus, Ammianus and the* Epitome de Caesaribus *between 358 and 378, along with further Thoughs on the Date and Nature of the «Kaisergeschichte»*, «Classical Philology» 100 (2005), 166-192 (un titolo che giustamente Paschoud giudica «long comme un train de marchandises américain», tuttavia dimenticando di avere avuto solo parole di lode, dodici anni prima, per B. BLECKMANN, *Die Reichskrise des III. Jahrhunderts in der spätantiken und byzantinischen Geschichtschreibung. Untersuchungen zu den nachdionischen Quellen der Chronik des Johannes Zonaras*, München 1992: vd. sopra); ID., *Eunape, Pierre le Patrice, Zosime, et l'histoire du fils du roi barbare réclamé en otage*, in Mélanges en l'honneur d'Yvette Duval, Paris 2000, 55-63 = ID., *Eunape, Olympiodore et Zosime...*, 395-402; ID., *Eunape, Olympiodore, Zosime...*, 493-497 (*Conclusions*, ove l'Autore enumera le tesi da lui date a tutt'oggi per certe).

Cameron ha preferito optare *tout court* per il passaggio, dopo Graziano (con Valentiniano II o, forse, già con il pio anti-imperatore cristiano Magno Massimo), dall'appellativo imperiale di *pontifex maximus* (pagano) a quello (più equivoco e ancora per secoli usato dagli imperatori cristiani) di *pontifex inclitus*. Pertanto, fu proprio grazie a questo lieve mutamento semantico che si conservarono ancora a lungo quelle funzioni del pontificato massimo – legate alla tradizione giuridica del paganesimo piuttosto che alla ritualità e ancora meno alle sue credenze religiose – che continuavano a rivestire una certa importanza agli occhi dei sovrani. Quello di *pontifex maximus*, di fatto, era stato uno fra i titoli ufficiali degli imperatori da Augusto in avanti (sebbene forse, nel IV secolo, assunto ormai automaticamente assieme agli altri titoli imperiali, senza una cerimonia vera e propria). Su tale punto mi trovo d'accordo con Cameron, e credo sia questo l'assunto più importante per parlare anche a questo proposito, fra IV e VI secolo, di continuità (formale) e di mutamento (sostanziale) al tempo stesso.

Non penso tuttavia che, per arrivare a una conclusione siffatta, sia indispensabile negare storicità a tutto il discorso di Zosimo, appoggiandosi precipuamente al fatto che abbiamo qui a che fare con un «notoriously unreliable Greek historian writing more than a century after the event»[3]. A mio modo di vedere, si tratta di una questione di metodo applicata a un caso specifico: è infatti quasi sempre più economico, nel formulare un'ipotesi, scegliere una soluzione costruttiva e semplice piuttosto che una distruttiva e complicata. E ho sempre condiviso con Arnaldo Momigliano il coraggio del dubbio persistente, piuttosto che le incrollabili e spesso

---

[3] AL. CAMERON, *The Imperial Pontifex...*, 341. Prima della fine del XVI secolo gli studiosi avevano sempre rifiutato di credere che un imperatore cristiano potesse avere accettato un titolo pagano; e soltanto fra Cinque e Seicento Cesare Baronio, di fronte a esplicite testimonianze epigrafiche del contrario, aveva ammesso il fatto, tuttavia interpretandolo in senso filo-cristiano (gli imperatori fra Costantino e Valentiniano I – benché ormai cristiani ad eccezione di Giuliano – avrebbero infatti accettato tale sacerdozio per vanificare le iniziative pagane in ámbito religioso: cfr. *ibid.* [sopra, nota 1], 341-342 con nota 4). Ma Jacques Godefroy, Antoine Pagi e Louis-Sébastien Le Nain de Tillemont (tanto per citare alcuni fra i più rinomati studiosi del Cinque e Seicento) continuarono a considerare un calunniatore il pagano Zosimo; finché verso la metà del Settecento (1740-1743) Joseph Bimart de la Bastie non dimostrò una volta per tutte che le testimonianze epigrafiche in merito erano irrefutabili, e che Graziano doveva quindi essere considerato il primo imperatore cristiano che avesse a un certo punto rifiutato formalmente di fregiarsi con il titolo di *pontifex maximus*, giusta la testimonianza di Zosimo: cfr. F. PASCHOUD, ed. di Zosimo, II/2 (cit. oltre, nota 8), 419 (nota 174).

perentorie certezze di un Ronald Syme o di un François Paschoud, i quali, a mio avviso, hanno finito talora per attribuire agli autori antichi tratti evidenti della personalità loro propria[4]. Senza dubbio – questo è un limite che ha bloccato, almeno in parte, il mio apprezzamento per un certo tipo di *Quellenforschung* – ho sempre nutrito un limitato interesse per le indagini riguardanti fonti perdute di cui poco o nulla si conosce oltre al titolo (se non altro, delle *Storie* di Eunapio possediamo non pochi frammenti), o che addirittura vengono presupposte sulla base di convergenze (spesso opinabili) fra opere conservate ma – abbastanza curiosamente – mai menzionate da autori antichi a noi giunti (come scriveva Arnaldo Momigliano già nel 1969 a proposito di *Ammianus Marcellinus and the Historia Augusta* di Ronald Syme, «dieci indizi cattivi non fanno un argomento buono»)[5].

Fonti del genere forse talora esistettero davvero (*Ignotus* dietro l'*Epitome de Caesaribus* e/o la *Enmann Kaisergeschichte* – opere breviaristiche più volte prolungate o *auctae*? – alle spalle di Aurelio Vittore, Festo, Eutropio, del *Chronicon* geronimiano e della *Historia Augusta*); ma troppo spesso esse somigliano a fantasmi evanescenti, ectoplasmi che fluttuano fra le divergenti opinioni dei diversi studiosi, e che stanno tutt'al più a testimoniare l'esistenza di un certo filone storiografico ormai cancellato: Cordo, Onesimo, lo stesso Mario Massimo, Eusebio «di Nantes», Sulpicio Alessandro, Renato Profuturo Frigerido, Turdulo Gallicano, Fabio Cerylliano, alcune effemeridi anonime, Claudio Eustenio, Teochio, Callicrate di Tiro/Callinico di Petra e così via (secondo Ronald Syme *bogus names* nella maggior parte, ossia nomi di mera fantasia quando menzionati dalla *Historia Augusta*: un'affermazione della quale però egualmente

---

[4] Si veda anche F. MILLAR, *The Path of the Polymath*, «Times Literary Supplement», 28 gennaio 1977, 99-100, il quale ha riconosciuto a Momigliano il merito di avere insinuato il dubbio nella storiografia inglese (anche se non pare che Momigliano gradisse la qualifica di *polymath* assegnatagli da Millar, ossia di erudito con una sottesa denuncia di dispersività: cfr. la lettera a Fergus Millar – allievo di Syme –, rimasta inedita ma della quale egli inviò copia ad alcuni colleghi, resa ora nota da G.W. BOWERSOCK, *Momigliano and his Critics*, in *Memoria di Arnaldo Momigliano nel centenario della nascita (Scuola Normale di Pisa, 18 ottobre 2008)*, in preparazione per la stampa (ho avuto il testo dall'Autore in anteprima, in qualità di *discussant* della Relazione stessa).

[5] A. MOMIGLIANO, *Ammiano Marcellino e la* Historia Augusta *(a proposito del libro di Ronald Syme)*, «Atti della Accademia delle Scienze di Torino, Classe di Scienze Morali» 103 (1968-1969), 423-436 = ID., *Quinto Contributo alla storia degli studi classici e del mondo antico*, I, Roma 1975, I, 93-103 e partic. 98; vd. pure ID., recensione in inglese al medesimo libro, «English Historical Review» 84 (1969), 566-569 = ID., *Quinto Contributo...*, 104-108 e partic. 105.

diffido, in certi casi essendosi rivelata falsa)[6]. In verità gli autori antichi

---

[6] Cfr. S. MAZZARINO, *La* Historia Augusta *e la «EKG»*, in *Atti del Colloquio patavino sulla* Historia Augusta, Roma 1963, 29-40; J. SCHLUMBERGER, *Die* Epitome de Caesaribus. *Untersuchungen zur heidnischen Geschichtsschreibung des 4. Jahrhuderts n.Chr.*, München 1974 (con l'importante recensione di F. PASCHOUD, *Deux ouvrages récents sur l'*Epitome de Caesaribus *et* Aurelius Victor, «Revue des études latines» 53 [1975], 86-98 e spec. 86-94); ID., *Die verlorenen «Annalen» des Nicomachus Flavianus: ein Werk über Geschichte der römischen Republik oder die Kaiserzeit?*, in *Historia-Augusta-Colloquium 1982-1983...*, 305-329; A. BALDINI, *Ricerche sulla «Storia» di Eunapio...*; ID., *Storie perdute*, Bologna 2000; ID., *Ancora sulla* devotio *di Claudio il Gotico*, in *Historiae Augustae Colloquium Perusinum*, a cura di G. BONAMENTE, Bari 2002, 11-31; ID., *Evagrio versus Zosimo. Considerazioni di storiografia a margine della «questione costantiniana»*, «Mediterraneo Antico» 7 (2004), 349-372; ID., *Ricerche di tarda storiografia (da Olimpiodoro di Tebe)*, Bologna 2004 (con la recensione di F. PASCHOUD, *Questions d'historiographie tardive: à propos de deux ouvrages récents*, in «Antiquité Tardive» 13 [2005] 363-376 e partic. 372-376); ID., *Una versione pagana del sacco di Roma del 410 e una smentita cristiana: considerazioni storiografiche*, in *Romani e barbari. Incontro e scontro di culture. Atti del Convegno (Bra, 11-14 aprile 2003)*, a cura di S. GIORCELLI BERSANI, Torino 2004, 84-104; ID., *Considerazioni in tema di* Annales *e di* Historia Augusta, in *Historiae Augustae Colloquium Barcinonense. Atti dei Convegni Internazionali sulla* Historia Augusta, a cura di G. BONAMENTE, M. MAYER, Bari 2005, 15-46; ID., *Storia senza storia (IV-V secolo d.C.)*, «Classica (Brazil)» 19 (2006), 7-18; ID., *Tra* Historia Augusta *e* Storia Romana *di Q. Aurelio Memmio Simmaco*, in *Historiae Augustae Colloquium Bambergense. Atti dei Convegni Internazionali sulla* Historia Augusta, a cura di G. BONAMENTE, H. BRANDT, Bari 2007, 9-34; ID., *Un nucleo di fronda storiografica nel senato di Roma tra IV e VI secolo*, in *Istituzioni, carismi ed esercizio del potere (IV-VI secolo d.C.)*, a cura di G. BONAMENTE e R. LIZZI TESTA, Bari 2010, 31-49; V. NERI, *Medius Princeps*, Bologna 1992, 210-282 e spec. 275 ss.; B. BLECKMANN, *Die Reichskrise...*; ID., *Bemerkungen zu den «Annales» des Nicomachus Flavianus*, «Historia» 44 (1995), 38-66; R.W. BURGESS, *Principes cum tyrannis: Two Studies on the «Kaisergeschichte» and Its Tradition*, «Classical Quarterly» n.s. 43 (1993), 491-500 (l'Autore pensa sia probabile una identificazione della *Enmann Kaisergeschichte* [d'ora innanzi *EKG*] con l'opera di Eusebio di Nantes); ID., *A Common Source...*; F. PASCHOUD, lavori dal 1975 in avanti, citati a nota 2; G. ZECCHINI, *Ricerche di storiografia latina tardoantica*, Roma 1993, e spec. ID., *L'*Origo Constantini imperatoris, *ibid.*, 29-38; *Da Nicomaco Flaviano a Memmio Simmaco: la fine della storiografia classica in Occidente*, *ibid.*, 51-64 (due contributi nei quali l'Autore ha formulato l'ipotesi che si possa riconoscere la *EKG* nella prima parte – costantiniana – dell'*Anonimo Valesiano*, ipotesi che Paschoud, nel 2006, ha considerato nell'insieme superata: cfr. ID., *Eunape, Olympiodore, Zosime...*, 315-316); *La fine della storiografia galloromana: Sulpicio Alessandro e Renato Profuturo Frigerido*, *ibid.*, 241-250; vd. inoltre ID., *Qualche ulteriore riflessione su Eusebio di Nantes e l'«EKG»*, in *Historiae Augustae Colloquium Genevense...*, 331-344 (con *status quaestionis*); ID., *Latin Historiography: Jerome, Orosius and the Western Chronicles*, in *Greek and Roman Hitoriography in Late Antiquity: Fourth to Sixth Century A.D.*, a cura di G. MARASCO, Leiden-Boston 2003, 317-345 (con la recensione di F. PASCHOUD, *Questions*

che la tradizione ha selezionato attraverso i secoli non sono sempre stati i più grandi; bensì quelli considerati più utili, significativi per come avevano saputo imporre la propria versione dei fatti con una certa semplicità ovvero semplificazione, quali che fossero l'epoca e la provenienza dei materiali trascelti. Il mio scetticismo e disagio si sono peraltro mescolati spesso (quasi in pari misura, direi) con un'ammirazione sincera per tali funambolismi filologici, dei quali mi riconosco personalmente incapace. Ma dopo questa premessa, a mio avviso doverosa, torniamo al passo di Zosimo in questione.

Senza dubbio il pagano Zosimo è l'unica fonte a noi giunta a parlarci di questo rifiuto della veste pontificale da parte di Graziano, quasi un secolo e mezzo dopo che una delegazione di senatori pagani avrebbe offerto in dono al giovane imperatore cristiano – probabilmente con deliberato intento propagandistico – una veste da indossare durante le funzioni pontificali. Per di più, com'è noto, si tratta di un racconto filtrato attraverso copie della *Storia nuova* derivate tutte dal codice vaticano greco 156, non privo di lacune e per secoli inaccessibile[7]. Dal punto di vista testuale, peraltro, non sussistono qui difficoltà particolari, e il passo ora centrale suona come segue:

---

d'historiographie tardive...); M. MAZZA, *La cosiddetta «digressione antimonarchica» in Zosimo I,5,2-4. Qualche breve nota ed un'ipotesi*, in Synodia. *Studia humanitatis Antonio Garzya septuagenario ab amicis atque discipulis dicata*, a cura di U. CRISCUOLO, R. MAISANO, Napoli 1997, 669-686 e partic. 682-686 (il quale ipotizza una derivazione diretta di Zos. I, 1-46 dagli *Annales* di Nicomaco Flaviano Sr.); L. CRACCO RUGGINI, *La storiografia latina da Ammiano Marcellino a Cassiodoro (e anche più in là): documenti, relitti e fantasmi reinterpretati*, «Cassiodorus» 3 (1997), 175-187 e partic. 180-185; S. RATTI, *Jérôme et Nicomaque Flavien: sur les sources de la «Chronique» pour les années 357-364*, «Historia» 46 (1997), 479-508; ID., *La lecture chrétienne du «Bréviaire» d'Eutrope (9, 2-5) par Jérôme et Orose*, «Latomus» 56 (1997), 264-278; ID., *La «Chronique» de Jérôme: opus tumultuarium?*, ibid., 58 (1999) 861-871; ID., *Les sources de la «Chronique» de Jérôme pour les années 357-364: nouveaux éléments*, in *L'historiographie de l'Église des premiers siècles*, a cura di B. PROUDERON, Y.-M. DUVAL, Paris 2001, 425-450; ID., *Jérôme et l'ombre d'Ammien Marcellin*, in *Historiae Augustae Colloquium Barcinonense...*, 233-247; ID., *Nicomaque Flavien senior et l'auteur de l'«Histoire Auguste»*, in *Historiae Augustae Colloquium Bambergense. Atti dei Convegni Internazionali sulla* Historia Augusta, a cura di G. BONAMENTE, H. BRANDT, Bari 2007, 305-317 (ove l'Autore propone addirittura d'identificare gli *Annales* di Nicomaco Flaviano Sr. con la *Historia Augusta*); ultime annotazioni in ID., *394: fin de la rédaction de l'Histoire Auguste?*, «Antiquité Tardive» 16 (2008), 335-348; J.H.W.G. LIEBESCHÜTZ, *Pagan Historiography and the Decline of the Empire*, in *Greek and Roman Historiography...*, 177-218 (con l'importante recensione di F. PASCHOUD, *Questions d'historiographie tardive...*, 368-372) .

[7] L. CRACCO RUGGINI, *La fine dell'impero e le trasmigrazioni dei popoli*, in *La Storia. I grandi problemi dal Medioevo all'età contemporanea*, a cura di N. TRANFAGLIA, M.

«Quando dunque i pontefici, secondo l'uso, portarono a Graziano la veste [pontificale], egli non accettò la loro richiesta, ritenendo trattarsi di un ornamento esteriore non adatto per un cristiano; e quando la veste fu restituita ai sacerdoti, si dice che il più importante per rango fra costoro dichiarasse: "Se il sovrano non vuole essere chiamato pontefice, ci sarà presto un pontefice massimo"» (e dunque un altro imperatore, di nome Massimo)[8].

Si tratta ovviamente di un gioco di parole fondato su di una profezia *post eventum*, ossia l'usurpazione di Magno Massimo in Gallia dopo l'uccisione quivi di Graziano ad opera dei suoi sostenitori. E la notizia è in funzione di un preteso disegno provvidenziale pagano, che avrebbe punito con la morte il Principe cristiano proprio per il suo «empio» rifiuto di figurare apertamente pontefice massimo[9].

Mi sembra invece lambiccata l'ipotesi per la prima volta formulata da François Paschoud oltre trent'anni or sono[10], secondo la quale si tratterebbe non solo di una tesi accettabile, ma sarebbe riconoscibile in essa un ulteriore, «profetico» gioco di parole allusivamente imperniato su Graziano mancato *pontifex maximus* e, per intervento di una Provvidenza punitrice pagana, *suo sanguine pontem infecturus* (un *hapax*; e *inficere* è, in ogni caso, un'espressione – come ha notato Alan Cameron – soprattutto culta). Secondo fonti ecclesiastiche bizantine del V secolo inoltrato, infatti, Graziano sarebbe stato catturato e forse anche ucciso dal generale Andragazio a Lione il 25 agosto 383, mentre attraversava un ponte durante il tentativo di riparare nel Norditalia (nella tradizione manoscritta di Zosimo, verosi-

---

Firpo, II: *Il Medioevo, 2. Popoli e strutture politiche*, Torino 1986, 1988, pp. 1-52 e partic. 28 (ripubblicato, con aggiornamenti bibliografici ma paginazione identica, Milano 1993). Sulle lacune – autentiche ovvero supposte – della *Storia nuova*, cfr. F. Paschoud, *Zosime et la fin de l'ouvrage historique d'Eunape...* (sopra, nota 2), 129 ss.; R.J. Penella, *Greek Philosophers and Sophists in the Fourth Century A.D. Studies in Eunapius of Sardis*, Leeds 1990, 144-145.

[8] Zos. IV, 36, 5, ed. a cura di F. Paschoud, II/2, Paris 1979, 302 (testo greco con traduzione francese a fronte): Τῶν οὖν ποντιφίκων κατὰ τὸ σύνηθες προσαγαγόντων Γρατιανῷ τὴν στολὴν ἀπεσείσατο τὴν αἴτησιν, ἀθέμιτον εἶναι Χριστιανῷ τὸ σχῆμα νομίσας· τοῖς τε ἱερεῦσι τῆς στολῆς ἀναδοθείσης φασὶ τὸν πρῶτον ἐν αὐτοῖς τεταγμένον εἰπεῖν· «εἰ μὴ βούλεται ποντίφεξ ὁ βασιλεὺς ὀνομάζεσθαι, τάχιστα γενήσεται ποντίφεξ μάξιμος».

[9] Cfr. V. Messana, *La politica religiosa di Graziano*, Roma 1998, 82-91 (*2.2: La rinunzia al titolo di* pontifex maximus, con *status quaestionis* ivi); T.D. Barnes, *Ambrose and Gratian*, «Antiquité Tardive» 7 (1999), 165-174.

[10] *Cinq Études...*; il medesimo Autore, nel suo commento del 1979, 405 (nota 164), ipotizza qui anche l'anti-datazione da parte di Zosimo della celebre normativa teodosiana del 391-392 (*C Th* XVI, 10, 10 e 16).

milmente per un errore di scrittura, *Lugdunum* appare deformato in *Singidunum*: ma la testimonianza appare in ogni caso abbastanza chiara)[11].

Pontifex/ποντίφεξ (ἀρχιερεύς = γεφυροποιός, γεφυραῖος) senza dubbio si collega – come Paschoud afferma – con un'etimologia latina; però è testimoniato anche in almeno due fonti greche tarde. Nella seconda metà del IV secolo (380/381?) il termine ricorre infatti nella libera traduzione greca del *Breviario* di Eutropio fatta da Peanio[12]; e Giovanni Lido

---

[11] SOCR. *Hist. Eccl.*, V, 11, 7-8, *GCS* 285-286; SOZOM. *Hist. Eccl.* VII, 13, 8-9, *GCS* 318 (ovviamente, trattandosi di fonti cristiane, l'eventuale connessione fra ponte e pontefice massimo è in ogni caso taciuta); ma Ambrogio di Milano – contemporaneo agli avvenimenti, che aveva seguito con particolare attenzione (cfr. T.D. BARNES, *Ambrose and Gratian...*, 165-174) – si limita ad affermare che Graziano era stato ucciso a tradimento durante un banchetto (*Expl. Ps. XII*, 61,23, *CSEL* 64, 392): un'affermazione senza dubbio degna di maggiore fiducia. Sulla morte di Graziano cfr. ad esempio N.B. MCLYNN, *Ambrose of Milan: Church and Court in a Christian Capital*, Berkeley-Los Angeles-London 1994, 152-155.

[12] PAIAN. II, 25 (ὁ γὰρ ἀρχιερεύς, ὁ καλούμενος παρ'αυτοῖς [scil. ʹΡωμαίοις] πόντιφεξ [sic], *MGH AA* II, 45). Peanio era nato ad Antiochia da nobile e facoltosa famiglia siriaca; fu allievo di Libanio, condiscepolo di Eutropio nella scuola di Libanio e in quella del rivale Acacio di Cesarea di Palestina (zio di Eutropio e professore ad Antiochia fino al 361), più tardi libero traduttore in greco del *Breviario* di Eutropio, il senatore pagano probabilmente nato a Bordeaux e bilingue per ragioni forse familiari, che nel 369 (mentr'era *magister memoriae* in nella *Pars Orientis*) dedicò all'imperatore (Valente oppure Valentiniano I) la propria opera storica, nel 371-372 fu *proconsul Asiae* e nel 387 *consul posterior* accanto a Valentiniano II. Su Peanio cfr. E. MALCOVATI, *Le traduzioni greche di Eutropio*, «Rendiconti dell'Istituto Lombardo, Classe di Lettere, Scienze morali e storiche» 77, s. III 8 (1943-1944), 273-304; P. VENINI, *Peanio traduttore di Eutropio*, «Memorie dell'Istituto Lombardo, Classe di Lettere, Scienze morali e storiche» 37 (1981-1983), 421-447; G. MATINO, *Due traduzioni greche di Eutropio*, in *Politica, cultura e religione nell'impero romano (secoli IV-VI) tra Oriente e Occidente. Atti del Secondo Convegno dell'Associazione di Studi Tardoantichi (Milano, 11-13 ottobre 1990)*, a cura di F. CONCA, I. GUALADRI, G. LOZZA, Napoli 1993, 227-238 (con ulteriore bibliografia su Peanio a nota 2); su Eutropio e la sua carriera politica, in generale *Prosopography of the Later Roman Empire* (d'ora innanzi *PLRE*), I (260-395), a cura di A.H.M. JONES, J.R. MARTINDALE, J. MORRIS, Cambridge 1971, *s.v.* «Eutropius» 2, 317; sulla probabile nascita bordolese del personaggio (fondata sulla testimonianza del gallico e contemporaneo Marcello Empirico) cfr. L. CRACCO RUGGINI, *Politici intellettuali di Roma fra IV e VI secolo: connotazioni ideologiche della cultura greca in Occidente*, in *Politica, cultura e religione...*, 41-58 e spec. 55-56 (con ulteriore bibliografia a nota 46); EAD., *Iatrosofistica pagana, «filosofia» cristiana e medicina (IV-VI secolo)*, in Consuetudinis amor. *Fragments d'histoire culturelle (II*^{e}*-VI*^{e} *siècle). Mélanges en l'honneur de Jean-Pierre Callu*, a cura di F. CHAUSSON, É. WOLFF, Roma 2003, 189-216 e spec. 208-212 (con note 38 e 40); per la diffusa convinzione circa l'origine greco-orientale di Eutropio cfr. invece per esempio G. BONAMENTE, *Giuliano l'Apostata e il* Breviarium *di Eutropio*, Roma 1986, spec. 17-45 (*La personalità*

– ben più noto – testimonia poi nel medesimo senso in età giustinianea[13]. Secondo Paschoud, invece, l'ulteriore gioco di parole su *pontifex - suo sanguine pontem infecturus* (del quale Zosimo non avebbe comunque afferrato il senso conferitogli dalla fonte-modello) rafforzerebbe l'ipotesi circa l'esistenza di una fonte storica latina oggi perduta: un *Ignotus* posteriore al 410, ovvero gli *Annales* di Virio Nicomaco Flaviano, il cui titolo è menzionato dall'iscrizione romana apposta nel 431 per ricordarne la riabilitazione della memoria ottenuta allora dai discendenti, dopo molte insistenze, presso Valentiniano III e Teodosio II.

---

dell'autore); ID., *Minor Latin Historians of the Fourth Century A.D.*, in *Greek and Roman Historiography...*, 85-125 e spec. 103-112; J. HELLENGUARC'H, curatore dell'ed. di Eutropio nella Collection «G. Budé», Paris 1999, VIII-IX.

[13] *De mens.* III, 21, *CSHB* 41-42, ove l'autore parla dei γεφυραῖοι /*pontifices*, così chiamati all'origine gli ἀρχιερεῖς che compivano i riti sacri a Pallade in Tessaglia su di un ponte che attraversava lo *Spercheios* (Zosimo parla invece del Peneo – oggi Salamvria –, affermando che i sacerdoti compivano allora i riti in onore degli dèi su di un ponte dal momento che i templi ancora non esistevano). Un'altra tradizione greca, conservata da uno scolio nel manoscritto veronese dell'*Eneide* virgiliana e da Servio, affermava invece che una statua della dea – il Palladio autentico – sarebbe scesa dal cielo su di un ponte che attraversava il Cefisso, non lungi da Atene (SERV. *Ad Aen.* II, v. 166: A. PELLIZZARI, *Servio. Storia, cultura e istituzioni nell'opera di un grammatico tardoantico*, Firenze 2003, 50-51; AL. CAMERON, *The Imperial Pontifex...*, 345 [nota 14]). Nei secoli precedenti *pontifex* era stato reso più esattamente con γεφυροποιός: PLUT. *Numa* 9, il quale enumera varie etimologie di ποντίφικες correnti al tempo suo: o nel senso di δυνατοί, ποτήντες, perché al servizio degli dèi che erano potenti (cfr. pure VARRO, *De lingua Lat.* V, 83, il quale riferisce l'opinione del *pontifex maximus* Quinto Scevola – console nel 95 a.C. – su *pontifex* da *posse et facere*, pur affermando di preferire personalmente la derivazione di *pontifex* da *pontem facere*); o perché addetti a distinguere ciò che «era possibile» da ciò che non lo era nell'ámbito delle funzioni sacre; o perché γεφυροποιοί, cioè costruttori dell'antichissimo ponte ligneo sul Tevere di cui erano custodi e sul quale eseguivano i riti sacri da tempo immemorabile (una spiegazione che Plutarco giudica comunque «risibile» in quanto non collegabile con Numa Pompilio, dal momento che il ponte Sublicio era stato completato soltanto da Anco Marcio, nipote di Numa). Sull'argomento vd. approfondimenti in L. CRACCO RUGGINI, *Costantino e il Palladio*, in *Roma Costantinopoli Mosca. Atti del Seminario Da Roma alla terza Roma (Roma, 21-23 aprile 1981)*, Napoli 1983, 241-251 e partic. 246-247 (nota 21); J. CHAMPEAUX, *Les pontifes romains et l'entretien du pont Sublicius*, «Bulletin de la Société Nationale des Antiquaires de France» (2002 [2008]), 117-128. Per meglio comprendere l'età di transizione giustinianea, più in generale M. MAAS, *John Lydus and the Roman Past. Antiquarianism and Politics in the Age of Giustinian*, London-New York 1992; M. MAZZA, *Giovanni Lido,* De Magistratibus: *sull'interpretazione delle magistrature romane nella Tarda Antichità*, in *Omaggio a Rosario Soraci. Politica, retorica e simbolismo del primato*, a cura di F. ELIA, Catania 2004, II, 219-258 = ID., *Tra Roma e Costantinopoli. Ellenismo Oriente Cristianesimo nella Tarda Antichità*, Catania 2009, 269-299.

La citazione epigrafica di un documento ufficiale come la lettera dei due imperatori a me sembra tuttavia escludere un'approssimazione nel titolo; mentre la dedica dell'opera storica flavianea a Teodosio I – che l'iscrizione afferma sollecitata dall'imperatore cristiano in persona quando Flaviano ancora godeva del favore imperiale come *quaestor sacri palatii* e poi come prefetto al pretorio d'Italia e d'Illirico nel 389-392 circa (appena conclusa l'usurpazione di Magno Massimo, con il quale si erano invece incautamente compromessi molti senatori romani, fra cui il consuocero stesso di Flaviano, Quinto Aurelio Simmaco)[14] – dovrebbe a sua volta escludere la presenza in tale opera storica di un colorito polemico fortemente ideologizzato in senso filo-pagano, quale ne fosse poi il contenuto «annalistico»-breviaristico: storia repubblicana? imperiale? o entrambe? si tratta in ogni caso di supposizioni fragili e indimostrabili, checché molti Autori moderni continuino a pensarne. Anche Rufino, nella sua *Historia Ecclesiastica*, sembra pertanto fornire un sostegno all'idea di una presa di posizione «politico»-religiosa tardiva da parte del pagano Flaviano[15].

---

[14] Per ulteriore documentazione rimando a L. CRACCO RUGGINI, *Il paganesimo romano tra religione e politica (384-394 d. C.): per una reinterpretazione del* Carmen contra paganos, «Memorie dell'Accademia Nazionale dei Lincei, Classe di Scienze morali, storiche e filologiche», s. VIII, 23, 1 (1979), 1-144 e spec. 47-74. *Ibid.*, 70-71 (con nota 206), è ricordato fra l'altro SYMM. *Ep.* II, 34 – anteriore al 389 in quanto Flaviano risulta libero da cariche e ritirato a vita privata –, in cui il celebre oratore rimprovera con una certa durezza l'amico per avere manifestato l'intenzione di disertare gli *Hilaria* in onore della Gran Madre Frigia – 15-27 marzo –, anteponendo i proprî interessi familiari (per tale epistola vd. pure G.A. CECCONI, *Commento storico al libro II dell'epistolario di Q. Aurelio Simmaco, con introduzione, testo, traduzione e indici*, Pisa 2002, 91 [testo], 120 [trad. it.], 257-261 [comm.]; M. KAHLOS, *Vettius Agorius Praetextatus. A Senatorial Life in Between*, Roma 2002, 90, ove l'Autrice sembra prendere i rimbrotti simmachiani a Flaviano soltanto come una deliberata manifestazione di diligenza cultuale, peraltro sorridente): segno evidente in ogni caso, direi, che ancora in questi anni il paganesimo di Flaviano era lontano dagli apici che avrebbero invece caratterizzato la sua «conversione» politica nel 394, secondo la testimonianza soprattutto di RUFIN. *Hist. Eccl.* XI, 33, *GCS* (*Eusebius Werke*, II/2) 1037-1038 (il quale parla di Flaviano Sr. come di un *eruditus admodum vir* che avrebbe anche potuto cavarsela, ma si sarebbe suicidato vergognandosi per l'errore commesso più che per la colpa in se stessa) e di Paulin. *Vita Ambrosii* 26, 3 e 31, 2; A. BALDINI, *Un nucleo di fronda...*, testo corrispondente a nota 26.

[15] *CIL* VI, 1783 = *ILS* 2948 + AÉ 1971, 13, nr. 24: titolo marmoreo, apposto dal nipote Appio Nicomaco Destro (prefetto urbano fra il 427 e il 431), che riporta il messaggio al senato di Roma con il quale i due imperatori della stirpe teodosiana – ammoniti *potius quam sponte* – per onorare il figlio Virio Nicomaco Jr. riabilitarono nel 431 la memoria del padre Virio Nicomaco Flaviano, 37 anni dopo l'appoggio da costui accordato contro Teodosio I all'usurpatore filo-pagano Eugenio nel 394 (sconfitto il

Appare inoltre difficile sostenere che Virio Nicomaco Flaviano fornisse la medesima versione che per la prima volta a noi risulta comparire attorno alla metà del V secolo nelle *Storie Ecclesiastiche* di Socrate e di Sozomeno, circa l'uccisione di Graziano su di un ponte a Lione a seguito di una romanzesca macchinazione di Andragazio. In ogni caso (non dimentichiamo che, sul contenuto dei perduti *Annales* flavianei, sono state formulate soltanto ipotesi, per di più in reciproco contrasto), costui fu un contemporaneo degli eventi, non diversamente dall'ex *clarissimus* romano Aurelio Ambrogio, vescovo di Milano, secondo il quale l'uccisione a tradimento di Graziano in Gallia avvenne invece durante un banchetto (*Explanatio Psalmorum XII*, del 394/397 circa). Tanto Ambrogio quanto Flaviano, entrambi diversamente coinvolti, dovevano pertanto essere meglio informati che non i due storici ecclesiastici bizantini, posteriori di decennî e privi d'informazioni dirette sugli eventi occidentali.

Paschoud ritiene che della fonte latina si sarebbe servito il greco Eunapio nelle sue *Storie*, seguito poi da Zosimo al tempo di Anastasio. Lasciamo pure da parte il fatto che nulla prova l'uso di fonti latine sia nella *Storia nuova* di Zosimo (peraltro *ex advocatus fisci*, che in quanto funzionario imperiale il latino doveva conoscerlo, ma che probabilmente preferì attingere i fatti narrati a due soli autori come lui grecofoni, Eunapio fino al 404 e Olimpiodoro in seguito)[16], sia – soprattutto – nel suo principale

---

5-6 settembre dello stesso anno alla battaglia del Frigido, accompagnandosi al suicidio di Flaviano stesso: F. Paschoud, *Chronique pour un mille six centième anniversaire: le Frigidus en ébullition*, «Antiquité Tardive» 5 [1997], 275-280 [recensione a *Westillyricum und Nordostitalien in der spätrömischen Zeit*, a cura di R. Bratož, Ljubljana 1996, *Atti* del Colloquio tenuto a Zemono in Slovenia nel 1994]); C.W. Hedrick Jr., *History and Silence. Purge and Rehabilitation of Memory in Late Antiquity*, Austin (Texas) 2000, spec. 237-240. Vd. pure *CIL* VI, 1782 = *ILS* 2947, iscrizione sottostante alla statua dedicatagli, forse nel 394 stesso, dal nipote acquisito Q. Fabio Memmio Simmaco nella casa avita sul Celio (gemella e speculare all'epigrafe in onore del padre Q. Aurelio Simmaco, consuocero e amico fraterno di Virio Nicomaco Flaviano, *CIL* VI, 1699 = *ILS* 2946), in cui Flaviano Sr. è ricordato come *historicus disertissimus*. Per Rufino nella sua *Historia Ecclesiastica* vd. sopra, nota 14. Anche Rita Lizzi Testa (*Alle origini della tradizione pagana su Costantino e il senato romano (Amm. Marc. 21.10.8 e Zos. 2.32.1)*, in *Transformations of Late Antiquity. Essays for Peter Brown*, a cura di P. Rousseau, M. Papoutsakis, London 2009, 85-127) ritiene che Virio Nicomaco Flaviano, dedicando i propri *Annales* a Teodosio I, dovesse essere interessato a compiacere l'imperatore cristiano (non diversamente, del resto, da Ammiano Marcellino) e che quindi la sua opera non potesse essere caratterizzata da un'aperta apologetica pagana.

[16] Risulta abbastanza perspicuo che Olimpiodoro fu adottato da Zosimo come fonte principale da V, 26 in avanti: su questo punto concordo pienamente con F. Paschoud e A. Baldini.

modello, le ampie – troppo ampie – *Storie* perdute di Eunapio, un sofista neoplatonico tardo che, come Libanio e molti altri retori del tempo[17], non sembra volesse mai apprendere il latino e farne uso, per dichiarate ragioni ideologiche.

La profezia su Graziano ucciso su di un ponte dopo aver declinato il dono della veste pontificale da parte di una delegazione di senatori pagani non risulta comunque testimoniata da fonti latine coeve. Si tratta di un'ipotesi che leggiamo per la prima volta in Friedrich Sylburg, quando questi pubblicò a Francoforte la prima edizione completa della *Storia nuova* zosimiana[18]. È possibile che essa fosse già stata elaborata da certa propaganda filopagana di alcuni decenni posteriori agli avvenimenti; ma le eventuali tracce trovano riscontro soltanto nella tradizione bizantina. Ciò non significa peraltro escludere l'esistenza, più in generale, di fonti latine filo-senatorie e filo-pagane oggi perdute alle spalle di storici tardi e familiari con la lingua latina nella fattispecie (come l'*Epitome de Caesaribus*, Aurelio Vittore, Festo, Eutropio, lo scrittore della *Historia Augusta*[19], lo stesso Ammiano Marcellino e così via). Vuol dire semplicemente che io rimango scettica circa una loro influenza diretta su autori bizantini come Eutropio e Zosimo (diverso il caso dell'intelligente e preciso Olimpiodoro, che il latino e le vicende occidentali conobbe da vicino e forse anche, in riferimento a personaggi vissuti a cavallo dei due secoli, con accenni a avvenimenti anteriori al 404, data ufficiale d'inizio delle sue annotazioni storiche secondo il più tardo riassunto del patriarca Fozio, che ancora nel IX secolo lo leggeva per intero)[20].

---

[17] Cfr. spec. LIBAN. *Epp.* 1004, 4 del 391 a Quinto Aurelio Simmaco (una cui lettera aveva letto tramite interprete) e 1036, 4-7 del 393 a Postumiano (rampollo di una celebre famiglia senatoria romana composta da membri sia cristiani sia pagani e raccomandato da Simmaco a Eutropio nell'*Ep.* III, 48), che nel 392 gli aveva mandato una lettera di condoglianze per la morte di suo figlio Cimone: lo prega di scrivergli la prossima volta in greco, dal momento che padroneggiava bene anche tale lingua: *PLRE*, I *s.v.* «Postumianus» 3, 718-719.

[18] Già L. CRACCO RUGGINI, *Il paganesimo romano...*, 5-6 (con nota 4).

[19] Anche i controlli informatici sullo stile delle varie *Vitae* sembrano oggi condurre a ipotizzate un autore unico per tutte le biografie imperiali della *Historia Augusta*, benché questa si auto-proclami scritta da diversi personaggi: M. MARRIOTT, *The Authorship of the* Historia Augusta – *Two Computer Studies*, «Journal of Roman Studies» 69 (1979), 65-77, con le precisazioni di D. SANSONE, *ibid.*, 80 (1990), 174-177.

[20] *Bibl. cod. 80*, ed. a cura di R. HENRY, I, Paris 1959, 166-187. I ben 22 libri di Olimpiodoro sono stati riassunti da Fozio in altrettante pagine dell'ed. HENRY; e P.A. BRUNT, *On Historical Fragments and Epitomes*, «Class. Quart.» 74 (1980), 482-485, ha giustamente insistito sul fatto che occorre maneggiare sempre con grande cautela l'estratto di un'opera perduta più ampia, in quanto esso ha filtrato vistosamente l'originale con la

Sono qui esonerata dall'offrire ulteriori particolari sull'argomento, essendo sufficiente rimandare al contributo di Alan Cameron più volte citato, esaustivo per fonti e per bibliografia[21]. Personalmente ritengo tuttavia che Zosimo, con ogni probabilità, derivi qui da Eunapio l'utilizzo di uno scritto antiquario più antico sui pontefici, già da quest'ultimo inserito in una digressione «provvidenzialistica» (mentre Alan Cameron – sulle orme di Wolf Liebeschütz – è convinto che si debba risalire piuttosto a una fonte antiquaria usata direttamente da Zosimo: gli argomenti addotti sono possibili, non però dirimenti)[22]. Concordo con Paschoud sul fatto che molteplici interpretazioni provvidenzialistiche pagane già esistevano nel IV secolo sia in Oriente sia in Occidente (per rendersene conto, basta leggere la celeberrima *Relatio* III di Simmaco del 384 o i *Discorsi* 24 e 30 di Libanio, del 379 e 386 rispettivamente), senz'aspettare il sacco alariciano di Roma nel 410[23]. Ma accantonando la sofisticata proposta interpretativa sylburghiana avanzata da Paschoud e accettando invece in larga misura la minuta analisi di Alan Cameron, penso che Zosimo abbia qui tramandato una notizia non di semplice fantasia, bensì autentica nel suo nocciolo, anche se adorna di fronzoli eruditi non sempre credibili.

Tutto ciò, come ho detto, poteva già trovarsi nella principale fonte storico-narrativa di Zosimo, Eunapio appunto. L'interpretazione provvidenzialistica poteva essergli giunta anche solo per via orale, attraverso i canali di una propaganda filo-pagana allora ampiamente circolante in tutto l'impero[24]. E tali spunti erano collegabili con facilità a notizie sui *pontifices*

---

possibilità di alterarne strutture e messaggi, più o meno consapevolmente: e ciò appare tanto più probabile qui, ove il riassunto è opera, a secoli di distanza, di un lettore come il patriarca Fozio (pur attento, nel complesso). Sulla data iniziale dell'opera storica di Olimpiodoro cfr. F. PASCHOUD, *Le début de l'ouvrage historique d'Olympiodore...*

[21] Inclusa l'improbabile ipotesi, formulata per la prima volta da K.-L. NÖTLICHS, *Die gesetzgeberischen Massnahmen der christlichen Kaiser des vierten Jahrhunderts gegen Häretiker, Heiden und Juden* (Universität-Dissertation), Köln 1971, 198-202, che fosse stato piuttosto il pio Teodosio a declinare per la prima volta il titolo di pontefice massimo cui allude Zosimo o, quanto meno, a convincere Graziano ad emularlo: discussione e bibliografia in AL. CAMERON, *The Imperial Pontifex...*, 351-352 (con note 39-40).

[22] J.H.W.G. LIEBESCHÜTZ, *Pagan Historiography...*; più in generale L. CRACCO RUGGINI, *Zosimo, ossia il rovesciamento delle «Storie Ecclesiastiche»*, «Augustinianum» 16 (1976), 23-36.

[23] Così J.H.W.G. LIEBESCHÜTZ, *Pagan Historiography...*, 191-201; vd. invece F. PASCHOUD, *L'intolérance chrétienne vue et jugée par les païens*, «Cristianesimo nella storia» 11 (1990), 545-577.

[24] J.H.W.G. LIEBESCHÜTZ, *Pagan Historiography...*, ha enumerato nove digressioni che Zosimo avrebbe derivato da Eunapio; ma F. PASCHOUD, ed. di Zosimo, I, Paris 1971, 2002², LXXII-LXXIV, ne fornisce un elenco più nutrito. Sono comunque d'accordo

attinte all'opera di un antiquario greco, utilizzato in seguito anche da Giovanni Lido (non però in funzione ideologica come in Eunapio). L'emulazione fra Romani e Greci – che proprio allora si andava accentuando – appare del resto già evidente anche a proposito dell'etimologia di *pontifex* nelle fonti latine e greche menzionate da Plutarco nel II secolo d.C.[25]. A mio parere è probabile che la digressione antiquario-«provvidenzialistica» già si trovasse nelle *Storie* di Eunapio perché esse erano state assai più dotte ed ampie: Zosimo vi attinse sopprimendo molti *excursus* (non tutti, però) e abbreviando fortemente il modello, con ogni verisimiglianza senza darsi pensiero di allargare ulteriormente le proprie letture.

Resto dunque convinta della sostanziale storicità (non certo dell'importanza epocale) della decisione grazianea di rifiutare la veste che gli era stata offerta dai senatori pagani di Roma. Innanzi tutto non è affatto detto, mi pare, che il declinare un abbigliamento speciale per esercitare il tradizionale pontificato massimo, da parte del Principe cristiano, significasse automaticamente anche il rifiuto della carica stessa (come la maggioranza degli studiosi ritiene), bensì soltanto della pubblicità propagandistica che la delegazione senatoria pagana intendeva conferire all'assunzione imperiale del sommo sacerdozio romano, in una congiuntura particolarmente delicata della politica religiosa imperiale. Il testo di Zosimo non autorizza infatti ad andare oltre.

Quando poi collocare l'evento? Quando Graziano visitò la capitale nell'estate del 376 e papa Damaso lo esortava a un più attivo impegno cristiano? Oppure (forse meglio, a mio avviso) quando nel 382/383 il giovane Principe già si trovava a Milano sotto l'influenza di Ambrogio e aveva deciso di far asportare l'altare della Vittoria dalla *Curia Iulia* in Roma, rifiutando perciò di ricevere la delegazione di senatori pagani che dall'Urbe si era recata a Milano per condolersene[26]? Graziano risulta infatti ancora fregiato del titolo di *pontifex maximus*, assieme con il padre e con lo zio, in un'iscrizione del 369 tuttoggi visibile sul ponte Cestio[27].

---

con quanto ha scritto Paschoud nel 1992 recensendo il volume di Ochoa (sopra, nota 2): «Le temps est venu de laisser Eunape un peu tranquille».

[25] Vd. sopra, nota 13; AL. CAMERON, *The Imperial Pontifex...*, 344.

[26] AL. CAMERON, *Gratian's Repudiation of the Pontifical Robe*, «Journal of the Roman Studies» 58 (1968), 96-102, che ha optato per il 382/383; F. PASCHOUD, *Cinq Études...*, 65-79, e ID., ed. di Zosimo... II/2, 419-420, propenso invece al 376 e incline a considerare un *terminus ante quem* la *Gratiarum actio* di Ausonio del 379 (oltre, nota 30); da escludere in ogni caso il 367, quando Graziano divenne Augusto ad Amiens accanto al padre Valentiniano I, ad appena 8 anni.

[27] *CIL* VI, 1175 = *ILS* 771; AL. CAMERON, *The Imperial Pontifex...*, 351 (con nota 32).

E ancora nella seconda metà del 379 egli viene apostrofato come *pontifex* dal poeta Decimius Magnus Ausonius (però ambiguamente, da cristiano tiepido qual'egli in effetti era)[28] proprio nel discorso di ringraziamento all'imperatore che lo aveva nominato console dal 1° gennaio e che certo egli non intendeva in alcun modo contrariare[29]. Le fonti pagane nel loro insieme, in ogni caso, non hanno mai considerato il regno di Graziano un tornante decisivo nella cristianizzazione dell'impero, come poi quello di Teodosio in Zosimo stesso, secondo quanto ha giustamente notato Alan Cameron[30] (per quanto non sembri accettabile ritenere che Zosimo parlasse di Graziano per errore quando si trattava invece di Teodosio stesso, come ha suggerito Karl-Ludwig Nötlich)[31].

Secondo certa propaganda filo-pagana di fine IV-inizi V secolo il rifiuto del cristiano Graziano sarebbe stato in ogni caso adeguatamente punito, come si è già detto. E per la sua presunta provvidenzialità questa era senza dubbio un'informazione tale da richiamare l'attenzione di Eunapio/Zosimo ben più delle misure anti-pagane di Graziano, di cui la *Storia nuova* zosimiana non reca infatti traccia. Pure a livello legislativo, del resto, le misure anti-pagane emanate da Graziano nel 382 non sono pervenute affatto; e noi le conosciamo soltanto attraverso i riferimenti ad esse nella *Relatio* III di Quinto Aurelio Simmaco e nelle epistole di Ambrogio 17-18 *PL* 16 = 72-73 *CSEL* 82, 3, durante la contesa *de ara Victoriae* (384 d.C.)[32]. In primo luogo tali disposizioni furono probabilmente più limitate

---

[28] L. CRACCO RUGGINI, *Simmaco, Ausonio e l'enigma del numero tre*, in Polyanthema. *Studi di letteratura cristiana antica offerti a S. Costanza*, I, Messina 1989, 167-176.
[29] *Gratiarum actio*, VII,35 e IX,42; F. PASCHOUD, *Cinq études*..., 73, il quale parla di «équivoque voulue»; R.P.H. GREEN, *The Work of Ausonius*, Oxford 1991², 545, 547; AL. CAMERON, *The Imperial Pontifex*..., 361 (con nota 81).
[30] Cfr. già L. CRACCO RUGGINI, *Zosimo*...
[31] Vd. sopra, nota 21.
[32] Rimando a questo proposito all'analisi approfondita di R. LIZZI TESTA, *Christian Emperor, Vestal Virgins, and Priestly Colleges: Reconsidering the End of Roman Paganism*, «Antiquité Tardive» 15 (2007), 251-262 (il testo, all'origine, è stato letto all'Oxford Centre for Late Antiquity durante il seminario *Late Antique Religion and Politics: from Rome to Berlin*, 29-30 settembre 2007); EAD., *Dal conflitto al dialogo: nuove prospettive sulle relazioni tra pagani e cristiani in Occidente alla fine del IV secolo*, in *Trent'anni di studi sulla tarda antichità: bilanci e prospettive (Associazione di Studi Tardoantichi, Napoli, 21-23 novembre 2007)*, a cura di U. CRISCUOLO, L. DE GIOVANNI, Napoli 2009, 167-190 e EAD., *La Chiesa, i domini, i rustici pagani: strategie di conversione in Occidente (IV-VI secolo)*, in *Quid sit christianum esse. Le problème de «la christianisation du monde antique». Colloque organisé par H. Inglebert, B. Dumézil, S. Destephen à l'Université de Paris X – Nanterre (26-28 Mai 2008)* (spec. testo corrispondente alle note 79-82, ove l'Autrice, con buoni argomenti, sostiene che i *constituta*

di quanto non si soglia credere, come di recente si è sottolineato. In secondo luogo, i compilatori dei *Codici* preferirono forse «dimenticare» misure anti-pagane che i successori di Graziano, pur cristiani, avevano ancora ampiamente disatteso. Infine – e, direi, soprattutto – l'iniziativa di Graziano nel 382 appariva legata a un'ideologia di primato dell'Urbe amplificata nel solco della sola tradizione romana, che ben poco doveva interessare i giuristi della corte costantinopolitana e ancora meno gli storici bizantini, cristiani o pagani che fossero. Per il rifiuto della veste pontificale da parte di Graziano nel racconto di Zosimo non mi sembra quindi il caso di scomodare, come ha invece proposto anni or sono Polymnia Athanassiadi, una fonte di propaganda neoplatonica diversa da Eunapio medesimo. E l'interpretazione da me proposta consente di meglio inscrivere la testimonianza zosimiana nel contesto degli avvenimenti storico-religiosi del tempo[33].

---

divi Gratiani cui allude *CTh* XVI, 10, 20 – del 415 – non sono identificabili *tout court* con le disposizioni grazianee del 382 menzionate nel 384 da Simmaco e Ambrogio, come per solito si suol fare), entrambi in preparazione per la stampa (ringrazio l'Autrice per avermene dato copia in anteprima, discutendone con me e autorizzandomi a farne uso).

[33] Cfr. P. ATHANASSIADI, *Damascius: The Philosophical History. Text with Translation and Notes*, Athens 1999, 350-357 (*Appendix III: Who Was Count Zosimos?*) e spec. 354-355; vd. pure AL. CAMERON, *The Imperial Pontifex...*, 348-349. Sul provvidenzialismo di Eunapio/Zosimo cfr. L. CRACCO RUGGINI, *Zosimo...*; EAD., *Sofisti greci nell'Impero Romano (a proposito di un libro recente)*, «Athenaeum» n.s. 49 (1971), 402-425. Quivi ho sostenuto – e continuo tuttora ad esserne convinta, in base alle considerazioni concrete già addotte nel 1972, 1973 e 1976, a mio avviso lette un po' frettolosamente da chi in seguito le ha criticate – che Zosimo conservasse una certa autonomia rispetto alle *Storie* di Eunapio (con i loro prolungamenti e/o edizioni inclusi, per cui cfr. spec. F. PASCHOUD, *Eunapiana...*, con ulteriore bibliografia ivi): non però nella forma espositiva, spesso assai prossima a quella del proprio modello, come si può dedurre dai frammenti delle *Storie* (diligentemente raccolti di A. BALDINI, *Ricerche sulla «Storia» di Eunapio...*, accompagnandoli con l'analisi dei luoghi corrispondenti nella *Storia nuova* zosimiana); e neppure nella sostanza dei fatti narrati, che in molti casi Zosimo sembra attingere a Eunapio quasi tali e quali, pur abbreviando grandemente il racconto e sopprimendo molti fronzoli (ma conservandone – spesso deliberatamente – la scarsa attenzione per gli aspetti cronologici e geografici, per cui cfr. A. BALDINI, *Ricerche sulla «Storia» di Eunapio...*, 19-74; F. PASCHOUD, *Questions d'historiographie tardive...ibid.*, 373, oltre a introdurre altri errori che Paschoud via via segnala nel proprio commento all'edizione di Zosimo nelle Belles Lettres: in questo senso aveva ragione FOZIO, *Bibl. Cod. 98* [Zosimo], ed. a cura di R. HENRY, Paris 1960, II, 65-66, quando già affermava che Zosimo non faceva che «riscrivere» Eunapio – ...μεταγράψαι τὴν [scil. ἱστορί αν] Εὐναπίου, τῷ συντόμῳ μόνον διαφέρουσαν – in forma ovviamente abbreviata, ossia più semplice e leggibile anche da non specialisti). Zosimo sembra invece mostrare una certa originalità nella cornice ideologica generale, più pragmatica di quella

Ancora a mio avviso, i successori di Graziano continuarono in seguito ad accettare, fra gli altri titoli, anche quello di *pontifex* (probabilmente *pontifex inclitus* come ha proposto di recente Cameron, piuttosto che *pontifex maximus*, una titolatura tradizionalmente pagana, che s'incontra fino a poco

---

di Eunapio, sebbene egualmente pagana e, in una certa misura, provvidenzialista. La tendenza a considerare Zosimo parzialmente autonomo rispetto a Eunapio è presente anche (ma adducendo argomentazioni differenti, spesso dubbie) in R.T. RIDLEY, *Eunapius and Zosimus*, «Helikon» 9-10 (1969-1970), 574-592; R.C. BLOCKLEY, *Zosimus, The First Historian of Rome's Fall*, «American Historical Review» 76 (1971), 412-441; ID., *Was the First Book of Zosimus' New History Based on More than Two Sources?*, «Byzantion» 50 (1980), 393-402; J.A. OCHOA, *La transmisiòn...*, 230-289 e spec. 281-282;G. FOWDEN, *The Last Days of Costantine: Oppositional Versions and Their Influence*, «Journal of Roman Studies» 84 (1994), 146-170 (con risultati ancora oggi considerati «aberranti» da A. BALDINI, *Un nucleo di fronda storiografica...*; l'Autore – come già Blockley nel 1980: vd. subito sopra – ha sostenuto la presenza in Zosimo di una pluralità di fonti: *contra* pure F. PASCHOUD, *Zosime ei Constantin...* [sopra, nota 2]); J.H.W.G. LIEBESCHÜTZ, *Pagan Historiography...* Sia F. PASCHOUD (spec. *Cinq Études...* 209-210, e ID., *Zosime et la fin de l'ouvrage...*, con rimando spec. a L. CRACCO RUGGINI, *Simboli di battaglia ideologica nel Tardo Ellenismo (Roma, Atene, Costantinopoli; Numa, Empedocle, Cristo)*, in *Studi Storici in onore di Ottorino Bertolini*, I, Pisa 1972, 177-300 e partic. 32-34 dell'estratto = 208-210, 81-83 = 251-253, 100-106 = 276-282, 116-119 = 292-295), sia – al suo seguito, ma con maggiore prudenza – A. BALDINI, *Ricerche sulla «Storia» di Eunapio...*, 41-42 (con note 47 e 49) mi hanno rimproverato un fondamentale difetto di metodo, in quanto avrei ignorato l'inevitabile diversità di prospettiva intercorrente tra la fonte biografica eunapiana (pervenuta) e l'opera storica dello stesso autore, giunta solo in pochi frammenti più o meno significativi (o, comunque, significativi diversamente che per Zosimo, il quale operò la selezione): secondo i calcoli di Paschoud, i 14 libri delle *Storie* eunapiane – di cui sono pervenuti frammenti per una decina di pagine a stampa nell'ed. Henry oltre al trasunto di FOZIO, *Bibl. cod.* 77 (Collection «G. Budé»...) I, 158-160 – rappresenterebbero circa il 7% del totale: cfr. ID., *Cinq Études...*, 211). Su ciò potrei anche essere d'accordo in linea di massima (ma ricordando quanto affermava un autore del IV secolo avanzato come Giuliano – pur egli neoplatonico secondo gli insegnamenti della scuola di Atene – che fare storia significa conoscere le verità passate alla luce dei valori filosofici e religiosi del presente: cfr. W.E. KAEGI, *The Emperor Julian's Assessment of the Significance and Function of History*, «Proceedings of the American Philological Society» 108 [1964] 29-38; e neppure dimenticando quanto ha affermato Paschoud stesso circa la commistione di generi in Ammiano Marcellino: ID., *Questions d'historiographie tardive...*, 364). Di fatto, nei contributi sopra menzionati, io ho appoggiato le mie osservazioni quasi esclusivamente all'analisi di alcuni frammenti delle *Storie* eunapiane (*frr*. 12, 48, 55, 75,1, 80, 82, ecc. nell'ed. dei *FHG*, IV, Paris 1851, a cura di C. MÜLLER), avvalendomi delle *Vitae sophistarum* (ed. a cura di G. GIANGRANDE, Roma 1956) soltanto là ov'esse risultano convergere ideologicamente con tali frammenti (magari ad altro proposito), e confrontando poi tali passi con quelli dell'opera storica di Zosimo: ciò che a me pare abbastanza legittimo.

prima fra quelle ufficiali complete, a noi note soprattutto per via epigrafica), sia per conservatorismo rituale (però ormai deideologizzato e tutt'altro che esibito), sia per volontà di accontentare tutti; e forse anche per scaramanzia, data la pessima fine cui era andato incontro Graziano dopo avere osato intaccare apertamente la tradizione enfatizzata da certa propaganda pagana, di cui soltanto Zosimo è il portavoce a noi giunto (sia pure a stento). Il silenzio che avrebbe circondato di estrema riservatezza il persistere di tale consuetudine non autorizza in ogni caso a escluderne l'esistenza.

Di fatto, il titolo di *pontifex* applicato a imperatori s'incontra saltuariamente anche in seguito, per esempio in una lettera di Marciano e Valentiniano III del 7 febbraio 452 e in un'altra di Anastasio al senato di Roma nel 516 (*pontifex inclitus*); nelle acclamazioni popolari a Marciano e a Teodosio II negli *Atti* del concilio di Calcedonia; e già nel 410 il pagano Tertullus, console di poco rilievo (*umbratilis*) durante l'usurpazione di Prisco Attalo, proprio attraverso l'assunzione del titolo di *pontifex* espresse ai senatori romani la sua speranza di diventare presto imperatore (così intese per esempio il passo di Orosio in merito anche Paolo Diacono nella sua *Historia Romana*; e a mio parere si tratta di una controprova importante)[34]. Il fatto che Eunapio e Zosimo scrivessero proprio fra gli inizî del V secolo e quelli del VI almeno in parte spiega in chiave di replica polemica filo-pagana la deliberata sottolineatura circa l'origine tradizionale di questa titolatura imperiale, della quale anche i cristiani mostravano allora di volersi impossessare.

Agli inizi del VI secolo (507 circa) Ennodio ben a ragione poteva comunque proclamare che gli antenati erano stati chiamati invano *divi* e *pontifices*[35], chiaramente alludendo anche alla perdurante – e parallela – sopravvivenza della *consecratio* imperiale, proclamata dal senato almeno fino alla morte di Teodosio incluso (quindi anche di Graziano) per le valenze squisitamente laiche e politiche implicite in tale prassi, che i senatori di Roma continuavano gelosamente a custodire[36]. Del resto, anche

---

[34] Cfr. *Acta conciliorum oecumenicorum*, II, 3, 2 e II,1,1, ed. a cura di E. SCHWARTZ, Berlin-Leipzig 1936, 87-88 e 54; *Coll. Avell.*, nr. 113, *CSEL* 35, 106-107; per Tertullo, OROS. *Hist. adversus paganos*, VII, 42, 8; PAUL. DIAC. *Hist. Rom.* XIII, 1, *MGH AA*, II, 196 (*Tertullus consul, qui se futurum principem in senatu gloriatus est, pari nihilominus exitu periit*); *PLRE* II (*395-527*), a cura di R. MARTINDALE, Cambridge 1980, s.v. «Tertullus» 1, 1059. Per ulteriori approfondimenti cfr. AL. CAMERON, *The Imperial Pontifex...*

[35] *Pan. Theoderici* 17, *MGH AA*, VII, 213.

[36] L. CRACCO RUGGINI, *Apoteosi e politica senatoria nel IV s. d. C.: il dittico dei Symmachi al British Museum*, «Rivista Storica Italiana» 89 (1977), 425-489 + 2 tavv., con approfondimenti ivi.

della *consecratio* (la cui persistenza è confermata da innumerevoli fonti) si potevano interpretarne i risvolti religiosi in senso tanto pagano quanto cristiano, data l'equivocità dei suoi aspetti sacrali e il fatto che il *divus* così onorato non fosse propriamente ritenuto un *deus* (la distinzione, con sfumature diverse, affiora a quest'epoca in autori di opposte fedi come Giuliano, Servio, Agostino, la *Historia Augusta*)[37].

La presenza pontificale era ancora ritenuta essenziale per qualsiasi tipo di consacrazione nelle *Institutiones* di Giustiniano, pubblicate nel 533: ma senza dubbio il significato appare già cristiano, applicato più genericamente a vescovi. In ogni caso, come ben a ragione ha osservato Iiro Kajanto, è sempre necessario distinguere, di volta in volta, l'uso alternativo di espressioni quali *pontifex, pontifex summus, pontifex inclitus, pontifex maximus*. Quest'ultimo titolo, durante tutta la prima età cristiana, era stato considerato offensivo (per esempio da Tertulliano, che nei primi lustri del III secolo aveva designato *pontifex maximus* papa Callisto per irrisione)[38], quindi fu evitato in quanto chiaramente ancora pagano. Soltanto nel Rinascimento il titolo di *pontifex maximus*, ormai da tempo svuotato di qualsivoglia valenza pagana, venne risuscitato in riferimento ai papi. *Pontifex* e *summus pontifex* invece – collegandosi direttamente alla Bibbia greca e poi latina (soprattutto nella versione *Afra*) come indicazione del sommo sacerdozio ebraico – ἀρχιερεύς, *pontifex* – già nel IV-V secolo furono applicati tanto a Cristo quanto a certi vescovi: si potrebbero ricordare Giovanni Cassiano per Cristo, Paolino di Nola per Agostino, l'epitaffio di Sidonio Apollinare per il vescovo stesso). Riferite ai papi (vescovi di Roma), entrambe le espressioni s'incontrano in iscrizioni e in testi letterarî cristiani quanto meno da Liberio (intorno al 360) fino a Leone Magno, Gregorio Magno (epitaffio funebre) e così via[39].

Gli imperatori cristiani continuarono dunque a essere designati *pontifices* nelle loro titolature complete fino a che il numero dei sudditi pagani fu significativo (per quanto le attestazioni ne siano soltanto saltuarie), anche se forse non pochi cristiani già allora dovevano scandalizzarsene. Alcuni

---

[37] *Ibid.*, 451-452 (con nota 92 e fonti ivi); più in generale G.W. BOWERSOCK, *The Imperial Cult. Perceptions and Resistence*, in *Jewish and Christian Self-Definition*, III (*Self-Definition in the Graeco-Roman World*), a cura di B.F. MEYERS, E.P. SANDERS, London 1982, 171-182 (testo) e 238-241 (note).

[38] *Pudicit.* 1,6.

[39] I. KAJANTO, Pontifex Maximus *as Title of the Pope*, «*Arctos*. Acta Philologica Fennica» 15 (1981), 37-52; AL. CAMERON, *The Imperial Pontifex*..., 361 (con nota 80), ove si ricorda l'uso di *pontifex* in riferimento già a papa Liberio (*Coll. Avell.*, nr. 12, CSEL 35, nr. 1, 1-5).

poteri dei pontefici, infatti, si rivelavano ancora utili. Mi trovo comunque d'accordo con Alan Cameron sul fatto che tale prassi, «though not false, [...] is nevertheless a misleading perspective. It is important to clear that the *pontifex maximus* was both more and less than a "high priest"»[40]. Gli imperatori cristiani del IV-V secolo non enfatizzarono certo né, probabilmente, svolsero mai i compiti sacrificali spettanti al pontefice di rango più elevato; però le mansioni di questo sacerdozio erano innumerevoli: la titolatura dovette quindi permanere, per lo meno a mio avviso, soprattutto in collegamento con significati «politici» in senso lato (includendo anche cerimonie collegate a culti sia pubblici sia privati) piuttosto che con aspetti attinenti alla fede, proprio come nel caso, cronologicamente e qualitativamente parallelo, della *consecratio*, in una sorta di patronato su tutti i cittadini, pagani o cristiani che fossero (continuò per esempio ad essere di competenza imperiale, in collegamento con il pontificato, l'autorizzazione al trasporto di salme – come nel caso del retore gallico Aemilius Magnus Arborius, uno zio di Ausonio defunto a Costantinopoli –, ovvero il controllo su certe cerimonie religiose o ludico-religiose)[41].

Fu pertanto grazie a tali funzioni di controllo delle cose di religione attraverso il pontificato massimo che gli Augusti cristiani da Costantino in avanti monopolizzarono il ruolo di mediatori religiosi in tutto l'impero. E ciò dovette favorire grandemente la trasformazione semantica di *pontifex maximus* in *pontifex inclitus*, anziché spingere verso la semplice soppressione del titolo pagano (la svolta decisiva dovette aver luogo fra il tempo del pagano Giuliano e quello del cristianissimo Graziano)[42]. Il mutamento non fu quindi una meccanica «sopravvivenza pagana»[43] di carattere antiquario-lessicale, bensì un'evoluzione lenta, consapevolmente orientata e in sostanza già avverata nel corso del V secolo secondo una «reinterpretazione» cristiana.

Tutto ciò è uno fra i tanti segni di permeabilità e di continuità fra paganesimo e cristianesimo, sfociando nella parziale cristianizzazione seman-

---

[40] AL. CAMERON, *The Imperial Pontifex*..., 356-357, ove l'Autore enumera svariate funzioni pontificali.
[41] Ritorniamo per certi versi alle tesi di Cesare Baronio (per le quali vd. sopra, nota 3); in generale S.R.F. PRICE, *Rituals and Power: The Roman Imperial Cult in Asia Minor*, Cambridge 1984, 36-69; R. GORDON, *The Veil of Power. Emperors, Sacrificers and Benefactors*, in *Pagan Priests: Religion and Power in the Ancient World*, a cura di M. BEARD, J. NORTH, London 1990, 201-231.
[42] AL. CAMERON, *The Imperial Pontifex*..., 359 (con nota 69) e 361.
[43] C. CAPIZZI, *L'imperatore Anastasio I (491-518). Studio sulla sua vita, la sua opera e la sua personalità*, Roma 1969, 242 e *passim*.

tica di realtà attinenti a funzioni che continuavano a rivestire una qualche importanza, nonostante l'ottica del tutto mutata da cui ormai si guardava ad esse. Si trattava invero di aspetti con valenze precipuamente amministrative e cerimoniali, che non potevano venire soppresse da un giorno all'altro se non a prezzo di gravi turbative politiche e sociali, come proprio l'esperienza di Graziano aveva insegnato.

Fu dunque questo uno fra i mutamenti graduali che passarono quasi inavvertiti, avendo trovato un felice incontro fra tradizioni antichissime e mentalità del tutto nuove. Come ha insegnato Peter Brown[44], anche in questo caso fu il cristianesimo ad essere conquistato dal mondo, piuttosto che viceversa.

---

[44] *La fine del mondo antico. Da Marco Aurelio a Maometto*, Torino 1974 (dall'ed. inglese, London 1971).

SILVIA ORLANDI

Gli ultimi sacerdoti pagani di Roma: analisi della documentazione epigrafica

Numerosi studi in questi ultimi anni sono stati dedicati ad un tema giustamente considerato cruciale nella storia dell'Impero romano come quello della «fine del paganesimo»[1]. Particolare attenzione è stata data alla religiosità o, meglio, ai comportamenti religiosi dei membri dell'aristocrazia, considerati da alcuni gli ultimi paladini di una «lotta» contro il Cristianesimo ormai imperante, e da altri come gli stanchi epigoni dell'antica religione, sopravvissuta solo come parte integrante della cultura tradizionale in cui tutti i rappresentanti – pagani e cristiani – degli strati più elevati della popolazione si erano formati[2].

Sono state utilizzate le seguenti abbreviazioni bibliografiche:
CHRISTOL, *Essai* = M. CHRISTOL, *Essai sur l'évolution des carrièeres sénatoriales dans la 2ᵉ moitié du IIIᵉ s. ap. J.-C.*, Paris 1986.
EAOR, VI = S. ORLANDI, *Epigrafia anfiteatrale dell'Occidente Romano*, VI. *Roma. Anfiteatri e strutture annesse, con una nuova edizione e commento delle iscrizioni del Colosseo*, Roma 2004.
LTUR = *Lexicon Topographicum Urbis Romae*, a cura di E. M. STEINBY, I-VI, Roma 1993-2000.
PORENA, *Origini* = P. PORENA, *Le origini della prefettura del pretorio tardoantica*, Roma 2003.
RÜPKE, *Fasti* = J. RÜPKE, *Fasti sacerdotum*, Stuttgart 2005.
Per periodici e sillogi epigrafiche le abbreviazioni sono quelle indicate sul sito www.edr-edr.it.

[1] Sull'importanza di questo tema restano valide le osservazioni di A. MOMIGLIANO, *Il cristianesimo e la decadenza dell'Impero romano*, in *Il conflitto tra paganesimo e cristianesimo nel secolo IV*, a cura di A. MOMIGLIANO, Torino 1968, 5-19.

[2] Si vedano, ad esempio, solo per citare alcuni dei numerosissimi studi dedicati all'argomento, H. BLOCH, *A new document of the last pagan revival in the West*, «Harv. Theol. Rev.» 38 (1945), 199-244 e *La rinascita pagana in Occidente alla fine del secolo IV*, in *Il conflitto tra paganesimo e cristianesimo nel secolo IV*, a cura di A. MOMIGLIANO, Torino 1968, 199-224; A. MARCONE, *La fine del paganesimo a Roma: per un'interpretazione politica*, in *Studi offerti ad Anna Maria Quartiroli e Domenico Magnino*, Pavia 1987, 53-59, ora ripubblicato in *Di Tarda Antichità. Scritti scelti*, Milano 2008, 54-59; A. FRASCHETTI, *Trent'anni dopo: il conflitto fra paganesimo e cristianesimo nel*

In molti di questi studi si fa largo uso delle fonti epigrafiche, da sempre considerate particolarmente attendibili (anche se non propriamente «oggettive») perché giunte sino a noi direttamente, senza mediazioni, e perché il loro contenuto era sottoposto, in quanto «scritture esposte», al vaglio del controllo sociale. Le epigrafi contenenti dediche sacre a divinità tradizionali e orientali, interventi edilizi su templi, menzioni di cerimonie e sacerdozi pagani sono state, dunque, utilizzate per dimostrare il lungo perdurare dei culti tradizionali tra i rappresentanti dell'aristocrazia urbana[3] anche dopo il regno di Costantino e la loro progressiva scomparsa nel corso del V secolo. Ma anche il «silenzio» delle iscrizioni è stato utilizzato nello stesso ambito di ricerca[4], interpretando l'assenza delle cariche religiose nelle epigrafi relative a magistrati romani tardoimperiali esposte in luoghi pubblici come frutto della volontà di relegare alla sola sfera privata

---

secolo IV, in *Pagani e cristiani da Giuliano l'Apostata al sacco di Roma*, a cura di F.E. CONSOLINO, Soveria Mannelli 1995, 5-14; A. CAMERON, *The last pagans of Rome*, in *The Transformations of Urbs Roma in Late Antiquity*, a cura di W.V. HARRIS, Portsmouth 1999, 109-121, con le osservazioni di C.W. HEDRICK JR., *History and Silence. Purge and Rehabilitation of Memory in Late Antiquity*, Austin 2000, 47-54; inoltre, sempre *exempli gratia*, F. PASCHOUD, *Les étapes d'une perte d'identité: les défenseurs du paganisme officiel face au naufrage de leur monde (312-410)*, in *Identità e valori: fattori di aggregazione e fattori di crisi nell'esperienza politica antica*, a cura di A. BARZANÒ ET AL., Roma 2001, 227-240; M.R. SALZMAN, *The Making of a Christian Aristocracy. Social and Religious Change in the Western Roman Empire*, Cambridge 2002 (con le recensioni di R.W. MATHISEN, in «Ill. Journ. Class. Trad.» 9, 2002-2003, 257-278 e di A. MARCONE, in «Athenaeum» 93, 2005, 758-759) ; B. ENJUTO SÁNCHEZ, *Los sacerdocios paganos: elemento de inclusión e integración de los homines novi en el ordo senatorius del s. IV d. C.? El caso de Tatianus*, «Stud. Histor. Hist. Ant.» 21 (2003), 159-176; R. LIZZI TESTA, *Christian Emperor, Vestal Virgins and priestly colleges: reconsidering the end of Roman paganism*, «Ant. Tard.» 15 (2007), 251-262; R. LIZZI TESTA, *Augures et pontifices: Public Sacral Law in Late Antique Rome (fourth to fifth centuries AD)*, in *The Power of Religion in Late Antiquity*, a cura di A. CAIN e N. LENSKY, Ashgate 2009, in corso di stampa, e soprattutto R. LIZZI TESTA, *Dal conflitto al dialogo: nuove prospettive sulle relazioni tra pagani e cristiani in Occidente alla fine del IV secolo*, in *Trent'anni di studi sulla tarda antichità: bilanci e prospettive (Napoli, 21-23 novembre 2007)*, a cura di U. CRISCUOLO, L. DE GIOVANNI, Napoli 2009, 167-190.

[3] Diverso il caso dell'aristocrazia municipale e dei sacerdozi locali, la cui analisi esula dalle finalità del presente lavoro.

[4] Oltre che per ricostruire la sequenza cronologica delle cariche civili e religiose all'interno di un *cursus honorum*: così nei volumi della *Prosopography of the Later Roman Empire* e, ad esempio, in S. CONTI, *Il collegio dei pontefici sotto gli imperatori cristiani*, in *Forme di aggregazione nel mondo romano*, a cura di E. LO CASCIO, G.D. MEROLA, Bari 2007, 363-377.

il ricordo di culti che, nel corso del IV secolo, avevano ormai perso il loro tradizionale valore civico[5].

Si è tuttavia trascurato che il significato di un testo epigrafico può essere compreso pienamente solo se si tiene conto dell'ambito in cui era originariamente inserito. La distinzione tra luoghi di destinazione pubblici e privati è, sì, fondamentale, perché diverso era il ruolo delle iscrizioni esposte nell'uno e nell'altro contesto, essendo diversi i possibili destinatari del messaggio in esse contenuto e, di conseguenza, i mezzi adottati per comunicarlo. Ma si deve tener conto anche del fatto che le iscrizioni non sono solo testi, ma «monumenti iscritti», la cui tipologia varia: l'analisi delle loro caratteristiche consente di individuare diverse «classi» di epigrafi, che seguono, fatte poche eccezioni, dei criteri comuni – dettati dall'uso – nella scelta dei canoni espressivi, adattando di volta in volta lessico e formulario a questa sorta di «leggi non scritte».

Ci si può dunque chiedere se i silenzi della documentazione epigrafica in materia di sacerdozi pagani vadano effettivamente considerati dei «silenzi eloquenti», o non siano piuttosto il frutto di una convenzione che semplicemente non prevedeva la loro menzione in tutti i «generi» di iscrizioni. Ho scelto di verificare tale ipotesi su un campione di materiale numericamente non illimitato, ma quantitativamente e qualitativamente significativo: tutte le iscrizioni, classificate nella tabella che segue, relative ai prefetti urbani elencati da A. Chastagnol, *Les Fastes de la Préfecture de Rome au Bas-Empire*, Paris 1962 (cui corrisponde il numero indicato nella prima colonna della tabella) e noti non esclusivamente da fonti giuridiche o letterarie, con l'aggiunta delle scoperte epigrafiche più recenti[6].

---

[5] Di questo argomento si è anche discusso nel corso di una tavola rotonda presieduta da M.R. Salzman, tenutasi il 27 maggio 2008 a Villa Aurelia, nel corso della quale sono stati presentati alcuni capitoli del libro, ancora inedito, di AL. CAMERON, *The Last Pagans of Rome*.

[6] La scelta di raccogliere e sistematizzare un nucleo consistente di documenti (in questo caso iscrizioni) nasce anche da un'osservazione di P. VILAR, *Sviluppo economico e analisi storica*, Roma-Bari 1978, 131: «La storia spirituale di una società non può fondarsi che sul testo in serie. Non che l'opera fuori serie (e ancor meno il capolavoro) sia fuori della storia, ma il diffondersi nello spazio sociale d'un tema intellettuale, il successo che gli riserva un pubblico, gli strumenti di diffusione che gli sono offerti, danno la misura della forza collettiva d'una inquietudine, d'un interesse, d'una volontà. Ogni attento raggruppamento cronologico di testi in serie, ogni individuazione di affinità nel caos delle pubblicazioni, fa dunque parte degli strumenti validi della ricerca storica» (citato da N. BAGLIVI, *Le trasformazioni letterarie, culturali e politico-religiose in età tardoantica*, «Vichiana», IV s., 8 [2006], 348).

Alcune premesse e avvertenze: nella tabella sono stati tenuti in considerazione (e segnalati in grassetto) anche i personaggi sicuramente o probabilmente cristiani, perché la documentazione ad essi relativa, pur non essendo, evidentemente, significativa per i sacerdozi pagani, può comunque costituire un valido confronto per il modo di indicare titoli e cariche nelle varie tipologie di testo e di contesto qui considerate.

Sono stati invece esclusi alcuni documenti che, per il loro stato di conservazione o la particolare natura del testo o del supporto, avrebbero rischiato di «falsare» le informazioni contenute nella tabella, immettendovi dati incerti o di difficile classificazione. Sono state sistematicamente escluse:

– tutte le iscrizioni troppo frammentarie per poter essere integrate con certezza (specialmente se la lacuna riguarda la parte del testo contenente titoli e cariche del personaggio menzionato);

– tutte le iscrizioni in cui il nome del personaggio considerato compare solo in espressioni dal valore «cronologico», come le datazioni consolari o, nel caso delle iscrizioni dell'Africa Proconsularis o dell'Achaia, le formule del tipo *ille proconsule* o *proconsulatu illius*; cfr. anche *CIL*, VI 40793 (*...regente urbi praefectura(m) Ceionio Rufio Volusiano, v. c., ex praef. praet., praef. urb.*) e *AE* 1981, 878 (datata dall'espressione *praefectura praetorio* seguita da quattro nomi in genitivo);

– le iscrizioni su *instrumentum*, in cui, per le dimensioni limitate del supporto e la stessa funzione del testo, i nomi dei personaggi appaiono spesso accompagnati dal solo titolo di rango *v(ir) c(larissimus)* e solo raramente da nomi di cariche: è il caso, ad esempio, della *fistula aquaria* con il nome di Q. Flavius Maesius Egnatius Lollianus (*CIL*, XV 1688), del *signaculum* di Aurelius Celsinus (*CIL*, XV 8151), o del bollo laterizio (*CIL*, XV 1705) e di quello che viene comunemente interpretato come un collare di cane (*CIL*, XV 7199) relativi a Q. Clodius Hermogenianus Olybrius; sono invece stati inclusi i due pesi campione che riportano la dicitura dell'avvenuto controllo da parte dei prefetti Turcius Apronianus e Q. Clodius Hermogenianus Olybrius, con la stessa formula (*ex auctoritate*) presente nell'intestazione degli editti, anch'essi compresi nella tabella;

– le iscrizioni relative ai *loca* del Colosseo, in cui i titolari dei posti riservati sul podio dell'anfiteatro – molti dei quali identificabili con i prefetti della tabella – vengono indicati con il loro nome, a volte accompagnato dal titolo di rango, ma – almeno per quanto riguarda l'epoca che qui ci interessa – non dalle cariche che avevano rivestito[7].

---

[7] Sulle caratteristiche di queste iscrizioni vd. *EAOR*, VI, 191-521.

Sono inoltre stati esclusi alcuni documenti che per la loro particolare natura escono dai canoni consueti e contengono informazioni non facilmente inseribili all'interno di una schema tradizionale come quello proposto dalla tabella:

– *CIL*, VI 37118 e 41314: si tratta di due documenti affini tra loro, in cui una serie di personaggi di rango senatorio – molti dei quali identificabili in quanto titolari di cariche databili tra la fine del III e i primi decenni del IV secolo sono elencati, in nominativo, senza alcuna altra indicazione. Il fatto che nel primo frammento i nomi siano seguiti da una somma di denaro piuttosto elevata (400.000 sesterzi) ha indotto a pensare che si tratti, in entrambi i casi, di liste di contributori coinvolti da Massenzio in un versamento straordinario per affrontare la carestia seguita alla rivolta di Domizio Alessandro o, più genericamente, per far fronte alle ingenti spese richieste dalla sua politica edilizia, ma non si può escludere che si tratti, invece, di finanziatori di un'opera pubblica costruita in età tetrarchica, come suggerisce l'uso dei sesterzi piuttosto che dei denari. Il criterio con cui i nomi dei personaggi si succedevano nelle due liste, certamente non casuale considerata la natura fortemente gerarchica della mentalità romana, rimane incerto: dal momento che non erano ricordati secondo l'ordine in cui rivestirono cariche civili, rimane la possibilità che fossero elencati semplicemente in ordine di anzianità o in base alla data della loro cooptazione in un collegio sacerdotale. Benché non manchino confronti in tal senso, mi pare azzardato considerare senz'altro tutti i personaggi menzionati nelle due liste quali membri di un collegio sacerdotale pagano[8].

– *CIL*, VI 40776, base dal Foro di Traiano con epistola dell'imperatore Costantino al Senato, in cui L. Aradius Valerius Proculus signo Populonius, p. u. 337-338 (*PLRE*, I Proculus 11), compare solo come *c. v.*: si tratta, infatti, di un testo non originariamente concepito come scrittura esposta, e che non può, quindi, essere considerato significativo per individuare i canoni del linguaggio epigrafico.

– *CIL*, X 407 = *InscrIt*, III, 1, nr. 17 + *SupplIt*, n.s., 3, 76-77 nr. 5: una lista di proprietari di *fundi* da *Volcei*, in Lucania, in cui Cossinius Rufinus e L. Turcius Apronianus compaiono solo nell'intestazione[9].

---

[8] Come fa Rüpke, *Fasti*, in part. 868-869, che propende per quello dei *septemviri epulonum*; vd. in proposito *EAOR*, VI, 266, cui si aggiunga R. Behrwald, *Die Stadt als Museum? Die Wahrnehmung der Monumente Roms in der Spätantike*, Berlin 2009, 139, nt. 46.

[9] Su quest'iscrizione vd. E. Champlin, *The Volcei Land-register*, in «Amer. Journ. Anc. Hist.» 5 (1980), 13-18 e, da ultimo, P. Porena, *Problemi di cronologia costantiniana*.

In definitiva, il materiale esaminato permette di avere un campione di 279 epigrafi per un totale di 80 personaggi, che si dispongono in un arco cronologico che va dal 290 al 423.

Dal materiale così raccolto emerge un quadro variegato ed interessante, da cui si ricavano sia conferme che elementi di novità.

Innanzi tutto, appare evidente la diversità delle iscrizioni provenienti dalla parte ellenofona dell'Impero: nelle iscrizioni onorarie in lingua greca, spesso in versi, è generalmente scarso l'interesse per le cariche pubbliche rivestite dall'onorato, ricordate nei loro elementi strettamente necessari a fornire un inquadramento logico e cronologico alle virtù civiche, morali e culturali che vengono presentate come le vere motivazioni della dedica. Il destinatario è per lo più ricordato con il semplice titolo di lamprotatos, che lo qualifica come membro dell'ordine senatorio, eventualmente accompagnato dalla carica di anthypatos (*proconsul*), con o senza la specificazione della provincia, che spesso, nei testi in versi, viene resa con una circonlocuzione. Un caso particolare è costituito dal complesso di iscrizioni onorarie poste alla fine del IV secolo da un unico personaggio, Dositeo, nel pretorio di Gortina, in cui i destinatari, tutti senatori, sono ricordati con il rango che avevano al momento della dedica, che fossero magistrati in carica o ex magistrati, con una precisione solitamente aliena dallo spirito greco, che fa di questo gruppo di documenti un caso a sé[10]. Prima ancora che politica, dunque, la diversità delle due *partes* dell'Impero era culturale: un'antica tradizione, un'altra mentalità, un diverso modo di concepire il rapporto con le istituzioni stanno alla base delle forme scelte dalla popolazione di lingua greca per ricordare l'opera dei magistrati romani[11] e, in queste condizioni, non sorprende di non trovare alcuna menzione di sacerdozi nella documentazione epigrafica di provenienza orientale, che evidentemente non aveva interesse per questo tipo di notazione, e i cui «silenzi» non possono, quindi, essere utilizzati per dimostrare la progressiva scomparsa delle testimonianze relative alla pratica della religione tradizionale.

L'imperatore, Vettius Rufinus e il Senato, «Ant. Tard.» 13 (2005), 235-237, con altra bibliografia.

[10] Lo studio più completo rimane quello di M. Guarducci, *Le iscrizioni del pretorio di Gortina*, «Riv. Ist. Naz. Arch. Art.» 1 (1929), 154-170, cui si aggiunga, da ultimo, G. De Tommaso, *Nota su alcune iscrizioni del pretorio di Dositeo*, in *Gortina, V. 1, Lo scavo del pretorio (1989-1995)*, a cura di A. Di Vita, Padova 2000, 384-388.

[11] Oltre al classico studio di L. Robert, *Hellenica. Recueil d'épigraphie, de numismatique et d'antiquités grecques*, IV. *Épigrammes du Bas-Empire*, Paris 1948, vd., da ultimo, F.A. Bauer, *Virtuelle Statuensammlungen*, in *Statuen in der Spätantike*, 86-92.

Per quanto riguarda l'Occidente, il dato più interessante che emerge dalla documentazione così raccolta è una costante tanto chiara quanto, credo, non adeguatamente valorizzata: la menzione dei sacerdozi pagani (i cui casi sono evidenziati nella tabella con uno sfondo grigio) si trova SOLO in alcuni tipi di iscrizioni che, non a caso, provengono per la maggior parte da Roma:
– epigrafi onorarie direttamente destinate al titolare dei sacerdozi;
– testi di carattere sepolcrale o comunque destinati ad essere esposti in un sepolcro[12];
– dediche sacre a divinità tanto del pantheon tradizionale quanto orientali.

Un caso a sé è costituito dall'iscrizione *CIL*, VI 2153, di incerta classificazione: si tratta di un frammento di lastra marmorea, attualmente perduto, contenente i resti di una lista di personaggi in nominativo, dei quali i primi due qualificati come *XVviri sacris faciundis*, altri due come *pontifices maiores*, il quarto come *philosophus* e l'ultimo come semplice *v(ir) c(larissimus)*. La presenza di titolari di sacerdozi diversi accanto a personaggi privi di qualifiche ufficiali sembra escludere che possa trattarsi dei fasti di un collegio sacerdotale, mentre rimane aperta – anche alla luce delle osservazioni fatte in questa sede – la possibilità che si tratti di una dedica collettiva ad una qualche divinità, il cui nome è andato perduto con la parte superiore della lastra.

In tutti gli altri casi, appare evidente che la mancata menzione delle cariche sacerdotali sia, più che una rinuncia dettata da considerazioni di ordine politico, una scelta imposta dai canoni della comunicazione epigrafica, che prevedevano che tali informazioni dovessero essere presenti solo in alcune categorie di iscrizioni.

È chiaro, ad esempio, che, più spesso di quanto accada nell'epigrafia altoimperiale[13], quando il titolare dei sacerdozi non era il diretto destinata-

---

[12] Tra i pochi testi sicuramente riconoscibili come tali rientra anche l'iscrizione *CIL*, VI 1419b = 41224 (tit. II), esclusa dalla tabella perché troppo incerta e frammentaria, in cui è verosimilmente da riconoscere l'epigrafe funeraria di T. Flavius Postumius Titianus (nr. 15).

[13] Quando comunque quest'uso non è abituale: esempi come quello di Caninia Galla da Tarragona, definita, nella sua iscrizione sepolcrale (*CIL*, II 4129 cfr. p. 972 = *RIT* 137), figlia di un *XVvir sacris faciundis* e nipote e affine di *VIIviri epulonum* (vd. G. ALFÖLDY, *Inschriften und Biographie in der römischen Welt*, in *Biographie und Prosopographie. Internationales Kolloquium zum 65. Geburtstag von Anthony R. Birley*, a cura di K. VÖSSING, Stuttgart 2005, 33-34), o quello di Cassia Cornelia Prisca, *pontificis uxor*, da Formia (su cui vd., da ultima, A. ARNALDI, *Donne e vita cittadina nel Lazio*

rio di un'iscrizione, ma un suo parente (padre, marito, suocero, avo)[14], la sua menzione era accompagnata solo dal titolo di rango di *clarissimus*[15] o, al massimo, da una o due delle sue cariche più significative, non essendo più ritenuti necessari, in quel contesto, altri elementi di identificazione. Si pensi, ad esempio, all'epigrafe funeraria per la moglie di Attius Insteius Tertullus (*CIL*, VIII 876: vd. nr. 17), in cui il nostro personaggio, come dedicante, appare solo come *v. c.*, o all'epitaffio della moglie di Clodius Celsinus signo Adelphius (*CIL*, VI 1712: vd. nr. 55), dove ad accompagnare il nome del marito è la qualifica di ex prefetto urbano. Significativi anche il complesso delle dediche poste per onorare L. Turcius Apronianus signo Asterius, prefetto urbano del 362-363 (nr. 65), in cui si ricorda che anche il padre, L. Turcius Apronianus (nr. 42) era stato *praef. urb.*, e la serie di statue erette ai suoi antenati da Anicius Acilius Glabrio Faustus (nr. 128) nel «foro di famiglia», dove il dedicante si qualifica solo come *v. c.*. Del tutto particolare il caso dell'iscrizione posta in Campidoglio per Caeionius Rufius Albinus (nr. 39), in cui la volontà del Senato di onorare sommamente questo personaggio per i suoi altissimi meriti passava anche attraverso il ricordo di suo padre Caeionius Rufius Volusianus (nr. 21), qualificato con ben tre cariche: consolato ordinario, prefettura urbana (entrambe per due volte) e prefettura del pretorio.

Per quanto riguarda, più in generale, le iscrizioni apposte sui monumenti onorari dedicati ai rappresentanti dell'aristocrazia senatoria in ambito urbano, effettivamente si nota, ed è stata già fatta rilevare[16], una tendenza a menzionare sempre meno le cariche sacerdotali nelle dediche esposte in luoghi pubblici, per riservarle piuttosto alle epigrafi riconducibili ad un ambito privato. L'ultimo sacerdote pagano ad essere onorato pubblicamente è L. Aurelius Avianius Symmachus signo Phosphorius (nr. 66), la cui iscrizione, incisa sulla base della statua postagli nel Foro di Traiano negli ultimi decenni del IV secolo, lo ricorda come *pontifex maior* e *XVvir sacris faciundis*; in seguito, tutte le testimonianze epigrafiche relative a sacerdoti dei culti tradizionali provengono da contesti di tipo privato, sia

---

meridionale, in *Donne e vita cittadina nella documentazione epigrafica*, Faenza 2005, 224-227) sono piuttosto eccezionali.

[14] Cfr. anche il caso dell'iscrizione *CIL*, VIII 25990, posta a Thubursicum Bure da un *procurator* di C. Caeionius Rufius Volusianus signo Lampadius (nr. 67), in cui questo personaggio è qualificato semplicemente come *c(larissimus) v(ir)*.

[15] O *consularis*, come nel caso della dedica formiana *CIL*, X 6084, posta per la moglie di L. Aelius Helvius Dionysius (nr. 11), che allora era *corrector Campaniae*.

[16] Ad es. da H. NIQUET, *Monumenta virtutum...*, 175-185 e da R. LIZZI TESTA, *Dal conflitto al dialogo...*

che si tratti di dediche poste nelle *domus* degli onorati – come nel caso della statua dedicata a Q. Aurelius Symmachus (nr. 90) nella sua casa sul Celio – sia che si tratti di testi di carattere funerario, come nel caso del famoso epitaffio per Vettius Agorius Praetextatus (nr. 69).

In ogni caso, mentre non si registra alcuna differenza tra l'età dei Tetrarchi e della dinastia costantiniana e l'epoca successiva (delle 20 iscrizioni con cariche sacerdotali qui considerate, 11 sono anteriori al 350 e 9 posteriori), è significativo che nessuna attestazione epigrafica di sacerdozi pagani, qualunque sia la tipologia dell'iscrizione su cui compare, scenda oltre gli ultimi anni del IV secolo, a conferma del punto di svolta segnato dai provvedimenti legislativi di Graziano e Valentiniano II che, se anche non abolirono né gli *amplissima collegia*, né i culti tradizionali[17], ne resero comunque difficile la sopravvivenza.

Ma quel che più interessa in questa sede è la circostanza che quando un personaggio pone una dedica imperiale o cura l'esecuzione di lavori pubblici in quanto titolare di una carica, nell'iscrizione relativa compare solo tale carica, a indicare – com'è logico che sia – il ruolo, la veste in cui si era compiuta una determinata azione, indipendentemente dalle cariche, civili e religiose, rivestite in passato[18]. È significativo, ad esempio, che quando T. Flavius Postumius Titianus (nr. 15) erige un tempio del Sole a Como (testimoniato da *AE* 1914, 249), lo fa in quanto *corrector Italiae*, benché, come sappiamo da un'altra iscrizione, più tarda, posta in suo onore nella sua *domus*, egli fosse anche *pontifex dei Solis*: è possibile che, come propongono gli autori della *PLRE*, il pontificato del Sole gli sia stato conferito solo dopo la *correctura Italiae*, ma non escluderei che tale sacerdozio non sia presente nell'iscrizione di Como semplicemente perché la tipologia di quest'ultima non lo prevedeva. Gli esempi in questo senso si potrebbero moltiplicare: M. Caeionius Iulianus signo Kamenius (nr. 37) quando restaura un acquedotto nel territorio di *Abellinum*, lo fa in quanto *consu-*

---

[17] Vd. in proposito N. BELAYCHE, Ritus et cultus *ou* superstitio? *Comment les lois du Code Théodosien (IX et XVI) de Constantin à Théodose parlent des pratiques religieuses traditionnelles*, in *Le Code Théodosien. Diversité des approches et nouvelles perspectives*, Rome 2009, 191-208; in particolare sul collegio pontificale F. VAN HAEPEREN, *Le collège pontifical (III a.C. – IV p.C.)*, Brussels 2002, 84-88. Sul perdurare di alcuni aspetti della religione pagana ancora nel VI secolo vd. G. BINAZZI, *La sopravvivenza dei culti tradizionali nell'Italia tardoantica e altomedievale*, Perugia 2008, 35-68 e le ultime pagine di R. LIZZI TESTA, *Dal conflitto al dialogo...*, cui si aggiunga ora EAD., *La conversione dei* cives*, l'evangelizzazione dei rustici: alcuni esempi fra IV e VI secolo*, in *Città e campagna nei secoli altomedievali*, Spoleto 2009, 115-150.

[18] Vd. già, in questo senso, R. LIZZI TESTA, *Augures et pontifices*..., e R. LIZZI TESTA, *Dal conflitto al dialogo*...

laris Campaniae, gli interventi di Q. Flavius Maesius Egnatius Lollianus signo Mavortius (nr. 45) alla *statio aquarum* nel Foro Romano sono da lui eseguiti in veste di *curator aquarum et Minuciae*, gli stessi Memmius Vitrasius Orfitus signo Honorius (nr. 59) e Vettius Agorius Praetextatus (nr. 69), che pure conosciamo come titolari di numerosi sacerdozi pagani, quando restaurano, rispettivamente, il tempio di Apollo (*CIL*, VI 45) e il Portico degli Dei Consenti (*CIL*, VI 102) agiscono in qualità di prefetti urbani. Fatte poche eccezioni[19], allo stesso modo si spiegano anche i casi in cui il nome del dedicante compare accompagnato da due cariche: nelle dediche poste a Costantino da C. Caeionius Rufius Volusianus (*CIL*, VI 1140: vd. nr. 21) e da Amnius Manius Casonius Nicomachus Anicius Paulinus signo Honorius (*CIL*, VI 1142: vd. nr. 38), ad esempio, entrambi i personaggi figurano come *cos. ord. praef. urb.* perché in quel momento rivestivano contemporaneamente prefettura urbana e consolato ordinario.

In queste condizioni, è evidente che le numerose epigrafi erette da prefetti e altri magistrati urbani, governatori di distretti italici e titolari di incarichi provinciali per onorare gli imperatori regnanti o ricordare i loro interventi di restauro e abbellimento di luoghi pubblici non possono essere utilizzate per dimostrare, con il loro «silenzio» in materia di sacerdozi, la scomparsa di ogni traccia della religione tradizionale dagli spazi pubblici in cui tali epigrafi erano esposte[20]: in esse i dedicanti apparivano solo con la carica che rivestivano in quel momento perché questo era l'unico tipo di informazione che quel genere di testi prevedeva e richiedeva, esattamente come solo con questa carica appaiono i nomi dei prefetti urbani nelle intestazioni degli editti da loro emanati o nelle iscrizioni apposte sui *pondera* da loro controllati in qualità di garanti di pesi e misure campione[21].

Anche l'apparente eccezione costituita dall'iscrizione relativa ad un intervento sul tempio della *Magna Mater* a Cartagine, operato da L. Aradius Valerius Proculus signo Populonius in qualità di *augur, pontifex maior*,

---

[19] Come la dedica agli imperatori Massimiano e Costanzo posta da Nummius Tuscus, che si qualifica sia come prefetto urbano che come *curator aquarum et Minuciae* (*CIL*, VI 31378B: vd. nr. 12), o la serie di basi erette da C. Caeionius Rufius Volusianus signo Lampadius, in cui alla carica di *praef. urb.* viene a volte premessa la specifica di *ex praef. praet.* (vd. nr. 67).

[20] C. LEPELLEY, *Le lieu des valeurs communes. La cité terrain neutre entre païens et chrétiens dans l'Afrique romain tardive*, in *Idéologies et valeurs civiques dans le monde romain. Hommage a Claude Lepelley*, a cura di H. INGLEBERT, Paris 2002, 271-285 parla, a proposito della documentazione africana, di «neutralità» degli spazi civici.

[21] Su questo aspetto della loro attività vd. A. CHASTAGNOL, *La préfecture urbaine a Rome sous le Bas-Empire*, Paris 1960, 330-332.

XVvir sacris faciundis e *pontifex Flavialis* (*CIL*, VIII 24521: vd. nr. 40), si configura, in realtà, innanzi tutto come dedica sacra a Cibele e Attis, cui si aggiunge la menzione di lavori edilizi in cui, peraltro, data la frammentarietà del testo, non è chiaro il ruolo del nostro personaggi[22]. E le dediche sacre costituiscono, appunto, l'altra tipologia di iscrizioni, oltre alle onorarie e alle sepolcrali, in cui si concentra, almeno per quanto riguarda la documentazione qui raccolta ed esaminata, la menzione dei sacerdozi pagani, a sottolineare il ruolo ufficiale del dedicante nelle pratiche della religione tradizionale – non necessariamente ad evidenziare l'adesione fideistica a tali culti che, semplicemente, nella religione romana non era richiesta. Ben si comprende, ad esempio, come nella dedica alla Sibilla posta nell'antro di Cuma da Fabius Titianus (*AE* 1893, 124: vd. nr. 43), la qualifica di *XVvir sacris faciundis*, cioè di membro del collegio sacerdotale addetto alla consultazione dei Libri Sibillini[23], non solo sia presente, ma compaia prima del consolato ordinario e della prefettura urbana[24].

Al contrario, è significativo il confronto con la dedica che M. Iunius Casonius Nicomachus Anicius Faustus Paulinus pone nel santuario di Ercole all'Ara Massima (*CIL*, VI 315: vd. nr. 9), dove, come in altri docu-

---

[22] A restauri al portico del tempio pensa S. CONTI, *Scambi culturali e persistenze: il paganesimo nell'Africa Proconsolare cristiana*, in *L'Africa Romana*, XVI, Roma 2006, 885; cfr. la dedica a Mercurio che lo stesso personaggio pose nella sua casa sul Celio (*AE* 1987, 102), in cui compare solo come *XVvir sacris faciundis*. Un'ulteriore eccezione sembra essere costituita dalla nuova iscrizione pubblicata da I. DI STEFANO MANZELLA, *Iscrizioni latine fra età augustea ed epoca tardoantica*, in *L'antica basilica di San Lorenzo in Damaso, II: I materiali*, a cura di C.L. FROMMEL, M. PENTIRICCI, Roma 2009, 32-37, in cui il senatore Plotius Faustus restaura un *opus* non identificato in qualità di *pontifex et rector decuriae Herculae*, verosimilmente nella seconda metà del IV secolo.

[23] Sulle ultime vicende di questi libri vd. L. CRACCO RUGGINI, *L'ordine naturale sconvolto e la morte di un mondo nella storiografia tardoantica*, «Riv. Stor. Ital.» 114 (2002), 830 nt. 31 e M. MONACA, *La Sibilla a Roma. I Libri Sibillini fra religione e politica*, Cosenza 2005, 87-93.

[24] Cfr. il caso della dedica alla *Magna Mater* posta nel *Phrygianum* del Vaticano da Clodius Hermogenianus Caesarius (*CIL*, VI 499: vd. nr. 75). Per questo gruppo di iscrizioni vd., da ultimo, C.J. GODDARD, *The evolution of pagan sanctuaries in Late Antique Italy (fourth-sixth centuries A.D.): a new administrative and legal framework. A paradox*, in *Les cités de l'Italie tardo-antique (IVe-VIe siècle). Institutions, économie, société, culture et religion*, a cura di M. GHILARDI, C. J. GODDARD, P. PORENA, Rome 2006, 294. In generale, sulle caratteristiche e le funzioni delle iscrizioni sacre nel mondo greco-romano vd. M. BEARD, *Writing and religion: Ancient literacy and the function of the written word in Roman religion*, in *Literacy in the Roman world*, Ann Arbor 1991, 47-48.

menti riconducibili allo stesso culto²⁵, compare in qualità di *praetor urbanus*. Evidentemente in questo caso era più funzionale sottolineare il ruolo ufficiale dei dedicanti, che agivano in veste di magistrati e come tali erano ricordati nelle iscrizioni che di queste cerimonie erano testimonianza.

Da tutto quanto detto finora, emerge abbastanza chiaramente che anche in epigrafia, come in letteratura, esistevano dei «generi», che prevedevano l'uso di canoni espressivi diversi – tradizionalmente riconosciuti anche se non ufficialmente codificati – per cui certi elementi erano o non erano presenti a seconda del tipo di comunicazione che si intendeva trasmettere. Così, ad esempio, sulla base di una statua recuperata da un edificio in rovina e restaurata era importante evidenziare il nome del magistrato che, in qualità di titolare di quella carica, aveva operato tale recupero²⁶, e non raccontare tutta la sua storia, mentre sulla base della statua che a quello stesso personaggio poteva essere eretta nell'atrio della sua casa, la sola carica del momento non sarebbe stata sufficiente ed era importante sintetizzare tutta la sua carriera per ripercorrere le tappe che avevano portato a quell'onore: a un diverso orizzonte d'attesa corrispondevano diverse strategie espositive²⁷.

Tali conclusioni acquistano forza anche maggiore se si considera che esse trovano piena conferma nella documentazione di età precedente, quando la presenza o l'assenza dei sacerdozi pagani nei testi delle iscrizioni non poteva essere determinata dall'influenza della religione cristiana. Gli stessi dati, infatti, si ricavano dall'analisi sistematica delle testimonianze epigrafiche relative ai senatori della seconda metà del III secolo, raccolte da M. CHRISTOL, *Essai sur l'évolution des carrières sénatoriales dans la 2ᵉ moitié du IIIᵉ s. ap. J.-C.*, Paris 1986. Gli esempi si potrebbero moltiplicare, ma

---

²⁵ *CIL*, VI 312-318 (cui si può aggiungere un'iscrizione inedita nota solo da tradizione manoscritta, su cui vd. *EAOR*, VI, 266); su questo gruppo di dediche vd. A. PIGANIOL, *Les origines du Forum Boarium*, «Mél. Arch. Hist.» 29 (1909), 110-117 e G. CRESSEDI, *Il Foro Boario e il Velabro*, «Bull. Comm. Arch. Rom.» 89 (1984), 268 nr. 19.

²⁶ In particolare, sull'attività dei prefetti urbani vd., da ultimo, R. BEHRWALD, *Die Stadt als Museum?...*, 140-146.

²⁷ Vd. anche, sulla differenza tra testi biografici e iscrizioni con *cursus honorum* in età altoimperiale, W. ECK, *Auf der Suche nach Personen und Persönlichkeiten. Cursus honorum un Biographie*, in *Biographie und Prosopographie...*, 53-72, cui si aggiunga ora ID., *The are no cursus honorum Inscriptions. The Function of the cursus honorum in Epigraphic Communication*, «Scripta Classica Israelica» 28 (2009), 79-92; cfr. le osservazioni di L. CRACCO RUGGINI, *Simmaco e la poesia*, in *La poesia tardoantica: tra retorica, teologia e politica*, Messina 1984, 477-521, in part. 491 sul controllo stilistico come esigenza sociale commisurata alla qualità dell'interlocutore e a ciò che questi politicamente e culturalmente rappresenta.

particolarmente significativo mi sembra quello costituito dal dossier relativo a T. Flavius Postumius Varus, prefetto urbano del 271[28]: nella sua iscrizione sepolcrale (*CIL*, VI 1417 cfr. p. 4695) trovano posto, oltre alle sue cariche civili, quelle sacerdotali di *augur* e *XVvir*, ma quando compare come dedicante nell'iscrizione onoraria del suo avo M. Postumius Festus (*CIL*, VI 1416 cfr. pp. 4694-4695) si qualifica solo come *consularis*, e quando, all'inizio della sua carriera, aveva restaurato un tempio di Diana in Britannia, l'aveva fatto in qualità di *legatus* (*RIB*, 316).

Il quadro non cambia se si estende l'analisi a personaggi non inclusi nella tabella perché non rivestirono la prefettura urbana: lo stesso fenomeno si riscontra anche per i titolari di altre cariche. Si confronti, ad esempio, da un lato il complesso delle iscrizioni onorarie e sepolcrali relative ad Alfenius Ceionius Iulianus signo Kamenius, che menzionano tutte le sue cariche e tutti i suoi sacerdozi[29] e, dall'altro, la documentazione relativa all'attività edilizia di numerosi governatori dell'Italia tardoantica, come il ciclo di statue poste a ornamento del Foro di Aquileia intorno al 360 da Septimius Theodulus, ricordato solo come *corrector Venetiae et Histriae*[30], o le iscrizioni relative agli interventi evergetici dei *consulraes Siciliae*[31].

Meno significativa, invece, la possibilità di istituire confronti con il periodo successivo ai primi decenni del V secolo, quando il generale declino dell'epigrafia porta ad una progressiva scomparsa anche a Roma, come già in precedenza era accaduto altrove, dei «generi» di iscrizioni qui considerati, ed in particolare delle iscrizioni onorarie che affidavano il compito di ricordare i meriti del destinatario alla ricostruzione del suo *cursus honorum*, sostituite da testi meno «canonici» e più aperti all'influenza del linguaggio della cancelleria imperiale e della poesia[32]. Piuttosto, sarebbe

---

[28] CHRISTOL, *Essai*, 193-195 nr. 27.

[29] Si tratta delle dediche esposte nella sua *domus CIL*, VI 1675 e 31940 = 41331, e dell'epigrafe sepolcrale rinvenuta nei suoi possedimenti nella zona delle Paludi Pontine *ILS* 1264, su cui vd. H. NIQUET, *Monumenta virtutum...*, 180.

[30] Su cui vd., da ultimo, C. WITSCHEL, *Statuen auf spätantike Platzanlagen in Italien und Afrika*, in *Statuen in der Spätantike*, 130-131.

[31] Recentemente raccolte e commentate da L. MAIMONE ANSALDO PATTI, *Munificentia publica. Manifestazioni evergetiche nella Sicilia tardoantica*, «Koinonia» 30-31 (2006-2007), 261-274.

[32] Vd. in proposito R. DELMAIRE, *Un genre en voie de disparition: les cursus épigraphiques au Bas-Empire*, in *Le monde romain à travers l'épigraphie: méthodes et pratiques*, a cura di J. DESMULLIEZ e C. HOËT-VAN CAUWENBERGHE, Lille 2005, 247-270; più in generale, sulla scomparsa della statuaria nel Tardo Antico vd. R. COATES-STEPHENS, *The Reuse of Ancient...*, 183-184.

interessante poter istituire un puntuale confronto con il formulario delle iscrizioni di apparato degli edifici cristiani, spesso opera di evergeti altolocati, che però agiscono, non in quanto titolari di magistrature, ma come fedeli: di qui la scelta di tacere completamente del proprio ruolo nella società, o di ricordarlo sotto forma di «sintesi di un percorso illustre», in cui pari dignità è riconosciuta alle cariche passate e a quelle presenti[33].

Benché, dunque, i dati che emergono da quest'analisi possano ulteriormente essere ampliati ed approfonditi, mi pare che trovi conferma l'assunto iniziale, per cui di fronte ad un'iscrizione non ci si deve chiedere tanto cosa dica (o soprattutto cosa non dica), quanto come funzioni. Solo considerandole non puri testi ma strumenti di comunicazione i cui meccanismi espressivi passano anche attraverso la forma che il contenuto assume, gli obiettivi che si pone e il contesto in cui si inserisce, le epigrafi possono essere comprese e «sfruttate» in tutte le loro potenzialità.

---

[33] Ad es. in *CIL*, VI 41400 i lavori relativi alla basilica di S. Pietro risultano eseguiti da Rufius Viventius Gallus, *v. c. et inl., ex praef. urb.* (su cui vd. *EAOR*, VI, 488-489). Sul formulario di questo tipo di iscrizioni vd. Y. DUVAL e L. PIETRI, *Évergetisme et épigraphie dans l'Occident chrétien (IVe-VIe s.)*, in *Actes du Xe Congrès Internationl d'épigraphie grecque et latine (Nîmes, 4-9 octobre 1992)*, a cura di M. CHRISTOL e O. MASSON, Paris 1997, 372-396; è inoltre in corso di preparazione un'edizione digitale delle iscrizioni di apparato degli edifici ecclesiastici romani da pare di Antonella Daniela Agostinelli, con la supervisione di Antonio Enrico Felle (informazioni sul sito http://epidoc.sourceforge.net/projects.shtml).

GLI ULTIMI SACERDOTI PAGANI DI ROMA 439

TABELLA.

Nr.	Prefetto	Iscrizione	Provenienza	Cont.	Tipologia	Ruolo	Cariche	Sacerd.
1	L. Turranius Gratianus p. u. 289-290 (*PLRE*, I Gratianus 3)[1]	*CIL*, III 6103	Athenae	pubbl.	dedica imperiale	ded.	corr. Achaiae	no
		CIL, VI 1128 = 31241 cfr. p. 4326	Roma, Foro Romano	pubbl.	dedica imperiale	ded.	praef. urb.	no?[2]
5	Ti. Claudius Aurelius Aristobulus p. u. 295-296 (*PLRE*, I Aristobulus)[3]	dossier di almeno 9 iscrizioni[4]	Madauros e altre località dell'Africa Proconsularis	pubbl.	opere pubbliche (tempio di Ercole, terme, ecc.)	ded.	procos. Africae	no
7	Afranius Hannibalianus p. u. 297-298 (*PLRE*, I Hannibalianus)	*ILS* 8929 = *ILBulg*, I, 2, 8a[5]	Oescus (Moesia)	pubbl.	dedica imperiale	ded.	praef. praet.	no
8	L. Artorius Pius Maximus p. u. 298-299 (*PLRE*, I Maximus 43)[6]	*AE* 1939, 58 = *IGLS* 2771	Heliopolis (Syria)	pubbl.	dedica imperiale	ded.	leg. Aug. pr. pr.	no
		J.-P. Rey-Coquai, *Inscriptions grecques et latines de Tyr*, Beyrouth 2006, nrr. 22-23	Tyrus	pubbl.	dediche imperiali	ded.	leg. Aug. pr. pr.	no
		CIL, III 14195, 27 = *IK* 12, 307	Ephesus	pubbl.	dedica imperiale	ded.	procos. Asiae	no
		IK 13, 621[7]	Ephesus	pubbl.	iscrizione onoraria	dest.	lamprotatos anthypatos	no

9	M. Iunius Caesonius Nicomachus Anicius Faustus Paulinus p. u. 299-300 (*PLRE*, I Faustus 6 e Paulinus 17)	*CIL*, VI 315	Roma, santuario di Ercole all'Ara Maxima	pubbl.	dedica sacra (a Ercole)	ded.	praet. urbanus	no
10	Pompeius Appius Faustinus p. u. 300-301 (*PLRE*, I Faustinus 7)	*CIL*, VI 314 d	Roma, santuario di Ercole all'Ara Maxima	pubbl.	dedica sacra (a Ercole)	ded.	praet. urbanus	no
		CIL, X 4785	Teanum Sidicinum	pubbl.	dedica imperiale	ded.	corr. Campaniae	no
11	L. Aelius Helvius Dionysius p. u. 301-302 (*PLRE*, I Dionysius 12)[8]	*CIL*, VI 255-256	Roma, Campo Marzio	pubbl.	dediche sacre (al Genio imp.) + opera pubblica (porticus)[9]	ded.	curator operum publicorum	no
		CIL, VI 773 cfr. p. 4301	Roma	pubbl.	dedica sacra (a Tiberino) + opera pubblica (lavori idraulici)	ded.	curator aquarum	no
		CIL, VIII 12459	Maxula	pubbl.	iscrizione onoraria	dest.	procos. Africae	no
		CIL, X 6084[10]	Formiae	pubbl.	iscrizione onoraria per la moglie	marito del dest.	consularis vir, corr. Campaniae	no
		CIL, VI 1673 = 31901a cfr. p. 4730	Roma	?	iscrizione onoraria	dest.	cursus honorum	sì [11]

12	Nummius Tuscus p. u. 302-303 (*PLRE*, I Tuscus 1)	*CIL*, VI 31378 B cfr. p. 4344	Roma, *domus* sul Quirinale[12]	priv.	dedica imperiale	ded.	praef. urb., cur. aquarum et Minuciae	no
13	Iunius Tiberianus p. u. 303-304 (*PLRE*, I Tiberianus 7)[13]	*AE* 1967, 477 = *IK* 12, 305[14]	Ephesus	pubbl.	dediche imperiali	ded.	procos. Asiae	no
15	T. Flavius Postumius Titianus p. u. 305-306 (*PLRE*, I Titianus 9)[15]	*CIL*, VI 1418 cfr. p. 4695	Roma, *domus* sul Quirinale[16]	priv.	iscrizione onoraria	dest.	cursus honorum	sì[17]
		AE 1914, 249[18]	Comum	pubbl.	opera pubblica (tempio del Sole)	ded.	corr. Italiae	no
16	C. Annius Anullinus p. u. 306-307 (*PLRE*, I Anullinus 3)[19]	*CIL*, VIII 1411 = 14910 = *ILTun* 1308 = *AE* 1942/3, 82	Thignica	pubbl.	dedica imperiale	ded.	procos. Africae	no
17	Attius Insteius Tertullus p. u. 307-308 (*PLRE*, I Tertullus 6)	*CIL*, V 2818	Patavium	pubbl.	dedica imperiale	ded.	corr. Venetiae et Histriae	no
		CIL, VIII 876	Villa di M'hammedia (Africa Proconsularis)	priv.	iscrizione funeraria per la moglie	ded.	solo v.c.	no?[20]
		CIL, VI 1696 cfr. pp. 4736-4737	Roma, *domus* sulla Velia?[21] sede della prefettura urbana?[22]	?	iscrizione onoraria	dest.	cursus honorum (in forma di elogium)	no

442

#	Nome	Riferimento	Luogo		Tipo		Posizione	
		CIL, VI 1697 cfr. p. 4737	Roma, vicino al Colosseo	?	iscrizione onoraria	dest.	cursus honorum	?[23]
19	Aurelius Hermogenes p. u. 309-310 (PLRE, I Hermogenes 8)	CIL, III 7069 = IK 3, 98	Ilium	pubbl.	dedica imperiale o opera pubblica	ded.	procos.	no
20	C. Caeionius Rufius Volusianus p. u. 310-311 e 313-315 (PLRE, I Volusianus 4)[24]	CIL, VI 1707 cfr. p. 4740	Roma, chiesa di S. Pudenziana (in reimpiego)	?	iscrizione onoraria	dest.	cursus honorum	?[25]
		CIL, VI 1708 = 31906 = 41318[26]	Roma, Campidoglio	pubbl.	iscrizione onoraria del figlio (vd. sotto nr. 39)	padre del dest.	bis cos. ord., bis praef. urb., praef. praet.	no
		CIL, X 1655	Puteoli	pubbl.	dedica imperiale	ded.	corrector	no
		CIL, X 304*[27]	Puteoli	pubbl.	iscrizione onoraria	dest.	corrector Campaniae	no
		CIL, VI 1140 cfr. p. 4328	Roma, Foro di Traiano	pubbl.	dedica imperiale	ded.	cos. ord. praef. urb.	no
		CIL, VI 2153[28]	Roma, in reimpiego	?	?	?[29]	no	sì[30]
22	Q. Aradius Rufinus p. u. 312-313 (PLRE, I Rufinus 10)	CIL, VIII 14688-14689[31]	Thuburnica	?	dediche sacre (al Sole e alla Luna)	ded.	cos. (suff.)	no
26	C. Vettius Cossinius Rufinus p. u. 315-316 (PLRE, I Rufinus 15)[32]	CIL, X 5061	Atina	pubbl.	iscrizione onoraria	dest.	cursus honorum	sì[33]

Gli ultimi sacerdoti pagani di Roma

				priv.?[35]	dedica sacra (al Sole?)	ded.	praef. urb.	sì[36]
27	Ovinius Gallicanus p. u. 316-317 (*PLRE*, I Gallicanus 3)	*CIL*, VI 32040 cfr. p. 4806[34]	Roma				praef. urb.	no
		CIL, VI 1155 cfr. p. 4330	Roma, Foro Romano	pubbl.	dedica imperiale	ded.	praef. urb.	no
		CIL, X 4785	Teanum Sidicinum	pubbl.	dedica imperiale	ded.	cur.	no
33	Publilius Optatianus signo Porphyrius p. u. 329 e 333 (*PLRE*, I Optatianus 3)	*AE* 1931, 6 = *SEG*, XI 810	Sparta	pubbl.	iscrizione onoraria	dest.	solo lamprotatos anthropos	no
35	Sex. Anicius Paulinus p. u. 331-333 (*PLRE*, I Paulinus 15)	*CIL*, VI 1680 cfr. pp. 4732-4733	Roma, villa (?) sulla via Latina	priv.	onoraria? sepolcrale?	dest.	cursus honorum	no
		CIL, VI 1681 cfr. p. 4733	Roma	?	sepolcrale?	dest.	cursus honorum	?[37]
		CIL, VI 1651 cfr. pp. 4725-4726	Roma, terme Deciane sull'Aventino	pubbl.	opera pubblica (stauta)	ded.	praef. urb.	no
37	M. Caeionius Iulianus signo Kamenius p. u. 333-334 (*PLRE*, I Iulianus 26)[38]	*AE* 1939, 151 = *AE* 1983, 194	Abellinum	pubbl.	opera pubblica (acquedotto)	ded.	cons. Campaniae	no
		CIL, VIII 25525	Bulla Regia	pubbl.?	iscrizione onoraria	dest.	procos. Africae	no
		CIL, VIII 15269	Thubursicu Bure	pubbl.	opera pubblica	ded.	procos. Africae	no

38	Amnius Manius Caesonius Nicomachus Anicius Paulinus signo Honorius p. u. 334-335 (*PLRE*, I Paulinus 14)[39]	*ILAlg* I, 4011 = *AE* 1922, 16	Madauros	?	iscrizione onoraria	dest.	c. v. (con riferimento al suo proconsolato)	no
		CIL, VI 1683 cfr. p. 4733	Roma, Foro di Traiano	pubbl.	iscrizione onoraria	dest.	cursus honorum	no
		CIL, VI 1682 cfr. p. 4733	Roma	?	iscrizione onoraria	dest.	cursus honorum	no
		CIL, VI 1652 cfr. p. 4726	Roma, Celio	pubbl.	opera pubblica (statua)	ded.	praef. urb.	no
		CIL, VI 1141 cfr. pp. 4328-4329	Roma, Foro Romano	pubbl.	dedica imperiale	ded.	cos. ord., praef. urb.	no
		CIL, VI 1142 cfr. p. 4329	Roma, in reimpiego	pubbl.	dedica imperiale	ded.	cos. ord., praef. urb.	no
39	Caeionius Rufius Albinus p. u. 335-337 (*PLRE*, I Albinus 14)	*CIL*, VI 1708 = 31906 = 41318	Roma, Campidoglio	pubbl.	iscrizione onoraria	dest.	cos.[ord., praef. urb.]	no[40]
40	L. Aradius Valerius Proculus signo Populonius p. u. 337-338 (*PLRE*, I Proculus 11)	*CIL*, VI 1684 cfr. pp. 4733-4734	Roma, *domus* sul Celio[41]	priv.	tabula patronatus	dest.	praeses prov. Val. Byzacenae	no

Gli ultimi sacerdoti pagani di Roma

		CIL, VI 1690-1691 e 1694 cfr. pp. 4735-4736	Roma, domus sul Celio	priv.	iscrizioni onorarie	dest.	cursus honorum	sì[42]
		CIL, VI 1692-1693 cfr. pp. 4735-4736	Roma, domus sul Celio	priv.	iscrizioni onorarie in versi (CLE 892 e 325)	dest.	no	no
		CIL, VIII 24521	Carthago	pubbl.	dedica sacra (a Cibele e Attis) + opera pubblica (portico del tempio?)	ded.	cursus honorum	sì
		AE 1987, 102[43]	Roma, domus sul Celio	priv.	dedica sacra (a Mercurio)	ded.	solo v. c.	sì[44]
41	Maecilius Hilarianus p. u. 338-339 (PLRE, I Hilarianus 5)[45]	CIL, VIII 1179	Utica	pubbl.	dedica imperiale	ded.	procos. Africae	no
		CIL, VIII 12524	Carthago	pubbl.	dedica imperiale	ded.	procos. Africae	no?[46]
		CIL, VI 32016 = 37116 = 41320	Roma, Foro Romano	pubbl.	opera pubblica? (statua?)	ded.	cos. ord.	no?[47]
42	L. Turcius Apronianus p. u. 339 (PLRE, I Apronianus 9)	CIL, VI 1768-1769 cfr. pp. 4755-4756	Roma, domus sull'Esquilino[48]	priv.	iscrizioni onorarie del figlio	padre del dest.	v. c., praef. urb.	no
		CIL, VI 1772 cfr. p. 4756	Roma, domus sull'Esquilino	priv.	iscrizione onoraria del figlio	padre del dest.	c. m. v., praef. urb.	no

	CIL, XIV 3582-3583	Tibur	pubbl.	opera pubblica	padre del ded.	praef. urb.	no
	CIL, XI 6218	Fanum	pubbl.	dedica imperiale + opera pubblica (arco)	padre del ded.	praef. urb.	no
	CIL, VI 1717 cfr. p. 4742	Roma, fuori Porta Flaminia	priv.?	iscrizione onoraria	dest.	cursus honorum	no
43 Fabius Titianus p. u. 339-341 e 350-351 (*PLRE*, I Titianus 6)[49]	CIL, VI 1653; 31879-31881; 37107-37108 cfr. pp. 4726-4727	Roma, Foro Romano	pubbl.	opera pubblica (statue)	ded.	cos., praef. urb.	no
	CIL, III 12330[50]	Traiana (Thracia)	pubbl.	dedica imperiale	ded.	praef. praet.	no
	CIL, VI 1654 cfr. p. 4727	Roma, Celio	pubbl.	opera pubblica (statua)	ded.	pref. urb. iterum	no
	CIL, VI 1166 a cfr. p. 4331	Roma, Terme di Tito	pubbl.	dedica imperiale	ded.	cos. ord., praef. urb. iterum	no
	CIL, VI 41335 a	Roma, Terme di Tito	pubbl.	opera pubblica (statua)	ded.	praef. urb.	no
	CIL, VI 1167 cfr. p. 4331	Roma	pubbl.	dedica imperiale	ded.	cos. ord., praef. urb. iterum	no
	AE 1893, 124 = *ILS* 8983	Cuma	priv.[51]	dedica sacra (alla Sibilla?)	ded.	cos. ord., praef. urb. iterum	sì[52]
	IK 13, 666C	Ephesus	pubbl.	iscrizione onoraria	dest.	lamprotatos anthypatos	no

Gli ultimi sacerdoti pagani di Roma

44	Aurelius Celsinus p. u. 341-342 e 351 (*PLRE*, I Celsinus 4)	*ILTun* 757 = *AE* 1929, 60 = *AE* 1992, 1799	Pagus Mercurialis (Africa Proconsularis)	pubbl.	dedica imperiale	ded.	procos. Africae	no
45	Q. Flavius Maesius Egnatius Lollianus signo Mavortius p. u. 342 (*PLRE*, I Lollianus 5)[53]	*CIL*, VI 36951 cfr. pp. 4354-4355	Roma, Foro Romano	pubbl.	dedica imperiale + opera pubblica (statio aquarum)	ded.	cur. aquar. et Miniciae	no
		CIL, VI 40782 A	Roma, in reimpiego	?	dedica imperiale	ded.	praef. urb.	no
		CIL, VI 1723 + 1757 = 37112 cfr. p. 4819	Roma, *domus* sull'Aventino[54]	priv.	iscrizione onoraria	dest.	cursus honorum	no[55]
		CIL, X 1695-1696 + *EphEp*, VIII 365 = *ILS* 1224 a-c	Puteoli	pubbl.	iscrizioni onorarie	dest.	cursus honorum	sì[56]
		CIL, X 4752	Suessa	pubbl.	iscrizione onoraria	dest.	cursus honorum	sì
46	Aco (o Aconius) Catullinus signo Philomathius p. u. 342-344 (*PLRE*, I Catullinus 3)	*CIL*, II 2635[57]	Asturica	priv.?[58]	dedica sacra (a Giove)	ded.	vir consularis, praeses prov. Callaeciae	no
		CIL, VI 1780 cfr. pp. 4759-4760	Roma	priv.?	iscrizione onoraria (forse post mortem) della figlia	padre del dest.	v.c., ex praef. et cos.ord.	no

47	Q. Rusticus p. u. 344-345 (*PLRE*, I Rusticus 2)	*CIL*, VI 1165 cfr. p. 4331	Roma, Campo Marzio	pubbl.	opera pubblica (terme di Agrippa)	cur.	praef. urb.	no
49	M. Maecius Memmius Furius Baburius Caecilianus Placidus p. u. 346-347 (*PLRE*, I Placidus 2)[59]	*CIL*, X 1700	Puteoli	pubbl.	iscrizione onoraria	dest.	cursus honorum	si[60]
55	Clodius Celsinus signo Adelphius p. u. 351 (*PLRE*, I Celsinus 6 e 7)[61]	*CIL*, VI 1712 = *ILCV* 1850 cfr. p. 4741	Roma, chiesa di S. Anastasia	priv.	iscrizione sepolcrale della moglie	ded.	ex praefectis urbis	no
		CIL, IX 1576	Beneventum	pubbl.	iscrizione onoraria	dest.	corrector	no
		CIL, VIII 7011 = *ILAlg*, II 587	Cirta (Numidia)	pubbl.	dedica imperiale	ded.	consularis Numidiae	no
57	Septimius Mnasea p. u. 352 (*PLRE*, I Mnasea)	*CIL*, VI 41344	Roma, in reimpiego	pubbl.	opera pubblica?[62]	ded.	praef. urb.	?[63]
58	Naeratius Cerealis p. u. 352-353 (*PLRE*, I Cerealis 2)	*CIL*, VI 1158 cfr. p. 4330	Roma, Foro Romano	pubbl.	dedica imperiale	ded.	praef. urb.	no
		CIL, VI 1744 = 31916 cfr. pp. 4749-4750	Roma, balnea sull'Esquilino	pubbl.	opera pubblica (statue nei balnea)	ded.	praef. urb.	no
		CIL, VI 1745 cfr. p. 4750	Roma, *domus* sull'Esquilino?[64]	priv.?	iscrizione onoraria	dest.	cursus honorum	no

Gli ultimi sacerdoti pagani di Roma

#	Nome	Riferimento	Luogo	pubbl./priv.	Tipo	ded./dest.	Descrizione	si/no
59	Memmius Vitrasius Orfitus signo Honorius p. u. 353-356 (*PLRE*, I Orfitus 3)	*CIL*, X 7200	Thermae Selinuntiae (Sicilia)	pubbl.	opera pubblica (statio del cursus publicus)	ded.	consularis Siciliae	no
		CIL, VI 1159 cfr. pp. 4330-4331 = *CIL*, XIV 461	Ostia	pubbl.	opera pubblica (statue)	ded.	praef. urb.	no
		CIL, VI 45 e D. AMBAGLIO, in *Museo dell'Istituto di Archeologia. Materiali*, 3, Milano 1987, 197-199	Roma, Campo Marzio[65]	pubbl.	dediche sacre (ad Apollo) + opera pubblica (restauro del tempio)	ded.	bis praef. urb.	no
		CIL, VI 1161-1162; 1168; 31395 cfr. pp. 4331-4332 e 4345	Roma, Foro Romano	pubbl.	dediche imperiali	ded.	praef. urb. iterum	no
		CIL, VI 1739-1742 cfr. pp. 4748-4749	Roma, *domus* sul Celio[66]	priv.	iscrizioni onorarie	dest.	cursus honorum	si[67]
60	Flavius Leontius p. u. 355-356 (*PLRE*, I Leontius 22)[68]	*CIL*, VI 31397 cfr. p. 4345	Roma, Foro Romano	pubbl.	dedica imperiale	ded.	preaf. urb.	no
		CIL, VI 1160 cfr. p. 4331	Roma, Aventino	pubbl.	dedica imperiale	ded.	preaf. urb.	no
62	Iunius Bassus signo Theotecnius p. u. 359 (*PLRE*, I Bassus 15)[69]	*CIL*, VI 32004 = 41341 a-b	Roma, Grotte Vaticane	priv.	iscrizione sepolcrale	dest.	v. c. + riferimento alla sua prefettura urbana	no

		AE 1964, 203 = AE 1975, 370[70]	Aqua Viva (Tuscia)	priv.	iscrizione onoraria del figlio	padre del dest.	praef. praet., cos. ord.	no
64	Valerius Maximus p. u. 361-362 (*PLRE*, I Maximus 17)	*CIL*, VI 31401 cfr. p. 4345	Roma, in reimpiego	?	dedica imperiale	ded.	praef. urb.	no
65	L. Turcius Apronianus signo Asterius p. u. 362-363 (*PLRE*, I Apronianus 10)[71]	*CIL*, VI 1770-1771 cfr. p. 4756 e *CIL*, VI 41327	Roma	pubbl.	editto		praef. urb.	no
		CIL, VI 1655 a-b cfr. p. 4727 e *CIL*, VI 40782 B	Roma	pubbl.	opera pubblica? (statue?)	ded.	praef. urb.	no
		J. Spon, *Miscellanea eruditae antiquitatis*, Lyon 1685, p. 303	Roma?	pubbl.	peso campione		praef. urb.	no
		CIL, VI 1768-1769 cfr. pp. 4755-4756	Roma, *domus* sull'Esquilino[72]	priv.	iscrizioni onorarie	dest.	cursus honorum	sì[73]
66	L. Aurelius Avianius Symmachus signo Phosphorius p. u. 364-365 (*PLRE*, I Symmachus 3)	*CIL*, VI 36954 B cfr. p. 4355	Roma	pubbl.	dedica imperiale	ded.	praef. annonae	no
		AE 1988, 217[74]	Ostia (in reimpiego)	pubbl.	dedica imperiale	ded.	praef. ann.	no?[75]

Gli ultimi sacerdoti pagani di Roma 451

	CIL, VI 31402-31404 cfr. pp. 4345-4346[76]	Roma, ponte di Valentiniano	pubbl.	dedica imperiale + opera pubblica (ponte)	ded.	ex praef. urb.	no
	CIL, VI 1698 cfr. p. 4737	Roma, Foro di Traiano	pubbl.	iscrizione onoraria (post mortem)	dest.	cursus honorum (in forma di elogium)	sì[77]
67 C. Caeionius Rufius Volusianus signo Lampadius p. u. 365-366 (PLRE, I Volusianus 5)	CIL, VIII 25990	Thubursicum Bure	priv.[78]	iscr. posta da un suo *procurator*	patrono del ded.	solo c. v.	no
	CIL, VI 512	Roma, Phrygianum del Vaticano	priv.	dedica sacra (alla Magna Mater) posta dal figlio	padre del ded.	ex praef. praet., ex praef. urb.	no
	AE 1945, 55 + AE 1955, 180 = CCCA, III, nr. 366	Ostia	priv.?	dedica sacra (ad Attis)	ded.	v. c., ex praefectis	no[79]
	CIL, VI 846 = SIRIS, nr. 434 = CIMRM, nr. 466	Roma, Aventino	priv.?	dedica sacra	ded.	solo v. c.	sì[80]
	CIL, VI 3866 = 31963 cfr. p. 4770	Roma	pubbl.	opera pubblica (castellum dell'Aqua Claudia)	ded.	ex praef. praet., praef. urb.	no
	CIL, VI 794 e 1171-1173 cfr. p. 4332	Roma, terme di Caracalla	pubbl.	dediche imperiali	ded.	praef. urb. (in un caso anche praef. praet.)	no

	CIL, VI 1170 cfr. p. 4332	Roma, terme di Caracalla	pubbl.	opera pubblica (statua)	ded.	ex praef. praet., praef. urb.	no
	CIL, VI 1174 e 36955 cfr. p. 4332 e 4355	Roma, Foro Romano	pubbl.	dediche imperiali	ded.	praef. urb.	no
69 Vettius Agorius Praetextatus p. u. 367-368 (*PLRE*, I Praetextatus 1)[81]	*AE* 1928, 48	Tespi	pubbl.	iscrizione onoraria in versi	dest.	anthypatos	no
	CIL, VI 102	Roma, Foro Romano	pubbl.	opera pubblica (portico degli Dei Consenti)	ded.	praef. urb.	no
	CIG, II 2594 = *ICret*, IV 316	Gortyna	pubbl.	iscrizione onoraria	dest.	lamprotatos apo eparchon[82]	no
	CIL, VI 1777 cfr. p. 4757[83]	Roma, *domus* sull' Aventino[84]	priv.	iscrizione onoraria post mortem	dest.	cursus honorum	no
	CIL, VI 1778 cfr. p. 4757	Roma, *domus* sepolcro?	priv.?	iscrizione onoraria post mortem	dest.	cursus honorum	sì
	CIL, VI 1779 cfr. pp. 4757-4759	Roma	priv.?	iscrizione sepolcrale	dest.	cursus honorum	sì[85]
	CIL, VI 1780 cfr. pp. 4759-4760	Roma, in reimpiego	priv.?	iscrizione onoraria (?) per la moglie	marito del dest.	v. c., praef., cos. design.	no
	CIL, VI 2145 = 32408[86]	Roma, sull'Esquilino?	priv.?	iscrizione onoraria per la Vestale Coelia Concordia		solo v. c.	no

70	Q. Clodius Hermogenianus Olybrius p. u. 368-370 (*PLRE*, I Olybrius 3)[87]	*CIL*, VI 1713 cfr. p. 4741	Roma, presso il teatro di Marcello?	priv.?	iscrizione onoraria (posta dal fratello)	dest.	solo v. c.	no
		CIL, VI 1714 cfr. p. 4741	Roma, domus sull'Esquilino?[88]	priv.?	iscrizione onoraria per la moglie	marito del dest.	cursus honorum	no
		CIL, X 6083	Formiae	pubbl.	iscrizione onoraria	dest.	consularis Campaniae	no
		CIL, VIII 1860 = 16505 = *ILAlg*, I 3052	Theveste	pubbl.	opera pubblica (arco)	ded.	procos. Africae	no
		J. Spon, *Miscellanea eruditae antiquitatis*, Lyon 1685, p. 303	Roma?	pubbl.	peso campione		praef. urb.	no
		CIL, VI 1657 cfr. p. 4727	Roma, S. Pietro in Vincoli	pubbl.	opera pubblica (statua)	ded.	praef. urb.	no
71	P. Ampelius p. u. 371-372 (PLRE, I Ampelius 3)	A. M. Woodward, *Excavations at Sparta*, «Ann. Brit. Sch. Ath.», 30 (1932), 217-220 e *AE* 1929, 19[89]	Sparta	pubbl.	opere pubbliche	ded.	lamprotatos anthypatos	no
		IG, XII 9, 907	Chalkis	pubbl.	editto		lamprotatos anthypatos	no
		IG, IV 53	Aigina	pubbl.?	iscrizione onoraria in versi	dest.	no	no

454 SILVIA ORLANDI

		IG, V 1, 455	Amyklaion	pubbl.?	iscrizione onoraria in versi	dest.	no
		AE 1933, 33b = *ILTun* 1538 B	Mustis	pubbl.	opera pubblica	cur.	procos. Africae	no
74	Flavius Eupraxius p. u. 374 (*PLRE*, I Eupraxius)	*CIL*, VI 1177 cfr. p. 4332	Roma	pubbl.	opera pubblica (Forum)[90]	cur.	praef. urb.	no
75	Clodius Hermogenianus Caesarius p. u. 374 (*PLRE*, I Caesarius 7)	*CIL*, VI 499 = *CCCA* III, 228	Roma, Phrygianum del Vaticano	priv.?	dedica sacra (alla Magna Mater)	ded.	procos. Africae, praef. urb.	sì[91]
76	Tanaucius Isfalangius p. u. 374-375 (*PLRE*, I Isfalangius)	*CIL*, VI 1672 cfr. p. 4730	Roma, Aventino	pubbl.	opera pubblica (statue)	ded.	praef. urb.	no
77	Tarracius Bassus p. u. 375-376 (*PLRE*, I Bassus 21)	*CIL*, VI 1766 = 31894 = 41328	Roma	pubbl.	editto	ded.	praef. urb.	
79	Furius Maecius Gracchus p. u. 376-377 (*PLRE*, I Gracchus 1 3)	*CIL*, XIV 3594[92]	Tibur	**pubbl.**	opera pubblica (statua)	ded.	corr. Flaminiae et Piceni	no
		CIL, VI 1709 = 31907 cfr. p. 4740	Roma	priv.?	iscrizione onoraria per il padre	ded.	solo v. c.	no

Gli ultimi sacerdoti pagani di Roma

#	Nome	Fonte	Luogo	pubbl.	tipo	ded./dest.	titolo	
80	Gabinius Vettius Probianus p. u. 377 (*PLRE*, I Probianus 4)	*CIL*, VI 11156b = 1658c, cfr. p. 4330; 1658, cfr. p. 4727; 3864 a-c = 31883-31885, cfr. pp. 4769; 31886 = 37105, cfr. p. 4792; 41337-41338	Roma, Foro Romano	pubbl.	opera pubblica (statue)	ded.	praef. urb.	no
		AE 1933, 195 = *ICret*, IV 319	Gortyna	pubbl.	iscrizione onoraria	dest.	lamprotatos ... apò eparchon[93]	no
82	Flavius Hypatius p. u. 378-379 (*PLRE*, I Hypatius 4)	*CIG* 2596 = *ICret*, IV 317	Gortyna	pubbl.	iscrizione onoraria	dest.	lamprotatos apòypaton kai apò eparchon tou paitoriou[94]	no
84	**Anicius Paulinus p. u. 380** (*PLRE*, I Paulinus 12)[95]	***AE* 1933, 193 = *ICret*, IV 320**	**Gortyna**	**pubbl.**	**iscrizione onoraria**	**dest.**	**lamprotatos apò anthypaton kai apò eparchon[96]**	**no**
		AE 1972, 75b[97]	Capua	pubbl.?	iscrizione onoraria	dest.	procos. Campaniae, praef. urb.	no
85	L. Valerius Septimius Bassus p. u. 379/383 (*PLRE*, I Bassus 20)[98]	*CIL*, VI 1184a cfr. p. 4333	Roma, Foro Romano	pubbl.	dedica imperiale	ded.	praef. urb.	no
87	**Valerius Severus p. u. 382** (*PLRE*, I Severus 29)[99]	***CIG*, II 2595 = *ICret*, IV 315**	**Gortyna**	**pubbl.**	**iscrizione onoraria**	**dest.**	**lamprotatos eparchos...[100]**	**no**
88	Anicius Auchenius Bassus p. u. 382 (*PLRE*, I Bassus 11)	*CIL*, VI 1679 cfr. p. 4732	Roma, Foro di Traiano	pubbl.	iscrizione onoraria	dest.	cursus honorum (in forma di elogium)	no

456 SILVIA ORLANDI

			?	dedica sacra (cristiana)		solo v. c.	
	CIL, XIV 1875 = *ILCV* 91	Ostia			ded.	solo v. c.	no
	CIL, X 6656	Antium	pubbl.	opera pubblica (terme)	ded.	procos. Campaniae	no
	CIL, X 3843	Capua	pubbl.	opera pubblica?	ded.	procos. Campaniae	no
	CIL, IX 1568-1569	Beneventum	pubbl.	iscrizioni onorarie	dest.	procos. Campaniae	no
	CIL, XIV 2917	Praeneste	pubbl.	iscrizione onoraria	dest.	procos. Campaniae	no
	CIL, X 5651	Fabrateria Vetus	pubbl.	iscrizione onoraria	dest.	[procos. Campaniae]	no
	CIG 2597 = *ICret*, IV 314	Gortyna	pubbl.	iscrizione onoraria	dest.	anthypatos Kampanias[101]	no
	AE 1892, 143 = *ILS* 8984	Neapolis	pubbl.	iscrizione onoraria	dest.	procos. Campaniae, praef. urb.	no
90	Q. Aurelius Symmachus signo Eusebius p. u. 384-385 (*PLRE*, I Symmachus 4)	*CIL*, VI 1699 cfr. pp. 4737-4738	Roma, *domus* sul Celio[102]	priv.	iscrizione onoraria	dest.	cursus honorum	sì[103]
		CIL, VIII 24584	Carthago	pubbl.	opera pubblica (statua)	ded.	procos. Africae	no
92	Sextius Rusticus Iulianus p. u. 387-388 (*PLRE*, I Iulianus 37)[104]	*CIL*, VIII 995 = 12455	Carpis	pubbl.	dedica imperiale	ded.	procos. Africae	no

GLI ULTIMI SACERDOTI PAGANI DI ROMA

#	Nome	Riferimento	Luogo		Tipo		Carica	
		CIL, VIII 1447 = 15256	Thubursicum Bure	pubbl.	opera pubblica (tempio?)	ded.	procos. Africae	no
		CIL, VIII 12537	Carthago	pubbl.	opera pubblica	ded.	procos. Africae	no
93	Sex. Aurelius Victor p. u. 388-389 (*PLRE*, I Victor 13)	*CIL*, VI 1186 cfr. p. 4333	Roma, Foro di Traiano	pubbl.	dedica imperiale	ded.	praef. urb.	no
94	Caeionius Rufius Albinus p. u. 389-391 (*PLRE*, I Albinus 15)[105]	*CIL*, VI 3791 a-b = 31413-31414, cfr. pp. 4338-4339; 36959-36960, cfr. pp. 4355-4356	Roma, Foro Romano	pubbl.	dediche imperiali	ded.	praef. urb.	no
95	Faltonius Probus Alypius p. u. 391 (*PLRE*, I Alypius 13)[106]	*CIL*, VI 1185 cfr. p. 4333	Roma, Colosseo	pubbl.	dedica imperiale	ded.	praef. urb.	no
		CIL, VI 31975 cfr. p. 4798	Roma, Campo Marzio	?	iscrizione onoraria	dest.	praef. urb.	no
96	Flavius Philippus p. u. 391 (*PLRE*, I Philippus 8)	*CIL*, VI 1728 e 31912 cfr. p. 4745	Roma	pubbl.	opera pubblica (ninfeo)	ded.	praef. urb.	no
97	Nicomachus Flavianus p. u. 393-394, 399-400 e 408 (*PLRE*, I Flavianus 14)[107]	*CIL*, VI 1783 cfr. pp. 4760-4761	Roma, Foro di Traiano	pubbl.	iscrizione onoraria (con *oratio* imperiale)	figlio del dest.	cursus honorum	no
		ILS 8985 = *AE* 1894, 89	Neapolis	pubbl.	iscrizione onoraria	dest.	cursus honorum	no
		CIL, VI 40798	Roma, Foro di Cesare	pubbl.	dedica imperiale	ded.	praef. urb.	no

#	Name	Reference	Location		Type		Role	
98	Fabius Pasiphilus p. u. 394/395 (*PLRE*, I Pasiphilus 2)	*CIL*, X 1692 e 1694	Puteoli	pubbl.	opera pubblica (macellum e basilica)	ded.	agens vicem praef. praet.	no
99	Basilius p. u. 395 (*PLRE*, I Basilius 3)	*CIL*, VI 41333	Roma, Foro di Cesare	pubbl.	opera pubblica (statua)	ded.	praef. urb.	no
104	**Quintilius Laetus p. u. 398-399** (*PLRE*, I Laetus 2)[108]	*CIL*, IX 4051	Carseoli	**pubbl.**	**opera pubblica (restauro di acquedotto)**	**ded.**	**[praef. urb.]**	**no**
107	**Flavius Macrobius Longinianus p. u. 401/402** (*PLRE*, II Longinianus)	*CIL*, VI 1188-1190 = 31257, cfr. p. 4334	Roma, porte delle Mura Aureliane	**pubbl.**	**opera pubblica (mura e porte)**	cur.	praef. urb.	no
		ICUR, II nr. 19 = *ILCV* 92	Roma, S. Anastasia	**pubbl.**	**opera pubblica (battistero)**	ded.	praef. urb.	no
108	Caecina Decius Albinus p. u. 402 (*PLRE*, I Albinus 10)	*AE* 1909, 223 = *AE* 1933, 159 = *AE* 1989, 784	Theveste	pubbl.	opera pubblica (arco)	ded.	consularis Numidiae	no
		ILAlg, II 619-622	Cirta	pubbl.	opera pubblica (acquedotto)	ded.	consularis Numidiae	no
		AE 1913, 23	Djemila	pubbl.	opera pubblica (basilica?)	ded.	[consularis Numidiae]	no
		CIL, VI 1192 cfr. p. 4334	Roma, Aventino	pubbl.	dedica imperiale	ded.	praef. urb.	no
109	Postumius Lampadius p. u. 403/408 (*PLRE*, II Lampadius 7)	*CIL*, X 3860	Capua	pubbl.	iscrizione onoraria	dest.	consularis Campaniae	no

GLI ULTIMI SACERDOTI PAGANI DI ROMA 459

	CIL, X 1704	Puteoli	pubbl.	opera pubblica	ded.	consularis Campaniae	no
	CIL, VI 9920	Roma, Campo Marzio	pubbl.	editto		praef. urb.	
110 Flavius Peregrinus Saturninus p. u. 403-407 (PLRE, II Saturninus 7)	CIL, VI 1727 cfr. pp. 4744-4745	Roma, Foro di Traiano	pubbl.	iscrizione onoraria	dest.	cursus honorum (in forma di elogium)	no
111 Flavius Pisidius Romulus p. u. 405-406 (PLRE, I Romulus 5)	CIL, VI 1731, cfr. p. 4746 e 31987, cfr. p. 4800	Roma, Foro Romano	pubbl.	iscrizioni onorarie per Stilicone	cur.	praef. urb.	no
115 Gabinius Barbarus Pompeianus p. u. 408-409 (PLRE, II Pompeianus 2)	CIL, VIII 969	Neapolis (Africa)	pubbl.	opera pubblica	cur.	procos. Africae	no
119 Naeratius Palmatus p. u. 412 (PLRE, I Palmatus 2 e PLRE, II Palmatus 1)[109]	CIL, X 7124	Syracusae	pubbl.	opera pubblica (teatro)	ded.	[consularis Siciliae]	no
120 Flavius Annius Eucharius Epiphanius p. u. 412-414 (PLRE, II Epiphanius 7)	CIL, VI 1718 cfr. pp. 4742-4743	Roma, Foro Romano	pubbl.	opera pubblica (secretarium senatus)[110]	ded.	praef. urb.	no
122 Caecina Decius Aginatius Albinus p. u. 414 (PLRE, II Albinus 7)	CIL, VI 1659, cfr. pp. 4727-4728 e CIL, VI 1703, cfr. pp. 4738-4739	Roma, Aventino	pubbl.	opera pubblica (terme)	ded.	praef. urb.	no

123	Arrius Maecius Gracchus p. u. 415 (*PLRE*, I Gracchus 2 e *PLRE*, II Gracchus)	*CIL*, X 520	Salernum	pubbl.	iscrizione onoraria	dest.	solo v. c.	no
125	**Rufius Antonius Agrypnius Volusianus** p. u. 417-418 (*PLRE*, II Volusianus 6)[111]	*CIL*, VI 1661 cfr. p. 4728	Roma	pubbl.	opera pubblica (statua)	ded.	praef. urb.	no
		CIL, VI 1194 cfr. p. 4334	Roma, Foro di Traiano	pubbl.	dedica imperiale	ded.	praef. urb.	no
		CIL, VI 41385	Roma, Foro di Cesare	pubbl.	opera pubblica (statua)	ded.	praef. urb.	no
126	Aurelius Anicius Symmachus p. u. 418-420 (*PLRE*, II Symmachus 6)[112]	*CIL*, VI 1719 cfr. p. 4743	Roma	pubbl.?	iscrizione onoraria per Flavio Costanzo	ded.	praef. urb.	no
		CIL, VI 1193 cfr. p. 4334	Roma, teatro di Pompeo	pubbl.	dedica imperiale	ded.	praef. urb.	no
		CIL, VI 36962 cfr. p. 4356	Roma, Foro Romano	pubbl.	opera pubblica	ded.	[praef. urb.]	?[113]
		CIL, XIV 4719	Ostia	pubbl.	opera pubblica (macellum)	ded.	praef. urb.	no
127	Petronius Maximus p. 420-421 (*PLRE*, II Maximus 22)	*CIL*, VI 1749 cfr. pp. 4750-4751	Roma, Foro di Traiano	pubbl.	iscrizione onoraria	dest.	cursus honorum (in forma di elogium)	no
		CIL, VI 1660 cfr. p. 4728	Roma, teatro di Marcello	pubbl.	opera pubblica (statue)	ded.	praef. urb.	no

	CIL, VI 36956, cfr. p. 4355 e CIL, VI 37109-37110, cfr. p. 4818	Roma, Foro Romano	pubbl.	opera pubblica (statue)	ded.	praef. urb.	no
	CIL, VI 1197-1198 cfr. p. 4335	Roma, Celio	priv.?	dedica imperiale + opera pubblica (foro privato)[114]	ded.	IIII praef., bis cos. ord.	no
128 Anicius Acilius Glabrio Faustus p. u. 421-423 (*PLRE*, II Faustus 8)[115]	*CIL*, XIV 2165	Aricia	pubbl.	iscrizione onoraria	dest.	cursus honorum	no
	CIL, VI 1676 cfr. pp. 4731-4732	Roma, Circo Flaminio	pubbl.	opera pubblica	ded.	praef. urb.	no
	CIL, VI 1677 cfr. p. 4732	Roma, Foro Boario	pubbl.	opera pubblica	ded.	praef. urb.	no
	CIL, VI 1678 cfr. p. 4732	Roma, Campo Marzio (foro privato)[116]	priv.	iscrizione onoraria per il padre	ded.	solo v. c.	no
	CIL, VI 1767 cfr. pp. 4754-4755	Roma, Campo Marzio (foro privato)	priv.	iscrizione onoraria per il suocero	ded.	solo v. c.	no
	CIL, VI 37119 = 41389 a[117]	Roma, Campo Marzio (foro privato)	priv.	iscrizione onoraria per il bisnonno	ded.	solo v. c.	no
129 Iunius Valerius Bellicius p. u. 423 (*PLRE*, II Bellicius)[118]	*CIL*, VI 31959 = 37114 cfr. p. 4819 e *CIL*, VI 40803	Roma, sede della prefettura urbana	pubbl.	opera pubblica (restauro della sede della prefettura)	ded.	praef. urb.	no

Note alla tabella

[1] Incerto se a questo personaggio o a suo figlio (come pensano gli autori della *PLRE*, I Gratianus 4 e RÜPKE, *Fasti*, 1330 nr. 3302) si riferisca una dedica inedita a Ercole, nota solo da tradizione manoscritta, in cui compare come dedicante il *praetor urbanus* L. Turranius Venustus Gratianus (vd. in proposito *EAOR*, VI, 264-267).
[2] L'iscrizione, a rigore, è frammentaria, ma il confronto con altre basi onorarie dello stesso tipo rende pressoché certa la sola menzione della prefettura urbana.
[3] Su questo personaggio vd. anche PORENA, *Origini*, 73-89.
[4] Raccolte in PORENA, *Origini*, 82-85
[5] Recentemente ristudiata da PORENA, *Origini*, 106-133.
[6] Vd. anche CHRISTOL, *Essai*, 143 nr. 5.
[7] Vd. anche F.A. BAUER, *Stadt, Platz und Denkmal in der Spätantike. Untersuchungen zur Ausstattung des öffentlichen Raums in den spätantiken Städten Rom, Konstantinopel und Ephesos*, Mainz 1996, 424.
[8] Il nome di questo personaggio, eraso, accompagnato dalla qualifica di *pontifex*, verosimilmente *dei Solis*, potrebbe essere restituito nella problematica iscrizione *CIL*, VI 2153, secondo T.D. BARNES, *The New Empire of Diocletian and Constantine*, Cambridge-London 1982, 121. Vd. anche CHRISTOL, *Essai*, 139 nr. 2.
[9] P. GROS, in *LTUR*, IV, 148-149, s. v. Porticus Pompei.
[10] Vd. anche R. ZUCCA, *Le basi onorarie di Formiae*, «Formianum», IV (1996), 55 nr. 24.
[11] *Pont. dei Solis*: vd. RÜPKE, *Fasti*, 729-730 nr. 467.
[12] F. GUIDOBALDI, in *LTUR*, II, 146-147 s. v. Domus: Nummii.
[13] Vd. anche CHRISTOL, *Essai*, 206 nr. 38.
[14] Vd. anche F.A. BAUER, *Stadt, Platz und Denkmal...*, 424.
[15] A questo personaggio si riferisce anche l'iscrizione – verosimilmente sepolcrale – *CIL*, VI 1419b = 41224 (tit. II), esclusa perché il testo è molto frammentario e non se ne conosce il contesto originario (è stata rinvenuta reimpiegata nelle catacombe di Callisto), ma che contiene l'interessante riferimento a un altro sacerdozio: quello di *duodecemvir urbis Romae* (su cui vd. RÜPKE, *Fasti*, 25).
[16] F. GUIDOBALDI, in *LTUR*, II, 163 s. v. Domus: Postumii.
[17] *Pont. dei Solis, augur*: vd. RÜPKE, *Fasti*, p. 994 nr. 1705.
[18] Recentemente ripubblicata da A. SARTORI, *Le iscrizioni romane. Guida all'esposizione*, Como 1994, 74.
[19] Sulla problematica identificazione di questo personaggio con il prefetto urbano del 312 e con il prefetto del pretorio di Severo e Massenzio vd. PORENA, *Origini*, 237-254.
[20] L'iscrizione è frammentaria.
[21] F. GUIDOBALDI, in *LTUR*, II, 186-187, s. v. Domus: Attius Insteius Tertullus.
[22] F. COARELLI, in *LTUR*, IV, 160, s. v. Praefectura Urbana. Su questo argomento vd. ora M. E. MARCHESE, *La Prefettura Urbana a Roma. Un tentativo di localizzazione attraverso le epigrafi*, «Mél. Ec. Fr. Rom. Ant.» 119 (2007), 613-634.
[23] L'iscrizione è frammentaria.
[24] A questo personaggio si riferisce anche il frammento di *cursus honorum CIL*, VI 41319, escluso perché troppo lacunoso e rinvenuto in luogo incerto. Incerto anche se a lui o a uno dei suoi discendenti si riferiscano le iscrizioni africane ILAfr 365 e *AE* 1949, 59. Su Volusianus vd. anche PORENA, *Origini*, 259-272, in part. 265-267 (su *CIL*, VI 41319).
[25] L'iscrizione è frammentaria, però il testo lo definisce *religiosissimus*.
[26] Cui si aggiunga ora M. BUONOCORE, *Mommsen ~ Seeck: un rapporto non facile. A*

proposito dell'auctoritas senatoria del 336/7 d. C. (CIL, VI, 1708 = 31906 = 41318), «Stud. Rom». 53 (2005), 596-615.

[27] Quest'iscrizione, per molto tempo considerata un falso (così ancora la *PLRE*, I, p. 977), è stata recentemente riabilitata da A. GIARDINA, *Le due Italie nella forma tarda dell'impero*, in *Società romana e impero tardoantico*, a cura di A. GIARDINA, Roma-Bari 1986, I, 14-15 (cfr. anche *CIL*, VI p. 4740).

[28] Ripubblicata da T.D. BARNES, *The New Empire of Diocletian and Constantine*, Cambridge-London 1982, 121.

[29] Il suo nome compare in una lista di personaggi menzionati in nominativo.

[30] *XVvir sacris faciundis*: vd. RÜPKE, *Fasti*, 868-869 nr. 1129.

[31] Ma non è certo che le iscrizioni si riferiscano a questo personaggio.

[32] Su questo personaggio vd. anche CHRISTOL, *Essai*, 253-254 nr. 59 e, da ultimo, P. PORENA, *Problemi di cronologia costantiniana...*, 230-246.

[33] *Pont. dei Solis, augur, salius Palatinus*: vd. RÜPKE, *Fasti*, 1364 nr. 3470.

[34] Ma cfr. P. PORENA, *Problemi di cronologia costantiniana...*, 244-245, che fa notare come non sia certo se la base si riferisca a questo personaggio o a un altro *Rufinus*.

[35] Vd. r. 10: *voti conpos*.

[36] *Augur, pont. dei Solis*: degna di nota l'assenza della carica di *salius Palatinus* (vd. sopra, note 39-40).

[37] Il testo dell'iscrizione, frammentario, lo definisce *benignus* e *sanctus*. Secondo la *PLRE*, I, 680 potrebbe essere cristiano; così anche RÜPKE, *Fasti*, 1241-1242 nr. 2859, che parla di una conversione. Contra T.D. BARNES e R.W. WESTALL, *The conversion of the Roman aristocracy in Prudentius' Contra Symmachum*, «Phoenix» 45 (1991), 50-61, che identificano, invece, il personaggio menzionato da Prudenzio con Anicius Paulinus p. u. 380 (vd. sotto, nr. 84).

[38] A questo personaggio potrebbe riferirsi anche l'iscrizione onoraria *CIL*, VIII 14431 da Gasr Mezuâr (*Africa Proconsularis*), esclusa perché troppo frammentaria.

[39] A questo personaggio si riferisce anche l'iscrizione *CIL*, VI 40775, esclusa perché troppo frammentaria.

[40] Il testo dell'iscrizione lo definisce *philosophus*.

[41] F. GUIDOBALDI, in *LTUR*, II, 36-37, s. v. Domus: Aradii.

[42] *Augur, pont. maior, XVvir s.f., pont. Flavialis*: vd. RÜPKE, *Fasti*, 778 nr. 707.

[43] Ripubblicata, con aggiornamenti, in S. PANCIERA, *Epigrafi, epigrafia, epigrafisti. Scritti vari editi e inediti (1956-2005) con note complementari e indici*, Roma 2006, 1119-1136.

[44] Solo *XVvir s. f.*.

[45] Vd. anche *EAOR*, VI 267-269 e RÜPKE, *Fasti*, 1125 nr. 2319.

[46] L'iscrizione è frammentaria.

[47] L'iscrizione è frammentaria.

[48] F. GUIDOBALDI, in *LTUR*, II, 204-205, s. v. Domus: Turcii; vd. anche R. COATES-STEPHENS, *The Reuse of Ancient Statuary in Late Antique Rome and the End of the Statue Habit*, in *Statuen in der Spätantike*, a cura di F. A. BAUER e C. WITSCHEL, Wiesbaden 2007, 179.

[49] A questo personaggio si riferiscono anche l'iscrizione urbana *CIL*, VI 3866 a = 32055 e la dedica imperiale di Efeso *IK* 13, 666D (in latino), entrambe escluse perché troppo frammentarie, nonché un'iscrizione inedita di Delfi citata dalla *PLRE*, I, 918.

[50] Su quest'iscrizione vd. recentemente PORENA, *Origini*, 491.

[51] Il testo contiene la formula *votum libens solvit*, che fa pensare ad una dedica posta a titolo privato in seguito allo scioglimento di un voto.

[52] *XVvir s. f.* (N.B. prima delle cariche): vd. RÜPKE, *Fasti*, 974 nr. 1603.

⁵³ Incerto se a questo personaggio o al prefetto urbano del 254 si riferisca la dedica a Ercole dall'Esquilino *CIL*, VI 30895 (su cui vd. ora *SupplIt – Imagines, Roma*, 2, nr. 2897).
⁵⁴ F. GUIDOBALDI, in *LTUR*, II, 132, s. v. Domus: Q. Flavius Maesius Egnatius Lollianus s. Mavortius.
⁵⁵ Però il testo lo definisce *religiosus*.
⁵⁶ *Augur publicus p. R. Q.*: vd. RÜPKE, *Fasti*, 993 nr. 1698.
⁵⁷ Recentemente ripubblicata da M.A. RABANAL ALONSO e S.M. GARCÍA MARTÍNEZ, *Epigrafía romana de la provincia de León: revisión y actualización*, León 2001, 100-101 nr. 43.
⁵⁸ La dedica fu posta *pro salute sua suorumque*.
⁵⁹ A questo personaggio si riferisce anche un'iscrizione inedita di Delfi citata dalla *PLRE*, I, 705.
⁶⁰ *Pont. maior, augur, XVvir s. f.*: vd. RÜPKE, *Fasti*, 1126 nr. 2323.
⁶¹ Su questo personaggio e sua moglie vd. ora T.D. BARNES, *An urban prefect and his wife*, «Class. Quart.» 56 (2006), 249-256.
⁶² Si tratta di un epistilio.
⁶³ L'iscrizione, attualmente irreperibile, è lacunosa.
⁶⁴ F. GUIDOBALDI, in *LTUR*, II, 79, s. v. Domus: Naeratius Cerealis.
⁶⁵ A. VISCOGLIOSI, in *LTUR*, I, 51, s. v. Apollo, aedes in Circo.
⁶⁶ F. GUIDOBALDI, in *LTUR*, II, 149, s. v. Domus: Memmius Vitrasius Orfitus s. Honorius.
⁶⁷ *Pont. Vestae, XVvir s.f., pont. Solis*: vd. RÜPKE, *Fasti*, 1150 nr. 2433.
⁶⁸ A questo personaggio si riferisce forse anche *CIL*, VI 31396 = 40781, ma il suo nome è completamente integrato.
⁶⁹ Incerto se a questo personaggio o ad Anicius Auchenius Bassus p. u. 382 (vd. sotto, nr. 88) si riferisca un frammento di epistilio rinvenuto recentemente nel Foro di Traiano, su cui vd. E. LA ROCCA, *La nuova immagine dei Fori Imperiali. Appunti in margine agli scavi*, «Mitt. Deutsch. Arch. Inst. (Römisch.)» 108 (2001), 181-184 e J. LIPPS, *Zur Datierung der spätantiken Portikus des Caesarforums. Literarische Quellen und archäologischer Befund*, «Mitt. Deutsch. Arch. Inst. (Römisch.)» 114 (2008), 398-399.
⁷⁰ Cui si aggiungano A. CAMERON, *The funeral of Iunius Bassus*, «Zeitschr. Pap. Ep.» 139 (2002), 288-292 e PORENA, *Le origini*, 342-356.
⁷¹ È possibile, ma non certo, che a questo personaggio si ricerischi il *carmen* con dedica a Libero *CIL*, VI 462, recentemente ripubblicato da M. G. SCHMIDT, *Textkritische Beiträge zu Carmina Latina Epigraphica*, «Rend. Pont. Ac. Arch.» 72 (1999-2000), 325-329, su cui vd. anche M.G. GRANINO, in *LTUR – Suburbium*, III, 232, s.v. Liberi Patris lous.
⁷² F. GUIDOBALDI, in *LTUR*, II, 204-205, s. v. Domus: Turcii.
⁷³ *XVvir s. f.*: vd. RÜPKE, *Fasti*, 1330 nr. 3298.
⁷⁴ Recentemente ripresa da G.A. CECCONI, *Avianio Simmaco, Costante e l'andamento delle carriere senatorie nel tardo impero*, «Stud. Doc. Hist. Iur.» 62 (1996), 343-355.
⁷⁵ Il testo termina con «vacat».
⁷⁶ Cui si aggiunga R. LIZZI, *Senatori, popolo, papi*, Bari 2004, 447-454.
⁷⁷ RÜPKE, *Fasti*, 798 nr. 808.
⁷⁸ *In his praediis*.
⁷⁹ Però il testo lo definisce *tauroboliatus*.
⁸⁰ *Pater ierofanta, profeta Isidis, pontifex Solis*: vd. RÜPKE, *Fasti*, 869 nr. 1130.
⁸¹ A questo personaggio si riferiscono anche *CIL*, VI 1779 a e 1781, escluse perché troppo incerte e frammentarie. Possibile, ma non certo, che a Pretestato si riferisca anche

un'iscrizione onoraria rinvenuta in una villa in Valdarno, pubblicata da F. BERTI e G.A. CECCONI, *Vettio Agorio Pretestato in un'epigrafe inedita del Valdarno?*, «Ostraka» 6 (1997), 15-21.

[82] Traduzione greca di *ex praefectis urbis Romae*.

[83] Sul complesso delle iscrizioni *CIL*, VI 1777-1780 vd., in particolare, H. NIQUET, *Monumenta virtutum titulique*, Stuttgart 2000, 237-252, cui si aggiungano G. POLARA, *Iscrizioni e propaganda: il cippo tombale di Pretestato*, in *Letteratura e propaganda nell'Occidente latino da Augusto ai regni romano-barbarici*, a cura di F.E. CONSOLINO, Roma 2000, 107-126 e M. KAHLOS, *Vettius Agorius Praetextatus. A Senatorial Life in Between*, Helsinki-Rome 2002, 216-225.

[84] F. GUIDOBALDI, in *LTUR*, II, 164, s. v. Domus: Vettius Agorius Praetextatus; vd. anche R. COATES-STEPHENS, *The Reuse of Ancient Statuary...*, 179.

[85] *Augur, pontifex Vestae, pontifex Solis, quindecemvir, curialis Herculis, sacratus Libero et Eleusiniis, hierophanta, neocorus, tauroboliatus, pater patrum*: vd. RÜPKE, *Fasti*, 1363-1364 nr. 3468.

[86] Su cui vd. ora R. FREI-STOLBA, *Coelia Concordia, la dernière Grand Vierge Vestale, et la partecipation des femmes au discours politique du IVe s. apr. J.-C.*, in *Les femmes antiques entre sphère privée et sphère publique*, a cura di R. FREI-STOLBA, A. BIELMAN e O. BIANCHI, Bern 2003, 281-315; S. CONTI, *Tra integrazione ed emarginazione: le ultime Vestali*, «Stud. Histor. Hist. Ant.» 21 (2003), 217.

[87] Della sua adesione alla fede cristiana sappiamo da varie fonti (*Coll. Avell.* 8-10 e Prud., *c. Symm.*, I 554-557), citate dalla *PLRE*, I, 641.

[88] F. GUIDOBALDI, in *LTUR*, II, 148-149, s. v. Domus: Q. Clodius Hermogenianus Olybrius.

[89] Tutti i testi epigrafici relativi al proconsolato di Ampelio sono riportati da E. GROAG, *Die Reichsbeamten von Achaia in spätrömischer Zeit*, Budapest 1946, 42.

[90] L. CHIOFFI, in *LTUR*, II, 311-312, s. v. Forum Palatini, cui si aggiunga F.A. BAUER, *Einige weniger bekannte Platzanlagen im spätantiken Rom*, in *Pratum Romanum. Richard Krautheimer zum 100. Geburtstag*, Wiesbaden 1997, 45-46.

[91] *XVvir s. f. + taurobolio crioboliogue perfecto*: vd. RÜPKE, *Fasti*, 882 nr. 1194.

[92] Vd. ora *SupplIt – Imagines, Latium Vetus*, 1, nr. 885.

[93] Traduzione greca di *ex praefectis urbis*.

[94] Traduzione greca di *ex consule et ex praefectis praetorio*.

[95] Della sua adesione al cristianesimo sappiamo da Prud., *C. Symm.*, I, 558. Vd. in proposito T.D. BARNES e R.W. WESTALL, *The conversion of the Roman aristocracy...*, 50-61.

[96] Traduzione greca di *ex proconsule et ex praefectis urbis*.

[97] Ora ripubblicata da L. CHIOFFI, *Museo Provinciale Campano di Capua. La raccolta epigrafica*, Capua 2005, 109, nr. 111.

[98] A questo personaggio si riferisce anche l'iscrizione *CIL*, VI 37132, esclusa perché troppo frammentaria

[99] Potrebbe essere cristiano, se è sua la famosa lucerna con l'iscrizione *Dominus legem dat* (*ILCV* 1592).

[100] Traduzione greca di *praefectus urbis*.

[101] Traduzione greca di *proconsul Campaniae*.

[102] F. GUIDOBALDI, in *LTUR*, II, 183-184, s. v. Domus: Q. Aurelius Symmachus s. Eusebius; vd. anche R. COATES-STEPHENS, *The Reuse of Ancient Statuary...*, 180.

[103] *Pont. maior*: vd. RÜPKE, *Fasti*, 811 nr. 876.

[104] A questo personaggio si riferisce anche *CIL*, VI 41343, esclusa perché troppo frammentaria.

[105] A questo personaggio si riferisce anche *CIL*, VI 41334, esclusa perché troppo frammentaria.

[106] Vd. anche *EAOR*, VI, 460.

[107] A questo personaggio si riferisce anche l'iscrizione onoraria dal Foro di Cesare *CIL*, VI 41384, esclusa perché troppo frammentaria; sulla documentazione epigrafica relativa a suo padre Virius Nicomachus Flavianus – che in *CIL*, VI 1783 non viene ricordato come *pontifex maior*, carica presente invece nell'iscrizione onoraria di ambito privato CIL, VI 1782 – vd. C.W. HENRICK JR., *History and Silence. Purge and Rehabilitation of Memory in Late Antiquity*, Austin 2000, in part. 17-18 e 35.

[108] Sulla sua adesione al cristianesimo vd. *PLRE*, I, 493.

[109] A questo personaggio si riferiscono anche alcune iscrizioni probabilmente relative a un restauro della *curia* (*CIL*, VI 37128 cfr. pp. 4821-4822 e *CIL*, VI 40803 a), escluse perché troppo incerte e frammentarie.

[110] Tra il 410 e il 418 si colloca anche un restauro della curia eseguito, verosimilmente in qualità di prefetto urbano, da Fl. Ianuarius, noto da una serie di frammenti di epistilio (*CIL*, VI 41378), che consentono di ricostruire un testo che originariamente doveva essere piuttosto lungo ed interessante, ma qui escluso perché troppo lacunoso.

[111] Sulla sua conversione al cristianesimo in punto di morte vd. A. CHASTAGNOL, *Le senateur Volusien et la conversion d'une famille de l'arisotocratie romaine au Bas-Empire*, «Rev. Et. Anc.» 58 (1956), 241-253.

[112] A questo personaggio si riferisce anche l'iscrizione *CIL*, VI 41376, esclusa perché troppo frammentaria. Vd. anche *EAOR*, VI, 511-512.

[113] L'iscrizione è frammentaria.

[114] C. LEGA, in *LTUR*, II, 312, s. v. Forum Petronii Maximi, cui si aggiunga F.A. BAUER, *Einige weniger bekannte Platzanlagen...*, 37-41.

[115] A questo personaggio si riferisce anche un frammento di iscrizione onoraria dal Foro di Augusto (*CIL*, VI 41390), che conserva parte del suo *cursus honorum*, esclusa perché troppo frammentaria.

[116] E. PAPI, in *LTUR*, II, 346, s. v. Forum Sibidi, cui si aggiunga F.A. BAUER, *Einige weniger bekannte Platzanlagen...*, 29-37.

[117] Su cui vd. ora H. NIQUET, *Monumenta virtutum...*, 253-259.

[118] A questo personaggio si riferisce verosimilmente anche un'iscrizione relativa ad un restauro del Colosseo (*CIL*, VI 32085, ripubblicata in *EAOR*, VI, 67-86), esclusa perché la restituzione del suo nome rimane ipotetica ed il testo è molto lacunoso.

Rita Lizzi Testa

Legislazione imperiale e reazione pagana: i limiti del conflitto

La convinzione che la legislazione antipagana, e quella di Teodosio I in particolare, abbia avuto un peso decisivo nell'assicurare il trionfo del cristianesimo, da Gibbon a Burckhard e per quasi tutto il Novecento senza soluzione di continuità, è stata condivisa da chiunque si sia occupato in vario modo della fine del paganesimo[1]. Oggi, tuttavia, è messa in discussione da un'ampia riflessione sulla reale efficacia delle leggi imperiali in generale e, in modo particolare, di quelle emanate contro il culto e i collegi religiosi tradizionali. I risultati delle ricerche più recenti sulla natura e i fini del Codice Teodosiano in quanto compilazione[2], così come l'analisi di alcune costituzioni-chiave, insistono sul valore geograficamente limitato della maggior parte delle disposizioni imperiali[3]. Le stesse misure antipagane, lungi dall'essere espressione di una politica religiosa autonoma,

---

[1] La generalità di tale opinione è stata sottolineata da P. Brown, *Christianization and Religious Conflict*, in *Cambridge Ancient History*, eds. Av. Cameron, P. Garnsey, XIII: *The Late Empire A. D. 337-425*, Cambridge 2000, 632-664, spec. 633; per un quadro della tradizione storiografica sviluppatasi dall'Ottocento ai nostri giorni, in riferimento alla funzione svolta dalle misure legislative di Graziano, R. Lizzi Testa, *Christian Emperor, Vestal Virgins, and Priestly Colleges: reconsidering the End of Roman Paganism*, «AnTard» 15 (2007), 251-262, spec. 252. Alcune eccezioni si segnalano a partire dagli anni Ottanta del Ventesimo secolo: R. Mac Mullen, *Christianising the Roman Empire (AD100-400)*, New Haven 1984, 95.

[2] T. Honoré, *The Making of the Theodosian Code*, «ZSS RA» 103 (1986), 133-222; *Part I. Compilation*, in *The Theodosian Code*, eds. J. Harries, I. Wood, London 1993, 17-94; J. Matthews, *Laying Down the Law: A Study of the Theodosian Code*, New Haven 2000.

[3] Le costituzioni avevano di solito applicazione limitata all'area geografica della quale i funzionari nominati erano responsabili: così già G.I. Luzzatto, *Ricerche sull'applicazione delle costituzioni imperiali nelle province*, in *Scritti di diritto romano in onore di C. Ferrini*, a cura di G.G. Archi, Milano 1946, 265-293; J. Gaudemet, *Le partage legislatif dans la seconde moitié du IVe siècle*, in *Studi in onore di P. De Francisci*, 2 Milano 1956, 319-354; e, più recentemente, B. Sirks, *From the Theodosian to the Justinian Code*, in *AARC* 6, Perugia 1986, 265-302.

anche quando minacciassero enormi pene, erano per lo più frutto delle sollecitazioni di questo o quel funzionario e raramente erano applicate con rigore; per la loro occasionalità e la stringente contingenza, la forte contradditorietà, una finalità diretta a convertire più con la logica delle minacce che con l'uso reale della forza, difficilmente esse potrebbero aver agito come fattore di conversione, persuadendo i cittadini dell'Impero e gli «ultimi pagani di Roma» a mutare la propria fede[4].

Che questo fosse il caso anche della legislazione antipagana di Teodosio sembrerebbe confermato dalla scarsa rilevanza che le fonti contemporanee attribuirono all'impegno legislativo di quell'imperatore: esaltato in parallelo a Costantino per aver portato a compimento il processo di smantellamento del culto pagano che da quello era stato avviato, Teodosio fu elogiato per averlo realizzato grazie a virtù come *fides*, *pietas*, *castitas* e ad altre manifestazioni filocristiane[5], non per quella capacità di emanare e rendere effettive le leggi antipagane, su cui si è indirizzata l'attenzione degli studiosi moderni. Anche dopo la pubblicazione del Codice Teodosiano, lo *scholastikòs* Sozomeno si preoccupò di citare solo una piccola

---

[4] Questa, in sostanza, la posizione di R.M. ERRINGTON, *Christian Accounts of the Religious Legislation of Theodosius I*, «Klio» 79 (1997)/2, 398-443. Con attenzione alla terminologia religiosa, che compare nelle costituzioni del IV secolo, D. HUNT, *Christianising the Roman Empire*, in *The Theodosian Code...*, 143-158. Con posizione sfumata, J. HARRIES, *Law Empire in Late Antiquity*, Cambridge 1999, 77-98. Sulle difficoltà di tracciare le linee di una coerente «politica religiosa imperiale» nelle costituzioni raccolte nel decimo *titulus* del sedicesimo libro del Codice Teodosiano (*de paganis, sacrificiis et templis*), N. McLYNN, *Pagans in a Christian Empire*, in *A Companion to Late Antiquity*, ed. P. ROUSSEAU, Oxford 2009, 572-587, spec. 574-575. Per la produzione legislativa contro gli eretici in particolare, si vedano ora le importanti riflessioni di M.V. ESCRIBANO, *Los emperadores repiensan sus leyes: rectificaciones y revocaciones en* Codex *Theodosianus 16,5*, in *Istituzioni, carismi ed esercizio del potere (IV-VI secolo d. C.). Convegno Internazionale, Perugia 25-27 giugno 2008*, a cura di R. LIZZI TESTA, G. BONAMENTE, Bari 2010, 207-226.

[5] V. NERI, *La figura di Costantino negli scrittori cristiani dell'età di Onorio*, in *Simblos. Scritti di storia antica*, Bologna 1995, 229-264. Diverso, tuttavia, è ciò che fu detto di Costantino: secondo Eusebio, le leggi stesse divennero più cristiane sotto tale imperatore, avendo questi rimodellato l'antica legislazione per renderla «più santa»: Eus. *Vita Const.* 4, 26. Naturalmente il dibattito moderno sull'argomento è ampio: vd. T.D. BARNES, *Constantine and Eusebius*, Cambridge, MA-London 1981, 52 e più recentemente, per l'influenza del cristianesimo sulla legislazione relativa alla famiglia, A. GIARDINA, *The family in the Late Roman World*, in *Cambridge Ancient History*, XIV: *Late Antiquity: Empire and Successors, A. D. 425-600*, eds. Av. CAMERON, B. WARD-PERKINS, M. WHITBY, Cambridge 2000, 392-415.

parte di quelle misure, e per di più in modo impreciso e con notevoli sfasature cronologiche[6].

Non intendo in questo breve contributo discutere nel suo complesso tale modello interpretativo. In generale, esso ha il merito di liberare l'immagine dell'Impero tardoantico da alcuni di quei caratteri che la supposta superproduzione legislativa di imperatori autocrati gli aveva attribuito, quali il dirigismo economico, l'oppressione fiscale, il centralismo burocratico, la corruzione dilagante[7]: caratteristiche queste, che sembrano piuttosto coniate negli ultimi decenni dell'Ottocento, in analogia agli effetti provocati dalle soluzioni autoritarie del neonato impero federale tedesco, guidato dal «cancelliere di ferro» e dal suo Kaiser[8]. Tuttavia, il tipo di relazione tra imperatore, leggi e sudditi che il nuovo modello prefigura – tale per cui l'imperatore, privo di ogni progettualità politica, emana solo rescritti su richiesta e con la coscienza della loro sostanziale inefficacia – sembra contenere alcuni ovviabili eccessi.

Per rimanere nei limiti della legislazione antipagana di Teodosio e delle conseguenze che poté produrre, la difficoltà nell'esprimere certezze assolute dovrebbe nascere in primo luogo proprio dalla considerazione che, per sua natura, la compilazione teodosiana ha conservato solo una piccola parte della produzione legislativa del periodo. In alcuni casi quelle che, al confronto delle leggi conservate, paiono discrasie o confusioni degli storici ecclesiastici, potrebbero viceversa derivare dalla loro conoscenza anche di testi diversi da quelli conservati nella compilazione. Per fare pochi esempi, gli autori del Codice Teodosiano preferirono eliminare il cosiddetto Editto di tolleranza emanato da Valentiniano I *in exordio imperii*[9];

---

[6] R.M. ERRINGTON, *Christian Account...*, 398-443.

[7] T. HONORÉ, *Roman Law AD 200-400: From Cosmopolis to Rechtstaat?*, in *Approaching Late Antiquity: The Transformation from Early to Late Empire*, eds. S. SWAIN, M. EDWARDS, Oxford-New York 2004, 109-132.

[8] R. LIZZI TESTA, *L'aristocrazia senatoria e la corte dell'imperatore: l'ottica rovesciabile di centro e periferia al tempo di Valentiniano I*, in *Poteri centrali e poteri periferici nella tarda antichità. Confronti conflitti*, a cura di L. DI PAOLA, D. MINUTOLI, Firenze 2007, 109-130, spec. 110-111.

[9] I compilatori del Codice Teodosiano non ne eliminarono però la menzione in *CTh* 9, 16, 9 (371 Mai. 29 *ad senatum: Haruspicinam ego nullum cum maleficiorum causis habere consortium iudico neque ipsam aut aliquam praeterea concessam a maioribus religionem genus esse arbitror criminis. Testes sunt leges a me in exordio imperii mei datae, quibus unicuique, quod animo inbibisset, colendi libera facultas tributa est. Nec haruspicinam reprehendimus, sed nocenter exerceri vetamus*), permettendo così di conoscerne il contenuto. La disposizione fu di grande importanza per rendere noto l'orientamento politico-religioso di Valentiniano I: R. LIZZI TESTA, *Senatori, popolo,*

e, se Ambrogio – costretto dalle circostanze – non avesse citato il rescritto di Valentiniano I in base al quale dovevano essere i vescovi a giudicare i vescovi su questioni di fede, senza interferenze da parte dell'imperatore, non avremmo alcuna informazione su tale importante delibera imperiale[10]. Nell'uno e nell'altro caso, il mutamento dei rapporti tra imperatore e Chiesa, per come essi erano evoluti nell'epoca di Teodosio II, dovette convincere i compilatori del Codice Teodosiano dell'inutilità di riportare leggi che erano state superate dai fatti.

Non diversamente, il poco interesse riservato alle misure antipagane o antieretiche di Teodosio da autori come Ambrogio, Agostino, Rufino, persino Sozomeno – benché quest'ultimo avesse dato programmatica assicurazione di considerare come parte essenziale della propria narrazione le leggi «emanate per stabilire e onorare la religione cattolica»[11] – potrebbe non essere semplicemente dovuto al fatto che essi le giudicavano poco significative quale strumento di conversione[12]. Riconoscere il ruolo preponderante della legislazione imperiale in materia di cristianizzazione avrebbe significato attribuire a motivi esterni il compimento di un disegno divino (di cui la sconfitta del politeismo era parte integrante), che si credeva già realizzato con la venuta di Cristo sulla terra. In base a tale fiducia, ogni martirio celebrava di nuovo il sacrificio di Cristo e ne iterava le vittorie sul Male e sulla menzogna. Non solo, dunque, in seguito alla conversione di Costantino, ovvero ancora sotto Teodosio, ma persino subito dopo il martirio di Lorenzo durante la persecuzione di Valeriano nel 258, parve lecito descrivere come già avvenuta la fuga dei demoni da tutte le regioni della terra, la vittoria totale sugli idoli del paganesimo, la distruzione di tutti i loro templi, ovvero la diserzione del tempio di Vesta, la conversione di

---

papi. *Il governo di Roma al tempo dei Valentiniani*, Bari 2004, 229-235 e Appendice II, 251-252.

[10] Una disposizione su tale soggetto fu citata da Ambrogio a proprio sostegno, nella lettera inviata a Valentiniano II nel marzo 386 per dare legittimità al proprio rifiuto di presentarsi davanti al concistoro e di sottoporsi a un confronto dottrinale con il vescovo omeo Mercurino Aussenzio, di cui giudice arbitrale sarebbe stato il giovane imperatore Valentiniano II: Ambr. *Ep.* 75 (Maur. 21), 2; 4- 5: *Haec enim verba rescripti sunt hoc est sacerdotes de sacerdotibus voluit iudicare*. Sul significato del rescritto, l'occasione in cui fu emesso e quella in cui Ambrogio fu spinto a citarlo, R. Lizzi Testa, *La* certatio *fra Ambrogio e Mercurino Aussenzio, ovvero a proposito di una deposizione mancata*, in *Ambrogio e la sua basilica*, «Studia Ambrosiana» 3 (2009), 39-68, spec. 39 e 60.

[11] Soz. *HE* 1, 8, 14.

[12] Così, invece, R.M. Errington, *Christian Accounts...*, 406, specialmente per quanto riguarda la narrazione di Rufino e di Socrate.

Luperci e Flamini, la fine di ogni sacrificio cruento, la sconfitta definitiva dell'empietà[13]. Giudicati di volta in volta come racconti tendenziosi, di cui tuttavia alcuni sono parsi storicamente più credibili di altri, essi sono espressione di una rappresentazione cristiana della storia della salvezza per la quale il trionfo della Chiesa era semplicemente preordinato[14].

Alla stessa concezione appartiene l'idea che lotta e conflitto erano inevitabili quanto la vittoria finale: era essa stessa parte dell'immaginario cristiano, frutto di una visione del mondo e della storia che i cristiani erano avvezzi ad esprimere in forme di opposizione binaria: cristiani-pagani, *religio-superstitio*, unico vero Dio-moltitudine di demoni, verità-menzogna, luce-tenebre, Gerusalemme-Babilonia, città-deserto, templi dei demoni-chiese di Dio, cultura pagana-religione cristiana[15]. Si trattava di strategie retoriche utili a costruire, mantenere, consolidare un'identità cristiana costantemente minacciata dal vivere nel mondo; favorirono un'interpretazione delle vicende contemporanee, in cui gli accadimenti reali erano inestricabilmente connessi con quanto si credeva realizzato per l'intervento provvidenziale di Dio: dell'efficacia di tali rappresentazioni, a stento gli studiosi riescono a distaccarsi.

Attribuire all'attività legislativa imperiale la vittoria del cristianesimo sul paganesimo significava, inoltre, assegnare all'imperatore un ruolo, che la Chiesa della fine del IV secolo non desiderava più riconoscergli. Chi si mostra convinto della pura contingenza delle singole emanazioni legislative non può dimenticare che altrettanto contingente e soggetto a variazioni fu il modo in cui i cristiani descrissero la funzione dell'imperatore nella Chiesa. Alcuni autori dimenticarono persino le compromissioni ariane di Costantino – su cui ancora pochi anni prima non aveva saputo tacere il ben poco diplomatico Gerolamo[16] –, pur di elogiare in termini appropria-

---

[13] PRUD. *Perist.* 2.1-20. Sul significato della rappresentazione prudenziana, vd. ora R. LIZZI TESTA, *La conversione dei «cives», la evangelizzazione dei «rustici»: alcuni esempi fra IV e VI secolo*, in *Città e campagna. LVI Settimana di Studio (Spoleto 27 marzo-1aprile 2008)*, Spoleto 2009, 115-150.

[14] P. BROWN, *Christianization...*, 634-635.

[15] M. KAHLOS, *Debate and Dialogue. Christian and Pagan Culture c. 360-430*, Aldershot, 2007, 1-10. Vedi già C. SOTINEL, *La disparition des lieux de culte païens en Occident. Enjeux et méthode*, in *Hellénisme & Christianisme*, eds. M. NARCY, E. REBILLARD, Villeneuve d'Ascq 2004, 35-55, spec. 53, sulla «necessità» dei cristiani di trovare templi da distruggere e pratiche pagane da combattere per poter rinnovare l'attualità del trionfo del cristianesimo.

[16] HIER. *Chron.* 234 c (Helm): *Constatinus extremo vitae suae tempore ab Eusebio Nicomedensi episcopo baptizatus in Arrianum dogma declinat. A quo usque in praesens tempus ecclesiarum rapinae et totius orbis est secuta discordia.*

ti, confrontandolo al primo imperatore cristiano, il *religiosus Theodosius*. Tuttavia, alla fine del IV secolo, come la lode di Costantino fu costruita esaltando non il principe, ma la *fides* prodotta in lui da Dio attraverso i chiodi ricevuti dalla croce di Cristo – che sua madre e non lui, aveva trovato –[17], così l'appena defunto Teodosio fu apprezzato soprattutto per essersi fatto strumento della volontà divina: solo grazie a Dio, egli aveva conseguito la vittoria definitiva sull'ultimo rigurgito di paganesimo, perché era Dio a garantire la permanenza vittoriosa al potere dell'imperatore, che si era fatto ricettacolo di vera *fides*; allo stesso modo, solo Dio poteva assicurare che quel potere fosse trasmesso agli eredi legittimi[18]. Siamo ben lontani dalla rappresentazione eusebiana di Costantino isapostolo, intermediario tra il Re del cielo e la terra degli uomini, imitatore dello stesso Figlio incarnato, o *Logos*[19].

Alla fine del IV secolo, dunque, il terreno era ben preparato perché Rufino descrivesse l'epoca di Teodosio come il tempo decisivo per il collasso del culto pagano: culto, che non le leggi imperiali distrussero, ma che *naturaliter* venne meno durante il regno di quell'imperatore. Nacque infatti con Rufino quel mito della fine improvvisa del paganesimo, intorno

---

[17] AMBR. *De obitu Theodosii* 48, 10-13 e 50, 1-4: per la digressione con cui Ambrogio chiuse il suo discorso avviando la leggenda dell'*inventio* della vera croce da parte di Elena, madre di Costantino, si veda W. STEIDLE, *Die Leichenrede des Ambrosius für Kaiser Theodosius und die Helena-Legende*, «Vigiliae Christianae» 32 (1978), 94-112, spec. 94; F. CONSOLINO, *Il significato dell'inventio crucis nel de obitu Theodosii*, «Annali della Facoltà di Lettere e Filosofia» V (1984) Firenze 1985, 161-180, spec. 176-177; J.W. DRIJVERS, *Helena Augusta: the Mother of Constantine the Great and Her Finding of the True Cross*, Leiden 1992; H.J.W. DRIJVERS, J.W. DRIJVERS, *The Finding of the True Cross. The Judas Kyriakos Legend in Syriac. Introduction Text and Translation*, Louvain 1997.

[18] Per l'evoluzione del pensiero cristiano, soprattutto in Ambrogio e, nella parte orientale dell'Impero, in Giovanni Crisostomo, vd. G. BONAMENTE, *Apoteosi e imperatori cristiani*, in *I cristiani e l'impero nel IV secolo. Colloquio sul cristianesimo nel mondo antico. Atti del Convegno (17-18 dic. 1987)*, a cura di G. BONAMENTE, A. NESTORI, Macerata 1988, 107-142, spec. 133; P. SINISCALCO *Gli imperatori romani e il cristianesimo nel IV secolo*, in *Legislazione imperiale e religione nel IV secolo,* a cura di J. GAUDEMET, P. SINISCALCO, G.L. FALCHI, Roma 2000, 67-120, spec. 99-100; R. LIZZI TESTA, *The Late Antique Bishop: Image and Reality*, in *A Companion to Late Antiquity*, 525-538, spec. 525-526. Per il carattere provvidenziale e miracoloso della vittoria del principe cristiano, che la consegue per la sua *pietas*, si veda M. FORLIN PATRUCCO, *Il tema politico della vittoria e della croce in Ambrogio e nella tradizione ambrosiana*, in *Paradoxos Politeia. Studi patristici in onore di Giuseppe Lazzati*, Milano 1979, 410-413. Per la trasmissione del potere del sovrano *pius* ai legittimi eredi, vd. anche AMBR. *De fide* 2, 16, 141.

[19] EUS. *Vita Const.* 4, 71, 2; *Laus Constantini* 2, 3-5.

al quale tanta storiografia moderna e contemporanea ha tentato di ricostruire i particolari storici della inevitabile parabola dell'antica religione romana. Molti studiosi tuttavia non hanno dato il giusto peso al fatto che il racconto cristiano dell'età di Onorio – dominato dalla grave crisi della presa di Roma di Alarico, dopo i primi segni di una divisione delle due *partes Imperii* – «aveva bisogno di porre un punto fermo agli eventi di un secolo ondeggiante»[20], e che tale narrazione significativamente non fece dell'opera di Teodosio, bensì del tempo in cui quegli aveva regnato, il momento finale di un processo avviato dalla conversione di Costantino.

La consapevolezza che la ricostruzione cristiana della storia è ben più che un semplice racconto tendenzioso, da cui estrapolare di volta in volta alcuni dati storicamente più verisimili, come impedisce di accreditare *tout court* la fede di Rufino in una «caduta di botto» (*conlapsus est*) del paganesimo, infine venuto meno sotto il pio Teodosio, altrettanto rende difficile credere che proprio le leggi emanate da quell'imperatore – ancorché suscitare la reazione degli «ultimi pagani di Roma» –, abbiano potuto decidere la fine del politeismo antico.

La brillante analisi cui Malcom Errington ha assoggettato la *Cunctos populos*, mostrando al confronto con il testo di Sozomeno che i compilatori del Codice Teodosiano ne divisero il testo in due rubriche, così snaturandone la stesura originaria e rendendo non perspicui i motivi reali per cui Teodosio era stato spinto a emanarla[21], conferma in modo definitivo quanto già altri in precedenza, sulla base di osservazioni diverse, avevano intuito. Lungi dal voler imporre a tutti i sudditi una fede definita per legge[22], Teodosio rivolse al popolo di Costantinopoli, ma soprattutto al suo al

---

[20] Così P. Brown, *Christianization*..., 634, parafrasando il titolo *The Wavering Fourth Century* del quarto capitolo di P. Chuvin, *A Chronicle of the Last Pagans*, Cambridge, MA, 1990, 36.

[21] R.M. Errington, *Christian Accounts*..., 411-416. Il contesto in cui maturò la decisione di Teodosio di emanare la *Cunctos populos* è dato da Soz. *HE* 7, 4, che razionalizza Socr. *HE* 5, 6, 3, secondo cui Teodosio si sarebbe accertato dell'ortodossia di Acolio prima di permettergli di battezzarlo. Il racconto di Sozomeno (soprattutto Soz. *HE* 7, 4, 5-6) permette di ricostruire il testo originale della disposizione, che fu diviso dai compilatori del Codice Teodosiano in due parti: *CTh* 16, 1, 2 e *CTh* 16, 2, 25, infatti, furono emanate nello stesso luogo (Tessalonica) il 28 febbraio (non il 27) del 380: W. Ensslin, *Die Religionspolitik des Kaisers Theodosius der Grossen*, «Sitzungsberichte der Bayerischen Akademie der Wissenschaften. Philosophisch-historische Klasse» 2 (1953), 16, n. 1; A. Lippold, *s. v. Theodosius* I (10), in *RE Suppl.*, XIII (1973), 956-958.

[22] Come si è creduto a causa dell'inserimento di *CTh* 16, 1, 2 nella rubrica *de fide catholica* del Codice Teodosiano, che il Codice di Giustiniano pose come prima della rubrica

clero in quanto principale responsabile della perpetuazione dell'eresia[23], indicazioni precise del culto che egli voleva fosse osservato nelle chiese della città, ove in pochi mesi si sarebbe trasferito. Non si trattava, pertanto, di un editto generale volto a definire l'ortodossia cristiana, come hanno creduto quanti l'hanno celebrata come «uno dei documenti più significativi nella storia europea»[24], bensì di una misura di circostanza per ristabilire l'ordine nella capitale orientale[25]; abbiamo altrove tentato d'individuare chi, nel 380, avrebbe potuto avere interesse a sollecitarne l'emissione[26].

Ed era per certo un rescritto, non una legge generale valevole per tutto l'Impero, anche la disposizione con cui Graziano, due anni dopo, avendo fatto rimuovere l'altare della Vittoria nella curia del senato, ridusse alcune importanti prerogative delle Vestali: Ambrogio stesso precisò che i privilegi dei pagani erano stati aboliti a Roma mediante rescritti[27]. Il testo legislativo non è pervenuto, ma un confronto tra i documenti pertinenti alla

---

De summa Trinitate et de fide catholica et ut nemo de ea publice contendere audeat (*CI* 1, 1, 1). I più tardi compilatori eliminarono la frase *nec conciliabula eorum ecclesiarum nomen accipere*, perché non più rilevante nel VI secolo, mentre essa viceversa esprime bene la volontà di Teodosio di proteggere la piccola comunità nicena da quanti «fuori di mente e insani» (*dementes vesanosque*) occupavano allora le chiese della capitale orientale.

[23] Come indica *CTh* 16, 2, 25 (*Qui divinae legis sanctitatem aut nesciendo confundunt aut neglegendo violant et offendunt, sacrilegium committunt*), che i compilatori del Codice Teodosiano inserirono nella rubrica *de episcopis, ecclesiis et clericis*.

[24] Così anche S. Williams, G. Friell, *The Empire at Bay*, London 1994, 53; al contrario, vedi ora R.M. Errington, *Roman Imperial Policy from Julian to Theodosius*, Chapel Hill 2006, 218.

[25] Già C. Pietri, *Damase et Théodose, communion orthodoxe et géographie politique*, in *Epéktasis. Mélanges Danielou*, Paris 1972, 627-34, spec. 628 = Id., *Christiana Respublica. Éléments d'une enquête sur le christianisme antique* (CÉFR, 234), II Roma 1997, 347-354.

[26] R. Lizzi Testa *La politica religiosa di Teodosio I. Miti storiografici e realtà storica*, «Rend. Mor. Acc. Lincei» s. 9 (1996)/7, 323-61, spec. 339-348, ove si suggerisce che *CTh* 16, 1, 2 fu formulata su indicazione di Acolio vescovo di Tessalonica, per rispondere alle richieste della piccola comunità nicena di Costantinopoli, alla cui guida Teodosio volle porre Gregorio di Nazianzo, dopo aver congedato l'omeo Demofilo. Gregorio, oltreché a Basilio, era legato ai generali di salda fede nicena (Saturnino, Ricomere e Vittore), i quali avevano suggerito a Graziano, dopo Adrianopoli, il richiamo del generale Teodosio, in quanto particolarmente esperto della situazione logistica del fronte orientale, ove l'esercito di Valente era stato annientato dai Goti.

[27] Ambr. *Ep.* 72 (Maur. 17), 5: *Sed haec (scl. privilegia) si iam sublata non essent, auferenda tuo imperio comprobarem. At cum per totum orbem a pluribus retro principibus inhibita interdictaque sint, Romae autem a fratre clementiae tuae, augustae memoriae Gratiano, fidei verae ratione sublata sint et datis antiquata rescriptis, ne, quaeso, vel fideliter statuta convellas vel fraterna praecepta rescindas.*

cosiddetta «questione *de ara Victoriae*», consente di credere che allora Graziano non bloccò i finanziamenti per i sacrifici pubblici, né abrogò le immunità per tutti i collegi sacerdotali romani, né confiscò i *fundi templorum* in tutto l'Impero, bensì bloccò alcuni privilegi di cui godevano le sole Vestali di Roma[28].

A dominare la tradizione antica e le opinioni degli studiosi anche contemporanei è stata, tuttavia, l'interpretazione che il vescovo di Milano seppe dare dell'episodio, suggerendola al lettore della sua raccolta epistolare – pubblicata intorno al 395[29] – anche visivamente. La disposizione a trittico della sua prima lettera a Valentiniano II, della *Relatio III* di Quinto Aurelio Simmaco e della sua seconda lettera all'imperatore, concepita come una risposta al testo del senatore pagano, doveva far dimenticare che si era trattato di una questione ufficiale dibattuta in senato, di cui il prefetto aveva riferito con la sua *Relatio* all'imperatore. L'episodio è trasformato in un confronto personale tra sé e Simmaco, tra la vecchia *superstitio* e la nuova *religio*, in cui i doni un tempo concessi ai sacerdoti dell'antico culto – e allora aboliti – erano raffrontati alla trascuratezza in cui erano tenute le Vergini cristiane, cui niente era garantito dall'imperatore, e i sacerdoti del vero Dio, assoggettati a forti restrizioni legislative[30]. In un quadro dominato dal conflitto tra due mondi e due sistemi religiosi non più conciliabili, le reali misure di Graziano sfumavano in un complesso di provvedimenti generali, identificati non per se stessi, bensì da una serie di azioni sacrileghe, che Valentiniano avrebbe commesso, se avesse accettato di abrogarli:

---

[28] Questo il risultato di una recente rilettura di AMBR. *Epp.* 72 (Maur. 17) e 73 (Maur. 17); *Ep. extra collectionem* 10 (Maur. 57), che Ambrogio scrisse nel 394 ad Eugenio, del breve cenno contenuto in *De obitu Valent.* 19, al confronto con SYMM. *Rel.* III: cfr. R. LIZZI TESTA, *Christian Emperor...*, 251-262.

[29] Sulla natura del X Libro della corrispondenza ambrosiana, che fu probabilmente Ambrogio stesso a pubblicare, si veda ora soprattutto J.H.W. LIEBESCHUETZ, C. HILL, *Ambrose of Milan. Political Letters and Speeches* (translated with an introduction and notes), Liverpool 2005, 36-46 e, per l'introduzione alle lettere qui esaminate, 61-63; 69-70; 78-80. Segue l'impostazione tradizionale R.M. ERRINGTON, *Roman Imperial Policy...*, 123 e 124 ove si suggerisce l'ipotesi, del tutto condivisibile, che l'iniziativa dei tagli al culto pagano fosse stata suggerita a Graziano dal prefetto urbano Anicius Auchenius Bassus.

[30] Ai preti cristiani, i quali non potevano più ricevere beni in eredità o in legati dalle vedove (*CTh* 16, 2, 20 del 30 Luglio 370 e *CTh* 16, 2, 22 del 1 dicembre 372), era stato imposto di rinunciare al patrimonio se avessero voluto godere delle immunità fiscali (*CTh* 12, 1, 99 da Milano il 18 Aprile 383 e *CTh* 12, 1, 104 da Constantinopoli il 7 Novembre 383).

costruire altari e finanziare i sacrifici profani, dare privilegi ai sacerdoti pagani e fornire fondi per i sacrifici tradizionali[31].

Accettando l'interpretazione ambrosiana, diffusa e vulgata dal sunto degli avvenimenti offertone nei primi decenni del V secolo da Paolino di Milano nella *Vita Ambrosii* – un testo la cui circolazione fu amplissima a partire dalla sua pubblicazione[32] –, la stessa disposizione, che secondo Simmaco vietava alle Vestali di ricevere terre in eredità[33], è stata considerata di portata generale e tale da ordinare l'incameramento dei *fundi templorum* di tutto l'impero nella *res privata* imperiale. Si è creduto, infatti, che a quella disposizione del 382 si riferissero i *constituta Gratiani* richiamati in una costituzione emanata a Ravenna da Onorio il 30 agosto 415[34]. Questo testo, viceversa, fornisce un'ottima prova del fatto che le costituzioni erano per lo più emanate in vista di situazioni locali, rimanendo per decenni inosservate. Dimostra anche, però, che una volta pubblicati, alcuni provvedimenti potevano essere richiamati a distanza di anni e, se necessario, fatti applicare retroattivamente. Tale procedimento, anche se in modo niente affatto lineare, agì sul processo di cristianizzazione: pur lentamente, si lasciò che venisse alterata la topografia urbana tradizionale, che le chiese si moltiplicassero e arricchissero, che il gruppo cattolico si consolidasse mentre il ceto dei sacerdoti pagani era vieppiù marginalizzato.

Priva del nome del destinatario, poiché risponde a una serie di situazioni verificatesi a Cartagine, *CTh* 16, 10, 20 avrà avuta l'intitolazione che le attribuisce il Codice di Giustiniano: al popolo di quella città, dunque,

---

[31] AMBR. *Ep.* 72 (Maur. 17), 3; 4; 9; *Ep. extra coll.* 10 (Maur. 57), 3-5; *Ep.* 73 (Maur. 18), 11-16.

[32] Il testo di Paolino ebbe una fortuna eccezionale a partire dall'età antica, essendo anche tra le pochissime opere latine tradotte in greco nell'VIII-IX secolo. Per le edizioni antiche e moderne, si veda *Paolino di Milano. Vita di S. Ambrogio*, a cura di M. PELLEGRINO, Roma 1961, 24-47, da completare con lo studio di L. RUGGINI, *Sulla fortuna della «Vita Ambrosii»*, «Athenaeum» 41 (1963), 98-110.

[33] SYMM. *Rel.* III, 13: *agros etiam verginibus et ministris deficientium voluntate legatos fiscus retentat.*

[34] *CTh* 16, 10, 20 = *Cod. Iust.* I, 11, 5: *popolo Carthaginiensi. Omnia loca, quae sacris error veterum deputabit, secundum divi Gratiani constituta nostrae rei iubemus sociari ita ut ex eo tempore, qui inhibitus est publicus sumptus superstitioni deterrimae exhiberi, fructus ab incubatoribus exigantur. Quod autem ex eo iure ubicumque ad singulas quasque personas vel precedentium principum largitas vel nostra maiestas voluit pervenire, id in eorum patrimoniis aeterna firmitate perduret. Quod non tam per Africam quam per omnes regiones in nostro orbe positas custodiri decernimus.* Per l'interpretazione tradizionale di tale costituzione, R. DELMAIRE, *Les lois religieuses des empereurs romains de Constantin à Théodose II (312-438). I. Code Théodosien Livre XVI*, Paris 2005, 460-462 con bibliografia.

fu rivolta. *Omnia loca, quae sacris error veterum deputavit* ha senz'altro il valore non di templi *tout court*, bensì di *fundi templorum*, essendo il valore di *deputavit* (utilizzato in due passi della costituzione) specifico per indicare non ciò che «apparteneva» ai templi, ma era stato messo a loro disposizione dall'imperatore[35]. Essa chiedeva che fosse reso funzionante un provvedimento di Graziano, che evidentemente aveva ordinato trenta anni prima l'annessione alla *res privata* delle terre dei templi di Cartagine.

Tale disposizione, infatti, si comprende solo alla luce delle misure che già Valentiniano I aveva adottato, al fine di abrogare le iniziative prese da Giuliano nei confronti di alcuni templi, che Costantino o i suoi figli avevano privato delle proprie rendite, venduti o regalati a chiese e privati[36]. Nel dicembre 364, infatti, il padre di Graziano aveva ordinato di trasferire di nuovo alla *res privata principis* tutti i beni *cum omni iure* che, appartenenti al patrimonio imperiale, erano stati attribuiti ai templi *per arbitrium divae memoriae Iuliani*[37]. L'anno successivo, evidentemente a fini applicativi e su richiesta, Valentiniano I precisò al *comes rerum privatarum Orientis* Caesarius, che si dovevano riportare sotto il controllo della *res privata* tutti i terreni e le pertinenze templari che, risultando allora in

---

[35] R. DELMAIRE, *Largesses sacrées et res privata. L'aerarium impérial et son administration du IVe au VIe siècle*, Roma 1989, p. 645. Sulle procedure di controllo e incameramento delle terre dei municipi e dei templi, che cominciano ad essere registrate nelle fonti a partire dai Severi, C.J. GODDARD, *The evolution of pagan sanctuaries in Late Antique Italy (fourth-sixth centuries A. D): a new administrative and legal framework. A paradox*, in *Les cités de l'Italie tardo-antique (IVe-VIe siècle). Institutions, économie, société, culture et religion*, eds. M. GHILARDI, C.J. GODDARD, P. PORENA, Roma 2006, 281-308.

[36] Per la devoluzione dei beni dei templi alle chiese, EUS. *VC* 3, 53, 56; 4, 28. Secondo gli autori più tardi, come Teofane, Cedreno e il *Chronicon Paschale*, questa sarebbe stata una misura generale: A. PIGANIOL, *L'Empire chrétien (325-395)*, Paris 1972², 57. Libanio (*Or.* 30, 38) ricordò che Costanzo II «diede in dono i templi ai propri cortigiani, come fossero stati cavalli, o schiavi, o cani, o coppe d'oro». Costantino, invece, aveva interdetto le petizioni sui beni dei templi (*CTh* 10, 10, 24), ma gli imperatori potevano donarli (LIB. *Or.* 17, 7; Amm. 22, 4, 3; cfr. *CTh* 16, 10, 20; 11, 20, 6) o venderli (*CI* 11, 70, 4): cfr. G. BONAMENTE, *Sulla confisca dei beni mobili dei templi in epoca costantiniana*, in *Costantino il Grande: dall'antichità all'Umanesimo* I, Macerata 1992, 171-201.

[37] *CTh* 5, 13, 3 *ad* Mamertinum (*PPO Italiae, Illyrici et Africae*), il 23 dicembre 364, da Milano: *Universa quae ex patrimonio nostro per arbitrium divae memoriae Iuliani in possessionem sunt translata templorum, sollicitudine sinceritatis tuae cum omni iure ad rem privatam nostram redire mandamus*; su cui *La legislazione di Valentiniano e Valente (364-375)* (Materiali per una palingenesi delle costituzioni tardo-imperiali, s. II, 4), a cura di F. PERGAMI, Milano 1993, 10-11 e 123.

iure templorum, erano state venduti o donati da diversi principi[38]. *Loca* e *praedia*, già parte del patrimonio del principe, finiti in possesso di privati per vendita o donazione, dovevano tornare alla *res privata*. Se la prima costituzione intendeva porre riparo alla politica con cui Giuliano aveva restituito *possessiones publicae* alle città e ai templi che ne erano stati privati, svincolando entrambe dai diritti del *res privata*, con la seconda si volevano annullare gli effetti di quella alienazione di beni templari (e forse persino di qualche tempio), che Costanzo II – forse imitando il padre – aveva perseguito.

Non conosciamo l'entità né dell'uno né dell'altro processo. D'altra parte, pur nei pochi anni di regno, Giuliano sembra avesse agito rapidamente, cercando di sanare i casi più eclatanti sottoposti alla sua attenzione[39]. La disposizione di Valentiniano I, dunque, pur con notevoli varianti regionali, dovette riguardare un certo numero di situazioni. Entrambe le

---

[38] *CTh* 10, 1, 8: *Universa loca vel praedia, quae nunc in iure templorum sunt quaeque a diversis principibus vendita vel donata sunt retracta, ei patrimonio, quod privatum nostrum est, placuit adgregari*. Per la datazione al 4 febbraio 365, vd. *La legislazione di Valentiniano...*, 7-11. L'ingiunzione di aggregare *universa loca vel praedia* al *patrimonium* (*patrimonium quod privatum nostrum est*), laddove in *CTh* 5, 13, 3 si ordinava di restituirli alla *res privata*, fa pensare a una già avvenuta fusione tra *patrimonium* e *res privata*: G. Bonamente, *Le città nella politica di Giuliano l'Apostata*, «Ann. Fac. Lett. e Filos. Macerata», XVI (1983), 35-65, spec. 66; E. Pack, *Städte und Steuern in der Politik Julians. Untersuchungen zu den Quellen eines Kaiserbildes*, Bruxelles 1986, 115-223; 229- 242.

[39] Per la politica di Giuliano, concretizzatasi in un editto inviato al prefetto del pretorio di Costantinopoli, smembrato in più rubriche del *Codex Theodosianus* (*CTh* 10, 3, 1; 11, 16, 10 e 23, 2 ; 12, 1, 50; 13, 1, 4; *CI* 11, 70, 2), vd. G. Bonamente, *Le città...*, 46-57. Anche il rescritto di Valente al *praeses* d'Asia mostra che per le municipalità si era tornati allo *status quo antea*, attribuendo di nuovo solo una parte (nel caso specifico un terzo) dei redditi dei *fundi* cittadini, sotto diretta sorveglianza del governatore. R. Delmaire, *Largesses sacrées...*, 643, sembra ritenere che Giuliano non tentò di restituire beni che, appartenenti un tempo alle città o ai templi, erano ormai gestiti dalla *res privata*, ma che semplicemente attribuì a qualche tempio *fundi* della *res privata*, con una sorta d'intervento evergetico in favore di questa o quella istituzione: Valentiniano I, dunque, avrebbe ordinato di restituire solo quei *fundi*. Cfr. ora G. Bonamente, *Politica antipagana e sorte dei templi da Costantino a Teodosio II*, in *Trent'anni di studio sulla Tarda Antichità: bilanci e prospettive. Congresso dell'Associazione di Studi Tardoantichi (Napoli 21-23 novembre 2007)*, a cura di U. Criscuolo, L. De Giovanni, Napoli 2009, 25-59. Giuliano tentò anche di far ricostruire alcuni templi demoliti da coloro, che ne avevano utilizzato i materiali per le proprie abitazioni private (Lib. *Or.* 18, 126; Amm. 22, 5, 2): l'azione si limitò probabilmente alla parte orientale dell'Impero, ove la depredazione doveva aver avuto maggior effetto: J.J. Arce, *Reconstrucciones de templos paganos en epoca del emperador Juliano (361-363 d. c.)*, «RSA» V (1975), 201-215.

costituzioni provocarono contestazioni e liti giudiziarie, come mostra un cursorio riferimento in un *Tractatus* di Zenone di Verona, vescovo forse di origine africana[40], il cui episcopato potrebbe essersi esteso tanto da permettergli di conoscere e fiancheggiare l'operato di Ambrogio[41], ma il cui inizio si colloca senz'altro intorno al 350/360[42]. Rivolto ai *domini* cristiani, Zenone ne denunciava il comportamento ipocrita: essi che conoscevano ogni zolla, ogni sassolino ed ogni sarchiello delle proprietà dei vicini, solo ignoravano i templi fumanti dei propri campi, che dissimulando volevano conservare. E non mancava giorno, che non imbastissero processi per impedire che venisse loro strappato il diritto dei templi[43]. In un sermone in cui vizi consueti e immorali pratiche pagane erano elencati con qualche topicità, il riferimento ai *fana fumantia* custoditi con dissimulazione e alle liti portate in tribunale (il termine *litigatis* è tecnico in tal senso), al fine di non perdere il *ius templorum*, paiono un riferimento diretto alla situazione innescata dalle costituzioni di Valentiniano I[44].

---

[40] Tale provenienza è stata supposta dalla particolare devozione da lui mostrata al martire di Cesarea di Mauretania Arcadio (ZENO, *Tract.* I, 39, p. 107-110) e dalla sua familiarità con le opere di Cipriano, Tertulliano e Lattanzio: *PChBE* 2 (Italie, 313-604), éd. C.-L. PIETRI, Rome 2000, 2377, n. 4.

[41] Già i fratelli Ballerini (PL 11, c. 335, n. 21), la cui edizione del 1739 fu accolta dal Migne nella *Patrologia Latina*, avevano notato una certa somiglianza tra ZENO, *Tract.* 14, 8, p. 59, 74-77 e *De officiis* II, 70 (cfr. II, 71 e 136-137), in cui Ambrogio ricordava di aver alienato gli arredi sacri della chiesa milanese per riscattare i prigionieri di guerra. Per quanto tale confronto non porti a conclusioni perentorie circa la supposta somiglianza tra i due testi, altri punti del trattato spingono pure a datarlo tra il 378 e il 379: R. LIZZI, *Fra prosopografia e antichità veronesi: il* consularis Venetiae et Histriae *Valerius Palladius*, «RIL» 122 (1988), 145-164, spec. 160-163.

[42] La durata dell'episcopato di Zenone fu tradizionalmente fissata tra il 362 e il 380 (Migne, PL 11, c. 81). A. BIGELMAIR, *Zeno von Verona*, Münster 1904, 51, lo restrinse di nove anni, calcolandone la lunghezza in base al numero dei differenti sermoni pasquali. La nuova edizione critica di B. Loefstedt (CC 22, Turnoult 1971), facendo conoscere meglio la natura della raccolta zenoniana, ha reso inconsistenti quelle argomentazione: *PChBE* 2 (Italie)..., 2376-2377.

[43] ZENO, *Tract.* I, 25, 10, 75: *Hic quaerite, Christiani, sacrificium vestrum an esse possit acceptum, qui vicinarum possessionum omnes glebulas, lapillos et sarculos nostis, in praediis autem vestris fumantia undique sola fana non nostis, quae, si vera dicenda sunt, dissimulando subtiliter custoditis. Probatio longe non est. Ius templorum ne quis vobis eripiat, cotidie litigatis.*

[44] Per i fratelli Ballerini, il *ius templorum* avrebbe indicato il diritto del *dominus* a concedere ai propri contadini l'autorizzazione a praticare nel proprio tempio i culti tradizionali (PL 11, c. 357-358), ma il confronto portato con *CTh* 16, 10, 12 (che Zenone comunque non poteva conoscere, essendo emanata l'8 novembre 392 a Costantinopoli), non sembra appropriato: anche in questa costituzione, infatti, *omnia loca... si*

Considerate le resistenze che incontrarono, le disposizioni di Valentiniano I dovettero essere largamente disattese: Graziano, dunque, iterò l'ingiunzione paterna, intervenendo laddove fosse necessario. I *constituta Gratiani* richiamati da Onorio dovevano essere un provvedimento rivolto ai templi di Cartagine: la riprova che quello di Graziano era stato un rescritto valevole solo per quella città, infatti, è nell'ordine di estenderne l'applicazione a tutta la parte occidentale dell'Impero, chiaramente espresso nel testo del 415[45].

Rispetto alle costituzioni della seconda metà del IV secolo, novità significative compaiono in quella del 415. Mentre in precedenza i *fundi*, che Giuliano aveva affidato alla gestione dei templi, dovevano essere ricondotti alla *res privata* e altrettanto era disposto per *loca* e *praedia* venduti o donati nel periodo precedente, Onorio lasciava cadere il principio della restituzione dei beni templari assegnati ai privati. Le contestazioni dei proprietari cristiani, cui Zenone accennava, non erano evidentemente cessate nel tempo e, non essendo state quelle disposizioni applicate, dopo trenta anni, l'imperatore riconosceva che le rendite di quei *loca*, attribuite ai privati o alla Chiesa dalla generosità dei principi precedenti o dalla propria Maestà, sarebbero rimaste in eterno nel loro patrimonio[46]. Sotto il controllo della *res privata*, in sostanza, sarebbero dovuti confluire i *fundi* che appartenevano ai templi pubblici di Cartagine, evidentemente già implicati nella disposizione di Graziano, e quelli di alcuni collegi pagani, menzionati di seguito[47]; poiché il godimento che i templi ne avevano tratto era da considerarsi usurpato, i responsabili

---

in iure turificantium è utilizzato per indicare la proprietà dei *loca* da parte di coloro che vi sacrificano. N. Tamassia, *Postille storiche e giuridiche alle opere di Zenone vescovo di Verona*, in Id., *Scritti di storia giuridica*, Padova 1964, 237-247, invece, lo identificò con i diritti dei proprietari sui proventi del culto officiato nei propri *fana*, ma tali proventi erano il frutto, più o meno occasionale, del *ius templorum*, non potevano coincidere con il *ius* stesso, che è dunque da intendersi come il diritto a mantenere quella proprietà, che Valentiniano I aveva allora rivendicato alla *res privata*.

[45] CTh 16, 10, 20 (= CI I, 11, 5): *Quod non tam per Africam quam per omnes regiones in nostro orbe positas custodiri decernimus*.

[46] CTh 16, 10, 20 (= CI I, 11, 5): *Quod autem ex eo iure ubicumque ad singulas quasque personas vel precedentium principum largitas vel nostra maiestas voluit pervenire, id in eorum patrimoniis aeterna firmitate perduret. Quod non tam per Africam quam per omnes regiones in nostro orbe positas custodiri decernimus. 2. Ea autem, quae multiplicibus constitutis ad venerabilem ecclesiam voluimus pertinere, Christiana sibi merito religio vindicabit, ita ut...*

[47] La costituzione è stata molto studiata per i riferimenti ai *sacerdotales paganae superstitionis* e ai *Frediani*: per tali collegi, bibliografia citata da R. Delmaire, *Les lois religieuses...*, 460-462 e *Annexe IV*, 492-494.

avrebbero dovuto rimborsare al fisco i proventi di una trentina d'anni. Nello spazio di una generazione, molti cambiamenti si lasciano cogliere nelle relazioni tra principe e *domini*: gli interessi del fisco cedevano a quelli di alcuni proprietari cristiani, fra cui le chiese. Ed inoltre, quella che per Valentiniano era stata una misura di tipo prettamente economico, al fine di rimpinguare la *res privata*, nel corso di un trentennio si era articolata sussumendo alcuni temi propri della polemica antipagana e trasformandosi in qualcosa di molto diverso. Omelie, lettere, sermoni vescovili avevano guidato le tappe di tale evoluzione.

Non diverse per natura, fini, ma anche per un'eventuale applicazione in un'area più vasta di quella prevista al momento dell'emissione, furono pure le costituzioni antipagane del 391-392: nel febbraio 391 furono proibiti i sacrifici, il culto delle statue e l'accesso ai templi[48]; seguendo l'interpretazione degli storici ecclesiastici, nel giugno dello stesso anno se ne sarebbe favorita la distruzione[49]; nel novembre 392, ogni forma di culto pagano fu messa al bando, dai sacrifici pubblici di animali alle offerte private d'incenso, di ghirlande, di vino; pesanti multe erano minacciate fino alla confisca della proprietà e alla pena capitale[50]. Poiché esse iterarono, in breve intervallo di tempo, divieti sempre più rigidi contro ogni manifestazione pagana, a una lunga tradizione storiografica sono parse espressione della programmatica volontà imperiale di smantellare ogni manifestazione pubblica dell'antico politeismo[51].

---

[48] *CTh* 16, 10, 10 (24 febbraio 391) *ad Albinum PPO*: l'*inscriptio* è errata perché all'epoca Ceionius Rufius Albinus era *PVR* (cfr. *PLRE* 1, s. v. Albinus 15) e altre leggi sono indirizzate a lui in qualità di prefetto urbano. Data la menzione, nel testo, di governatori provinciali, R. DELMAIRE, *Les lois religieuses...*, 439, n.7 suggerisce che quella riportata nel Codice Teodosiano fosse la copia indirizzata al prefetto di Roma di un testo di portata più generale destinato al prefetto del pretorio. Cautele circa il valore e l'efficacia generale di questa disposizione furono già espresse da J. GAUDEMET, *La condemnation des pratiques païennes en 391*, in *Epektasis. Mélanges offerts au cardinal Jean Daniélou*, Paris 1972, 597-602, spec. 600.

[49] *CTh* 16, 10, 11 (16 giugno 391) *Evagrio praefecto Augustali et Romano comiti Aegypti*: ma per l'interpretazione di questa costituzione, in relazione al racconto di Rufino, Socrate, Sozomeno, vedi oltre.

[50] *CTh* 6, 10, 12 (8 novembre 392) *Flavio Rufino PPO Orientis*.

[51] Giudicate unanimamente «una sentenza di morte del paganesimo»: E. STEIN, *Histoire du Bas-Empire*, I: *De l'état romain à l'état byzantin, 284-476)*, Paris 1949-1959, 209; J.R. PALANQUE, *Saint Ambrose et l'Empire romain. Contribution à l'histoire des rapports de l'Eglise et de l'état à la fin du quatriéme siècle*, Paris 1933, 251; A. PIGANIOL, *L'Empire chrétien...*, 285; P. CHUVIN, *A Chronicle...*, 69; A.D. LEE, *Pagans and Christians in Late Antiquity: a Sourcebook*, London-New York 2000, 123.

Viceversa, si suggerisce oggi, che nessuna di quelle disposizioni ebbe portata generale e furono tutte, piuttosto, misure di circostanza. Quella inviata nel febbraio 391 intendeva forse regolare il comportamento religioso di alcuni ufficiali pubblici, non necessariamente solo pagani, in seguito a qualche denuncia[52]. La costituzione al prefetto augustale e al *comes* d'Egitto, nel giugno 391, è parsa incitare alla distruzione dei templi, solo perché è stata impropriamente identificata con la legge che, secondo Rufino, Socrate, e in modo indiretto anche Sozomeno, avrebbe autorizzato l'abbattimento del Serapeo di Alessandria[53]; della lunga legge al prefetto del pretorio d'Oriente Rufino, che giungeva a comminare persino la pena di morte a chi consultasse le viscere di animali dopo averli immolati, si è sottolineata la stretta relazione con le vicende personali del funzionario cui fu rivolta[54]. L'interpretazione recente di tale legislazione ne ha saputo restituire, meglio che nel passato, il profilo storico e una più credibile funzione all'interno della procedura legislativa tardoantica; non ne esaurisce, però, il significato in quanto strumento di cristianizzazione. Alcune considerazioni intendono mostrarlo.

La costituzione inviata nel giugno 391 al prefetto augustale e al *comes* d'Egitto deve essere svincolata dalla concreta distruzione del tempio di Serapide in Alessandria, almeno in termini di causa e d'effetto: il tempio, infatti, non fu abbattuto nel 391, come a lungo si è creduto, bensì l'anno successivo[55]. Come riportata dal Codice Teodosiano, inoltre, essa non autorizzava alcuna violenza contro i templi e, nel ribadire il divieto assoluto di compiere sacrifici, era inviata a chiarire in che modo potesse essere applicata anche in Alessandria la costituzione rivolta pochi mesi prima ad Albino[56]. Più che autorizzare l'assalto al Serapeo, può averne dunque creato le premesse, favorendo l'eplosione di contrasti tra gli elementi più estremisti del gruppo pagano e cristiano. Il *pròstagma* di cui parla Socrate,

---

[52] R.M. Errington, *Christian Accounts...*, 425.

[53] *Ibid.*, 425-429.

[54] *Ibid.*, 431-432.

[55] J. Hahn, Vetustus error extinctus est. *Wann wurde das Sarapeion von Alexandria zerstört?*, «Historia» 55 (2006), 368-383; Id., *The Conversion of the Cult Statues: the Destruction of the Serapeum 392 A.D.: and the transformation of Alexandria into the «Christ-Loving» city*, in *From Temple to Chrurch: Destruction and Renewal of Local Cultic Topography in Late Antiquity*, eds. J. Hahn, St. Emmel, U. Gotter, Leiden-Boston 2008, 335-365, spec. 344.

[56] N. McLynn, *Ambrose of Milan. Church and Court in a Christian Capital*, Berkeley-Los Angeles-London 1994, 332-333, ha suggerito che Teofilo può aver esercitato le dovute pressioni sui due funzionari, dopo aver saputo da informatori romani della legge del 24 febbraio 391.

che Rufino definisce *rescriptum*, non può tuttavia identificarsi con *CTh* 16, 10, 11. Ottenuto, secondo entrambi gli storici ecclesiastici, quando il conflitto aveva raggiunto livelli elevati di scontri ripetuti e cruenti, lungi dall'essere una legge generale, fu probabilmente una misura di ordine pubblico inviata in un secondo momento, qualche mese dopo il giugno 391. Il riconoscimento della santa devozione mostrata dai cristiani assassinati, ma pure l'esortazione a non perseguire i colpevoli, se si fossero ravveduti, suonano come indicazioni di squisito tenore politico. Né diversa, nell'intento dell'imperatore, doveva essere l'ingiunzione a eliminare quel culto degli idoli, che costituiva la vera causa del conflitto; generica nella formulazione, fu facilmente interpretata come incitamento a distruggere statue e templi[57]. Questo secondo rescritto, peraltro, non fu registrato dai compilatori del Codice per la sua portata strettamente locale[58].

La stessa costituzione rivolta ad Evagrio e Romano, benché priva di quella risonanza universale cui un tempo le si riconosceva, non fu tuttavia senza effetti sul processo di cristianizzazione della città di Alessandria: effetti beninteso indiretti, ma concreti e tangibili nel corso di pochi decenni, se solo si tiene conto delle immense ricchezze che Teofilo e il suo successore Cirillo furono in grado d'investire per promuovere le fortune politiche della sede alessandrina sullo scenario internazionale; in massima parte provenivano dai templi egiziani, urbani e agresti, che – secondo il racconto di Socrate e gli epigrammi di Pallada – il vescovo riuscì a depredare[59]; né è noto che Teofilo abbia subito alcuna conseguenza legale per la dissacrazione degli arredi sacri pagani o per gli atti di vandalismo perpetrati contro varii templi, dopo quello di Serapide[60].

In modo affine, non mi pare si possa mettere in dubbio che la costituzione emanata a Costantinopoli nel 392 avesse motivazioni politiche e che, messa subito in forza, fosse stata richiesta e fatta applicare da Rufino per distruggere l'odiato Taziano, una volta sostituito nella prefettura, suo figlio Proculo e il gruppo di sostenitori lici che avevano dominato la

---

[57] Per i rapporti tra il testo di Soz. *HE* 7, 15, unico a citare i nomi dei due ufficiali egiziani che avrebbero informato l'imperatore dei disordini di Alessandria, con Eun. *Vitae Soph.* 6, 11, 1-7, che però chiama Evagrius col nome di Evetios, R.M. Errington, *Christian Accounts...*, 425-426. Vedi anche sull'episodio e il rapporto tra le fonti A. Baldini, *Problemi della tradizione sulla «distruzione» del Serapeo di Alessandria*, «RSA» 15 (1985), 97-152.
[58] Ruf. *HE* 11, 22, Soc. *HE* 5, 16, 1; cfr. Soz. *HE* 7, 15 e Theod. *HE* 5, 22.
[59] Ottima analisi in J. Hahn, *The Conversion of the Cult Statues...*, 352-360.
[60] G. Bonamente, *Prefetti del pretorio, vescovi e governatori all'opera nell'applicare la legislazione*, in *Poteri centrali e poteri periferici...*, 13-34, spec. 31.

capitale durante l'assenza di Teodosio[61]. La legge, la quarta ottenuta da Fl. Rufino neppure due mesi dopo l'insediamento come prefetto, colpiva chiunque, di qualunque ceto sociale o dignità, fosse sorpreso in ambiente urbano a compiere in pubblico sacrifici animali, o ad adorare nella propria dimora con incenso o ghirlande i propri penati; l'*extispicium* era passibile di laesa maestà anche se la consultazione delle viscere non avesse riguardato la vita del principe.

Nella seconda parte, inoltre, conteneva precisi riferimenti ai riti che si potessero effettuare in campagna: venerare con incenso una statua, addobbare un albero, elevare un altare di terra, rendeva colpevole di *violata religio*; le proprietà che qualcuno avesse dimostrato cultualmente attive (*quae turis constiterit vapore fumasse*), se appartenenti al responsabile dei sacrifici, sarebbero state confiscate. Qualora a compiere il sacrificio in templi pubblici o in case e campi estranei fosse stato un dipendente, costui doveva essere multato di 25 libbre d'oro; al proprietario o al funzionario connivente era riservata una pena pecuniaria pari a quella comminata al diretto colpevole. Il controllo era affidato ai governatori, ai *defensores civitatis*, ai curiali; per incuria, questi ultimi, potevano essere denunciati ai tribunali; gli altri, invece, se dissimulando (*si vindictam dissimulatione distulerint*) avessero lasciato impuniti i colpevoli sarebbero stati multati, con i membri del loro ufficio, di 30 libbre d'oro[62]. Con tali disposizioni, dunque, comportamenti cultuali «erronei» divenivano punibili persino con la morte; qualunque diritto a conservare la proprietà privata poteva essere messo a repentaglio dalla denuncia che vi fossero compiuti atti sacrileghi; la *coniventia* di *domini* e amministratori era punita alla stregua dell'attività cultuale espressamente rilevata.

Poiché già il 22 agosto di quell'anno Arbogaste aveva dichiarato Eugenio imperatore[63], la costituzione probabilmente non fu neppure diffusa in Occidente[64]. Essa, tuttavia, fu richiamata alla morte di Teodosio da una

---

[61] *PLRE* 1, s. v. Fl. Eutolmius Tatianus 5, 876-878 e s. v. Fl. Rufinus 18, 778-781; cfr. già J.F. Matthews, *Western Aristocracies and Imperial Court* (A. D. 364-425), Oxford 1975 (rist. an. 1990), 113; 135.

[62] Sul tenore di *CTh* 16, 10, 12, molto studiata (presenta anche il primo impiego di *gentilis* nel senso di pagano), si vedano L. De Giovanni, *Chiesa e Stato nel Codice Teodosiano. Saggio sul libro XVI*, Napoli, 2000⁵, 128-130; P. Chuvin, *A Chronicle...*, 69-71; S. Montero, *Política y adivinación en el Bajo Imperio Romano: emperadores y harúspices (193 d.C – 408 d.C.)*, Bruxelles 1991, 139-140; R. Delmaire, *Les lois religieuses...*, 442-446.

[63] *Fasti Vind. Priores* 517 (*Chron. Min.* I, 298).

[64] Viceversa, molti autori ne fanno la causa precipitante della cosiddetta «reaction païenne» che avrebbe condotto al Frigido: oltre a Piganiol e Alföldi, vedi più recentemente

costituzione che, confermandone il contenuto, minacciava un'applicazione più rigida della legge: accanto agli altri funzionari e ai curiali, che nel 392 erano stato implicati nel controllo, nel 395 anche i *procuratores* furono chiamati in causa per la repressione del culto pagano ed eretico nelle terre della *res privata* imperiale[65]. Nel testo legislativo si riconosceva apertamente che era stato difficile far applicare la misura emanata nel 392, e l'ambito di vigore della seconda legge dovette rimanere ugualmente limitato alla prefettura d'Oriente. Ciononostante, non può non colpire che nelle omelie di alcuni vescovi norditalici – come Massimo di Torino e Gaudenzio di Brescia – pronunciate proprio in quegli anni, si presenti con insistenza il tema della *coniventia* e della *dissimulatio* dei *domnedii*, sui cui possedimenti erano espletati riti demoniaci.

Anche Zenone di Verona aveva alluso alla responsabilità, che i proprietari cristiani avevano, del perpetuarsi dei culti pagani nei *loca* e *praedia*, di cui volevano mantenere la proprietà (*ius templorum*) anche se rivendicati dal fisco[66]. Massimo, tuttavia, era esplicito sulle colpe dei *domini*, sottolineando che col tacere, o rimanendo indifferenti, essi mostravano di apprezzare ciò che era compiuto. La loro *conscientia* equivaleva alla *coniventia*, un atteggiamento che se denunciato era passibile di ripercussioni legali[67]. E, tra il 402 e il 408, Gaudenzio assimilava la tolleranza di quanti permettevano che nei propri possedimenti si adorassero gli idoli, mantenendo in piedi i templi dei demoni e gli altari del diavolo, con crimini come *adulterium, stuprum, homicidium, raptum*, che la legislazione puniva come *laesa maiestas*[68].

S. WILLIAMS, G. FRIEL, *The Empire at Bay*, London 1994, 125. La pensa invece destinata anche all'Occidente L. CRACCO RUGGINI, *Il paganesimo romano fra religione e politica (384-394 d. C.): per una reinterpretazione del «Carmen contra paganos»*, «MANL (Cl. Sc. Mor., St. e Filol.)», VIII, 23, 1, Roma 1979, 1-144, spec. 57.

[65] *CTh* 16, 10, 13 (7 agosto 395 allo stesso Rufino): *...scituri quidquid divi genitoris nostri legibus est in ipsos (scl. ereticos et paganos) vel supplicii vel dispendii constitutum nunc acrius exsequendum. Sciant autem moderatores provinciarum nostrarum... procuratores possessionum nostrarum...*

[66] ZENO, *Tract.* I, 25, 10, 75: *supra*, n. 43.

[67] MAX. TAUR. *S.* CVI, 1-2: *si non conscientia, vel coniventia maculare – maculat enim coniventia eum qui [...] dissimulando permisit* (r. 16-18); *reos nos statuimus si non operatione sceleris at tamen dissimulationis adsensu* (r. 26-28); cfr. *S.* CVII, 1, r. 10-19: *Quisquis enim intellegit in re sua exerceri sacrilegia nec fieri prohibet, quodammodo ipse praecepit. Tacendo enim et non arguendo, consensum praebuit immolanti. [...] dum enim taces, placet tibi quod facit rusticus tuus, quod si non faceret, forsitan displiceret.*

[68] GAUD. BRIX. *Tract.* 13, 28 databile al 402 o al 408 in quanto l'attacco imminente dei barbari di paragr. 21 è probabilmente quello di Alarico. Per l'estensione della *maiestas*

Massimo citava un *imperiale praeceptum*, giunto infine ad ammonire i fedeli dopo le continue esortazioni del vescovo[69]. Essendo stato variamente identificato, si è anche pensato a una legge del 399, che ordinava la distruzione dei templi agresti[70]. Inviata da Damasco al *PPOOrientis* Eutychianus, di quella tuttavia ci sono note solo le disposizioni relative a strutture templari pubbliche. Sia Massimo, sia le costituzioni del 392 e del 395, invece, si rivolgevano ai *domini* richiamandoli al dovere di abrogare ogni forma di culto nelle loro proprietà. E come nel 395 si ammetteva implicitamente che gli ordini affidati all'esecuzione di governatori e curiali erano stati evasi, così Massimo esprimeva la sua disillusione sulla possibilità che l'*imperiale praeceptum* avesse reale applicazione[71]. Sebbene forse non diffuse in Occidente, come la partizione legislativa allora in vigore indurrebbe a credere, si ha però l'impressione che quelle due leggi costantinopolitane fossero note a Massimo e a Gaudenzio, così da dar loro l'impressione di possedere ormai strumenti legislativi efficaci per fare pressione sui proprietari locali, iterando dal pulpito le minacce impugnabili in tribunale su denuncia.

Nel 407, inoltre, una costituzione indirizzata a Curtius, prefetto del pretorio d'Italia, prevedendo che gli edifici sacri della *res privata* imperiale sarebbero stati convertiti ad *usus adcommodos*, ordinò che i *domini* fossero forzati a distruggere quelli su cui si vantavano diritti privati (*domini destruere cogantur*), e conferì ai vescovi locali l'autorità di contrastare i banchetti rituali e altro genere di cerimonie pagane[72]. Pur da osservatori

---

(punibile con la morte) ai crimini indicati, vd. già *CTh* 11, 36, del 314 o 315 e 9, 38, 7 del 384.

[69] Max. Taur. *S.* CVI, 2, r. 48- 49: *Post nos admonuit imperiale praeceptum. Videte quanta divinitas sit derogatio haec humanae potestatis adiectio!*

[70] Così *Maximus Taurinensis. Sermones*, ed. A. Mutzenbecher, (CC 23), Turnhout 1962, XXXIII, ove si richiama *CTh* 16, 10, 16 (10 luglio 399: *Si qua in agris templa sunt, sine turba ac tumultu diruantur*). In base a tale suggerimento, E.M. Sironi, *Dall'oriente in Occidente: i santi Sisinnio, Martirio e Alessandro martiri in Anaunia*, Sanzeno 1989, 140-141, colloca nel 399 i *SS*. 105 e 106 pensando che quest'ultimo fosse recitato il 15 agosto 399, giorno in cui sarebbe caduta la seconda celebrazione dei martiri anuaniensi.

[71] Max. Taur. *Sermo* CVI extr., 2, p. 418: *Principes quidem tam boni christiani leges pro religione promulgant, sed eas exsecutores non exerunt conpetenter: et ideo exuto a culpa principe exsecutor remanet in reatu, qui si acrimoniam legis exerceat, et ipse peccato absolvitur et pro salute multorum aeterna mercede donabitur.*

[72] *Sirm.* 12: *Arae locis omnibus destruantur omniaque templa in possessionibus nostris ad usus adcommodos transferantur; domini destruere cogantur...* Il testo conservato in *CTh* 16, 10, 19, con la data 15 novembre 408 (da Roma, *ad Curtium PPO Italiae*) è un estratto di *Sirm.* 12 (come 16, 5, 43) emanata il 15 novembre 407, quando Curtius è

periferici, i vescovi dunque raccoglievano informazioni e creavano opinione; con la loro attività omiletica ed epistolare si rivolgevano ai principi, influendo talvolta sul dettato delle leggi e ottenendone degli aggiustamenti normativi, come la costituzione del 407 sembrerebbe mostrare. Pure la sua efficacia probabilmente rimase limitata a singoli casi, forse solo quelli per i quali l'intervento legislativo era stato richiesto. Di per sé, è difficile precisare persino quale tipo di *facultas*, in particolare, fosse data ai vescovi da Onorio: *haec ipsa*, infatti, potrebbe riferirsi solo agli ultimi elementi del testo – i banchetti in onore del rito sacrilego tenuti in luoghi nefasti –, ovvero più in generale, al complesso delle attività descrittevi, compresa la distruzione dei templi agresti che i privati erano sollecitati a compiere[73].

Di quest'ultima opinione non sembra essere stato Agostino. Pur consapevole che *idola* erano occultati un po' ovunque – *abscundunt in terra, abscundunt in spelunca, abscundunt in cavernis [...] illi a timore legum abscundunt* –[74], ammetteva tuttavia che sarebbe stato più opportuno infrangerli nei cuori, piuttosto che nelle proprietà dei pagani, non avendone la facoltà[75]; era lecito, invece, e anche necessario distruggerli sulle proprie terre, se si era cristiani, e tanto più se ve ne fossero nelle terre della Chiesa[76]. È possibile, tuttavia, che Agostino recitasse quel sermone prima che la legge del 407 fosse emanata, prima che i *comites* Gaudenzio e Giovio

---

ancora attestato come prefetto, allorché nel 408 l'ufficio fu ricoperto da Longinianus e poi da Theodorus: R. DELMAIRE, *Les lois religieuses...*, 454-457.

[73] Sirm. 12: *Simulacra, si qua etiam nunc in templis fanisque consistunt [...] suis sedibus evellantur... Aedificia ipsa templorum, quae in civitatibus vel oppidis vel extra oppida sunt ad usum publicum vindicetur. Arae locis... transferantur, domini destruere cogantur. Non liceat omnino in honorem sacrilegi ritus funestioribus locis exercere convivia vel quicquam sollemnitatis agitare. Episcopis quoque locorum haec ipsa prohibendi ecclesiasticae manus tribuimus facultatem; iudices autem viginti librarum auri poena constringimus et pari forma officia eorum, si haec eorum fuerint dissimulatione neglecta.* Mentre F.R. TROMBLEY, *Hellenic Religion and Christianization c. 370-529*, Leiden 1995, 29-30, pensa che ai vescovi fosse stata dato il potere di contrastare l'organizzazione dei banchetti funebri, e L. DE GIOVANNI, *Il libro XVI nel Codice...*, 136, parla di banchetti pagani nei templi, P. BROWN, *La coercizione religiosa nel basso impero romano*, in *Religione e società nell'età di sant'Agostino*, Torino 1975, 287-316, spec. 304, ritiene che i vescovi potessero intervenire anche nella distruzione dei santuari pagani.

[74] AUG. *S. Mayence* 60, 8 (a. 399-405), in F. DOLBEAU, *Vigt-six sermons au peuple d'Afrique*, Paris 1996, 48.

[75] AUG. *S.* 62, 17.

[76] AUG. *S.* 62, 18.

fossero inviati da Onorio a distruggere *templa* e *simulacra* a Cartagine[77], prima ancora che due concili cartaginesi nel 401 (il 16 giugno e il 13 settembre rispettivamente) avessero richiesto l'intervento imperiale per eliminare ogni possibile traccia di paganesimo in Africa.

I vescovi riuniti in quei concili specificavano che, tra le *reliquiae idolatriae*, dovessero essere compresi boschi ed alberi sacri e sottolineavano che i templi agresti, oppure collocati in luoghi remoti e nascosti, non erano di alcun ornamento[78]. L'allusione è significativa: una costituzione dell'agosto 399 che, nella copia conservata nel Codice Teodosiano è rivolta a due funzionari che governavano la Spagna e la Gallia del Sud, aveva espresso l'esigenza di tutelare templi ed opere di pregio in quanto *publicorum operum ornamenta*[79]. Benché le costituzioni continuassero ad avere una funzione contingente, la circolazione delle notizie attraverso le lettere di comunione, i rapporti interecclesiali, i viaggi dei molti che si spostavano da una chiesa all'altra dell'Impero, arricchivano la conoscenza delle costituzioni emanate in regioni anche lontane dalla propria prefettura. I vescovi africani conoscevano la disposizione spagnola e, precisando che demolire i templi agresti non significava violarla, mostravano di volerne dare corretta applicazione.

Non sempre la Corte reagì positivamente alle pressioni della Chiesa, ed è certo che nessun imperatore romano, prima che Giustiniano si risolse a imporre il battesimo ai «pochi sopravvissuti pagani»[80], pensò di emanare una legge generale, valida e applicabile in tutto l'Impero, per cancellare il politeismo. Il destino e l'efficacia delle singole misure antipagane continuò a riposare sullo zelo di chi volesse impegnarsi a denunciarne la violazione. Talvolta e in alcuni luoghi, però, ciò poteva verificarsi con grande determinazione; in altri casi la legge rimaneva lettera morta. Non tutte le disposizioni pertanto ebbero la stessa efficacia, non tutte suscitarono lo

---

[77] Aug. *de civ. Dei* 18, 54: in tal senso, C. Lepelley, *Une forme religieuse du patriotisme municipal: le culte du Génie de la cité dans l'Afrique romaine*, in Id., *Aspects de l'Afrique romaine. Les citées, la vie rurale, le christianisme*, Bari 2001, 49, n. 48; ma si tratta di templi pubblici, non quelli di privati cittadini. Una datazione differente, al 407-408 è data da A. La Bonnardière, *Recherches de chronologie augustinienne*, Paris 1965, in connessione con la costituzione a Curtius.

[78] *Conc. Carthaginiense* (16 iunii 401), c. 58 e *conc. Carthaginiense* (13 sept. 401), c. 84.

[79] *CTh* 16, 10, 15 (29 gennaio 399, o meglio il 29 agosto 399) *Macrobio vicario Hispaniarum et Procliano vicario quinque provinciarum: Sicut sacrificia prohibemus, ita volumus publicorum operum ornamenta servari. Ac ne sibi aliqua auctoritate blandiantur, qui ea conantur evertere, si quod rescriptum, si qua lex forte praetendatur...* Per i destinatari e la data della costituzione, R. Delmaire, *Les lois religieuses...*, 450-451.

[80] *CI* I, 11, 10, 1-4.

stesso interesse. Il conflitto, a parte rare occasioni, rimase limitato a reazioni individuali. Sostenere che la legislazione antipagana fu in generale ignorata perché non applicabile, o che le leggi furono dimenticate – dopo aver realizzato un fine immediato – finché i compilatori del Teodosiano non le riesumarono[81], è un eccesso interpretativo. Provvedimenti puramente locali ebbero talvolta un impatto che neppure l'imperatore, emanandoli, aveva calcolato. Potevano, infatti, essere richiamati a distanza di anni (come nel caso dei *constituta Gratiani*), se una nuova opportunità ne avesse rinverdito la memoria.

È quanto accadde, a mio parere, quando nel 408 Agostino si trovò ad affrontare la violenza donatista. Egli sollecitò allora alcuni funzionari, perché confermassero la normativa contro eretici e pagani in vigore durante il governo di Stilicone, che alcuni volevano decaduta con la sua eliminazione il 22 agosto 408[82]. La costituzione fu indirizzata nel 409 a Flavius Mallius Theodorus, *PPO Italiae, Illyrici et Africae*[83]. Comminava la pena di morte a quanti, facendo irruzione in una chiesa, avessero apportato offesa a ministri e sacerdoti, disturbata la cerimonia in corso, o arrecato danni allo stesso luogo di culto. Il testo specificava che sarebbe stato necessario catturare la maggior parte dei colpevoli qualora fosse stata l'intera moltitudine ad aver commesso il sacrilegio: e questo anche in assenza di formale denuncia. Specificando che i rei dovessero essere perseguiti d'ufficio, si dava ai vescovi la possibilità di non denunciare apertamente quanti avevano provocato danni ai sacerdoti o alle Chiese: in tal modo essi si sarebbero mostrati caritatevoli verso gli stessi persecutori[84].

---

[81] R.M. ERRINGTON, *Christian Accounts...*, 435; ID., *Roman Imperial Policy...*, 248.

[82] AUG. *Ep.* 97, 2 a Olimpio, che aveva sostituito Stilicone nella carica di *magister militum*, dopo aver tramato contro di lui: *ut opus tuum bonum diligentissima acceleretur instantia, quo noverint inimici Ecclesiae leges illas, quae de idolis confringendis et haereticis corrigentis vivo Stilichone in Africam missae sunt, ex voluntate Imperatoris piissimi et fidelissimi constitutas*; cfr. anche AUG. *Ep.* 100 a Donato, proconsole d'Africa dal 408 al 410. Una delegazione di vescovi africani si era recata a Ravenna durante l'inverno per domandare la conferma delle precedenti disposizioni, ottenendo *Sirm.* 14, che i compilatori del Codice Teodosiano divisero in due: *CTh* 16, 2, 31 e *CTh* 16, 5, 46. Da quest'ultima risulta confermata la data del 15 gennaio 409, nonostante il manoscritto indichi il 412 – per erronea lettura dei consolati di Onorio e Teodosio II – e *CI* 1, 3, 10 ripeta l'errore.

[83] *CTh* 16, 2, 31 indirizzata a Flavius Mallius Theodorus (*PLRE* 2, s. v. Theodorus 9, 1086-1087), il quale fu proconsole d'Africa nel 396, *PPO Galliarum* nel 396-397, per la seconda volta *PPO Italiae, Illyrici et Africae*, dal 13 settembre 408 al 15 gennaio 409, come indicano le leggi a lui indirizzate nel 408-409.

[84] Sulla costituzione, si veda J.-L. MAIER, *Le dossier du donatisme*, II (*De Julien l'Apostat à saint Jean Damascène, 361-750*) (TU, 135), Berlin 1989, n. 90: L. DE GIOVANNI,

È esattamente quanto Agostino desiderava. Una sua lettera del 411-412, ove si ricordano le vicissitudini dei donatisti che erano stati catturati e avevano confessato, conferma che anche una costituzione applicabile in tutta la prefettura governata dal suo destinatario, poteva essere suggerita da situazioni specifiche, in riferimento alle quali veniva subito messa in forza. Alcune note del vescovo d'Ippona, inoltre, sembrano indicare che nel richiedere la disposizione del 409, il vescovo avesse tenuto presente la dinamica provocata dall'emanazione di una disposizione, in regioni lontane dalla propria, in seguito al conflitto scatenatosi non tra donatisti e cattolici, bensì tra cattolici e pagani, e di cui aveva conoscenza per vie diverse dalla normale pubblicazione di una legge. Esortando infatti Marcellino a esporre in pubblico i verbali ufficiali redatti contro i donatisti, lo pregava di affiggere anche la lettera con cui egli implorava il giudice di sottoporli a pena più mite di quella capitale[85]. Se il proconsole non avesse accettato il suo intervento, egli avrebbe tentato di ottenere clemenza dall'imperatore. Sapeva infatti che, già alcuni anni prima in Val di Non, i pagani colpevoli di aver ucciso tre leviti – ora venerati come martiri – si erano salvati per l'intercessione del vescovo[86].

Molto probabilmente una legge di tenore simile a quella richiesta dai vescovi africani contro i donatisti era stata sollecitata da Vigilio di Trento nel 397/398, con la specifica clausola che i colpevoli fossero perseguiti d'ufficio, riservandosi l'opportunità d'intercedere per loro presso i giudici o l'imperatore[87]. Nota ad Agostino, anche se non conservata nel Codice perché intesa solo a risprintinare l'ordine pubblico nel distretto di Trento, la disposizione doveva essere stata ottenuta per il tramite del padre di Flavius Mallius Theodorus – dello stesso nome, tanto da essere con lui

---

Chiesa e stato..., 42-44; Y. Rivière, *Les délateurs sous l'Empire romain*, Rome 2002, 295-298; R. Delmaire, *Les lois religieuses...*, 180-183.

[85] Aug. *Ep.* 139, 2: *Si proconsul vel simul ambo in illos estis sententiam prolaturi [...] tamen si necesse fuerit, etiam Gestis iubete allegari epistolas meas, quas de hac re singulas vobis mittendas putavi.*

[86] Aug. *Ep* 139, 2: *Scio enim in causa clericorum Anaunensium, qui occisi a gentilibus, nunc martyres honorantur, Imperatorem rogatum facile concessisse ne illi qui eos occiderant et capti iam tenebantur, poena simili punirentur.*

[87] Sulla funzione della *lenitas* come strumento di conversione, Aug. *Ep* 139, 2: *in tanta quippe crudelitate, quaecumque praeter sanguinem vindicta processerit, magna lenitas apparebit.* Sugli effetti prodotti in Val di Non dal comportamento del vescovo: Vig. *Ep.* II, (edd. E. Menestò, in A. Quacquarelli, I. Rogger, *I martiri della Val di Non e la reazione pagana alla fine del IV secolo*, Trento 1985, 169: *sed iam crescit damno fecundior, leto vivacior, laetior post moerorem*).

confuso –[88], dal 397 al 399 a capo della medesima prefettura retta poi dal figlio. Theodorus padre era sicuramente legato ad Agostino, che gli dedicò il *De Beata Vita*, ma era anche membro religiosamente attivo di quegli ambienti ecclesiastici milanesi, che avevano gestito con Vigilio di Trento la pubblicizzazione dell'evento e la circolazione delle reliquie dei tre martiri[89].

---

[88] J.-L. MAIER, *Le dossier du donatisme...*, 162-168, confonde il figlio con il padre omonimo.

[89] La carriera e l'attività di quest'uomo, che fu console nel 399, è ben nota, essendo menzionato molte volte nel V libro delle lettere di Quinto Aurelio Simmaco e nelle costituzioni del Codice Teodosiano; un panegirico fu scritto in suo onore, all'epoca del consolato, da Claudiano, che celebrò tutti gli uffici avuti fino ad allora, menzionando come esempio della sua fervida attività letteraria il *De metris* dedicato al figlio: *PLRE* 1, s. v. Fl. Mallius Theodorus 27, 900-902. Sull'episodio della Val di Non, cfr. R. LIZZI, *Vescovi e strutture ecclesiastiche nella città tardoantica (l'Italia Annonaria nel IV-V secolo d.C.)*, Como 1989, 59-85; EAD., *L'Eglise, les* domini, *les païens* rustici: *quelques stratégies pour la christianisation de l'Occident (IVe-VIe siècle)*, in *Quid sit christianum esse. Le problème de «la christianisation du monde antique». Colloque organisé par Hervé Inglebert, Bruno Dumézil et Sylvain Destephen à l'Université de Paris X-Nanterre, les 26-27-28 mai 2008*, in stampa.

CARLOS MACHADO

Roman aristocrats and the christianization of Rome

At some point during the year 400, Jerome addressed a letter to his Roman friend Oceanus[1]. The letter praised the recently deceased Fabiola, a woman whose wealth and family placed her right at the top of late Roman society[2]. Besides being a close associate, Fabiola had led an eventful life. Divorced from her first husband, she remarried and, following the death of her second husband, she dedicated herself to works of charity and prayer. She spent some time in Jerusalem and Bethlehem, after which she returned to Rome[3]. While living in the old imperial capital, Jerome noted, her plans to built a *xenodochium* in Portus coincided with those of his friend, the Christian aristocrat Pammachius. Rather than competing for glory, their competition was fuelled by philanthropy[4]. On joining forces, they founded a centre for the reception and hospitality of strangers that was known all around the world[5].

I would like to thank the Alexander von Humboldt Stiftung, who generously funded my research. I am also grateful to the organizers of the conference for their invitation, and especially to Rita Lizzi, for her incentive and hospitality. Robert Coates-Stephens, Lucy Grig, and Bryan Ward-Perkins helped me with comments and suggestions, while the text was read and much improved (as always) by Elizabeth O'Keeffe Machado.

[1] JER. *Ep.* 77. J. Labourt suggested in his edition for the G. Budé collection that the letter was written in the summer. For Oceanus, see *PLRE* I, Oceanus and *PCBE* 2 (Italie), Oceanus.

[2] On Fabiola, see *PLRE* I, Fabiola and *PCBE* 2 (Italie), Fabiola 1: she descended from the *gens Fabia*, and must have died in 399.

[3] See E.D. HUNT, *Holy Land Pilgrimage in the Later Roman Empire AD 312-460*, Oxford 1984, 191 for the context of her return.

[4] JER. *Ep.* 77.10: «*erat haec inter utrumque contentio, quis humanitate superaret*».

[5] The identification of this foundation as a centre for the reception of travellers was recently questioned by H. DEY, Diaconiae, xenodochia, hospitalia *and monasteries:* «*social security*» *and the meaning of monasticism in Early Medieval Rome*, «Early Medieval Europe» 16 (2008), 407. For this foundation, see R. SANTANGELI VALENZANI, *Pellegrini, senatori e papi. Gli* xenodochia *a Roma tra il V e il IX secolo*, «Rivista

Jerome's eulogy of Fabiola is an important document for our understanding of the social and religious transformations that involved the city of Rome in the 4th and 5th c. The appropriate lifestyle to be adopted by Christian aristocrats, the troubled standing of married and divorced women in ascetic circles, the role played by widows, these were questions to which Jerome returned in various letters to his Roman correspondents[6]. What is perhaps more important is that the many acts of charity which characterized Fabiola, «honour of the Christians»[7], are here placed in their religious, geographic, and social contexts. Her actions were motivated by her love of Christ, to whom she «owed her soul»[8]. Her donations benefitted clerics and lay men and women in different provinces of the Empire, and not just in Rome. Rather than isolated from the society to which she belonged, Fabiola's pious initiatives were available to other aristocrats also, and had important repercussions well beyond the narrow group of Christian enthusiasts to which Jerome is usually associated by scholars.

Jerome's letter to Oceanus illustrates the close links between aristocratic circles and members of the Church. It also indicates the impressive transformations set in motion by the conversion of Roman aristocrats to Christianity[9]. The development of Christian Rome was a complex and multi-faceted process, involving elements as diverse as the affirmation of the Church as an institution, the development of a new religious topography, and the adherence to new codes of behaviour, as well as the construction of a new self-image for the city and its population[10].

The aim of this article is to discuss these issues by focusing on a specific social group, the peers of Fabiola and Oceanus. Recent years have witnessed a surge in studies of aristocratic involvement in the development of

---

dell'istituto nazionale d'archeologia e storia dell'arte», s. III, 19-20 (1996-1997), 204-205.

[6] See, of a long bibliography, S. REBENICH, *Hieronymus und sein Kreis. Prosopographische und sozialgeschichtliche Untersuchungen*, Stuttgart 1992, ch. 2. More recently, J. CURRAN, *Pagan City and Christian Capital. Rome in the Fourth Century*, Oxford 2000, ch. 7.

[7] *Ep.* 77.2: «*laudem Christianorum*».

[8] To paraphrase Jerome: *Ep.* 77.11.

[9] On this subject, see P. BROWN, *Aspects of the Conversion of the Roman Aristocracy*, «Journal of Roman Studies» 51 (1961), 1-11; also M. SALZMAN, *The Making of a Christian Aristocracy*, Cambridge, Mass. 2002.

[10] The bibliography is unending: see C. PIETRI, *Roma Christiana. Recherches sur l'Église de Rome, son organisation, sa politique, son idéologie de Miltiade à Sixte III (311-440)*, Rome 1976, 2 vols. Also S. DIEFENBACH, *Römische Erinnerungsräume. Heiligenmemoria und kollektive Identitäten in Rom des 3. bis 5. Jahrhunderts n. Chr.*, Berlin 2007.

late Roman Christianity, bringing into sharp focus the role of this group in different aspects of Christian life[11]. Rather than focusing on the process of Christianization of Rome *per se*, what I intend to do here is to discuss two inter-related questions: how did Roman aristocrats react to the historical transformations that we, on hindsight, call the Christianization of Rome? More importantly, to what extent – and how – did the new religion fit into this group's strategies for achieving, exercising, and displaying power[12]? It would be impossible to answer these questions in a definitive way, especially in such a short space. What I will do instead is to discuss the involvement of aristocrats in the construction of three specific religious complexes: the basilica of S. Sebastiano on the via Appia, the basilica of S. Stefano on the via Latina, and the basilica of S. Peter in the Vatican. By construction, I refer not only to the actual physical process of building, but also to the ideological and symbolic processes involved in the definition of these spaces. We might then be able to form a more coherent picture of the role played by Rome's social and political elite in the making of *Roma Christiana*.

1. S. Sebastiano and the celebration of aristocratic Christianity

The church of S. Sebastiano on the via Appia is the best preserved of all 4th c. funerary basilicas (fig. 1)[13]. A large circus-shaped church (30.5 x 73.4 m), the late antique *Basilica Apostolorum* (re-dedicated to S. Sebastian in the late 6th-early 7th c.) was built over an area that had been used, at least since the late 1st c AD, as a burial ground[14]. The area acquired renewed

---

[11] For example: *Religion, Dynasty and Patronage in Early Christian Rome, 300-900*, ed. by K. COOPER, J. HILLNER, Cambridge 2007 and K. BOWES, *Private Worship, Public Values, and Religious Change in Late Antiquity*, Cambridge 2008.

[12] «Strategy», in this case, refers to a set of structured practices unconsciously adopted by members of a group with a specific aim. For a discussion of this concept, see P. BOURDIEU, *Stratégies de reproduction et modes de domination*, «Actes de la Recherche en Sciences Sociales» 105 (1994), 3-12.

[13] On the architecture and meaning of these buildings, see M. TORELLI, *Le basiliche circiformi di Roma. Iconografia, funzione, simbolo*, in «*Felix temporis reparatio*», ed. by G. SENA CHIESA, A. ARSLAN, Milan 1992, 203-217 and E. LA ROCCA, *Le basiliche cristiane «a deambulatorio» e la sopravvivenza del culto eroico*, in «*Aurea Roma*». *Dalla città pagana alla città cristiana*, ed. E. LA ROCCA, S. ENSOLI, Rome 2000, 204-220.

[14] For a good introduction to the complex, see A. FERRUA, *S. Sebastiano f.l.m. e la sua catacomba*, Rome 1968. See also R. KRAUTHEIMER, S. CORBETT, in *Corpus Basilicarum Christianarum Romae*, vol. 4, ed. by R. KRAUTHEIMER, Vatican City 1970, 99-147. See

importance after the middle of the 3rd c., when the earlier cemetery was buried, and a complex known as «triclia», or *memoria apostolorum*, was built on top of it. Consisting of a *memoria*, a porticus, and a fountain, the complex was already identified in Antiquity as the temporary resting place of the remains of the apostles Peter and Paul[15]. A reference in the *Feriale ecclesiae Romanae*, from 354, suggests that the relics of the apostles had been moved to this site during the persecution of 258, and this is supported by a large number of graffiti attesting to their veneration at this site[16].

The cemetery of the via Appia became a focal point for Christian worship and for the construction of a specifically Christian identity in late 3rd c. Rome[17]. This makes it all the more astonishing that we have no textual evidence for the construction of the basilica in the first half of the 4th c. It is impossible to know when construction started but there is reasonable evidence to suggest that building works were completed in the 340s, if not earlier. This includes inscriptions recording burials inside the church and especially a monogram carved in the threshold, most likely that of Constantine's son, Constans (emperor between 337-350)[18]. When bishop Damasus (366-384) celebrated the presence of the apostles in one of his most famous epigrams, the *Basilica Apostolorum* was already a few decades old[19]. Another epigram by Damasus celebrated the martyr Eutychius, and fragments of other Damasan inscriptions were found in the same area[20].

It is not surprising that a bishop like Damasus, whose contested election had undermined so much of his authority, should pay such attention

---

also A.M. NIEDDU, *La Basilica Apostolorum sulla via Appia e l'area cimiteriale circostante*, Vatican City 2009, which was not yet available for me at the time of writing.

[15] See L. SPERA, *Il paesaggio suburbano di Roma dall'antichità al medioevo. Il comprensorio tra le vie Latina e Ardeatina dalle mura Aureliane al III miglio*, Rome 1999, 219-20; also A.M. NIEDDU, *«Catacumbas coemeterium» (cimitero sopraterra)*, in *Lexicon Topographicum Urbis Romae – Suburbium*, vol. 2, ed. by A. LA REGINA, Rome 2004, 82-83.

[16] *Feriale ecclesiae Romanae*, l.l. 15-16 (MGH AA IX, p.71), with useful discussion in C. PIETRI, *Roma Christiana*..., 366-368; for the graffiti, see ICUR n.s. V, 12907-13096.

[17] Discussed by S. DIEFENBACH, *Römische Erinnerungsräume*..., 38-80, esp. 41-43 for the graffiti.

[18] See evidence and discussion in A. FERRUA, *Lavori a S. Sebastiano*, «Rivista di Archeologia Cristiana» 37 (1961), 203-36, esp. 227-31 for the monogram.

[19] *Hic abitasse prius santos cognoscere debes nomina quisq(ue) Petri pariter Pauliq(ue) requiris*: ICUR n.s. V, 13273=ILCV 951. Also *Epigrammata Damasiana*, ed. by A. FERRUA, Vatican City 1942, n. 20.

[20] See *Epigrammata Damasiana*, ns. 21 (Eutychius) and 22-23 (fragmentary inscriptions).

to the basilica on the via Appia[21]. Different acts of martyrs, as well as the *Liber Pontificalis*, attest to the importance of this site in the construction of different Christian memories in the 5th and 6th c. (when most of these texts were composed), a process that was already underway in the 4th c[22]. It was important for the bishop of Rome to affirm his position in a place that was, after all, connected to the very foundations of his Church. The Christian community gathered here on the 29th of June every year to celebrate its most important martyrs[23].

The importance of the *Basilica Apostolorum* and its site made this area an important burial ground for contemporaries. As with other such complexes, the interior of the basilica and the area around it was a densely occupied cemetery. The tombs found inside the basilica proper were generally of similar size and type («alla cappuccina»), which suggests a certain degree of social homogeneity. However, a number of inscriptions suggest, by their content and lettering, the presence of wealthier commissioners as well[24]. A large mausoleum, adjacent to the southern side of the apse, housed thirteen tombs before it received the relics of the Pannonian bishop Quirinus in the early 5th c., and was later known as the church of S. Quirinus (fig. 1: A)[25].

The occupation of the basilica as a burial ground was contemporary to its construction. Inscriptions record burials as early as the 340s, and the same is suggested by the architectural analysis of the tombs. Almost immediately, the southern side of the basilica was also occupied by grand mausolea, with elaborate architecture and rich decoration[26]. The first structure seen by visitors arriving at the church was a round mausoleum built into the hill, with a diameter of 13.3 m and a round roof (fig. 1: B). The structure, which partially survives, was preceded by a double apsed

---

[21] On the bishopric of Damasus, see C. PIETRI, *Damase, évêque de Rome*, in *Saecularia Damasiana*, Vatican City 1986, 29-58.

[22] As discussed by K. COOPER, *The martyr, the* matrona *and the bishop: the matron Lucina and the politics of martyr-cult in fifth- and sixth-century Rome*, «Early Medieval Europe» 8 (1999), 308-315. For a consideration of Damasus' policy, see M. SÁGHY, *Scinditur in partes populos: Pope Damasus and the Martyrs of Rome*, «Early Medieval Europe» 9 (2000), 273-87.

[23] See esp. C. PIETRI, *Roma Christiana...*, 365-80.

[24] See A. FERRUA, *Lavori a S. Sebastiano*, 206; also A. M. NIEDDU, *«Catacumbas coemeterium»...*, 85-86 and L. SPERA, *Il paesaggio suburbano di Roma...*, 225-229.

[25] See A.M. NIEDDU, *«Quirini ecclesia»*, in *Lexicon Topographicum Urbis Romae – Suburbium*, vol. 4, ed. by A. LA REGINA, Rome 2006, 294-297.

[26] See A.M. NIEDDU, *«Catacumbas coemeterium»...*, 83-84.

vestibule, and decorated with marble[27]. The monument is typologically similar to the mausoleum of the empress Helena on the via Labicana, also adjacent to a funerary basilica; its size, architecture, and decoration suggest a particularly wealthy commissioner. The fragment of an inscribed marble architrave found inside it helps us identify the owners of this monument. The fragment, with the dimensions of 1.63 x 0.44 x 0.30 m. was most likely part of a monumental entrance. This is also suggested by the dimension of the letters, 0.28 m high, as well as by the inscription itself: «Urani[---]»[28]. It was recently suggested that the mausoleum belonged to a funerary association, and the inscription would have cosmic associations[29]. A more plausible explanation is that the mausoleum belonged to the Uranii, a family that occupied important positions in the administration of Italy from the time of Constantine onwards, rising from the rank of *perfectissimi* to the clarissimate[30]. If this is the case, the fact that the Uranii built their funerary monument before reaching the clarissimate (at that time the highest rank of the Roman aristocracy) would be a good example of how building could be incorporated into the aristocratic strategies for self-legitimation and social advancement in a Christian context[31].

Christianity, we should not forget, offered to aristocrats the possibility of being buried in publicly frequented monuments, something they had not enjoyed since the beginning of the Principate. Although early imperial senators and other members of the Roman elite continued to build magnificent tombs inside their suburban *villae* and *horti* (spaces frequented by clients, friends, and associates)[32], there is nothing that might have had as

---

[27] L. SPERA, *Il paesaggio suburbano di Roma...*, 233; A.M. NIEDDU, «*Catacumbas coemeterium*»..., 84; also of the same author, see «*Uraniorum sepulchri*», in *Lexicon Topographicum Urbis Romae – Suburbium*, vol. 5, ed. by A. LA REGINA, Rome 2008, 214.

[28] ICUR n.s. V, 13659a.

[29] A.M. NIEDDU, «*Catacumbas coemeterium*»..., 85; also ID., «*Uraniorum sepulchri*»....

[30] On the Uranii, see *PLRE* I, Uranius 4 (*v.p.*, *corrector Flaminiae et Piceni* in 325) and Uranius 5 (initially *v.p.*, later *v.c.*). This identification had already been suggested by M. TORELLI, *Le basiliche circiformi di Roma...*, 205. More unlikely is the identification of these Urani as the family of S. Ambrose, suggested by De Rossi and accepted by, for example, F. TOLOTTI, *Memorie degli apostoli* in catacumbas, Vatican City 1953, 268.

[31] Although the precise dating of the mausoleum remains unknown, it was certainly a near contemporary of the basilica itself: see A. FERRUA, *Lavori a S. Sebastian...*, 217. ICUR n.s. V, 13296, dated to 349, was found inserted into the floor of the structure in 1885, but it might have been moved there.

[32] For early imperial Rome, see the remarks of N. PURCELL, *Tomb and Suburb*, in *Römische Gräberstrassen. Selbstdarstellung – Status – Standard*, ed. by H. VON HESBERG, P. ZANKER, Munich 1987, 32-40. B. BORG, *Bilder für die Ewigkeit oder glanzvoller Auftritt? Zum Repräsentationsverhalten der stadtrömischen Eliten im dritten Jahr-*

great an impact on contemporaries as the tombs around S. Sebastiano, for example.

These mausolea should be seen as part of the physical context in which the celebration of martyrs took place. Prudentius illustrates this point in his *Peristephanon*, when he says that the «ornaments of the senate», once pagan priests, now eagerly kissed the thresholds of apostles and martyrs[33]. The conversion of important senatorial families, with long and distinguished histories, is a theme that also appears in his *Contra Symmachum*, where the Probi, Anicii, and Gracchi appear paying tributes to the martyrs[34]. By entering spaces like the *Basilica Apostolorum*, these powerful aristocrats left a strong impression in the imagination of Christian writers such as Prudentius and Jerome. However, the monuments and inscriptions on display did not celebrate the city's martyrs and its bishops only: they also celebrated these same aristocratic families.

The problem is, of course, how to visualize these Christian celebrations. Ammianus Marcellinus famously criticized the daily processions of members of senatorial families, who crossed the city surrounded by attendants and clients, dressed in great splendour[35]. The mere presence of aristocrats in the streets of the city was a spectacular sight, a fact that conflicted with values expected from committed Christians. Jerome specifically praised Asella for passing unnoticed when visiting the tombs of the martyrs, and emphasised the importance of not seeking attention when fulfilling the precepts of a Christian life[36].

The life of Melania tells us that she insisted on attending the celebrations of S. Lawrence in Rome with her mother, and it is unlikely that two such important women, one of them pregnant, would have passed unnoticed among the crowd[37]. Such processions took place in days of celebration, and these constituted ideal occasions for the dramatic appearances of aristocrats. Peter Brown observed that celebrating saints also involved enjoying these events, even if parts of the clergy were not exactly happy

---

hundert nach Christus, in *Statuen in der Spätantike*, ed. by F.A. BAUER, C. WITSCHEL, Wiesbaden 2007, 53-63 shows that the monumentality of these tombs was actually increased in the course of the 3rd c.

[33] *Perist*. 2.517-20: *Ipsa et senatus lumina, quondam luperci aut flamines, apostolorum et martyrum exosculantur limina.*

[34] *C. Symm.* 1.548-65.

[35] AMM. MARC. 14.6.9; 14.9.16-17.

[36] See respectively JER. *Ep.* 24.4 (to Asella) and 22.16, 27, and 32 (to Eustochium).

[37] *V. Mel. Gr.* 6; also *V. Mel. Lat.* 5.3.

with the excesses of these festive occasions³⁸. This is more relevant when we consider the fact that just like S. Sebastiano, other shrines of martyrs surrounded the city, built along the main roads leading to Rome. Papal works and the memory of the martyrs could reinforce the standing of senatorial families, who in turn brought attention and attendants to these festivals. Besides martyrs, Christians also witnessed the glory of families like the Uranii.

Taking part in the celebration of martyrs, or being buried next to them, should not be seen merely as a form of aristocratic self-aggrandizement. Celebrating one's (or a family's) power and standing was certainly a legitimate concern of Christian aristocrats, but what made their presence in the shrines of martyrs so meaningful to contemporaries was the fact that they shared the same beliefs, doctrinal differences notwithstanding. As Peter Brown reminds us, «[b]urial besides the saints was not only an occasion for the rich and for the clergy to show their special status in the community: for some pious persons, it marked the end of a life characterized by continuous efforts to imitate their chosen saints»³⁹. The same is true with respect to the patronage of religious foundations, as can be seen when considering another complex, the church dedicated to the apostle Stephen on the via Latina.

2. S. Stefano on the via Latina and the Nature of aristocratic patronage

At the beginning of the 5th c., there were few aristocratic families whose support was as eagerly sought as that of Anicia Faltonia Proba⁴⁰. The family's wealth, religious commitment, and ecclesiastical connections placed the Anicii in a prominent position within the Christian community. Correspondents of Jerome, Augustine, and Pelagius, among others, they were involved in the theological controversies that rocked Rome and North Africa at the beginning of the 5th c.⁴¹ In 432, the Roman bishop Celesti-

---

[38] P. BROWN, *Enjoying the Saints in Late Antiquity*, «Early Medieval Europe» 9 (2000), 1-24.

[39] Ivi, 13-14.

[40] On Proba and her family, see *PLRE* I, Proba 3 and *PCBE* 2 (Italie), Proba 2. For what follows, see A. A. KURDOCK, *Demetrias* ancilla dei: *Anicia Demetrias and the problem of the missing patron*, in *Religion, Dynasty and Patronage...*, 190-224.

[41] See, for these links, A. KURDOCK, *Demetrias* ancilla dei...; for the theological controversies, see P. BROWN, *The patrons of Pelagius: the Roman aristocracy between East and West*, «Journal of Theological Studies» n.s. 21 (1970), 56-72.

ne reminded Theodosius II of the many properties in the East donated by Proba to the support of the clergy, the poor, and monasteries[42].

The wealth and position of Proba found a suitable heir in the figure of her granddaughter Demetrias. Having embraced virginity while still a teenager in 414, she remained an active supporter of asceticism for her entire life, both by observing it and supporting others[43]. When Jerome wrote to her in 414, he characterized her as one of the wealthiest and noblest women in the Roman world[44]. The properties and influence of Demetrias put her in a position from where she enjoyed considerable freedom to choose how, where, and on what to invest her resources. However, most studies of Demetrias have failed to consider her as an active patron, emphasising the letters she received from male ecclesiastical figures[45]. As a result, the most famous project sponsored by Demetrias, the building of a church dedicated to the martyr Stephen on the via Latina, is rarely discussed in the context of her social standing and strategies[46].

As the *Liber Pontificalis* records it, during the pontificate of Leo (440-461), «Demetrias the servant of God built a basilica to S. Stephen on her estate at the 3rd mile of the Via Latina»[47]. The basilica and the property in which it was built were excavated by Lorenzo Fortunati in 1857, and although most of the complex was subsequently spoliated and buried, leaving only the basilica itself standing, there is enough evidence to discuss the nature of the project (fig. 2)[48]. As the excavations revealed, the basilica

---

[42] *Acta Conc. Oec.* I.2, p. 90 (ed. E. Schwartz). These donations should be seen in the light of P. Brown, *Augustine and a Crisis of Wealth in Late Antiquity*, «Augustinian Studies» 36 (2005), 5-30.

[43] See for example the comments of Pelagius, *Ep. ad Demetriadem* 14.1-2 (in *The Letters of Pelagius and his Followers*, ed. and transl. R. Rees, Suffolk 1991, 50-51).

[44] Jer. *Ep.* 130.1.

[45] A. Kurdock, *Demetrias* ancilla dei ..., 191.

[46] A. Kurdock herself only mentions it in passing: ivi, 223-224. But see now K. Bowes, *Private Worship, Public Values...*, 94-96 and V. Fiocchi Nicolai, *Il ruolo dell'evergetismo aristocratico nella costruzione degli edifici di culto cristiani nell'hinterland di Roma*, in *Archeologia e società tra tardoantico e alto medioevo*, ed. by G. P. Brogiolo and A. Chavarria Arnau, Mantua 2007, 107-126.

[47] *LP* I, p. 238 (ed. L. Duchesne). For bibliography and sources, see now G. Bartolozzi Casti, «*Sancti Stephani Basilica (via Latina)*», in *Lexicon Topographicum Urbis Romae – Suburbium*, vol. 5, ed. by A. La Regina, Rome 2008, 106-109.

[48] See on the excavations L. Fortunati, *Relazione generale degli scavi e scoperte fatte lungo la via Latina*, Rome 1859. More recently, specifically on the basilica, see R. Krautheimer, in *Corpus Basilicarum Christianarum Romae*, vol. 4, ed. by R. Krautheimer, Vatican City 1970, 230-242 and G. Sorrenti, *Roma. La basilica paleocristiana di Santo Stefano in via Latina*, «Bollettino di Archeologia» 41-42 (1996), 253-267.

was built inside a very large private villa next to the via Latina (fig. 3: A). Fortunati found lavishly decorated rooms, with marble revetment on the walls, mosaic floors, and frescoes. On the northern side of the complex (fig. 3: B), a large apsidal room with many fragments of herms and statues of classical subject, style, and date was discovered. Although the chronology of the complex remains uncertain, the building techniques used in different parts (*opus reticulatum*, *latericium*, and *listatum*) suggest a long history, stretching back at least to the beginning of the Empire. This is supported by the inscribed *fistulae aquariae* found in the property, which allowed Filippo Coarelli to trace the transmission of the property through different aristocratic families from the beginning of the 2nd c. onwards[49].

It is not clear when the property passed into the hands of the Anician family. Coarelli suggests the late 3rd-early 4th c., based on the discovery of an inscription of Sextus Anicius Paulinus, consul in 325: "To Sextus Anicius Paulinus, proconsul of Africa twice, consul, urban prefect"[50]. The inscription was found covering a tomb *inside* the basilica (with the corpse *in situ*), which leaves us with two options: either the corpse of Paulinus was moved there after the foundation of the basilica, or the church was earlier than the foundation as recorded in the *Liber Pontificalis*[51]. The removal of corpses was a controversial issue in Late Antiquity, being prohibited by imperial legislation. Nonetheless, bishops and patrons were extremely interested in the movement of relics, and permission for such initiatives could be sought from the imperial court. Such a possibility should not be ruled out in the case of a family as powerful as the Anicii[52]. On the other hand, chapels and private churches were a common feature of properties of wealthy Christians, and one would expect the family of Demetrias to have provided for their spiritual needs in their villa[53]. The dating of the surviving structure is not secure, as the use of *opus listatum* was common

---

[49] For the *fistulae*, see CIL XV, 7535 and 7561. See F. COARELLI, *L'Urbs e il suburbio*, in *Società romana e impero tardoantico*, vol. 2, ed. by A. GIARDINA, Bari 1986, 47-48.

[50] CIL VI, 1680: *Sexto Anicio Paulino, procons(uli) Africae bis, co(n)s(uli), praef(ecto) urb(i)*. See F. COARELLI, *L'Urbs e il suburbio*, 38-39.

[51] See L. FORTUNATI, *Relazione generale...*, 13.

[52] Legislation collected in *Cod. Theod.* 9.17. For a discussion of these laws in a Christian context, see G. CLARK, *Translating Relics: Victricius of Rouen and fourth-century debate*, «Early Medieval Europe» 10 (2001), 164-166.

[53] On private churches, see now K. BOWES, *Private Worship, Public Values...*, 78 (for Rome) and 147-151 (rural properties). This possibility had already been suggested in passing by R. LANCIANI, *Pagan and Christian Rome*, Cambridge, Mass. 1893, 116.

throughout Late Antiquity, and this question must remain open[54]. In any case, the presence of the inscription and tomb of Paulinus, possibly the first high-ranking senator to convert to Christianity, emphasises the familial nature of S. Stefano[55].

The dynastic character of S. Stefano on the via Latina was reinforced by its architectural setting: the church was located inside the residential part of the villa, probably adapting a courtyard surrounded by columns (the base of one can still be seen incorporated into the apse wall), and opened onto a large peristyle (fig. 3: C) accessible from the via Latina[56]. Furthermore, the villa was still in use when the church was built, as suggested not only by the traces of wall and floor decoration found *in situ*, but also by the statues and sculptural fragments found in different rooms[57]. We cannot be certain of the motivations that led Demetrias to choose this specific site for her foundation. Demetrias must have had plenty of properties from which to choose for the foundation of a church, and her choice of site seems to be quite atypical. As Vincenzo Fiocchi Nicolai observed, the number of aristocratic foundations in the suburbs of Rome was strikingly low, especially when we consider their involvement in the *Urbs*, or even further away in Lazio[58].

As should be clear by now, the short reference in the *Liber Pontificalis* presents a much simplified version of the circumstances surrounding the foundation of S. Stefano. In order to form a clearer picture of what type of foundation we are dealing with, it is better to consider the dedicatory inscription found during the excavations:

> «When the virgin Amnia Demetrias leaving this world brought to a close her last day (yet not truly dying) she gave to you, Pope Leo, these final vows, that this sacred house arise. The trust of her command is fulfilled, yet it is more glorious to fulfil a vow of another than one's own. Stephen, who first in the

---

[54] For a good description of the remains, see G. SORRENTI, *Roma. La basilica paleocristiana...*, 258-259: different building techniques, presumably from different periods, coexist, and even the type of *opus listatum* changes: most walls are made of one course of tufa to one of brick, but the exterior wall of the southern aisle has two courses of tufa to one of brick. Note that even the flooring is of uncertain date.

[55] According to PRUD. *C. Symm.* 1.552-553, it was a «*generosus Anicius*». See also *PLRE* I, Paulinus 15.

[56] See V. FIOCCHI NICOLAI, *Il ruolo dell'evergetismo aristocratico...*, 111.

[57] See L. FORTUNATI, *Relazione generale...*, 3-6 (who announced, on p. 4 n. 5 that «[q]ueste sculture sono tutte ancora nel Magazzino di Città, e per vederle o contrattarne l'acquisto, si deve dimandare al Fortunati, via Due Macelli n. 94») and also G. SORRENTI, *Roma. La basilica paleocristiana...*, 256.

[58] V. FIOCCHI NICOLAI, *Il ruolo dell'evergetismo aristocratico...*, 107.

world was carried away by savage death, and reigns in the height of heaven, illuminates the summit [of the work]. By order of the bishop, the presbyter Tigrinus oversaw it, honourable in mind, work, and faith»[59].

As the inscription tells us, the foundation was carried out by the Roman bishop, fulfilling the last vow of Demetrias. Construction of the church was overseen by Tigrinus, a presbyter, following episcopal instructions. This presbyter is the same one whose funerary inscription was first seen near the via Latina, a man responsible for works in many churches[60]. Demetrias' last vows were fulfilled in a rather professional way, under the general direction of the bishop and the close supervision of a «specialist» subordinated to him. Episcopal control would help explain the fact that the basilica of S. Stefano also had a baptistery with a fountain, next to its apse (marked with arrow in fig. 3). In other words, this foundation had an important pastoral function, and as such must have followed the intentions of the bishop himself, and not only those of its aristocratic patron[61].

We should be careful, however, not to push the case for episcopal control too hard. Demetrias' personal piety played a crucial role in the definition of the project. The choice of the martyr Stephen as patron of the basilica seems to have been due to her interests, and not Leo's. Demetrias was in North Africa when the relics of Stephen arrived there in 416, an event that attracted great attention from contemporaries[62]. That the cult of the martyr was a central element in the planning of the church is indicated by the presence of a crypt and (probably) a *fenestella confessionis*[63]. The

---

[59] ICUR n.s. VI, 15764: *Cum mundum li[nqu]ens Dem[etri]as Amn[ia virgo]/ cla[ud]eret extremum non morit[ura diem,]/ [hae]c tibi, pap[a L]eo, votorum extrem[a suorum]/ [trad]idit, ut s[a]crae surgeret aula d[omus]./ M[a]ndati comple[t]a fides, sed glor[ia maior]/ [al]terius votum [s]olvere quam propr[ium.]/ In[lus]trat culmen Steph[a]nus qui primus in or[be]/ [r]aptus mort[e t]ruci regn[a]t in arc[e poli.]/ [Pr]aesulis ha[ec nut]u Tigrinus pr[esbyter instans]/ excolit ins[ig]nis mente labor[e fide].* My translation owes to A. KURDOCK, *Demetrias ancilla dei...*, 223, but differs mainly in the fact that she used the text as restored in ILCV 1765 (superseded by ICUR).

[60] ICUR n.s. VI, 15842: *diversis reparo tecta sacrata locis.* See *PCBE* 2 (Italie), Tigrinus.

[61] As argued by V. FIOCCHI NICOLAI, *Il ruolo dell'evergetismo aristocratico...*, 110. On episcopal control over aristocratic foundations see J. HILLNER, *Clerics, Property and Patronage: The Case of the Roman Titular Churches*, «Antiquité Tardive» 14 (2006), 59-68 and also of the same author, *Families, patronage, and the titular churches of Rome, c. 300-c. 600*, in *Religion, Dynasty and Patronage...*, 225-261.

[62] Noted by A. KURDOCK, *Demetrias ancilla dei...*, 223.

[63] See G. BARTOLOZZI CASTI, «*S. Stephani Basilica (via Latina)*», 108; V. FIOCCHI NICOLAI, *Il ruolo dell'evergetismo aristocratico...*, 111; for the importance of the cult of the

phrasing of the inscription, as well as the reference in the *Liber Pontificalis*, emphasise the connection between the church and the piety of the *virgo* Demetrias, *ancilla dei*.

S. Stefano on the via Latina is a good example of the impact that aristocrats could have on the Christianization of Rome. The size of the basilica (fig. 3: A), c. 29 x 19 m (plus an apse with a diameter of c. 8.5 m), together with the decoration, the presence of a baptistery, and the cult of the proto martyr Stephen, attest to the importance of the church in 5th c. Rome's religious life. At the same time, the fact that it was located in a private villa, the association with Demetrias' veneration of Stephen, and the tomb of her ancestor Paulinus, show that pastoral care was not necessarily at odds with family celebration. A number of inscriptions attest to the late antique use of this basilica as a funerary space. The Latin epitaph of a *vir spectabilis* from 530-533 refers explicitly to the association between the church and the martyr, indicating that Demetrias' piety remained an important factor in the choice of this church as a burial ground[64].

The association between Demetrias and her church, celebrated in the *Liber Pontificalis* and in the dedicatory inscription remained strong even after the site was abandoned[65]. The Roman breviary still mentioned this association in the context of the celebration of pope Leo, until its revision in 1960[66]. Foundations like the church dedicated to Stephen immortalized their aristocratic patrons, while helping to shape what we now call «Christian Rome»[67]. Powerful laics and the ecclesiastical hierarchy might have had different agendas, but these were not necessarily contradictory. Rather than the complex on the via Latina, the interaction between these two groups can best be appreciated in the most prestigious martyr-shrine of Rome, the basilica of the prince of the apostles.

---

martyr, see also S. EPISCOPO, *L'ecclesia baptismalis nel suburbio di Roma*, in *Atti del VI Congresso Nazionale di Archeologia Cristiana*, Florence 1986, 307. There are no remains of the *fenestella*, as the altar is badly damaged: G. SORRENTI, *Roma. La basilica paleocristiana...*, 263.

[64] ICUR n.s. VI, 15785: *[Martyris invicti Stepha]ni requiscis in aula*; *PLRE* II, Maurianus. See also ICUR n.s. VI, 15765, 15809, 15833, 15840a,c, 15857a-e, 15876, and 15884.

[65] The last references to the church are from the Middle Ages, see G. BARTOLOZZI CASTI, «*S. Stephani Basilica (via Latina)*», 106.

[66] Cited by K. KRABBE (ed. and transl.), *Epistula ad Demetriadem de vera humilitate*, Washington 1965, 6.

[67] A point made by K. BOWES, *Private Worship, Public Values...*, 70.

3. Clerics and Laics: the basilica of S. Peter

Although there is no real consensus about when the basilica dedicated to the apostle Peter in the Vatican was built, there is no doubt that it was an imperial foundation[68]. The evidence available, from inscriptions to the *Liber Pontificalis*, confirms its Constantinian inception (the date of completion remains uncertain), and scholars have shown that it was part of a wider building programme that transformed the city and its self-image[69]. Furthermore, there is no doubt that identification of the image of Peter with the bishop of Rome was a cornerstone of episcopal ideology[70]. To a large extent, the Vatican basilica represents the association of imperial and episcopal interests that still defines our image of late antique Rome, an imperial capital turned into the centre of the Christian world.

The image of S. Peter's as a joint project of imperial and episcopal authorities is largely justified, and it is perhaps for this reason that most studies concentrate on the original, Constantinian phase of the basilica. And yet, it is striking to realize the extent to which members of the Roman aristocracy intervened in and appropriated this space. This is clear in the case of the baptismal fountain built by Damasus. A structure of undeniable importance in terms of pastoral care, it was also an instrument in Damasus' policy of emphasising the unity of his church following his troubled election[71]. It is not clear where the baptistery was located, but we do know from an inscription found in the area that it was decorated by the *clarissima femina* Anastasia and her husband[72]. It was probably her son,

---

[68] See, of an ever-expanding bibliography, R. KRAUTHEIMER, A. FRAZER, in *Corpus Basilicarum Christianarum Romae*, vol. 5, ed. by R. KRAUTHEIMER, Vatican City 1970, 165-279. Also useful and more succinct, J. TOYNBEE, J. WARD-PERKINS, *The Shrine of St. Peter*, London 1956, 195-239.

[69] For an appreciation of Constantine's programme and S. Peter's role in it, see R. KRAUTHEIMER, *Rome. Profile of a City, 312-1308*, Princeton 1980, 26-28. The evidence is discussed in great detail in C. PIETRI, *Roma Christiana...*, 51-69. G. BOWERSOCK recently suggested that the basilica was the work of Constans, and not Constantine: *Peter and Constantine*, in «Humana Sapit». *Études d'antiquité tardive offertes à Lellia Cracco Ruggini*, ed. by J.-M. CARRIÉ, R. LIZZI TESTA, Turnhout 2002, 209-217; the only positive evidence for this suggestion, however, is a brick-stamp discovered in the apse, which could well be from a late phase of the works.

[70] Discussed in C. PIETRI, *Roma Christiana...*, 272-401.

[71] As attested to by the inscription, *Epigrammata Damasiana*, n. 4 = ICUR n.s. II, 4096: *Una Petri sedes, unum verumq(ue) lavacrum.*

[72] CIL VI, 41331a=ICUR n.s. II, 4097. See A. SILVAGNI, *Intorno ad un gruppo di iscrizioni del IV e V secolo appartenenti alla Basilica Vaticana*, «Bullettino della comissione archeologica comunale di Roma» 57 (1929), 145. For the location of the baptistery,

Gallus Anastasiae natus, who paid for important works in the church a few years later, as we know from an inscription[73].

In the mid-5th c., another Anastasia, married to Flavius Avitus Marinianus (consul in 423), was responsible for the elaborate mosaic decoration of the facade, at the request of bishop Leo[74]. As in the case of S. Stefano, here too aristocrats worked in close cooperation with bishops, complementing their works or attending to their requests. What is particularly striking in the case of the Vatican basilica is the fact that all these works seem to have been connected to one same family, as the repetition of names indicates. It has been suggested that the family of Anastasia descended from the Caesar Gallus, nephew of Constantine himself, a hypothesis that would explain the reappearance of the name in the late 4th century as patron of the basilica[75]. The most prestigious martyr-shrine in Rome could thus be converted into a space for the celebration of one aristocratic family, its links to the ecclesiastical hierarchy and possibly even to the original imperial builder of the church. The fact that a son of Marinianus and the 5th c. Anastasia called Rufius Viventius Gallus, a former urban prefect, fulfilled a vow «*pro beneficiis domini apostoli*», possibly on the altar or even on the apostolic tomb, is perhaps the best testimonial to the continued importance and prestige of this family[76].

There was a close association between the patronage of Christian structures and the social and political standing of aristocrats, as the inscriptions recording works by the family of Anastasia indicate. The early 6th c. author of the *Gesta de Xysti purgatione*, a fictitious account of a process moved against bishop Xystus III (432-440) by members of the Roman Senate, included Flavius Marinianus as one of the leaders of the anti-papal faction. In doing this, this anonymous author was probably influenced by the

---

see A. COSENTINO, *Il battesimo a Roma: edifici e liturgia*, in *Ecclesiae Urbis. Atti del congresso internazionale di studi sulle chiese di Roma*, vol. 1, ed. by F. GUIDOBALDI, A. GUIGLIA GUIDOBALDI, Vatican City 2002, 135.

[73] CIL VI, 41336a = DE ROSSI, ICUR II, p. 148 n. 15. See A. SILVAGNI, *Intorno ad un gruppo di iscrizioni...*, 137. For a different identification, see *PLRE* II, Gallus 3.

[74] CIL VI, 41397a = ICUR n.s. II, 4102; on the inscription and mosaic decoration, see now P. LIVERANI, *Saint Peter's, Leo the Great and the Leprosy of Constantine*, «Papers of the British School at Rome» 76 (2008), 155-72.

[75] Originally by A. SILVAGNI, *Intorno ad un gruppo di iscrizioni...*, 146; the suggestion is expanded and convincingly supported by F. Chausson, *Une soeur de Constantin: Anastasia*, in «*Humana Sapit*»..., 146-148.

[76] CIL VI, 41400 = ICUR n.s. II, 4782. For Rufius Viventius Gallus and Marinianus, see (besides works cited) S. ORLANDI, *Epigrafia anfiteatrale dell'Occidente romano*, vol. 6, Rome 2006, 488-489 and 494-495.

prestige of the consul and his family in ecclesiastical life[77]. As the case of Anastasia's husband suggests, Roman aristocrats were inextricably linked with papal politics, and the basilica of S. Peter was inevitably involved in this process.

In 533, the Ostrogothic king Athalaric addressed a letter to bishop John II, regulating papal elections on the basis of a former decision of the Senate. Another letter, sent to the urban prefect Salventius, asked him to inform the members of the Curia that the senatorial decision, as well as the royal edict, would be recorded on marble slabs and placed in the *atrium* of S. Peter's[78]. *Atria* were common elements in the architecture of basilicas in the late Roman world[79]. They served a variety of functions, both architectural and social; in churches, as well as in houses and palaces, these spaces were designed to shelter, direct, and impress visitors. In this case, a joint intervention by the Ostrogothic king and the Senate in matters of church politics were to be displayed in monumentalized form in a complex that was intimately related to the position and power of the bishop himself. Roman aristocrats had been involved in ecclesiastical politics since at least the middle of the 4th century[80]. The decision of Athalaric, in support of a senatorial decree, should not be seen as an exceptional measure, but as part of the normal relations between political and ecclesiastical elites in Rome.

But it is to funerals, the ultimate form of aristocratic self-representation, that we must turn in order to appreciate the extent to which aristocrats were involved with this space[81]. We know from a letter of Paulinus of Nola how Pammachius was able to celebrate his wife's funeral in Saint Peter's[82]. There we read of the crowds of poor men and women gathered inside the church, in the *atrium*, and even before the steps that led to it.

---

[77] For this controversial document, see G. ZECCHINI, *I Gesta de Xysti purgatione e le fazioni aristocratiche a Roma alla metà del V secolo*, «Rivista di Storia della Chiesa in Italia» 34 (1980), 60-74.

[78] CASS. *Var.* 9.15 (to John II) and 9.16 (to urban prefect).

[79] See J.-C. PICARD, *L'atrium dans les églises paléochrétiennes d'Occident*, in *Actes du XIe Congrès international d'archéologie chrétienne*, Rome 1989, 1451-1468.

[80] A point well discussed in R. LIZZI TESTA, *Senatori, popolo, papi. Il governo di Roma al tempo dei Valentiniani*, Bari 2004.

[81] I follow here some of the ideas developed in greater detail in C. MACHADO, *The city as stage: aristocratic commemoration in late antique Rome*, in *Les frontières du profane dans l'Antiquité tardive*, ed. by C. SOTINEL, E. REBILLARD, Rome (forthcoming).

[82] PAUL. *Ep.* 13.11. See discussion of this letter in L. GRIG, *Throwing parties for the poor: poverty and splendour in the late antique Church*, in *Poverty in the Roman World*, ed. by M. ATKINS, R. OSBORNE, Cambridge 2006, 145-161.

Paulinus' letter shows us how allusions to the gospels, the decoration of the basilica, and the generosity of Pammachius contributed to make this a special occasion. Although we have no evidence for it, it is likely that she was buried in the Vatican basilica or in its vicinity.

Although the Vatican was an important and prestigious burial ground, there is no definitive evidence for the burial of a Roman bishop in the area before Leo in 461. Even during the 5th c. bishops frequently chose other locations for their tombs, and it is only from the death of Simplicius (483) onwards that we can see a clear trend in this direction[83]. The situation is similar for members of the imperial family, and it was only in the 5th c. that the first imperial burials took place at S. Peter's, most famously in the mausoleum known later as the tomb of S. Petronilla[84]. In other words, during the 4th and for most of the 5th c. aristocratic tombs and funerals were among the most conspicuous memorials and commemorations taking place in the area.

The funeral of the urban prefect Iunius Bassus, who died in office in 359, must have been as impressive as that of Pammachius' wife[85]. His sarcophagus was discovered in 1597, and as Alan Cameron showed, the inscription on top of the sarcophagus refers to a *iustitium*, an officially declared period of public mourning in the city[86]. Bassus was buried in his family tomb, which was still in use until at least the mid-5th century[87]. More importantly, the funerary monument of the Bassi was located inside the basilica, in front of the altar of the crypt, and it is a striking example of *depositio ad martyres*, possibly carried out before the basilica had been completed[88].

The main area used for aristocratic burials seems to have been immediately behind the basilica. At the time of the great destructions carried out by Nicholas V (1452), Maffeo Vegio reported seeing a number of grand tombs, and part of the cemetery was still visible in the early 16th c., when

---

[83] See J.-C. PICARD, *À propos des sépultures papales jusqu'au début du VIIIe siècle*, «Antiquité Tardive» 1 (1993), 240. The *Liber Pontificalis* records the burial of 1st and 2nd c. bishops next to S. Peter, but as Picard notes (234) this might be a 5th c. fabrication.

[84] See M. JOHNSON, *Late Antique Imperial Mausolea*, (PhD Diss.), Princeton 1986, 118. For full discussion and bibliography, see F. PAOLUCCI, *La tomba dell'imperatrice Maria e altre sepulture di rango di età tardoantica a San Pietro*, «Temporis Signa» 3 (2008), 225-252.

[85] On Bassus, see *PLRE* I, Bassus 15.

[86] A. CAMERON, *The Funeral of Junius Bassus*, «Zeitschrift für Papyrologie und Epigraphik» 139 (2002), 288-292, correcting CIL VI, 41341a.

[87] *LP* I, 232.

[88] See F. PAOLUCCI, *La tomba dell'imperatrice Maria...*, 249.

large sarcophagi were found[89]. It is not clear how old this cemetery was, since Vegio mentions the presence of pagan tombs. The area available must have been extended during the pontificate of Damasus, when works were carried out to drain the hill to protect the tombs from flooding[90]. It was probably the Damasan works that made it possible for the construction of the grandest aristocratic mausoleum connected to S. Peter's, the mausoleum of Petronius Probus and his family.

The description made by Vegio is our main source of information about this tomb[91]. The *templum Probi* (as he called it) was grand and noble, decorated with many marble columns and inscriptions, including the famous metrical inscription celebrating Probus and his wife Proba (grandparents of Demetrias). At the time of Vegio, the mausoleum could not be entered from any side, and it was probably thanks to demolition works that the many treasures reported by a pilgrim in the middle of the 15th c. were found[92]. Further information can be gathered from the plan drawn by Tiberio Alfarano in the 2nd half of the 16th c. (marked with arrow in fig. 4). The tomb of the Probi is here shown as a basilica (12x18 m.) with apse and three naves separated by pillars[93]. The location of the tomb was also striking, having been built as an (partially or completely) underground complex, back-to-back with the apse of the Vatican basilica. In other words, it was right next to the *martyrium* of Peter himself.

The location and splendour of the Anician mausoleum would have been enough to single it out as one of the most important structures in the Vatican complex. But it was the name and standing of Petronius Probus and his family that made it such a powerful presence in late antique Rome.

---

[89] M. VEGIO, *De rebus antiquis memorabilibus basilicae S. Petri Romae*, in *Codice topografico della città di Roma*, vol. 4, ed. by R. VALENTINI, G. ZUCCHETTI, Rome 1953, 385 (also in DE ROSSI, ICUR II, 349). See also P. LIVERANI, *La topografia antica del Vaticano*, Vatican City 1999, 148 and F. PAOLUCCI, *La tomba dell'imperatrice Maria...*, 248.

[90] As recorded in *Epigrammata Damasiana*, n. 3: *Cingebant latices monte[m teneroq(ue) meatu]/ corpora multorum cineres [adq(ue) ossa rigabant]*.

[91] See M. VEGIO, *De rebus antiquis...*, 384-385 (DE ROSSI, ICUR II, 347-349). Also R. LANCIANI, *Storia degli scavi di Roma*, vol. 1, Rome 1989, 64. A useful discussion can be found in F. PAOLUCCI, *La tomba dell'imperatrice Maria...*, 245-248.

[92] Cited by P. LIVERANI, *La topografia antica del Vaticano...*, 147-148.

[93] For the architecture of the tomb, see the description in T. ALFARANO, *De Basilicae Vaticanae antiquissima et nova structura*, ed. M. CERRATI, Roma 1914. Particularly useful are R. KRAUTHEIMER, *The crypt of Sta. Maria in Cosmedin and the* mausoleum *of Probus Anicius*, in *Essays in Memory of Karl Lehmann*, ed. by F. FREEMAN SANDLER, New York 1964, 171-175, and P. LIVERANI, *La topografia antica del Vaticano*, 147-148. Liverani shows certain doubts with respect to Alfarano's plan, but see Krautheimer on p. 174.

The inscription copied by Vegio celebrates Probus, distinguished by his wealth, family, and titles, brought closer to Christ after his death[94]. As John Matthews observed, «the epitaph almost persuades us that Probus had simply received yet another promotion in his political career»[95]. The sarcophagus of Probus and his wife, showing a man and a woman kneeling before a *traditio legis* scene, now in the grotte Vaticane, was found here. Another large sarcophagus, showing Christ in front of city gates, now in the Louvre, is also reported as coming from this mausoleum[96]. Antonio Bosio attributes other sarcophagi with similar motifs to this tomb, a possibility that would fit the description of Vegio[97]. This was a family tomb, a fitting memorial to one of the most influential men in the late 4th c. and his descendants.

The strong familial links between members of the Anician family were also celebrated through the dedication of five statues to Probus and his wife by their children: Anicius Probinus, Anicius Probus, and Anicius Hermogenianus Olybrius (with his wife Anicia Iuliana)[98]. The dedicatory inscriptions record the personal virtues and political accomplishments of the parents, while also commemorating the political successes of the children. The statues were dedicated in 395, when Probinus and Olybrius were appointed joint consuls, in spite of their young age[99]. This initiative was repeated a decade later, when Anicius Probus was made consul, and a few verses were added to one of the statue-bases[100]. The statues were dedicated, therefore, after the death of Probus, which probably took place in 388 when he was exiled in Thessalonica.

The statues of Probus and his wife have long disappeared, but the bases on top of which they were originally set up were first recorded as in the gardens of the Palazzo Cesi, right by S. Peter's. The first member of the Cesi family to expand its collection of antiquities was cardinal Paolo Emilio, born in 1481, when works for the construction of the basilica were already

---

[94] CIL VI, 1756b=ICUR n.s. II, 4219. On Probus, see *PLRE* I, Probus 5.
[95] In J. MATTHEWS, *Western Aristocracies and Imperial Court, AD 364-425*, Oxford 1975, 195.
[96] See J. DRESKEN-WEILAND, *Sarkophagbestattungen des 4.-6. Jahrhunderts im Westen des römischen Reiches*, Rome 2003, 377-378.
[97] See A. BOSIO, *Roma Sotterranea*, Rome 1632, 55.
[98] CIL VI, 1752-1756 (+ pp.4751-4752)
[99] *PLRE* I, Probinus 2 and Olybrius 1.
[100] CIL VI, 1754, dedicated to Proba. For the date of the consulship, see *PLRE* II, Probus 11.

under way[101]. It is reasonable to suggest that the bases, with the statues they originally supported, were originally dedicated in the mausoleum of Probus, a possibility that is supported by the posthumous character of the inscriptions[102]. If this is correct, the mausoleum of the Anicii would have been a splendid monument, full of political and religious resonances.

It was not uncommon for aristocrats to receive posthumous dedications of statues, in private and public places. Iunius Bassus, who was also buried in S. Peter's, was honoured with a statue in his family's villa at Falerii Novi (modern province of Viterbo)[103]. In Rome, a statue was dedicated to Nicomachus Flavianus in the forum of Trajan decades after his death[104]. There are also earlier examples to which we can compare the *templum Probi* in Rome itself: tombs richly decorated with marble columns and inscriptions, populated by the remains and the likenesses of members of a prestigious family. The tomb of Marcus Artorus Geminus, in Trastevere, is one such example; the tomb of Priscilla, on the via Appia, described by Statius in his *Silvae*, is another[105].

The location of the statues dedicated by the children of Probus in the family tomb, if correct, would also provide us with a date and a context for the inauguration of such a splendid dynastic monument: the consulship of the brothers Probinus and Olybrius in 395. The choice of the sons of Probus as consuls must be seen in the context of the political turmoil in the West, following the victory of Theodosius over Eugenius. Roman aristocrats were deeply involved in this usurpation, and the court had to struggle to legitimise the new regime of the young Honorius – who would, incidentally, be the first emperor buried in S. Peter's[106]. When composing the panegyric read in honour of the two young consuls, Claudian made copious references to their deceased father, and the political overtones of the epitaph, mentioned earlier, also make more sense in this context. The descendants of Petronius Probus would remain loyal supporters of both

---

[101] See R. Lanciani, *Storia degli Scavi...*, IV (1992) 111-26, for the Museo Cesi.

[102] A possibility already suggested by A. Bosio, *Roma Sotterranea*, 55.

[103] *AE* 1964, 203 = *Supplementa Italica* 1, *Falerii* 13 (from 364).

[104] CIL VI, 1783 (from 431).

[105] See F. Silvestrini, *Sepulcrum Marci Artori Gemini*, Rome 1987 (esp. pp. 73-79 for the statues). Also Stat. *Silv.* 5.1.221-36. For a general discussion, see H. Wrede, *Die Ausstattung stadtrömischer Grabtempel und der Übergang zur Körperbestattung*, «Römische Mitteilungen» 85 (1978), 411-433.

[106] See A. Cameron, *Claudian. Poetry and Propaganda at the Court of Honorius*, Oxford 1970, 31-32.

the imperial court and of orthodoxy, for the decades to come. They certainly deserved a place in their religion's main space of worship.

4. Conclusion

During the excavations of the Constantinian presbytery of S. Peter's in the middle of the 20th c., a large marble slab was found re-used in a later (undated) phase of the pavement. The slab contained the funerary inscription of the *vir clarissimus* Eventius, who died in 407[107]. Eventius was a lawyer, adlected into the Senate and sent to Gaul as provincial governor. The inscription is the only source we have for his life and career, and must have come from the basilica itself. Eventius was a humbler senator, buried in a simpler monument than that of Petronius Probus, yet still managing to find space in this prestigious complex[108]. The mausoleum of Probus, in the meantime, had become the stuff of legend: in the Middle Ages, it was identified as the *Confessio* of Peter, the crypt to where he withdrew to pray before his martyrdom[109].

As the discussion of the Vatican basilica showed, Roman aristocrats played a crucial role in the making of Christian Rome. This role was much broader than merely paying for building projects and the embellishment of churches. It involved being a fully committed member of the Christian community, taking part in its debates, festivities, and cultic practices. Being a Christian was an option open to all, but it was something that men and women of different social and economic standing experienced in different ways. Both Eventius and Probus could be accommodated within the same community.

Aristocrats left a lasting mark on the Christianization of Rome through their works, rituals, and memorials. Aristocratic initiatives cannot be understood if we do not consider their social and political standing in conjunction with their religious commitment. This is made clearer in the case of the foundation of S. Stefano on the via Latina by Demetrias, a project that owed as much to her personal piety as to her family wealth. Scholars have recently questioned the relationship between the interests of laic pa-

---

[107] *AE* 1953, 200; see also B.M. APOLLONJ GHETTI ET AL., *Esplorazioni sotto la confessione di S. Pietro in Vaticano*, vol. 1, Vatican City 1951, 172.
[108] See *PLRE* II, Eventius 1.
[109] Cited by M. VEGIO, *De rebus antiquis...*, 384.

trons and ecclesiastic control over their foundations[110], but the case of S. Stefano is important precisely because it shows that these should not be seen as conflicting factors. In the Vatican basilica, aristocratic donations were specifically combined to ecclesiastical projects, and it is striking to notice that although the area was intensely used for the commemoration of powerful families, this did not stop it from becoming a symbol of papal power.

The importance of aristocrats in the Christianization of Rome can also be seen in a chronological sense. The grand mausolea built around S. Sebastiano were contemporary with the basilica, just as the tomb of Iunius Bassus was built around the same date as the completion of the basilica of S. Peter. It seems clear that aristocrats played a crucial role after the initial boom of the Constantinian period; a role that, although never quite as dramatic as that of imperial patrons, was important for being stable and more closely connected to ecclesiastical agendas. This role continued into the 5th c., when Demetrias and Leo pushed for the Christianization of the suburbs South of Rome.

It would be interesting, in this sense, to consider these same questions for the period after the Byzantine invasion (in 535) and especially after the pontificate of Gregory I (590-604), when the relationship between the Roman aristocracy and the ecclesiastical elite seems to have changed in a dramatic fashion. However, this would be well beyond the limits of this discussion. What the examples discussed here suggest is that, if emperors and bishops should remain the main characters in our narrative of the Christianization of Rome, there was a period between the end of the Constantinian dynasty and the Byzantine invasion of Italy when the Roman aristocracy played a leading role in this story.

---

[110] Most forcefully by J. HILLNER, *Clerics, Property and Patronage...*, and also *Families, patronage, and the titular churches of Rome*.

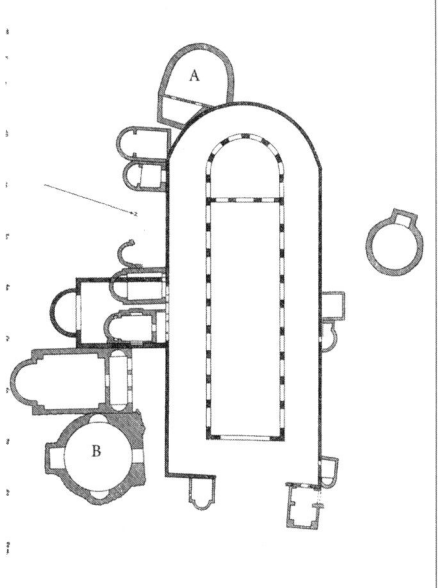

Fig. 1. *The* Basilica Apostolorum *and surrounding mausolea (adapted from E. La Rocca, in* Aurea Roma, *2000, 205).*

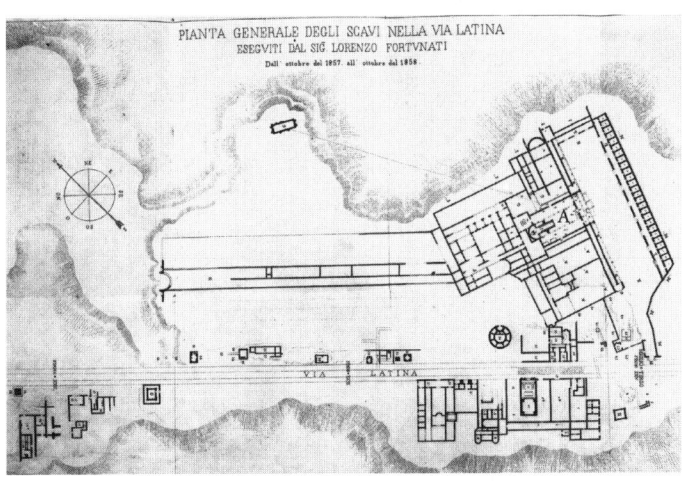

Fig. 2. *The villa of Demetrias on the via Latina (from L. Fortunati,* Relazione generale..., *1859).*

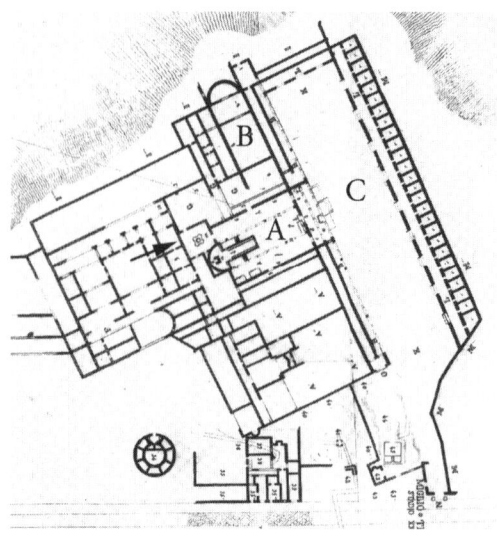

FIG. 3. *The villa of Demetrias, detail (adapted from L. Fortunati,* Relazione generale..., *1859)*.

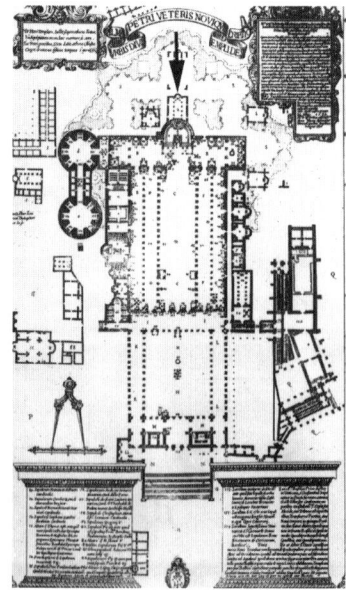

FIG. 4. *Basilica of S. Peter and the mausoleum of Probus (adapted from T. Alfarano,* De Basilicae Vaticanae..., *1914)*.

ALAN CAMERON

Vergil and his commentators

Arnaldo Momigliano once remarked that it was not so much pagan historians that disturbed Augustine, who «knew where to look for the real enemy», as «the idealization of the Roman past which he found in fourth-century Latin antiquarians... and commentators». This, he argued, is why Augustine «went back to the sources of their antiquarianism, and primarily to Varro, in order to undermine the foundations of their work»[1].

This is basically true, though not quite in the way most people have assumed. My subject this afternoon will be Vergil and his commentators, and their knowledge of Varro. Vergil has often been proclaimed the «pagan bible». Perhaps *Roman* bible, in the sense that Homer was the Greek bible, a text regarded by all educated people as canonical, the source of all knowledge and a continuing subject of exegesis. But hardly a *pagan* bible.

It was once taken for granted that Macrobius and Servius were pillars of what used to be called a pagan reaction, and though people are more sceptical now about pagan reactions, Nicholas Horsfall has recently written of the «passionately heated religious climate under which details of pagan cult in Virgil were discussed in late antiquity». He is right to point out that Macrobius and Servius «represent two readings of Vergil more interested than the poet himself in religious detail»[2]. But that does not mean that they had a religious purpose. The key factor here is that this interest of the Vergil commentators in ritual detail does not begin with Macrobius and Servius, nor with their source Donatus, nor even with his source, Aemilius Asper. Indeed, the first ancient critic to raise the issue was a man who might actually have known Vergil himself, Hyginus, a

---

[1] *Conflict between Paganism and Christianity*, ed. by A. MOMIGLIANO, Oxford 1963, 98-99.
[2] *Virgil, Aeneid 3: A Commentary*, ed. by N. HORSFALL, Leiden 2000, 59-60; and in «CR» 41 (1991), 242.

freedman of Augustus and friend of Ovid, described by Gellius as «not ignorant of pontifical law». No fewer than four of the nine quotations from his *De Vergilio* are concerned with ritual language, of which three already reveal the same exaggerated insistence on Vergil's ritual accuracy that is so characteristic of Servius and Macrobius.

But while Hyginus and the fourth-century commentators shared a preoccupation with Vergil's ritual language, there is nonetheless an essential difference between their approaches. Hyginus accused Vergil of error in his references to Roman cult and ritual, whereas the later commentators saw him as an expert in all areas of Roman religion, repeatedly characterising him as *sacrorum peritus*. Three other of Hyginus's nine surviving notes accuse Vergil of error of one sort or another, while for Servius and Macrobius Vergil *never* makes errors. Macrobius explicitly states more than once that Vergil was both expert and infallible in all matters. Servius too claims universal expertise for him, and many passages imply infallibility, though he does not make the point explicitly.

When and how did this remarkable doctrine of Vergilian infallibility arise? There can be little doubt that it gradually developed out of the response to the many early attacks on Vergil. First-century critics compiled lists of his plagiarisms (*furta*), others accused him of faults (*vitia*) both stylistic and moral, not to mention inconsistencies and ignorance of various sorts. A fascinating article by Sergio Casali has shown that Ovid's «Aeneid» (*Metamorphoses* 13) reflects some evidently very early criticisms otherwise known from later commentators[3]. Perhaps the most interesting thing about the response to this polemic is that, instead of just accepting some criticisms and ignoring the rest, Vergil's more single-minded admirers set out to refute them systematically, in part because from an early date the reception of Vergil was influenced by the reception of Homer. The fullest response we know of was published by Asconius († 88 AD) under the title *Contra obtrectatores Vergilii*. All these works have perished, but substantial traces survive in parts of Macrobius. To judge from his commentary on Cicero, Asconius's responses were probably balanced and judicious, but it is clear that some admirers felt obliged to defend Vergil against *all* criticisms, at any cost.

It is understandable that modern readers have been tempted to link debates in the *Saturnalia* about cult details in Vergil with the pagan/Christian conflicts of the fourth and fifth centuries. But ignorance of ritual was

---

[3] S. CASALI, *Correcting Aeneas's Voyage: Ovid's Commentary on Aeneid 3*, in «TAPA» 137 (2007), 181-210.

one of the very earliest criticisms made of Vergil. It was because Hyginus and other early critics accused Vergil of ignorance in ritual matters that his defenders were tempted to exaggerate his pontifical and augural expertise. In consequence, as early as the second century sacral law had simply become one of the areas of Vergil's omniscience. There is no sign that Macrobius and Servius treated it any differently from the others. As for the «debates» about Vergil's knowledge of sacral law, as Ribbeck saw long ago, they are no more than an inescapable element of any dialogue. The issues were long settled (in Vergil's favour), and the polemic simply lifted from the pro- and anti-Vergilian literature of the first century.

Indeed, this literature was surely one of the factors in his decision to cast the material he had collected in the form of a dialogue in the first place. In the interest of verisimilitude, whenever he could Macrobius liked to add a bit of cut and thrust to the often interminable learned lists he put in the mouths of his interlocutors. For example, he neatly divided a couple of passages of continuous exposition copied from Gellius between two of his speakers[4]. The first-century pro- and anti-Vergil literature was tailor-made to fit the cut and thrust of a dialogue. The polemical tone of these pamphleteers was ideal for his purpose. All had to do was divide up the two sides between different interlocutors. Clear traces of this first-century polemic are still present in Macrobius's section on Vergil's debt to Homer, which juxtaposes countless parallels between Homer and Vergil. After beginning with extravagant praise of Vergil's erudition, in several individual cases Macrobius condemns his «shameful inferiority», obviously here copying from an anti-Vergil pamphlet.

The obvious candidate for delivering the attacks on Vergil was the stock dialogue character of the uninvited guest, a disagreeable person whose function was to provoke the other interlocutors to discuss topics that would not otherwise have arisen among likeminded guests. The single most influential element in the «pagan reaction» reading of the *Saturnalia* has in fact always been Macrobius's uninvited guest, the boorish Euangelus, who repeatedly attacks Vergil. Few have been able to resist the assumption that he is meant to represent Christian hostility to the «pagan culture» venerated by the rest of the company[5]. This is a complete misunderstanding of Macrobius's purpose.

---

[4] R.A. KASTER, *Macrobius and Servius: Verecundia and the grammarian's function*, in «Harvard Studies in Class. Philology» 84 (1980), at 240-242.

[5] Most recently C. ANDO, *The Palladium and the Pentateuch*, «Phoenix» 55 (2001), 369-410 at 389

In the first place, this interpretation presupposes that Euangelus is immediately identifiable as a Christian. This is simply not so. The name itself might *seem* to suggest a Christian, yet it is not in fact a common Christian name. Like the names of all the other interlocutors, it is not a fictitious name, but the name of a real person taken from Symmachus's correspondence, a man Symmachus describes as a trouble-maker – obviously the reason Macrobius selected him for the role of uninvited guest.

More important, a number of passages in the *Saturnalia* unmistakably portray him as a practising pagan, a pagan (moreover) who claims to know more about pontifical law than Praetextatus himself. We are undoubtedly meant to think of him as a serious, well-informed pagan, only differing from the other interlocutors in his (rather surprising) hostility to Vergil. No one depreciated Vergil like that in the fifth century, not even Augustine. While criticizing Vergil's treatment of the pagan gods, Augustine never entirely lost his deep love for the poet who had once meant so much to him. The fact that it is Vergil who is the main object of Euangelus's hostility is not a reflection of contemporary attitudes to Vergil, much less Christian hostility to pagan culture. It is simply a reflection of Macrobius's first- and second-century sources, skilfully adapted to provide a foil for his own glorification of Vergil.

Anyone who takes the trouble to look carefully at what Euangelus is actually given to say will discover that he nowhere depreciates anything «pagan» about Vergil. Rather he claims to judge Vergil by stricter standards than the other interlocutors. He constantly and aggressively casts doubt on what he sees as exaggerated claims made for Vergil's scholarly attainments. Ironically enough, most modern readers of Vergil would agree with his general position, if not his actual arguments. For example, at *Sat.* i. 24. 9: «all that remains for you people to do now is to proclaim Vergil an orator as well» – which is (of course) exactly what they proceed to do, indeed had been doing since the early second century. In late antiquity it was heresy to doubt that Vergil was the supreme orator (a striking illustration of the assimilation of Vergilian to Homeric criticism: Homer too was universally regarded as the supreme orator). Tiberius Claudius Donatus goes so far as to claim that it should be rhetors, not grammatici, who taught Vergil.

Whether it is Greek literature, rhetoric or pontifical law, Euangelus is just a foil in the literary frame Macrobius chose to demonstrate Vergil's omniscience. Let us take a closer look at one of his questions together with the answer put in Praetextatus's mouth. After listening to an interpretation by Praetextatus that postulated considerable knowledge of pontifical law on Vergil's part, Euangelus loses his temper: «I too have attended lectures on pontifical law, and from what I know of it I shall establish Vergil's ignorance of the discipline.» After citing *Aen.* iii. 21, where Aeneas sacrifices a bull (*taurus*) to Jupiter, he quotes one passage from Ateius Capito forbidding the sacrifice of a bull (*taurus*) to Jupiter; and another from Antistius Labeo laying down that a *taurus* may only be sacrificed to Neptune, Apollo and Mars. That is to say, Euangelus is clearly presented as an authority on pontifical law – and so unmistakably as a pagan. In defence of Vergil, Praetextatus admits that Aeneas made the wrong sacrifice, but points out that a terrible portent followed the sacrifice. Vergil's mistake (he claims) was *deliberate*, a neat way of foreshadowing the terrible portent that follows, a detail (he implies) that would be picked up by learned readers. Servius has the same explanation, and adds further cases of supposedly deliberate mistakes in rituals that foreshadow bad outcomes. It is an argument that cannot fail, reminiscent of Gibbon on Salvian («the calamities of the wicked are judgments, and those of the righteous trials»). If Vergil gets a ritual right, that proves how learned he was. If he gets it wrong, the mistake is deliberate!

The truth is that Servius and Macrobius were not in the least interested in Roman cult in and for itself, and actually knew very little about it. Their only concern was proving that Vergil's ritual descriptions were never mistaken – except when they were deliberately mistaken. While insisting that Vergil was an unsurpassed expert on sacral law, their lack of real interest in the subject is proved by the fact that, when they came across mistakes they couldn't explain as deliberate, they were often satisfied with astonishing weak explanations. For example, that Vergil referred to the sacrifice of a female rather than male victim «for the sake of euphony» (DS on *Aen.* viii. 641).

Is it possible that late antique Vergilian commentators read the pagan/Christian issues of their own day into their beloved Vergil? Perhaps the most intriguing Macrobian conception is Vergil the *pontifex maximus*. In i. 24 he represents his interlocutors mapping out the course of their future discussions. Symmachus announces that he will cover rhetoric in Vergil. Next comes Praetextatus:

> «Of all the high qualities for which Vergil is praised, my constant reading of his poems leads me to admire the great learning with which he has observed the rules of pontifical law in many different parts of his work, as if he had made a special study of it. If my discourse does not prove unequal to so lofty a topic, I undertake to show that our Vergil may fairly be regarded as a *pontifex maximus* (i. 24. 16)».

It is tempting to link this passage with Gratian's supposed repudiation of the title of *pontifex maximus*. Taken by itself, it might well seem an attractive notion that pagans assigned to Vergil the religious duties rejected by the imperial pontifex. But by 382 it had been three quarters of a century since Christian emperors had played this role. More important, the long discourse of Praetextatus that follows makes it clear that the reference is not to religious secrets or respect for the gods, but simply to details in the Vergilian text alleged to reflect the minutiae of pontifical law – the province of the *pontifex*. Even in chapters that appear to be straightforward discussions of textual points, the underlying purpose is always to argue for the reading that implies the deepest knowledge of cult practice. For example, at *Aen*. v. 238, where the best MSS offer *extaque...proiciam*, Servius (misguidedly) insists that the correct reading is *porriciam*, quoting obscure pontifical writers in support, texts we are asked to believe Vergil had at his fingertips. For Macrobius, the key factor is the learning displayed by the citation. In context, *pontifex maximus* has less the modern associations of «high priest» than «religious expert».

The emphasis on details of sacrifice and ritual we find in Macrobius and Servius has no connection with the living pagan cult of the age in which they lived. Their interest was purely antiquarian. They were simply not interested in what we would call the *religious* issues involved in Vergil's cult references. Above all, there is not the slightest indication that they were responding to Christian criticisms of Vergil.

But if that is really so, you are no doubt thinking, why is it that the antipagan polemic in Augustine's *City of God* devotes so much space to Vergil and Varro? The choice of Vergil is obvious enough: the ever popular poet of empire, whose *Aeneid* is full of those references to pagan cult we have seen Macrobius and Servius discussing. But were people still reading Varro? According to Robert Markus (among many others), Varro's *Antiquitates* «carried weighty authority in fifth-century pagan circles such as the... group represented in Macrobius's *Saturnalia*»[6]. But did they? And which pagans? Certainly not Symmachus, who mentions Varro just once in his extensive correspondence.

Macrobius and Servius do indeed often appeal to the authority of Varro's many works. But if you study these citations, you will discover that they are invariably at second, third or fourth hand. Neither Macrobius nor Servius had ever seen an original work of Varro, least of all his *Human*

---

[6] Response in *Religion and Superstition in Latin Literature*, ed. by A.H. SOMMERSTEIN, Bari 1996, 77-80.

and Divine Antiquities. Macrobius cites that work only 8 times, five of them to illustrate points in Vergil. The fact that some passages are quoted in the same words by both Macrobius and Servius proves that both got their citations from a common source, not an original text.

Augustine, however, clearly sought out a complete text of Varro's *Antiquities* and read all 16 books. His more than 80 citations are at first hand. Since Macrobius wrote after Augustine, it is naturally tempting to wonder whether he made any attempt to answer Augustine's often very unfair use of Varro. There is no indication of anything of the sort. In any case, he could not (as Augustine could) have reconsidered any given passage of Varro in context and reformulated his argument to take account of objections. More important, he could not have offered any sort of informed rebuttal of any of Augustine's anti-Varronian arguments because he had no first-hand knowledge of the passages on which Augustine had based those arguments.

There is not the slightest indication that either Servius or Macrobius had any thought of defending the old gods and their rites against Augustine's mockery. For example, Augustine made particular fun of Stercutius, the god of manure (*CD* 18. 15). Servius lists him along with a series of other deities with no less trivial functions (on *Geo.* 1. 21). A defensive pagan would have been well advised quietly to drop the god of manure.

Very few of Augustine's Varro quotations find any parallel in Servius or Macrobius. That is to say, there is no indication that either of them was interested in discussing any of his (often unfair and misleading) arguments based on Varro. Complete texts of Varro's *Antiquitates* cannot have been easy to come by in the fifth century. But if Augustine managed to get hold of one in remote Hippo Regius, Macrobius, writing in Rome, could surely have done so if he had really looked. What does it mean that Macrobius did not take the trouble to track down and actually read a work that had always been an important resource for any serious Roman antiquarian, and had now been transformed by Augustine into a central text in the battle against paganism? Apparently Varro meant no more to him than the scores of other republican writers he so lovingly excerpted.

No less instructive in a different way is the long chapter on Janus and Saturnus (*Sat.* i. 7). According to Macrobius, Janus was originally a king of Italy, and the story that he had two faces and so could see both behind and before him is «undoubtedly a reference to the foresight and shrewdness of the king» (i. 7. 20). At some point Saturnus arrived, and, after learning from him the art of husbandry, Janus rewarded Saturnus by sharing the kingdom with him. When Saturnus died Janus devised religious honors for him (21-24). This is pure euhemerism. In earlier centuries some pagans had been attracted by the idea that (at least some) gods were originally just outstanding men deified by a grateful posterity. But from the second century on Christians siezed on euhemerism as a neat way of attacking pagans through one of their own. It would have been a bad mistake for any pagan apologist to present a euhemeristic account of Janus and Saturnus as if it were no more than historical fact. So why does Macrobius do just this? The explanation must be that he were simply reproducing, without any agenda of his own, what we know to have been Varro's approach, as we can reconstruct it from Augustine. DS and Servius claim that Faunus too was originally a mortal, with a DS note explicitly citing Varro. A pagan whose goal was to respond, however indirectly, to Augustine's criticisms would hardly have so casually conceded so central a point in contemporary Christian polemic.

Not the least of the reasons Augustine turned to Varro was (I suggest) precisely that *nobody* was actually reading him any more. He was no longer a text that people read but an authority scholars appealed to, almost always (as Augustine, an experienced reader of texts, could easily see) at second or third hand. Of his more than 70 works in more than 600 volumes, only one has survived complete. Nonius Marcellus, who preserves almost all of the 600 surviving fragments of Varro's *Menippean Satires*, might seem an exception. At least one copy of this extraordinary work must have survived into the fourth century, but even so it can hardly be said that Nonius *read* them. He quotes them, a line or so at a time, for details of morphology or vocabulary. What mattered was Varro's opinion, usually as reported in some later work, on whether this or that noun was masculine or feminine, or made its genitive in this way or that. In a word, what mattered was *auctoritas Varronis*, a formula we encounter constantly in the grammarians. It was enough that Varro was known to have said this rather than that. Macrobius and Servius constantly appeal to Varro, on a variety of topics, but obviously it was his authority in religious affairs that worried Augustine. He knew the Vergil commentators intimately (citing Asper, Cornutus and Donatus by name), and must have been disturbed at how often Varro was invoked to explain some cult detail in Vergil. For educated Romans, the combined authority of Vergil and Varro was irresistible. Augustine's brainwave was to sit down and actually *read* this great authority from cover to cover, and show those who appealed to him so trustingly, whether pagans or Christians, what laughable nonsense it was.

The anti-pagan polemic of Augustine's *City of God* has always puzzled thoughtful readers, overwhelmingly concerned as it is with the religion of the Roman republic as reconstructed from Varro and illustrated by Vergil. Some have argued that Augustine was out of touch with living, contemporary paganism. This is very is hard to believe in a man who devoted so much thought and serious research to the problem of paganism. The solution is surely that contemporary paganism was not his target. He cannot realistically have expected pagans even to read, much less be persuaded by so massive and polemical a work. What worried Augustine was not the few remaining pagans, but contemporary Christians, many of them recent converts, not yet baptized, disturbed by the sack of Rome, people whose motives and sincerity alike he considered suspect. It was disturbing that such people continued to devote so much of their formative years to Vergil.

Not the least of the reasons Augustine eventually came to disapprove so strongly of the poet he had once loved so deeply was that, as a former student and teacher himself, he knew only too well that, for Christians and pagans alike, the *Aeneid* remained much more than a mythological poem about the founder of Rome. The heady aura of paganism continued to linger around Vergil's poems and (especially) his commentators long after the last pagans were gone.

Silenti epiloghi

PAOLO LIVERANI

I vescovi nell'edilizia pubblica

Il tema che affronto è stato già toccato nell'ambito di inquadramenti più ampi[1], il che mi esime dal riprendere analiticamente tutta la documentazione e mi spinge invece a concentrarmi sulla messa a fuoco di alcuni dettagli meno considerati, che mi sembrano presentare un certo interesse.

Basandosi sull'epigrafia di lingua greca Anna Avramea[2] ha schematizzato i diversi ruoli dei vescovi nell'edilizia pubblica e soprattutto in quella civile: in età pre-giustinianea la studiosa considera essenzialmente due casi, distingue cioè tra le costruzioni finanziate dall'imperatore e quelle a carico dello stesso vescovo o meglio della diocesi. A partire da Giustiniano, invece, l'epigrafia conosce sfumature più variate e la casistica di questo periodo vede il vescovo investito di responsabilità di diverso tipo: da un patrocinio puramente spirituale, a una responsabilità morale come intermediario, a una responsabilità diretta, che può essere autonoma o in rappresentanza della città e che può interessare sia il finanziamento che la direzione dei lavori.

Questo maggiore coinvolgimento dei vescovi nelle opere pubbliche è abbastanza ovvio se si tiene presente la legislazione di questo periodo, che

---

[1] C. CAPIZZI, *L'imperatore Anastasio I (491-518): Studio sulla sua vita, la sua opera e la sua personalità*, Roma 1969; F.R. TROMBLEY, *War And Society in Rural Syria c. 502-613 A.D.: Observations on the Epigraphy*, in *Byzantine and Modern Greek Studies* XXI (1997), 154-209; D. FEISSEL, *L'évêque, titres et fonctions d'après les inscriptions grecques jusqu'au VIIe siècle*, in *Actes du XIe Congrès international d'archéologie chrétienne (Lyon, Vienne, Grenoble, Genève et Aoste 21-28 septembre 1986)*, Città del Vaticano-Rome 1989, 801-828, specialmente 820-824; A. AVRAMEA, *Les constructions profanes de l'évêque dans l'épigraphie et les textes d'orient*, in *Actes du XIe Congrès international d'archéologie chrétienne...*, 829-834; J.H.W.G. LIEBESCHUETZ, *The Rise of the Bishop in the Christian Roman Empire and the Successor Kingdoms*, «Electrum» I (1997), 120; ID., *The Decline and Fall of the Roman City*, Oxford 2001, 61, 111, 145-155, 157; C. RAPP, *Holy Bishops in Late Antiquity. The Nature of Christian Leadership in an Age of Transition*, Berkeley-Los Angeles-London 2005, 220-223.

[2] A. AVRAMEA, *Les constructions profanes...*, infra.

tra il V e la metà del VI secolo affida ai vescovi compiti sempre maggiori di supervisione e di indirizzo nell'amministrazione civica[3]. Il fenomeno tuttavia non può considerarsi una conseguenza automatica e necessaria di questi provvedimenti: esso è infatti molto più evidente nella metà orientale dell'impero piuttosto che in quella occidentale, dove sembra di poter osservare una divisione più rigorosa tra ambito civile e compiti propriamente ecclesiastici[4].

Per delineare più in dettaglio i passi di questa evoluzione, è utile cercare di comprendere – almeno nelle grandi linee – come avvenisse la conduzione di un'opera edile. A tal fine – oltre alla documentazione già discussa nei contributi a cui accennavo – si può considerare quella relativa all'erezione di basiliche cristiane: anche questi edifici possono essere considerati opere di interesse pubblico, in quanto approfittano di cospicui finanziamenti imperiali e sono soggette a procedure amministrative simili a quelle adottate per le costruzioni di interesse civile. Un approccio di questo tipo permette di valorizzare documenti relativamente antichi – risalenti cioè al IV e al V secolo – e di entrare più a fondo in alcuni meccanismi amministrativi dell'impero.

Vorrei cominciare dall'esame del dossier relativo al cantiere della seconda basilica di S. Paolo fuori le mura a Roma, quella teodosiana. In questo caso – benché il vescovo abbia un parte decisamente minoritaria – è possibile entrare in dettaglio nell'organizzazione e nella conduzione del lavoro. Il punto di partenza è il rescritto inviato nel 386 da Valentiniano II, Arcadio e Teodosio al *praefectus urbi* Sallustio[5] con le disposizioni per l'erezione della nuova basilica in sostituzione di quella costantiniana, ormai insufficiente.

Quel che ci interessa in questo contesto sono le dettagliate prescrizioni che vengono impartite al prefetto sulle procedure da seguire. Sallustio aveva già inviato alla corte una relazione sulla situazione del terreno; successivamente avrebbe dovuto:

---

[3] Partecipazione alla scelta del *defensor civitatis*: *C I* 1, 55, 8 pr (409), 1, 55, 11 (509); partecipazione alla scelta di *curator* e *sitona*: *C I* 1, 4, 17; 10, 27, 3 (491-505); partecipazione al collegio dei revisori dei conti civici e compiti di ispezione sugli edifici pubblici: *C I* 1, 4, 26 (531); *Nov.* 128,16 (545).

[4] C. Rapp, *Holy Bishops...*, 132.

[5] *Epistulae Imperatorum Pontificum aliorum inde ab a. CCCLXVII usque ad a. DLIII datae Avellanae quae dicitur collectio*, CSEL XXXV, ed. O. Guenther, I, Pragae-Vindobonae-Lipsiae 1895, 46-47, n. 3. Il rescritto si data entro il 6 luglio 386, data della prima costituzione indirizzata a Piniano, successore di Sallustio: *CTh* 6, 35, 13 = *C I* 12, 28, 4.

1) prendere contatti con il vescovo di Roma, il clero e la comunità cristiana per discutere a fondo la costruzione;

2) chiedere l'autorizzazione al *senatus populusque Romanus* per le modifiche della situazione stradale circostante, imposte dall'ampliamento della basilica;

3) far redigere un progetto dagli architetti;

4) inviare a corte, per l'approvazione del finanziamento sulle casse imperiali, una *synopsis operis construendi* – una stima cioè dell'opera da costruire – e un computo analitico di tutti i costi secondo i prezzi correnti a Roma[6].

Possediamo, inoltre, un'importante iscrizione incisa sulla base di una colonna della basilica[7], che ne commemora la parziale consacrazione[8] il 18 novembre 390[9]. Secondo questo testo, il lavoro era stato eseguito *administrante Fl(avio) Filippo vir[o] clarissimo]*, mentre risulta *[curato]re Fl(avio) Anastasio [v(iro) c(larissimo), t]rib(uno) praetoria[no]*. Il primo

---

[6] *Synopsis operis construendi fideli tendatur examine sumptuumque omnium iuxta pretia rerum, quae [sunt] in sacratissima urbe, praetaxatio plenius ordinetur atque ad nostram clementiam debita maturitate referatur.* «Venga offerta una stima dell'opera da costruire con esame accurato e sia disposta una valutazione preliminare con la massima completezza di ogni spesa secondo i prezzi vigenti a Roma e venga riferita alla nostra clemenza nella dovuta perfezione».

[7] ICUR II, 4778 c; ILCV 1857; G. Filippi, in *Pietro e Paolo. La storia, il culto, la memoria* (cat. della mostra Roma 2000), Milano 2000, 228-229, n. 101.

[8] H. Brandenburg, *Beobachtungen zur architektonischen Ausstattung der Basilica von S. Paolo fuori le Mura in Rom*, in *Vivarium. Festschrift für Christian Gnilka*, «Jahrbuch für Antike und Christentum», Ergänzungsband XXX (2002), 83-84 (nota 3); Id., *Die Basilica S. Paolo fuori le mura, der Apostel-Hymnus des Prudentius (Peristeph. XII) und die architektonische Ausstattung des Baues*, in *Ecclesiae Urbis (Atti Congr. Int. di studi sulle Chiese di Roma [IV-X secolo], Roma 4-10 settembre 2000)*, Città del Vaticano 2002, 1530; Id., *Le prime chiese di Roma. IV-VII secolo*, Milano 2004, 122. L'inaugurazione definitiva dovette avvenire solo nel 403-404, cfr. P. Liverani, *La cronologia della seconda basilica di S. Paolo f.l.m.*, in *Scavi e scoperte recenti nelle chiese di Roma (Atti della giornata di studi, Pontificio Istituto di Archeologia Cristiana, 13 marzo 2008)*, a cura di H. Brandenburg e F. Guidobaldi, Città del Vaticano, in corso di stampa.

[9] La data risulta da una integrazione di G.B. De Rossi, *Musaici cristiani e saggi dei pavimenti delle chiese di Roma anteriori al secolo XV*, Roma 1872-1899, commento alla tav. XIII, p. 2 del fascicolo (non numerata). La datazione al 390 proposta da A. Chastagnol, *Sur quelques documents relatifs à la basilique de Saint Paul-hors-les-murs*, in *Mélanges Piganiol*, I, Paris 1966, 420-436 (ristampato in *Aspects de l'antiquité tardive, Saggi di storia antica*, VI Roma 1994, 309-327) può essere respinta alla luce della migliore lettura dell'iscrizione proposta da G. Filippi, in *Pietro e Paolo...*, 228-229, n. 101.

doveva avere la responsabilità amministrativa, mentre il secondo doveva essere l'architetto direttore dei lavori[10].

Sul sommoscapo della stessa colonna era invece l'iscrizione che ricordava papa Siricio[11], senza attribuirgli particolari compiti, ma evidentemente dandogli la responsabilità spirituale dell'opera e forse quella morale, se vogliamo ipotizzare che la ricostruzione fosse avvenuta in seguito a una sua richiesta all'imperatore[12]. La dedica vera e propria, d'altra parte, sarebbe stata collocata qualche anno dopo e ricordava Teodosio e Onorio, gli imperatori che avevano ordinato la costruzione[13].

---

[10] P. LIVERANI, *Basilica di S. Paolo*, basilica nova, basilica Piniani, «Boreas» XXVI (2003), 73-81.

[11] ICUR II, 4778 a ILCV 1857; G. FILIPPI, in *Pietro e Paolo...*, 229, n. 102.

[12] La basilica dovette essere ricostruita non solo per l'insufficienza della vecchia chiesa, che era di dimensioni estremamente ridotte e non poteva contenere il grande afflusso di pellegrini, ma anche per equipararla al modello di S. Pietro in Vaticano. Una simile preoccupazione è fortemente romana e rientra nel programma della *concordia apostolorum* promosso con forza in quegli anni dalla sede romana. Gli ultimi anni hanno visto una fioritura molto vivace di studi sull'evoluzione architettonica della basilica: cfr. G. FILIPPI, S. DE BLAAUW, *San Paolo fuori le mura: la disposizione liturgica fino a Gregorio Magno*, «Mededelingen van het Nederlands instituut te Rome» LIX (2000), 5-25; H. BRANDENBURG, *Beobachtungen...*, 83-107; ID., *Die Basilica S. Paolo...*, 1525-1578; G. FILIPPI, *La tomba di S. Paolo e le fasi della Basilica tra il IV e il VII secolo. Primi risultati di indagini archeologiche e ricerche d'archivio*, «Bollettino dei Monumenti, Musei e Gallerie Pontificie» XXIV (2004), 187-224; H. BRANDENBURG, *Die Architektur der Basilika San Paolo fuori le mura. Das Apostelgrab als Zentrum der Liturgie und des Märtyrerkultes*, «Mitteilungen des Deutschen Archäologischen Instituts, Römische Abteilung» CXII (2005-2006), 237-275; G. FILIPPI, *Die Ergebnisse der neuen Ausgrabungen am Grab des Apostels Paulus. Reliquienkult und Eucharistie im Presbyterium der Paulsbasilika*, ibid., 277-292; ID., *La tomba di San Paolo alla luce delle recenti scoperte*, in *Il culto di San Paolo nelle chiese cristiane e nella tradizione maltese (Atti simposio int., Malta 26-27.6.2006)*, a cura di G. AZZOPARDI, s.l. 2006, 3-12, tavv. alle pp. 99-106; M. DOCCI, *San Paolo fuori le Mura. Dalle origini alla basilica delle origini*, Roma 2006; G. FILIPPI, *Recenti ricerche nella Basilica di San Paolo fuori le mura*, in *Il complesso basilicale di Cimitile. Patrimonio culturale dell'umanità? Der basilikale Komplex in Cimitile. Ein Weltkulturerbe?*, a cura di M. DE MATTEIS e A. TRINCHESE, Oberhausen 2007, 123-137; ID., *La tomba di S. Paolo. I dati archeologici del 2006 e il taccuino Moreschi del 1850*, «Bollettino dei Monumenti, Musei e Gallerie Pontificie» XXVIII (2008), 321-348; P. LIVERANI, *La cronologia della seconda basilica di S. Paolo f.l.m.*, in *Atti della giornata di studi «Scavi e scoperte recenti nelle chiese di Roma» (Pontificio Istituto di Archeologia Cristiana 13 marzo 2008)*, a cura di H. BRANDENBURG, F. GUIDOBALDI, Città del Vaticano, in corso di stampa.

[13] ICUR II, 4780; per la discussione cfr. P. LIVERANI, *La cronologia...* Durante la ricostruzione ottocentesca della basilica l'iscrizione fu riportata sulla sommità dell'arcone trionfale, ma in realtà non sappiamo dove si trovasse, poiché le sillogi che la tramandano non ne specificano la collocazione, mentre nelle incisioni che raffigurano i mosaici

Riassumendo possiamo suddividere le responsabilità della costruzione della basilica attribuendo a diversi attori i vari ruoli:
- al papa la responsabilità spirituale e una serie di indicazioni in fase di progetto, in qualità di primo utente dell'opera;
- all'imperatore la decisione politica e il finanziamento;
- al PUR l'alta sovrintendenza e il coordinamento;
- a Flavio Filippo la gestione amministrativa;
- a Flavio Anastasio la direzione tecnica.

Come si vede siamo di fronte a un organigramma abbastanza articolato, che possiamo provare ad applicare anche ai cantieri di altre basiliche finanziate dall'imperatore a cominciare già dall'inizio del IV secolo[14] (tabella 1).

Tab. 1. *Schema delle responsabilità in alcuni cantieri edilizi tra IV e VI sec.*

impresa edile	progetto / dir. tecnica	data progetto	fondi	amministrazione	fonti
Gerusalemme, bas. del S. Sepolcro	vescovo Macario; arch. Zenobio	326 o poco dopo	provinciali + imperiali	*Dracilianus PPO*; governatore della provincia	Eus., *VC* 3.31; Theophan., *Chronogr.* A. 5825
bas. di Mamre	vescovi di Palestina e Fenicia	326 o poco dopo	provinciali + imperiali	*Acacius comes*	Eus., *VC* 3.52-53
bas. di Costantina	vescovo di Costantina	330 ca.	fisco imperiale	*consularis Numidiae*	*CSEL* XXVI app. X, 215

---

prima dell'incendio ottocentesco (G.G. CIAMPINI, *Vetera Monimenta*, I Romae 1690, tav. LXVIII; R. KRAUTHEIMER, S. CORBETT, A. FRAZER, *Corpus Basilicarum Christianarum Romae* V, Città del Vaticano 1977, fig. 132) l'iscrizione è già perduta. G.B. DE ROSSI, *Musaici cristiani...*, commento alla tav. XIII, p. 4 del fascicolo (non numerata), ipotizzava si trovasse nell'abside con buoni argomenti.

[14] Per una discussione di dettaglio dei dati qui elencati R. KRAUTHEIMER, *The Ecclesiastical Building Policy of Constantine*, in *Costantino il Grande, dall'antichità all'umanesimo (Atti del Colloquio, Macerata 18-20.12.1990)*, a cura di G. BONAMENTE e F. FUSCO, II Macerata 1993, 509-552; P. LIVERANI, *Progetto architettonico e percezione comune in età tardoantica*, «Bulletin antieke beschaving» LXXVIII (2003), 173-188; IDEM, *L'architettura costantiniana, tra committenza imperiale e contributo delle élites locali*, in *Konstantin der Große. Geschichte – Archäologie – Rezeption (Akten des Internationales Kolloquiums, 10.-15. Oktober 2005, Trier)*, a cura di A. DEMANDT e J. ENGEMANN, Trier 2007, 235-244.

impresa edile	progetto / dir. tecnica	data progetto	fondi	amministrazione	fonti
Roma, bas. di S. Paolo f.l.m.	(vescovo); Flavius Anastasius vc [t]rib. praetoria[no] [curato]re	386	imperiali	Flavius Philippus vc administrante	CSEL XXXV, 46-47, n. 3; ICUR II, 4778
Gaza, bas. Eudossiana	Eudossia; arch. Rufino di Antiochia	402	Eudossia	Porfirio vesc. di Gaza	Marc. Diac., Vita Porfyrii
Dara - Anastasiopolis	vescovo Tommaso; patrizio Calliopium	505-506	imperiali	vescovo Tommaso (+ presbiteri e diaconi)	Ps.- Zach., HE 7.6; Marc. Comes, a. 518, MGH, AA XI, 100
Gerusalemme, bas. di S. Maria Theotokos (Nea)	arch. Teodoro	530	tesoriere imp. per la Palestina	Pietro, patriarca di Gerusalemme; Barachos, vesc. di Bakatha	Proc., Aed. 5.6; Cyr. Skythop., Vita Sabae 72-73

Procediamo in ordine cronologico: per la costruzione della basilica del S. Sepolcro disponiamo della lettera del 326 inviata da Costantino a Macario, vescovo di Gerusalemme[15]: la costruzione viene realizzata sotto la responsabilità del prefetto del pretorio per l'oriente, il governatore locale provvede alla mano d'opera e alla maggior parte dei materiali, mentre i marmi, le colonne e l'oro per le dorature sono forniti dall'imperatore, il progetto viene approntato sotto la responsabilità del vescovo, coadiuvato dall'architetto Zenobio[16].

Questo caso deve essere simile ad altri due coevi sui quali le fonti sono un po' meno dettagliate. Il primo è la costruzione della basilica di

---

[15] Eus. Vita Const. 3.31.1-3.
[16] Theophan., Chronogr. a. 5825, ed. De Boor 1883, 33; cfr. anche Chron. miscellaneum, ed. Brooks, CSCO, Scriptores Syri Versio, s. III, IV.2, 101. F.W. Deichmann, Waren Eustathios und Zenobios die Architekten der Grabeskirche?, «Byzantinische Zeitschrift» LXXXII (1989), 221-224, ha chiarito i malintesi relativi al presbitero Eustathios, che nulla ha a che fare con questa costruzione. Si può aggiungere però che la dizione sintetica di Teofane, secondo cui Zenobio avrebbe eretto «il Martyrium a Gerusalemme su comando di Costantino», non precisa se si debba intendere che l'architetto sia stato incaricato dalla corte imperiale, ovvero se l'ordine imperiale riguardasse l'erezione della basilica, lasciando aperta la possibilità che la scelta dell'architetto fosse dovuta al vescovo di Gerusalemme.

Mamre[17]: qui il ruolo di intercessione viene svolto dalla suocera Eutropia, il progetto viene affidato da Costantino ai vescovi di Palestina e Fenicia sotto la direzione amministrativa del comes Acacius. Il secondo è la costruzione della basilica di Costantina in Numidia[18]: la richiesta parte dal vescovo e sembra di capire che a questi venga affidata la responsabilità del progetto, mentre l'amministrazione va al *consularis Numidiae*.

Passiamo alla basilica Eudossiana di Gaza, pagata e patrocinata dall'imperatrice Eudossia. In questo caso la fonte, la Vita di Porfirio scritta da Marco Diacono[19], è più problematica: si tratta infatti di una rielaborazione più tarda dell'opera originale, per cui alcuni dettagli possono rispecchiare una situazione successiva[20]. Secondo la narrazione, Eudossia fornisce fondi, marmi e colonne al vescovo, grata per la profezia della nascita del figlio Teodosio II. Il vescovo Porfirio inizia a discutere la costruzione con il clero e i laici della città, ma Eudossia invia uno schema di progetto che risolve dubbi e discussioni. Questa procedura viene presentata come eccezionale, il che implica che di regola il progetto veniva realizzato sul posto. La direzione tecnica dei lavori viene affidata all'architetto Rufino di Antiochia, mentre la gestione dei fondi imperiali sembra attribuita al vescovo stesso.

Infine va esaminato un caso dell'età di Giustiniano, interessante perché possiamo affiancare alle notizie di Procopio[21] quelle fornite indipendentemente da Cirillo di Scitopoli nella Vita di S. Saba[22]. Si tratta della basilica di Gerusalemme dedicata a Maria Theotokos[23], la cosiddetta *Nea*. Questo

---

[17] Eus., *Vita Const.* 3.52-53. Bibliografia in A. Ovadiah, *Corpus of the Byzantine Churches in the Holy Land*, Bonn 1970, 131-133, n. 135; A. Ovadiah, C. Gómez de Silva, *Supplementum to the «Corpus of the Byzantine churches in the Holy Land», 2. Updated material on churches discussed in the corpus*, «Levant» XIV (1982), 153, n. 41.

[18] CSEL XXVI (1893) app. X, 217.

[19] Marcus Diaconus, *Vita Porfyrii episcopi Gazensis*, (ed. H. Grégoire, M.-A. Kugener, Paris 1930). Cfr. R. van Dam, *From Paganism to Christianity at Late Antique Gaza*, «Viator» XVI (1985), 1-20; C.A.M. Glucker, *The City of Gaza in the Roman and Byzantine Period*, Oxford 1987.

[20] Il caso forse per prudenza non sarebbe dovuto essere inserito nella tabella 1, che comprende per il resto dati tratti da fonti più affidabili, tuttavia nel peggiore dei casi la narrazione presenta quelle che dovevano essere considerate le procedure usuali e in questo senso potrà essere considerata di complemento al resto dell'evidenza raccolta.

[21] Proc., *De Aedificiis* 5.6.

[22] Cyr. Skythop., *Vita Sabae* 72-73.

[23] Sulla chiesa cfr. F.-M. Abel, *Jérusalem*, in F. Cabrol, H. Leclercq, *Dictionnaire d'archéologie chrétienne et de liturgie* VII.2 (1927), 2337-2346; J.P. Milik, *La topographie de Jérusalem vers la fin de l'époque Byzantine*, «MélBeyrouth» XXXVII (1960-61), 145-151; N. Avigad, *A Building Inscription of the Emperor Justinian and the Nea in*

progetto era stato già avviato autonomamente da Elia, patriarca di Gerusalemme, che aveva gettato le fondamenta, ma era stato cacciato dalla sua sede e sostituito con Giovanni. Il ruolo di intercessione presso l'imperatore viene svolto dal santo abate Saba, il progetto e la direzione tecnica dei lavori è affidato all'architetto Teodoro, inviato da Costantinopoli; gli esattori imperiali di Palestina forniscono i fondi necessari, la direzione amministrativa dell'impresa è delegata all'ordinario del luogo, l'arcivescovo Pietro, patriarca di Gerusalemme, ma la direzione dei lavori è attribuita a Barachos, vescovo di Bakatha. Siamo di fronte a una ripartizione delle responsabilità amministrative su due livelli. Che tuttavia si tratti di un regime amministrativo straordinario è chiarito da un'iscrizione[24] relativa a una grande cisterna realizzata, ancora a spese di Giustiniano, pochi anni dopo, quando la basilica era ormai regolarmente funzionante e dotata di un suo proprio clero: l'opera infatti in questo caso fu curata dal presbitero Costantino, l'igumeno della *Nea*[25].

Questi esempi sono importanti ma in fondo, trattandosi dell'erezione di basiliche cristiane è abbastanza logico trovare un coinvolgimento anche amministrativo del vescovo che usufruirà del nuovo edificio. Ci si può chiedere quindi se e quanto questo modello sia applicabile anche a imprese di edilizia civile finanziate su fondi pubblici in cui sia coinvolto il vescovo.

Già abbiamo osservato come un edificio ecclesiastico – la basilica di S. Paolo a Roma – viene costruita da una amministrazione civile, ma con lo

---

Jerusalem. (Preliminary Note), «Israel Exploration Journal» XXVII (1977), 145-151; ID., *Discovering Jerusalem*, Jerusalem 1980, 229-246; A. OVADIAH, C. GÓMEZ DE SILVA, *Supplementum to the «Corpus of the Byzantine churches in the Holy Land», 1. Newly discovered churches*, «Levant» XIII (1981), 200-261, 221-222, n. 24; K. BIEBERSTEIN, *Die Porta Neapolitana, die Nea Maria und die Nea Sophia in der Neapolis von Jerusalem. Beobachtungen zur Stadtentwicklung in byzantinischer und frühharabischer Zeit*, «Zeitschrift des Deutschen Palästina-Vereins» CV (1989), 117; Y. TSAFRIR, *Procopius and the Nea Church in Jerusalem*, «Antiquité tardive» VIII (2000), 149-164.

[24] N. AVIGAD, *A Building Inscription...* (= ID., *A Building Inscription Justinian and the «Nea» Church in Jerusalem*, «Quadmoniot» X (1979), 80-83 = ID., *Die Entdeckung der «Nea» genannten Marienkirche in Jerusalem*, «Antike Welt» X (1989)/3, 31-35); SEG XXVII 1977, n. 1015; P. FIGUEIRAS, in *Actes XI Congrès International d'Archéologie Chrétienne 1986*, Città del Vaticano – Rome 1989, 1781, fig. 2: Κ(αὶ) τοῦτο τὸ ἔργον ἐφιλοτιμήσατο ὁ εὐσεβ(έστατος) ἡμῶν βασιλεὺς Φλ(άουιος) Ἰουστινιανὸς προνοίᾳ κ(αὶ) σπουδῇ Κωνσταντίνου ὁσιωτά(του) πρεσβ(υτέρου) κ(αὶ) ἡγουμέ(νου) ἰνδ(ικτιῶνος) ιγ' ++. Cfr. anche D. FEISSEL, *Les édifices de Justinien au témoignage de Procope et de l'épigraphie*, «Antiquité tardive» VIII (2000), 99-100, n. 63.

[25] Abbiamo conferma da Giovanni Mosco che Costantino fosse l'igumeno della basilica: PG 87, c. 2857.

stesso schema di ripartizione delle responsabilità. Possiamo portare però anche un esempio eclatante di edilizia civile su larga scala in cui il vescovo svolge un ruolo protagonista e in cui i meccanismi gestionali e amministrativi sembrano essere gli stessi. Alludo alla costruzione della città di Dara decisa dall'imperatore Anastasio per dotarsi di una piazzaforte a ridosso del confine persiano, uno degli scenari più delicati di quell'epoca. Non si tratta dell'unico caso di edilizia militare che coinvolga vescovi[26], tuttavia è certamente quello meglio documentato dalle fonti[27]. Zaccaria di Mitilene[28] narra come l'imperatore coinvolse Tommaso, vescovo di Amida, il quale fece eseguire dei rilevamenti topografici del villaggio necessari per il progetto. L'imperatore acquistò il villaggio, che era tributario del vescovo, e affidò a quest'ultimo la direzione dei lavori, assumendosi tutte le spese e inviando inoltre manodopera specializzata. Quest'ultimo dettaglio viene confermato archeologicamente dall'utilizzo nelle mura di una tecnica detta *opus punicum*, del tutto inusuale in quest'area geografica[29].

I lavori procedettero con estrema rapidità, nonostante i tentativi persiani di arrestarli, e il vescovo si servì della collaborazione di due dei suoi presbiteri e di tre diaconi. Oltre alle mura vennero realizzate delle terme pubbliche, una chiesa, un magazzino, un acquedotto e grandi cisterne. Si dovettero risolvere problemi di ingegneria assai complessi dovuti al fatto che il fiume *Cordessus* (o *Kordes* in greco) attraversava la città e dunque il percorso delle mura.

È interessante notare come la nostra fonte si preoccupi di precisare che il vescovo inviò una formale attestazione che tutto il denaro ricevuto era

---

[26] I casi attestati dalle fonti sono raccolti in C. CAPIZZI, *L'imperatore Anastasio...*; F.R. TROMBLEY, *War And Society...*; A. AVRAMEA, *Les constructions profanes...*, 829-834; J.H.W.G. LIEBESCHUETZ, *The Decline and Fall...*, 61, 111, 145-155, 157; C. RAPP, *Holy Bishops...*, 220-223; F.R. TROMBLEY, J.W. WATT, *The Chronicle of Pseudo-Joshua the Stylite*, Liverpool 2000, XLVIII-XLIX, 106.

[27] La bibliografia è vasta: si vedano J. CROW, B. CROKE, *Procopius and Dara*, «Journal of Roman Studies» LXXIII (1983), 143-159; M. WHITBY, *Procopius' description of Dara («Buildings» II 1-3)*, in *The defence of the Roman and Byzantine East* II, a cura di P. FREEMAN e H. KENNEDY, Oxford 1986, 737-783; J. RIST, *Der Bau des ostsyrischen Stadt Dara (Anastasiupolis). Überlegungen zum Eigengut in der Kirchengeschichte des Ps.-Zacharias Rhetor*, in *Syriaca II*, a cura di M. TAMCKE, Münster 2004, 243-66.

[28] *Hist. Eccl.* VII.6 (ed. F.J. HAMILTON, E.W. BROOKS 1899, 164-168); assai più laconiche le altre fonti: PS.-JOS. STYL., *Chron.* 90 (trad. F.R. TROMBLEY, J.W. WATT, *The Chronicle...*, 109); *Chron. Zuqnin.*, a. 505-506 (trad. A. HARRAK, *The Chronicle of Zuqnīn, Parts III and IV A.D. 488-775*, Toronto 1999, 42, con ulteriori fonti).

[29] J. CROW, B. CROKE, *Procopius and Dara...*, 154; E. ZANINI, *La cinta muraria di Dara. Materiali per un'analisi stratigrafica*, in *Costantinopoli e l'arte delle province orientali*, a cura di F. DE MAFFEI, C. BARSANTI e A. GUIGLIA GUIDOBALDI, Roma 1990, 229-264.

stato impiegato nelle opere edili e che l'imperatore gli diede riscontro con solenni dichiarazioni che né lui né i suoi successori avrebbero chiesto ulteriore conto delle somme spese. Un importante elemento è aggiunto dalla cronaca del conte Marcellino[30], secondo il quale i lavori sarebbero stati diretti dal patrizio antiocheno *Calliopium*, il quale avrebbe sovrainteso al tracciamento delle mura. La apparente divergenza delle fonti può essere risolta considerando il vescovo Tommaso (e i suoi collaboratori) come responsabile della gestione amministrativa e *Calliopium* degli aspetti logistici e della direzione tecnica[31].

In sintesi si riproduce lo schema già visto per le altre imprese edilizie in cui la decisione politica e il sostegno finanziario spettano all'imperatore, la gestione amministrativa e l'impostazione del progetto – si ricordi l'esecuzione preliminare dei rilievi – al vescovo, la direzione tecnica a *Calliopium*, un personaggio che aveva già una notevole esperienza in ambito militare e logistico[32]. In questo caso, il fatto che sul posto non esistesse alcuna unità amministrativa statale e che il villaggio fosse di proprietà della chiesa di Amida ha reso quasi inevitabile la scelta di una ampia delega al vescovo. Nella stessa regione, inoltre, sono noti altri casi di interventi su mura e fortificazioni diretti da vescovi nello stesso periodo, come a Edessa, a Birta e in altri fortilizi minori[33].

Riassumendo i dati finora raccolti, appare evidente come l'intervento dei vescovi in collaborazione con le autorità civili per imprese edilizie è ben attestato e segue delle prassi che, nelle linee generali, non devono differire da quelle usuali nell'amministrazione imperiale. La collaborazione può avvenire a vari livelli e la responsabilità può essere spirituale, morale, progettuale o amministrativa. L'opportunità e i modi di un tal coinvolgimento episcopale sono determinati da una serie di elementi variabili, ma soprattutto dal carattere della costruzione, dalla disponibilità di unità amministrative affidabili sul posto e dalle situazioni di emergenza.

In altre parole ciò significa che, lungi dal sostituire l'amministrazione civile ordinaria, i vescovi svolgono una funzione di supplenza straordinaria, anche se relativamente frequente. Dove un'amministrazione funziona regolarmente – come nel caso della Roma teodosiana – anche una basilica cristiana come quella di S. Paolo può essere realizzata dalle autorità

---

[30] MARCELL. COMES, ad. a. 518, 3, ed. MOMMSEN, *MGH AA* XI, 100.

[31] B. CROKE, *Marcellinus on Dara: A Fragment of His Lost «De Temporum Qualitatibus et Positionibus Locorum»*, «Phoenix» XXXVIII (1984)/1, 77-88.

[32] B. CROKE, *Marcellinus on Dara...*, *Appendix*, 86-89.

[33] PS.-JOS. STYL., *Chron.* 87, 91 (trad. F.R. TROMBLEY, J.W. WATT, 106, 110); *IGLSyr* 1607, 270 (Add. II 381), 9135.

civili competenti, coinvolgendo il vescovo solo nella fase progettuale per il semplice motivo che egli rappresenta la comunità che utilizzerà la struttura stessa.

Per il resto si può ricordare come la media dei vescovi sembra venisse considerata di affidabilità maggiore dei funzionari imperiali[34] e ovviamente l'assunzione di responsabilità nel campo dell'edilizia pubblica non può essere separata da quel processo che vede attribuire ai vescovi crescenti responsabilità civiche, man mano che la struttura amministrativa curiale diveniva meno efficiente. Tuttavia quel che emerge dagli esempi sopra riportati è che un simile coinvolgimento avviene già fin dall'età costantiniana, quando la struttura amministrativa civica era ancora sufficientemente solida. Dunque si deve ritenere che, a fianco delle cause di ordine culturale e sociale più volte evidenziate, i motivi in base ai quali i vescovi vennero coinvolti precocemente in questa specifica responsabilità siano legati soprattutto alle loro funzioni peculiari di sovrintendenza e amministrazione della comunità cristiana, nell'ambito delle quali non era infrequente che dovessero assumersi autonomamente la cura di provvedere all'erezione o alla manutenzione degli edifici sacri o profani necessari alla vita della comunità e del clero diocesano.

---

[34] C. RAPP, *Holy Bishops...*, 249.

BÉATRICE CASEAU

Le crypto paganisme
et les frontières du licite: un jeu de masques?

Avec la fermeture des temples et l'interdiction officielle des sacrifices, une période nouvelle s'ouvre pour les adeptes des cultes traditionnels[1]. Leurs dévotions se font en privé, en secret ou encore elles prennent des formes détournées[2]. Le conformisme religieux s'impose de plus en plus, surtout pour ceux qui veulent faire carrière et le soupçon d'une conversion de façade progresse en même temps. Comme le faisait remarquer Alan Cameron à propos d'Augustin, apparaît alors une catégorie de personnes qu'une historiographie ancienne a appelé des «demi-chrétiens»[3], qui sont

---

[1] *Les lois religieuses des empereurs romains de Constantin à Théodose (312-438). Code Théodosien (Livre XVI)*, éd. T. MOMMSEN, trad. J. ROUGÉ, introduction et notes R. DELMAIRE, Paris 2005; P. CHUVIN, *Chronique des derniers païens. La disparition du paganisme dans l'empire romain du règne de Constantin à celui de Justinien*, Paris 2009$^{(2)}$; R. DELMAIRE, *La législation sur les sacrifices au IVe siècle: un essai d'interprétation*, «Revue d'histoire du droit français et étranger» 82 (2004)/3, 319-334; R.M. ERRINGTON, *Christian Accounts of the Religious Legislation of Theodosius*, «Klio» 79 (1997), 423-427; G. BOWERSOCK, *Hellenism in Late Antiquity*, Cambridge 1990. Jean Gascou, Vincent Déroche, David Frankfurter et Michel Perrin ont relu cet article et contribué par leur science et leurs stimulantes remarques à l'améliorer, qu'ils en soient chaleureusement remerciés.

[2] D. FRANKFURTER, *Religion in Roman Egypt: Assimilation and Resistance*, Princeton 1998; L. FOSCHIA, *Shifting Pagan and Christian Cult Places in Late Antiquity: from Monumentalization to Cryptocult and vice versa*, in *Actes du Symposium on Mediterranean Archaeology (SOMA), Fifth Annual Meeting of Post-Graduate Researchers, Univ. Liverpool, 23-25 février 2001*, Oxford 2002, 105-111.

[3] Le terme est assez ancien, fort utilisé dans les années 50, mais il a été repris en 2005 dans un livre de L. BROTTIER, *L'appel des «demi-chrétiens» à la vie angélique. Jean Chrysostome prédicateur, entre idéal monastique et réalité mondaine*, Paris 2005. Chez cet auteur, Jean Chrysostome, le terme désigne en principe des chrétiens d'origine juive, plutôt que des convertis du paganisme venus au christianisme par opportunisme et de manière superficielle. La question a été reprise lors du colloque *«Quid est christianum esse?». Le problème de la christianisation du monde antique*, Nanterre 26-28 Mai 2008 par M. PERRIN, *«Crevit hypocrisis». Limites d'adhésion au christianisme dans l'Antiquité tardive: entre histoire et historiographie* (à paraître).

l'objet d'une attention toute particulière de la part des prédicateurs, évêques ou moines. Dans les communautés chrétiennes des Ve et VIe siècles, les auteurs ecclésiastiques, moines et évêques, manifestent leur souci d'imposer non seulement un christianisme orthodoxe mais aussi un comportement chrétien. La chasse aux comportements déviants est alors ouverte, elle concerne en particulier les élites cultivées qui ont conservé un goût pour la culture classique et qui sont soupçonnées de crypto paganisme[4]. Plus grave encore que ces soupçons et que les pressions qu'ils entraînent, l'accusation de pratiques païennes ou magiques devient un instrument politique permettant de se débarrasser de personnes concurrentes ou gênantes. On voit alors se faire un amalgame entre accusations de paganisme et accusation de magie, dans le but d'obtenir une condamnation à mort des accusés. Le climat s'assombrit donc aux VIe et VIIe siècles, obligeant ceux qui pourraient être visés à des stratégies de prudence, ce qui a pu conduire certains d'entre eux à se débarrasser d'objets compromettants comme les statues divines, à afficher une distance moqueuse à l'égard de la culture religieuse antique ou à donner des gages de piété.

Nous analyserons d'abord quelles furent les stratégies mises en œuvre par les adeptes des cultes traditionnels pour vénérer les divinités, de manière secrète, sans être découverts, puis nous examinerons comment la fluidité religieuse liée aux conversions et à la multiplicité des appartenances possibles engendre une incertitude sur l'identité religieuse réelle des individus. Enfin, nous étudierons le soupçon de crypto paganisme qui peut naître facilement et parfois entraîner un procès, voire une condamnation.

1. Les stratégies de survie des adeptes des cultes traditionnels

On constate un changement dans les pratiques religieuses des adeptes des cultes interdits. Le premier est un repli sur la sphère privée où il est possible, si l'on contrôle bien sa maisonnée, de faire tranquillement un certain nombre de gestes rituels sans être inquiété. Comme Shénouté le fait remarquer, tant que les adeptes des cultes traditionnels se contentaient de vénérer les astres, en se tournant vers le soleil, la lune et les étoiles, ils pouvaient le faire sans être inquiétés. Mais dès lors qu'ils voulaient offrir des sacrifices, cela nécessitait sans doute quelques précautions. Il était

---

[4] V. DÉROCHE, *Quelques interrogations à propos de la Vie de Syméon Stylite le Jeune*, «Eranos» 94 (1996), 65-83, compare le phénomène des «paganisants» à celui des «judaïsants».

simple de faire brûler quelques grains d'encens ou d'offrir une libation chez soi. Un sacrifice dans l'âtre pouvait passer inaperçu, mais non un sacrifice sanglant. Les personnes visées par la surveillance appartenaient à la haute société. Elles disposaient de *lararia*, et possédaient des statues des dieux, devant lesquelles était pratiqué un culte domestique. Offrir des sacrifices aux divinités représentées par leurs statues était nécessairement moins discret et laissait des traces, ne seraient-ce que les offrandes de fleurs ou les cendres de l'encens brulé. Les gestes sacrificiels étaient connus et facilement interprétables. Même un sacrifice végétal ne passait pas nécessairement inaperçu si, au lieu d'être pratiqué dans les champs, en l'absence de témoins, il se déroulait à la maison, en présence de serviteurs. La difficulté était donc de pouvoir compter sur un silence complice dans sa maison, comme l'apprit à des dépens Gèsios, ce gouverneur de Thébaïde[5], retiré sur ses terres dans la région de Panopolis qui fut probablement dénoncé comme crypto païen par quelqu'un de sa maison[6]. Il tenta de convaincre le terrible Shénouté de sa bonne foi, de son respect des lois et de sa conversion au christianisme en l'invitant à venir voir qu'il n'y avait pas dans sa maison d'idoles ou d'autels suspects. Shénouté fit donc la démarche de venir une première fois dans la maison de Gèsios pour y constater en effet l'absence de tout objet compromettant. Mais c'était sans compter sur les informateurs qui indiquèrent à Shénouté dans quelle pièce fermée au second étage de la maison, il trouverait une collection de statues divines, soigneusement mise à l'abri par Gèsios. Une seconde expédition, s'apparentant à un cambriolage nocturne, livra à Shénouté lesdits objets. Regroupée dans une pièce fermée, ces «idoles démoniaques», pour reprendre l'expression de Shénouté, n'étaient pas de simples statues orne-

---

[5] L'identité du personnage dénoncé par Shénouté a fait l'objet de nombreuses recherches, S. EMMEL, *From the Other Side of the Nile: Shenoute and Panopolis*, dans *Perspectives on Panopolis. An Egyptian Town from Alexander the Great to the Arab Conquest*, éds. A. EGBERTS, B.P. MUHS, J. VAN DER VLIET, Leyde 2002, 95-113; H. BEHLMER, *Historical Evidence from Shenoute's «De extremo Judicio»*, dans *Sesto Congresso Internazionale di Egittologia. Atti*, éds. G.M. ZACCONE, T.R. DI NETRO, Turin 1993, t. 2, 11-19; dossier de textes dans H.J. THISSEN, *Zur Begegnung von Christentum und «Heidentum». Shenoute und Gessios*, «Enchoria», 19-20 (1992-1993), 155-164.

[6] S. EMMEL, *Shenoute of Atripe and the Christian Destruction of Temples in Egypt: Rhetoric and Reality*, dans *From Temple to Church. Destruction and Renewal of Local Cultic Topography in Late Antiquity*, éds. J. HAHN, S. EMMEL, U. GOTTER, Leyde 2008, 161-201; ID., *From the Other Side of the Nile...*, 95-113.

mentales puisque des lampes avait été allumées devant elles[7] et qu'elles provenaient d'un temple mis à mal par une attaque de Shénouté[8].

La cachette de Gèsios n'était pas aussi efficace que certaines caches de statues, qui ont été fouillées par des archéologues. Ainsi dans la maison dite des statues à Carthage, on a retrouvé des statues protégées par un mur, dans une pièce scellée[9]. Les chrétiens savaient que de telles pratiques avaient cours. Quodvultdeus par exemple dit avoir vu «dans un coin de la province Abaritane, tirer de grottes et de cavernes d'antiques idoles qui y avaient été cachées»[10].

Si la maison privée n'était pas nécessairement un lieu sûr, les temples désertés et parfois détruits, pouvaient aussi être surveillés. Le même Gèsios avait été surpris à mettre des roses dans un sanctuaire récemment brûlé par Shenouté. Ce geste fut pris pour un sacrifice, ce qu'il était probablement. La nostalgie que certains adeptes des cultes anciens pouvaient avoir à l'égard des temples poussaient certains à visiter ces lieux désormais interdits[11]. Une visite furtive pouvait être pour eux une occasion de manifester leur fidélité aux divinités ancestrales.

On retrouve un écho de pratiques sacrificielles continuées dans les temples, dans une lettre que Publicola adressa à Augustin en 398, pour laquelle nous avons la réponse d'Augustin. Publicola était inquiet de la

---

[7] SHENOUTE, *Que nos yeux*, trad. S. EMMEL, *Shenoute of Atripe and the Christian destruction*, 186; attaque du temple d'Atripe commentée, 142-143

[8] D. FRANKFURTER, *Iconoclasm and Christianization in Late Antique Egypt: Christian Treatments of Space and Image*, dans *From Temple to Church...*, 135-159. A. CAMERON, *Poets and pagans in Byzantine Egypt*, dans *Egypt in the Byzantine World (300-700)*, éd. R. BAGNALL, Cambridge 2007, 41 écrit: «Uneducated monks were not only unable to distinguish between cult statues and mythological art. They would have denied the very existence of such a distinction. In some cases at least they were probably raiding the sculpture gardens of well-to-do Christians». Il doute que les moines aient pu identifier statue de culte et statue ornementale, et qu'ils aient établi une distinction, ce qui est sans doute juste, mais ils pouvaient se rendre compte si des couronnes de fleurs avaient été déposées, ou de l'encens brûlé ou des lampes allumées. Il est polémique et probablement inexact de les assimiler tous à des gens analphabètes, comme le récent débat sur la culture de Shénouté le montre.

[9] S. ANGHEL, *Cachettes of Marble. Hiding and Protecting Statuary in Late Antiquity*, oral communication AIA 2009.

[10] QUODVULTDEUS, *Livre des promesses et des prédictions de Dieu*, III, 38, 45, éd. et trad. RENÉ BRAUN, Paris 1964, 578-599: *Noui quoque ipse in quadam parte Abaritanae prouinciae de spelaeis et cauernis ita antiqua producta simulacra quae fuerant absconsa*.

[11] M. TARDIEU, *Les paysages reliques: routes et haltes syriennes d'Isidore à Simplicius*, Louvain 1990.

contamination que les sacrifices pouvaient causer aux éléments naturels et des contacts qu'il pourrait avoir avec des aliments contaminés par des sacrifices. Il révèle par ses questions qu'il appartient à une époque de transition. Certains temples ont été fermés, mais n'ont pas pour autant perdu leur caractère sacré, d'autres continuent de fonctionner: «Est-ce qu'un chrétien doit boire de l'eau d'un puits qui se trouve dans un temple qui a été désaffecté? Si dans le temple qui rend un culte aux idoles se trouve un puits ou une fontaine et que rien ne soit fait dans ce puits ou cette fontaine, est-ce qu'un chrétien doit y puiser ou boire de l'eau?»[12] se demande-t-il. Publicola en chrétien consciencieux sait que tout ce qui a été clairement offert en sacrifice ne doit pas être touché, mais il explore les frontières de cet interdit. Jusqu'où va la contamination du sacré païen ? Publicola se demande «est-ce qu'un chrétien, en connaissance de cause, peut acheter un légume ou un fruit quelconque, venu d'un jardin ou d'une possession des idoles ou de leurs prêtres, et en manger ?»[13]. Les scrupules de Publicola révèlent que certains temples étaient encore fréquentés, de même qu'il donne à penser que des sacrifices avaient lieu dans les thermes où certaines statues divines se trouvaient. En 399, un texte publié à Padoue prévoit que les idoles des temples, qui malgré l'interdiction absolue de sacrifices, reçoivent un culte seront déposées et placées sous le contrôle des autorités impériales[14]. Un texte similaire, de peu postérieur, fut affiché à Rome en 407. Il ordonne que les statues des temples qui continuent à recevoir un culte soient arrachées de leur socle[15].

---

[12] AUGUSTIN, *Ep.* 46, 14 de Publicola à Augustin, éd. AL. GOLDBACHER, *S. Aureli Augustini Hipponiensis Episcopi Epistulae*, Vienne 1898, 123-129, à 127: *Si licet de fonte bibere uel de puteo, ubi de sacrificio aliquid missum est? si de puteo, quod in templo est et desertum factum est, debet inde Christianus bibere? si in templo, quod colitur, idoli puteus ibi sit uel fons et nihil ibi factum sit in eodem puteo uel fonte, si debet haurire aquam inde Christianus et bibere?*; trad. fr. dans C. LEPELLEY, *La diabolisation du paganisme et ses conséquences psychologiques: les angoisses de Publicola, correspondant d'Augustin*, dans *Impies et païens entre Antiquité et Moyen Age*, textes réunis par L. MARY et M. SOT, Paris 2002, 81-96.

[13] *Ep.* 46, 18 de Publicola à Augustin, *ibid.*, 128: *Si de horto uel de possessione idolorum uel sacerdotum eorum debet Christianus sciens holus emere uel aliquem fructum et inde edere?*

[14] *Codex Theodosianus*, 16, 10, 18, dans *Les lois religieuses...*, 454: *depositis sub officio idolis discreptatione habita, quibus etiam nunc patuerit cultum uanae superstitionis inpendi.*

[15] *Codex Theodosianus*, 16, 10, 19, *ibid.*, 454: *Simulacra, si qua etiamnunc in templis fanisque consistunt et quae alicubi ritum uel acceperunt uel accipiunt paganorum, suis sedibus euellantur, cum hoc repetita sciamus seapius sanctione decretum.*

Comme les temples étaient parfois sous surveillance, la recherche de lieux discrets, plus éloignés des centres habités fut donc une alternative appréciée. Les archéologues ont pu constater la renaissance d'anciens sanctuaires archaïques, situés dans des montagnes ou dans des forêts. On a ainsi retrouvé en Grèce plusieurs grottes qui servirent de lieux de culte tardifs, postérieurement à la fin du IVe siècle[16]. La présence d'offrandes, surtout de lampes votives en grand nombre est le révélateur de l'utilisation de ces lieux à des fins cultuelles. Ces lampes achetées au marché pouvaient porter des signes chrétiens, un signe de l'évolution de la société, une évolution que ceux qui les déposaient dans ces grottes n'appréciaient peut-être pas pleinement ou pas du tout. Ce n'est pas un hasard si des évêques comme Césaire d'Arles dénoncent les cultes rendus aux sources ou aux arbres. Dans un sermon pour exhorter le peuple, il écrivait: «Je vous exhorte de nouveau à détruire tous les sanctuaires païens, où que vous en trouviez. Ne rendez pas de culte aux arbres; ne priez pas auprès des fontaines; [...] Si quelqu'un sait que près de sa maison se trouvent des autels ou un sanctuaire païen, ou des arbres auxquels on rend un culte païen, qu'il s'applique à les abattre, à les mettre en pièces, ou à les couper à la racine»[17].

Il y avait enfin des moyens détournés de continuer à rendre un hommage aux divinités sans enfreindre la loi et sans se cacher, par exemple par l'organisation de banquets. Cette forme de patronage pouvait permettre de conserver aux divinités la sympathie de ceux qui bénéficiaient d'un repas gratuit pour les fêtes traditionnelles. De nouveau, les évêques ne s'y sont pas trompés. Ceux réunis à Carthage en 401 demandèrent l'interdiction des banquets aux autorités civiles:

> «La suppression des banquets païens est encore demandée. Contrairement aux commandements de Dieu se font, en de nombreux endroits, des banquets qui

---

[16] B. CASEAU, *The Fate of Rural Temples in Late Antiquity and the Christianisation of the Countryside,* dans *Recent Research on the Late Antique Countryside,* éds. W. BOWDEN, L. LAVAN, C. MACHADO, Leyde 2004, 105-144; quelques exemples: H. LAUTER, H. LAUTER BUFE, *Ein attisches Höhenheiligtum bei Varzika,* dans *Festschrift zum 60. Geburtstag von Werner Böser,* Karlsruhe 1986, 304-305; C. WELLER ET AL., *The Cave at Vari,* «American Journal of Archaeology», 7 (1903), 335-349; *Placing the Gods. Sanctuaries and Sacred Space in Ancient Greece,* éds. S. ALCOCK, R. OSBORNE, Oxford 1994; *Lieux sacrés, lieux de culte, sanctuaires. Approches terminologiques, méthodologiques, historiques et monographiques,* éd. A. VAUCHEZ, Rome 2000.

[17] CÉSAIRE D'ARLES, *Sermon,* 14, 4, éd. et trad. M.-J. DELAGE, Paris 1971, 438-439; sur les pratiques rituelles dans les bois sacrés: O. DE CAZENOVE, *Suspension d'ex-voto dans les bois sacrés,* dans O. DE CAZENOVE, J. SHEID, *Les bois sacrés,* Naples 1993, 111-126.

sont un héritage du paganisme. Aussi les païens entraînent-ils les chrétiens à les célébrer. Ce qui est comme une nouvelle persécution, mais occulte, en un temps où les empereurs sont chrétiens. On demande donc que ces banquets soient interdits et proscrits des villes et des campagnes sous peine d'amende. En particulier ne craint-on pas de commettre ces abus même aux jours anniversaires des martyrs et dans leurs propres sanctuaires. Ces mêmes jours, il est honteux de le dire, des danseurs produisent leurs exhibitions indécentes jusque dans les rues et les places. Ils portent ainsi atteinte à l'honneur du mariage et à la pudeur de beaucoup de femmes qui viennent faire leurs dévotions en ces saints jours. C'est tout juste s'ils ne les font pas fuir de l'entrée même des lieux saints de la religion»[18].

La crainte qui est ici exprimée est bel et bien le pouvoir attractif de telles cérémonies sur les chrétiens, puisque certains de ces banquets ont même lieu dans les sanctuaires des martyrs. Ce que redoutent les évêques ce sont des formes de va-et-vient entre l'ancienne et la nouvelle religion[19]. Ces mouvements ne sont pas nouveaux, puisqu'ils sont déjà signalés dans la lettre de Pline à Trajan[20], mais ils ont manifestement continué par la suite[21]. Les empereurs légifèrent sur les conversions de façade. Ils auto-

---

[18] *Concile de Carthage*, c.60 (adopté en 401 et repris lors du concile de 419), *Discipline générale antique*, éd. et trad. P.P. JOANNOU, t. I, 2, *Les canons des synodes particuliers*, Rome 1962, 297-298: *Illud etiam petendum, ut quoniam contra praecepta divina convivia multis in locis exercentur, quae ab errore gentili attracta sunt, ita ut nunc a paganis christiani ad haec celebranda cogantur, ex qua re temporibus christianorum imperatorum persecutio altera fieri occulte iveatur: vetari talia iubeant et de civitatibus et de possessionibus imposita poena prohibere. Maxime cum etiam in natalibus beatissimorum martyrum per nonnullas civitates et in ipsis locis sacris talia committere non reformident; quibus diebus etiam, quod pudoris est dicere, saltationes sceleratissimas per vicos atque plateas exercent, ut matronalis honor et innumerabilium foeminarum pudor devote venientium ad sacratissimum diem injuriis lascivientibus appetatur, ut etiam ipsius sanctae religionis pene fugiatur accessus*; GÉLASE, *Lettre contre les lupercales*, éd. et trad. G. POMARÈS, Paris 1959.

[19] E. KARABELIAS, *Apostasie et dissidence religieuse à Byzance de Justinien Ier jusqu'à l'invasion arabe (variations byzantines sur l'intolérance)*, «Islamochristiana» 20 (1994), 41-74; *Les syncrétismes religieux dans le monde méditerranéen antique. Actes du colloque international en l'honneur de Franz Cumont*, éds. C. BONNET, A. MOTTE, Rome 1999.

[20] PLINE LE JEUNE, *ep.* 96 dans *Lettres, Livre X*, éd. et trad. M. DURRY, Paris 1972, 74.

[21] S.G. WILSON, *Leaving the Fold. Apostates and Defectors in Antiquity*, Minneapolis 2004; M. PERRIN, *De quelques homologies entre ralliements confessionnels en régime chrétien et adhésions au christianisme dans l'antiquité tardive*, dans *Religioni in contatto nel Mediterraneo antico. Modalità di diffusione e processi di interferenza. Atti del III colloquio «Le religioni orientali nel mondo greco e romano», Loveno di Menaggio (Como), 26-28 mai 2006*, éds. C. BONNET, S. RIBICHINI, D. STEUERNAGEL, «Mediterranea» 4 (2007), 263-280.

risent les Juifs à retourner à leur ancienne religion, s'ils se sont convertis «par dissimulation hypocrite et non par esprit de foi»[22].

Tant que les cultes étaient pratiqués légalement et ouvertement, il était facile de repérer ceux des chrétiens qui y participaient. Un chrétien nouvellement converti qui se serait rendu à un sacrifice, ou qui aurait participé à une grande procession aurait sans doute du s'expliquer sur sa motivation à devenir chrétien. Les parrains des catéchumènes devaient en particulier veiller à ce que leur filleul soit clairement détaché de ces anciennes pratiques. Mais dès lors que les cultes sont interdits et pratiqués en secret, les moyens de contrôle simples disparaissent et le spectre du crypto paganisme apparaît.

2. La fluidité religieuse aux VIe-VIIe siècles

On peut constater cette fluidité religieuse dans les recueils de miracles des sanctuaires chrétiens. Il était dans l'intérêt des sanctuaires de rendre manifeste leur capacité à offrir guérison et conversion à une très grande diversité de personnes, venues de tous les horizons religieux[23]. Il est donc naturel de trouver dans les recueils de miracles des exemples de guérison pour des chrétiens d'une foi différente de celle du sanctuaire, pour des non chrétiens, juifs ou païens qui se convertissent, ce qui leur permet d'obtenir la guérison. Il importait aux compilateurs de montrer la puissance d'attraction du sanctuaire en donnant une origine géographique lointaine à certains de leurs visiteurs. Riches et pauvres se côtoient face à la maladie. Les recueils montrent l'universalité du pouvoir de guérir des saints en fournissant des exemples qui reflètent la diversité sociale et religieuse contemporaine[24].

---

[22] *Codex Theodosianus*, XVI, 8, 23, dans *Les lois religieuses...*, 404-406: *non id deuotione fidei, sed obreptione simulandum.*

[23] V. Déroche, *Pourquoi écrivait-on des recueils de miracles? L'exemple des miracles de saint Artémios*, dans *Les saints et leur sanctuaire à Byzance. Textes, images et monuments*, éds. C. Jolivet-Lévy, M. Kaplan, J.-P. Sodini, Paris 1993, 95-116; P. Maraval, *Fonction pédagogique de la littérature hagiographique d'un lieu de pèlerinage: l'exemple des Miracles de Cyr et Jean*, dans *Hagiographies, cultures et sociétés*, Paris 1981, 383-397.

[24] J. Gascou, *Religion et identité communautaire à Alexandrie à la fin de l'époque byzantine d'après les Miracles des saints Cyr et Jean*, dans *Alexandrie Médiévale*, vol. 3, Le Caire 2008, 69-88.

On apprend aussi dans ces recueils la place que tient la médecine religieuse dans la société de la fin de l'Antiquité. Les textes hagiographiques soulignent que face à la maladie, les malades ou leurs parents essayaient différents types de médecine, médecine hippocratique, dans sa version savante ou populaire, et médecine religieuse, traditionnelle ou chrétienne. L'offre médicale s'était diversifiée avec le développement des hospices et des hôpitaux[25]. La recherche de la guérison tendait à abolir les frontières mentales entre ces différentes offres médicales. La capacité d'accueil des malades existait dans de nombreux sanctuaires, qui disposaient au moins de portiques, et souvent de résidences pour les pèlerins et les malades[26]. Il était toujours possible de tenter sa chance dans un sanctuaire, sans qu'il soit requis de partager la foi du clergé du lieu. Bien plus, la venue d'un non croyant ou d'un hérétique était une forme d'hommage rendu aux saints du lieu et une occasion de prosélytisme pour les clercs. Les hérétiques étaient repérés à cause de leur refus de prendre la communion[27]. Rien n'obligeait un malade à prendre la communion avec les fidèles du lieu, mais le choix de rester à part était significatif et interprété.

On dispose d'un assez grand nombre de recueils de miracles provenant de sanctuaires de guérisons à la fin de l'Antiquité[28]. Ils sont composés de récits, souvent assez brefs, autour de la maladie d'une personne particulière, de sa venue au sanctuaire en vue d'obtenir la guérison, et de la décision des saints d'accorder ou non le miracle demandé. La plupart des recueils sont anonymes, mais on a le nom de l'auteur pour certains. Sophrone, futur patriarche de Jérusalem, a lui-même fait l'expérience d'une guérison

---

[25] P. HORDEN, *Hospitals and Healing from Antiquity to the Later Middle Ages*, Aldershot 2008; V. NUTTON, *From Galen to Alexander, aspects of medicine and medical practice in Late Antiquity,* dans *Symposium on Byzantine Medicine*, éd. J. SCARBOROUGH, «DOP» 38 (1984), 1-14.

[26] B. CASEAU, *Ordinary Objects in Christian Healing Sanctuaries*, dans *Late Antique Archaeology: Objects in Use,* éd. L. LAVAN, Leyde 2008, 625-654; A.T. CRISLIP, *From Monastery to Hospital. Christian Monasticism and the Transformation of Health Care in Late Antiquity*, Ann Arbor 2005; M. LOPEZ SALVA, *Actividad asistencial y terapéutica en el Kosmidion de Constantinopla*, dans «*Epigeios ouranos». El cielo en la tierra. Estudios sobre el monasterio bizantino*, éd. P. BADENAS, Madrid 1997, 131-145.

[27] B. CASEAU, *«Sancta sanctis»: Normes et gestes de la communion entre Antiquité et haut Moyen âge*, dans *Pratiques de l'eucharistie dans les Églises d'Orient et d'Occident*, éds. N. BÉRIOU, B. CASEAU, D. RIGAUX, Paris 2009, 371-420.

[28] H. DELEHAYE, *Les recueils antiques de miracles des saints*, Bruxelles 1925; A.J. FESTUGIÈRE, *Sainte Thècle, Saints Côme et Damien, Saints Cyr et Jean (extraits), Saint Georges traduits et annotés. Collections grecques de miracles*, Paris 1971; J.F. HALDON, *The miracles of Artemios and contemporary attitudes: context and significance*, dans *The Miracles of St. Artemios*, éds. V.S. CRISAFULLI, J.W. NESBITT, Leyde 1997, 45-55.

miraculeuse dans le sanctuaire de deux saints médecins, martyrs, les saints anargyres Cyr et Jean, à Menouthis, en Égypte[29]. Il compose un recueil de 70 miracles opérés par les deux saints médecins, les *Thaumata*, dans le but de promouvoir la réputation du sanctuaire chrétien implanté en un lieu où, encore vers 480, se pratiquaient secrètement des sacrifices aux divinités selon la *Vie de Sévère* par Zacharie le Scholastique qui signale un temple d'Isis autrefois célèbre mais désormais enfoui le sable. L'origine du sanctuaire chrétien est complexe à retracer, en raison de sources contradictoires et amendées. L'une des traditions fait remonter le culte de Cyr et Jean à Cyrille d'Alexandrie et à la lutte contre le paganisme, mais l'analyse philologique des textes attribués à Cyrille, la mention d'églises dédiées à des saints et l'implantation du tombeau dans l'église même montrent que ces textes ne sont sans doute pas antérieurs au VIe siècle ou ont été falsifiés[30]. Au temps où Sophrone compose ce recueil de miracles, peu après 610 et bien avant son accession à l'épiscopat en 634, le sanctuaire est aux mains d'un clergé chalcédonien, dans une Égypte largement monophysite. Le sanctuaire de Cyr et Jean[31] est probablement assez modeste en comparaison de celui de saint Ménas[32], situé de l'autre côté d'Alexandrie, et dont la renommée, que l'on peut suivre à travers la dispersion des ampoules portant l'image du saint, a traversé les mers[33]. Les sanctuaires et les monastères restés aux mains des chalcédoniens ont décliné depuis l'époque de la création d'une Église monophysite autonome sous Justinien. Il faut donc lire ces miracles de guérison en tenant compte de la concurrence

---

[29] J. GASCOU, *Sophrone de Jérusalem, Miracles des Saints Cyr et Jean*, Paris 2006; C. VON SCHÖNBORN, *Sophrone de Jérusalem. Vie monastique et confession dogmatique*, Paris 1972, 64-66 et 105.

[30] J. GASCOU, *Les origines du culte de Cyr et Jean*, «Analecta Bollandiana» 127 (2007), 241-281 (première version sur http://halshs.archives-ouvertes.fr); J. GASCOU, *Encore une fois sur l'onomastique ecclésiale ancienne*, dans «*Anthropos laïkos*». *Mélanges Alexandre Faivre*, éds. M.-A. VANNIER, O. WERMELINGER, G. WURST, Fribourg 2000, 119-130. Une synthèse de l'ancienne chronologie que j'avais suivie dans des articles précédents se trouve dans D. MONTSERRAT, *Pilgrimage to the shrine of SS Cyrus and John at Menouthis in Late Antiquity*, dans *Pilgrimage and Holy Space in Late Antique Egypt*, éd. D. FRANKFURTER, Leyde 1998, 257-279.

[31] Il est actuellement sous les eaux, une fouille sous-marine a repéré le lieu: F. GODDIO, M. CLAUSS, *Egypt's Sunken Treasures, Exhibition Catalogue*, Munich 2006.

[32] P. GROSSMANN, *Abu Mina. A Guide to the Ancient Pilgrimage Center*, Le Caire 1986.

[33] M. GILLI, *Le ampolle di San Mena. Religiosità, cultura materiale e sistema produttivo*, Rome 2002; J. WITT, *Menasampullen, Staatliche Museen zu Berlin-Preussischer Kulturbesitz, Skulpurensammlung und Museum für Byzantinische Kunst*, Wiesbaden 2000; P. LOPREATO, *Le ampolle di San Menas e la diffusione del suo culto nell'alto Adriatico*, dans *Aquileia e l'oriente mediterraneo*, Udine 1977, 411-428.

entre Église monophysite et Église chalcédonienne qui bénéficie encore à cette date du soutien impérial byzantin[34].

Au début du VIIe siècle, la population de l'Empire byzantin est officiellement chrétienne, puisque, en dehors de la petite minorité juive qui a un statut particulier, les autres religions ne sont pas licites[35]. A moins d'être un étranger de passage, il n'est pas permis d'être zoroastrien ou manichéen, par exemple. Il est aussi illégal d'être païen, depuis qu'une série de lois en 529 exige que tous ceux qui ne sont pas encore baptisés soient instruits dans la foi chrétienne. Elle complète le dispositif d'interdiction des cultes traditionnels qui à la fin du IVe siècle avait fermé les temples, interdit les sacrifices, et les autres rituels en l'honneur des dieux traditionnels. S'il n'est plus possible, et même dangereux, de se déclarer un adepte des antiques divinités, on peut être soupçonné de fidélité de cœur à la religion ancestrale, voire même de transgression des interdits en matière de sacrifice ou de pratiques dites «païennes». Ce soupçon de crypto paganisme transparaît dans le recueil de Sophrone. Dans un monde où il est convenu que toute personne est chrétienne, le jeu identitaire consiste à deviner à quelle sorte de chrétien on a affaire: s'agit-il d'un hérétique ou d'un faux chrétien, resté attaché aux anciens cultes? Les miracles de Cyr et Jean fournissent plusieurs exemples de cette quête identitaire. On perçoit que toute anomalie de comportement donne aussitôt naissance au soupçon, sans qu'il soit possible de démêler le vrai du faux. Le sanctuaire accueille une multiplicité de personnes, et, en cette époque de fluidité religieuse, de transferts d'un groupe à un autre, il est important pour les sanctuaires de lier guérison avec orthodoxie. Il est en particulier fréquent d'attribuer l'échec d'une guérison à une hétérodoxie, et la guérison à une

---

[34] S. DAVIS, *The Early Coptic Papacy: the Egyptian Church and its Leadership in Late Antiquity*, Le Caire 2005; V. DÉROCHE, *Études sur Léontios de Néapolis*, Uppsala 1995.

[35] Renforcement du dispositif juridique contre les non chrétiens résumé dans B. FLUSIN,*Triomphe du christianisme et définition de l'orthodoxie*, dans *Le monde byzantin, I. L'empire romain d'Orient (330-641)*, éd. C. MORRISON, Paris 2004, 51-54. Sur la période théodosienne, J. HAHN, *Gewalt und religiöser Konflikt*, Berlin 2004. Pour une évaluation différente de la vitalité des cultes païens en Égypte, R. BAGNALL, *Models and Evidence in the Study of religion in Late Roman Egypt*, dans *From Temple to Church...*, 23-41; J. HAHN, *The conversion of cult statues: the destruction of the Serapeum 392 A.D. and the Transformation of Alexandria into the «Christ-Loving» City*, dans *From Temple to Church...*, 335-365. A l'origine du débat, R. BAGNALL, *Egypt in Late Antiquity*, Princeton 1993, 269; 275-289; D. FRANKFURTER, *Religion in Roman Egypt: Assimilation and Resistance*, Princeton 1988.

conversion, mais ce qui ressort principalement de ces récits, c'est l'incertitude sur la foi réelle des visiteurs.

Prenons quelques exemples pour illustrer ce propos. Le miracle 54 raconte l'histoire d'un jeune garçon, issu d'une famille de philosophes de Damas et devenu épileptique. Le père du garçon, après avoir réalisé l'impuissance des disciples d'Hippocrate envoie son enfant avec sa mère au sanctuaire de Cyr et Jean. On peut noter que le premier réflexe du père est de recourir aux médecins. La médecine religieuse est un dernier recours. Sophrone fait le récit du rituel d'incubation et de la méthode recommandée par les saints pour obtenir la guérison:

> «Les martyrs les reçurent à leur arrivée et, peu de temps après, accomplirent la guérison et les renvoyèrent. Ils apparurent donc à la mère de l'enfant pendant qu'elle dormait et lui ordonnèrent de l'oindre de sa main, des cheveux aux orteils, de graisse de porc, ayant eu recours à un plan divin, parce qu'ils avaient à cœur de soigner l'âme de cette femme. En effet, on prétendait en effet que Joulia (tel était son nom) avait un défaut de foi, inclinait aux erreurs païennes et s'abstenait de viande de porc à cause de la mort d'Adonis. Ces rumeurs étaient-elles vraies? Cette réputation était-elle fausse? Dieu le sait ainsi que les martyrs qui donnèrent cet ordre. Elle s'abstenait de viande de porc: c'était une évidence indiscutable. Pour quelle raison n'en mangeait-elle pas? Personne, *à moins qu'il ne fût de ses intimes*, ne le savait. En tout cas, la maladie de l'enfant la contraignait à exécuter l'ordre»[36].

L'enfant est guéri et Sophrone conclut: «Quant à la mère, je pense qu'elle profita du miracle, s'il y avait vraiment en elle ce défaut, à moins qu'elle ne fut quelqu'un de tout à fait impie et insensé»[37].

Les méthodes des saints pour guérir les fidèles sont souvent insolites ou même drôles. Les recueils insistent sur la différence entre les médicaments prescrits par les médecins et les remèdes qu'indiquent en songe les saints anargyres. Il faut éviter la confusion et permettre d'attribuer la guérison à une intervention miraculeuse et non au médicament[38]. Leurs remèdes se distinguent non seulement des médicaments de la médecine

---

[36] SOPHRONE DE JÉRUSALEM, *Miracles des saints Cyr et Jean*, 54, 6-7, dans *Los Thaumata de Sofronio*, éd. N. FERNANDEZ, Madrid 1975, 369; trad. J. GASCOU, *Sophrone de Jérusalem...*, 189.

[37] SOPHRONE DE JÉRUSALEM, *Miracles des saints Cyr et Jean*, 54, 8, dans *Los Thaumata de Sofronio*, 370; trad. J. GASCOU, *Sophrone de Jérusalem...*, 189.

[38] B. CASEAU, *Parfum et guérison dans le christianisme ancien et byzantin: des huiles parfumées au myron des saints byzantins*, dans *Les Pères de l'Eglise face à la science médicale de leur temps*, éds. V. BOUDON-MILLOT, B. POUDERON, Y.M. BLANCHARD, Paris 2005, 141-191; A. VAKALOUDI, *Illnesses, Curative Methods and Supernatural Forces in the Early Byzantine Empire (4th-7th C. A.D.)*, «Byzantion» 73 (2003), 172-200.

savante, qui comportent souvent des ingrédients onéreux à base d'épices et de gommes résines, mais aussi des recettes magiques qui utilisent des ingrédients rares comme des parties d'animaux sauvages (ibis, crocodiles)[39]. Les saints, au contraire, recommandent souvent des ingrédients faciles à trouver sur place comme de l'huile des lampes du sanctuaire, de la kérôtè, une sorte de cire, du pain, de l'eau... Dans le miracle 54, le remède est de la graisse de porc, car, tout en soignant l'enfant, il vise en fait la mère dont le comportement alimentaire est différent des autres visiteurs du sanctuaire: son refus du porc est en soi une anomalie et c'est ce qui retient l'attention de Sophrone. Si le remède prescrit par les saints est précisément de la graisse de porc, ce ne peut être qu'en relation avec son refus à elle: c'est elle qui est visée à travers la maladie et la guérison de son fils. Bien que cette femme soit venue au sanctuaire, qu'elle y ait pratiqué le rituel d'incubation avec et pour son fils, et obéi aux ordres, un soupçon pèse sur elle. Malgré cela, son comportement alimentaire perturbe. Il est non conformiste, donc il doit cacher quelque chose, que seuls ses intimes connaissent. Ce qui ressort de ce texte, c'est l'incertitude sur la manière d'interpréter ce refus du porc. Curieusement, Sophrone ne suit pas la piste juive. Il lui préfère une piste païenne, en lien avec le culte d'Adonis. Les fêtes en l'honneur d'Adonis comportaient des offrandes végétales – les fameux jardins d'Adonis –[40], des pains particuliers aux épices[41]. Y avait-il chez les fidèles, souvent des femmes, un refus de la viande de porc pour pleurer la mort d'Adonis tué, selon la légende, par un sanglier? C'est ce que suggère Sophrone, mais on peut le soupçonner d'inventer et de préférer suivre une piste religieuse païenne et grecque pour dénoncer les attachements secrets à d'anciens cultes.

---

[39] L.R. LIDONNICI, *Beans, Fleawort, and the Blood of a Baboon: Recipe Ingredients in Greco-Roman Magical Materials*, dans *Magic and Ritual in the Ancient World*, éds. P. MIRECKI, M. MEYER, Leyde 2002, 359-377; ID., *Single-Stemmed Wormwood, Pinecones and Myrrh: Expense and Availability of Recipes Ingredients in the Greek Magical Papyri*, «Kernos» 14 (2001), 61-91; *Encyclopédie religieuse de l'Univers végétal. Croyances phytoreligieuses de l'Égypte ancienne*, II, éd. S. AUFRÈRE, Montpellier 2001; J. SCARBOROUGH, *The Pharmacology of Sacred Plants, Herbs, and Roots*, dans *Magica Hiera: Ancient Greek Magic and Religion*, éds. C.A. FARAONE, D. OBBINK, Oxford 1991, 138-174; A. TOUWAIDE, *La thérapeutique par la magie dans l'Égypte gréco-romaine*, «Revue d'histoire de la pharmacie», 38 n. 290 (1991), 349-350.

[40] M. DÉTIENNE, *Les jardins d'Adonis*, Paris 1972, évoque le refus de la viande chez les Pythagoriciens. Pour Adonis, pas d'offrande de viande mais plutôt de plantes.

[41] THÉOCRITE, *Idylle*, 15; J.D. REED, *Arsinoe's Adonis and the Poetics of Ptolemaic Imperialism*, «Transactions of the American Philological Association» 130 (2000), 319-351.

3. Sophrone et la mise au pas de l'élite cultivée, imprégnée de tradition classique

Sophrone vise en fait particulièrement les élites qui restaient attachées à la culture grecque classique. Comme G. Bowersock le faisait justement remarquer, en milieu alexandrin, les références au paganisme grec à cette époque sont le fait de chrétiens cultivés, une sorte de plaisir de l'érudition qui les met au dessus du commun et révèle leur éducation[42]. Sophrone est hostile à cette forme de culture hybride. Il cherche à rabaisser l'orgueil de cette élite sociale qui se permet des opinions personnelles en matière religieuse et qui n'hésite pas à dénoncer certains abus du culte des saints. Ainsi, d'une riche femme d'Alexandrie, une certaine Athanasia, fille de clarissimes, qui émet des doutes sur les saints Cyr et Jean, dont elle note que ce ne sont pas des martyrs bien identifiés[43], Sophrone écrit: «Inclinait-elle, sous l'emprise de quelque égarement, aux illusions païennes, lorsqu'elle déchirait ainsi les saints? [...] Je ne saurais me prononcer»[44]. Il lance le soupçon, alors même qu'il n'en a pas de preuve, simplement sur un désaccord concernant le culte de ces deux saints. J. Gascou fait remarquer qu'il s'agit d'une démarche d'intimidation, à l'égard des incrédules[45].

Époque dangereuse que ce début du VIIe siècle, où l'accusation de paganisme pouvait causer du tort, voire même conduire à une condamnation. Le soupçon tombait facilement sur ceux qui manifestaient une opposition aux idées dominantes, tandis que la rumeur pouvait être un instrument de vengeance personnelle. Sophrone rapporte à ce sujet le cas d'un argyroprate de Constantinople, peut-être dénoncé par des concurrents comme païen et qui s'est ainsi retrouvé en prison. Cet homme du nom d'Agapios

> «paganisait ouvertement, vénérait les idoles et adorait la créature au lieu du créateur. Convaincu de cette exécrable impiété, il fut arrêté dans la ville impériale et châtié pour ce motif. Contre toute attente, il échappe au glaive de la Justice, non pas par un changement d'opinion (car personne ne l'en aurait blâmé), mais par de nombreuses distributions d'or (acte d'extrême impiété);

---

[42] G. Bowersock, *Late antique Alexandria*, dans *Alexandria and Alexandrianism*, Malibu 1996, 266: «Wherever purely classical Greek paganism turns up in literature or art [...] it appears to be an elegant or erudite pleasure of Christians».

[43] A. Papaconstantinou, *Le culte des saints en Égypte des Byzantins aux Abbassides. L'apport des inscriptions et des papyrus grecs et coptes*, Paris 2001, 135-136.

[44] Sophrone de Jérusalem, *Miracles des saints Cyr et Jean*, 29, dans *Los Thaumata de Sofronio*, 298-302; trad. J. Gascou, *Sophrone de Jérusalem...*, 97-101.

[45] J. Gascou, *Sophrone de Jérusalem...*, 98, n. 564.

non pas par la mansuétude des lois [...] mais par la cupidité des défenseurs de la légalité»[46].

Après ces mésaventures, il s'installe à Alexandrie et tombe malade. Atteint de paralysie, devant l'incapacité à trouver du soulagement auprès des médecins, on lui conseille d'aller chercher la guérison auprès de Cyr et Jean les martyrs: «ils pourraient le délivrer de son mal, s'il allait les trouver plein de foi et de larmes»[47]. Agapios agit alors par conformisme religieux, par crainte d'une nouvelle dénonciation. Sophrone le considère comme un crypto païen, qui s'enfonce dans le mensonge. Il écrit à son sujet:

> «Craignant que ces gens ne découvrent son paganisme s'il ne voulait pas aller voir les saints (car ce maudit feignait d'être chrétien et d'être revêtu de la toison de la brebis, même si cet impie était un loup véritablement reconnu), Agapios se rangea à leur avis et fit signe qu'il partirait, pensant par ce comportement échapper aux hommes et duper les martyrs, comme s'ils n'avaient pas de nos affaires une connaissance d'origine divine»[48].

Sophrone décrit donc le comportement d'un homme qui se fait passer pour chrétien, et qui en adopte les habitudes mais sans adhérer pour autant dans son for intérieur au christianisme. Il agit par peur, ce qui le pousse au conformisme religieux.

> «Peu de temps après, il est reconnu sous son vrai jour par les malades, car, feignant d'être hérétique, il refusait de participer aux vivifiants mystères, ce qui soulevait contre lui beaucoup de murmures dans le public du sanctuaire. Il s'en rendit compte. Voulant se laver des soupçons, il participa aux saints mystères du Christ. Dès qu'il eut communié, un démon féroce se jeta sur lui, comme Satan entra dans le traître Judas, après qu'il eût pris le pain que lui avait donné le Sauveur après l'avoir trempé»[49].

Le texte décrit une crise d'épilepsie, accompagnée de convulsions. Ses gens, explique Sophrone, le voyant mal en point, décident de le ramener chez lui, mais il meurt avant d'avoir atteint Alexandrie. Les sanctuaires

---

[46] SOPHRONE DE JÉRUSALEM, *Miracles des saints Cyr et Jean*, 32, 1, dans *Los Thaumata de Sofronio*, 308; trad. J. GASCOU, *Sophrone de Jérusalem...*, 110-111.

[47] SOPHRONE DE JÉRUSALEM, *Miracles des saints Cyr et Jean*, 32, 5, dans *Los Thaumata de Sofronio*, 310; trad. J. GASCOU, *Sophrone de Jérusalem...*, 112.

[48] SOPHRONE DE JÉRUSALEM, *Miracles des saints Cyr et Jean*, 32, 6, dans *Los Thaumata de Sofronio*, 310; trad. J. GASCOU, *Sophrone de Jérusalem...*, 112.

[49] SOPHRONE DE JÉRUSALEM, *Miracles des saints Cyr et Jean*, 32, 9, dans *Los Thaumata de Sofronio*, 311; trad. J. GASCOU, *Sophrone de Jérusalem...*, 113.

n'aimaient pas que les malades viennent mourir chez eux et ils renvoyaient parfois ceux qui étaient sur le point de rendre l'âme. Agapios, tel que le présente Sophrone, vécut en homme traqué, d'abord accusé de paganisme, échappant à la justice, se faisant passer pour hérétique pour ne pas céder au conformisme, et cédant finalement pour ne pas être mal traité. Le récit nous apprend que dans l'Égypte du début du VIIe siècle, il est préférable d'être hérétique que païen. Les lois sont sévères à l'encontre des hérétiques, mais elles ne sont que rarement appliquées, alors que les lois contre les croyances ou les sacrifices païens peuvent l'être.

Parmi les personnes facilement soupçonnées de crypto paganisme, il faut citer les lettrés. Sophrone évoque le cas d'un certain Némésiôn, un aristocrate, fier de sa «science des doctrines païennes et des inepties qu'on étudie avec leur aide»[50]. Il était, en somme, féru d'astrologie. Cela suffit à en faire, aux yeux de Sophrone, un crypto païen. Il écrit à son sujet:

> «Compté soi-disant au nombre des chrétiens, sectateur irréfléchi de ceux qui admettent la fatalité, il faisait de ce fait l'expérience du châtiment qui leur a été réservé: il est privé à juste titre de ses yeux corporels, avec lesquels il observait malignement le ciel, et regardait superstitieusement le mouvement du chœur des astres, oubliant son baptême et tout ce qu'il avait promis alors au Christ»[51].

Ce châtiment est d'autant plus sévère que Némésion est lui-même un instrument de guérison pour une autre personne frappée de cécité, mais on trouve ici un récit étiologique, dont la fonction est la mise en garde des chrétiens contre les traditions astrologiques, de même que le récit précédent mettait en garde contre le fait de prendre la communion imprudemment.

Parmi les lettrés, ceux que Sophrone condamne par dessus tout sont les iatrosophistes, car ils étaient à la fois praticiens et enseignants. Il voit en eux des êtres arrogants et ne manque pas une occasion de rappeler leur incapacité à soigner et le coût élevé de leurs consultations. Comme Jean Gascou le souligne Sophrone dénonce les médecins théoriciens, non les praticiens: il «ne s'en prend pas à l'art médical ou au médecin en eux-mêmes, mais au dogmatisme naturaliste, achrétien ou antichrétien, sur lequel s'appuyait inévitablement la médecine de son temps»[52]. Sophrone inclut

---

[50] SOPHRONE DE JÉRUSALEM, *Miracles des saints Cyr et Jean*, 28, 1, dans *Los Thaumata de Sofronio*, 294; trad. J. GASCOU, *Sophrone de Jérusalem...*, 92.

[51] SOPHRONE DE JÉRUSALEM, *Miracles des saints Cyr et Jean*, 28, 6, dans *Los Thaumata de Sofronio*, 296; trad. J. GASCOU, *Sophrone de Jérusalem...*, 94.

[52] J. GASCOU, *Introduction*, dans J. GASCOU, *Sophrone de Jérusalem...*, 20.

donc dans son recueil de miracles un récit qui concerne précisément un iatrosophiste, du nom de Gèsios.

> «Notre Gésios était un très savant sophiste, non qu'il portât la toge parce qu'il professait la rhétorique, mais parce qu'il était un maître de l'art médical. Il l'enseignait méthodiquement et y avait acquis de la célébrité auprès des étudiants de l'époque. Ce savant, exalté dans les discours, médecin s'exprimant par les plus belles paroles, n'était pas indemne, le trois fois malheureux, de la superstition païenne, comme le disaient ceux qui connaissaient bien son cas. Il se moquait ouvertement de son baptême contraint, auquel il s'assujettit en effet par peur des menaces impériales. En remontant du divin bassin, il récita avec impiété ce fameux passage d'Homère: "Ajax mourut après qu'il eût bu l'onde amère".Une fois donc initié aux très divins (mystères), dissimulant par-devers lui cette impiété, il se moquait sans cesse des chrétiens, au prétexte qu'ils vénéraient le Christ d'une manière absolument déraisonnable, qu'ils étaient les esclaves de ses divins préceptes. Il éructait honteusement bien d'autres choses du même genre, et, tirées du magasin de méchanceté de son cœur, proférant de méchantes paroles»[53].

Sophrone dénonce Gésios[54] comme un chrétien qui reste attaché à son ancienne religion et qui a reçu le baptême par convenance mais non par conviction, et qu'on peut donc rattacher à la catégorie des crypto païens. Naturellement, si ce Gésios se trouve dans le recueil c'est qu'il tombe malade du dos, sans que ses collègues ne puissent le soigner. En désespoir de cause, il se rend au sanctuaire de Ménouthis où les saints inventent pour lui une épreuve sur mesure: «Prends un bât d'âne et revêts-le en t'en ceignant les parties souffrantes, épaules, cou et dos. Fais à midi le tour complet de notre sanctuaire en criant à haute voix: "je suis fou et très sot"». L'humour n'est pas absent des recueils de miracles et ce récit est sans nul doute destiné à faire rire les lecteurs, en tournant en dérision de savant médecin et son arrogance païenne. Le malheureux médecin se résout à ce remède humiliant et obtient sa guérison. L'humiliation lui a été utile. On notera que Gèsios n'est pas puni pour son incrédulité supposée. Il est vrai que le soupçon de son attachement aux traditions religieuses traditionnelles anciennes venait probablement de sa culture littéraire et de

---

[53] SOPHRONE DE JÉRUSALEM, *Miracles des saints Cyr et Jean*, 30, 2, dans *Los Thaumata de Sofronio*, 302; trad. J. GASCOU, *Sophrone de Jérusalem...*, 102.

[54] J. Gascou suggère même que le nom de Gèsios n'est pas choisi au hasard par Sophrone, mais qu'il est une sorte d'équivalent de crypto païen; E. WATTS, *The Enduring Legacy of the Iatrosophist Gessius*, «Greek, Roman, and Byzantine Studies» 49 (2009), 113-133.

ses réflexions philosophiques. Il n'avait pas à son actif une condamnation pour paganisme, contrairement à Agapios.

Un dernier exemple tiré des *Miracles* de Sophrone illustre comment le passé païen pouvait être utilisé pour rendre compte d'une maladie. Sophrone raconte un miracle qui concerne un jeune homme frappé de cécité alors qu'il venait de communier. Cette soudaine cécité aurait été causée par un blasphème du jeune homme qui a fait entendre, juste après avoir communié, un «bruit retentissant pareil à un terrible éclat de tonnerre, un bruit qui fit aussitôt trembler tous les gens qui étaient là et le voyaient, et de leurs oreilles, bien malgré eux, l'entendaient»[55]. Sophrone nous explique qu'il a commis par ce bruit un acte sacrilège et abominable, un acte cultuel propre à certains rituels païens, où le bruit nasal serait équivalent au chant d'hymnes. N'ayant pas lui-même fait l'expérience de tels rituels, il cite Porphyre à l'appui de sa démonstration. Il s'agirait d'un «bruit inventé pour le culte des démons», et selon J. Gascou qui commente après A.J. Festugière l'épisode, il pourrait être considéré comme une forme d'apostasie[56]. D'autres attestations de ce ronflement sont dûment notées, qui montrent que ce bruit était compris dans les milieux alexandrins comme une sorte d'injure. C'était visiblement une manifestation de colère, une marque de dédain, injurieuse pour la personne à qui elle était adressée. Le papyrus Col. VIII 42 datant du Ve siècle et provenant de Karanis présente le cas d'un homme qui fait un tel bruit alors qu'on lui réclame une somme d'argent: περιερρόγχασεν μοι[57]. Il s'agit d'un cas de résistance à l'impôt. Le mot semble proche de ῥέγχος», qui se réfère à un bruit fait avec le nez ou la gorge, qui correspond plus ou moins à notre ricanement et qui est considéré comme grossier. Une femme se plaint de ce que son mari «lui lance de nombreuses insultes au visage et à travers son nez»[58]. Une inscription datée du IVe ou Ve siècle, retrouvée sur une table de jeu d'Appia demande que «soit enduit de suie celui qui fait des bruits de nez»

---

[55] SOPHRONE DE JÉRUSALEM, *Miracles des saints Cyr et Jean*, 31, 1, dans *Los Thaumata de Sofronio*, 306; trad. J. GASCOU, *Sophrone de Jérusalem...*, 107.

[56] J. GASCOU, *Sophrone de Jérusalem...*, 108 n. 618.

[57] J.R. REA, *P. Col. VIII 242: Caranis in the Fifth Century*, dans *Proceedings of the 20th Int. Congress of Papyrologists*, Copenhagen 1994, 269 et 271 note 4-5, cite un ouvrage où le diable fait ce bruit devant Jésus: *Diaboli Jesus Christo contradicto*, 4-10, éd. A. VASSILIEV.

[58] *P. Oxy* VI, 903, l. 21-22, IVe siècle, καὶ πολλὰ ἀσελγήματα λέγων εἰς πρόσωπόν μου καὶ διὰ τῆς ῥινὸς αὐτοῦ. V. Déroche me signale la présence du mot ῥινοκτυπέω dans les *Miracles d'Artemios*, à propos d'un homme très en colère: *Miracle* 26, 150, l. 3-4 avec commentaire et autres références, dans *The Miracles of St. Artemios*, 270.

(ἀσβολόθη ὁ ῥονχά)⁵⁹. Le bruit d'inspirer l'air par le nez a été l'objet de différents commentaires, mais toutes les interprétations antiques s'orientent vers la moquerie, le dédain, l'insulte⁶⁰. L'interprétation religieuse de ce bruit est le fait de Sophrone, qui précise que la portée du grognement a échappé aux pèlerins présents dans l'église, dans la mesure où c'est un bruit courant: «beaucoup de chrétiens font de même, ne pensant pas blasphémer, je suppose, mais ignorant complètement le sens de l'acte [...] et que c'est une invention digne de l'impiété des païens»⁶¹. De tels grognements, rapporte Sophrone à un public ignorant, étaient pratiqués par les païens lors de leurs sacrifices. Sophrone se lance alors dans une description ironique et cocasse de sacrifices au cours desquels les fidèles rivalisaient entre eux pour faire des bruits nasaux. Mais on sent une utilisation quelque peu forcée, voire même inventive du passé, qui permet de tourner en dérision les païens, tout en attribuant à la persistance de leur influence toute maladie soudaine. Le passé païen est ainsi instrumentalisé, Sophrone s'appuyant sur une autorité en la personne de Porphyre, pour faire rire ses lecteurs tout en leur instillant une dose d'inquiétude à l'idée de se livrer à des gestes dont la portée démoniaque leur échappe. De fait les savants contemporains n'ont pas trouvé trace d'un tel cérémonial chez Sophrone. Campbell Bonner était allé jusqu'à écrire quelques pages sur ce passage en précisant: «The patriarch is not likely to have invented it, though he may have represented an ancient local oddity as a regular feature of Greek sacrificial procedure». On peut au contraire soupçonner Sophrone d'avoir bel et bien inventé un rituel païen d'un comique grossier pour éloigner ses lecteurs, membres de l'élite chrétienne, des traditions antiques. Le goût de l'élite sociale alexandrine et plus largement égyptienne pour les représentations et les poèmes en l'honneur des divinités grecques conti-

---

⁵⁹ D. Feissel, *Chroniques d'épigraphie grecque, 1987-2004*, Paris 2006, 116 à propos de l'inscription 330 retrouvée dans la cour d'une maison au sud du village Carsamba, dans la région d'Appia publiée dans MAMA X. *Monuments from Appia and the Upper Tembris Valley, Cotiaeum, Cadi, Synaus, Ancyra, Sidera and Tiberiopolis, recorded by C.W.M. Cox, A. Cameron, J. Cullen*, eds. B. Levick, S. Mitchell, J. Potter, M. Waelkens, Londres 1993, 107.
⁶⁰ C. Bonner, *A Tarsian Peculiarity (Dio Prus. Or. 33) with an unnoticed fragment of Porphyry*, «Harvard Theological Review» 35 (1942)/1, 1-11; Pouderon-Bost, *Le ronflement des Tarsiens. L'interprétation du discours XXXIII de Dion de Pruse*, «Revue des études grecques» 113 (2000)/2, 636-651.
⁶¹ Sophrone de Jérusalem, *Miracles des saints Cyr et Jean*, 31, 2, dans *Los Thaumata de Sofronio*, 306; trad. J. Gascou, *Sophrone de Jérusalem...*, 108.

nuait à se manifester[62], comme les poèmes de Dioscore d'Aphrodite[63] ou les tapisseries et mosaïques[64] ornant leurs maisons le prouvent[65]. Même dans des maisons ordinaires, dans lesquelles on a trouvé des images chrétiennes, les fouilles ont mis au jour des objets en os ou en ivoire portant l'image de Dionysos[66]. Il est probable que ces images avaient perdu leur portée religieuse au profit de la valeur ornementale, même s'il reste difficile d'évaluer cette désacralisation des objets religieux païens[67]. On a pu noter une mise à distance ironique dans la manière d'évoquer[68] ou de représenter certaines scènes mythologiques, comme Leda et le cygne, ou des idoles en posture ridicule sur les tissus égyptiens de cette époque[69]. Mais, inversement, des représentations chrétiennes étaient très empreintes de traditions antiques[70]. Sophrone est très au fait de ce goût pour la culture classique autour de lui, mais il refuse de ne voir en elle qu'une culture séculière. Il n'approuve pas le côté hybride de cette culture qui mêle des références religieuses classiques et chrétiennes. Par ce petit récit amusant, il invite ses lecteurs à tourner en dérision les rituels religieux antiques et à

---

[62] A. CAMERON, *Poets and Pagans* ..., 21-46.

[63] J.-L. FOURNET, *L'hellénisme dans l'Égypte du VIe siècle. La bibliothèque et l'œuvre de Dioscore d'Aphrodité*, Le Caire 1999; ID., *L'«homérisme» à l'époque protobyzantine: l'exemple de Dioscore d'Aphrodité*, «Ktema» 20 (1995), 301-315: «L'utilisation d'Homère se fait au second degré: par elle, on manifeste sa culture en même temps qu'on se réclame d'un hellénisme, qui n'est plus géographique, politique ni religieux, mais linguistique et culturel».

[64] G.W. BOWERSOCK, *Mosaics as History. The Near East from Late Antiquity to Islam*, Cambridge, Ma 2006.

[65] Sur le goût des Alexandrins pour les statues ornementales des divinités grecques, C. HAAS, *Hellenism and opposition to Christianity in Alexandria*, dans *Ancient Alexandria between Egypt and Greece*, ed. W.V. HARRIS, G. RUFFINI, Leyde 2004, 217-229; sur le décor, L. TÖRÖK, *Transfigurations of Hellenism. Aspects of Late Antique Art in Egypt*, Leyde 2005.

[66] M. RODZIEWICK, *Les habitations romaines tardives d'Alexandrie à la lumière des fouilles polonaises à Kôm el-Dikka*, Varsovie 1984, 148, 172, 332-333.

[67] B. CASEAU, *«Polemein Lithois». La désacralisation des espaces et des objets religieux païens durant l'Antiquité tardive*, in *Le sacré et son inscription dans l'espace à Byzance et en Occident. Etudes comparées*, éd. M. KAPLAN, Paris 2001, 61-123.

[68] W. LIEBESCHUETZ, *Pagan Mythology in the Christian empire*, «International Journal of the Classical Tradition» 2 (1995)/2, 193-208.

[69] H. TORP, *Leda Christiana: the Problem of the Interpretation of Coptic Sculture with Mythological Reliefs*, «Acta ad archaeologiam et artium historiam pertinentia», IV (1969), 10-112; E. DAUTERMAN MAGUIRE, H. MAGUIRE, *Other Icons. Art and Power in Byzantine Secular Culture*, Princeton 2007, 116.

[70] S. MCNALLY, *Syncretism in Panopolis? The Evidence of the «Mary Silk» in the Abegg Stiftung*, dans *Perspectives on Panopolis*..., 145-164.

se détourner de cette intégration culturelle d'éléments religieux du passé païen. La pratique littéraire de se moquer des rituels religieux païens était ancienne et avait gagné ses lettres de noblesse auprès des apologistes[71]. Comme ses prédécesseurs, il a recours au rire et au ridicule pour opérer ce détachement. Dès lors qu'il s'agit de se moquer des païens, il n'est plus nécessaire de fournir un récit crédible[72]. Il suffit de le rendre drôle et de l'appuyer sur une référence littéraire. Par ce récit comme par celui de la femme qui refusait de manger du porc, Sophrone pimente son récit édifiant par une once satirique.

L'épisode révèle que l'ambition de Sophrone n'est rien moins que de refaçonner la culture de ces gens, en faisant table rase non seulement des croyances mais aussi des pratiques déviantes ou idolâtres. Il veut de plus imposer un comportement exemplaire lors des liturgies chrétiennes, or les homélies nous apprennent que les fidèles n'étaient pas toujours parfaitement recueillis:

«Ce ne sont pas seulement les enfants que je vois jouer, dans votre ville, au milieu de l'église par mauvaise habitude, mais aussi des femmes d'un certain âge et des hommes mûrs. Comme des chevaux sauvages, ils sautent et piaffent au-dedans et au-dehors, de sorte que le lieu de culte des croyants n'est plus séparé des débordements»[73].

Sophrone attribue comme cause à la maladie, un vice de l'âme, un thème classique de la littérature chrétienne qui associe volontiers péché et maladie[74]. Mais il va plus loin encore s'il invente des pratiques païennes, soit qu'il les ait imaginées, soit qu'il les ait tirées de lectures savantes, à la manière de Nonnos de Panopolis[75]. On mesure le changement opéré depuis le IVe siècle. L'ennemi visé n'est plus le culte païen lui-même, mais la pureté de la foi chrétienne. La majorité des exemples concerne

---

[71] B. CASEAU, *Rire des dieux*, dans *La dérision au Moyen Âge: de la pratique sociale au rituel politique*, éds. E. CROUZET-PAVAN, J. VERGER, Paris 2007, 117-141.

[72] QUODVULTDEUS, *Livre des promesses...*, III, 38, 43, éd. R. BRAUN, 572-573, dénonce les mécanismes de certains sanctuaires, et rapporte l'histoire invraisemblable d'un dragon mécanique, près de Rome, auquel les païens sacrifiaient des vierges consacrées, et qui fut démoli par un moine.

[73] F. RILLIET-MAILLARD, *Une homélie sur le début du jeûne attribuée à Mar Jean*, dans *ANTIDWRON, Hommage à M. Geerard pour célébrer l'achèvement de la Clavis Patrum Graecorum*, Wetteren 1984, 57-72, à 70-71.

[74] *Les Pères de l'Eglise face à la science médicale de leur temps*, éds. V. BOUDON-MILLOT, B. POUDERON, Y.-M. BLANCHARD, Paris 2005.

[75] P. CHUVIN, *Mythologie et géographie dionysiaques. Recherches sur l'œuvre de Nonnos de Panopolis*, Clermont-Ferrand 1991.

des chrétiens qui sont soupçonnés de crypto paganisme. Les raisons du soupçon peuvent être minces. Par principe, tout attachement aux pratiques religieuses des anciens cultes, et toute manifestation d'un goût trop prononcé pour la littérature classique entrainait une forme de condamnation morale et une dénonciation d'hypocrisie ou de conversion de façade au christianisme.

Quelles étaient les conséquences de ces soupçons? Dans le sanctuaire de Ménouthis, les conséquences n'étaient pas très menaçantes, mais, en d'autres lieux, une accusation de pratiques païennes pouvaient être instrumentale pour ruiner une réputation, entraver une carrière ou même conduire à un procès et à une condamnation. Les constitutions impériales étaient très sévères à l'encontre de ceux qui continueraient à offrir des sacrifices. Leur mise en application n'était nullement systématique. Il eut été coûteux et irréaliste de poursuivre en justice tout paysan faisant une offrande végétale, ou même tout lettré visitant d'anciens sanctuaires. Mais le potentiel de nuisance de ces lois n'échappa pas à ceux qui voulaient opérer la chute de personnalités en vue. Dans le cadre des conflits christologiques, elles furent mises à profit pour ruiner la réputation d'un évêque, et pour entacher la validité de son credo.

En milieu nestorien, Mar Abraham, successeur de Narsaï († 503), à la tête de l'école de Nisibe (circa 510-569), fut accusé de crypto paganisme:

> «Certaines fois des hommes mauvais, frères de nom l'accusèrent et dirent 'il adore les idoles et il sacrifie aux astres'. Car le saint avait une image de Notre-Seigneur et le signe de la Croix et, quand il se levait pour l'office, il commençait par réciter trois antiennes devant cette image, puis il saluait la Croix. On fit courir le bruit que cette sainte image était une idole. Lorsque les habitants de la ville étudièrent cette affaire et quand on sut que c'était une calomnie, alors (ces frères) prirent la fuite»[76].
>
> «Les méchants répandirent le bruit dans la ville que cette machination avait pour but de faire adorer son idole à quiconque entrait sans sa maison; ils disaient qu'elle était cachée en face de la porte, dans les murailles. Lorsque les fidèles vinrent et trouvèrent que la Croix était peinte en face de l'entrée de la

---

[76] BARHADBESABBA ARBAIA, *Histoire des saints pères persécutés à cause de la vérité*, éd. F. NAU, *Documents pour servir à l'histoire de l'Eglise nestorienne. La seconde partie de l'Histoire de Barhadbesabba Arbaia*, Paris 1913, 624. Sur cet auteur et les débats d'identification, A.H. BECKER, *Fear of God and the Beginning of Wisdom. The School of Nisibis and the Development of Scholastic Culture in Late Antique Mesopotamia*, Philadelphia 2006, 100-101. Pour E.R. HAYES, *L'école d'Edesse*, Paris 1930, 13, c'était l'évêque de Holvan au VIe siècle.

porte, Satan entra dans les calomniateurs au point de leur faire dire: « L'idole est cachée derrière la croix»[77].

Les chalcédoniens n'étaient pas plus épargnés que les nestoriens par ce genre d'accusation. En 579, toute une série de personnalités d'Antioche se trouva accusée d'avoir participé à des sacrifices païens. Il s'agissait de membres de l'élite administrative et ecclésiastique. Parmi eux, on comptait Rufin, un prêtre d'Antioche, le gouverneur et procurateur d'Edesse, Anatolius, ainsi que son secrétaire Théodore, le patriarche d'Antioche, Grégoire (570-593) et le futur patriarche d'Alexandrie, Euloge. Ils furent accusés de crypto paganisme, les accusations allant de la célébration de fêtes en l'honneur de Zeus à celle de sacrifice humain. Grégoire, comme Euloge, furent en effet accusés d'avoir sacrifié de nuit, à Daphné, un jeune garçon. La «preuve» de cette horrible transgression fut, selon Jean d'Ephèse, que la terre avait tremblé.

Sur les accusations de 579 et le procès de Grégoire, nous disposons non seulement du témoignage hostile de Jean d'Ephèse[78] mais aussi de celui favorable d'Évagre[79], qui servit d'avocat à Grégoire. Tandis que Jean d'Ephèse s'indigne devant l'indifférence supposée de l'empereur face aux accusations portées contre le patriarche d'Antioche, Évagre s'indigne que des calomnies aient entaché la réputation de l'évêque et il souligne qu'il a gagné son procès. Il nous révèle les puissants ennemis qu'avait Grégoire en Syrie, et leur capacité à manipuler la foule.

Dans le récit de Jean d'Ephèse, on constate que toutes les personnes accusées voient leur vie complètement bouleversée par l'accusation. L'un d'eux, le prêtre Rufin va aller jusqu'à se suicider. Les autres s'échappent et cherchent un abri. Le gouverneur cherche refuge dans la maison de l'évêque, où il est arrêté avec son secrétaire, ce qui le sauve du lynchage. Le patriarche Grégoire, bloqué dans son palais, n'ose pas pénétrer dans sa cathédrale en pleine semaine sainte et ne consacre pas le saint *myron* alors qu'il est seul habilité à le faire. De fait, la «population» d'Antioche à qui

---

[77] BARHADBESABBA ARBAIA, *Histoire des saints pères...*, 625; autres exemples d'accusations de cryptopaganisme à cause des images, G. DAGRON, *Holy Images and Likeness*, «DOP» 45 (1991), 22-33.

[78] JOHN OF EPHESUS, *The Third Part of the Ecclesiastical History*, translated by R. PAYNE SMITH, Oxford 1860, 210-218.

[79] ÉVAGRE D'ÉPIPHANIE, *Histoire ecclésiastique*, VI, 7, éd. J. BIDEZ, L. PARMENTIER, Londres 1898, réimpr. Amsterdam 1964, p. 225-226, trad. A.-J. FESTUGIÈRE, «Byzantion» 45 (1975), 450-452; V. DÉROCHE, *Quelques interrogations à propos de la Vie de Syméon Stylite le Jeune*, «Eranos» 94 (1996), 65-83.

la révélation de la cause du tremblement de terre a été faite – le sacrifice humain nocturne de Daphné par le patriarche chalcédonien – est horrifiée et prête à rendre justice elle-même. Il fallut fermer la cathédrale pour éviter qu'elle ne soit envahie par la foule. Accuser quelqu'un d'avoir fait un sacrifice était un puissant moyen de se débarrasser d'un ennemi. Le risque le plus grand était en effet le lynchage, car la peur et la colère que de telles pratiques pouvaient engendrer dans la «population» si celle-ci était adroitement manipulée pouvait suffire à créer une émeute et à obtenir la mort des accusés avant même qu'un examen de leur cas n'ait lieu. On aimerait savoir quelle est cette foule anonyme et qui la manipule. Mais ce que cherche avant tout à montrer Jean d'Ephèse, c'est la collusion entre pouvoir impérial, administration civile et clergé chalcédonien. La foule joue un rôle important dans le récit. Elle représente la justice du peuple qui ne se laisse pas acheter par l'argent, contrairement à la justice impériale. Elle reste anonyme, mais représente dans le récit le doigt de Dieu qui punit les impies en leur donnant une mort violente. Il s'agit bien d'un règlement de compte sur fond de querelle christologique[80].

Dans le récit de Jean d'Ephèse, la foule intervient non seulement à Antioche mais aussi à Constantinople où ont été transférés les prévenus. Il ne s'agit donc pas d'un simple conflit local ou plus exactement dans la mesure où il y a un enjeu théologique, le conflit local pour le contrôle de la Syrie est naturellement étendu à la capitale qui représente l'empire. Dans la capitale aussi l'intervention de la foule est sollicitée: l'émeute s'organise avec la fermeture des boutiques. La population indignée par l'inertie de la justice impériale qu'elle soupçonne de vouloir innocenter ou gracier les accusés se rend d'abord auprès du patriarche pour qu'il exige la condamnation des accusés. La foule des émeutiers menace de mort le patriarche mais montre sa piété en reculant toutefois à l'idée de commettre un sacrilège en brulant la cathédrale. Elle se rend ensuite au palais de Placidia où les accusés avaient été enfermés. Le but du récit est de montrer la collusion du patriarche avec le pouvoir impérial chalcédonien[81].

En cette fin du VIe siècle, les accusations de pratiques païennes peuvent causer du tumulte politique mais conduisent rarement à une conviction. Jean d'Ephèse rapporte que la population de Constantinople était persua-

---

[80] R. DEVREESE, *Le patriarcat d'Antioche depuis la Paix de l'Église jusqu'à la conquête arabe*, Paris 1945.
[81] On trouve une confirmation de la confiance dont jouissait le patriarche Grégoire auprès de Maurice dans l'*Histoire* de THÉOPHYLACTE SIMOCATTA, IV, 14, 6 et dans l'*Histoire ecclésiastique* d'ÉVAGRE, V, 21

dée de l'indifférence non seulement de l'empereur mais aussi de celle du patriarche, une sorte de coalition des élites qui savent à quoi s'en tenir au sujet de ce genre d'accusations et qui y voient le moyen de règlement de compte. De fait, le pouvoir impérial était peu enclin à donner crédit à de semblables accusations, sauf si cela pouvait l'arranger.

Les accusations de pratiques païennes fusionnent à cette époque avec celles de pratiques magiques, ce qui doit conduire à une grande prudence dans l'interprétation des données. La question qui se pose est la suivante: peut on prendre les accusations de magie ou de pratiques païennes, ou même les condamnations comme la preuve d'une pratique effective de la magie ou de rituels des anciens cultes par les personnes impliquées? Ces sources peuvent-elles, comme cela a été souvent fait, être utilisées pour dresser un tableau de la diversité religieuse et du maintien des traditions cultuelles traditionnelles? La question se pose en particulier pour les accusations portées contre des membres du haut clergé chrétien. Anastasia Vakaloudi, qui s'est penché sur ces questions concluait que le clergé chrétien était très fortement impliqué dans toutes les sortes de magie[82]. Elle en prenait pour preuve les textes conciliaires interdisant le recours aux magiciens aux membres du clergé ainsi que plusieurs accusations portées contres des évêques et des prêtres à la fin de l'Antiquité. La question se pose toutefois de savoir s'il est possible et avisé de prendre ces accusations comme preuves de pratiques magiques réelles sans tenir compte du contexte particulier à chacune et sans prendre en considération la signification et les enjeux de ces accusations. Les accusations de magie sont utilisées en effet au cours de l'antiquité romaine comme instrument de normalisation politique ou sociale. Elles ne servent pas seulement à résoudre des tensions sociales ou des crises personnelles comme le montre Fritz Graf[83], elles peuvent aussi servir d'arme politique visant à discréditer une ou plusieurs personnes. L'accusation de magie est une arme précise, qui permet de porter atteinte à un individu ou à un petit groupe. Elle est plus efficace que l'accusation d'hérésie pour obtenir une condamnation. C'est précisément parce que les pratiques magiques étaient fréquentes et difficiles à distinguer des pratiques médicales ou des gestes de piété, qu'il était possible d'accuser quelqu'un de magie sans qu'il soit aisé à cette personne de se défendre. Alors que les risques encourus pour une fausse accusation

---

[82] A. VAKALOUDI, *Religion and Magic in Syria and Wider Orient in the Early Byzantine Period*, «Byzantinische Forschungen» 26 (2000), 255-280; ID., *H Mageia*, Athènes 2001.
[83] F. GRAF, *La magie dans l'Antiquité gréco-romaine*, Paris 2004.

de magie étaient importants pour l'accusateur selon le droit civil, il parait clair que vers la fin de l'Antiquité, une certaine impunité s'est développée. Parallèlement, l'aspect très politique de ces diverses accusations n'a pas échappé à la justice impériale, qui a pris de moins en moins au sérieux ces accusations, percevant très justement ce qu'elles avaient de partial. Devant l'inefficacité croissante des accusations de magie pour obtenir une condamnation par la justice et donc la mise en prison ou à mort de l'accusé, les accusateurs ont cherché à manipuler les foules. Puisque la justice se lavait les mains d'accusations biaisées, la justice populaire allait se charger de condamner à mort les personnes accusées. Plusieurs épisodes de violence urbaine sont liés à la propagation de rumeurs que d'immondes pratiques sacrificielles avaient eu lieu[84]. Les anciennes rumeurs de sacrifice humain, perpétrés en particulier contre des enfants, qui circulaient autrefois pour stigmatiser le rituel eucharistique chrétien, visent désormais des villageois que l'on accuse de pratique païennes illicites[85].

4. Se protéger des rumeurs

Dans pareil climat, il devint important de ne pas prêter le flanc à la rumeur et la question de se débarrasser des objets trop marqués, comme une collection de statues des divinités se posait pour les familles les plus riches. De telles collections étaient devenues compromettantes et pouvaient donner naissance à une rumeur. Il ne restait en principe que des statues divines d'ornement mais on peut concevoir qu'il était opportun de se débarrasser même de ce genre de statues. La distinction entre statue divine cultuelle et statue divine d'ornement existait sans doute au temps de la splendeur des cérémonies religieuses païennes mais elle a cessé d'être pertinente avec la fermeture des temples et la désacralisation des idoles. Dans la mesure où les statues ornementales pouvaient recevoir des sacrifices, un soupçon de pratiques illicites pouvait naître de leur simple présence. C'est sans doute ce qui explique la mise au rebut de plusieurs collections de statues retrouvées enfouies ou jetées dans des puits. A Athènes, un groupe de maisons bâties au IVe siècle sur l'Aréopage et abandonnées dans les années

---

[84] C. HAAS, *Alexandria in Late Antiquity. Topography and Social Conflict*, Baltimore 1997.

[85] J. RIVES, *Human Sacrifice among Pagans and Humans*, «Journal of Roman Studies» 85 (1995), 65-85. Rumeur à l'encontre de villageois: D.W. JOHNSON, *A Panegyric on Macarius, bishop of Tkôw, Attributed to Dioscorus of Alexandria*, Louvain 1980.

530-550 a livré, lors des fouilles, de nombreuses statues parmi lesquelles se trouvaient un portrait d'Antonin le Pieux, une statue d'Hercule, une autre d'Hermès, les têtes de Némésis et d'Hèlios, une Nike, mais aussi une statuette de philosophe assis, celle d'un homme barbu et deux statues de femmes. C'est l'ensemble des sculptures qui a donc été l'objet d'un rejet[86]. Ces sculptures ont été retrouvées, soit soigneusement déposées dans des puits, ce qui suppose un désir de protection de ces objets, soit dans des remblais de construction, ce qui se comprend plutôt comme une mise au rebut. On a rapproché l'une de ces maisons de la description que donne, dans sa *Vie de Proclus*, Marinus de Neapolis d'une maison possédant un sanctuaire domestique et de nombreuses niches abritant des statues[87]. Le philosophe néoplatonicien Proclus (412-485) était resté attaché à la pratique religieuse traditionnelle et à la vénération des divinités grecques. L'hypothèse que la maison aurait peut-être appartenu au philosophe est fondée sur des éléments de description du texte de Marinus. Cette maison aurait de plus servi à la pratique clandestine de sacrifices et de banquets religieux. On a retrouvé, sous le sol d'une des pièces, plusieurs statues de divinités païennes ainsi qu'une tombe d'animal (un cochon) entouré d'offrandes votives, datées du Ve siècle. La prudence est de mise cependant, le fait de trouver trace d'un cochon sacrifié peut être le reste d'un rituel païen de fondation de maison et n'indique pas que le résident de cette maison était Proclus[88]. La statuaire représentant des dieux ou des philosophes ne permet pas de conclure qu'il s'agisse d'une maison païenne ou d'une maison de philosophe[89]. Il s'agit plus sûrement d'une indication de statut social que d'un marqueur identitaire religieux.

On peut peut-être trouver un indice de l'état d'esprit des habitants de la maison à l'époque du rejet de la statuaire, dans la manière dont les statues

---

[86] A. Frantz, *The Athenian Agora*, vol. XXIV, Princeton 1988, 41.
[87] Marinus de Neapolis, *Proclus ou Sur le bonheur*, éd. et trad. H.D. Saffrey, A. Segonds, Paris 1991; A. Karivieri, *The House of Proclus on the Southern Slope of the Acropolis: A Contribution*, in *Post Herulian Athens. Aspects of Life and Culture in Athens, A.D. 267-529*, ed. P. Castrén, Helsinki 1994, 109-139.
[88] P. Castrén, *Paganism and Christianity in Athens and Vicinity during the Fourth to the Sixth centuries A.D.*, in *The Idea and Ideal of the Town between Late Antiquity and the Early Middle Ages*, ed. G.P. Brogiolo, B. Ward-Perkins, Leyde, 1999, 211-223; L.E. Baumer, *Klassische Bildwerke für tote Philosophen? Zu zwei spätklassischen Votivskulpturen aus Athen und ihrer Wiederverwendung in der späten Kaiserzeit*, «AK» 44 (2001) 55-69 (*non vidi*).
[89] J.-P. Sodini, *L'habitat en Grèce à la veille des invasions*, in *Villes et peuplement dans l'Illyricum protobyzantin*, Rome 1984, 341-397; Id., *Habitat de l'Antiquité tardive*, in «Topoi» 7 (1997), 535-577.

ont été finalement traitées. Il ne peut servir que dans le cas où les statues ont été endommagées avant d'être jetées, ce qui indique un rejet clair de l'objet, peut-être attribuable à une motivation religieuse (chrétienne et plus tard musulmane). Les archéologues distinguent la mise à l'abri et la mise au rebut en fonction de la manière dont les statues ont été enfouies. L'une des maisons fouillées sur l'Aréopage a été réutilisée par une famille qui a souhaité en modifier le décor. La christianisation de la maison s'est accompagnée d'un nettoyage de ce qui restait d'images des divinités: retrait de certaines mosaïques, humiliation d'une statue d'Athéna retournée et placée de façon à ce qu'elle se fasse piétiner, décapitation des têtes de Dionysios et des nymphes sur un bas-relief. Rien n'indique si ces objets avaient ou non une signification religieuse aux yeux des derniers habitants à les avoir conservés, mais il est clair que les nouveaux résidents les ont jugés dangereuses. La pratique consistant à enfouir une statue la face contre terre sous un mur ou un seuil semble correspondre à un rituel d'humiliation, puisqu'un tel procédé a été utilisé, par exemple, lors de la conversion du temple d'Aphrodite à Aphrodisias vers le milieu du Ve siècle[90]. On constate alors une véritable humiliation de la statue qui est traitée comme une idole vaincue et non pas comme une sculpture ornementale.

La vindicte contre les statues ne touchait pas seulement les statues divines, mais aussi les statues honorifiques, mais il faut pouvoir cerner les circonstances particulières de leur rejet pour interpréter la signification du geste et le relier ou non au danger de l'accusation de cryptopaganisme[91]. Aphrodisias a révélé un groupe de statues représentant des philosophes dont le sort n'a guère été meilleur que celui de statues divines humiliées. Elles ornaient, au Ve siècle, un bâtiment, qui servait peut-être d'école philosophique. Au VIe siècle, elles étaient devenues importunes: les marbres ont été jetés dans une petite allée, non sans avoir été décapités et brisés puis dispersés. Les nouveaux occupants des lieux voulurent sans doute se débarrasser de ces objets compromettants, qui rappelaient l'ancienne fonction du bâtiment et célébraient la sagesse païenne[92].

Le mouvement d'abandon des statues mises au rebut s'intensifie entre la fin du Ve siècle et le VIIe siècle. A Scythopolis, lors de l'abandon du bain oriental, daté des années 515/516, l'hypocauste fut rempli de statues.

---

[90] R. CORMACK, *Byzantine Aphrodisias. Changing the Map of a City*, in «Proceedings of the Cambridge Philosophical Society 214», n.s. 24 (1990), 26-41.

[91] B. CASEAU, *Buried Statues and Religious Intolerance*, in *Late Antique Statuary*, éd. L. LAVAN, (*Late Antique Archaelogy*), Leiden (a paraître).

[92] R.R.R. SMITH, *Late Roman Philosopher Portraits from Aphrodisias*, «Journal of Roman Studies» 80 (1990), 127-155.

De nombreux fragments provenant de statues de différente taille y ont été retrouvés, le plus souvent sans tête. D'autres statues ont été découvertes sous le sol d'une nouvelle construction entreprise sur les lieux, la salle dite de Silvanus, parmi lesquelles une statue de Dionysos grandeur nature dont les yeux, le nez et la bouche avaient été mutilés et une statue d'empereur dont seul le torse fut mis à jour. Le portrait de la Gorgone Méduse qui ornait sa cuirasse avait été buriné.

Les témoignages archéologiques d'enfouissement de statues divines ne sont pas exempts d'ambiguïté. Une importante collection de statues a été de la sorte enfouie au début du VIIe siècle dans la région d'Antioche, et si les circonstances exactes ne sont pas connues (on peut aussi penser à l'invasion perse), il semble plausible de rattacher ce geste au climat de suspicion évoqué ci-dessus. D.M. Brinkerhoff a suggéré que la collection retrouvée à Antioche avait été constituée pour satisfaire les besoins religieux d'une famille demeurée païenne, mais force est de constater que cette collection était composite et contenait aussi bien des statues impériales que des statues divines. Il n'y a guère de moyen d'être sûr d'un crypto paganisme dans ce cas, d'autant que la date de l'enfouissement protecteur des statues semble osciller entre le VIe et le VIIe siècle. S'il y avait dans certaines maisons de véritables sanctuaires clandestins comme celui de Ménouthis dont la découverte derrière une armoire nous est racontée par Zacharie le Scholastique dans la *Vie de Sévère*[93], la majorité des collections de statues antiques appartenaient à de riches chrétiens qui aimaient à s'entourer de beaux objets antiques sans pour autant être des cryptopaïens[94].

Les frontières du licite ont donc changé entre le Ve et le VIIe siècles. Il était possible au Ve siècle de se constituer d'importantes collections de statues divines, venues pour certaines des temples fermés[95], tandis qu'aux VIe et VIIe siècles, leur conservation pouvait se révéler dangereuse. Pour

---

[93] Zacharie le Scholastique, *Vie de Sévère*, éd. M.A. KUGENER, Paris 1904, 27-32. Sur cet épisode daté du milieu du Ve siècle: E. WIPSCYSKA, *La christianisation de l'Egypte aux IVe-VIe siècles. Aspects sociaux et ethniques*, «Aegyptus» 68 (1988), 117-164; C. HAAS, *Alexandria in Late Antiquity. Topography and Social Conflict*, Baltimore 1997.

[94] M. MUNDELL MANGO, *Art Collecting in Byzantium*, «Etudes balkaniques. Cahiers Pierre Belon» 2 (1995), 139-160; N. HANNESTAD, *Tradition in Late Antique Sculpture. Conservation, Modernization, Production*, Aarhus 1994; C. ROUÉCHÉ, *The Image of Victory*, «Travaux et Mémoires (Mélanges G. Dagron)» 14 (2002), 527-546.

[95] S. BASSET, *The Urban Image of Late Antique Constantinople*, Cambridge 2004.

les familles de l'élite sociale[96], posséder des images des divinités ou des livres de magie pouvait alors nourrir un soupçon de cryptopaganisme et attirer des ennuis. Le risque de se faire accuser était suffisamment réel pour conduire à des modifications du comportement ou du décor. Certes, s'il y avait poursuites, le motif réel de procès était le plus souvent à chercher ailleurs, dans les enjeux de pouvoir, les conflits d'intérêts économiques ou les conflits théologico-politiques. L'accusation de paganisme était un prétexte.

Pour le reste de la société, la mise en garde contre le cryptopaganisme conduisait plus rarement à un procès mais plutôt à des sanctions ecclésiastiques. Les listes de pratiques païennes interdites servaient aux clercs à définir une frontière du licite et du sacrilège et à tenter de modeler un comportement chrétien purifié des scories du passé. À un siècle de différence, et séparés par une grande distance géographique, l'univers mental de Sophrone († 638/639) n'est pas éloigné de celui de Césaire d'Arles (†542)[97]. Il s'agit d'un monde où on qualifie de païen ce qu'on veut voir disparaître ou s'effacer. Césaire, par exemple, s'en prend aux danses et aux ripailles. Dans un «sermon indispensable pour les paroisses», il écrit:

> «Ces pauvres malheureux qui ne craignent ni ne rougissent de se livrer à des danses et à des pantomimes, juste devant les basiliques des saints, même s'ils arrivent chrétiens à l'église, en repartent païens; car cette habitude de danser est un reste des pratiques païennes».

Et il ajoute qu'on peut perdre le sacrement du baptême:

> «Si vous voyez des gens rendre un culte à des sources ou à des arbres, et comme je l'ai déjà dit, consulter aussi magiciens, devins ou enchanteurs, suspendre même sur eux ou sur les leurs des phylactères diaboliques, des grimoires magiques, des herbes ou de l'ambre, faites-leur des reproches très sévères, car quiconque a commis ce péché perd le sacrement du baptême»[98].

---

[96] Vers 510, accusation de pratique magique, emprisonnement et fuite de Basilius et Praetextatus, des hommes de haut rang: GRÉGOIRE LE GRAND, *Dialogues*, I, 4, 3, éd. A. DE VOGÜÉ, trad. P. ANTIN, Paris 1979, 38-40; CASSIODORE, *Variae*, IV, 22-23.

[97] W. KLINGSHIRN, *Caesarius of Arles: the Making of a Christian Community in Late Antique Gaul*, Cambridge 1994; R. MARKUS, *From Caesarius to Boniface: Christianity and Paganism in Gaul*, dans *Le septième siècle: changements et continuités*, éds. J. FONTAINE, J.N. HILLGARTH, Londres, 1992, 154-168; P.R.L. BROWN, *The Rise of Western Christendom*, Cambridge 1996.

[98] CÉSAIRE D'ARLES, *Sermon* 13, 5, éd. et trad. M.-J. DELAGE, Paris 1971, 426-427.

Ces collections d'interdits présents dans les homélies ou dans le droit canonique ont longtemps servi à reconstituer ce que devait être la vie religieuse dans les campagnes avant la christianisation. Il est préférable d'y voir des éléments du comportement religieux des chrétiens contemporains de ces écrits. Il est très difficile d'affirmer que ces chrétiens avaient conscience de transgresser la frontière du licite en agissant ainsi. Nous ne disposons que du témoignage des clercs comme Sophrone ou Césaire qui n'hésitent pas à stigmatiser comme pratiques païennes tout ce qui leur paraît contraire à un comportement chrétien idéal.

Le crypto paganisme recouvre donc deux phénomènes différents. Il sert à définir les pratiques religieuses secrètes d'adeptes des cultes traditionnels, une fois ceux-ci interdits. Jusqu'au VIe siècle, il reste possible de se définir comme adepte de ces cultes, même si la pratique sacrificielle ou la visite des temples est interdite. Mais, ensuite, tout byzantin non juif doit être, au moins nominalement, un chrétien, pour éviter les ennuis. Certaines des demandes de baptême sont alors faites par conformisme social plutôt que par adhésion personnelle à la foi chrétienne.

Le crypto paganisme concerne aussi les pratiques dévotionnelles que les évêques désapprouvent et rejettent hors de la sphère du christianisme. La liste des interdits et des pratiques ainsi condamnées n'est nullement fixe et elle peut changer avec le temps, comme on a pu le voir concernant la possession de statues divines. Elle peut n'avoir qu'un rapport très lointain avec les anciens cultes traditionnels des divinités dites païennes. Certaines de ces pratiques sont nées ou se sont développées après l'interdiction des sacrifices, comme les dépôts de lampes votives sur d'anciens lieux de cultes archaïques, longtemps abandonnés et visités de nouveau en raison de leur inaccessibilité aux foules chrétiennes indiscrètes. D'autres sont plus ambiguës et relèvent de pratiques magico-religieuses de protection dont l'identité religieuse reste difficile à déterminer, ou encore de pratiques festives. Quelle est la portée religieuse d'une chanson à Bacchus, à la suite d'un banquet bien arrosé? Les évêques de la fin de l'Antiquité tout comme ceux du haut Moyen Âge, soucieux de la *cura animarum* ont dressé leur propre liste d'interdits. Elle n'est pas nécessairement la même pour un paysan et pour l'élite sociale, mais elle tend au même but qui est de faire pression pour christianiser les fidèles et les pousser à rompre toute forme d'attache avec les pratiques religieuses et la culture antique.

GIORGIO CRACCO

Un conflitto dentro il cristianesimo.
L'apporto di Gregorio Magno
alla storia religiosa dell'Occidente

1. «Se non salvò l'Impero, almeno in Occidente», tuttavia salvò – soggetto è il cristianesimo – «molti elementi della civiltà romana»; nel senso che favorì per più versi la «romanizzazione dei Barbari», e li mise «in grado di convivere con i cittadini dell'Impero romano»[1].

Non so se fu un giudizio di questo genere a far passare nelle «tendenziose» edizioni Einaudi (di un Giulio Einaudi che amava, per sua stessa dichiarazione, la storia «relativa»)[2] un volume come quello inventato in un contesto anglosassone da Arnaldo Momigliano, che opportunamente stiamo ricordando a 40 anni di distanza dalla sua apparizione in Italia. Difatti tutto il saggio introduttivo a questo volume – che mantiene la sua forza anche dopo i decenni di studi che lo hanno seguito – sembra fatto apposta per mostrare che il cristianesimo o la Chiesa (i due termini sono spesso usati come sinonimi) non fu affatto «responsabile della caduta dell'Impero», come invece aveva sostenuto già nel Settecento Edward Gibbon. Né fu sua colpa se nei propri ranghi confluirono sia «le menti più creative» sia «chi amava il potere»; se furono i vescovi, ben più che i militari e i burocrati, a fare argine potente, in tempi di invasioni barbariche, contro il terrore e l'insicurezza; se perfino il monachesimo – che era «qualcosa di propriamente suo» (ossia del cristianesimo) – si rivelò «una forza costruttiva della società», capace addirittura di aprire «un nuovo capitolo nella storia intellettuale d'Europa».

Insomma – ecco la conclusione di Momigliano –, «la superiorità del cristianesimo sul paganesimo, dal punto di vista del dinamismo e dell'efficienza», era già chiara nel secolo IV»; ovvero toccò ai Cristiani – ai Cri-

---

[1] A. MOMIGLIANO, *Introduzione: Il cristianesimo e la decadenza dell'Impero romano*, in *Il conflitto tra paganesimo e cristianesimo nel IV secolo*, saggi a cura dello stesso, trad. it. Torino 1968 (London 1963), 3-19, partic. 18.
[2] *Presentazione dell'Editore*, in *Storia d'Italia, Volume primo: I caratteri originali*, Torino, 1972, XIX-XXXVI, partic. XXV.

stiani che avevano scoperto «un ponte tra la barbarie e la civiltà»[3] –, e non già ai pagani, che con i Barbari non avevano saputo interloquire, scrivere la storia successiva dell'Occidente.

La lezione di Momigliano – uno studioso che sapeva laicamente apprezzare il ruolo delle religioni – non fu del tutto compresa; tant'è vero che, invece di cercare, sulle sue tracce, come accadde che poi, realmente, il paganesimo quasi disparve a fronte di una cristianizzazione talmente forte da permeare in profondità le istituzioni, la società e la cultura dell'Europa altomedievale – perché è un fatto che l'Europa divenne cristiana (così come poi buona parte dell'Oriente divenne musulmana), si preferì favoleggiare, ideologicamente, di un blocco di potere (alto clero, aristocrazia romana e guerrieri barbari) che dall'alto, specie in Gallia e in Italia, finì per imporsi a forza sulle masse, da sempre e tenacemente attaccate invece alle loro ataviche tradizioni folkloriche, ossia pagane[4]. Come se il nocciolo duro della storia tardoantica continuasse a essere il paganesimo, e la novità cristiana avesse avuto la sola funzione di occultarlo e comprimerlo temporaneamente dall'alto. Temporaneamente, perché poi, lungo i secoli successivi, le *traditions folkloriques* sarebbero riesplose, anche sotto forma di «eresie», prendendosi la rivincita sul cristianesimo (un modo come un altro per affermare le radici «pagane» d'Europa).

Il fatto è che questa storiografia ideologica, e tutta consegnata alle strutture, cui mancavano le categorie di base per apprezzare la novità del cristianesimo – non conosceva ciò che per Momigliano era irrinunciabile: la scienza dell'individuo, la biografia; né mai fu in grado di approdare davvero, come fece ancora Momigliano, alla «sapienza straniera» –[5], dominò per anni, specie in Italia, dove programmaticamente si intendeva separare, una volta per tutte, la storia del Paese dalla storia della Chiesa; e ad essa, ben pochi seppero sottrarsi (donde la scarsa eco che ebbe, appunto in Italia, il volume da cui siamo partiti). Tra questi pochi, oltre allo stesso Momigliano, è da citare anche uno studioso italiano oggi quasi dimenticato, Paolo Lamma, scomparso troppo presto, ancor giovane (poco oltre i 40 anni), nella primavera del 1961, solo pochi mesi dopo essere stato chia-

---

[3] A. MOMIGLIANO, *Introduzione*..., 12-18.
[4] Alludo soprattutto a un contributo che fece scuola in Italia e nel mondo: J. LE GOFF, *Culture cléricale et traditions folkloriques dans la civilisation mérovingienne*, «Annales E.S.C.», 22 (1967), 780-781, trad. it. in ID., *Tempo della Chiesa e tempo del mercante e altri saggi sul lavoro e la cultura nel Medioevo*, Torino 1977, 193-207.
[5] Alludo a due classici libri di A. MOMIGLIANO, *Lo sviluppo della biografia greca*, trad. it., Torino 1974 (1971); *Saggezza straniera. L'Ellenismo e le altre culture*, trad. it., Torino 1980 (1975).

mato alla cattedra di Storia medievale nella Facoltà di Lettere e Filosofia dell'Università di Padova.

2. Lamma merita tuttavia di essere ricordato: sia per la sua attitudine, allora rara – e registrata con disagio anche dalla coeva storiografia di osservanza cattolica[6] –, a guardare alle singole persone (solo lui poteva tracciare, ad esempio, un certo profilo di Raingarda di Montboissier, la madre di Pietro il Venerabile) e a mettere a confronto tra loro mondi diversi per cogliere ciò che li univa (penso ai due volumi *Comneni e Staufer*)[7], sia per aver studiato anche, e con apporti non propriamente di margine, il tema e l'epoca che qui ci riguardano, ossia i rapporti tra paganesimo e cristianesimo tra IV e VI secolo.

Fin dal 1947 aveva scritto un breve contributo dal titolo poco accademico: *Cultura e vita nell'esperienza di Cassiodoro*. Nulla a che fare, sia chiaro, con i prestigiosi lavori che Momigliano dedicherà in seguito allo stesso personaggio e al suo mondo, dove peraltro tale specifico contributo viene esplicitamente ricordato insieme con altri dello stesso studioso: il *Teoderico* del 1951, *with a good bibliography* (e Momigliano, di bibliografia, se ne intendeva parecchio) e le *Ricerche sulla storia e la cultura del VI secolo* dell'anno precedente, che contenevano – ed è un altro apprezzamento non da poco – *an important essay* sullo storico Agazia[8].

---

[6] P. ZERBI, *A proposito di tre recenti libri di storia. Riflessioni sopra alcuni problemi di metodo*, «Aevum», 31 (1957), 492-531, partic. 507-518. Ciò che si sentiva insidiato, dal fatto di mettere al centro l'interesse per gli «incontri» e per le «reazioni» (la nota riguardava in primo luogo l'*Arnaldo da Brescia* di A. FRUGONI) era da un lato il primato delle «gerarchie» e dall'altro il quasi dogma dell'autosufficienza dell'Occidente in quanto raggiunta «unità spirituale e culturale».

[7] P. LAMMA, *La madre di Pietro il Venerabile*, «Studium», 54 (1958), 740-751, ripubblicato in «Bullettino dell'Istituto storico italiano per il medioevo e Archivio muratoriano», 75 (1963), 173-178; Raingarda compare anche nell'ultimo libro di Lamma, uscito qualche giorno dopo la sua morte (non riuscì a vederlo stampato): *Momenti di storiografia cluniacense*, Roma 1961, 191; ID., *Comneni e Staufer. Ricerche sui rapporti fra Bisanzio e l'Occidente*, Roma 1955-57. Un tema, quest'ultimo, che per Lamma «valeva bene la vita di uno storico» (per riprendere le parole di A. FRUGONI, *Commemorazione di Paolo Lamma*, in P. LAMMA, *Oriente e occidente nell'Alto Medioevo. Studi storici sulle due civiltà*, Padova 1968, XIII-XXV, partic. XXII.

[8] A. MOMIGLIANO, *Cassiodorus and Italian Culture of his Time* (1955); *Gli Anicii e la storiografia latina del VI sec. D. C.* (1956); *Cassiodoro* (voce del *Biografico degli Italiani* pubblicata nel 1978, ma scritta nel 1971): cfr. ID., *Secondo Contributo alla storia degli studi classici*, Roma 1960, 191-253, partic. 221, 225, 229; *Sesto Contributo alla storia degli studi classici e del mondo antico*, II, Roma 1980, 487-508.

Ma ecco che cosa, in tema di opzioni religiose, Lamma scriveva di Cassiodoro, che tra l'altro, circa un trentennio prima di Gregorio Magno, si trovò a risiedere per circa 8 anni (546-554) – come spesso accadeva, appunto, a esponenti di grandi e meno grandi famiglie senatorie –, a Costantinopoli: «per lunghi anni il cristianesimo non entrò come elemento vitale nella fisionomia del ministro, sia come uomo di cultura che come politico»; considerava «l'elemento religioso e la forza della Chiesa dal di fuori, come momenti del gioco politico da reggere e da dominare a seconda delle circostanze». Solo dopo la crisi del regime gotico intravvide il Dio cristiano, «la patria celeste»; e guardò alla Chiesa non solo come a un «un fattore di potenza», ma anche come a «un mondo di certezze» che può dare speranza a «un animo turbato e deluso»[9].

Si noti: Lamma non parlava di «conversione», di passaggio dal paganesimo al cristianesimo, magari con il filtro della storiografia tradizionale (quella della teutonica *Bekehrung*)[10], bensì di un ampliamento di orizzonti, di una conquista di senso, che il suo personaggio per primo connotava (la produzione di Lamma ha un carattere di fondo: l'auscultazione diretta e intensiva dei testi)[11]; perché – questa l'esperienza che lui trovava testimoniata in Cassiodoro – «l'erudizione, la filologia, la scienza», lungi dall'essere rinnegate (succederà poi con Gregorio Magno), o scadere a lavoro «fine a se stesso, di pura conservazione», diventano una via per «vedere più a fondo», e quindi «meritare» la rivelazione (questo verbo «meritare» è significativo: apre tutto un orizzonte nuovo)[12]. Ovvero, la cultura «secolare» che veniva dal passato poteva confluire, quasi senza traumi o conflitti, nella cultura cristiana. Momigliano, con espressione un po' ruvida, concluderà: Cassiodoro fu uno di quegli «uomini migliori» che finirono per lavorare «per la Chiesa, non per lo Stato»[13].

Questo profilo che Lamma disegnò di Cassiodoro ci serve non poco, come oltre vedremo, per introdurre Gregorio Magno, che appartiene alla generazione a lui successiva, proprio per il tema che qui interessa: quello del conflitto non solo tra paganesimo e cristianesimo, ma anche di un

---

[9] P. LAMMA, *Cultura e vita nell'esperienza di Cassiodoro*, «Studium», 48 (1947), 234-241. Ma qui si cita da ID., *Oriente e Occidente*, 173-186.

[10] Si veda in proposito l'*Introduzione* di M. MAZZA alla trad. ital. del libro di A.D. NOCK, *La conversione. Società e religione nel mondo antico*, Roma-Bari 1974, VII-XXXVII.

[11] Pur avendo conosciuto Lamma solo per pochi mesi, posso testimoniare un fatto: si portava a casa, uno dopo l'altro, i tomi della *Patrologia Graeca*, per leggerli a tappeto.

[12] P. LAMMA, *Oriente e Occidente*..., 184.

[13] A. MOMIGLIANO, *Introduzione*..., 14.

conflitto emergente all'interno del cristianesimo. E non basta: ora, sempre per introdurre Gregorio, ci serve anche un altro profilo lasciato ancora da Lamma, che ci riporta in Oriente, a Costantinopoli, nel cuore dell'Impero: quello del giurista-storico Agazia, uno che scriveva le sue *Historiae* forse negli anni stessi in cui Gregorio Magno svolgeva il suo compito di apocrisiario sul Bosforo (579/585-586 c.)[14] (allora, quando Lamma scriveva, erano rari gli studiosi che sapevano e volevano occuparsi comparativamente di due mondi diversi e lontani come Roma e Bisanzio).

Su Agazia, Averil Cameron, in una monografia sempre valida del 1970, restava ancora in dubbio, come del resto precedenti studiosi, «se era pagano o cristiano»[15]. Ma Lamma, in merito, aveva già dato una sua risposta netta e decisa: «apertamente, aveva concluso, certo no», Agazia non fu un pagano; si fosse protestato tale, o soltanto non fosse stato battezzato, avrebbe violato la legislazione giustinianea vigente nell'Impero: quella che assimilava i pagani agli eretici peggiori e li puniva, giusta un editto del 529, con l'esclusione dallo Stato e con la spoliazione di ogni bene[16]. Non risulta peraltro che Agazia abbia subito condanne o sia caduto in disgrazia. Ma – continua Lamma –, se Agazia apertamente non poteva dichiararsi pagano e tale mai si dichiarò, «nel cuore forse lo fu, come infiniti altri, quel tanto che esigeva, per sopravvivere, la cultura laica di origine e di tradizioni classiche»; ed è certo inoltre che disdegnava «il radicalismo religioso»[17].

Lamma dava molta importanza a questo paganesimo che resisteva impavido sotto l'ufficialità cristiana, al punto da documentarne l'incidenza reale nella vita e nella storia. Agazia, egli osserva, aveva gli occhi bene aperti sul suo tempo, attraversato oltretutto da catastrofi immani come pestilenze e terremoti (specie il terremoto del 557); ma non si lasciò affatto coinvolgere dalle reazioni di segno religioso, anche eccessive, che ne scaturivano. Sì, il terrore dilagante di una fine prossima incentivava conversioni, fughe dal mondo, atti straordinari di giustizia e di pietà; ma poi – è il suo commento –, una volta passato il pericolo, «subito i più tornavano ai

---

[14] P. LAMMA, *Ricerche sulla storia e la cultura del vi secolo*, II: *Oriente e Occidente nell'opera storica di Agazia*, ora in ID., *Oriente e Occidente...*, 90-131.

[15] AV. CAMERON, *Agathias*, Oxford 1970, 89.

[16] P. LAMMA, *Oriente e Occidente...*, 126-130. Lamma parla solo di «legislazione giustinianea» senza entrare nel merito: cfr. ora P. MARAVAL, *La politique religieuse de Justinien*, in *Histoire du Christianisme des origines à nos jours*, III, *Les Églises d'Orient et d'Occident*, sous la responsabilité de L. PIETRI, Paris 1998, 393-395.

[17] P. LAMMA, *Oriente e Occidente...*, 126-127.

costumi soliti»[18]. Come a dire: ci si converte, ci si ricorda del Dio cristiano e si ha paura dei suoi castighi solo quando le cose precipitano; in tempi normali gli uomini vivono come se Dio non esistesse; con l'implicita deduzione: che razza di fede è mai questa!

Il che è segno, conclude Lamma, che Agazia, pur vivendo dentro un Impero ufficialmente cristiano del quale amava tessere la storia – un Impero, in ogni caso (è giusto ricordarlo), talmente vasto e composito (quasi un migliaio di diocesi) che non può certo essere ridotto alla sola capitale – , si sentiva, come del resto altri grandi personaggi della burocrazia e della cultura del suo tempo (ad esempio, un Giovanni Lido), sempre interno alla tradizione romano-pagana, laica e secolare: una tradizione che pensava di avere tutti i titoli per guidare in proprio lo Stato e la società, e anche per interpretare la storia, senza bisogno di ricorrere alla cultura cristiana. La quale semmai, con le sue irrazionalità, con la sua tendenza a valorizzare i Barbari (ecco l'attacco, forse diretto a Cassiodoro, *qui origines gothicas historiam fecit esse Romanam*), rappresentava una novità pericolosa, insomma «la getica stoltezza» (con questa espressione, Agazia tirava in ballo probabilmente un autore a lui coevo, Giordane, che non gli piaceva punto)[19].

Tutto questo fa dire a Lamma che, sul piano della cultura, fino a tutto il VI secolo, Oriente e Occidente sembrano seguire un percorso diverso se non divergente: il primo, l'Oriente, dove non a caso l'Impero continuava ad avere forza, privilegiava la continuità con le antiche tradizioni, che erano ufficialmente cristiane e di fatto ancora pagane (Agazia ne è perfetto interprete); il secondo, l'Occidente, che trovandosi pressoché abbandonato e in balia dei Barbari sperimentava invece l'insufficienza di quelle antiche tradizioni e si orientava sempre più vistosamente sulla novità cristiana (interprete ne è Cassiodoro). Il quale Cassiodoro tuttavia, pur optando alla fine per la cultura cristiana, mai rinunciò a quella pagana. Ma alla fine questa rinuncia ci fu: e ne fu interprete Gregorio Magno. Per approdare a quale altra cultura?

3. Nel tentativo inquadrare, dal punto di vista del rapporto paganesimo-cristianesimo, un personaggio come Gregorio, sul quale (è pleonastico dirlo) in questi ultimi trent'anni le ricerche si sono moltiplicate a valanga (segno che costituisce, e continua a costituire, un problema), parto – anche

---

[18] *Ibid.*, 127-129.
[19] *Ibid.*, 94-95.

se può apparire una partenza anomala – da un argomento *ex silentio*: invano si cercherebbe nella sua produzione una linea portante, evidentissima ad esempio in Agostino e in Paolo Orosio, che si può sintetizzare con l'espressione connotante tanto il *De civitate Dei* del primo quanto le *Historiae* del secondo: *adversus Paganos*. Gregorio non ebbe affatto, come problema prioritario – altro segno della sua diversità rispetto ad Agostino –, quello dello scontro polemico o dell'aspra resa dei conti con il paganesimo. Si può anzi dire, quasi paradossalmente – è un primo dato da evidenziare –, che egli fu così poco antipagano da sentirsi a lungo, a sua volta, addirittura quasi un «pagano».

Mi spiego meglio: la sua prima e più grande opera, i *Moralia in Iob* un'opera riscritta e rifinita, dopo il primitivo abbozzo tracciato a Costantinopoli, sino alla fine della vita –, è incentrata, autobiograficamente (Gregorio si impersona di volta in volta – già mi è accaduto di osservarlo – in personaggi della grande tradizione mediterranea) su Giobbe, che fu un principe pagano. Giobbe, infatti, nella sua qualità di *vir gentilis*, *vir saecularis*, fu nel contempo uomo di pietà, che però mai interruppe, per quanto travolto da tragedie di ogni sorta, il suo rapporto con Dio (*qui legem non novit et tamen tenuit, qui praecepta vitae quae scripta non acceperat custodivit*)[20]. Come a dire: ancor prima di farsi tutto e solo «cristiano», Gregorio – anche lui un «principe» tormentato, che cercava un rapporto con Dio – aveva sentito il bisogno di esplorare le grandi tradizioni religiose dell'umanità che venivano da un lontano passato, quelle ebraico-pagane; e non gli faceva specie identificarsi con un «eroe» che era pagano.

Si può aggiungere che, con molta probabilità, Gregorio «scoprì» Giobbe proprio negli anni in cui visse a Costantinopoli, dove questo «eroe» era per così dire alla moda: non per nulla Eustratius, scrivendo un *Bíos* del patriarca Eutichio in quegli stessi anni, lo celebrò come «in tutto simile a Giobbe sia per le tante disgrazie che gli accaddero, sia per la forza con cui le affrontò»[21]. Gregorio conobbe personalmente Eutichio e anche, come vedremo, ne prese le distanze in tema di resurrezione dei corpi; ma intanto è importante notare come entrambi avessero almeno una certezza in comune: che anche il vecchio paganesimo aveva qualcosa da insegnare ai cristiani. E del resto, per quanto riguarda Gregorio, non gli dispiacque,

---

[20] *Moralia*, XIV, 1. Rinvio in merito a miei contributi: *Gregorio «morale»: la costruzione di una identità*, in *Gregorio Magno nel XIV Centenario della morte (Atti dei Convegni Lincei 209)*, Roma 2004, 171-98; *Gregorio Magno e i «Libri dei Re»* (con L. CRACCO RUGGINI), in *Transformations of Late Antiquity. Essays for Peter Brown*, eds. P. ROUSSEAU, M. PAPOUTSAKIS, Farnham, 2009, 223-258, partic. 238.
[21] *PG* 86, col. 2278.

anche da vescovo di Roma, rifarsi talvolta ai *mores* pagani: come quando ricordò ai suoi *sacerdotes* l'*antiqua consuetudo*, tipica dei *Gentiles* – una consuetudine non solo antica, ma anche da imitarsi – di non lucrare sulle sepolture[22].

Non meraviglia allora se nella bibliografia gregoriana – quella diligentemente ricostruita da Robert Godding –, che sappiamo diluviale ed estesa a un'infinità di aspetti di Gregorio Magno (anche aspetti non necessari), non si trova affatto, se non erro, un titolo comprensivo come *Gregorio Magno e il paganesimo* (mentre si trova – il che è spiegabile – il titolo *Saint Benoît et le paganisme*); e resta leggenda (una leggenda tra l'altro parecchio tardiva) l'idea di un Gregorio *destroyer of Pagan idols*[23]. Davvero Gregorio, neppure dopo il 595, mai si concentrò, come già era accaduto ad Agostino e a Paolo Orosio, nella lotta a oltranza contro il paganesimo. Parlo del dopo il 595, perché allora assunse, anche con iniziative clamorose, il ruolo di pastore e missionario delle «genti» e fu esplicitamente richiesto di pronunciarsi in merito alle tenaci persistenze pagane che si riscontravano presso gli Angli[24].

Di ciò s'è accorto di recente, pur a proposito d'altro, uno studioso che, memore di una celebre direttiva inviata da Gregorio ai missionari in Bretagna – «i templi degli déi presso quella gente non bisogna affatto distruggerli; basterà abbattere gli idoli che ci sono in essi» –, ha rilevato come nulla costui avesse fatto, dentro Roma che era la sua sede, per trasformare in chiese i templi pagani. E in effetti, non lui, ma il successore Bonifacio, nel 609, un quinquennio dopo la sua morte, prese l'iniziativa di adattare il Pantheon a chiesa dedicandolo a Maria e a tutti i martiri[25]. Nessuna particolare bellicosità, dunque, sembra nutrire Gregorio nei confronti dei pagani; semmai, tolleranza e rispetto. E si tratta di un atteggiamento che induce a scavare nei testi per capire di più.

---

[22] Il riferimento a *Gen.* 23 (come Abramo trovò sepoltura a Sara presso gli Hetei) compare in due lettere del *Registrum*: VIII, 3 e 35 (II, 4 e 38 dell'ediz. MGH). Interessante un passo della seconda: *Si ergo tantae considerationis paganus vir fuit, quanto magis nos, qui sacerdotes dicimur, hoc facere non debemus?*

[23] R. Godding, *Bibliografia di Gregorio Magno (1890-1989)*, Roma 1990, nn. 1326, 1327 (due contributi di J. Laporte), 2442. Ma cfr. anche i nn. 1187, 2275.

[24] G. Cracco, *Alle origini dell'Europa cristiana: Gregorio Magno*, in *Il Papato e l'Europa*, cura di G. De Rosa e G. Cracco, Soveria Mannelli 2001, 13-54, partic. 45-46.

[25] M. Wallraff, *Templi pagani e chiese cristiane. Continuità e discontinuità ai tempi di Gregorio Magno e dei suoi successori*, in «*Per longa maris intervalla». Gregorio Magno e l'Occidente mediterraneo fra tardoantico e altomedioevo. Atti del Convegno Internazionale di studi, Cagliari 17-18 dicembre 2004*, a cura di L. Casula, G. Mele, A. Piras, con la collab. di L. Armando, Cagliari 2006, 419-426.

4. Non è facile tuttavia rinvenire dati ulteriori. Già è ben noto che di una «vera e propria biografia» di Gregorio non si può parlare se non a partire dagli anni successivi al 573, ossia posteriori alla sua «conversione», come se in precedenza – ma si tratta di un lungo periodo, circa 33 anni, essendo egli nato attorno al 540 – neppure fosse esistito. Altrettanto noto è il fatto che la sua «conversione» non significò affatto passaggio dal paganesimo al cristianesimo, bensì fuga dal mondo, per raggiungere «il porto sicuro della vita monastica»[26]. Ovvia deduzione: convertendosi, Gregorio non rifiuta il paganesimo – difatti egli era già un cristiano, un battezzato –, bensì un'esperienza cristiana che non gli bastava più in quanto avvertita tutt'uno con il «mondo» e pericolosamente complice dello stesso. Egli era preoccupato, in altri termini, di denunciare implicitamente, con la sua opzione, un problema interno al cristianesimo: l'alterità e anzi irriducibilità di questa *religio* rispetto al mondo.

Markus, tuttavia, definisce Gregorio come un «convertito», anzi «un contemplativo in un mondo in tempesta»[27]. Un'immagine corretta, ci sembra, oltre che utile: perché fa capire, fra l'altro, la differenza rispetto a Cassiodoro che una generazione prima si era convertito, come sappiamo, non già per negare il mondo di cui era figlio, bensì per dargli un'anima cristiana, diventando quindi «un contemplativo in un mondo riconciliato». Ma nel contempo un'immagine anche deviante: perché in qualche modo maschera il conflitto che Gregorio implicitamente denunciava con il suo ritiro, tra cristianesimo e mondo, lo riduce a un caso di coscienza personale, e quindi nulla spiega rispetto alla successiva storia dello stesso Gregorio. Dirò di più: fosse rimasto, costui, allo stadio della conversione-fuga, non credo saremmo qui ancora a parlare di lui: non sarebbe andato a Costantinopoli; non sarebbe diventato vescovo di Roma; e, ove avesse lasciato traccia di sé, lo avremmo, al massimo, catalogato tra gli *holy men* della sua epoca, ossia tra quei transfughi dal mondo di allora, che però furono incapaci di incidere in qualche modo sul mondo stesso o addirittura di cambiarlo.

Gregorio, invece, per quanto interiormente combattuto, andò a Costantinopoli, accettò il compito di vescovo di Roma, e quindi fu uno – già lo possiamo dire – che seppe alla fine incidere sul suo mondo e anzi lo trasformò. Ma tutto ciò per il fatto che in certo modo tradì la sua scelta monastica, e continuò a tradirla per tutta la vita lasciandosi strappare

---

[26] R.A. MARKUS, *Gregorio Magno e il suo mondo*, trad. it. Milano 2001 (Cambridge 1997), 4, 12-13.
[27] *Ibid.*, 3 ss.

dall'isolamento. Lo sottolineo perché una certa storiografia lo ha spesso descritto come un monaco mancato e come un protettore di monaci che continuava a fare il monaco[28]. No, Gregorio, pur con rammarico e nostalgia, a un certo punto lasciò per sempre il *buen retiro* monastico, e rientrò nel mondo. Non già in un mondo generico, bensì, per non pochi anni, in quello dell'Oriente romano: che era lo stesso di Agazia, dell'intellettuale ufficialmente cristiano ma nella sostanza ancora e sempre pagano, sicuro della forza della *ratio*, impermeabile al «mistero» e agli «entusiasmi» religiosi.

Appunto, fu a stretto contatto con il mondo elitario d'Oriente, solo ufficialmente cristiano, che Gregorio, non più monaco, pur vivendo in una comunità di monaci o comunque di amanti della vita monastica, si trovò a convivere per più anni. A convivere e anche a interagire: gli toccò infatti familiarizzarsi con i vertici del potere; vestire i panni dell'apocrisiario, ossia del «diplomatico» – cosa che ben sapeva fare: da laico aveva ben percorso tutto il *cursus* senatorio fino alla prefettura urbana –, e quindi intessere rapporti frequenti con il «palazzo», ossia con la corte imperiale, per discutere di strategie, di spedizioni navali, di corpi armati da dislocare in Occidente invece che lungo i confini orientali; e ciò con lo scopo (per questo era stato inviato a Costantinopoli da papa Pelagio) di difendere o ricuperare le Chiese dell'Occidente minacciate o invase dai Barbari, a partire da quella di Roma. E per giunta con la frustrazione di muoversi a vuoto: nulla, nessun aiuto politico-militare, riuscì a ottenere, nonostante una permanenza durata la bellezza di sette anni (e il fallimento della sua missione lo segnò per tutta la vita).

Soprattutto, durante il periodo costantinopolitano, Gregorio si trovò a fare i conti con un mondo che scoprì ben presto diverso, troppo diverso dal suo: per la cultura, anzi per le culture allora vivaci nella capitale, mentr'egli non riconosceva più alcuna cultura umana, ma solo la parola di Dio; per la mentalità delle classi alte che si sentivano investite e protette da Dio ai fini del dominio del mondo («combatte con noi l'Eterno», avrebbe dichiarato un generale del tempo per incitare i soldati alla battaglia)[29], mentr'egli ogni giorno constatava (e lo denunciò negli stessi *Moralia*) quanto i

---

[28] Importante in merito il lavoro, ancora oggi istruttivo, di C. DAGENS, *Saint Grégoire le Grand. Culture et expérience chrétienne*, Paris 1977, che discute a lungo sia il tema della conversione, sia quello del «monachesimo» di Gregorio. Per quest'ultimo, per quando condizionato dal precedente dei «monaci diventati vescovi» (come anche Agostino), l'Autore percepisce che al centro della spiritualità di Gregorio si trovano non già i monaci bensì personaggi universali come Giobbe (438-439).

[29] P. LAMMA, *Oriente e Occidente...*, 90-131, partic. 99.

membri di quelle classi fossero invece lontani da Cristo, ignari del Vangelo[30]. Dovette perfino onorare un imperatore che, sulla scia di Costantino, governava, in nome di Dio – *mìmesis* di Dio, re e sacerdote nello stesso tempo –[31], un Impero *sacratissimum*, meritando i titoli di *piissimus*, *christianissimus*; ma che in realtà – come in seguito sperimenterà di persona – poteva rivelarsi anche «tiranno»: fu il caso di Maurizio, della cui morte violenta Gregorio riterrà giusto gioire[32]; e in cuor suo già si era accorto dell'impossibilità di un governo diretto di Dio sul mondo.

Di solito, chi ha studiato i *Moralia*, che sono l'unica eco diretta del Gregorio costantinopolitano, poco valorizza queste «differenze»; e insiste sul suo persistente profilo monastico, sulla sua separatezza rispetto al mondo che pure doveva fronteggiare: come se tra il Gregorio ritirato a Roma sul Celio nel suo monastero domestico e il Gregorio apocrisiario sul Bosforo non ci fosse stacco alcuno. Con la conseguenza di ridurre i medesimi *Moralia* a «conferenze monastiche», quasi a un *vademecum* per chi dal mondo era fuggito per sempre[33]. Mentre è di evidenza palmare che i *Moralia* – ne è spia anche l'assenza di un lessico specifico (mancano, si è osservato, termini come *abbas*, *monachus* e derivati)[34] –, superano di gran lunga l'ambito monastico o la fase monastica di una vita e impostano un problema cruciale che riguardava sì la persona dello stesso Gregorio – «è forse un disegno della divina provvidenza (scrisse nella dedica a Leandro) che io colpito dal Male commenti la storia di Giobbe colpito dal Male» –, ma insieme tutti gli uomini, di allora e di ogni tempo[35]: come essere cristiani, veri cristiani «in un mondo in tempesta» (ripetiamo le parole di Markus); ovvero come affrontare il Male della storia, anche il Male estremo (oggi diremmo: anche Auschwitz), continuando ad avere fede in Dio[36]. Non per nulla i *Moralia* rimasero opera aperta, quasi «agende» (si

---

[30] G. Cracco, *Gregorio «morale»*..., 185-186.
[31] Si ricordi, oltre ai classici lavori di G. Dagron, anche un contributo di M. Mazza, *L'uso del passato: temi della politica in età giustinianea*, in *Alle soglia della classicità. Il Mediterraneo tra tradizione e innovazione. Studi in onore di Sabatino Moscati*, a cura di E. Acquaro, Pisa-Roma 1998, 307-329, partic. 325-329.
[32] *Registrum*, XIII, 34, maggio 603 (II, 397 dell'edizione MGH).
[33] Si veda l'*Introduction* di R. Gillet all'edizione e traduzione dei *Moralia* in *SC* 32, Paris 1950.
[34] P. Pellegrini, *«Militia Clericatus Monachici ordines». Istituzioni ecclesiastiche e società in Gregorio Magno*, Roma 2008, 150.
[35] P. Siniscalco, *Qualche nota sulla fortuna dei «Moralia» di Gregorio Magno*, in *«Per longa maris intervalla»*..., 363-377, partic. 375-376.
[36] G.E. Rusconi, *Come se Dio non ci fosse. I laici, i cattolici e la democrazia*, Torino 2000, 67-88, partic. 67 («Dov'era Dio ad Auschwitz?»), 71 ss. («L'esperienza di Giob-

passi il termine anacronistico)[37] in cui Gregorio riversò riflessioni e ripensamenti per tutta la vita, specie da quando fu fatto vescovo e patriarca dell'Occidente.

Come essere cristiani, appunto. Si tratta infatti – parlo sempre dei *Moralia* – di un'opera che documenta un conflitto in atto non tanto tra le due *Partes Imperii* – quella dell'Oriente e quella dell'Occidente – quanto tra due opposte visioni religiose, che ormai si facevano strada dentro la romanità di tradizione costantiniana. Si facevano strada perché la crisi dell'Impero si acuiva in rapporto alle «genti» che premevano da fuori e da dentro; e si trattava di decidere con quali armi affrontarle e possibilmente conquistarle: nel caso di Gregorio, non tanto armi materiali, che semplicemente mancarono (non già aiuti militari, ma solo diffidenze e intralci vennero dall'Oriente) quanto armi ideali. Ovvero, una volta constatato che l'Impero mai avrebbe saputo o potuto liberare l'Occidente dai Barbari, si poneva il problema se per convivere in qualche modo con essi era utile il cristianesimo dell'Impero, che era un paganesimo travestito (come mostra il caso di Agazia), o un cristianesimo diverso, che però era tutto da inventare. Dentro i *Moralia*, di questo cristianesimo diverso, già emerge qualcosa; ma sempre in riferimento al mondo romano di Costantinopoli. Il problema, tuttavia, era l'Occidente, con i Barbari alle porte di Roma e la città in preda alle fame e alle malattie: dentro questa ben diversa realtà – ben diversa rispetto all'Oriente – quale cristianesimo andava proposto?

5. Una fonte come i *Moralia* non può essere addotta come unica e di per sé decisiva per individuare il cristianesimo di Gregorio: non solo perché si tratta di un'opera di genere invincibilmente esegetico, ma anche di un'opera che è sì, per quanto sappiamo, la prima a lui sicuramente attribuibile, ma anche, per certi versi, la più «lavorata» in quanto riscritta, rivista, letteralmente aggiustata per tutta la vita. E attraverso il tempo, con di mezzo un'esperienza da vescovo di Roma (impensabile negli anni di Costantinopoli), più di qualche aspetto può essere stato di proposito cambiato, mascherato, o semplicemente lasciato cadere. Occorre dunque allargare lo sguardo ad altri testi gregoriani, quelli prodotti negli anni cruciali in cui

---

be-Israele»: «Giobbe non è solo il portatore del destino particolarissimo dell'ebraismo, ma il simbolo dell'umanità in quanto tale»). Rusconi dipende da M. SUSMAN, *Das Buch Hiob und das Schicksal des jüdischen Volches*, Frankfurt a. Main 1996.

[37] Alludo alle *Agende del patriarca* ANGELO GIUSEPPE RONCALLI, ora edite e annotate a cura di E. GALAVOTTI, in due volumi, Bologna 2008 (Edizione nazionale dei diari di Angelo Giuseppe Roncalli – Giovanni XXIII, 6 – Pace e Vangelo).

Gregorio esordisce come vescovo di Roma (il ruolo che era stato forzato di assumere), ossia tra il 590 e il 594.

Sono anni che, come dimostrano questi stessi testi (visti tuttavia non già partitamene ma nel loro insieme organico), grondano (se ci si passa l'espressione) di novità. In primo luogo, Gregorio si rifiuta di essere un vescovo della tradizione, e del vescovo s'impegna a disegnare un profilo ideale che è tutto ricalcato sul *Nuovo Testamento*: dove si privilegia non certo la funzione di custode della fede proclamata nei grandi Concili, bensì quella del «buon pastore». Non per nulla nella lettera *synodica* con cui Gregorio si accreditò di fronte agli altri Patriarchi, solo 19 righe sono dedicate alla *confessio fidei*, e quasi 300 alla figura del pastore. Il quale è colui che non può tacere perché deve parlare di Dio, e quindi s'innalza a predicatore e profeta; e colui che sa guardare al cielo ma non dimentica la terra, dove deve caricarsi sulle spalle le tragedie del suo popolo (*Intus Dei arcana considerat, foris onera carnalium portat*)[38]. E, sia detto per inciso, la *Regula pastoralis* che ne fu tratta perde smalto e spessore se non si tiene conto del perché e in rapporto a che cosa essa fu concepita, ossia della sua genesi in funzione della *Synodica*.

In secondo luogo, Gregorio si mette a predicare al popolo. Non è questa, ovviamente, una novità: l'omiletica cristiana disponeva già di una lunga e anche maestosa tradizione. Ma è una novità il fatto che Gregorio predichi il Vangelo e soltanto il Vangelo, e lo predichi non da una cattedra solenne bensì mettendosi sullo stesso piano degli ascoltatori, in termini quasi confidenziali («un diretto colloquio con voi»), per mostrare come Gesù è venuto al mondo non per porsi al di sopra o alla testa degli uomini bensì per essere accanto a ogni uomo, e diventargli «amico»: Egli «passa accanto a noi»; quando preghiamo, «prende posto nel nostro cuore»; ma non dobbiamo chiedergli «la ricchezza, ma la luce», come fece il cieco: «Signore che io veda». Gesù, se gli chiediamo la luce, allora concede, fa anche il miracolo: «la tua fede ti ha salvato»[39].

Potremmo addurre ben altre espressioni, tutte fresche di Vangelo (solo di recente si è acquisito che, quanto a *vita vere evangelica*, Gregorio anticipa di parecchi secoli Francesco d'Assisi)[40]; ma è sicuro che in età tar-

---

[38] G. CRACCO, *Vangelo e strutture ecclesiali in Gregorio Magno (a partire dalla Sinodica)*, in *Gregorio Magno e la Sardegna. Atti del Convegno Internazionale di Studio, Sassari, 15-16 aprile 2005*, a cura di L.G.G. RICCI, Firenze 2007, 31-58, partic. 42-47.

[39] Omelia XXI, 1; II, 5-7. Seguo la trad. it. a cura di G. CREMASCOLI, Torino 1968, 211-212, 63-65.

[40] Sull'idea del Gregorio «evangelico» – ripresa anche da C. DAGENS, *Saint Grégoire le Grand inspirateur d'une nouvelle culture chrétienne à l'aube du Moyen Age*, in *Gre-*

doantica mai si era sentito presentare un Cristo così: un Cristo sussurrato con amore al cuore e all'angoscia di tutti, specie degli umili. Oggi diremmo che Gregorio aveva una capacità eccezionale di comunicare e di coinvolgere chiunque (anche a dispetto della sua fragilità fisica, della sua debole voce): come neppure Agostino; e come, invece, Maometto, colui che, pochi anni dopo Gregorio, seppe ugualmente, pur in diverso contesto, raccogliere «attorno a sé i deboli, molti giovani e persino schiavi»[41].

In terzo luogo, Gregorio, che pur aveva una spiccata predilezione per l'esegesi, come dimostrano i *Moralia* (e ancor più lo dimostra l'ultima grande opera da lui lasciata, l'*In primum Regum*), decise di *interrumpere* l'*expositionis studium*[42] per dedicarsi al *Miracula Patrum Italicorum*, che non sono né una banale raccolta di *exempla*, né tanto meno di *pre-exempla*, come categorizza Le Goff[43], bensì una vera e propria aretalogia, come i Vangeli (una vera novità per l'Occidente, anche come genere letterario)[44] – in quattro libri, come i quattro Vangeli[45] –, collocata a ridosso della sua epoca, nel pieno del «vissuto» contemporaneo.

Dovremmo soffermarci anche sulla produzione delle *Lettere*, che per quanto documenti ufficiali, sono eco e talora, riproposizione puntuale di quanto si legge nelle *Omelie* e perfino (ciò che spesso è sfuggito) degli stessi *Dialogi* (oltre ne daremo prova): come a dire che anche le *Lettere* sono cariche di novità. Ma ci sembra di aver già accumulato dati sufficienti a conferma del fatto che sin dall'inizio del pontificato Gregorio s'impe-

---

gorio Magno nel XIV Centenario della morte, 209-220 – è fondato il contributo mio e di mia moglie cit. *supra*, nota 20.

[41] J. VAN ESS, *Prospettive islamiche*, in H. KÜNG, J. VAN ESS, H. VON STIETENKRON, H. BECHERT, *Cristianesimo e religioni universali. Introduzione al dialogo con islamismo, induismo e buddismo*, trad. it., Milano 1986, 20.

[42] Certamente Gregorio aveva una spiccata predilezione per l'esegesi, che tornerà a coltivare soprattutto dopo il 595 – *magnum nobis, sicut nostis, erat in verbo Dei solacium*, scriverà nell'aprile del 598 al vescovo di Ravenna: *Registrum*, VIII, 18 dell'ediz. dei *MGH*, II, 20 –; ma nei primi anni del pontificato, trovò necessario *interrumpere expositionis studium* per dedicarsi ai *Dialogi*, ai *Sermones*, alle *Lettere* (*Dialogi*, Proemio, 9, nell'ediz. curata da A. DE VOGÜÉ in SC 260, 1979, II, 16-17, con nota 9).

[43] G. CRACCO, *Gregorio Magno autore mariano: un'altra immagine del papa nella cultura tardomedievale*, in *Chiesa, vita religiosa, società nel medioevo italiano. Studi offerti a Giuseppina De Sandre Gasparini*, a cura di M. ROSSI e G.M. VARANINI, Roma 2005, 253-270.

[44] *Dialogi*, Proemio, 9, nell'ediz. curata da A. DE VOGÜÉ in SC 260, 1979, II, 16-17, con nota 9.

[45] L. CRACCO RUGGINI, *Gregorio Magno, Agostino e i quattro Vangeli*, in *Miscellanea di studi agostiniani in onore di P. Agostino Trapé, OSA*, «Augustinianum» 25 (1985), 255-263.

gnò a gettare le basi di un cristianesimo nuovo, o comunque in gran parte inedito rispetto al più vasto mondo religioso mediterraneo.

Entrando ora nel merito delle novità, ci si accorge che ne emerge una in particolare, attinente al nostro tema. Sappiamo dai *Moralia* che per Gregorio il paganesimo non era più un pericolo attuale. E invece, a leggere i *Dialogi*, lo ridiventa, come se fosse improvvisamente rinato dalle ceneri, come mostrano alcuni episodi che però sono nel contempo anche dati significativi.

Giunto al *castrum* di Cassino, Benedetto s'imbatte in un *vetustissimum fanum* in cui, *ex antiquorum more gentilium*, «una stupida comunità di rustici rendeva culto ad Apollo». Per giunta, nelle vicinanze dello stesso *castrum*, si trovavano ancora molti *infideles* che «da pazzi insistevano con i sacrifici sacrileghi agli Dei dei boschi»[46]. *Gentiles, infideles*: il senso del passo, da far risalire direttamente a Gregorio per il fatto che trova riscontri coevi (come subito vedremo), non lascia dubbi: parla di un paganesimo che ancora esiste, ma esiste come fenomeno residuale, sopravvivenza «insana» e per menti «insane» (quelle contadine); e quindi da spazzare via, senza tolleranza o pietà. Si può far notare quanto questa violenta reazione di Benedetto – *contrivit idolum, subvertit aram, succidit lucum* –, sia agli antipodi della tolleranza permissiva suggerita dallo stesso Gregorio più tardi, nel 601, in rapporto alle *durae mentes* degli Angli[47]. Ma intanto questa avversione c'è (in Gregorio, a seconda delle congiunture, si trovano anche atteggiamenti differenziati se non contraddittori), e non può essere trascurata. Tanto più che trova conferma, come si diceva, in una lettera del *Registrum* cronologicamente di poco posteriore (maggio 594) al passo suddetto, relativa alla Sardegna.

Nella grande isola, con sorpresa di Gregorio, anche battezzati continuavano ad *immolare idolis*; e nel contempo quella che potremmo chiamare una «minoranza etnica», i Barbaricini – definiti «rustici», *insensata animalia* –, adoravano legni e pietre *pravae gentilitatis more*. Il loro *dux*, tuttavia, già era stato battezzato, e la loro conversione, come si deduce dal contesto, era solo questione di tempo e di buona volontà dei vescovi dell'isola[48].

Esisteva, dunque, ancora esisteva, durante i questi primi anni di pontificato di Gregorio, un paganesimo «insensato» e «contadino», per quanto

---

[46] *Dialogi*, II, 8 , 10 (II, 166-168).
[47] *Nam duris mentibus simul omnia abscidere impossibile esse non dubium est*: *Registrum*, XI, 56 (II, 330-331).
[48] IV, 27 (I, 261-262).

residuale e in via di estinzione, che induceva il patriarca di Roma a reagire con intolleranza e repressione. Una reazione non usuale in Gregorio, ma forse da connettere con la scoperta preoccupata di un altro tipo di paganesimo, che proprio in quei mesi si manifestava non già come spento relitto del passato o stolta tradizione contadina, bensì come fenomeno nuovo e irrompente con la furia di un uragano. Si tratta dei Longobardi «pagani», identificati appunto come tali – *gentiles viri* – negli stessi *Dialogi*, che compaiono nell'episodio riguardante Santolo, un prete della provincia di Norcia, il quale li dovette affrontare mentre cercavano di spremere olive nel frantoio senza riuscirci (ignoravano, da Barbari, anche il minimo di tecnica agricola); e in più si capisce che più ostili ai cristiani non potevano essere: avevano dato alla fiamme, come nulla fosse, la chiesa di S. Lorenzo martire[49].

Di questi «pagani», a differenza di quelli incontrati da Benedetto o scoperti in Sardegna, Gregorio si mostra non tanto preoccupato quanto terrorizzato, come prova la visione che sempre nei *Dialogi* attribuisce al vescovo Redento: una voce apocalittica, quella del martire Iutico apparsogli a mezzanotte durante il dormiveglia, per tre volte pronunciò un lugubre annuncio: *Finis venit universae carni*. E in effetti – commenta Gregorio – da quando l'*effera Langobardorum gens*, uscendo dalla sua terra, si era riversata lungo la penisola italica portando flagelli – *depopulatae urbes, eversa castra, concrematae ecclesiae [...] desolata ab hominibus praedia [...] occupaverunt bestiae loca, quae prius multitudo hominum tenebat* –, la fine del mondo non solo si diceva stesse per succedere: era già avvenuta[50].

Val la pena di soffermarsi su questo celebre lamento, più spesso citato, anche rifiutato[51], che analizzato, per osservare che anche Gregorio, quando lo dettò (forse nel 593, agli inizi del suo pontificato), con i Longobardi che assediavano Roma, pare convinto che la nuova ondata di barbari-pagani

---

[49] *Dialogi*, III, 37, 2-4 (II, 412-414).
[50] *Ibid.*, III, 38, 2-4 (II, 428-430).
[51] L. Duchesne, *I primi tempi dello Stato pontificio*, trad. it., II ediz. con Introduzione di G. Miccoli, Torino 1967 (1947) partic. pp. 13. L'Autore, che vedeva Gregorio come «il principale rappresentante della politica di rassegnazione che ammetteva la divisione dell'Italia fra l'Impero e i Longobardi», non s'incanta di fronte alla testimonianza dello stesso Gregorio, che mascherava, a suo giudizio, risvolti politici: «questo stile evangelico non deve illuderci»; e quasi difende i Longobardi: che cosa mai potevano fare gli invasori se non depredare? Del resto, sono frequenti, nella storiografia, gli avvertimenti a non cadere nella trappola di Gregorio dando credito «ingenuo» a quello che disse e fece scrivere: F. Mores, *«Per intendere questi tempi bisogna essere un poco Monsignore»: I Longobardi e la Chiesa Romana secondo Louis Duchesne*, «Rivista di storia della Chiesa in Italia» 62 (2008), 113-160, partic. 133.

(due termini per lui allora equivalenti) stesse per sommergere davvero il mondo romano-cristiano. E in effetti, proprio in quei mesi, esattamente nell'aprile dello stesso 593, l'espressione catastrofica *Eversae urbes, castra eruta, ecclesiae destructae, nullus in terra nostra cultor inhabitat* ricorre anche, e di poco mutata, in una lettera al clero di Milano transfuga a Genova per salvarsi dai Longobardi, che si era scelto come nuovo vescovo un proprio membro, Costanzo; e ricorre ancora – ulteriore prova dell'*unité des tous ses écrits*[52] – nel contesto apocalittico di un mondo ridotto allo stremo, anzi ai *paucissimi*, sui quali incombeva la fine[53]. Nulla, infatti, sembrava poter fermare i barbari-pagani dilaganti per l'Italia.

Proviamo a mettere insieme i diversi elementi sin qui evidenziati: Gregorio propone, da vescovo, un nuovo cristianesimo; e lo propone contestualmente all'emergere di una nuova ondata di paganesimo – quello rappresentato dai Longobardi invasori – capace di distruggere l'intero mondo cristiano. Ci sembra evidente la relazione tra i due fatti. Sia chiaro: nessun automatismo scontato o a senso unico. Gregorio, di fronte all'irrompere dei nuovi «pagani», reagisce come può, muovendosi su tutti i fronti: cerca aiuti anche militari per scongiurare il tracollo; confida nei poteri esistenti, nell'imperatore, nell'esarca che lo rappresentava in Italia. Tenta perfino, con abile mossa, di far breccia tra i «pagani» rivolgendosi a Teodolinda, regina dei Longobardi, che proprio pagana non era, ma ostile ai Cattolici sì: per convincerla che Giustiniano, ossia il legittimo potere imperiale, mai aveva rinnegato la fede di Calcedonia[54]. Ma con esito nullo. Finché si trovò e si sentì solo; costretto ad affrontare, da solo, la «fine del mondo».

Da solo? Tutt'altro: nell'ora più difficile, quando toccò con mano il fallimento dei poteri terreni – il nesso Impero-Chiesa, di cui erano fieri i suoi predecessori come Leone Magno –, egli s'accorse di poter disporre di un potere del tutto «altro», e ben altrimenti salvifico: quello che gli veniva dalla sua esperienza di asceta e di pastore, ossia da quel Gesù dei Vangeli di cui andava parlando al popolo e che diceva vicino, anzi pronto a entrare nel cuore di tutti. Non era, questo Gesù, il Dio maestoso del *basileus*, ma il compagno, anzi l'«amico» di tutti.

Stiamo parlando dell'emergere, in Gregorio, di una cultura nuova, ben diversa da quella conservativa e dotta di un Cassiodoro, che sconfessa, con il suo evangelismo, la precedente cultura, quella romano-cristiana o costantiniano-giustinianea, coinvolgendo di conseguenza interlocutori

---

[52] Una unità già felicemente individuata da C. Dagens, *Saint Grégoire le Grand*, 435.
[53] *Registrum*, III, 29 (I, 186-187).
[54] *Ibid.*, IV, 4 (I, 236-237); IV, 33 (I, 268-269).

nuovi: gli umili (come si diceva), i *sine litteris*, tanto romani quanto barbari, e cambiando in prospettiva la storia dell'Occidente.

6. Si tratta, in effetti, di «nuovo modo di accostarsi alla religione», che occorre meglio precisare. Un modo che non si arrestava – direbbe un autore moderno come Ronald Knox, che peraltro di Gregorio mai si accorse – alle «forme» e ai «riti esteriori», perché era «un affare di cuore». Espressioni siffatte sembrano di per sé ben lontane da Gregorio, anche perché tipiche di una cultura di tanti secoli dopo che, stanca di rassicuranti ricette come quella della grazia che non annulla la natura ma la perfeziona, audacemente parla di una grazia che «ha distrutto la natura» e sorpassato «il miserabile intelletto dell'uomo» (altro che *fides et ratio*)[55]. Ma, a parte che neppure Gregorio fu mai attaccato alle forme e ai riti, e sicuramente disdegnò il pensiero e la parola degli uomini per fare spazio solo a Dio, alla sua parola, perfino alla sua «lingua», è da dire quello che significò di fatto, per lui, l'approdo a questa nuova cultura. Significò, per riprendere un'espressione dello stesso Knox, che «Davide non deve vestire l'armatura di Saul»[56].

Mi spiego meglio: di fronte a quei barbari-pagani che erano i Longobardi, fosse stato, Gregorio, quello che non fu mai, ovvero un uomo della corte di Costantinopoli – un alto funzionario, un generale, o anche il patriarca –, avrebbe tanto più confidato in Dio quanto più si sentiva in pericolo; e non avrebbe avuto dubbi sul fatto che alla fine, «Dio è con noi», perché – secondo l'idea, anzi la teologia politica allora dominante in Oriente – Dio non poteva non venire in soccorso dei «suoi», di un Impero cristiano che era comunque «suo», nel senso che egli stesso l'aveva voluto e amava preservarlo intatto e vittorioso per la guida e la salvezza del mondo. Quel teorico Gregorio «orientale», a ben pensarci, avrebbe anche mobilitato Maria, la Madre di Dio, che proprio in quell'epoca, vedi caso, fu eletta in Costantinopoli a protettrice della capitale (lo stesso imperatore Maurizio istituì, nell'anno 600, la festa dell'Assunzione), e come tale sarà poi vista combattere al tempo di Eraclio, nel 626, in veste di eroico guer-

---

[55] R.A. KNOX, *Enthusiasm. A Chapter in the History of Religion*, Oxford 1950, trad. it. con il titolo *Illuminati e carismatici. Una storia dell'entusiasmo religioso*, Bologna 1970, 9-10.
[56] *Ibid.*, 10.

riero (come già la dea Atena in difesa dell'antica Atene), sulle mura della città assediata, per terrorizzare e respingere gli invasori[57].

E invece no: Gregorio non è più, se mai lo era stato, l'uomo del «Dio con noi», della Vergine e delle schiere celesti che scendono in terra per difendere con la spada sguainata la città dei Romano-Cristiani; non è insomma un romano-cristiano da corte orientale; è invece – ecco il fatto nuovo di cui si diceva – un uomo che alla fine accetta gli eventi (nel caso concreto, perfino la fine del mondo romano-cristiano) e si mette a riflettere sul significato ad essi soggiacente, ossia sul rapporto dei Cristiani con il mondo.

Una riflessione che non è esagerato definire profetica, se non rivoluzionaria, nella sua radicalità: che importa, osserva nello stesso passo dei *Dialogi* sopra citato, se i flagelli distruggono tutto? Distruggono in realtà solo cose transeunti, tutto ciò che garantisce il benessere materiale. Ma questo colpisce solo chi crede che il benessere sia tutto, che esista solo la vita in questo mondo e neanche si chiede se «l'anima continui a vivere dopo la morte del corpo». Non può colpire invece quanti proprio nel pieno delle catastrofi si sentono, e non certo paradossalmente, come confortati: perché, vedendo dissolversi i *temporalia*, più comprendono di doversi orientare verso gli *aeterna*; e hanno una prova in più che una vita futura li attende[58].

Espressioni solo consolatorie e topiche, in fondo coerenti con lo stile «basso» e «plebeo» – *such silly stuff*, per dirla con Francis Clark[59] – spesso rimproverato all'autore dei *Dialogi*? Oppure, più propriamente, una ripresa estremizzata dell'idea, mutuata da Agostino, di un Dio che nella storia resta coinvolto e sulla storia scatena la sua ira per punire i malvagi?[60] In primo luogo, è da notare il fatto che quelle espressioni ricorrono pressoché immutate e perfino dilatate, anche nella già citata e coeva lettera al clero di Milano, ossia in un atto ufficiale rimasto nel *Registrum*. Anche qui – ed è

---

[57] G. CRACCO, *«Nescio virum»: alle origini del culto mariano in Occidente*, in *Pensiero e sperimentazioni istituzionali nella «Societas Christiana» (1046-1250). Atti della sedicesima Settimana internazionale di studio, Mendola, 26-31 agosto 2004*, a cura di G.C. ANTENNA, Milano 2007, 487-519, partic. 501-502.

[58] *Tanto ergo nos necesse est instantius aeterna quaerere quanto a nobis cognoscimus velociter temporalia fugisse. Despiciendus a nobis hic mundus fuerat etiam si blandiretur, si rebus prosperis demulceret animum. At postquam tot flagellis premitur, tanta adversitate fatigatur, tot nobis cotidie dolores ingeminat, quid nobis aliud quam ne diligatur clamat?*: *Dialogi*, III, 38, 4-5 (II, 430-432).

[59] F. CLARK, *The Pseudo-Gregorian Dialogues*, Leiden 1987, I, 7-8.

[60] C. TAYLOR, *A Secular Age*, Cambridge-London 2007, 105 e *passim*: l'Autore adotta l'espressione *hyper-Augustinianism*.

la diversità rispetto alla tradizione – Gregorio continua a sostenere, appunto, che in vista della fine del mondo, quando i flagelli diventano intollerabili (è il momento, come aveva detto nei *Moralia*, del terribile «silenzio di Dio»), non resta che piangere sulle colpe commesse e fare penitenza. Così, aggiunge, il Giudice eterno, «quanto più vedrà che ci siamo puniti da soli, tanto più ci accoglierà nella sua grazia»[61]. Ovvero, Gregorio sposta l'asse della storia dal tempo all'eternità.

E questo spostamento non può essere lasciato nel vago: vuol dire che Gregorio (e qui si coglie l'impatto concreto del suo nuovo cristianesimo) non ha più fiducia nella positività del mondo terreno, neppure nella sua sopravvivenza – una fiducia che ad esempio ad Agostino, per quanto conscio della *senectus mundi*, specie a seguito del sacco di Roma del 410, mai venne meno del tutto (la Città non stava *in parietibus*, ma, appunto, *in civibus*)[62] –, ed è anche pronto a lasciarlo andare al suo destino. Vuol dire che il vero mondo che di conseguenza prospettava diventa l'aldilà; e ciò ancora una volta in armonia con il Gesù dei Vangeli che aveva proclamato in termini inequivoci: «Il mio regno non è di questo mondo».

Si può anche dire che per affrontare il male della storia (quello che più colpisce e fa soffrire, lo rileva egli stesso, soprattutto i deboli, gli indifesi), Gregorio non conta su resistenze cieche, su respingimenti violenti; non erige barricate o muraglie; «non veste – per riprendere l'immagine di Knox – l'armatura di Saul»; resta il Davide che si è fatto. E invita per giunta a guardarsi dentro, per capire dove e come anche le vittime possono aver sbagliato, e sbagliato al punto da provocare, seppure indirettamente,

---

[61] *In interitum ergo rerum omnium pensare debemus nil fuisse quod amavimus. Adpropinquantem itaque aeterni iudicis diem sollecita mente conspicite et terrorem illius paenitendo prevenite. Delictorum omnium maculas fletibus lavate. Iram quae aeterna inminet temporali lamento compescite. Pius enim conditor noster, cum ad iudicium venerit, tanto nos maiore gratia consolabitur quanto nunc conspicit quod a nobis nostra delicta puniuntur*: *Registrum*, III, 29 (I, 187). Per il «silenzio di Dio», cfr. il passo dei *Moralia*, XXXIV.

[62] Si veda la sfumata analisi di F. PASCHOUD, *Roma aeterna. Études sur le patriotisme romain dans l'Occident latin à l'époque des grandes invasions*, Rome 1967, 234-275. Tuttavia, a parte il celebre *Sermo de excidio urbis*, è certo che anche le due *civitates* furono pensate come realtà di questo mondo, «finché non le separi l'ultimo Giudizio», e con la prospettiva che la *civitas Dei* potesse crescere e allargarsi, anche con il *bellum iustum*, fino a fare del mondo una sola e «romana» cristianità: L. ALICI, *Introduzione* a AURELIO AGOSTINO, *La città di Dio*, Milano 1990, II ediz., 31 ss. Anche P. BROWN, nel memorabile capitolo 25 del suo *Agostino d'Ippona*, trad. it., Torino 1971 (London 1967), 294, afferma che «Agostino dava per scontata la sopravvivenza dell'Impero romano».

il male medesimo; prospettando infine per tutti – buoni o malvagi, persecutori e vittime, vincitori e vinti – il Giudice eterno che tutti attende sulla soglia dell'altra *patria*: una *patria* che quindi non si può ascrivere, data la presa che trovò nella cultura dei secoli, a fatua invenzione.

Siamo di fronte, in effetti, a un connotato essenziale del nuovo cristianesimo di Gregorio, che va connesso con il contesto altamente drammatico, da fine dei tempi, sopra evocato. Per essere più chiari: Gregorio non approda all'aldilà se non dopo aver visto dissolversi l'aldiqua, la patria terrena; non «vede» né descrive l'aldilà in termini icastici se non dopo aver sperimentato che ben pochi cristiani, per via dell'attaccamento a questa vita, sapevano o credevano *quod anima post carnem vivat*[63], e che lo stesso corpo poteva risorgere. E invece staccare, anzi sradicare gli uomini da un mondo transeunte e di continuo esposto alla rovina, orientarli verso un aldilà concepito come il luogo del benessere eterno, e far capire per giunta che esiste una *constant interpenetration of this world and the next*, ossia che le sofferenze di quaggiù sono davvero in rapporto con le gioie di lassù: questa la *greatest novelty* che Gregorio introduce nella cultura del suo mondo[64].

Una novità – non sorprenda il richiamo – analoga a quella che il profeta dell'Oriente, Maometto, di lì a pochi anni, proclamerà a sua volta contrapponendo, da un lato, gli infedeli, «la gran parte della gente», che, sazi del mondo di quaggiù, «ironizzano con superiorità: Per noi c'è solo questa vita, la presente. Si vive. Si muore. È il tempo che passa che ci uccide»; e dall'altro i fedeli, che invece riconoscono di doversi alla fine presentare al cospetto di Dio, di un Dio che dà la vita e dà la morte, e che giudicherà

---

[63] All'interlocutore dei *Dialogi* Pietro, che gli aveva segnalato come anche cristiani avessero dubbi circa l'esistenza di una vita eterna dopo la morte del corpo, Gregorio risponde: «È arduo convincerli, ma per quanto sarò capace, cercherò di dimostrare *quod anima post carnem vivat*: III, 38, 5 (II, 432). Questo il passo finale del III libro dei *Dialogi* che funge da introduzione al IV libro, ossia di quel libro che più ha contribuito, con le sue «grossolane» descrizioni dell'oltretomba, a mettere in dubbio l'autenticità dei Dialogi. In effetti anch'io penso che questo quarto libro sia quello più «infiltrato», più «addomesticato» dagli *scriptores*; fors'anche il più «tradito». E ciò perché, a ben riflettere, il *quod anima post carnem vivat* – che nella tradizione manoscritta ha fatto circolare questo libro anche da solo sotto il titolo *De aeternitate animae* – è per Gregorio solo il prolegomeno di un'idea ben più ampia e complessa: quella della resurrezione della carne stessa (cfr. oltre).

[64] J.N. HILLGARTH, *Eschatological and Political Concepts in the Seventh Century*, in *Le septième siècle, Changements et continuités. Actes du Colloque bilatéral franco-britannique tenu au Warburg Institute le 8-9 juillet 1988*, London 1992, 212-235, partic. 230-231.

«nel giorno della resurrezione», perché «ognuno riceva ricompensa delle sue azioni»[65].

E la novità di Gregorio va connessa con un'altra, altrettanto grande, che a lui risale: la visione dell'uomo salvato, ricongiunto con il suo Dio. Difatti, se l'approdo all'aldilà diventa il fine della storia, si trattava di capire quale sarebbe stata, appunto, la sorte dell'uomo, dell'uomo di carne, dopo la morte, una volta giunto all'aldilà. Nei *Moralia* compare a un certo punto il ricordo di un clamoroso dibattito da lui sostenuto in Costantinopoli con Eutichio, il grande patriarca di Costantinopoli forse nel 582-583. Il quale Eutichio, da raffinato teologo qual era, tutto imbevuto di cultura ellenica, aveva sostenuto che sì, l'uomo risorgerà, ma non nella carne – anche il paolino *Caro non prodest quicquam* pesava, eccome – bensì come entità «impalpabile, più sottile del vento e dell'aria». E Gregorio non ci sta e reagisce seccamente, con le parole stesse di Giobbe: No, «nell'ultimo giorno io uscirò dalla terra e sarò coperto dalla mia pelle e nella mia carne vedrò il mio Dio. Proprio io lo vedrò, i miei occhi lo vedranno». Sennonché questo «proprio io» lo poteva dire, secondo Gregorio, ogni persona, e tanto più chi nella sua pelle e nella sua carne più aveva patito le ferite della miseria, delle violenze e delle malattie (questo, adducendo esempi, egli andava predicando al popolo).

È pensabile che il passo in questione, di per sé così poco adatto a un testo di esegesi, sia stato inserito non già a Costantinopoli bensì più tardi, a Roma, quando, pressato dai nuovi barbari-pagani, Gregorio «inventò» l'altro mondo, e abbozzò fra l'altro il IV libro dei *Dialogi*. Ma a parte questo, non si può non notare come questo aldilà di Gregorio fosse tanto in linea con il suo evangelismo che associava – le *Omelie* ne sono la prova evidente – il quaggiù alla Croce e il lassù alla risurrezione, quanto sensibile alle attese dell'umanità sofferente della sua epoca. La quale umanità, proprio perché fatta soprattutto di tanti Lazzaro (e Dio – predicava Gregorio – conosce il nome dei poveri come Lazzaro, non già quello dei ricchi «epuloni»)[66], non poteva che «vedersi» nel Paradiso di Gregorio, popolato di uomini veri che con i loro occhi, coperti dalla loro pelle e nella loro carne, godevano della compagnia di un Dio risorto con il corpo. Non già, dunque – come aveva scritto Agostino –, in un non immaginabile «cielo del cielo del Signore», in una dimora «immersa nella contemplazione delle tue delizie, senza distacchi né evasioni, mente pura»: una dimora

---

[65] Sura XLV, 22, 24, 26.
[66] *Omelia* 40, 3.

infinitamente lontana, di cui null'altro si può predicare se non che sarà *in fine sine fine*[67].

E dire che l'«umanità» di Gregorio ha riscosso lo scetticismo ironico di studiosi moderni in quanto espressione di un Occidente di «pecore e pastori» che finisce per sfigurare di fronte all'Oriente dei pensatori «alti»[68]; per non dire dell'accusa mossa allo stesso Gregorio di aver facilitato la *barbarisation* e la *folklorisation du sacré*[69]. In realtà Gregorio non faceva che respingere precocemente e per primo – a breve arriverà anche il Paradiso di Maometto, che è un «giardino di delizie» traboccante di umane «felicità»[70] – il processo da tempo in atto tanto di ellenizzazione quanto di romanizzazione del cristianesimo (due tendenze ancor oggi allignanti ai vertici della Chiesa cattolica), per far spazio solo al Dio degli *Atti*, quello che «non fa distinzione di persone», e può essere quindi anche il Dio dei Barbari, degli stessi Longobardi (e poi anche degli Angli): la riscoperta della missione è organicamente connessa con l'invenzione di una vita eterna, anzi di «quella» vita eterna, che tutti attende.

---

[67] Si tratta dello spazio riservato ai *cives civitatis tuae*, collocato *in coelestibus super ista coelestia*: SANT'AGOSTINO, *Confessioni*, XII, XI, 12, a cura di M. SIMONETTI, V, Milano 2001, II ediz., 18-19. Ma si veda anche il *De civitate Dei*, XXII, 30, laddove si parla del grande sabato del Signore, dell'ottavo giorno eterno che ingenera quiete eterna nell'anima e nel corpo: *Ibi vacabimus et videbimus, amabimus et laudabimus. Ecce quod erit in fine sine fine. Nam qui alius noster est finis nisi pervenire ad regnum cuius nullus est finis?*

[68] Si tratta della «gerarchia» delineata nella conclusione del pur valido contributo di Y.-M. DUVAL, *La discussion entre l'apocrysiaire Grégoire et le patriarche Eutychios au sujet de la résurrection de la chair. L'arrière-plan doctrinal oriental et occidental*, in *Grégoire le Grand. Actes publiés par* J. FONTAINE, R. GILLET, S. PELLISTRANDI, Paris 1986, 347-366 (dal quale abbiamo tratto dati e citazioni).

[69] J. LE GOFF, *«Vita» et «preexemplum» dans le 2e livre des «Dialogues» de Grégoire le Grand*, in *Hagiographies Cultures et Sociétés, IVe-XIIe siècle. Actes du Colloque organisé à Nanterre et à Paris (12-15 mai 1979)*, par E. PATLAGEAN, P. RICHÉ, Paris 1981, 105-117, partic. 109.

[70] Sura XLIV, 51-57: «Ma i devoti vivranno in luogo sicuro, in mezzo a gannat e a sorgenti. Vestiranno di seta e broccato, saranno collocati in faccia gli uni degli altri, e gli daremo per spose le huri dagli occhi grandissimi. Ivi chiederanno soavemente ogni specie di frutta. Morte più non gusteranno dopo la prima morte [...] Ecco una gioia senza barriere»; LV, 48-56 («Incontreranno in delizie amorose le belle dallo sguardo innocente, che nessuno, uomo o spiritello, avrà mai deflorato prima d'allora»); LXXVIII, 32-35: «Parchi e vigne, vergini dal seno turgido, coetanee e calici ricolmi. Ivi saranno bandite futili chiacchiere, né vi saranno menzogne».

7. Ma a questo punto credo di aver illustrato a sufficienza, se non altro per taluni aspetti, la novità cristiana portata da Gregorio: una novità che ebbe effetti indubbi sull'emergere in Occidente – specie in Italia, in Spagna, in Inghilterra (meno in Gallia, che più risentì, come scrisse Agazia, della romanità orientale)[71] – di un cristianesimo non più romano-politico, ma soltanto religioso, anzi evangelico. Un cristianesimo che, come poi l'islamismo di Maometto (non a caso frutto dell'altra grande discendenza abramitica, quella dei figli del deserto)[72], s'incentra unicamente sulla fede in un Dio trascendente (pur diversamente trascendente: il Dio vicino di Gregorio, il Dio lontano di Maometto), che comunque farà giustizia solo nell'aldilà.

Non ho insistito invece abbastanza sul fatto dei conflitti che tale novità suscitò tra gli stessi cristiani. Gregorio, del resto, fu tanto compreso, al suo tempo e anche nella posterità, dalle masse umili e dai popoli non romani quanto frainteso e perfino negato dai colti e dalle Chiese dell'Occidente: a cominciare dai suoi «figli» spirituali, che gli stettero accanto e misero per iscritto, spesso *valde inutilius*, ogni sua parola[73]; e dallo stesso clero di Roma, che non vide l'ora di liberarsi di lui e di coprirlo con una *damnatio memoriae*. Per non parlare dei *basileis* di Costantinopoli, dei tanti *reges* e imperatori di Occidente, e perfino dei tanti vescovi di Roma, primo tra tutti Gregorio VII, che si fecero portatori di un cristianesimo diverso se non rovesciato rispetto al suo, come se Cristo avesse detto: «Il mio regno è di questo mondo». Attraverso i secoli, Gregorio continuò a essere un segno di contraddizione, al punto da alimentare, come in età moderna, vere e proprie «guerre»[74].

E ancora oggi il giudizio su di lui è diviso: tra chi giunge perfino a censurarne o a negarne le opere, e chi lo vede invece come risorsa preziosa da ricuperare nell'interesse dello stesso papato[75], fino a immaginarlo presente in controluce, com'è accaduto di recente, in un papa finalmente «cri-

---

[71] P. LAMMA, *Ricerche sulla storia e la cultura del VI secolo*, 97-98.
[72] M. DOUSSE, *L'Islam et la necessaire dualité du monotheisme abrahamique*, «Rivista di storia e letteratura religiosa», 45 (2009), 119-138.
[73] L. CRACCO RUGGINI, G. CRACCO, *Gregorio Magno e i «Libri dei Re»*..., 244 ss.
[74] G. CRACCO, *Storiografia*, in *Enciclopedia Gregoriana. La vita, l'opera e la fortuna di Gregorio Magno*, a cura di G. CREMASCOLI, A. DEGL'INNOCENTI, Firenze 2008, 331-344, partic. 339.
[75] H. KÜNG, *La Chiesa*, trad. it. Brescia 1969, partic. p. 545: «Se l'ulteriore sviluppo del papato fosse corso nello spirito evangelico ed ecumenico di Gregorio Magno, si sarebbero potute evitare molte cose, e non ultima la divisione fra oriente e occidente».

stiano» e «conciliare» come Giovanni XXIII[76]. Personalmente lo vedrei presente, per certi aspetti, in un altro papa «cristiano» e «conciliare», per quanto finora poco riconosciuto, Giovanni Paolo I[77]. Ma è un'illusione: come potrebbero papi «tridentini» (rubo l'aggettivo a Melloni)[78] rispecchiare un Gregorio che «papa», nel senso tradizionale del termine, non fu mai, né poteva esserlo[79]? Il conflitto dentro il cristianesimo, anche nell'età secolare, o forse già postsecolare[80], che stiamo vivendo, resta fatalmente aperto.

---

[76] A. MELLONI, *Papa Giovanni. Un cristiano e il suo concilio*, Torino 2009, 78-79: sulle tracce di una frase di Küng (contributo cit. nella nota precedente, 545): «La figura moderna che fa da riscontro a Gregorio Magno è Giovanni XXIII».

[77] Sono in corso di stampa gli Atti del Convegno tenuto, per iniziativa dell'Istituto per ricerche di storia sociale e religiosa di Vicenza, a Canale d'Agordo-Vicenza-Venezia il 24-26 settembre 2008, dove si può leggere anche un mio contributo: *Modelli di papi e idee sul papato negli scritti di Albino Luciani*.

[78] A. MELLONI, *Papa Giovanni...*, 19-23.

[79] G. CRACCO, *Cristianesimo e storia: il nodo del Medioevo*, «Nuova Iniziativa Isontina», 49 (2008), 28-38, partic. 34-36. Importante, per ripensare il ruolo del vescovo di Roma, quanto ha scritto M. POIRIER, *L'évêque, les clercs, le peuple. La structure d'una communauté chrétienne au milieu du IIIe siècle en Occident, d'après les oeuvres de saint Cyprien*, «Bulletin de la Société nationale des Antiquaires de France 2002», 54-78, partic. 56-64. Non utile, in questa direzione, il contributo di C. PAPINI, *Da vescovo di Roma a sovrano del mondo. L'irresistibile ascesa del papato romano al potere assoluto. Frammenti di storia del papato dalle origini al secolo VII*, Torino 2009, 321 ss.

[80] Cfr. G. CRACCO, T. TREU, *From Vicenza to Astana*, in *Kazakhstan. Religions and Society in the History of Central Eurasia*, ed. by G.L. BONORA, N. PIANCIOLA, P. SARTORI, Torino 2009, 11-16; G. MANNION, *Chiesa e postmoderno. Domande per l'ecclesiologia del nostro tempo*, trad. it. Bologna 2009 (Collegeville, MN, 2007).

PETER BROWN

Concluding remarks

This conference took place in an environment which is close, both on the map and in the feel of its quiet mountain beauty, to the Cassiciacum of Augustine. Better still, it took place in the Monastery of Bose where it is still possible to breathe, on the intellectual level, the sharp autumn air of Cassiciacum as Augustine wished it to be. Like the monastery of Bose, in its rare combination of scholarly endeavor and gentle solitude, we also have breathed a little of the air of that Cassiciacum. We have shared in a common search for truth for which Cassiciacum itself remained (for Augustine) an apposite symbol – *in monte incaseato, monte tuo, monte uberi* – a «mountain of rich milk [...] a mountain of abundance» (*Confessions* IX.iii.5: *Psalm* 67:16).

We have had our abundance. In the first place, we have found ourselves thinking thoughts which were unthinkable in 1958. Fifty years is a long time in the historiography of a field such as that of Late Antiquity. I think that it has become plain to us that the *Warburg Lectures* have a double aspect. In retrospect, they are rightly held to mark a starting point in the study of the last centuries of the ancient world. But we are also reminded that the lectures represent, very faithfully, the point of rest to which previous traditions had come at the time when they were delivered in 1958. The contributions of many of the leading participants stand, now, like great boulders from which the momentum imparted by the scholarship of previous decades (of the 1930s and 1940s) had already ebbed. They stand there at the end their career. Even at the time, they represented the summing up, with warm and magisterial certainty, of what was known and what was thought to be thinkable in the late 1950s.

And yet the paradox of this remarkable series is that historians of the genius of Momigliano, Jones and others were able, from these viewing points, to point to prospects in the study of late antiquity that have taken us far beyond the horizons which their lectures could have envisioned.

Thus, when Arnaldo Momigliano challenged us in his *Introduction* to take up the study of the social history of the Christian church in the fourth and fifth centuries, I am struck by the fact that not a single «basic fact» concerning the social and economic condition of the Latin West to which he appealed, with characteristic succinctness (as if these facts were certain and known to all) has survived intact. No modern social and economic history of the late Roman world could be content with the brisk summary of Rostovtzeff and Pirenne on which Momigliano based his presentation of the problem of the role of the Christian church in late Roman society. But it was Momigliano who saw the problem. The challenge that he delivered has remained with us ever since[1].

For this reason, the conference has proved an invaluable occasion to measure exactly the distance covered by scholarship between 1958 and the present day. This has little to do with the mere increase of knowledge. We are dealing with more vertiginous distances. What were presented, in 1958, as assured ways of thinking about the past have, in many cases, ceased to be convincing. They have been replaced by perspectives and by approaches for which the speakers in 1958 had no room in their own thoughts. A realization of this sense of distance between ourselves and the lecturers of 1958 should be cherished. It is an indication that we also do not know what will be thinkable in 2058. The one thing of which we can be certain is that we will still be hard at work. When, for instance, Hervé Inglebert demonstrates the inapplicability of the clear division of historical genres which Momigliano took for granted in his presentation of the relations between pagan and Christian historians in the fourth century, we know that we still have a lot to do: «La question de la christianisation de l'historiographie est donc à repenser totalement. Il y faudra bien un autre demi-siècle».

One comes to conferences to hear a challenge such as that.

Not only have many of the perspectives and basic modes of categorization used by the lecturers of 1958 become strange to us. An entire crowd of new characters have silently stepped on the stage of late antiquity. Pagans and Christians in the fourth century – and most of the best-known of them in Rome – seemed a sufficiently vivid cast at that time. But they are dwarfed by the number of possible interlocutors who have been discovered by scholars of Late Antiquity in the last fifty years. Allow me to use the privilege of extempore speech simply to single out one obvious

---

[1] P. Brown, «*Through the Eye of a Needle»: Wealth and the Formation of Latin Christianity, ca.350-ca.550* (to appear): see P. Brown, «*Per la cruna dell'ago»: la formazione della cristianità occidentale*, «Rivista di storia e letteratura religiosa» (to appear).

absence in the cast of 1958. There are no late antique Jews in the Warburg Lectures.

To emphasize this lacuna is not merely to redress a disciplinary and a confessional lacuna. It takes us to the center of how we define «conflict» in a late Roman society. Recent work on the relations between pagans and Christians which has come to include the Jews has changed our views on that theme. It has shown that it is now possible to use our knowledge of the attitudes and vicissitudes of the Jewish communities in many late antique regions to gain a more differentiated picture of the relation between religious groups and of the balance of coexistence and intolerance in a late antique society than we would from accounts that are limited to the relations between pagans and Christians alone. I am thinking of Hagith Sivan's *Palestine in Late Antiquity*[2] and of the work of Angelos Chaniotis on the Jewish community of Aprodisias in Caria, to which I referred in my own presentation[3]. A study of the end of paganism in Rome viewed from the angle of the Jewish community of Venosa (perched in prime wool country in the rolling Murge of Puglia), whose notables quietly outlived the Sack of Rome of 410 and the end of the Western Empire in 476, would look very different – should we ever come near to discovering it – from the hectic narratives that have come down to us from Christian sources.

For what the lectures of 1958 and the papers that we have presented in 2008 have in common is that they all pose the problem of change. One thing can be said with certainty. Paganism did end. A change happened. But the nature and rhythm of the changes which led to that end remain tantalizingly opaque to us. Here I particularly welcomed the analogy invoked by Wolfgang Liebeschuetz to describe the end of sacrifice at Antioch in the course of the fourth century – the end of smoking in public spaces in Europe and America. I remember how, in May of 2008, a conference took place on Christianization at the Université de Nanterre (which many of those present here attended)[4]. It took place in a lecture hall which bore the proud notice: «Nanterre, université sans tabac». It was like reading again Eusebius of Caesarea's triumphalist account of Constantine's foundation of Constantinople as a «city without sacrifice». It made one wonder at the

---

[2] H. Sivan, *Palestine in Late Antiquity*, Oxford 2008.
[3] A. Chaniotis, *The Conversion of the Temple of Aphrodite at Aphrodisias in Context*, in *From Temple to Church. Destruction and Renewal of Local Cultic Topography in Late Antiquity*, ed. J. Hahn, S. Emmel, U. Gotter, Leiden 2008, 243-273.
[4] *Quid est christianum esse? Le problème de la «christianisation du monde antique»*, ed. H. Inglebert, S. Destephen, B. Dumezil, Université de Paris-Ouest, Nanterre, 26-29 mai 2008.

complexity of the process which accounted for the appearance of this one, neat placard in a modern class room. An entire history of modern culture, of modern science and of modern state-building lay behind its appearance. Can we ever hope to re-capture its equivalent – the processes that led to the end of sacrifice in a distant, late Roman world and the meaning to contemporaries of this sudden lacuna?

What makes it particularly difficult for us, of course, is that there is one thing which we do not know (or very seldom know) about persons in the distant past. We do not know what they thought about the future. Let me put it simply. If I were to be given the use of a time-machine so as to return to the reign of Constantine, and were, indeed, granted an interview by that most interesting monarch, I would not waste valuable viewer-time asking him if he was a Christian. He would have told me that at great length; and there might have been little that he would have told me that I could not already have learned from the books of my friend Timothy Barnes. By half way through, I would have been extremely bored. Rather, I would have asked him – and, indeed, any Christian who was willing to be interviewed – what he or she thought that the future of the Chritian religion might be. In an age of change, and for a man who undoubtedly set himself up as an agent of change (as did Constantine) the issue was how far reaching these changes were imagined to be and what would be their effect in future ages. How did Constantine (or indeed any other of his contemporaries) measure the horizons of the possible for the future?

To ask this question of Constantine is, in fact, to ask it of the entire Christianity of his age. For we know a lot about the Christianity of Constantine, from his own statements. But we know surprisingly little about the Christianity of his age. Bluntly: could any of the protagonists have envisaged a world without pagans? If so, when did they come to do so? The answer may have been that nobody did – or, at least, nobody did until, perhaps, at the earliest, the age of Augustine[5]. Pagans, Jews and Christians (for all they knew) might have found themselves living side by side in the *saeculum* until the Second Coming of Christ. This was an event to which many Christians of the fourth century paid greater attention than we often allow. Such a view of the future would have saved the Christian Church, in effect, from the dangerous responsibility of a triumph in this world. One wonders whether this abrupt and discontinuous view of the future acted as

---

[5] P. BROWN, *Conversion and Christianization: the case of Augustine*, in *The Past Before Us. The Challenge of Historiographies in Late Antiquity*, ed. C. STRAW, R. LIM, Turnhout 2004, 103-117, at 110-114.

an implicit brake on the expectations aroused by Constantine's measures. They were not perceived as aimed at a real future. They were, rather, perceived as the first steps, on earth, of a triumph whose concrete effects did not need to be followed out on earth. They gestured towards the Coming of Christ. But it was this coming which would rid the world of the enemies of the Church – not the work of bishops and emperors to which we give such close attention in the fourth century.

Let me use the licence of an extempore commentator to suggest that we pay more attention to the sense of time of fourth century persons, pagans and Christians alike, before we impose on them a narrative of events driven by our own, modern sense of historical process. Many persons, Christian, pagan and Jewish alike, lacked our sense of hurry. As late as the fifth century, in many regions, their reaction to the conversion of Constantine in 312 might have been not unlike the magnificently offhand reply of Chairman Mao, who, when asked by a devotee whether he thought that the French Revolution was important, answered abruptly: «It is too early to tell».

There were many papers delivered at this conference where we are taken into a different time-rhythm. The classical literary tradition and the structures of education move at different pace from that imposed upon the fourth century by the notion of a conflict between pagans and Christians. The more they are studied – as by Professors Agosti and Chuvin – the more we realize that profound changes did, indeed, take place in late antique literature. But they took place among persons for whom it is almost always «Too early to tell» whether the conversion of Constantine, and, indeed, the rise of Christianity itself, was the most important agent of change. I particularly appreciated the more flexible view of the options open to Christian and pagan members of the teaching profession implied by the paper of Professor Cecconi. Faced by hitherto unknown phenomena such as the Christian poetry of the *Bodmer Papyrus* and in the light of more intensive work on late antique authors – such as Nonnos of Panopolis[6] – we seem to be dealing with a creativity that is driven less by any notion of religious conflict as by the spirit of artistic competition – constant, exuberant competition with the past and with contemporaries of any or all religions. The attitude is closer to that of the intense atmosphere of competition among the rival painters' workshops in the Rome of Caravaggio than to any imagined conflict of Christianity and paganism. We need only think of the newly discovered poems placed on the wall of a school room at Trimithis in the distant Dakhleh Oasis, in south western

---

[6] D. HERNÁNDEZ DE LA FUENTE, *Bakkhos Anax: un estudio sobre Nono de Panópolis*, Madrid 2008.

Egypt, to catch something of the pulse of competitive *ingegno* working its way up from the most distant provinces to the centers of late antique literary production[7].

This does not mean that, in certain areas, religious conflict did not happen and that venerable religious institutions did not disappear. But we have gained a healthy uncertainty as to the exact manner in which this happened. There was a time when it was sufficient to recite the Theodosian Code alongside the careers of Christian bishops of known weight and ferocity (such as Ambrose) to explain the end of public paganism in the West. Little of this certainty has survived modern scrutiny. This can be seen from the trenchant contributions of Professor Lizzi, and of the others which touch on the fate and functions of the traditional Roman priesthoods.

Yet we still have to face the fact that many areas of the later empire were characterized by intense religious conflict. This conflict might be delimited in its impact, in many regions and in many niches of society, by the massive and diffuse weight of the values of the *saeculum*. For many members of the elites, the very fact of seeing the world in terms of confessional divisions involved a novel and unwelcome adjustment of perspective. Claude Lepelley's North Africa is a classic example of one such region. Yet, for all the robustness of the earthly city in that province (to which Lepelley returns again with characteritic erudition and affection) North Africa also experienced outbursts of religious hatred and coercion, in connection with the divisions of its local Christians, that were without parallel in the Latin West. The book of my friend and colleague at Princeton, Brent Shaw – soon to appear under the title of *Sacred Violence: Sectarian Hatred and African Christians in the Age of Augustine* (Cambridge University Press) – uses the abundant sources related to the origin and suppression of the Donatist schism to write one of the most searching studies that I have ever read of the role of emotion in the politics of an ancient society.

It is with Brent Shaw's study in mind that I would like to end by drawing attention to two issues in the study of late antiquity which were allowed to linger only in the background of the Warburg Lectures of 1958. They have not been allowed to emerge as clearly, perhaps, as they should in subsequent discussions of the relations between pagans and Christians. I refer to the notorious intellectual ferocity of late antiquity and to the remarkable quickening of the pace of textuality which we now see to be a significant feature of the period. These were prominent features of the society and culture of

---

[7] R. CRIBIORE ET AL., *A teacher's dipinto from Trimithis (Dakhleh Oasis)*, «Journal of Roman Archaeology» 21 (2008), 171-192.

the fourth century. Yet, in 1958, they were not so much ignored as taken for granted. The authors of the lectures had recently emerged from an age of ideologies. They were the products of societies where traditional Christianity was omnipresent. They assumed that they knew religious dogmatism and religious intolerance when they saw it. Persons of liberal temperament, they regretted it. They were concerned to explain why there seemed to be more of it in the fourth century than in earlier periods. But that religious dogmatism was there caused them no surprise. Nor did the textual infrastructure of late Roman culture interest them in its own right. Last pagans did what they should do – they copied the classics. That was all that needed to be said.

Yet, over the years, both these two background features have ceased to be taken for granted. They have become puzzling to us. I would like to make an appeal for the return of a more «propositional» approach to late antiquity. We have to enter more deeply than we have done into the metaphysical and theological concerns which drove many late antique persons. We have been reluctant to do this. We have not wished to fall back into the mere reproduction of confessional opinions. For this is often all that is offered to late antique historians by those who accuse them of not taking «seriously» the theological and intellectual preoccupations of the age. Doxography of this kind (frequently offered in a tone of ill-disguised superiority) is no substitute for history.

But we do have to take seriously why the late antique period is a period marked by such remarkable and by such abrasive intellectual fervor. On this issue, I have always treasured the remarks of Aline Rousselle in her synthesis (with Jean-Michel Carrié) of the crisis of the third century, *L'empire romain en mutation. Des Sévères à Constantin 192-337*. In a few golden pages, she seizes the essence of the religious mood of the third century. It was not an «Age of Anxiety» as E.R. Dodds would have it. It was an Age of Understanding. Its religious ferment was characterized by the sudden release of the intellect upon religious issues: «Recrudescence de réflexion [...] d'explication constructive... Un puissant besoin de justificiation... une explicitation du croire»[8].

It is this search for intellectual comprehensibility and consequentiality, whether in pre-existing traditions or in new faiths, which makes late antiquity such an exciting period. The speculation on the exact role of the hero between gods and men, posed in the *Heroikos* of Philostratus (as shown by Francisco Marshall) is an early example of this new mood. The theories

---

[8] A. ROUSSELLE, J.M. CARRIÉ, *L'empire romain en mutation. Des Sévères à Constantin 192-337*, Paris 1999, 436-437.

of theurgy in the schools of Jamblichus and Proclus, and their intimate connection with basic metaphysical issues of the relation between spirit and matter (as demonstrated by Sergio Knipes), shows this passion for coherence at work in the later centuries of the ancient world.

The more we study late antiquity, the more we stumble on intense, unfinished intellectual conversations. The barely exploited genre of *Questions and Answers* to which Yannis Papadoyannakis and his colleagues have recently drawn our attention shows an eastern Christianity constantly adjusting its imaginative world under the pressure of innumerable questions, raised so as to resolve the doubts of believers[9]. The genre continues deep into the Byzantine Middle Ages. Here we see the manner in which the drive towards an «explicitation du croire», to which Aline Rousselle drew attention in the third century continued to work, like the bacillus of a yoghourt, throughout the Greek Christianity of the late antique and Byzantine periods. It is a reminder that societies can maintain a high level of religious intellectualism – one thinks of the fierce debates conducted in the great Buddhist monasteries of northern India and Central Asia at just this time[10] – without necessarily enjoying the reputation for tolerance which modern persons like to associate with intellectual endeavor.

Indeed, as the work of Michel Perrin has come to make increasingly plain, not all conversations were supposed to have happy issues[11]. Perrin rightly insists on the dogmatic and contestational quality of Christian catechetical teaching in this period. For good or ill, *homo dogmaticus* was not a creature safely limited to the higher levels of the Christian hierarchy. *Homo dogmaticus* was regarded as the desired end product of the socialization of every Christian. Schooled by doctrinal catechesis, every Christian was expected to emerge from the bapstismal font bearing a full battery of answers to discharge against the rivals of his or her church.

---

[9] Y. PAPADOYANNAKIS, *Instruction by Question and Answer in Late Antiquity: the Case of Late Antique Erotapokriseis*, in *Greek Literature in Late Antiquity: Dynamism, Didacticism, Classicism*, ed. S. JOHNSON, Aldershot 2006, 91-105.

[10] On the fierce debates conducted in northern India by the Chinese pilgrim, Xuan Zhang, in around 620 (where he was rewarded for his victory by being paraded on the elephant of the local raja, to the shame of his Indian contestants who moved to another monastery!): *The Life of Hieuen-Tsiang by Shaman Hwui-li*, ch. V, transl. S. BEAL, London 1911, 180.

[11] M. PERRIN, *A propos de la participation des fidèles aux controverses doctrinaux de l'antiquité tardive*, «Antiquité Tardive» 9 (2001), 179-199 and ID., Arcana mysteria *ou ce que cache la religion. De certains pratiques de l'arcane dans le christianisme antique*, in *Religionen – Die religiöse Erfahrung*, ed. M. RIEDL, T. SCHABERT, Würzburg 2008, 119-141.

For this reason, I sympathize with the disquiet expressed by Wolfgang Liebeschuetz. To speak of the relation of religious groups in late antiquity in terms of «identity formation» alone may be too inert a description of the aims of preachers such as John Chrysostom, as he strove to instill Christian norms of thought and behavior in his hearers. He did not only teach Christians how to remain different from pagans and Jews. He taught them to feel different *sub specie aeternitatis* – to feel eternally right in a world where it was possible to be eternally wrong. One may not approve of such a formation. But part of the secret of religious intolerance in this period is precisely that it could be shared by all. These hard, conflictual propositions (generated by a fierce wish for total answers) circulated more widely up and down the social scale and evoked more enthusiasm than would have been the case in an intellectuallly less inquisitive society, where the speculations of the few took place at a distance from the uneducated crowd. Such stratification of intellectual commitment was the formula for a tolerant society. But it was not what late antiquity was like.

And all parties were prepared to say *scripta manent.* We are dealing with a world awash with textuality. Perhaps we have only come to realize the strangeness of this phenomenon because our own cultural infrastructure has suddenly crumbled as a result of the cybernetic revolution of our days. In a world where books themselves can no longer be taken for granted, the strangeness of the books of late antiquity has suddenly caught our attention. Here we have a textual equivalent (which also emerged in the third century) to the remarkable drive towards cognitive order to which Aline Rousselle drew attention. Allow me to refer to the book of a friend and colleague and of our joint student, Anthony Grafton and Megan Williams, *Christianity and the Transformation of the Book*[12].

As Augustine said, when referring to the fulfillment of Biblical prophecies in his own time: *cottidie codices dominici venales sunt* – «The books of the Lord are out there every day on the open market»[13]. Indeed, the effort of reading and producing so many new books gave a novel tempo to later antiquity as a whole. Each book would be read with a sense of imagined opponents reading over one's shoulder. One only need look at the new edition of the *Monogenes* of Macarius Magnes to realize that one is not faced with a straight forward interchange between a pagan and a

---

[12] A. GRAFTON, M. WILLIAMS, *Christianity and the Transformation of the Book*, Cambridge, MA, 2006.
[13] AUGUSTINE, *Sermon Dolbeau* 5.14 [7]. 339, ed. F. DOLBEAU, *Vingt-Six Sermons au Peuple d'Afrique*, Paris 1996, 447.

Christian. It is a course in the reading of the Gospels framed in the form of answers to an imagined pagan critic[14].

We have entered the age of the book. For the Manichees, the final triumph of the preaching of Mani was imagined to take the form of a Gathering of the Books:

> «Thousands of books will be saved. They will come into the hands of the righteous .. Not one will be lost... They will kiss them and say: "Oh wisdom. I rejoice that the books have come into the hands of the believers".
> You will find little girls being taught to write and singing psalms and reading»[15].

We have recently come to re-live a little of the Manichaean excitement for the book. When we look at a late antique manuscript, we are more aware than we once were that we are not looking only at a routine feature of an unchanging cultural world. We can catch in it some of the same strangeness with which we now view an e-book. We are looking at the humble roots of a cultural revolution whose intensity, in the late antique period, we had only begun to gauge in 1958.

Altogether, we still have a lot to learn. With this, Rita, I think that we can safely retire to lunch, to gather energy, in this our Cassiciacum, for the next fifty years.

---

[14] MACARIUS MAGNES, *Le Monogénès*, ed. R. GOULET, Paris 2006.
[15] *Manichaean Homilies*, transl. N.A. PEDERSEN, *Manichaean Homilies: With a Number of Unpublished Fragments*, Turnhout 2006, 25 and 31, cited in E. IRICINSCHI, «*A Thousand Books will be Saved*»: *Manichaean Writings and Religious Propaganda in the Roman Empire*, in *Jewish and Christian Scripture as Artifact and Canon*, ed. C. EVANS, D. ZACHARIAS, Edinburgh 2009, 261-272, at 270.

Indici dei nomi

Indice dei nomi antichi

Abele: 200n., 201n.
Abraham / Abramo: 150, 173, 200n., 201n., 202, 365, 580n.
Acacius (comes): 533, 535
Acolio (vescovo di Tessalonica): 353 e n., 473n., 474n.
Aemilius Asper: 517, 524
Agapios: 554, 555, 556, 558
Agazia / Agatias: 575, 577 e n., 578, 582, 584, 596
Agostino / St Augustin / Augustine / Aurelius Augustinus: 10n., 34 e n., 35, 41, 47, 48n., 82, 85, 88, 93n., 95, 96n., 100n., 104 e n., 105, 164 e n., 165, 167, 169, 174 e n., 190 e n., 191 e n., 192 e n., 223n., 230, 231n., 236n., 239, 251n., 256, 257 e n., 259n., 263, 265 e n., 267, 268, 284n., 288, 289, 320n., 322n., 346, 358 e n., 359 e n., 360 e n., 364n., 368n., 369n., 370, 395n., 421, 470, 487 e n., 488n., 489 e n., 490 e n., 491, 500, 501n., 517, 520, 522, 523, 524, 525, 541, 544, 545n., 579, 580, 582n. 586 e n., 591, 592 e n., 594, 595n., 599, 602 e n., 604, 607 e n.
Agrestio Cromazio (PVR della Passio s. Sebastiani): 245, 260
Alarico: 358n., 360, 473, 485n.

Alessandro Magno / Alexander the Great / Alexandre (Roman d'): 49n., 98, 58, 101 e n., 174, 181, 191 n., 251n., 331n., 347, 367, 543n.
Alessandro Severo / Severus Alexander / Alexandre Sévère: 102 e n., 173, 174, 175, 334, 364n., 365n., 369, 370n., 384
Ambrose / s. Ambrogio / Aurelius Ambrosius: 18 e n., 74, 106, 157 n., 190 e n., 226n., 242n., 283, 284, 316, 322, 348 e n., 349 e n., 350, 351, 352 e n., 353 e n., 354n., 355 e n., 356 e n., 357n., 361, 365n., 369n., 409n., 410n., 412, 413, 416, 417, 418n., 470 e n., 472n., 474 e n., 475n., 476 e n. 479 e n., 481n., 482n., 498n., 604
Ammianus / Ammien / Ammiano Marcellino: 19n., 20n., 94, 95n., 100 e n., 101, 102n., 104, 105, 106, 107, 111n., 116, 128, 131, 135n., 142n., 143n., 147n., 149n., 150 e n., 157n., 226n., 276n., 314n., 315n., 317n., 347n., 348n., 357n., 362, 368n., 378 e n., 382, 383 e n., 384 e n., 386, 388, 403n., 404n., 406 e n., 408n., 413n., 414, 419n., 499
Amphilochio Iconiense: 229 e n.
Anastase / Anastasio: 375n., 413, 420, 422n., 529n., 537 e n.

Nell'indice non sono considerati i nomi che ricorrono una sola volta e quelli indicizzati nella tabella del saggio di Silvia Orlandi.

Anastasia (clarissima femina): 506, 507, 508
Andragazio: 409, 413
Anicia Faltonia Proba: 500 e n., 501, 510, 511n.
Anicius Auchenius Bassus (PVR 382): 383, 475
Anicius Probus (cos 406): 511, 512
Anonimo / Author / Autore Histoire Auguste / Scriptor Historiae Augustae / Storia Augusta): 20 e n., 93n., 94, 95n., 102 e n., 107, 173, 174, 340n., 363 e n., 364 e n., 365 e n., 366 e n., 367 e n., 369 e n., 370, 381n., 382n., 385 e n., 387n., 388n., 394n., 403n., 404n., 406 e n., 407n., 408n., 414 e n., 421
Antioco (re di Siria): 57, 62
Antoine / Antonio (monaco): 94, 96n., 206
Aphraate: 96n., 161
Apollinarii: 197, 199, 235
Apollonius of Tyana / Apollonio di Tiana: 174, 175, 180 e n., 181, 365
Aradius Valerius Proculus (PVR 337-338): 275, 429, 434
Arbogaste: 354n., 356, 484
Arcadius / Arcadio: 189, 227n., 286, 287, 348n., 360 e n., 530
Areta (vescovo di Cesarea): 125 e n., 126
Aristotle / Aristote: 85 e n., 101n., 113, 114, 330n.
Arius / Ario: 74n., 80, 89, 349, 351
Arnobius / Arnobio: 236n., 358, 359n.
Asella: 499 e n.
Athanasius / Athanase d'Alexandrie / Atanasio: 81, 87n., 94, 95n., 96n., 206, 228, 349n., 351n., 353, 390 e n.
Attius Insteius Tertullus: 432, 462n.
Augusto / Auguste / Augustus: 80n., 101, 102n., 105, 106, 181 e n., 331n., 339, 364n., 365n., 370n., 387 e n., 405, 465n., 466, 518

Aurelianus / Aurélien / Aureliano (imperatore romano: 364n., 370n., 381n., 385
Ausone / Ausonio / Decimius Magnus Ausonius: 98, 226n., 347n., 416n., 417 e n., 422

Basil / Basilio / Basilius: 24 e n., 111n., 123, 124 e n., 125, 126 e n., 127, 128, 141 e n., 201, 225n., 227, 353, 474n.
Boniface / Bonifacio (papa): 570n., 580
Bouttios (Boutios) of Antioch: 329n., 331

Caino: 196, 200 n., 201n.
Caligula: 181, 387
Callisto (papa e martire): 297, 421, 462n.
Caracalla: 175, 364n.
Cassiodoro / Cassiodorus: 239, 408n., 570n., 575 e n., 576 e n., 578, 581, 589
Ceionio (Caeionius) Rufius Albinus (PVR 389-391): 362n.,432, 481n., 482
Celsus / Celse / Celso: 39n., 87 e n., 88, 102, 173 e n., 232n., 237, 252
Césaire d'Arles / Caesarius / Cesario: 241 e n., 546 e n., 570 e n.
Christ / Christus / Cristo / Jesus / Gesù: 24n., 49n., 71, 72 e n., 73, 74 e n., 75, 76n., 82 e n., 83 e n., 84 e n., 86, 89, 105, 106, 145, 151, 157, 159, 160, 161 e n., 162, 172n., 173 e n., 174 e n., 176 n., 177n., 183 e n., 184, 189 e n., 190 e n., 199, 200n., 201 n., 204 e n., 205 e n., 206n., 207n., 209, 211 e n., 221, 223, 231, 232, 237, 245, 257, 259, 261 e n., 264, 292, 297, 309, 311, 317, 322, 325, 342, 343, 346, 351, 352, 359, 365 e n., 421, 470, 472, 482n., 494, 499n., 511, 551n., 555, 556, 557, 558n., 583, 585, 586, 589, 592, 596, 602, 603

Chronographe de 354: 94, 96n., 97, 107
Chrysanthius (neoplatonist): 110, 111n.
Cicéron / Cicerone / Cicero: 103, 239, 518
Cirillo / Cyril / Cyrill / Cyrille (vescovo di Alessandria): 120, 159, 160, 209 e n., 210n., 364n., 483, 550
Claudien / Claudio Claudiano / Claudian: 218n., 354n., 355n., 357n., 375 e n., 491n., 512 e n.
Claudio / Claudius (imperatore romano, 41-54): 58n., 159
Claudius / Claudio il Gotico (imperatore romano, 268-270): 364n., 370n., 407n.
Claudius Mamertinus / Claudio Mamertino: 109n., 117n., 128 e n., 375 e n., 379n., 387, 477n.
Clement of Alexandria / Clemente Alessandrino: 77, 297
Commodus / Commodo: 87, 179, 181, 364n.
Constance II / Costanzo / Constantius / Konstantius II: 73, 100, 111n., 113 e n., 114, 121, 122, 123, 143n., 145n., 189, 275, 276 e n., 279, 283, 311, 312, 342, 345 e n., 346 e n., 347 e n., 348, 349n., 351n., 355, 356, 361, 362, 367n., 378n, 383, 384, 391n., 477n., 478
Constantia (figlia postuma di Costanzo II): 384 e n.
Costante / Constans: 344n., 464n., 496, 506n.
Costantino / Constantine / Constantin / Constantinus / Konstantin: 12, 42 e n., 44, 48, 50n., 70 e n., 73 e n., 74 e n., 79n., 80 e n., 88, 89, 93, 94, 95n., 97n., 100, 104n., 105, 106, 107, 117n., 131n., 132, 134, 135n., 136n., 137, 141, 142 e n., 143 e n., 145 e n., 146 e n., 147, 151, 152, 154, 158, 159, 161, 162, 166n., 172, 225, 246, 247, 250, 251, 253, 258, 273, 274 e n., 275, 277, 279, 287, 297, 309n., 312n., 321, 326, 336, 339 e n., 340 e n., 341 e n., 342 e n., 343 e n., 344 e n., 345, 346 e n., 347 e n., 348, 349 e n., 350 e n., 351 e n., 352 e n., 355, 356, 357, 359 e n., 360 e n., 361 e n., 362n., 364, 365 e n., 366n., 367, 369 e n., 370, 376n., 377, 379 e n., 380 e n., 388 e n., 389, 394, 395, 404n., 405n., 407n., 411n., 413n., 419n., 422, 426, 429, 433n., 434, 462n. 463n. 468 e n., 470, 471, 472 e n., 473, 476n., 477 e n., 478n., 496, 498, 506n., 507 e n., 533n., 534 e n., 535, 541n., 583, 601, 602, 603, 605 e n.
Costanzo Cloro: 340, 344n., 434n.
Costanzo III / Constantius: 360, 361n., 477n., 478
Crispo: 350, 351
Curetius: 274, 275
Curtius (PPO Italiae et Africae 407-408): 486 e n., 488n.
Cyprian / s. Cipriano: 82, 211, 353, 479n.

Damase / Damasus / Damaso: 20n., 106, 348, 349, 350, 416, 474n., 496, 497n., 506, 510
Daniele (il profeta): 63n., 105, 157 e n., 203, 208n., 329
Demetrias: 500n., 501 e n., 502, 503, 504 e n., 505 e n., 510, 513, 514, 515, 516
Destro / Dexter (Nummius Aemilianus): 236 e n.
Didymus / Didymos il Cieco: 174 e n.
Diocletian / Diocleziano / Dioclétien / Diocletianus / Diokletian: 142, 147, 180, 182 e n., 183n., 245, 258, 273, 364 e n., 366 e n., 379 e n., 380 n., 385, 387n., 389n., 462n., 463n.
Dion Cassius / Cassio Dione / Cassius Dio: 102n., 352n., 363n., 364n., 366n., 387n.

Dioscoro di Afrodito / Dioscore / Dioscorus: 198, 213 e n., 560 e n.
Domitius Zenofilus (senatore): 274, 275

Elagabal / Elagabalo / Heliogabalus / Heliogabal / Eliogabalo: 102n., 365n., 369 e n., 381n.
Elena / Helen / Helena: 347n., 351, 377, 472n., 498
Ennius: 101, 102n.
Enmannsche (Enmann) Kaisergeschichte / EKG: 95n., 102n., 363n., 366n., 404n., 406, 407n.
Ennodio: 239, 240 e n., 420
Ephrem Syrus / Ephraem of Nisibis: 100, 109 e n., 117n., 135, 137, 138 e n., 139, 157 e n., 158, 159 e n., 161n.
Euagrius (vescovo di Antiochia): 318, 319
Euangelus: 519-521
Eudocia / Eudossia: 198, 203, 207n., 208 e n., 210, 211, 212 e n., 534, 535
Eugenio / Eugenius: 353, 354n., 356 e n., 412n., 475n., 484, 512
Eugippius / Eugippio: 50, 266 e n.
Eunape / Eunapius / Eunapio : 93n., 102, 103n., 104-106, 111n., 112n., 148n., 354n., 368n., 370 e n., 403n., 404n., 406, 407n., 409n., 413, 414, 415 e n., 416 e n., 417, 418 e n., 419n., 420, 483n.
Eusebio (vescovo di Cesarea di Cappadocia nel 362): 123, 124 e n., 125, 126, 127
Eusebio (vescovo di Nantes): 406, 407n.
Eusebio (vescovo di Nicomedia): 350 e n., 471n.
Eusebius (vescovo di Vercelli): 74, 353
Eusebius / Eusèbe (bishop of Rome in Julian Romance): 132, 133, 134, 136n., 140, 141n., 142n., 147, 148

Eusebius / Eusebio / Eusèbe (vescovo di Cesarea di Palestina): 42 e n., 44, 45 e n., 48, 73 e n., 74n., 76, 78 e n., 88, 90, 94, 95n., 96n., 97n., 98, 100 e n., 103, 105, 106, 131, 143n., 180 e n., 209n., 231n., 232, 297, 328, 339, 340 e n., 342, 343 e n., 344, 347n., 366n., 412n., 468n., 601
Eustazio / Eusthatius (vescovo di Sebastia): 126 e n., 127n.
Eutichio patriarca di Costantinopoli: 579, 594
Eutrope / Eutropio / Eutropius: 94, 95n., 100, 101, 106, 350n., 359n., 362, 367n., 368n., 388 e n., 404n., 406, 408, 410 e n., 411n., 414 e n.
Evagrius (Praefectus Augustalis): 481n., 483 e n.
Evagrius Scolastichus / Evagrio: 334 e n., 407n., 563 e n., 564n.
Eventius (vir clarissimus): 513 e n.

Fabiola: 493 e n., 494
Fausta (moglie di Costantino): 350, 351
Festus / Festo: 94, 95n., 100, 106, 404n., 406, 414
Filocalo (calendario di): 361n., 367
Flavianus (vescovo di Antiochia): 318, 319, 325 e n.
Flavius Anastasius / Flavio Anastasio (vir clarissimus): 531, 533, 534
Flavio Filippo / Flavius Philippus (vir clarissimus): 531, 533, 534
Flavio Giuseppe / Flavius Josèphe: 57 e n., 62 e n., 65, 96n., 238
Flavius Avitus Marinianus (cos. 423): 507 e n.
Flavius Mallius Theodorus (cos. 399): 284n., 487n., 489 e n., 490, 491n.
Flavius Philostratus: 171, 172 e n., 173n., 174 e n., 175 e n., 176n., 177, 178, 179 e n., 180 e n., 183, 388n., 605
Flavius Saturninus: 293, 294, 304

Fozio (patriarca): 211, 414 e n., 415n., 418n., 419n.

Galerius / Galère: 78, 102n., 379 e n.
Galla Placidia: 355n., 360 e n., 361 e n.
Gallus Caesar: 317, 324, 507
Gaudentius (notarius): 276 e n.
Gaudentius / Gaudenzio (vescovo di Brescia): 190n., 485, 486
Gélase de Césarée / Gelasio: 95n., 96n., 238
Gèsios (iatrosophist): 543, 544, 557 e n.
Giovanni / Jean di Gaza: 199n., 219 e n.
Giulio Cesare: 81 e n., 339, 367, 466
Giusta Grata Onoria: 361 e n.
Giustiniano / Justinian / Justinien: 219n., 332, 333 e n., 334, 345n., 361, 389 e n., 390 e n., 411n., 421, 467n., 473n., 476, 488, 529, 535 e n., 536 e n., 541n., 547n., 550, 577 n., 589
Gratianus / Gratienne / Graziano: 281, 282, 283, 284n., 285, 286, 322, 348, 355 e n., 356, 360 e n., 362 e n., 382, 383, 384, 385, 386, 403 n., 404, 405 e n., 408, 409 e n., 410n., 413, 414, 415n., 416 e n., 417, 418 e n., 419, 420, 422, 423, 433, 462, 467n., 474 e n., 475 e n., 476 e n., 477, 480, 489, 522
Gratianus son of Theodosius / Graziano: 355 e n., 360 e n.
Grégoire (patriarche d'Antioche): 563; 564n.
Grégoire de Nazianze / Gregory / Gregorio di Nazianzo / Gregorius: 100, 113n., 123 e n., 124 e n., 125, 126 e n., 135 e n., 157, 158, 194, 195, 196 e n., 197 e n., 198 e n., 199, 200-202 e n., 206 e n., 213, 214, 225 n., 227, 228, 318n., 349, 368 e n., 474n.
Gregory the Great / Gregorio Magno / Grégoire le Grand: 39n., 258, 265n., 289, 421, 514, 532n., 570n., 573, 576, 577, 578, 579 e n., 580 e n., 581 e n., 582 e n., 583 e n., 584, 585 e n., 586 e n., 587, 588 e n., 589 e n., 590, 591, 592, 593 e n., 594, 595 e n., 596 e n., 597 e n.

Hadrian / Hadrianus / Adriano: 175, 344 n., 360, 364n., 370n.
Hegesippus / Egesippo: 78 e n.
Hermas (the Shepherd) / Erma: 76, 200, 201n.; 202n., 238n.
Hérodies / Herodianus / Erodiano: 363n., 364n., 388n.
Hesiod / Esiodo: 178, 205
Hierocles (governor of Egypt): 180 e n., 181
Hilary of Poitier / Hilaire de Poitier / Ilario: 74, 96n., 351 e n.
Himerius / Himerios (athenian sophist): 111 e n., 112 e n.
Homer / Omero / Homère: 148, 175, 176, 180, 201, 202 e n., 207n., 209, 210, 211 e n., 213-215, 216 e., 217, 218, 221, 236, 517, 518, 519, 520, 557
Honorius / Onorio: 107, 218n., 284n., 286, 287, 350n., 355n., 360 e n., 375 e n., 389, 468n., 473, 476, 480, 487, 488, 489n., 512 e n., 532
Hosius / Ossius: 73, 351n.
Hyginus: 517-519

Iamblichus / Giamblico / Jamblique: 110, 163, 164, 165n., 166, 167, 168 e n., 169 e n., 232 e n., 606
Ibas di Edessa: 161 e n.
Hilary / Hilaire / Ilario / Hilarius: 74, 96n., 351 e n.
Illus (ufficiale imperiale): 312n., 327 e n.
Ipazia: 210 e n.
Isidoro (filosofo): 233 e n., 544n.
Iunius Bassus (PVR 359): 464n., 509 e n., 512, 514
Iunius Tiberianus: 385n., 394n.

Jean Lydus / John Lydus / Giovanni Lido: 389 e n., 390 e n., 410, 411n., 416, 578

Jérôme / Jerome / Hieronymus / Gerolamo / Girolamo: 94, 96n., 98, 100n., 105, 188 e n., 189 e n., 190 e n., 191, 236 e n., 237n., 238, 346n., 347n., 350 e n., 364n., 404n., 407n., 408n., 471 e n., 493, 494 e n., 499, 500, 501

John Chrysostomus / Crisostomo: 7, 109 n., 116n., 117n., 192, 230n., 236 e n., 309, 313 e n., 314, 316 e n., 317 e n., 318 e n., 319, 320 e n., 321, 322, 323, 324 e n., 325 e n., 326, 328, 333, 336, 337, 345n., 346 e n., 347, 348, 349n., 350, 354n., 360, 364n., 370, 472n., 541n., 607

John of Ephesus / Jean (bishop and ecclesiastic historian): 332n., 334 e n., 563 e n., 564

John the Baptist / Giovanni Battista: 75, 353n.

Jovian / Gioviano: 133, 134, 135, 136n., 138, 139 e n., 141 e n., 143 e n., 144 e n., 145 e n., 146 e n., 147, 148, 149, 151, 152 e n., 153 e n., 154, 155n., 157, 158, 159, 160, 161, 162, 347 e n.

Julian / Julien / Iulianus / Giuliano l'Apostata: 6, 12, 37n., 70n., 100, 101, 102, 104, 106, 109 e n., 110 e n., 111 e n., 112 e n., 113 e n., 114 e n., 115 e n., 116 e n., 117 e n., 118, 119 e n., 120 e n., 121 e n., 122, 123 e n., 124, 125, 127 e n., 128, 131 e n., 132 e n., 133 e n., 134 e n., 135 e n., 136 e n., 137 e n., 138n., 139 e n., 140 e n., 141 e n., 142 e n., 143 e n., 144 e n., 145 e n., 146 e n., 147 e n., 148 e n., 149 e n., 150 e n., 151 e n., 152 e n., 153 e n., 154 e n., 155 e n., 156 e n., 157 e n., 158, 159 e n., 160n., 161n., 162 e n., 163, 170 e n. 175, 176 e n., 177, 182, 183 e n., 199, 232, 233 e n., 236n., 237, 276 e n., 277, 278, 279, 283, 309 e n., 310 e n., 311 e n., 313 e n., 314n., 315 e n., 316, 317, 318, 324, 331, 336, 337, 345n., 346 e n., 347n., 348 e n., 349 e n., 354n., 357n., 364, 367e n., 368 e n., 369 e n., 386, 387, 388n., 405n., 410n., 419n., 421, 422, 426n., 474n., 477, 478 e n., 480, 489n.

Justin: 77, 85n., 173

Lactance / Lattanzio / Lactantius: 82, 93n., 94, 96 e n., 97, 103, 105, 183 e n., 236n., 238n., 264n., 329n., 331, 364n., 379n., 479n.

Leone Magno / Leo: 421, 503, 504 e n., 505, 507 e n., 509, 514, 589

Leontius: 327 e n.

Libanius / Libanios / Libanio: 51n., 100, 101 e n., 104, 111n., 113, 116 e n., 117 e n., 118 e n., 119, 125, 127, 166n., 197, 198n., 211n., 229 e n., 230n., 309 e n., 310 e n., 311n., 312n., 314, 315 e n, 316, 317, 325n.. 326, 327, 328n., 368, 369n., 376, 377, 390, 393, 410n., 414, 415, 477n.

Liberius / Liberio: 74, 351 e n., 421 e n.

Licinio / Licinius: 80n., 350, 376n., 377n.

Live / Livio: 94, 101, 102n., 105, 106, 262, 287

Lollianus (PVR 342): 392n, 428, 434, 464n.

Longinianus: 395n., 487n.

Lucien / Luciano: 103, 250n.

Lucifer : 74, 351n.

Lucius Aurelius Avianius Symmachus (signo Phosphorius): 432, 450

Maccabei / Maccabees / Maccabées: 57, 62n., 318n., 320 e n.

Macrobius / Macrobe / Macrobio: 19, 20n., 238n., 279, 280, 362 e n., 517, 518, 519 e n., 520, 521, 522, 523, 524

Magno Massimo / Maximus: 356 e n., 405, 409, 412
Malalas: 7, 144n., 309, 314n., 326, 327 e n., 328 e n., 329 e n., 330 e n., 331 e n., 332 e n., 333 e n., 334 e n., 336
Manlius Crepereius Scipio Vincentius: 286, 287
Maometto: 423n., 586, 593, 595, 596
Marcellianus (dux per Valeriam): 384 e n.
Marcellinus comes: 538 e n.
Marcion of Sinope: 86, 87
Marcus Artorus Geminus: 512 e n.
Marcus Aurelius / Marc Aurèle: 86n., 166n., 364, 365, 366 e n., 367, 369, 370n., 387, 423n.
Marco Diacono / Marcus Diaconus: 535 e n.
Marinus de Neapolis: 567 e n.
Marius Maximus / Mario Massimo: 102n, 404n., 406
Martin of Tours: 180, 353n.
Maurizio (imperatore) / Maurice: 564n., 583, 590
Maximian / Maximianus / Maximien / Massimiano: 142, 144n., 147, 182 e n., 258, 364n., 375n., 379 e n., 434
Maximin Daia / Massimino Daia: 102, 232
Maximus of Ephesus: 111 e n., 148n.
Maximus Taurinensis / Massimo: 191 e n., 192, 485 e n., 486 e n.
Menandor Rhetor / Menandre le Rhéteur: 375n., 376, 391n.

Nero / Néron: 139n., 176n., 181
Nicomachus Flavianus / Nicomaco Flaviano / Nicomaque Flavien (Virius Nicomachus Flavianus Sr.): 20, 95n., 356, 362n., 403n., 404n., 407n., 408n., 411, 412n., 413 e n., 466n., 512
Nilo di Ancyra: 198, 233n.
Nonno / Nonnos di Panopoli: 194 e n., 195n., 196 e n., 192, 200, 202, 203 e n., 205 e n., 208 e n., 209 e n., 215, 216 e n., 217, 218 e n., 219, 220, 224 e n., 330 n., 561 e n., 603
Numa: 359n., 411n., 419n.

Oceanus: 493 e n., 494
Olympiodore /Olimpiodoro /Olympiodorus: 103n., 169n., 354n., 403n., 404n., 407n., 413 e n., 414 e n., 415n.
Optat de Milev: 96n., 274, 276 e n., 279
Oribasius (physician): 111 e n.
Origen / Origenes: 39n., 74n., 75n., 84n., 88, 173 e n., 225n., 231n., 232n., 237n.
Orosio / Orose / Orosius: 93n., 95, 96n., 100, 103n., 104, 131, 354n., 407n., 408n., 420 e n., 579, 580
Ovid: 518 e n.

Pammachius: 493, 508, 509
Paolino da Milano: 412n., 476 e n.
Paolino da Nola /Paulinus: 230, 231 e n., 421, 508 e n., 509
Patricio (centonista): 211, 212n.
Paul le Silentiaire / Paolo Silenziario: 6, 199n., 215, 216, 217, 218, 219 e n., 220 e n., 221, 222, 223, 224
Pausanias (periegeta): 171 e n., 172
Peanio (traduttore del Breviarium): 410 e n.
Pegasius / Pegasios (vescovo cristiano): 115 e n., 116
Pelagius / Pelagio: 500 e n., 501n.
Philo /Philon: 85 e n., 387n.
Philestorigio: 111n., 112n., 152n., 157n.
Pierre le Patrice (Leoquelle): 95n., 403n., 404n.
Pietro il Venerabile: 575 e n.
Pilate / Pilato / Pilatus: 102, 232, 356
Piniano: 530n., 532n.

Pisander of Laranda / Pisandro di Laranda: 198n., 330n.
Plato / Platon: 33n., 71, 114n., 133, 166, 169n., 236
Pline Junior: 387n., 547 e n.
Plinio il Vecchio / Pline: 9, 223n., 387n.
Plotinos / Plotin / Plotinus / Plotino: 166 e n., 167, 168 e n., 169n., 388n.
Porfirio (vescovo di Gaza): 534, 535
Porphyre / Porphyry / Porphirius / Porphyrios / Porfirio: 102, 103, 163, 167 e n., 168n., 174 e n., 177, 237, 558, 559 e n.
Praetextatus / Pretestato / Vettius Agorius Praetextatus: 20, 182n., 238n., 362n., 412n., 433, 434, 464n., 465n., 520, 521, 522, 570n.
Praxeas (grammarian): 86 e n., 87 e n.
Priscus (filosofo neoplatonico): 111 e n.
Probino e Olibrio / Anicius Probinus and Anicius Hermogenianus Olybrius (coss. 395): 354n., 511 e n., 512
Proclus / Proclos / Proclo: 166, 167 e n., 168 e n., 169 e n., 208, 209, 233n., 567 e n., 606
Procopius / Procopio di Cesarea: 333 e n., 534, 535 e n., 536n., 537n.
Prohaeresius: 112 e n.
Propertius: 181 e n.
Prudence / Prudenzio / Prudentius: 104, 105, 106, 232 e n., 391n., 463n., 499, 531n.
Ps. -Joshua Styl.: 537n., 538n.
Ps. -Philon: 94, 96n., 97
Publicola: 544, 545 e n.
Publilius Ceionius (Caeionius) Caecina Albinus: 279, 280-282, 481

Quintus Aurelius Symmachus (signo Eusebius) / Quinto Aurelio Simmaco: 19, 20, 24 e n., 362 e n., 365, 378 n., 381, 382 e n., 385n., 412 e n., 413n., 414n., 415, 417 e n., 418n., 433, 436n., 463 n., 465 e n., 475, 476, 491, 499, 520, 521, 522
Quirinus (Pannonian bishop): 497 e n.
Quodvultdeus: 284n., 544 e n., 561n.

Rabbula (vescovo di Edessa): 138, 160, 161 e n.
Raingarda di Montboisier: 575 e n.
Romulus / Romolo (re di Roma): 100n., 106, 340n., 358 e n.
Rufin / Fl. Rufino / Fl. Rufinus (PPO Orientis 393): 376, 377, 391n., 393, 481n., 482, 483, 484 e n., 485n.
Rufin d'Aquilée / Rufinus / Rufino: 95n., 96n., 103n., 236n., 351 e n., 412 e n., 413n., 470 e n., 472, 473, 481, 482, 483
Rufino di Antiochia (architetto): 534, 535
Rufius Viventius Gallus (PVR nella metà del V sec.): 438n., 507 e n.

s. Acacio: 345, 347
s. Babylas / Babila: 157n., 230n., 236n., 316 e n., 317, 318n., 324
s. Benedetto: 265, 266, 587, 588
ss. Cyr et Jean / ss. Ciro e Giovanni: 210, 548n., 549n., 550 e n., 551, 552 e n., 554 e n., 555 e n., 556n., 557n., 558n., 559n.
s. Francis of Assisi / Francesco d'Assisi: 75n., 585
s. Giovanni (Evangelista) / S. Giovanni: 84, 194, 203 e n., 205, 208 e n., 209, 301n., 302, 307, 355n., 360
ss. Giovanni e Paolo: 301, 307
S. Lorenzo / s. Lorenzo / Laurentius / Laurent / Lawrence: 380, 381n., 399, 435n., 470, 499, 588
S. Marcellino e Pietro (catacomba): 174, 297, 305
s. Paul / Paulus / S. Paul / S. Paolo: 71 e n., 76 e n., 106, 157n., 189 e n., 238 e n., 346n., 496 e n., 508n., 530, 531n.,

532n., 534, 536, 538
s. Pietro / Pierre / S. Pietro / Peter: 81, 106, 173, 189 e n., 302, 360, 438n., 453, 495, 496 e n., 506 e n., 507n., 508, 509 e n., 510 e n., 511, 512, 513 e n., 514, 516, 531n., 532n.
s. Saba: 534, 535 e n., 536
s. Sebastiano / Sebastianus (martire) / S. Sebastiano (basilica): 6, 245 e n., 246, 250, 258, 259, 260, 261 e n., 262, 263 e n., 264, 265, 266, 267, 269, 495 e n., 496n., 497n., 498n., 499, 500, 514
s. Severinus / san Severino: 50 e n., 265, 266 e n.
s. Stephen / S. Stefano (protomartire): 161, 495, 500, 501n., 503, 504 e n., 505 e n., 507, 513, 514
Salluste / Sallustio: 94, 240
Saturninus Sallustius (Salutius) Secundus: 112, 176, 368, 530 e n.
Scipio: 362, 395, 396n.
Septimius Severus / Septime Sévère: 175, 363n., 364n. 370n., 379 n.
Servio / Servius: 234n., 358 e n., 367, 368n., 387n., 411n., 421, 517, 518, 519 e n., 521, 522, 523, 524
Sévérien de Gabala: 389 e n., 390 e n.
Severus / Sévère (vita di): 209, 234, 550, 569 e n.
Sextus Anicius Paolinus (cos. 325): 502 e n., 503 e n., 505
Sextus Aurelius Victor / Aurelio Vittore: 94, 95, 105, 106, 131, 362, 366n., 388 e n., 406, 407n., 414n.
Sextus Claudius Petronius Probus: 510, 511 e n., 512, 513, 516
Shapur: 133, 134, 135, 138, 139, 142n., 143n., 144, 146 e n., 147, 153, 159
Shenoute of Atripe / Shénouté: 23 e n., 207n., 208, 542, 543 e n., 544 e n.
Sibyl (Sibilla cumana): 65n., 435 e n.
Socrate (storico ecclesiastico) / Sokrates: 103n., 107, 120n., 126n., 128n., 142n., 145n., 146n., 152n., 157n., 197, 208, 235 e n., 345n., 346n., 353n., 368n., 410n., 473n., 481n., 482, 483
Sophrone de Jérusalem / Sofronio: 549, 550 e n., 551, 552 e n., 553, 554 e n., 555 e n., 556 n., 557 e n., 558 e n., 559 e n., 560, 561, 570, 571
Sozomène / Sozomenus / Sozomeno: 103n., 122 e n., 125 e n., 128 e n., 142n., 145n., 146n., 152n., 157n., 197n., 208, 345n., 346n., 353n., 410n., 413, 468, 470 e n., 481n., 482, 483n.
Stilicone: 218n., 489 e n.
Sulpicio Alessandro / Sulpicius Alexander: 404n., 406, 407n.
Sulpice Sévère / Sulpicio Severo: 93n., 105, 351n.
Svétone / Svetonio / Suetonius: 102n., 352n., 387n.
Sylvester (actus): 350, 351n.
Synesius of Cyrene / Sinesio: 18 e n., 19n., 94n., 195n.

Tacito / Tacite: 32n., 37n., 60 e n., 94, 102n., 106
Tatien / Tatian / Taziano: 77, 85n., 102
Taziano / Flavius Eutolmius Tatianus (cos. 391): 198, 426n., 483, 484n.
Tertullian / Tertulliano: 77, 78 e n., 79, 82, 86, 87 e n., 232n., 236n., 421, 479n.
Tertullus (cos. 410): 420 e n.,
Themistius: 110 e n., 112, 113 e n., 114 e n., 115 e n., 143n.
Théodoret de Cyr / Theodoret / Theoderet / Teodoreto: 96n., 102, 103n., 184n., 242n., 326 e n., 331n., 336n., 337, 364n., 483n.
Théodose I / Teodosio / Theodosius : 93, 100, 104n., 106, 113n., 135n., 143n., 236, 282, 283, 284, 286, 287,

312, 322, 325 e n., 346n., 348 e n., 349n., 350 e n., 351, 352 e n., 353 e n., 354 e n., 355 e n., 356 e n., 357 e n., 359 e n., 360 e n., 361, 362, 365, 370, 375 e n., 386, 389n., 393, 412 e n., 413n., 415n., 417, 433n., 467, 468 e n., 469, 472 e n., 473 e n., 474n., 484, 512, 530, 532

Théodose senior / Teodosio: 355, 362 e n., 380 e n., 381n.,

Theodosius / Teodosio (nobilissimus puer): 360 e n.

Theodosius II / Teodosio : 50n., 117n., 211, 287, 309, 314, 316, 360, 372n., 411, 420, 433n., 470, 476n., 478n., 489n., 501, 535, 541 n.

Theophanes / Teofane (storico): 332n., 333n., 477n., 533, 534n.

Theophilos of Alexandria / Teofilo: 23, 482n., 483

Thucydides / Tucidide: 17, 202

Tibère / Tiberius: 105, 159, 331n., 387n.

Tigrinus (presbyter): 504 e n.

Tommaso (vescovo di Amida): 534, 537, 538

Trajan / Traianus / Traiano: 181, 331n., 364, 366n., 370n., 387, 429, 432, 464n., 512, 547

Tranquillino (martire): 245, 260, 262, 263

Ulpius Egnatius Faventinus: 280, 281
Uranius / Uranii: 498 e n., 500

Valens / Valente: 100, 146n., 152n., 235, 285, 286, 315n., 317 e n., 345, 348, 350n., 410n., 474n., 477n., 478n.

Valentinien I / Valentiniano I/: 279, 280, 282, 283, 285, 286, 347, 348, 355 e n., 356n., 360 e n. , 388n., 395 e n., 403n., 405n., 410n., 416n., 469 e n., 470, 475n., 477 e n., 478 e n., 479, 480 e n., 481

Valentinien II / Valentiniano II: 283, 348 e n., 352n., 355 e n., 356, 357, 381, 405, 410n., 433, 470n., 475, 530

Valentiniano III: 360, 361 e n., 411, 420, 470n.

Valeriano: 344, 470

Varron / Varro: 98, 517, 522, 523, 524, 525

Victricius of Rouens:188n., 502n.

Vigilantius: 188 e n., 189 e n., 190

Vigilio (vescovo di Trento) / Vigilius: 490 e n., 491

Virgile / Vergil / Vergilius / Virgilio: 7, 94, 180, 181, 231n., 240, 329, 330n., 358n., 517 e n., 518, 519, 520, 521, 522, 523, 524, 525

Vitaliano / Vitalianus: 196, 197n.

Volusianus (p.u. 365) / Ceionius Rufius Volusianus / Volusiano / Volusien: 132, 428, 432 e n., 434 e n., 462n., 466n.

Zaccaria (profeta): 203, 208n., 261
Zaccaria Scolastico: 209, 234, 537
Zenobio (architetto): 533, 534 e n.
Zenone (vescovo di Verona): 479 e n., 480 e n., 485 e n.
Zonaras: 346n., 347n., 403n., 404n.
Zosime / Zosimus / Zosimo: 105, 152n., 349n., 354n., 366n., 367n., 384 e n., 403 e n., 404 e n., 405 e n., 407n., 408 e n., 409 e n., 411 e n., 413 e n., 414, 415 e n., 416 e n., 417 e n., 418 e n., 419n., 420

Indice dei nomi moderni

Abel F.-M.: 535n.
Accorinti D.: 203n., 208n., 212n.
Acquaro E.: 583n.
Adorno T.L.W.: 33n.
Adrados F.R.: 347n.
Adunka E.: 71n., 72n., 74n.
Agosti G.: 195n., 196n., 197n., 198n., 199n., 200n., 201n., 203n., 204n., 206n., 208n., 209n., 210n., 211n., 213n., 214n., 242n., 603
Agostinelli A.D.: 438n.
Aiello V.: 351n.
Aitken A.B.: 172n., 175n.
Aland K.: 339 e n.
Al-Azmeh A.: 52 e n.,53 e n., 54 e n.
Albenhausen A.: 349n.
Alberigo G.: 90n.
Alcock S.E.: 171n., 546n.
Alexander J.J.G.: 381n.
Alfarano T.: 510 e n., 516
Alföldi A.: 378n., 379n., 381 e n., 382 e n., 387 e n., 388 e n., 484n.
Alici L.: 592n.
Allen P.: 334n.
Aloni A.: 195n.
Alpi F.N.: 314n.
Altheim F.: 28
Amata G.: 340n.
Amato E.: 195n., 196n.
Amedick R.: 372n., 373n., 374n., 377n.
Amerise M.: 343n.
Amici A.: 344n., 355n., 361n.

Ando C.: 52n., 380n., 519n.
Anghel S.: 544n.
Angiolani S.: 127n., 369n.
Antenna G.C.: 591n.
Apollonj Ghetti B.M.: 513n.
Arce J.J.: 344n., 478n.
Archi G.G.: 467n.
Armando L.: 580n.
Armiseren- Marchetti M.: 396n.
Armstrong A.H.: 168 e n., 264n.
Arnaldi A.: 431n.
Arslan E.A.: 391n., 495n.
Assemani J.S.: 161n.
Assmann J.: 89n.
Athanassiadi-Fowden P.: 109n., 111n., 114n., 149n., 193n., 362n., 367n., 418 e n.
Atiya A.S.: 141n.
Atkins M.: 508n.
Auerbach E.: 265n.
Aufrère S.: 553n.
Augusta Boularot S.: 331n.
Averincev S.: 193n.
Avigad N.: 535n., 536n.
Avramea A.: 529 e n., 537n.
Azéma Y.: 326n.
Azzopardi G.: 532n.

Bäbler B.: 120n.
Bachofen J.J.: 63 e n.
Badenas P.: 549n.
Badewien J.: 87n.
Baglivi N.: 378n.

Bagnall R.: 194n., 209n., 371n., 544n., 551n.
Bainbridge W.S.: 256n.
Baldini A.: 403n., 407n., 412n., 413n., 418n., 419n., 483n.
Ballerini G.: 479n.
Ballerini P.: 479n.
Balmelle C.: 293n.
Balty J.: 302n., 315n.
Bandy A.C.: 390n.
Banfi A.: 28n., 65, 66
Baratte F.: 377 e n.
Barb A.A.: 19 e n., 34, 163 e n., 164 e n., 165 e n., 166, 167, 168, 169
Barbero A.: 100n.
Barceló P.: 349n.
Barchiesi A.: 195n.
Barnes T.D.: 111n., 112n., 349n., 409n., 410n., 462n., 463n., 464n., 465n., 468n., 602
Barone G.: 353n., 354n.
Baronio C.: 405n., 422n.
Barrate F.: 372n.
Barsanti C.: 537n.
Bartalucci A.: 240 e n.
Bartholomew P.: 381n.
Bartolozzi Casti G.: 501n., 504n., 505n.
Barzanò A.: 426n.
Basset S.: 569n.
Batiffol P.: 339 e n.
Bauer F.A.: 430n., 462n., 463n., 465n., 466n., 499n.
Baumer L.: 233n., 567n.
Baumgarten I.: 119n., 170n.
Baumstark A.: 138 e n., 139 e n.
Baur F.C.: 45
Bayet J.: 339 e n.
Baynes N.: 45, 378n.
Beal S.: 606n.
Beard M.: 422n., 435n.
Beatrice P.F.: 210n., 332n.
Beaucamp J.: 331n.
Becatti G.: 379n.

Bechert H.: 586n.
Becker A.H.: 161n., 562n.
Behlmer H.: 543n.
Behrwald R.: 429n., 436n.
Belayche N.: 119n., 170 e n., 238n., 371n., 433n.
Ben Abed-Ben Khader A.: 286 e n.
Bengston H.: 29n.
Ben-Horin U.: 141n.
Benjamin W.: 64 e n.
Béranger J.: 358n.
Béranger-Badel A.: 238n.
Berenson MacLean J.K.: 172n., 173n., 175n.
Berger P.: 381n.
Bériou N.: 549n.
Berkhof H.: 73n.
Bernardi J.: 123n., 124 e n., 125n., 126n., 129n., 135n., 368n.
Bernays J.: 64 e n.
Berry M.: 181n.
Bertacchi L.: 300n.
Berti F.: 465n.
Berti S.: 25n., 38n., 59n.
Bertolini O.: 359n., 419n.
Berve H.: 27
Betz H.D.: 172n., 173n.
Bianchi Bandinelli R.: 294, 379n.
Bianchi O.: 465n.
Bickell G.: 161n.
Bickermann E.: 64 e n., 344n., 352n., 358n.
Bidez J.: 151n., 232n., 313n., 334n., 345n., 563n.
Bielman A.: 465n.
Biermann M.: 352n., 354n.
Bigelmair A.: 479n.
Bimart de la Bastie J.: 405n.
Binazzi G.: 433n.
Binder G.: 174n.
Bing G.: 11, 42
Biondo F.: 48
Birley A.R.: 95n., 363n., 431n.
Birman P.: 23n.

Bisconti F.: 293, 373n., 374 e n.
Blanc C.: 316n.
Blanchard Y.M.: 552n., 561n.
Bleckmann B.: 403n., 404n.
Bloch H.: 17 e n., 19 e n., 34, 194n., 226 e n., 425n.
Blockley R.C.: 419n.
Blum G.G.: 161 n.
Bode C.: 28n.
Bof R.: 245n.
Boillat M.: 404n.
Bolgiani F.: 82n., 83n., 84n.
Bollati G.: 26, 30 e n., 31 e n.
Bonamente G.: 95n., 127n., 339n., 340n., 341n., 342n., 343n., 344n., 345n., 346n., 351n., 352n., 354n., 356n., 357n., 358n., 359n., 361n., 362n., 363n., 364n., 366n., 367n., 368n., 380n., 407n., 408n., 410n., 468n., 472n., 477n., 478n., 483n., 533n.
Bonifay M.: 286
Bonino G. D.: 31, 32n.
Bonnafé A.: 222 e n.
Bonner C.: 166 e n., 382n., 403n., 559 e n.
Bonnet C.: 547n.
Bonora G.L.: 597n.
Bookmann H.: 349n.
Borg B.: 498n.
Böser W.: 546n.
Bosio A.: 511 e n., 512n.
Bost J.-P.: 275n., 559n.
Boudon-Millot V.: 552n., 561n.
Bouffartigue J.: 114n., 119n.
Bourdieu P.: 495n.
Bowden H.: 181n., 182n.
Bowden W.: 546n.
Bowersock G.W.: 22 e n., 44 e n., 49n., 66n., 109n., 111n., 112n., 119n., 139n., 149n., 175n., 176n., 194 e n., 203n., 406n., 421n., 506n., 541n., 554 e n., 560n.
Bowes K.: 495n., 501n., 502n., 505n.
Bowie E.L.: 176n.

Boyarin D.: 51n.
Brandenburg H.: 302n., 531n., 532n.
Brandes W.: 147n.
Brändle R.: 346n.
Brandt H.: 363n., 407n., 408n.
Bratož R.: 413n.
Brauch T.: 113n.
Braudel F.: 36n.
Braun R.: 135n., 136n., 368n., 544n., 561n.
Bregman J.: 163n.
Bréhier L.: 339 e n.
Bremmer J.N.: 165n.
Brenk B.: 301n.
Brennecke H.C.: 121, 122 e n., 123 e n.
Brice W.: 150n.
Bringmann K.: 109n., 111n., 147n., 149n.
Brinkerhoff D.M.: 569
Brinton C.: 70n.
Brock S.P.: 136n., 157n., 331n.
Brogiolo G.P.: 501n., 567n.
Brooks E.W.: 534n., 537n.
Brottier L.: 313n., 541n.
Brown P.: 10 e n., 19n., 22n., 23n., 34 e n., 35 e n., 41n., 44, 47, 48, 49 e n., 52, 171n., 192n., 207n., 247 e n., 248 e n., 249, 259 e n., 265n., 291, 302, 323n., 325n., 343n., 349n., 371n., 413n., 423, 467n., 471n., 473n., 487n., 494n., 499, 500 e n., 501n., 570n., 579n., 592n., 600n., 602n.
Browning R.: 147n., 149n.
Bruggisser P.: 182n., 358n.
Brunt P.A.: 414n.
Buckler W.H.: 333n.
Budé G.: 152n., 403, 411n., 419n., 493n.
Buonaiuti E.: 12, 69, 71, 74n., 75 e n., 76 e n., 77 e n., 78 e n., 79 e n., 80 e n., 81 e n., 89
Buonocore M.: 462n.
Burckhardt J.: 42, 467
Burgess R.W.: 95n., 404n.

Burian J.: 364n., 366n.
Buxton R.: 179n.

Cabouret B.: 309n., 376n., 391n.
Cabrol F.: 343n., 535n.
Caffiero M.: 353n.
Caimi J.: 390n.
Calderone S.: 341n., 343n., 344n., 367n.
Callu J.-P.: 101 e n., 391n., 393, 410n.
Caltabiano M.: 378n.
Cameron Alan: 19n., 20n., 182n., 194 e n., 195n., 203 e n., 207n., 208 e n., 226n., 227 e n., 234n., 362n., 371n., 403 e n., 405 e n., 409, 411n., 415 e n., 416n., 417 e n., 418n., 419, 420n., 421n., 422 e n., 426n., 427n., 464n., 509 e n., 512n., 541, 544n., 559n., 560n.
Cameron Averil.: 10n., 40n., 41n., 48n., 49n., 52n., 192n., 194n., 199n., 343n., 467n., 468n., 577 e n.
Canivet P.: 136n., 326n.
Cantimori D.: 27 e n., 28, 33 e n.
Cantimori E.: 33 e n.
Capizzi C.: 422n., 529n., 537n.
Capodiferro A.: 379n.
Caprara M.: 208n.
Caprino C.: 28n., 29
Caprioglio S.: 30 e n.
Carandini A: 379n.
Carena C.: 35 e n.
Carile A.: 340n.
Carletti C.: 296
Carrié J.-M.: 342n., 371n., 376n., 506n., 605 e n.
Casali S.: 518 e n.
Caseau B.: 546n., 549n., 552n., 560n., 561n., 568n.
Casel O.: 71n.
Castrén P.: 567n.
Casula L.: 580n.
Cavallo G.: 200n., 201n.
Cavarzer A.: 195n.

Cecconi G.A.: 197n., 242n., 395 e n., 412n., 464n., 465n., 603
Cerati R.: 25n.
Ceresa-Gastaldo A.: 237n.
Cérfaux L.: 339 e n.
Cerrati M.: 510n.
Chabod F.: 28 e n.
Chabot J.-B.: 332n.
Chadwick H.: 39 e n.
Champeaux J.: 411n.
Champlin E.: 429n.
Chaniotis A.: 24 e n., 601 e n.
Chantraine P.: 219n., 342n.
Charlesworth M.P.: 27
Charlier M.-T.: 389n.
Chastagnol A.: 274n., 382 e n., 383 e n., 385n., 386n., 389n., 394n., 427, 434n., 466n., 531n.
Châtelain T.: 404n.
Chausson F.: 410n., 507n.
Chauvot A.: 375n.
Chavarria Arnau A.: 501n.
Chenu M.-D.: 70n., 90n.
Chevalier P.: 293n.
Chin C.M.: 227n., 234n.
Chioffi L.: 465n.
Christol M.: 274, 275, 425n., 436, 452n., 462n., 463n.
Chuvin P.: 194 e n., 213n., 219n., 224n., 330n., 473n., 481n., 484n., 541n., 561n., 603
Ciampini G.G.: 533n.
Ciccolella F.: 195n.
Clark F.: 591 e n.
Clark G.: 188n., 502n.
Clarke E.G.: 169 e n.
Classen C.J.: 357n.
Clauss M.: 341n., 344n., 358n., 550n.
Clemente G.: 25n., 26n., 41 e n.
Coarelli F.: 462n., 502 e n.
Coates-Stephens R.: 437n., 463n., 465n., 493n.
Conca F.: 410n.
Congourdeau M.H.: 390n.

Consolino F.E.: 70n., 345n., 352n., 426n., 465n., 472n.
Conti S.: 110n., 426n., 435n, 465n.
Contini R.: 135n.
Conybeare F.C.: 180n.
Cooper K.: 245n., 246n., 250n., 258n., 259n., 264n., 266n., 495n., 497n.
Corbett S.: 495n.
Corbier M.: 286
Cormack R.: 568n.
Cornell T.: 63n.
Cortés D.: 74n.
Cosentino A.: 507n.
Courcelle P.: 34
Cox C.W.M.: 559n.
Cox Miller P.: 264n.
Cracco G.: 299n., 580n., 583n., 585n., 586n., 591n., 596n., 597n.
Cracco Ruggini L.: 10n., 20 e n., 25n., 40n., 41n., 43 e n., 70n., 299n., 342n., 353n., 354n., 358n., 359n., 362n., 365n., 367n., 368n., 369n., 378n., 379n., 380 e n., 381n., 396n., 399, 408n., 410n., 411n., 412n., 414n., 415n., 417n., 418n., 419n., 420n., 435n., 436n., 476n., 485n,. 506n., 579n., 586n., 596n.
Cramer W.: 150n.
Crawford M.: 40n., 43n., 63n.
Cremascoli G.: 585n., 596n.
Cressedi G.: 436n.
Cribiore R.: 200 e n., 209n., 230n., 604n.
Crisafulli V.S.: 549n.
Crisci E.: 202n.
Criscuolo U.: 111n., 135n., 370n., 408n., 417n., 426n., 478n.
Crislip A.T.: 549n.
Cristante L.: 200n., 214n.
Croce B.: 10, 25 e n., 41, 43n., 60n., 74n., 594
Croke B.: 327n., 328n., 329n., 537n., 538n.
Crouzet-Pavan E.: 561n.

Crow J.: 537n.
Cullen J.: 559n.
Cumont F.: 63 e n., 73n., 547n.
Curran J.R.: 22n., 378n., 494n.
Cuscito G.: 291n., 293 e n., 294n., 296

D'Azeglio M.: 25
D'Elia S.: 360n.
Dagens C.: 582n., 585n., 589n.
Dagron G.: 20n., 113n., 233 e n., 242n., 371n., 569n., 583n.
Dal Covolo E.: 365n.
Dalla Torre Del Tempio di Sanguinetto G.: 374n.
Daly L.J.: 115n.
Daniélou J.: 209n., 474n., 481n.
Darras-Worms A.L.: 390n.
Dassmann E.: 143n.
Dauphin C.: 302n.
Dauterman Maguire E.: 560n.
Davis S.: 551n.
De Blaauw S.: 532n.
de Broglie A.: 80n.
de Cazenove O.: 546n.
De Giovanni L.: 342n., 417n., 426n., 478n., 484n., 487n., 489n.
De Luca G.: 26
De Maffei F.: 537n.
De Martino E.: 28n., 65, 66 e n.
De Matteis M.: 532n.
De Mille C.B.: 254
de Polignac F.: 179 e n.
De Rosa G.: 580n.
De Rossi G.B.: 498n., 507n., 510n., 531n., 533n.
De Salvo L.: 341n., 355n.
De Sanctis F.: 25 e n., 27, 41, 56n., 59
de Ste Croix G.: 45
De Stefani C.: 208n., 209n.
De Tommaso G.: 430n.
de Vogué: 266n., 570n., 586n.
Degli'Innocenti A.: 596n.
Deichmann F.W.: 534n.
Delage M.-J.: 546n., 570n.

Delehaye H.: 258, 324n., 549n.
Delmaire R.: 437n., 476n., 477n., 478n., 480n., 481n., 484n., 487n., 488n., 490n., 541n.
Delmas L.: 301n.
Demandt A.: 183n., 533n.
Demoen K.: 197n., 198n., 206n.
Demougeot E.: 384n.
Demougin S.: 389n.
den Boeft J.: 135n., 142n., 143n., 147n., 149n., 150n., 157n., 198n., 403n.
den Hengst D.: 135n., 142n., 143n., 147n., 150n., 157n., 403n.
Derda T.: 209n.
Déroche V.: 541n., 542n., 558n.
Desmulliez J.: 437n.
Dessau H.: 110n., 273n.
Destephen S.: 11n., 417n., 491n., 601n.
Détienne M.: 553n.
Devijver H.: 389n.
Devos P.: 149n.
Devreese R.: 564n.
Dey H.: 493n.
Di Donato R.: 26n., 31n., 40 e n., 41n., 44n., 50n., 57n., 58n.
Di Netro T.R.: 543n.
Di Paola L.: 469n.
Di Santo E.: 236n.
Di Stefano Manzella I.: 435n.
Diefenbach S.: 349n., 494n., 496n.
Diesenberger M.: 266n.
Dillon J.M.: 169n.
Dionisotti C.: 26, 38 e n., 56n., 58n., 60n.
Dittrich U.-B.: 384n.
Docci M.: 532n.
Dodds E.R.: 32, 47, 165, 166 e n., 167, 605
Doignon J.: 100n.
Dolbeau F.: 20 e n., 360n., 395n., 607n.
Dopsch A.: 45, 48
Dörrie H.: 209n.

Douglas M.: 267 e n.
Dousse M.: 596n.
Downey G.: 324n., 326n., 327n.
Drake H.A.: 49n., 336n.
Dresken-Weiland J.: 511n.
Drijvers H.J.W.: 136n., 137n., 138 e n., 139 e n., 140n., 145n., 151n., 159n., 161n., 472n.
Drijvers J.W.: 6, 131, 132, 134, 135n., 136 e n., 138 e n., 140 e n., 142 e n., 143n., 144, 145n., 146, 147n., 148, 150 e n., 152, 154 e n., 156 e n., 157n., 158 e n., 160 e n., 162, 472n.
Droysen J.G.: 59, 63, 64 e n.
Duby G.: 392n.
Duchesne L.: 75n., 501n., 588n.
Ducos M.: 286
Dumézil B.: 11n., 417n., 491n., 601n.
Dumézil G.: 30n., 63 e n.
Dummer J.: 197n., 235n.
Dundes A.: 172n.
Dupuis X.: 286
Durry M.: 547n.
Duval N.: 274n., 293n., 302n., 352n.
Duval Y.-M.: 95n., 100n., 356n., 378n., 404n., 408n., 438n., 595n.

Eck W.: 436n.
Edbrooke Jr. R.O.: 378n.
Edwards M.: 195n., 234n., 469n.
Egberts A.: 193n., 543n.
Einaudi G.: 12, 14, 26, 28 e n., 29 e n., 30n., 32 e n., 33 e n., 34 e n., 36 e n., 573
Eitrem S.: 167 e n., 168, 173n.
Ekroth G.: 171n.
Elia F.: 345n., 411n.
Elm S.: 51n.
Elsner J.: 208n.
Engemann J.: 533n.
Enjuto Sánchez B.: 426n.
Ensoli S.: 301n., 495n.
Ensslin W.: 154n., 358n., 360n., 382 e n., 473n.

Episcopo S.: 505n.
Eppinger A.: 171n., 182n.
Erbse H.: 331n.
Errington R.M.: 113n., 115n., 349n., 468n., 470n., 473, 475n.
Escribano M.V.: 468n.
Estienne S.: 387n.
Evans C.: 608n.

Faber R.: 71n.
Falchi G.L.: 472n.
Fantuzzi M.: 199n.
Faraone C.A.: 553n.
Farina R.: 340n., 343n.
Fatti F.: 121n., 126n., 345n.
Fayant M.-C.: 219n., 221
Fears J.R.: 344n.
Feissel D.: 529n., 536n., 559n.
Felle A.E.: 438n.
Fentress L.: 371n.
Ferchiou N.: 277, 278n., 285
Ferguson E.: 312n.
Fernandez N.: 552n.
Ferrini C.: 467n.
Ferrua A.: 495n., 496n.
Festugiére A.-J.: 116n., 166, 549n., 558, 563n.
Fevrier C.: 381n.
Février P.A.: 191n.
Fiey J.-M.: 152n.
Filip I.: 214n.
Filippi G.: 531n.
Finley M.: 64 e n.
Fiocchi Nicolai V.: 501n., 503 e n., 504n.
Firpo M.: 409n.
Fixot M.: 286 e n.
Flamant J.: 362n.
Flinterman J.J.: 175n., 180n.
Flusin B.: 551n.
Fobelli M.L.: 219n., 221
Foerster R.: 123n., 125n., 127n., 128n., 198n., 212n., 376n.
Fogelin R.J.: 249n.

Fontaine J.: 226 e n., 378n., 570n., 595n.
Forlin Patrucco M.: 353n., 472n.
Fortunati L.: 501 e n., 502 e n., 503n. 515, 516
Foschia L.: 541n.
Foucault M.: 98
Fournet J.-L.: 194n., 202n., 212n., 213 e n., 560n.
Fowden G.: 52n., 166 e n., 419n.
Fowler W.: 63
Francesio M.: 118n.
Franchi De' Cavalieri P.: 342n.
Frankfurter D.: 207n., 541n., 550n.
Frantz A.: 567n.
Fraschetti A.: 70n., 362n., 372n., 378n., 379n., 389
Fraser P.M.: 47n.
Frazer A.: 506n., 533n.
Frazer J.: 171 e n.
Freeman P.: 537n.
Freeman Sandler F.: 510n.
Frei-Stolnba R.: 465n.
Friell G.: 474n., 485n.
Frizzi G.: 35n.
Frommel C.L.: 435n.
Frugoni A.: 575n.
Fubini G.: 33n., 59n.
Fuhrmann M.: 352n.
Fuller R.H.: 173n.
Furman D.E.: 21n.
Fusco F.: 341n., 380n., 533n.

Gabba E.: 58n.
Gaddis M.: 49n.
Gaeta G.: 75n.
Gaisbauer A.: 71n., 75n.
Gaiser E.: 235n.
Galavotti E.: 584n.
Gallay P.: 124n.
Galletier E.: 375n., 378n.
García Martínez S.M.: 464n.
Garnsey P.: 192n., 467n.
Garstad B.: 329n., 331n.

Gärtner H.: 112n.
Garzetti A.: 36
Gascou J.: 274n., 286, 541n., 548n., 550n., 552n., 554 e n., 555n., 556 e n., 557n., 558 e n., 559n.
Gasperini L.: 360n.
Gaudemet J.: 355n., 467n., 472n., 481n.
Gauthier N.: 377n., 378n.
Gemeinhardt P.: 230
Gemelli A.: 26, 38
Gendre Loutsch M.: 404n.
Germino E.: 233n.
Getto G.: 36n.
Ghedini F.: 175n., 299n., 387n.
Ghetta M.: 299
Ghilardi M.: 395n., 435n., 477n.
Giangrande G.: 419n.
Giardina A.: 51n., 379n., 395 e n., 463n., 468n., 502n.
Giarrizzo G.: 28n.
Gibbon E.: 33, 34, 45 e n., 46, 47, 61 e n., 247 e n., 467, 521, 573
Gibbs M.: 27n.
Gigante M.: 25n., 28n.
Gigli D.: 194n., 198n., 203n., 204n.
Gillet R.: 583n., 595n.
Gilli M.: 550n.
Gillot J.: 31n.
Gilsenan M.: 264n.
Ginzburg C.: 28n., 66n.
Giorcelli Bersani S.: 407n.
Giovanni Paolo I: 597
Girardet K.M.: 350n., 351n.
Giuffrida C.: 343n.
Giuliano: 37n., 373n.
Glucker C.A.M.: 535n.
Glück A.: 190n.
Goddard C.J.: 372n., 377n., 388n., 394n., 395n., 435n., 477n.
Godding R.: 580 e n.
Goddio F.: 550n.
Godefroy J.: 405n.
Goldbacher Al.: 545n.

Goldsworthy A.: 52n.
Golega J.: 210n.
Gollancz H.: 132n., 133n., 134n., 136 e n., 138 e n., 142n., 143n., 144n., 145n., 146n., 147n., 148n., 149n., 150n., 151n., 152n., 153n., 154n., 155n., 156n., 159n., 160n., 162n.
Gombrich E.: 19 e n., 37n.
Gómez de Silva C.: 535n., 536n.
Gonnelli F.: 198n., 206n., 209n.
Gonzalez-Galvez A.: 111n.
Goodburn R.: 381n.
Gorbachev M.: 21
Gordon R.: 422n.
Gotter U.: 23n., 482n., 543n., 601n.
Gottheil R.J.H.: 136n.
Goulet R.: 608n.
Grabar A.: 296, 297n., 300n.
Grabar O.: 49n.
Graf F.: 565n.
Grafton A.: 26n., 27n., 40n., 43 e n., 45n., 46n., 607 e n.
Gramsci A.: 33n., 74n.
Granata G.: 25n., 64n.
Granino M.G.: 464n.
Grassigli G.L.: 300n., 302n.
Greco C.: 208n.
Green R.P.H.: 417n.
Grégoire H.: 535n.
Gregorutti C.: 294
Gregory J.: 245n., 264n.
Grelle F.: 395 e n.
Griffin F.: 314n.
Griffith S.H.: 109n., 160 e n.
Grig L.: 493n., 508n.
Grillet B.: 316n.
Groag E.: 465n.
Gronewald M.: 174n.
Gros P.: 462n.
Gross K.: 349n.
Grossmann P.: 550n.
Gruen E.S.: 51n.
Gualadri I.: 410n.
Guarducci M.: 430n.

Guénée B.: 371 e n.
Guenther O.: 530n.
Guidi I.: 161n.
Guidobaldi F.: 462n., 463n., 464n., 465n., 507n., 531n., 532n.
Guiglia Guidobaldi A.: 507n., 537n.
Guinot J.-N.: 316n.
Gwynn D.H.: 48n.

Haas C.: 560n., 566n., 569n.
Hadas M.: 172n.
Hadot P.: 164n.
Haffner M.: 211n.
Hahn J.: 23 e n., 24 e n., 50n., 116n., 117n., 157n., 309n., 320n., 482n., 483n., 543n., 551n., 601n.
Hall S.G.: 343n.
Halsall G.: 52n.
Hamilton F.J.: 537n.
Hammerstaedt J.: 364n.
Hannestad N.: 569n.
Hanson R.P.C.: 312n.
Harkins P.W.: 318n.
Harl M.: 321n.
Harrak A.: 537n.
Harries J.: 467n., 468n.
Harris W.V.: 182n., 426n., 560n.
Hartog F.: 98
Haubold J.: 328n.
Hayes E.R.: 562n.
Heather P.: 52n., 110n., 113n.,114n.
Hedrick Jr. C.W.: 413n., 426n., 466n.
Heer F.:12, 69, 70 e n., 71 e n., 72 e n., 73 e n., 74 e n., 75n., 82 e n., 83, 84, 90
Hegel G.W.F.: 59
Heikel I.A.: 73n.
Heiler F.: 339 e n.
Heimgartner M.: 346n.
Hellenguarc'h J.: 411n.
Henig M.: 292n.
Henry R.: 414n., 418n., 419n.
Hernández de la Fuente D.: 603n.
Héron de Villefosse A.: 275

Hershbell J.P.: 169n.
Hilhorst A.: 198n.
Hill C.: 475n.
Hillgarth J.N.: 570n., 593n.
Hillner J.: 495n., 504n., 514n.
Himmelmann N.: 372n., 377
Hitler A.: 70 e n., 84 e n.
Hoët-Van Cauwenberghe C.: 437n.
Hoffmann J.G.E.: 132n., 133n., 136 e n., 140
Hölscher T.: 182n.
Honoré T.: 467n., 469n.
Hopkins K.: 180 e n.
Horden P.: 549n.
Hörling E.: 330n.
Horsfall N.: 517 e n.
Hose M.: 195n.
Hume D.: 247, 248, 249 e n., 267
Humfress C.: 390n.
Hunt E.D.: 468n., 493n.
Hunter D.G.: 337n.
Hurst A.: 200n., 211n.
Huskinson J.: 328n.

Inglebert H.: 11n., 95n., 96n., 99n., 101n., 108n., 226n., 274n., 329n., 417n., 491n., 600, 601n.
Iricinschi E.: 608n.
Isnardi-Parente M.: 59n.
Isola A.: 360n.

Jacobs A.S.: 51n.
Jacobs C.: 404n.
Jaczynowska M.: 182n.
James W.: 251 e n., 252
Janon M.: 274, 275
Jedin H.: 90n.
Jeffreys E.: 327n., 328n.
Jeffreys M.: 327n.
Jesnick L.: 297n.
Joannou P.P.: 126n., 547n.
Johnson D.W.: 566n.
Johnson M.: 509n.
Johnson S.F.: 194n., 606n.

Jolivet-Lèvy C.: 548n.
Jones A.H.M.: 18 e n., 22, 23n., 34, 42 e n., 46, 47 e n., 48n., 49 e n., 50, 229n., 241n., 385n., 386n., 410n., 599
Jones C.: 175n., 177n.
Jürgensen K.: 349n.

Kaariainen K.: 21n.
Kaegi W.E.: 419n.
Kahlos M.: 187n., 190n., 193n., 313n., 322n., 326n., 336n., 362n., 412n., 465n., 471n.
Kajanto I.: 403n., 421 e n.
Kalavrezou-Maxeiner I.: 388n.
Kaldellis A.: 240n.
Kaniuth A.: 343n.
Kantorowitz E.: 371 e n.
Kaplan M.: 548n.
Karabelias E.: 547n.
Karivieri A.: 567n.
Kasser R.: 200n.
Kaster R.A.: 519n.
Kennedy H.: 537n.
Kern O.: 331n.
Khanoussi M.: 273n., 277
Kienast D.: 384n.
Kierdorf W.: 341n.
Kinch K.F.: 379n.
Klein B.: 238n.
Klein R.: 378n.
Klingshirn W.E.: 120n., 241n., 570n.
Klugkist A.C.: 136n.
Klutz T.E.: 192n.
Knipe S.: 606
Knöpfler D.: 404n.
Knox R.: 590 e n., 592
Kolb F.: 183n., 349n., 363n.
Kolde A.: 211n.
Kosseleck R.: 98
Kotila H.: 191n.
Kotter B.: 390n.
Krautheimer R.: 346n., 465n., 495n., 501n., 506n., 510n., 533n.

Kreider A.: 253n., 256, 257 e n.
Krueger J.: 70n.
Küng H.: 586n., 596n., 597n.
Kugener M.-A.: 326n., 535n., 569n.
Kurdock A.: 500n., 501n., 504n.

La Conte M.G.: 241n.
La Regina A.: 496n., 497n., 498n., 501n.
La Rocca C.: 259n.
La Rocca E.: 301n., 464n., 495n., 515
Labourt J.: 493n.
Laistner M.L.W.: 236n.
Lamma P.: 574, 575 e n., 576 e n., 577 e n., 578
Lanciani R.: 502n., 510n., 512n.
Larsen D.B.: 165n., 168 e n.
Laubscher H.P.: 379n.
Lauter Bufe H.: 546n.
Lauter H.: 546n.
Lavan L.: 546n., 549n, 568n.
Lavarene M.: 391n.
Lavenant R.: 136n.
Le Bonniec H.: 283n.
Le Goff J.: 574n., 586, 595n.
Le Nain de Tillemont L.-S.: 405n.
Leclercq H.: 343n., 535n.
Lee A.D.: 481n.
Lega C.: 466n.
Lehnen J.: 378n.
Lehoux F.: 371 e n.
Lenski N.: 146n.
Lepelley C.: 191n., 273n., 274n., 277, 281n., 288n., 312n., 371n., 380n., 389 e n.394n., 395n., 434n., 488n., 545n., 604
Lepschy G.: 30
Levenson D.B.: 157n.
Levick B.: 559n.
Levis-Sullam S.: 57n.
Leyser C.: 265n., 266n.
Lidonnici L.R.: 553n.
Liebeschuetz W.: 11, 95n., 230n., 310n., 313n., 315n., 323n., 330n.,

334n., 408n., 415 e n., 419n., 475n., 529n., 537n., 560n., 601, 607
Lieu S.N.C.: 109n., 117n.
Lightfoot J.L.: 332n.
Ligota C.R.: 63n.
Lim R.: 602n.
Lippold A.: 473n.
Lipps J.: 464n.
Liverani P.: 291n., 371n., 375n., 380n., 381n., 507n., 510n., 531n., 532n., 533n.
Livrea E.: 194n., 201n., 203n., 208n., 209n.
Lizzi Testa R.: 9n., 11n., 20 e n., 126n., 284n., 335n., 342n., 345n., 346n., 348n., 349n., 352n., 353n., 354n., 355n., 356n., 365n., 367n., 371n., 413n., 417n., 426n., 432n., 433n., 464n., 467n., 468n., 469n., 470n., 471n., 472n., 474n., 475n., 479n., 491n., 493n., 506n., 508n., 604
Lloyd S.: 150n.
Lo Cascio E.: 426n.
Loefstedt B.: 479n.
Lofland J.: 255 e n.
Long J.: 227 e n.
Lopez Salva M.: 549n.
Lopreato P.: 550n.
Loriot X.: 238n.
Löwith K.: 33n.
Lowry J.M.P.: 168 e n.
Lowther Clarke W.: 24 e n.
Lozza G.: 410n.
Lucchi G.: 380, 398
Lugaresi L.: 225n., 369n.
Lukinovich A.: 210n., 211n.
Luzzatto G.I.: 467n.
Luzzatto M.T.: 234n.

Maas M.: 390n., 411n.
MacCormak S.G.: 344n., 371n.
MacDonald A.: 162n.
Machado C.: 171n., 508n., 546n.
MacMullen R.: 166n., 236n., 238n., 251, 252 e n., 253, 254, 256 e n., 262, 263, 467n.
Madec G.: 395n.
Magdelaine C.: 213n.
Maguire H.: 560n.
Maier G.-L.: 489n., 491n.
Maimone Ansaldo Patti L.: 437n.
Maioli M.G.: 22n., 298n.
Maisano R.: 408n.
Malcovati E.: 410n.
Mallon J.: 283n.
Malosse P.-L.: 111n., 311n.
Mango C.: 346n., 347n.
Mango Mundell M.: 569n.
Mangoni L.: 27n., 28n.
Mannheim R.: 265n.
Mannion G.: 597n.
Marasco G.: 93n., 340n., 363n., 407n.
Maraval P.: 73n., 548n., 577n.
Marchese M.E.: 462n.
Marcone A.: 41 e n., 44 e n., 46 e n., 48n., 52n., 70n., 193n., 208n., 291n., 294n., 425n., 426n.
Marcuse H.: 37
Marin E.: 377n.
Markiewiecz T.: 209n.
Markschies C.: 235n.
Markun H.: 75n.
Markus R.: 104, 105n., 120n., 288 e n., 289 e n., 309n., 314 e n., 334n., 522, 570n., 581 e n., 583
Marotta V.: 388n., 394 e n.
Marriott M.: 414n.
Marrou H.-I.: 18 e n., 19n., 22 e n., 34, 41 e n., 42, 47, 48 e n., 194n., 225n., 298n.
Martin J.P.: 238n., 315n.
Martindale J.R.: 410n., 420n.
Mary L.: 545n.
Masetti C.: 30n.
Masson O.: 438n.
Mastino A.: 380n.
Mathews T.: 300n.
Mathisen R.W.: 187n., 426n.

Matino G.: 410n.
Matthews J.F.: 147n., 323n., 378n., 467n., 484n., 511 e n.
Matting H.: 183n.
Mattingly, H.: 388n.
Maurin L.: 275n.
Mauss M.: 65, 66n.
Maxwell J.I.: 313n., 320 e n.
Mayer M.: 407n.
Mazza M.: 116n., 343n., 408n., 411n., 576n., 583n.
Mazzarino S.: 47, 48n., 50, 97, 407n.
Mazzoleni D.: 293n., 295
McCormick M.: 371n.
McGuckin J.: 135n., 209n., 210n.
McLynn N.: 18 e n., 410n., 468n., 482n.
McNally S.: 560n.
Mehmet II: 222
Mele G.: 580n.
Melloni A.: 9, 90n., 597 e n.
Menestò E.: 490n.
Menis G.C.: 302n.
Merisalo O.: 190n.
Merola G.D.: 426n.
Mertol Tulum A.: 222n.
Meslin M.: 315n.
Messana V.: 409n.
Métivier S.: 127n.
Metzger C.: 372n., 377 e n.
Meyer B. F.: 421n.
Meyer E.: 28, 29, 30, 31 e n., 32 e n., 33, 36n.
Meyer M.: 553n.
Meyers B.F.: 421n.
Mezuâr G.: 463n.
Mian F.: 300n.
Miccoli G.: 26n., 588n.
Micheli M.E.: 373n.
Miguèlez Cavero L.: 195n.
Milanovic C.: 196n., 197n.
Miles R.: 51n., 288 e n., 328n.
Milik J.P.: 535n.
Millar F.: 51n., 151n., 154n., 157n., 372 e n., 376n., 406n.

Miller P.C.: 264n.
Miller P.N.: 26n., 63n., 69n.
Milman D.: 247
Minutoli D.: 469n.
Mirecki P.: 553n.
Misson J.: 116n., 117n.
Mitchell S.: 559n.
Mocsy A.: 384n.
Momigliano A.: 9, 10, 11 e n., 12 e n., 14, 17 e n., 18 n., 25 e n., 26 e n., 27 e n., 28 e n., 29 e n., 30 e n., 31 e n., 32 e n., 33 e n., 34 e n., 35 e n., 36 e n., 37 e n., 38 e n., 39 e n., 40 e n., 41 e n., 42 e n., 43 e n., 44 e n., 45 e n., 46 e n., 47, 48, 49, 50, 51, 52, 53, 55, 56n., 57 e n., 58 e n., 59 e n., 60 e n., 61, 62, 63 e n., 64 e n., 65 e n., 66 e n., 67, 69 e n., 70 e n., 89 e n., 93 e n., 94, 95 e n., 96n., 97, 98, 99, 101, 104, 107, 131, 163n., 226n., 248, 291 e n., 329n., 335, 382 e n., 405, 406 e n., 517 e n., 573 e n., 574 e n., 575 e n., 576 e n., 599, 600
Momigliano F.: 26
Mommsen T.: 361n., 462n., 541n.
Monaca M.: 435n.
Monat P.: 183n.
Moncur D.: 110n., 113n.
Montero S.: 484n.
Montesquieu C.L.: 28, 47
Montserrat D.: 550n.
Moon S.M.: 255
Moosa M.: 335n., 337n.
Mores F.: 588n.
Moreschini C.: 198n.
Morghen R.: 75n.
Morin G.: 265n.
Morpurgo A.D.: 30, 31, 32, 33n., 34, 35
Morris J.: 410n.
Morrison C.: 551n.
Mortley R.: 95n.
Moscati S.: 583n.
Moser E.: 223n.
Moss C.A.: 314n.

Motte A.: 547n.
Müller C.: 419n.
Müller W.F.: 71n., 72n.
Muhlberger S.: 329n.
Muhs P.B.: 193n., 543n.
Mulders J.: 188n.
Muraviev A.: 136n., 137n., 138, 139n., 140 e n., 141n., 159n.
Murdoch I.: 28n.
Murray G.: 166
Murray M.: 166n.
Murray O.: 43 e n., 63n.
Muth S.: 299
Mutzenbecher A.: 486n.

Namier L.B.: 27, 37n.
Narcy M.: 471n.
Nau F.: 562n.
Neri V.: 349n., 350n., 351n., 352n., 360n., 367n., 407n., 468n.
Nesbitt J.W.: 549n.
Nesselrath H.-G.: 120n., 197n., 235n.
Nestori A.: 343n., 472n.
Nichtweiss B.: 82n., 84n.
Nieddu A.M.: 496n., 497n., 498n.
Niquet H.: 432n., 437n., 465n., 466n.
Nock A.D.: 112n., 251 e n., 252, 368n., 576n.
Nöldeke T.: 135 e n., 137 e n., 138 e n., 139, 140, 141n., 143n., 144n., 146n., 158n.
Norelli E.: 202n.
Norman A.F.: 111n., 117n., 309n., 325n.
North J.: 42n., 422n.
Nötlichs K.-L.: 415n., 417
Nutton V.: 549n.

O'Donnel J.: 50n., 52n.
O'Keeffe Machado E.: 493n.
Obbink D.: 553n.
Oberg E.: 229n.
Ochoa J.A.: 403n., 416n.
Onida P.P.: 340n., 342n.

Orlandi S.: 10n.
Ortalli J.: 298n., 299n.
Osborne R.: 508n., 546n.
Ostrogorski G.: 28, 32n.
Ovadiah A.: 535n., 536n.
Overbeck J.J.: 161n.

Pace V.: 291n.
Pack E.: 119n., 127n., 478n.
Pagi A.: 405n.
Pailler J.-M.: 225n.
Palanque J.-R.: 80n., 481n.
Palla R.: 202n.
Palmer A.-M.: 232n.
Panciera S.: 463n.
Pani Ermini L.: 345n.
Paolucci F.: 509n., 510n.
Papaconstantinou A.: 554n.
Papadoyannakis Y.: 606 e n.
Papi E.: 466n.
Papini C.: 74n., 597n.
Papoutsakis M.: 136n., 138n., 140n., 143n., 146n., 349n., 413n., 579n.
Parente F.: 59n., 75n., 251n.
Parmentier L.: 334n., 563n.
Parrish D.: 293n.
Paschoud F.: 354n., 403 e n., 404n., 405n., 406, 407n., 408n., 409 e n., 410, 411, 413 e n., 415 e n., 416n., 417n., 418n., 419n., 426n., 592n.
Patlagean E.: 595n.
Pavan M.: 299n.
Pavese C.: 33n.
Payen P.: 225n.
Pazdernik C.: 390n.
Pecer O.: 201n.
Pedersen N.A.: 608n.
Peeters P.: 161n.
Pellegrini P.: 583n.
Pellegrino M.: 476n.
Pellistrandi S.: 595n.
Pellizzari A.: 411n.
Penella R.P.: 112n., 113n., 114n., 120n., 156n., 409n.

Pentiricci M.: 435n.
Pereira Leite M.: 23n.
Perelli R.: 354n.
Perels H.-U.: 85n.
Pergami F.: 477n.
Perrin M.: 541n., 547n., 606 e n.
Perrot M.: 392n.
Perry B.E.: 139n.
Petazzoni R.: 28
Peterson E.: 12, 69, 71, 73n., 74n., 81, 82 e n., 83 e n., 84 e n., 85 e n., 86 e n., 87 e n., 88 e n., 89 e n.
Petit P.: 229 e n., 230n., 309n., 310n., 311n., 312n.
Peyras J.: 275n.
Pfeiffer R.: 219n.
Pfister F.: 173n.
Piana G.: 90n.
Pianciola N.: 597n.
Picard G.: 283n., 508n., 509n.
Piccinini P.: 341n.
Piepenbrink K.: 227 e n.
Pieri P.: 27
Pietri C.: 474n., 479n., 494n., 496n., 497n., 506n.
Pietri L.: 438n., 479n., 577n.
Piganiol A.: 80n., 436n., 477n., 481n., 484n., 531n.
Pighi G.B.: 392n.
Pincherle A.: 75n.
Pinzone A.: 340n.
Piras A.: 580n.
Pirelli R.: 391n.
Pirenne H.: 45, 48, 69, 600
Pohl W.: 266n.
Poirier M.: 597n.
Polara G.: 240n., 465n.
Polverini L.: 25n., 40n., 41n., 56n., 70n.
Pomarès G.: 547n.
Ponchiroli D.: 30, 31n.
Popper K.: 37n.
Porena P.: 371n., 395n., 425n., 429n., 435n., 462n., 463n., 464n., 477n.

Potter J.: 559n.
Pouderon B.: 552n., 559n., 561n.
Pradels W.: 346n.
Praet D.: 251n.
Prato C.: 128n.
Préchac F.: 391n.
Prestige G.L.: 198n.
Pretagostini R.: 199n,
Previtali G.: 37n.
Prévot F.: 377n., 378n.
Price R.: 51n., 312n., 422n.
Pricoco S.: 237n.
Prinzivalli E.: 340n.
Prouderon B.: 408n.
Purcell N.: 498n.

Quacquarelli A.: 237n., 490n.
Queyrel F.: 233n.

Rabanal Alonso M.A.: 464n.
Rallo Freni R.A.: 240n.
Rapp C.: 353n., 529n., 530n., 537n., 539n.
Raschle C.R.: 356n.
Ratti S.: 408n.
Ravà M.: 75n.
Ravenhill P.L.: 264n.
Rawlings L.: 181n., 182n.
Rea J.R.: 558n.
Rebecchi F.: 376n.
Rebenich S.: 343n., 346n., 355n., 494n.
Rebillard E.: 51n., 471n., 508n.
Reed J.D.: 553n.
Rees R.: 182n., 183n., 501n.
Regali M.: 368n.,
Reinink G.J.: 136n., 138n., 140n.
Rendic-Miocevic D.: 376n.
Reverdin O.: 200n.
Rey A.L.: 211n., 212n.
Rey-Coquais J.-P.: 315n., 439
Ribichini S.: 547n.
Ricci L.G.G.: 585n.
Richardson Jr. L.: 181n.

Riché P.: 231n., 595n.
Richer J.: 135n., 136n., 368n.
Ridley R.T.: 419n.
Riedl M.: 606n.
Riegl A.: 48
Rigaux D.: 549n.
Rilliet-Maillard F.: 561n.
Rinaldi G.: 236n., 368n.
Ripoll G.: 293n.
Rist J.: 537n.
Ritter S.: 181n.
Rives J.: 566n.
Rivière Y.: 490n.
Robert L.: 224n., 430n.
Roberts C.: 42
Robinson D.M.: 333n.
Rochow I.: 334n.
Roddaz J.-M.: 275n.
Rodziewick M.: 560n.
Rogger I.: 490n.
Rohrbacher D.: 103n.
Romano A.: 51n.
Roncalli A.G. (Giovanni XXIII): 584n., 597 e n.
Rosan L.J.: 167 e n., 168
Rose H.J.: 173n.
Rosen K.: 111n., 123n., 136n., 147n., 149n., 344n., 351n., 352n., 366n., 367n.
Rossi G.: 360n.
Rossi M.: 586n.
Rostovtzeff M.: 46, 47, 69, 600
Roth C.: 56n.
Rothaus R.: 187n., 190n.
Roucole S.: 286
Roueché C.: 20 e n., 569n.
Rougé J.: 210n., 541n.
Rousseau P.: 349n., 413n., 468n., 579n.
Rousselle A.: 376n., 605 e n., 606, 607
Routledge e Kegan Paul ed.: 35
Rudhardt J.: 200n.
Rüpke J.: 315n., 425n., 429n., 462n., 463n., 464n., 465n.

Ruffini G.: 560n.
Ruggieri G.: 82n., 90n.
Rusconi G.E.: 583n., 584n.
Russel D.A.: 375n., 391n.

Sabbah G.: 95n., 384n.
Saffrey H.D.: 567n.
Sághy M.: 497n.
Saglio E.: 223n.
Sainsbury M.: 249n.
Salama P.: 278, 279
Salamon M.: 334n.
Saliou C.: 331n.
Salomies O.: 286, 287
Salvatorelli L.: 75n., 79n.
Salway P.: 292n.
Salzman M.R.: 259n., 315n., 336n., 361n., 426n., 427n., 494n.
Samarin W.J.: 264n.
Sanders E.P.: 421n.
Sandwell I.: 309n., 311n., 321n., 328n.
Sansone D.: 414n.
Sansterre J.-M.: 73n.
Santangeli Valenzani R.: 493n.
Santoni A.: 32n.
Saradi H.: 314n.
Sartori A.: 462n.
Sartori P.: 597n.
Sartre J.P.: 28n.
Sasso G.: 60n.
Scaligero G.G.: 31n.
Scarborough J.: 549n., 553n.
Schabert T.: 606n.
Schäfer A.: 235n.
Schamp J.: 195n., 390n.
Schatkin M.A.: 230n., 316n.
Scheichl S.P.: 71n.
Scheid J.: 371n., 375n., 392, 393, 397, 546n.
Scheindler A.: 208n.
Schembra R.: 212n.
Schenkl H.: 115n.
Schindler A.: 82n.
Schirollo L.: 26n.

Schliemann H.: 178, 179n.
Schlumberger J.: 407n.
Schmidt M.G.: 282, 464n.
Schmitt C.: 74n., 88, 89
Schmitt-Pantel P.: 392n.
Schneider H.: 219n.
Schoeps H.J.: 70n.
Scholem G.: 31, 64 e n., 65
Schöllgen G.: 115n.
Schubert P.: 203n.
Schulten P.N.: 344n.
Schwartz E.: 501n.
Schwartz J.: 363n.
Schwarz S.: 51n.
Scorza Barcellona F.: 353n.
Scott R.: 327n.
Scullard H.H.: 27
Seeck O.: 115n., 117n., 378n., 381n., 384n., 462n.
Segal J.B.: 151n., 161n., 172n.
Segonds A.: 567n.
Selby-Bigge L.A.: 249n.
Sellew P.: 174n.
Sena Chiesa G.: 495n.
Serafini A.: 343n.
Seston W.: 73n., 80n., 274n., 379n.
Settis S.: 201n., 387n.
Shahid I.: 52n.
Shaw B.: 49n., 604
Shaw G.: 169 e n.
Shepardson C.: 109n.
Shils E.: 21 e n.
Shorrock R.: 216n.
Sichtermann H.: 301n.
Silvagni A.: 506n., 507n.
Silvestrini F.: 512n.
Simon M.: 182n.
Simonetti M.: 351n., 595n.
Simonsohn S.: 31n.
Sindoni A.: 355n.
Sini F.: 340n.
Siniscalco P.: 345n., 472n., 583n.
Sirks B.: 467n.
Sironi E.M.: 486n.

Sivan H.S.: 157n., 187n., 601 e n.
Skeat T.C.: 42n.
Smith A.: 167 e n., 168 e n.
Smith J.Z.: 192n.
Smith N.: 172n.
Smith R.P.: 334n., 354n., 563n.
Smith R.R.R.: 116n., 233 e n., 568n.
Smolak K.: 204n.
Snodgrass A.: 179n.
Sodini J.-P.: 548n., 567n.
Soler E.: 311n., 315n., 319n., 324n., 335n.
Solmi S. : 27, 28n.
Solmsen F.: 174n.
Sommerstein A.H.: 522n.
Soraci R.: 345n., 355n., 411n.
Sordi M.: 349n., 352n., 353n.
Sorrenti G.: 501n., 503n.
Sot M.: 545n.
Sotinel C.: 293n., 300n., 471n., 508n.
Spencer D.: 181n.
Spera L.: 496n., 497n., 498n.
Speyer W.: 174n.
Springer C.P.E.: 206n.
Squarcini F.: 232n.
Sraffa P.: 37n.
Staehelin E.: 80n.
Stark R.: 50n., 192n., 254 e n., 255 e n., 256 e n., 261, 263, 267
Steidle W.: 472n.
Stein E.: 481n.
Steinberg J.:70n.
Steinberg M.P.: 25n., 44n.
Steinby E.M.: 379n., 425n.
Steinrück M.: 195n.
Stella F.: 195n.
Stemberger G.: 156n.
Stern H.: 363n.
Stern J.: 330n.
Steunernagel D.: 547n.
Stevens C.E.: 42n.
Stoltenberg G.: 349n.
Stramaglia A.: 201n.
Stratton K.B.: 165n.

Straub J.: 365n., 368n., 378n., 403n.
Strauss L.: 64 e n.
Straw C.: 602n.
Strothmann M.: 345n.
Stroumsa G.: 28n., 69n., 89n., 241n.
Stupperich R.: 171n.
Sturzo L.: 74n.
Susman M.: 584n.
Swain S: 195n., 234n., 469n.
Sykes D.A.: 198n.
Syme R.: 14, 20n., 27, 30 e n., 406 e n.
Szidat J.: 360n.

Tamassia N.: 480n.
Tambiah S.: 264n.
Tamcke M.: 537n.
Tantillo I.: 371n.
Tardieu M.: 164n., 544n.
Tavarnesi L.: 232n.
Taylor C.: 591n.
Teatini A.: 380n.
Teitler H.C.: 135n., 142n., 143n., 147n., 150n., 157n., 403n.
Teja R.: 379n.
Thélamon F.: 191n., 237n.
Thomas Y.: 371n.
Thompson E.A.: 18 e n.
Thompson L.L.: 173n.
Thomson R.W.: 139n.
Thraede K.: 143n., 204n.
Thurn I.: 327n.
Tirone C.: 346n.
Tolotti F.: 498n.
Tondriau J.: 339 e n.
Torelli M.: 495n.
Török L.: 208n., 560n.
Torp H.: 560n.
Touwaide A.: 553n.
Tovar S.T.: 202n.
Toynbee A.: 18, 29
Toynbee J.M.C.: 292n., 506n.
Tranfaglia N.: 408n.
Trapé A.: 586n.
Travis W.: 177n.

Treu T.: 597n.
Treves P.: 27
Treves R.: 28n.
Trinchese A.: 532n.
Tripet C.: 404n.
Troeltsch E.: 46, 69
Trombley F.R.: 312n., 313n., 322n., 326n., 327n., 333n., 487n., 529n., 537n., 538n.
Trouillard J.: 168 e n.
Trout D.: 231n.
Trzcionka S.: 165n.
Tse-tung Mao: 603
Turcan R.: 364n., 381n., 387 e n.
Turchi N.: 82n.
Turi G.: 28n.
Tursun B.: 222 e n.

Ugenti V.: 369n.
Uglione R.: 360n., 365n.

Vainio R.: 190n.
Vakaloudi A.: 552n., 565 e n.
Valentini R.: 510n.
van Bekkum W.J.: 136n.
van Dam R.: 127n., 535n.
Van den Ven P.: 333n.
van der Vliet J.: 193n., 543n.
Van Deun P.: 95n.
Van Emmel S.: 23 e n., 482n., 543n., 544n., 601n.
van Esbroeck M.: 136n., 137n., 140, 141n., 149n.
Van Ess J.: 586n.
van Haelst J.: 201
Van Haeperen F.: 433n.
van Liefferinge C.: 169 e n.
van Minnen P.: 193n.
van Paverd F.: 325n.
Vanderspoel J.: 113n., 114n., 115n., 143n.
Vannier M.-A.: 550n.
Vanstiphout H.L.J.: 136n.
Varanini G.M.: 586n.

Vasiliev A.: 28
Vauchez A.: 546n.
Vegio M.: 509, 510 e n., 511, 513n.
Venini P.: 410n.
Ventura L.: 57n.
Venturi F.: 27, 29, 31
Vera D.: 24n., 362n., 378n., 383 e n., 385n., 386n.
Verger J.: 561n.
Vergone G.: 293, 294, 295, 296
Vessereau J.: 391n.
Vessey M.: 120n.
Veyne P.: 379n., 393 e n.
Vian F.: 194n., 196n., 202n., 213n., 215, 216, 217n.
Vielberg M.: 116n., 197n., 235n.
Vigourt A.: 238n.
Vilar P.: 427n.
Villette J.: 302n.
Vincelli M.: 227
Viscogliosi A.: 464n.
Vitiello M.: 378n.
Vivanti C.: 26, 31 e n., 32 e n., 33 e n., 34n., 35 e n., 36n., 37 e n.
Völker H.: 111n.
Voltaire J.J.: 47
Von den Steinen W.: 70n.
Von Haeling R.: 369n.
von Harnack A.: 46, 69, 83 e n.
von Hesberg H.: 498n.
von Humboldt A.: 171n., 493n.
von Schönborn C.: 550n.
von Stietenkron H.: 586n.
Vössin G.K.: 431n.

Waelkens M.: 559n.
Walker Bynum C.: 188n.
Wallraff M.: 580n.
Walter H.: 183n.
Warburg A.: 19 e n., 184 e n.
Ward-Perkins B.: 52n., 468n., 493n.
Watt J.W.: 537n., 538n.
Watts E.J.: 112n., 557n.
Weber W.: 373 e n., 374n., 377 e n.

Weil E.: 26n.
Weller C.H.: 171n., 546n.
Wenger A.: 390n.
Wermelinger O.: 550n.
Werner M.: 73n.
Westall R.W.: 463n., 465n.
Westernik L.G.: 125n., 168, 169n.
Whitby M.: 51n., 113n., 468n., 537n.
Whitley J.: 179n.
Whittow M.: 52n.
Wiebe F.J.: 315n.
Wienand J.: 349n.
Wiessner G.: 314n.
Wilamowitz U.: 29n., 31
Wiles M.F.: 141n.
Wilken R.L.: 120n., 318n.
Williams M.: 607 e n.
Williams S.: 474n., 485n.
Wilpert G.: 294, 372n., 373n., 374 e n., 375, 377 e n., 396, 397
Wilson A.: 375n., 391n.
Wilson S.G.: 547n.
Winckelmann O.: 96n., 379n.
Winkelmann F.: 95n., 345n.
Wintjes J.: 310n., 315n.
Wipszycka E.: 209n., 569n.
Wirth G.: 143n.
Wiseman P.: 52n.
Witakowski W.: 332n.
Withmarsh T.: 180 e n.
Witschel C.: 437n., 463n., 499n.
Witt J.: 550n.
Wlosok A.: 344n.
Wöhrle G.: 116n.
Wood I.: 467n.
Woods D.: 183n.
Worn K.A.: 202n.
Wrede H.: 512n.
Wright W.: 114n., 138 e n., 151n., 313n.
Wurst G.: 550n.

Yarnold E.J.: 141n.
Yarrow S.: 264n.

Zaccone G.M.: 543n.
Zacharias D.: 608n.
Zadé R.: 318n.
Zamagni G.M.: 12n.
Zambelli M.: 359n.
Zanini E.: 537n.
Zanker P.: 498n.
Zecchini G.: 354n., 508n.

Zelzer M.: 353n.
Zerbi P.: 575n.
Zimmermann M.: 102n.
Zinsli S.C.: 369n.
Zoroddu D.: 211n.
Zucca R.: 462n.
Zucchetti G.: 510n.

Autori

GIANFRANCO AGOSTI, Università di Udine, Italy
GIORGIO BONAMENTE, Università di Perugia, Italy
PETER BROWN, Princeton University, NJ, USA
ALAN CAMERON, Columbia University, NY, USA
AVERIL CAMERON, Keble College, Oxford, UK
BEATRICE CASEAU, Université Paris-Sorbonne; Collège de France, France
GIOVANNI ALBERTO CECCONI, Università di Firenze, Italy
PIERRE CHUVIN, Université de Paris-Ouest Nanterre-La Défense, France
GUIDO CLEMENTE, Università di Firenze, Italy
KATE COOPER, University of Manchester, UK
GIORGIO CRACCO, Istituto di Storia di Vicenza, Italy
LELLIA CRACCO RUGGINI, Accademia Nazionale de Lincei, Roma
JAN WILLEM DRIJVERS, University of Groningen, The Netherlands
FEDERICO FATTI, Università di Perugia, Italy
CHRISTOPHE J. GODDARD, UMI 3199 Transitions – Cnrs-New York University, France-USA
HERVÉ INGLEBERT, Université de Paris-Ouest Nanterre-La Défense, France
JOHANNES HAHN, Westfälische Wilhelms-Universität Münster, Germany
MAIJASTINA KAHLOS, University of Helsinki, Finland
SERGIO KNIPE, Cambridge University, UK
CLAUDE LEPELLEY, Université de Paris-Ouest Nanterre-La Défense, France
WOLF LIEBESCHUETZ, University of Nottingham, UK
PAOLO LIVERANI, Università di Firenze, Italy
RITA LIZZI TESTA, Università di Perugia, Italy
CARLOS MACHADO, Universidade de São Paulo, Brazil
ARNALDO MARCONE, Università di Roma Tre, Italy
FRANCISCO MARSHALL, Universidade Federal do Rio Grande do Sul (UFRGS), Porto Alegre, Brazil
ALBERTO MELLONI, Università di Modena e Reggio Emilia, Italy
SILVIA ORLANDI, Università Sapienza di Roma, Italy
GIANMARIA ZAMAGNI, Westfälische Wilhelms-Universität Münster, Germany

Christianity and History
Series of the John XXIII Foundation for Religious Studies in Bologna
edited by Prof. Dr. Alberto Melloni (Fondazione per le scienze religiose Giovanni XXIII, Bologna)

Alberto Melloni; Riccardo Saccenti (Eds.)
In the Image of God
Foundations and Objections within the Discourse on Human Dignity. Proceedings of the Colloquium Bologna and Rossena (July 2009) – in Honour of Pier Cesare Bori on his 70th Birthday

In the last years, starting from the study of the foundations of human rights, Pier Cesare Bori has focused his research on the exegesis of *Genesis* 1, 26-28, according to which man is created in the image of God. In the Christian framework the *imago Dei* has led to different interpretations: a charismatic and eschatological, an ontological and a functional one. To solve the contradictions between these different exegesis of *imago Dei* Bori has suggested to consider a larger context, looking not only at the Christian tradition, but also at the other monotheisms, cultures and religions. The proceedings here presented are the result of this attempt to develop new approaches to the study of the topic of *imago Dei*. It has been undertaken by an international group of scholars from different research fields (history, theology, hermeneutics, philosophy, exegesis) during a few days of scientific exchange and dialogue.
Bd. 8, 2010, 424 S., 39,90 €, br., ISBN 978-3-643-10456-4

LIT Verlag Berlin – Münster – Wien – Zürich – London
Auslieferung Deutschland / Österreich / Schweiz: siehe Impressumsseite

Alberto Guasco; Raffaella Perin (Eds.)
Pius XI: Keywords
International Conference Milan 2009
The documents of Pius XI's pontificate from the Vatican Secret Archives, recently accessible for the first time, establish new perspectives of research and analysis. International experts and junior specialists discuss here the Roman point of view concerning the most important issues in the international scene between the two world wars and offer new outlooks and interpretations marking a substantial step forward in research.
Bd. 7, 2010, 440 S., 34,90 €, br., ISBN 978-3-643-90027-2

LIT Verlag Berlin – Münster – Wien – Zürich – London
Auslieferung Deutschland / Österreich / Schweiz: siehe Impressumsseite

Alberto Melloni (Ed.)
Giuseppe Dossetti
Studies on an Italian Catholic Reformer

Giuseppe Dossetti is a name barely known outside Italy. Some may remember his role within the Christian Democratic Party in the early years of the Italian Republic. Readers familiar with the history of the Second Vatican Council may have heard his name as one of its most important ghost writers and theologians. However, to most, his biography remains more or less unknown. One the purposes by the John XXIII Foundation – created by Dossetti in 1953 – was to fill this gap with papers presented to the 2006 Bologna conference, for the decennial of Dossetti's death. Among them the most important for an international readership are gathered in this volume.
Bd. 6, 2008, 296 S., 34,90 €, br., ISBN 978-3-8258-1313-0